Fodor's 2012

W9-BNA-091

ENGLAND

Fodor's Travel Publications   New York, Toronto, London, Sydney, Auckland
www.fodors.com

FODOR'S ENGLAND 2012
Editor: Linda Cabasin

Editorial Contributor: Mark Sullivan
Writers: Robert Andrews, Paul Cannon, Sarah Christie, Christi Daugherty, Astrid deRidder, Damian Harper, Julius Honnor, Erin Huebscher, Kate Hughes, Jack Jewers, Michelle Rosenberg, Ellin Stein, Alex Wijeratna

Production Editor: Evangelos Vasilakis
Maps & Illustrations: Mark Stroud, David Lindroth, Inc., Ed Jacobus, *cartographers;* Bob Blake, Rebecca Baer, *map editors;* William Wu, *information graphics*
Design: Fabrizio La Rocca, *creative director;* Guido Caroti, *art director;* Tina Malaney, Nora Rosansky, Chie Ushio, Jessica Walsh, *designers;* Melanie Marin, *associate director of photography*
Cover Photo: Hadrian's Wall, Housesteads: SIME/eStockPhoto
Production Manager: Angela L. McLean

ISBN 978-0-679-00952-8

ISSN 1558870X

SPECIAL SALES
This book is available at special discounts for bulk purchases for sales promotions or premiums. Special editions, including personalized covers, excerpts of existing books, and corporate imprints, can be created in large quantities for special needs. For more information, write to Special Markets/Premium Sales, 1745 Broadway, MD 3-1, New York, NY 10019, or e-mail specialmarkets@randomhouse.com.

AN IMPORTANT TIP & AN INVITATION
Although all prices, opening times, and other details in this book are based on information supplied to us at press time, changes occur all the time in the travel world, and Fodor's cannot accept responsibility for facts that become outdated or for inadvertent errors or omissions. So **always confirm information when it matters,** especially if you're making a detour to visit a specific place. Your experiences—positive and negative— matter to us. If we have missed or misstated something, **please write to us.** Share your opinion instantly through our online feedback center at fodors.com/contact-us.

PRINTED IN CHINA

10 9 8 7 6 5 4 3 2 1

CONTENTS

Fodor's Features

MAPS

ABOUT THIS BOOK

Our Ratings

At Fodor's, we spend considerable time choosing the best places in a destination so you don't have to. By default, anything we recommend in this book is worth visiting. But some sights, properties, and experiences are so great that we've recognized them with additional accolades. Orange **Fodor's Choice** stars indicate our top recommendations; black stars highlight places we deem **Highly Recommended;** and **Best Bets** call attention to top properties in various categories. Disagree with any of our choices? Care to nominate a new place? Visit our feedback center at www.fodors.com/contact-us.

Hotels

Hotels have private bath, phone, and TV, and do not offer meals unless we specify that in the review. We always list facilities but not whether you'll be charged an extra fee to use them.

> For expanded hotel reviews, visit **Fodors.com**

Restaurants

Unless we state otherwise, restaurants are open for lunch and dinner daily. We mention dress only when there's a specific requirement and reservations only when they're essential or not accepted—it's always best to book ahead.

Credit Cards

We assume that restaurants and hotels accept credit cards. If not, we'll note it in the review.

Budget Well

Hotel and restaurant price categories from £ to £££££ are defined in the opening pages of the respective chapters. For attractions, we always give standard adult admission fees; reductions are usually available for children, students, and senior citizens.

Listings
★ Fodor's Choice
★ Highly recommended
⊠ Physical address
✛ Directions or Map coordinates
🕭 Mailing address
☎ Telephone
⊕ On the Web
✉ E-mail

🎟 Admission fee
🕙 Open/closed times
Ⓤ Tube stations
🚫 No credit cards

Hotels & Restaurants
🏨 Hotel
🛏 Number of rooms
🛀 Facilities
🍽 Meal plans
✗ Restaurant
🔑 Reservations
👔 Dress code
🚭 Smoking

Outdoors
⛳ Golf
⛺ Camping
Other
👪 Family-friendly
⇨ See also
⊠ Branch address
☞ Take note

Experience
England

1

ENGLAND TODAY

England is the biggest part of the United Kingdom (or U.K.), the nation that also includes Scotland, Wales, Northern Ireland, and the Channel Islands. Some but not all of these are also part of Great Britain (or just Britain), which is made up of the contiguous regions of England, Scotland and Wales on the main British isle. While England, Scotland, and Wales are all part of Britain and the U.K., Wales and Scotland are not part of England, and vice versa. The three are separate countries within the United Kingdom. Although it's about the size of Louisiana, England has a population 12 times as large: 51 million people find space to live on its green rolling hills and in its shallow valleys and crowded cities.

Coalition Country

The current government in the United Kingdom is a coalition government. In the last election in 2010, no single party won more than 50 percent of the vote, so the leading vote-winner, the Conservative party, joined together with a small moderate party, the Liberal Democrats, to form a government led by Prime Minister David Cameron, a Conservative, and Deputy Prime Minister Nick Clegg, a Liberal Democrat.

This uncomfortable alliance between two parties that had long been political enemies is controversial with some voters because both parties are forced to compromise on complex issues: nobody gets everything they want. Caught up, as so much of the world is, in the ongoing global economic crisis, the United Kingdom has been cutting back on government spending, at the same time that it also needs to spend more than £9 billion on the Olympic Games being held in London in summer 2012. The necessary fiscal belt tightening has kept the government wrapped up in controversy and fighting off one political crisis after another as those who stand to lose fight back.

But this country loves a good controversy and adores a juicy scandal. Analyzing how the different political parties respond to everything from changing London double-decker bus designs to tabloid news-gathering techniques to cutting back on public sector pensions is a national hobby. There has been much to debate: in summer 2011, the five days of riots and looting that broke out in a number of cities in England after a police shooting in London have caused widespread discussion about everything from police methods to the motives of the looters and the use of social networking.

Olympics 2012

The entire city of London, and much of southern England, is likely to be packed solid from July 27 through August 12 for the summer Olympics. The Olympic Village will be in the neighborhood of Stratford in far east London (not to be confused with Stratford-upon-Avon in central England), and most events will take place there. The country's been planning for this a long time, so expect more than a little Olympic-mania. *(For more information, see the box on the London 2012 Summer Olympics in Chapter 2.)*

The Royals Reinvented

How things have changed for the Windsor family. Essentially a figurehead monarchy but with a symbolic political role, the royal family has teetered on the brink of obsolescence for more than a decade now. After the death of Princess Diana in 1997 and the royal scandals and divorces that littered the late 20th century, the idea of ending the monarchy's political

role—and its government subsidy—was widely discussed publicly. Maintaining the royal family costs the country £42 million (more than $65 million) each year, and that amount was increasingly difficult to justify as the popularity of the family—aside from the beloved Queen—plummeted.

It's not surprising, then that some in the media maintain that when Prince William married the appealing Catherine Middleton he saved the monarchy. Half the country watched the wedding—and the rest of the world paid attention, too—and the young couple's popularity is enormous. In particular, polls show that younger people, those who previously had the least interest in the monarchy, are changing their opinions.

In 2012, the Queen celebrates her Diamond Jubilee, the 60th year of her reign. The country has been given a national holiday in her honor (Tuesday, June 5) and there will, no doubt, be royal parties aplenty to celebrate her majesty's continued longevity. All of this is likely only to make her subjects even fonder of her, and to push once common conversations about doing away with the monarchy out of the picture.

Fashionable Britannia

Known for their quirky, creative, and bold style, British fashion designers have been influential on a global stage for decades. If anything, sales have grown in recent years as international fashion editors and stylists discover them.

Whether it's from top-of-the-line companies like Burberry and Aquascutum or from individual designers such as Jasper Conran, Karen Millen, and the late Alexander McQueen, clothes and furnishings made by British designers are sought

after by moneyed shoppers. According to a 2010 report commissioned by the British Fashion Council, the British fashion industry is worth £21 billion and growing.

Kate Middleton has vowed to promote British fashion, and often wears clothes by British designers. Her influence should not be underestimated: an off-the-rack beige "bandage" dress—from the British clothing company Reiss—that she wore when she met President Obama and the First Lady sold out within hours, and demand crashed the company's Web site.

Last Call for Alcohol

According to published studies, Britain is only the 12th-heaviest drinking nation in Europe, but on a Friday night in any town center that rating can be hard to believe. The British refer to some busy towns after 11 pm as "no-go areas," packed with raucous, drunken young people stumbling out of pubs for late-night food and then making their hiccuping way home on public transportation. Even normally staid towns, such as Harrogate in Yorkshire and Rochester in Kent, can take on a spring-break atmosphere after the pubs close on a Friday night. Seaside towns tend to have the most problems, including Bristol, Newquay, and Hastings.

The main cause, experts say, is a binge-drinking culture, particularly among the young. While, overall, Britain may rank quite low in drinking studies, for people under 25 the results are quite different. A recent study ranked British youth as the third heaviest drinkers in their age group in Europe. Previous programs to change this have failed to make much impact. Now government programs are underway to try and change the nation's gulp-it-down approach to alcohol, but that process will take time.

WHAT'S WHERE

The following numbers refer to chapters.

2 London. Not only Britain's financial and governmental center but also one of the world's great cities, London has mammoth museums, posh palaces, double-decker buses, and iconic sights such as Big Ben. Intriguing villagelike neighborhoods from Notting Hill to Bloomsbury call out to be explored; when you need a break, pop into a pub or relax in one of the city's sprawling parks.

3 The Southeast. This compact green and pleasant region within day-trip distance of London takes in Canterbury and its cathedral, funky seaside Brighton, the appealing towns of Rye and Lewes, Dover's white cliffs, and castles such as Bodiam, Leeds, and Hever. Noted gardens as different as smaller, romantic Sissinghurst and large-scale Wisley add to the mix.

4 The South. Hampshire, Dorset, and Wiltshire are quintessential English countryside, with gentle hills and green pastures. Explore the stone circles at Stonehenge and Avebury, and take in Winchester (Jane Austen country) and Salisbury, and Lyme Regis and the fossil-rich Jurassic Coast.

5 The West Country. Somerset, Devon, and Cornwall are sunnier and warmer than the rest of the country, with sandy beaches. Cornwall has lush gardens and stunning coast, Bristol is a vibrant city, and Wells and Exeter are pretty towns. Take in the brooding heaths and moors of Exmoor and Dartmoor, too.

6 The Thames Valley. London's commuter belt takes in Windsor, where the Queen spends time, and Eton. Then there are the spires of Oxford and peaceful river towns such as Henley and Marlow; in all of these, you have the opportunity for some relaxing river excursions. Among the stately homes not to be missed are over-the-top Blenheim Palace and Waddesdon Manor.

7 Bath and the Cotswolds. The grand Georgian town of Bath is one of England's highlights, with the Roman Baths and golden-stone 18th- and 19th-century architecture. Nearby, pretty as a picture, the Cotswolds region is justly famous for tranquil, stone-built villages, such as Chipping Campden, Stow-on-the-Wold, and Tetbury. Notable gardens include those at Hidcote Manor and Sudeley Castle.

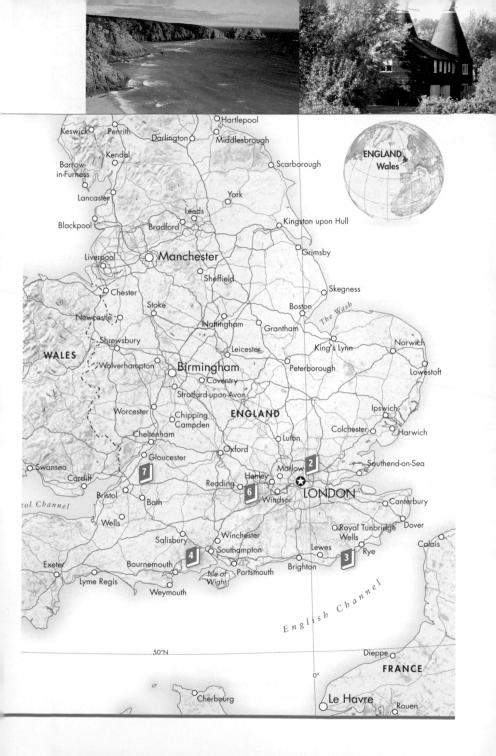

WHAT'S WHERE

8 Stratford-upon-Avon and the Heart of England. One hundred miles north of London, Stratford-upon-Avon is the place to see Shakespeare's birthplace and watch his plays, and Warwickshire has Warwick and Kenilworth castles, too. Nearby Birmingham offers a modern urban experience. You can explore the Industrial Revolution museums of Ironbridge Gorge, Ludlow's half-timber buildings, medieval Shrewsbury, and popular Chester.

9 Lancashire and the Peaks. Liverpool rides the Beatles' coattails but, like Manchester, has transformed its warehouses and docks into sleek hotels, restaurants, and shops. Buzzing nightlife and excellent museums are highlights in both cities. The Peak District has great walking and stately homes such as Chatsworth and Haddon Hall.

10 The Lake District. A popular national park, this is a startlingly beautiful area of craggy hills, wild moorland, stone cottages, and glittering silvery lakes. Nature lovers and hikers crowd the area in summer. Among the literary high points are Wordsworth's and Beatrix Potter's homes.

11 East Anglia. The biggest lure in this green, flat, low-key region is Cambridge, with its medieval halls of learning. The countryside is dominated by the cathedrals of Ely and Norwich and by time-warp towns such as Lavenham. Coastal spots from Aldeburgh to Wells-next-the-Sea add a salty flavor.

12 Yorkshire. This wilder part of England has great appeal for lovers of the outdoors, but ancient walled York is also a center of attention. To York's west are the moors and dales that inspired the Brontës, and in east Yorkshire the moors collide with the sea at salty towns such as Whitby. Leeds is a reviving urban center.

13 The Northeast. Travelers can walk in the footsteps of Roman soldiers along Hadrian's Wall in this remote northern region. Bamburgh and Dunstanburgh castles guard the coast; Alnwick Castle has stunning gardens. The small city of Durham is a medieval gem, a contrast to modern Newcastle.

14 Wales. Clinging to the western edge of England, Wales is green and ruggedly beautiful, with mountains and magnificent coastline. Except for Cardiff and Swansea, this is a rural country, with three national parks. Wales is also known for its castles.

55°N

Londonderry

NORTHERN IRELAND

Donegal

Omagh

Sligo

Lisburn

Galway

IRELAND

Shannon

Limerick

Kilkenny

Waterford

Cork

50°N

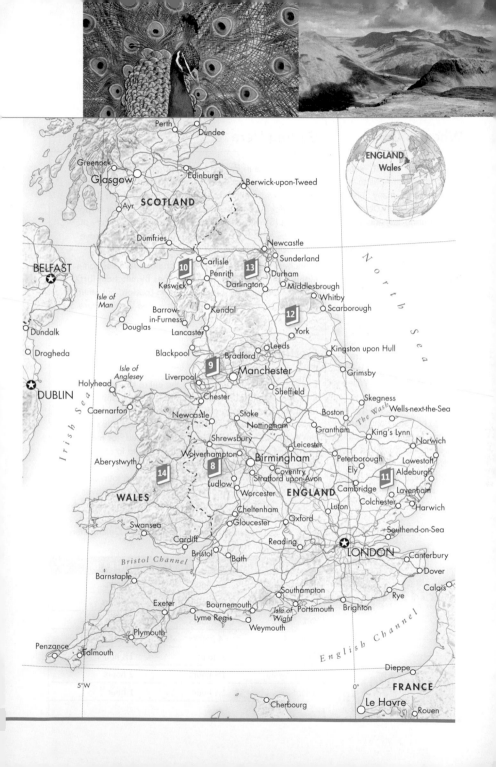

ENGLAND
Wales

SCOTLAND

Perth
Dundee
Greenock
Glasgow
Edinburgh
Ayr
Berwick-upon-Tweed

Dumfries
Newcastle
BELFAST
Carlisle
Sunderland
10
Penrith
13
Durham
Keswick
Darlington
Middlesbrough
Isle of
Man
Whitby
Barrow-
in-Furness
Kendal
Scarborough
Dundalk
Douglas
Lancaster
12
York
Drogheda
Blackpool
Bradford
Leeds
Kingston upon Hull
Isle of
Anglesey
9
Liverpool
Manchester
Grimsby
DUBLIN
Holyhead
Chester
Sheffield
Skegness
Caernarfon
Newcastle
Stoke
Boston
Wells-next-the-Sea
Nottingham
The Wash
Shrewsbury
Grantham
King's Lynn
Aberystwyth
Wolverhampton
Leicester
Norwich
14
8
Birmingham
Peterborough
Lowestoft
Coventry
Ely
11
Aldeburgh
Ludlow
Stratford-upon-Avon
Cambridge
Lavenham
WALES
Worcester
ENGLAND
Colchester
Harwich
Cheltenham
Luton
Swansea
Gloucester
Oxford
Southend-on-Sea
Cardiff
Reading
LONDON
Canterbury
Bristol Channel
Bristol
Bath
Dover
Barnstaple
Calais
Southampton
Rye
Exeter
Bournemouth
Portsmouth
Brighton
Lyme Regis
Isle of
Wight
Weymouth
English Channel
Penzance
Plymouth
Falmouth
Dieppe
5°W
0°
FRANCE
Le Havre
Cherbourg
Rouen
North Sea
Irish Sea

ENGLAND PLANNER

When to Go

The English tourist season peaks from mid-April to mid-October, and many historic houses close from October to Easter. During July and August, accommodations in popular resorts and areas are in high demand. In 2012, the London Olympics take place July 27 to August 12. The winter cultural season in London is lively. Hotel rates are lower then, too. Spring and fall can be good alternatives, as prices are still below high-season rates, and crowds are thinner. Generally, the climate in England and Wales is mild. Summer temperatures can reach the mid-80s, but it's more likely to be cooler and cloudier than you expect. In winter there can be heavy frost, thin snow, thick fog, and rain, rain, rain. Here are average daily maximum and minimum temperatures for two cities.

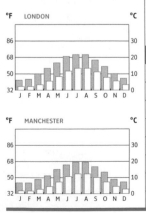

Getting Here

You can arrive in England by plane, train, or boat, and there are many places to disembark. Most international flights arrive at either London's Heathrow Airport (LHR) or at Gatwick Airport (LGW). A third, much smaller airport, Stansted (STN), handles mainly European and domestic traffic, as does Luton Airport (LLA). These airports have good train and bus options for getting into London.

Manchester (MAN) in northwest England handles some flights from the United States, as does Birmingham (BHX) in the Midlands. Most people fly into London, but other airports can be useful. *For more details, see Getting Here and Around in Travel Smart England.*

Getting Around

England is not a large country: the entire United Kingdom (including England, Scotland, Wales, and Northern Ireland) is about the size of Oregon, so you're less likely to fly within the country. The country's train and bus systems are extensive and relatively well maintained; for major towns and cities, there is generally no need to rent a car. To see castles and historic houses—which may be far from towns—you may have to rent a car or join a tour. Driving is on the left, and gas (petrol) is expensive at just over $5 a gallon. Train tickets tend to be two to three times more expensive than bus fares, but trains are usually at least twice as fast as buses. *For more details, see Getting Here and Around in Travel Smart England.*

FROM LONDON TO	BY CAR	BY TRAIN
Newquay, Cornwall	6½ hours	5 hours
The Lake District	5½ hours	4 hours
York	3½ hours	2 hours
Liverpool	4 hours	3 hours
Bath	2 hours	1½ hours
The Cotswolds	1½ hours	2 hours
Oxford	1½ hours	1 hour

Restaurants: The Basics

What you should eat in England depends on where you are, as food is surprisingly regional. Fresh seafood dominates the coastal areas, but lamb and beef lead the way in the inland regions. Local cuisine is also affected by ethnic communities. Although England is increasingly a foodie country with a good restaurant scene, the strongest food culture is limited to major cities and a few regions, most notably London and the Southeast.

In the rural north—Cumbria, Yorkshire, and Northumberland—you'll get hearty meals in family-friendly pubs and inns. York and Harrogate have better options, and Leeds has a burgeoning food scene. Look for local lamb and beef. Birmingham, in the Midlands, is famous for its Indian restaurants serving spicy curries. In Cornwall, Devon, and Dorset, it's all about great fresh seafood. However, don't overlook Cornish pasties (hand-size meat-and-potato pies), sold everywhere. *For details and a price-category chart, see Eating Out in Travel Smart England.*

Lodging: The Basics

London is in part about sleek, modern hotels, where enormous amounts of money get you relatively small amounts of space. One way to get a good deal is to book a chain—such as Millennium or Premier—online well in advance. Check for off-season deals, too. Budget hotels in London can be so unattractive that it's better to look for a special offer at a better chain.

In major towns, you have more options than in rural areas. Hotels are harder to come by in the countryside, and you may stay in a small bed-and-breakfast attached to a pub. Prices may be half or less of what you'll pay in London. Some B&Bs are gorgeous, and many are in handy locations; others are neither, so be careful. B&Bs are popular with British travelers and can be a great way to meet locals. You might also stay in an old coaching inn from the stagecoach era. There are modern twists on the theme, with chains operating cheap modern hotels with bland pub-restaurants. Some older hotels can be old-fashioned but also less pricey.

House and apartment rentals, in cities or in the countryside, can be a good, sometimes cheaper alternative to hotels. *For details and a price-category chart, see the Lodging Primer in this chapter and Accommodations in Travel Smart England.*

Saving Money

Here are ways to start pinching your pennies.

■ Take advantage of free breakfasts if your hotel or B&B offers them. Or grab a croissant at a coffee shop.

■ Many pubs serve lunches for less than £10; most restaurants offer cheap lunch deals.

■ Make one meal a prepared sandwich from a grocery store or sandwich shop.

■ In London, consider staying in a house or apartment. Outside London, stay in a B&B or small guesthouse.

■ Check the Web sites of major chains for deals, especially in the off-season.

■ Buy a prepaid Oyster Card in London to save on the Tube and buses.

■ Ask about family tickets at major sights.

■ Get your culture kicks in free national museums.

■ Check out a sightseeing pass such as the Great British Heritage Pass.

■ Purchase a BritRail train pass or regional passes.

Visitor Information

These sites have information useful for planning.

Contacts VisitBritain (⊕ www.visitbritain.com). **VisitEngland** (⊕ www.visitengland.com).

ENGLAND
TOP ATTRACTIONS

London
(A) Packed with enough treasures and pleasures, London entices with superb museums, royal pageantry, and exciting theater, shopping, and nightlife. Its iconic sights include the Houses of Parliament, Westminster Abbey, the Tower of London, and the British Museum, but parks and pubs offer satisfying diversions as well. (⇨ *See Chapter 2.)*

Hampton Court Palace
(B) This Thames-side redbrick palace was built by and for Cardinal Wolsey. But Henry VIII coveted it, so it became a splendid royal home. Hampton Court, a half hour from London by train, has grand Tudor kitchens, sprawling gardens, and a tricky maze. (⇨ *See Chapter 2.)*

Stonehenge and Avebury
(C) Prehistoric monuments dot England's landscape, silent but tantalizing reminders of the distant past. Of these, the great circle of stones at Stonehenge is one of the country's icons. Nearby, the Avebury Stone Circles surround part of a village and are also deeply intriguing. (⇨ *See Chapter 4.)*

Brighton and Its Seafront
(D) England is more than stately homes and pretty towns. This longtime seaside resort lives it up with classic seaside fun as well as the eccentric Royal Pavilion. Good shopping and restaurants, plus energetic nightlife, keep the action going. (⇨ *See Chapter 3.)*

Bath
(E) Exquisitely preserved but entertaining, this Georgian town still centers on the hot mineral springs that made it the fashionable spa for the wealthy in the 18th and early 19th centuries. Streets lined with Palladian buildings made of golden limestone, an ancient abbey, boutiques, and the ruined Roman baths give Bath real character. (⇨ *See Chapter 7.)*

Hadrian's Wall

(F) Begun in AD 122, the thick stone wall built by the Emperor Hadrian across the rugged far north of the country is a remarkable survivor from Roman Britain, where it protected Roman soldiers from invading tribes. Biking, hiking, and horseback riding are wonderful ways to explore. (⇨ *See Chapter 13.*)

Oxford and Cambridge

(G) It's hard to choose a favorite between these two ancient university towns. Oxford is larger and more cosmopolitan, but lovely with its fairytale cityscape of steeples and towers. In Cambridge, you can stroll through the colleges, visit the university's museums, and relax in the city's pubs. (⇨ *See Chapters 6 and 11.*)

Coastal Cornwall

(H) The coasts of Cornwall, in the far southwest, are beloved by many (too many, in summer) for different reasons. The rugged northern coast has cliffs that drop to tiny coves and beaches; ruined, cliff-top Tintagel Castle and Padstow with its lively harbor are here. The south coast has resort towns such as Penzance and arty St. Ives. (⇨ *See Chapter 5.*)

Cotswold Villages

(I) Marked by rolling uplands, green fields, and limestone cottages with prim flower beds, the Cotswolds, 100 mi west of London, make a peaceful getaway. There's little to do in idyllic villages, but that's the point. Exquisite gardens and stately homes add further charm. (⇨ *See Chapter 7.*)

Lake District

(J) Sprawling across northwest England, this area of 16 major lakes and jagged mountains inspired Romantic poets. You can hike the trails or view the mountains from a boat, or visit the retreats of Wordsworth and Beatrix Potter. (⇨ *See Chapter 10.*)

QUINTESSENTIAL ENGLAND

Pints and Pubs

Pop in for a pint at a pub to encounter what has been the center—literally the "public house"—of English social life for centuries. The basic pub recipe calls for a variety of beers on draft—dark creamy stouts like Guinness; bitter, including brews such as Tetley's and Bass; and lager, the blondest and blandest of the trio—a dartboard, oak paneling, and paisley carpets. Throw in a bunch of young suits in London, a generous dash of undergrads in places such as Oxford or Cambridge, and, in rural areas, a healthy helping of blokes around the television and ladies in the corner sipping their *halves* (half pints) and having a *natter* (gossip). In smaller pubs, listen in and enjoy the banter among the regulars—you may even be privy to the occasional *barney* (harmless argument). Join in if you care to, but remember not to take anything too seriously—a severe breach of pub etiquette. Make your visit soon: the encroachment of gastro-pubs (bar-restaurant hybrids) is just one of the forces challenging traditional pub culture.

Daily Rags

To blend in with the English, stash your street map or your cell phone, slide a folded newspaper under your arm, and head for the nearest park bench or café. Lose yourself in any one of the national dailies for often well-written insight into Britain's worldview. The phone-hacking scandal of 2011 caused various resignations and shut down the *News of the World*—but also provided yet more for the press to write about. For a dose of melodrama, choose the tabloid *Sun*. The headlines are hard to miss—"Prince's Cheating Scandal" and "Empire Strikes Bark: Dogs Dress Up as Vader"—and you can assume that the topless model on Page 3 has helped rather than hindered the paper's success. The biweekly *Private Eye* offers British wit at its best, specializing

If you want to get a sense of contemporary English culture, and indulge in some of its pleasures, start by familiarizing yourself with the rituals of daily life. Here are a few highlights—things you can take part in with relative ease.

in political cartoons, parodies, and satirical reporting.

A Lovely Cuppa

For almost four centuries, the English and tea have been immersed in a love affair passionate enough to survive revolutions, rations, tariffs, and lattes, but also soothing, as whistling kettles across the nation mark moments of quiet comfort in public places and in homes and offices. The ritual known as "afternoon tea" had its beginnings in the early 19th century, in the private chambers of the duchess of Bedford, where she and her "ladies of leisure" indulged in afternoons of pastries and fragrant blends. But you don't need to dress up to lift your pinky to sip the steamy brew. Department stores and tearooms across the nation offer everything from simple tea and biscuits to shockingly overpriced spreads with sandwiches and cakes that would impress even the duchess herself. And if tea is not your cup of tea,

don't worry; there's no shame for those who prefer coffee with their scones and clotted cream.

Sports Fever

Whoever says England is not an overtly religious country has not considered the sports mania that has descended here, and not merely because of the 2012 Olympic Games in London. Whether water events (such as Henley, Cowes, and the Head of the River Race) or a land competition (the Grand National steeplechase, the Virgin London Marathon, a good football match), most bring people to the edge of their seats—or more often the living room couch. To partake in the rite, you'll need Pimm's (the drink for swank spectators of the Henley Royal Regatta) or beer (the drink for most everything else). You may experience the exhilaration yourself—which, you'll probably sense, is not for the love of *a* sport, but for the love of *sport* itself.

IF YOU LIKE

Castles and Stately Homes

Exploring the diversity and magnificence of England's castles and stately homes, from Norman towers to Palladian palaces, can occupy most of a blissful vacation. Whether world famous or less visited, owned by royalty, aristocratic families, or the National Trust, each abode has tales to tell about history or domestic life. Castles and houses are spread around the nation (with fewer stately homes in Cornwall and the Lake District), but certain clusters may help your planning. Note that most stately homes are open only from spring through fall. England's southeastern coast is lined with sturdy castles; nearby but inland, around Royal Tunbridge Wells, are treasure houses such as Hever Castle and Knole. West of Salisbury are Wilton House, Stourhead, and Longleat, and the Cotswolds have a rich assortment. England's north has gems from Peak District manors to castles on the remote northeastern coast. London visitors won't miss out, either: Buckingham and Kensington palaces, the Tower of London, and Hampton Court Palace and Windsor Castle lie within easy reach. If your itinerary extends to Wales, look for Edward I's "iron ring" of castles, including Caernarfon and Conwy.

Blenheim Palace, Thames Valley. This baroque extravaganza is touted as England's only rival to Versailles.

Holkham Hall, East Anglia. A splendid 60-foot-tall marble entryway and salons filled with old masters distinguish this Palladian house.

Petworth House, the Southeast. One of the National Trust's glories is known for art from J.M.W. Turner.

Idyllic Villages

Year after year, armies of tourists with images of green meadows, thatched roofs, and colorful flower beds flock to England's countryside, for good reason. Most will find their way to famously adorable towns along the Thames, magical seaside resorts in the West Country, and a smattering of fairy-tale hamlets in the Cotswolds—an area in west-central England renowned for its golden and gray-stone cottages. However, torrential tourist traffic has made these once-quintessentially quaint areas a little *too* accessible for some at times. Steer clear of busy Cotswolds towns such as Broadway in summer (especially on weekends); Winchcombe and Snowshill are more unspoiled options. Choose a weekday to visit the Thames Valley towns, which attract Londoners. To avoid some crowds, consider the pastoral flatlands of East Anglia beyond Cambridge, where historic villages remain relatively undiscovered, or explore the Norfolk coast. The rural parts of the West Midlands have tranquil landscapes and towns, or head to Wales, with its mountainside hamlets and sleepy seaside resorts.

Lavenham, East Anglia. This village is full of Tudor buildings, the former houses of wool merchants and weavers.

Ludlow, Stratford-upon-Avon and the Heart of England. Medieval and Georgian buildings cluster below a castle in this town, whose restaurants have made it a foodie favorite.

Whitby, Yorkshire. A ruined abbey and a cliff-lined harbor combine with a rich fishing and whaling legacy to enhance this coastal gem.

Glorious Gardens

Despite being cursed with impertinent weather and short summers, English gardeners will gladly grab a gardening tool and attack a misbehaving rose garden for just a few short months of enjoyment. The Tudors were the first to produce gardens that were more than strictly utilitarian, and since then French, Italian, Dutch, and even Japanese ideas have been imported and adapted to suit the national aesthetic. A pilgrimage to a garden is an essential part of any spring or summer trip, whether you visit a large educational garden such as Kew Gardens near London or the West Country's Eden Project; a period gem such as Arts and Crafts Hidcote Manor in the Cotswolds; or gardens that are part of a stately home and as lovely as the house. Green havens thrive all over England, but perhaps the most fertile hunting grounds are in Oxfordshire, Gloucestershire (including the Cotswolds), and Kent (the "Garden of England"). Some of these visions of paradise have limited hours, and most close in winter; they're all worth the trip.

Sissinghurst Castle Garden, Southeast. Vita Sackville-West's masterpiece, set within the remains of a Tudor castle, is busy in summer but also spectacular in autumn.

Stourhead, South. One of the country's most impressive house-and-garden combinations is an artful 18th-century sanctuary with a tranquil lake, colorful shrubs, and grottoes.

Wisley, Southeast. The Royal Horticultural Society's garden splendidly blends the pretty and the practical in its inspirational displays and glasshouses.

Urban Excitement

London has everything a world capital should have—rich culture and history, thrilling art and theater scenes, world-class restaurants and sensational shopping—along with crowds, traffic, and high prices. It shouldn't be missed, but if you appreciate modern cities, fall out of the tourist trap and spend time in some of England's reviving urban centers, including those in its former industrial heartland, where blossoming multiculturalism has paved the way for a unique vibe. Football (soccer) fans might take in a match in Manchester or Liverpool, two bitter sporting rivals in the Northwest, or join hordes of fans to watch the game at a local pub. Manchester's museums are excellent, and its downtown (rebuilt after a 1996 IRA bombing) is worth a look, as are its famous clubs. Liverpool claims the Beatles sites and the stellar museums of the Albert Dock; its stint as the European Union's Capital of Culture in 2008 produced dramatic changes. See what's gentrifying in Birmingham, the country's second-largest city and a cultural force in England.

Brighton, Southeast. Bold, bright, and boisterous are the words to describe a seaside charmer that has everything from the dazzling Royal Pavilion to the trendy shops of the Lanes.

Bristol, West Country. With its lively waterfront and homegrown music talent, this youthful city has vibrant nightlife as well as a long history.

Leeds, Yorkshire. Another northern, former industrial city polishing its Victorian buildings, Leeds is known for its shopping arcades and youthful music scene.

Ancient Mysteries

Stone circles as well as ancient stone and earthen forts and mounds offer intriguing hints about Britain's mysterious prehistoric inhabitants. The country's southwestern landscape, particularly the Salisbury Plain, Dorset, and the eastern side of Cornwall, has a notably rich concentration of these sites, perplexing mysteries that human nature compels us to try to solve. Stonehenge, the stone circle begun 5,000 years ago, stands on the wide Salisbury Plain; crowds detract from the magic, so arrive early or late to appreciate the monument's timeless power. Hypotheses about its purpose range from the scientific (ancient calendar) to the fantastic (a gift from extinct giants). Other relics—chambered tombs and mounds—dot the Avebury area to the north. Equally enigmatic are Maiden Castle, a colossal prehistoric hill fort near Dorchester, and the nearby figure of a giant carved into the hillside overlooking Cerne Abbas. Sometimes the setting of these ancient creations, such as Castlerigg Stone Circle in the Lake District, is as awesome as the surviving remains.

Avebury Stone Circles, South. Large and marvelously evocative, these circles surround part of the village of Avebury. You can walk right up to the stones here.

Stanton Drew Circles, West Country. Use your imagination to visualize the vast size of the two avenues of standing stones, three rings, and burial chamber that now lie in a field.

Vale of the White Horse, Thames Valley. The gigantic horse here was actually carved into the chalky hillside around 1750 BC.

Wonderful Walks

England seems to be designed with walking in mind—footpaths wind through the contours of the landscape, and popular routes are well endowed with cozy bed-and-breakfasts and pubs. Your decisions will be what kind of landscape you prefer (coast or countryside, flat or mountainous) and how long a hike you want, though you can often do just part of a long-distance trail such as the Thames Path. Ramble through one of England's national parks (which are sprinkled with towns), and you'll generally find well-maintained trails and handy maps at local tourist information centers. The country's most famous walking spots are in the Lake District, from a short meander to a major mountain trek—but beware of summer congestion. Yorkshire's dales and moors are also popular. Cross the border to Wales, where the Brecon Beacons offer windswept uplands with easy paths, and ferocious peaks in Snowdonia National Park promise challenging hikes. Wherever you hike, always be prepared for storms or fogs. Check out ⊕ *www.nationaltrail. co.uk* for inspiration and advice.

Borrowdale, Lake District. Have a color-pencil kit handy to capture the beauty of the dramatically verdant valleys and jagged peaks.

Peak District, Lancashire and the Peaks. Its rocky outcrops and vaulting meadows make some people say this is the country's most beautiful national park.

South West Coast Path, West Country. Spectacular is the word for the 630-mi trail that winds from Minehead in Somerset to Poole Harbour in Dorset.

Thrilling Theater

There's no better antidote to an overdose of stately homes and glorious gardens than a face-to-face encounter with another British specialty, the theater. London is the heart and soul of the action: here companies famous and lesser known consistently churn out superb productions, from musicals and monologues to comedies and avant-garde dramas. Be sure to sample theater outside London, wherever you travel. Pre- or post-London tours often take place in Bath's Regency-era Theatre Royal, and the Stephen Joseph Theatre in Yorkshire premieres many of Alan Ayckbourn's plays. Stratford-upon-Avon may be the Bard's hometown, but festivals all over the country celebrate Shakespeare's work—the best are the Ludlow Festival in the Welsh Borders and London's Shakespeare Under the Stars at Regent's Park. Brighton Dome and Windsor's Theatre Royal specialize in pantomime—theatrical entertainment with puppetry, slapstick, and music. Theatrical arts are often a major component of English festivals: see musicals at the Exeter Festival (West Country) and street theater at the Harrogate International Festival (Yorkshire). Try a university production; you may see the next big star.

Minack Theatre, West Country. This open-air theater in coastal Cornwall, near Land's End and Penzance, nuzzles the slope of a sandy cliff.

Royal Shakespeare Company, Stratford-upon-Avon and the Heart of England. Seeing any play by the Bard performed in Stratford is a treat in the renovated Royal Shakespeare Theatre.

Yvonne Arnaud Theatre, Guildford, the Southeast. The productions at this theater on an island often travel to London.

Country-House Hotels

In all their luxurious glory, country-house hotels are an essential part of the English landscape, particularly in the southern part of the country. Whether you choose a converted castle, Elizabethan manor, or neoclassical retreat, these are places to indulge yourself and escape, however briefly (most are pricey), most realities of modern life. Some hotels are traditional in style, with flowery fabrics and polished wood furniture; a newer breed juxtaposes modern design with the traditional architecture. At some hotels, spas and sports—and even, alas, meeting facilities—are becoming more elaborate, but service is less stuffy. If you can't spend a night, consider just having dinner; notable chefs are turning up in more hotel kitchens. In the Thames Valley, splurge at Cliveden or Coworth Park, dress up for dinner at Hartwell House, or indulge in French cuisine at Le Manoir aux Quat' Saisons. The West Country's concentration includes Bovey Castle and Gidleigh Park in Dartmoor National Park, and the Cotswolds are prime ground for these retreats. One tip: ask if a wedding party will be using the hotel during your stay; these can take over a smaller establishment.

Calcot Manor, Bath and the Cotswolds. Luxury and opulence join with family-friendly amenities at this Cotswolds retreat that mixes traditional and modern style.

Miller Howe, Lake District. Stunning views of Windermere, Arts and Crafts touches, and superior service are part of the appeal at this retreat.

Victoria at Holkham, East Anglia. In the shadow of stately Holkham Hall, this Eastern-inspired hideaway provides a colorful seaside escape.

FLAVORS OF ENGLAND

The New Food Scene

England has never lacked a treasure store of nature's bounty: lush green pastures, fruitful orchards, and the encompassing sea. Over the past few decades, dowdy images of English cooking have been sloughed off, and a new focus on the land and a new culinary confidence and expertise are exemplified by the popularity of celebrity chefs such as Rick Stein, Heston Blumenthal, Gordon Ramsay, and Jamie Oliver. The chefs are only one indicator of change: all over the country, artisanal food producers and talented cooks are indulging their passion for high-quality, locally sourced ingredients.

Food festivals, farmers' markets (some organic), and farm shops have sprung up in more cities and towns. Alongside the infiltration of supermarkets, much opposed by some people, comes a more discriminating attitude to food supplies. Outdoor-reared cows, sheep, and pigs; freshly caught fish; and seasonal fruits and vegetables provide a bedrock upon which traditional recipes are tempered with cosmopolitan influences. The contemporary English menu takes the best of Mediterranean and Asian cuisine and reinterprets it with new enthusiasm.

Natural Bounty

Meat. Peacefully grazing cattle, including Aberdeen Angus, Herefordshire, and Welsh Black varieties, are an iconic symbol of the English countryside. When hung and dry-aged for up to 28 days, this beef is at its most flavorsome. Spring lamb is succulent, and salt-marsh lamb from Wales and the Lake District, fed on wild grasses and herbs, makes for a unique taste. Outdoor-reared and rare breeds of pig, such as Gloucester Old Spot, often provide the breakfast bacon.

Game. In the fall and winter, pheasant, grouse, partridge, and venison are prominent on restaurant menus, served either roasted, in rich casseroles, or in pies. Duck (particularly the Gressingham and Aylesbury breeds), rabbit, and hare are available all year round.

Seafood. The traditional trio of cod, haddock, and plaice is still in evidence, but declining fishing stocks have brought other varieties to prominence. Hake, bream, freshwater trout, wild salmon, sardines, pilchards, and mackerel are on the restaurant table, along with crab, mussels, and oysters. The east and Cornish coasts are favored fishing grounds.

Dairy produce. The stalwart Cheddar, Cheshire, Double Gloucester, and Stilton cheeses are complemented by traditional and experimental cheeses from small, local makers. Some cheeses come wrapped in nettles or vine leaves, others stuffed with apricots, cranberries, or herbs. Dairies are producing more sheep and goat cheeses, yogurts, and ice creams.

Preserved foods. Marmalade is a fixed item on the breakfast menu, and a wide variety of jams, including the less usual quince, find their place to the teashop table. Chutneys made from apples or tomatoes mixed with onions and spices are served as an accompaniment to cheese, either at the end of a meal or as part of a pub lunch.

Cask ales. The increased interest in the provenance of food extends to beer, encouraging microbreweries to develop real or cask ales: beer that is unfiltered and unpasteurized, and that contains live brewer's yeast. The ales can be from kegs or bottles as well as casks, and they range from the pale amber, through fruity, to the full-bodied. The Casque Mark outside pubs signals their availability.

Traditional Dishes

Fish and chips. This number-one seaside favorite not only turns up in every seaside resort, but in fish-and-chip shops and restaurants throughout the land. Fish, usually cod, haddock, or plaice, is deep-fried in a crispy batter and served with thick french fries (chips) and, if eaten out, wrapped up in paper. The liberal sprinkling of salt and vinegar and "mushy" (processed) peas are optional.

Meat pies and pasties. Pies and pasties make a filling lunch. Perhaps the most popular is steak and kidney pie, combining chunks of lean beef and kidneys mixed with braised onions and mushrooms in a thick gravy, topped with a light puff- or short-pastry crust. Other combinations are chicken with mushrooms or leek and beef slow-cooked in ale (often Guinness). Cornish pasties are filled with beef, potato, rutabaga, and onions, all enveloped in a circle of pastry folded in half.

Shepherd's and cottage pie. Instead of a pastry crust, these classic pub dishes have a lightly browned mashed-potato topping over stewed minced meat and onions in a rich gravy. Shepherd's pie uses lamb, cottage pie beef.

Sausages. "Bangers and mash" are sausages with mashed potatoes and onion gravy; they are most commonly made with pork, but sometimes beef or lamb. The original Lincolnshire sausage consists of pork flavored with sage. Cumberland sausage comes in a long coil and has a peppery taste.

Black pudding. In this dish, associated with Lancashire, Yorkshire, and the Midlands, onions, pork fat, oatmeal, herbs and spices are blended with the blood from a pig. At its best this dish has a delicate, crumbly texture and can be served at breakfast or as a starter to a meal.

Meals Not to Be Missed

Full English breakfast. Setting you up for the rest of the day, the "full English" is a three-course affair. Starting with orange juice, cereals, porridge, yogurt or stewed fruit, it's followed by any combination of sausages, eggs, bacon, tomatoes, mushrooms, black pudding, baked beans, and fried bread. The feast finishes with toast and marmalade and tea or coffee. Less fattening alternatives to the fry-up are kippers, smoked haddock, or boiled eggs. Some cafés serve an all-day breakfast.

Ploughman's lunch. Crusty bread, English cheese (perhaps farmhouse Cheddar, blue Stilton, crumbly Cheshire, or waxy red Leicester), and tangy pickles with a side salad garnish make up a delicious light lunch, found in almost every pub.

Tea in the afternoon. Tea, ideally served in a country garden on a summer afternoon, ranks high in the list of England's must-have experiences. You may simply have a scone with your tea, or you can opt for a more ample feast: sandwiches made with wafer-thin slices of ham, smoked salmon or cucumber, scones with jam and clotted cream, and an array of homemade cakes served with properly brewed tea.

Roast dinners. On Sunday, the traditional roast dinner is still popular. The meat, either beef, pork, lamb, or chicken, is served with roast potatoes, carrots, seasonal green vegetables, and Yorkshire pudding, a savory batter baked in the oven until crisp, and then topped with a rich, dark, meaty gravy. Horseradish sauce and English mustard are on hand for beef; a mint sauce accompanies lamb.

ENGLAND LODGING PRIMER

If your England dreams involve staying in a cozy cottage with a tidy garden, here's some good news: you won't have to break the bank. Throughout the country, you'll find stylish lodging options—from good-value hotels and intimate bed-and-breakfasts to chic apartments and unique historic houses—in all price ranges.

For a price chart, resources and contacts, and information on hotel grading and booking, see Travel Smart England.

Hotels

England is a popular vacation destination, so be sure to reserve hotel rooms weeks (months for London) in advance. The country has everything from budget chain hotels to luxurious retreats in converted country houses. In many towns and cities you will find old inns that are former coaching inns, which served travelers as they journeyed around the country in horse-drawn carriages and stagecoaches.

Apartments and House Rentals

For a home base with cooking facilities and roomy enough for a family, consider renting furnished "flats" (the word for apartments in England). These are popular in cities and towns throughout the country and can save you money. They also provide more privacy than a hotel or B&B.

Cottages and other houses are available for weekly rental in all areas. These vary from quaint older homes to brand-new buildings in scenic surroundings. For families and large groups, they offer the best value-for-money accommodations, but because they are often in isolated locations, a car is vital. Living Architecture offers stays in one-of-a-kind architect-designed country houses. Lists of rental properties are available free of charge from VisitBritain. You may find discounts

of up to 50% on rentals during the off-season (October through March).

Bed-and-Breakfasts

A special English tradition, and the backbone of budget travel, B&Bs are usually in a family home. Typical prices (outside London) range from £45 to £100 a night. They vary in style and grace, but these days most have private bathrooms. B&Bs range from the ordinary to the truly elegant. Guesthouses are a slightly larger and sometimes more luxurious version of the same thing.

Some Tourist Information Centres in cities and towns can help you find and book a B&B even on the day you show up in town. There are also many private services. *For reservation services in London, see the Where to Stay section in Chapter 2.*

Farmhouses

Over the years farmhouses have become popular; their special appeal is the rural experience, whether in Cornwall or Yorkshire. Consider this option only if you are touring by car, since farmhouses may be in remote locations. Prices are generally reasonable. Ask VisitBritain for the booklet "Stay on a Farm" or contact Farm Stay UK. Regional tourist boards may have information as well.

Historic Buildings

Looking for a unique experience and want to spend your vacation in a Gothic banqueting house, an old lighthouse, or maybe in an apartment at Hampton Court Palace? Several organizations, such as the Landmark Trust, National Trust, English Heritage, and Vivat Trust, have specially adapted historic buildings to rent. Many of these have kitchens.

GREAT ITINERARIES

HIGHLIGHTS OF ENGLAND: UNFORGETTABLE IMAGES

12 days

London

Day 1. The capital is just the jumping-off point for this trip, so choose a few highlights that grab your interest. If it's the Changing of the Guard at Buckingham Palace, check the time to be sure you catch the pageantry. If Westminster Abbey appeals to your sense of history, arrive as early as you can. Pick a museum (many are free, so you needn't linger if you don't want to), whether it's the National Gallery on Trafalgar Square, the British Museum in Bloomsbury, or a smaller gem like the Queen's Gallery. Stroll Hyde Park or take a boat ride on the Thames before you find a pub or Indian restaurant for dinner. End with a play; the experience of theatergoing may be as interesting as whatever work you see.

Windsor

Day 2. Resplendent with centuries of treasures, Windsor Castle is favored by the Queen, and has been by rulers for centuries. Tour it to appreciate the history and wealth of the monarchy. The State Apartments are open if the Queen is not

in residence, and 10 kings and queens are buried in magnificent St. George's Chapel. Time permitting, take a walk in the adjacent Great Park. If you can splurge for a luxurious stay (versus making Windsor a day trip from London), head up the valley to Cliveden, the Thames Valley's most spectacular hotel.

Logistics: Trains from Paddington and Waterloo stations leave about twice hourly and take less than one hour. Green Line buses depart from the Colonnades opposite London's Victoria Coach Station.

Salisbury and Stourhead

Day 3. Visible for miles around, Salisbury Cathedral's soaring spire is an unforgettable image of rural England. See the Magna Carta in the cathedral's Chapter House as you explore this marvel of medieval engineering, and walk the town path to get the view John Constable painted. Pay an afternoon visit to Stourhead to experience the finest example of the naturalistic 18th-century landscaping for which England is famous; the grand Palladian mansion here is a bonus.

Logistics: For trains to Salisbury from Windsor Riverside, head back to London's Clapham Junction to catch a train on the Western England line.

Bath and Stonehenge

Day 4. Bath's immaculately preserved, golden-stone Georgian architecture helps you recapture the late 18th century. Take time to stroll; don't miss the Royal Crescent (No. 1 may be open, allowing you to view a period interior), and sip the Pump Room's vile-tasting water as Jane Austen's characters might have. The Roman Baths are an amazing remnant of the ancient empire, complete with curses left by soldiers. Today you can do as the Romans did as you relax in the warm mineral waters at the Thermae Bath Spa. There's plenty to do in Bath (museums, shopping, theater), but you might make an excursion to Stonehenge (by car or tour bus). Go early or late to avoid the worst crowds at Stonehenge, and use your imagination—and the good audio guide—to appreciate this enigma.

Logistics: Trains and buses leave hourly from Salisbury to Bath.

The Cotswolds

Day 5. Antiques-shop in fairy-tale Stow-on-the-Wold and feed the ducks at the brook in Lower Slaughter for a taste of the mellow stone villages and dreamy green landscapes for which the area is beloved. Choose a rainy or off-season day to visit Broadway or risk jams of tourist traffic. Another great experience is a walk on the Cotswold Way or any local path.

Logistics: Drive to make the best of the beautiful scenery. Alternatively, opt for a guided tour bus.

Oxford and Blenheim Palace

Day 6. Join a guided tour of Oxford's glorious quadrangles, chapels, and gardens to get the best access to these centuries-old academic treasures. This leaves time for a jaunt to Blenheim, a unique combination of baroque opulence (inside and out) and naturalistic parkland, the work of the great 18th-century landscape designer Capability Brown. For classic Oxford experiences, rent a punt or join students and go pub-crawling around town.

Logistics: Hourly trains depart from Bath for Oxford. Buses frequently depart from Oxford's Gloucester Green for Blenheim Palace.

Stratford-upon-Avon

Day 7. Skip this stop if you don't care about you-know-who. Fans of Shakespeare can see his birthplace and Anne Hathaway's Cottage (walking there is a delight), and then finish with a memorable performance at the Royal Shakespeare Company's magnificently renovated main stage. Start the day early and be prepared for crowds.

Logistics: From Oxford there are direct trains and more frequent Stagecoach bus service.

Shrewsbury to Chester

Day 8. Head north to see the half-timber buildings of Shrewsbury, one of the best preserved of England's Tudor towns. Strolling is the best way to experience it. In Chester the architecture is more or less the same (though not always authentic), but the Rows, a series of two-story shops with medieval crypts beneath, and the fine city walls are sights you can't pass by. You can walk part or all of the city walls for views of the town and surrounding area.

Logistics: For Shrewsbury, change trains at Birmingham. The train ride to Chester is 55 minutes.

The Lake District

Days 9 and 10. In the area extending north beyond Kendal and Windermere, explore the English lakes and beautiful surrounding mountains on foot in the Lake District

National Park. This area is jam-packed with hikers in summer and on weekends, so rent a car to seek out the more isolated routes. Take a cruise on Windermere or Coniston Water, or rent a boat, for another classic Lakeland experience. If you have time for one Wordsworth-linked site, head to Dove Cottage; you can even have afternoon tea there.

Logistics: Train to Liverpool, with a switch in either Windermere or Oxenholme.

York

Day 11. This historic cathedral city is crammed with 15th- and 16th-century buildings, but don't miss magnificent York Minster, with its stunning stained glass, and the medieval streets of the Shambles. Take your pick of the city's museums or spend time shopping; have tea at Betty's or unwind at a pub. The energetic can take a walk along the top of the several miles of city walls.

Logistics: By train, switch in Carlisle and Newcastle for the four-hour journey. Buses take twice as long.

Cambridge

Day 12. Spend the afternoon touring King's College Chapel and the Backs—gardens and sprawling meadows—and refining your punting skills on the River Cam. The excellent Fitzwilliam Museum, full of art and antiquities, is another option, as is the Polar Museum. To relax, join the students for a pint at one of the many pubs.

Logistics: For train service, switch at Leeds and again at Peterborough or Stevenage. Trains leave Cambridge for London frequently.

TIPS

❶ Train travelers should keep in mind that regional "Rovers" and "Rangers" offer unlimited train travel in one-day, three-day, or weeklong increments. See ⊕ *www.nationalrail. co.uk/promotions/* for details. Also check out BritRail passes, which must be purchased before your trip.

❷ Buses are time-consuming, but more scenic and cheaper than train travel. National Express offers discounts including fun fares—fares to and from London to various cities (including Cambridge) as low as £1 if booked more than 24 hours in advance. Or check out low-cost Megabus.

❸ To cut the tour short, consider skipping Chester and Shrewsbury and proceed to the Lake District from Stratford-upon-Avon on day eight. Likewise, you can consider passing up a visit to Cambridge if you opt for Oxford. You can add the time to your London stay.

❹ It's easy to visit Stonehenge from Salisbury, as well as from Bath, whether you have a car or want a guided excursion.

❺ Buy theater tickets well in advance for Stratford-upon-Avon.

GREAT ITINERARIES

STATELY HOMES AND LANDSCAPES TOUR

11 days

Hampton Court Palace

Day 1. Start your trip royally at this palace a half hour from London by train. It's two treasures in one: a Tudor palace with magnificent baroque additions by Christopher Wren. As you walk through cobbled courtyards, Henry VIII's State Apartments, and the enormous kitchens, you may feel as if you've been whisked back to the days of the Tudors and William and Mary. A quiet stroll through the 60 acres of immaculate gardens—the sculpted yews look like green gumdrops—is recommended. Be sure to get lost in the 18th-century maze—if it's open (diligent maintenance leads to occasional closures). It's easy to spend a whole day here, so start early.

Logistics: Tube to Richmond, then Bus R68; or catch the train from Waterloo to Hampton Court Station.

Knole and Ightham Mote

Days 2 and 3. Clustered around Royal Tunbridge Wells south of London is the highest concentration of stately homes in England, and, as if that weren't enough, the surrounding fields and colorful orchards are often wrapped in clouds of mist, creating a picture-perfect scene. We've picked two very different homes to visit, leaving you plenty of time to tour at a leisurely pace. Knole, Vita Sackville-West's sprawling childhood home, has dark, baroque rooms and a famous set of silver furniture. Ightham Mote, a smaller, moated house, is a vision from the Middle Ages. Its rooms are an ideal guide to style changes from the Tudor to Victorian eras. Spend the evening at one of the many good restaurants in Royal Tunbridge Wells.

Logistics: Take the Hastings-bound train from London's Charing Cross to Tunbridge Wells, then the bus to Knole. There is no public transportation to Ightham Mote.

Petworth House

Day 4. Priceless paintings by Gainsborough, Reynolds, and Turner (19 by Turner alone) embellish the august rooms of Petworth House, present-day home to Lord and Lady Egremont and one of the National Trust's treasures. Check out Capability Brown's 700-acre deer park or the Victorian kitchens, and for the perfect lunch, peruse the offerings in the winding lanes of Petworth town. Head to Chichester for the evening, along a route passing through the rolling grasslands and deep valleys of the South Downs.

Logistics: Train to Chichester, switching in Redhill, then bus to Petworth.

Wilton House

Day 5. Base yourself in Salisbury for two days, taking time to see the famous cathedral with its tall spire and to walk the town path for the best view of it. Visit neoclassical Wilton House first, where the exquisite Double Cube Room contains a spectacular family portrait by Van Dyck and gilded furniture that accommodated Eisenhower when he contemplated the Normandy invasion here. On your way back make a detour to Stonehenge to view the wide-open Salisbury Plain and ponder the enigmatic stones.

Logistics: Take a train from Chichester to Salisbury, with a switch in Cosham; then bus it to Wilton House.

Stourhead to Longleat House

Day 6. Day-trip west from Salisbury to Stourhead, to experience perhaps the most stunning house-garden combination in the country, and either spend the day here (climb Alfred's Tower for a grand view of the house) or leave some time for nearby Longleat House—a vast, treasure-stuffed Italian Renaissance palace complete with safari park and a devilish maze. If you want to see the safari park, you'll need plenty of time here. Once back in Salisbury, relax in one of New Street's many cafés.

Logistics: Bus to Warminster for Longleat; for Stourhead, take the train to Gillingham from Salisbury.

Blenheim Palace

Day 7. Home of the dukes of Marlborough and birthplace of Winston Churchill, Blenheim Palace uniquely combines exquisitely designed parklands (save time to walk) and one of the most ornate baroque structures in the world. After your visit, have afternoon tea at Blenheim Tea Rooms in the adorable village of Woodstock. Overnight in Oxford; do your own pub crawl.

Logistics: From Salisbury, change at Bath or Basingstoke for Oxford, then catch a bus to Blenheim.

Snowshill Manor and Sudeley Castle

Days 8 and 9. Here you can take in the idyllic Cotswold landscape, a magical mix of greenery and mellow stone cottages and ancient churches (built with wool-trade money), along with some famous buildings. Spend the first night in Broadway to explore nearby Snowshill Manor—with its delightfully eccentric collection of Tibetan scrolls, Persian lamps, and samurai armor—in the unspoiled village of Snowshill. If you have a car, don't linger in busy Broadway. Instead, head to Chipping Campden, one of the best-preserved Cotswolds villages, which nestles in a secluded valley. Move to another charming town, Winchcombe, on the second day. Take a stroll past honey-color stone cottages and impeccably well-kept gardens. Visit Sudeley Castle, once home to Catherine Parr (Henry VIII's last wife), a Tudor-era palace with romantic gardens (only a few rooms are now open to the public). Another option near Winchcombe is Stanway House, a Jacobean manor owned by Lord Neidpath; hours are limited, but this timeworn home and its gabled gatehouse is typically English.

Logistics: Take a train from Oxford to Moreton-in-Marsh for Broadway; from Broadway, walk to Snowshill Manor; for Sudeley Castle, take a bus from Broadway to Winchcombe, then walk.

Chatsworth House, Haddon Hall, and Hardwick Hall

Days 10 and 11. For the final stops, head north, east of Manchester, to a more dramatic landscape. In or near the craggy Peak District, where the gentle slopes of the Pennine Hills begin their ascent to Scotland, are three of England's most renowned historic homes. Base yourself in Bakewell, and spend your first day taking in the art treasures amassed by the dukes of Devonshire at Chatsworth House. The gardens, grounds, shops, and farmyard exhibits make it easy to spend a day here. If you have any time left over, get out of Bakewell and take a walk in the hills of the Peak District National Park (maps are available at the town's tourist information center).

On the second day, devote the morning to the crenellations and boxy roofs of medieval Haddon Hall, a quintessentially English house. Give your afternoon to Hardwick Hall, an Elizabethan stone mansion with a facade that is "more glass than wall"—a truly innovative idea in the 16th century. Its collections of period tapestries and embroideries are remarkable reminders of the splendor of the age.

Logistics: Take a train back to Oxford and then up to Manchester for the connection to Buxton; then catch a bus to Bakewell.

London

WORD OF MOUTH

"Do you know about the Ceremony of the Keys at the Tower of London? Tickets are free, and attendees are limited to a small group. Check out www.hrp.org.uk in advance. It is a very authentic ceremony they do every evening at sunset to lock up the Tower. They explain it as they go."

—PeaceOut

WELCOME TO LONDON

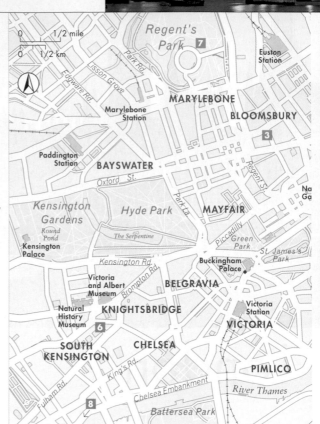

TOP REASONS TO GO

★ **The abbey and the cathedral:** The pillars of Westminster Abbey stand around the final resting place of the people who built Britain. To the east, St. Paul's Cathedral takes the breath away.

★ **Buckingham Palace:** Not the prettiest royal residence, but a must-see for the glimpse it affords of modern royal life. The Queen's Gallery is next door.

★ **Tower of London:** The Tower is London at its majestic, idiosyncratic best. This is the heart of the kingdom, with foundations dating back nine centuries.

★ **Museum marvels:** The National Gallery has old masters, the Tate Modern the latest thing. Treasures from around the globe fill the British Museum. These are just a few top museums.

★ **A city of villages:** London has dozens of neighborhoods, bursting with life. Parks, shops, pubs: walk around and make the city your own.

1 Westminster and Royal London. This is the place to embrace the "tourist" label. Snap pictures of the mounted Horse Guards, play with the pigeons in Trafalgar Square, and visit stacks of art in the national galleries. It's well worth braving the crowds to wander ancient Westminster Abbey and its historic bounty.

2 Soho and Covent Garden. More sophisticated than seedy these days, the heart of London puts Theaterland, strip joints, Chinatown, and the trendiest of film studios side by side. Nearby Charing Cross Road is a bibliophile's dream; hectic hordes fill Leicester Square, London's answer to Times Square.

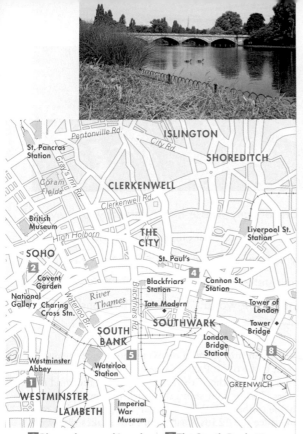

GETTING ORIENTED

London grew from a wooden bridge built over the Thames in the year AD 43 to its current 600 square mi and 7 million souls in haphazard fashion, meandering from its two official centers: Westminster, seat of government and royalty, to the west, and the City, site of finance and commerce, to the east. In this city of urban villages, the neighborhoods continue to evolve. If the city's great parks such as Hyde Park are, in Lord Chatham's phrase, "the lungs of London," then the River Thames remains its backbone.

3 Bloomsbury and Legal London. The literary and left-wing set that made Bloomsbury world famous has left its mark, and the area remains the heart of brainy London. Stop for a good while in the incomparable British Museum.

4 The City. London's Wall Street might be the oldest part of the capital, but thanks to futuristic skyscrapers and a sleek Millennium Bridge, it looks like the newest. Fans of ages gone by won't be disappointed, however: head for St. Paul's Cathedral, Tower Bridge, and the Tower of London.

5 The South Bank. The Royal National Theatre and Royal Festival Hall, the National Film Theatre, Shakespeare's Globe, and the Tate Modern make this area a creative hub. Take it all in from the London Eye.

6 Kensington, Knightsbridge, and Mayfair. The museums are awe-inspiring; the Science Museum and the Natural History Museum are the most fun for children. Flash your cash at Harrods and Harvey Nichols..

7 Regent's Park and Hampstead. London becomes noticeably calmer and greener as you head north from Oxford Street. This area will provide a taste of how laid-back (moneyed) Londoners can be.

8 Up and Down the Thames. The quaint Thames-side streets of Greenwich have some brilliant sights, Christopher Wren architecture, and the Greenwich Meridian Line. Other excursions include Kew Gardens and Hampton Court Palace.

Updated by Astrid deRidder, Damian Harper, Julius Honnor, Erin Huebscher, Jack Jewers, Michelle Rosenberg, Ellin Stein, and Alex Wijeratna

London is an ancient city whose history greets you at every turn; it's also one of the coolest cities in the world. If the city contained only its famous landmarks—the Tower of London, Big Ben, Westminster Abbey, Buckingham Palace—it would still rank as one of the world's top cities. But London is so much more.

To gain a sense of its continuity, stand on Waterloo Bridge at sunset. To the east, the great globe of St. Paul's Cathedral glows golden in the fading sunlight as it has since the 17th century, still majestic amid the modern glass towers. To the west stand the mock-medieval ramparts of Westminster, home to the "Mother of Parliaments," which has met here or hereabouts since the 1250s. Past them both snakes the swift, dark Thames, which flowed past the Roman settlement of Londinium nearly 2,000 years ago.

The city beckons with great museums, royal pageantry, and history-steeped houses. There's no other place like it in its medley of styles, in its mixture of the green loveliness of parks and the modern gleam of neon. Modern-day London largely reflects its tangled medieval layout. Even Londoners, most of whom own a dog-eared copy of an indispensable A–Z street finder, get lost in their own city.

You should not only visit St. Paul's Cathedral and the Tower of London, but also set aside some time for random wandering; the city repays every moment spent exploring on foot. Walk in the city's backstreets and mews, around Park Lane and Kensington. Pass up Buckingham Palace for Kensington Palace. Take in the National Gallery, but don't forget London's "time machine" museums, such as the 19th-century home of Sir John Soane. Abandon the city's chain stores for its wonderful markets.

Today the city's art, style, fashion, and dining scenes, not to mention its financial muscle, make headlines around the world. London's chefs have become superstars. Its fashion designers have conquered Paris, avant-garde artists have caused waves at the Royal Academy of Arts, the raging after-hours scene is packed with music mavens ready to catch the Next Big Thing, and the theater continues its tradition of radical, shocking productions. In 2012, the city is hosting the summer Olympics and the Queen's Diamond Jubilee.

Then there's that greatest living link with the past—the Royal Family. Don't let the tag of "typical tourist destination" stop you from enjoying the pageantry of the Windsors: the Changing of the Guard, at Buckingham Palace and at Whitehall, is one of the greatest free shows in the world.

Be prepared to be taken by surprise. The great 18th-century author Samuel Johnson said that a man who is tired of London is tired of life. Armed with energy and curiosity, you can find, to quote Dr. Johnson again, "in London all that life can afford."

LONDON PLANNER

WHEN TO GO
The heaviest tourist season runs mid-April through mid-October, with another peak around Christmas—though the tide never really ebbs. Spring is the time to see the royal London parks and gardens at their freshest; fall to enjoy near-ideal exploring conditions. In late summer, be warned: air-conditioning is rarely found in places other than department stores, modern restaurants, hotels, and cinemas in London, although it's really needed for only a few days. Winter can be rather dismal, but all the theaters, concerts, and exhibitions go full speed ahead.

Avoid the February and October "half-terms" when schools in the capital take a break for a week and nearly all attractions are flooded by children. Arriving at the start of August can be a very busy time, and the weather makes Tube travel a nightmare. Shopping in central London the week before Christmas is an idea best left only to desperate Londoners who have forgotten to buy presents.

In 2012 the Olympics will be held in London from July 27 to August 12. Expect the city to be unusually crowded, with hotel rooms at a premium and various roads closed. There will also be crowds during the Queen's Diamond Jubilee celebrations during the first weekend in June.

GETTING HERE AND AROUND

ADDRESSES
Central London and its surrounding districts are divided into 32 boroughs—33, counting the City of London. More useful for finding your way around, however, are the subdivisions of London into postal districts. The first one or two letters give the location: N means north, NW means northwest, etc.

AIR TRAVEL
For information about airports and airport transfers, see Getting Here and Around in Travel Smart England.

BUS TRAVEL
Buses, or "coaches," as privately operated bus services are known here, operate mainly from London's Victoria Coach Station to more than 1,200 major towns and cities. *For information, see Getting Here and Around in Travel Smart England.*

In central London, Transport for London (TfL) buses are traditionally bright red double- and single-deckers. Not all buses run the full length of their route at all times, so check with the driver. In central London you must purchase tickets from machines at bus stops along the routes before you board. The main bus stops have a red TfL symbol on a white background. When the word "Request" is written across the sign, you must flag the bus down. Buses are a good way to see the town, but don't take one if you're in a hurry.

A flat-rate fare of £2 applies for all bus fares. If you buy a one-day Travelcard for Tube, bus and train, it covers all journeys. You can also get an Oystercard, an electronic smart card that you load with money, which is then deducted each time you use the card on buses or the Tube: a single fare is £1.30. A 7-Day Bus Pass for zones 1 through 4 is £17.80 but must be bought before boarding from one of the machines at bus stops, most newsagents, or underground stations. Children ages 11–15 travel free on buses as long as they order an Oystercard at least four weeks before they travel.

Traveling without a valid ticket makes you liable for an on-the-spot fine (£50, £25 if paid within three weeks), or you can be charged with a criminal offense. For more information, there are Transport for London Travel Information Centres at the following Tube stations: Euston, Liverpool Street, Piccadilly Circus, Victoria, and Heathrow. Most are open in daytime only.

Night Buses can prove helpful for travel in London from 11 pm to 5 am—these buses add the prefix "N" to their route numbers. You may have to transfer at one of the Night Bus nexuses: Victoria, Westminster, and either Piccadilly Circus or Trafalgar Square. For safety reasons, avoid sitting alone on the top deck of a Night Bus.

Contact Transport for London (☎ 020/7222–1234 ⊕ www.tfl.gov.uk).

CAR TRAVEL

The major approach roads to London are six-lane motorways. Motorways (from Heathrow, M4; from Gatwick, M23 to M25, then M3; Stansted, M11) are usually the faster option for getting in and out of town, although rush-hour traffic is horrendous. Stay tuned to local radio stations for updates.

The simple advice about driving in London is: don't. The city never had a central street plan, and the result is a chaotic winding mass, made no easier by the one-way street systems. During the Olympics there will be lane restrictions and traffic diversions, so driving will be even trickier. If you must drive, remember to drive on the left and stick to the speed limit (30 mph on most city streets, 20 mph near schools and in some residential areas).

A "congestion charge" is levied on all vehicles entering central London (bounded by the Inner Ring Road and "C" road markings note the area) on weekdays from 7 am to 6 pm, excluding bank holidays. You can pay up to 90 days in advance, or by midnight on the day of travel (£10) or by midnight on the following day (£12). You can pay by phone, mail, or Internet, or at retail outlets (look for signs), except for following day payments, which can only be paid via the Web site or call center. There are no tollbooths; cameras monitor the area. The penalty for not paying is stiff: £120 (£60 if paid within two weeks). For current information, check ⊕ *www.cclondon.com.*

TAXI TRAVEL
Taxis are expensive, but if you're with several people they can be practical. Hotels and main tourist areas have taxi ranks; you can also hail taxis on the street. If the yellow "For Hire" sign is lighted on top, the taxi is available. Drivers often cruise at night with their signs unlighted, so if you see an unlighted cab, keep your hand up. Generally fares start at £2.20 for the first minute and increase by units of 20p, and then increase at varying amounts depending on time of day, distance traveled, and taxi speed. Surcharges are added around Christmas and New Year's days. Fares also go up between 10 pm and 6 am. Tips are extra, usually 10% to 15% per ride. The average cost for a journey within central London is £10.70.

TRAIN TRAVEL
London has eight major train stations, each serving a different area of the country, all accessible by Underground or bus. Trains are operated by a number of private companies, but National Rail Enquiries acts as a central rail information number. *For further information on train travel, see Getting Here and Around in Travel Smart England.*

Contact National Rail Enquiries (☎ 0845/748–4950 ⊕ www.nationalrail.co.uk).

UNDERGROUND (TUBE) TRAVEL
London's extensive Underground (Tube) system has color-coded routes, clear signs, and extensive connections. Trains run out into the suburbs, and all stations are marked with the London Underground circular symbol. (In Britain, the word "subway" means "pedestrian underpass.") Some lines have branches (Central, District, Northern, Metropolitan, and Piccadilly), so be sure to note which branch is needed for your destination. Electronic platform signs tell you the final stop and route of the next train and how many minutes until it arrives. London is divided into six concentric zones (ask at Underground ticket booths for a map and booklet, which give details of the ticket options). Tube fares are determined by how many zones the journey covers and whether it includes the most expensive central Zone 1. The more zones your trip crosses, the higher the fare. Most tourist sights are within Zone 1, but some are not—Kew Gardens, for example, is in Zone 4. If you travel into a zone for which you do not have the right ticket, you can purchase an "extension" to your own ticket at the ticket office by the barriers. This usually costs a pound, and merely equalizes your fare. Buy an Oystercard (*see Bus Travel*) for fare reductions; it is a huge money-saver, since for single fares a flat fee of £4 applies across all six zones, even if you're traveling one stop.

If you're traveling on the Tube as well as the bus, consider an off-peak one-day Travelcard (£6.60 for zones 1 and 2, more for farther zones), which allows unrestricted travel on buses *and* Tubes after 9:30 am and all day on weekends and national holidays. "Peak" Travelcards—those for use before 9:30 am—are more expensive (£8.00 for zones 1 and 2, more for farther zones). Children under 11 travel free on the tube and buses after 9:30 am.

The tube begins running just after 5 am Monday through Saturday; the last services leave central London between midnight and 12:30 am. On Sunday, trains start two hours later and finish about an hour earlier. Normally you should not have to wait more than 10 minutes in central areas. Lines may be closed or partially suspended for engineering works on weekends, especially in the run-up to the Olympics—check the TfL Web site or boards in stations. Most tube stations are not accessible for people with disabilities. Travelers with disabilities should get the free leaflet "Access to the Underground," which lists the stations that are.

Contact Transport for London (☎ 020/7222–1234 ⊕ www.tfl.gov.uk).

DISCOUNTS AND DEALS

All national collections (such as the Natural History Museum, Science Museum, Victoria & Albert Museum) are free, a real bargain for museumgoers. The London Pass, a smart card, offers entry to more than 50 top attractions, such as museums and tours on boats and buses. The charge is £43 for one day, which drops to £15.60 per day for those with weekly passes. The London Pass is available by phone, online, or from the Britain Visitor Centre and Tourist Information Centre branches. *For other discounts, see Sightseeing Passes in Essentials in Travel Smart England.*

Contact London Pass (☎ 0870/242–9988, 0166/448–5020 from U.S. ⊕ www.londonpass.com).

TOUR OPTIONS
BOAT TOURS

The Thames Clippers commuter river service stops at 10 piers between the London Eye/Waterloo and Greenwich, with peak-time extensions to Putney in the west and Woolwich Arsenal in the east. The Waterloo–Woolwich commuter service runs every 20 minutes from 6 am–1 am on weekdays, 8:30 am–midnight on weekends. Tickets are £5.50, with discounts for Oystercard and Travelcard holders. There is also a special Tate-to-Tate express, a 20-minute trip between Tate Modern and Tate Britain that costs £5. Boats run every 40 minutes from 10 to 5. A £12.60 River Roamer ticket offers unlimited river travel from 10 to 10 weekdays and 8 am–10 pm on weekends.

Year-round, but more frequently from April to October, sightseeing cruises leave from central London piers going downstream to the Thames Barrier via Canary Wharf and upstream to Hampton Court (mainly in summer). Most launches seat between 100 and 250 passengers, and provide a commentary on points of interest. River trips may last from one to four hours. A £14.50 River Rover ticket combines one-day DLR travel with hop-on, hop-off travel on City Cruises riverboats between Westminster, Waterloo, Tower, and Greenwich piers.

The tranquil side of London can be found on narrow boats that cruise the city's two canals, the Grand Union and Regent's Canal; most vessels operate on the latter, which runs between Little Venice in the west (nearest Tube: Warwick Avenue on the Bakerloo Line) and Camden Lock (about 200 yards north of Camden Town Tube station). Fares start at £9 for 1½-hour round-trip cruises.

Contacts **Bateaux London** (☎ *020/7695–1800* ⊕ *www.bateauxlondon.com*).
Canal Cruises (☎ *0208/440–8962* ⊕ *www.londoncanalcruises.com*). **Jason's
Trip (Regent's Canal)** (☎ *020/7286–3428* ⊕ *www.jasons.co.uk*). **London Duck
Tours** (☎ *0207/928-3132* ⊕ *www.londonducktours.co.uk*). **London River Services** (☎ *0207/930–4097* ⊕ *www.tfl.gov.uk*). **Thames Clippers** (☎ *0870/781–
5049* ⊕ *www.thamesclippers.com*). **Thames Cruises** (☎ *0207/928–9009*
⊕ *www.thamescruises.com*). **Thames River Boats** (☎ *0207/930–2062*
⊕ *www.wpsa.co.uk*). **Thames River Services** (☎ *0207/930–4097*
⊕ *www.thamesriverservices.co.uk*).

BUS TOURS

Guided sightseeing tours in double-decker buses, which are open-top in
summer, are a good introduction to the city, as they cover all the main
central sights. Numerous companies run daily bus tours that depart
(usually starting between 8:30 and 9 am) from central points. You
may board or alight at any stop, and reboard on the next bus. Tickets,
purchased from the driver, are good all day. Prices vary according to
the tour, although £23 is the benchmark.

Green Line, Evan Evans, and National Express offer day excursions by
bus to places within easy reach of London, such as Hampton Court,
Oxford, Stratford, and Bath.

Contacts **Big Bus Tours** (☎ *0207/233–9533* ⊕ *www.bigbustours.com*). **Evan
Evans** (☎ *0207/950–1777, 800/422–9022 in U.S.* ⊕ *www.evanevans.co.uk*).
Green Line (☎ *0844/801–7261* ⊕ *www.greenline.co.uk*). **National Express**
(☎ *0871/781–8181* ⊕ *www.nationalexpress.com*). **Original London Sightseeing Tour** (☎ *0208/877–1722* ⊕ *www.theoriginaltour.com*).

PRIVATE GUIDES

Black Taxi Tour of London is a personal tour by cab direct from your
hotel. The price is per cab, so the fare can be shared among as many
as five people. An introductory two-hour tour is £100 by day, £110 by
night. You can hire a Blue Badge–accredited guide (trained by the tourist
board) for walking or driving tours.

Contacts **Black Taxi Tour of London** (☎ *020/7935–9363*
⊕ *www.blacktaxitours.co.uk*). **Blue Badge tour guides** (☎ *020/7403–1115*
⊕ *www.blue-badge-guides.com*).

WALKING TOURS

One of the best ways to get to know London is on foot. If horror and mystery are your interest, try walks with a Jack the Ripper or ghost theme,
or Blood and Tears walks (not suitable for younger children). Other
themed tours include Secret London, The Beatles, Sherlock Holmes,
Gandhi, Dickens—you name it. Context London's expert docents lead
small groups on walks with art, architecture, and similar themes. London Walks hosts more than 100 walks every week on themes, including
a Thames pub walk, Literary Bloomsbury, and Spies and Spycatchers.

Contacts **Blood and Tears Walk** (☎ *07905/746-733* ⊕ *www.shockinglondon.
com*). **Context London** (☎ *020/193-9158, 800/691-6036 in U.S.*
⊕ *www.contexttravel.com/london*). **London Discovery Tours** (☎ *0208/530–
8443* ⊕ *www.discovery-walks.com*). **London Walks** (☎ *0207/624–3978*

⊕ www.walks.com). **Shakespeare City Walk** (☎ 07905/746733
⊕ www.shakespeareguide.com).

VISITOR INFORMATION

You can get good information at the Travel Information Centres at Victoria Station and St. Pancras International train station. These are helpful if you're looking for brochures for London sights, or if something's gone wrong with your hotel reservation—as they have a useful reservations service. There are also Travel Information Centres at Euston and Liverpool Street train stations, Heathrow Airport, and Piccadilly Circus. The Britain and London Visitor Centre is a worthwhile stop for travel, hotel, and entertainment information. There are Tourist Information Centres for the City of London, Greenwich, and various outer boroughs of London. London & Partners, the city's tourist board, has a helpful Web site, ⊕ *www.visitlondon.com*, with links to other sites; you can also book a hotel on the site. The London 2012 Web site has Olympics-related information from transportation to tickets.

Information Britain and London Visitor Centre (✉ 1 Regent St., Piccadilly Circus, Piccadilly ☎ 0870/156-6366 ⊕ www.visitlondon.com). **King's Cross/ St. Pancras Travel Information Centre** (✉ LUL Western Ticket Hall, Euston Rd., King's Cross ☎ No phone). **London & Partners** (⊕ www.visitlondon.com). **London Olympics 2012** (☎ 0845/267–2012 ⊕ www.london2012.com). **Victoria Station Travel Information Centre** (✉ Opposite Platform 8, Victoria Station Forecourt, Victoria ☎ No phone).

EXPLORING LONDON

Westminster and the City contain many of the grand buildings that have played a central role in British history: the Tower of London and St. Paul's Cathedral, Westminster Abbey and the Houses of Parliament, Buckingham Palace, and the older royal palace of St. James's.

Within a few minutes' walk of Buckingham Palace lie St. James's and Mayfair, neighboring quarters of elegant town houses built for the nobility during the 17th and early 18th centuries and now notable for shopping opportunities. Westminster Abbey's original vegetable patch (or convent garden), which became the site of London's first square, Covent Garden, is now a popular stop.

Hyde Park and Kensington Gardens, preserved by past kings and queens for their own hunting and relaxation, create a swath of parkland across the city center. A walk across Hyde Park brings you to the museum district of South Kensington, with the Natural History Museum, the Science Museum, and the Victoria & Albert Museum. The South Bank has many cultural highlights: the theaters of the South Bank Centre, the Tate Modern, and the reconstruction of Shakespeare's Globe theater. The London Eye observation wheel here gives stunning city views, or you can walk across the Millennium or Hungerford Bridge. Farther downstream is the gorgeous 17th- and 18th-century symmetry of Greenwich, and its maritime attractions.

A classic photo op: don't miss the cavalry from the Queen's Life Guard at Buckingham Palace.

WESTMINSTER AND ROYAL LONDON

If you have time to visit only one part of London, this is it. Westminster and Royal London might be called "London for Beginners." If you went no farther than these few acres, you would have seen many of the famous sights, from the Houses of Parliament, Big Ben, Westminster Abbey, and Buckingham Palace, to two of the world's greatest art collections, in the National and Tate Britain galleries. You can truly call this area Royal London, since it is bounded by the triangle of streets that make up the route that the Queen usually takes when journeying from Buckingham Palace to Westminster Abbey or to the Houses of Parliament on state occasions. The three points on this royal triangle are Trafalgar Square, Westminster, and Buckingham Palace. Naturally, in an area that regularly sees the pomp and pageantry of royal occasions, the streets are wide and the vistas long. This is concentrated sightseeing, so pace yourself. For a large part of the year, much of Royal London is floodlighted at night, adding to the theatricality of the experience.

GETTING HERE   Trafalgar Square—easy to access and smack dab in the center of the action—is a good place to start. Take the Tube to Embankment (District and Circle lines) and walk north until you cross the Strand, or alight at Charing Cross (Bakerloo, Jubilee, and Northern lines), where the Northumberland Avenue exit deposits you on the southeast corner of the Square.

PLANNING
YOUR TIME   You could spend a lifetime absorbing the rich history of this part of London. More practically, try to leave at least two days if you want to dip into the full gamut of attractions without feeling horribly rushed. If Royal London is what you want, make a day of Buckingham Palace

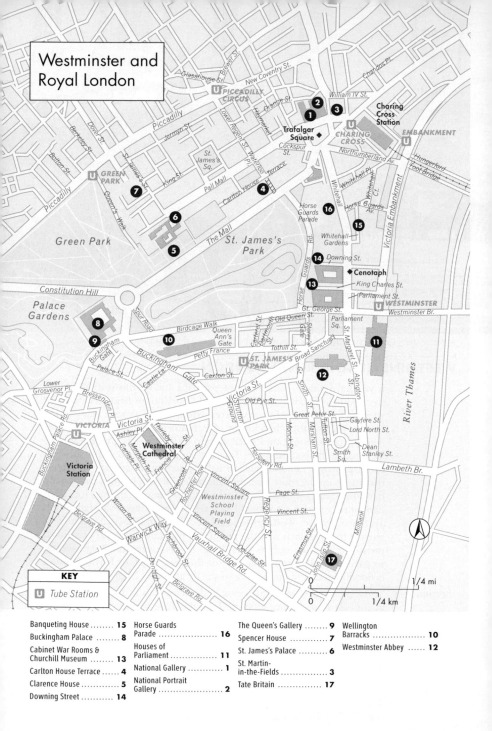

Westminster and Royal London

Green Park

St. James's Park

Palace Gardens

Trafalgar Square

Cenotaph

Westminster Cathedral

Victoria Station

River Thames

Westminster School Playing Field

KEY

U *Tube Station*

0   1/4 mi

0   1/4 km

or Westminster Abbey, the Queen's Gallery, and the Guards Museum at Wellington Barracks. If you've a more constitutional bent, visit the Houses of Parliament and the Cabinet War Rooms.

TOP ATTRACTIONS

Fodor'sChoice
★
Buckingham Palace. It's rare to get a chance to see how the other half—well, other minute fraction—lives and works. But when the Queen heads off to Scotland on her annual summer holiday (you can tell because the Union Jack flies above the palace instead of the Royal Standard), the palace's 19 State Rooms open up to visitors (although the north wing's private apartments remain behind closed doors). With fabulous gilt moldings and walls adorned with masterpieces by Rembrandt, Rubens, and other old masters, the State Rooms are the grandest of the palace's 775 rooms.

Inside the palace, the **Grand Hall,** followed by the **Grand Staircase** and **Guard Room,** gives a taste of what's to follow: marble, gold leaf galore, and massive, twinkling chandeliers. Don't miss the theatrical **Throne Room,** with the original 1953 coronation throne, or the sword in **The Ballroom,** used by the Queen to bestow knighthoods and other honors. Royal portraits line the **State Dining Room,** and the **Blue Drawing Room** is splendor in overdrive. The alabaster-and-gold plasterwork of the **White Drawing Room** is a suitable crescendo on which to end the tour.

The **Changing of the Guard,** also known as **Guard Mounting,** remains one of London's best free shows and culminates in front of the palace. Marching to live bands, the old guard proceeds up the Mall from St. James's Palace to Buckingham Palace. Shortly afterward, the new guard approaches from Wellington Barracks. Then within the forecourt, the captains of the old and new guards symbolically transfer the keys to the palace. ■TIP➜ Get there by 10:30 am to grab a spot in the best viewing section at the gate facing the palace, since most of the hoopla takes place behind the railings in the forecourt. ⊠ *Buckingham Palace Rd., St. James* ☏ *020/7766–7300* ⊕ *www.royalcollection.org.uk* ☉ *Late July–late Sept., daily 9:45–6 (last admission 3:45); times subject to change; check Web site before visiting* ⊡ *£17* Ⓤ *Victoria, St. James's Park, Green Park.*

Ⓒ
★
Cabinet War Rooms & Churchill Museum. It was from this small warren of underground rooms—beneath the vast government buildings of the Treasury—that Winston Churchill and his team directed troops in World War II. Designed to be bombproof, the whole complex has been preserved almost exactly as it was when the last light was turned off at the end of the war. Every clock shows almost 5 pm, and the furniture, fittings, and paraphernalia of a busy, round-the-clock war office are in situ, down to the colored map pins.

An absorbing addition to the Cabinet War Rooms is the **Churchill Museum,** a tribute to the stirring politician and defiant wartime icon. Different zones explore his life and achievements—and failures, too—through objects and documents, many of which, such as his personal papers, had never previously been made public. ⊠ *Clive Steps, King Charles St., Westminster* ☏ *020/7930–6961* ⊕ *www.iwm.org.uk* ⊡ *£14.95, includes audio tour* ☉ *Daily 9:30–6; last admission 5; disabled access* Ⓤ *Westminster.*

GREAT ITINERARIES

London overflows with choices: from exploring local pubs and tearooms to taking in great theater and concerts, it's easy to fill a day. A stroll through a quiet neighborhood or a ride on the Thames may be as satisfying as seeing a world-famous museum. Below are suggestions for different experiences.

CROWNING GLORIES

This regal runaround packs more into a day than most cities can offer in a week. Hit Westminster Abbey early to avoid the crowds, then cut through St. James's Park to catch the Changing of the Guard at 11:20 at Buckingham Palace. Take a quick detour to the Tudor delights of St. James's Palace, before a promenade down the Mall past the Regency glory of Carlton House Terrace and through Admiralty Arch to Trafalgar Square. Choose from the treasures of the National Gallery, the Who's Who of the National Portrait Gallery, or a brass rubbing in the crypt of St. Martin's-in-the-Fields. This leaves a stroll down Whitehall—past Downing Street, Horse Guards Parade, and Banqueting House—to the Houses of Parliament, where you have the option of prebooking a tour, or trying to get in to see a debate. If you have any time or energy left, stroll through Hyde Park to Kensington Palace, childhood home of Queen Victoria, and (for aspiring princesses everywhere) the Royal Dress Collection.

MUSEUM MAGIC

London has one of the finest collections of museums in the world, and many are free. Some resemble hands-on playgrounds that will keep children and adults amused for hours; others take a more classical approach. One of the latter is the British Museum in Bloomsbury, an Aladdin's cave of treasures from across the world. While in the area, pop into the nearby museum of architect Sir John Soane.

Alternatively, South Kensington's "Museum Mile" on Cromwell Road houses a triple-whammy that makes for a substantial day's-worth of diversion: the Victoria & Albert Museum, the Natural History Museum, and the Science Museum.

RETAIL THERAPY

It's not hard to shop 'til you drop in London's West End. Start with the upscale on New Bond Street, an awesome sweep of expense and elegance. In the afternoon, head to Oxford Street, which encompasses four Tube stations and is unbeatable for mass-market shopping. Run the gauntlet of designers, cheap odds and ends, department stores, and ferocious pedestrians: it's seriously busy.

A more sedate but utterly fashionable experience can be found in Knightsbridge, wandering between Harvey Nichols and Harrods department stores. Head south down Sloane Street to Sloane Square and head out along King's Road, with boutiques galore. To dip into the ever-expanding world of urban chic, try an afternoon in the lively Portobello street market in Notting Hill, where you can pick up remnants of various bygone ages: glassware, furniture, art, and clothes.

Horse Guards Parade. Once the tilt-yard of Whitehall Palace, where jousting tournaments were held, the Horse Guards Parade is now notably mainly for the annual Trooping the Colour ceremony, in which the Queen takes the salute, her official birthday tribute, on the second Saturday in June. (Like Paddington Bear, the Queen has two birthdays; her real one is on April 21.) At the Whitehall facade of Horse Guards, the changing of two mounted sentries known as the **Queen's Life Guard** provides what may be London's most popular photo opportunity. The ceremony lasts about half an hour. ⊠ *Whitehall, Whitehall* ☎ *020/7930–4832* ⊙ *Changing of the Queen's Life Guard at 11 am Mon.–Sat. and 10 am Sun.; inspection of the Queen's Life Guard daily at 4 pm* Ⓤ *Westminster.*

> **A VIEW TO REMEMBER**
>
> The most romantic view of the Houses of Parliament is from the opposite (south) side of the river, especially dramatic at night when the spires, pinnacles, and towers are floodlighted green and gold— a fairy-tale vision only missing the presence of Peter Pan and Wendy on their way to Neverland.

Fodor's Choice ★ **Houses of Parliament.** If you want to understand some of the centuries-old traditions and arcane idiosyncrasies that make up constitutionless British parliamentary democracy, the Palace of Westminster, as the complex is still properly called, is the place to come. The architecture in this 1,100-room labyrinth impresses, but the real excitement lies in stalking the corridors of power. A palace was first established on this site by Edward the Confessor in the 11th century. William II started building a new palace in 1087, and this gradually became the seat of English administrative power. However, the current building dates from the 19th century, when fire destroyed the rest of the complex in 1834.

Visitors aren't allowed to snoop too much, but the **Visitors' Galleries** of the House of Commons do afford a view of democracy in process when the banks of green-leather benches are filled by opposing MPs (members of Parliament). When they speak, it's not directly to each other but through the Speaker, who also decides who will get time on the floor. Elaborate procedures notwithstanding, debate is often drowned out by raucous jeers. When MPs vote, they exit by the "Aye" or the "No" corridor, thus being counted by the party "tellers."

Westminster Hall, with its remarkable hammer-beam roof, was the work of William the Conqueror's son William Rufus. It's one of the largest remaining Norman halls in Europe, and its dramatic interior was the scene of the trial of Charles I.

After the 1834 fire, the **Clock Tower** was completed in 1858, and contains the 13-ton bell known as **Big Ben**. At the southwest end of the main Parliament building is the 323-foot-high Victoria Tower. ■**TIP→** The only guided tour nonresidents can go on is the paid-for (£14) tour offered on Saturday or during August and September. ⊠ *St. Stephen's Entrance, St. Margaret St., Westminster* ☎ *020/7219–4272 or 0844/847–1672* ⊕ *www.parliament.uk/visiting* ⊠ *Free; £14 Aug. and Sept. tours (weekdays) and Sat. through the year (must book ahead)* ⊙ *Call to confirm hrs* Ⓤ *Westminster.*

Fodor's Choice
★ **National Gallery.** Standing proudly on the north side of Trafalgar Square is one of the world's supreme art collections, with more than 2,300 masterpieces on show. Picasso, van Gogh, Michelangelo, Leonardo, Monet, Turner, and more—all for free.

This brief selection is your jumping-off point, but there are hundreds more, enough to fill a full day. In chronological order: (1) **Van Eyck** (circa 1395–1441), *The Arnolfini Portrait*—a solemn couple holds hands, the fish-eye mirror behind them mysteriously illuminating what can't be seen from the front view. (2) **Holbein** (1497–1543), *The Ambassadors*—two wealthy visitors from France stand surrounded by what were considered luxury goods at the time. Note the elongated skull at the bottom of the painting, which takes shape when viewed from an angle. (3) **Leonardo da Vinci** (1452–1519), *The Virgin and Child*—this exquisite black-chalk "Burlington Cartoon" has the master's most haunting Mary. (4) **Constable** (1776–1837), *The Hay Wain*—rendered overfamiliar by too many greeting cards, this is the definitive image of golden-age rural England. (5) **Turner** (1775–1851), *Rain, Steam and Speed: The Great Western Railway*, an astonishing whirl of rain, mist, steam, and locomotion (spot the hare). (6) **Caravaggio** (1573–1610), *The Supper at Emmaus*—a cinematically lightened, freshly resurrected Christ blesses bread in an astonishingly domestic vision from the master of chiaroscuro. (7) **Seurat** (1859–91), *Bathers at Asnières*—this static summer day's idyll is one of the pointillist extraordinaire's best-known works. (8) **Botticelli** (1445–1510), *Venus and Mars*—Mars sleeps, exhausted by the love goddess, oblivious to the lance wielded by mischievous cherubs. ■TIP➔ One-hour free, guided tours start at the Sainsbury Wing daily at 11:30 and 2:30. ⊠ *Trafalgar Sq.* ☎ *020/7747–2885* ⊕ *www.nationalgallery.org. uk* ✉ *Free, charge for special exhibitions; audio guide £3* ☉ *Sun.–Thurs. 10–6, Fri. 10–9* Ⓤ *Charing Cross, Embankment, Leicester Square.*

Ⓒ **National Portrait Gallery.** A suitably idiosyncratic collection that presents
Fodor's Choice
★ a potted history of Britain through its people, past and present, this museum is an essential stop for all history and literature buffs, where you can choose to take in a little or a lot. The spacious, bright galleries are accessible via a state-of-the-art escalator. Pop into Portrait Explorer in the IT Gallery for computer-aided exploration. At the summit, the Portrait Restaurant (open an hour after gallery closing times on Thursday and Friday) will delight skyline aficionados. ■TIP➔ Here you'll see one of the best landscapes for real: a panoramic view of Nelson's Column and the backdrop along Whitehall to the Houses of Parliament.

Galleries are arranged chronologically from Tudor times on the second floor forward to contemporary Britain. In the Tudor Gallery—a modern update—on a Tudor long hall—is a Holbein cartoon of Henry VIII. Joshua Reynolds's self-portrait hangs in the refurbished 17th-century rooms; portraits of notables, including Shakespeare, the Brontë sisters, Jane Austen, and the Queen are always on display. ⊠ *St. Martin's Pl., Covent Garden* ☎ *020/7312–2463, 020/730–0555 recorded switchboard information* ⊕ *www.npg.org.uk* ✉ *Free, charge for special exhibitions; £3 audiovisual guide* ☉ *Mon.–Wed. and weekends 10–6, Thurs. and Fri. 10–9, last admission 45 mins before closing* Ⓤ *Charing Cross, Leicester Sq.*

Where to See the Royals

The Queen and the Royal Family attend approximately 400 functions a year, and if you want to know what they are doing on any given date, turn to the *Court Circular*, printed in the major London dailies, or check out the Royal Family Web site, ⊕ *www.royal.gov.uk*, for the latest events on the Royal Diary. The Queen's Diamond Jubilee, marking 60 years on the throne, will be held June 2–5, 2012. Trooping the Colour is usually held on the second Saturday in June, to celebrate the Queen's official birthday. This spectacular parade begins when she leaves Buckingham Palace in her carriage and rides down the Mall to arrive at Horse Guards Parade at 11 exactly. To watch, just line up along the Mall with your binoculars.

Another time you can catch the Queen in all her regalia is when she and the Duke of Edinburgh ride in state to Westminster to open the Houses of Parliament. The famous gilded coach, such an icon of fairy-tale glamour, parades from Buckingham Palace, escorted by the brilliantly uniformed Household Cavalry—on a clear day, it's to be hoped, for this ceremony takes place in late October or early November, depending on the exigencies of Parliament.

But perhaps the most relaxed, least formal time to see the Queen is during Royal Ascot, held at the racetrack near Windsor Castle—a short train ride out of London—usually during the third week of June (Tuesday–Friday). After several races, the Queen invariably walks down to the paddock on a special path, greeting race goers as she proceeds.

★ **The Queen's Gallery.** The former chapel at the south side of Buckingham Palace is now a temple of art and rare and exquisite objects, acquired by kings and queens over the centuries. Although Her Majesty herself is not the personal owner, she has the privilege of holding these works for the nation. Step through the splendid portico (designed by John Simpson) into elegantly restrained, spacious galleries whose walls are hung with some truly great works. An excellent audio guide takes you through the treasures. ■TIP→ The E-gallery allows the user to open lockets, remove a sword from its scabbard, or take apart the tulip vases. ⊠ *Buckingham Palace, Buckingham Palace Rd., St. James's* ☎ *020/7766–7301* ⊕ *www.royal.gov.uk* ⌫ *£8.50 with free audio guide, joint ticket with Royal Mews £15* ⊗ *Daily 10–5:30; last admission 4:30* Ⓤ *Victoria, St. James's Park, Green Park.*

Ⓒ **St. James's Park.** With three palaces at its borders (the Palace of Westminster, the Tudor **St. James's Palace,** and Buckingham Palace), St. James's Park is acclaimed as the most royal of the royal parks. It's London's smallest, most ornamental park, as well as the oldest; once marshy water meadows, the land was acquired by Henry VIII in 1532 as a royal deer-hunting park (with dueling and sword fights forbidden); the public was always allowed access. James I improved the land and installed an aviary and zoo (complete with crocodiles). Charles II (after his exile in France, where he admired Louis XIV's formal Versailles Palace landscapes) had formal gardens laid out, with avenues, fruit orchards, and

Historic Westminster Abbey is a beautiful setting for any choral performance.

a canal. ⊠ *The Mall or Horse Guards approach, or Birdcage Walk, St. James's* ⊕ *www.royalparks.gov.uk* ⊙ *Daily 5 am–midnight* Ⓤ *St. James's Park, Westminster.*

♺ ★ **Tate Britain.** The stately neoclassical building may not be as ambitious as its sibling Tate Modern on the south bank, but Tate Britain's bright galleries lure only a fraction of the Modern's crowds. A great place for exploring British art from 1500 to the present, the museum also hosts the annual Turner Prize exhibition, with its accompanying furor over the state of contemporary art, from about October to January each year. First opened in 1897, funded by the sugar magnate Sir Henry Tate, the museum includes the Linbury Galleries on the lower floors, which stage temporary exhibitions (which can get busy), whereas the upper floors show the permanent collection. You can find classic works by Constable, Gainsborough, Stubbs, David Wilkie, Francis Bacon, Duncan Grant, Barbara Hepworth, and Ben Nicholson—and an outstanding display from J.M.W. Turner in the Clore Gallery, including many later vaporous and light-infused works such as *Sunrise with Sea Monsters.* You can catch the Tate-to-Tate shuttle boat to the Tate Modern from the nearby riverside. ⊠ *Millbank, Westminster* ☎ *020/7887–8888* ⊕ *www.tate.org.uk/britain* ⊠ *Free, exhibitions £5–£11* ⊙ *Daily 10–6, last entry at 5, 10–10 1st Friday of month* Ⓤ *Pimlico (signposted 5-min walk).*

Fodor's Choice ★ **Westminster Abbey.** A monument to the nation's rich—and often bloody and scandalous—history, the abbey rises on the Thames skyline as one of London's most iconic sites. The mysterious gloom of the lofty medieval interior is home to more than 600 statues, tombs, and commemorative tablets. About 3,300 people, from kings to composers to wordsmiths, are buried in the abbey. It has been the scene of 15 royal weddings (Prince William's marriage to Kate Middleton on April 29, 2011 is the most recent) and no fewer than 38 coronations—the first in 1066, when William the Conqueror was made king here.

There's only one way around the abbey, and as there will almost certainly be a long stream of shuffling tourists at your heels, you'll need to be alert to catch the highlights. Enter by the north door then turn around and look up to see the **painted-glass rose window**, the largest of its kind.

As you walk east toward the apse you'll see the **Coronation Chair**, at the foot of the Henry VII Chapel, which has been briefly graced by nearly every regal posterior since Edward I ordered it in 1301. Farther along, the exquisite confection of the Henry VII's Lady Chapel is topped by a magnificent fan-vaulted ceiling. The wooden seats are known as stalls, carrying the heraldic banners of knights. The tomb of Henry VII lies behind the altar; his queen, Elizabeth of York, is also here. The bodies of the so-called Princes in the Tower—Edward V and Richard—are also believed to be buried here. Elizabeth I is buried above arch enemy Mary Tudor in the tomb just to the north, while Mary Queen of Scots if buried in the tomb to the south. In front of the **High Altar**, which was used for the funerals of Princess Diana and the Queen Mother, is a black-and-white marble pavement laid in 1268. The intricate Italian Cosmati work contains three Latin inscriptions, one of which states that the world will last for 19,683 years.

Continue through the South Ambulatory to the **Chapel of St. Edward the Confessor**, which contains the shrine to the pre-Norman king. Because of its great age, you must join one of the vergers' tours to be admitted to the chapel (details available at the admission desk; there is a small charge), or attend Holy Communion within the shrine on Tuesdays at 8 am).

To the left, you'll find **Poets' Corner**. Geoffrey Chaucer was the first poet to be buried in Poets' Corner in 1400. Other statues and memorials include: William Shakespeare, D.H. Lawrence, T.S. Eliot, and Dylan Thomas as well as non-poets, including Laurence Olivier and a statue of George Frederick Handel; look out for the 700-year old wall frescoes. A door from the south transept and south choir aisle leads to the calm of the **Great Cloisters**. Watch for the headstones of 26 monks who died in 1348, during the Black Death. A café can be also found in the cloisters.

The medieval Chapter House is adorned with 14th-century frescoes and a magnificent 13th-century tiled floor, one of the finest surviving tiled floors in the country. The King's Council met here between 1257 and 1547. Near the entrance is Britain's oldest door, dating from the 1050s. Take a left out of the Chapter House to visit the **Abbey Museum**, which houses a collection of deliciously macabre effigies made from the death masks and actual clothing of Charles II and Admiral Lord Nelson (complete with eye patch). Past the museum, the **Little Cloister** is a quiet haven, and just beyond, the **College Garden** is a delightful diversion. On the west side of the abbey, the **Dean's Yard** is the best spot for a fine view of the massive flying buttresses above.

Continue back to the nave of the abbey. In the choir screen, north of the entrance to the choir, is a marble **monument to Sir Isaac Newton.** If you walk towards the West Entrance, you'll see **a plaque to Franklin D. Roosevelt**—one of the Abbey's very few tributes to a foreigner. The poppy-wreathed Grave of the Unknown Warrior commemorates soldiers who lost their lives in both world wars; nearby is a portrait of Richard II.

Arrive early if possible, but be prepared to wait in line to tour the abbey. Photography is not permitted. ⊠ *Broad Sanctuary, Westminster* ☎ *020/7222–5152* ⊕ *www.westminster-abbey.org* ⊠ *Abbey and museum £15 adults; children under 11 free if accompanied by adult; free audio tour* ☉ *Abbey, weekdays 9:30–3:30; closes 1 hr after last admission. Museum, daily 10:30–4. Cloisters daily 8–6. College Garden, Apr.–Sept., Tues.–Thurs. 10–6; Oct.–Mar., Tues.–Thurs. 10–4. Chapter House, daily 10–4. Services may cause changes to hrs, so call ahead* Ⓤ *Westminster.*

WORTH NOTING

Banqueting House. Built on the site of the original Tudor Palace of White-hall, which was (according to one foreign visitor) "ill-built, and nothing but a heap of houses," James I commissioned Inigo Jones, one of England's great architects, to undertake a grand building. Influenced during a sojourn in Italy by Andrea Pa lladio's work, Jones brought Palladian sophistication and purity back to London with him. The resulting graceful and disciplined classical style of Banqueting House, completed in 1622, must have stunned its early occupants. In the quiet vaults beneath, James would escape the stresses of being a sovereign with a glass or two. ⊠ *Whitehall, Westminster* ☎ *020/3166–6154 or 020/3166–6155, 020/3166–6153 concert information* ⊕ *www.hrp. org.uk* ⊠ *£4.80, includes audio guide, concerts from £20* ☉ *Mon.– Sat. 10–5, last admission 4:30. Closed Christmas wk. Liable to close at short notice for events so calling first is advisable* Ⓤ *Charing Cross, Embankment, Westminster.*

Carlton House Terrace. A glorious example of Regency architect John Nash's genius, Carlton House Terrace was built between 1812 and 1830, under the patronage of George IV (Prince Regent until George III's death in 1820). Today Carlton House Terrace houses the Royal College of Pathologists (No. 2), the Royal Society (No. 6), whose members included Isaac Newton and Charles Darwin, the Turf Club (No. 5), and, at No. 12, the **Institute of Contemporary Arts,** better known as the ICA. ⊠ *The Mall, St. James's* Ⓤ *Charing Cross.*

Clarence House. The London home of Queen Elizabeth the Queen Mother for nearly 50 years, Clarence House is now the Prince of Wales' and the Duchess of Cornwall's residence. The Regency mansion was built by John Nash for the Duke of Clarence, who found living in St. James's Palace quite unsuitable. Since then it has remained a royal home for princesses, dukes, and duchesses, including the present monarch, Queen Elizabeth, as a newlywed before her coronation. Like Buckingham Palace, Clarence House is open only in August and September and tickets must be booked in advance. ⊠ *Clarence House, St. James's Palace, St. James's* ☎ *020/7766–7303* ⊕ *www.royalcollection.org.uk* ⊠ *£8.50* ☉ *Aug. and Sept.* Ⓤ *Green Park.*

Downing Street. Looking like an unassuming alley but for the iron gates at both its Whitehall and Horse Guards Road approaches, this is the location of the famous **No. 10,** London's modest version equivalent of the White House. The Georgian entrance is deceptive, though, since the old house now leads to a large mansion behind it, overlooking the Horse Guards Parade. ⊠ *Whitehall, Whitehall* Ⓤ *Westminster.*

St. James's Palace. With its solitary sentry posted at the gate, this surprisingly small palace of Tudor brick was once a home for many British sovereigns, including the first Elizabeth and Charles I, who spent his last night here before his execution. Today it's the working office of another Charles—the Prince of Wales. ⊠ *Friary Court, St. James's* ⊕ *www.royal. gov.uk* Ⓤ *Green Park.*

Ⓒ **St. Martin-in-the-Fields.** One of London's best-loved and most welcoming of churches, in a splendid 18th-century building designed by James Gibbs, has been enhanced both inside and out by refurbishment work; the building's array of functions continues unabated. Hearing a concert here (daytime rehearsals are free) is a treat. The crypt is a hive of activity, with a café and shop, plus the **London Brass-Rubbing Centre,** where you can make your own life-size souvenir knight, lady, or monarch from replica tomb brasses, with metallic waxes, paper, and instructions from about £4.50. ⊠ *Trafalgar Sq., Covent Garden* ☎ *020/7766–1100, 020/7839–8362 brass rubbings; 020/7766–1122 evening-concert credit-card bookings* ⊕ *www.smitf.org* ☒ *Concerts £6–£22; Church audio tour £3.50* ◐ *Mon.–Sat. 8–6, Sun. 8–6 for worship; café Mon. and Tues. 8–8, Wed. 8–7, Thurs.–Sat. 8–9, Sun. 11–6* Ⓤ *Charing Cross, Leicester Sq.*

Spencer House. Ancestral abode of the Spencers—Diana, Princess of Wales's family—this is perhaps the finest example of an elegant 18th-century town house extant in London. Reflecting his passion for the Grand Tour and classical antiquities, the first Earl Spencer commissioned architect John Vardy to adapt designs from ancient Rome for a magnificent private palace. Vardy was responsible for the lavish Palm Room, which boasts a spectacular screen of columns covered in gilded carvings that resemble gold palm trees. The house is open only on Sunday (closed January and August), and only to guided tours. ⊠ *27 St. James's Pl., St. James's* ☎ *020/7499–8620* ⊕ *www.spencerhouse.co.uk* ☒ *£9* ◐ *Sept.– Dec. and Feb.–July, Sun. 10:30–5:45, last tour 4:45; tour leaves approx. every 25 mins; tickets on sale Sun. at 10:30* Ⓤ *Green Park.*

Ⓒ **Wellington Barracks.** These are the headquarters of the Guards Division, the Queen's five regiments of elite foot guards (Grenadier, Coldstream, Scots, Irish, and Welsh) who protect the sovereign and patrol her palaces dressed in tunics of gold-purled scarlet and tall bearskin caps. If you want to learn more about the guards, visit the **Guards Museum,** which has displays on all aspects of a guardsman's life in conflicts dating back to 1642; the entrance is next to the Guards Chapel. Next door is the **Guards Toy Soldier Centre,** a great place for a souvenir. ⊠ *Wellington Barracks, Birdcage Walk, Westminster* ☎ *020/7414–3428* ⊕ *www. theguardsmuseum.com* ☒ *£4* ◐ *Daily 10–4; last admission 3:30* Ⓤ *St. James's Park.*

CLOSE UP

The 2012 London Olympic Games

After Beijing's mind-boggling display at the 2008 Olympic Games, the baton was passed to London for the 2012 Olympic Games (⊕ www. london2012.com), to be held July 27 to August 12, 2012. London's handover performance at the Beijing Olympics curtain call—featuring a double-decker bus and umbrella-toting commuters—was a typically English affair: slapstick, tongue-in-cheek, and devoid of bombast. The unmistakable message was: come to London and enjoy yourself.

HOTELS AND FLIGHTS
London has more than 100,000 hotel rooms but you will need to book your room as far ahead as you can, especially if you want to be near the Olympic Park. Air tickets are also going to be snapped up close to the event.

GETTING AROUND
More than £17 billion has been earmarked for transport development in the run-up to the 2012 Games in this city that sees 20 million trips daily on the transport system. Served by five airports, London has the world's second largest (and oldest) underground system, but pre-Olympics development saw the extension of the East London line (May 2010) and the Docklands Light Railway, the upgrading and modernization of all underground stations, investment on the Jubilee Line (serving Olympic facilities) to handle extra capacity, and a high-rail link between St. Pancras International and Stratford International for the Olympic Park, shuttling spectators to the Games in seven minutes from central London. New cycle and walking lanes are also planned to encourage healthier modes of transportation.

London, however, remains one of the most congested cities in Europe.

BUYING TICKETS
Tickets for the London Olympics 2012 go on sale in 2011 and will generally be available until the start of each event unless sold out. Advance tickets start to go on sale beginning March 15 to April 26, 2011, through the Authorized Ticket Reseller, Cosport (⊕ cosport.com), or through the various offices of the National Olympic Committees of the International Olympic Committee (⊕ www.olympic. org). Tickets will include free public transport on the day of the event.

NEW LONDON?
The 2008 Olympic Games in Beijing further marked the long-heralded shift eastward of the world economic axis. Back in London for the first time since 1948, the Olympic Games return to a nation increasingly at ease with its decreased global stature but just as eager to put on a show. Drawing on impressive reserves of cosmopolitan verve, creativity, and sheer élan, London aims to host the Olympic Games in striking fashion. The 2012 Olympics will be about showing why London remains one of the world's most-loved and cosmopolitan cities. The jigsaw-style logo for the London Olympics may have polarized opinion, but the Games have been applauded for their promise to revitalize areas of East London and swing the spotlight of global attention back to town. The Games are also an occasion to showcase some dramatic new architecture. And Olympic visitors are expected to bring as much as £2.2 billion to the local economy in 2012, fueling the London feel-good factor.

2

UNDER CONSTRUCTION
London has focused its Olympic energies on transforming the deprived East London, where the Olympic Park is under construction, but the occasion has been seized on to overhaul public transport, to showcase some sparkling new architecture, and to convert some well-known landmarks into Olympic venues.

A spectacular crop of new architecture—the 945-foot (288-meter) "Helter-Skelter" Bishopsgate Tower, 740-foot (228-meter) Leadenhall Building "Cheese Grater," and 1,020-foot (310-meter) "Shard of Glass"—is set to inject fresh adrenaline into London's streetscapes.

A curvilinear £303-million piece of eye candy due for completion in 2011, the **Aquatics Centre** will be a centerpiece of London's Olympics display. Designed by Iraqi architect Zaha Hadid, the center's wavelike form is impressive and inspirational.

The **Olympic stadium's** design has divided opinion, with critics making unfavorable comparisons with Beijing's iconic Bird's Nest, but supporters have pointed to the 80,000-capacity stadium's ability to be dismantled as a major plus point.

OLYMPIC VENUES
Most big-ticket events will take place in the Olympic Park but some medals will be vied for in more unusual settings, many that are open to the public today. A number of events take place outside London, such as sailing in Weymouth Pay and Portland Harbour.

Athletics events will all take place in the 80,000-capacity **Olympics Stadium.**

Gymnasts and basketball finalists will be limbering up in the **O2 Arena,** to be temporarily rechristened the **North Greenwich Arena 1**; badminton contestants and rhythmic gymnasts will aim for glory in the North Greenwich Arena 2.

The Beach Volleyball competition will be held in **Horse Guard's Parade** in Whitehall, a beach ball's toss from Downing Street and next to St. James's Park.

Road Cycling takes to **Regent's Park.** (For great views of the park and Central London head to nearby Primrose Hill.)

Football (soccer) matches will kick off in 90,000-seat **Wembley Stadium,** the home of the English National Football team.

Triathlon contestants and Marathon swimmers will make a splash in the Serpentine in **Hyde Park.**

Swimming and diving will be held in the astonishing form of the signature **Aquatics Centre.**

Lovely **Greenwich Park** is the venue for Equestrian events and Modern Pentathlon.

In Woolwich, shooting will be staged at the **Royal Artillery Barracks,** while **Lord's Cricket Ground** will host archery.

Tennis can really only be held at one venue—**Wimbledon**—with its famous grass courts, but rowers, canoeists, and kayakers will be heading off to **Eton Dorney,** near Windsor Castle.

SOHO AND COVENT GARDEN

Once a red-light district, the Soho of today delivers more "grown-up" than "adult" entertainment. Its theaters, restaurants (including those in Chinatown), pubs, and clubs merge with the first-run cinemas of Leicester Square and the venerable venues (Royal and English National Operas) of Covent Garden to create the mega-entertainment district known as the West End. During the day Covent Garden's historic piazza is packed with shoppers and sightseers, while Soho reverts to the business side of its lively, late-night scene—ad agencies, media, film distributors, actors, agents, and casting agents all looking for each other.

A quadrilateral bounded by Regent Street, Coventry and Cranbourn streets, Charing Cross Road, and the eastern half of Oxford Street encloses Soho. This appellation, unlike the New York City neighborhood's similar one, is not an abbreviation of anything, but a blast from the past—derived from the shouts of "So-ho!" that royal huntsmen in Whitehall Palace's parklands were once heard to cry.

The Covent Garden Market became the Covent Garden Piazza in 1980. It was originally the "convent garden" belonging to the Abbey of St. Peter at Westminster (later Westminster Abbey), and still functions as the center of a neighborhood—one that has always been alluded to as "colorful." After centuries of magnificence and misery, Covent Garden became London's vegetable and flower market in the 19th century. When the produce moved to the Nine Elms Market in Vauxhall in 1974, the glass-covered market halls took on new life with stores and entertainment. Today it bustles with tourists and shoppers.

GETTING HERE Take any train to the Piccadilly Circus station (on the Piccadilly and Bakerloo lines or Leicester Square and Northern lines for Soho). Get off at Covent Garden on the Piccadilly Line for Covent Garden and Embankment (Bakerloo, Northern, District, and Circle lines) or Charing Cross (Northern, Bakerloo, and main railway lines) for the area south of the Strand.

PLANNING You can comfortably tour all the sights in Covent Garden in a day. Visit
YOUR TIME the small but perfect Courtauld Institute Gallery on Monday before 2 pm when it's free. That leaves plenty of time to visit the marketplace, watch the street entertainment, and do a bit of shopping, with energy left over for a night on the town (or "on the tiles," as the British say) in Soho.

TOP ATTRACTIONS

Courtauld Institute Gallery. One of London's most beloved art collections, the Courtauld is to your left as you pass through the archway into the grounds of the beautifully restored, grand 18th-century classical **Somerset House.** Founded in 1931 by the textile magnate Samuel Courtauld to house his remarkable private collection, this is one of the world's finest impressionist and postimpressionist galleries, with artists ranging from Bonnard to van Gogh. ⊠ *Somerset House, Strand, Covent Garden* ☎ *020/7848–2526* ⊕ *www.courtauld.ac.uk* 🖃 *£5, free Mon. 10–2, except bank holidays* ۞ *Daily 10–6; last admission 5:30* Ⓤ *Covent Garden, Holborn, Temple.*

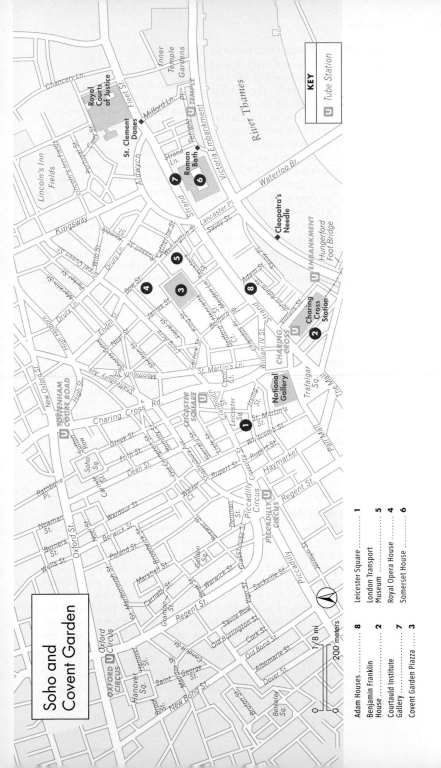

Soho and Covent Garden

KEY

U Tube Station

0
0   200 meters
0
0   1/8 mi

⚙ **Covent Garden Piazza.** Once home to London's main flower market, and former stomping ground of *My Fair Lady*'s Eliza Doolittle, the market building around which Covent Garden pivots is known as the Piazza. Inside, the shops are mostly higher-class clothing chains, plus several restaurants and cafés and knick-knack stores that are good for gifts. One particular gem is Benjamin Pollock's Toyshop at No. 44 in the market. Established in the 1880s,

it sells delightful toy theaters. There's the superior **Apple Market** for crafts on most days, too. On the south side of the Piazza, the indoor **Jubilee Market,** with its stalls of clothing, army-surplus gear, and more crafts and knickknacks, has a distinct flea-market feel. By the church in the square, street performers—from global musicians to jugglers and mimes—play to the crowds, as they have done since the first English Punch and Judy Show, staged here in the 17th century. ⊠ *Covent Garden* Ⓤ *Covent Garden.*

★ **Somerset House.** An old royal palace once stood on the site, but it was eventually replaced by this 18th-century building, the work of Sir William Chambers (1726–96), during the reign of George III. It was built to house government offices, principally those of the Navy. For the first time in more than 100 years, these gracious rooms are on view, including the Seamen's Waiting Hall and the Nelson Stair. In addition, the Navy Commissioners' Barge has returned to dry dock at the Water Gate. The rooms are on the south side of the building, by the river. The **Courtauld Institute Gallery** occupies most of the north building, facing the busy Strand. ⊠ *The Strand, Covent Garden* ☎ *020/7845–4600* ⊕ *www.somerset-house.org.uk* ✉ *Embankment Gallery £5, Courtauld Gallery £5, other areas free* ☉ *Daily 10–6; last admission 5:30* Ⓤ *Charing Cross, Waterloo, Blackfriars.*

WORTH NOTING

The Adam Houses. All that remains of what was once a regal riverfront row of houses on a 3-acre site, connected by arches and streets below grade, are a few of the structures, but such is their quality that they are worth a detour off the Strand to see. The work of 18th-century Scottish architects and interior designers (John, Robert, James, and William Adam, known collectively as the Adam brothers), the original development was damaged in the 19th century during the building of the embankment, and mostly demolished in 1936 to be replaced by an art deco tower. Nos. 1–4 Robert Street and Nos. 7 and 10 Adam Street are the best. At the **Royal Society of Arts** (⊠ *8 John Adam St.* ☎ *020/7930–5115* ⊕ *www.thersa.org* ✉ *Free* ☉ *1st Sun. of month, 10–1*), you can see a suite of Adam rooms; no reservations are required. ⊠ *The Strand, Covent Garden* ☉ *Closed weekends* Ⓤ *Charing Cross, Embankment.*

Benjamin Franklin House. Opened to the public for the first time in 2006, this architecturally significant 1730 house is the only surviving

Pure street theater: you can't miss the buskers performing in the streets of Soho and Covent Garden.

residence of American statesman, scientist, writer, and inventor Benjamin Franklin, who lived and worked here for 16 years preceding the American Revolution. The restored Georgian town house has been left unfurnished, the better to show off the original features—18th-century paneling, stoves, beams, bricks, and windows. ⊠ *36 Craven St., Covent Garden* ☎ *020/7839–2006, 020/7925–1405 booking line* ⊕ *www.benjaminfranklinhouse.org* ◺ *£7* ☉ *Wed.–Sun. noon–5.*

Leicester Square. Looking at the neon of the major movie houses, the fast-food outlets, and the disco entrances, you'd never guess that this square (pronounced *Lester*) was a model of formality and refinement when it was first laid out around 1630. By the 19th century it was already bustling and disreputable, and although today it's not a threatening place, you should still be on your guard, especially at night—any space so full of people is bound to attract pickpockets, and Leicester Square certainly does. Although it retains some residual glamour as the site of red-carpet film premieres, Londoners generally tend to avoid this windswept plaza, crowded as it is with suburban teenagers, wandering backpackers, and mimes. ■ TIP→ One landmark worth visiting is tkts, the Society of London Theatre ticket kiosk, which sells half-price tickets for many of that evening's performances. ⊠ *Covent Garden* Ⓤ *Leicester Sq.*

London Transport Museum. Housed in the old flower market at the southeast corner of Covent Garden, this stimulating museum includes the interactive features that explain why London was the first world city. As you watch the crowds gawk at the horse-drawn trams (and the piles of detritus that remained behind), the ever-fascinating steam locomotives, and trolley buses from the past, you're not sure who's enjoying it more, children or adults. ✉ *Covent Garden Piazza* ☎ *020/7379–6344* ⊕ *www. ltmuseum.co.uk* ⬛*£10* ☉ *Sat.–Thurs. 10–6 (last admission 5:15), Fri. 11–6 (last admission 5:15)* Ⓤ *Leicester Sq., Covent Garden.*

Royal Oper. London's premier opera and ballet venue was designed in 1858 by E.M. Barry, son of Sir Charles, the House of Commons architect, and is the third theater on the site. ✉ *Bow St., Covent Garden* ☎ *020/7240–1200* ⊕ *www.royalopera.org* Ⓤ *Covent Garden.*

BLOOMSBURY AND LEGAL LONDON

The hub of intellectual London, Bloomsbury is anchored by the British Museum and the University of London, which houses—among other institutions—the internationally ranked London School of Economics and the School of Oriental and African Studies. As a result, the streets and cafés around Bloomsbury's Russell Square are often crawling with students and professors engaged in heated conversation, while literary agents and academics surf the shelves of the antiquarian bookstores nearby.

The character of an area of London can change visibly from one street to the next. Nowhere is this so clear as in the contrast between fun-loving Soho and intellectual Bloomsbury, a mere 100 yards to the northeast, or between arty, trendy Covent Garden and—on the other side of Kingsway—sober Holborn (pronounced *hoe*-bun). Bloomsbury is known for its famous flowering of literary-arty bohemia, personified during the first three decades of the 20th century by the clique known as the Bloomsbury Group, including Virginia Woolf, E. M. Forster, Vanessa Bell, and Lytton Strachey. Holborn, filled with ancient buildings of the legal profession, is more interesting and beautiful than you might suppose. The Great Fire of 1666 razed most of the city but spared the buildings of legal London, and all of Holborn oozes history. Leading landmarks here are the Inns of Court, where the country's top solicitors and barristers have had their chambers for centuries.

GETTING HERE   You can easily get to where you need to be on foot in Bloomsbury, and the Russell Square Tube stop on the Piccadilly Line leaves you right at the corner of Russell Square. The best Tube stops for the Inns of Court are Holborn on the Central and Piccadilly lines or Chancery Lane on the Central Line. Tottenham Court Road on the Northern and Central lines or Russell Square (Piccadilly Line) are best for the British Museum.

PLANNING   Bloomsbury can be seen in a day, or in half a day, depending on your
YOUR TIME   interests. If you plan to visit the Inns of Court as well as the British Museum, and you'd also like to get a feel for the neighborhood, then you may devote an entire day to this literary and legal enclave, or come back on another day to visit the vast British Museum. You can also pick up a "Museum Mile" map, which marks all the museums in this area, and use it to plan your path.

TOP ATTRACTIONS

Fodor's Choice   **British Museum.** With a facade like a great temple, this celebrated trea-
★   sure house, filled with plunder of incalculable value and beauty from around the globe, occupies an immense Greco-Victorian building that makes a suitably grand impression. Inside are some of the greatest relics

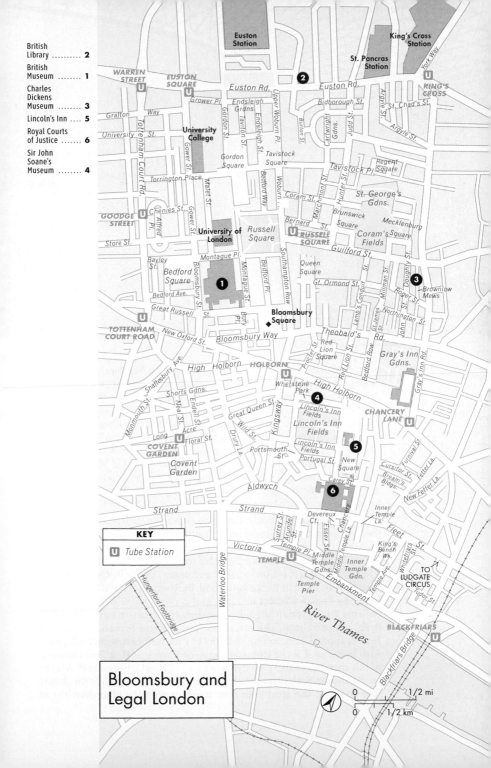

Bloomsbury and Legal London

KEY

🚇 Tube Station

The massive, glass-roofed Great Court in the British Museum has a couple of cafés.

of humankind: the Parthenon Sculptures (Elgin Marbles), the Rosetta Stone, the Sutton Hoo Treasure—almost everything, it seems, but the Ark of the Covenant. The three rooms that comprise the **Sainsbury African Galleries** are a must-see in the Lower Gallery—together they present 200,000 objects, highlighting such ancient kingdoms as the Benin and Asante. The museum's focal point is the **Great Court,** a brilliant modern design with a vast glass roof that reveals the museum's covered courtyard. The revered **Reading Room** has a blue-and-gold dome. If you want to navigate the highlights of the almost 100 galleries, join the free **eyeOpener** 30- to 40-minute tours by museum guides (details at the information desk).

The collection grew quickly, thanks to enthusiastic kleptomaniacs after the Napoleonic Wars—most notoriously the seventh Earl of Elgin, who acquired the marbles from the Parthenon and Erechtheion in Athens during his term as British ambassador in Constantinople. Here follows a highly edited résumé (in order of encounter) of the British Museum's greatest hits: close to the entrance hall, in Room 4, is the **Rosetta Stone,** found by French soldiers in 1799, and carved in 196 BC by decree of Ptolemy V in Egyptian hieroglyphics, demotic (a cursive script developed in Egypt), and Greek. This inscription provided the French Egyptologist Jean-François Champollion with the key to deciphering hieroglyphics. Also in Room 4 is the Colossal statue of Ramesses II, a 7-ton likeness of this member of the 19th dynasty's (ca. 1270 BC) upper half. Maybe the **Parthenon Sculptures** should be back in Greece, but while the debate rages on, you can steal your own moment with the Elgin Marbles in

Room 18. Carved in about 400 BC, these graceful decorations are displayed along with a high-tech exhibit of the Acropolis.

Upstairs are some of the most popular galleries, especially beloved by children: Rooms 62–63, where the **Egyptian mummies** live. Nearby are the glittering 4th-century **Mildenhall Treasure** and the equally splendid 8th-century Anglo-Saxon **Sutton Hoo Treasure** (with magnificent helmets and jewelry). A more prosaic exhibit is that of Pete Marsh, sentimentally named by the archaeologists who unearthed the **Lindow Man** from a Cheshire peat marsh; poor Pete was ritually slain in the 1st century, and lay perfectly pickled in his bog until 1984. The **Korean Foundation Gallery** (Room 67) delves into the art and archaeology of the country, including a reconstruction of a sarangbang, a traditional scholar's study. ⊠ *Great Russell St., Bloomsbury* ☎ *020/7323–8000* ⊕ *www.britishmuseum.org* ✉ *Free; donations encouraged* ⊗ *Museum Sat.–Wed. 10–5:30, Thurs. and Fri. 10–8:30. Great Court Sun.–Wed. 9–6, Thurs.–Sat. 9 am–11 pm* Ⓤ *Russell Square.*

Charles Dickens Museum. This is the only one of the many London houses Charles Dickens (1812–70) inhabited that is still standing, and it would have had a real claim to his fame in any case because he wrote *Oliver Twist* and *Nicholas Nickleby* and finished *Pickwick Papers* here between 1837 and 1839. The house looks exactly as it would have in Dickens's day, complete with first editions, letters, and a tall clerk's desk (where the master wrote standing up, often while chatting with visiting friends and relatives). ⊠ *48 Doughty St., Bloomsbury* ☎ *020/7405–2127* ⊕ *www.dickensmuseum.com* ✉ *£5* ⊗ *Daily 10–5; last admission 4:30* Ⓤ *Chancery La., Russell Sq.*

Lincoln's Inn. There's plenty to see at one of the oldest, best preserved, and most attractive of the Inns of Court—from the Chancery Lane Tudor brick gatehouse to the wide-open, tree-lined, atmospheric Lincoln's Inn Fields and the 15th-century chapel remodeled by Inigo Jones in 1620. ⊠ *Chancery La., Bloomsbury* ☎ *020/7405–1393* ⊕ *www.lincolnsinn. org.uk* ✉ *Free* ⊗ *Gardens weekdays 7–7, chapel weekdays noon–2:30; public may also attend Sun. service in chapel at 11:30 during legal terms* Ⓤ *Chancery La.*

★ **Sir John Soane's Museum.** Sir John (1753–1837), architect of the Bank of England, bequeathed his house to the nation on condition that nothing be changed. He obviously had enormous fun with his home: in the Picture Room, for instance, two of Hogarth's *Rake's Progress* series are among the paintings on panels that swing away to reveal secret gallery pockets with even more paintings. Everywhere mirrors and colors play tricks with light and space, and split-level floors worthy of a fairground fun house disorient you. ⊠ *13 Lincoln's Inn Fields, Bloomsbury* ☎ *020/7405–2107* ⊕ *www.soane.org* ✉ *Free, Sat. tour £5* ⊗ *Tues.–Sat. 10–5; also 6–9 on 1st Tues. of month* Ⓤ *Holborn.*

WORTH NOTING

British Library. Formerly in the British Museum, the collection of around 18 million volumes now has a home in state-of-the-art surroundings. The library's greatest treasures are on view to the general public: Magna Carta, a Gutenberg Bible, Jane Austen's writings, Shakespeare's First

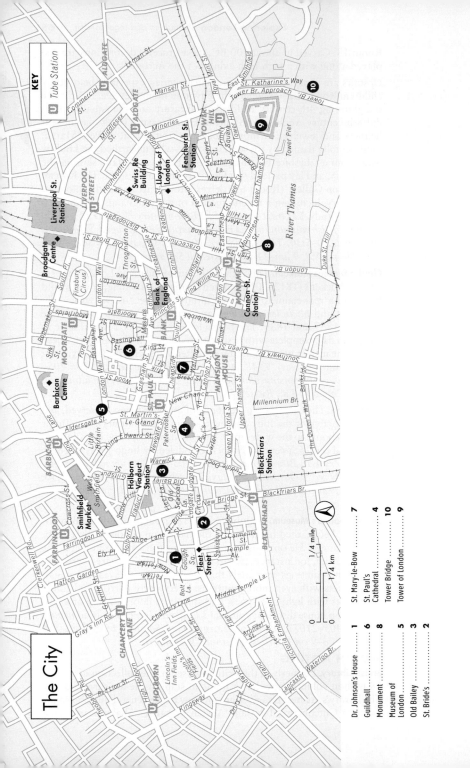

The City

KEY

U Tube Station

Dr. Johnson's House **1**
Guildhall **6**
Monument **8**
Museum of
London **5**
Old Bailey **3**
St. Bride's **2**

St. Mary-le-Bow **7**
St. Paul's
Cathedral **4**
Tower Bridge **10**
Tower of London........ **9**

Folio, and musical manuscripts by G.F. Handel as well as Sir Paul McCartney are on display in the Sir John Ritblat Gallery. ⊠ *96 Euston Rd., Bloomsbury* ☎ *0870/7412–7332* ⊕ *www.bl.uk* ⌦ *Free, donations appreciated, charge for special exhibitions* ⊙ *Mon. and Wed.–Fri. 9:30–6, Tues. 9:30–8, Sat. 9:30–5, Sun. and bank holiday Mon. 11–5* Ⓤ *Euston, Euston Sq., King's Cross.*

Royal Courts of Justice. Here is the vast Victorian Gothic pile of 35 million bricks containing the nation's principal law courts, with 1,000-odd rooms running off 3½ mi of corridor. And here are heard the most important civil law cases—that's everything from divorce to fraud, with libel in between. You can sit in the viewing gallery to watch any trial you like. ⊠ *The Strand, Bloomsbury* ☎ *020/7947–6000* ⊕ *www.hmcourtsservice.gov.uk* ⌦ *Free* ⊙ *Weekdays 9–4:30; during Aug. there are no sittings and public areas close at 2:30* Ⓤ *Temple.*

THE CITY

The City, as opposed to the city, is the capital's fast-beating financial heart. Behind a host of imposing neoclassical facades lie the banks and exchanges whose frantic trade determines the fortunes that underpin London—and the country. But the "Square Mile" is much more than London's Wall Street—the capital's economic engine room also has currency as a religious and political center. St. Paul's Cathedral has looked after Londoners' souls since the 7th century, and the Tower of London—that moat-surrounded royal fortress, prison, and jewel house—has taken care of beheading them. The City's maze of backstreets is also home to a host of old churches, marketplaces, and cozy pubs.

Twice the City has been nearly wiped off the face of the earth. The Great Fire of 1666 necessitated a total reconstruction, in which Sir Christopher Wren had a big hand, contributing not only his masterpiece, St. Paul's Cathedral, but 49 additional parish churches. The second wave of destruction was dealt by the German bombers of World War II. The ruins were rebuilt, but slowly, and with no overall plan, leaving the City a patchwork of the old, the new, the interesting, and the flagrantly awful. Since a mere 8,000 or so people call it home, the nation's financial center is deserted on weekends, with restaurants shuttered.

Crossing the Millennium Bridge from the Tate Modern to St. Paul's is one of the finest walks in London for views of the river and the cathedral that towers over it.

GETTING HERE The City is well served by a concentrated selection of underground stops. St Paul's and Bank, on the Central Line, and Mansion House, Cannon Street, and Monument, on the District and Circle lines, deliver visitors to the heart of the City. Liverpool Street and Aldgate border the City's eastern edge, while Chancery Lane and Farringdon lie to the west. Barbican and Moorgate provide easy access to the theaters and galleries of the Barbican, while Blackfriars, to the south, leads to Ludgate Circus and Fleet Street.

PLANNING The "Square Mile" is as compact, making it easy to dip into the City
YOUR TIME for an afternoon stroll. For full immersion in the Tower of London,

set aside half a day, especially if seeing the Crown Jewels is a priority. Allow an hour minimum each for the Museum of London, St. Paul's Cathedral, and the Tower Bridge. On weekends, the City is nearly deserted, making it hard to find lunch—and yet this is when the major attractions are at their busiest. So if you can manage to come on a weekday, do so.

TOP ATTRACTIONS

Monument. Commemorating the "dreadful visitation" of the Great Fire of 1666, this is the world's tallest isolated stone column. It is the work of Sir Christopher Wren and Dr. Robert Hooke, who were asked to erect it "on or as neere unto the place where the said Fire soe unhappily began as conveniently may be." ⊠ *Monument St., The City* ☎ *020/7626–2717* ⊕ *www.themonument.info* ⌹ *£3; combined ticket with Tower Bridge exhibition £8* ⊙ *Daily 9:30–5:30, last admission 5* Ⓤ *Monument.*

↻
★ **Museum of London.** If there's one place to absorb the history of London, from 450,000 BC to the present day, it's here: Oliver Cromwell's death mask, Queen Victoria's crinoline gowns, Selfridges' Art deco elevators, and the London's Burning exhibition are just some of the goodies. The museum appropriately shelters a section of the 2nd- to 4th-century London wall, which you can view from a window inside. Permanent displays include "London Before London," "Roman London," "Medieval London," and "Tudor London." The Galleries of Modern London, which opened in 2010 following a £20 million modernization, are enthralling. Experience the "Expanding City," "People's City," and "World City" galleries, each one dealing with a section of London's history from 1666 until the 21st century. ⊠ *London Wall, The City* ☎ *020/7001–9844* ⊕ *www.museumoflondon.org.uk* ⌹ *Free* ⊙ *Mon.– Sun. 10–6; last admission 5:30* Ⓤ *Barbican, St. Paul's.*

St. Bride's. According to legend, the distinctively tiered steeple of this Christopher Wren–designed church gave rise to the shape of the traditional wedding cake. One early couple inspired to marry here were the parents of Virginia Dare, the first European child born in colonial America in 1587. ⊠ *Fleet St., The City* ☎ *020/7427–0133* ⊕ *www. stbrides.com* ⌹ *Free* ⊙ *Weekdays 8–6, Sat. 11–3, Sun. for services only 10–1 and 5–7:30* Ⓤ *St. Paul's, Blackfriars.*

St. Mary-le-Bow. This church is a classic City survivor; various versions have stood on the site since the 11th century. In 1284 a local goldsmith took refuge here after committing a murder, only to be killed inside the church by enraged relatives of his victim. The church was abandoned for a time afterward, but started up again, and was rebuilt in its current form after the Great Fire. ⊠ *Cheapside, The City* ☎ *020/7248–5139* ⊕ *www.stmarylebow.co.uk* ⊙ *Mon.–Wed. 7–6, Thurs. 7–6:30, Fri. 7–4; closed weekends* Ⓤ *Mansion House, St. Paul's.*

QUICK BITES The **Café Below** (☎ *020/7329–0789* ⊕ *www.cafebelow.co.uk*), in St. Mary-le-Bow's Norman crypt, is packed with City workers weekdays from 7:30 am until 9 pm for a menu covering breakfasts, scrumptious light lunches, and delicious dinners.

Fodor's Choice
★ **St. Paul's Cathedral.** St. Paul's is simply breathtaking—even more so since it was spruced up for its 300th anniversary in 2008. The dome, the world's third largest, is easily recognizable through the skyline from many an angle around London. The structure is Sir Christopher Wren's masterpiece, completed in 1710 after 35 years of building, and, much later, miraculously spared (mostly) by World War II bombs. When you enter and see the dome from the inside, it may seem smaller

> **MUSICAL FRICTION**
>
> The organ at St. Paul's, with its cherubs and angels, was not installed without controversy. The mighty instrument proved a tight fit, and the maker, known as Father Schmidt, and Wren nearly came to blows. Wren was reputed to have said he would not adapt his cathedral for a mere "box of whistles."

than you expected. It *is* smaller, and 60 feet lower than the lead-covered outer dome. Beneath the lantern is Wren's famous epitaph, which his son composed and had set into the pavement, and which reads succinctly: "Lector, si monumentum requiris, circumspice"—"Reader, if you seek his monument, look around you." The epitaph also appears on Wren's memorial in the Crypt. Up 259 spiral steps is the **Whispering Gallery,** an acoustic phenomenon; you whisper something to the wall on one side, and a second later it transmits clearly to the other side, 107 feet away. Ascend to the **Stone Gallery,** which encircles the base of the dome. Farther up (280 feet from ground level) is the small **Golden Gallery,** around the dome's highest point. From both these galleries (if you have a head for heights) you can walk outside for a spectacular panorama of London. The climb up the spiraling steps can be fun for older kids.

The remains of the poet John Donne, who was dean of St. Paul's for his final 10 years (he died in 1631), are in the south choir aisle. The vivacious choir-stall carvings nearby are the work of Grinling Gibbons, as are those on the organ, which Wren designed and Handel played. Behind the high altar is the **American Memorial Chapel,** dedicated in 1958 to the 28,000 GIs stationed in the United Kingdom who lost their lives in World War II. Among the famous whose remains lie in the **Crypt** are the duke of Wellington and Admiral Lord Nelson. The Crypt also has a gift shop and a café. ⊠ *St. Paul's Churchyard, The City,* ☎ *020/7236–4128* ⊕ *www.stpauls.co.uk* ✉ *£12.50, (cost includes multimedia guides and guided tours)* ⊗ *Cathedral Mon.–Sat. 8:30–4 (last admission at 4), Shop Mon.–Sat. 8:30–5, (Wed. 9–5), Sun. 10–4:30, Crypt Café Mon.–Sat. 9–5, Sun. noon–4* Ⓤ *St. Paul's.*

☺ **Tower Bridge.** Despite its medieval, fairy-tale appearance, this is a Victorian youngster. Constructed of steel, then clothed in Portland stone, the Horace Jones masterpiece was deliberately styled in the Gothic persuasion to complement the Tower next door. The **Tower Bridge Exhibition** is a child-friendly tour where you can discover how one of the world's most famous bridges actually works. ⊠ *Tower Bridge Rd., The City* ☎ *020/7403–3761* ⊕ *www.towerbridge.org.uk* ✉ *£7* ⊗ *Apr.–Sept., daily 10–6:30; Oct.–Mar., daily 9:30–6; last admission 30 min before closing* Ⓤ *Tower Hill.*

🔄 **Tower of London.** *See the highlighted feature in this section.*

Fodor's Choice

★

WORTH NOTING

Dr. Johnson's House. This is where Samuel Johnson lived between 1748 and 1759, compiling his famous dictionary in the attic as his health deteriorated. Built in 1700, the elegant Georgian residence, with its paneled rooms and period furniture, is where the Great Bear (as he was known) compiled his *Dictionary of the English Language.* After soaking up the atmosphere, repair around the corner in Wine Office Court to the famed **Ye Olde Cheshire Cheese** pub, once Johnson and Boswell's favorite watering hole. ✉ *17 Gough Sq., The City* ☎ *020/ 7353–3745* ⊕ *www.drjohnsonshouse.org* ☜ *£4.50* ⊙ *May–Sept., Mon.–Sat. 11–5:30; Oct.–Apr., Mon.–Sat. 11–5; closed bank holidays* Ⓤ *Holborn, Chancery La.*

Guildhall. The Corporation of London, which oversees The City, has ceremonially elected and installed its lord mayor here for the last 800 years. The Guildhall was built in 1411, and though it failed to avoid either the 1666 or 1940 flames, its core survived. To the right of Guildhall Yard is the **Guildhall Art Gallery,** which includes portraits of the great and the good, cityscapes, famous battles, and a slightly cloying pre-Raphaelite section. The construction of the gallery led to the exciting discovery of London's only **Roman amphitheater,** which had lain underneath Guildhall Yard undisturbed for more than 1,800 years. ✉ *Aldermanbury, The City* ☎ *020/7606–3030, 020/7332–3700 gallery* ⊕ *www.cityoflondon. gov.uk* ☜ *Free; gallery and amphitheater £2.50* ⊙ *Mon.–Sat. 9:30–5; gallery Mon.–Sat. 10–5, Sun. noon–4, last admission 4:30 or 3:30* Ⓤ *St. Paul's, Moorgate, Bank, Mansion House.*

Old Bailey. If you're lucky, this is the place to watch the real-life drama of justice in action in one of the 16 courtrooms that are open to the public. Previous trials have included those of Crippen and Christie, two of England's most notorious wife murderers, as well as the controversial trial of Oscar Wilde. The present-day **Central Criminal Court** is where Newgate Prison stood from the 12th century right until the beginning of the 20th century. The most famous feature of the solid Edwardian building is the 12-foot gilded statue of Justice perched on top; she was intended to mirror the dome of St. Paul's. ✉ *Newgate St., The City* ☎ *020/7248–3277 information* ⊕ *www.cityoflondon.gov. uk* ⊙ *Public Gallery weekdays 10–1 and 2–5 (approx.); line forms at Newgate St. entrance or in Warwick St. Passage; closed bank holidays and day after* Ⓤ *St. Paul's.*

Continued on page 78

THE TOWER OF LONDON

The Tower is a microcosm of the city itself—a sprawling, organic hodgepodge of buildings that inspires reverence and terror in equal measure. See the block on which Anne Boleyn was beheaded, marvel at the Crown Jewels, and pay homage to the ravens who keep the monarchy safe.

An architectural patchwork of time, the oldest building of the complex is the fairytale White Tower, conceived by William the Conqueror in 1078 as both a royal residence and a show of power to the troublesome Anglo-Saxons he had subdued at the Battle of Hastings. Today's Tower has seen everything, as a palace, barracks, a mint for producing coins, an armoury, and the Royal menagerie (home of the country's first elephant). The big draw is the stunning opulence of the Crown Jewels, kept on-site in the heavily fortified Jewel House. Most of all, though, the Tower is known for death: it's been a place of imprisonment, torture, and execution for the realm's most notorious traitors as well as its martyrs. These days, unless you count the killer admission fees, there are far less morbid activities taking place in the Tower, but it still breathes London's history and pageantry from its every brick and offers hours of exploration.

TOURING THE TOWER

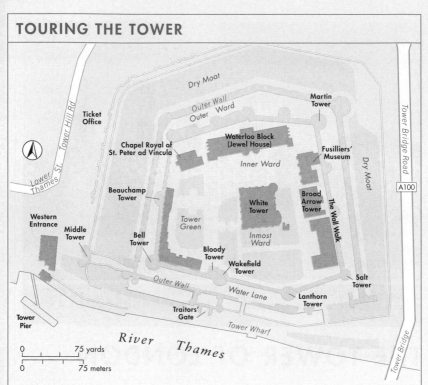

Dry Moat

Outer Wall
Outer Ward

Martin
Tower

Ticket
Office

Chapel Royal of
St. Peter ad Vincula

Waterloo Block
(Jewel House)

Fusilliers'
Museum

Inner Ward

Dry Moat

Beauchamp
Tower

White
Tower

Broad
Arrow
Tower

The Wall Walk

A100

Western
Entrance

Middle
Tower

Tower
Green

Inmost
Ward

Bell
Tower

Bloody
Tower

Wakefield
Tower

Salt
Tower

Outer Wall

Water Lane

Lanthorn
Tower

Tower
Pier

Traitors'
Gate

Tower Wharf

River Thames

Tower Hill Rd

Lower Thames St.

Tower Bridge Road

Tower Bridge

0   75 yards

0   75 meters

Entry to the Tower is via the **Western Entrance** and the **Middle Tower,** which feed into the outermost ring of the Tower's defenses.

Water Lane leads past the dread-inducing **Traitors' Gate,** the final point of entry for many Tower prisoners.

Toward the end of Water Lane, the **Lanthorn Tower** houses by night the ravens rumored to keep the kingdom safe, and by day a timely high-tech reconstruction of the Catholic Guy Fawkes's plot to blow up the Houses of Parliament in 1605.

The **Bloody Tower** earned its name as the apocryphal site

of the murder of two young princes, Edward and Richard, who disappeared from the Tower after being put there in 1483 by their uncle, Richard III. Two little skeletons (now in Westminster Abbey) were found buried close to the White Tower in 1674 and are thought to be theirs.

The **Beauchamp Tower** housed upper-class miscreants: Latin graffiti about Lady Jane Grey can be glimpsed today on its walls.

Like a prize gem set at the head of a royal crown, the **White Tower** is the center-piece of the complex. Its four towers dominate the Inner

GOLD DIGGER?

Keep your eyes peeled as you tour the Tower: according to one story, Sir John Barkstead, goldsmith and Lieutenant of the Tower under Cromwell, hid £20,000 in gold coins here before his arrest and execution at the Restoration of Charles II.

Ward, a fitting and forbidding reminder of Norman strength at the time of the conquest of England.

Once inside the White Tower, head upstairs for the **Armouries,** where the biggest attraction, quite literally,

ROYAL BLING

The Crown of Queen Elizabeth, the Queen Mother, from 1937, contains the exotic 105-carat Koh-i-Noor (mountain of light) diamond.

Jewel House, Waterloo Barracks

TIME KILLERS

Some prisoners managed to keep themselves plenty amused: Sir Walter Raleigh grew tobacco on Tower Green, and in 1561 suspected sorcerer Hugh Draper carved an intricate astronomical clock on the walls of his Salt Tower cell.

is the suit of armor worn by a well-endowed Henry VIII. There is a matching outfit for his horse.

Other fascinating exhibits include the set of Samurai armor presented to James I in 1613 by the emperor of Japan, and the tiny set of armor worn by Henry VIII's young son Edward.

The **Jewel House** in **Waterloo Block** is the Tower's biggest draw, perfect for playing pick-your-favorite-crown from the wrong side of bul-

letproof glass. Not only are these crowns, staffs, and orbs encrusted with heavy-duty gems, they are invested with the authority of monarchical power in England, dating back to the 1300s.

Outside, pause at **Tower Green,** permanent departure point for those of noble birth. The hoi polloi were dispatched at nearby Tower Hill. The Tower's most famous female victims—Anne Boleyn, Margaret Countess of Salisbury, Catherine Howard, and Lady Jane Grey—all went this "priviledged" way.

Behind a well-kept square of grass stands the **Chapel Royal of St. Peter ad Vincula,** a delightful Tudor church and final resting place of six beheaded Tudor bodies. ■TIP➔ **Visitors are welcome for services and can also enter after 4:30 pm daily.**

The **Salt Tower,** reputedly the most haunted corner of the complex, marks the start of the **Wall Walk,** a bracing promenade along the stone spiral steps and battlements of the Tower that looks down on the trucks, taxis, and shimmering high-rises of modern London.

The Wall Walk ends at the **Martin Tower,** former home of the Crown Jewels and now host to the crowns and diamonds exhibition that explains the art of fashioning royal headwear and tells the story of some of the most famous stones.

On leaving the Tower, browse the **gift shop,** and wander the wharf that overlooks the Thames, leading to a picture-postcard view of Tower Bridge.

WHO ARE THE BEEFEATERS?

First of all, they're Yeoman Warders, but probably got the nickname "beefeater" from their position as Royal Bodyguards which entitled them to eat as much beef as they liked. Part of the "Yeoman of the Guard," started in the reign of Edmund IV, the warders have formed the Royal Bodyguard as far back as 1509 when Henry VIII left a dozen of the Yeoman of the Guard at the Tower to protect it.

Originally, the Yeoman Warders also served as jailers of the Tower, doubling as torturers when necessary. (So it would have been a Beefeater tightening the thumb screws, or ratchetting the rack another notch on some unfortunate prisoner. Smile nicely.) Today 36 Yeoman Warders (men and women since 2007), along with the Chief Yeoman Warder and the Yeoman Gaoler, live within the walls of the Tower with their families, in accommodations in the Outer Ward. They stand guard over the Tower, conduct tours, and lock up at 9:53 pm every night with the Ceremony of the Keys.

■ TIP➔ Free tickets to the Ceremony of the Keys are available by writing several months in advance; check the Tower Web site for details.

HARK THE RAVENS!

Legend has it that should the hulking black ravens ever leave, the White Tower will crumble and the kingdom fall. Charles II, no doubt jumpy after his father's execution and the monarchy's short-term fall from grace, made a royal decree in 1662 that there should be at least six of the carrion-eating nasties present at all times. There have been some close calls. During World War II, numbers dropped to one, echoing the precarious fate of the war-wracked country. In 2005, two (of eight) died over Christmas when Thor—the most intelligent but also the largest bully of the bunch—killed new recruit Gundolf, named after the Tower's 1070 designer. Pneumonia put an end to Bran, leaving lifelong partner Branwen without her mate.

■ DID YOU KNOW? In 1981 a raven named Grog, perhaps seduced by his alcoholic moniker, escaped after 21 years at the Tower. Others have been banished for "conduct unbecoming."

The six that remain, each one identified by a colored band around a claw, are much loved for their fidelity (they mate for life) and their cheek (capable of 440 noises, they are witty and scolding mimics). It's not only the diet

of blood-soaked biscuits, rabbit, and scraps from the mess kitchen that keeps them coming back. Their lifting feathers on one wing are trimmed, meaning they can manage the equivalent of a lop-sided air-bound hobble but not much more. For the first half of 2006 the ravens were moved indoors full-time as a preventive measure against avian flu but have since been allowed out and about again. In situ they are a territorial lot, sticking to Tower Green and the White Tower, and lodging nightly by Wakefield Tower. They've had free front-row seats at all the most grisly moments in Tower history—Anne Boleyn's execution included.

■ TIP➔ Don't get too close to the ravens: they are prone to pecking and not particularly fond of humans, unless you are the Tower's Raven Master.

And *WHAT* are they wearing?

A **pike** (or halberd), also known as a partisan, is the Yeoman Warder's weapon of choice. The Chief Warder carries a staff topped with a miniature silver model of the White Tower.

Anyone who refers to this as a costume will be lucky to leave the Tower with head still attached to body: this is the ceremonial uniform of the Yeoman Warders, and it comes at a cool £13,000 a throw.

The black Tudor **bonnet** is made of velvet; the blue undress consists of a felt top hat, with a single Tudor rose in the middle.

This **Tudor-style ruff** helps date the ceremonial uniform, which was first worn in 1552.

Insignia on a Yeoman Warder's upper right arm denote the rank he carried in the military.

The **medals** on a Yeoman Warder's chest are more than mere show: all of the men and women have served for at least 22 years in the armed forces.

This version of the **royal livery** bears the insignia of the current Queen ("E" for Elizabeth) but originally dates from Tudor times. The first letter changes according to the reigning monarch's Christian name; the second letter is always an "R" for *rex* (king) or *regina* (queen).

Slits in the **tunic** date from the times when Beefeaters were expected to ride a horse.

Red socks and **black patent shoes** are worn on special occasions. Visitors are more likely to see the regular blue undress, introduced in 1858 as the regular working dress of the Yeoman Warders.

The **red lines down the trousers** are a sign of the blood from the swords of the Yeoman Warders in their defense of the realm.

(IN)FAMOUS PRISONERS OF THE TOWER

Anne Boleyn   Lady Jane Grey   Sir Walter Raleigh

Sir Thomas More. A Catholic and Henry VIII's friend and chancellor, Sir Thomas refused to attend the coronation of Anne Boleyn (Henry VIII's second wife) or to recognize the multi-marrying king as head of the Church. Sent to the Tower for treason, in 1535 More was beheaded.

Anne Boleyn. The first of Henry VIII's wives to be beheaded, Anne, who failed to provide the king with a son, was accused of sleeping with five men, including her own brother. All six got the chop in 1536. Her severed head was held up to the crowd, and her lips were said to be mouthing prayer.

Margaret, Countess of Salisbury. Not the best-known prisoner in her lifetime, she has a reputation today for haunting the Tower. And no wonder: the elderly 70-year-old was condemned by Henry VIII in 1541 for a potentially treacherous bloodline (she was the last Plantagenet princess) and hacked to death by the executioner after she refused to put her head on the block like a common traitor and attempted to run away.

Queen Catherine Howard. Henry VIII's fifth wife was locked up for high treason and infidelity and beheaded in 1542 at age 20. Ever eager to please, she spent her final night practicing how to lay her head on the block.

Lady Jane Grey. The nine-days-queen lost her head in 1554 at age 16. Her death was the result of sibling rivalry gone seriously wrong, when Protestant Edward VI slighted his Catholic sister Mary in favor of Lady Jane as heir, and Mary decided to have none of it.

Guy Fawkes. The Roman Catholic soldier who tried to blow up the Houses of Parliament and kill the king in the 1605 Gunpowder plot was first incarcerated in the chambers of the Tower, where King James I requested he be tortured in ever-worsening ways. Perhaps unsurprisingly, he confessed. He met his seriously grisly end in the Old Palace Yard at Westminster, where he was hung, drawn, and quartered in 1607.

Sir Walter Raleigh. Once a favorite of Elizabeth I, he offended her by secretly marrying her Maid of Honor and was chucked in the Tower. Later, as a conspirator against James I, he paid with his life. A frequent visitor to the Tower (he spent 13 years there in three stints), he managed to get the Bloody Tower enlarged on account of his wife and growing family. He was finally executed in 1618 in Old Palace Yard, Westminster.

Josef Jakobs. The last man to be executed in the Tower was caught as a spy when parachuting in from Germany and executed by firing squad in 1941. The chair he sat in when he was shot is preserved in the Royal Armouries' artifacts store.

FOR FURTHER EVIDENCE . . .

A trio of buildings in the Inner Ward, the **Bloody Tower, Beauchamp Tower,** and **Queen's House,** all with excellent views of the execution scaffold in Tower Green, are the heart of the Tower's prison accommodations and home to a permanent exhibition about notable inmates.

TACKLING THE TOWER (without losing your head)

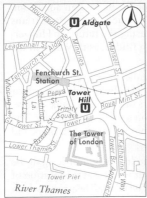

✉ H.M. Tower of London, Tower Hill ☎ 0844/482-7777, 0844/482-7799 tickets ⊕ www.hrp.org.uk 💷 £19.80, children 16 and under £9.50, children under 5 free. Family tickets (2 adults, 3 children) £55 🕓 Mar.–Oct., Tues.–Sat. 9–5:30, Sun. and Mon. 10–5:30; last admission at 5. Nov.–Feb., Tues.–Sat. 9–4:30, Sun. and Mon. 10–4:30; last admission at 4 Ⓤ Tower Hill

■ TIP➜ You can buy tickets from automatic kiosks on arrival, or up to seven days in advance at any Tube station. Avoid lines completely and save by booking discounted tickets online.

MAKING THE MOST OF YOUR TIME: Without doubt, the Tower is worth two to three hours. A full hour of that would be well spent by joining one of the Yeoman Warders' tours (included in admission). It's hard to better their insight, vitality, and humor—they are knights of the realm living their very own fairytale castle existence.

The Crown Jewels are worth the wait, the White Tower is essential, and the Medieval Palace and Bloody Tower should at least be breezed through.

■ TIP➜ It's best to visit on weekdays, when the crowds are smaller.

WITH KIDS: The Tower's centuries-old cobblestones are not exactly stroller-friendly, but strollers are permitted inside most of the buildings. If you do bring one, be prepared to leave it temporarily unsupervised (the stroller, that is—not your child) outside the White Tower, which has no access. There are baby-changing facilities in the Brick Tower restrooms behind the Jewel House. Look for regular free children's events such as the Knight's school where children can have a go at jousting, sword-fighting, and archery.

■ TIP➜ Tell your child to find one of the Yeoman Warders if he or she should get lost; they will in turn lead him or her to the Byward Tower, which is where you should meet.

IN A HURRY? If you have less than an hour, head down Wall Walk, through a succession of towers, which eventually spit you out at the Martin Tower. The view over modern London is quite a contrast.

TOURS: Tours given by a Yeoman Warder leave from the main entrance near Middle Tower every half-hour from 10–4, and last about an hour. Beefeaters give occasional 30-minute talks in the Lanthorn Tower about their daily lives. Both tours are free.

THE SOUTH BANK

Culture, history, sights: the South Bank has it all. High-caliber art, music, film, and theater venues sit alongside the likes of an aquarium, historic warships, and Borough Market, a foodie favorite. Pedestrians cross between the north and south banks using the futuristic Hungerford Bridge and the curvaceous Millennium Bridge, as they take in the compelling views of the Thames.

The Tate Modern is the star attraction, installed in a 1930s power station, with the eye-catching Millennium Bridge linking its main door across the river to the City. Near the theaters of the South Bank Centre, the London Eye observation wheel gives you a flight over the city. The South Bank of the Thames isn't beautiful, but this area of theaters and museums has Culture with a capital C.

It's fitting that so much of London's artistic life should once again be centered on the South Bank—in the past, Southwark was the location of theaters, taverns, and cockfighting arenas. The Globe Theatre, in which Shakespeare acted and held shares, was one of several here. In truth the Globe was as likely to stage bear-baiting as Shakespeare, but today, at the reconstructed "Wooden O," you can see only the latter. Be sure to take a walk along Bankside, the embankment along the Thames from Southwark to Blackfriars Bridge.

GETTING HERE For the South Bank use Westminster station on the Jubilee or Northern line, from where you can walk across Westminster Bridge; Embankment on District, Circle, Northern, and Bakerloo lines, where you can walk across Hungerford Bridge; or Waterloo on the Jubilee, Northern, and Bakerloo lines, where it's a five-minute walk to the Royal Festival Hall. In the east, alternatively, use Tower Gateway on the Docklands Light Railway (DLR). London Bridge on the Northern and Jubilee lines is but a five-minute stroll from Borough Market and Southwark Cathedral.

PLANNING
YOUR TIME The South Bank sprawls; block out visiting times based on locations and your interests. The Imperial War Museum demands a couple of hours; the Tate Modern deserves a whole morning or afternoon to do justice to temporary exhibitions and the permanent collection. The Globe Theatre requires about two hours for the exhibition theater tour and two to three hours for a performance. Finish with drinks or dinner at the Oxo Tower or a stroll west along the riverbank and then across Hungerford Bridge.

TOP ATTRACTIONS

🕑 **Imperial War Museum.** Despite its title, this museum of 20th-century war-
★ fare does not glorify bloodshed but emphasizes understanding through evoking what life was like for citizens and soldiers alike through the two world wars and beyond. There's an impressive amount of hardware at the main entrance with accompanying interactive material, including a Battle of Britain Spitfire, a German V2 rocket, tanks, guns, and submarines—and from here you can peel off to the various sections of the museum. Sights, sounds, and smells are used to re-create the uncomfortable Trench Experience in the World War I gallery. ⊠ *Lambeth Rd., South Bank* ☎ *020/7416–5000* ⊕ *www.iwm.org.uk* ⊠ *Free (charge for special exhibits)* ⊗ *Daily 10–6* Ⓤ *Lambeth North.*

2

☺ **London Eye.** To mark the start of the new millennium, architects David
★ Marks and Julia Barfield conceived an entirely new vision: a beautiful
and celebratory structure that would allow people to see this great city
from a completely new perspective—on a giant wheel. The London Eye
is the largest observation wheel ever built and among the top 10 tallest
structures in London. ■TIP➜ Buy your ticket online, over the phone, or at
the ticket office in advance to avoid the long lines. The London Eye sightseeing cruise also departs here for a 40-minute cruise of the Thames.
⊠ *Jubilee Gardens, South Bank* ☎ *0870/990–8883* ⊕ *www.londoneye.*
com ☎ *£17.95, cruise £12* ☼ *June and Sept., daily 10–9; July and Aug.,*
daily 10–9:30; Oct.–Mar., daily 10–8 Ⓤ *Waterloo.*

Oxo Tower. Long a London landmark to the insider, the Art deco–era
Oxo building has graduated from its former incarnations as a power-
generating station and warehouse into a vibrant community of artists'
and designers' workshops, a pair of restaurants, and five floors of community homes. There's an observation deck for a super river vista. ⊠ *Barge-*
house St., South Bank ☎ *020/7021–1686* ⊕ *www.oxotower.co.uk* ☎ *Free*
☼ *Studios and shops Tues.–Sun. 11–6* Ⓤ *Blackfriars, Waterloo.*

☺ **Shakespeare's Globe Theatre.** A spectacular theater, this is a replica of
Fodor's Choice Shakespeare's open-roof, wood-and-thatch Globe Playhouse (built in
★ 1599 and burned down in 1613), where most of the Bard's great plays
premiered. For several decades, American actor and director Sam Wana-
maker worked ceaselessly to raise funds for the theater's reconstruction, 200 yards from its original site, using authentic materials and
techniques. His dream was realized in 1997. At the plays, "ground-
lings"—those with £5 standing-only tickets—are not allowed to sit
during the performance. You can reserve an actual seat, though, on any
one of the theater's three levels, but you will want to rent a cushion for
£1 (or bring your own) to soften the backless wooden benches. The
show must go on, rain or shine, warm or chilly—so come prepared
for anything. Umbrellas are banned, but you can bring a raincoat or
buy a cheap Globe rain poncho, which doubles as a great souvenir.
Throughout the year, you can tour the theater as part of the **Shake-**
speare's Globe Exhibition, a museum under the theater (the entry is
adjacent) that provides background material on the Elizabethan theater
and the construction of the modern-day Globe. Admission also includes
a tour of the theater. On matinee days, the tour visits the archaeological
site of the nearby (and older) Rose Theatre. ⊠ *21 New Globe Walk,*
Bankside, South Bank, ☎ *020/7902–1400 box office, 020/7401–9919*
New Shakespeare's Globe Exhibition ⊕ *www.shakespeares-globe.org*
☎ *Exhibition & Globe Theatre Tour £10.50 (£2 reduction with valid*
performance ticket; ticket prices for plays vary, £5–£35 ☼ *Exhibition*
May–early Oct., daily 10–5; mid-Oct.–Apr., daily 9–12:30 and 1–5;
plays May–early Oct., call for performance schedule Ⓤ *Southwark, then*
walk to Blackfriars Bridge and descend the steps; Mansion House,
then cross Southwark Bridge; Blackfriars, then walk across Blackfriars
Bridge; St. Paul's, then cross Millennium Bridge.

Southwark Cathedral. Pronounced "Suth-uck," this is the second-oldest
Gothic church in London, after Westminster Abbey, with parts dating
back to the 12th century. Look for the gaudily renovated 1408 tomb

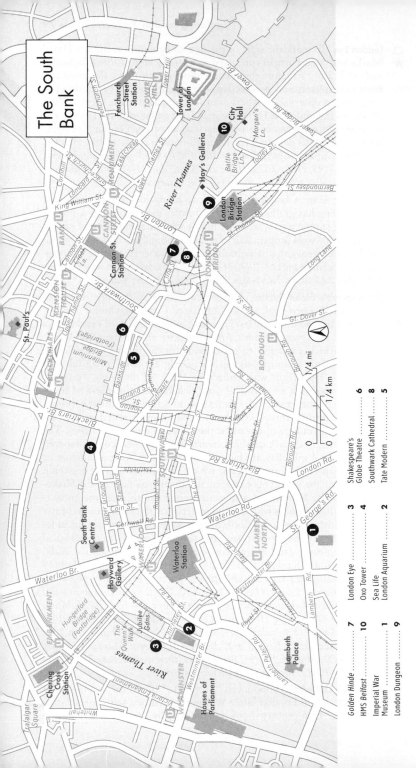

The South Bank

of the poet John Gower, friend of Chaucer, and for the Harvard Chapel. Another notable buried here is Edmund Shakespeare, brother of William. ⊠ *London Bridge, South Bank* ☎ *020/7367–6700* ⊕ *www. southwark.anglican.org* ⊠ *Free, suggested donation £4* ⊙ *Daily 8–6* Ⓤ *London Bridge.*

<table>
<tr><td>**WHEN TO GO**</td></tr>
<tr><td>Avoid going to the Tate Modern on weekends, when visitor numbers are at their greatest. Visit during the week or join the cool crowd on Friday evenings, when it's open until 10.</td></tr>
</table>

Fodor's Choice ★ **Tate Modern.** This spectacular art museum took something functional—a 1930's power station—and made it a place for creativity. Today, it is one of the greatest new museums devoted to modern and contemporary art. Besides a permanent collection that ranges from Matisse to the most-talked-about British upstarts and is not grouped by artist, but arranged thematically—Landscape, Still Life, and the Nude—the museum hosts its latest barnstorming exhibition, often a talking point at smart dinner parties across the art world.

The vast **Turbine Hall** is a dramatic entrance point used to showcase big, audacious installations that tend to generate a lot of publicity. Past highlights include a massive glowing sun and, perhaps most bizarrely, a long crack in the floor. The **Material Gestures** galleries on Level 3 feature an impressive offering of post–World War II painting and sculpture. Room 7 contains a breathtaking collection of Rothkos and Monets; there are also paintings by Matisse, Pollock, and Picasso, and newer works from the likes of the sculptor Anish Kapoor.

Head to the Restaurant on Level 7 or the Espresso Bar on Level 4 for stunning vistas of the Thames. The view of St. Paul's from the Espresso Bar's balcony is one of the best in London. ⊠ *Bankside, South Bank* ☎ *020/7887–8888* ⊕ *www.tate.org.uk/modern* ⊠ *Free, charge for special exhibitions* ⊙ *Sun.–Thurs. 10–6, Fri. and Sat. 10–10 (last admission to exhibitions 45 min before close)* Ⓤ *Blackfriars, Southwark.*

WORTH NOTING

Ⓒ **Golden Hinde.** Sir Francis Drake circumnavigated the globe in this little galleon, or one just like it. This exact replica made a 23-year round-the-world voyage—much of it spent along U.S. coasts, both Pacific and Atlantic—and has settled here to continue its educational purpose. ⊠ *Units 1 & 2, Pickfords Wharf, Clink St., South Bank* ☎ *020/7403– 0123* ⊕ *www.goldenhinde.com* ⊠ *£6* ⊙ *Daily 10–5:30* Ⓤ *London Bridge, Mansion House.*

Ⓒ **HMS Belfast.** At 613 feet, this is one of the largest and most powerful cruisers the Royal Navy has ever had. It played an important role in the D-Day landings off Normandy, left for the Far East after the war, and has been moored in the relative calm of the Thames since 1971. ⊠ *Morgan's La., Tooley St., South Bank* ☎ *020/7940–6300* ⊕ *hmsbelfast.iwm.org.uk* ⊠ *£12.95, children under 16 free* ⊙ *Mar.–Oct., daily 10–6; Nov.–Feb., daily 10–5; last admission 1 hr before closing* Ⓤ *London Bridge.*

Ⓒ **London Dungeon.** Here's the goriest, grisliest, most gruesome attraction in town, where realistic waxwork people are subjected in graphic detail to all the historical horrors the Tower of London merely tells you about.

Perhaps the most shocking thing here is the mass of children lined up roaring to get in every day—kiddies absolutely adore this place, but some nervous types may find it too frightening (and that goes for the adults, too). ■TIP→ Expect long lines on weekends and during school holidays. Booking online will save at least £5. ⊠ *28–34 Tooley St., South Bank* ☎ *0871/7403-7221* ⊕ *www.thedungeons.com* ⊠ *£23* ⊘ *Daily; opening times vary slightly, week by week, but generally Sept.–Mar. 10–5; Mar.– Sept. 9:30–6; Aug. 9:30–7; phone to confirm times* Ⓤ *London Bridge.*

☾ **Sea Life London Aquarium.** The curved, colonnaded, neoclassic hulk of County Hall once housed London's local government administration (now at the Norman Foster–designed City Hall building farther downriver by Tower Bridge). Now it's where you can catch a dark and thrilling glimpse of the waters of the world, focused around a superb three-level aquarium full of sharks and stingrays, among other common and rarer breeds. ⊠ *County Hall, Riverside Bldg., Westminster Bridge Rd., South Bank* ☎ *0871/663-1678* ⊕ *www.sealife.co.uk* ⊠ *£16* ⊘ *Mon.–Thurs. 10–6, last admission 5; Fri.–Sun. 10–7, last admission 6* Ⓤ *Westminster, Waterloo.*

KENSINGTON, KNIGHTSBRIDGE, AND MAYFAIR

Splendid houses with pillared porches, as well as fascinating museums, stylish squares, and glittering antiques shops, line the streets of this elegant area of the Royal Borough of Kensington. Also here is Kensington Palace (the former home of both Diana, Princess of Wales, and Queen Victoria), which put the district literally on the map back in the 17th century. To Kensington's east is one of the highest concentrations of important artifacts in London, the "museum mile" of South Kensington. Kensington first became the *Royal* Borough of Kensington (and Chelsea) when William III, who suffered from the Thames mists over Whitehall, decided in 1689 to buy Nottingham House in the rural village of Kensington. By the time Queen Anne was on the throne (1702–14), Kensington was overflowing. In a way, it still is, since most of its grand houses have been divided into apartments, or are serving as embassies.

Hyde Park and Kensington Gardens together form by far the biggest of central London's royal parks. It's probably been centuries since any major royal had a casual stroll here, but the parks remain the property of the Crown, and it was the Crown that saved them from being devoured by the city's late-18th-century growth spurt.

Around the borders of Hyde Park are several of London's most beautiful and posh neighborhoods. To the south of the park and a short carriage ride from Buckingham Palace is the splendidly aristocratic enclave of Belgravia. Its white-stucco buildings and grand squares—particularly Belgrave Square—are Regency-era jewels. On the eastern border of Hyde Park is Mayfair, which gives Belgravia a run for its money as London's wealthiest district.

GETTING HERE   There's good Tube service to these areas. On the Central Line, Marble Arch and Bond Street (also Jubilee Line) take you to the heart of Mayfair; the Hyde Park Corner stop on the Piccadilly line is at the southeast corner of the park, near Apsley House. South Kensington and

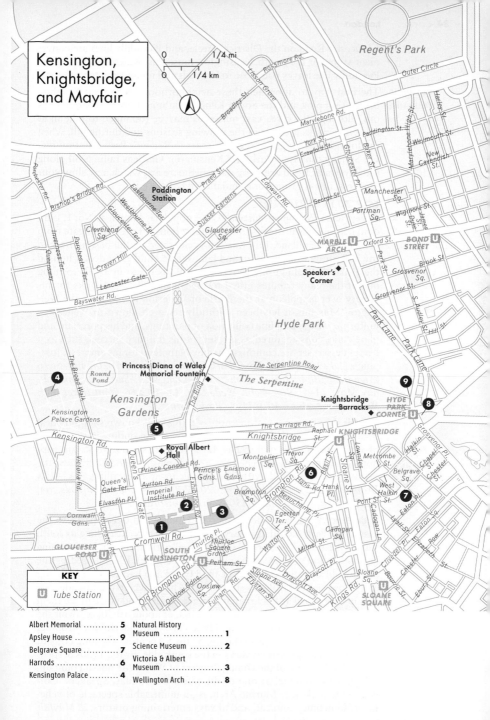

Kensington, Knightsbridge, and Mayfair

0   1/4 mi

0   1/4 km

Regent's Park

Outer Circle

Rossmore Rd.

Lisson Grove

Broadley St.

Marylebone Rd.

York St.

Crawford St.

Paddington St.

Gloucester Pl.

Baker St.

Harley St.

New Cavendish St.

Weymouth St.

Manchester Sq.

Portman Sq.

George St.

Wigmore St.

James St.

MARBLE ARCH [U]   Oxford St.   BOND STREET [U]

Brook St.

Grosvenor Sq.

Grosvenor St.

Park St.

S. Audley St.

Park Lane

Praed St.

Eastbourne Ter.

Paddington Station

Bishop's Bridge Rd.

Westbourne Ter.

Gloucester Ter.

Sussex Gardens

Edgware Rd.

Gloucester Sq.

Cleveland Sq.

Craven Hill

Lancaster Gate

Bayswater Rd.

Rochester Rd.

Porchester Ter.

Inverness Ter.

Queensway

Speaker's Corner

Hyde Park

The Broad Walk

The Ring

Round Pond

Princess Diana of Wales Memorial Fountain

The Serpentine Road

The Serpentine

Kensington Palace Gardens

Kensington Gardens

4 ●

9 ●

HYDE PARK CORNER [U]

8 ●

Knightsbridge Barracks

The Carriage Rd.

Knightsbridge

KNIGHTSBRIDGE

Kensington Rd.

Victoria Rd.

Gloucester Rd.

5 ●

Royal Albert Hall

Prince Consort Rd.

Queen's Gate Ter.

Queen's Gate

Ayrton Rd.

Imperial Institute Rd.

Prince's Gdns.

Elvaston Pl.

Cornwall Gdns.

GLOUCESTER ROAD [U]

Cromwell Rd.

SOUTH KENSINGTON [U]

Thurloe Pl.

Thurloe Square Gdns.

Pelham St.

Old Brompton Rd.

Onslow Gdns.

Onslow Sq.

Fulham Rd.

Enismore Gdns.

Montpelier Sq.

Trevor Sq.

Raphael St.

Basil St.

Sloane St.

Hans Rd.

Hans Pl.

Metcombe St.

Lowndes St.

West Halkin St.

Halkin St.

Belgrave Sq.

Chapel Pl.

Chester St.

Grosvenor Pl.

7 ●

Pont St.

Cadogan Ln.

Eaton Pl.

Eaton Sq.

Cliveden Pl.

Elizabeth St.

Chester Row

Eaton Sq.

Cadogan Sq.

Sloane Ave.

Draycott Ave.

Milne St.

Walton St.

Egerton Ter.

Brompton Sq.

Brompton Rd.

Beauchamp Pl.

6 ●

Draycott Pl.

Sloane Sq.

Kings Rd.

SLOANE SQUARE [U]

Elstan St.

1 ●

2 ●

3 ●

KEY

[U] Tube Station

Gloucester Road on the District, Circle, and Piccadilly lines are convenient stops for the South Kensington museums; Knightsbridge on the Piccadilly line leaves you close to Harrods and many retail temptations.

PLANNING
YOUR TIME
The best way to approach these neighborhoods is to treat Knightsbridge shopping and the South Kensington museums as separate days out, although the three vast museums may be too much to take in at once. The parks are best in the growing seasons and during fall, when the foliage is turning; the summer roses in Regent's Park are stunning. On Sunday the Hyde Park and Kensington Gardens railings all along the Bayswater Road are hung with mediocre art, which may slow your progress; this is prime perambulation day for locals.

TOP ATTRACTIONS

★ **Apsley House (Wellington Museum).** Once popularly known as No. 1, London, because it was the first and grandest house at the old tollgate from Knightsbridge village, this was long celebrated as the best address in town. Built by Robert Adam and later refaced and extended, it housed the Duke of Wellington from 1817 until his death in 1852, forming one of the many tributes gifted to the "Iron Duke" in thanks for his victory over Napoléon at the Battle of Waterloo in 1815. As the Wellington Museum, it has been faithfully restored, down to Wellesley's uniforms, weapons, a fine collection of paintings, and his porcelain and plate collections acquired as a result of his military success, such as a Sévres dessert service commissioned by Napoléon for his empress, Josephine. ✉ *149 Piccadilly, Hyde Park Corner, Mayfair* ☎ *020/7499–5676* ⊕ *www.english-heritage.org.uk* ⏱ *Mar.–Oct., Wed.–Sun. and bank holiday Mon. 11–5; Nov.–Feb., Wed.–Sun. 11–4* ⬛*£6, joint ticket with Wellington Arch £7.40* Ⓤ *Hyde Park Corner.*

Harrods. Just in case you don't notice it, this well-known shopping destination frames its domed terra-cotta Edwardian outline in thousands of white lights each night. The 4.5-acre store's sales weeks are top-notch, and inside it's as frenetic as a stock-market floor. Don't miss the extravagant Food Hall, with its stunning art nouveau tiling. ✉ *87–135 Brompton Rd., Knightsbridge* ☎ *0207/730–1234* ⊕ *www.harrods.com* ⏱ *Mon.–Sat. 10–8, Sun. 11:30–6* Ⓤ *Knightsbridge.*

Hyde Park. Along with the smaller St. James's and Green parks to the east, Hyde Park started as Henry VIII's hunting grounds. Along its south side runs Rotten Row, once Henry's royal path to the hunt—the name is a corruption of *route du roi* (route of the king). It's still used by the Household Cavalry, who live at the Hyde Park Barracks—a high-rise and a low, ugly, red block—to the left. This is where the brigade that mounts the guard at Buckingham Palace resides, and you can see them leave to perform their duty, in full regalia, at about 10:30, or await the return of the guard about noon. Hyde Park is wonderful for strolling, watching the locals, or just relaxing by the Serpentine, the long body of water near its southern border. On the south side, by the 1930s Serpentine Lido, is the site of the Diana, Princess of Wales' Memorial Fountain, a good spot to refuel at one of the cafés. On Sunday, Speakers' Corner, in the park near Marble Arch, is an unmissable spectacle of vehement, sometimes comical, and always entertaining orators. ✉ *Mayfair*

These ice-skaters outside the Natural History Museum in South Kensington are making the best of London's winter.

☎ *020/7298–2141* ⊕ *www.royalparks.gov.uk* ⊙ *Daily 5 am–midnight* Ⓤ *Hyde Park Corner, Knightsbridge, Lancaster Gate, Marble Arch.*

🐦 **Kensington Gardens.** More formal than neighboring Hyde Park, Kensington Gardens was first laid out as palace grounds for William III. He was attracted to the location for its clean air and tranquility, and subsequently commissioned Sir Christopher Wren for the splendid **Kensington Palace.** To the north of the palace complex is the early-20th-century **Sunken Garden.** Nearby is George Frampton's beloved 1912 *Peter Pan.* The **Round Pond** is a magnet for model-boat enthusiasts and duck feeders. The fabulous **Diana, Princess of Wales' Memorial Playground** has specially designed structures and areas on the theme of J.M. Barrie's Neverland. ✉ *Kensington* ⊕ *www.royalparks.gov.uk* ⊙ *Daily 6 am–dusk* Ⓤ *Kensington High Street, Lancaster Gate, Queensway, South Kensington.*

★ **Kensington Palace.** Not as splendid as Buckingham Palace, or as famous as Hampton Court, Kensington Palace is the most intimate of London's great royal residences. Bought in 1689 by Queen Mary and King William III, it was converted into a palace by Sir Christopher Wren and Nicholas Hawksmoor. Royals have been living here ever since, most famously Princess Diana, in the private part of the palace. The State Apartments, however, are open to the public and now house a temporary exhibition, "The Enchanted Palace," which evokes the seven princesses who have lived at KP through innovative installations that utilize gowns, artifacts, and soundscapes.

The palace is home to the **Royal Ceremonial Dress Collection,** including royal raiments ranging from the elaborate (an 18th-century mantua— a dazzling court dress with a 6-foot-wide skirt) to the downright odd

(King George III's socks). Also look for the King's Staircase, with its panoramic trompe l'oeil painting, and the King's Gallery, with royal artworks in a jewelbox setting of rich red damask walls, intricate gilding, and a beautiful painted ceiling. Outside, the grounds are almost as lovely as the palace itself.

From January 3, 2012 to March 25, 2012, the palace will be completely closed while a renovation is finished. The "new" palace will showcase four new exhibitions that unfold the palace saga: Queen Victoria (with the theme "love, duty and loss"); William and Mary and Queen Anne ("the private life of the Queen"); George II ("the curious world of the court"); and princesses Diana and Margaret ("it's not easy being a princess"). ⊠ *The Broad Walk, Kensington Gardens, Kensington* ☏ *0844/482–7799 advance booking, 0844/482–7777 information, 0203/166–6000 from outside U.K.* ⊕ *www.hrp.org.uk* ☐ *£12.50* ⊙ *Mar.–Sept., daily 10–6; Oct.–Feb., daily 10–5; last admission 1 hr before closing* Ⓤ *Queensway, High Street Kensington.*

Ⓒ ★ **Natural History Museum.** The outrageously ornate terra-cotta facade of this enormous Victorian museum is strewn with relief panels, depicting living creatures to the left of the entrance and extinct ones to the right. It's an appropriate design, for within these walls lie more than 70 million different specimens. The museum is full of cutting-edge exhibits, with all the wow-power and interactives necessary to secure interest from younger visitors. The **Dinosaur Gallery** (Gallery 21) contains plenty of real-life dino bones, fossils—and some extremely long teeth. A dizzyingly tall escalator takes you into a giant globe in the **Earth Galleries,** where there's a choice of levels—and Earth surfaces—to explore. Don't leave without checking out the earthquake simulation in Gallery 61. ⊠ *Cromwell Rd., South Kensington* ☏ *0207/942–5000* ⊕ *www. nhm.ac.uk* ☐ *Free (some fees for special exhibitions)* ⊙ *Daily 10–5:50, last admission at 5:30* Ⓤ *South Kensington.*

Ⓒ ★ **Science Museum.** This, one of the three great South Kensington museums, stands next to the Natural History Museum in a far plainer building. It has loads of hands-on exhibits, with entire schools of children apparently decanted inside to interact with them; but it is, after all, painlessly educational. Don't dismiss the Science Museum as just for kids, though. Highlights include the Launch Pad gallery, which demonstrates basic laws of physics; *Puffing Billy,* the oldest steam locomotive in the world; and the actual *Apollo 10* capsule. ⊠ *Exhibition Rd., South Kensington* ☏ *0870/870–4868* ⊕ *www.sciencemuseum.org.uk* ☐ *Free, charge for cinema shows and special exhibitions* ⊙ *Daily 10–6* Ⓤ *South Kensington.*

Ⓒ ★ **Victoria and Albert Museum.** Always referred to as the V&A, this huge museum is devoted to the applied arts of all disciplines, all periods, and all nationalities. Full of innovation, it's a wonderful, generous place to get lost in. First opened as the South Kensington Museum in 1857, it was renamed in 1899, in honor of Queen Victoria's late husband, and has since grown to become one of the country's best-loved cultural institutions. Many collections at the V&A are presented not by period, but by category—textiles, sculpture, jewelry, and so on. Nowhere is the benefit of this more apparent than in the **Fashion Gallery** (Room 40), where formal 18th-century court dresses are displayed alongside the haute couture styles of contemporary designers, creating an arresting sense of visual continuity. The **British Galleries** (rooms 52–58), devoted to British art and design from 1500 to 1900, are full of beautiful diversions—among them the Great Bed of Ware (immortalized in Shakespeare's *Twelfth Night*). ■**TIP**➔ The V&A is a notoriously difficult building to navigate, so be sure to pick up a free map. There are stacks of them at each entrance. ✉ *Cromwell Rd., South Kensington* ☎ *0207/942–2000* ⊕ *www.vam.ac.uk* 🎫 *Free* ⊙ *Sat.–Tues. 10–5:45, Fri. 10–10* Ⓤ *South Kensington.*

WORTH NOTING

Albert Memorial. This gleaming, neo-Gothic shrine to Prince Albert created by George Gilbert Scott epitomizes the Victorian era. Albert's grieving widow, Queen Victoria, had this elaborate confection (including a 14-foot bronze statue of the prince) erected on the spot where his Great Exhibition had stood a decade before his early death, from typhoid, in 1861. ✉ *Kensington Gore, Hyde Park, Kensington.*

Belgrave Square. This is the heart of Belgravia, the epicenter of posh aristocratic London. The square, as well as the streets leading off it, is genuine grand territory and has been since it was built in the mid-1800s. ■**TIP**➔ Traffic really whips around Belgrave Square, so be careful.

Wellington Arch. Opposite the Duke of Wellington's mansion, Apsley House, this majestic stone arch surveys the busy traffic rushing around Hyde Park Corner. Designed by Decimus Burton and built in 1828, it was created as a grand entrance to the west side of London and echoes the design of that other landmark gate, Marble Arch. ✉ *Hyde Park Corner, Mayfair* ☎ *020/7930–2726* ⊕ *www.english-heritage.org.uk* 🎫 *£3.50* ⊙ *Apr.–Oct., Wed.–Sun. 10–5; Nov.–Mar., Wed.–Sun. 10–4* Ⓤ *Hyde Park Corner.*

REGENT'S PARK AND HAMPSTEAD

Besides lovely Regent's Park and its attractions, this area is the showcase for some of the most aristocratic architecture in the world, thanks to the town houses of John Nash, 19th-century design whiz. They provide the setting for some splendid sights, from Keats House to—Strawberry Beatles Forever!—Abbey Road, the favorite studio of the Fab Four. Northwards lies Hampstead, which continues its historic tradition of providing a haven for literati and some of the most stunning town-house architecture in England (think any Merchant Ivory film) while Primrose Hill is home to models and movie stars. Excellent bookshops, contemporary boutiques, and cozy cafés line tree-shaded blocks.

GETTING HERE   To get to Regent's Park, take the Bakerloo Line to Regent's Park Tube station or, for Primrose Hill, the Chalk Farm stop on the Northern Line. Reaching Hampstead by Tube is as easy as it looks: Simply take the Edgware branch of the Northern Line to the Hampstead station, or the overground North London line to Hampstead Heath. The south side of Hampstead Heath can also be reached by the Gospel Oak station on the North London line.

Depending on your pace and inclination, Regent's Park and Hampstead can realistically be covered in a day. It might be best to spend the morning in Hampstead, then head south toward Regent's Park in the afternoon so that you're closer to central London come nightfall, if that is where your hotel is located.

TOP ATTRACTIONS

Jewish Museum. Reopened in 2010 after a £10-million refurbishment, this museum traces the history of the Jewish people in Britain from medieval times to the present day, although most of the exhibits date from the 17th century—when Cromwell repealed the laws against Jewish settlement—and later. The collection is spread over four galleries. "History: A British Story" provides a general overview of British Jewish people over the centuries, through a mix of rare artifacts and interactive displays, including a re-creation of a Victorian street from what was then the Jewish Quarter of East London. ⊠ *Raymond Burton House, 129–131 Albert St., Camden Town* ☎ *020/7284–7384* ⊕ *www.jewishmuseum.org.uk* ⊡ *£7* ⊙ *Sun.–Wed. 10–5, Thurs. 10–9, Fri. 10–2. Last admission 30 min before closing. Closed Sat. and on major Jewish festivals* Ⓤ *Camden Town.*

Keats House. Here you can see the plum tree under which the young Romantic poet composed "Ode to a Nightingale," many of his original manuscripts, his library, and other possessions he managed to acquire in his short life. He left this house in September, moved to Rome, and died of consumption there, in early 1821, at age 25. ∎**TIP→** Picnics can be taken into the grounds during the summer. ⊠ *Wentworth Pl., Keats Grove, Hampstead* ☎ *020/7332–3868* ⊕ *www.keatshouse.cityoflondon.gov.uk* ⊡ *£5* ⊙ *Apr.–Oct., Tues.–Sun. 1–5; Nov.–Mar., Fri.–Sun. 1–5; closed Good Friday and Christmas wk* Ⓤ *Hampstead; North London Line overground: Hampstead Heath from Highbury & Islington.*

☾ ★ **Kenwood House.** This gracious Georgian villa was first built in 1616 and remodeled by Robert Adam between 1764 and 1779. Adam refaced most of the exterior and added the splendid library, which, with its curved painted ceiling, rather garish coloring, and gilded detailing, is the highlight of the house for decorative arts and interior design buffs. What is not to be missed here is the **Iveagh Bequest,** a collection of paintings that the Earl of Iveagh gave the nation in 1927, including a wonderful self-portrait by Rembrandt and works by Reynolds, Van Dyck, Hals, Gainsborough, and Turner. Top billing goes to Vermeer's *Guitar Player,* considered by some to be one of the most beautiful paintings in the world. In front of the house, a lawn slopes down to a little lake crossed by a trompe-l'oeil bridge—all in perfect 18th-century upper-class taste. ⊠ *Hampstead La., Hampstead* ☎ *020/8348–1286* ⊕ *www.english-heritage.org.uk* ⊡ *Free* ⊙ *House daily except Dec. 24–26 and Jan. 1, 11:30–4. Gardens daily dawn–dusk* Ⓤ *Golders Green, then Bus 210.*

☾ ★ **Regent's Park.** Cultivated and formal—compared with the relative wildness of Hampstead Heath—Regent's Park was laid out in 1812 by John Nash, in honor of the Prince Regent (hence the name), who was later crowned George IV. The idea was to re-create the feel of a grand country residence close to the center of town, with all those magnificent

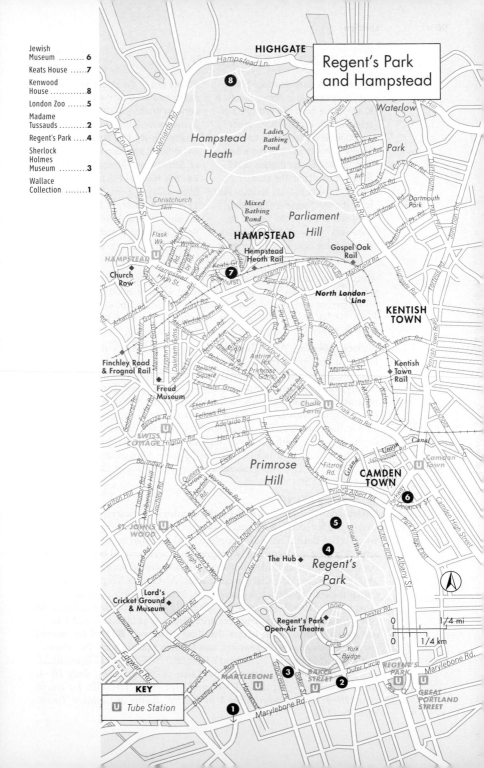

HIGHGATE

Regent's Park and Hampstead

Hampstead Ln.

8

Waterlow

Hampstead
Heath

Ladies
Bathing
Pond

Park

N. End Way

Spaniards Rd.

Highgate

Oakeshott Ave.

Makepeace Ave.

Landsdowne
Ave.

Swains La.

St. Albans Rd.

Chester Rd.

Highgate Rd.

Dartmouth

Dartmouth

Christchurch
Hill

Heath St.

West Heath Rd.

Mixed
Bathing
Pond

Parliament
Hill

Croftdown

Dartmouth
Park

Dartmouth Pk. Rd.

Highgate Rd.

Flask
Wk.

Willow Rd.

HAMPSTEAD

Church
Row

HAMPSTEAD

Hampstead High St.

Keats Grove

Hempstead
Heath Rail

7

Downshire Hill

Constantine Rd.

Agincourt Rd.

Savernake Rd.

Gospel Oak
Rail

Mansfield Rd.

Parliament
Hill

North London
Line

KENTISH
TOWN

Kentish Town Rd.

Fleet Rd.

Parliament Hill

Arkwright Rd.

Finchley Rd.
& Frognal Rail

Netherhall Gdns.

Fitzjohn's Ave.

Maresfield Gdns.

Daleham Gdns.

Lyndhurst Rd.

Thurlow Rd.

Wedderburn Rd.

Belsize Park Gdns.

Ornan Rd.

Belsize
Square

Lancaster Grove

Freud
Museum

Eton Ave.

Fellows Rd.

Adelaide Rd.

Antrim
Rd.

England's La.

Haverstock Hill

Prince of Wales Rd.

Malden Rd.

Grafton Rd.

Queen's
Crescent

Ryland Rd.

Prince
of Wales Rd.

Marsden St.

Kentish Town Rd.

Leighton Rd.

Gaisford St.

Kentish
Town
Rail

SWISS
COTTAGE

Finchley Rd.

Belsize Rd.

Goldhurst Terr.

Fairfax Rd.

Hilgrove Rd.

Henry's Rd.

Elsworthy Rd.

Fellows Rd.

Chalk
Farm

Chalk Farm Rd.

Union

Canal

Boundary Rd.

Queen's Grove

Carlton Hill

Loudoun Rd.

Abbey Rd.

Hartland Rd.

Primrose
Hill

Regent's Pk. Rd.

Primrose Hill Rd.

Elsworthy Rd.

King Henry's Rd.

Gloucester Ave.

Fitzroy
Rd.

Regent's Pk. Rd.

Oval Rd.

Grand

Jamestown

Parkway

CAMDEN
TOWN

Camden
Town

6

Delancey St.

Camden High Street

Park Village East

ST. JOHN'S
WOOD

Acacia Rd.

St. John's
Wood High St.

Wellington Rd.

Finchley Rd.

Grove End Rd.

Woronzow Rd.

Avenue Rd.

Ordnance Hill

St. John's
Wood Ter.

Allitsen Rd.

Prince Albert Rd.

Outer Circle

5

Broad
Walk

Prince Albert Rd.

Outer Circle

Albany St.

Park Village East

4

The Hub ◆

*Regent's
Park*

Lord's
Cricket Ground
& Museum

St. John's Wood Rd.

Hamilton Terr.

Lodge Rd.

St. John's Wood Rd.

Park Rd.

Gloucester Pl.

Outer Circle

Inner
Circle

Regent's Park
Open-Air Theatre ◆

Chester Rd.

York
Bridge

0 — 1/4 mi

0 — 1/4 km

REGENT'S
PARK

Marylebone Rd.

GREAT
PORTLAND
STREET

Lisson Grove

Rossmore Rd.

3

BAKER
STREET

2

Edgware Rd.

Church St.

Broadley St.

Harewood

MARYLEBONE

Gloucester Pl.

Baker St.

Marylebone Rd.

KEY

🅄 *Tube Station*

1

A TRIP TO ABBEY ROAD

For countless Beatlemaniacs and baby boomers, No. 3 Abbey Road is one of the most beloved spots in London. Here, outside the legendary Abbey Road Studios, is the most famous zebra crossing in the world, immortalized on the Beatles' 1969 *Abbey Road* album. The studios are closed to the public, but tourists like to Beatle-ize themselves by taking the same sort of photo. One of the best—and safer—ways Beatle lovers can enjoy the history of the group is to take one of the smashing walking tours offered by the **Original London Walks** (☎ *020/7624-3978* ⊕ *www.walks.com*), including **The Beatles In-My-Life Walk** (11:20 am at the Marylebone Underground on Saturday and Tuesday) and **The Beatles Magical Mystery Tour** (Wednesday at 2 pm, Thursday at 11 am, and Sunday at 10:55 am at Underground Exit 3, Tottenham Court Road), which cover nostalgic landmark Beatles spots in the city.

white-stucco terraces facing in on the park. Your nostrils should lead you to **Queen Mary's Gardens,** a fragrant 17-acre circle that riots with 400 different varieties of roses in summer. ⊠ *Marylebone Rd., Regent's Park* ☎ *020/7486–7905* ⊕ *www.royalparks.gov.uk* ⊠ *Free* ☉ *5 am–dusk* Ⓤ *Baker St., Regent's Park, Great Portland St.*

Wallace Collection. Assembled by four generations of marquesses of Hertford and given to the nation by the widow of Sir Richard Wallace, illegitimate son of the fourth, this collection of art and artifacts is important, exciting, undervisited—and free. Look for Rembrandt's portrait of his son, the Rubens landscape, Gainsborough and Romney portraits, the Van Dycks and Canalettos, the French rooms, and of course the porcelain. The highlight is Fragonard's *The Swing*, which conjures up the 18th century's let-them-eat-cake frivolity better than any other painting around. ⊠ *Hertford House, Manchester Sq., Marylebone* ☎ *020/7563–9500* ⊕ *www.wallacecollection.org* ⊠ *Free* ☉ *Daily 10–5* Ⓤ *Bond St.*

WORTH NOTING

London Zoo. The zoo, owned by the Zoological Society of London (a charity), opened in 1828 and peaked in popularity during the 1950s, when more than 3 million people passed through its turnstiles every year. A recent modernization program has seen several big attractions open up, with a definite focus on wildlife conservation, education, and the breeding of endangered species. At Gorilla Kingdom you can watch the four resident gorillas—Effie, Mjukuu, Bobby, and Zaire—at close range. Also popular is the Clore Rainforest Lookout, home to tiny primates such as marmosets and golden lion tamarins and a large collection of other rain-forest-dwelling creatures. ■TIP➔ For animal encounter sessions with keepers, and feeding times, check the information board at admission. ⊠ *Regent's Park* ☎ *020/7722-3333* ⊕ *www.zsl.org* ⊠ *£16.20–£19.80 depending on season* ☉ *Nov.–Feb., daily 10–4; Mar.–1st wk in Sept., daily 10–6; mid-Sept.–Oct. 10–5:30; 1st wk in Nov. 10–4:30; last admission 1 hr before closing* Ⓤ *Camden Town, then Bus 274.*

2

☺ **Madame Tussauds.** One of London's busiest sights, this is nothing more and nothing less than the world's premier exhibition of lifelike wax-work models of celebrities. Madame T. learned her craft while making death masks of French Revolution victims, and in 1835 set up her first show of the famous ones near this spot. Top billing still goes to the murderers in the Chamber of Horrors, who stare glassy-eyed at visitors—one from an electric chair, one sitting next to the tin bath where he dissolved several wives in quicklime. ■**TIP**➡ Beat the crowds by calling in advance for timed entry tickets or by booking online. ✉ *Marylebone Rd., Regent's Park* ☎ *0870/400–3000 for timed entry tickets* ⊕ *www. madame-tussauds.com* ✇ *£14–£28 according to time; call or check Web site. Combination ticket with London Eye, London Dungeons, and London Aquarium from £57.50* ⊗ *Weekdays 9–5:30 (last admission); weekends 9:30–6 (last admission)* Ⓤ *Baker St.*

Sherlock Holmes Museum. Outside Baker Street station, by the Marylebone Road exit, is a 9-foot-high bronze statue of the celebrated detective. Nearby is number 221B Baker Street—the address of Arthur Conan Doyle's fictional detective. Inside, Mrs. Hudson, "Holmes's housekeeper," conducts you into a series of Victorian rooms full of Sherlock-abilia. ✉ *221B Baker St., Regent's Park* ☎ *020/7224–3688* ⊕ *www.sherlock-holmes.co.uk* ✇ *£6* ⊗ *Daily 9:30–6* Ⓤ *Baker St.*

UP AND DOWN THE THAMES

Downstream—meaning seaward, or east—from central London, Greenwich has enough riches, especially if the maritime theme is your thing, that you should allow a very full day to see them. Upstream, the royal palaces and grand houses that dot the area were built not as town houses but as country residences with easy access to London by river; Hampton Court Palace is the best and biggest of all.

GREENWICH

8 mi east of central London.

Greenwich makes an ideal day out from central London, thanks to its historic and maritime attractions. Sir Christopher Wren's Royal Naval College and Inigo Jones's Queen's House reach architectural heights; the Old Royal Observatory measured time for the entire planet; and the Greenwich Meridian divides the world in two. You can stand astride it with one foot in either hemisphere. The National Maritime Museum will appeal to seafaring types, and landlubbers can stroll the parkland that surrounds the buildings, the pretty 19th-century houses, and the weekend crafts and antiques markets.

Once, Greenwich was considered remote by Londoners, with only the river as a direct route. With transportation links in the form of the Docklands Light Railway (DLR) and the Tube's Jubilee Line, getting here is easy and inexpensive. The quickest route to maritime Greenwich is the Tube to Canary Wharf and the Docklands Light Rail to the Greenwich stop. However, river connections to Greenwich make the journey memorable. On the way, the boat glides past famous London sights and the ever-changing Docklands.

Among the botanical splendors of Kew Gardens is the Waterlily House.

★ **National Maritime Museum.** Following a millennial face-lift, one of Greenwich's star attractions has been completely updated to make it one of London's most enjoyable museums. Its glass-covered courtyard of beautifully grand stone, dominated by a huge revolving propeller from a powerful frigate, is reminiscent of the British Museum. The collection spans seascape paintings to scientific instruments, interspersed with the heroes of the waves. A permanent Nelson gallery contains the uniform he wore, complete with bloodstain, when he met his end in 1805. ■TIP➔ The museum has a good café with views over Greenwich Park. Nearby, the Queen's House, a magnificent Inigo Jones building, has an excellent collection of maritime-themed art. ⊠ *Romney Rd., Greenwich* ☎ *020/8858–4422* ⊕ *www.nmm.ac.uk* ⊠ *Free* ☉ *Daily 10–5; last admission 30 min before closing* Ⓤ *DLR: Greenwich.*

QUICK BITES

With excellent vista of the Thames, there is no more handsomely situated pub in Greenwich than the **Trafalgar Tavern** (⊠ *Park Row* ☎ *020/8858–2909* ⊕ *www.trafalgartavern.co.uk*). Featured in Charles Dickens's *Our Mutual Friend,* it's still as grand a place to have a pint and some (upscale) pub grub as it ever was.

★ **Old Royal Naval College.** Begun by Christopher Wren in 1694 as a rest home for ancient mariners, it became instead a school for young ones in 1873. Today the University of Greenwich and Trinity College of Music have classes here. Architecturally, you'll notice how the structures part to reveal the **Queen's House** across the central lawns. Behind the college are two more buildings you can visit: the **Painted Hall,** the college's dining hall, derives its name from the baroque murals of

2

William and Mary (reigned 1689–95; William alone 1695–1702) and assorted allegorical figures. ⊠ *Old Royal Naval College, King William Walk, Greenwich* ☎ *020/8269–4747* ⊕ *www.oldroyalnavalcollege.org* ✉ *Free, guided tours £5* ⊗ *Painted Hall and chapel daily 10–5 (Sun. chapel from 12:30); grounds 8–6* Ⓤ *DLR: Greenwich.*

Ranger's House. This handsome, early-18th-century villa, which was the Greenwich Park ranger's official residence during the 19th century, is hung with Stuart and Jacobean portraits. But the most interesting diversion is the Wernher Collection, more than 700 works of art with a northern European flavor, amassed by diamond millionaire Julius Wernher at the turn of the 20th century. Wernher's American wife, Birdie, was a strong influence and personality during the belle époque, which is easy to imagine from her striking portrait by Sargent. ⊠ *Chesterfield Walk, Greenwich Park, Greenwich* ☎ *020/8853–0035* ⊕ *www.english-heritage.org.uk* ✉ *£6* ⊗ *Apr.–Sept., Mon.–Wed. guided tours only, 11:30 and 2:30, Sun. 11–5; call ahead to confirm* Ⓤ *DLR: Greenwich; no direct bus access, only to Vanbrugh Hill (from east) and Blackheath Hill (from west).*

⏱ **Royal Observatory.** Since 1884, the ultimate standard for time around
★ the world has been set here: Greenwich is on the prime meridian at 0° longitude. Why was Greenwich adopted as the international standard? The reason was due to Britain's preeminence as a naval power. A redesign in 2007 split the observatory into two sites—one devoted to the study of the stars, the other to the study of time—and added new exhibition spaces.

There's a planetarium, and if you come with children, don't miss the high-technology rooms of the **Astronomy Galleries,** where cutting-edge touch screens and interactive programs give young explorers the chance to run their own space missions to Ganymede, one of Jupiter's moons. **Flamsteed House** holds the Time Galleries, with the Maritime Clocks of John Harrison; he won the Longitude Prize in the 18th century for solving the problem of accurate timekeeping at sea and greatly improved navigation. ⊠ *Romney Rd., Greenwich* ☎ *020/8858–4422* ⊕ *www.rog. nmm.ac.uk* ✉ *Free, planetarium shows £6* ⊗ *Daily 10–5 (May–Aug., Meridian courtyard until 6); last entry 30 min before closing; last planetarium show 4* Ⓤ *DLR: Greenwich.*

HAMPTON COURT PALACE
20 mi southwest of central London.

⏱ **Hampton Court Palace.** Today the royal palace that sits beside the slow-
Fodor's Choice moving Thames gives you two palaces for the price of one: The mag-
★ nificent Tudor redbrick mansion that was begun in 1514 by Cardinal Wolsey to impress the young Henry, and the larger 17th-century baroque offering, for which the graceful south wing was designed by Christopher Wren of St. Paul's fame. The first buildings of Hampton Court belonged to a religious order founded in the 11th century and were expanded over the years by its many subsequent residents, none more important than Henry VIII and his six wives. Henry spent a king's ransom (today's equivalent of £18 million or $27.5 million) expanding and refurbishing the palace.

If Tudor takes your fancy, wander through the **State Apartments,** hung with priceless paintings, and on to the wood-beamed magnificence of **Henry's Great Hall,** lined with tapestries and the mustiness of old, before taking in the strikingly azure ceiling of the **Chapel Royal.** Topping it all is the Great House of Easement, a lavatory that could sit 28 people at a time.

Feel a chill in the air? Watch out for the ghost of Henry VIII's doomed fifth wife, Catherine Howard, who literally lost her head yet apparently still screams her way along the **Haunted Gallery.** The latter-day baroque transformers of the palace, William and Mary, maintained beautiful **King's and Queen's Apartments, Georgian Rooms,** and fine collections of porcelain.

The gardens here are lovely, and don't miss the famous maze, its ½ mi of pathways among clipped hedgerows still fiendish to negotiate. There's a trick, but we won't give it away here: it's much more fun to go and lose yourself. ■TIP→ Avoid the queue and save by buying your tickets online. ⊠ *Hampton Court Palace, East Molesley, Surrey* ☎ *0844/482–7799 tickets, 0844/482–7777 information* ⊕ *www. hrp.org.uk/hamptoncourtpalace* ⊠ *£14* ☉ *Late Mar.–Oct., daily 10–6 (last ticket sold at 5; last entry to maze at 5:15); Nov.–late Mar., daily 10–4:30 (last ticket sold at 3:30; last entry to maze at 3:45); check Web site before visiting* Ⓤ *Richmond, then Bus R68; National Rail, South West: Hampton Court Station, 35 min from Waterloo (most trains require change at Surbiton).*

KEW GARDENS
6 mi southwest of central London.

Kew Gardens. Enter Kew Gardens and you are enveloped by blazes of color, extraordinary blooms, hidden trails, magnificent buildings, and centuries of endeavor aimed at getting to grips with the mysteries of plants that entrance, medicate, and excite. Even today academics are hard at work on more than 300 scientific projects across as many acres, researching everything from the cacti of eastern Brazil to the yams of Madagascar. Two great 19th-century greenhouses—the **Palm House** and the **Temperate House**—are filled with exotic blooms, and many of the plants have been there since the final glass panel was fixed into place. The crazy **Pagoda,** more than 150 feet tall and visible for miles around, is the star turn. ■TIP→ Guided tours with natureloving volunteers leave daily from the Guides' desk inside Victoria Plaza at 11 and 2. ⊠ *Royal Botanic Gardens, Kew, Richmond, Surrey (main entrance is between Richmond Circus and traffic circle at Mortlake Rd.)* ☎ *020/8332–5655* ⊕ *www.kew.org* ⊠ *£13.50* ☉ *Feb., daily 9:30–5:30; Mar.–Aug., weekdays 9:30–6:30, weekends 9:30–7:30; Sept. and Oct., 9:30–6; Nov.–Feb. 9:30–4:15* Ⓤ *Kew Gardens.*

Kew Palace and Queen Charlotte's Cottage. To this day quietly domestic Kew Palace remains the smallest royal palace in the land. The house and gardens offer a glimpse into the 17th century. Originally known as the Dutch House, it was bought by King George II to provide more room in addition to the White House (another royal residence that used to exist on the grounds) for the extended Royal Family. In spring there's a romantic haze of bluebells. ⊠ *Kew Gardens, Kew* ⊕ *www.hrp.org.uk* ✉*£5, in addition to ticket for Kew Gardens* ☉ *Apr.–Sept., Tues.–Sun. 10–5, Mon. 11–5* ⓤ *Kew Gardens.*

QUICK BITES

The Original Maids of Honour (⊠ *288 Kew Rd., Kew* ☎ *020/8940–2752* ⊕ *www.theoriginalmaidsofhonour.co.uk),* the most traditional of Old English tearooms, is named for the famous tarts invented here and still baked by hand on the premises. Tea is served daily 2:30–6. They also serve lunch daily, in two sittings at 12:30 and 1:30. Or opt for take-out to picnic at Kew Gardens or on Kew Green.

WHERE TO EAT

Use the coordinate (✛ B2) at the end of each listing to locate a site on the corresponding map.

London rivals New York, Paris, and Tokyo as one of the best places to eat in the world right now. The sheer diversity of restaurants here is unparalleled. Among the city's 6,700 restaurants are see-and-be-seen hot spots, casual ethnic eateries, innovative gastro-pubs, and shrines to haute cuisine.

To measure London's spectacular culinary rise, note that it was once a common dictum that the British ate to live, whereas the French lived to eat. The best of British food—local, seasonal, wild, and regional—is now all the rage and appears on more menus by the day. Waste not, want not "nose-to-tail" eating—where every last scrap of meat is deemed fair game for the plate—has made a spectacular comeback at St. John in Clerkenwell, and fits perfectly with the new age of austerity. Meanwhile, the haute cuisine scene powers blithely on. A Heston Blumenthal protégé sets the standard at Dinner by Heston Blumenthal; Marcus Wareing wows at the Berkeley; Brett Graham is cooking on gas at The Ledbury; and Hélène Darroze does it for the girls at the Connaught.

For cheap eats, don't miss the city's unofficial dish, the ubiquitous Indian curry. The quality of other global cuisines also has grown remarkably in recent years, with London becoming known for its Thai, Italian, Spanish, Chinese, and North African restaurants. With all of the choice, traditional British food, when you track it down, appears as just one more exotic cuisine in the pantheon.

Whatever eating experience you seek, London can likely deliver. From dirt-cheap street food to posh multicourse meals, the city has become a destination for gustatory adventurers. We've uncovered the best of the best, so dig in, and enjoy!

PRICES AND SAVING MONEY

London is not an inexpensive city. A modest lunch for two can cost £40 (about $60) and the £100-a-head dinner is not so taboo. Damage-control strategies include making lunch your main meal—the top places have bargain lunch menus, halving the price of evening à la carte—and ordering a second appetizer instead of an entrée, to which few places object. Note that an appetizer, usually known as a "starter" or "first course," is sometimes called an "entrée," as it is in France, and an entrée in England is dubbed the "main course" or simply "mains."

Indian and other international restaurants have always been a good money-saving bet here. Sandwich shops and chains proliferate. *See Local Chains Worth a Taste box for the best bets.* Seek out fixed-price menus, and watch for hidden extras on the check: cover, bread, or vegetables charged separately, and service. Many restaurants exclude service charges from the menu (which the law obliges them to display outside), then add 10% to 12.5% to the check, or else stamp "Service not included" along the bottom, in which case you should add the 10% to 12.5% yourself. Don't pay twice for service.

WHAT IT COSTS IN POUNDS					
	£	££	£££	££££	£££££
AT DINNER	under £10	£10–£16	£17–£23	£24–£32	over £32

Prices are per person for a main course, excluding drinks, service, and V.A.T.

ST. JAMES'S AND MAYFAIR

ST. JAMES'S

££££
BRITISH
✕ **Wiltons.** Blue bloods, aristocrats, and the well-to-do blow the bank at this 1742 bastion of fine dining. Gentlemen are required to wear a jacket for lunch and dinner at this clubby time capsule and ode to all things English. Posh patrons take half-a-dozen finest Colchester oysters, followed by grilled Dover sole on the bone, or fabulous game in season, like woodcock, grouse, and teal. Old-fashioned savories like anchovies on toast are also enjoyed. Service is formal and discreet. ⊠ *55 Jermyn St., St. James's* ☎ *020/7629–9955* ⊕ *www.wiltons.co.uk* ⌖ *Reservations essential* ⌂ *Jacket required* ⊙ *Closed weekends* Ⓤ *Green Park* ✛ *D3.*

£££
AUSTRIAN
✕ **The Wolseley.** The whole of London seems to love the spectacle and grand elegance at this Viennese-style café on Piccadilly. The brasserie begins its long days with breakfast at 7 am and stays serving until midnight. Linger for Hungarian goulash, Viennese boiled beef *Tafelspitz* (with apple sauce and sour cream), codlike whiting, chopped liver, flaked haddock kedgeree rice, Matjes herrings, or Wiener schnitzel. For dessert, go for apple strudel or *kaiserschmarren*—a pancake with stewed fruit and raisins. ⊠ *160 Piccadilly, St. James's* ☎ *020/7499–6996* ⊕ *www.thewolseley.com* Ⓤ *Green Park* ✛ *D4.*

MAYFAIR

£££
ITALIAN
✕ **Cecconi's.** Wedged strategically between Savile Row, Cork Street, and Old Bond Street, and across from the Royal Academy on Burlington Gardens, this fashionable Italian brasserie is where the jet set come for breakfast, brunch, and *cicchetti* (Italian tapas) and return later for something more substantial. Ilse Crawford's green-and-brown interior is a stylish backdrop for classics like veal Milanese, Venetian calves' liver, crab ravioli, and tiramisu. Note: This is a good place for a pit stop during a West End shopping spree. ⊠ *5A Burlington Gardens, Mayfair* ☎ *020/7434–1500* ⊕ *www.cecconis.co.uk* Ⓤ *Green Park, Piccadilly Circus* ✛ *D3.*

BEST BETS FOR LONDON DINING

2

Where can I find the best food London has to offer? Fodor's writers and editors have selected their favorite restaurants by price, cuisine, and experience in the lists below. In the first column, the Fodor's Choice properties represent the "best of the best" across price categories. You can also search by neighborhood for excellent eating experiences—just peruse our complete reviews on the following pages.

Hibiscus, ££££, p. 100
Le Gavroche, £££££, p. 100
Koffmann's, £££, p. 110
The Ledbury, ££££, p. 113

INDIAN

Rasoi, £££££, p. 112
Tayyabs, £, p. 108

ITALIAN

Bocca di Lupo, £££, p. 102
Cecconi's, £££, p. 96
L'Anima, £££, p. 107

Fodor'sChoice★

Busaba Eathai, £, p. 103
Dean Street Townhouse, £££, p. 103
Dinner by Heston Blumenthal, £££££, p. 110
Giaconda Dining Room, ££, p. 103
Goodman, £££, p. 100
Great Queen Street, £££, p. 105
Harwood Arms, ££, p. 109
Hix, £££, p. 104
Hunan, £££, p. 109
Marcus Wareing at the Berkeley, £££££, p. 111
The Ledbury, ££££, p. 113
The Orange, ££, p. 109
Scott's, ££££, p. 101
St. John, £££, p. 108
Viajante, £££, p. 108

By Price

£

Busabe Eathai, p. 103
Côte, p. 103

Golden Hind, p. 102
Tayyabs, p. 108
Wahaca, p. 106

££

Giaconda Dining Room, p. 103
Harwood Arms, p. 109
Magdalen, p. 109
The Orange, p. 109

£££

Bistrot Bruno Loubet, p. 108
Boundary, p. 107
Cecconi's, p. 96
Dean Street Townhouse, p. 103
Great Queen Street, p. 105
Hereford Road, p. 113
Hix, p. 104
Koffmann's, p. 110
Moro, p. 107
Viajante, p. 108

££££

Hibiscus, p. 100
La Petite Maison, p. 100

The Ledbury, p. 113
Scott's, p. 101
Wiltons, p. 96

£££££

Dinner by Heston Blumenthal, p. 110
Hélène Darroze at the Connaught, p. 100
Le Gavroche, p. 100
Savoy Grill, p. 106

By Cuisine

MODERN BRITISH

Great Queen Street, £££, p. 105
Harwood Arms, ££, p. 109
Hereford Road, £££, p. 113
Hix, £££, p. 104
St. John, £££, p. 108

FRENCH

Bistrot Bruno Loubet, £££, p. 108
Hélène Darroze at the Connaught, £££££, p. 100

By Experience

HOT SPOTS

Dean Street Townhouse, £££, p. 103
Dinner by Heston Blumenthal, £££££, p. 110
Hix, £££, p. 104
Cecconi's, £££, p. 96
Scott's, ££££, p. 101

BEST GASTROPUBS

The Cow, £££, p. 112
Great Queen Street, £££, p. 105
Harwood Arms, ££, p. 109
The Orange, ££, p. 109

MOST HISTORIC

Rules, ££££, p. 105
Simpson's Tavern, £, p. 107
Sweetings, £££, p. 107

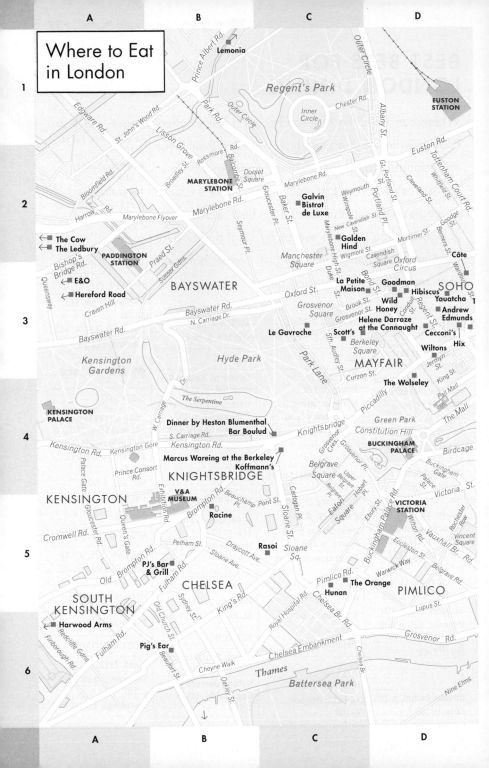

Where to Eat in London

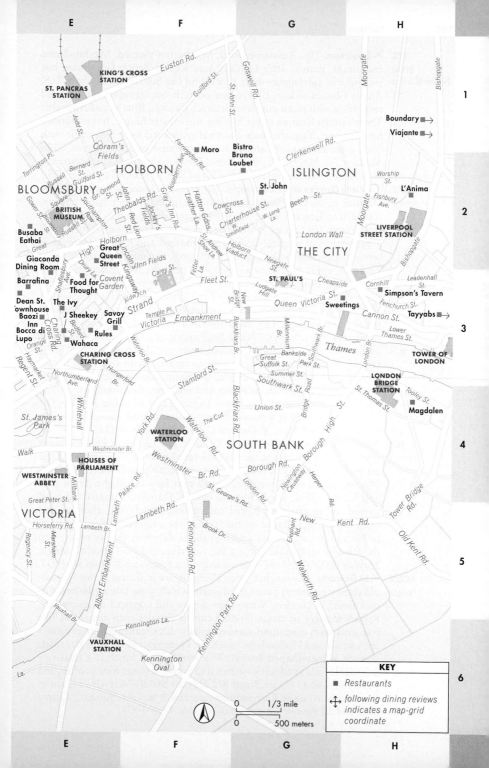

£££ ✕**Goodman.** This Russian-owned, Manhattan-themed, Mayfair-based
STEAK   restaurant, named after Chicago jazz legend Benny Goodman, has
Fodor'sChoice   everyone in agreement—here you'll find the best steaks in town. U.S.
★   Angus T-bones, sirloin, rib eye, and porterhouses compete for taste and
tenderness with prime cuts from Ireland, Canada, Britain, and Australia.
There's token Russian sweet herring and lobster bisque, but everyone's
here for one thing: the juicy charcoal grilled steaks, which come with
fries, creamed spinach, and luscious béarnaise or Stilton sauce. ✉ *26
Maddox St., Mayfair* ☎ *020/7499–3776* ⊕ *www.goodmanrestaurants.
com* ⚞ *Reservations essential* ☾ *Closed Sun.* Ⓤ *Oxford Circus* ✛ *D3.*

£££££ ✕**Hélène Darroze at the Connaught.** The crème de la crème flock to Hélène
FRENCH   Darroze at the Connaught for dazzling regional French haute cuisine,
served in an Edwardian wood-paneled hotel dining room. Taking inspiration from Les Landes in southwest France, Darroze sallies forth with
a procession of magical dishes. Spit-roasted and flambéed grouse is
served delightfully pink, with duck foie gras, and mini–Brussels sprouts.
To finish, enjoy Madagascar chocolate ganache with *galangal* (Asian
root) crème brûlée. Note that the prices are high: £35 for lunch, and
£75 or £85 for the set dinners. ✉ *The Connaught, Carlos Pl., Mayfair*
☎ *020/3147–7200* ⊕ *www.the-connaught.co.uk* ⚞ *Reservations essential* 🎩 *Jacket required* ☾ *Closed Sun. and Mon.* Ⓤ *Green Park* ✛ *C3.*

££££ ✕**Hibiscus.** French chef Claude Bosi excels at one of London's finest
MODERN FRENCH   modern French restaurants, tucked away on Maddox Street in Mayfair. Bosi's effortless cuisine is sure to impress with frogs' leg fricas-
sée, Cornish pollock with clams, Glenham salmon with eucalyptus,
or Lyonnaise tripe with cuttlefish and pig's ear. Rice soufflé and pineapple sorbet will send you home happy. ✉ *29 Maddox St., Mayfair*
☎ *020/7629–2999* ⊕ *www.hibiscusrestaurant.co.uk* ☾ *No lunch Sat.
Closed Sun. and Mon.* Ⓤ *Oxford Circus, Piccadilly* ✛ *D3.*

£££ ✕**La Petite Maison.** American in London star Gwyneth Paltrow blogs
FRENCH   that La Petite Maison is her all-time favorite London restaurant, and
no wonder—there's nothing on the impeccably well-sourced French
Mediterranean and Provençale menu that fails to delight. Try a crab
and lobster salad, a soft Burrata cheese, Datterini tomato and basil
spread, or an aromatic baked turbot with artichokes, chorizo, and
white wine sauce. Based on the style of the original La Petite Maison
in Nice in France, dishes come to the table when they're ready, and
the friendly staff make for a convivial vibe. ✉ *53–54 Brook's Mews,
Mayfair* ☎ *020/7495–4774* ⊕ *www.lpmlondon.co.uk* Ⓤ *Bond St.* ✛ *D3.*

£££££ ✕**Le Gavroche.** Master chef judge Michel Roux Jr. thrives at this 44-year-
FRENCH   old clubby basement haven in Mayfair, which some rate as the best formal dining in London. With silver domes and unpriced ladies' menus,
Roux's mastery of classic French cuisine dazzles with signatures like
foie gras with cinnamon-scented crispy duck pancake, langoustines
with snails and Hollandaise sauce, or Pyrennean lamb with *flageolets*
(French kidney-shaped beans). The weekday set lunch is a relatively
affordable treat at £48.90—with a half bottle of wine, water, coffee, and
petits fours. ✉ *43 Upper Brook St., Mayfair* ☎ *020/7408–0881* ⊕ *www.
le-gavroche.co.uk* ⚞ *Reservations essential* 🎩 *Jacket required* ☾ *Closed
Sun. and 10 days at Christmas* Ⓤ *Marble Arch* ✛ *C3.*

A juicy burger and fries are simple pleasures at meat specialist Goodman.

££££
SEAFOOD
Fodor's Choice
★

✕ **Scott's.** This is where the A-list come to dine. Founded in 1851, and reborn as a glamorous seafood haven and oyster bar, Scott's draws movers-and-shakers and the beautiful people who pick at Cumbrae oysters, Dublin Bay prawns, and Stargazy pie (Cornish pie with fish heads gazing out of a pastry crust). Standouts like cod with chorizo, ray wings, and brown butter or padron peppers are to die for. Prices are super high, but not to worry: this really is *the* hottest joint in town. ✉ *20 Mount St., Mayfair* ☎ *020/7495–7309* ⊕ *www.scotts-restaurant. com* ⌲ *Reservations essential* Ⓤ *Bond St.* ✛ *C3.*

£££
MODERN
EUROPEAN

✕ **Wild Honey.** Wild Honey's notable set lunch or pre- and posttheater evening deals (£19.95–£22.95) are wildly popular. Book ahead at this wood-paneled clublike salon, with bright modern pictures and comfy booths, in swanky Mayfair. Try the tasty Exmouth crab and white peach, Marseille bouillabaisse, Dorset plaice with Swiss chard, panna cotta, or signature wild honey ice cream with crushed honeycomb. The food is unpretentious, and all 50-odd wines come in handy third-of-a-bottle carafes. ✉ *12 St. George St., Mayfair* ☎ *020/7758–9160* ⊕ *www. wildhoneyrestaurant.co.uk* Ⓤ *Oxford Circus* ✛ *D3.*

MARYLEBONE

£££
BISTRO

✕ **Galvin Bistrot de Luxe.** The hard-working Galvin brothers blaze a trail for the deluxe bistro concept on a no-man's-land stretch of Baker Street in Marylebone. Feted chefs Chris and Jeff forsake Michelin stars and cut loose under the brasserie banner. Loyal fans and a more mature crowd enjoy impeccable service in a handsome slate floor and mahogany-paneled salon. There's no finer crab lasagna around, and mains punch above their weight: gilthead bream, calves liver with Morteaux sausage, stuffed pig's trotter, and the veal kidneys with girolles mushrooms are all a triumph. The £17.50 set lunch or £19.50 early evening dinners (6–7 pm) are unbeatable and there's monthly live Sunday evening jazz performed by the students from the nearby Royal Academy of Music. ⊠ 66 *Baker St., Marylebone* ☎ *020/7935–4007* ⊕ *www.galvinrestaurants. com* Ⓤ *Baker St.* ✣ *C2.*

£ ✕**Golden Hind.** You'll find some of the best fish-and-chips in London
SEAFOOD   at the Golden Hind, a British chippy (a shop serving traditional fish and chips) in a retro 1914 Art deco café, off Marylebone High Street. Locals and tourists alike love the fresh calamari, skate wings, and fish cakes, but it's the perfect—nongreasy—deep-fried or steamed battered cod, plaice, and haddock from Grimsby, the classic hand-cut chips, and mushy peas that are the big draw. It's corkage-free BYO and it's open noon–3 pm weekdays and 6–10 pm Monday through Saturday. ⊠ *73 Marylebone La., Marylebone* ☎ *020/7486–3644* ⍩ *BYOB* ⊘ *No lunch Sat. Closed Sun.* Ⓤ *Bond St.* ✣ *C2.*

SOHO AND COVENT GARDEN

SOHO

££ ✕**Andrew Edmunds.** Rustic food at realistic prices defines this perpetu-
MEDITERRANEAN   ally jammed, Dickensian, softly lighted romantic Soho restaurant—though it could be larger and the wooden bench seats more forgiving. Tucked away behind Carnaby Street, it's a favorite with the Soho media crowd that come for daily changing, fixed-price lunch menus. Starters and main courses draw on the taste of Ireland, the Mediterranean, and Middle East. Pigeon breast, Roquefort soufflé, and swordfish with basil mayonnaise are all hale and hearty. ⊠ *46 Lexington St., Soho* ☎ *020/7437–5708* ⌂ *Reservations essential* Ⓤ *Oxford Circus, Piccadilly Circus* ✣ *D3.*

£ ✕**Baozi Inn.** Vintage Chairman Mao posters and paraphernalia deco-
CHINESE   rate the interior of this hole-in-the-wall Sichuan café on a busy side street in Chinatown. Baozi steamed buns—pork and onion, or shrimp and radish—are house specials, and there's dragon wonton broth or Chengdu pork dumplings with chili oil (£5.50). Try ginger juice spinach (£4.90), or peace and happiness noodle soup, topped with duck, garlic, and Chinese toon tree shoots (£6.50). Tables are cramped, turnover is fast, and service is speedy. ⊠ *25 Newport Ct., Soho* ☎ *020/7287–6877* ⌂ *Reservations not accepted* Ⓤ *Leicester Sq.* ✣ *E3.*

££ ✕**Barrafina.** Soho's favorite tapas bar on Frith Street is modeled on Cal
SPANISH   Pep the famed tapas bar in Barcelona, and similarly has only a few (23 in total) raised counter seats. It's a no-reservations spot and there will likely be a wait, but the authentic tapas are worth it. Nosh on shrimp, chorizo, quail, sardines, and octopus, or classics like cured Jabugo ham and Spanish tortillas. You can check out the scene—or who's waiting in line—at the Barrafina webcam. ⊠ *54 Frith St., Soho* ☎ *020/7440–1463* ⊕ *www.barrafina.co.uk* ⌂ *Reservations not accepted* Ⓤ *Tottenham Court Rd.* ✣ *E3.*

£££ ✕**Bocca di Lupo.** The place is always packed, tables are jammed too
ITALIAN   close together, and the acoustics are particularly lousy, but everyone comes for the brilliant regional Italian cuisine. Set in an unlikely street

off Soho's red-light district, here you'll find succession of small plates and dishes from Bologna to Veneto. Try fried anchovies, grilled red prawns, lamb *prosciutto*, cannellini beans, or rustic pork and foie gras sausages. You may not be able to hear yourselves speak, but at least the amazing milk-free espresso ice cream makes up for the loss. ⊠ *12 Archer St., Soho* ☎ *020/7734–2223* ⊕ *www.boccadilupo.com* ⚅ *Reservations essential* ☯ *Closed Sun.* Ⓤ *Piccadilly Circus* ✛ *D3.*

£ ✕ **Busaba Eathai.** It's top Thai nosh for little money at this no-reservations
THAI eatery in the heart of Soho. Fitted with wooden bench seats and hard-
Fodor's Choice wood tables, this flagship restaurant has communal dining, rapid ser-
★ vice, and a fast-moving queue. The menu includes noodles, curries, soups, and stir-fries. Pour yourself a lemongrass tea, then try the chicken with shiitake, cuttlefish curry, or vermicelli with prawns, squid, and scallops. It's always handy as a shopping pit stop. ⊠ *106–110 Wardour St., Soho* ☎ *020/7255–8686* ⊕ *www.busaba.com* ⚅ *Reservations not accepted* Ⓤ *Tottenham Court Rd.* ✛ *E2.*

£ ✕ **Côte.** Where else can you get a surprisingly good three-course
FRENCH French meal for £11.95? The Côte French brasserie—softly lighted and smoothly decked out with grey and white striped awning, ban-quettes, and Parisian-style round tables—does just the trick, and offers these deals weekdays from 3 pm until 7 pm, and weekends noon to 6 pm. With four choices per course, you'll find all your favorites: Bay-onne ham, beef Bourguignon, Les Landes chicken, *moules marinières* (steamed mussels with white wine), tuna Niçoise, minced beefsteak haché patties, and crème caramel. ⊠ *124–126 Wardour St., Soho* ☎ *020/7287–9280* ⊕ *www.cote-restaurants.co.uk* Ⓤ *Tottenham Court Rd., Piccadilly Circus* ✛ *D3.*

£££ ✕ **Dean Street Townhouse.** It's impossible not to feel glamorous at this
BRITISH packed and buzzing restaurant, attached to the stylish hotel of the same
Fodor's Choice name. Soft lighting, dark-wood floors, red banquettes, raised bar seats
★ and walls crammed with monochromes by Brit artists Tracy Emin and Mat Collishaw create a hip atmosphere for London's good-looking media elite. No-frills, no-fuss retro-British favorites include smoked haddock soufflé, fish fingers, or toad-in-the-hole, plus sherry trifle, trea-cle tart, and bread-and-butter pudding. You'll find buttered crumpets for afternoon tea, as well as a high tea service, and weekend brunch, plus a few celebrities dotted around the place, too. ⊠ *69–71 Dean St., Soho* ☎ *020/7434–1775* ⊕ *www.deanstreettownhouse.com* ⚅ *Reserva-tions essential* Ⓤ *Tottenham Court Rd.* ✛ *E3.*

££ ✕ **Giaconda Dining Room.** A gastro-landmark with an indie spirit on Den-
MODERN mark Street's Tin Pan Alley (think Bowie, Marley, and the Clash), the
EUROPEAN friendly Australian-run two-room dining room may only seat 35, but
Fodor's Choice the eclectic menu is inspired. Chef Paul Merrony sends out mighty start-
★ ers—creamed shallots with horseradish, crab linguine, or lamb with cocoa beans—and a full range of luscious main entrées at extremely low prices. Try the fish cakes, pig's trotters, salmon and fennel, or hearty dishes like veal kidneys, Italian pork sausage stew, or ham-hock hash with a fried egg on top. ⊠ *9 Denmark St., Soho* ☎ *020/7240–3334* ⊕ *www.giacondadining.com* ☯ *No lunch Sat. Closed Sun. and Mon.* Ⓤ *Tottenham Court Rd.* ✛ *E4.*

LOCAL CHAINS WORTH A TASTE

When you're on the go or don't have time for a leisurely meal, you might want to try a local chain restaurant or sandwich bar. The ones listed below are well priced and are the best in their category.

✕ **Busaba Eathai:** It's always jam-packed at these five Thai canteen supremos where you'll find Thai noodles, rice dishes, and spicy all-in-one meals in a bowl in sultry dark-wood surrounds. ⊕ www.busaba.com.

✕ **Byron:** Bright and child-friendly, this 10-strong line of superior hamburger joints storms the market with its delicious Aberdeen Angus Scotch hamburgers, onion rings and fries. ⊕ www.byronhamburgers.com.

✕ **Café Rouge:** A classic 30-strong French bistro chain that's been around for ages and does great prix-fixe deals—so uncool that it's now almost fashionable. ⊕ www.caferouge.co.uk.

✕ **Carluccio's Caffè:** The Carluccio's chain of 22 all-day Italian café/bar/food shops are freshly sourced, family-friendly, and make for brilliant pasta and salad stops on a shopping spree. ⊕ www.carluccios.com.

✕ **Ed's Easy Diner:** Overdose on milk shakes, ice-cream floats, chili dogs, and made-to-order hamburgers at this chain of shiny, retro 1950s-theme American diners. ⊕ www.edseasydiner.com.

✕ **Le Pain Quotidien:** Try tartine open sandwiches and salads at the communal wooden tables. There are 16 branches, including at the stunning St. Pancras station and Eurostar terminus. ⊕ www.lepainquotidien. co.uk.

✕ **Pizza Express:** Serving classic thin-crust pizzas, old-favorite Pizza Express is everywhere (there are nearly 100 in London). The Soho branch has a famed livejazz program. ⊕ www.pizzaexpress.com.

✕ **Pret A Manger:** London's high-street take-out supremo isn't just for store-made sandwiches: there are wraps, toasties, noodles, sushi, salads, fruit, and teacakes, too. ⊕ www.pret.com.

✕ **Ranoush Juice:** Shawarma lamb kebabs are the draw at these mirrored late-night kebab and juice bars (open 8 am to 3 am daily). They also serve falafel, meze, and tabbouleh. ⊕ www.maroush.com.

✕ **Strada:** Stop at this 28-strong chain for authentic hand-stretched pizzas baked over a wood fire, plus classic pastas, steaks, and risottos. It's cheap, stylish, and packed. ⊕ www.strada.co.uk.

✕ **Wagamama:** Londoners drain bowls of noodle soup at this child-friendly chain. ⊕ www.wagamama. com

£££
BRITISH
Fodor's Choice
★

✕ **Hix.** Hix, a spiffy Soho establishment on Brewer Street that oozes class, style, and panache, serves brilliant but simple British fare: think flat-iron steak with a huge chunk of bone marrow, Aryshire veal with Mendip snails, or *gurnard* (a white fish) with cockles and sea *purslane* (green leaves). You can also find epic feasts for the whole table, such as goose, chop, and oysters, or suckling pig, plus riffs on classics, like rabbit and crayfish Stargazy pie. Check out Brit artists Sarah Lucas and Damian Hirst mobiles, plus old-fashioned bar billiards, kilim rugs, and

2

famed mixologist Nick Strangeway's cocktails in the winning basement bar. ⊠ *66–70 Brewer St., Soho* ☏ *020/7292–3518* ⊕ *www.hixsoho. co.uk* ⌕ *Reservations essential* Ⓤ *Piccadilly Circus* ⊹ *D3.*

££ ✕ **Yauatcha.** It's all-day dim sum at this superbly lighted slinky Soho
CHINESE classic. Well designed by Christian Liaigre—with black granite floors, aquarium, candles, and a starry ceiling—the food is a match for the seductive setting. There's wicked dim sum (try prawns or scallops), crispy duck rolls, silver cod, fancy cocktails, tea and colorful cakes in the first-floor tearoom. Note the quick table turns, and ask to dine in the more romantic basement at night. ⊠ *15 Broadwick St., Soho* ☏ *020/ 7494–8888* ⊕ *www.yauatcha.com* ⌕ *Reservations essential* Ⓤ *Oxford Circus* ⊹ *D3.*

COVENT GARDEN

£££ ✕ **Great Queen Street.** Expect crowds at Covent Garden's leading gas-
MODERN BRITISH tropub that showcases classic British dishes in a burgundy and bare
Fodor's Choice oak-floor-and-table setting. Old-fashioned offerings like pressed tongue,
★ mackerel and gooseberry, Old Spot pork, and mussels and brown crab on toast may be revived from a bygone era, but Londoners absolutely adore them. Venison pie and dishes for the whole table—like seven-hour shoulder of lamb—are highly convivial. There's little for nonmeat eaters, and no dinner Sunday. ⊠ *32 Great Queen St., Covent Garden* ☏ *020/7242–0622* ⌕ *Reservations essential* ☉ *No dinner Sun.* Ⓤ *Covent Garden, Holborn* ⊹ *E2.*

£££ ✕ **The Ivy.** The A-list tend to spurn the Ivy for other hot spots like Scott's,
BRITISH J Sheekey, and Hix, but it's still hard to get a table here. A mix of TV stars and out-of-towners dine on Moroccan spiced lamb and smoked *aubergine* (eggplant), salmon fish cakes, eggs Benedict, and English classics like shepherd's pie and *kedgeree* (curried rice with flaked haddock, parsley, and boiled egg) in a handsome stained-glass and wood-paneled dining salon. For midrange West End star spotting this is a prime spot. If you can't score a reservation, try walking in for a table at the last moment—it's been known to work. ⊠ *1–5 West St., Covent Garden* ☏ *020/7836–4751* ⊕ *www.the-ivy.co.uk* ⌕ *Reservations essential* Ⓤ *Covent Garden* ⊹ *E3.*

£££ ✕ **J Sheekey.** West End theater and movie stars slip into this famous
SEAFOOD seafood haunt as an alternative to Scott's or Hix. Linked with nearby Theaterland and Shaftesbury Avenue, J Sheekey is one of Londoners' all-time favorite West End haunts. It charms with warm wood paneling, showbiz monochromes, a warren of alcove tables, and lava-rock bar tops. Opt for Arctic herring, Dover sole, Cornish sardines, monkfish, or famous Sheekey fish pie. Have champagne and West Mersea oysters at the original mirrored oyster bar for the ultimate in true romance, or enjoy the £25.50 weekend set lunch. ⊠ *28–32 St. Martin's Ct., Covent Garden* ☏ *020/7240–2565* ⊕ *www.j-sheekey.co.uk* Ⓤ *Leicester Sq.* ⊹ *E3.*

££££ ✕ **Rules.** Come here to escape the 21st century. Opened by Thomas Rule
BRITISH in 1798, London's oldest restaurant has hosted everyone from novelist Charles Dickens to actor Laurence Olivier and the current Prince of Wales. This most traditional of English dining salons has plush red banquettes and lacquered yellow walls crammed with old oil paintings,

Fried calamari is typically delicious fare at Busaba Eathai, a good-value Thai favorite.

antique clocks, prints, engravings, and Victorian cartoons. Try pricey and historic British dishes—steak-and-kidney pie, perhaps, or roast beef and Yorkshire pudding—for a taste of the 18th century. ✉ *35 Maiden La., Covent Garden* ☎ *020/7836–5314* ⊕ *www.rules.co.uk* Ⓤ *Covent Garden* ✛ *E3.*

£££££
GRILL

✕ **Savoy Grill.** You can feel the history at this 1889 art deco power-dining salon at the Savoy, which has hosted everyone from Oscar Wilde and Winston Churchill to Marilyn Monroe and Audrey Hepburn. Nowadays, business blue bloods and top-end tourists enjoy the Grill's famous table-side daily trolley, which might have roast rack of pork, or traditional roast beef Wellington. T-bone, rib-eye, and porterhouse steaks sizzle straight off the flame grill. Puddings like mandarin baked Alaska are from a bygone age. ✉ *The Savoy, 100 Strand, Covent Garden* ☎ *020/7592–1600* ⊕ *www.gordonramsay.com/thesavoygrill* ⚑ *Reservations essential* Ⓤ *Charing Cross, Covent Garden.* ✛ *E3.*

£
MEXICAN

✕ **Wahaca.** Expect a wait for the fab-value Mexican street food at this brightly colored Covent Garden favorite. Mud walls and bench seats make for buzzy basement surroundings, but it's the cheap £3.85–£8.95 tacos, enchiladas, quesadillas, and burritos that pull in the student crowds. A £19.95 spread for two will produce a feast of broad bean quesadillas, pork tacos, slaw, green rice, black beans, and guacamole, but note that reservations aren't taken and that it's often full by 6:30 pm. ✉ *66 Chandos Pl., Covent Garden* ☎ *020/7240–1883* ⊕ *www.wahaca.co.uk* ⚑ *Reservations not accepted* Ⓤ *Charing Cross* ✛ *E3.*

THE CITY AND ENVIRONS

THE CITY

£££ ✕ **Boundary.** Design guru and restaurateur Sir Terence Conran scores
FRENCH a bull's-eye at Boundary in über-fashionable Hoxton–Shoreditch. A
theatrical glass-fronted open kitchen and sparkling lighting, acoustics,
and Technicolor seats, make this plush 100-plus seat basement French
brasserie the *glamorati's* east-end destination of choice. The menu's a
wish list of crowd-pleasers designed to impress: shellfish bisque, escar-
gots à la Bourguignonne, *cassoulet Toulousain* (haricot bean stew with
pork, lamb, duck, and garlic sausage), *lapin à la moutarde* (rabbit with
mustard), and roast Les Landes chicken. ✉ *2–4 Boundary St., entrance
at 9 Redchurch St., The City* ☎ *020/7729–1051* ⊕ *www.theboundary.
co.uk* ⌕ *Reservations essential* ☽ *No lunch Mon.* Ⓜ *Liverpool St.* ✛ *H1.*

£££ ✕ **L'Anima.** Brilliant Southern Italian cuisine in a love-it-or-loathe-it
ITALIAN modern glass-fronted box of a restaurant characterizes the scene at
L'Anima. Chef Francesco Mazzei draws inspiration from Sicily, Sar-
dinia, and Calabria, and works the floor, bar, and clear-fronted kitchen
like the proud owner he is. Simple, modern dishes like wild mushroom
and black truffle *tagliolini* are near perfection, as is the wood-roasted
turbot with clams—as succulent as you could wish. Dessert puddings,
like cappuchino tiramisu, are *belissimo*; the wines are mainly Italian.
✉ *1 Snowden St., The City* ☎ *020/7422–7000* ⊕ *www.lanima.co.uk*
☽ *Closed Sun.* Ⓤ *Liverpool St.* ✛ *H2.*

£££ ✕ **Moro.** Up from the City, near Clerkenwell and Sadler's Wells con-
MEDITERRANEAN temporary dance theater, is Exmouth Market, a cluster of cute shops,
a few delis, an Italian church, and fine restaurants like Moro. The
menu includes a mélange of Spanish and North African flavors. Spiced
meats, Serrano ham, salt cod, and wood-fired and char-grilled offerings
are the secret to Moro's success. Wood-roasted sea bass with capers
and fennel sauce stands out. Sidle up to the zinc bar, or squeeze into a
tiny table and lean in—it's noisy here. ✉ *34–36 Exmouth Market, The
City* ☎ *020/7833–8336* ⊕ *www.moro.co.uk* ⌕ *Reservations essential*
☽ *Closed Sun.* Ⓤ *Farringdon* ✛ *F1.*

£ ✕ **Simpson's Tavern.** This Dickensian back-alley City chophouse was
BRITISH founded in 1757 and is as raucous as the day it opened. It draws pin-
striped City folk, who love the boardinghouse scene and old-school
grub: oxtail stew, steak-and-kidney pie, potted shrimp (brown shrimp
preserved in a pot of butter), and "stewed cheese" house special (cheese
on toast with Béchamel sauce). The grumpy service and shared oak
bench stalls are all part of the charm. Note that it's open weekdays only
from noon until 3. ✉ *38½ Cornhill, at Ball Ct., The City* ☎ *020/7626–
9985* ⊕ *www.simpsonstavern.co.uk* ☽ *Closed weekends. No dinner*
Ⓤ *Bank* ✛ *H3.*

£££ ✕ **Sweetings.** Established in 1889, Sweetings is a remnant from the
SEAFOOD old imperial City of London heyday. There are some things Sweetings
doesn't do: reservations, dinner, coffee, weekends. It does, however,
do seafood. Not far from St. Paul's Cathedral, it's patronized by self-
assured City gents who drink tankards of Black Velvet (Guinness and
champagne) and eat soused herrings, roe on toast, and skate wings
with black butter at linen-covered raised counters. The oysters are fresh

and desserts like spotted dick and syrup pudding are classic favorites. ✉ *39 Queen Victoria St., The City* 🕾 *020/7248–3062* ⌖ *Reservations not accepted* ☾ *Closed weekends. No dinner* Ⓤ *Mansion House* ✛ *G3*.

£ ✕ **Tayyabs.** Blythe City bankers and medics from the Royal London
PAKISTANI Hospital swamp this no-reservations high-turnover Pakistani curry canteen in Whitechapel. Expect a wait after dark, and bear in mind that it's corkage-free BYO, jam-packed, noisy, and maddeningly chaotic. Nonetheless, prices are cheap and you can gorge handsomely for £17 on minced meat seekh kebabs, karahi prawns, or marinated and char-grilled lamb chops. ✉ *83 Fieldgate St., The City* 🕾 *020/7247–9543* ⊕ *www.tayyabs.co.uk* ⌖ *Reservations not accepted* ⛾ *BYOB* Ⓤ *Aldgate East* ✛ *H3*.

CLERKENWELL

£££ ✕ **Bistrot Bruno Loubet.** Beloved French chef Bruno Loubet creates so
FRENCH many distinctive dishes, it's hard to decide which ones to choose. Deliciously pink quail comes with pistachio and soft egg-yolk ravioli, and guinea fowl *boudin blanc* sausage sits perfectly with leek fondue and chervil source. You'll find stewed beef daube Provençale, crêpe Suzette in a shiny copper pan, and Pernod floating island, all served in a ground-floor dining room with retro lamps and artifacts overlooking St. John's Square. Watch out for the £30 three-course foragers' menu, which may include hedge sorrel, dill pollen, dandelion, and *marsh samphire* (an edible green plant that grows by the sea). ✉ *The Zetter, 86–88 Clerkenwell Rd, Clerkenwell* 🕾 *020/7324–4455* ⊕ *www.bistrotbrunoloubet. com* ⌖ *Reservations essential* Ⓜ *Farringdon St.* ✛ *G2*.

£££ ✕ **St. John.** Foodies travel the world for chef Fergus Henderson's ultra-
BRITISH British nose-to-tail cooking at this no-frills stark-white converted
Fodor's Choice smokehouse in Clerkenwell. His chutzpah is laudable: One appetizer
★ is pigskin, and others, like ox heart or pig spleen and bacon, are marginally less extreme. Signature dishes like bone marrow and parsley salad, or chitterlings with dandelion appear stark on the plate but arrive with aplomb. Expect an all-French wine list and finish with quince jelly and Jersey cream or half a dozen golden Madeleines. ✉ *26 St. John St., Clerkenwell* 🕾 *020/7251–0848* ⊕ *www.stjohnrestaurant.com* ☾ *No dinner Sun.* Ⓤ *Farringdon* ✛ *H2*.

THE EAST END

£££ ✕ **Viajante.** It's a massive schlep from the West End to Viajante in Beth-
MODERN nal Green, but chef Nuno Mendes's ultra-contemporary, avant-garde
EUROPEAN cuisine is the hottest, most exciting in London—bar none. Armed with
Fodor's Choice tweezers in a fascinating open-kitchen, Mendes creates 3- to 12-course
★ extravaganzas (£24–£150) in the serene converted former Bethnal Green Town Hall. Unlikely tastes, textures, and flavors abound—like iced green tea and Japanese purple shiso herb leaves, or Thai basil panna cotta—but everything excels, and looks like high art. Expect rare micro-herbs and local urban-foraged goodies, such as wood sorrel, sweet violets, and honeysuckle. Our advice is simple: Go! ✉ *Town Hall Hotel, Patriot Sq., East End* 🕾 *020/7871–0461* ⊕ *www.viajante. co.uk* ⌖ *Reservations essential* Ⓤ *Bethnal Green Tube/rail, Cambridge Heath rail* ✛ *H1*.

THE SOUTH BANK

££
MODERN BRITISH

✕ **Magdalen.** South of the river between London and Tower bridges, and a hop and a skip from the London Assembly headquarters, Magdalen is a self-assured beacon of class in an up-and-coming part of town. It specialized in inventive modern British cuisine at keen prices; fried calves brain (£7.50), braised Welsh lamb (£15.50), wild turbot and cockles (£18), and cow's curd and honey for £6 will hardly break the bank. With dark-wood and aubergine-color surroundings, sit back with a clever 70-bottle wine list that carries 19 by the carafe. ✉ *152 Tooley St., South Bank* ☎ *020/7403–1342* ⊕ *www.magdalenrestaurant.co.uk* ⊗ *No lunch Sat. Closed Sun.* Ⓤ *London Bridge* ✛ *H4.*

KENSINGTON, CHELSEA, AND KNIGHTSBRIDGE

KENSINGTON

££
AMERICAN

✕ **PJ's Bar & Grill.** Enter PJ's and assume the Polo Joe lifestyle: wooden floors and stained glass, a slowly revolving propeller from a 1919 Vickers Vimy flying bomber, and vintage polo gear galore. The place is packed, relaxed, and efficient, and the menu, which includes all-American staples like organic steaks, salads, and brownies, pleases all except vegetarians. Weekend brunch is a must with the wealthy Chelsea jet set. ✉ *52 Fulham Rd., Kensington* ☎ *020/7581–0025* ⊕ *www.pjsbarandgrill.co.uk* Ⓤ *South Kensington* ✛ *B5.*

CHELSEA

££
MODERN BRITISH
Fodor'sChoice
★

✕ **Harwood Arms.** Modern British game doesn't get any better—or more inventive—than at this unassuming gastro pub. The co-owner Mike Robinson shoots all the venison on the menu in season, and you'll find a catalogue of awesome dishes like Berkshire roe deer with Douglas fir sausages or whole North Yorkshire grouse with watercress. Tuck into stout-soaked beef cheeks with Herefordshire snails, or wood pigeon with pickled apricots. Some dishes are served on a slab of wood, and there are popular carve-your-own whole-roast joints for the entire table. ✉ *27 Walham Grove, Chelsea* ☎ *020/7386–1847* ⊕ *www.harwoodarms.com* ⌕ *Reservations essential* ⊗ *No lunch Mon.* Ⓤ *Fulham Broadway* ✛ *A6.*

£££
CHINESE
Fodor'sChoice
★

✕ **Hunan.** There's no menu at this quirky, top-rated family-run Chinese restaurant in Pimlico. Instead diners state their preferences to owner-chef Peng, or his son Michael, and sit back, relax, and plough through a succession of highly tasty items to share. A seasoned crowd might enjoy 14 to 18 unfailingly delicious dishes like Hunan water-fried dumplings, sliced duck, pork broth, crispy frogs' legs, pig's ears and tongues, and crab noodle soup. There's no real logic to what you might receive, but portion sizes are generous, and the not knowing is all part of the fun. ✉ *51 Pimlico Rd., Chelsea* ☎ *020/7730–5712* ⊕ *www.hunanlondon.com* ⌕ *Reservations essential* ⊗ *Closed Sun.* Ⓤ *Sloane Sq.* ✛ *C5.*

££
MODERN BRITISH
Fodor'sChoice
★

✕ **The Orange.** The handsome Orange gastropub in Pimlico gets everything right, which seems appropriate because most nights and weekends the place is full. It's light and airy, with stripped wood, an ochra color–scheme, and mini-potted orange trees; service is noticeably smiley and well-mannered. Try the chicken liver parfait and wood-fired pizzas, or enjoy a leisurely Sunday roast like Castle of Mey beef, Kilravock pork, or chicken with sage and bacon, all served with duck-fat roast potatoes, Yorkshire pudding, and braised red cabbage. ⊠ *37–39 Pimlico Rd., Chelsea* ☎ *020/7881–9844* ⊕ *www.theorange.co.uk* ⌖ *Reservations essential* Ⓤ *Sloane Sq.* ✚ *C5.*

££
MODERN BRITISH

✕ **The Pig's Ear.** Heir to the throne Prince William once came with friends and split the bill in the first-floor dining room at this classic Sloaney boho-chic gastropub off the King's Road. Elbow in for space at the crowded ground-floor pub area, or choose a more formal vibe in the dark wood-paneled salon upstairs. You'll find creative dishes on a short menu, like pig's ear, Cornish crab, wild mallard, lamb neck, veal and bone marrow and braised pork belly, which are all typical, and executed . . . royally. ⊠ *35 Old Church St., Chelsea* ☎ *020/7352–2908* ⊕ *www.thepigsear.info* Ⓤ *Sloane Sq.* ✚ *B6.*

£££
BRASSERIE

✕ **Racine.** There's an upscale buzz at this star of the Brompton Road dining scene, not far from the V&A museum, Harrods department store, and Holy Trinity Brompton church. This smooth-running chic French brasserie excels in doing simple things well—and not overcharging. Chef Henry Harris's classics like melted Raclette cheese, roast partridge, paté-like Middlewhite pork rillette, and rack of lamb all hit the high notes. Many of the patrons are wealthy local regulars, and the £15–£17.50 set lunch or early evening dinners (6–7:30 pm) are deservedly popular. ⊠ *239 Brompton Rd., Chelsea* ☎ *020/7584–4477* ⊕ *www. racine-restaurant.com* Ⓤ *South Kensington* ✚ *B3.*

KNIGHTSBRIDGE

£££
FRENCH

✕ **Bar Boulud.** Star chef Daniel Boulud successfully mixes the best of French high-end brasserie fare with a dash of gourmet burgers and fries, at this popular ground-level haunt in the Mandarin Oriental. Small-board platters of the most delicate Gilles Verot charcuterie, or chunky Beaujolaise sausages with Lyonnaise mashed potatoes are followed by fist-sized New York hamburgers in a sesame seed bun with *pommes frites* on the side. The appealing grazing menu and informal wait staff make for a friendly and convivial vibe in a handy spot opposite the Harvey Nichols department store. ⊠ *Mandarin Oriental Hyde Park, 66 Knightsbridge, Knightsbridge* ☎ *020/7201–3899* ⊕ *www.barboulud.com/barbouludlondon.html* ⌖ *Reservations essential* Ⓤ *Knightsbridge* ✚ *C4.*

£££££
BRITISH
Fodor's Choice
★

✕ **Dinner by Heston Blumenthal.** Medieval and historically inspired English dishes executed with modern precision is the draw at Heston Blumenthal's London outpost. The "Meat Fruit" starter (c.1500) is shaped like a mandarin, and encases creamy chicken liver parfait. Beef Royale (c.1720) of Angus rib is cooked sous-vide in a water bath for 72 hours at 56°C to create a layered depth of flavor. Other historic treats include, "Rice and Flesh" (c.1390), featuring calf's tail and red wine, and a dish called "Salamagundy" (c.1720), with chicken oysters, bone marrow, and horseradish cream. ⊠ *Mandarin Oriental Hyde Park, 66 Knightsbridge, Knightsbridge* ☎ *020/7201–3833* ⊕ *www.dinnerbyheston.com* ⌖ *Reservations essential* Ⓤ *Knightsbridge* ✚ *C4.*

£££
FRENCH

✕ **Koffmann's.** Perfectly seared scallops with black squid ink and gelatinous pig's trotters stuffed with sweetbreads and morel mushrooms are

LONDON'S BEST CURRIES

Curry has become England's surrogate national dish and in London you'll find some of the best.

✕ **Dishoom** is modeled on the Persian-run all-day Irani cafés of Victorian Bombay and it skillfully churns out marvelous street food, from naan bread and roti wraps, to masala Bombay sausages. Average price of dinner for two: £24. ✉ *12 Upper St. Martin's La., Covent Garden* ☎ *020/7420–9320* ⊕ *www.dishoom. com* Ⓤ *Leicester Sq.*

✕ **Hot Stuff** in Vauxhall offers some of the best-loved and best-priced curries in London. Run by the Dawood family, it's a BYO café with two tables. Home-cooked specials include rice and king prawn *biryani*, thick chicken bhuna curry, and chili paneer cubed white cheese. Average price of dinner for two: £24. ✉ *19 Wilcox Rd., South Bank* ☎ *020/7720–1480* ⊕ *www.eathotstuff.com* 🍴 *BYOB* Ⓤ *Vauxhall.*

✕ **Indian Zing's** chef-owner Manoj Vasaikar woos the west London curry mafia with updated eclectic Indian cuisine. Try Khyber Pass shoulder of lamb or duck with Chettinad spices. Average price of dinner for

two: £65. ✉ *236 King St., Hammersmith* ☎ *020/8748–5959* ⊕ *www. indianzing.co.uk* Ⓤ *Hammersmith.*

✕ **Rasoi's** chef-owner Vineet Bhatia prepares modern Indian cuisine at this special occasion Chelsea town house, where fans swoon over skewered scallops, tandoori salmon, and Keralean lamb lasagne. Average price of dinner for two: £160. ✉ *10 Lincoln St., Knightsbridge* ☎ *020/72251–1881* ⊕ *www. rasoirestaurant.co.uk* Ⓤ *Sloane Sq.*

✕ **Tayyabs** attracts queues for its Pakistani curries, grilled meats, and spicy seekh kebabs at this throbbing Whitechapel mecca. Average price of dinner for two: £30. ✉ *83 Fieldgate St., The City* ☎ *020/7247–9543* ⊕ *www.tayyabs.co.uk* 🍴 *BYOB* Ⓤ *Aldgate East.*

✕ **Trishna's** £34.50, five-course tasting menus are the way to enjoy this Mumbai-inspired seafood specialist in Marylebone. Try shrimp with carom seed, minted bream, tiger prawns, fish curry, and spiced king crab. Average price for dinner for two: £95. ✉ *15–17 Blandford St., Marylebone* ☎ *020/79351–5624* ⊕ *www. trishnalondon.com* Ⓤ *Bond St.*

two all-time French classics at Pierre Koffmann's eponymous last-hurrah at the Berkeley. Coaxed out of retirement and in his early sixties, and the antithesis of a celebrity chef, Koffmann showcases 35 years of experience and the best of regional Gascony cuisine in a well-appointed basement setting. Try his snail with mushrooms and mash, roast wild duck à l'orange, and his feather-light pistachio soufflé with pistachio ice cream. ✉ *The Berkeley, Wilton Place, Knightsbridge* ☎ *020/7235–1010* ♦ *Reservations essential* Ⓤ *Knightsbridge* ✛ *C4.*

£££££
MODERN
EUROPEAN
Fodor's Choice
★

✕ **Marcus Wareing at the Berkeley.** Relentless master chef Marcus Wareing vies to be the best in London at his eponymous restaurant at the Berkeley. Opulently designed by David Collins—all clarets, carpet, and burgundy leather seats—Wareing pulls out all the haute cuisine stops with a succession of world-class dishes. Standouts include Orkney scallops with blueberries, a fine chunk of Scottish halibut with charred leeks

Harwood Arms has a modern take on Scotch eggs, a classic British dish.

or Anjou pigeon with Amaretti. An oozing hot chocolate *moëlleux* pudding with salted caramel, or lemon crème with spiced brioche are absolutely flawless, and the wine list includes page after page of famous names. ✉ *The Berkeley, Wilton Pl., Knightsbridge* ☎ *020/7235–1200* ⊕ *www.the-berkeley.co.uk* ⚱ *Reservations essential* ♥ *Closed Sun. No lunch Sat.* Ⓤ *Knightsbridge* ✛ *C4.*

£££££   ✕ **Rasoi.** Chef-proprietor Vineet Bhatia showcases the finest new Indian
INDIAN cuisine at this tony Victorian town-house restaurant off the King's Road. Ring the door bell before entering at this super-seductive venue, which is decked with colorful Indian silks, prints, masks, bells, and ornaments. Bhatia pushes the boundaries with signatures like wild mushroom rice with tomato ice cream, lamb lasagna with coconut chutney, or grilled lobster dusted with cocoa and sour spices. Prices are extreme, but don't leave without sampling chai panna cotta or the famous warm chocolate samosas. ✉ *10 Lincoln St., Knightsbridge* ☎ *020/7225–1881* ⊕ *www. rasoirestaurant.co.uk* Ⓤ *Sloane Sq.* ✛ *C5.*

NOTTING HILL AND BAYSWATER

NOTTING HILL

£££   ✕ **The Cow.** A popular boho-chic gastropub, the Cow comprises a faux-
MODERN BRITISH Dublin 1950s backroom saloon that serves Fines de Claires oysters, *whelks and winkles* (sea snails and gastropods), and whole Dorset crab. Upstairs the chef whips up Brit specialties like deviled lamb with artichokes, Stilton cheese and hazelnut salad, black bream, and sea trout

with shrimp. Notting Hill locals love the house special in the packed bar: draft cold Guinness with a pint of prawns and mayonnaise (£5.25). ✉ *89 Westbourne Park Rd., Notting Hill* ☎ *020/7221–0021* ⊕ *www. thecowlondon.co.uk* Ⓤ *Westbourne Park* ✢ *AZ.*

££ ✕ **E&O.** The global jet set and fashionistas hang out here, one of London's most successful hip bar scene and restaurant, off Portobello Road street market. E&O means "Eastern and Oriental," and the mix of Chinese, Japanese, Vietnamese, and Thai dishes includes a slew of figure-friendly, low-carb vegetarian options. Don't skip the lychee martinis, miso black cod, chili tofu, Thai rare beef, papaya salad or green fried rice; the sea bass sashimi is fresh. There are pavement tables and curbside bench seats to watch the world go by on Portobello. ✉ *14 Blenheim Crescent, Notting Hill* ☎ *020/7229–5454* ⊕ *www.rickerrestaurants. com/eando* Ⓤ *Ladbroke Grove* ✢ *A3.*

ASIAN

££££ ✕ **The Ledbury.** Australian-born chef Brett Graham's fantastic fine-dining housed in a handsome high-ceiling dining room, full of drapes, mirrors, and leather seats continues to impress. The £40 weekend set lunch is a tour de force that weaves from monkfish and truffle purée to ceviche of scallops and seaweed, to Pyrennean lamb with Chinese artichokes. Graham is known for his desserts, so finish with unusual olive oil panna cotta and fig leaf ice cream. Excellent service and a confident sommelier round out this winning proposition. ✉ *127 Ledbury Rd., Notting Hill* ☎ *0207/7792–9090* ⊕ *www.theledbury.com* Ⓤ *Westbourne Park* ✢ *A2.*

MODERN FRENCH

Fodor's Choice

★

BAYSWATER

£££ ✕ **Hereford Road.** Chef and co-owner Tom Pemberton mans the front-of-house grill at this must-visit Bayswater favorite, which specializes in pared-down British fare. With an accent on well-sourced regional and seasonal ingredients, many dishes are as unfussy as you'll find. Work your way though razor clams and lovage, smoked eels with horseradish, and buttermilk pudding. ✉ *3 Hereford Rd., Bayswater* ☎ *020/7727–1144* ⊕ *www.herefordroad.org* Ⓤ *Bayswater, Queensway* ✢ *A3.*

MODERN BRITISH

REGENT'S PARK AND HAMPSTEAD

££ ✕ **Lemonia.** Primrose Hill's favorite Greek Cypriot restaurant, vine-decked and taverna-style Lemonia is large and light, and always packed with hungry North London customers. Besides an endless supply of small-dish *mezédes* dips and starters, there are rustic mains like baked lamb in lemon, and beef stewed in red wine. Expect Greek hospitality, hordes of locals, loads of noise, and the boho chic Primrose Hill set. Top-value weekday three-course lunch is £10.50. ✉ *89 Regent's Park Rd., Regent's Park* ☎ *020/7586–7454* ⊗ *No lunch Sat. No dinner Sun.* Ⓤ *Chalk Farm* ✢ *B1.*

GREEK

PUBS AND AFTERNOON TEA

PUBS

The city's pubs, public houses, or "locals" dispense beer, good cheer, and casual grub in settings that range from ancient wood-beam rooms to ornate Victorian interiors to utilitarian modern rooms. Pubs in the capital are changing: 90-year-old licensing laws have finally been modernized, gastro-pub fever is sweeping London, and smoking in all pubs has been illegal since 2007. At many places, char-grills are being installed in the kitchen out back, and up front the faded wallpapers are being replaced by abstract paintings. Some showcase nouveau pub grub, but whether you have Moroccan chicken or the usually dismal ploughman's special, do order a pint. Note that American-style beer is called "lager" in Britain, whereas the real British brew is "bitter" (usually served cellar temperature, which is cooler than room temperature but not actually chilled). Order up your choice in two sizes—pints or half pints. Some London pubs also sell "real ale," which is less gassy than bitters and, many would argue, has a better flavor.

The list below offers a few pubs selected for central location, historical interest, a pleasant garden, music, or good food, but you might just as happily adopt your own temporary local.

BLOOMSBURY

★ **The Lamb.** Charles Dickens and his contemporaries drank here, but today's enthusiastic clientele make sure this intimate and eternally popular pub avoids the pitfalls of feeling too old-fashioned. For private chats at the bar, you can close the delicate etched-glass "snob screen" to the bar staff, opening it only when you fancy another pint. ⊠ *94 Lamb's Conduit St., Bloomsbury* ☎ *020/7405–0713* Ⓤ *Russell Sq.*

★ **Museum Tavern.** Across the street from the British Museum, this friendly and classy Victorian pub makes an ideal resting place after the rigors of the culture trail. Karl Marx unwound here after a hard day in the Library. He could have spent his *Kapital* on any of seven well-kept beers available on tap. ⊠ *49 Great Russell St., Bloomsbury* ☎ *020/7242–8987* Ⓤ *Tottenham Court Rd.*

THE CITY

Fodor'sChoice
★ **Black Friar.** A step from Blackfriars Tube stop, this spectacular pub has an Arts-and-Crafts interior that is entertainingly, satirically ecclesiastical, with inlaid mother-of-pearl, wood carvings, stained glass, and marble pillars all over the place. In spite of the finely lettered temperance tracts on view just below the reliefs of monks, fairies, and friars, there is a nice group of ales on tap from independent brewers. ⊠ *174 Queen Victoria St., The City* ☎ *020/7236–5474* Ⓤ *Blackfriars.*

Ye Olde Cheshire Cheese. Yes, it's full of tourists, but it's also an extremely historic pub (it dates from 1667, the year after the Great Fire of London), and it deserves a visit for its sawdust-covered floors, low wood-beam ceilings, and the 14th-century crypt of Whitefriars' monastery under the cellar bar. This was the most regular of Dr. Johnson's and Dickens's *many* locals. ⊠ *145 Fleet St., The City* ☎ *020/7353–6170* Ⓤ *Blackfriars.*

CLERKENWELL

Fodor's Choice
★

Jerusalem Tavern. Owned by the well-respected St. Peter's Brewery from Suffolk, the Jerusalem Tavern is one-of-a-kind, small and endearingly eccentric. Ancient Delft-style tiles meld with wood and concrete in a converted watchmaker and jeweler's shop dating back to the 18th century. The beer, both bottled and on tap, is some of the best available anywhere in London. It's often busy, especially after work. ⊠ *55 Britton St., Clerkenwell* ☎ *020/7490–4281* Ⓤ *Farringdon.*

THE EAST END

Prospect of Whitby. Named after a ship, this is London's oldest riverside pub, dating from around 1520. Once upon a time it was called the Devil's Tavern because of the lowlife criminals—thieves and smugglers—who congregated here. Ornamented with pewter ware and nautical objects, this much-loved "boozer" is often pointed out from boat trips up the Thames. ⊠ *57 Wapping Wall, East End* ☎ *020/7481–1095* Ⓤ *Wapping.*

KNIGHTSBRIDGE

★

The Nag's Head. It's best not to upset the landlord in this classic little mews pub in Belgravia—he runs a tight ship, and no cell phones are allowed. If that sounds like misery, the lovingly collected Victorian artifacts (including antique penny arcade games), high-quality beer, and old-fashioned pub grub should make up for it. ⊠ *53 Kinnerton St., Belgravia* ☎ *020/7235–1135* Ⓤ *Hyde Park Corner.*

MAYFAIR

The Running Horse. Wood paneling gives this smart Mayfair pub an authentic feel, although the bright art deco lights may seem a bit out of place. Pub grub is served, and it's a pleasant stopover during your jaunt around the elegant neighborhood. ⊠ *50 Davies St., Mayfair* ☎ *020/7493–1275* ⊕ *www.therunninghorselondon.co.uk* Ⓤ *Bond St.*

HAMPSTEAD

Spaniards Inn. Ideal as a refueling point when you're on a Hampstead Heath hike, this historic oak-beam pub has a gorgeous garden, scene of the tea party in Dickens's *Pickwick Papers*. Dick Turpin, the highwayman, frequented the inn. Before Dickens's time, Shelley, Keats, and Byron hung out here as well. It's extremely popular, especially on Sunday, when Londoners roll in. It's also very dog-friendly—there's even a dog wash in the garden. ⊠ *Spaniards Rd., Hampstead* ☎ *020/8731–8406* ⊕ *www.thespaniardshampstead.co.uk* Ⓤ *Hampstead.*

SOUTHBANK

Fodor's Choice
★

Anchor & Hope. One of London's most popular gastropubs, the Anchor & Hope doesn't take reservations (except for Sunday lunch), meaning queuing would-be diners snake around the red-walled, wooden-floored pub, kept happy by some good real ales and a fine wine list as they wait for hours for a table. The food is old-fashioned English (think salt cod, tripe, and chips) with a few modern twists. ⊠ *36 The Cut, South Bank* ☎ *020/7928–9898* Ⓤ *Southwark.*

COVENT GARDEN

Lamb & Flag. This refreshingly ungentrified 17th-century pub was once known as the Bucket of Blood because the upstairs room was used as a ring for bare-knuckle boxing. Now it's a friendly—and bloodless— pub, serving food (lunch only) and real ale. It's on the edge of Covent Garden, off Garrick Street. ⊠ *33 Rose St., Covent Garden* ☎ *020/7497– 9504* Ⓤ *Covent Garden.*

★ **White Hart.** This elegant, family-owned pub on Drury Lane is one of the best places to mix with cast and crew of the stage. A female-friendly environment, a cheery skylight above the lounge area, a late license, and above-average pub fare make the White Hart a particularly sociable spot for a drink. ⊠ *191 Drury La., Covent Garden* ☎ *020/7242–2317* ⊕ *www.whitehartdrurylane.co.uk* Ⓤ *Holborn, Covent Garden, Tottenham Court Rd.*

AFTERNOON TEA

Taking afternoon tea is the height of cool in London right now. From Kate Moss to Cameron Diaz, everyone wants to sit up straight, stick their pinkie out, and sip hot tea in the company of friends and family— and preferably in the warm embrace of an established hotel tea salon.

So, what is afternoon tea, exactly? It means real tea (Earl Grey, English Breakfast, Ceylon, Darjeeling or Assam Indian, or Chinese) brewed in a china pot, and served with china cups and saucers, milk, lemon, and silver spoons, between 3 and 5:30 pm. In grand places (with grand prices), there should be elegant finger foods on a three-tiered silver tea stand: crustless sandwiches on the bottom; fruit scones with Devonshire clotted cream and strawberry jam in the middle; and rich fruitcake, shortbread, patisseries, macaroons, and fancies on top. Tea-goers dress up in posh hotels, and conversation (by tradition) avoids politics and religion.

Brown's Hotel. This classic Mayfair town-house hotel sets the standard at the English Tea Room, where one of London's best-known Afternoon Teas is served (Afternoon Tea £35, Champagne Tea £45). ⊠ *33 Albermarle St., Mayfair* ☎ *020/7493–6020* ☉ *Tea weekdays 3–6, weekends 1–6* Ⓤ *Green Park.*

Café at Sotheby's. What could be better than perusing the famous Mayfair auction house before afternoon tea? Breakfasts are from 9:30 am, then teas from 3 pm; teas are available from £6.50 (including tea cakes and scones) and up to £18.75 for Champagne Tea. ⊠ *Sotheby's, 34 New Bond St., Mayfair* ☎ *020/7293–5077* ⤳ *Reservations essential* ☉ *Tea weekdays 3–4:45* Ⓤ *Green Park.*

The Dorchester. Amid a maze of marble and gold leaf, afternoon tea in the Promenade is best taken on comfy sofas and to the sound of the resident pianist. Teas are £35.50, £45.50 for Champagne Tea, and £49.50 for High Tea (with light bites like salmon and Cromer crab). Book well ahead. ⊠ *53 Park La.* ☎ *020/7629–8888* ⤳ *Reservations essential* ☉ *Tea daily 2:30 and 4:45* Ⓤ *Hyde Park Corner.*

Fortnum & Mason. Upstairs at the revamped 300-year-old Queen's grocers, three set teas are ceremoniously served: Afternoon Tea (sandwiches, scones, and cakes: £34), old-fashioned High Tea (the traditional nursery meal, with scrambled eggs and salmon: £36), and Champagne Tea (price according to Champagne). Hours: teas, Monday–Saturday noon to 8, Sun. noon to 6. ✉ *St. James's Restaurant, 4th fl., 181 Piccadilly, St. James's* ☎ *020/7734–8040* ⊙ *Tea Mon.–Sat. 2–7, Sun. noon–4:30* Ⓤ *Green Park.*

The Ritz. At the Ritz tea is served in the impressive Palm Court, with marble tables and Louis XIV chaises complete with musical accompaniment, giving the last morsel of Edwardian London. Afternoon Tea is £39 and Champagne Tea £50. Reserve two to three months ahead and remember to wear a jacket and tie. ✉ *150 Piccadilly, St. James's* ☎ *020/7300–2309* ⚇ *Reservations essential* ⊙ *Tea daily 11:30, 1:30, 3:30, 5:30, 7:30* Ⓤ *Green Park.*

Looking for a few other options? Fashionistas quaff designer pâtisserie among low seats and chandeliers at **Palour at Sketch** (✉ *9 Conduit St., Mayfair* ☎ *0870/777–4488* ⊕ *www.sketch.uk.com*) for £9.50. The **Wolseley** on Piccadilly (✉ *160 Piccadilly, St. James's* ☎ *020/7499–6996* ⊕ *www.thewolseley.com*) does gooey pastries and fine Ceylon tea for £21. The airy, 18th-century **Orangery** near Kensington Palace is a great spot for tea: cost is £15–£33.

WHERE TO STAY

Use the coordinate (✛ B2) at the end of each listing to locate a site on the corresponding map.

Few of the world's great cities have such an awkwardly mismatched hotel scene as London. At one end of the scale, you have luxury and glamour like nowhere else—legendary, iconic places like the Savoy, the Dorchester, and Claridge's. But at the other extreme lie terrible service, outdated facilities, and painfully poor value for money. The kicker, for London, is that there hasn't been a huge amount to choose from in between.

The good news is that things are improving. If all you want is a decent, basic, and (reasonably) inexpensive place to stay in the center of town, good bets are to be found in convenient neighborhoods like Bloomsbury and Kensington. Even better are the small but growing numbers of budget boutique hotels and B&Bs to be found just outside the center, such as the delightful Church Street Hotel, the bohemian 66 Camden Square, and the chic Stylotel. These have few frills but buckets of charm, so long as you don't mind the (sometimes lengthy) Tube or bus rides to get there.

There are also chains, such as Premier and Millennium, both of which have rooms for under £100 per night. And even such uber-trendy enclaves as the Hoxton and Dean Street Townhouse offer great bargains if you know what to look for. Wherever you decide to stay, however, book as far in advance as you can. You can sometimes get last-minute deals, but don't rely on it—or else you're liable to find yourself slumming, breaking the bank, or both.

BEST BETS FOR LONDON LODGING

Fodor's offers a selective listing of high-quality lodging experiences at every price range, from the city's best budget motel to its most sophisticated luxury hotel. Here, we've compiled our top recommendations by price and experience. The very best properties—in other words, those that provide a particularly remarkable experience in their price range—are designated in the listings with the Fodor's Choice logo.

Fodor's Choice ★

Church Street Hotel, ££, p. 134

Claridge's, ££££– £££££, p. 124

The Connaught, £££££, p. 125

The Dorchester, £££££, p. 125

The Generator, £, p. 130

The Hoxton, ££–£££, p. 132

Mandarin Oriental Hyde Park, £££££, p. 136

Number Sixteen, £££–££££, p. 135

One Aldwych, £££££, p. 127

Renaissance Chancery Court, ££££– £££££, p. 131

The Rookery, ££££– £££££, p. 132

The Savoy, £££££, p. 127

The Stafford London by Kempinski, ££££– £££££, p. 124

The Zetter, ££££, p. 132

Best by Price

£

66 Camden Square, p. 138

Church Street Hotel, p. 134

Stylotel, p. 137

££

B&B Belgravia, p. 120

Harlingford Hotel, p. 130

Premier Travel Inn County Hall, p. 134

£££

The Hoxton, p. 132

Millennium Gloucester, p. 135

Number Sixteen, p. 135

££££

Claridge's, p. 124

Hazlitts, p. 127

The Rookery, p. 132

The Zetter, p. 132

£££££

Athenaeum Hotel and Apartments, p. 124

The Savoy, p. 127

The Dorchester, p. 125

Mandarin Oriental Hyde Park, p. 136

One Aldwych, p. 127

Best by Experience

BEST SPAS

One Aldwych, £££££, p. 127

Claridge's, ££££– £££££, p. 124

Mandarin Oriental, £££££, p. 136

BEST HISTORIC HOTELS

Claridge's, ££££– £££££, p. 124

The Dorchester, £££££, p. 125

The Rookery, ££££– £££££, p. 132

BUSINESS TRAVELERS

Ramada Hotel and Suites Docklands, ££, p. 132

Millennium Gloucester, £££, p. 135

The Zetter, ££££, p. 132

BEST CONCIERGE

The Dorchester, £££££, p. 125

Mandarin Oriental Hyde Park, £££££, p. 136

Claridge's, ££££– £££££, p. 124

MOST ROMANTIC

Number Sixteen, £££–££££, p. 135

The Rookery, ££££, p. 132

Dean Street Townhouse, ££££–£££££, p. 127

MOST KID-FRIENDLY

Mint Hotel Westminster, ££££, p. 120

Premier Travel Inn County Hall, ££, p. 134

Vandon House Hotel, ££, p. 120

WHERE SHOULD I STAY?

	NEIGHBORHOOD VIBE	PROS	CONS
Westminster and Royal London	This historic section, aka "Royal London," is home to major tourist attractions like Buckingham Palace.	Central area near tourist sites; easy Tube access; considered a safe area to stay.	Mostly expensive lodging options; few restaurants and entertainment venues nearby.
St. James and Mayfair	Traditional, old money; a mixture of the business and financial set with fashionable shops.	In the heart of the action; some of London's best hotels are found here.	Pricey part of town; the city-that-never-sleeps buzz makes peace and quiet hard to come by.
Soho and Covent Garden	A tourist hub with endless entertainment on the streets and in theaters and clubs—it's party central for young adults.	Buzzing area with plenty to see and do; late-night entertainment abounds; wonderful shopping district.	The area tends to be noisy at night; few budget hotels; keep your wits about you at night, and watch out for pickpockets.
Bloomsbury, Holborn, Hampstead, and Islington	Diverse area that is part bustling business center and part tranquil respite with tree-lined streets and meadows.	Easy access to Tube, and 15 minutes to city center; major sights, like British Museum are here; buzzing nightlife in Islington.	Busy streets filled with honking trucks and roving students; the area around King's Cross can be sketchy—avoid it at night.
The City and South Bank	London's financial district, where most of the city's banks and businesses are headquartered.	Central location with easy transportation access; great hotel deals in South Bank; many major sights nearby.	It can be as quiet as a tomb after 8 pm; many nearby restaurants and shops close over the weekend.
East End	Increasingly trendy area east of the town center, with a great arts scene.	Great for art lovers, shoppers, and business execs with meetings in Canary Wharf.	Still a transitional area, parts of Hoxton can be a bit dodgy at night; 20-minute Tube ride from central London.
Kensington, Chelsea, and Knightsbridge	This is one of London's most upscale neighborhoods and a center of London's tourist universe. A glittering galaxy of posh department stores, boutiques, and fabulous hotels.	Diverse hotel selection; great area for meandering walks; superb shopping district. London's capital of high-end shopping with Harrods; easy Tube access; gorgeous architecture.	Depending on where you are, the nearest Tube might be a hike; residential area might be too quiet for some. Few budget hotel or restaurant options; beware of pickpockets.
Notting Hill and Bayswater	Plenty of hotel options in an upscale, trendy area favored by locals and tourists.	Hotel deals abound in Bayswater; gorgeous greenery in Hyde Park; great shopping districts.	Few budget lodging options; residential areas may be too quiet at night for some.
Regent's Park and Hampstead	A mix of arty, fashionable districts with a village-like feel in other places.	Good access to central London; easy to fall in love with this part of town.	Surprisingly easy to stray into "edgier" neighborhoods.

You should confirm *exactly* what your room costs before checking in. British hotels are obliged by law to display a price chart at the reception desk; study it carefully. In January and February you can often find reduced rates, and large hotels with a business clientele have frequent weekend packages. The usual practice these days in all but the cheaper hotels is for quoted prices to cover room alone; breakfast, whether Continental or "full English," costs extra. V.A.T. (Value Added Tax—sales tax) follows the same rule, with the most expensive hotels excluding a hefty 20%; middle-of-the-range and budget places include it in the initial quote.

WHAT IT COSTS IN POUNDS				
£	££	£££	££££	£££££
FOR TWO PEOPLE	under £80	£80–£140	£141–£200	£201–£300	over £300

Prices reflect the rack rate of a standard double room for two people in high season, including 20% V.A.T. Check online for off-season rates and special deals or discounts.

WESTMINSTER AND ROYAL LONDON

For expanded hotel reviews, visit Fodors.com.

WESTMINSTER

£££–££££
HOTEL
C

Mint Hotel Westminster. In a rather stark steel-and-glass building steps from the Tate Britain, this member of a small U.K. chain has some rooms with spectacular views of Big Ben and the London Eye; extras like floor-to-ceiling windows and flat-screen TVs complement the contemporary monochrome guest rooms. **Pros:** amazing views; lots of high-tech toys, including iMac computers. **Cons:** with more than 400 rooms, you're just a number. ⊠ *30 John Islip St., Westminster* ☎ *020/7630–1000* ⊕ *www. minthotel.com* ⟿ *444 rooms, 16 suites* ⟿ *In-room: a/c, Wi-Fi. In-hotel: restaurant, room service, bar, gym, parking* Ⓤ *Pimlico* ✛ *F5.*

£–££
HOTEL

Vandon House Hotel. Popular with students, backpackers, and families on a budget, this simply decorated hotel is close to Westminster Abbey and Buckingham Palace; the accommodations on offer are the very definition of cheap and cheerful. **Pros:** handy location; comfortable beds. **Cons:** simple decor; few extras; some rooms share bathrooms. ⊠ *1 Vandon St., Westminster* ☎ *020/7799–6780* ⊕ *www.vandonhouse. com* ⟿ *32 rooms* ⟿ *In-room: no a/c, Wi-Fi. In-hotel: bar* ⟲*Breakfast* Ⓤ *St. James's Park* ✛ *F5.*

VICTORIA

££
B&B/INN

B&B Belgravia. This modern guesthouse a short walk from Victoria Station has cool all-white decor—white chairs and walls, white pillars and desks, white linens and towels; it all looks a bit ethereal, which is what they're aiming for. **Pros:** nice extras like free use of a laptop in the hotel lounge; coffee and tea always available. **Cons:** bathrooms and rooms are small; no hotel restaurant or bar. ⊠ *64–66 Ebury St., Victoria* ☎ *020/7259–8570* ⊕ *www.bb-belgravia.com* ⟿ *17 rooms* ⟿ *In-room: no a/c. In-hotel: Wi-Fi* ⟲*Breakfast* Ⓤ *Knightsbridge* ✛ *E5.*

Claridge's

The Connaught

The Dorchester

The Stafford London by Kempinski

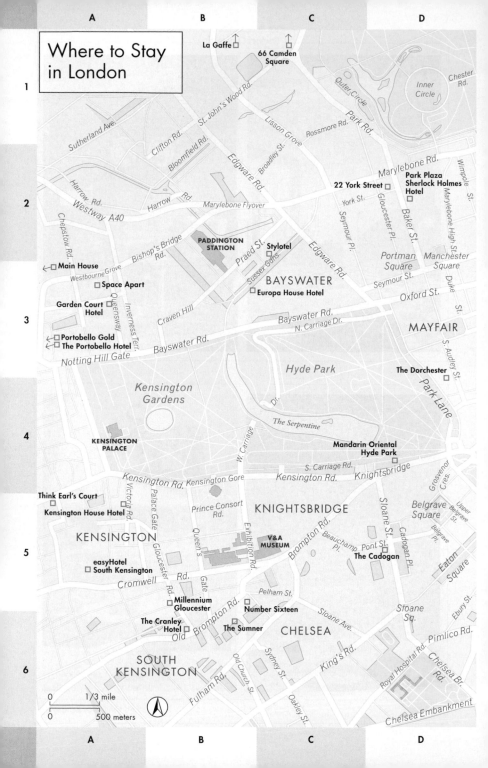

Where to Stay in London

A

1
La Gaffe ↑
66 Camden Square ↑

Sutherland Ave.
Clifton Rd.
St. John's Wood Rd.
Bloomfield Rd.
Edgware Rd.
Lisson Grove
Broadley St.
Rossmore Rd.
Park Rd.
Outer Circle
Inner Circle
Chester Rd.

2
Harrow Rd.
Westway A40
Harrow Rd.
Marylebone Flyover
Marylebone Rd.
York St.
22 York Street
Seymour Pl.
Gloucester Pl.
Baker St.
Park Plaza Sherlock Holmes Hotel
Wimpole St.
Marylebone High St.

Chepstow Rd.
Bishop's Bridge Rd.
PADDINGTON STATION
Praed St.
Stylotel
Sussex Gdns.
Edgware Rd.
Portman Square
Manchester Square
Seymour St.
Duke St.

Main House
Westbourne Grove
Space Apart
Europa House Hotel
BAYSWATER
Oxford St.
MAYFAIR

3
Garden Court Hotel
Queensway
Inverness Terr.
Craven Hill
Bayswater Rd.
N. Carriage Dr.

Portobello Gold
The Portobello Hotel
Bayswater Rd.
Notting Hill Gate

Kensington Gardens

Hyde Park
The Serpentine
Dr.

The Dorchester
Park Lane
S. Audley St.

4
KENSINGTON PALACE
W. Carriage Dr.
Mandarin Oriental Hyde Park

Kensington Rd.
Kensington Gore
S. Carriage Rd.
Kensington Rd.
Knightsbridge
Grosvenor Cres.

5
Think Earl's Court
Kensington House Hotel
Victoria Rd.
Palace Gate
Prince Consort Rd.
KNIGHTSBRIDGE
Brompton Rd.
Beauchamp Pl.
Pont St.
Sloane St.
The Cadogan
Belgrave Square
Upper Belgrave St.
Belgrave Pl.
Cadogan Pl.
Eaton Square

KENSINGTON
Gloucester Rd.
Queen's Gate
Exhibition Rd.
V&A MUSEUM

easyHotel South Kensington
Cromwell Rd.
Millennium Gloucester
Pelham St.
Number Sixteen
Sloane Ave.
Sloane Sq.
Ebury St.

The Cranley Hotel
Brompton Rd.
Old
The Sumner
CHELSEA
King's Rd.
Pimlico Rd.
Royal Hospital Rd.
Chelsea Br.
Chelsea Rd.

6
SOUTH KENSINGTON
Fulham Rd.
Old Church St.
Sydney St.
Oakley St.
Chelsea Embankment

0   1/3 mile
0   500 meters

B   **C**   **D**

£££££   📷 **The Goring.** Buckingham Palace is just around the corner, and visiting
HOTEL   VIPs use the Goring as a convenient, suitably dignified base for royal
occasions. **Pros:** comfortable beds; spacious rooms. **Cons:** price is too
high for what you get; decor is a bit fussy. ✉ *15 Beeston Pl., Grosvenor Gardens, Victoria* ☎ *020/7396–9000* ⊕ *www.thegoring.com* ⬅ *68
rooms, 6 suites* ♿ *In-room: a/c, Internet. In-hotel: restaurant, room
service, bar, gym, parking* Ⓤ *Victoria* ✛ *E5.*

££–£££   📷 **Lime Tree Hotel.** On a street filled with budget hotels, the homey Lime
HOTEL   Tree stands out for its gracious proprietors, the Davies family, who also
act as concierges. **Pros:** friendly and cheap; great location. **Cons:** some
rooms are up several flights of stairs, and there's no elevator; family rooms
don't allow kids under five. ✉ *135–137 Ebury St., Victoria* ☎ *020/7730–
8191* ⊕ *www.limetreehotel.co.uk* ⬅ *25 rooms* ♿ *In-room: no a/c, Wi-Fi.
In-hotel: some age restrictions* 🍽 *Breakfast* Ⓤ *Victoria* ✛ *E5.*

££   📷 **Studios @ 82.** These self-catering apartments represent fantastic value
B&B/INN   for money; after checking in at the main B&B, you're left entirely to
your own devices in the newly converted apartments. **Pros:** great price;
lovely location; all the independence of self-catering. **Cons:** lots of
stairs and no elevator. ✉ *64–66 Ebury St., Victoria* ☎ *020/7259–8570*
⊕ *www.bb-belgravia.com* ⬅ *9 apartments* ♿ *In-room: no a/c, Wi-Fi*
🍽 *Breakfast* Ⓤ *Knightsbridge* ✛ *E5.*

ST. JAMES'S AND MAYFAIR

For expanded hotel reviews, visit Fodors.com.

ST. JAMES'S

£££££–£££££   📷 **Claridge's.** Stay here, and you're staying at a hotel legend with one of
HOTEL   the world's classiest guest lists around. The friendly staff are not in the
☺   least condescending, and the rooms are never less than luxurious. **Pros:**
Fodor's Choice   serious luxury everywhere—this is an old-money hotel; kids won't be
★   bored, with comics, books, and DVDs to help keep them amused. **Cons:**
it's a bit pretentious—the guests in the hotel bar can be almost cartoon-
ishly snobbish. ✉ *Brook St., St. James's* ☎ *020/7629–8860, 866/599–
6991 in U.S.* ⊕ *www.claridges.co.uk* ⬅ *203 rooms* ♿ *In-room: a/c,
Wi-Fi. In-hotel: restaurant, bar, gym, spa, parking* Ⓤ *Bond St.* ✛ *E3.*

£££££–£££££   📷 **The Stafford London by Kempinski.** This is a rare find: a posh hotel that
HOTEL   is equal parts elegance and friendliness; it's hard to check in without
Fodor's Choice   meeting the gregarious manager, and his unshakable cheeriness must
★   be infectious, for the staff are also upbeat and helpful. **Pros:** great staff;
big, luxurious rooms; quiet location. **Cons:** traditional decor is not to
all tastes; men must wear jackets in the bar. ✉ *St. James's Pl., St. James's*
☎ *020/7493–0111* ⊕ *www.kempinski.com/london* ⬅ *81 rooms* ♿ *In-
room: a/c, Wi-Fi. In-hotel: restaurant, bar* Ⓤ *Green Park* ✛ *E4.*

MAYFAIR

£££££–£££££   📷 **Athenaeum Hotel and Apartments.** This grand hotel overlooking Green
HOTEL   Park offers plenty for the money; rooms are both comfortable and lavishly decorated, with deeply comfortable Hypnos beds, plasma-screen
TVs, luxurious fabrics, and original contemporary artworks. **Pros:**
peaceful park views; handy for Buckingham Palace and Piccadilly; great
value for elegant setting. **Cons:** some rooms could use a decor update;

bathrooms are almost all small. ⊠ *116 Piccadilly, Mayfair* ☎ *020/7499–3464* ⊕ *www.athenaeumhotel.com* ⤵ *111 rooms, 46 suites and apartments* ⚙ *In-room: a/c, kitchen (some), Wi-Fi. In-hotel: restaurant, room service, bar, gym, spa* ⫶⦿⫶ *Breakfast* Ⓤ *Green Park* ⊹ *E4.*

£££££ 🛏 **Brown's Hotel.** Founded in 1837 by James Brown, Lord Byron's "gen-
HOTEL tleman's gentleman," this hotel, made up of 11 Georgian town houses,
holds a treasured place in London society. **Pros:** elegant space; attentive service. **Cons:** everything costs here. ⊠ *34 Albemarle St., Mayfair*
☎ *020/7493–6020* ⊕ *www.brownshotel.com* ⤵ *88 rooms, 29 suites*
⚙ *In-room: a/c, Internet. In-hotel: restaurants, room service, bar, gym,*
spa Ⓤ *Green Park* ⊹ *E3.*

£££££ 🛏 **The Connaught.** Many of the classic Connaught touches (the grand
HOTEL oak staircase, for example, and the small, elegant bars) remain, but
Fodor'sChoice the hotel has a modern look since a thorough 2007 renovation. **Pros:**
★ legendary hotel; great for star-spotting. **Cons:** history comes at a price;
bathrooms are tiny. ⊠ *Carlos Pl., Mayfair* ☎ *020/7499–7070* ⊕ *www.*
the-connaught.co.uk ⤵ *92 rooms* ⚙ *In-room: a/c, Wi-Fi. In-hotel: res-*
taurants, room service, bars, gym, spa, business center, parking Ⓤ *Bond*
St. ⊹ *E3.*

£££££ 🛏 **The Dorchester.** The glamour level is off the scale here with 1,500
HOTEL square yards of gold leaf and 1,100 square yards of marble; bedrooms
Fodor'sChoice (some not as spacious as you might expect) have Irish linen sheets on
★ canopied beds, brocades, velvets, and Italian marble and etched-glass
bathrooms with exclusive toiletries created by Floris. **Pros:** historic
luxury; lovely views of Hyde Park; top-notch star spotting. **Cons:** traditional look is not to all tastes; prices are high. ⊠ *Park Lane, Mayfair*
☎ *020/7629–8888* ⊕ *www.thedorchester.com* ⤵ *195 rooms, 55 suites*
⚙ *In-room: a/c, Internet. In-hotel: restaurants, bar, gym, spa, Wi-Fi,*
parking Ⓤ *Marble Arch, Hyde Park Corner* ⊹ *D3.*

MARYLEBONE

££ 🛏 **22 York Street.** This Georgian town house has a cozy, family feel
B&B/INN with polished pine floors and plenty of quilts and antiques. **Pros:**
handy guesthouse in a great location for shoppers. **Cons:** price is a bit
steep for what is, in the end, a glorified B&B. ⊠ *22 York St., Mayfair*
☎ *020/7224–2990* ⊕ *www.22yorkstreet.co.uk* ⤵ *10 rooms* ⚙ *In-room:*
no a/c. In-hotel: bar ⫶⦿⫶ *Breakfast* Ⓤ *Baker St.* ⊹ *D2.*

£££–££££ 🛏 **Park Plaza Sherlock Holmes Hotel.** This was once a rather ordinary
HOTEL Hilton, until somebody had the idea of exploiting the Sherlock Holmes
connection (the fictional detective had his home on Baker Street); making it a boutique hotel; adding a beautiful bar for a bit of local buzz,
and—presto!—the place took off like a rocket. **Pros:** nicely decorated;
good location for fans of shopping and Holmes. **Cons:** have to walk
through the bar to get to reception; not well soundproofed from the
noisy street. ⊠ *108 Baker St., Marylebone* ☎ *020/7486–6161* ⊕ *www.*
sherlockholmeshotel.com ⤵ *119 rooms* ⚙ *In-room: a/c, Wi-Fi. In-*
hotel: restaurant, room service, bar, gym, spa Ⓤ *Baker St.* ⊹ *D2.*

Fodor's Choice ★

Renaissance Chancery Court

One Aldwych

The Generator

SOHO AND COVENT GARDEN

For expanded hotel reviews, visit Fodors.com.

SOHO

£££–££££
HOTEL

🖼 **Dean Street Townhouse.** An adjunct to the private member's club, Soho House, and much beloved of the glitterati, this chic boutique hotel offers a discreet, unpretentious, but oh-so-stylish place to stay in the heart of Soho. **Pros:** über-cool; an amazing bargain if you can get the one cheap room. **Cons:** at full rate you're paying more for the address than what you get; rooms at the front can be noisy, especially on weekends. ✉ 69–71 Dean St., Soho ☎ 020/7434–1775 ⊕ www.deanstreettownhouse. com ♿ In-room: a/c, Wi-Fi. In-hotel: restaurant, bar Ⓤ Leicester Sq., Tottenham Court Rd. ✛ F3.

££££–£££££
HOTEL

🖼 **Hazlitt's.** Three connected early-18th-century houses, one of which was the last home of essayist William Hazlitt (1778–1830), make up this charming Soho hotel. **Pros:** great for art and antiques lovers; historic atmosphere; truly beautiful and relaxed. **Cons:** no in-house restaurant; breakfast is extra; no elevators. ✉ 6 Frith St., Soho ☎ 020/7434–1771 ⊕ www.hazlittshotel.com ⟿ 20 rooms, 3 suites ♿ In-room: a/c, Wi-Fi. In-hotel: room service, parking, some pets allowed Ⓤ Tottenham Court Rd. ✛ F3.

COVENT GARDEN

£££££
HOTEL
Fodor'sChoice
★

🖼 **One Aldwych.** Flawlessly designed inside an Edwardian building, One Aldwych is coolly eclectic, with an artsy lobby, feather duvets, Italian linen sheets, and ample elegance; it's an understated blend of contemporary and classic, resulting in pure, modern luxury. **Pros:** understated (and underwater) luxury; ultra-cool atmosphere. **Cons:** all this luxury doesn't come cheap; fashionable ambience not always relaxing; design sometimes verges on form over function. ✉ 1 Aldwych, Covent Garden ☎ 020/7300–1000 ⊕ www.onealdwych.co.uk ⟿ 93 rooms, 12 suites ♿ In-room: a/c, kitchen (some), Wi-Fi. In-hotel: restaurants, room service, bars, pool, gym, spa, parking Ⓤ Charing Cross, Covent Garden ✛ G3.

£££££
HOTEL
Fodor'sChoice
★

🖼 **The Savoy.** Reopened in late 2010 after a £220 million renovation, the Savoy is one of London's most famous hotels—and undoubtedly one of its best, too. **Pros:** historic hotel; gorgeous location; luxurious surroundings; less snooty than many others of its pedigree. **Cons:** everything comes with a price tag (even Wi-Fi); bedrooms can be surprisingly noisy; particularly on lower floors. ✉ Strand, Covent Garden ☎ 020/7836–4343, 800/257–7544 in U.S. ⊕ www.the-savoy.com ♿ In-room: a/c, Wi-Fi. In-hotel: restaurants, bars, room service, gym, pool, parking Ⓤ Covent Garden, Charing Cross ✛ G3.

BLOOMSBURY AND LEGAL LONDON

For expanded hotel reviews, visit Fodors.com.

BLOOMSBURY

£
HOTEL

🖼 **Alhambra Hotel.** One of the best bargains in Bloomsbury, this family-run hotel has singles as low as £50 and doubles as low as £60; the place is not fancy, but it certainly is cheap. **Pros:** low price; friendly service;

RENTALS, B&BS, AND HOME EXCHANGES

APARTMENT RENTALS

For a home base that's roomy enough for a family and that comes with cooking facilities, consider renting furnished "flats" (the British word for apartments). These can save you money, especially if you're traveling as a family or with a group. If you're interested in home exchange, but don't feel like sharing, some home-exchange directories list rentals as well. If you want to deal directly with local agents, get a personal recommendation from someone who has used the company.

International Agents Hideaways International (✉ 767 Islington St., Portsmouth, NH ☎ 603/430–4433 or 800/843–4433 ⊕ www.hideaways. com) offers boutique hotels, tours, and cruises. Its offerings in London are extremely exclusive. Annual membership is $195.

Interhome (✉ c/o ResortQuest, 2860 State Rd. 84, Suite 116–PMB 214, Fort Lauderdale, FL ☎ 800/882–6864 ⊕ www.interhome.us) has dozens of rather pricey, but luxurious, flats all over London starting at about £400 per week, rising to more than 10 times that for those with money to burn.

Villanet (✉ 1251 N.W. 116th St., Seattle, WA ☎ 206/417–3444 or 877/250–4366 ⊕ www.rentavilla. com) has hundreds of flats in residential neighborhoods all over London, with prices starting at about £1,000 per week.

The Villas International (✉ 17 Fox La., San Anselmo, CA ☎ 415/499–9490 or 800/221–2260 ⊕ www. villasintl.com) agency has exclusively priced flats all over London that start around £1,800 per week—some sleep up to 10 people.

Local Agents Acorn Apartments (✉ Ground Fl., 19 Bedford Pl. ☎ 020/7636–8325 ⊕ www.acorn-apartments.co.uk) offers attractive small central apartments starting at around £100, however the Web site is not very good and it may be easier to call for information.

The Apartment Service (✉ 5 Francis Grove, Wimbledon ☎ 020/8944–1444 ⊕ www.apartmentservice.com) specializes in executive apartments for business travelers in and around The City, so prices are high, but so is the level of quality. Aside from a few super-cheap places in parts of town you wouldn't want to stay in, prices start at £74 per night for a one-bedroom near the Olympic Village, rising to £585 per night for a four-bedroom near Buckingham Palace.

At Home in London (✉ 70 Black Lion La., Hammersmith ☎ 020/8748–1943 ⊕ www.athomeinlondon. co.uk) has rooms in private homes in Knightsbridge, Kensington, Mayfair, Chelsea, and West London. Prices average around £80 a night per room, making this a great alternative to budget hotels.

The Bed and Breakfast Club (✉ Suite 192, 405 Kings Rd., Chelsea ☎ 0870/803–4414 ⊕ www. thebedandbreakfastclub.co.uk ☞ There's a 2.5% fee for using a credit card; debit cards incur no fees; the full price of room must be paid in advance. Check cancellation policies carefully) offers delightful little London flats in Knightsbridge, Kensington, and Chelsea. Most properties are available for £60–£125 per night with full English breakfasts.

Stay in the properties of Londoners who are temporarily away with **Coach House London Vacation Rentals** (⊠ *2 Tunley Rd., Balham* ☎ *020/8133–8332* ⊕ *www.rentals. chslondon.com* ☞ *Payment by credit card only; 10% deposit required*). Attractive apartments and houses are primarily in Notting Hill, Kensington, and Chelsea, and most cost around £125 per night. The minimum booking of five to seven nights is a bit limiting, though, and you must make a substantial security deposit (usually between £200 and £1,000).

Landmark Trust (☎ *01628/825–925* ⊕ *www.landmarktrust.org.uk*) has London apartments in unusual and historic buildings; prices start at around £100 a night, but many buildings require a minimum stay of seven days.

Uptown Reservations (☎ *020/7937–2001* ⊕ *www. uptownres.co.uk*) accepts only upscale addresses, and specializes in hosted homes or apartments for Americans, often business executives. Nearly all the homes on its register are in Knightsbridge, Belgravia, Kensington, and Chelsea. Prices start at £105 per person, per night. Bookings must be made over the phone. A nonrefundable deposit is required.

BED-AND-BREAKFASTS

The main benefit of staying in a B&B is that the price is usually cheaper than a hotel room of comparable quality, and you receive more personal service. If you book a room in a privately owned house through an agency, prices start as low as £70 a night, and go up for more central neighborhoods and larger and more luxurious homes.

Contacts Host & Guest Service can find you a room in London as well as the rest of the United Kingdom. It's a great way to find bargains, knowing that all have been vetted by the agency, but the Web site functionality is a bit creaky. ⊠ *103 Dawes Rd., Fulham* ☎ *020/7385–9922* ⊕ *www. host-guest.co.uk* ☞ *Full payment in advance.*

London B&B has some truly spectacular—and some more modest—homes in central London. Most cost $130–$150 per night. You can check many of them online, but you have to call to find out prices. ⊠ *437 J St., Suite 210, San Diego, CA* ☎ *800/872–2632* ⊕ *www. londonbandb.com* ☞ *30% deposit required.*

HOME EXCHANGES

If you would like to exchange your home for someone else's, join a home-exchange organization, which will send you its updated listings of available exchanges for a year and will include your own listing in at least one of them.

Exchange Clubs HomeLink International (⊠ *2937 NW 9th Terr., Fort Lauderdale, FL* ☎ *954/566–2687* or *800/638–3841* ⊕ *www.homelink. org*); $119 yearly for a listing and online access.

Intervac U.S (✉ *Box 590504, San Franciso, CA 94159* ☎ *800/756– 4663* ⊕ *www.intervacus.com*); $99 yearly for a listing and online access.

great location. **Cons:** very much a no-frills option; some rooms have shared bathrooms. ✉ *17–19 Argyle St., Bloomsbury* ☎ *020/7837–9575* ⊕ *www.alhambrahotel.com* ⇄ *52 rooms* 🛇 *In-room: no a/c, no phone, Wi-Fi. In-hotel: parking* ¡⊚¡ *Breakfast* Ⓤ *King's Cross* ✛ *G1.*

££
B&B/INN

🔝 **Arosfa Hotel.** The friendly owners and interesting historical background (the property once was the home of pre-Raphaelite painter Sir John Everett Millais) sets this B&B apart from the Gower Street hotel pack. **Pros:** friendly staff; check-in from 7 am; good location for museums and theaters. **Cons:** some rooms are very small; few services. ✉ *83 Gower St., Bloomsbury* ☎ *020/7636–2115* ⊕ *www.arosfalondon. com* ⇄ *15 rooms* 🛇 *In-room: no a/c, Wi-Fi. In-hotel: bar* ¡⊚¡ *Breakfast* Ⓤ *Goodge St.* ✛ *F2.*

£
HOSTEL
Fodor's Choice
★

🔝 **The Generator, London.** This is where the young, enthusiastic traveler comes to find fellow partyers. Set in a former police barracks, the decor makes the most of the bunk beds and dim lighting. **Pros:** funky, youthful attitude; great location. **Cons:** bar is crowded and noisy; party atmosphere is not for everyone. ✉ *MacNaghten House, Compton Pl. off 37 Tavistock Pl., Bloomsbury* ☎ *020/7388–7666* ⊕ *www.generatorhostels.com/london* ⇄ *214 beds* 🛇 *In-room: no a/c, no phone, no TV. In-hotel: restaurant, bars, business center, parking* ¡⊚¡ *Breakfast* Ⓤ *Russell Sq.* ✛ *F1.*

££
HOTEL

🔝 **Harlingford Hotel.** The Harlingford is by far the sleekest and most contemporary of the Cartwright Gardens hotels; bold color schemes and beautifully tiled bathrooms enliven the family-run place. **Pros:** good location; friendly staff; wider breakfast choice than many small London hotels. **Cons:** rooms are quite small; no elevator. ✉ *61–63 Cartwright Gardens, Bloomsbury* ☎ *020/7387–1551* ⊕ *www.harlingfordhotel.com* ⇄ *43 rooms* 🛇 *In-room: no a/c, Internet. In-hotel: bar, tennis court* ¡⊚¡ *Full breakfast* Ⓤ *Russell Sq.* ✛ *F1.*

£–££
HOTEL

🔝 **Jenkins Hotel.** This small, moderately priced hotel has a classic Georgian exterior that belies its simply designed interior. **Pros:** good location for theaters and restaurants. **Cons:** thin mattresses; very small bathrooms; cheaper rooms have shared bathroom; lots of stairs but no elevator. ✉ *45 Cartwright Gardens, Bloomsbury* ☎ *020/7387–2067* ⊕ *www. jenkinshotel.demon.co.uk* ⇄ *14 rooms* 🛇 *In-room: no a/c, Internet* ¡⊚¡ *Breakfast* Ⓤ *Russell Sq., King's Cross, Euston* ✛ *F1.*

££–£££
HOTEL

🔝 **The Portland Hotel.** Just around the corner from leafy Russell Square, the Portland is one of several hotels on the same street that are owned by the same Grange Hotels chain. This occasionally means that you can book into one hotel and actually end up staying in another, and while the quality is comparable, not all amenities are the same—so be quite clear of your requirements when you book. **Pros:** great location; large rooms; kitchenettes free you from restaurants. **Cons:** restaurant located in neighboring hotel means walk down the street to breakfast. ✉ *31–32 Bedford Pl., Bloomsbury* ☎ *020/7580–7088* ⊕ *www.grangehotels.com* ⇄ *18 rooms* 🛇 *In-room: no a/c, kitchen, Internet. In-hotel: restaurant* Ⓤ *Holborn Rd.* ✛ *G2*

£££–££££
HOTEL

🔝 **Rough Luxe.** Bloomsbury's quirkiest hotel is, as its name implies, a strange combination of shabby chic and swanky luxury; in a 19th-century building near King's Cross train station in a neighborhood

UNIVERSITY ROOMS

UNIVERSITY RESIDENCE HALLS
University student dorms (Halls of Residence) can be ideal for single travelers as well as those on a tight budget who want to come to London in summer when deals on other lodgings are scarce. Walter Sickert Hall has year-round lodging in its "executive rooms" (six single and three twin), and breakfast is even delivered to your room. Beds are usually available for a week around Easter, and from mid-June to mid-September in all the university accommodations around town. As you might expect, showers and toilets are shared.

Contacts City University Hall of Residence: Walter Sickert Hall

(✉ *Graham St.* ☎ *020/7040–8037* ⊕ *www.city.ac.uk/ems*) has rooms starting at £21 per person, per night. **London School of Economics Vacations** (☎ *020/7955–7575* ⊕ *www.lsevacations.co.uk*) costs around £50 for a double without a toilet to £72 for a double with a toilet. You can choose from a variety of rooms in their many halls of residence around London. The LSE also rent out self-catering apartments starting at around £90 per night. **University College London** (✉ *Residence Manager, Campbell House, 5–10 Taviton St.* ☎ *020/7679–2000* ⊕ *www.ucl.ac.uk/residences*) is open from mid-June to mid-September.

locals would describe as "dodgy," its rooms have been renovated to keep bits of their old battered walls and flooring in place so that the elegant new beds, designer lighting, and original artwork are cast in stark relief. **Pros:** art and design lovers will be dazzled; it's all very avant-garde. **Cons:** not everybody likes avant-garde; no restaurant or bar; neighborhood is a bit scary; some rooms share baths. ✉ *1 Birkenhead St., Bloomsbury* ☎ *0207/837–5338* ⊕ *www.roughluxe.co.uk* ↷ *10 rooms* ⚅ *In-room: no a/c, no TV (some), Wi-Fi.* Ⓜ *King's Cross* ✛ *G1.*

£££   ☶ **Thistle Bloomsbury Park Hotel.** A block away from leafy Russell Square
HOTEL   and a short stroll from the British Museum, the location of the Thistle Bloomsbury Park Hotel is outstanding, though once you get past the handsome frontage and gleaming lobby, everything seems decidedly more average—though not necessarily in a bad way. **Pros:** affordable option in a great location; good deals and discounts; family rooms cost only slightly more than doubles. **Cons:** small rooms; tired decor; cheap furnishings. ✉ *126 Southampton Row, Bloomsbury* ☎ *0871/376–9007* ⊕ *www.thistle.com* ↷ *95 rooms* ⚅ *In-room: no a/c, Wi-Fi. In-hotel: restaurant, bar* ⍩ *Breakfast* Ⓤ *Russell Sq.* ✛ *G2.*

HOLBORN

££££–£££££   ☶ **Renaissance Chancery Court.** This landmark structure, built by the
HOTEL   Pearl Assurance Company in 1914, houses a beautiful Marriott hotel;
Fodor'sChoice   so striking is the architecture that the building was featured in the film
★   *Howards End.* **Pros:** gorgeous space; great spa; your every need catered to. **Cons:** area is deserted at night and on weekends. ✉ *252 High Holborn, Holborn* ☎ *020/7829–9888* ⊕ *www.marriott.com* ↷ *342 rooms, 14 suites* ⚅ *In-room: a/c, Internet. In-hotel: restaurant, room service, bar, gym, spa* Ⓤ *Holborn* ✛ *G2.*

THE CITY

For expanded hotel reviews, visit Fodors.com.

££££-£££££
HOTEL
Fodor's Choice
★

The Rookery. This beautiful 1725 town house, surrounded by office buildings, is tucked away down a discreet alleyway in the heart of London's business district. **Pros:** absolutely unique and beautiful; helpful staff; good deals to be had in the off-season. **Cons:** breakfast costs extra. ⊠ *12 Peter's La., at Cowcross St., The City* ☎ *020/7336–0931* ⊕ *www. rookeryhotel.com* ↝ *30 rooms, 3 suites* ⚅ *In-room: a/c, Internet. In-hotel: room service, bar, parking* Ⓤ *Farringdon* ✛ *H2.*

££££
HOTEL
Fodor's Choice
★

The Zetter. By day, nothing but business suits buzz through the area between Holborn and Clerkenwell, and by night, the ties are loosened and it's all oh-so-trendy. **Pros:** big rooms; lots of gadgets; free Wi-Fi; gorgeous "Rainforest" showers. **Cons:** rooms with good views cost more. ⊠ *86–88 Clerkenwell Rd., Holborn* ☎ *020/7324–4444* ⊕ *www. thezetter.com* ↝ *59 rooms* ⚅ *In-room: a/c, Internet. In-hotel: restaurant, room service, bar* Ⓤ *Farringdon* ✛ *H2.*

THE EAST END

For expanded hotel reviews, visit Fodors.com.

£££-££££
HOTEL

Andaz. This swanky, upscale hotel owned by the Hyatt group opened in 2007 and immediately made headlines for its modern, masculine design and unconventional approach; instead of checking in at a desk, guests sit in a lounge while a staff member with a handheld computer takes their information. **Pros:** nice attention to detail; guests can borrow an iPod from the front desk; no standing in line to check in. **Cons:** sparse decor is not for all. ⊠ *40 Liverpool St., East End* ☎ *020/7961–1234* ⊕ *london. liverpoolstreet.andaz.hyatt.com* ↝ *267 rooms* ⚅ *In-room: a/c, Wi-Fi. In-hotel: restaurant, room service, bar, gym, parking* Ⓤ *Liverpool St.* ✛ *H2.*

££-£££
HOTEL
Fodor's Choice
★

The Hoxton Hotel. This trendy, East London hotel sits in the eponymous neighborhood and is designed to reflect the funky galleries and small boutiques for which the area is known. **Pros:** cool-looking place; price includes one hour of free international calls; every night five rooms in this hotel are priced at £1, but you'll need to join the mailing list. **Cons:** restaurant and bar can be crowded in the evening; area is a bit off the beaten tourist track. ⊠ *81 Great Eastern St., East End* ☎ *020/7550–1000* ⊕ *www.hoxtonhotels.com* ↝ *205 rooms* ⚅ *In-room: a/c, Internet, Wi-Fi. In-hotel: restaurant, room service, bar* ⦿l *Breakfast* Ⓤ *Old St.* ✛ *H1.*

££
HOTEL

Ramada Hotel and Suites Docklands. Built in a dramatic waterfront location, this modern hotel is in the rejuvenated Docklands area of East London. **Pros:** waterfront views. **Cons:** hotel lacks character; area is quiet on weekends; about a 20-minute Tube ride to central London. ⊠ *ExCel, 2 Festoon Way, Royal Victoria Dock, East End* ☎ *020/7540–4820* ⊕ *www.ramadadocklands.co.uk* ↝ *224 rooms* ⚅ *In-room: a/c, Internet. In-hotel: restaurant, room service, bar, gym* ⦿l *Breakfast* Ⓤ *Old St.* ✛ *H3.*

£££-£££££
HOTEL

Town Hall Hotel. This building used to be one of London's living ghosts—an art deco Town Hall that was abandoned by the city in the early 1980s and literally untouched until it was turned into a chic hotel

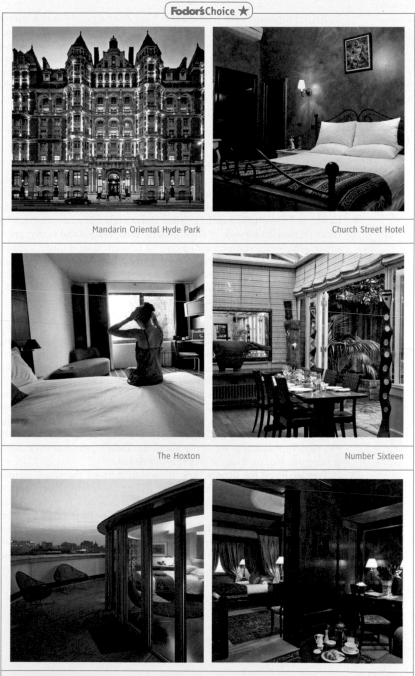

Fodor'sChoice ★

Mandarin Oriental Hyde Park

Church Street Hotel

The Hoxton

Number Sixteen

The Zetter

The Rookery

in 2010. Fortunately the new owners have done a good job in keeping the building's more elegant original features, while creating a stylish and modern new place to stay in a neglected corner of the East End. **Pros:** beautifully designed; lovely staff; close to a Tube station; big discounts for weekend stays. **Cons:** not a great part of town; far from tourist sights. ⊠ *Patriot Square, Bethnal Green, East End* ☎ *020/7657–8080* ⊕ *www.townhallhotel.com* ⚷ *In-room: a/c, Wi-Fi. In-hotel: restaurant, room service, bar, pool, spa, gym* Ⓤ *Bethnal Green* ✥ *H2.*

THE SOUTH BANK

For expanded hotel reviews, visit Fodors.com.

££   🍽 **Church Street Hotel.** Above a popular tapas restaurant, this immensely
HOTEL   welcoming boutique hotel is like a ray of sunshine in gritty South Lon-
Fodor'sChoice   don; each room is individually decorated in rich, bold tones and authen-
★   tic Central American touches, from elaborately painted crucifixes to tiles that were handmade in Guadalajara. **Pros:** unique and funky; great breakfasts; lovely staff; closer to central London than it might appear. **Cons:** not a great part of town; would suit adventurous young things more than families; far from a Tube station; some rooms have shared bathroom. ⊠ *29–33 Camberwell Church St., South East* ☎ *020/7961–1234* ⊕ *www.churchstreethotel.com* ⌁ *267 rooms* ⚷ *In-room: a/c, Wi-Fi. In-hotel: restaurant, bar* Ⓤ *Oval St.* ✥ *H6.*

£££–££££   🍽 **London Marriott Hotel County Hall.** Housed in part of what was, until
HOTEL   the 1980s, the seat of London's government, this grand hotel on the Thames has perhaps the most iconic view of any in London: right next door is the London Eye, and directly across the River Thames are Big Ben and the Houses of Parliament. **Pros:** handy location for South Bank arts scene, London Eye and Westminster; great gym; good weekend discounts. **Cons:** decor is overdone; breakfasts are pricey; rooms facing Parliament inevitably cost extra. ⊠ *County Hall, Westminster Bridge Rd., South Bank* ☎ *020/7928–5200* ⊕ *www.marriott.com* ⌁ *200 rooms* ⚷ *In-room: a/c, Wi-Fi. In-hotel: restaurants, room service, bars, pool, gym, spa, parking* Ⓤ *Westminster* ✥ *G4.*

££   🍽 **Premier Travel Inn County Hall.** Although part of the same former
HOTEL   County Hall complex as the London Marriott Hotel County Hall, it
☾   shares none of its spectacular riverside views; that said, it is every bit as convenient a location, and decidedly cheaper, too. **Pros:** good location for the South Bank; bargains to be had if you book in advance. **Cons:** denied great views by other buildings nearby; limited services. ⊠ *Belvedere Rd., South Bank* ☎ *0871/527–8648* ⊕ *www.premiertravelinn.com* ⌁ *313 rooms* ⚷ *In-room: no a/c, Internet. In-hotel: restaurants, bar, parking* Ⓤ *Westminster* ✥ *G4.*

KENSINGTON, CHELSEA, AND KNIGHTSBRIDGE

For expanded hotel reviews, visit Fodors.com.

KENSINGTON

£££
HOTEL
The Cranley Hotel. Old-fashioned British propriety is the overall feeling here at this small, Victorian town-house hotel; high ceilings, huge windows, and a pale, creamy color scheme make the bedrooms light and bright. **Pros:** good-size rooms; friendly staff; free evening nibbles are a nice touch. **Cons:** steep stairs into lobby; no restaurant. ⊠ *10–12 Bina Gardens, South Kensington* ☎ *020/7373–0123* ⊕ *www.thecranley.com* ↝ *29 rooms, 5 suites, 4 apartments* ⚘ *In-room: a/c, Internet. In-hotel: parking* Ⓤ *Gloucester Rd.* ✥ *B6.*

£
HOTEL
easyHotel South Kensington. This budget hotel, which opened in 2005 as London's first "pod hotel," has 34 tiny rooms, all with a double bed, private bathroom, and little else. **Pros:** amazing price; safe and pleasant space. **Cons:** not for the claustrophobic; six floors, no elevator; no services; everything costs extra, from a TV in your room (£5 per day), to Wi-Fi (£3 per hour) and even fresh towels (£1 each). ⊠ *14 Lexham Gardens, Kensington* ☎ *020/7216–1717* ⊕ *www.easyhotel.com* ↝ *34 rooms* ⚘ *In-room: no a/c, no phone* Ⓤ *Gloucester Rd.* ✥ *A5.*

££–£££
HOTEL
Kensington House Hotel. This refurbished 19th-century town house off High Street Kensington has streamlined rooms with a creamy, contemporary look. **Pros:** attractive design; relaxing setting; free Wi-Fi. **Cons:** rooms are small; bathrooms are minuscule; the elevator is Lilliputian. ⊠ *15–16 Prince of Wales Terr., Kensington* ☎ *020/7937–2345* ⊕ *www. kenhouse.com* ↝ *41 rooms* ⚘ *In-room: no a/c, Wi-Fi. In-hotel: room service, bar, parking* ⦿ *Breakfast* Ⓤ *High Street Kensington* ✥ *A5.*

££–£££
HOTEL
Millennium Gloucester. Refurbished in 2007, the hotel has a sleek lobby with polished wood columns, a warming fireplace, and glittering chandeliers; guest rooms are done in neutral creams and earth tones, and blond-wood desks and leather chairs have a blandly masculine look. **Pros:** good deals available if you book in advance. **Cons:** lighting in some bedrooms is a bit too subtle; public areas and restaurant can get crowded. ⊠ *4–18 Harrington Gardens, Kensington* ☎ *020/7373–6030* ⊕ *www.millenniumhotels.co.uk/millenniumgloucester* ↝ *143 rooms* ⚘ *In-room: a/c, Wi-Fi. In-hotel: restaurant, room service* ⦿ *Breakfast* Ⓤ *Gloucester Rd.* ✥ *B5.*

£££–££££
HOTEL
Fodor's Choice
★
Number Sixteen. A more boutique-style offering from the same people behind the elegant Charlotte Street Hotel, Number Sixteen is a lovely luxury guesthouse just around the corner from the Victoria & Albert Museum. **Pros:** just the right level of helpful service; decor is gorgeous. **Cons:** there's no restaurant; small elevator. ⊠ *16 Sumner Pl., South Kensington* ☎ *020/7589–5232, 800/553–6674 in U.S.* ⊕ *www.firmdale. com* ↝ *42 rooms* ⚘ *In-room: no a/c (some), Wi-Fi. In-hotel: room service, bar* ⦿ *Breakfast* Ⓤ *South Kensington* ✥ *B5.*

£££–££££
HOTEL
The Sumner. This elegant Georgian town house on a quiet residential street is the kind of place where you can feel yourself relaxing the minute you enter. **Pros:** small enough that the staff knows your name. **Cons:** services are limited but prices high. ⊠ *5 Sumner Pl., South Kensington* ☎ *020/7723–2244* ⊕ *www.thesumner.com* ↝ *20 rooms* ⚘ *In-room: a/c,*

Internet. In-hotel: room service, parking ¶⊙∣ *Breakfast* Ⓤ *South Kensington* ♣ *B6.*

££–£££
RENTAL

⁜ **Think Earl's Court.** Accommodations in this part of town more commonly pretend they're in Kensington rather than neighboring Earl's Court, but don't be fooled by the name—these brand new serviced apartments are a stone's throw from Kensington High Street. **Pros:** brand new building; self-catering offers greater independence. **Cons:** payment is made when you book; biggest apartments are two-bedroom, so not really geared to families. ⊠ *26A Adam and Eve Mews, Kensington* ☎ *0845/602–9437 or 020/7795–6880* ⊕ *www.think-apartments.com* ⤳ *133 rooms* ♿ *In-room: a/c, kitchen, Wi-Fi* Ⓤ *High Street Kensington* ♣ *A5.*

CHELSEA

££££–£££££
HOTEL

⁜ **The Cadogan Hotel.** This is one of London's most historically naughty hotels; it was once the home of Lillie Langtry, a scandalous actress and King Edward's mistress in the 1890s. **Pros:** luxurious but not stuffy; friendly staff; great location for shopping. **Cons:** rooms are quite small, as are the bar and restaurant. ⊠ *75 Sloane St., Chelsea* ☎ *020/7235–7141* ⊕ *www.cadogan.com* ⤳ *65 rooms* ♿ *In-room: a/c, Wi-Fi. In-hotel: restaurant, room service, bar, tennis courts* Ⓤ *Sloane Sq.* ♣ *D5.*

KNIGHTSBRIDGE

£££££
HOTEL
Fodor's Choice
★

⁜ **Mandarin Oriental Hyde Park.** Stay here, and the three greats of Knightsbridge—Hyde Park, Harrods, and Harvey Nichols—are at your doorstep. Built in 1880, the Mandarin Oriental is one of London's most elegant hotels. **Pros:** amazing views of Hyde Park; excellent service. **Cons:** nothing here comes cheap; you must dress for dinner (and lunch and breakfast). ⊠ *66 Knightsbridge, Knightsbridge* ☎ *020/7235–2000* ⊕ *www.mandarinoriental.com/london* ⤳ *177 rooms, 23 suites* ♿ *In-room: a/c, Wi-Fi. In-hotel: restaurants, room service, bar, gym, spa, parking* Ⓤ *Knightsbridge* ♣ *D4.*

NOTTING HILL AND BAYSWATER

For expanded hotel reviews, visit Fodors.com.

NOTTING HILL

££
HOTEL

⁜ **TheMain House.** A brass lion door knocker marks Main House's Victorian front door, typical of Notting Hill. With just four rooms, this hotel offers nothing but a good night's sleep in a Victorian home. **Pros:** unusual option; great location. **Cons:** few rooms mean it books up far in advance; two-night minimum stay; no room service. ⊠ *6 Colvile Rd., Notting Hill* ☎ *020/7221–9691* ⊕ *www.themainhouse.com* ⤳ *4 rooms* ♿ *In-room: a/c (some), Wi-Fi (some). In-hotel: parking* ¶⊙∣ *Breakfast* Ⓤ *Notting Hill Gate* ♣ *A3.*

££££–£££££
HOTEL

⁜ **The Portobello Hotel.** One of London's most famous hotels, the little Portobello (formed from two adjoining Victorian houses) is seriously hip and attracts scores of celebrities. **Pros:** stylish; great for celebrity spotting; good location. **Cons:** most rooms are quite small; may be too eccentric for some. ⊠ *22 Stanley Gardens, Notting Hill* ☎ *020/7727–2777* ⊕ *www.portobello-hotel.co.uk* ⤳ *24 rooms* ♿ *In-room: no a/c* *(some), Internet. In-hotel: restaurant, room service, bar ☺ Closed 10 days at Christmas* ¶Ol *Breakfast* Ⓤ *Notting Hill Gate* ✥ *A3.*

£–££
B&B/INN

▦ **Portobello Gold.** This no-frills B&B in the heart of the Portobello Road antiques area is on the floor above the pub and restaurant of the same name; flat-screen TVs are mounted on the wall, and the beds take up almost the entire tiny room in the doubles. **Pros:** great location; laid-back atmosphere; good advance deals. **Cons:** rooms are tiny; can be noisy; no elevator. ✉ *95–97 Portobello Rd., Notting Hill* ☎ *020/7460–4910* ⊕ *www.portobellogold.com* ⇥ *6 rooms, 1 apartment* ♿ *In-room: a/c, Wi-Fi. In-hotel: restaurant, room service, bar* ¶Ol *Breakfast* Ⓤ *Notting Hill Gate* ✥ *A3.*

BAYSWATER

£
B&B/INN

▦ **Europ Hotel.** This modest family-run B&B near Hyde Park is a decent, unfussy alternative to overpriced, impersonal chain hotels. **Pros:** bargain price; close to two Tube stations. **Cons:** dated decor; few amenities; no elevator. ✉ *151 Sussex Gardens, Bayswater* ☎ *020/7723–7343* ⊕ *www.europahousehotel.com* ⇥ *20 rooms* ♿ *In-room: no a/c* Ⓤ *Paddington, Lancaster Gate* ✥ *C3.*

£–££
HOTEL

▦ **Garden Court Hotel.** This small hotel is formed from two 19th-century town houses in a quiet garden square; rooms with toilet and shower cost an extra £30, and a hot breakfast also ups the bill. **Pros:** lovely garden; lots of charm; new elevator makes the upper floors more pleasant. **Cons:** not all rooms have private baths; some rooms need updating. ✉ *30–31 Kensington Gardens Sq., Bayswater* ☎ *020/7229–2553* ⊕ *www.gardencourthotel.co.uk* ⇥ *12 rooms, 10 with bath* ♿ *In-room: no a/c. In-hotel: bar, some pets allowed* ¶Ol *Breakfast* Ⓤ *Bayswater, Queensway* ✥ *A3.*

££
HOTEL

▦ **Space Apart Hotel.** This Georgian hotel near Hyde Park is a great find with 30 studio apartments that have all been recently renovated in stellar style. **Pros:** the price is right; the larger suites have space for four people. **Cons:** no in-house restaurant or bar; minimum two-night stay required. ✉ *32–37 Kensington Gardens Sq., Bayswater* ☎ *0207/908–1340* ⊕ *www.aparthotel-london.co.uk* ⇥ *30 rooms* ♿ *In-room: a/c, no phone, kitchen, Wi-Fi* Ⓜ *Bayswater* ✥ *A3.*

£
HOTEL

▦ **Stylotel.** Just around the corner from Paddington station, this is a wry, funky-looking little place that conceals a smoothly run operation underneath its rather camp exterior. **Pros:** bargain price; helpful staff; unique style. **Cons:** style will be too unique for some; small bedrooms and bathrooms; serves breakfast only—you have to eat out every night; Web site is frequently down, which makes booking online a challenge. ✉ *160–162 Sussex Gardens Sq., Bayswater* ☎ *0207/223–1026* ⊕ *www.stylotel.com* ♿ *In-room: no a/c, Wi-Fi (paid). In-hotel: parking* Ⓜ *Paddington, Edgware Rd* ✥ *C2.*

REGENT'S PARK AND HAMPSTEAD

For expanded hotel reviews, visit Fodors.com.

££
HOTEL

▦ **La Gaffe.** Italian Bernardo Stella has welcomed people back to these early-18th-century row houses, a short walk up one of Hampstead's magnificent hills, for more than 20 years. **Pros:** pretty area of town;

friendly staff. **Cons:** bathrooms have showers only; few services; no elevator. ✉ *107–111 Heath St., Hampstead* ☎ *020/7435–8965* ∰ *www. lagaffe.co.uk* ⊅ *18 rooms, 3 suites* ⬠ *In-room: no a/c. In-hotel: restaurant, bar, laundry facilities, parking* ⎟⊙⏐ *Breakfast* Ⓤ *Hampstead* ✢ *B1.*

CAMDEN TOWN

££
B&B/INN

🏠 **66 Camden Square.** This beautiful B&B is run by an architect and his wife, so it comes as no surprise to find that the space within is tastefully done; the owners, Sue and Roger Davis, are gracious and personable hosts, with an encyclopedic knowledge of what the area has to offer in terms of pubs, restaurants, and nightlife. **Pros:** lovely owners; unique place; inexpensive. **Cons:** few extras; bathrooms not en suite (but not shared either); maximum stay of one week; no Web site. ✉ *66 Camden Sq., Camden Town* ☎ *020/7485–4622* ⊅ *35 rooms, 3 suites* ⬠ *In-room: no a/c, Wi-Fi. In-hotel: parking* Ⓤ *Camden Rd.* ✢ *C1.*

NIGHTLIFE AND THE ARTS

London is a veritable utopia for excitement junkies, culture fiends, and those who like to party. Most who visit London will be mesmerized by the city's energy, which reveals itself in layers. Whether you prefer a romantic evening at the opera, rhythm and blues with fine French food, the gritty guitar riffs of east London, a pint and gourmet pizza at a local gastro-pub, or swanky cocktails and sushi at London's sexiest lair, the U.K. capital is sure to feed your fancy. Admission prices are not always bargain-basement, but when you consider how much a London hotel room costs, the city's arts and nightlife diversions are a bargain.

NIGHTLIFE

As is true of nearly all cosmopolitan centers, the pace with which bars and clubs go in and out of fashion in London is mind-boggling. The dreaded velvet rope has been usurped by the doorbell-ringing mystique of members-only drinking clubs; and the understated glamour of North London's Primrose Hill, which makes movie stars feel so at ease, might be considered dull by the über-trendy club goers of London's East End.

BLOOMSBURY, FITZROVIA

BARS

All Star Lanes. One of London's most chic bars is an unlikely combination—it's in a sleek underground retro bowling alley in the heart of literary Bloomsbury. Here, surrounded by 1950s Americana, you can sit on the red leather seats and choose from the largest selection of bourbons in London. DJs play on Friday and Saturday nights and there are also locations in Bayswater and Brick Lane. ✉ *Victori, Bloomsbury Pl., Bloomsbury* ☎ *020/7025–2676* ∰ *www.allstarlanes.co.uk* ⏱ *Mon.– Wed. 5 pm–11:30 pm, Thurs. 5–midnight, Fri. and Sat. noon–2 am, Sun. noon–11* Ⓤ *Holborn.*

Fodor's Choice
★

Crazy Bear. This sexy basement bar with cowhide stools and croc-skin tables feels like Casablanca in Fitzrovia. As you enter Crazy Bear, a spiral staircase leads to a mirrored parlor over which presides a 1947

Murano chandelier. But don't let the opulence fool you: Waitstaff here are warm and welcoming to an all-ages international crowd abuzz with chatter. The menu advertises high quality Thai, Chinese, and Japanese food alongside the drinks. ✉ *26–28 Whitfield St., Fitzrovia* ☎ *020/7631–0088* ⊕ *www.crazybeargroup.co.uk* ☉ *Sun.–Wed. noon–midnight, Thurs.–Sat. noon–1 am* Ⓤ *Goode St.*

THE EAST END
DANCE CLUBS
Fabric. This sprawling subterranean club is now a firm fixture on the London scene. "Fabric Live" hosts drum 'n' bass, dubstep, and hip-hop crews and live acts on Friday; international big-name DJs play slow, sexy bass lines and cutting-edge music on Saturday. The devastating sound system and "bodysonic" dance floor ensure that bass riffs vibrate through your entire body. ■**TIP→** Get there early to avoid a lengthy queue, and don't wear a suit. ✉ *77A Charterhouse St., East End* ☎ *020/7336–8898* ⊕ *www.fabriclondon.com* 🎟 *£13–£16* ☉ *Fri. 10 pm–6 am, Sat. 11 pm–8 am, Sun. 11 pm–6 am* Ⓤ *Farringdon.*

Cargo. Housed under a series of old railway arches, this vast brick-wall bar, restaurant, dance floor, and live-music venue pulls a young, international crowd with its hip vibe and diverse selection of music. Long tables bring people together, as does the food, which draws on global influences and is served tapas-style. ✉ *83 Rivington St., Shoreditch* ☎ *020/7739–3440* ⊕ *www.cargo-london.com* 🎟 *Free–£20* ☉ *Mon.–Thurs. noon–1 am, Fri. noon–3 am, Sat. 6 pm–3 am, Sun. 1 pm–midnight* Ⓤ *Old St.*

KENSINGTON, CHELSEA, AND KNIGHTSBRIDGE
BARS
Fodor'sChoice ★ **The Blue Bar at the Berkeley Hotel.** With low-slung gray-blue walls this hotel bar is ever so slightly sexy. Immaculate service, an excellent cocktail list—try the Sex in the City—and a trendy David Collins design, make this an ideal spot for a secretive tête-à-tête, complete with jazzy music in the background. ✉ *Wilton Pl., Knightsbridge* ☎ *020/291–1680* ⊕ *the-berkeley.co.uk* ☉ *Mon. 4 pm–1 am, Tues.–Sat. 9 am–1 am, Sun. 4–11 pm* Ⓤ *Knightsbridge.*

JAZZ AND BLUES
606 Club. Expect a civilized Chelsea club that showcases mainstream and contemporary jazz by well-known British-based musicians. ■**TIP→** You must eat a meal in order to consume alcohol, so allow for an extra £20. Reservations are advisable. Sunday lunchtime jazz takes place once or twice a month; call ahead. ✉ *90 Lots Rd., Chelsea* ☎ *020/7352–5953* ⊕ *www.606club.co.uk* 🎟 *£8–£12 music charge added to bill* ☉ *Mon. 7:30 pm–12:30 am, Tues.–Thurs. 7 pm–12:30 am, Fri. and Sat. 8 pm–1:30 am, Sun. 7 pm–midnight* Ⓤ *Earl's Court, Fulham Broadway.*

NOTTING HILL
DANCE CLUBS
★ **Notting Hill Arts Club.** Rock stars like Liam Gallagher and Courtney Love have been seen at this small basement club-bar. An alternative crowd swills beer to eclectic music that spans Asian underground, hip-hop, Latin-inspired funk, deep house, and jazzy grooves. What it lacks in

looks it makes up for in mood. ✉ *21 Notting Hill Gate, Notting Hill* ☎ *020/7460–4459* ⊕ *www.nottinghillartsclub.com* 🖃 *Free–£8* ☉ *Weekdays 7 pm–2 am, Sat. 4 pm–2 am, Sun. 4 pm–1 am* Ⓤ *Notting Hill Gate.*

ST. JAMES'S AND MAYFAIR

BARS

★ **American Bar.** Festooned with a chin-dropping array of club ties, signed celebrity photographs, sporting mementos, and baseball caps, this sensational hotel cocktail bar has superb martinis. ■**TIP**➜ Jacket required. ✉ *Stafford Hotel, 16–18 St. James's Pl., St. James's* ☎ *020/518–1253* ⊕ *www.thestaffordhotel.co.uk* ☉ *Weekdays 11:30–11, weekends noon–11* Ⓤ *Green Park.*

Fodor'sChoice ★ **Claridge's Bar.** This elegant Mayfair meeting place remains unpretentious even when it brims with beautiful people. The bar has an art deco heritage made hip by the sophisticated touch of designer David Collins. A library of rare champagnes and brandies as well as a delicious choice of traditional and exotic cocktails—try the Flapper or the Black Pearl—will occupy your taste buds. Request a glass of vintage Cristal in the Macanudo Fumoir. ✉ *55 Brook St., Mayfair* ☎ *020/7629–8860* ⊕ *www.claridges. co.uk* ☉ *Mon.–Sat. noon–1 am, Sun. noon–midnight* Ⓤ *Bond St.*

DANCE CLUBS

Fodor'sChoice ★ **Vendome Mayfair.** This classy club draws a trendy crowd for house music, colorful furnishings, and futuristic designs with '70s retro disco decor. The revolving DJ booth at the center of the club, the Renaissance-like entrance, the individually themed booths, and the faux snakeskin banisters shout out pure decadence. ✉ *85 Piccadilly, Mayfair* ☎ *020/495–2595* ⊕ *www.vendomemayfair.com* 🖃 *£20* ☉ *Mon., Tues., and Thurs. 10 pm–3 am, Fri. and Sat. 10 pm–4 am.*

BRIXTON AND SOUTH BANK

BARS

★ **Dogstar.** This popular South London hangout is frequented by local hipsters and counterculture types. It was the first DJ bar in the world and has since enjoyed a fabulous reputation. The vibe at this "surrealist boudoir" is unpretentious, with top-name DJs playing cutting-edge sounds every night (free Tuesday–Thursday). ✉ *389 Coldharbour La., Brixton* ☎ *020/7733–7515* ⊕ *www.antic-ltd.com/dogstar* 🖃 *Free–£8* ☉ *Tues.–Thurs. 4 pm–2 am, Fri. 4 pm–4 am, Sat. noon–4 am, Sun. noon–2 am* Ⓤ *Brixton.*

DANCE CLUBS

Ministry of Sound. It's more of an industry than a club, with its own record label, online radio station, and international DJs. The stripped-down warehouse-style club has a super sound system and pulls in the world's most legendary names in dance. There are chill-out rooms, two bars, and three dance floors. ✉ *103 Gaunt St., South Bank* ☎ *020/740–8600* ⊕ *www.ministryofsound.com* 🖃 *£15–£23* ☉ *Fri. 10:30 pm–6 am, Sat. 11 pm–7 am* Ⓤ *Elephant & Castle.*

ECLECTIC MUSIC

Fodor'sChoice ★ **O2 Academy Brixton.** This legendary Brixton venue has seen it all—mods and rockers, hippies and punks. Despite a capacity for almost 5,000 people, this refurbished Victorian hall with original Art deco fixtures retains a clublike charm; it has plenty of bars and upstairs seating. ✉ *211 Stockwell Rd., Brixton* ☎ *020/7771–3000* ⊕ *www.brixton-academy.co.uk* 💷 *£10–£50* ◷ *Opening hrs vary* Ⓤ *Brixton.*

SOHO AND COVENT GARDEN

BARS

★ **Le Salon Bar.** Renowned chef Joël Robuchon's intimate, relaxed, and elegant bar with red undertones is in the same premises as his L'Atelier and La Cuisine restaurants. New cocktails await you, as the drink menu changes every six months, with new flavors and textures sure to entice your taste buds. If you're feeling generous, treat yourself to an unforgettable dinner at the restaurant pre- or post-drinks—try the Fois Gras Chaud. ✉ *13–15 West St., Leicester Square* ☎ *020/7010–8600* ⊕ *www.joel-robuchon.com* ◷ *Mon.–Sat. 2:30 pm–2 am, Sun. 2:30 pm–10:30 pm* Ⓜ *Leicester Sq.*

★ **Nordic.** With shooters called "Husky Poo" and "Danish Bacon Surprise" and crayfish tails and meatballs on the smorgasbord menu, Nordic takes its Scandinavian feel the whole way. This secluded, shabby-chic bar serves many couples cozied up among travel brochures promoting the Viking lands. If you can't decide what to drink, the cocktail roulette wheel on the wall may help. ✉ *25 Newman St., Soho* ☎ *020/7631–3174* ⊕ *www.nordicbar.com* ◷ *Mon.–Thurs. noon–11 pm, Fri. noon–midnight, Sat. 6 pm–midnight* Ⓤ *Tottenham Court Rd.*

Sketch. At this esoteric living room bar one seat never looks like the next. A patisserie during the day, the exclusive Parlour Bar exudes plenty of rarefied charm while the intimate East Bar at the back is reminiscent of a sci-fi film set. ✉ *9 Conduit St., Soho* ☎ *020/7659–4500* ⊕ *www. sketch.uk.com* ◷ *Parlour Bar Mon.–Thurs. 6:30–10 pm, Fri. and Sat. 6:30–9 pm, members only after 9 pm; East Bar Mon.–Thurs. 6 pm–1 am, Fri. and Sat. 6 pm–2 am* Ⓤ *Oxford Circus.*

COMEDY AND CABARET

Amused Moose. This Soho basement/retro nightclub is widely considered the best place to see breaking talent as well as household names doing "secret" shows. Ricky Gervais, Eddie Izzard, and Russell Brand are among those who have graced this stage, and every summer a handful of the Edinburgh Fringe comedians preview here. The bar is open late (and serves food), and there's a DJ and dancing until 5 am after the show. Tickets are often discounted with a printout from their Web site, and shows are mainly on Saturday. ✉ *Moonlighting, 17 Greek St., Soho* ☎ *020/7287–3727* ⊕ *www.amusedmoose.com* 💷 *£9 and up* ◷ *Doors open at 7:30 pm* Ⓤ *Tottenham Court Rd.*

★ **Comedy Store.** Known as the birthplace of alternative comedy, this is where the United Kingdom's funniest stand-ups have cut their teeth before being launched onto prime-time TV. Comedy Store Players, a team with six comedians doing improvisation with audience suggestions, entertain audiences on Wednesday and Sunday; the Cutting Edge team steps in every Tuesday; and on the last Monday of every month the King Gong show (£5) hits the stage, where amateur comedians try their luck. Thursday, Friday, and Saturday have the best stand-up acts. There's also a bar with food. ■ **TIP→** Tickets can be booked through Ticketmaster or over the phone. Note that children under 18 are not admitted to this venue. ⊠ *1A Oxendon St., Soho* ☎ *0844/847–1728* ⊕ *www.thecomedystore.co.uk* ⊟ *£13–£18* ⏱ *Shows daily 8 pm, with extra shows Fri. and Sat. at midnight* Ⓤ *Piccadilly Circus, Leicester Sq.*

THE GAY SCENE

Fodor's Choice
★

Friendly Society. This haute moderne hot spot hops with activity almost any night of the week; the basement feels a bit like something out of *Star Trek* with its white-leather pod seats. The place is known for being gay yet female-friendly. ⊠ *79 Wardour St., Soho* ☎ *020/7434–3805* ⏱ *Weekdays 4–11, Sat. 2–11, Sun. 2–10:30* Ⓤ *Leicester Sq.*

Fodor's Choice
★

Heaven. With by far the best light show on any London dance floor, Heaven is unpretentious, loud, and huge, with a labyrinth of rooms, bars, and live-music parlors. Friday and Saturday nights there's a gay comedy night (£10 in advance, 7–10 pm). If you go to just one gay club, Heaven should be it. ⊠ *The Arches, Villiers St., Covent Garden* ☎ *020/7930–2020* ⊕ *www.heaven-london.com* ⊟ *£4–£12* ⏱ *Mon. 11 pm–6 am, Tues.–Thurs. 11 pm–5 am, Wed. 10:30 pm–4 am, Fri. 11 pm–5 am, Sat. 10:30 pm–5 am* Ⓤ *Charing Cross, Embankment.*

★

The Shadow Lounge. This fabulous little lounge and dance club glitters with faux jewels and twinkling fiber-optic lights over its sunken dance floor, which comes complete with pole for those inclined to do their thing around it. It has a serious A-list celebrity factor, with the glamorous London glitterati camping out in the VIP booth. Members are given entrance priority when the place gets full, especially on weekends, so show up early or prepare to queue. Free entry on Monday. ⊠ *5 Brewer St., Soho* ☎ *020/7287–7988* ⊕ *www.theshadowlounge.co.uk* ⊟ *£5–£10* ⏱ *Mon.–Sat. 10 pm–3 am* Ⓤ *Leicester Sq.*

JAZZ AND BLUES

Fodor's Choice
★

Pizza Express Jazz Club Soho. One of the capital's most ubiquitous pizza chains also runs a great Soho jazz venue. The dimly lighted restaurant hosts top-quality international jazz acts every night. The Italian-style thin-crust pizzas are good, too, though on the small side. ⊠ *10 Dean St., Soho* ☎ *0845/602–7017* ⊕ *www.pizzaexpresslive.com* ⊟ *£10–£25* ⏱ *Daily from 11:30 am for food; music 7:30 pm–11 pm* Ⓤ *Tottenham Court Rd.*

REGENT'S PARK, CAMDEN, AND HAMPSTEAD

DANCE CLUBS

★

KOKO. This Victorian theater, formerly known as Camden Palace, has seen acts from Charlie Chaplin to Madonna, and genres from punk to rave. Updated with lush reds not unlike a cockney Moulin Rouge, this is still one of London's most stunning venues. Sounds of live indie rock, cabaret, funky house, and club classics keep the big dance floor moving, even when it's not heaving. ⊠ *1A Camden High St., Camden Town* ☎ *0870/432–5527* ⊕ *www.koko.uk.com* ⊟ *£3–£20* ⏱ *Opening hrs vary, depending on shows* Ⓤ *Mornington Crescent.*

ECLECTIC

★

Union Chapel. This beautiful old chapel has excellent acoustics and sublime architecture. The beauty of the space and its impressive multicultural programming have made it one of London's best musical venues, especially for acoustic shows. Performers have included Björk, Beck, and Goldfrapp, though now you're more likely to hear lower-key

London's dance clubs present all kinds of live music in venues both large and small.

alternative country, world music, and jazz. ⊠ *Compton Terr., Islington* ☎ *020/7226–1686* ⊕ *www.unionchapel.org.uk* ⊠ *Free–£25* ☉ *Opening hrs vary* Ⓤ *Highbury & Islington.*

JAZZ AND BLUES

★ **Jazz Café.** A palace of high-tech cool in bohemian Camden—it remains an essential hangout for fans of both the mainstream end of the repertoire and hip-hop, funk, rap, and Latin fusion. Book ahead if you want a prime table overlooking the stage, in the balcony restaurant. ⊠ *5 Pkwy., Camden Town* ☎ *020/7688–8899 restaurant reservations, 0870/060–3777 standing tickets* ⊕ *www.jazzcafe.co.uk* ⊠ *£10–£25* ☉ *Daily 7 pm–2 am* Ⓤ *Camden Town.*

ROCK

★ **Barfly Club.** At one of the finest small clubs in the capital, punk, indie guitar bands, and new metal rock attract a nonmainstream crowd. Weekend club nights upstairs host DJs (and live bands) who rock the decks. The Baryfly's sister club, **The Fly**, is at 36/38 New Oxford Street. ⊠ *49 Chalk Farm Rd., Camden Town* ☎ *020/7688–8994* ⊕ *www.barflyclub. com* ⊠ *£5–£8* ☉ *Mon. and Tues. 7–midnight, Wed. and Thurs. 7 pm–2 am, Fri. and Sat. 7 pm–3 am* Ⓤ *Camden Town, Chalk Farm.*

WESTMINSTER

BARS

Cinnamon Club. In the basement of what was once Old Westminster Library, the Club Bar of this contemporary Indian restaurant (treat yourself to a superb curry) has Bollywood scenes playing on a large screen, Asian-theme cocktails (mango mojitos, Delhi mules), delicious bar snacks, and a clientele that includes fashionable young politicos. Upstairs, the Library Bar also serves cocktails through the day. ✉ *The Old Westminster Library, Great Smith St., Westminster* ☎ *020/7222–2555* ⊕ *www.cinnamonclub.com* ☾ *Mon.–Sat. 6–11:45 pm* Ⓤ *Westminster.*

THE ARTS

"All the world's a stage," said Shakespeare, and whether you prefer your art classical or modern, or as a contemporary twist on a time-honored classic, you'll find that London's vibrant cultural scene holds its own on the world stage. Divas sing original-language librettos at the Royal Oper, Shakespeare's plays are brought to life at the reconstructed Globe Theatre, and challenging new writing is produced at the Royal Court. Whether you feel like the lighthearted extravagance of a West End musical or the next shark-in-formaldehyde at the White Cube, the choice is yours.

To find out what's showing now, the weekly magazine *Time Out* (issued every Tuesday) is invaluable. The *Evening Standard* carries listings, many of which are available online at ⊕ *www.thisislondon.co.uk*. London's widely available free newspapers are also worth checking out, as are many Sunday papers, and the Saturday *Independent, Guardian,* and *Times.* You can pick up the free fortnightly *London Theatre Guide* from hotels and tourist-information centers.

CLASSICAL MUSIC

Whether it's a concert by cellist Yo-Yo Ma or a Mozart requiem by candlelight, it's possible to hear first-rate musicians in world-class venues almost every day of the year. The London Symphony Orchestra is in residence at the Barbican Centre, although other top orchestras—including the Philharmonia and the Royal Philharmonic—also perform here. The Barbican also hosts chamber-music concerts, with celebrated orchestras such as the City of London Sinfonia. Wigmore Hall, a lovely venue for chamber music, is renowned for its song recitals by up-and-coming young singers. The Southbank Centre has an impressive international music season, held in the Queen Elizabeth Hall and the small Purcell Room as well as in the Royal Festival Hall, now completely refurbished. Full houses are rare, so even at the biggest concert halls you should be able to get a ticket for £12. If you can't book in advance, arrive at the hall an hour before the performance for a chance at returns.

■**TIP**→ Lunchtime concerts take place all over the city in smaller concert halls, the big arts-center foyers, and churches; they usually cost less than £5 or are free, and feature string quartets, singers, jazz ensembles, or gospel choirs. St. Martin-in-the-Fields is one popular location. Performances usually begin about 1 pm and last one hour.

Henry Wood Promenade Concerts. A great British tradition since 1895, the "Proms" run eight weeks, from July to September, at the Royal Albert Hall. Despite an extraordinary quantity of high-quality concerts, it's renowned for its (atypical) last night: a madly jingoistic display of singing "Land of Hope and Glory," Union Jack–waving, and general madness. Demand for last-night tickets is so high that you must enter a lottery. For regular Proms, tickets run £5–£90, with hundreds of standing tickets for £5 available at the hall on the night of the concert. ■TIP➜ The last night is broadcast in Hyde Park on a jumbo screen, but even here a seat on the grass requires a paid ticket that can set you back around £25. ⊕ *www.bbc.co.uk/proms.*

Barbican Centre. Home to the **London Symphony Orchestra** (⊕ *www. lso.co.uk*) and frequent host of the English Chamber Orchestra and the BBC Symphony Orchestra, the Barbican has an excellent season of big-name virtuosos. ⊠ *Silk St., East End* ☎ *020/7638–8891 box office* ⊕ *www.barbican.org.uk* Ⓤ *Barbican, Moorgate.*

★ **Royal Albert Hall.** Built in 1871, this splendid iron-and-glass–dome auditorium hosts music programs in a wide range of genres, including top-flight pop artists, as well as being the home of Europe's most democratic music festival, the Proms. The hall is also open daily for daytime guided tours (£8). ⊠ *Kensington Gore, Kensington* ☎ *020/7589–8212* ⊕ *www. royalalberthall.com* Ⓤ *South Kensington.*

★ **St. Martin-in-the-Fields.** Popular lunchtime concerts (free but £3.50 donation suggested) are held in this lovely 1726 church, as are regular evening concerts. You can sit in on many rehearsals for free. ■TIP➜ Stop for a snack at the Café in the Crypt. ⊠ *Trafalgar Sq., Covent Garden* ☎ *020/7766–1100* ⊕ *www.stmartin-in-the-fields.org* Ⓤ *Charing Cross.*

Southbank Centre. Both the Philharmonia and the London Philharmonic orchestras are based here, and other venues host smaller-scale music performances; the Queen Elizabeth Hall has chamber orchestras and top-tier soloists, and in the intimate Purcell Room you can listen to chamber music and solo recitals. ⊠ *Belvedere Rd., South Bank* ☎ *020/7960–4200* ⊕ *www.southbankcentre.org.uk* Ⓤ *Waterloo.*

Fodor's Choice ★ **Wigmore Hall.** Hear chamber music and song recitals in this charming hall with near-perfect acoustics. Don't miss the midmorning Sunday concerts. ⊠ *36 Wigmore St., Marylebone* ☎ *020/7935–2141* ⊕ *www. wigmore-hall.org.uk* Ⓤ *Bond St.*

CONTEMPORARY ART

In the 21st century, the focus of the city's art scene has shifted from the past to the future. Helped by the prominence of the Tate Modern, London's contemporary art scene has never been so high profile. In publicly funded exhibition spaces like the Barbican Gallery, the Hayward Gallery, the Institute of Contemporary Arts, and the Serpentine Gallery, London now has a modern-art environment on a par with Bilbao and New York. Young British Artists (YBAs, though no longer as young as they once were) Damien Hirst, Tracey Emin, and others are firmly planted in the public imagination. The celebrity status of British artists is in part thanks to the annual Turner Prize, which always stirs up controversy in the media during a monthlong display of the work, usually at Tate Britain.

The South Bank's Tate Modern may house the giants of modern art, but East London is where the innovative action is. There are dozens of galleries in the fashionable spaces around Old Street, and the truly hip have already moved even farther east, to areas such as Bethnal Green. The Whitechapel Art Gallery and Jay Jopling's influential White Cube in Hoxton Square remain at the epicenter of the new art establishment and continue to show exciting work by emerging British artists.

Barbican Centre. Innovative exhibitions of 20th-century and current art and design are shown in the Barbican Gallery and the **Curve** (✉ *Usually free* ☉ *Mon., Thurs.–Sun. 11–8, Tues. and Wed. 11–6).* ✉ *Silk St., The City* ☎ *020/7638–8891* ⊕ *www.barbican.org.uk* ✉ *Prices vary with exhibition (some free), tickets cheaper if booked online in advance* ☉ *Mon., Thurs.–Sun. 11–8, Tues. and Wed. 11–6* Ⓤ *Barbican.*

★ **Hayward Gallery.** This modern art gallery is a classic example of 1960s Brutalist architecture. It's part of the Southbank Centre and is one of London's major venues for contemporary art exhibitions. ✉ *Belvedere Rd., Southbank Centre, South Bank* ☎ *08703/800–400* ⊕ *www.hayward.org.uk* ✉ *Prices vary with exhibition (some free)* ☉ *Sat.–Thurs. 10–6, Fri. 10–10* Ⓤ *Waterloo.*

Institute of Contemporary Arts. Housed in an elegant John Nash–designed Regency terrace, the ICA's three galleries have changing exhibitions of contemporary visual art. The ICA also programs performance, film, new media, literary talks, and photography. There's an arts bookstore, cafeteria, and bar. ✉ *Nash House, The Mall, St. James's* ☎ *020/7930–3647* ⊕ *www.ica.org.uk* ✉ *Free* ☉ *Daily noon–7:30, Thurs. noon–9* Ⓤ *Charing Cross.*

Lisson. Owner Nicholas Logsdail represents about 40 blue-chip artists, including minimalist Sol Lewitt and Dan Graham, at arguably the most respected gallery in London. The gallery is most associated with New Object sculptors like Anish Kapoor and Richard Deacon, many of whom have won the Turner Prize. A branch down the road at 29 Bell Street features work by younger, up-and-coming artists. ✉ *52–54 Bell St., Marylebone* ☎ *020/7724–2739* ⊕ *www.lissongallery.com* ✉ *Free* ☉ *Weekdays 10–6, Sat. 11–5* Ⓤ *Edgware Rd., Marylebone.*

Royal Academy of Arts. Housed in an aristocratic mansion and home to Britain's first art school (founded in 1768), the academy is best known for its blockbuster special exhibitions. The annual Summer Exhibition has been a popular London tradition since 1769. ✉ *Burlington House, Mayfair* ☎ *020/7300–8000* ⊕ *www.royalacademy.org.uk* ✉ *From £8, prices vary with exhibition* ☉ *Daily 10–6, except Fri. 10–10* Ⓤ *Piccadilly Circus.*

Saatchi Gallery. Charles Saatchi's ultramodern gallery devoted to leading contemporary artists occupies all 70,000 square feet of the duke of York's HQ building in Chelsea and has a bookshop and café-bar. ✉ *Duke of York's HQ, Sloane Sq., Chelsea* ☎ *020/7823–2332* ⊕ *www.saatchi-gallery.co.uk* ✉ *Free* Ⓤ *Sloane Sq.*

Serpentine Gallery. Built in 1934 as a tea pavilion in Kensington Gardens, the Serpentine has an international reputation for exhibitions of modern and contemporary art. Man Ray, Henry Moore, Andy Warhol, Bridget Riley, Damien Hirst, and Rachel Whiteread are a few of the artists who have had exhibits here. The annual Summer Pavilion, designed by a different leading architect every year, is always worth catching. ✉ *Kensington Gardens, South Kensington* ☎ *020/7402–6075* ⊕ *www.serpentinegallery.org* ✉ *Free* ☉ *Daily 10–6* Ⓤ *South Kensington, Knightsbridge.*

Fodor's Choice **Tate Modern.** This converted power station is one of the largest modern-
★ art galleries in the world, so give yourself ample time to take it all in.
The permanent collection includes work by all the major 20th-century
artists, though only a fraction is shown at any one time. There are also
blockbuster touring shows and solo exhibitions of international artists. ■TIP➔ The bar on the top floor has gorgeous views overlooking the
Thames and St. Paul's Cathedral. ⊠ *Bankside, South Bank* ☎ *020/7887–
8888* ⊕ *www.tate.org.uk* ⊠ *Free–£12.50* ⊗ *Sun.–Thurs. 10–6, Fri. and
Sat. 10–10* Ⓤ *Southwark.*

Victoria Miro Gallery. This important commercial gallery has exhibited
some of the biggest names on the British contemporary art scene—Chris
Ofili, the Chapman brothers, Peter Doig, to name a few. ⊠ *16 Wharf
Rd., Islington* ☎ *020/7336–8109* ⊕ *www.victoria-miro.com* ⊠ *Free*
⊗ *Tues.–Sat. 10–6* Ⓤ *Old St., Angel.*

★ **White Cube.** Jay Joplin's influential gallery is housed in a 1920s light-
industrial building on Hoxton Square. Many of its artists are Turner
Prize stars—Hirst, Emin, Hume, et al.—and many live in the East End,
which supposedly has the highest concentration of artists in Europe.
Farther west, White Cube has a second gallery in a striking building
in Mason's Yard, St. James's. ⊠ *48 Hoxton Sq., Hoxton* ☎ *020/7930–
5373* ⊕ *www.whitecube.com* ⊠ *Free* ⊗ *Tues.–Sat. 10–6* Ⓤ *Old St.*

★ **Whitechapel Art Gallery.** Established in 1897 and newly expanded, this
large, independent East End gallery is one of London's most innovative
and consistently interesting. Jeff Wall, Bill Viola, Gary Hume, and Janet
Cardiff have exhibited here and there is an interesting program of events
as well as an excellent restaurant. Closed Monday. ⊠ *80–82 Whitechapel
High St., Shoreditch* ☎ *020/7522–7888* ⊕ *www.whitechapel.org* ⊠ *Free*
⊗ *Tues., Wed., Fri.–Sun. 11 am–6 pm, Thurs. 11 am–9 pm* Ⓤ *Aldgate East.*

DANCE

The **English National Ballet** and visiting international companies usually
perform at the London Coliseum and at Sadler's Wells.

The **Royal Ballet,** world renowned for its classical excellence, as well as
innovative contemporary dance from several companies and scores of
independent choreographers, can be seen at the Royal Oper.

Encompassing the newly refurbished **Royal Festival Hall,** the Southbank
Centre has a seriously good contemporary dance program that hosts top
international companies and important U.K. choreographers, as well as
multicultural offerings from Japanese Butoh and Indian Kathak to hip-
hop. The **Place** and the **Lilian Bayliss Theatre** at Sadler's Wells are where
you'll find the most daring, cutting-edge performances.

The biggest annual event is **Dance Umbrella** (☎ *020/8741–4040* ⊕ *www.
danceumbrella.co.uk*), a four-week season in October that hosts international and British-based artists at various venues across the city.

The following theaters are the key dance venues. Check weekly listings
or ⊕ *www.londondance.com* for current performances and fringe venues.

DANCE BOX **London Coliseum** (⊠ *St. Martin's La., Covent Garden* ☎ *020/7632–8300*
OFFICES ⊕ *www.eno.org* Ⓤ *Leicester Sq.*).

The Proms at Royal Albert Hall have standing tickets for £5 on the night of the concerts.

The Place (✉ *17 Duke's Rd., Bloomsbury* ☎ *020/7121–1100* ⊕ *www. theplace.org.uk* Ⓤ *Euston*).

Fodor's Choice ★ **Royal Opera** (✉ *Bow St., Covent Garden* ☎ *020/7304–4000* ⊕ *www.roh. org.uk* Ⓤ *Covent Garden*).

Fodor's Choice ★ **Sadler's Wells** (✉ *Rosebery Ave., Islington* ☎ *0844/412–4300* ⊕ *www. sadlers-wells.com* Ⓤ *Angel*).

Southbank Centre (✉ *Belvedere Rd., South Bank* ☎ *020/7960–4200* ⊕ *www.southbankcentre.co.uk* Ⓤ *Waterloo, Embankment*).

FILM

There are many lovely movie theaters in London and several that are committed to nonmainstream cinema, notably the National Film Theatre. Most of the major houses, such as the Odeon Leicester Square and the Empire, are in the Leicester Square–Piccadilly Circus area, where tickets average £15. Monday and matinees are often cheaper, at around £6–£10, and there are also fewer crowds.

★ ☺ **BFI Southbank.** With easily the best repertory programming in London, the three cinemas and studio at what was previously known as the National Film Theatre are effectively a national film center run by the British Film Institute. They show more than 1,000 titles each year, favoring art-house, foreign, silent, overlooked, classic, noir, and short films over Hollywood blockbusters. After a recent rejuvenation and expansion, the center also has a gallery, bookshop, and "mediatheque," where visitors can watch film and television from the National Archive. This is one of the venues for the Times BFI London Film Festival; throughout the year there are minifestivals, seminars, and guest speakers. ■ TIP→ Members

(£40) get priority bookings (useful for special events) and £1.40 off each screening. ✉ *Belvedere Rd., South Bank* ☎ *020/7928–3535 information, 020/7928–3232 box office* ⊕ *www.bfi.org.uk* Ⓤ *Waterloo.*

★ **Curzon Soho.** This comfortable cinema runs an artsy program of mixed repertoire and mainstream films. There are also branches in Mayfair, Bloomsbury, Chelsea, and Richmond. Members (£50) get discounts. ✉ *99 Shaftesbury Ave., Soho* ☎ *0871/703–3988* Ⓤ *Piccadilly Circus, Leicester Sq.* ✉ *38 Curzon St., Mayfair* ☎ *0871/703–3989* ⊕ *www. curzoncinemas.com* Ⓤ *Green Park.*

☾ **The Electric Cinema.** This refurbished Portobello Road art house screens
★ mainstream and international movies. The emphasis is on comfort, with leather sofas, armchairs, footstools, and mini–coffee tables for your tapas-style food and wine. Saturday matinees for kids are popular. The Electric now has an equally sumptuous sister cinema in east London— the Aubin, on Redchurch Street. ✉ *191 Portobello Rd., Notting Hill* ☎ *020/7908–9696* ⊕ *www.electriccinema.co.uk* Ⓤ *Ladbroke Grove, Notting Hill Gate.*

OPERA

The two key players in London's opera scene are the Royal Oper (which ranks with the Metropolitan Oper in New York) and the more innovative English National Opera (ENO), which presents English-language productions at the London Coliseum. Only the Theatre Royal, Drury Lane, has a longer theatrical history than the Royal Oper—the third theater to be built on the site since 1858.

Despite occasional performances by the likes of Björk, the Royal Oper struggles to shrug off its reputation for elitism and ticket prices that can rise to £200. It is, however, more accessible than it used to be—the cheapest tickets are under £10. Conditions of purchase vary; call for information. Prices for the ENO are generally lower, ranging from around £17 to £85. You can get same-day balcony seats for as little as £5.

Almeida Opera is a festival that showcases new and often cutting-edge opera. In summer, the increasingly adventurous Opera Holland Park presents the usual chestnuts alongside some obscure works under a newly enlarged canopy in leafy Holland Park.

OPERA BOX **Almeida Theatre** (✉ *Almeida St., Islington* ☎ *020/7359–4404* ⊕ *www.*
OFFICES *almeida.co.uk* Ⓤ *Angel*).

English National Opera (✉ *St. Martin's La., Covent Garden* ☎ *0871/911–0200* ⊕ *www.eno.org* Ⓤ *Leicester Sq.*).

Opera Holland Park (✉ *Holland Park, Kensington High St., Kensington* ☎ *0845/230–9769* ⊕ *www.operahollandpark.com* Ⓤ *Kensington High St.*).

Fodor'sChoice **Royal Opera** (✉ *Bow St., Covent Garden* ☎ *020/7304–4000* ⊕ *www.*
★ *royalopera.org* Ⓤ *Covent Garden*).

THEATER

In London the play really *is* the thing, ranging from a long-running popular musical like *Mamma Mia!,* a groundbreaking reworking of Pinter, imaginative physical theater from an experimental company like *Complicite,* a lavish Disney spectacle, or a small fringe production above a pub. West End glitz and glamour continue to pull in the audiences, and so do the more innovative productions. Only in London will a Tuesday matinee of the Royal Shakespeare Company's *Henry IV* sell out a 1,200-seat theater.

In London the words radical and quality or classical and experimental are not mutually exclusive. The Royal Shakespeare Company (⊕ *www. rsc.org.uk*) and the National Theatre (⊕ *www.nationaltheatre.org.uk*) often stage contemporary versions of the classics. The Almeida, Battersea Arts Centre (BAC), Donmar Warehouse, Royal Court Theatre, Soho Theatre, and Old Vic attract famous actors and have excellent reputations for new writing and innovative theatrical approaches. These are the venues where you'll see an original production before it becomes a hit in the West End or on Broadway (and for a fraction of the cost).

The London theater scene remains vibrant throughout the summer months. Open-air productions of Shakespeare are particularly well served, whether in the faithful reconstruction of the Elizabethan Globe Theatre or under the stars in Regent's Park's Open Air Theatre.

Theatergoing isn't cheap. Tickets less than £10 are a rarity, although designated productions at the National Theatre have seats at this price. At the commercial theaters you should expect to pay from £15 for a seat in the upper balcony to at least £25 for a good one in the stalls (orchestra) or dress circle (mezzanine). However, last-minute returns available on the night may provide some good deals. Tickets may be booked through ticket agents, at individual theater box offices, or over the phone by credit card. Be sure to inquire about any extra fees—prices can vary enormously, but agents are legally obliged to reveal the face value of the ticket if you ask. All the larger hotels offer theater bookings, but they tack on a hefty service charge. ■TIP➜ Be very wary of ticket touts (scalpers) and unscrupulous ticket agents outside theaters and working the line at tkts, a half-price ticket booth (⊕ www.tkts.co.uk).

Ticketmaster ((☎ *0844/277–4321* ⊕ *www.ticketmaster.co.uk*) sells tickets to a number of different theaters, although they charge a booking fee. For discount tickets, **Society of London Theatre** (☎ *020/7557–6700*) operates **tkts**, a half-price ticket booth (⊕ *www.tkts.co.uk*) on the southwest corner of Leicester Square, and sells the best available seats to performances at about 25 theaters. It's open Monday–Saturday 10–7, Sunday noon–3; there's a £2.50 service charge (included in the price). Major credit cards are accepted.

THEATERS

★ **Almeida Theatre.** This Off–West End venue premieres excellent new plays and exciting twists on the classics, often featuring high-profile actors. The Almeida Opera Festival in July has an adventurous program of new opera and musical theater. ⊠ *Almeida St., Islington* ☎ *020/7359–4404* ⊕ *www.almeida.co.uk* Ⓤ *Angel, Highbury & Islington.*

★ **BAC.** Battersea Arts Centre has a reputation for producing innovative new work. Check out Scratch, a spring festival of low-tech cabaret theater by emerging artists where the audience provides feedback on works-in-progress. Tuesday shows usually have pay-what-you-can entry. ✉ *176 Lavender Hill, Battersea* ☎ *020/7223–2223* ⊕ *www.bac. org.uk* Ⓤ *British Rail: Clapham Junction.*

Barbican Centre. Built in 1982, the Barbican Centre puts on a number of performances by British and international theater companies as part of its year-round **B.I.T.E.** (Barbican International Theatre Events), which also features groundbreaking performance, dance, drama, and musical theater. ✉ *Silk St., The City* ☎ *020/7638–8891* ⊕ *www.barbican.org. uk* Ⓤ *Barbican.*

Fodor's Choice **Donmar Warehouse.** Hollywood stars often perform here in diverse and ★ daring new works, bold interpretations of the classics, and small-scale musicals. Under current Artistic Director Michael Grandage, who succeeded Sam Mendes, Nicole Kidman, Gwyneth Paltrow, and Ewan McGregor have all been featured. ✉ *41 Earlham St., Covent Garden* ☎ *0844/871–7624* ⊕ *www.donmarwarehouse.com* Ⓤ *Covent Garden.*

★ **National Theatre.** Interspersed with the three theaters, the 1,120-seat Olivier, the 890-seat Lyttelton, and the 300-seat Cottesloe, is a multi-layered foyer with exhibitions, bars, and restaurants, and free entertainment. Musicals, classics, and new plays are performed by a top-flight company. Some shows offer £10 ticket deals. ✉ *Southbank Centre, Belvedere Rd., South Bank* ☎ *020/7452–3000 box office, 0207/452–3400 information* ⊕ *www.nationaltheatre.org.uk* ✄ *Tour £5.90* ☉ *Foyer Mon.–Sat. 9:30 am–11 pm; 75-min tour backstage up to 6 times daily weekdays, twice on Sat., often on Sun.* Ⓤ *Waterloo.*

The Old Vic. Who would have thought it? This grand old theater, former haunting grounds of such stage legends as John Gielgud, Vivien Leigh, Peter O'Toole, Richard Burton, and Judi Dench is now masterminded by noted American actor Kevin Spacey. Even though Laurence Olivier called this grand 1818 Victorian theater his favorite, the theater had suffered decades of financial duress. Before being shut down, however, the Old Vic was brought under the ownership of a dedicated trust headed by Spacey. His production record so far has been spotty but there are high hopes, at this writing, for his interpretation of Shakespeare's *Richard III.* ✉ *The Cut, Southwark* ☎ *0844/871–7628* ⊕ *www. oldvictheatre.com* Ⓤ *Waterloo.*

Fodor's Choice **Open Air Theatre.** On a warm summer evening, classical theater in the ★ pastoral and royal Regent's Park is hard to beat for magical adventure. Enjoy a supper before the performance, a bite during the intermission on the picnic lawn, or drinks in the spacious bar. ✉ *Inner Circle, Regent's Park* ☎ *0844/826–4242* ⊕ *www.openairtheatre.org* Ⓤ *Baker St., Regent's Park.*

★ **Royal Court Theatre.** Britain's undisputed epicenter of new writing, the RCT is now 50 years old and continues to produce gritty British and international drama. ■**TIP➜** Don't miss the best deal in town—10-pence standing tickets go on sale one hour before each performance, and there are £10 tickets on Monday. ✉ *Sloane Sq., Chelsea* ☎ *020/7565–5000* ⊕ *www. royalcourttheatre.com* Ⓤ *Sloane Sq.*

Fodor's Choice **Shakespeare's Globe Theatre.** Making world headlines when the Globe ★ "reopened" in 1996 to wide acclaim, this faithful reconstruction of the open-air playhouse where Shakespeare worked and wrote many of his greatest plays marvelously re-creates the 16th-century theatergoing experience. Standing room in the "pit" right in front of the stage costs £5. The season runs April through October. ✉ *21 New Globe Walk, Bankside, South Bank* ☎ *020/7401–9919* ⊕ *www.shakespeares-globe. org* Ⓤ *Southwark, then walk to Blackfriars Bridge and descend steps; Mansion House, then cross Southwark Bridge; Blackfriars, then walk across Blackfriars Bridge; St. Paul's, then cross Millenium Bridge.*

Soho Theatre. This sleek theater in the heart of Soho is devoted to fostering new writing and is a prolific presenter of work by emerging writers and comedy performance. ✉ *21 Dean St., Soho* ☎ *0207/478–0100* ⊕ *www.sohotheatre.com* Ⓤ *Tottenham Court Rd.*

Tricycle Theatre. The Tricycle is committed to the best in Irish, African-Caribbean, Asian, and political drama, and the promotion of new plays. There is also a gallery and cinema. ✉ *269 Kilburn High Rd., Kilburn* ☎ *020/7328–1900 information, 020/7328–1000 box office* ⊕ *www. tricycle.co.uk* Ⓤ *Kilburn.*

Young Vic. Ensconced in a new home near Waterloo, big names perform here alongside young talent, often in daring, innovative productions of classic plays. ✉ *66 The Cut, Waterloo, South Bank* ☎ *020/922–2922* ⊕ *www.youngvic.org* Ⓤ *Waterloo.*

SHOPPING

As befits one of the great trading capitals of the world, London's shops have been known to boast, "You name it, we sell it." Finding and buying "it" can be a delight (the private fitting rooms at couturier Vivienne Westwood) or a trial (mobbed Oxford Street on a Saturday morning). No matter where you head in this city, you'll find you can melt as much plastic as your wallet can stand. You can shop like royalty at Her Majesty's glove maker, run down a leather-bound copy of Wuthering Heights at a Charing Cross bookseller, or find flea-market goodies on Portobello Road. Whether out for fun—there's nothing like those amazing street markets to stimulate the acquisitive juices—or for fashion, London can be the most rewarding of hunting grounds.

Although it's impossible to pin down one particular look that defines the city, homegrown designers like Vivienne Westwood, Matthew Williamson, Paul Smith, and Alice Temperley stand out for their quirky, eccentric designs. London is, after all, the city that introduced punk, miniskirts, and Mod fashion to the world. If you're after a more traditional look, however, head to Jermyn Street and Savile Row, which still retain their old-world look and feel—and there's no better place in the city to buy custom-made shirts and suits. If your budget can't stretch to Savile Row, no problem. The city's High-street chain stores like Topshop, Oasis, Reiss, and French Connection are excellent places to pick up designs straight from the catwalk, at a fraction of the price. And don't forget London's markets, known for their size, variety, and sheer street theater.

Apart from bankrupting yourself, the only problem you may encounter is exhaustion. London's shopping districts are spread out all over the

LONDON'S SPECTATOR SPORTS

London will host the 2012 Olympics, but don't expect to see many city inhabitants practicing their javelin throws in Hyde Park. Sport in the capital comes into its own when it's watched, rather than participated in. You'll most easily witness London's fervent sporting passions in front of a screen in a pub with a pint in hand. And those passions run deep.

CRICKET

★ **Lord's** (✉ *St. John's Wood Rd., St. John's Wood* ☎ *020/7432-1000* ⊕ *www.lords.org* Ⓤ *St. John's Wood*) has been hallowed turf for worshippers of England's summer game since 1811. Tickets are hard to come by: obtain an application form and enter the ballot (lottery) to purchase tickets. Forms are sent out in early December or you can apply online. Test Match tickets cost between £25 and £95. Cheaper county matches (Middlesex plays here) can usually be seen by lining up on match day.

FOOTBALL

Three of London's football (soccer) clubs competing in the **Premier League** and the Football Association's FA Cup are particularly popular, though not always correspondingly successful: **Arsenal** (✉ *Emirates Stadium, Datyon Park* ☎ *020/7704-4040* ⊕ *www. arsenal.com* Ⓤ *Arsenal*), **Chelsea** (✉ *Stamford Bridge, Fulham Rd., Fulham* ☎ *0871/984-1905* ⊕ *www. chelseafc.co.uk* Ⓤ *Fulham Broadway*), and **Tottenham Hotspur** (*"Spurs"* ✉ *White Hart La., 748 High Rd., Tottenham* ☎ *0844/499-5000* ⊕ *www. tottenhamhotspur.com* Ⓤ *National Rail: White Hart La.*). Try to buy tickets well in advance, and don't get too carried away by the excitement a vast football crowd can generate.

TENNIS

The **Wimbledon Lawn Tennis Championships** (☎ *020/8944-1066* ⊕ *www.wimbledon.org*), the most prestigious of the four Grand Slam tournaments, is also one of London's most eagerly awaited annual events. There's a lottery system for advance purchase; check the Web site. You can purchase tickets online for the next day's matches throughout the tournament.

city, so do as the locals do. Plan your excursion with military precision, taking in only one or two areas in a day, and stop for a hearty English lunch with a glass of wine or a pint at a pub.

BLOOMSBURY, HOLBORN, AND ISLINGTON

ANTIQUES

★ **London Silver Vaults.** Housed in a basement vault, this extraordinary space holds stalls from more than 30 silver dealers. Products range from the spectacular to the over-the-top, but you can also pick up smaller items, from a set of Victorian cake forks to a teaspoon or candlesticks. ■ **TIP→** Most of the silver merchants actually trade out of room-size, underground vaults, which were originally rented out to London's upper crust to store their valuables. ✉ *53–64 Chancery La., Holborn* ☎ *020/7242-3844* ⊕ *www.thesilvervaults.com* ☉ *Closed Sat. after 1, and Sun.* Ⓤ *Chancery La.*

STATIONERY

Paperchase. The stationery superstore of London, Paperchase sells writing paper in every conceivable shade and in a dozen mediums. There are lovely cards, artists' materials, notebooks, and loose stationery. The three-floor store has a café. ✉ *213–215 Tottenham Court Rd., Bloomsbury* ☎ *020/7467–6200* ⊕ *www.paperchase.co.uk* Ⓤ *Goodge St.*

THE CITY AND SOUTH BANK

ART GALLERY

★ **Lesley Craze Gallery.** This serene gallery displays jewelry by some 100 young designers from around the world, with a strong British bias, featuring both precious and semiprecious stones. There's also a textiles room showcasing unusual and colorful handmade scarves, bags, and cushions. Prices are reasonable. ✉ *33–35A Clerkenwell Green, Clerkenwell* ☎ *020/7608–0393* ⊕ *www.lesleycrazegallery.co.uk* ⊙ *Closed Sun.; open Mon. in Nov. and Dec. only* Ⓤ *Farringdon.*

Bargehouse. Many varied artisans have to pass rigorous selection procedures to set up in the prime riverside workshops where they make, display, and sell their work. There are around 30 studios, spread over two floors. The Oxo Tower Restaurant & Brasserie on the top floor is expensive, but with its fantastic view of London, it's worth popping up for a drink. ✉ *Oxo Tower Wharf, Bargehouse St., South Bank* ☎ *020/7401–4255* ⊙ *Closed Mon.* Ⓤ *Southwark, Waterloo.*

STREET MARKETS

★ **Borough Market,** a foodie's delight that continues to get better and better, carries whole-grain, organic everything, mainly from Britain but with an international flavor. Don't make any other lunch plans: there's plenty to eat on the spot. Wild boar sausages? Handmade Indian condiments? It's all here. ✉ *Borough High St., South Bank* ⊙ *Thurs. 11–5, Fri. noon–6, Sat. 8–5* Ⓤ *London Bridge, Borough.*

THE EAST END

CLOTHING

★ **Junky Styling.** This brand was launched by designers Annika Sanders and Kerry Seager, who used to "deconstruct" old clothing when they wanted something unique to wear clubbing. The highly original (and eco-friendly) garments, for both men and women, are funky but retain the sophistication of their tailored origins. ✉ *12 Dray Walk, The Old Truman Brewery, 91 Brick La., Spitalfields* ☎ *020/7247–1883* ⊕ *www.junkystyling.co.uk* Ⓤ *Liverpool St., Aldgate East.*

★ **The Laden Showroom.** Sienna Miller, Victoria Beckham, and Noel Gallagher are among the celebs who regularly check out emerging talent at this East End showroom for young designers. The store retails the work of more than 70 new designers, some selling one-off items—so the look you find is likely to be original. ✉ *103 Brick La., Spitalfields* ☎ *020/7247–2431* ⊕ *www.laden.co.uk* Ⓤ *Shoreditch High St.*

REGENT'S PARK

CAMDEN TOWN
cheap second-hand and club gear

CLERKENWELL
a historical hotspot for crafts and design

BLOOMSBURY

MARYLEBONE
small shops in village-like setting

HOXTON & SHOREDITCH
edgy young designers

NOTTING HILL
antiques, vintage clothing, and boho boutiques

OXFORD CIRCUS
global flagships, department stores, and street style on Carnaby

SOHO
books abound on Charing Cross Road

BAYSWATER

COVENT GARDEN
an urban-wear mecca around Seven Dials

MAYFAIR
catwalk names on Bond St., trad tailors on Savile Row

HYDE PARK

ST JAMES'S
old-fashioned specialists, from hatters to shirtmakers

Green Park

St. James's Park

KNIGHTSBRIDGE
luxe labels and, of course, Harrods

WESTMINSTER

BELGRAVIA

River Thames

LAMBETH

VICTORIA

CHELSEA
the King's Rd. spans fashion to furniture

0   1/2 mile
0   1/2 km

GREAT SPOTS TO SHOP

Portobello Road Market. Whether you are a serious antiques buyer or just want to browse the stalls and people-watch, Portobello Road is London's most dynamic market.

Liberty. Look for an outstanding collection of clothing crafted from its famous prints and furniture, as well as cutting-edge fashion.

Dover Street Market. This concept store is a combination art gallery and department store, and also hosts design retrospectives.

Hamleys. With floor after floor of treasures for every child on your list, this is *the* London toy shop.

Rellik. Celebs love Rellik for its superb collection of vintage clothing, ranging from classic Dior to Vivienne Westwood.

Mint. Fans of contemporary furniture and housewares should head to Mint, which showcases the work of both leading and up-and-coming designers.

HATS

★ **Bernstock Speirs.** Paul Bernstock and Thelma Speirs turn traditional hats on their head with street-smart trilbies and knitted hats that feature unusual colors and quirky details. ⊠ *234 Brick La., Spitalfields* ☎ *020/7739–7385* ⊕ *www.bernstockspeirs.com* Ⓤ *Liverpool St., Bethnal Green.*

MUSIC

★ **Rough Trade East.** Whereas some London record stores are struggling, this veteran indie-music specialist seems to have gotten the formula right. In 2007 it opened this spacious new East End branch that's as much a hangout as a shop, complete with a stage for live gigs, a café, and even Internet access. ⊠ *Dray Walk, Old Truman Brewery, 91 Brick La., Spitalfields* ☎ *020/7392–7788* Ⓤ *Liverpool St.*

STREET MARKETS

Spitalfields, the covered market (once London's wholesale meat market), is at the center of this area's boho revival. The original building has been restored to its Victorian splendor, and a modern shopping complex that respects its character has been developed around it, with a covered area housing additional stalls. Wares include crafts, retro clothing, handmade rugs, soap, and cakes. And, from Spanish tapas to Thai satays, it's possible to eat your way around the world. ⊠ *Brushfield St., East End* ⊙ *Stalls Thurs. and Fri. 10–4, Sun. 9–5; restaurants weekdays 11–11, Sun. 9–5, retail shops daily 11–7* Ⓤ *Liverpool St., Aldgate, Aldgate East.*

KENSINGTON, CHELSEA, KNIGHTSBRIDGE, AND BELGRAVIA

ACCESSORIES

★ **Anya Hindmarch.** Exquisite leather bags and personalized, printed canvas totes are what made Hindmarch famous, along with her hit 2007 "I'm Not A Plastic Bag" eco-creation. Her designs are sold at Harrods and Harvey Nichols, but in her stores you can see her complete collection

Bring your appetite to Borough Market on the South Bank; it's a foodie favorite.

of bags and shoes. ✉ *157–158 Sloane St., Belgravia* ☎ *020/7730–0961* ⊕ *www.anyahindmarch.com* Ⓤ *Sloane Sq., Knightsbridge.*

★ **Lulu Guinness.** Famous for her flamboyantly themed bags (think the satin "bucket" topped with roses or the elaborately beaded red snakeskin "lips" clutch), Guinness also showcases vintage-inspired vanity cases, shoes, beauty products, and bed linens in this frilly little shop. ✉ *3 Ellis St., Belgravia* ☎ *020/7823–4828* ⊕ *www.luluguinness.com* ⊙ *Closed Sun.* Ⓤ *Sloane Sq.*

Philip Treacy. Treacy's magnificent hats are annual showstoppers on Ladies Day at the Royal Ascot races and regularly grace the glossy magazines' society pages. In addition to the extravagant, haute couture hats handmade in the atelier, ready-to-wear hats and bags are also for sale. ✉ *69 Elizabeth St., Belgravia* ☎ *020/7730–3992* ⊕ *www.philiptreacy.co.uk* ⊙ *Closed Sun.* Ⓤ *Sloane Sq.*

CLOTHING: MENSWEAR

★ **Bamford & Sons.** The men's and boys' wear at Bamford & Sons combines
⟳ the British heritage of tailoring and fabrics with a suave modernity. Dashing city wear, romantically nonchalant country clothes, plus fine leather and cashmere accessories are all available. There is also a small but exquisite women's collection ✉ *31 Sloane Sq., Chelsea* ☎ *020/7881–8010* Ⓤ *Sloane Sq.*

CLOTHING: WOMEN'S

★ **Agent Provocateur.** Created by Vivienne Westwood's son, these shops purvey sexy, naughty-but-nice lingerie in gorgeous fabrics and lace. The original shop is in the almost-red-light area of Soho, but there are now branches across the city—and across the Atlantic. Selections are also available in Harrods, Harvey Nichols, and Selfridges. ⊠ *16 Pont St., Knightsbridge* ☎ *020/7235-0229* ⊕ *www.agentprovocateur.com* ⊗ *Closed Sun.* Ⓤ *Knightsbridge, Sloane Sq.*

★ **Jigsaw.** Popular with women in their twenties through forties, Jigsaw toes the line between trendy and classic (similar to Banana Republic). Prices are reasonable for feminine dresses, practical T-shirts, and knitwear in high-quality fabrics and distinctive yet subtle colors. There are several other branches around town. Girls get in on the act, too, with their own line, Jigsaw Junior. ⊠ *The Chapel, Duke of York Sq., King's Rd., Chelsea* ☎ *020/730-4404* ⊕ *www.jigsawonline.com* Ⓤ *Sloane Sq.*

Rigby & Peller. Those who love luxury lingerie shop here for brands like Prima Donna and Aubade, as well as R&P's own line. Quality is excellent and the service much friendlier than you might expect. There are a number of stores across town, all of which are open on Sunday except the Conduit Street location. ⊠ *13 Kings Rd., Chelsea* ☎ *0845/076-5545* ⊕ *www.rigbyandpeller.com* Ⓤ *Sloane Sq.*

DEPARTMENT STORES

Fodor's Choice
★ **Harrods.** A fabled encyclopedia of luxury brands, this Knightsbridge institution has more than 300 departments and 20 restaurants, all spread over 1 million square feet. If you approach Harrods as a tourist attraction rather than a fashion store, you won't be disappointed. Focus on the spectacular food halls, the huge ground-floor perfumery, the marble-clad accessory rooms, and the theme park–like Egyptian Room—at the bottom of the nearby Egyptian escalator there's a commemorative memorial to Diana and Dodi (whose father owns Harrods). ■ TIP→ Be prepared to brave the crowds (avoid visiting on a Saturday if you can), and be prepared to pay if you want to use the bathroom on some floors (!). ⊠ *87–135 Brompton Rd., Knightsbridge* ☎ *020/7730-1234* ⊕ *www.harrods.com* Ⓤ *Knightsbridge.*

★ **Harvey Nichols.** While visiting tourists flock to Harrods, true London fashionistas shop at Harvey Nichols, or "Harvey Nicks" as it's called. The fashion and accessories departments are outstanding, carrying designs from Prada to 3.1 Phillip Lim. The furniture and housewares are equally gorgeous (and pricey), but bargains abound during the twice-annual sales in January and July. The Fifth Floor restaurant is a place to see and be seen, but if you're after a quick bite, pick up a sandwich and some chocolates from the Foodmarket or Daylesford Organic. ⊠ *109–125 Knightsbridge, Knightsbridge* ☎ *020/7235-5000* ⊕ *www.harveynichols.com* Ⓤ *Knightsbridge.*

HOUSEHOLD

★ **The Conran Shop.** This is the domain of Sir Terence Conran, who has been informing British taste since 1960s. Home enhancers from furniture to stemware—both handmade and mass produced, by famous names and young designers—are displayed in a suitably gorgeous building that is a modernist design landmark in its own right. Both the flagship store and the branch on Marylebone High Street are bursting with great gift ideas. ⊠ *Michelin House, 81 Fulham Rd., South Kensington* ☎ *020/7589-7401* ⊕ *www.conranshop.co.uk* Ⓤ *South Kensington.*

Fodor's Choice
★ **Mint.** Owner Lina Kanafani has scoured the globe to stock an eclectic mix of furniture, art, ceramics, and home accessories. Mint also showcases works by up-and-coming designers and sells plenty of limited edition and one-off pieces. If you don't want to ship a couch home, consider a miniature flower vase or a handmade ceramic pitcher. ✉ 2 *North Terr., South Kensington* ☎ *020/7225–2228* ⊕ *www.mintshop. co.uk* Ⓤ *South Kensington.*

2

JEWELRY
★ **Butler & Wilson.** Long before anybody ever heard the word bling, this shop was marketing the look—in diamanté, colored rhinestones, and crystal—to movie stars and secretaries alike. Specialists in bold costume jewelry, they've added semiprecious stones to the collections and the look is anything but subtle, so it may not suit all tastes unless you're in the market for a rhinestone Union Jack pin. Even if you're not a fan, the shop is worth a visit for its vintage (and vintage-influenced) clothes. There's also another shop at 20 South Molton Street. ✉ *189 Fulham Rd., South Kensington* ☎ *020/7352–3045* ⊕ *www.butlerandwilson. co.uk* Ⓤ *South Kensington.*

Melissa McArthur Jewellry. Tucked between Vivienne Westwood's shop and the Bluebird in Chelsea, this small but mighty jewelry store is a must-see on the King's Road. With everything handmade in-house using precious and semiprecious gems (don't forget the pearls), stocking up on gifts for female loved ones is easy here. The price points are also very reasonable for such eternally wearable and gorgeous items. ✉ *378 King's Rd., Chelsea* ☎ *020/7351–1551* ⊕ *www.mmjlondon.com* Ⓤ *Sloane Sq.*

NOTTING HILL

CLOTHING
Aimé. French-Cambodian sisters Val and Vanda Heng-Vong launched this shop to showcase the best of French clothing and designer housewares. Expect to find fashion by Isabel Marant, Antik Batik, and A.P.C. You can also pick up scents by Esteban and a well-edited collection of ceramics. Just next door at 34 Ledbury Road, Petit Aimé sells children's clothing. ✉ *32 Ledbury Rd., Notting Hill* ☎ *020/7221–7070* ⊕ *www. aimelondon.com* Ⓤ *Notting Hill Gate.*

CLOTHING: VINTAGE
Fodor's Choice
★ **Rellik** is favored by the likes of Kate Moss and originally began as a street stall on Portobello Road. Today vintage hunters looking to splurge can find a selection of YSL, Chanel, and Dior, as well as items from lesser-known designers. Prices range from £30 to £1,000. ✉ *8 Golborne Rd., Notting Hill* ☎ *020/8962–0089* ⊕ *www.relliklondon.co.uk* Ⓤ *Westbourne Park.*

MUSIC
Music & Video Exchange. This store—actually a conglomeration of several shops on Notting Hill Gate—is a convenient destination for seekers of unusual and mainstream chart music as well as classical and pop. Rare records and CDs are upstairs, the soul and dance branch is at No. 42, and the classical branch is at No. 36. There are also branches

in Soho, Greenwich, and Camden. ⊠ *38 Notting Hill Gate, Notting Hill* ☎ *020/7243–8574* ⊕ *www.mveshops.co.uk* Ⓤ *Notting Hill Gate.*

STREET MARKETS

Fodor'sChoice **Portobello Market,** London's most famous market, still wins the prize for
★   the all-round best. There are 1,500 antiques dealers here, so bargains are still possible. Nearer Notting Hill Gate, prices and quality are highest; the middle is where locals buy fruit and vegetables and hang out in trendy restaurants. Under the Westway elevated highway is a great flea market, and more bric-a-brac and bargains appear as you walk toward Golborne Road. Take Bus 52 or the Tube here, and arrive early to beat the crowds. ⊠ *Portobello Rd., Notting Hill* ☉ *Fruit and vegetables Mon.–Wed. and Fri. 8–5, Thurs. 8–1; food market and antiques Sat. 8–6* Ⓤ *Ladbroke Grove, Notting Hill Gate.*

ST. JAMES'S, MAYFAIR, AND MARYLEBONE

ANTIQUES

★   **Alfie's Antique Market.** A large and exciting labyrinth on four floors, it has dealers specializing in anything and everything, but particularly in vintage clothing, decorative accessories, and furniture. Highlights include the fabulous collection of cocktail dresses and kitsch bar accessories at the Girl Can't Help It, and Vincenzo Caffarrella's spectacular Italian lighting. There's also a rooftop restaurant if you need a coffee break. In addition to the market, this end of Church Street is lined with excellent antiques shops. ⊠ *13–25 Church St., Marylebone* ☎ *020/7723–6066* ☉ *Closed Sun. and Mon.* Ⓤ *Edgware Rd.*

ACCESSORIES

★   **Swaine Adeney Brigg.** This shop has been selling practical supplies for country pursuits since 1750. Not just for the horsey set, the store has golf umbrellas, walking sticks, and hip flasks—all beautifully crafted and ingenious. Or pick up your own Poet Hat, the iconic hat worn by Harrison Ford in every Indiana Jones film, and which the company has been making since the 1890s. ⊠ *54 St. James's St., St. James's* ☎ *020/7409–7277* ⊕ *www.swaineadeney.co.uk* ☉ *Closed Sun.* Ⓤ *Green Park.*

BEAUTY

Fodor'sChoice **Floris.** One of the most beautiful shops in London, Floris boasts gleam-
★   ing glass-and-Spanish-mahogany showcases from the Great Exhibition of 1851. As well as beautifully packaged soaps, bath essences, perfumes, and its famous rose-scented mouthwash, gift possibilities include goose-down powder puffs and cut-glass atomizers. ⊠ *89 Jermyn St., St. James's* ☎ *0845/702–3239* ⊕ *www.florislondon.com* ☉ *Closed Sun.* Ⓤ *Piccadilly Circus.*

Space NK. A cult favorite among beauty product fiends, this upscale chain boasts more than 20 locations throughout London. The minute you step inside, you're surrounded by very luxurious and sought-after brands like Kate Somerville, Chantecaille, and Rodial. ⊠ *83a Marylebone High St., Marylebone* ☎ *020/7486–8791* ⊕ *www.spacenk.co.uk* Ⓤ *Baker St.*

2

BOOKS AND STATIONERY

Fodor'sChoice **Hatchards.** This is London's oldest bookshop, open since 1797 and
★ beloved by writers themselves (customers have included Oscar Wilde,
Rudyard Kipling, and Lord Byron) thanks to its cozy, independent
character. Independence, however, is a matter of appearance only—
Hatchards is owned by the same corporate giant as the omnipresent
Waterstone's chain. Nevertheless, you can revel in its old-fashioned
charm while perusing the well-stocked shelves lining the winding
stairs. The staff has retained old-fashioned helpfulness, too. ⊠ *187
Piccadilly, St. James's* ☎ *020/7439–9921* ⊕ *www.hatchards.co.uk*
Ⓤ *Piccadilly Circus.*

★ **Smythson of Bond Street.** Hands down, this is the most elegant stationer
in Britain. No hostess of any standing would consider having a leather-
bound guest book made by anyone else, and the shop's distinctive pale-
blue–page diaries and social stationery are thoroughly British. Bespoke
stationery sets come with a form and a sample so that recipients can
personalize their gift. Smythson also produces a small range of leather
handbags and purses. There are branches on Sloane Street within Harvey Nichols, Harrods, and even at Selfridges. ⊠ *40 New Bond St., Mayfair* ☎ *020/7629–8558* Ⓤ *Bond St., Green Park.*

Waterstone's. For book buying as a hedonistic leisure activity, the mon-
ster-size store near Piccadilly Circus caters to all tastes. Sip a gin-and-
tonic or get a bite while browsing through a book and admiring the view
from the top floor until 9 pm at the 5th View Bar & Food. Waterstone's
is the country's leading book chain, and they've pulled out all the stops
to make their flagship as comfortable and relaxed as a bookstore can be.
⊠ *203–206 Piccadilly, Mayfair* ☎ *020/7851–2400* ⊕ *www.waterstones.
com* Ⓤ *Piccadilly Circus.*

CERAMICS

Emma Bridgewater. Peruse this shop for fun and funky casual plates,
mugs, jugs, and breakfast tableware embellished with polka dots, hens,
hearts and flowers, amusing mottoes, or matter-of-fact labels (sugar or
coffee). Other locations include Fulham and Chiswick. ⊠ *81a Marylebone High St., Marylebone* ☎ *020/7486–6897* Ⓤ *Baker St.*

CLOTHING

Fodor'sChoice **Dover Street Market.** Visiting this six-floor emporium isn't just about
★ buying; with its arty displays and eccentric mix of merchandise, it is
as fascinating as any gallery. The creation of Comme des Garçons'
Rei Kawakubo, it showcases all of the label's collections for men and
women alongside other designers such as Lanvin, Alaïa, and exclusive
Japanese lines, plus curiosities including antique medical specimens,
avant-garde art books, and vintage couture. You never know what you
will find, which is half the fun. ■**TIP➜** An outpost of the Rose Bakery
on the top floor makes for a yummy break. ⊠ *17–18 Dover St., Mayfair* ☎ *020/7518–0680* ⊕ *www.doverstreetmarket.com* ☾ *Closed Sun.*
Ⓤ *Green Park.*

Choices, choices: there are plenty of prints—and much else—at the Portobello Road Market.

CLOTHING: MENSWEAR

★ **Ozwald Boateng.** Ozwald Boateng's (pronounced Bwa-teng) is one of the funkiest tailors working on Savile Row these days. His made-to-measure suits in eye-popping colors (even the more conservative suits sport bright silk linings), luxurious fabrics, and leading-edge styling have been worn by rock and club-land luminaries including Jamie Foxx, Mick Jagger, and Laurence Fishburne. ⊠ *30 Savile Row, Mayfair* ☎ *020/7440–5231* ⊕ *www.ozwaldboateng.co.uk* ⊙ *Closed Sun.* Ⓤ *Piccadilly Circus.*

★ **Turnbull & Asser.** This is *the* custom shirtmaker, dripping exclusivity from every fiber—after all, Prince Charles is a client and James Bond wore the shirts on film. At least 28 separate measurements are taken, and the cloth, woven to their specifications, comes in 1,000 different patterns—the cottons feel as good as silk. The first order must be for a minimum of six shirts, starting from £180 each. There are less expensive, though still exquisite, ready-to-wear shirts available as well as jackets, cashmeres, suits, ties, and accessories like pajamas perfect for the billionaire who has everything. ⊠ *71–72 Jermyn St., St. James's* ☎ *020/7808–3000* ⊕ *www.turnbullandasser.com* ⊙ *Closed Sun.* Ⓤ *Green Park.*

CLOTHING: WOMEN'S WEAR

★ **Browns.** This shop—actually a series of small shops on South Molton Street—was a pioneer designer boutique in the 1970s and continues to talent-spot the newest and best around. Browns also has its own label, a bargain outlet at No. 50, and a designer bridal boutique at 11–12 Hinde Street. There is also a smaller boutique at 6C Sloane Street, and another at 59 Book Street, off New Bond Street, which solely sells

2

shoes. ✉ *24–27 South Molton St., Mayfair* ☎ *020/7514–0000* ⊕ *www. brownsfashion.com* ☽ *Closed Sun.* Ⓤ *Bond St.*

Fenwick. A haven of realistically priced fashion, Fenwick is found in a shopping area where most things cost the earth. Five floors of chic clothes and accessories for men and women, lingerie, and home furnishings highlight lesser known and emerging designers from all over Europe. ✉ *163 New Bond St., Mayfair* ☎ *020/7629–9161* ⊕ *www. fenwick.co.uk* Ⓤ *Bond St.*

Vivienne Westwood. This is where it all started: the designer still represents the apex of high-style British couture. Head for the Conduit Street flagship for all the collections. The small Davies Street boutique sells only the Gold Label and made-to-measure couture. ✉ *44 Conduit St., Mayfair* ☎ *020/7439–1109* Ⓤ *Oxford Circus* ✉ *Original boutique, 430 King's Rd., Chelsea* ☎ *020/7352–6551* ☽ *Closed Sun.* Ⓤ *Sloane Sq.*

DEPARTMENT STORES

★ **Browns.** Launched in the 1970s, mini-department store Browns caters to the very label-conscious customer. You will find men's and women's fashion from Alexander McQueen and Marni and Chloe, as well as lesser-known designers like Nicholas Kirkwood and jewelry by Muriel Grateau. ✉ *24–27 South Molton St., Mayfair* ☎ *020/7514–0000* ⊕ *www.brownsfashion.com* Ⓤ *Bond St.*

Fodor's Choice
★ **Liberty.** With a wonderful black-and-white mock-Tudor facade, Liberty is a peacock among the chain-store pigeons on Regent Street. In the 19th century, Liberty's designers, leaders in the art nouveau and aesthetic movements, created classic fabric and home-furnishing designs. Those Liberty prints are still world famous today, and grace fashionable goods, from silk kimonos to embossed leather bags, wallets, and photo albums. Inside, the store is a labyrinth of nooks and crannies stuffed with goodies. Fashion, for men and women, focuses on high quality and beautiful fabric. ✉ *Regent St., Mayfair* ☎ *020/7734–1234* ⊕ *www. liberty.co.uk* Ⓤ *Oxford Circus.*

Marks & Spencer. You'd be hard-pressed to find a Brit who doesn't have something in their closet from Marks & Spencer (or "M&S" as it's affectionately known). It occasionally scores a fashion hit with its Per Una and Autograph lines, but the best buys are the classics, such as cashmere and wool sweaters, socks and underwear, and believe it or not, machine-washable suits. The food department at M&S is consistently superb, and a great place to pick up a sandwich or premade salad on the go. (Look for their M&S Simply Food stores all over town.) ✉ *458 Oxford St., Marylebone* ☎ *020/7935–7954* ⊕ *www.marksandspencer. com* Ⓤ *Marble Arch.*

Fodor's Choice
★ **Selfridges.** This giant, bustling store gives Harvey Nichols a run for its money as London's leading fashion department store. It's packed to the rafters with clothes for everyone in the family, from midprice lines to the latest catwalk names. The store continues to break ground with its striking modern design—especially the men's and women's high-fashion Superbrands sections, and the ground-floor Wonder Room, which showcases extravagant jewelry and luxury gifts. The frenetic cosmetics department is, according to the store, the largest in Europe.

■**TIP→** Take a break with a glass of wine from the Wonder Bar, or pick up some rare tea in the Food Hall as a gift. ✉ *400 Oxford St., Marylebone* ☎ *0800/123–400* ⊕ *www.selfridges.com* Ⓤ *Bond St.*

FOOD

Fortnum & Mason. Although it's the Queen's grocer, this store is, paradoxically, the most egalitarian of gift shops. It has plenty of irresistibly packaged luxury foods, stamped with the gold "By Appointment" crest, for less than £10, which make ideal gifts. The gleaming food hall spans two floors, and there's also a sleek wine bar designed by David Collins. The rest of the store is devoted to upscale gifts, toiletries, and housewares. Afternoon tea is also offered at the restaurants here. ✉ *181 Piccadilly, St. James's* ☎ *020/7734–8040* ⊕ *www.fortnumandmason. com* Ⓤ *Green Park.*

JEWELRY

★ **Asprey.** Exquisite jewelry and gifts are displayed in a discreet and very British environment at the "global flagship" store, designed by Lord Foster and British interior designer David Mlinaric. The setting oozes money, good taste, and comfort. If you're in the market for an immaculate 1930s cigarette case, a crystal vase, a lizard-bound diary, or a pair of pavé diamond and sapphire earrings, you won't be disappointed. Bespoke jewelry is available as well. ✉ *167 New Bond St., Mayfair* ☎ *020/7493–6767* ⊕ *www.asprey.com* Ⓤ *Green Park.*

★ **Kabiri.** A dazzling array of exciting contemporary jewelry by emerging and established designers from around the world is packed into this small shop. There is something to suit most budgets and tastes, from flamboyant statement pieces to subtle, delicate adornment. Look out for British talent Johanne Mills, Scott Stephen, and Tatty Devine, among many others. ✉ *37 Marylebone High St., Marylebone* ☎ *020/7224– 1808* ⊕ *www.kabiri.co.uk* Ⓤ *Baker St.*

SHOES

★ **Beatrix Ong.** This young designer trained under Jimmy Choo, and her collection is just as sexy and bold. Her Burlington Arcade shops sells a ready-to-wear collection of strappy sandals and stilettos, and brides-to-be are also well catered to. ✉ *200/206 Regent St., Mayfair* ☎ *020/979– 1100* ⊕ *www.beatrixong.com* Ⓤ *Oxford Circus.*

★ **Rupert Sanderson.** Designed in London and made in Italy, Sanderson's elegant shoes have been a huge hit in fashion circles. Ladylike styles, bright colors, smart details, and a penchant for peep toes are signature elements. Prices reflect the impeccable craftsmanship. There's now a tiny outpost next to Harrods at 2A Hans Road. ✉ *33 Bruton Pl., Mayfair* ☎ *0207/491–2220* ⊕ *www.rupertsanderson.com* ☉ *Closed Sun.* Ⓤ *Bond St., Green Park.*

SOHO AND COVENT GARDEN

BOOKS AND PRINTS

Fodor's Choice
★
Foyles. Today Foyles' five floors carry almost every title imaginable. The store stocks everything from popular fiction to military history, sheet music, medical tomes, opera scores, and fine arts. Store-within-a-store Ray's Jazz has a cool café. ⊠ *113–119 Charing Cross Rd., Soho* ☎ *020/7437–5660* Ⓤ *Tottenham Court Rd.* ⊠ *Royal Festival Hall, South Bank* ☎ *020/7437–5660* Ⓤ *Waterloo.*

★ **Grosvenor Prints.** London's largest collection of 17th- to early-20th-century prints includes a good selection of rare, early Americana. The main emphasis is on London views and architecture as well as sporting and decorative prints. It's an eccentric collection, with prices ranging from £5 into the thousands. ⊠ *19 Shelton St., Covent Garden* ☎ *020/7836–1979* ⊕ *www.grosvenorprints.com* ◷ *Closed Sun.* Ⓤ *Covent Garden.*

CLOTHING

★ **Paul Smith.** British classics with colorful and irreverent twists define Paul Smith's collections for both women and men. Beautifully tailored men's suits in exceptional fabrics might sport flamboyant linings or unusual detailing. Women's lines tend to take familiar and traditional British ideas and turn them on their heads with humor and color. ⊠ *40–44 Floral St., Covent Garden* ☎ *020/7379–7133* ⊕ *www.paulsmith.co.uk* Ⓤ *Covent Garden.*

CLOTHING: WOMEN'S WEAR

★ **Koh Samui.** Named for a Thai island resort, this shop stocks designer clothes for the kind of hip young woman who thinks nothing of flying there for a week's detox at the drop of a hat. ⊠ *65–67 Monmouth St., Covent Garden* ☎ *020/7240–4280* Ⓤ *Covent Garden.*

Office. Inexpensive but imaginative takes on catwalk looks are the stock in trade at this popular chain. Styles for men and women feature trend-conscious shapes and funky patterns and finishes. Upscale sibling stores Poste (⊠ *10 South Molton St.*) and Poste Mistress (⊠ *61–63 Monmouth St.*) stock cutting-edge designer shoes for men and women, respectively. ⊠ *57 Neal St., Covent Garden* ☎ *020/7379–1896* ⊕ *www.office.co.uk* Ⓤ *Covent Garden.*

Fodor's Choice
★
Topshop. Plenty of foreign fashion editors make Topshop their first port of call when visiting London for this standby has successfully made the transition from "cheap and cheerful" to genuine fashion hot spot (with mostly affordable prices). Clothing and accessories are geared to the younger, trendier end of the market; Topman brings the same fashion approach to clothing for men. ■TIP→ If the crowds become too much, head to one of the smaller Topshops in town, such as the Kensington High Street branch. ⊠ *214 Oxford St., Soho* ☎ *020/927–7634* ⊕ *www.topshop.com* Ⓤ *Oxford Circus* ⊠ *42–44 Kensington High St., Kensington* ☎ *020/7938–1242* Ⓤ *High Street Kensington.*

TOYS

Fodor's Choice ★ ☺ **Benjamin Pollock's Toyshop.** Robert Louis Stevenson was a fan who wrote, "If you love art, folly, or the bright eyes of children, speed to Pollock's." Magical toy theaters (most of the antique theaters or toy scenery now cost a fortune, but there are some nice "new" reproductions that are reasonable in cost) are the main stock in trade, but nostalgic puppets, mechanical toys, and paper dolls are also available. ⊠ *44 The Market, Covent Garden* ☎ *020/7379–7866* Ⓤ *Covent Garden.*

TOYS

Fodor's Choice ★ ☺ **Hamleys.** Every London child puts a trip to Hamleys at the top of his or her wish list. A Regent Street institution, the shop has demonstrations, a play area, a café, and every cool toy on the planet—as soon as it's launched. The huge stock, including six floors of toys and games for children and adults, ranges from traditional teddy bears to all the latest technological gimmickry. It's a mad rush at Christmastime, but Santa's grotto is one of the best in town. ⊠ *188–196 Regent St., Soho* ☎ *0871/704–1977* ⊕ *www.hamleys.com* Ⓤ *Oxford Circus, Piccadilly Circus.*

The Southeast

WORD OF MOUTH

"Brighton can be done by train. Also, I am not a twenty-something clubber and have enjoyed the area both as a child and as a forty-something adult. Kids love the seaside, and Brighton is quintessentially British, which is what most visitors to these shores are looking for."

—RM67

WELCOME TO THE SOUTHEAST

TOP REASONS TO GO

★ **Bodiam, Dover, Hever, and Herstmonceux castles:** Take your pick: the most evocative castles in a region filled with them dazzle you with their fortitude and fascinate you with their histories.

★ **Brighton:** With its nightclubs, sunbathing, and funky atmosphere, this is the quintessential modern English seaside city.

★ **Canterbury Cathedral:** This massive building, a textbook of medieval architecture, inspires awe with its soaring towers and flagstone corridors.

★ **Treasure houses:** Here is one of England's richest concentrations of historic homes: among the superlatives are Petworth House; sprawling Knole; Ightham Mote; and Chartwell.

★ **Amazing gardens:** Gardens of all kinds are an English specialty, and at Sissinghurst and Wisley, as well as in the gardens of Hever Castle and Chartwell, you can easily spend an entire afternoon wandering through acres of floral exotica.

1 Canterbury, Dover, and Environs. Dover's distinctive chalk-white cliffs plunging hundreds of feet into the sea are just a part of this region's dramatic coastal scenery. Don't miss Canterbury's medieval town center, dominated by its massive cathedral.

2 Rye, Lewes, and Environs. Medieval villages dot the hills along this stretch of Sussex coastline. The centerpiece is Rye, a pretty hill town of cobbled streets lined with timbered homes. Lewes, with its crumbling castle, is another gem.

GETTING ORIENTED

3

For sightseeing purposes, the Southeast can be divided into four sections. The eastern part of the region takes in the cathedral town of Canterbury, as well as the port city of Dover. The next section stretches along the southern coast from the medieval hill town of Rye to picturesque Lewes. A third area reaches from the coastal city of Brighton inward to Chichester and to sprawling Guildford. The fourth section takes in the spa town of Royal Tunbridge Wells and western Kent, where stately homes and castles dot the farmland. Larger towns in the area can be easily reached by train or bus from London for a day trip. To visit most castles, grand country homes, or quiet villages, though, you need to rent a car or join a tour.

3 Brighton, the Sussex Coast, and Surrey. Funky, lively Brighton perfectly melds Victorian architecture with a modern vibe that includes the best shopping and dining on the coast. Outside town are beautiful old homes such as Petworth House and even a Roman villa.

4 Tunbridge Wells and Environs. From Anne Boleyn's regal childhood abode at Hever Castle to the medieval manor at Ightham Mote, this area is rich with grand houses. Spend a couple of days exploring them; Tunbridge Wells is a comfortable base.

TEA TIME IN ENGLAND

Tea is often called the national drink, and for good reason. Most people start their day with "a cuppa," have tea breaks in the afternoon, and a cup after dinner. Join in by lifting a cup, or try a cream tea with a scone or a fancier formal afternoon tea.

Relaxing with tea and a scone with clotted cream and jam is a civilized pastime (above); cucumber sandwiches at afternoon tea (top right); tea store (right, bottom)

It's hard to imagine a time when tea wasn't part of English culture. But there was no tea in Europe until the 1600s, when Portuguese and Dutch traders began introducing it. Charles II and his wife, Catherine of Braganza, were tea drinkers. When coffeehouses in London began serving the drink in the mid-17th century, it was seen as an expensive curiosity. By the early 18th century tea was sold in coffeehouses all over the country, and consumed by all classes. The duchess of Bedford is credited with popularizing formal afternoon tea in the early 1800s. Dinner in those days was often not served until after 8 pm, so a light meal in late afternoon was welcome. The tradition faded when more people began working in offices in the 20th century—though the love of tea remains.

WHICH TEA?

England's most popular tea is English Breakfast tea, a full-bodied blend of black teas. Second in line is Earl Grey: oil of bergamot orange creates an elegant perfume, but it's an acquired taste. Assam is one of the major teas blended into English Breakfast, and it tastes similar, if a bit more brisk. By contrast, Darjeeling is light and delicate; it's perfect for afternoons.

3

CREAM TEA

In popular tourist areas in Britain, signs everywhere advertise "cream tea." This is the national shorthand for "tea and scones." The "cream" part is delectable clotted cream—a cream so thick it has a texture like whipped butter. Some scones are fruity and have raisins or dried cranberries; others are more like a cross between American biscuits and shortbread. Along with the cream, you'll usually be offered jam. It's customary to put both jam and cream on the scone, treating the cream like butter.

Cream teas are widely offered in areas favored by travelers, such as Stratford-upon-Avon, the Cotswolds, Devon, and Canterbury. In those regions you'll see it advertised in pubs, restaurants, and dedicated tea shops. Cream tea is a casual afternoon affair: think of it as a coffee break, with tea. Your tea will likely be a teabag rather than loose tea. The cost is usually from £3 to £7.

AFTERNOON TEA

A pricey treat reserved for vacations and special occasions, afternoon tea (called "high tea" in America, but not in England, where that term referred to a meal between 5 and 7 pm) is served in upscale hotels in London, but also in Oxford, Cambridge, and Brighton, or anywhere popular with travelers. Along with tea—and you can choose from a variety of teas—you'll be served finger sandwiches (cucumber, egg and watercress, and smoked salmon) and scones, as well as tiny cakes and pastries. These will usually be brought on tiered plate stands, with sweet options higher up and savory on the lower level.

Tea will be brewed in a china pot and served with china cups and saucers; milk and lemon are accompaniments.

Afternoon tea is generally offered between 3 and 5:30 pm and can last for hours. It's generally quite formal, and most people dress up for the occasion. Expect to spend from £17 to £50.

TEA IN THE SOUTHEAST

In Brighton, afternoon tea at the elegant **Grand Hotel** (⊠ *Kings Rd.* ☎ *01273/ 224300* ⊕ *www.grandbrighton.co.uk*) is a local tradition. Dress up to fit in. In Canterbury, afternoon tea at **Michael Caine's** at the Abode Hotel (⊠ *High St.* ☎ *01227/ 766266* ⊕ *www.abodehotels.co.uk*) has all the requisite teas, sandwiches, cakes and scones.

Very good cream teas are served in the tea rooms at all National Trust–run houses and gardens, as well as at most other historic estates open to the public. In the Southeast, the cafés at **Chartwell, Dover Castle, Knole, Wisley, Sissinghurst Castle Gardens,** and **Bodiam Castle** all offer excellent, affordable cream teas.

—*by Christi Daugherty*

TEA PALACE

Updated
by Christi
Daugherty

Surrey, Kent, and Sussex form the breadbasket of England, where bucolic farmland stretches as far as the eye can see. Once a favorite destination of English nobility, this region is rich with history, visible in the great castles and stately homes that dot the countryside. Its cities are similarly historic, especially ancient Canterbury, with its spectacular cathedral and medieval streets. Along the coast, funky seaside towns have a more relaxed attitude, especially artsy Brighton, where artists and musicians use the sea as inspiration for their work.

Although it is close to London (both Surrey and Kent reach all the way to London's suburbs) and is one of the most densely populated areas of Britain, the Southeast feels far away from the big city. In Kent, acres of orchards burst into a mass of pink-and-white blossoms in spring, while Dover's white cliffs and brooding castle have become symbols of Britain. Historic mansions, such as Petworth House and Knole, are major draws for travelers, and lush gardens such as Vita Sackville-West's Sissinghurst and the Royal Horticultural Society's Wisley attract thousands to their vivid floral displays.

Because the English Channel is at its narrowest here, a great deal of British history has been forged in the Southeast. The Romans landed in this area and stayed to rule Britain for four centuries. So did the Saxons—*Sussex* means "the land of the South Saxons." The biggest invasion of them all took place here when William ("the Conqueror") of Normandy defeated the Saxons at a battle near Hastings in 1066, changing the island forever.

SOUTHEAST PLANNER

WHEN TO GO

It's best to visit in spring, summer, or early fall. Many privately owned castles and mansions are open only between April and September or October. Failing that, the parks surrounding the stately houses are often open all year. If crowds tend to spoil your fun, avoid August, Sunday, and national holidays, particularly in Canterbury and the seaside towns.

PLANNING YOUR TIME

With the exception of Brighton, you can easily see the highlights of each of the towns in less than a day. Brighton has more to offer, and you should allot at least two days to take it all in. Consider basing yourself in one town while exploring a region. For example, you could stay in Brighton and take in Lewes on a day trip. Base yourself in Rye for a couple of days while exploring Winchelsea, Battle, Hastings, and Herstmonceux Castle. Tunbridge Wells is a great place to overnight if you plan on exploring the many stately homes and castles nearby.

GETTING HERE AND AROUND

AIR TRAVEL

Heathrow is very convenient for Surrey, but Gatwick Airport is a more convenient gateway for Kent. The rail station inside Gatwick has trains to Brighton and other major towns, and you can take a taxi from Heathrow to Guildford for around £40.

BUS TRAVEL

National Express buses serve the region from London's Victoria Coach Station. Trips to Brighton and Canterbury take two hours; to Chichester, about three hours. Megabus runs buses at budget prices from Victoria Coach Station to many of the same destinations as National Express and can be cheaper, although luggage limits are strict.

Bus service between towns can be useful but is often intermittent. Out in the country, don't expect buses more often than once every half hour or hour. Sometimes trains are a better option; sometimes they're much worse. Traveline is the best central place to call for bus information, and local tourist information centers can be a big help.

Contacts **Megabus** (⊕ *www.megabus.co.uk*).

National Express (☎ *0871/781–8181* ⊕ *www.nationalexpress.com*).
Traveline (☎ *0871/200–2233* ⊕ *www.traveline.org.uk*).

CAR TRAVEL

Traveling by car is the best way to get to the stately homes and castles in the region. Having a car in Canterbury or Brighton, however, is a nuisance; you'll need to park and walk. Major routes radiating outward from London to the Southeast are, from west to east, M23/A23 to Brighton (52 mi); A21, passing by Royal Tunbridge Wells to Hastings (65 mi); A20/M20 to Folkestone (58 mi); and A2/M2 via Canterbury (56 mi) to Dover (71 mi).

TRAIN TRAVEL

Trains are the fastest and most efficient way to travel to major cities in the region, but they do not stop in many small towns. From London, Southeastern trains serve Sussex and Kent from Victoria and Charing Cross stations, and South West trains travel to Surrey from Waterloo Station. Getting to Brighton takes about 1 hour, to Canterbury about 1½ hours, and to Dover almost 2 hours. A Network Railcard costing £25, valid throughout the southern and southeastern regions for a year, entitles you and three companions to one-third off many off-peak fares.

Contacts **National Rail Enquiries** (☎ *0845/748–4950* ⊕ *www.nationalrail. co.uk/railcard*). **Network Railcard** (⊕ *www.railcard.co.uk*).

RESTAURANTS

If you're in a seaside town, look for that great British staple, fish-and-chips. Perhaps "look" isn't the word—just follow your nose. On the coast, seafood, much of it locally caught, is a specialty. Try local smoked fish (haddock and mackerel), or the succulent local oysters. Inland, sample fresh local lamb and beef. In cities such as Brighton and Tunbridge Wells there are numerous restaurants and cafés, but out in the countryside your options will be limited largely to pubs.

HOTELS

All around the coast, resort towns stretch along beaches, their hotels standing cheek by jowl. Of the smaller hotels and guesthouses only a few remain open year-round; most do business only from mid-April to September or October. Some hotels have all-inclusive rates for a week's stay. Prices rise in July and August, when the seaside resorts can get solidly booked, especially Brighton. (On the other hand, hotels may drop rates by up to 40% off season.) Places in Brighton may not take a booking for a single night in summer or on weekends.

WHAT IT COSTS IN POUNDS					
	£	££	£££	££££	£££££
Restaurants	under £10	£10–£14	£15–£19	£20–£25	over £25
Hotels	under £70	£70–£120	£121–£160	£161–£220	over £220

Restaurant prices are per person for a main course or equivalent combination of smaller dishes at dinner excluding tax. Hotels prices reflect the rack rate of a standard double room for two people in high season, including 20% V.A.T. Check online for off-season rates and special deals or discounts.

VISITOR INFORMATION

Tourist boards in the main towns can help with information, and many will also book local accommodations.

Contacts **Southeast England Tourist Board** (☎ *023/8062–5400* ⊕ *www.visitsoutheastengland.com*).

CANTERBURY, DOVER, AND ENVIRONS

The cathedral city of Canterbury is an ancient place that has attracted travelers since the 12th century. Its magnificent cathedral, the Mother Church of England, remains a powerful draw. Even in prehistoric times, this part of England was relatively well settled. Saxon settlers, Norman conquerors, and the folk who lived here in late-medieval times all left their mark. From Canterbury there's rewarding wandering to be done in the gentle Kentish countryside between the city and the busy port of Dover. Here the landscape ravishes the eye in spring with apple blossoms, and in autumn with lush fields ready for harvest. It is a county of orchards, market gardens, and round oasthouses with their tilted, pointed roofs; they were once used for drying hops, but now many are pricey homes.

CANTERBURY

56 mi southeast of London.

Just mention Canterbury, and most people are taken back to memories of high-school English classes and Geoffrey Chaucer's *Canterbury Tales,* about medieval pilgrims making their way to Canterbury Cathedral. Judging from the tales, however, in those days Canterbury was as much a party town as it was a spiritual center.

The city has been the seat of the Primate of All England, the archbishop of Canterbury, since Pope Gregory the Great dispatched St. Augustine to convert the heathen hordes of Britain in 597. The height of Canterbury's popularity came in the 12th century, when thousands of pilgrims flocked here to see the shrine of the murdered archbishop St. Thomas à Becket. This southeastern town became one of the most visited in England, if not Europe. Buildings that served as pilgrims' inns (and that survived World War II bombing of the city) still dominate the streets of Canterbury's center, though it's tourists who flock to this city of about 40,000 people today.

Budget problems have caused prices at city museums to skyrocket. If you plan to see more than one, stop in at the tourist office to find out if a combination ticket might be cheaper.

GETTING HERE AND AROUND

The fastest way to reach Canterbury from London is by train. Southeastern trains to Canterbury run every half hour in peak times from London's Charing Cross Station. The journey takes around 1½ hours. Canterbury has two centrally located train stations, Canterbury East Station (a 5-minute walk from the cathedral square) and Canterbury West Station (a 10-minute walk from the cathedral).

National Express and Megabus buses bound for Canterbury depart several times a day from London's Victoria Coach Station. Trips to Canterbury take around two hours, and drop passengers near the train stations. If you're driving, take the A2/M2 to Canterbury from London (56 mi). Park in one of the signposted parking lots at the edge of the town center.

Canterbury has a small, walkable town center. Although the town has good local bus service, you're unlikely to need it. Most major tourist sites are on one street that changes name three times—beginning as St. George's Street and then becoming High Street and St. Peter's Street.

Canterbury Guild of Guides provides walking tours with expert guides. Tours (£6) are at 11 am every day between Easter and October, with an additional tour at 2 pm in July and August. VisitBritain offers an MP3 tour of Canterbury (£5) that you can download from its Web site.

TIMING
The town tends to get crowded around religious holidays—particularly Easter weekend—and on other national holiday weekends. If you'd rather avoid the tour buses, try visiting midweek.

ESSENTIALS
Visitor and Tour Information Canterbury (✉ 12–13 Sun St. ☎ 01227/378100 ⊕ www.canterbury.co.uk).

Canterbury Guild of Guides (✉ Arnett House, Hawks La. ☎ 01227/459779 ⊕ www.canterbury-walks.co.uk) **VisitBritain.** ⊕ www.visitbritain.com).

EXPLORING
TOP ATTRACTIONS
Fodor's Choice
★
Canterbury Cathedral. The focal point of the city was the first of England's great Norman cathedrals. Nucleus of worldwide Anglicanism, the Cathedral Church of Christ Canterbury (its formal name) is a living textbook of medieval architecture. The building was begun in 1070, demolished, begun anew in 1096, and then systematically expanded over the next three centuries. When the original choir section burned to the ground in 1174, another replaced it, designed in the new Gothic style, with tall, pointed arches. The cathedral is popular, so arrive early or late in the day to avoid the crowds. You can just walk around, or you can buy a guidebook with an overview of the building's history, use an audio guide for the most detail, or take a tour.

The cathedral was only a century old, and still relatively small, when Thomas à Becket, the archbishop of Canterbury, was murdered here in 1170. Becket, a defender of ecclesiastical interests, had angered his friend Henry II, who was heard to exclaim, "Who will rid me of this troublesome priest?" Thinking they were carrying out the king's wishes, four knights burst in on Becket in one of the side chapels and killed him. Two years later Becket was canonized, and Henry II's subsequent submission to the authority of the Church, and his penitence helped establish the cathedral as the center of English Christianity.

Becket's tomb, destroyed by Henry VIII in 1538 as part of his campaign to reduce the power of the Church and confiscate its treasures, was one of the most extravagant shrines in Christendom. In **Trinity Chapel,** which held the shrine, you can still see a series of 13th-century stained-glass windows illustrating Becket's miracles. So hallowed was this spot that in 1376, Edward, the Black Prince, warrior son of Edward III and a national hero, was buried near it. The actual site of Becket's murder is down a flight of steps just to the left of the nave. In the corner, a second flight of steps leads down to the enormous Norman **undercroft,** or

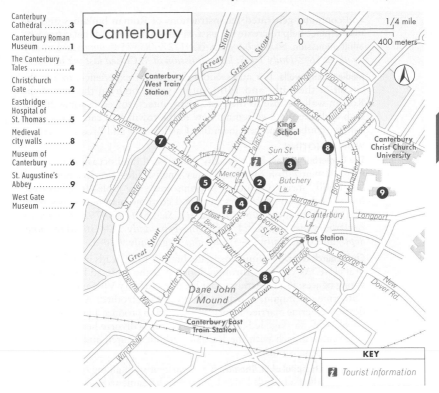

Canterbury

Canterbury
West Train
Station

Kings
School

Sun St.

Canterbury
Christ Church
University

Mercery La.

Butchery La.

Hawk's La.

Beer Court La.

Canterbury La.

Bus Station

Dane John Mound

Canterbury East Train Station

3

KEY

Tourist information

vaulted cellarage, built in the early 12th century. A row of squat pillars whose capitals dance with animals and monsters supports the roof.

If time permits, explore the **cloisters** and the small monastic buildings to the north of the cathedral. The 12th-century octagonal water tower is still part of the cathedral's water supply. The Norman staircase in the northwest corner of the Green Court dates from 1167 and is a unique example of the architecture of the times. ⊠ *Cathedral Precincts* ☎ *01227/762862* ⊕ *www.canterbury-cathedral.org* 🎟 *£9, free for services and ½ hr before closing; £5 for tour; £3.50 for audio guide* ⊙ *Easter–Sept., Mon.–Sat. 9–5:30, Sun. 12:30–2:30; Oct.–Easter, Mon.–Sat. 9–5, Sun. 12:30–2:30. Last entry ½ hr before closing. Restricted access during services.*

QUICK BITES

The Custard Tart (⊠ *35A St. Margaret's St.* ☎ *01227/785178*), a short walk from the cathedral, serves freshly made sandwiches, pies, tarts, and cakes, along with steaming cups of tea and coffee. You can take your choice upstairs to the seating area. It's not open for dinner.

Canterbury Roman Museum. Belowground, at the level of the remnants of Roman Canterbury, this museum features colorful mosaic Roman pavement and a hypocaust—the Roman version of central heating. Displays of excavated objects (some of which you can hold in the Touch the Past area) and computer-generated reconstructions of Roman buildings and the marketplace help re-create the past. ■ **TIP→** Up to four kids get in free with adult admission. ✉ *Butchery La.* ☎ *01227/785575* ⊕ *www.canterbury. co.uk* 🎫 *£6* ⊙ *Daily 10–5; last admission at 4. Closed last wk in Dec.*

Medieval city walls. For an essential Canterbury experience, follow the circuit of the 13th- and 14th-century walls, built on the line of the Roman walls. Those to the east survive intact, towering some 20 feet high and offering a sweeping view of the town. You can access these from a number of places, including Castle Street and Broad Street.

WORTH NOTING

☺ **The Canterbury Tales.** It's a kitschy audiovisual (and occasionally olfactory) dramatization of 14th-century English life—touristy but popular. You'll "meet" Chaucer's pilgrims and view tableaus illustrating five tales. In summer, actors in period costume play out scenes from the town's history. ✉ *St. Margaret's St.* ☎ *01227/479227* ⊕ *www. canterburytales.org.uk* 🎫 *£8* ⊙ *Nov.–Feb., daily 10–4:30; Mar.–June, Sept., and Oct., daily 10–5; July and Aug., daily 9:30–5.*

Christchurch Gate. This immense gate, built in 1517, leads into the cathedral close. As you pass through, look up at the sculpted heads of two young figures: Prince Arthur, elder brother of Henry VIII, and the young Catherine of Aragon, to whom Arthur was betrothed. After Arthur's death, Catherine married Henry. Her failure to produce a male heir after 25 years of marriage led to Henry's decision to divorce her, creating an irrevocable breach with the Roman Catholic Church and altering the course of English history.

Eastbridge Hospital of St. Thomas. The 12th-century building (which would now be called a hostel) lodged pilgrims who came to pray at the tomb of Thomas à Becket. It's a tiny place, fascinating in its simplicity. The refectory, the chapel, and the crypt are open to the public. ✉ *25 High St.* ☎ *01227/471668* ⊕ *www.eastbridgehospital.org.uk* 🎫 *£1* ⊙ *Mon.–Sat. 10–5; last admission at 4:30.*

☺ **Museum of Canterbury.** The medieval Poor Priests' Hospital is the site of this local museum, where exhibits provide an overview of the city's history and architecture from Roman times to World War II. It's a quirky place that covers everything and everyone associated with the town, including the Blitz, the mysterious death of the 16th-century writer Christopher Marlowe, and the British cartoon characters Bagpuss and Rupert Bear. Kids get in free with their parents. ✉ *20 Stour St.* ☎ *01227/475202* ⊕ *www.canterbury.co.uk* 🎫 *£8* ⊙ *Daily 10–5; last admission at 4.*

St. Augustine's Abbey. Augustine, England's first Christian missionary, was buried here in 597, at one of the oldest monastic sites in the country. The site remained intact for nearly 1,000 years, until Henry VIII seized the abbey in the 16th century, destroying some of the original buildings and converting others into a royal manor for his fourth wife, Anne of Cleves. It's now made up of beautiful ruins that give a good idea of what it must have looked like when it was intact. A free audio tour vividly puts events into context. ✉ *Longport* ☎ *01227/378100* ⊕ *www.english-heritage.org.uk* 🎫 *£4.80* ⊙ *Apr.–June, Wed.–Sun. 10–5; July and Aug., daily 10–6; Sept.–Mar., Sun. 11–5.*

Impressive both inside and out, ancient Canterbury Cathedral dominates the town.

West Gate Museum. In medieval times, Canterbury had seven gatehouses guarding entry to the city, but only this one survives, complete with its twin castelled towers. It contains a small museum with medieval bric-a-brac and armaments once used by the city guard, as well as more-contemporary weaponry. The building became a jail in the 14th century, and you can view the tiny prison cells. ■TIP➔ Climb to the roof for a panoramic view of the city. ⊠ *St. Peter's St.* ☎ *01227/789576* ⊕ *www.canterbury.co.uk* ✉ *£4* ☉ *Tues.–Sun. 11–12:30 and 1:30–3:30.*

WHERE TO EAT

£ ✕ **City Fish Bar.** Long lines and lots of satisfied finger-licking attest to
BRITISH the deserved popularity of this excellent fish-and-chips outlet in the center of town. Everything is freshly fried, the batter crisp and the fish tasty; the fried mushrooms are also surprisingly good. There's no seating, so your fish is wrapped up in paper and you eat it where you want, perhaps in the park. This place closes at 7. ⊠ *30 St. Margaret's St.* ☎ *01227/760873* ▭ *No credit cards.*

£££ ✕ **The Goods Shed.** Next to Canterbury West Station, this vaulted wooden
BRITISH space with stone-and-brick walls was a storage shed in Victorian times. Now it's a farmers' market with a restaurant that has wooden tables and huge arched windows overlooking the market and a butchers' stall. It's well known for offering fresh Kentish food—from locally caught fish and smoked meats to local cider and bread baked in-house. Whatever is fresh that day appears on the menu, whether it's grilled bass with brown shrimp or roasted goose with turnips and prunes. The food is reliably good, but service is slow. ⊠ *Station Rd. W.* ☎ *01227/459153* ⊕ *www.thegoodsshed.net* ☉ *Closed Mon. No dinner Sun.*

££££ ✗ **Michael Caines.** Canterbury's most sought-after tables are at Michael
MODERN FRENCH Caines (named not for the actor, but for the chef with a similar name).
Fodor's Choice This light-filled eatery in the trendy Abode Canterbury, with its pine
★ tables, white walls, and sophisticated country style, packs in the foodies. Modern French cuisine is the main attraction—true aficionados will
reserve the chef's table in the kitchen to watch the staff in action. Dishes
change weekly but look for treats such as panfried red mullet with
aubergine caviar, roasted scallops with vanilla parsnip puree, or roasted
sirloin of Kentish beef with truffle potatoes. The seven-course tasting
menu (£68) is great for special occasions. There's a glass-enclosed wine
room and an adjoining champagne bar, ensuring that the wine is as good
as the food. ⊠ *30–33 High St.* ☎ *01227/766266* ⊕ *www.michaelcaines.
com* ⌲ *Reservations essential.*

££ ✗ **Old Brewery Tavern.** Although it's part of a hotel, this pub has a sepa-
BRITISH rate entrance leading to a room with polished floors, wooden tables,
and whitewashed stone. The menu and kitchen are overseen by top chef
Michael Caines, so it's a good place to try his food at a more reasonable price (a two-course lunch is £10). The atmosphere is relaxed and
casual, except on weekend nights when the music gets turned up for the
party crowd. Expect reliably good comfort food—juicy burgers, crispy
fish-and-chips, or sirloin steak grilled to order. The courtyard is perfect
for alfresco dining. ⊠ *Abode Canterbury, High St.* ☎ *01227/826682*
⊕ *www.michaelcaines.com.*

££ ✗ **Old Buttermarket.** A colorful, friendly old pub near the cathedral, the
BRITISH Buttermarket is a great place to grab a hearty lunch, including consistently tasty meat pies. There's been a pub on this site for more than
500 years, so although the current building is a few hundred years
younger than that, it's carrying on a fine tradition. You can indulge in
a fresh English ale from the changing selection while sampling a creamy
chicken and leek pie or a steaming steak and ale pie. Other choices
are fish-and-chips and wild mushroom–and–pea risotto. ⊠ *39 Burgate*
☎ *01227/462170* ⊕ *www.nicholsonspubs.co.uk.*

WHERE TO STAY
For expanded reviews, visit Fodors.com.

££–£££ ⊟ **Abode Canterbury.** This glossy boutique hotel inside the old city
HOTEL walls offers an up-to-date style in traditional Canterbury. **Pros:** central
location; luxurious handmade beds; great restaurants and bars. **Cons:**
one of the priciest hotels in town; bar gets quite crowded. ⊠ *High St.*
☎ *01227/766266* ⊕ *www.abodehotels.co.uk* ⌁ *73 rooms* ⌂ *In-room:
a/c, Internet. In-hotel: restaurants, bar, parking.*

££ ⊟ **Canterbury Cathedral Lodge.** Small and modern, this hotel tucked
HOTEL away within the grounds of the cathedral has quiet, soothingly decorated rooms with white walls and exposed oak trim. **Pros:** outstanding location; incredible views; free access to the cathedral. **Cons:** no
restaurant; few services. ⊠ *The Precincts* ☎ *01227/865350* ⊕ *www.
canterburycathedrallodge.org* ⌁ *35 rooms* ⌂ *In-room: no a/c, Wi-Fi*
⏻⏽ *Breakfast.*

££ ⊟ **Ebury Hotel.** Family-run, this hotel earns raves for its laid-back atti-
HOTEL tude and comfortable accommodations inside two big Victorian buildings. **Pros:** cozy lounge; comfortable rooms. **Cons:** a bit of a walk to the

town center; no elevator. ⊠ *65–67 New Dover Rd.* ☎*01227/768433* ⊕ *www.ebury-hotel.co.uk* ↪*15 rooms* ♿ *In-room: no a/c. In-hotel: restaurant, bar, pool* ⦿*Breakfast.*

£££–££ **B&B/INN**

🖫 **Magnolia House.** A lovely walled garden enhances this bed-and-breakfast in a Georgian house, where the bedrooms have floral motifs and traditional furnishings. **Pros:** adorable house; friendly atmosphere. **Cons:** a bit of a walk to the town center; some rooms are small; no elevator. ⊠*36 St. Dunstan's Terr.* ☎*01227/765121* ⊕ *www. magnoliahousecanterbury.co.uk* ↪*7 rooms* ♿ *In-room: no a/c, Wi-Fi. In-hotel: some age restrictions* ⦿*Breakfast.*

££ **B&B/INN**

🖫 The White House. Reputed to have been the place in which Queen Victoria's head coachman came to live upon retirement, this handsome Regency building sits on a quiet road off St. Peter's Street. **Pros:** historic house; spacious rooms; family-friendly atmosphere. **Cons:** a bit outside the center; no restaurant; no elevator. ⊠*6 St. Peter's La.* ☎*01227/761836* ⊕ *www.canterburybreaks.co.uk* ↪*9 rooms* ♿ *In-room: no a/c, Wi-Fi. In-hotel: bar* ⊟*No credit cards* ⦿*Breakfast.*

NIGHTLIFE AND THE ARTS

NIGHTLIFE Canterbury is home to a popular university, and the town's many pubs and bars are busy, often crowded with college-age folks.

Alberry's Wine Bar (⊠*St. Margaret's St.* ☎*01227/452378*), with late-night jazz and hip-hop and a trendy crowd, is the coolest place in town.

The **Parrot** (⊠*3–9 Church La.* ☎*01227/762355*) is a pub known for its real ales—at least six kinds are available at any time—and its convivial setting in an old wood-beam building.

Thomas Becket (⊠*21 Best La.* ☎*01227/464384*), a traditional English pub, has a fire crackling in winter, copper pots hanging from the ceiling, and a friendly crowd. It serves good pub lunches.

THE ARTS The two-week-long, mixed-arts **Canterbury Festival** (☎*01227/452853* ⊕ *www.canterburyfestival.co.uk*) fills the town with color and music every October.

The **Gulbenkian Theatre** (⊠*Giles La.* ☎*01227/769075*), outside the town center at the University of Kent, mounts all kinds of plays, particularly experimental works, and is a venue for dance performances, concerts, comedy shows, and films.

The **New Marlowe** (⊠*St. Margaret's St.* ☎*01227/787787*) reopened in 2011 after a massive renovation, has great sight lines and excellent acoustics. Expect popular and innovative theater and music.

SHOPPING

Canterbury's medieval streets are lined with shops, perfect for an afternoon of rummaging. The best are in the district just around the cathedral. The King's Mile, which stretches past the cathedral and down Palace Street and Northgate, is a good place to start.

925 (⊠*57 Palace St.* ☎*01227/785699*) has a great selection of handmade silver jewelry.

Burgate Antiques (⊠*23 Palace St.* ☎*01227/456500*) is a rambling shop full of fine British and French antiques, mostly Georgian and Victorian, with both high-end and less expensive selections. It's a great place to nose around on a rainy day.

Crowthers of Canterbury (✉ *1 The Borough* ☎ *01227/763965*) is for music lovers, as it carries an extensive selection of musical instruments, gifts, and sheet music.

Hawkin's Bazaar (✉ *34 Burgate* ☎ *01227/785809*) carries an exceptional selection of traditional and modern toys and games.

BROADSTAIRS

17 mi east of Canterbury.

Like other Victorian seaside towns such as Margate and Ramsgate on this stretch of coast, Broadstairs was once the playground of vacationing Londoners. Today grand 19th-century houses line the waterfront. In the off-season Broadstairs is peaceful, but day-trippers pack the town in July and August.

Park your car in one of the town lots, and strike out for the crescent beach or wander down the residential Victorian streets. Make your way down to the amusement pier and try your hand in one of the game arcades. You can grab fish-and-chips to go and eat it on the beach.

Charles Dickens spent many summers in Broadstairs between 1837 and 1851 and wrote glowingly of its bracing freshness. During 2012, the 200th anniversary of his birth, many local activities are planned.

GETTING HERE AND AROUND

By car, Broadstairs is about a two-hour drive (78 mi) from London, off A256 on the southeast tip of England. Trains run from London's St. Pancras Station to Broadstairs once an hour; it's a 90-minute trip. Broadstairs Station is off The Broadway in the town center. National Express buses travel to Broadstairs from London several times a day; the journey takes about three hours.

ESSENTIALS

Visitor Information Broadstairs (✉ *6B High St.* ☎ *01843/862242* ⊕ *www.visitbroadstairs.co.uk*).

EXPLORING

Dickens House Museum. This house was originally the home of Mary Pearson Strong, on whom Dickens based the character of Betsey Trotwood, David Copperfield's aunt. Dickens lived here from 1837 to 1839 while writing *The Pickwick Papers* and *Oliver Twist*. Some rooms have been decorated to look as they would have in Dickens's day, and there's a reconstruction of Miss Trotwood's room as described by Dickens. ✉ *2 Victoria Parade* ☎ *01843/861232* ⊕ *www.dickensfellowship.org* 🖼 *£3.50* 🕐 *Apr.–Oct., daily 2–5.*

WHERE TO STAY

For expanded reviews, visit Fodors.com.

£–££
HOTEL
📷 **Number 68.** Charming decor and a friendly atmosphere are the pluses of this sweet Edwardian house a five-minute walk from central Broadstairs. **Pros:** close to the sea; tasty breakfasts; free Wi-Fi. **Cons:** minimum stay required; tough cancellation policy. ✉ *68 West*

Cliff Rd. ☎ *01843/609459* ⊕ *www. number68.co.uk* ⌐3 *rooms* ⚒ *In-room: no a/c, Wi-Fi. In-hotel: some age restrictions* ⊟ *No credit cards* ⍥ *Breakfast.*

NIGHTLIFE AND THE ARTS
Each June Broadstairs holds a **Dickens Festival** (☎ *01843/861827* ⊕ *www.broadstairsdickensfestival. co.uk*), lasting about a week, with readings, people in Dickensian costume, a Dickensian cricket match, a Victorian bathing party, and vaudeville, among other entertainments.

3

DEAL

18 mi south of Broadstairs.

The large seaside town of Deal, known for its castle, is famous in history books as the place where Caesar's legions landed in 55 BC, and it was from here that William Penn set sail in 1682 on his first journey to the American colony he founded, Pennsylvania.

GETTING HERE AND AROUND
Southeastern trains travel to Deal every 30 minutes from London's St. Pancras Station. The journey takes 90 minutes. You can also hop aboard a National Express bus from London's Victoria Coach Station, but the trip takes about an hour longer.

ESSENTIALS
Visitor Information Deal Tourist Information Centre (✉ *Landmark Centre, High St.* ☎ *01304/369576* ⊕ *www.deal.gov.uk*).

EXPLORING
Deal Castle. Erected in 1540 and intricately built to the shape of a Tudor rose, Deal Castle is the largest of the coastal defenses constructed by Henry VIII. A moat surrounds its gloomy passages and austere walls. The castle museum has exhibits about prehistoric, Roman, and Saxon Britain. ✉ *Victoria Rd.* ☎ *01304/372762* ⊕ *www.english-heritage.org. uk* ⌐*£4.80* ⊗ *Apr.–Sept., daily 10–6.*

Walmer Castle and Gardens. One of Henry VIII's fortifications, this castle was converted in 1708 into a residence for the lord warden. Made up of four round towers around a circular keep, the castle has sprawling lavender gardens with gorgeous ocean views. Among its famous lord wardens were William Pitt the Younger; the duke of Wellington, hero of the Battle of Waterloo, who lived here from 1829 until his death here in 1852 (a small museum contains memorabilia); and Sir Winston Churchill. The drawing and dining rooms are open to the public except when the lord warden is in residence. ✉ *A258, 1 mi south of Deal* ☎ *01304/364288* ⊕ *www.english-heritage.org.uk* ⌐*£7.30* ⊗ *Mar. and Oct., Wed.–Sun. 10–4; Apr.–Sept., daily 10–6.*

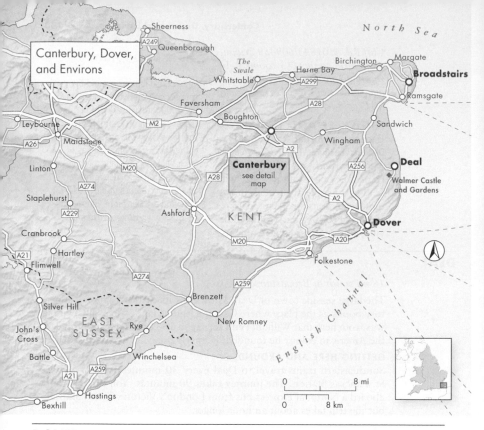

Canterbury, Dover,
and Environs

DOVER

8 mi south of Deal, 78 mi east of London.

The busy passenger port of Dover has for centuries been Britain's gateway to Europe and is known for the famous white cliffs. You may find the town itself disappointing; the savage bombardments of World War II and the shortsightedness of postwar developers left the city center an unattractive place. Roman legacies include a lighthouse adjoining a stout Anglo-Saxon church.

GETTING HERE AND AROUND

National Express buses depart from London's Victoria Coach Station for Dover every hour and a half. The journey takes about two hours and 40 minutes. Drivers from London take the M20, which makes a straight line south to Dover. The 76-mi journey should take around two hours. Southeastern trains leave London's Charing Cross Station every 20 minutes or so for Dover Priory Station in Dover. The trip is an hour and 45 minutes.

For the best views of the cliffs, you need a car or taxi; it's a long way to walk from town.

ESSENTIALS

Visitor Information Dover (✉ *The Old Town Gaol, Biggin St.* ☎ *01304/205108* ⊕ *www.whitecliffscountry.org.uk*).

EXPLORING

☺ ★ **Dover Castle.** Spectacular and with plenty to explore, Dover Castle, towering high above the ramparts of the white cliffs, is a mighty medieval castle that has served as an important strategic center over the centuries, even in World War II. Most of the castle, including the keep, dates to Norman times. It was begun by Henry II in 1181 but incorporates additions from almost every succeeding century. There's a lot to see besides the castle rooms, and many of the exhibits will appeal to kids, including the Siege of 1216, the Princess of Wales Regimental Museum, and Castle Fit for a King. ■**TIP→** Tour the secret wartime tunnels, a medieval and Napoleonic-era system that was used again during World War II. ✉ *Castle Rd.* ☎ *01304/211067* ⊕ *www.english-heritage. org.uk* ☑ *£16* ⊘ *Feb. and Mar., daily 10–4; Apr.–Sept., daily 10–6; Oct., daily 10–5; Nov.–Jan., Thurs.–Mon. 10–4.*

Roman Painted House. Believed to have been a hotel, this structure includes some Roman wall paintings, along with the remnants of an ingenious heating system. ✉ *New St.* ☎ *01304/203279* ⊕ *www. theromanpaintedhouse.co.uk* ☑ *£3* ⊘ *Apr.–Sept., Tues.–Sat. 10–5, Sun. 1–5.*

★ **White Cliffs.** Plunging hundreds of feet into the sea, Dover's chalk-white cliffs are an inspirational site and a symbol of England. They stay white because of the natural process of erosion. Because of this, you must be cautious when walking along the cliffs—experts recommend staying at least 20 feet from the edge. The best places to see the cliffs are at Samphire Hoe, St. Margaret's Bay, or East Cliff & Warren Country Park. Signs will direct you from the roads to scenic spots. ■**TIP→** The visitor center at Langdon Cliffs has 5 mi of walking trails with some spectacular views.

WHERE TO STAY

For expanded reviews, visit Fodors.com.

£–££
HOTEL

🏨 **Premier Inn Dover.** By the waterfront, this modern hotel has spacious, quiet rooms and a handy restaurant and bar. **Pros:** affordable rates; great location. **Cons:** busy neighborhood; hotel restaurant is only so-so. ✉ *Marine Court, Marine Parade* ☎ *0871/527–8306* ⊕ *www.premierinn. com* 🛏 *100 rooms* ♿ *In-room: no a/c, Wi-Fi. In-hotel: restaurant, parking* ¶◯¶ *Breakfast.*

HENRY VIII'S CASTLES

Why did Henry VIII rapidly (1539–42) build sturdy forts along the southern coast? After enraging the pope and Europe's Catholic monarchs with his marriages and by seizing control of the wealthy monasteries, he prepared for an impending French invasion. (It never came.) Today you can bike or walk along the beachfront between Deal and Walmer castles.

3

The majestic White Cliffs of Dover are a national icon.

RYE, LEWES, AND ENVIRONS

From Dover the coast road winds west through Folkestone (a genteel resort, small port, and Channel Tunnel terminal), across Romney Marsh (famous for its sheep and, at one time, its ruthless smugglers), and on to the delightful medieval town of Rye. The region along the coast is noted for Winchelsea, the history-rich sites of Hastings, Herstmonceux, and Bodiam, and the Glyndebourne Opera House festival, based outside Lewes, a town celebrated for its architectural heritage. One of the three steam railroads in the Southeast services part of the area: the Romney, Hythe, and Dymchurch Railway.

RYE

68 mi southeast of London, 34 mi southwest of Dover.

★ With cobbled streets and ancient timbered dwellings, Rye is an artist's dream. It was an important port town until the harbor silted up and the waters retreated more than 150 years ago; now the nearest harbor is 2 mi away. Virtually every building in the little town center is intriguingly historic. Rye is known for its many antiques stores and also for its sheer pleasantness. This place can be easily walked without a map, but the local tourist office has an interesting audio tour of the town as well as maps.

GETTING HERE AND AROUND
If you're driving to Rye, take the M20 to A2070. There's no direct route by train; take a Southeastern train from Charing Cross or Victoria Station to Ashford and change for the Rye train, which runs every hour or so.

ESSENTIALS

Visitor Information Rye (⊠ *The Heritage Centre, Strand Quay* ☎ *01797/226696* ⊕ *www.rye-tourism.co.uk*).

EXPLORING

TOP ATTRACTIONS

★ **Bodiam Castle.** Immortalized in paintings, postcards, and photographs, the ruins of Bodiam Castle rise out of the distance like a piece of medieval legend. Its turrets, battlements, wooden portcullis, glassy moat, and 2-foot-thick walls survive, but all that was within them is long gone. Built in 1385 to withstand a threatened French invasion, it was "slighted" (partly demolished) during the English Civil War of 1642–46 and has been uninhabited ever since. Still, you can climb the towers to take in sweeping countryside views, and kids can run around the castle. The castle, 12 mi west of Rye, schedules organized activities for kids during school holidays. ⊠ *Off B2244, Bodiam* ☎ *01580/830196* ⊕ *www.nationaltrust.org.uk* ⊒ *£6* ⊙ *Mid-Feb.–Oct., daily 10:30–5; Nov. and Dec., Wed.–Sun. 11–4 or dusk; Jan.–mid-Feb., weekends 11–4; last admission 1 hr before closing.*

Church of St. Mary the Virgin. At the top of the hill at the center of Rye, this classic English village church is more than 900 years old and encompasses a number of architectural styles. The turret clock dates to 1561 and still keeps excellent time. Its huge pendulum swings inside the church nave. ■ **TIP →** Climb the tower for amazing views of the surrounding area. ⊠ *Church Sq.* ⊙ *Daily 10–4.*

★ **Great Dixter House and Gardens.** Combining a large timber-frame hall with a cottage garden on a grand scale, this place will get your green thumbs twitching. The house dates to 1464 (you can tour a few rooms) and was restored in 1910 by architect Edwin Lutyens, who also designed the garden. From these beginnings, the late horticulturist and writer Christopher Lloyd, whose home this was, developed a series of creative, colorful "garden rooms" and a dazzling herbaceous Long Border that continue to be inspirational. The house is 9 mi northwest of Rye. ⊠ *Off A28, Northiam* ☎ *01797/252878* ⊕ *www.greatdixter.co.uk* ⊒ *£10; gardens only, £8* ⊙ *Apr.–Oct., Tues.–Sun. 11–5 (house 2–5).*

Mermaid Street. One of the town's original cobbled streets heads steeply from the top of the hill to the former harbor. Its name, according to local lore, came from the night a sailor who had sipped a few too many walked down it. He swore he heard a mermaid call him down to the sea. ■ **TIP →** Take a stroll here to see the many ancient buildings that make it one of the town's most scenic streets.

Ypres Tower. Down the hill past Church Square, Ypres Tower was originally built as part of the town's fortifications (now largely gone) in 1249; it later served as a prison. The stone chambers hold a rather random collection of local items, such as smuggling bric-a-brac and shipbuilding mementos. ⊠ *Gungarden* ☎ *01797/226728* ⊒ *£3, includes Rye Castle Museum* ⊙ *Apr.–Oct., Thurs.–Mon. 10:30–1 and 2–5; Nov.–Mar., daily 10:30–3:30; last admission 30 mins before closing.*

WORTH NOTING

Chapel Down Winery. English wine? Indeed, the English wine industry is beginning to be taken more seriously. For a change of pace, head several miles north of Rye to see one of Britain's leading wine producers. You can visit the wine shop and explore the herb gardens for free. Book in advance and you can also take an hour-long guided tour of the rest of the grounds. ⊠ *Off B2082, Small Hythe* ☎ *01580/766111* ⊕ *www.englishwinesgroup.co.uk* ☝ *£9 tour* ☺ *June–Sept., daily 10–5; May and Oct., weekends 10–5.*

Lamb House. Something about Lamb House, an early-18th-century dwelling, attracts writers. The novelist Henry James lived here from 1898 to 1916. E. F. Benson, onetime mayor of Rye and author of the witty *Lucia* novels (written in the 1920s and 1930s), was a later resident. The ground-floor rooms contain some of James's furniture and personal belongings. ⊠ *West St.* ☎ *01580/762334* ⊕ *www.nationaltrust.org.uk* ☝ *£4.30* ☺ *Apr.–Oct., Thurs. and Sat. 2–6; last admission at 5:30.*

Rye Castle Museum. The diminutive Rye Castle Museum, below the remains of the castle wall, displays watercolors and examples of Rye pottery, for which the town was famous. ⊠ *3 East St.* ☎ *01797/226728* ⊕ *www.ryemuseum.co.uk* ☝ *£3, includes Ypres Tower* ☺ *Apr.–Oct., Thurs.–Mon. 2–5, weekends 10:30–1 and 2–5; last admission 30 mins before closing.*

Winchelsea. Like Rye, Winchelsea perches prettily atop its own small hill amid farmland. The town's historic houses, some with clapboards, are surrounded with gardens. Look for the splendid (though damaged) church built in the 14th century with Caen stone from Normandy. This was once a walled town, and some original town gates still stand. Winchelsea was built on a grid system devised in 1283, after the sea destroyed an earlier settlement at the foot of the hill. The sea later receded, leaving the town high and dry. The town is 2 mi southwest of Rye.

WHERE TO EAT

£££
SEAFOOD

✕ **Fish Café**. One of Rye's most popular restaurants occupies a brick building that dates to 1907, but the interior has been redone in a sleek, modern style. The ground-floor café has a relaxed atmosphere, and upstairs is a more formal dining room. Most of the seafood here is caught nearby, so it's very fresh. Sample the shellfish platter with oysters, whelks, winkles, shrimp, and crab claws, or try the grilled squid with bok choy. Reservations are recommended for dinner. ⊠ *17 Tower St.* ☎ *01797/222226* ⊕ *www.webbesrestaurants.co.uk* ☺ *Closed Mon. Oct.–Apr. No dinner Sun.*

£
ITALIAN

✕ **Simply Italian**. In a prime location near the marina, this popular Italian eatery packs in the crowds on weekend nights with its inexpensive classic pasta-and-pizza dishes. The atmosphere is cheerful and bright, and the food is straightforward and unfussy. Try tagliatelle with salmon in a creamy sauce, or grilled lemon sole with white wine sauce. Good pizza picks are the *quarto stagioni*, with mushrooms, salami, and peppers on a crisp crust, and pizza *reale* with red peppers, spinach, goat cheese, and red onion. ⊠ *The Strand* ☎ *01797/226024* ⊕ *www.simplyitalian.co.uk.*

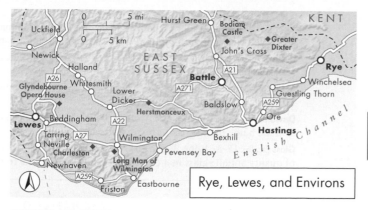

Rye, Lewes, and Environs

WHERE TO STAY

For expanded reviews, visit Fodors.com.

£££–££££ ⌂ **The George.** This attractive hotel on Rye's main road takes a boutique
HOTEL   approach, mixing modern pieces cleverly with antiques in a sprawling
Georgian building. **Pros:** elegant room design; very central. **Cons:** main-
street location makes street noise unavoidable; bar can get crowded and
a bit raucous. ⊠ *98 High St.* ☎ *01797/222114* ⊕ *www.thegeorgeinrye.
com* ⤳ *24 rooms* ⚭ *In-room: no a/c, Internet. In-hotel: restaurant, bar*
⎮◯⎮ *Breakfast.*

££–£££   ⌂ **Jeake's House.** Antiques fill the cozy bedrooms of this rambling 1689
B&B/INN house, where the snug, painted-and-paneled parlor has a wood-burning
stove for cold days. **Pros:** pleasant atmosphere; delicious breakfasts;
winter discounts. **Cons:** Mermaid Street is steep and cobbled; books up
far in advance. ⊠ *Mermaid St.* ☎ *01797/222828* ⊕ *www.jeakeshouse.
com* ⤳ *11 rooms, 10 with bath* ⚭ *In-room: no a/c. In-hotel: bar, some
pets allowed, some age restrictions* ⎮◯⎮ *Breakfast.*

££££   ⌂ **The Mermaid.** Once the headquarters of a smuggling gang, this classic
HOTEL   half-timber inn has been in business for six centuries; its sloping floors,
oak beams, low ceilings, and a huge open hearth testify to its roots in
the 15th century. **Pros:** city's most historic hotel; full of period charm;
good restaurant. **Cons:** some parts need refurbishment; price is high for
what's on offer; it's allegedly haunted. ⊠ *Mermaid St.* ☎ *01797/223065*
⊕ *www.mermaidinn.com* ⤳ *31 rooms* ⚭ *In-room: no a/c. In-hotel: restaurant, bar* ⎮◯⎮ *Breakfast.*

£££   ⌂ **White Vine House Hotel.** Occupying a building from the late 1500s,
HOTEL   this small guesthouse shows a traditional approach in features such as
wood-paneled lounges with warming fireplaces. **Pros:** beautiful building; soothing decor; a fireplace to warm your toes. **Cons:** main street
location can be a bit noisy; price is high for so few services. ⊠ *24 High
St.* ☎ *01797/224748* ⊕ *www.whitevinehouse.co.uk* ⤳ *7 rooms* ⚭ *In-
room: no a/c, Wi-Fi. In-hotel: restaurant* ⎮◯⎮ *Breakfast.*

SHOPPING

Rye has great antiques shops, perfect for an afternoon of rummaging, with the biggest cluster at the foot of the hill near the tourist information center.

Black Sheep Antiques (✉ *72 The Mint* ☎ *01797/224508*) has a superior selection of antique crystal and silver.

Collectors Corner (✉ *2 Market Rd.* ☎ *01797/225796*) sells a good mix of furniture, art, and silver.

David Sharp Pottery (✉ *55 The Mint* ☎ *01797/222620*) specializes in the ceramic name plaques that are a feature of the town.

Glass Etc. (✉ *18-22 Rope Walk* ☎ *01797/226600*) has a glorious collection of quality antique glass in a colorful, friendly shop by the train station.

HASTINGS

12 mi southwest of Rye, 68 mi southeast of London.

In the 19th century Hastings became one of England's many popular spa resorts. Tall Victorian row houses painted in lemony hues still cover the cliffs around the deep blue sea, and the views from the hilltops are extraordinary. The old town, on the east side of the city, offers a glimpse into the city's 16th-century past. Hastings has been through difficult times in recent decades, and the town developed a reputation as a rough place. In 2010, vandals burned down its beautiful Victorian amusement pier, so there are still issues. All visitors may notice, though, is that it's handsome, if tattered, and that the seafront has all the usual English accoutrements—fish-and-chips shops, candy stores, shops selling junk, miniature golf, and rocky beaches that stretch for miles.

THE BATTLE OF HASTINGS

When William of Normandy attacked King Harold's army in 1066, a vicious battle ensued. Harold's troops had just successfully fended off the Vikings near York and marched across the country to take on the Normans. Utterly exhausted, Harold never stood a chance, and William became known as William the Conqueror. It's worth noting that, though it was called the Battle of Hastings, the skirmish actually took place 6 mi away at a town now called, well, Battle.

GETTING HERE AND AROUND

If you're driving to Hastings from London (70 mi), take A21. Trains travel to Hastings every 30 minutes or so from London's Charing Cross and St. Pancras stations; the journey takes just under two hours. The station, Hastings Warrior Square, is in the town center, within easy walking distance of most sights. National Express buses travel from London to Hastings about twice a day in about 3½ hours.

ESSENTIALS

Visitor Information Hastings (✉ *Queens Sq., Priory Meadow* ☎ *01424/781111* ✉ *2 The Stade* ☎ *01424/781111* ⊕ *www.visit1066country.com*).

EXPLORING

Carr Taylor Vineyards is well known locally for its traditional methods of bottled fermentation, known as *Méthode Champenoise*. The store also stocks fruit wines, ranging from strawberry to apricot, and mead—a wine of medieval origin—made following a *very* sweet recipe involving fermented grapes, apple juice, and honey. Take the A21 north from Hastings for 3 mi, turn onto the A28, and follow the signs. ⊠ *Westfield, Hastings* ☎ *01424/752501* ⊕ *www.carr-taylor.co.uk* ☞ *£1.50* ⊙ *Daily 10–5; closed last wk of Dec.*

BEACH HUTS

As English as clotted cream, rows of tiny, cheerfully painted, one-room wooden beach huts brighten the shoreline in Sussex (look for them at the edges of Hastings and Brighton) and elsewhere. The huts originated in the Victorian wheeled bathing machines that were rolled into the water so that women could swim modestly behind them. Eventually the wheels came off, and they and similar structures became favored for storage and as a windbreak. Most huts lack electricity or plumbing but are beloved for their adorableness. Some are rented; others are owned, and prices can be quite high.

☺ **Hastings Castle.** Take a thrilling ride up the West Hill Cliff Railway from George Street precinct to the atmospheric ruins of the Norman fortress now known as Hastings Castle, built by William the Conqueror in 1069. All that remains are fragments of the fortifications, some ancient walls, and a number of gloomy dungeons. Nevertheless, you get an excellent view of the chalky cliffs, the rocky coast, and the town below. ⊠ *West Hill* ☎ *01424/781112* ☞ *£3.75* ⊙ *Easter–Sept., daily 10–5; Oct.–Easter, daily 11–3; last admission 30 mins before closing.*

☺ **Smuggler's Adventure.** Waxworks and exhibits recall the history of smuggling in this labyrinth of caves and passages a 5- or 10-minute walk above Hastings Castle. You can spend about an hour here. ⊠ *St. Clement Caves* ☎ *01424/422964* ⊕ *www.smugglersadventure.co.uk* ☞ *£7.40* ⊙ *Easter–Sept., daily 10–5:30; Oct.–Easter, daily 11–4:30; last admission 30 mins before closing.*

WHERE TO EAT AND STAY

£ ✕ **Blue Dolphin.** The crowds line up all day to make their way into this

SEAFOOD small fish-and-chips shop just off the seafront, down near the fish shacks. Although the atmosphere is humble, reviewers consistently rank the battered fresh cod and haddock and huge plates of double-cooked fries as among the best in the country. Everything is steaming fresh, and it's all cheaper if you get it to take out. ⊠ *61 High St.* ☎ *01424/425778* ⊟ *No credit cards* ⊙ *No dinner.*

£ 🖼 **Eagle House Hotel.** This guesthouse in St. Leonards-on-Sea, just west

HOTEL of Hasting's city center, is a quirky place with somewhat dated décor, but the guest rooms have nice antique details. **Pros:** quiet neighborhood; historic house. **Cons:** furnishings are a bit worn; service is hit or miss. ⊠ *12 Pevensey Rd., St. Leonards-on-Sea* ☎ *01424/430535* ⊕ *www. eaglehousehotel.co.uk* ☞ *18 rooms* ☪ *In-room: no a/c. In-hotel: restaurant* ⏱ *Breakfast.*

££–£££   ☷ **Hastings House.** In Warrior Square at the edge of Hastings near St.
HOTEL   Leonards-on-Sea, this renovated boutique guesthouse in a Victorian
          house takes a funky, modern approach. **Pros:** spacious rooms; near the
          sea. **Cons:** no restaurant; few services. ⊠ *9 Warrior Sq., St. Leonards-*
          on-Sea ☎ *01424/422709* ⊕ *www.hastingshouse.co.uk* ⊷ *8 rooms* ⚬ *In-*
          room: no a/c, Wi-Fi ⫯⊙⫯ *Breakfast.*

£££–££££   ☷ **Zanzibar International Hotel.** This quirky hotel pays homage to exotic
HOTEL   destinations with its large guest rooms, each designed with an interna-
          tional theme. **Pros:** spacious rooms; water views; breakfasts begin with
          a glass of champagne. **Cons:** a bit over the top; high prices for this town;
          nonrefundable deposit required. ⊠ *9 Everfield Pl., St. Leonards-on-Sea*
          ☎ *01424/460109* ⊕ *www.zanzibarhotel.co.uk* ⊷ *9 rooms* ⚬ *In-room:*
          no a/c, Internet. In-hotel: bar, some age restrictions ⫯⊙⫯ *Breakfast.*

BATTLE

7 mi northwest of Hastings, 61 mi southeast of London.

Battle is the actual site of the crucial Battle of Hastings, at which,
on October 14, 1066, William of Normandy and his army trounced
King Harold's Anglo-Saxon army. Today it's a sweet, quiet town, and
a favorite of history buffs.

GETTING HERE AND AROUND

Southeastern trains arrive from London's Charing Cross and Canon
Street stations every half hour. The journey takes 90 minutes. National
Express buses travel daily from London's Victoria Coach Station. The
trip takes around 2½ hours.

ESSENTIALS

Visitor Information Battle (⊠ *High St.* ☎ *01424/773721*
⊕ *www.visit1066country.com*).

EXPLORING

Battle Abbey. This great Benedictine abbey erected by William the Conqueror still conveys the sense of past conflict. A memorial stone marks
the high altar, which stood on the spot where Harold II was killed.
Despite its historical significance, this abbey was not spared Henry
VIII's wrath, and it was largely destroyed during his dissolution of
the monasteries. Films and interactive exhibits engage kids as well as
adults. You can also take the 1-mi-long walk around the edge of the
battlefield and see the remains of many of the abbey's buildings. ⊠ *High*
St. ☎ *01424/775705* ⊕ *www.english-heritage.org.uk* ⊠ *£7.30* ⊙ *Apr.–*
Sept., daily 10–6; Oct.–Mar., daily 10–4.

★   **Herstmonceux.** A banner waving from one tower and a glassy moat
⟳   crossed by what was, surely, once a drawbridge—this fairy-tale castle
       has everything except knights in shining armor. The redbrick struc-
       ture was originally built by Sir Roger Fiennes (ancestor of actor Ralph
       Fiennes) in 1444, although it was altered in the Elizabethan age and
       again early in the 20th century, after it had largely fallen to ruin. Can-
       ada's Queen's University owns the castle, so only part of it is open
       for guided tours once or twice a day (except Saturday). Highlights
       include the magnificent ballroom, a medieval room, and the stunning

Elizabethan-era staircase. When school is not in session, the castle rents out its small, plain guest rooms for £75 per night. ■**TIP→** Explore the formal walled garden, lily-covered lakes, and miles of woodland—the perfect place for a picnic on a sunny afternoon. There's also a hands-on science center for kids. The castle is 8 mi southwest of Battle. ☒ *Off A271, Hailsham* ☎ *01323/834481* ⊕ *www.herstmonceux-castle.com* ☒ *Castle tours £2.50, grounds £6* ⊗ *Mid-Apr.–Sept., daily 10–6; Oct., daily 10–5; last admission 1 hr before closing.*

WHERE TO EAT AND STAY

£££

MODERN FRENCH

✕ **The Sundial.** This 17th-century brick farmhouse with views of the South Downs is home to a popular Modern French restaurant run by chef Vincent Rongier and his wife, Mary. Wood-beamed rooms and white tablecloths provide a backdrop for the imaginative choices on the changing menu, such as roasted John Dory fillet served with chicory braised with orange, or panfried sea bass served with lobster ravioli. Praline mousse cake served with orange panna cotta is just one of the memorable desserts. The eatery is near the castle in Herstmonceux, 8 mi southwest of Battle. ☒ *Gardner St., Herstmonceux* ☎ *01323/832217* ⊕ *www.sundialrestaurant.co.uk* ⊗ *Closed Mon. No dinner Sun.*

£

B&B/INN

⌂ **Fox Hole Farm.** On a working farm about 2 mi outside Battle, this pretty wood-and-brick bed-and-breakfast is known for its soothing country views. **Pros:** peaceful views; relaxing atmosphere. **Cons:** outside town; small, so tends to book up. ☒ *Kane Hythe Rd.* ☎ *07801/668669* ◺ *3 rooms* ⌂ *In-room: no a/c. In-hotel: parking* ⊟ *No credit cards* ⊗ *Closed Jan.–Mar.* ⦿❘ *Breakfast.*

EN
ROUTE

Wilmington, 9 mi southwest of Herstmonceux Castle on A27, has a famous landmark that people drive for miles to see. High on the downs to the south of the village (signposted off A27), a 226-foot-tall white figure, known as the **Long Man of Wilmington,** is carved into the chalk; he has a staff in each hand. His age is a subject of great debate, but some researchers think he might have originated in Roman times.

LEWES

★

24 mi east of Battle, 8 mi northeast of Brighton, 54 mi south of London.

The town nearest to the celebrated Glyndebourne Opera House, Lewes is so rich in architectural history that the Council for British Archaeology has named it one of the 50 most important English towns. A walk is the best way to appreciate its steep streets and appealing jumble of building styles and materials—flint, stone, brick, tile—and the secret lanes (called "twittens") behind the castle, with their huge beeches. Here and there are smart antiques shops, good eateries, and secondhand-book dealers. Most of the buildings in the center date to the 18th and 19th centuries.

Something about this town has always attracted rebels. It was once the home of Thomas Paine (1737–1809), whose pamphlet *Common Sense* advocated that the American colonies break with Britain. It was also favored by Virginia Woolf and the Bloomsbury Group, early-20th-century countercultural artistic innovators.

Today Lewes's beauty and proximity to London mean that the counter-culture crew can't really afford to live here anymore, but its rebel soul still peeks through, particularly on Guy Fawkes Night (November 5), the anniversary of Fawkes's foiled attempt to blow up the Houses of Parliament in 1605. Flaming tar barrels are rolled down High Street and into the River Ouse; costumed processions fill the streets. The night here is enthusiastically anti-Catholic (Fawkes was a Catholic fanatic), if a bit tongue-in-cheek. Although the pope is burned in effigy, figures from popular culture are also burned, in the spirit of (dark-humored) fun.

GETTING HERE AND AROUND

If you're driving to Lewes from London, take the M23 south. The 57-mi journey takes around an hour and 45 minutes. Southern trains run direct to Lewes from Victoria Station every 30 minutes or so on the Brighton line. It may be faster to take a train to Brighton and change to the regional service for Lewes. There's no easy way to get to Lewes by bus; you need to take a National Express or Megabus to Brighton and change to a regional bus line.

ESSENTIALS

Visitor Information Lewes (⊠ *187 High St.* ☎ *01273/483448* ⊕ *www.lewes.gov.uk*).

EXPLORING

Ⓒ **Anne of Cleves House.** This 16th-century structure, a fragile-looking, timber-frame building, holds a small collection of Sussex ironwork and other items of local interest, such as Sussex pottery. The house was part of Anne of Cleves's divorce settlement from Henry VIII, but she never lived in it. There are medieval dress-up clothes for kids. To get to the house, walk down steep, cobbled Keere Street, past lovely Grange Gardens, to Southover High Street. ⊠ *52 Southover High St.* ☎ *01273/474610* ⊕ *www.sussexpast.co.uk* ⊠ *£4.40, £9.20 includes Lewes Castle* ☉ *Mar.–Oct., Tues.–Thurs. 10–5, Sun., Mon., and holidays 11–5.*

Charleston. Art and life mixed at Charleston, the farmhouse Vanessa Bell—sister of Virginia Woolf—bought in 1916 and decorated with Duncan Grant (who resided here until 1978), fancifully painting the walls, doors, and furniture. The house became a refuge for writers and artists of the Bloomsbury Group and displays colorful ceramics and textiles of the Omega Workshop—in which Bell and Grant participated—and paintings by Picasso and Renoir as well as by Bell and Grant. You view the house on a guided tour (there may be a wait) except on Sunday. ⊠ *Off A27, 7 mi east of Lewes, Firle* ☎ *01323/811265* ⊕ *www.charleston.org.uk* ⊠ *£9; gardens only, £3* ☉ *Apr.–June, Sept., and Oct., Wed.–Sun. 1–5; July and Aug., Wed.–Sat. noon–5, Sun. 1–5.*

Lewes Castle. High above the valley of the River Ouse stand the majestic ruins of Lewes Castle, begun in 1100 by one of the country's Norman conquerors; it took 300 years to complete. The castle's barbican holds a small museum with archaeology collections, a changing temporary exhibition gallery, and a bookshop. There are panoramic views of the town and countryside. ⊠ *169 High St.* ☎ *01273/486290* ⊕ *www.sussexpast. co.uk* ⊠ *£6.40, £9.20 includes Anne of Cleves House* ☉ *Tues.–Sat. 10–5:30 or dusk; Sun., Mon., and holidays 11–5:30 or dusk; last admission 30 mins before closing; closed Mon. in Jan.*

A mixture of architectural styles and good shops make Lewes a wonderful town for a stroll.

Monk's House. Of interest to Bloomsbury fans, Monk's House was the home of novelist Virginia Woolf and her husband, Leonard Woolf, who purchased it in 1919. Leonard lived here until his death in 1969. Rooms in the small cottage include Virginia's study and her bedroom. Artists Vanessa Bell (Virginia's sister) and Duncan Grant helped decorate the house. ⊠ *C7 off A27, 3 mi south of Lewes, Rodmell* ☎ *01323/870001 (c/o Alfriston Clergy House)* ⊕ *www.nationaltrust.org.uk* ⊑ *£4.20* ⊙ *Apr.–Oct., Wed. and Sat. 2–5:30.*

WHERE TO EAT

££ ✕ **The Real Eating Company.** This light-filled restaurant has big windows
CAFÉ overlooking the bustling shopping street outside. The heavy wood tables are perfect for lingering over a long lunch of home-style cooking. Try the poached-egg muffins with hollandaise and smoked salmon, or the kedgeree (smoked fish with rice and curry spices), a traditional dish that's hard to find on other menus. There are also more-comfort-food options like hamburgers and macaroni and cheese. Great cakes and strong tea help to make this a good afternoon resting spot. ⊠ *18 Cliff High St.* ☎ *01273/402650* ⊕ *www.real-eating.co.uk* ⊙ *No dinner Mon.–Wed.*

£ ✕ **Robson's of Lewes.** Good coffee, fresh produce, and delicious pastries
CAFÉ have made this coffee shop very popular with locals. A light-filled space with wood floors and simple tables creates a pleasant, casual spot to enjoy a cup of joe with breakfast, a scone, or a light sandwich or salad lunch. You can also order to go. ⊠ *22A High St.* ☎ *01273/480654* ⊙ *No dinner.*

WHERE TO STAY

For expanded reviews, visit Fodors.com.

££
B&B/INN

Berkeley House. A smart town house in one of Lewes's Georgian terraces, this place has spacious rooms and a roof terrace and guest lounge where you can unwind. **Pros:** warm atmosphere; great breakfast. **Cons:** rooms are a bit bland; nothing fancy here. ⊠ *2 Albion St.* ☎ *01273/476057* ⊕ *www.berkeleyhousehotel.co.uk* ⟋*3 rooms* ⟋ *In-room: no a/c, Wi-Fi* ⟋ *Breakfast.*

£££
HOTEL

Crossways Hotel. Near the Long Man of Wilmington, this small hotel in a whitewashed house with 2 acres of gardens is decorated in warm, upbeat colors that contrast with the lovely antique furniture. ⊠ *Lewes Rd., Polegate* ☎ *01323/482455* ⊕ *www.crosswayshotel.co.uk* ⟋*7 rooms, 1 cottage* ⟋ *In-room: no a/c. In-hotel: restaurant* ⟋ *Breakfast.*

££££
B&B/INN

Horsted Place. On 1,100 acres, this luxurious Victorian manor house was built as a private home in 1850; it was owned by a friend of Queen Elizabeth until the 1980s, and she was a regular visitor. **Pros:** historic building; amazing architecture; lovely gardens. **Cons:** too formal for some; creaky floors bother light sleepers. ⊠ *Little Horsted* ✛ *2½ mi south of Uckfield, 6 mi north of Lewes* ☎ *01825/750581* ⊕ *www. horstedplace.co.uk* ⟋*15 rooms, 5 suites* ⟋ *In-room: no a/c, Wi-Fi. In-hotel: restaurant, tennis court* ⟋ *Breakfast.*

££££
B&B/INN

The Shelleys. The lounge and dining room in this 17th-century building are on the grand scale, furnished with antiques that set the tone for the rest of the lovely building. **Pros:** historic atmosphere; good, French-influenced cuisine. **Cons:** service a bit spotty; securing a table at the restaurant can be tough. ⊠ *High St.* ☎ *01273/472361* ⊕ *www. the-shelleys.co.uk* ⟋*19 rooms* ⟋ *In-room: no a/c, Wi-Fi. In-hotel: restaurant, bar* ⟋ *Breakfast.*

NIGHTLIFE AND THE ARTS

NIGHTLIFE

Lewes has a relatively young population and a nightlife scene to match; there are also many lovely old pubs.

Try the **Brewers' Arms** (⊠ *91 High St.* ☎ *01273/475524*), a good pub with a friendly crowd.

The **King's Head** (⊠ *9 Southover High St.* ☎ *01273/474628*), a traditional pub, has a good menu with game and fish dishes.

THE ARTS

Glyndebourne Opera House (⊠ *Off A26, Glyndebourne* ✛ *Near Lewes* ☎ *01273/813813* ⊕ *www.glyndebourne.com*) is one of the world's leading opera venues. Nestled beneath the downs, Glyndebourne combines first-class productions, a state-of-the-art auditorium, and a beautiful setting. Seats are *very* expensive (£25–£140) and often difficult to acquire, but they're worth every penny to aficionados, some of whom wear evening dress and bring a hamper for a picnic in the gardens. The main season runs from mid-May to the end of August. The Glyndebourne Touring Company performs here in October, when seats are cheaper and slightly easier to obtain.

SHOPPING

Antiques shops offer temptation along the busy High Street. Lewes also has plenty of tiny boutiques and independent clothing stores vying for your pounds.

Adamczewski (⊠ *88 High St.* ☏ *01273/470105*) is a marvelous throwback to the days when everything was made by hand. Its homemade soaps, scents, and even hand-hewn brooms are works of art.

Cliffe Antiques Centre (⊠ *47 Cliffe High St.* ☏ *01273/473266*), a great place for one-stop antiques shopping, carries a fine mix of vintage English prints, estate jewelry, and art at reasonable prices.

Classic bone china and antique glass are the center of attention at **Louis Potts & Co.** (⊠ *43 Cliffe High St.* ☏ *01273/472240*).

3

BRIGHTON, THE SUSSEX COAST, AND SURREY

The self-proclaimed belle of the coast, Brighton is upbeat, funky, and endlessly entertaining. Outside town the soft green downs of Sussex and Surrey hold stately homes you can visit, including Arundel Castle and Petworth House. Along the way, you'll discover the largest Roman villa in Britain, the bustling city of Guildford, and Chichester, whose cathedral is a poem in stone.

BRIGHTON

9 mi southwest of Lewes, 54 mi south of London.

For more than 200 years, Brighton has been England's most interesting seaside city, and today it is more vibrant, eccentric, and cosmopolitan than ever. A rich cultural mix—Regency architecture, specialty shops, sidewalk cafés, lively arts, and a flourishing gay scene—makes it unique and unpredictable.

In 1750 physician Richard Russell published a book recommending seawater treatment for glandular diseases. The fashionable world flocked to Brighton to take Dr. Russell's "cure," and sea bathing became a popular pastime. Few places in the south of England were better for it, since Brighton's broad beach of smooth pebbles stretches as far as the eye can see. It has been popular with sunbathers ever since.

The next windfall for the town was the arrival of the Prince of Wales (later George IV). "Prinny," as he was called, created the Royal Pavilion, a mock-Asian pleasure palace that attracted London society. Visitors followed, triggering a wave of villa building, and today the elegant terraces of Regency houses are among the town's greatest attractions. The coming of the railroad set the seal on Brighton's popularity: the *Brighton Belle* brought Londoners to the coast within an hour.

Londoners still flock to Brighton. Add them to the many local university students, and you have a trendy, young, laid-back city that does, occasionally, burst at its own seams. Property values have skyrocketed, but all visitors may notice is the good shopping and restaurants, attractive (if pebbly) beach, and wild nightlife. Brighton is also the place to go if you're looking for hotels with offbeat design and party nights.

GETTING HERE AND AROUND

Brighton-bound National Express and Megabus buses depart from London's Victoria Coach Station. The trip takes about two hours. Southeastern trains leave from London's Victoria and Charing Cross stations

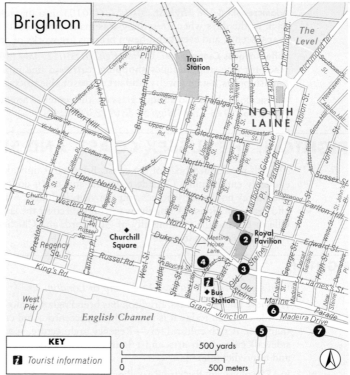

every 30 minutes. The journey takes just under an hour, and the trains stop at Gatwick Airport. By car from London, head to Brighton on the M23/A23. The journey should take about 1½ hours.

Brighton (and the adjacent Hove) sprawls in all directions, but the part of interest to travelers is fairly compact. None of the sights is more than a 10-minute walk from the train station. You can pick up a town map at the station. City Sightseeing has a hop-on, hop-off tour bus that leaves Brighton Pier every 20 to 30 minutes. It operates May through mid-September and costs £8.

TIMING

On summer weekends, the town is packed with Londoners looking for a day by the sea. Oceanfront bars can be rowdy, especially on national holidays when concerts and events bring in people. But summer is also when Brighton looks its best, and revelers pack the shops, restaurants, and bars. At other times, the town is much quieter. The Brighton Festival in May fills the town with music and other performances.

ESSENTIALS

Visitor and Tour Information Brighton (✉ *Royal Pavilion Shop, Royal Pavilion* ☎ */01273/290337* ⊕ *www.visitbrighton.com*).

City Sightseeing (☎ *01789/294466* ⊕ *www.city-sightseeing.com*).

EXPLORING

TOP ATTRACTIONS

Beach. The foundation of everything in Brighton is its broad beach, which spreads smoothly from one end of town to the other. In summer sunbathers, swimmers, and hawkers selling ice cream and toys pack the shore; in winter people stroll at the water's stormy edge, walking their dogs and searching for seashells. The water is bracingly cold, and the beach is covered in a thick blanket of large, smooth pebbles. ■TIP➜ If you plan on swimming, bring a pair of rubber swimming shoes, as the stones are hard on bare feet.

Brighton Museum and Art Gallery. The grounds of the Royal Pavilion contain this museum, whose buildings were designed as a stable block for the prince regent's horses. The museum has particularly interesting art nouveau and art deco collections. Look out for Salvador Dalí's famous sofa in the shape of Mae West's lips, and pause at the Balcony Café for its bird's-eye view over the 20th-century Art and Design Gallery. ✉ *Church St.* ☎ *03000/290900* ⊕ *www.brighton-hove-rpml.org. uk* ✆ *Free* ⊙ *Tues.–Sun. 10–5.*

★ **Brighton Pier.** Opened in 1899, the pier is an amusement park set above
☾ the sea. In the early 20th century it had a music hall and entertainment; today it has roller coasters and other carnival rides, as well as game arcades, clairvoyants, candy stores, and greasy-food stalls. In summer it is packed with children by day and teenagers by night. The skeletal shadow of a pier you can see off in the water is all that's left of the old West Pier. At the time of this writing, work was underway on a futuristic observation tower, called **i360,** where that pier once touched the shore. It is expected to be completed by summer 2012. ☎ *01273/609361* ⊕ *www.brightonpier.co.uk* ⊙ *Mid-Sept.–June, daily 11 am–10 pm; July–mid-Sept., daily 11 am–10:30 pm.*

The Lanes. This maze of tiny alleys and passageways was once the home of fishermen and their families. Closed to vehicular traffic, the area's narrow cobbled streets are filled with interesting restaurants, boutiques, and antiques shops. Fish and seafood restaurants line the heart of the Lanes, at Market Street and Market Square. ✉ *Bordered by West, North, East, and Prince Albert Sts.*

★ **Royal Pavilion.** The city's most remarkable building is this delightfully over-the-top domed and pinnacled fantasy. Planned as a simple seaside villa and built in the fashionable classical style of 1787 by architect Henry Holland, the Pavilion was rebuilt between 1815 and 1822 by John Nash for the prince regent (later George IV), who wanted an exotic, Eastern design with opulent Chinese interiors. Today period furniture and ornaments, some given or lent by the current Royal Family, fill the interior. The two great set pieces are the **Music Room,** styled in the form of a Chinese pavilion, and the **Banqueting Room,** with its enormous flying-dragon "gasolier," or gaslight chandelier, a revolutionary invention in the early 19th century. The gardens, too, have been restored to Regency splendor, following John Nash's naturalistic design of 1826. ■TIP➜ For an elegant time-out, retire to one of the Pavilion's bedrooms, where a tearoom serves snacks and light meals. ✉ *Old Steine*

George IV loved the sea at Brighton and built the flamboyant Royal Pavilion as a seaside escape.

☎ 03000/290900 ⊕ *www.royalpavilion.org.uk* 🖻 *£9.80* ⊙ *Oct.–Mar., daily 10–5:15; Apr.–Sept., daily 9:30–5:45; last admission 45 mins before closing.*

QUICK BITES
On the street adjacent to the bus station, and less than a five-minute walk from the Royal Pavilion, the **Mock Turtle** (⊠ *4 Pool Valley* ☎ *01273/ 328380*) is a great old-fashioned, homey café. Alongside a decent selection of teas and coffees are four types of rarebit, soups, and scones, as well as cakes and enormous doughnuts. It's closed Monday.

Steine. One of the centers of Brighton's action is the Steine (pronounced *steen*), a large open area close to the seafront. This was a river mouth until the Prince of Wales had it drained in 1793.

WORTH NOTING

ⓒ **Sea Life Centre.** Near Brighton Pier, this aquarium has many sea-dwelling creatures—from sharks to sea horses—in more than 30 marine habitats. It also has a giant-turtle convalescence center. Allow two hours for your visit. ⊠ *Marine Parade* ☎ *0871/423–2110* ⊕ *www.sealifeeurope.com* 🖻 *£16.20* ⊙ *Apr.–Oct., daily 10–5; Nov.–Mar., daily 10–4.*

ⓒ **Volk's Electric Railway.** Built by inventor Magnus Volk in 1883, this was the first public electric railroad in Britain. In summer you can take the 1¼-mi trip along Marine Parade. ⊠ *Marine Parade* ☎ *01273/292718* ⊕ *www.volkselectricrailway.co.uk* 🖻 *£1.90 one way, £3 round-trip* ⊙ *Apr.–Sept., weekdays 10:30–5, weekends 10:30–6.*

WHERE TO EAT

£ ✕ **Bill's Produce**. Even groceries seem
CAFÉ attractive at this casual, pleasant
coffee shop–restaurant–deli. On
tall shelves all around the light-filled
dining room, bottles of olive oil and
vinegars glisten alongside stacks
of fresh fruit, vegetables, baskets,
and flowers. Blackboards near the
counter list the day's specials: these
usually include a variety of salads,
sandwiches (your choice of fresh
breads), and a few hot dishes. For
mains, consider the goat cheese tart with tomatoes and pasta. Breakfast
is great here, too, but on weekends expect a line of hungry diners. ⊠ *The
Depot, 100 North Rd.* ☎ *01273/692894* ⊕ *www.billsproducestore.co.uk.*

£££ ✕ **Due South**. Arguably the finest dining option on Brighton's seafront,
SEAFOOD Due South is drawing young professionals who also appreciate its celebratory atmosphere. Big windows overlook the sea and let in plenty of
light. The menu changes monthly and showcases clever takes on classic
seafood dishes. You'll find everything from roasted pheasant (from a
local farm) to pan-roasted scallops (fresh off the boat each day). Even
the vegetables are sourced locally. Desserts are decadent. ⊠ *139 King's
Rd. Arches* ☎ *01273/821218* ⊕ *www.duesouth.co.uk.*

££ ✕ **Nia Café**. In the funky North Laine area, Nia has views down Trafal-
CAFÉ gar Street from its outdoor tables. Besides good coffees and leaf teas,
excellent café food is available all day, from steaming hot breakfasts
to simple sandwiches at lunch to more sophisticated dinners like goat
cheese tartlets or braised beef and butternut squash tagine. The decor
is coffee-shop chic, with wood tables, chairs, and floors; large windows
flood the room with light. Nia is near the station, which is handy if you
have time to kill before a train. ⊠ *87–88 Trafalgar St.* ☎ *01273/671371*
⊕ *www.nia-brighton.co.uk.*

££ ✕ **Pomegranate**. A contemporary Kurdish restaurant, Pomegranate takes
MIDDLE EASTERN a lighthearted, fun approach to Middle Eastern cuisine. Its small dining
area spreads over two floors and has large windows and exposed brick
walls; the staff encourages a friendly, relaxed atmosphere. The menu
sprawls and includes slow-roasted lamb with phyllo parcels stuffed
with nuts and apricots, beef stewed with pomegranates, and salmon on
grape leaves with cream sauce. For dessert, try the figs stuffed with walnuts and pomegranate. ⊠ *10 Manchester St.* ☎ *01273/628386* ⊕ *www.
eatpomegranates.com.*

££££ ✕ **Riddle and Finns**. A white-tiled room and bare metal tables greet you
SEAFOOD when you walk in this restaurant, but the sparkling chandeliers overhead indicate that all is not as it seems. The latest critics' darling in
Brighton calls itself a "Champagne oyster bar," and the elegant simplicity of its approach is impressive. Freshness and the sustainable sourcing
of the seafood on the menu are the calling cards. The house specialty
is oysters, offered eight different ways, hot or cold; a sampler plate lets
you sample them all. Other options include mixed shellfish marinière,

3

Brighton and the Regent

The term "Regency" comes from the last 10 years of the reign of George III (1811–20), who was deemed unfit to rule because of his mental problems. Real power was officially given to the prince of Wales, also known as the prince regent, who became King George IV and ruled until his death in 1830.

Throughout his regency, George spent grand sums indulging his flamboyant tastes in architecture and interior decorating—while failing in affairs of state.

The distinctive architecture of the Royal Pavilion is a prime, if extreme, example of the Regency style, popularized by architect John Nash (1752–1835) in the early part of the 19th century. The style is characterized by a diversity of influences—French, Greek, Italian, Persian, Japanese, Chinese, Roman, Indian—you name it. Nash was George IV's favorite architect, beloved for his interest in Indian and Asian designs and for his neoclassical designs, as evidenced in his plans for Regent's Park and its terraces in London.

boiled crab and lobster served cold, and smoked local mackerel with fennel and poached egg. The Champagne selection is pricey and interesting. It's open weekends for breakfast (and, yes, they serve oysters and champagne). ⊠ *12B Meeting House La.* ☎ *01273/323008* ⊕ *www. riddleandfinns.co.uk* ⌕ *Reservations essential.*

£££
MODERN BRITISH
✕ **Seven Dials.** A former bank houses a restaurant that's undeniably striking and surprisingly laid-back, given the elegance of the cooking. Sophisticated Modern British cuisine rules the menu, with main dishes including grilled rib-eye steak served with "proper chips" (well-cooked, hand-cut, chunky fries), and slow-roasted pork belly with savoy cabbage and pancetta. For dessert try the creamy lemon posset with fresh raspberries. ⊠ *1 Buckingham Pl.* ☎ *01273/885555* ⊕ *www. sevendialsrestaurant.co.uk* ⌕ *Reservations essential.*

££
VEGETARIAN
✕ **Terre à Terre.** This inspiring vegetarian restaurant is incredibly popular, so come early for a light lunch or later for a more sophisticated evening meal. The wood tables are modern but simple; it's the food that shines. Dishes span the globe in terms of their influences, so choose deep-fried corn cakes with avocado and chilies or carrot custard with pickled beets, then move on to braised tempeh with pumpkin polenta or dumplings with a Szechuan-style stir-fry. There's also an excellent collection of wines from around the globe. ⊠ *71 East St.* ☎ *01273/729051* ⊕ *www. terreaterre.co.uk* ⊘ *Closed Mon. No lunch Tues. and Wed. in winter.*

WHERE TO STAY
For expanded reviews, visit Fodors.com.

££–£££
B&B/INN
⌂ **Brighton Wave.** Chic and sleek, this hotel off the seafront but near Brighton Pier is all about relaxation. **Pros:** big, comfy beds; soothing decor. **Cons:** not a lot of privacy. ⊠ *10 Madeira Pl.* ☎ *01273/676794* ⊕ *www.brightonwave.com* ⇆ *8 rooms* ⌕ ⍀*Breakfast.*

£££–££££
HOTEL
⌂ **Drakes.** It's easy to miss the low-key sign for this elegant, modern hotel tucked away amid the frilly houses on Marine Parade; it's worth the trouble, because everything is cool, calm, and sleekly designed.

Pros: great attention to detail; well-designed bathrooms; excellent restaurant. Cons: can feel a bit cold; too trendy for some. ✉ *43–44 Marine Parade* ☎ *01273/696934* ⊕ *www.drakesofbrighton.com* ⌯ *20 rooms* ♿ *In-room: Internet. In-hotel: restaurant, bar.*

££££–£££££ 🖥 **Grand Hotel.** The city's most famous hotel, this seafront landmark is
HOTEL a huge, creamy Victorian wedding cake of a building dating from 1864.
★ Pros: as grand as its name; lovely sea views. Cons: a bit impersonal; lobby can be crowded with people taking tea. ✉ *King's Rd.* ☎ *01273/224300* ⊕ *www.devere.co.uk* ⌯ *200 rooms, 3 suites* ♿ *In-room: no a/c (some), Internet. In-hotel: restaurant, bar, pool, gym, some pets allowed* ᵗᵒᵗ *Breakfast.*

££–£££ 🖥 **Granville Hotel.** Three grand Victorian buildings facing the sea make
HOTEL up this hotel where the themed guest quarters include the pink-and-white Brighton Rock Room and the art deco Noël Coward Room. Pros: creative design; friendly staff; rambunctious atmosphere. Cons: rooms are a bit too quirky; can get noisy. ✉ *124 King's Rd.* ☎ *01273/326302* ⊕ *www.granvillehotel.co.uk* ⌯ *24 rooms* ♿ *In-room: no a/c, Internet. In-hotel: restaurant, bar, some pets allowed* ᵗᵒᵗ *Breakfast.*

££££ 🖥 **Hotel du Vin.** In the Lanes area, this outpost of a stylish chain has
HOTEL crisply modern rooms. Pros: gorgeous rooms; comfortable beds; excellent eatery. Cons: bar can get crowded; restaurant books up fast. ✉ *Ship St.* ☎ *01273/718588* ⊕ *www.hotelduvin.com* ⌯ *40 rooms, 3 suites* ♿ *In-room: no a/c, Wi-Fi. In-hotel: restaurant, bar.*

£££–££££ 🖥 **Nineteen.** A calm oasis of white, this guesthouse is filled with contem-
B&B/INN porary art and chic designer accessories. Pros: relaxing rooms; innovative design. Cons: not on the nicest street in town; a bit New Agey. ✉ *19 Broad St.* ☎ *01273/675529* ⊕ *www.hotelnineteen.co.uk* ⌯ *8 rooms* ♿ *In-room: no a/c, Wi-Fi. In-hotel: some pets allowed* ᵗᵒᵗ *Breakfast.*

££–£££ 🖥 **Oriental Brighton.** With a casual elegance that typifies Brighton, this
HOTEL Regency-era hotel sits close to the seafront; all this comes at a reasonable price that tends to attract a trendy thirtysomething crowd. ros: close to the beach; beautiful rooms; great prices. Cons: No restaurant; busy bar. ✉ *9 Oriental Pl.* ☎ *01273/205050* ⊕ *www.orientalbrighton. co.uk* ⌯ *9 rooms* ♿ *In-room: no a/c, no safe, no TV (some), Wi-Fi. In-hotel: bar, parking, some pets allowed* ᵗᵒᵗ *Breakfast.*

££–£££ 🖥 **Pelirocco.** Here the imaginations of designers have been given free rein,
HOTEL and the result is a vicarious romp through pop culture and rock and roll. Pros: quirky design; laid-back atmosphere; near the beach. Cons: too form-over-function; no hotel restaurant. ✉ *10 Regency Sq.* ☎ *01273/327055* ⊕ *www.hotelpelirocco.co.uk* ⌯ *18 rooms, 1 suite* ♿ *In-room: no a/c, Internet. In-hotel: bar, some age restrictions* ᵗᵒᵗ *Breakfast.*

NIGHTLIFE AND THE ARTS
NIGHTLIFE
Brighton is a techno hub, largely because so many DJs have moved here from London. Clubs and bars present live music most nights, and on weekends the entire place can be a bit too raucous for some tastes. There's a large and enthusiastic gay scene.

The popular **Above Audio** (✉ *10 Marine Parade* ☎ *01273/606906*), in an art deco building east of Brighton Pier, has a mix of house and underground music.

Specialty nights at the **Funky Buddha Lounge** (✉ *169 King's Rd. Arches* ☎ *01273/725541*) are at the forefront of Brighton's underground, with funk and acid disco blasting out to a fairly sophisticated crowd.

Small, friendly, and unfailingly funky, the **Jazz Place** (✉ *10 Ship St.* ☎ *01273/328439*), in the basement of Smugglers bar, can get a little cramped but makes up for it with cool, jazzy attitude.

The **Pussycat Club** (✉ *189–192 King's Rd. Arches* ☎ *08455/191909*), under the arches right on the beach, is one of Brighton's hottest clubs. Paint your face with glitter and dance, dance, dance.

THE ARTS

★ The three-week-long **Brighton Festival** (☎ *01273/706771* ⊕ *www. brightonfestival.org*), one of England's biggest and liveliest arts festivals, takes place every May in venues around town. The more than 600 events include drama, music, dance, and visual arts.

The **Brighton Dome** (✉ *New Rd.* ☎ *01273/709709*), just west of the Royal Pavilion, was converted from the prince regent's stables in the 1930s. It includes a theater and a concert hall that stage pantomime (a British theatrical entertainment with songs and dance) and classical and pop concerts.

The **Cinematheque** (✉ *9–12 Middle St.* ☎ *01273/384300*) screens sub-art-house oddities, obscurities, and rarities.

The elegant 1910 **Duke of York's Picture House** (✉ *Preston Circus* ☎ *01273/ 626261*), a 10-minute walk north of the main train station, shows art-house movies.

The **Theatre Royal** (✉ *New Rd.* ☎ *0844/871–7627*), close to the Royal Pavilion, has a gem of an auditorium that is a favorite venue for shows on their way to or fresh from London's West End.

SHOPPING

The main shopping area to head for is **the Lanes**, especially for antiques or jewelry. It also has clothing boutiques, coffee shops, and pubs.

Across North Street from the Lanes lies the **North Laine**, a network of narrow streets full of little stores, less glossy than those in the Lanes, but fun, funky, and exotic.

The Antique House (✉ *43 Meeting House La.* ☎ *01273/321684*) has a mix of pricey and affordable antiques spread over two floors.

Colin Page (✉ *36 Duke St.* ☎ *01273/325954*), at the western edge of the Lanes, stocks a wealth of antiquarian and secondhand books at all prices.

Curiouser & Curiouser (✉ *2 Sydney St.* ☎ *01273/673120*) is filled with unique, handmade jewelry, mostly sterling silver pieces with semiprecious stones.

The Lavender Room (✉ *16 Bond St.* ☎ *01273/220380*), a relaxing boutique, tempts with scented calendars, glittery handmade jewelry, and little things you just can't live without.

The **Pavilion Shop** (✉ *4–5 Pavilion Bldgs.* ☎ *01273/292798*), next door to the Royal Pavilion, carries well-designed toys, trinkets, books, and cards—all with a loose Regency theme—and high-quality fabrics, wallpapers, and ceramics based on material in the Pavilion itself.

The old-fashioned **Pecksniff's Bespoke Perfumery** (✉ *45–46 Meeting House La.* ☎ *01273/723292*) mixes and matches ingredients to suit your wishes.

Simultane (✉ *52 Ship St.* ☎ *01273/777535*), a boutique near the waterfront, displays women's fashions from its own label—contemporary looks inspired by the styles of the '40s and '50s—and clothing from other designers.

ARUNDEL

3

23 mi west of Brighton, 60 mi south of London.

The little hilltop town of Arundel is dominated by its great castle, the much-restored home of the dukes of Norfolk for more than 700 years, and an imposing neo-Gothic Roman Catholic cathedral—the duke is Britain's leading Catholic peer. The town itself is full of interesting old buildings and well worth a stroll.

GETTING HERE AND AROUND

Arundel is on the A27, about a two-hour drive south of central London. There are no direct trains from London, but you can take a Southern train from London Bridge Station and change at Three Bridges to an Arundel train. The trip takes about 90 minutes, and trains run every 30 minutes or so. No direct buses run from London, but you can take a National Express bus to Worthing or Chichester and change to a local bus to Arundel; that journey could easily take five hours, though.

ESSENTIALS

Visitor Information Arundel (✉ *1–3 Crown Yard Mews, River Rd.* ☎ *01903/882419* ⊕ *www.sussex-by-the-sea.co.uk*).

EXPLORING

Arundel Castle. Begun in the 11th century, this vast castle remains rich with the history of the Fitzalan and Howard families and with paintings by Van Dyck, Gainsborough, and Reynolds. It suffered destruction during the civil war and was remodeled during the 18th century and in the Victorian era, when it was reconstructed in the fashionable Gothic style. The keep, rising from its conical mound, is as old as the original castle (you can climb its 130 steps for great views of the River Arun and the area), and the barbican and the Barons' Hall date from the 13th century. Among the treasures are the rosary beads and prayer book used by Mary, Queen of Scots, in preparing for her execution. The newly redesigned formal garden is a triumph of order and beauty. Although the castle's ceremonial entrance is at the top of High Street, you enter at the bottom, close to the parking lot. ✉ *Mill Rd.* ☎ *01903/882173* ⊕ *www.arundelcastle.org* ✉ *£16; grounds only, £7.50* ⊙ *Apr.–Oct., Tues.–Sun. noon–5 (grounds open at 10); last admission at 4.*

WHERE TO EAT AND STAY

£ ✕ **Black Rabbit.** This renovated 18th-century pub outside Arundel is a

BRITISH find, and you must persevere along Mill Road to find it. Its location by the River Arun, with views of the castle and a bird sanctuary, makes it ideal for a summer lunch. There's a good selection of real ales and an all-day restaurant. ✉ *Mill Rd., Offham* ☎ *01903/882828.*

Brighton, the Sussex Coast, and Surrey

0   8 mi
0   8 km

£££££   **Amberley Castle.** The lowering of the portcullis every night at midnight
HOTEL   is a sure sign that you're in a genuine medieval castle. **Pros:** sleep in a
★   castle; putting course for golfers; lovely gardens and grounds. **Cons:**
        you have to dress for dinner. ⊠ *5 mi north of Arundel, off B2139,
        Amberley* ☎ *01798/831992* ⊕ *www.amberleycastle.co.uk* ➷ *20 rooms*
        ☐ *In-room: no a/c, Internet. In-hotel: restaurant, bar, tennis court, some
        age restrictions* ¶⊙¶ *Breakfast.*

   ££   **Norfolk Arms Hotel.** Like the cathedral and the castle in Arundel, this
HOTEL   18th-century coaching inn on the main street was built by one of the
        dukes of Norfolk. **Pros:** charming building; historic setting. **Cons:** many
        rooms are very small; decor is dated. ⊠ *22 High St.* ☎ *01903/882101*
        ⊕ *www.norfolkarmshotel.com* ➷ *34 rooms* ☐ *In-room: no a/c, Wi-Fi.
        In-hotel: restaurant, bars, some pets allowed* ¶⊙¶ *Breakfast.*

NIGHTLIFE AND THE ARTS

The **Arundel Festival** (☎ *01903/883690* ⊕ *www.arundelfestival.co.uk*)
presents dramatic productions and classical and pop concerts in and
around the castle grounds for 10 days in August or September.

CHICHESTER

10 mi west of Arundel, 66 mi southwest of London.

The Romans founded Chichester, the capital city of West Sussex, on the low-lying plains between the wooded South Downs and the sea. The city walls and major streets follow the original Roman plan. This cathedral town, a good base for exploring the area, is a well-respected theatrical hub, with a reputation for attracting good acting talent during its summer repertory season. North of town is Petworth House, a National Trust treasure house.

3

GETTING HERE AND AROUND

From London, take A3 south and follow exit signs for Chichester. The 67-mi journey takes slightly more than two hours; much of it is in on smaller highways. Southern trains run to Chichester every half hour from Victoria Station, with a travel time of about 90 minutes. Bus service from London requires a trip to Brighton or Portsmouth and a change to a regional service; the train is faster.

ESSENTIALS

Visitor Information Chichester (✉ *29A South St.* ☎ *01243/775888* ⊕ *www.visitchichester.org*).

EXPLORING

TOP ATTRACTIONS

Chichester Cathedral. Standing on Roman foundations, 900-year-old Chichester Cathedral has a glass panel that reveals Roman mosaics uncovered during restoration. Other treasures are the wonderful Saxon limestone reliefs of the raising of Lazarus and Christ arriving in Bethany, both in the choir area. Among the outstanding contemporary artworks are a stained-glass window by Marc Chagall, a colorful tapestry by John Piper, and a painting by Graham Sutherland. ✉ *West St.* ☎ *01243/782595* ⊕ *www.chichestercathedral.org.uk* 🎟 *£3 suggested donation* ☻ *Easter–Sept., daily 7:15–7; Oct.–Easter, daily 7:15–6. Tours Mon.–Sat. at 11:15 and 2:30.*

Fishbourne Roman Palace. In 1960, workers digging a water-main ditch uncovered a Roman wall; so began nine years of archaeological excavation of this site, the remains of the largest, grandest Roman villa in Britain. Intricate mosaics (including Cupid riding a dolphin) and painted walls lavishly decorate what is left of many of the 100 rooms of the palace, built in the 1st century AD, possibly for local chieftain Tiberius Claudius Togidubnus. It's a glimpse of high living, Roman-leader style. You can explore the sophisticated bathing and heating systems, and the only example of a Roman garden in northern Europe. An expansion has added many modern attributes, including a video reconstruction of how the palace might have looked. The site is ½ mi west of Chichester. ✉ *Salthill Rd., Fishbourne* ☎ *01243/785859* ⊕ *www.sussexpast.co.uk* 🎟 *£8* ☻ *Mar.–Oct., daily 10–5; Nov. and Dec., daily 10-4; Feb., Sun. daily 10–4.*

Fodor's Choice ★   **Petworth House.** One of the National Trust's greatest treasures, Petworth is the imposing 17th-century home of Lord and Lady Egremont and holds an outstanding collection of English paintings by Gainsborough, Reynolds, and Van Dyck, as well as 19 oil paintings by the great proponent of romanticism J. M. W. Turner, who often visited Petworth and immortalized it in luminous drawings. A 13th-century chapel is all that remains of the original manor house. The celebrated landscape architect Capability Brown (1716–83) added a 700-acre deer park. Other highlights include Greek and Roman sculpture and Grinling Gibbons wood carvings, such as those in the spectacular Carved Room. Six

A TEMPTING TOWN

After you visit Petworth House, take time to explore the small town of Petworth, with its narrow old streets and timbered houses. Temptation awaits, too: this is a center for fine antiques and collectibles, with many excellent shops.

rooms in the servants' quarters, among them the old kitchen, are also open to the public. A restaurant serves light lunches. You can reach the house off A272 and A283 (parking lots are off the latter); Petworth House is 13 mi northeast of Chichester and 54 mi south of London. Between 11 am and 1 pm visits are by guided tour only. ⊠ *Petworth* ☎ *01798/342207* ⊕ *www.nationaltrust.org.uk* 🖾 *£10.40; gardens only, £4* ⊗ *House mid-Mar.–early Nov., Sat.–Wed. 11–5; last admission at 4:30. Gardens Mar.–late Oct., Sat.–Wed. 11–6; Nov.–mid-Dec., Wed.–Sat. 10–3:30. Park daily 8–dusk.*

★ **Sculpture at Goodwood.** Twenty acres of woodland provide a backdrop for this collection of contemporary British sculpture specially commissioned by the Hat Hill Sculpture Foundation. A third of the approximately 40 exhibits change annually, and walks through green fields connect the pieces, sited to maximize their effect. It's a stimulating way to spend an afternoon. The park is 3 mi north of Chichester, signposted on the right off A286. Wear appropriate footwear because the site gets muddy. Allow about two hours to explore it. ⊠ *Hat Hill Copse, Goodwood* ☎ *01243/538449* ⊕ *www.sculpture.org.uk* 🖾 *£10* ⊗ *Apr.–Oct., Tues.–Sun. and national holidays 10:30–5.*

WORTH NOTING

Pallant House. Chichester's architecture is mainly Georgian, and its 18th-century stone houses give it a wonderful period appearance. One of the best is Pallant House, built in 1712 as a wine merchant's mansion. At that time its state-of-the-art design showed the latest in complicated brickwork and superb wood carving. Appropriate antiques and porcelains furnish the faithfully restored rooms. The **Pallant House Gallery,** attached to the house, showcases a small but important collection of mainly modern British art. Admission includes entry to the **Hans Fiebusch Studio,** nearby in St. Martin's Square, with an exact re-creation of the London studio of this exiled German artist (1898–1998) who was the last member of the so-called degenerate art group. ⊠ *9 N. Pallant* ☎ *01243/774557* ⊕ *www.pallant.org.uk* 🖾 *£7.50* ⊗ *Tues., Wed., Fri., and Sat. 10–5; Thurs. 10–8; Sun. and national holidays 12:30–5.*

🔆 **Weald and Downland Open Air Museum.** It's worth a stop in Singleton, a secluded village 5 mi north of Chichester, to see this excellent museum, a sanctuary for historical buildings dating from the 13th to 19th century. Among the 45 structures moved to 50 acres of wooded meadows are a cluster of medieval houses, a water mill, a Tudor market hall, and an ancient blacksmith's shop. ⊠ *A286* ☎ *01243/811363* ⊕ *www. wealddown.co.uk* ✍ *£9.50* ⊘ *Apr.–Oct., daily 10:30–6; Nov., Dec., and mid-Feb.–Mar., daily 10:30–4; Jan.–mid-Feb., weekends and Wed. 10:30–4:30; last admission 1 hr before closing.*

WHERE TO EAT AND STAY

£££

FRENCH

✕ **Comme Ça**. Its location, about a five-minute walk across the park from the Chichester Festival Theatre, makes this a popular spot for a meal before or after a performance. The dining room is relaxed and homey, with big windows and ceiling fans. The owner, Michel Navet, is French, and his chef produces sophisticated, authentic French dishes using fresh local produce. The menu changes regularly, but includes dishes like braised leg of venison in a strong red wine sauce, or grilled sole with lemon and olive oil. The fixed-price lunch menu offers two courses for £22; pretheater and bar menus are other options. ⊠ *67 Broyle Rd.* ☎ *01243/788724* ⊕ *www.commeca.co.uk* ⊘ *Closed Mon. No dinner Sun. No lunch Tues.*

££–£££

HOTEL

🛏 **Ship Hotel**. Originally the home of Admiral George Murray, one of Admiral Nelson's right-hand men, this architecturally interesting hotel is known for its flying (partially freestanding) staircase and colonnade. **Pros:** well-restored building; good location. **Cons:** rooms are small; not many amenities. ⊠ *North St.* ☎ *01243/778000* ⊕ *www.theshiphotel.net* ⌨ *36 rooms* ⌖ *In-room: no a/c, Internet. In-hotel: restaurant, bar, some pets allowed* ⫴⚫⫵ *Breakfast.*

NIGHTLIFE AND THE ARTS

The **Chichester Festival Theatre** (⊠ *Oaklands Park* ☎ *01243/781312* ⊕ *www.cft.org.uk*) presents classics and modern plays from May through September and is a venue for touring companies the rest of the year. Built in 1962, it has an international reputation for innovative performances and attracts theatergoers from across the country.

GUILDFORD

22 mi north of Petworth House, 35 mi north of Chichester, 28 mi southwest of London.

Guildford, the largest town in Surrey and the county's capital, has a lovely historic center with charming original storefronts. Gabled merchants' houses line the steep, pleasantly provincial High Street, where the remains of a Norman castle are tucked away in a peaceful garden, and the iconic clock on the old guildhall dates to the 1683. The outskirts of Guildford, and the area around the train station, are very busy and crowded, but once you make your way to the center it's a more peaceful, pleasant town. Guildford is a good place to base yourself if you're planning to visit Wisley, one of the Royal Horticultural Society's display gardens, 10 mi away.

GETTING HERE AND AROUND

From London, take A3 south and then exit onto the A31, following signs for Guildford. The 28-mi journey takes about an hour. Southwest trains run to Guildford every half hour from London's Waterloo Station; the trip takes about 40 minutes. Guildford Station in an unappealing

HIKING IN THE SOUTHEAST

A walk on the South Downs provides some panoramic views.

For those who prefer to travel on their own two feet, the Southeast offers long sweeps of open terrain that makes walking a pleasure. Ardent walkers can explore all or part of the **North Downs Way** (153 mi) and the **South Downs Way** (106 mi), following ancient paths along the tops of the downs—the undulating treeless uplands typical of the area. Both trails give you wide views over the countryside.

TRAILS ON THE DOWNS

The North Downs Way starts outside Guildford, in the town of Farnham, alongside the A31. (You can park at the train station.) It passes along the white cliffs of Dover and ends in the Dover town square. It follows part of the old Pilgrim's Way to Canterbury that so fascinated Chaucer.

The South Downs Way starts in Winchester, at Water Lane. It ends on the promenade in the seaside town of Eastbourne. Along the way it crosses the chalk landscape of Sussex Downs, with parts of the route going through deep woodland. Charming little villages serve the walkers cool ale in inns that have been doing precisely that for centuries.

The 30-mi (north–south) **Downs Link** joins the two routes. Along the Kent coast, the Saxon Shore Way, 143 mi from Gravesend to Rye, passes four Roman forts.

RESOURCES

Guides to these walks are available from the excellent Web site for **National Trails** (⊕ *www. nationaltrail.co.uk*). Tourist information offices throughout the region also have good information.

modern neighborhood with many busy roads. To get to the center, follow signs for High Street. National Express buses travel from London to Guildford every couple of hours; the trip takes 75 minutes.

ESSENTIALS

Visitor Information Guildford (✉ *14 Tunsgate* ☎ *01483/444333* ⊕ *www.guildford.gov.uk*).

EXPLORING

Guildford Museum. In the old castle building, this museum has exhibits on local history and archaeology, as well as memorabilia of Charles Dodgson, better known as Lewis Carroll, author of *Alice in Wonderland*. Dodgson spent his last years in a house on nearby Castle Hill. He is buried in the Mount Cemetery, up the hill on High Street. **Castle Arch**, all that remains of the entrance of the old castle, displays a slot for a portcullis. ✉ *Quarry St.* ☎ *01483/444751* ⊕ *www.guildfordmuseum. co.uk* 🎟 *Free* ☾ *Mon.–Sat. 11–5.*

☾ **Sculpture Park at Churt.** Set in a forested park 8 mi outside Guildford, this is a wild, fanciful place where giant metal spiders climb trees, bronze horses charge up hillsides, and metal girls and boys dance on lakes. You follow signposted paths across the parkland, spotting tiny sculptures up in trees, and walking through the legs of other more gigantic creations. Adults enjoy it as much as kids. The park is off the A287 between Guildford and Farnham. ✉ *Jumps Rd., Churt* ☎ *07831/500506* ⊕ *www. thesculpturepark.com* 🎟 *£6* ☾ *Daily 10–5.*

★ **Watts Gallery.** An extraordinary small museum that's often overlooked, Watts Gallery was built in tiny Compton in 1904 by the late-19th-century artist George Frederic Watts (1817–1904) to display his work. Recently opened after a major renovation, the gallery shines, with Watts' romantic, mystical paintings beautifully displayed. His massive sculptures are astonishing both for their size and the near-obsessive attention to detail. Mary, his wife and a devotee of the art nouveau style, designed a mortuary **chapel** nearby, covering the walls (inside and out) in elaborate paintings. It's about 50 yards away from the museum in the village cemetery. The museum is 3 mi south of Guildford. ✉ *Down La., Compton* ☎ *01483/810235* ⊕ *www.wattsgallery.org.uk* 🎟 *£6.50* ☾ *Tues.–Sat. 11–5, Sun. 1–5.*

Fodor's Choice **Wisley.** In a nation of gardeners and garden goers, Wisley is the Royal
★ Horticultural Society's innovative and inspirational 240-acre showpiece. Both an ornamental and scientific center, it claims to have greater horticultural diversity than any other garden in the world. The flower borders and displays in the central area, the rock garden and alpine meadow in spring, and the large, modern conservatories are just a few highlights, along with a garden center that sells more than 10,000 types of plants and an impressive bookstore. Near Woking, the garden is 10 mi northeast of Guildford. It's very easy to spend half a day or more here. ✉ *A3, Woking* ☎ *01483/224234* ⊕ *www.rhs.org.uk/gardens/ wisley* 🎟 *£10* ☾ *Mar.–Oct., weekdays 10–6, weekends and national holidays 9–6; Nov.–Feb., weekdays 10–4:30, weekends 9–4:30.*

WHERE TO EAT

££ ✕ **Café Rouge.** Part of a chain of inevitably charming and friendly
FRENCH French-style cafés, the Guildford branch is no exception. It's a great
place to stop for a coffee, or to have a full lunch or dinner. Menu stal-
warts include warming onion soup (with gooey Gruyère cheese) and the
meltingly good croque-monsieur sandwich, with ham and cheese. In the
evening, steak frites is a classic choice. The decent wine list is pleasantly
priced, and the coffee is excellent. ⊠ *8–9 Chapel St.* ☎ *01483/451221*
⊕ *www.caferouge.co.uk.*

£ ✕ **Gourmet Burger Kitchen.** Part of a chain of quality burger restaurants,
AMERICAN this very popular place does what it says on the label—good burgers
and not a lot else. You wait for a table, then order at the counter. All the
burgers are excellent: try the Pesterella, with pesto and mozzarella; the
Habernero, with spicy salsa; or the Wellington, with mushrooms and
horseradish sauce. The enormous milkshakes are tasty diet-busters. One
order of fries will be enough for two. ⊠ *10 Friary St.* ☎ *01483/572464*
⊕ *www.gbk.co.uk.*

££ ✕ **Loch Fyne.** Tucked away in one of Guildford's older buildings, this
SEAFOOD cleanly designed seafood restaurant has whitewashed walls and a casual
atmosphere. Loch Fyne is a reliably good, innovative chain dedicated
to using fresh, sustainable British seafood. Menu items change with
the seasons, but oysters (in season) lead the way and are served several
ways, although purists insists they are best served on the half shell. Main
courses include poached smoked haddock with mashed potatoes in a
whole-grain-mustard sauce, or char-grilled kiln-roasted salmon with
whisky sauce. ⊠ *Centenary Hall, Chapel St.* ☎ *01483/230550* ⊕ *www.
lochfyne.com.*

£ ✕ **Rumwong.** With an incredibly long menu, Rumwong has dozens of
THAI choices from all over Thailand. Tasty dishes include the fisherman's
soup, a spicy mass of delicious saltwater fish in a clear broth, or *yam
pla muek,* a hot salad with squid. The owners also run an Asian supermarket next door. ⊠ *16–18 London Rd.* ☎ *01483/536092* ⊕ *www.
rumwong.co.uk* ☯ *Closed Mon.*

WHERE TO STAY

For expanded reviews, visit Fodors.com.

£££–££££ ⌅ **Angel Posting House and Livery.** Guildford was once famous for its
HOTEL coaching inns, and this handsome 500-year-old hotel is the last to survive. **Pros:** historic building; lovely rooms. **Cons:** price is high for this
area; books up far in advance. ⊠ *91 High St.* ☎ *01483/564555* ⊕ *www.
angelpostinghouse.com* ↪ *21 rooms* ⌂ *In-room: no a/c, Wi-Fi. In-hotel:
restaurant, gym, spa, some pets allowed.* ⫶⊘⫶ *No meals.*

££ ⌅ **Old Great Halfpenny.** Surrounded by well-maintained grounds, this
B&B/INN 16th-century half-timbered house looks like something out of a picture
book. **Pros:** beautiful gardens; lovely old building; peace and quiet.
Cons: a 15-minute drive out of town. ⊠ *Halfpenny La., St. Martha*
✛ *5 mi north of Guildford* ☎ *01483/567835* ↪ *2 rooms* ⌂ *In-room:
no a/c* ⊟ *No credit cards* ⫶⊘⫶ *Breakfast.*

NIGHTLIFE AND THE ARTS

The **Yvonne Arnaud Theatre** (✉ *Millbrook* ☎ *01483/440000*), a horseshoe-shape building on an island in the River Wey, frequently previews West End productions. The smaller Mill Studio showcases more intimate productions.

TUNBRIDGE WELLS AND ENVIRONS: CASTLES AND STATELY HOMES

3

England is famous for its magnificent stately homes and castles, but many of them are scattered across the country, presenting a challenge for travelers. Within a 15-mi radius of Tunbridge Wells, however, in that area of hills and hidden dells known as the Weald, lies a wealth of architectural wonder in historic homes, castles, and gardens: Penshurst Place, Hever Castle, Chartwell, Knole, Ightham Mote, Leeds Castle, and lovely Sissinghurst Castle Garden.

ROYAL TUNBRIDGE WELLS

39 mi southeast of London.

Nobody much bothers with the "Royal" anymore, but Tunbridge Wells is no less regal because of it. Because of its wealth and political conservatism, this historic bedroom community has been the subject of (somewhat envious) British humor for years. Its restaurants and lodgings make it a convenient base for exploring the many homes and gardens nearby.

The city owes its prosperity to the 17th- and 18th-century passion for spas and mineral baths. In 1606 a mineral-water spring was discovered here, drawing legions of royal visitors looking for eternal health. Tunbridge Wells reached its zenith in the mid-18th century, when Richard "Beau" Nash presided over its social life. The buildings at the lower end of High Street are mostly 18th century, but as the street climbs the hill north, changing its name to Mount Pleasant Road, structures become more modern.

GETTING HERE AND AROUND

National Express buses headed to Kent and Tunbridge Wells depart from London's Victoria Coach Station several times a day. The trip takes about 90 minutes. Southeastern trains leave from London's Charing Cross Station every 30 minutes. The journey to Tunbridge Wells takes just under an hour. If you're traveling by car from London, head here on the A21; travel time is about an hour.

Tunbridge Wells sprawls in all directions, but the historic center is compact. None of the sights is more than a 10-minute walk from the main train station. You can pick up a town map at the station.

ESSENTIALS

Visitor Information Royal Tunbridge Wells (✉ *The Old Fish Market, the Pantiles* ☎ *01892/515675* ⊕ *www.visittunbridgewells.com*).

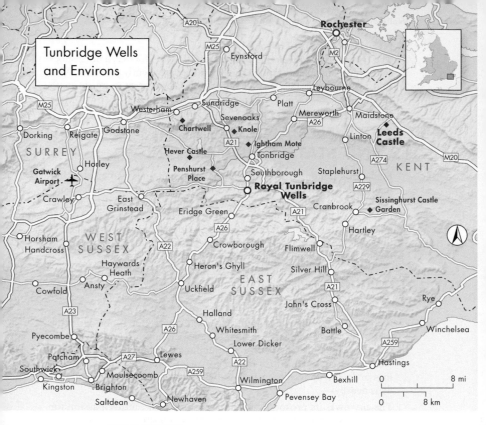

Tunbridge Wells
and Environs

EXPLORING

OFF THE
BEATEN
PATH

All Saints Church. This modest 13th-century church holds one of the glories of 20th-century church art. The building is awash with the luminous yellows and blues of 12 windows by Marc Chagall (1887–1985), commissioned as a tribute by the family of a young girl who was drowned in a sailing accident in 1963. The church is 4 mi north of Tunbridge Wells; turn off A26 before Tonbridge and continue a mile or so east along B2017. ⊠ *B2017, Tudeley* ☎ *0870/744–1456* ⊠ *Free* ☉ *Daily 9–6 or dusk.*

Church of King Charles the Martyr. Across the road from the Pantiles, this church dates from 1678, when it was dedicated to Charles I, who had been executed by Parliament in 1649. Its plain exterior belies its splendid interior; take special note of the beautifully plastered baroque ceiling. ⊠ *Chapel Pl.*

Pantiles. A good place to begin a visit is at the Pantiles, a famous promenade with colonnaded shops near the spring on one side of town. Its odd name derives from the Dutch "pan tiles" that originally paved the area. Now bordered on two sides by busy main roads, the Pantiles remains an elegant, tranquil oasis, and the site of the actual well. ■ **TIP→** You can still drink the waters when a "dipper" (the traditional water dispenser) is in attendance, from Easter through September.

WHERE TO EAT

£ ✕**Himalayan Gurkha.** It's not what you might expect to find in the cozy
ASIAN confines of Tunbridge Wells, but the Nepalese cuisine of this friendly
spot is popular with locals. Spicy mountain dishes are cooked with care
in traditional clay ovens or barbecued on flaming charcoal. Vegetarian
options are appealing, too. ⊠ *31 Church Rd.* ☎ *01892/527834* ⊕ *www.
himalayangurkha.com.*

£ ✕**Mount Edgcumbe Restaurant and Bar.** To some degree, the attraction of
BRITISH this casual restaurant above the old town center is the fact that it's in
a cave. Since it's carved out of the limestone foundation of the Mount
Edgcumbe Hotel it's a nice cave, though. Service can be a bit shaky,
but the food is pretty good. The menu, which changes regularly, serves
upscale versions of traditional English cuisine, including grilled fish
and steaks. The bar has a good selection of cask ales and lagers. ⊠ *The
Common* ☎ *01892/526823* ⊕ *www.mountedgcumbe.com.*

££££ ✕**Thackeray's House.** Once the home of Victorian novelist William
FRENCH Makepeace Thackeray, this mid-17th-century tile-hung house is now an
★ elegant restaurant known for creative French cuisine. A terrace accom-
modates alfresco dining in season. The menu changes daily, but often
lists such dishes as roasted partridge with creamed savoy cabbage. Desserts are butter-rich and delicious. The lunchtime menu du jour is a good
value at £16.50 for two courses. ⊠ *85 London Rd.* ☎ *01892/511921*
⊕ *www.thackerays-restaurant.co.uk* ۞ *Closed Mon. and last wk in Dec.
No dinner Sun.*

WHERE TO STAY

For expanded reviews, visit Fodors.com.

££££ ⬚ **Hotel du Vin.** An elegant sandstone house dating from 1762 has been
HOTEL transformed into a chic boutique hotel with polished wood floors and
luxurious furnishings. **Pros:** historic building; luxurious linens. **Cons:**
restaurant can get booked up; bar can be crowded. ⊠ *Crescent Rd. near
Mount Pleasant Rd.* ☎ *01892/526455* ⊕ *www.hotelduvin.com* ⇝ *34
rooms* ♿ *In-room: no a/c, Wi-Fi. In-hotel: restaurant, bars* ❙◎❙ *Breakfast.*

££ ⬚ **Smart & Simple Hotel.** This small place near the train station takes
HOTEL a modern approach with rooms that are small but nicely and mini-
mally decorated. **Pros:** handy location; free Wi-Fi. **Cons:** few services; no frills at all. ⊠ *54–57 London Rd.* ☎ *0845/4025744* ⊕ *www.
smartandsimple.co.uk* ⇝ *40 rooms* ♿ *In-room: no a/c, Wi-Fi. In-hotel:
gym* ❙◎❙ *Breakfast.*

££££ ⬚ **Spa Hotel.** Carefully chosen furnishings and details help maintain the
HOTEL country-house flavor of this 1766 Georgian mansion, although modern
touches like wireless Internet connections make it convenient. **Pros:** lap-
of-luxury feel; gorgeous views. **Cons:** very formal atmosphere; can be a
bit stuffy. ⊠ *Mount Ephraim* ☎ *01892/520331* ⊕ *www.spahotel.co.uk*
⇝ *69 rooms* ♿ *In-room: no a/c (some), Wi-Fi. In-hotel: restaurant, bar,
pool, tennis court, gym, spa, some pets allowed.*

PENSHURST PLACE

7 mi northwest of Royal Tunbridge Wells, 33 mi southeast of London.

GETTING HERE AND AROUND

To get to Penshurst, take the A26 north to Penshurst Road. The drive from Tunbridge Wells takes about 12 minutes. Bus 231 runs from Tunbridge Wells to Penshurst.

EXPLORING

★ **Penshurst Place.** At the center of the adorable hamlet of Penshurst stands this fine medieval manor house, hidden behind tall trees and walls. Although it has a 14th-century hall, Penshurst is mainly Elizabethan and has been the family home of the Sidneys since 1552, giving it particular historical interest. The most famous Sidney is the Elizabethan poet Sir Philip, author of *Arcadia*. The **Baron's Hall,** topped with a chestnut roof, is the oldest and one of the grandest halls to survive from the early Middle Ages. Family portraits, furniture, tapestries, and armor help tell the story of this house that was first inhabited in 1341 by Sir John de Pulteney, the very wealthy four-time London mayor. On the grounds are a toy museum, a gift shop, and the enchanting 11-acre walled Italian Garden, which displays tulips and daffodils in spring, roses in summer. The house is off Leicester Square; take time to study the village's late-15th-century half-timber structures adorned with soaring brick chimneys. To get here from Tunbridge Wells, take A26 and B2176. ⊠ *Off B2188* ☎ *01892/870307* ⊕ *www.penshurstplace.com* ⊠ *£10 for house and grounds; grounds only, £8* ⊙ *House Apr.–Oct., daily noon–4. Grounds daily 10:30–6.*

WHERE TO EAT AND STAY

££ ✕ **Spotted Dog.** This pub first opened its doors in 1520 and hardly
BRITISH appears to have changed. Its big inglenook fireplace and heavy beams give it character, the views from the hilltop are lovely, and the good food and friendly crowd make it a pleasure. Cheeses, meats, and beer are locally sourced. There's seating in the sunny garden in the summertime. The pub, which sells locally made ales, is 1.3 mi from Penshurst via the narrow B2188. ⊠ *Smarts Hill* ☎ *01892/870253* ⊕ *www.spotteddogpub.co.uk.*

££ ⊞ **Best Western Rose and Crown Hotel.** Originally a 16th-century inn,
HOTEL this hotel on the main street in Tonbridge has low-beam ceilings and Jacobean woodwork in the snug, inviting bar and the restaurant. **Pros:** atmospheric setting; public pool nearby. **Cons:** older rooms are quite small; annex rooms have less charm. ⊠ *125 High St., Tonbridge* ☎ *01732/357966* ⊕ *www.bestwestern.co.uk* ⊷ *56 rooms* ⟁ *In-room: no a/c, Wi-Fi. In-hotel: restaurant, bar, parking* ⦿ *Breakfast.*

HEVER CASTLE

3 mi west of Penshurst, 10 mi northwest of Royal Tunbridge Wells, 30 mi southeast of London.

GETTING HERE AND AROUND

Hever Castle best reached via the narrow, often one-lane B2026. From Tunbridge Wells, take A264 east then follow signs directing you north toward Hever.

EXPLORING

3

Fodor'sChoice **Hever Castle.** For some, 13th-century Hever Castle fits the stereotype of
★ what a castle should look like: all turrets and battlements, the whole encircled by a water lily–bound moat. Here, at her childhood home, the unfortunate Anne Boleyn, second wife of Henry VIII and mother of Elizabeth I, was courted and won by Henry. He loved her dearly for a time but had her beheaded in 1536 after she failed to give birth to a son. He then gave Boleyn's home to his fourth wife, Anne of Cleves, as a present. Famous though it was, the castle fell into disrepair in the 19th century. American millionaire William Waldorf Astor acquired Hever in 1903, and the Astor family owned it until 1983. Astor built a Tudor village to house his staff (it's now used for private functions) and created the stunning gardens, which include an excellent yew maze, a water maze, ponds, playgrounds, tea shops, gift shops, plant shops—you get the picture. There's a notable collection of Tudor portraits, and in summer activities are nonstop here, with jousting, falconry exhibitions, and country fairs, making this one of southern England's most rewarding castles to visit. ⊠ *Off B2026, Hever* ☎ *01732/865224* ⊕ *www.hevercastle. co.uk* 🖾 *£14; grounds only, £11.50* ☉ *Castle Apr.–Oct., daily noon–6; Mar., Wed.–Sun., noon–5; Nov. and Dec., Wed.–Sun. 11–5. Grounds Apr.–Oct., daily 10:30–6; Mar., Wed.–Sun. 10:30–4; Nov. and Dec., Thurs.–Sun. 10:30–4. Last admission 1 hr before closing.*

CHARTWELL

9 mi north of Hever Castle, 12 mi northwest of Tunbridge Wells, 28 mi southeast of London.

GETTING HERE AND AROUND

From Tunbridge Wells, take A21 north towards Sevenoaks, then turn east onto A25 and follow signs from there. You can travel to Chartwell by bus from the town of Sevenoaks. Take Go Coach 401, but check with the driver to make sure the bus passes near the mansion.

EXPLORING

Chartwell. A grand Victorian mansion with views over the Weald, Chartwell was the home of Sir Winston Churchill from 1924 until his death in 1965. Virtually everything has been kept as it was when he lived here, with his pictures, books, photos, and maps. There's even a half-smoked cigar that the World War II prime minister never finished. Churchill was an amateur artist, and his paintings show a different side of the crusty politician. Admission to the house is by timed ticket available only the day of your visit. ■TIP➔ Be sure to explore the rose gardens and take one of the walks in the nearby countryside. ⊠ *Off B2026, Westerham*

THE SOUTHEAST'S BEST HISTORIC HOUSES

Touring the Southeast's historic houses proves that no other country clings to the past with the tenacity of Britain. From modest manor houses to the sprawling stately homes of the aristocracy, each building has something to tell about private life or the history of the nation, and often the story is presented in an entertaining way.

Penshurst Place gracefully evokes the Elizabethan era (above); Bodiam Castle has a moat (right, top); Hever Castle claims Tudor connections (right, bottom).

Historic houses reveal the evolution of the country, from medieval fortresses planned for defense to architectural wonders that displayed the owner's power. In time, gardens and grounds became another way to display status. Times, however, changed. And the aristocratic rewards of owning tracts of countryside, art, and family treasures encountered reality in the 20th century, as cash flow and death taxes presented huge challenges. Private owners opened homes to the public for a fee, some with marketing flair. Hundreds of other homes and castles are now owned by the National Trust or English Heritage, organizations that raise part of the money needed to maintain them through entrance fees.

BEYOND THE HOUSE

The idea of exploring historic houses may inspire joy—or, frankly, boredom. If the latter, please don't give up: many houses have gardens and extensive grounds that make a great day out for garden lovers or walkers. You may be able to purchase a ticket that includes only the grounds. Some houses have so many activities aimed at kids that the whole family will find something to do.

CHOOSING A HOUSE

We admit it: there are almost too many houses to visit in the Southeast, but they are conveniently close to each other. Here are the prime characteristics of some top spots to help you decide.

Arundel Castle: Still a family home for the duke of Norfolk, Arundel has its Norman-era keep and Barons' Hall, as well as magnificent examples of Gothic-style domestic remodeling by the Victorians.

Bodiam Castle: For the castle fan: Bodiam has medieval turrets and an exquisite moat. It hasn't been inhabited since the 17th century and is partially ruined.

Chartwell: The National Trust owns this Victorian mansion, the former home of Winston Churchill. There's plenty of memorabilia, plus good woodland walks. Tours are by timed ticket.

Herstmonceux Castle: This moated 15th-century brick castle is romantic; a 20th-century rehab saved it. Only a few rooms are open (it's a school), but they and the extensive gardens and grounds are evocative.

Hever Castle: Turrets, battlements, and a moat set the mood: Hever dates to the 13th century but has a Tudor link as the childhood home of Anne Boleyn, Henry VIII's second wife. The American Astors restored it after 1903. Gardens and activities—jousting, fairs—keep things entertaining for the whole family.

Ightham Mote: Ideal for lovers of romantic antiquity, this 14-century manor house has an exquisite moat. The Great Hall is ancient, but there are Tudor and Victorian sections at this National Trust property.

Knole: Home of the Sackvilles and now a National Trust property, this sprawling Tudor house resembles a village. Furnishings are dark and florid, and include a set of 17th-century silver furniture. Writer and gardener Vita Sackville-West grew up here. Explore the deer park, too.

Leeds Castle: The setting of this castle on two islands on a lake is amazing. The inside reflects a 20th-century refurbishing by the last owner, and family activities are plentiful. You can eat and spend the night here, too, at themed events.

Penshurst Place: For more than 500 years this medieval manor house has been the family home of the Sidneys. The wood-beam medieval hall is famous, and the interior is Elizabethan. An 11-acre Italian garden and a toy museum are other interests.

Petworth House: Art lovers, take note: this sprawling 17th-century mansion has the National Trust's richest collections of paintings, including treasures by J.M.W. Turner, who visited here. Capability Brown's park is a draw, too.

Redbrick Herstmonceux Castle looks like something out of a fairy tale.

TIPS FOR VISITING

Keep in mind that houses and castles are unique. What you get for your entrance fee differs enormously. You may be free to wander at will, or you may be organized into groups like prisoners behind enemy lines. Sometimes the exterior of a building may be spectacular, but the interior dull. And the gardens and grounds may be just as interesting as (or more so than) the house. You can often pay separately for the house and grounds, so choose your admission ticket accordingly.

Consider the kids. More and more houses have activities or special events aimed at kids, especially in summer; some even have playgrounds.

Look into money-saving passes. If you plan to see lots of historic houses and castles, it might be cheaper to buy a pass, such as VisitBritain's Great British Heritage Pass, or to join an organization such as the National Trust (⇨ *Sightseeing Passes in Essentials in Travel Smart England*) and thus get free entry. Check entrance fees against your itinerary to see what you will save.

Check seasonal opening hours. Hours can change abruptly, so call the day before or check online. Many houses are open only from April to October, and they may have extremely limited hours. In other cases the houses have parks and gardens that are open much of the year. Consider a trip in shoulder seasons if you can't take the crowds that inevitably pack the most popular houses. Quite a few places are open during December with Christmas displays.

Plan your transportation. If you don't have a car, it's essential to plan transportation in advance. Some places are tucked deep in the countryside; others are more accessible.

Consider a stay at a property. To get even more up close and personal, you can rent a cottage from the **National Trust** (⊕ *www.nationaltrustcottages.co.uk*) or **English Heritage** (⊕ *www.english-heritage. org.uk/holidaycottages*). Some privately owned houses have cottages for rent on their estates; their Web sites generally have this information. The **Landmark Trust** (⊕ *www.landmarktrust.org.uk*) and **Vivat Trust** (⊕ *www.vivat-trust.org*) also have properties for rent.

DID YOU KNOW?

Visits to England's historic houses aren't just about looking at rooms from behind velvet ropes. Some places, including Hever Castle, offer plenty of family fun and activities including fairs and jousting displays.

☎ *01732/866368* ⊕ *www.nationaltrust.org.uk* ✉£*10.60; garden only, £5.30* ⊙ *Mid–Mar.–June and early Sept.–late Oct., Wed.–Sun. 11–5; July–early Sept., Tues.–Sun. 11–5; last admission at 4:15.*

KNOLE

8 mi east of Chartwell, 11 mi north of Royal Tunbridge Wells, 27 mi southeast of London.

GETTING HERE AND AROUND

To get to the town of Sevenoaks from Chartwell, drive north to Wester-ham, then pick up A25 and head east for 8 mi to A225. The route is well signposted. Southeastern trains travel from London's Charing Cross Station to Sevenoaks every 15 minutes. The journey takes about 30 minutes. Knole is a 20-minute walk from the train station.

EXPLORING

Fodor's Choice
★

Knole. The town of Sevenoaks lies in London's commuter belt, a world away from the baronial air of its premier attraction, the grand, beloved home of the Sackville family since the 16th century. Begun in the 15th century and enlarged in 1603 by Thomas Sackville, Knole, with its complex of courtyards and buildings, resembles a small town. You'll need most of an afternoon to explore it thoroughly. The house is noted for its tapestries, embroidered furnishings, and the most famous set of 17th-century silver furniture to survive. Most of the salons are in the pre-baroque mode, rather dark and armorial. The magnificently florid staircase was a novelty in its Elizabethan heyday. Vita Sackville-West grew up at Knole and set her novel *The Edwardians,* a witty account of life among the gilded set, here. Encircled by a 1,000-acre park where herds of deer roam free, the house lies in the center of Sevenoaks, opposite St. Nicholas Church. ⊠ *Off A225* ☎ *01732/450608* ⊕ *www. nationaltrust.org.uk* ✉ *House £10.40, gardens £5* ⊙ *Mar., weekends noon–4; Apr.–Oct., Wed.–Sun. noon–4. Gardens Apr.–Sept., Tues. 11–4. Last admission 30 mins before closing.*

IGHTHAM MOTE

7 mi southeast of Knole, 10 mi north of Royal Tunbridge Wells, 31 mi southeast of London.

GETTING HERE AND AROUND

The house sits 6 mi south of Sevenoaks. From Sevenoaks, follow A25 east to A227 and then follow the signs. At the village of Ivy Hatch follow signs to tiny Mote Road, which winds its way to the house. The 404 bus from Sevenoaks stops in Ivy Hatch periodically throughout the day, and you can walk to the house from there; the journey is slightly under a mile.

EXPLORING

★   **Ightham Mote.** Finding Ightham Mote requires careful navigation, but it's worth the effort to see a vision right out of the Middle Ages. To enter this outstanding example of a small manor house, you cross a stone bridge over a dreamy mote. This moat, however, does not relate to the "mote" in the name, which refers to the role of the house as a meeting place, or "moot." Built nearly 700 years ago, Ightham (pronounced

One of England's most notable stately homes, sprawling Knole displayed the power of the Sackvilles.

i-tem) Mote's magical exterior has changed little since the 14th century, but within you'll find that it encompasses styles of several periods, Tudor to Victorian. The Great Hall is an antiquarian's delight, both comfy and grand, and the Tudor chapel, drawing room, and billiards room in the northwest quarter are highlights. ⊠ *Off A227, Ivy Hatch, Sevenoaks* ☎ *01732/810378* ⊕ *www.nationaltrust.org.uk* 🎫 *£11* ⊗ *House Mid-Mar.–Oct., Thurs.–Mon. 11–5; Nov. and Dec., Thurs.–Sun. 11–3. Estate daily all yr, dawn–dusk.*

ROCHESTER

15 mi north of Ightham Mote, 28 mi southeast of London.

Positioned near the confluence of the Thames and the River Medway, this posh town has a history of Roman, Saxon, and Norman occupation, all of which have left architectural remains, including the vast castle at the town center. Novelist Charles Dickens called Rochester home for more than a decade, until his death in 1870. You can still stroll through the garden and see the exterior of the Swiss-style chalet where he wrote. Every December the city hosts the Dickensian Christmas Festival.

Across the river from Rochester is Chatham, with a noted maritime museum and the Dickens World theme park.

GETTING HERE AND AROUND

To drive to Rochester, take the M2, turning off on the A2. The journey from London should take about 45 minutes. Southeastern trains run from several London stations, including St. Pancras, Victoria, and Cannon Street. The journey trip takes around 40 minutes.

ESSENTIALS
Visitor Information Rochester (✉ *95 High St.* ☎ *01634/843666*
⊕ *www.visitkent.co.uk*).

EXPLORING

🐌 **Dickens World.** Filling an aluminum-clad hangar in a giant shopping center, Dickens World is a literary theme park. Inside is a small but beautifully designed Victorian London scene where you can walk down an alley and climb the stairs in period houses. There's a schoolroom with a fierce headmaster; a haunted house; and a (silly but fun) boat ride down a narrow canal that is loosely based on the story of Pip and Magwitch in *Great Expectations.* The 3-D film about Dickens is actually pretty good. This curiosity is popular for families with young children and for local school field trips. ✉ *Leviathan Way, Chatham* ☎ *01634/890421* ⊕ *www. dickensworld.co.uk* 🎫 *£13* ⊙ *Tues.–Sun. 10–5:30; last admission at 5.*

Historic Dockyard. The buildings and 47 retired ships at the 80-acre dockyard across the River Medway from Rochester constitute the country's most complete Georgian-to-early-Victorian dockyard. Fans of maritime history could easily spend a day at the exhibits and structures. The dockyard's origins go back to the time of Henry VIII; some 400 ships were built here over the centuries. There's a guided tour of the submarine HMS *Ocelot,* the last warship to be built for the Royal Navy at Chatham. ■ **TIP➔** Save your ticket, as it's good for a year. ✉ *Chatham* ☎ *01634/823807* ⊕ *www.chdt.org.uk* 🎫 *£15.50* ⊙ *Mid-Mar.–Oct., daily 10–6 (or dusk if earlier).*

Rochester Castle. The impressive ruins of Rochester Castle are a superb example of Norman military architecture. The keep, built in the 1100s using the old Roman city wall as a foundation, is the tallest in England. It's been shored up but left without floors, so that from the bottom you can see to the open roof and study the complex structure. At the shop you can pick up well-researched guides to the building. ✉ *Boley Hill* ☎ *01634/402276* ⊕ *www.english-heritage.org.uk* 🎫 *£5* ⊙ *Apr.–Sept., daily 10–6; Oct.–Mar., daily 10–4; last admission 30 mins before closing.*

Rochester Cathedral. In AD 604 Augustine of Canterbury ordained the first English bishop in a small cathedral on this site. The current cathedral, England's second oldest, is a jumble of architectural styles. Much of the original Norman building (1077) remains, including the striking west front, the highly carved portal, and the tympanum above the doorway. Some medieval art survives, including a 13th-century Wheel of Fortune on the choir walls; it's a reminder of how difficult medieval life was. ✉ *Boley Hill* ☎ *01634/843366* ⊕ *www.rochestercathedral.org* 🎫 *£2 donation suggested* ⊙ *Mon.–Sat. 7:30–6, Sun. 7:30–5.*

WHERE TO STAY
For expanded reviews, visit Fodors.com.

££   ▦ **Gordon House Hotel.** Across from the cathedral, this friendly guest-
HOTEL house in central Rochester retains some Victorian architectural details.
Pros: friendly staff; quiet rooms. **Cons:** some rooms are small; bathrooms are a bit old-fashioned. ✉ *91 High St.* ☎ *01634/814769* ⊕ *www. gordonhousehotel.net* ⇥ *12 rooms* ⚇ *In-room: no a/c. In-hotel: restaurant, bar* ▯◯▯ *Breakfast.*

NIGHTLIFE AND THE ARTS

Rochester sponsors a **Dickensian Christmas Festival** (☏ 01634/306000) on the first weekend in December. Thousands of people in period dress participate in reenactments of scenes from the author's novel *A Christmas Carol*. A candlelight procession, mulled wine and roasted chestnuts, and Christmas carols at the cathedral add to the celebration. Another important Dickens festival takes place in Broadstairs (40 mi east).

LEEDS CASTLE

12 mi south of Rochester, 19 mi northwest of Royal Tunbridge Wells, 40 mi southeast of London.

GETTING HERE AND AROUND

Just off the M20 motorway, signs direct you to Leeds Castle from every road in the area, so it's hard to miss.

EXPLORING

Leeds Castle. The bubbling River Medway runs through Maidstone, Kent's county seat, with its backdrop of chalky downs. Nearby, the fairy-tale stronghold of Leeds Castle commands two small islands on a peaceful lake. Dating to the 9th century and rebuilt by the Normans in 1119, Leeds (not to be confused with the city in the north of England) became a favorite home of many medieval English queens. Henry VIII liked it so much he had it converted from a fortress into a grand palace. The interior doesn't match the glories of the much-photographed exterior, although there are fine paintings and furniture, including many pieces from the 20th-century refurbishment by the castle's last private owner, Lady Baillie. The outside attractions are more impressive and include a maze, a grotto, an aviary of native and exotic birds, and woodland gardens. The castle is 5 mi east of Maidstone. ⊠ *A20* ☏ *01622/765400* ⊕ *www.leedscastle.org.uk* ✏ *£17.50* ☉ *Apr.–Oct., daily 10–5; Nov.– Mar., daily 10:30–4; last admission 30 mins before closing.*

SISSINGHURST CASTLE GARDEN

10 mi south of Leeds Castle, 53 mi southeast of London.

GETTING HERE AND AROUND

For those without a car, take a train from London's Charing Cross Station and transfer to a bus in Staplehurst. Direct buses operate on Tuesday, Friday, and Sunday between May and August; at other times, take the bus to Sissinghurst village and walk the remaining 1¼ mi. From Leeds Castle, make your way south on B2163 and A274 through Headcorn, and then follow signs.

EXPLORING

Fodor's Choice ★ **Sissinghurst Castle Garden.** One of the most famous gardens in the world, unpretentiously beautiful and quintessentially English, Sissinghurst rests deep in the Kentish countryside. The gardens, with 10 themed "rooms," were laid out in the 1930s around the remains of part of a moated Tudor castle by writer Vita Sackville-West (one of the Sackvilles of Knole; she grew up there) and her husband, the diplomat Harold Nicolson. Climb the tower to see Sackville-West's study and to get wonderful views of the garden and surrounding fields. You can also enter the house to see the library, with its echoes of Knole. ■TIP→ Visit in June and July, when the roses are in bloom. It's less busy later in the afternoon. The White Garden, with its snow-color flowers and silver-gray foliage, is a classic, and the herb garden and cottage garden reveals Sackville-West's knowledge of plants. There are woodland and lake walks, too, making it easy to spend a half day or more here. Stop by the big tea shop for a lunch that uses the farm's fruits and vegetables. If you'd like to linger, the National Trust is now renting the Priest's House on the property for a minimum stay of three nights: check ⊕ *www.nationaltrustcottages. co.uk*. ⊠ *A262, Cranbrook* ☎ *01580/710701* ⊕ *www.nationaltrust.org. uk* ☜ *£10* ⊘ *Mid-Mar.–Oct., Fri.–Tues. 10:30–5; last admission at 4:30.*

Biddenden Winery and Cider Works. About 3½ mi east of Sissinghurst on the A262, Biddenden Windery cultivates nine types of grapes on 22 acres, with a focus on the German Ortega, Huxelrebe, Bacchus, and Reichensteiner varieties. You can wander the grounds and sample wines, ciders, and apple juice. There are free tours once a month or so. It also rents out a loft with a kitchen by the week (from £260 per week in winter to £440 in summer). ⊠ *Biddenden* ☎ *01580/291726* ⊕ *www. biddendenvineyards.com* ☜ *Free* ⊘ *Mar.–late Dec., Mon.–Sat. 10–5, Sun. 11–5; Jan. and Feb., Mon.–Sat. 10–5. Closed Christmas wk.*

WHERE TO EAT AND STAY

£   ✕ **Claris's Tea Shop.** Claris's, near Sissinghurst Castle Garden, serves tra-
CAFÉ   ditional English teas in a handsome half-timber room. A cream tea includes scones and butter, clotted cream, preserves, and a pot of tea, or choose from cakes and toasted sandwiches. The garden is pleasant on sunny summer days, and a gift shop stocks china and glass. ⊠ *1–3 High St., Biddenden* ☎ *01580/291025* ⊕ *www.collectablegifts. net* ⊟ *No credit cards* ⊘ *Closed Mon.–Wed. No dinner.*

££   ▥ **Bishopsdale Oast.** This converted 18th-century double-kiln oasthouse
B&B/INN   (used for drying hops) makes an atmospheric place to stay in tiny Biddenden, near Sissinghurst. **Pros:** quiet and restful setting; owner is a chef so breakfasts are great; nice garden. **Cons:** some rooms are small; car needed to get around. ⊠ *Biddenden* ☎ *01580/291027* ☜ *www. bishopsdaleoast.co.uk* ☜ *5 rooms* ⚇ *In-room: no a/c. In-hotel: parking* ❑| *Breakfast.*

The South

WORD OF MOUTH

"Close to Avebury Stone Circles is West Kennet Long Barrow. You can park on the roadside and walk up to this, and then enter it. To actually be inside a 5,000-year-old manmade structure is amazing. There is also the Kennet Stone Avenue, Silbury Hill, and the museum in Avebury."

—julia_t

WELCOME TO THE SOUTH

TOP REASONS TO GO

★ **Salisbury Cathedral:** At one of England's most spectacular cathedrals, try a tour around the roof and spire for a fascinating angle on this must-see monument.

★ **Stonehenge:** At the right time of day (early or late is best), this mystical ring of stones can cast a memorable spell against the backdrop of Salisbury Plain.

★ **House and garden at Stourhead:** It's the perfect English combination. A Palladian mansion plus acres of parkland, landscaped in the 18th century, induce feelings of bliss.

★ **The New Forest:** Get away from it all in the South's most extensive wilderness—crisscrossed by myriad trails that are ideal for horseback riding, hiking, and biking.

★ **Literary trails:** Jane Austen, Thomas Hardy, and John Fowles have all made this part of Britain a happy stomping ground for book buffs, with a concentration of sights in Chawton, Dorchester, and Lyme Regis.

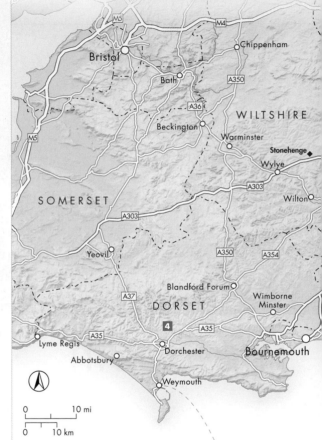

1 Winchester, Portsmouth, and Southampton. One of the region's most compelling and historically rich towns, Winchester, lies a short distance from the well-heeled villages of New Alresford and Chawton and the great south-coast ports of Portsmouth and Southampton.

2 Isle of Wight. Osborne House, near Cowes, and Carisbrooke Castle, outside Newport, have much historic interest. The picturesque east-coast resorts of Ryde and Ventnor contrast with the dramatic Needles, the island's most iconic landmark, on the western tip.

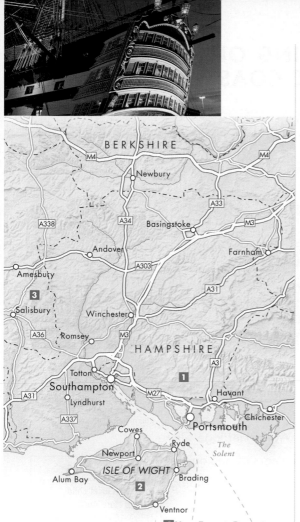

GETTING ORIENTED

The wide-open, wind-blown inland county of Wiltshire offers a sharp contrast to the tame, sequestered villages of Hampshire and Dorset and the bustle of the port cities of Southampton and Portsmouth. Spend your nights in the more compelling towns of Salisbury and Winchester instead of these cities. One draw outside Salisbury is Stonehenge; you're also near the stone circles at Avebury. From there you can swing south to the New Forest. The southern coast of Dorset has a couple of popular vacation resorts, Bournemouth and Weymouth, and ancient sites: Corfe Castle, Maiden Castle, and Cerne Abbas. Lyme Regis, at the center of the wide arc of Lyme Bay, is a vacation favorite. It provides a gateway to the Jurassic Coast, a World Heritage Site that stretches between Swanage in the east and Exmouth in Devon.

3 **Salisbury, Stonehenge, and Salisbury Plain.** A tour of Wiltshire kicks off in the cathedral city of Salisbury, close to Wilton, Stonehenge, and Avebury. Farther afield are the great estates of Stourhead and Longleat.

4 **New Forest, Dorset, and the South Coast.** The sparsely populated New Forest stretches between Southampton and Bournemouth. The route west passes Wimborne Minster, dominated by its church, and ruined Corfe Castle. South of the market towns of Shaftesbury and Sherbourne, Dorchester and Weymouth lead to Lyme Regis.

FOSSIL HUNTING ON THE JURASSIC COAST

Besides the dramatic beauty of the jagged cliffs and hidden coves, fossils and fossil hunting are the lure for visitors to the Jurassic Coast. The varied coastline is a World Heritage Site encompassing 185 million years of geological history, and constant erosion makes finding fossils a distinct possibility.

Scenery can distract you from fossil hunting on the beautiful Jurassic Coast (above); intriguing fossil finds (right, top); the coast near Charmouth (right, bottom).

A geological journey through time, the Jurassic Coast stretches for 95 mi between the younger, Cretaceous, chalk stacks at Studland Bay in Dorset in the east to the older, striking red Triassic cliffs at Exmouth (Devon) in the west. The earliest Jurassic cliffs of West Dorset formed in a tropical sea that flooded a vast desert. After the sea level dropped 140 million years ago, forest, swampland, and dinosaurs thrived, before the rising sea flooded the area once again. Fossils are continuously being uncovered here, and both amateurs and professionals have made many important finds here. Coastal towns and villages act as gateways to the site, offering tourist information, boat trips, and guided fossil walks.

MARY ANNING

In 1811 a local child named Mary Anning (1799–1847) dug out an ichthyosaur skeleton near Lyme Regis; it's now on display in London's Natural History Museum. Anning's obsession with Jurassic remains left her labeled locally as the "fossil woman." Throughout her life she made many valuable discoveries that were sought after by museums and collectors in Britain, Europe, and beyond.

WHEN TO GO

If you're intent on collecting fossils, consider visiting in winter when storms and rough seas encourage cliff erosion that sweeps fossils onto the beaches below. Search at low tide if you want the very best chance of making discoveries. Winter is not only wilder, but a lot quieter, too. In summer the seas are calmer and the weather is more reliable. Although summer is busier, the days are longer and buses more frequent—a plus if you're exploring the coastal path.

4

WHAT TO LOOK FOR

Fossil hunters should stick to the area around Charmouth (the beach below Stonebarrow Hill, east of Charmouth, is especially fruitful) and Lyme Regis. The rock here is rich in fossils of the creatures that lived in the Jurassic oceans, and is especially prone to rapid erosion. You are free to pick and chip at the rocks; no permit is needed.

Keep your eyes peeled on the shore at low tide and you may well find ammonites. These chambered cephalopods from the Jurassic era, related to today's nautilus, are usually preserved in either calcite or iron pyrite ("fool's gold"); shinier, more fragile specimens may be found in aragonite. Visit the museums in Lyme Regis and Dorchester to remind you what to look for: the lustrous spirals are similar in heft and size to a brass coin, most smaller than a 10p piece. Other common fossils include sea urchins, white oyster shells, and coiled worm tubes. Look out for belemnites, an extinct cephalopod.

SEEING THE COAST

The South West Coast Path National Trail, more than 600 mi long, passes through the area and is a great way to get closer to the Jurassic Coast. The CoastlinX53 bus travels along the Jurassic Coast from Poole to Weymouth and Exeter, and allows you to walk a section of the path and return by bus.

You can join a pro: information on guided walks is available from local tourist offices and the Lyme Regis Museum. Operators offer boat trips from gateway towns, an easy way to appreciate the coastline. See the boards at harbors, or ask at information centers. Fossil collector **Brandon Lennon** (☎ 07944/664757 ⊕ *www. lymeregisfossilsforsale.co.uk* ✉ *£7*) runs fossil-hunting expeditions with geologist Ian Lennon. A mile east of Lyme Regis, the **Charmouth Heritage Coast Centre** (☎ 01297/560772 ⊕ *www.charmouth. org* ✉ *£7 walks*) offers walks, kids' events, and a permanent exhibit. March through November, **Harry May** (☎ 07974/753287 ⊕ *www.mackerelfishinglymeregis.com* ✉ *£8*) operates mackerel fishing and sightseeing boat trips on the *Marie F* from the Cobb in Lyme Regis.

Updated by
Sarah Christie

Cathedrals, stately homes, stone circles—the South, made up of Hampshire, Dorset, and Wiltshire counties, holds all kinds of attractions, and not a few quiet pleasures. Two important cathedrals, Winchester and Salisbury (pronounced *sawls-bree*), are here, as are stately homes—Longleat, Stourhead, and Wilton House, among them—intriguing market towns, and hundreds of haunting prehistoric remains, two of which, Avebury and Stonehenge, should not be missed.

These are just the tourist-brochure superlatives. Anyone spending time in these parts should rent a bike or a car and set out to discover the back-road villages. Close to London, the green fields of Hampshire divide the cliffs and coves of the West Country from the hustle and bustle of the big city. Even if you have a coastal destination in mind, hit the brakes—there's plenty to see. One of the many historical highlights was when Alfred the Great, teaching religion and letters, made Winchester the capital of 9th-century England and helped lay plans for Britain's first navy, sowing the seeds of the Commonwealth. Winchester is dominated by its imposing cathedral, filled with the Gothic tombs of 15th-century bishops. This town is a good base for visiting quiet villages where many of England's literary greats lived or died. The road to Jane Austen's home at Chawton is a much-trodden path.

Beyond Hampshire and the New Forest lies the somewhat harsher terrain of Salisbury Plain. Two monuments, millennia apart, stand sentinel over the plain. One is the 404-foot-tall stone spire of Salisbury Cathedral, immortalized in oil by John Constable. Not far away is the most imposing and dramatic prehistoric structure in Europe: Stonehenge. The many theories about its construction and purpose only add to its mystical attraction.

Other districts have their own pleasures, and many have literary or historical associations. Turn your sights to the Dorset heathland, the countryside explored in the novels of Thomas Hardy. This district is spanned by grass-covered chalk hills—the downs—wooded valleys, meandering rivers, and meadows. Heaving beach resorts sit next to hidden coves, interspersed with unspoiled market towns and villages. Facing the sea are Lyme Regis, on the fossil-rich Jurassic Coast, and Cowes, on the Isle of Wight—Queen Victoria's favorite getaway—where colorful flags flutter from sleek yachts.

The South has been quietly central to England's history for well over 4,000 years, occupied successively by prehistoric man, the Celts, the Romans, the Saxons, the Normans, and the modern British. History continues to be made here. On D-Day, Allied forces sailed for Normandy from this coast; nearly 40 years later, British forces set out to recover the Falklands.

4

SOUTH PLANNER

WHEN TO GO

Places such as Stonehenge and Longleat House attract plenty of people at all times; bypass such sights on weekends, public holidays, or school vacations. Don't plan to visit the cathedrals of Salisbury and Winchester on a Sunday, when your visit will be restricted, or during services, when it won't be appreciated by worshippers. In summer the coastal resorts of Bournemouth and Weymouth are crowded; it may be difficult to find the accommodations you want. The Isle of Wight gets its fair share of summer visitors, especially during the weeklong Cowes Regatta in late July or early August. Because ferries fill up to capacity, you may have to wait for the next one. The New Forest is most alluring in spring and early summer (for the foaling season) and fall (for the colorful foliage), whereas summer can be busy with walkers and campers. In all seasons, take waterproof boots for the mud and puddles.

PLANNING YOUR TIME

The South has no obvious hub, though many people base themselves in one or both of the cathedral cities of Winchester and Salisbury and make excursions to nearby destinations. The coastal cities of Portsmouth and Southampton have their charms, but neither of these large urban centers is particularly attractive as an overnight stop. Busy Bournemouth, whose major sight is a Victorian-era museum, has quieter areas that are more conducive to relaxation. To escape the bustle, the New Forest, southwest of Southampton, offers space and semi-wilderness. It's easy to take a morning or afternoon break to enjoy the activities it offers, whether on foot, by bike, or on horseback. The Isle of Wight needs more time, and is worth exploring at leisure over at least a couple of days.

GETTING HERE AND AROUND

BUS TRAVEL

National Express buses at London's Victoria Coach Station on Buckingham Palace Road depart every one to two hours for Bournemouth (2½ hours), Southampton (2¼), and Portsmouth (2 hours), and every 2 to 3 hours for Winchester (1 hour, 40 minutes). There are three buses daily to Salisbury (about three hours). Bluestar and Stagecoach South operate a comprehensive service in the Portsmouth, Southampton, New Forest, Winchester, and Bournemouth areas. First and Wilts & Dorset serve

234 <   **The South**

Salisbury, Bournemouth, and Dorchester, and Southern Vectis covers
the Isle of Wight. Greyhound operates a daily bus service between Bul-
leid Way, near Victoria Coach Station, and Portsmouth, Southampton,
and Bournemouth. Wilts & Dorset offers both one-day Dayrider and
seven-day Network passes valid on all the company's bus routes. Ask
about the Megarider tickets offered by Stagecoach, Rover and Freedom tickets offered by Southern Vectis, and Freedom tickets offered
by Bluestar. Explorer tickets allow you unlimited travel on buses operated by different companies. Contact Traveline for all information on
routes and tickets.

Bus Contacts Bluestar (☎ 01983/827005 ⊕ www.bluestarbus.co.uk).
First (☎ 0870/010–6022 ⊕ www.firstgroup.com). **Greyhound** (☎ 0900/096–
0000 ⊕ www.greyhounduk.com). **National Express** (☎ 0871/781–8178
⊕ www.nationalexpress.com). **Southern Vectis** (☎ 01983/827000
⊕ www.islandbuses.info). **Stagecoach South** (☎ 0845/121–0170 ⊕ www.
stagecoachbus.com). **Traveline** (☎ 0871/200–2233 ⊕ www.traveline.org.uk).
Wilts & Dorset Bus Co. (☎ 01722/336855 ⊕ www.wdbus.co.uk).

CAR TRAVEL

On the whole, the region is easily negotiable using public transportation. But for rural spots, especially the grand country estates, a car is
useful. The well-developed road network includes M3 to Winchester
(70 mi from London) and Southampton (77 mi); A3 to Portsmouth (77
mi); and M27 along the coast, from the New Forest and Southampton
to Portsmouth. For Salisbury, take M3 to A303, then A30. A35 connects Bournemouth to Dorchester and Lyme Regis, and A350 runs
north to Dorset's inland destinations.

TRAIN TRAVEL

South West Trains serves the South from London's Waterloo Station.
Travel times average 1 hour to Winchester, 1½ hours to Southampton,
1¾ hours to Bournemouth, and 2¾ hours to Weymouth. The trip to
Salisbury takes 1½ hours, and Portsmouth about 1¾ hours. A yearlong
Network Railcard, valid throughout the South and Southeast, entitles
you and up to three accompanying adults to one-third off most train
fares, and up to four accompanying children ages 5–15 to a 60% discount off the full fare. It costs £25.

Train Contacts National Rail Enquiries (☎ 0845/748–4950 ⊕ www.
nationalrail.co.uk). **South West Trains** (☎ 0845/748–4950 or 0845/600–0650
⊕ www.southwesttrains.co.uk).

TOURS

The Guild of Registered Tourist Guides maintains a directory of qualified Blue Badge guides who can meet you anywhere in the region for
private tours. Local organizations such as Wessexplore can also arrange
Blue Badge tours. On the Isle of Wight, Southern Vectis operates open-
top bus tours.

Tour Information Guild of Registered Tourist Guides (☎ 020/7403–1115
⊕ www.blue-badge-guides.com). **Wessexplore** (☎ 01722/326304
⊕ www.dmac.co.uk/wessexplore).

RESTAURANTS

In summer, and especially on summer weekends, visitors can overrun the restaurants in small villages, so either book a table in advance or be prepared to wait. The more popular or upscale the restaurant, the more critical a reservation is. For local specialties, try fresh-grilled river trout or sea bass poached in brine, or dine like a king on New Forest's renowned venison. Hampshire is noted for its pig and sheep farming, and you might zero in on pork and lamb dishes on local restaurant menus. The region places a strong accent on seasonal produce, so venison, for example, is best sampled between September and February.

HOTELS

Modern hotel chains are well represented, and in rural areas you can choose between elegant country-house hotels, traditional coaching inns (updated to different degrees), and modest guesthouses. Some seaside hotels do not accept one-night bookings in summer. If you plan to visit Cowes on the Isle of Wight during Cowes Week, the annual yachting jamboree in late July or early August, book well in advance.

WHAT IT COSTS IN POUNDS					
	£	££	£££	££££	£££££
Restaurants	under £10	£10–£14	£15–£19	£20–£25	over £25
Hotels	under £70	£70–£120	£121–£160	£161–£220	over £220

Restaurant prices are per person for a main course or equivalent combination of smaller dishes at dinner excluding tax. Hotels prices reflect the rack rate of a standard double room for two people in high season, including 20% V.A.T. Check online for off-season rates and special deals or discounts.

Visitor Information Tourism South East (⊕ www.visitsoutheastengland.com). **Tourism South West** (⊕ www.visitsouthwest.co.uk).

WINCHESTER, PORTSMOUTH, AND SOUTHAMPTON

From the cathedral city of Winchester, 70 mi southwest of London, you can meander southward to the coast, stopping at the bustling ports of Southampton and Portsmouth to explore their maritime heritage. From either port you can strike out for the restful shores of the Isle of Wight, vacation home of Queen Victoria and thousands of modern-day Britons.

WINCHESTER

70 mi southwest of London, 12 mi northeast of Southampton.

Winchester is among the most historic of English cities, and as you walk the graceful streets and wander the many gardens, a sense of the past envelops you. Although it is now merely the county seat of Hampshire, for more than four centuries Winchester served as England's capital. Here, in AD 827, Egbert was crowned first king of England, and his successor, Alfred the Great, held court until his death in 899. After the

Norman Conquest in 1066, William I ("the Conqueror") had himself crowned in London, but took the precaution of repeating the ceremony in Winchester. William also commissioned the local monastery to produce the Domesday Book, a record of the general census begun in 1085. The city remained the center of ecclesiastical, commercial, and political power until the 13th century, when that power shifted to London. It may be England's ancient capital, but Winchester is also a thriving market town living firmly in the present, with its fair share of shops and eateries on High Street.

GETTING HERE AND AROUND

On a main train line and on the M3 motorway, Winchester is easily accessible from London. The train station is a short walk from the sights; the bus station is in the center, opposite the tourist office. The one-way streets are notoriously confusing, so find a parking lot as soon as possible. The city center is very walkable, and most of High Street is closed to vehicular traffic. A walk down High Street and Broadway will bring you to St. Giles Hill, which has a panoramic view of the city.

TIMING

The city is busier than usual during the farmers' market, the largest in the country, held on the second and the last Sunday of each month.

ESSENTIALS

Visitor and Tour Information Winchester (⊠ *The Guildhall, Broadway* ☎ *01962/840500* ⊕ *www.visitwinchester.co.uk*). **Winchester Tourist Guides** (⊕ *www.winchestertouristguides.com*).

EXPLORING
TOP ATTRACTIONS

City Museum. Across from the cathedral, the museum tells Winchester's past through displays of Celtic pottery, Saxon jewelry and coins, and reconstructed Victorian shops. It's an imaginative, well-presented collection that will appeal to children and adults alike—check out the Saxon costumes for kids to try on, local ceramics, and domestic and agricultural bits and pieces from the Middle Ages, and, on the top floor, some well-restored Roman mosaics. Pick up an audio guide at the entrance (£2) to get the most out of the museum. ⊠ *The Square* ☎ *01962/863064* ⊕ *www.winchester.gov.uk* ⊠ *Free* ⊙ *Tues.–Sat. 10–4, Sun. noon–4.*

Great Hall. A few blocks west of the cathedral, this hall is all that remains of the city's Norman castle, and is still used today for events and ceremonies. Here the English Parliament met for the first time in 1246; Sir Walter Raleigh was tried for conspiracy against King James I and condemned to death in 1603; and Dame Alice Lisle was sentenced to death by the brutal Judge Jeffreys for sheltering fugitives, after Monmouth's Rebellion in 1685. Occupying one corner of the Great Hall is a huge and gaudy sculpture of Queen Victoria, carved to mark her Golden Jubilee in 1887. But the hall's greatest relic hangs on its west wall: King Arthur's Round Table has places for 24 knights and a portrait of Arthur bearing a remarkable resemblance to King Henry VIII. In fact, the table dates back no further than the 13th century and was repainted by order of Henry on the occasion of a visit by the Holy Roman Emperor Charles V; the real Arthur was probably a Celtic chieftain who held off

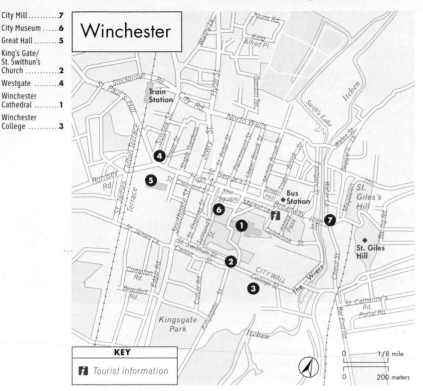

the invading Saxons after the fall of the Roman Empire in the 5th or 6th century. The Tudor monarchs revived the Arthurian legend for political purposes. Take time to wander through Queen Eleanor's Garden—a re-creation of a medieval noblewoman's shady retreat. ⊠ *Castle Hill* ☎ *01962/846476* ⊕ *www.hants.gov.uk/greathall* ⊑ *Free* ☉ *Daily 10–5.*

King's Gate. On St. Swithun Street on the south side of the Close, this structure was built in the 13th century and is one of two gates remaining from the original city wall. **St. Swithun's Church** is built over King's Gate.

★ **Winchester Cathedral.** The city's greatest monument, begun in 1079 and consecrated in 1093, presents a sturdy, chunky appearance in keeping with its Norman construction, so that the Gothic lightness within is even more breathtaking. Its tower, transepts, and crypt, and the inside core of the great Perpendicular nave, reveal some of the world's best surviving examples of Norman architecture. Other features, such as the arcades, the presbytery (behind the choir, holding the high altar), and the windows, are Gothic alterations carried out between the 12th and 14th century. Little of the original stained glass has survived, however, thanks to Cromwell's Puritan troops, who ransacked the cathedral in the 17th century during the English Civil War, but you can still see the sumptuously illuminated 12th-century Winchester Bible in the Library and Triforium Gallery.

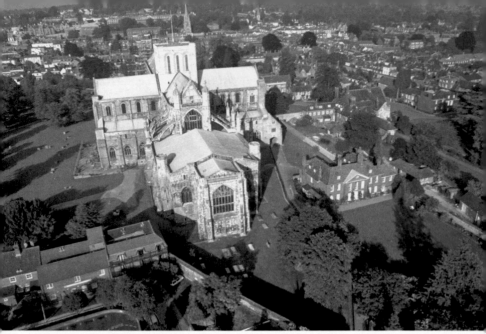

The historic city of Winchester, with its graceful cathedral, is well worth exploring.

Among the many well-known people buried in the cathedral are William the Conqueror's son, William II ("Rufus"), mysteriously murdered in the New Forest in 1100; Izaak Walton (1593–1683), author of *The Compleat Angler,* whose memorial window in Silkestede's Chapel was paid for by "the fishermen of England and America"; and Jane Austen, whose grave lies in the north aisle of the nave. The tombstone makes no mention of Austen's literary status, though a brass plaque in the wall, dating from 80 years after her death, celebrates her achievements, and modern panels provide an overview of her life and work. Firmly in the 20th century, Antony Gormley's evocative statue *Sound II* (1986) looms in the crypt, as often as not standing in water (as it was designed to do), because of seasonal flooding. You can also explore the bell tower—with views as far as the Isle of Wight in fair weather—and other recesses of the building on a tour. Special services or ceremonies may mean the cathedral is closed to visits, so call ahead. Outside the cathedral, explore the Close, the area that nearly envelopes the cathedral and contains neat lawns and the Deanery, Dome Alley, and Cheyney Court. ⊠ *The Close, Cathedral Precincts* ☏ *01962/857200* ⊕ *www.winchester-cathedral. org.uk* ✉ *Bell tower £6; combined entry to cathedral and bell tower £9* ◷ *Mon.–Sat. 9:30–5, Sun. 12:30–3. Library and Triforium Gallery Apr.–Oct., Mon. 2–4, Tues.–Sat. and national holidays 10:30–4; Nov.–Mar., Sat. 10:30–3:30. Free tours on the hr Mon.–Sat. 10–3, bell tower tours late May–Aug., Mon., Wed., and Fri. 2:15, Sat. 11:30 and 2:15; Sept.–late May, Wed. 2:15, Sat. 11:30 and 2:15.*

WORTH NOTING

City Mill. Set over the River Itchen, this working 18th-century water mill, complete with small island garden, is at the east end of High Street. The medieval mill on the site was rebuilt in 1743, remaining in use until the early 20th century. Restored by the National Trust, it still operates as a working mill on weekends, and you can purchase flour produced here in the gift shop. ✉ *Bridge St.* ☎ *01962/ 870057* ⊕ *www.nationaltrust.org. uk* ✉ *£3.60* ⊙ *Mid-Mar.–early Apr., late Apr.–May, mid-June–early July, and mid-Sept.–late Oct., Wed.–Sun. 10:30–5; mid-Apr., early June, mid-July–mid-Sept., and late Oct.–late Dec., daily 10:30–5.*

⟲ **Watercress Line.** New Alresford, 8 mi northeast of Winchester by A31 and B3046, is the starting point of the Watercress Line, a 10-mi railroad reserved for steam locomotives that runs to Alton. The line (named for the watercress beds formerly in the area) takes you on a nostalgic tour through reminders of 19th-century England. New Alresford has a village green crossed by a stream and some Georgian houses and antiques shops. ✉ *Railway station* ☎ *01962/733810* ⊕ *www.watercressline.co.uk* ✉ *£14* ⊙ *May–Sept., departures most days; Oct. and Dec.–Apr., weekends and national holidays.*

⟲ **Westgate.** At the top of High Street, this atmospheric fortified medieval structure was a debtor's prison for 150 years, and now holds a motley assortment of items relating to Tudor and Stuart times, displayed among the 16th-century graffiti by prisoners. Suits of armor—examples can be tried on—and the opportunity to make brass rubbings make it popular with kids, and you can take in a view of Winchester from the roof. ✉ *High St.* ☎ *01962/869864* ✉ *Free* ⊙ *Apr.–Oct., Mon.–Sat. 10–5, Sun. noon–5; early Feb.–Mar., Tues.–Sat. 10–4, Sun. noon–4.*

Winchester College. One of England's oldest "public" (i.e., private) schools was founded in 1382 by Bishop William of Wykeham, who has his own chapel in Winchester Cathedral. The school chapel is notable for its delicately vaulted ceiling. Among the buildings still in use is Chamber Court, center of college life for six centuries. Notice the "scholars"—students holding academic scholarships—clad in their traditional gowns. Call about tours, sometimes canceled due to college events. ✉ *College St.* ☎ *01962/621209* ⊕ *www.winchestercollege.co.uk* ✉ *£6* ⊙ *1-hr tours Mon., Wed., Fri., and Sat. 10:45, noon, 2:15, and 3:30; Tues. and Thurs. 10:45 and noon; Sun. 2:15 and 3:30.*

ST. SWITHUN WEATHER

St. Swithun (died AD 862) is interred in Winchester Cathedral, although he requested outdoor burial. Legend says that when his body was transferred inside from the cathedral's churchyard, it rained for 40 days. Since then, folk wisdom says that rain on St. Swithun's Day (July 15) means 40 more days of wet weather. (Elsewhere in England the name is usually spelled "Swithin.") Near St. Swithun's Church at King's Gate, at 8 College Street, is the house where Jane Austen died on July 18, 1817, three days after writing a comic poem about the legend of St. Swithun's Day (copies are usually available in the cathedral).

4

WHERE TO EAT

£££
MODERN BRITISH
✗ **The Bistro at Hotel du Vin.** Classic French and British fare is served with modern touches in this stylish bistro, converted from a redbrick Georgian town house. Dishes such as fillet of sea bass and char-grilled rib-eye steak are complemented by the many eclectic wine selections. In summer, food is served in the walled garden. The hotel's luxurious rooms (£££) are richly furnished in crisp modern style, with Oriental rugs enhancing the polished wooden floors. ⊠ *14 Southgate St.* ☎ *01962/841414* ⊕ *www.hotelduvin.com.*

£££
MODERN BRITISH
✗ **Chesil Rectory.** The timbered and gabled building may be Old English— 15th or 16th century—but the cuisine is contemporary, mixing classic recipes with local ingredients. Dishes might include seared Portland scallops, followed by braised shoulder of lamb or fish stew. Good-value fixed-price lunches and early-evening dinners are available. Service and the antique charm of the surroundings match the quality of the food. ⊠ *1 Chesil St.* ☎ *01962/851555* ⊕ *www.chesilrectory.co.uk* ⊘ *No dinner Sun.*

£
MODERN BRITISH
✗ **Ginger Two for Tea.** This bright and airy corner café is the place to come for a relaxed afternoon tea. White walls and wooden furniture lend it a modern, rustic feel. The kitchen serves simple lunches, locally baked cakes and pastries, and a variety of teas and coffees. Try such seasonal dishes as butternut squash soup, beet salad, or crepes with salmon. You'll find this place on a quiet road off High Street. ⊠ *29 St. Thomas St.* ☎ *01962/877733* ▭ *No credit cards* ⊘ *No dinner.*

£
BRITISH
✗ **The Royal Oak.** Quaff a half pint of draft bitter or dry cider at this lively traditional pub, which claims to be England's oldest bar. There's plenty of space to find a comfortable spot, including a secluded cellar with the remains of a Saxon wall. Bar meals, including roasts and burgers, are served until 9 pm. ⊠ *Royal Oak Passage off High St.* ☎ *01962/842701* ⊕ *www.theroyaloakwinchester.com.*

WHERE TO STAY

For expanded reviews, visit Fodors.com.

££
B&B/INN
★
⊡ **Enmill Barn.** Surrounded by gardens, this converted barn in peaceful countryside 3 mi west of the center of Winchester makes a good base for exploring villages and the South Downs. **Pros:** comfortable and spacious rooms; personal service; top-quality snooker and tennis facilities. **Cons:** guests share one breakfast table; rather remote location. ⊠ *Enmill La., Pitt* ☎ *01962/856740* ⊕ *www.enmill-barn.co.uk* ↘*3 rooms* ⌂ *In-room: no a/c, Wi-Fi (some). In-hotel: tennis court* ▭ *No credit cards* ⦿*Breakfast.*

£££££
HOTEL
⊡ **Lainston House.** Dating from 1668, this elegant country house in a 63-acre park is discreetly secluded, an obvious attraction for such eminent guests as Margaret Thatcher, who stayed here to write her memoirs. **Pros:** beautiful setting; attentive staff; sumptuous guest rooms and bathrooms. **Cons:** lower-priced rooms are drab; food sometimes disappoints. ⊠ *Woodman La. off B3049, Sparsholt* ☎ *01962/776088* ⊕ *www.lainstonhouse.com* ↘*41 rooms, 9 suites* ⌂ *In-room: no a/c (some), Wi-Fi. In-hotel: restaurant, tennis courts, gym, some pets allowed* ⦿*Breakfast.*

£££–££££
HOTEL
⊡ **Old Vine.** Blessed with an ideal location opposite the cathedral, this 18th-century inn has received a smart, modern makeover without losing any of its character. **Pros:** comfortable, elegant rooms; delicious

food. **Cons:** some rooms are small with no view; parking may be tricky to find. ✉ *8 Great Minster St.* ☎ *01962/854616* ⊕ *www. oldvinewinchester.com* ⌖ *4 rooms, 1 suite* ⚬ *In-room: no a/c, Internet. In-hotel: restaurant, bar, parking* ❧❘ *Breakfast.*

££   ⌕ **Wykeham Arms.** This old place,
HOTEL conveniently located near the cathedral and the college, has bedrooms that are cozy and full of quirky knickknacks. **Pros:** central location; quirky charm; lively bar. **Cons:** rooms above pub can be noisy; steep stairs; shabby in places. ✉ *75 Kingsgate St.* ☎ *01962/853834* ⊕ *www. fullershotels.com* ⌖ *13 rooms, 1 suite* ⚬ *In-room: no a/c, Wi-Fi. In-hotel: restaurant, bars, parking, some age restrictions* ❧❘ *Breakfast.*

> ## OPEN-AIR MARKETS
>
> Local markets provide a unique sense of place. Among the best is Winchester's, held in Middle Brook Street on the second and the last Sunday of each month. It specializes in local produce and goods. Also worth a look are Salisbury's traditional city market (Tuesday and Saturday); Southampton's Bargate Market for bric-a-brac (Friday), arts and crafts (first Saturday of each month), antiques (third Saturday), and local produce (second and fourth Saturday); and Dorchester's massive market of more than 500 stalls (Wednesday). The largest of all is just outside Wimborne Minster (Friday).

SHOPPING

King's Walk, off Friarsgate, has a number of stalls selling antiques, crafts, gift items, and bric-a-brac.

The Jays' Nest (✉ *King's Walk* ☎ *01962/865650*) specializes in jewelry, silver, and china.

Kingsgate Books and Prints (✉ *Kingsgate Arch, College St.* ☎ *01962/864710*) has a selection of secondhand books, maps, and prints.

The oldest bookshop in town, **P&G Wells** (✉ *11 College St.* ☎ *01962/ 852016*) has numerous books by and about Jane Austen, who took lodgings almost next door in 1817. It also has the region's largest selection of children's books.

CHAWTON

16 mi northeast of Winchester.

In Chawton you can visit the home of Jane Austen (1775–1817), who lived the last eight years of her life in the village; she moved to Winchester only during her final illness. The site has always drawn literary pilgrims, but with the ongoing release of successful films based on her novels, the town's popularity among visitors has grown enormously.

GETTING HERE AND AROUND

Hourly Stagecoach bus X64 service connects Winchester and New Alresford with Chawton. It's a 10-minute walk from the bus stop to Jane Austen's House. By car, take A31. Alternatively, take a 40-minute stroll along the footpath from Alton.

IN SEARCH OF JANE AUSTEN

Jane Austen used this tiny writing table at her home in Chawton.

Jane Austen country—a pleasant landscape filled with intimate villages—is where you can peer into decorous 18th- and early-19th-century society that she described with wry wit in such novels as *Emma, Persuasion, Sense and Sensibility,* and *Pride and Prejudice.* You can almost hear the tinkle of teacups raised by the likes of Elinor Dashwood and Mr. Darcy. Serious Janeites will want to retrace her life in the towns of Bath *(see Chapter 7), Chawton,* Winchester, and Lyme Regis.

BATH
Bath is the elegant setting that served as the backdrop for some of Austen's razor-sharp observations. She lived in Bath between 1801 and 1806, and although she wrote relatively little while she was here, she used it as a setting for *Northanger Abbey* and *Persuasion.* Bath's Jane Austen Centre explores her relationship with the city.

CHAWTON
About 83 mi southeast of Bath is this tiny Hampshire village, the heart of

Jane Austen country. Here you'll find the elegant but understated house where Austen worked on three of her novels. A former bailiff's cottage on her brother's estate, the house is now a museum that gives more than just a flavor of how she lived.

WINCHESTER
Driving southwest from Chawton, take A31 for about 15 mi to Winchester, where you can visit Austen's austere grave within the cathedral and view an exhibit about her life; then take in No. 8 College Street, where her battle with Addison's disease ended with her death on July 18, 1817.

LYME REGIS
Heading 110 mi southwest of Winchester you can visit Lyme Regis, the 18th-century seaside resort on the Devon border where Austen spent the summers of 1804 and 1805. Here, at the Cobb, the stone jetty that juts into Lyme Bay, poor Louisa Musgrove jumps off the steps known as Granny's Teeth—a turning point in Chapter 12 of *Persuasion.*

EXPLORING

★ **Jane Austen's House.** Here, in an unassuming redbrick house, Jane Austen wrote *Emma, Persuasion,* and *Mansfield Park,* and revised *Sense and Sensibility, Northanger Abbey,* and *Pride and Prejudice.* Now a museum, the house retains the atmosphere of restricted gentility suitable to the unmarried daughter of a clergyman. In the left-hand parlor, Jane would play her piano every morning, then repair to her mahogany writing desk in the family sitting room—leaving her sister, Cassandra, to do the household chores ("I find composition impossible with my head full of joints of mutton and doses of rhubarb," Jane wrote). In the early 19th century the road near the house was a bustling thoroughfare, and one traveler reported that a window view proved that the Misses Austen were "looking very comfortable at breakfast." Jane was famous for working through interruptions, but one protection against the outside world was the famous door that creaked. She asked that its hinges remain unattended to because they gave her warning that someone was coming. The museum often schedules readings and other special events, so call ahead. ⊠ *Signed off A31/A32 roundabout* ☎ *01420/83262* ⊕ *www.jane-austens-house-museum.org.uk* ⊠ *£7* ⊙ *Jan.–mid-Feb., weekends 10:30–4:30; mid-Feb.–May and Sept.–Dec., daily 10:30–4:30; June–Aug., daily 10–5; last admission 30 mins before closing.*

PORTSMOUTH

24 mi south of Chawton, 77 mi southwest of London.

Portsmouth's historic harbor, revitalized waterfront, and working port make it an energetic place. At the newly developed Gunwharf Quays you'll find the soaring Spinnaker Tower, as well as shops, restaurants, bars, and a contemporary art gallery. The main attraction for many travelers is the extraordinary collection of maritime memorabilia, including well-preserved warships from the Napoleonic era, at the Portsmouth Historic Dockyard, and other museums. For others, Portsmouth is primarily of interest for the ferries that set off from here to the Isle of Wight and more distant destinations.

GETTING HERE AND AROUND

The M27 motorway from Southampton and the A3 from London take you to Portsmouth. There are also frequent buses and trains that drop you off at the Hard, the main transport terminus. It's near the tourist information center and a few steps from the Historic Dockyard and Gunwharf Quays. Regular passenger ferries cross Portsmouth Harbour from the Hard for Gosport's Royal Navy Submarine Museum. Attractions in the nearby town of Southsea are best reached by car or by buses departing from the Hard.

ESSENTIALS

Visitor Information Portsmouth (⊠ *The Hard* ☎ *023/9282–6722* ⊕ *www.visitportsmouth.co.uk*). **Southsea** (⊠ *Clarence Esplanade, Southsea* ☎ *023/9282–6722* ⊕ *www.southsea.co.uk*).

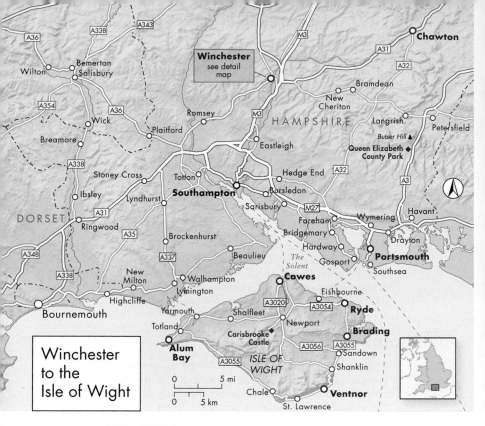

EXPLORING

TOP ATTRACTIONS

★ **D-Day Museum.** In the absorbing D-Day Museum, in nearby Southsea, an eclectic range of exhibits illustrates the planning and logistics involved in the D-Day landings, as well as the actual invasion on June 6, 1944. The museum's centerpiece is the Overlord Embroidery ("Overlord" was the code name for the invasion), a 272-foot-long embroidered cloth with 34 panels illustrating the history of World War II, from the Battle of Britain in 1940 to D-Day and the first days of the liberation. ✉ *Clarence Esplanade, Southsea* ☎ *023/9282–7261* ⊕ *www.ddaymuseum. co.uk* ✍ *£6.50* ⏱ *Apr.–Sept., daily 10–5:30; Oct.–Mar., daily 10–5; last admission 30 mins before closing.*

Fodor'sChoice **Portsmouth Historic Dockyard.** The city's most impressive attraction
★ includes an unrivaled collection of historic ships. The dockyard's youngest ship, **HMS *Warrior 1860*,** was England's first ironclad battleship. Admiral Nelson's flagship, **HMS *Victory*,** has been painstakingly restored to appear as it did at the battle at Trafalgar (1805). You can inspect the cramped gun decks, visit the cabin where Nelson entertained his officers, and stand on the spot where he was mortally wounded by a French sniper. Visits aboard the *Victory* are by guided tour only and may require a long wait. The *Mary Rose*, former flagship of the Tudor

navy, which capsized and sank in the harbor in 1545, was raised in 1982. Described in the 16th century as "the flower of all the ships that ever sailed," the *Mary Rose* is now housed in a special enclosure, where water continuously sprays her timbers to prevent them from drying out and breaking up. (As this book went to press, a new museum was being built to house the *Mary Rose*. It was expected to reopen in late 2012.)

The **Royal Naval Museum** has extensive exhibits about British naval hero Admiral Lord Horatio Nelson and the battle of Trafalgar, a fine collection of painted figureheads, and galleries of paintings and mementos recalling naval history from King Alfred to the present. **Action Stations**, an interactive attraction, gives insight into life in the modern Royal Navy and tests your sea legs with tasks such as piloting boats through gales. **Dockyard Apprentice** showcases the skills of the shipbuilders and craftsmen who constructed and maintained the naval vessels, with illustrations of rope making, sail making, caulking, signals, and knots. You should allow the best part of a day to tour all the attractions in the Historic Dockyard. ■ **TIP➜** The entrance fee includes a boat ride around the harbor. ⊠ *Historic Dockyard, Portsmouth Naval Base* ☎ *023/9272–8060* ⊕ *www.historicdockyard.co.uk* 🖃 *£19.90 includes harbor tour; valid for return visits* ⊙ *Apr.–Oct., daily 10–6; Nov.–Mar., daily 10–5:30; last admission 90 mins before closing.*

QUICK BITES

In the heart of the Historic Dockyard, **Boathouse No. 7** (⊠ *Victory Gate* ☎ *02392/839766* ⊕ *www.historicdockyard.co.uk*) is a family-friendly eatery in a converted 18th-century boathouse. The kitchen dishes out such classics as shepherd's pie and baked potatoes, as well as lighter options like freshly made sandwiches, salads, and soups. Kids can enjoy the "treasure trove" lunchbox filled with healthful snacks. A stone's throw from the *HMS Victory*, you can eat here without purchasing a ticket to the museums.

Spinnaker Tower. On the lively Gunwharf Quays development of shops and bars, Spinnaker Tower adds a striking visual focus to Portsmouth's skyline. The slender structure, with the form of a mast and billowing sail, rises to a height of 541 feet. An elevator whisks you to three viewing platforms 330 feet high, for thrilling all-around views over the harbor and up to 20 mi beyond. ⊠ *Gunwharf Quays* ☎ *023/9285–7520* ⊕ *www.spinnakertower.co.uk* 🖃 *£7.55* ⊙ *Sept.–July, daily 10–6; Aug., Sun.–Thurs. 10–7:30, Fri. and Sat. 10–6.*

WORTH NOTING

Explosion! In a former arms depot near Submarine World, Explosion! (the name given to the Museum of Naval Firepower) gathers together munitions, mines, and missiles in relating the history of armaments used at sea. The museum also tells the story of the locals who manufactured them. Interactive exhibits help you understand what it's like to do nautical things such as walk on a seabed. ⊠ *Priddy's Hard, Gosport* ☎ *023/9250–5600* ⊕ *www.explosion.org.uk* 🖃 *£10* ⊙ *Apr.–Oct., daily 10–5; Nov.–Mar., weekends 10–4; last admission 1 hr before closing.*

Millennium Promenade. Beginning outside the Spinnaker Tower, the Millennium Promenade meanders through Old Portsmouth and along the seafront. The 4-mi self-guided walk, marked by a rope pattern on the sidewalk, passes though the original port, where fishing boats still dock, and where press gangs forcibly enlisted young men for the Royal Navy in the 18th century. Follow it to Clarence Pier in Southsea. ✉ *Gunwharf Quays.*

Portchester Castle. Incorporating the walls of a Roman fort built more than 1,600 years ago, Portchester Castle claims the most complete set of Roman walls in northern Europe. In the 12th century a Norman castle (now in ruins) was built inside the impressive fortifications. From the keep's central tower you can take in a sweeping view of the harbor and coastline. ✉ *Off A27 near Fareham* ☎ *023/9237–8291* ⊕ *www.english-heritage.org.uk* 🎟 *£4.80* ☉ *Apr.–Sept., daily 10–6; Oct.–Mar., daily 10–4.*

RULING THE WAVES

Great Britain invested heavily in its Royal Navy to defend its shores and, eventually, to access its far-flung empire. The first dry dock in Europe was built in 1495 in Portsmouth, by order of Henry VII. His son Henry VIII greatly built up the navy early in his reign, but it was still a smaller force than the Spanish Armada, whose attack the English beat back famously in 1588, during the reign of Elizabeth I. It would take another century for England to make its navy the largest, and the world's most powerful, a rank it held up to World War II.

🅒 **Royal Navy Submarine Museum.** The highlight here is the tour of the World War II submarine HMS *Alliance,* from the cramped quarters to the engine room. The museum fills you in on submarine history and lets you view Portsmouth Harbour through a periscope. There are plenty of subs, weapons, and diving paraphernalia around the large site. From Portsmouth Harbour, take the ferry to Gosport and walk along Millennium Promenade past the huge sundial clock. ✉ *Haslar Jetty Rd., Gosport* ☎ *023/9251–0354* ⊕ *www.submarine-museum.co.uk* 🎟 *£10* ☉ *Apr.–Oct., daily 10–5:30; Nov.–Mar., daily 10–4:30; last tour 1 hr before closing.*

WHERE TO EAT AND STAY

For expanded reviews, visit Fodors.com.

££
BISTRO
✕ **Abarbistro.** A relaxed, modern bistro midway between Old Portsmouth and Gunwharf Quays, this place is ideal for a snack, a full meal, or just a drink. Seafood dishes, mostly sourced from Portsmouth's fish market right opposite, include *moules marinière,* fish cakes, and salmon steak in a creamy dill sauce; alternatively, opt for the sirloin steak and fries, or an asparagus-and–wild mushroom tartlet. You can sit indoors, in a garden at the back, or at Continental-style tables on the pavement. ✉ *58 White Hart Rd.* ☎ *023/9281–1585* ⊕ *www.abarbistro.co.uk.*

£££££
MEDITERRANEAN
★
✕ **Montparnasse.** Modern photographs on cinnamon walls add a contemporary touch to this relaxed but semiformal restaurant. The fixed-price menus (£31.50 and £36.50) may list sautéed pigeon breast and roasted lamb fillet, and desserts such as amaretto-and-mascarpone mousse with white coffee ice cream are to die for. Service is discreet but attentive and knowledgeable. Book a table downstairs for more atmosphere. ✉ *103 Palmerston Rd., Southsea* ☎ *023/9281–6754* ⊕ *www. bistromontparnasse.co.uk* ☉ *Closed Sun. and Mon.*

You can tour Admiral Nelson's famous flagship, the HMS *Victory*, at Portsmouth's Historic Dockyard.

££
B&B/INN

Fortitude Cottage. With sleek modern bedrooms done in white and neutrals, this friendly B&B provides top-class accommodation in two buildings in the center of Old Portsmouth, just yards from the waterside. **Pros:** central but quiet location; immaculate, modern rooms. **Cons:** stairs; some rooms have poor view. ⊠ *47–51 Broad St.* ☎ *023/9282–3748* ⊕ *www.fortitudecottage.co.uk* 🛏 *6 rooms* ⚒ *In-room: no a/c (some), Wi-Fi. In-hotel: parking, some pets allowed* ⦙〇⦙ *Breakfast.*

££
HOTEL

Westfield Hall. Portsmouth is well supplied with chain offerings, but this pleasant smaller establishment has personal service and character. **Pros:** reliably clean; hospitable staff; good breakfast. **Cons:** dated decor; thin walls; some smallish rooms. ⊠ *65 Festing Rd., off Eastern Parade* ☎ *023/9282–6971* ⊕ *www.whhotel.info* 🛏 *26 rooms* ⚒ *In-room: no a/c, Internet, Wi-Fi. In-hotel: restaurant, parking* ⦙〇⦙ *Breakfast.*

THE OUTDOORS

Queen Elizabeth Country Park, part of an Area of Outstanding Beauty in the South Downs, has 1,400 acres of chalk hills and shady beeches with 20 mi of scenic trails for hikers, cyclists, and horse riders. You can climb to the top of Butser Hill (888 feet) to take in a splendid view of the coast. The park lies 12 mi north of Portsmouth, and 4 mi south of the Georgian market town of Petersfield, in a wide valley between wooded hills and open downs. A visitor center has a theater, café, and shop. ⊠ *A3* ☎ *023/9259–5040* ⊕ *www3.hants.gov.uk/qecp* 🖃 *Free; parking £1, Sun. £1.50* 🕐 *Park open 24 hrs; visitor center Mar.–Oct., daily 10–5:30; Nov.–late Dec. and mid–late Jan., daily 10–4:30.*

SOUTHAMPTON

17 mi northwest of Portsmouth, 24 mi southeast of Salisbury, 77 mi southwest of London.

Southampton is England's leading passenger port, and as the home port of Henry V's fleet bound for Agincourt, the *Mayflower,* the *Queen Mary,* and the ill-fated *Titanic,* along with countless other great ocean liners of the 20th century, Southampton has one of the richest maritime traditions in England. Much of the city center is shoddy, having been hastily rebuilt after World War II bombing, but bits of the city's history peek out from between modern buildings. The Old Town retains its medieval air, and considerable parts of Southampton's castellated town walls remain. Other attractions include a decent art gallery, extensive parks, and a couple of good museums. The Southampton Boat Show, a 10-day event in mid-September, draws huge crowds.

GETTING HERE AND AROUND

Located on the M3 motorway from London and Winchester, and on the M27 from Portsmouth, Southampton is also easily accessed by bus or train from these cities. The bus and train stations are a few minutes' walk from the tourist office, and the main sights can be reached by foot.

ESSENTIALS

Visitor Information Southampton (⊠ *9 Civic Centre Rd.* ☎ *023/8083–3333* ⊕ *www.visit-southampton.co.uk*).

EXPLORING

God's House Tower. Incorporated in the town walls are a number of old buildings, including God's House Tower, originally a gunpowder factory and now an archaeology museum. Displays focus on the Roman, Saxon, and medieval periods of Southampton's history. ⊠ *Winkle St.* ☎ *023/8063– 5904* ⊕ *www.southampton.gov.uk* 🎟 *£2* ⊗ *Tues.–Sat. 10–4, Sun. 1–6.*

Mayflower Park and the Pilgrim Fathers' Memorial. This memorial was built to commemorate the departure of 102 passengers on the North America–bound *Mayflower* from Southampton on August 15, 1620. A plaque also honors the 2 million U.S. troops who left Southampton in World War II. ⊠ *Western Esplanade.*

Southampton Maritime Museum. Incongruously housed in a 14th-century wool warehouse, this museum brings together models, mementos, and pieces of furniture from the age of the great clippers and cruise ships, including a wealth of memorabilia relating to the *Titanic*—footage, photos, crew lists, and so on. Boat buffs will relish plenty of vital statistics dealing with the history of commercial shipping. ⊠ *Bugle St.* ☎ *023/8022–3941* ⊕ *www.southampton.gov.uk* 🎟 *£2.50* ⊗ *Early May–late Sept., weekdays 10–6, weekends 11–6; late Sept.–early May, weekdays 10–4, weekends 11–4.*

WHERE TO EAT AND STAY

For expanded reviews, visit Fodors.com.

£££
BRASSERIE
✕ **Oxford Brasserie.** Close to the docks, this informal place gets lively in the evening, but it's calmer at lunchtime. Fresh fish is always available (the fixed-price menus are a particularly good value), along with

Mediterranean fare. The tile floor and cream-color walls hung with paintings are straightforward and not gimmicky. ⊠ *33–34 Oxford St.* ☎ *023/8063–5043* ⊕ *www.theoxfordbrasserie.co.uk* ⊗ *No dinner Sun.*

££££–£££££   🛏 **TerraVina Hotel.** At this small and select boutique hotel outside the
HOTEL   city, the public areas invite lingering with their mix of contemporary
Fodor's Choice   and period furnishings. **Pros:** chic, well-appointed rooms; fantastic
★   food; attention to detail. **Cons:** some noise intrusion; a little remote
from Southampton. ⊠ *174 Woodlands Rd., Woodlands, Netley Marsh* ☎ *023/8029–3784* ⊕ *www.hotelterravina.co.uk* 🛏 *11 rooms* ♿ *In-room: a/c, Wi-Fi. In-hotel: restaurant, bar, pool.*

NIGHTLIFE AND THE ARTS

The **Mayflower** (⊠ *Commercial Rd.* ☎ *023/8071–1811* ⊕ *www.mayflower. org.uk*) is among the larger theaters outside London; the Royal Shakespeare Company and Barnum on Ice are among the organizations that have packed the house.

The **Nuffield** (⊠ *University Rd.* ☎ *023/8067–1771* ⊕ *www.nuffieldtheatre. co.uk*), at Southampton University, has a repertory company and also hosts national touring groups.

ISLE OF WIGHT

A slightly tattered, slightly romantic place, this island sometimes gets so crowded it seems that it might sink beneath the weight of the throngs of summer visitors. Its appealingly dusty Victorian look comes courtesy of Queen Victoria, who put the Isle of Wight (pronounced white) on the map by choosing it for the site of Osborne House. She lived here as much as she could, and ultimately she died here. Perhaps understandably, islanders are chauvinistic; like Tennyson, who lived here until tourist harassment drove him away, they resent the crowds of tourists. But every season the day-trippers arrive—thanks to the ferries and hydrofoils that connect the island with Southampton, Portsmouth, Southsea, and Lymington. People come to this 23-mi-long island for its vacation resorts—Ryde, Bembridge, Ventnor, Freshwater (stay away from tacky Sandown and Shanklin)—and its rich vegetation, narrow lanes, thatched cottages, curving bays, sandy beaches, and walking paths. The fabulous ocean air, to quote Tennyson, is "worth six pence a pint." All is not sea and sails, however. There is splendid driving to be done in the interior of the island, in such places as Brading Down, Ashley Down, Mersely Down, and along Military Road, and the occasional country house to visit, none more spectacular than Queen Vicky's Osborne House.

GETTING HERE AND AROUND

Wightlink operates a car ferry between the mainland and the Isle of Wight. The crossing takes about 30 minutes from Lymington to Yarmouth, 40 minutes from Portsmouth to Fishbourne. The company also operates catamaran service between Portsmouth and Ryde (20 minutes). Red Funnel runs a car ferry (one hour) and hydrofoil service (25 minutes) between Southampton and Cowes. Hovertravel runs a hovercraft shuttle between Southsea (Portsmouth) and Ryde (10 minutes). The island is covered by a good network of roads, and you can rely on a regular local bus

4

service. Southern Vectis, the local bus company, operates open-top tours between March and October. One goes to Dimbola Lodge, the Needles, and Alum Bay. You can board and disembark at different points for £10.

TIMING

Summer traffic slows things down considerably. Try to avoid Cowes Week in late July or early August and the two major rock festivals that take place in mid-June and mid-September.

ESSENTIALS

Bus and Tour Information **Southern Vectis** (☎ *01983/827000* ⊕ *www.islandbuses.info*).

Ferry Information **Hovertravel** (☎ *01983/811000 or 023/9281–1000* ⊕ *www.hovertravel.co.uk*). **Red Funnel** (☎ *0844/844–9988* ⊕ *www.redfunnel. co.uk*). **Wightlink** (☎ *0871/376–1000* ⊕ *www.wightlink.co.uk*).

COWES

7 mi northwest of Ryde.

If you embark from Southampton, your ferry will cross the Solent channel and dock at Cowes, near Queen Victoria's Osborne House. Cowes is a magic name in the sailing world because of the internationally known Cowes Week yachting festival (⊕ *www.cowesweek.co.uk*), held each July or August. At the north end of High Street, on the Parade, a tablet commemorates the 1633 sailing from Cowes of two ships carrying the first English settlers of the state of Maryland.

GETTING HERE AND AROUND

A car ferry and a hydrofoil shuttle passengers from Southampton. Southern Vectis runs numerous buses connecting Cowes with other destinations on the island.

ESSENTIALS

Visitor Information **Cowes** (✉ *Fountain Quay* ☎ *01983/813813* ⊕ *www.islandbreaks.co.uk*).

EXPLORING

★ **Carisbrooke Castle.** Standing above the village of Carisbrooke, this castle was built by the Normans and enlarged in Elizabethan times. It had its moment of historical glory when King Charles I was imprisoned here during the English Civil War. Note the small window in the north curtain wall through which he tried unsuccessfully to escape. A museum holds items from his incarceration. You can stroll along the battlements and visit the well house, where donkeys draw water from a deep well, as well as the Edwardian-style Princess Beatrice garden. The castle is about a mile southwest of the Isle of Wight's modern-day capital, Newport. From Cowes, take Bus 1 or 5 (1 from West Cowes, near Holmwood Hotel; 5 from East Cowes, near Osborne House) to Newport, from where you can walk (about 30 minutes) or pick up the 7 or 38 buses— it's about a 10-minute walk from the bus stop in The Mall, Carisbrooke. ✉ *Off B3401* ☎ *01983/522107* ⊕ *www.english-heritage. org.uk* 🎟 *£7.30* ☉ *Apr.–Sept., daily 10–5; Oct.–Mar., daily 10–4.*

Osborne House. Queen Victoria's beloved home, designed by Prince Albert after a villa in the stodgiest Italian Renaissance style, holds enormous interest for anyone drawn to the domestic side of history. After Albert's death in 1861 the queen spent much of her time here, mourning her loss in relative seclusion. In this massive pile, one sees the engineer manqué in Prince Albert and his clever innovations—including a kind of central heating—as well as evidence of Victoria's desperate attempts to give her children a normal but disciplined upbringing. A carriage ride will take you to the Swiss Cottage, a superior version of a playhouse built for the children. The antiques-filled rooms have scarcely been altered since Victoria's death here in 1901. The house and grounds—which can be quite crowded during July and August—were used as a location for the 1998 movie *Mrs. Brown.* ■TIP→ Book ahead for guided tours of the house and gardens. Buses 4 (from Ryde) and 5 (from Cowes and Newport) stop outside. ⊠ *Off A3021, 1 mi southeast of Cowes* ☎ *01983/200022* ⊕ *www.english-heritage.org.uk* 🎫 *£11.50* ☉ *Apr.– Sept., daily 10–6; Oct., daily 10–4; Nov.–Mar., Wed.–Sun. 10–4; pre-booked guided tours only, last tour at 2:30.*

4

WHERE TO STAY
For expanded reviews, visit Fodors.com.

££   🏨 **New Holmwood Hotel.** This Best Western hotel occupies an unrivaled
HOTEL   location above the western end of the Esplanade—ideal for watching yachters in the Solent. **Pros:** good sea views; friendly staff; within walking distance of passenger ferry. **Cons:** some rooms are small and dated; slightly run-down feel. ⊠ *Queens Rd., Egypt Point* ☎ *01983/292508* ⊕ *www.newholmwoodhotel.co.uk* ⤳ *24 rooms, 2 suites* ⚙ *In-room: no a/c, Wi-Fi. In-hotel: restaurant, bar, pool, some pets allowed* ⫚⍟ *Breakfast.*

RYDE

7 mi southeast of Cowes.

The town of Ryde has long been one of the Isle of Wight's most popular summer resorts, with several family attractions. After the construction of Ryde Pier in 1814, elegant town houses sprang up along the seafront and on the slopes behind, commanding fine views of the harbor. In addition to its long, sandy beach, Ryde has a large lake (you can rent rowboats and pedal boats) and children's playgrounds.

GETTING HERE AND AROUND
From Portsmouth, catamaran service takes about 20 minutes; from Southsea a hovercraft gets you to Ryde in 10 minutes. If you're driving from Cowes, take the A3021 to the A3054.

ESSENTIALS
Visitor Information Ryde (⊠ *81–83 Union St.* ☎ *01983/813813* ⊕ *www.islandbreaks.co.uk*).

WHERE TO EAT AND STAY

£££   ✕ **Seaview.** A strong maritime flavor defines this outstanding restaurant,
MODERN BRITISH   in the heart of a harbor village just outside Ryde. Choose between the
Fodor's Choice   two main dining areas, one a smaller Victorian room, the other bright
★   and modern, with tables spilling out into a conservatory. The kitchen

specializes in seafood and fresh island produce, much of it from the Seaview's own farm. You might start with the chicken-liver parfait and then move on to roast salmon fillet. Plainer, less expensive fish dishes and snacks can be ordered in the two congenial bars, one modern, one traditional. Pale brown tones and luxurious fabrics characterize the chic guest rooms in the adjoining hotel (££££). ⊠ *Seaview Hotel, High St., Seaview* ☎ *01983/612711* ⊕ *www.seaviewhotel.co.uk.*

££ **Lakeside Hotel.** Halfway between Cowes and Ryde, this modern hotel
HOTEL has a perfect location for exploring the northern part of the island. **Pros:** convenient location; comfortable rooms. **Cons:** can be noisy; patchy service. ⊠ *Wooton Bridge, Ryde* ☎ *01983/882266* ⊕ *www. lakesideparkhotel.com* ⤴ *44 bedrooms, 3 suites* ⅏ *In-room: a/c, Wi-Fi. In-hotel: restaurants, bar, pool, gym, spa, business center, parking* ⍾ *Breakfast.*

££££–£££££ **Priory Bay Hotel.** This hotel, part of which dates to medieval times,
HOTEL has been sympathetically developed in country-house style. **Pros:** quirky character; beautiful setting. **Cons:** shabby in places; inconsistent food and service; minimum stay required. ⊠ *Priory Dr., Seaview* ☎ *01983/ 613146* ⊕ *www.priorybay.com* ⤴ *18 rooms, 9 cottages* ⅏ *In-room: no a/c, Wi-Fi (some). In-hotel: restaurants, bar, golf course, pool, tennis courts, some pets allowed* ⍾ *Breakfast.*

BRADING

3 mi south of Ryde on A3055.

In Brading, St. Mary's Church, dating from Norman times, contains monuments to the local Oglander family, whose ancestor from Normandy served William the Conqueror. You can still see the old lockup, dating from 1750, complete with stocks and whipping post at the Town Hall.

GETTING HERE AND AROUND
To get here from Ryde, take the Island Line trains or local bus services.

ESSENTIALS
Contacts Island Line (☎ *0870/906–6649* ⊕ *www.southwesttrains.co.uk*).

EXPLORING
Brading Roman Villa. Housed within a striking wooden-walled, glass-roofed building, the remains of this substantial 3rd-century villa include walls, splendid mosaic floors, and a well-preserved heating system. The mosaics, depicting peacocks (symbolizing eternal life), gods, gladiators, sea beasts, and reclining nymphs, are a rare example of this type of floor preserved in situ in a domestic building. There's also a café at the site, 1 mi south of Brading. ⊠ *Morton Old Rd. off A3055* ☎ *01983/406223* ⊕ *www.bradingromanvilla.co.uk* ⌑ *£6.50* ⊙ *Daily 9:30–5; last entry at 4.*

VENTNOR

11 mi south of Ryde.

The south-coast resorts are the sunniest and most sheltered on the Isle of Wight. Handsome Ventnor rises from such a steep slope that the ground floors of some of its houses are level with the roofs of those across the road.

GETTING HERE AND AROUND

Local bus service connects Ventnor with the rest of the island.

EXPLORING

Isle of Wight Studio Glass. Not only famous for sailing and Victoriana, the Isle of Wight is also renowned for its glassmaking. The village of St. Lawrence, near Ventnor, has been home to Isle of Wight Studio Glass since 1973. Best known for its original designs, its pieces are sought after by collectors. You can watch glassmakers in action, or blow your own glass bubble. For £75 you can design and make your own paperweight. ✉ *Old Park, St. Lawrence* ☎ *01983/853526* ⊕ *www. isleofwightstudioglass.co.uk* ✆ *Nov.–May, weekdays 9–4.30, Sat. 10–4; June—Oct., weekdays 9–4.30, weekends 10–4.*

Ventnor Botanic Gardens. Laid out over 22 acres, these gardens contain more than 3,500 species of trees, plants, and shrubs. The impressive greenhouse includes banana trees and a waterfall, and a visitor center puts the subtropical and display gardens into context. ✉ *Undercliff Dr.* ☎ *01983/855397* ⊕ *www.botanic.co.uk* ✆ *Garden free, greenhouse £1* ✆ *Gardens always open. Visitor center Mar.–Oct., daily 10–5; Nov.–Feb., call to check.*

WHERE TO EAT

£££
MEDITERRANEAN
✕ **The Pond Café.** Overlooking a secluded, elongated pond in the hamlet of Bonchurch, a mile north of Ventnor, this quiet, understated restaurant is a good place to gently unwind. The simply furnished interior is compact and contemporary in style, and there are a few outdoor tables for eating alfresco when the weather permits. Come for a tea or coffee, or tuck in to brunch or a full meal. The set-price lunch menu (£18) includes such dishes as sautéed squid with chorizo, followed by wild-mushroom risotto with truffles or fillet of sea bass with salsify and champagne sauce. There are fresh-baked breads and homemade ice creams, among other toothsome desserts and a wide selection of cheeses. ✉ *Bonchurch Village Rd., Bonchurch* ☎ *01983/855666* ⊕ *www.thehambrough.com.*

ALUM BAY AND THE NEEDLES

19 mi northwest of Ventnor, 18 mi southwest of Cowes.

At the western tip of the Isle of Wight is the island's most famous natural landmark, the **Needles,** a long line of jagged chalk stacks jutting out of the sea like monstrous teeth, with a lighthouse at the end. It's part of the Needles Pleasure Park, which has mostly child-oriented attractions. Adjacent is **Alum Bay,** accessed from the Needles by chairlift. Here you can catch a good view of the "colored sand" in the cliff strata or take a boat to view the lighthouse. **Yarmouth,** a quaint fishing village is a 10-minute drive from Alum Bay.

GETTING HERE AND AROUND

Wightlink car and passenger ferries from Lymington dock at nearby Yarmouth. The spectacular A3055 runs along the southwest coast from Ventnor to Freshwater, the nearest town. From there you can follow the coast road to Alum Bay. Local bus services connect Freshwater with the rest of the island.

ESSENTIALS

Visitor Information **Yarmouth** (✉ *The Quay* ☎ *01983/813813* ⊕ *www.islandbreaks.co.uk*).

EXPLORING

Dimbola Lodge. This was the home of Julia Margaret Cameron (1815–79), the eminent Victorian portrait photographer and friend of Lord Tennyson. A gallery includes more than 60 examples of her work, including striking images of Carlyle, Tennyson, and Browning. There's also a room devoted to the various Isle of Wight rock festivals, most famously the five-day event in 1970 that featured the Who, the Doors, Joni Mitchell, and Jimi Hendrix. On the ground floor you'll find a bookshop and a good café for snacks and full meals. ✉ *Terrace La., Freshwater Bay* ☎ *01983/756814* ⊕ *www.dimbola.co.uk* 🎫 *£4* ⊗ *Mar.–Oct., Tues.–Sun. and national holiday Mon. 10–5; Nov.–Feb., Tues.–Sun. and national holiday Mon. 10–4; open daily during school summer vacation.*

SALISBURY, STONEHENGE, AND SALISBURY PLAIN

The roster of famous sights in this area begins in the attractive city of Salisbury, renowned for its glorious cathedral, and then loops west around Salisbury Plain, up to Avebury, and back to Stonehenge. A trio of stately homes reveals the ambitions and wealth of their builders—Wilton House with its Inigo Jones–designed state rooms, Stourhead and its exquisite gardens, and the Italian Renaissance pile of Longleat. Your own transportation is essential to see anything beyond Salisbury, other than Stonehenge or Avebury.

SALISBURY

24 mi northwest of Southampton, 44 mi southeast of Bristol, 79 mi southwest of London.

The silhouette of Salisbury Cathedral's majestic spire signals your approach to this historic city long before you arrive. Although the cathedral is the principal interest in the town, and the Cathedral Close one of the country's most atmospheric spots (best experienced on a foggy night), Salisbury has much more to see, not least its largely unspoiled—and relatively traffic-free—old center. Here are stone shops and houses that grew up in the shadow of the great church over the centuries. You're never far from any of the three rivers that meet here, or from the bucolic water meadows that stretch out to the west of the cathedral and provide the best views of it. Salisbury did not become important until the early 13th century, when the seat of the diocese was transferred

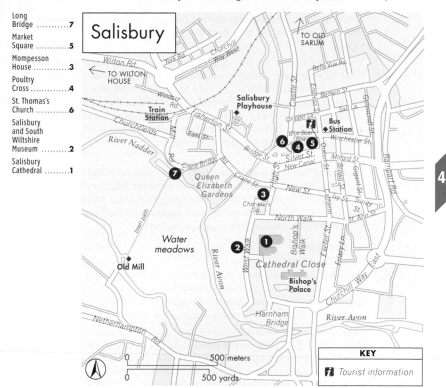

4

here from Old Sarum, the original settlement 2 mi to the north, of
which only ruins remain. In the 19th century, novelist Anthony Trollope
based his tales of ecclesiastical life, notably *Barchester Towers,* on life
here, although his fictional city of Barchester is really an amalgam of
Salisbury and Winchester. The local tourist office organizes walks—of
differing lengths for varying stamina—to lead you to the treasures. And
speaking of treasures, prehistoric Stonehenge is less than 10 mi away
and easily visited from the city.

GETTING HERE AND AROUND

Salisbury is on main bus and train routes from London and Southampton; regular buses also connect Salisbury with Winchester. The bus station is centrally located on Endless Street. Trains stop west of the center.
After negotiating a ring-road system, drivers will want to park as soon as
possible. The largest of the central parking lots is by Salisbury Playhouse.
The city center is compact, so you won't need to use local buses for most
sights. For Wilton, take Bus 3 from New Canal, near Market Square.

TIMING

Market Square hosts general markets every Tuesday and Saturday and
farmers' markets on the first and third Wednesday of the month. It's
also the venue for other fairs and festivals, notably the one-day Food
& Drink Festival in mid-September and the three-day Charter Fair in

October. The city gets busy during the arts festival in May and June, when accommodation may be scarce.

TOURS

The Stonehenge Tour has open-top buses leaving once or twice an hour all year from the train station and the bus station. Tickets cost £11, or £18 including admission to Stonehenge. Salisbury City Guides offers city tours, departing from the tourist office every day from April through September and on weekends the rest of the year. The cost is £4. Wessexplore has everything from walking tours to trips in luxury cars to a helicopter ride over Stonehenge.

ESSENTIALS

Visitor and Tour Information Salisbury (✉ *Fish Row off Market Sq.* ☎ *01722/334956* ⊕ *www.visitwiltshire.co.uk/salisbury*). **Salisbury City Guides** (☎ *01722/320349* ⊕ *www.salisburycityguides.co.uk*). **Stonehenge Tour** (☎ *01983/827005* ⊕ *www.thestonehengetour.info*). **Wessexplore** (☎ *01722/326304* ⊕ *www.dmac.co.uk/wessexplore*).

EXPLORING
TOP ATTRACTIONS

Cathedral Close. Salisbury's close forms probably the finest backdrop of any British cathedral, with its smooth lawns and splendid examples of architecture from many periods creating a harmonious background. Some of the historic houses are open to the public.

Mompesson House. One of Britain's most appealing Queen Anne houses, dating from 1701, sits on the north side of Cathedral Close. There are no treasures per se, but some fine original paneling and plasterwork, as well as a fascinating collection of 18th-century drinking glasses, are highlights. Tea and refreshments are served in a walled garden. ⊠ *The Close* ☎ *01722/335659* ⊕ *www.nationaltrust.org.uk* ⊠ *£5* ⊙ *Mid-Mar.–Oct., Sat.–Wed. 11–5; last admission at 4:30.*

Old Sarum. Massive earthwork ramparts in a bare sweep of Wiltshire countryside are all that remain of this impressive Iron Age hill fort, which was successively taken over by Romans, Saxons, and Normans (who built a castle and cathedral within the earthworks). The site was still fortified in Tudor times, though the population had mostly decamped in the 13th century for the more amenable site of New Sarum, or Salisbury. You can clamber over the huge banks and ditches and take in the bracing views over the chalk downland. ⊠ *Off A345, 2 mi north of Salisbury* ☎ *01722/335398* ⊕ *www.english-heritage.org.uk* ⊠ *£3.50* ⊙ *Apr.–June and Sept., daily 10–5; July and Aug., daily 9–6; Oct. and Mar., daily 10–4; Nov.–Jan., daily 11–3; Feb., daily 11–4.*

Salisbury and South Wiltshire Museum. Opposite the cathedral's west front, this excellent museum is in the King's House, parts of which date back to the 15th century (James I stayed here in 1610 and 1613). Models and exhibits at the Stonehenge Gallery arm you with helpful background information for a visit to the famous stones. Also on view are skeletons, collections of costumes, lace, embroidery, a Wedgwood pottery, and a collection of Turner watercolors, all dwarfed by the medieval pageant figure of St. Christopher, a 14-foot-tall giant, and his companion hobbyhorse, Hob Nob. A cozy café is in one of the oldest sections of the

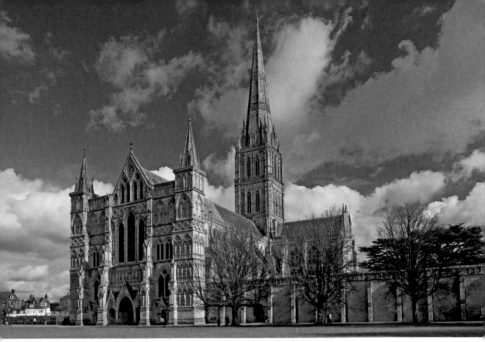

Salisbury Cathedral has a towering spire—the tallest in England—that you can tour.

building. ✉ *The King's House, 65 The Close* ☎ *01722/332151* ⊕ *www. salisburymuseum.org.uk* ✉ *£6* ⊗ *July and Aug., Mon.–Sat. 10–5, Sun. noon–5; Sept.–June, Mon.–Sat. 10–5.*

Fodor's Choice **Salisbury Cathedral.** Salisbury is dominated by the towering cathedral,
★ a soaring hymn in stone. It is unique among cathedrals in that it was
conceived and built as a whole, in the amazingly short span of 38 years
(1220–58). The spire, added in 1320, is the tallest in England and a
miraculous feat of medieval engineering—even though the point, 404
feet above the ground, is 2½ feet off vertical. For a fictional, keenly
imaginative reconstruction of the drama underlying such an achievement, read William Golding's novel *The Spire*. The excellent model of
the cathedral in the north transept, the "arm" of the church to your
left as you look toward the altar, shows the building about 20 years
into construction, and makes clear the ambition of Salisbury's medieval
builders. For all their sophistication, the height and immense weight
of the great spire have always posed structural problems. In the late
17th century Sir Christopher Wren was summoned from London to
strengthen the spire, and in the mid-19th century Sir George Gilbert
Scott, a leading Victorian Gothicist, undertook a major program of
restoration. He also initiated a clearing out of the interior and removed
some less-than-sympathetic 18th-century alterations. Despite this, the
interior seems spartan and a little gloomy, but check out the remarkable lancet windows and sculpted tombs of crusaders and other medieval heroes. The clock in the north aisle—probably the oldest working
mechanism in Europe, if not the world—was made in 1386.

With its art and gilded furniture, the Double Cube Room at Wilton House may well be one of England's most beautiful interiors.

The **cloisters** are the largest in England, and the octagonal **Chapter House** contains a marvelous 13th-century frieze showing scenes from the Old Testament. Here you can also see one of the four original copies of the **Magna Carta**, the charter of rights the English barons forced King John to accept in 1215; it was sent here for safekeeping in the 13th century. ■**TIP→** Join a free 45-minute tour of the church, leaving two or more times a day. There are also daily tours of the roof and spire (except on Sunday from October through April). For a peaceful break, the café in the cloister offers freshly baked cakes and pastries. ⊠ *Cathedral Close* ☎ *01722/555120* ⊕ *www.salisburycathedral.org.uk* ⊠ *Cathedral £5.50, tower tour £8.50, Chapter House free* ☉ *Cathedral Mon.– Sat. 9–5, Sun. noon–6 (excluding services). Chapter House Apr.–Oct., Mon.–Sat. 9:30–4:30, Sun. 12:45–5:30; Nov.–Mar., Mon.–Sat. 10–4:30, Sun. 12:45–4:30.*

★ **Wilton House.** The home of the 18th earl of Pembroke, Wilton House
☾ would be noteworthy if it contained no more than the magnificent 17th-century state rooms designed by Inigo Jones, Ben Jonson's stage designer and the architect of London's Banqueting House. John Webb rebuilt the house in neoclassical style after fire damaged the original Tudor mansion in 1647. In fine weather the lordly expanse of sweeping lawns that surrounds the house, bisected by the River Avon and dotted with towering oaks and a gracious Palladian bridge, is a quintessential English scene. Wilton House contains the Single Cube Room (built as a perfect 30-foot cube) and one of the most extravagantly beautiful rooms in the history of interior decoration, the aptly named Double Cube Room. The name refers to its proportions (60 feet long by 30 feet wide and 30

feet high), evidence of Jones's classically inspired belief that beauty in architecture derives from harmony and balance. The room's headliner is the spectacular Van Dyck portrait of the Pembroke family. Elsewhere at Wilton House, the art collection includes several other old master paintings, including works by Rembrandt and members of the Brueghel family. ■TIP→ Be sure to explore the extensive gardens; children will appreciate the large playground. The town of Wilton is 4 mi west of Salisbury. Buses 2, 13, 25, 26, 27 and Red 3 from Salisbury stop outside Wilton House. They depart every 10 to 15 minutes. ⊠ *Wilton, off A36 linking Salisbury to Bath* ☎ *01722/746714* ⊕ *www.wiltonhouse.co.uk* ⌑ *£14; grounds only, £5.50* ☉ *House Easter and May–Aug., Sun.–Thurs. 11:30– 4:30, last admission at 3:45; grounds Easter and May–Aug., daily 11–5; Sept., weekends 11–5, last admission at 4:30.*

> ## DOUBLE CUBE ROOM
>
> Adorned with gilded furniture by William Kent, Wilton House's Double Cube was where Eisenhower prepared plans for the Normandy invasion during World War II. It has been used in many films, including *The Madness of King George*, *Mrs. Brown*, the 2005 version of *Pride and Prejudice*, Emma Thompson's adaptation of *Sense and Sensibility*, and *The Young Victoria*.

4

WORTH NOTING

Long Bridge. For a classic view of Salisbury, head to the Long Bridge and the town path. From High Street walk west to Mill Road, which leads you across Queen Elizabeth Gardens. Cross the bridge and continue on the town path through the water meadows along which you can find the very spot where John Constable set down his easel to create that 19th-century icon, *Salisbury Cathedral,* now hung in the Constable Room of London's National Gallery.

Market Square. One of southern England's most popular markets fills this square on Tuesday and Saturday. Permission to hold an annual fair here was granted in 1221, and that right is still exercised for three days every October, when the Charter Fair takes place. A narrow side street links Poultry Cross to Market Square.

Poultry Cross. One of Salisbury's best-known landmarks, the hexagonal Poultry Cross is the last remaining of the four original medieval market crosses, and dealers still set up their stalls beside it. A cross on the site was first mentioned in 1307, and a poultry cross here was first named as such a century or so later. The canopy and flying buttresses were added in 1852. ⊠ *Silver St.*

St. Thomas's Church. This church contains a rare medieval doom painting of Judgment Day, the best preserved and most complete of the few such works left in Britain. Created around 1470 and covering the chancel arch, the scenes of heaven and hell served to instill the fear of damnation into the congregation. ■TIP→ It's best seen on a spring or summer evening when the light through the west window illuminates the details. ⊠ *St. Thomas's Sq., Silver St.* ☎ *01722/322537* ⊕ *www.stthomassalisbury. co.uk* ⌑ *Free* ☉ *Apr.–Oct., Mon.–Sat. 8:30–5, Sun. noon–6; Nov.–Mar., Mon.–Sat. 8:30–3, Sun. noon–6.*

QUICK BITES

A former granary, Fisherton Mill ⊠ *108 Fisherton St.* ☎ *01722/415121* ⊕ *www.fishertonmill.co.uk* houses artist studios and exhibition spaces showcasing paintings, sculptures, textiles, and jewelry. Enjoy a light lunch or Wiltshire cream tea in the well-regarded café.

WHERE TO EAT

££
INDIAN

✕ **Anokaa.** For a refreshingly modern take on Indian cuisine, try this bustling eatery a few minutes from the center. Classic recipes are taken as starting points for the artistically presented dishes, which include beef marinated in yogurt and rum, cinnamon-glazed duck breast stuffed with garlicky spinach, and black tiger prawns in a sauce of curry leaves and coconut oil. At lunchtime, choose from the buffet selection. The setting is contemporary and cosmopolitan, and service by staff in traditional dress is friendly and prompt. ⊠ *60 Fisherton St.* ☎ *01722/414142* ⊕ *www.anokaa.com.*

£
MODERN BRITISH

✕ **Boston Tea Party.** Specializing in quick, nourishing meals, this relaxed and child-friendly café serves hot and cold breakfasts, lunches, and afternoon snacks. Homemade meat and vegetarian burgers with interesting toppings like red-onion marmalade or chili sauce, come with potato wedges. The huge vegan Super Salad is enlivened with mango and avocado. Freshly roasted coffee and a wide selection of teas are a nice complement to the freshly baked cakes. You can eat upstairs in the spectacular Tudor great hall or the quieter side room. ⊠ *13 High St.* ☎ *01722/238116* ⊕ *www.bostonteaparty.co.uk* ⊗ *No dinner.*

££
BRITISH

✕ **Charter 1227.** Casual and friendly but upscale, with regal blue carpets and cream leather seats, this second-floor restaurant enjoys a prime position overlooking Market Square. The menu blends traditional British and Mediterranean dishes, such as scallops wrapped in pancetta and slow-braised lamb shank. There are good-value fixed-price lunches. ⊠ *7 Ox Row, Market Sq.* ☎ *01722/333118* ⊕ *www.charter1227.co.uk* ⊗ *Closed Sun. and Mon.*

££
BRITISH

✕ **Haunch of Venison.** This wood-panel tavern opposite the Poultry Cross has been going strong for more than six centuries. It is brimming with odd details, such as the mummified hand of an 18th-century card player still clutching his cards, found by workmen in 1903. You can fortify yourself with any of 80 or so malt whiskies or enjoy such substantial meals as spiced fried salmon and haunch of venison (naturally). Sit in the bar area or the stylish upstairs restaurant. ⊠ *1 Minster St.* ☎ *01722/411313* ⊕ *www.haunchofvenison.uk.com.*

£££££
BRITISH
★

✕ **Howard's House.** If you're after complete tranquillity, head for this early-17th-century house set on 2 acres of grounds in the Nadder Valley. The style is traditional and smart, and a terrace provides alfresco dining overlooking the tidy lawns in summer. Sophisticated contemporary fare makes up most of what's on the set-price menus, such as fillet of wild

FOOD AND DRINK FESTIVAL

Salisbury forces you to squeeze a lot in during its one-day **Food & Drink Festival** (☎ *01722/332241* ⊕ *www.salisburyfestival.co.uk*) in mid-September. There are wine and beer tents, a waiters' race, cooking demonstrations, barbecues, and festival menus in the restaurants. The main venue is Market Square.

Salisbury lives it up at the annual Salisbury International Arts Festival.

turbot with goat cheese gnocchi, and breast of guinea fowl with seared foie gras. Nine luxuriously furnished guest rooms (££££) may tempt you into forgoing the 10-mi drive back to Salisbury. ✉ *Off B3089, Teffont Evias* ☎ *01722/716392* ⊕ *www.howardshousehotel.co.uk.*

WHERE TO STAY

For expanded reviews, visit Fodors.com.

££ — B&B/INN — ⊞ **Cricket Field House.** As the name suggests, this ex-gamekeeper's cottage overlooks a cricket ground, allowing you to puzzle over the intricacies of the game at leisure. **Pros:** efficient, helpful management; quiet, well-maintained rooms. **Cons:** dated decor; on a busy road; lacks charm. ✉ *Wilton Rd.* ☎ *01722/322595* ⊕ *www.cricketfieldhousehotel.co.uk* ⇝ *17 rooms* ☍ *In-room: no a/c, Wi-Fi. In-hotel: parking, some age restrictions* ☝ *Breakfast.*

££ — B&B/INN — ⊞ **Rokeby Guest House.** Easy to find on the east side of town, this four-story Edwardian B&B has a spic-and-span, traditionally styled interior and a large, landscaped garden with a summerhouse and small gym. **Pros:** convenient location; helpful hosts; abundant and tasty breakfasts. **Cons:** not central; excess of patterned carpets and wallpaper. ✉ *3 Wain-a-Long Rd.* ☎ *01722/329800* ⊕ *www.rokebyguesthouse.co.uk* ⇝ *8 rooms* ☍ *In-room: no a/c, Wi-Fi. In-hotel: business center, parking, some age restrictions* ☝ *Breakfast.*

£–££ — B&B/INN — ⊞ **Wyndham Park Lodge.** This simple Victorian house in a quiet part of town (off Castle Street) provides an excellent place to rest and a delicious breakfast, as well as a garden. **Pros:** efficient and hospitable owners; convenient location; good breakfast. **Cons:** spotty Wi-Fi connection. ✉ *51 Wyndham Rd.* ☎ *01722/416517* ⊕ *www.wyndhamparklodge.*

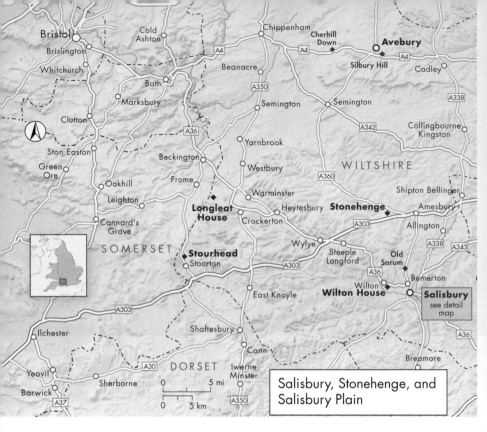

Salisbury, Stonehenge, and Salisbury Plain

co.uk 🛏 64 rooms ⚙ In-room: no a/c, Wi-Fi. In-hotel: business center,
parking ⦿ Breakfast.

NIGHTLIFE AND THE ARTS

★ The **Salisbury International Arts Festival** (✉ 87 Crane St. ☎ 0845/241–9651
⊕ www.salisburyfestival.co.uk), held in May and June, has outstanding
classical concerts, recitals, plays, and outdoor events.

The **Salisbury Playhouse** (✉ Malthouse La. ☎ 01722/320333) presents
high-caliber drama all year and is the main venue for the Salisbury
Arts Festival.

SHOPPING

Most of the shops are gathered around Market Square, venue for twice-
weekly markets and the annual Charter Fair, and along High Street,
where chain stores predominate.

Dauwalders (✉ 42 Fisherton St. ☎ 01722/412100) specializes in stamps,
coins, medals, and models, including some quirky gift ideas.

The **National Trust Shop** (✉ 41 High St. ☎ 01722/331884) has a range of
traditional gifts, from pottery to books, bags, ornaments, and fragrances.

SPORTS

Hayball Cyclesport (✉ 26–30 Winchester St. ☎ 01722/411378) rents
bikes for about £10 per day or £65 per week, with a £25 cash deposit.

STONEHENGE

8 mi north of Salisbury, 20 mi south of Avebury.

Fodor'sChoice **Stonehenge.** *For information about this site, see the feature Mysterious*
★ *Stonehenge in this chapter.*

AVEBURY

24 mi north of Stonehenge, 34 mi north of Salisbury, 25 mi northeast of Longleat, 27 mi east of Bath.

The village of Avebury was built much later than the stone circles that brought it fame; it has an informative museum. You can also explore a cluster of other ancient sites nearby.

4

GETTING HERE AND AROUND

From Salisbury, follow A345 north as far as Marlborough, then drive 7 mi west on A4, or take Wilts & Dorset Bus 5 to Pewsey, changing there to number 96 for Avebury (by bus, travel time is over 90 minutes).

ESSENTIALS

Visitor Information Avebury (✉ *Avebury Chapel, Green St.* ☎ *01672/539179* ⊕ *www.visitwiltshire.co.uk).*

EXPLORING

ℭ **Alexander Keiller Museum.** Archaeological finds from the Avebury area, and charts, photos, models, and home movies taken by archaeologist Alexander Keiller himself, put the Avebury Stone Circles and the site into context. Recent revelations suggest that Keiller, responsible for the excavation of Avebury in the 1930s, may have adapted the site's layout more in the interests of presentation than authenticity. The exhibits are divided between the **Stables Gallery,** showing excavated finds, and the more child-friendly, interactive **Barn Gallery.** ✉ *1 mi north of A4* ☎ *01672/539250* ⊕ *www.nationaltrust.org.uk* ⌕ *£4.90* ⊙ *Apr.–Oct., daily 10–6; Nov.–Mar., daily 10–4:30.*

★ **Avebury Stone Circles.** Surrounding part of Avebury village, the Avebury Stone Circles are one of England's most evocative prehistoric monuments—not so famous as Stonehenge, but all the more powerful for their lack of commercial exploitation. The stones were erected around 2850 BC, some several centuries after Stonehenge was started but more than 500 years before that much smaller site assumed its present form. As with Stonehenge, the purpose of this stone circle has never been ascertained, although it most likely was used for similar ritual purposes. Unlike Stonehenge, however, there are no certain astronomical alignments at Avebury, at least none that have survived. The main site consists of a wide, circular ditch and bank, about 1,400 feet across and more than half a mile around. Entrances break the perimeter at roughly the four points of the compass, and inside stand the remains of three stone circles. The largest one originally had 98 stones, although only 27 remain. Many stones on the site were destroyed centuries ago, especially in the 17th century when they were the target of religious fanaticism. Some were pillaged to build the thatched cottages you see flanking the fields. You can walk around the circles at any time; early

Continued on page 271

MYSTERIOUS STONEHENGE

A circle of giant stones sitting on the wide sweep of Salisbury Plan, Stonehenge is one of the most famous prehistoric sites in England. It still has the capacity to fascinate and move those who view it, but Stonehenge can also be perplexing. The site seems to ask more questions than it answers about its 5,000-year-long history, and its meaning and purpose are continually reevaluated and debated. With some context, you can experience Stonehenge as it once was: deeply mystical and awe-inspiring.

The medieval term Stonehenge means "hanging stones," and the huge stones seem to rest lightly on the ground. Yet they stand with a permanence that defies both the busy road nearby and the hordes of visitors—close to a million a year. There are other challenges to visiting besides crowds: you are kept on a paved path a short distance from the stones, and facilities are limited at present, with no good interpretive center. Timing your visit and taking advantage of what the site offers—including a good audio guide—are important.

It also helps to sort through the myths and theories, and to look at the landscape. Stonehenge was created in five stages between around 3000 BC and 1600 BC on Salisbury Plain, an area devoid of trees since the last ice age—but it was not a solitary construction. The UNESCO World Heritage Site of Stonehenge and Avebury (a nearby stone circle) covers almost 6,500 acres containing more than 350 burial mounds and prehistoric monuments.

Archaeologists are continually rewriting the site's history as they uncover more evidence about Stonehenge and the surrounding ancient structures.

—by Sarah Christie

Opposite: Theories about the sun and its alignment with Stonehenge continue to invite debate. Above: An aerial view provides perspective on the great stone circle.

VIEWING STONEHENGE TODAY

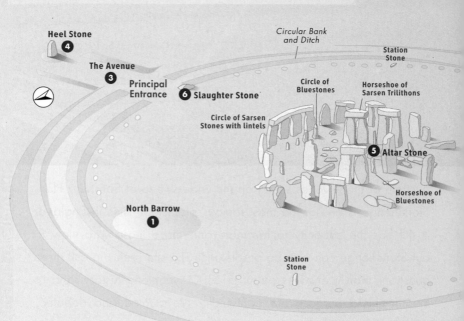

Heel Stone ❹

The Avenue ❸

Principal Entrance

❻ **Slaughter Stone**

Circular Bank and Ditch

Station Stone

Circle of Bluestones

Horseshoe of Sarsen Trilithons

Circle of Sarsen Stones with lintels

❺ **Altar Stone**

Horseshoe of Bluestones

North Barrow ❶

Station Stone

LAYOUT OF THE CIRCLE

Stonehenge today has an **outer circle of sarsen stones**, sandstone blocks from nearby Marlborough Downs. It is the only stone circle in England with lintels. The huge stones are around 13 feet high, 7 feet wide, and weigh about 25 tons each. This sarsen circle surrounds a smaller **circle of bluestones**, a dolerite stone that appears blue when wet.

Bluestones were the first stones at the site, brought from the Preseli Hills in West Wales 150 miles away.

Sarsen stones form the **trilithons**, the tall (over 20 feet) pairs of upright stones with lintels across the top, in the center of the circle, part of an **inner horseshoe of sarsen stones and bluestones.** The sandstone **Altar Stone** is also in the

center. The horseshoe's open end and central upright stones face midsummer sunrise and midwinter sunset.

The word "henge" refers to another feature of the site: a henge is a **circular earthwork bank with an internal ditch** surrounding flattened ground. Stonehenge is unusual in that the ditch is outside the earthwork bank.

OVER THE CENTURIES

Circular ditch with interior bank constructed; first bluestones brought from Wales

2850 BC Construction of nearby Avebury stone circles begins

2600 BC Large sarsen stones brought to Stonehenge

3000 BC   2800 BC   2600 BC   2400 B

Heel Stone

South Barrow

Secondary
Entrance

Aubrey Holes
2

1 North Barrow. The outer ditch and bank intersect with the largely unexcavated North Barrow, thought to have been a burial chamber. The barrow may predate Stonehenge.

2 Aubrey Holes. These 56 pits inside the outer bank, now with concrete markers, are named after John Aubrey, the antiquarian who identified them in 1666. Evidence from 2008 suggests they once contained bluestone uprights, and some were later used for burials.

3 The Avenue. The Avenue's parallel ditches and banks stretch over 2.8 km (1.7 mi) to Bluestonehenge, a smaller circle on the bank of the River Avon that once contained bluestones. It was discovered in 2010, but little remains. The natural banks at the beginning of the Avenue align with the midsummer solstice.

4 Heel Stone. This sarsen block stands at the entrance to the Avenue, on the edge of the current site. At midsummer solstice, the sun rises over the Heel Stone.

5 Altar Stone. Now recumbent, the great sandstone Altar Stone stood nearly 6 feet tall at the center of Stonehenge. Unlike the sarsen stones, it probably came from Milford Haven in Wales. Despite the name, its purpose

remains unknown. Today the stone is the centerpiece for rituals around the summer and winter solstice.

6 Slaughter Stone. This stone, originally upright, now lies within the northeast entrance, and may have formed part of a portal. It is stained a rusty red by rainwater acting on the iron in the stone, rather than by the blood of human sacrifice, as 18th-century legend says.

Trilithon standing stones

MOVING THE STONES
The first 80 bluestones were brought by sea and river over 150 miles from Wales after 3000 BC. People probably used rafts to transport the bluestones over water. The heavier sarsen stones were dragged about 25 miles over land from the Marlborough Downs, and tipped into pits dug in the chalk plain. It is likely that people used wooden rollers for transporting the stones, mounted on wooden "rails" that may have held ball bearings in grooves.

HOW MANY STONES?
Many of the site's original stones have been lost over the years to builders of roads and houses and souvenir hunters, and some have fallen down. However, out of the original 30 large sarsen uprights, 17 remain, with 3 of the 5 trilithons still standing. Forty-three bluestones are left from the original 80 or so, and other major stones remain at the site.

4

IN FOCUS MYSTERIOUS STONEHENGE

2400 BC The Avenue constructed, leading to Bluestonehenge at the River Avon

2200 BC Final rearrangement of bluestones into interior circle

1600 BC Concentric circles of Y and Z holes dug

| 2200 BC | 2000 BC | 1800 BC | 1600 BC |

LEGENDS, MYTHS, and CURRENT THEORIES

LEGENDARY STONEHENGE

Because of its prominence, Stonehenge has become steeped in myths assigning it any number of religious, mystical, and spiritual functions: it was built by the legendary Arthurian wizard Merlin, by the devil, giants, even aliens. The rebel queen Boudicca, who fought against the Romans, was said to have been buried at Stonehenge after the Romans fought the Druids, giving rise to the myth that the Druids built the stone circle to mark her tomb. One thing is certain: the Druids had nothing to do with the construction of Stonehenge, which had already stood for 2,000 years when they appeared.

WHO BUILT STONEHENGE?

The Neolithic and Bronze Age people who built Stonehenge, beginning around the time that the great pyramids in Egypt were built, had only hand tools for shaping the stones and their own manpower for moving them. No other stone circle contains such carefully shaped and meticulously placed stones. Some stones also show carvings of daggers and axes.

The first Neolithic people who worked at the site were semi-nomadic farmers who buried their dead in large, east-west facing barrows. Around 2400 BC, the more organized and sophisticated Beaker people invaded. Their name comes from their tradition of burying their dead with pottery (seen in displays at the Salisbury and South Wilshire Museum), and they may have been sun worshipers. The final group was the Wessex people, around 1600 BC, who probably made the carvings in the stones and finalized Stonehenge's structure.

NEW THEORIES

Recent excavations have put forward two major new theories about its purpose. Evidence from the Stonehenge Riverside Project, a major ongoing archaeological study running since 2003, indicates that it was a domain of the dead: both a burial ground and a memorial. Numerous burials have been found all over the site and the surrounding area. Stonehenge is joined to Durrington Walls, the world's largest known henge and a nearby ancient

Above: Many stones have fallen, but Stonehenge is still a powerful sight.

settlement, by the River Avon and the Avenue. The journey along the river to Stonehenge may have been a ritual passage from life to death.

Another theory is that Stonehenge was a place of healing, accounting for the number of burials with physical injury and disease found in the tombs here as well as the unusual number of people who were not native to the area. That the bluestones were brought from so far away suggests that they were thought to harbor great powers.

STONEHENGE AND THE SUN

Stonehenge's design offers a clue: pairs of Aubrey Holes align with the midsummer solstice axis, following the direction of the natural parallel chalk formations at the beginning of the Avenue. Perhaps this solar alignment with natural lines in the land caused the Neolithic people to revere this location. The centuries-old theory persists that Stonehenge was an astronomical observatory, a calendar, or a sun temple. It is fairly certain that it was a religious site, and worship here may have involved cycles of the sun.

On Summer Solstice (June 21), thousands gather to watch the sun rise over the Heel Stone. But the discovery of a neighboring stone to the Heel Stone questions even this, suggesting it may not itself have been a marker of sunrise, but part of a "solar corridor" that framed the sunrise. Ongoing archaeological research, not to mention speculation, continues to revise the story of Stonehenge.

EXPLORING NEARBY SITES

NEAR STONEHENGE

Hundreds of Neolithic monuments and barrows dot the landscape around Stonehenge. Excavations at **Durrington Walls**, a couple of miles northeast of Stonehenge off A345, have unearthed a substantial settlement dating from around 2500 BC, probably occupied by Stonehenge's builders. Although there is little left of most Neolithic sites today, concrete posts mark nearby **Woodhenge** (also off A345), which dates from around 2300 BC. Its long axis is aligned to the midsummer sunrise and the midwinter sunset. Admission and parking are free at both these sites.

AVEBURY AND ENVIRONS

Twenty-four miles to the north lie Avebury and the **Avebury Stone Circles**, the largest stone circles in the world (dating to around 2850 BC). You can walk freely among the stones — a major attraction for those who prefer the site to Stonehenge. **Silbury Hill**, the last of the great monuments, and **West Kennet Long Barrow**, a tomb, are close by.

Above, Silbury Hill

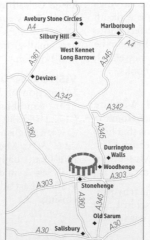

MAKING THE MOST OF YOUR VISIT

WHEN TO VISIT
Come early before the crowds arrive, or in the evening when the light is low and skies darkening. Summer weekends and school holidays can be especially crowded. Stonehenge is packed at Summer Solstice, when visitors stay all night to watch the sun rise. If you want to visit at this time, use the dedicated bus service from Salisbury.

English Heritage, which manages the site, can arrange access to the inner circle (not a guided tour) outside of regular hours; each group is 26 people maximum. This requires application and payment of £15.30 well in advance, as Stone Circle Access visits are popular. Apply by mail or fax, call the booking office at ☎ 01722/343834, or email ✉ stonecircleaccess@englishheritage. org.uk. The booking form is available at ⊕ www.english-heritage.org.uk.

The site plans a major development program. Until 2014, facilities remain limited to a visitor center, shop, and refreshment stand.

TIPS AND WHAT TO BRING
Since the stones are roped off, bring binoculars to see the prehistoric carvings on them. Spend a few hours: walk all around the site to get that perfect photo and to observe the changing light on the plain. The free audio guide is essential, and the shop sells plenty of books.

MAKING A DAY OF IT
The Salisbury and South Wiltshire Museum in Salisbury has finds from the site and burial reconstructions that help put Stonehenge into perspective. The smaller Alexander Keiller Museum in Avebury has finds from the area.

It's an easy drive between nearby prehistoric sites. Stonehenge is set in 1,500 acres of National Trust land with excel-

Avebury, Wiltshire

lent walks. The Great Stones Way will link Avebury with Stonehenge and will reach Salisbury; a 14-mi central stretch is open. The trail will be fully open by mid-2012.

GETTING HERE
By car, Stonehenge is 2 mi west of Amesbury off A344. The **Stonehenge Tour Bus** (⊕ www.thestonehengetour. info) departs from Salisbury rail and bus stations frequently; buses leave every half hour or hour. Tickets cost £11, or £18 with Stonehenge admission. Other options are a taxi or an organized tour. **Salisbury and Stonehenge Guided Tours** (⊕ www.salisbury-guidedtours.com ☎ 07775/674816 ✉ pat_shelley@btinternet.com) operates small-group tours from Salisbury and London.

VISITOR INFORMATION
✉ Junction of A303 and A344/A360, near Amesbury ☎ 0870/333–1181, 01722/343830 for after-hours access ⊕ www.english-heritage.org.uk ✍ £7.50 ☉ Mid-Mar.–May and Sept.–mid-Oct., daily 9:30–6; June–Aug., daily 9–7; mid-Oct.–mid-Mar., daily 9:30–4. Last admission 30 mins before closing.

morning and early evening are recommended. ✉ *1 mi north of A4* ☎ *No phone* ⊕ *www.english-heritage.org.uk* 🎟 *Free* ☉ *Daily.*

Cherhill Down. Four miles west of Avebury, on A4, Cherhill Down is a prominent hill carved with a vivid white horse and topped with a towering obelisk. It's one of a number of hillside etchings in Wiltshire, none of which dates back farther than the late 18th century. This one was put there in 1780 to indicate the highest point of the downs between London and Bath. The views from the top are well worth the half-hour climb. The best view of the horse is from A4, on the approach from Calne.

Kennet Stone Avenue. The Avebury monument lies at the end of Kennet Stone Avenue, a sort of prehistoric processional way leading to Avebury. The avenue's stones were spaced 80 feet apart, but only the half mile nearest the main monument survives intact. The lost stones are marked with concrete obelisks.

Silbury Hill. Rising 130 feet, this man-made mound dates from about 2500 BC and is the largest of its kind in Europe. Excavations beginning more than 200 years have provided no clue as to its original purpose, but the generally accepted notion is that it was a massive burial chamber. The viewing area, less than 1 mi east of Avebury, is only accessible during daylight hours. ✉ *A4.*

West Kennet Long Barrow. Prehistoric relics dot the entire Avebury area. The West Kennet Long Barrow is one of the largest Neolithic chambered tombs in Britain, dating from about 3250 BC. You can explore all around the site and also enter the tomb, which was used for over 1,000 years before the main passage was blocked and the entrance closed. More than 300 feet long, it has an elevated position with a great view of Silbury Hill and the surrounding countryside. It's about 1 mi east of Avebury. ✉ *A4.*

WHERE TO EAT AND STAY

££
BRITISH
✗**Waggon and Horses.** A 16th-century thatched building created in part with stones taken from the Avebury site, this traditional inn and pub is beside the traffic circle linking A4 and A361, a two-minute drive from the prehistoric circle. Dickens mentioned the building in the *Pickwick Papers.* Excellent lunches and dinners are served beside a fire; homemade dishes include steak, kidney, and ale pie, baked Camembert, and a smoked fish platter, or you can opt for a baguette. In high season it's something of a tourist hub. ✉ *Beckhampton* ☎ *01672/539418* ☉ *No dinner Sun. Oct.–May.*

£££
B&B/INN
🛏 **The Lodge.** Inside the Avebury Stone Circles, this charming inn's spacious rooms are full of character, thanks to the eclectic decor, rare prints, and antique furnishings. **Pros:** great views; comfortable rooms. **Cons:** not great for young children. ✉ *High St.* ☎ *01672/539023* ⊕ *www.aveburylodge.co.uk* 🛏 *2 rooms* ⚙ *In-room: no a/c, Wi-Fi. In-hotel: some age restrictions* ⵌ *Breakfast.*

££
B&B/INN
🛏 **Manor Farm.** Views of Avebury's monoliths straggling across the field greet you from the windows of this 18th-century farmhouse right in the heart of the village. **Pros:** ideal location; cozy and comfortable rooms; good breakfasts. **Cons:** often booked up; young children not accepted. ✉ *High St.* ☎ *01672/539294* ⊕ *www.manorfarmavebury.com* 🛏 *2 rooms without bath* ⚙ *In-room: no a/c. In-hotel: some age restrictions* ▭ *No credit cards* ⵌ *Breakfast.*

4

LONGLEAT HOUSE

31 mi southwest of Avebury, 6 mi north of Stourhead, 19 mi south of Bath, 27 mi northwest of Salisbury.

GETTING HERE AND AROUND

Longleat House is off A36 between Bath and Salisbury. The nearest train station is Warminster, about 5 mi away. Your best option is taking a taxi from there.

ESSENTIALS

Visitor Information Warminster (⊠ *Central car park, off Station Rd.* ☎ *01985/218548* ⊕ *www.visitwiltshire.co.uk*).

EXPLORING

★ **Longleat House.** Home of the marquess of Bath, Longleat House is one of
☾ southern England's most famous private estates, and possibly the most ambitiously, even eccentrically, commercialized, as evidenced by the presence of a drive-through safari park (open since 1966) with giraffes, zebras, monkeys, rhinos, and lions. The Italian Renaissance building was completed in 1580 (for more than £8,000, an astronomical sum at the time) and contains outstanding tapestries, paintings, porcelain, and furniture, as well as notable period features such as the Victorian kitchens, the Elizabethan minstrels' gallery, and the great hall with its massive wooden beams. Giant antlers of the extinct Irish elk decorate the walls, and free tours of the present Lord Bath's occasionally raunchy murals—described as "keyhole glimpses into my psyche," ranging from philosophical subjects to depictions of the Kama Sutra—can be booked separately at the front desk. Besides the safari park, Longleat has a butterfly garden, a miniature railway, an extensive (and fairly fiendish) hedge maze, and an adventure castle, all of which make it extremely popular, particularly in summer and during school vacations. ■ TIP→ You can easily spend a whole day here. Visit the house in the morning, when tours are more relaxed, and the safari park in the afternoon. A safari bus service is available (£6) for those arriving without their own transport. ⊠ *Off A362, Warminster* ☎ *01985/844400* ⊕ *www. longleat.co.uk* ⊠ *£26; house and grounds only, £12.90* ⊙ *House and park Mar., weekends 10–5; Apr.–mid-July and mid-Sept.–late Oct., weekdays 10–5, weekends 10–6; late July–early Sept., daily 10–7:30; early Nov., 10–4; Dec., weekends at various times, call in advance; last entry 1 hr before closing.*

WHERE TO STAY

For expanded reviews, visit Fodors.com.

££££–£££££
HOTEL

🎫 **Bishopstrow House.** This ivy-covered Georgian house has been converted into a refreshingly relaxed hotel that combines well-chosen antiques with modern amenities such as DVD players. **Pros:** country-house ambience; impressive suites; excellent leisure facilities. **Cons:** expensive extras; restaurant lacks charm. ⊠ *Boreham Rd., Warminster* ☎ *01985/212312* ⊕ *www.bishopstrow.co.uk* ⇴ *29 rooms, 2 suites* ⌂ *In-room: no a/c, Internet, Wi-Fi (some). In-hotel: restaurant, bar, pools, tennis courts, gym, spa, some pets allowed* ⊚⊙ *Breakfast.*

STOURHEAD

9 mi southwest of Longleat, 15 mi northeast of Sherborne, 30 mi west of Salisbury.

GETTING HERE AND AROUND

By car, you can reach Stourhead via B3092. It's signposted off the main road. From London, board at train to Gillingham and take a five-minute cab ride to Stourton.

ESSENTIALS

Visitor Information Warminster (✉ *Central car park, off Station Rd.* ☎ *01985/218548* ⊕ *www.visitwiltshire.co.uk*).

EXPLORING

Fodor's Choice ★ **Stourhead.** Close to the village of Stourton lies one of Wiltshire's most breathtaking sights—Stourhead, a country-house-and-garden combination that has few parallels for beauty anywhere in Europe. Most of Stourhead was built between 1721 and 1725 by Henry the Magnificent, the wealthy banker Henry Hoare. A fire gutted the center of the house in 1902, but it was reconstructed with only a few differences. Many rooms in the Palladian mansion contain Chinese and French porcelain, and some have furniture by Chippendale. The elegant library and floridly colored picture gallery were built for the cultural development of this exceedingly civilized family. Still, the house takes second place to the adjacent gardens designed by Henry Hoare II, which are the most celebrated example of the English 18th-century taste for "natural" landscaping. Temples, grottoes, and bridges have been placed among shrubs, trees, and flowers to make the grounds look like a three-dimensional oil painting. A walk around the artificial lake (1½ mi) reveals changing vistas that conjure up the 17th-century landscapes of Claude Lorrain and Nicolas Poussin; walk counterclockwise for the best views. ■TIP→ The best time to visit is early summer, when the massive banks of rhododendrons are in full bloom, but the gardens are beautiful at any time of year. You can get a fine view of the estate from Alfred's Tower, a 1772 folly (a structure built for picturesque effect). In summer there are occasional concerts, sometimes accompanied by fireworks and gondoliers on the lake. A restaurant and plant shop are on the grounds. All in all, it's easy to spend half a day here. ✉ *Off B3092, northwest of Mere, Stourton* ☎ *01747/841152* ⊕ *www.nationaltrust.org.uk* ✉ *£12.80; house only, £7.70; gardens only, £7.70; Alfred's Tower £3.10* ☉ *House and Alfred's Tower mid-Mar.–Oct., Fri.–Tues. 11–5 or dusk; last admission 30 mins before closing; gardens daily 9–7 or dusk.*

WHERE TO STAY

For expanded reviews, visit Fodors.com.

££ HOTEL ★ 🛏 **The Spread Eagle.** You can't stay at Stourhead, but this popular hostelry, built at the beginning of the 19th century inside the main entrance to Stourhead, is the next best thing. **Pros:** period character; easy and free access to Stourhead. **Cons:** needs some modernization; food can be disappointing. ✉ *Off B3092, northwest of Mere, Stourton* ☎ *01747/840587* ⊕ *www.spreadeagleinn.com* ⇌ *5 rooms* ⟳ *In-room: no a/c, Wi-Fi. In-hotel: restaurant, bar* ❑ *Breakfast.*

NEW FOREST, DORSET, AND THE SOUTH COAST

Tucked southwest of Southampton, the New Forest was once the hunting preserve of William the Conqueror and his royal descendants. Thus protected from the deforestation that has befallen most of southern England's other forests, this wild, scenic expanse offers great possibilities for walking, riding, and biking. West of here stretches the green, hilly, and largely unspoiled county of Dorset, the setting for most of the books of Thomas Hardy, author of *Far from the Madding Crowd* and other classic Victorian-era novels. "I am convinced that it is better for a writer to know a little bit of the world remarkably well than to know a great part of the world remarkably little," he wrote as he immortalized the towns, villages, and fields of this idyllically rural area, not least the county capital, Dorchester, an ancient agricultural center. North of here is the unspoiled market town of Sherbourne. Other places of historic interest such as Maiden Castle and the chalk-cut giant of Cerne Abbas are interspersed with the bustling seaside resorts of Bournemouth and Weymouth. You may find Lyme Regis (associated with another writer, John Fowles) and the villages along the route closer to your ideal of coastal England. The Jurassic Coast is the place to search for fossils.

LYNDHURST

26 mi southeast of Stonehenge, 18 mi southeast of Salisbury, 9 mi west of Southampton.

Lyndhurst is famous as the capital of the New Forest. Although some popular spots can get crowded in summer, there are ample parking lots, picnic areas, and campgrounds. Miles of trails crisscross the region.

GETTING HERE AND AROUND

From Salisbury, follow A36, B3079, and continue along A337 another 4 mi or so. To explore the depths of the New Forest, take A35 out of Lyndhurst (the road continues southwest to Bournemouth) or A337 south. The New Forest Tour, a hop-on, hop-off open-top bus, runs a circular route through the New Forest between mid-June and mid-September (adults £9 per day, tickets on board). There are eight departures daily, and the bus will stop anywhere. Regular bus services are operated by Bluestar and Wilts & Dorset; see Traveline for details.

Many parts of the New Forest are readily accessible by train from London via the centrally located Brockenhurst Station.

ESSENTIALS

Visitor and Tour Information Lyndhurst (✉ *Main Car Park, High St.* ☎ *023/8028–2269* ⊕ *www.thenewforest.co.uk*).

New Forest Tour (⊕ *www.thenewforesttour.info*).

EXPLORING

New Forest. This park consists of 150 square mi of open countryside interspersed with dense woodland, a natural haven for herds of free-roaming deer, cattle, and, most famously, hardy New Forest ponies.

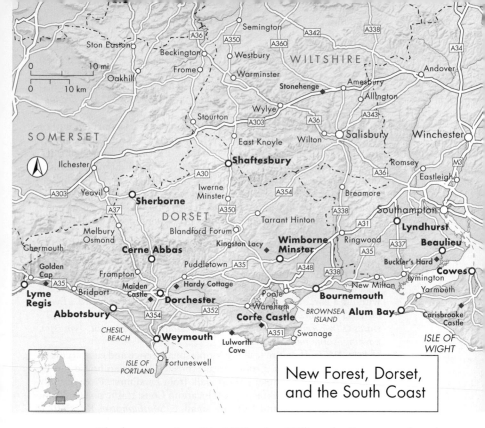

New Forest, Dorset, and the South Coast

The forest was "new" in 1079, when William the Conqueror cleared the area of farms and villages and turned it into his private hunting grounds. An extensive network of trails makes it a wonderful place for biking, walking, and horseback riding. ⊕ *www.thenewforest.co.uk*.

New Forest Museum. In the same building as the New Forest Centre, this museum contains fascinating and informative background on the region. The exhibits focus on the area's fauna, flora, and social traditions and are linked by quizzes, and there are other interactive elements that will keep children engaged. ⊠ *High St.* ☎ *023/8028–3444* ⊕ *www. newforestcentre.org.uk* ⊠ *£3.50* ⊗ *Daily 10–5; last entry at 4.*

St. Michael and All Angels. Lyndhurst's High Street is dominated by this redbrick, high Victorian church, which holds stained glass from William Morris's studio and a large fresco of the parable of the virgins by Frederick Leighton. Fans of Lewis Carroll's *Alice in Wonderland* should note that Alice Hargreaves (née Liddell), the inspiration for the fictional Alice, is buried in the churchyard. ⊠ *High St.* ☎ *023/8028–2154* ⊕ *www.newforestparishes.com*.

WHERE TO EAT AND STAY

££
BRITISH
✕ **White Buck Inn.** This traditional forest lodge makes a welcome stop for refreshment. The extensive menu relies on local seasonal fare, such as pork belly with a cider-and-apple sauce, and venison. In summer you

can sit in the spacious garden, where there are regular barbecues. Live Dixieland jazz plays on Thursday evenings. There are also seven guest rooms (££) ranging from functional to plush, all with garden views, and four of them themed along Elizabethan or Indian lines. ✉ *Bisterne Close, Burley, 7 mi west of Lyndhurst* ☎ *01425/402264* ⊕ *www.fullershotels.com.*

£££££ ⓘ **Chewton Glen.** Once the home of Captain Frederick Marryat, author
HOTEL of *The Children of the New Forest,* this early-19th-century country
★ house on extensive grounds ranks among Britain's most acclaimed— and most expensive—lodgings. **Pros:** classic English luxury; excellent restaurant; top-notch leisure facilities. **Cons:** dated in parts; patchy service in restaurant. ✉ *Christchurch Rd., New Milton* ☎ *01425/275341, 800/344–5087 in U.S.* ⊕ *www.chewtonglen.com* ⤴ *33 rooms, 25 suites* ♿ *In-room: Wi-Fi. In-hotel: restaurant, golf course, pools, tennis courts, gym, spa, business center.*

£££££ ⓘ **Lime Wood.** If you're pining for a discreet, luxurious hideaway in
HOTEL the heart of the New Forest, with top-notch food and uninterrupted
★ views, this welcoming country house hotel is hard to beat. **Pros:** great location; stylish decor; iPod dock in every room. **Cons:** hard to reach without a car; some rooms on the small side. ✉ *Beaulieu Rd., Lyndhurst* ☎ *02380/287177* ⊕ *www.limewoodhotel.co.uk* ⤴ *14 rooms, 15 suites* ♿ *In-room: a/c, Wi-Fi. In-hotel: restaurants, bar, pool, gym, spa, parking, some pets allowed.*

££ ⓘ **Rufus House.** If you're looking for personal service and easy access to
B&B/INN the New Forest, book a room at this turreted Victorian house run by a Japanese-Italian couple, a short walk from Lyndhurst. **Pros:** friendly owners; delicious breakfasts; great location. **Cons:** traffic noise in front rooms; some rooms and beds are small. ✉ *Southampton Rd.* ☎ *023/8028–2930* ⊕ *www.rufushouse.co.uk* ⤴ *8 rooms, 2 suites* ♿ *In-room: no a/c, Wi-Fi. In-hotel: some age restrictions* ⅋ *Breakfast.*

SPORTS AND THE OUTDOORS

Unspoiled, wild, yet accessible even to those not normally given to long walks or bike rides, the New Forest offers countless opportunities to explore the outdoors. Bike rental and horseback riding are widely available. Numerous trails lead through thickly wooded country, across open heaths, and through the occasional bog. With very few hills, it's fairly easy terrain, and rich with wildlife. You're almost guaranteed to see ponies and deer, as well as free-roaming cattle and pigs.

BIKING

The range of trails weaving through the New Forest makes this one of Britain's best terrains for off-road biking. For £14 per day you can rent bikes at **Cycle Experience** (✉ *2–4 Brookley Rd., Brockenhurst* ☎ *01590/624204*).

HORSEBACK RIDING

Burley Manor Riding Stables (✉ *Burley Manor Hotel, Ringwood Rd., Burley* ☎ *01425/403489*) caters to all levels. Hour-long rides are £30.

You can arrange a ride at **Forest Park Riding Centre** (✉ *Rhinefield Rd., Brockenhurst* ☎ *01590/623429*). The cost is £30 per hour.

WALKING

New Forest is crisscrossed with short, easy trails, as well as longer hikes. For an easy walk (about 4 mi), start from Lyndhurst and head directly south for Brockenhurst, a commuter village. The path goes through woods, pastureland, and heath—and you'll see plenty of New Forest ponies.

BEAULIEU

7 mi southeast of Lyndhurst.

The unspoiled village of Beaulieu (pronounced *byoo*-lee) has three major attractions in one at Beaulieu Abbey and is near the museum village of Buckler's Hard.

GETTING HERE AND AROUND

Beaulieu is best reached by car on B3056 from Lyndhurst or B3054 from Lymington. It's signposted off A326 from Southampton. Bus 112 connects Beaulieu to Lymington and Hythe.

EXPLORING

Beaulieu. With a ruined abbey, a stately home, and an automobile museum, Beaulieu can satisfy different interests. In 1204 King John established **Beaulieu Abbey** for the Cistercian monks, who gave their new home its name, which means "beautiful place" in French. It was badly damaged as part of the suppression of Catholicism during the reign of Henry VIII, leaving only the cloister, the doorway, the gatehouse, and two buildings. A well-planned exhibition in one building re-creates daily life in the monastery. **Palace House** incorporates the abbey's 14th-century gatehouse and has been the home of the Montagu family since they purchased it in 1538, after the dissolution of the monasteries. Inside you can see drawing rooms, dining halls, and fine family portraits. The present Lord Montagu is noted for his work in establishing the **National Motor Museum**, which traces the development of motor transport from 1895 to the present. You can see more than 250 classic cars and motorcycles. Museum attractions include a monorail, audiovisual presentations, and a trip in a 1912 London bus. ⊠ *Off B3056* ☎ *01590/612345* ⊕ *www.beaulieu.co.uk* ⊠ *Abbey, Palace House, and Motor Museum £16.50* ⊙ *Late May–late Sept., daily 10–6; late Sept.–late May, daily 10–5; last admission 30 mins before closing.*

Buckler's Hard. Among the area's more interesting attractions is this museum village 2 mi south of Beaulieu. This restored 18th-century hamlet is home to a fascinating **Maritime Museum** that tells the story of Lord Nelson's favorite ship, HMS *Agamemnon*. Exhibits and model ships trace the town's shipbuilding history. Also part of the museum are four building interiors in the hamlet that re-create 18th-century village life. Easter through October, you can take a cruise on the Beaulieu River. The **Master Builder's House Hotel** has a bar and restaurant. ⊠ *Off B3056* ☎ *01590/616203* ⊕ *www.bucklershard.co.uk* ⊠ *£5.95* ⊙ *Mar.–June, Sept., and Oct., daily 10–5; July and Aug., daily 10–5:30; Nov.–Feb., daily 10–4:30; last entry 30 mins before closing.*

4

EN ROUTE From Beaulieu, take any of the minor roads leading west through wide-open heathland to Lymington and pick up A337 for the popular seaside resort of Bournemouth, a journey of about 18 mi.

BOURNEMOUTH

26 mi southwest of Southampton, 26 mi south of Salisbury, 24 mi east of Dorchester.

Bournemouth has 7 mi of beaches, and the waters are said to be some of southern England's most pristine. The resort was founded in 1810 by Lewis Tregonwell, an ex-army officer. He settled near what is now the Square and planted the first pine trees in the distinctive steep little valleys—or chines—cutting through the cliffs to the Bournemouth sands. The scent of fir trees was said to be healing for consumption (tuberculosis) sufferers, and the town grew steadily.

Today, the city has expanded to swallow up neighboring settlements, making it a somewhat amorphous sprawl on first view. Its stodgier, more traditional side is kept in check by the presence of a lively student population—partly made up of foreign-language students from abroad. Gardens laid out with trees and lawns link the Square and the beach. This is an excellent spot to relax and listen to music wafting from the Pine Walk bandstand. Regular musical programs take place at the Pavilion and at the nearby Winter Gardens.

GETTING HERE AND AROUND

From the New Forest, take A35 or A31/A338 southwest to Bournemouth. The center of town is best explored on foot, but to reach East Cliff or Boscombe you'll need to drive or hop aboard the frequent local buses. Fast trains from London take about two hours.

ESSENTIALS

Visitor Information Bournemouth (✉ *Westover Rd. near bandstand* ☎ *0845/051–1701* ⊕ *www.bournemouth.co.uk*).

EXPLORING

Bournemouth Beach. With miles of beaches tucked beneath its cliffs, Bournemouth is said to enjoy some of the country's warmest sea temperatures. Taking the zigzag paths through the leafy public gardens, you can descend to the seafront, where Bournemouth Pier juts into the channel from the pristine sandy beach. If you're not tempted to swim, you can stroll the nearby promenade. Europe's first artificial **surf reef** was constructed here in 2009. The goal is to attract surf fans as well as create an area of calm water that's perfect for children—surfers, however, have reported that the reef is more suitable for bodyboarding than standing up. Windsurfing, sailing, and other water sports are also big here.

★ **Russell-Cotes Art Gallery and Museum.** Perched on East Cliff, this unusual late-Victorian mansion overflows with vintage paintings and miniatures, cases of butterflies, and treasures from Asia, including an exquisite suit of Japanese armor. Members of the Russell-Cotes family, wealthy hoteliers who traveled widely, collected the items. Fine landscaped gardens surround the house. ✉ *East Cliff* ☎ *01202/451858*

⊕ *www.russell-cotes.bournemouth.gov.uk* 🎫 *Free* ☉ *Tues.–Sun. and national holiday Mon. 10–5.*

St. Peter's. On the corner of Hinton Road stands this parish church, easily recognizable by its 200-foot-high tower and spire. Lewis Tregonwell, founder and developer of Bournemouth, is buried in the churchyard. Here, too, is the elaborate tombstone of Mary Shelley, author of *Frankenstein* and wife of the great Romantic poet Percy Bysshe Shelley, whose heart is buried with her. ⊠ *Hinton Rd.* ⊕ *www. stpetersbournemouth.org.*

WHERE TO EAT AND STAY

£££

SEAFOOD

✕ **WestBeach.** Superbly positioned right on the marine promenade, close to Bournemouth Pier, this place has views over sand and sea. It also serves the best seafood in town, whether grilled, baked, or in fish pies and stews. The menu usually lists halibut, sea bass, plaice, and shellfish (oysters, mussels, lobster). Non-fish dishes may include rib-eye steak and sesame mille-feuille with grilled sweet potato and eggplant. The simple wooden tables and large glass front lend a modern, minimalist feel, and there's a narrow deck for eating alfresco. In summer you can pick up baguettes, ice cream, and other snacks from the adjacent takeout. ⊠ *Pier Approach* 🕾 *01202/587785* ⊕ *www.west-beach.co.uk.*

£££

HOTEL

🛏 **The Urban Beach.** Once-sedate Bournemouth has been waiting a long time for the injection of contemporary style and energy provided by this funky boutique hotel. **Pros:** modern designer decor; friendly staff. **Cons:** not central; occasional noise intrusion. ⊠ *23 Argyll Rd., Boscombe* 🕾 *01202/301509* ⊕ *www.urbanbeachhotel.co.uk* 🖙 *12 rooms* ⚐ *In-room: no a/c, Wi-Fi. In-hotel: restaurant, bar, business center, parking* 🍴 *Breakfast.*

££

B&B/INN

🛏 **Wood Lodge Hotel.** Calm and sedate, this small hotel just 200 yards from the shore is a reliable choice. **Pros:** welcoming staff; close to beach. **Cons:** dated in places; some bathrooms need improving. ⊠ *10 Manor Rd., East Cliff* 🕾 *01202/290891* ⊕ *www.woodlodgehotel.co.uk* 🖙 *15 rooms* ⚐ *In-room: no a/c, Wi-Fi (some). In-hotel: restaurant, bar* 🍴 *Breakfast.*

WIMBORNE MINSTER

7 mi northwest of Bournemouth via A341.

GETTING HERE AND AROUND

To reach Wimborne Minster from central Bournemouth, take any main road heading west, following signs for A341 or A349, or take advantage of the regular bus service.

ESSENTIALS

Visitor Information Wimborne Minster (⊠ *29 High St.* 🕾 *01202/886116* ⊕ *www.ruraldorset.com*).

EXPLORING

Kingston Lacy. This grand 17th-century house was altered in the 19th century by Sir Charles Barry, co-architect of the Houses of Parliament in London. It holds a choice picture collection with works by Titian, Rubens, Van Dyck, and Velásquez, as well as the fabulous Spanish Room, lined with gilded leather and topped with an ornate Venetian

The ruins of Corfe Castle, destroyed during the 17th-century Civil War, are evocative after a winter snowfall.

ceiling. There's also a fine collection of Egyptian artifacts. Parkland with walking paths surrounds the house. ⊠ *B3082, 1½ mi northwest of Wimborne Minster* ☎ *01202/883402* ⊕ *www.nationaltrust.org. uk* 🖃 *£10.50; park and garden only, £5.25* ☉ *House mid-Mar.–Oct., Wed.–Sun. and national holiday Mon. 11–5, last admission at 4. Garden and park early Feb.–early Mar., Fri.–Sun. 10:30–4; mid-Mar.–Oct., daily 10:30–6; Nov.–late Dec., daily 10:30–4.*

Priest's House Museum. On the main square in a Tudor building with a garden, this museum includes rooms furnished in period styles and a Victorian kitchen. It also has Roman and Iron Age exhibits, including a cryptic, three-faced Celtic stone head. The garden displays agricultural and horticultural tools and holds a tearoom. ⊠ *23–27 High St.* ☎ *01202/882533* ⊕ *www.priest-house.co.uk* 🖃 *£3.50, free in Dec.* ☉ *Apr.–Oct., Mon.–Sat. 10–4:30; also open for 10 days before Christmas, 3 days at the end of Dec., and 1 wk in Feb.*

Wimborne Minster. The crenellated and pinnacled twin towers of Wimborne Minster present an attractive patchwork of gray and reddish-brown stone. The church's Norman nave has zigzag molding interspersed with carved heads, and the Gothic chancel has tall lancet windows. ■ TIP➔ See the chained library, a survivor from the days when books were valuable enough to keep locked up. Look out for the 14th-century astronomical clock on the inside wall of the west tower. ⊠ *High St.* ☎ *01202/884753* ⊕ *www.wimborneminster.org.uk* 🖃 *£2 suggested donation for church, 50p suggested donation for chained library* ☉ *Church Mar.–Dec., Mon.– Sat. 9:30–5:30, Sun. 2:30–5:30; Jan. and Feb., Mon.–Sat. 9:30–4, Sun.*

2:30–4. Chained library Easter–Oct., weekdays 10:30–12:30 and 2–4, Sat. 10:30–12:30; Nov.–Easter, Sat. 10–12:30.

WHERE TO EAT AND STAY

££

MEDITERRANEAN

✕ **Primizia.** Its tangerine walls, low ceiling, and tile floor lend this popular bistro an intimate feel. The regularly changing menu, which shows French and Italian influences, may include marinated crayfish tails or roasted butternut squash risotto with sweet peppers, pesto, and Parmesan. ✉ 26 W. Borough ☎ 01202/883518 ⊗ Closed Sun. and Mon. No lunch Tues. and Sat.

££–£££

HOTEL

⊞ **Museum Inn.** It's worth making the detour 10 mi north of Wimborne Minster to find this characterful inn known for fine contemporary British fare. **Pros:** pretty village location; great food. **Cons:** remote from Wimborne Minster. ✉ Farnham ☎ 01725/516261 ⊕ www.museuminn. co.uk ⤵ 8 rooms ⚐ In-room: no a/c, Wi-Fi (some). In-hotel: restaurant, bar, some pets allowed, some age restrictions ⦿ Breakfast.

CORFE CASTLE

25 mi south of Wimborne Minster, 15 mi south of Poole, 5 mi southeast of Wareham.

ESSENTIALS

Visitor Information Wareham (✉ Holy Trinity Church, South St. ☎ 01929/552740 ⊕ www.visitswanageandpurbeck.com).

EXPLORING

★ **Corfe Castle.** One of the most impressive ruins in Britain, Corfe Castle overlooks the appealing gray limestone village of the same name. The castle site guards a gap in the surrounding Purbeck Hills and has been fortified since at least 900. The present ruins are of the castle built between 1105, when the great central keep was erected, and the 1270s, when the outer walls and towers were built. It owes its ramshackle state to Cromwell's soldiers, who blew up the castle in 1646 during the Civil War, after Lady Bankes led its defense during a long siege. ✉ A351 ☎ 01929/481294 ⊕ www.nationaltrust.org.uk ⌂ £5.90 ⊗ Mar. and Oct., daily 10–5; Apr.–Sept., daily 10–6; Nov.–Feb., daily 10–4.

OFF THE
BEATEN
PATH

Clouds Hill. This brick-and-tile cottage served as the retreat of T.E. Lawrence (Lawrence of Arabia) before he was killed in a motorcycle accident on the road from Bovington in 1935. The house remains very much as he left it, with photos and memorabilia from the Middle East. It's particularly atmospheric on a gloomy day, as there's no electric light. ✉ 8 mi northwest of Corfe, off B3390, Wareham ☎ 01929/405616 ⊕ www.nationaltrust.org.uk ⌂ £4.50 ⊗ Mid-Mar.–Oct., Wed.–Sun. and national holiday Mon. 11–5 or dusk.

WHERE TO EAT AND STAY

££

BRITISH

★

✕ **The Fox.** An age-old pub, the Fox has a fine view of Corfe Castle from its flower garden. There's an ancient well in the lounge bar and more timeworn stonework in an alcove, as well as a pre-1300 fireplace. The bar cheerfully doles out soups and sandwiches, as well as steaks and fish dishes. This place is popular, and can get uncomfortably congested in summer. ✉ West St., Corfe ☎ 01929/480449.

££ ⊡ **Castle Inn.** This thatched hotel, 10 mi west of Corfe Castle, has a
HOTEL flagstone bar and other 15th-century features. **Pros:** close to Lulworth
Cove; historic vibe. **Cons:** shabby in places; some rooms are over the
noisy bar. ✉ *Main Rd., West Lulworth* ☎ *01929/400311* ⊕ *www.*
lulworthinn.com ⊋ *10 rooms* ⚭ *In-room: no a/c, Wi-Fi. In-hotel: bar,*
some pets allowed ⦿ *Breakfast.*

DORCHESTER

21 mi west of Corfe on A351 and A352, 30 mi west of Bournemouth,
43 mi southwest of Salisbury.

In many ways Dorchester, the Casterbridge of Thomas Hardy's novel
The Mayor of Casterbridge, is a traditional southern country town.
The town owes much of its fame to its connection with Hardy, whose
bronze statue looks westward from a bank on Colliton Walk. Born in
a cottage in the hamlet of Higher Bockhampton, about 3 mi northeast
of Dorchester, "Hardy country" includes a number of hidden-away
villages in the rolling hills of Dorest. Two important historical sites, as
well as his former residence, are a short drive from Dorchester.

Dorchester has many reminders of the Roman presence in the area. The
Romans laid out the town about AD 70, and a stroll along Bowling
Alley Walk, West Walk, and Colliton Walk follows the approximate line
of the original Roman town walls. On the north side of Colliton Park
lies an excavated Roman villa with a marvelously preserved mosaic
floor. High Street was tranquil in Hardy's day, but today it is usually
busy with vehicle traffic. To appreciate the town's contemporary character, pick up a walking itinerary from the tourist office, which will take
you past the main points of interest along quieter routes.

GETTING HERE AND AROUND

Dorchester can be reached from Corfe Castle via A351 and A352. From
Salisbury take A354. Park wherever you can (pay parking lots are scattered around the center) and explore the town on foot.

ESSENTIALS

Visitor Information Dorchester (✉ *11 Antelope Walk* ☎ *01305/267992*
⊕ *www.westdorset.com).*

EXPLORING

TOP ATTRACTIONS

Athelhampton House and Gardens. Fine 19th-century gardens enhance an
outstanding example of 15th-century domestic architecture at Athelhampton House and Gardens, 5 mi east of Dorchester. Thomas Hardy
called this place Athelhall in some of his writings, referring to the legendary King Aethelstan, who had a palace on this site. The current
house includes the Great Hall, with much of its original timber roof
intact, the King's Room, and the Library, with oak paneling and more
than 3,000 books. The 10 acres of landscaped gardens include a dozen
giant yew pyramids. ✉ *A35* ☎ *01305/848363* ⊕ *www.athelhampton.*
co.uk ⊡ *£10.75* ⊙ *Mar.–Oct., Sun.–Thurs. 10:30–5; Nov.–Feb., Sun.*
11–dusk.

CLOSE UP

Hardy's Dorset

Among this region's proudest claims is its connection with Thomas Hardy (1840–1928), one of England's most celebrated novelists. If you read some of Hardy's novels before visiting Dorset—re-created by Hardy as his part-fact, part-fiction county of Wessex—you may well recognize some places immediately from his descriptions. The tranquil countryside surrounding Dorchester is lovingly described in *Far from the Madding Crowd*, and Casterbridge, in *The Mayor of Casterbridge*, stands for Dorchester itself. Any pilgrimage to Hardy's Wessex begins at the author's birthplace in Higher Bockhampton, 3 mi east of Dorchester. Salisbury makes an appearance as "Melchester" in *Jude the Obscure*. Walk in the footsteps of Jude Fawley by climbing Shaftesbury—"Shaston"—and its steep Gold Hill, a street lined with cottages. Today many of these sights seem frozen in time, and Hardy's spirit is ever present.

Dorset County Museum. This labyrinthine museum contains ancient Celtic remains from nearby Maiden Castle and Roman remains from town, a rural crafts gallery, and a local-history gallery. It's better known for its large collection of Hardy memorabilia, and there's a gallery focusing on the nearby Jurassic Coast. ✉ *High West St.* ☎ *01305/262735* ⊕ *www.dorsetcountymuseum.org* 🎫 *£6.50* ⊙ *Apr.–Oct., Mon.–Sat. 10–5; Nov.–Mar., Tues.–Sat. 10–4.*

QUICK BITES

Drop into **Potters Café** (✉ *19 Durngate St.* ☎ *01305/260312*), occupying a 17th-century cottage, for teas and delicious cakes and pastries, as well as grilled ciabattas and lunches of fish pie or macaroni and cheese. The courtyard garden is pleasant in summer.

★ **Maiden Castle.** About 2 mi southwest of Dorchester, Maiden Castle is one of the most important pre-Roman archaeological sites in England. It's not an actual castle but an enormous hill fort of stone and earth with ramparts that enclose about 45 acres. England's mysterious prehistoric inhabitants built the fort some 4,000 years ago, and many centuries later it was a Celtic stronghold. In AD 43 invading Romans, under the general (later emperor) Vespasian, stormed the fort. Finds from the site are on display in the Dorset County Museum in Dorchester. To experience an uncanny silence and sense of mystery, climb Maiden Castle early in the day. Leave your car at the lot at the end of Maiden Castle Way, a 1½-mi lane. ✉ *A354.*

WORTH NOTING

🄲 **Dinosaur Museum.** The popular Dinosaur Museum has life-size models, interactive displays, and a hands-on Discovery Gallery. ✉ *Icen Way off High East St.* ☎ *01305/269880* ⊕ *www.thedinosaurmuseum.com* 🎫 *£6.95* ⊙ *Apr.–Sept., daily 10–5; Oct.–Mar., daily 10–4.*

Hardy's Cottage. The small thatch-and-cob cottage, where the writer was born in 1840, was built by his grandfather and is little altered since that time. From here Thomas Hardy would make his daily 6-mi walk to school in Dorchester. Among other things, you can see the desk at which the author completed *Far from the Madding Crowd*. Access is on foot only, via a woodland walk, or country lane from the parking lot. ✉ *½ mi south of Blandford Rd. (A35), Higher Bockhampton* ☎ *01305/262366* ⊕ *www.nationaltrust.org.uk* ✎ *£4.75* ☉ *Late Apr.–Oct., Wed.–Sun. and holiday Mon. 11–5 or dusk.*

Maumbury Rings. These remains of a Roman amphitheater on the edge of town were built on a prehistoric site that later served as a place of execution. (Hardy's *Mayor of Casterbridge* contains a vivid evocation of the Rings.) As late as 1706 a girl was burned at the stake here. ✉ *Maumbury Rd.*

Max Gate. Thomas Hardy lived in Max Gate from 1885 until his death in 1928. An architect by profession, Hardy designed the house himself, and visitors can now see the study where he wrote *Tess of the d'Urbevilles*, *The Mayor of Casterbridge,* and *Jude the Obscure.* The dining room, the drawing room, and the garden are open to the public. ✉ *Allington Ave., 1 mi east of Dorchester on A352* ☎ *01305/262538* ⊕ *www.nationaltrust.org.uk* ✎ *£43* ☉ *Apr.–Oct., Wed.–Sun. and holiday Mon. 11–5.*

OFF THE BEATEN PATH

Poundbury. Owned by the Duchy of Cornwall and under the aegis of the Prince of Wales, this settlement a mile west of Dorchester on B3150 is a showcase of Prince Charles's vision of urban planning and community living. The emphasis is on conservation and energy efficiency; private houses coexist with shops, offices, small-scale factories, and leisure facilities. Central Pummery Square is dominated by the colonnaded Brownsword Hall. Here you'll find Dorchester's Farmers' Market, held the first Saturday of the month.

WHERE TO EAT AND STAY

£

ITALIAN

✗ **Judge Jeffreys.** Relaxed and charming, this eatery occupies the former residence of Judge Jeffreys, a 17th-century hanging judge. The restaurant serves a reliable menu of Italian classics. Alongside the risottos, pastas, and pizzas, you'll also find crab cakes and *pollo siciliana* (char-grilled chicken breast). Both dining areas are paneled (dark at street level, lighter upstairs), with beamed ceilings, antique fireplaces, and swords on the walls. ✉ *6 High West St.* ☎ *01305/259678* ⊕ *www.loveprezzo.co.uk.*

££££

MODERN BRITISH

★

✗ **Yalbury Cottage.** A thatch roof and inglenook fireplaces add to the appeal of this 300-year-old cottage, 2½ mi east of Dorchester. The restaurant's three-course fixed-price menu (£34) of superior Modern British and European fare emphasizes seasonal local fare and might include seared Lyme Regis scallops, roast loin of lamb, or glazed duck breast. There are eight comfortable bedrooms (££) available in an extension overlooking gardens or fields. Lower Bockhampton is signposted off the A35, northeast of town. ✉ *Bockhampton La., Lower Bockhampton* ☎ *01305/262382* ⊕ *www.yalburycottage.com* ☉ *No dinner Sun. or Mon.*

££–£££

B&B/INN

▦ **The Casterbridge.** Small but full of character, this Georgian building from 1790 reflects its age with period furniture and elegance. **Pros:** central location; elegant period setting; good breakfasts. **Cons:** traffic noise in front rooms; annex rooms are small and lack character; limited parking. ✉ *49 High East St.* ☎ *01305/264043* ⊕ *www.thecasterbridge.co.uk* ⇆ *14 rooms* ⚐ *In-room: no a/c, Wi-Fi (some). In-hotel: bar, parking* ❙⊙❙ *Breakfast.*

SHOPPING

You can find Dorset delicacies such as Blue Vinney cheese (which some connoisseurs prefer to Blue Stilton) in the **Wednesday Market** (✉ *Fairfield parking lot, off Weymouth Ave.*).

THE OUTDOORS

From April through October the **Thomas Hardy Society** (☎ *01305/251501* ⊕ *www.hardysociety.org*) organizes walks that follow in the steps of Hardy's novels. Readings and discussions accompany the walks, which take most of a day.

CERNE ABBAS

4

6 mi north of Dorchester.

The village of Cerne Abbas, worth a short exploration on foot, has some Tudor houses on the road beside the church. Nearby you can also see the original village stocks.

GETTING HERE AND AROUND

Cerne Abbas is best reached by car from Dorchester to the south or Sherborne to the north via A352.

EXPLORING

Cerne Abbas Giant. The town's main claim to fame is the colossal and unblushingly priapic Cerne Abbas Giant, a figure cut in chalk on a hillside overlooking the village. The 180-foot-long giant carries a huge club, and may have originated as a tribal fertility symbol long before Roman times. His outlines are formed by 2-foot-wide trenches. The present giant is thought to have been carved in the chalk about AD 1200. The best place to view the figure is from the A352 itself, where you can park in any of numerous nearby turnouts. ✉ *A352* ⊕ *www. nationaltrust.org.uk.*

Cerne Abbey. This 10-century abbey is now a ruin, with little left to see except its old gateway, although the nearby Abbey House is still in use.

SHERBORNE

12 mi north of Cerne Abbas, 20 mi north of Dorchester, 15 mi west of Shaftesbury, 40 mi west of Wilton, 43 mi west of Salisbury.

Once granted cathedral status, until deferring to Old Sarum in 1075, this unspoiled market town is awash with medieval buildings built with the honey-color local stone. The focal point of the winding streets is the abbey church. Also worth visiting here are the ruins of the 12th-century Old Castle and Sherborne Castle with its grounds.

GETTING HERE AND AROUND

Hourly trains from Salisbury take 45 minutes to reach Sherborne. The station is at the bottom of Digby Road, near the abbey. Drivers should take A30, passing through Shaftesbury.

ESSENTIALS

Visitor Information Sherborne (✉ *3 Tilton Ct., Digby Rd.* ☎ *01935/815341* ⊕ *www.westdorset.com*).

EXPLORING

Shaftesbury. The model for the town of Shaston in Thomas Hardy's *Jude the Obscure* is still a small market town. It lies on a ridge overlooking Blackmore Vale—you can catch a sweeping view of the surrounding countryside from the top of Gold Hill, a steep relentlessly picturesque street lined with cottages. It has even appeared in TV commercials. Shaftesbury is 20 mi west of Salisbury and 15 mi east of Sherbourne.

Sherborne Abbey. The glory of Sherbourne Abbey, a warm, "old gold" stone church, is the delicate and graceful 15th-century fan vaulting that extends the length of the soaring nave and choir. ("I would pit Sherborne's roof against any contemporary work of the Italian Renaissance," enthused Simon Jenkins, in his *England's Thousand Best Churches*.) If you're lucky, you might hear "Great Tom," one of the heaviest bells in the world, pealing out from the bell tower. Guided tours are offered from April through September on Tuesday (10:30) and Friday (2:30), or by prior arrangement. ⊠ *Abbey Clos* ☎ *01935/812452* ⊕ *www.sherborneabbey. com* ⊠ *Free* ⊙ *Apr.–Sept., daily 8–6; Oct.–Mar., daily 8–4.*

Sherborne Castle. Built by Sir Walter Raleigh in 1594, this castle remained his home for 10 years before it passed to the custodianship of the Digby family. The interior has been remodeled in 19th-century Gothic style, and ceilings have splendid plaster moldings. After admiring the extensive collections of Meissen and Asian porcelain, stroll around the lake and landscaped grounds, the work of Capability Brown. The house is less than a mile southeast of town. ⊠ *Off A352* ☎ *01935/812072* ⊕ *www.sherbornecastle.com* ⊠ *£9.50; gardens only, £5* ⊙ *Apr.–Oct., Tues.–Thurs., Sun., and national holiday Mon. 11–5, Sat. 2–5; last admission at 4:30.*

WHERE TO STAY

For expanded reviews, visit Fodors.com.

£ ⚏ **The Alders.** A quiet, unspoiled village 3 mi north of Sherborne contains
B&B/INN this B&B, an old stone house with a walled garden. **Pros:** peaceful setting; relaxing massages; interesting artworks. **Cons:** a bit remote; nothing to do in evening. ⊠ *Off B3145, Sandford Orcas* ☎ *01963/220666* ⊕ *www.thealdersbb.com* ⤴ *3 rooms* ⅃ *In-room: no a/c, Wi-Fi* ⊟ *No credit cards* ⍩ *Breakfast.*

WEYMOUTH

8 mi south of Dorchester, 28 mi south of Sherbourne.

West Dorset's main coastal resort, Weymouth, is known for its sandy beaches and its royal connections. King George III began bathing here for his health in 1789, setting a trend among the wealthy and fashionable people of the day. Popularity left Weymouth with many fine buildings, including the Georgian row houses lining the Esplanade. Striking historical details clamor for attention: a wall on Maiden Street holds a cannonball that was embedded in it during the Civil War. Not far away, a column commemorates the launching of U.S. forces from Weymouth on D-Day.

Weymouth and its lively harbor offer the full bucket-and-spade seaside experience: donkey rides, sand castles, and plenty of fish-and-chips. Weymouth and Portland are hosting the 2012 Olympic sailing events.

GETTING HERE AND AROUND

You can reach Weymouth on frequent local buses and trains from Dorchester, or on less frequent services from Bournemouth. The bus and train stations are close to each other near King's Statue, on the Esplanade. If you're driving, take A354 from Dorchester and park on or near the Esplanade—an easy walk from the center—or in a lot near the harbor.

ESSENTIALS

Visitor Information Weymouth (✉ *The Pavilion, The Esplanade* ☎ *01305/785747* ⊕ *www.visitweymouth.co.uk*).

EXPLORING

Chesil Beach. A 5-mi-long peninsula jutting south from Weymouth leads to the Isle of Portland, well known for its limestone. The peninsula is the eastern end of the unique geological curiosity known as Chesil Beach—a 200-yard-wide, 30-foot-high bank of pebbles that decrease in size from east to west. The beach extends for 18 mi. A powerful undertow makes swimming dangerous, and tombstones in local churchyards attest to the many shipwrecks the beach has caused. There are walking and cycle trails along the rugged coastline.

WHERE TO EAT

££££
SEAFOOD

✗**Perry's.** In a Georgian town house right by the harbor, this busy restaurant specializes in simple dishes using the best local seafood. Try the lobster or scallops, or grilled fillet of sea bass with asparagus and a mussel, lemon, and vanilla sauce. Meat dishes, such as roast beef fillet and rump of lamb, are tasty, too. Set-price lunch menus are a good value. ✉ *The Harbourside, 4 Trinity Rd.* ☎ *01305/785799* ⊕ *www.perrysrestaurant.co.uk* ♥ *Closed Mon. No lunch Sat.*

£
FRENCH

✗**Time for Tea.** Tucked away from the busy harbor, this French-owned haven serves classics dishes and superlative Dorset cream teas. The onion or fish soup and *croque-monsieur* are favorites. If you're looking for an afternoon pit stop, try the substantial, and very English, afternoon tea selection with freshly baked cakes and scones. ✉ *8 Cove St.* ☎ *01305/777500* ♥ *No dinner.*

ABBOTSBURY

10 mi northwest of Weymouth.

Pretty Abbotsbury is at the western end of Chesil Beach and has a swannery. In other parts of the village, you can also visit a children's farm, housed in an impressive medieval barn, and subtropical gardens.

GETTING HERE AND AROUND

By car, take B3157 from Weymouth, or the steep and very minor road passing through Martinstown off A35 from Dorchester; the latter route has marvelous views of the coast.

Visitor Information Abbotsbury (✉ *Bellenie's Bakehouse, 11 Market St.*
☎ *01305/871990* ⊕ *www.abbotsbury.co.uk*).

EXPLORING

Abbotsbury Swannery. A lagoon outside the village serves as a famous breeding place for swans. Introduced by Benedictine monks as a source of meat in winter, the swans have remained for centuries, building new nests every year in the soft, moist eelgrass. Cygnets hatch between mid-May and late June. Try to visit during feeding time, at noon and 4 pm. ✉ *New Barn Rd.* ☎ *01305/871858* ⊕ *www.abbotsburyswannery.co.uk* 🖾 *£9.95* ⊗ *Apr.–Sept., daily 10–6; late Mar. and Oct., daily 10–5; last admission 1 hr before closing.*

LYME REGIS

19 mi west of Abbotsbury.

"A very strange stranger it must be, who does not see the charms of the immediate environs of Lyme, to make him wish to know it better," wrote Jane Austen in *Persuasion*. Judging from the summer crowds, most people appear to be not at all strange. The ancient, scenic town of Lyme Regis and the so-called Jurassic Coast are highlights of southwest Dorset. The crumbling seaside cliffs in this area are especially fossil rich.

GETTING HERE AND AROUND

Lyme Regis is off the A35, extending west from Bournemouth and Dorchester. Drivers should park as soon as possible—there are lots at the top of town—and explore the town on foot. First buses run here from Dorchester and Axminster, 6 mi northwest; the latter town is on the main rail route from London Waterloo and Salisbury.

ESSENTIALS

Visitor Information Lyme Regis (✉ *Guildhall Cottage, Church St.*
☎ *01297/442138* ⊕ *www.lymeregis.org*).

EXPLORING

Cobb. Lyme Regis is famous for its curving stone harbor breakwater, the Cobb, built by King Edward I in the 13th century to improve the harbor. The duke of Monmouth landed here in 1685 during his ill-fated attempt to overthrow his uncle James II. The Cobb figured prominently in the movie *The French Lieutenant's Woman*, based on John Fowles's novel set in Lyme Regis, as well as in the film version of Jane Austen's *Persuasion*.

🄲 **Dinosaurland Fossil Museum.** In a former church, this museum displays an excellent collection of local fossils and gives the background on regional geology and how fossils develop. Although the museum is aimed at children, most people find it informative. Ask here about guided fossil-hunting walks. The shop on the ground floor sells books and fascinating fossils from around the world. ✉ *Coombe St.* ☎ *01297/443541* ⊕ *www.dinosaurland.co.uk* 🖾 *£5* ⊗ *Mid-Feb.–mid-Oct., daily 10–4; mid-Oct.–mid-Feb., hrs vary, call ahead to check.*

Lyme Regis Museum. In a gabled and turreted Victorian building, this lively museum contains engaging items that illustrate the town's

Sunrise is lovely at the Cobb, the harbor wall built by Edward I in Lyme Regis.

maritime and domestic history, as well as a section on local writers and a good selection of local fossils. It also offers a series of fossil hunting walks throughout the year. ⊠ *Bridge St.* ☎ *01297/443370* ⊕ *www. lymeregismuseum.co.uk* ⌫ *£3.50* ⊘ *Easter–Oct., Mon.–Sat. 10–5, Sun. 11–5; Nov.–Easter, Wed.–Sun. 11–4.*

🔄 **Marine Aquarium.** This small but child-friendly museum offers the usual up-close look at creatures aquatic, from conger eels to spider crabs. ⊠ *End of the Cobb* ☎ *01297/444230* ⊕ *www.lymeregismarineaquarium. co.uk* ⌫ *£5* ⊘ *Mid-Mar.–Oct., daily 10–5.*

WHERE TO EAT AND STAY

£   ✕ **Bell Cliff.** This friendly little place at the bottom of Lyme's main street
BRITISH   makes a great spot for a light lunch or tea, although it can get noisy and cramped. Apart from teas and coffees, you can order seafood, including salmon, cod, and breaded plaice stuffed with prawns and mushrooms, or a gammon steak (a thick slice of cured ham) or leek-and-mushroom crumble. ⊠ *5–6 Broad St.* ☎ *01297/442459* ⊘ *No dinner during school terms.*

£££   ✕ **Hix Oyster & Fish House.** The finest oysters complement the grandest
SEAFOOD   views at this trendy, white-wall bistro on a height overlooking the Cobb. Seafood rules here, simply cooked and beautifully presented, from Cornish hake with clams to wild sea trout with asparagus and pea shoots. Non-fish-eaters have limited choices, but the dessert menu is extensive, including cider-brandy chocolate truffles, and buttermilk pudding. Book well ahead to sit by the floor-to-ceiling windows or on the small terrace. ⊠ *Cobb Rd.* ☎ *01297/446910* ⊕ *www.hixoysterandfishhouse. co.uk* ⌫ *Reservations essential* ⊘ *Closed Mon. Oct.–June.*

£££–££££ ⛶ **Alexandra**. Magnificently sited above the Cobb, the Alexandra com-
HOTEL bines contemporary decor with an old-fashioned, genteel air. **Pros:** great
garden; lovely views; deck overlooking the sea; central location. **Cons:**
cheaper rooms have no sea views; small bathrooms; restricted parking. ⊠ *Pound St.* ☎ *01297/442010* ⊕ *www.hotelalexandra.co.uk* 🖘 *24
rooms* ⟁ *In-room: no a/c, Internet, Wi-Fi (some). In-hotel: restaurants,
bar, business center, some pets allowed* ⊘ *Closed late Dec.–late Jan.*
⭑⦿⭑ *Breakfast.*

£ ⛶ **Coombe House**. Tucked away on one of the oldest lanes in Lyme
B&B/INN (dating from the 16th century), this simple B&B has genial hosts and
spacious, modern guest rooms in pastel shades. **Pros:** friendly owners;
pleasant rooms; central location. **Cons:** only two rooms; little parking.
⊠ *41 Coombe St.* ☎ *01297/443849* ⊕ *www.coombe-house.co.uk* 🖘 *2
rooms* ⟁ *In-room: no a/c, Wi-Fi* ⊟ *No credit cards* ⭑⦿⭑ *Breakfast.*

SPORTS AND THE OUTDOORS

The 72-mi **Dorset Coast Path** (☎ *01392/383560* ⊕ *www.southwestcoastpath.
com*) runs east from Lyme Regis to Poole, bypassing Weymouth and taking in the quiet bays, shingle beaches, and low chalk cliffs of the coast.
Some highlights are Golden Cap, the highest point on the south coast;
the Swannery at Abbotsbury; Chesil Beach; and Lulworth Cove (between
Weymouth and Corfe Castle). Villages and isolated pubs dot the route,
as do many rural B&Bs.

The West Country

WORD OF MOUTH

"Choose Cornwall if you want dramatic coastal scenery, tranquil villages and pubs, and wonderful gardens and museums. For castles, you could do a lot worse than Tintagel on the north coast and St. Michael's Mount in the southwestern tip of the county."

—Gordon_R

WELCOME TO
THE WEST COUNTRY

TOP REASONS
TO GO

★ **A coastal walk:** For high, dramatic cliff scenery, choose the Exmoor coast around Lynmouth or the coast around Tintagel. The South West Coast Path is 630 mi long.

★ **Riding or hiking on Dartmoor:** Escape to southern England's greatest wilderness—a treeless expanse dotted with rocky outcrops; there are many organized walks and pony-trekking operations.

★ **Seafood in Padstow:** Celebrity chef Rick Stein rules the roost in this small, pretty Cornish port, and any of his establishments will strongly satisfy.

★ **Tate St. Ives:** There's nowhere better to absorb the local arts scene than this offshoot of London's Tate in the pretty seaside town of St. Ives. A rooftop café claims views over Porthmeor Beach.

★ **A visit to Eden:** It's worth the journey west for Cornwall's Eden Project alone: a wonderland of plant life in a former clay pit. Two gigantic geodesic "biomes" are filled with flora.

1 Bristol, Wells, and North Devon. Bristol is filled with remnants of its long history, but you need to explore small towns like Wells and Glastonbury to get the full flavor of the region. West of here, Exmoor National Park has an unfettered, romantic appeal, with some entrancing coastline.

2 Cornwall. You're never more than 20 mi from the sea in this western outpost of Britain, and the maritime flavor imbues such port towns as Padstow and Falmouth. A string of good beaches and resort towns such as St. Ives pull in the summer crowds.

Barnstaple Bay

Clovelly

A361

Boscastle

Tintagel

Launceston

A30

Port Isaac

Padstow Bay

Padstow

2 CORNWALL

Bodmin

A388

Newquay

A390

A38

Perranporth

Fowey

Plymouth

St. Austell

St Austell Bay

Camborne   A30

Truro

St. Ives

St. Mawes

Penzance

Falmouth

Mousehole

English Channel

Bristol Channel

Clevedon
Bristol
Weston Super Mare
1

Lynmouth
Porlock
Dunster
A39
Wells
Glastonbury
A37

Exmoor National Park
Bridgwater
SOMERSET

Barnstaple
Taunton
A361

DEVON
A303

A377
M5
Honiton
DORSET
A35

A386
Exeter **4**
A30
Topsham

Okehampton
Chagford
Exmouth

Dartmoor National Park
A38 A380

3
Torbay
Paignton
Totnes
Brixham
Dartmouth
A379

0   12 mi

0   12 km

GETTING ORIENTED

Going from east to west, the counties of Somerset, Devon, and Cornwall make up the West Country. A circular tour of the West Country peninsula covers stark contrasts, from the bustling city of Bristol in the east to the remote and rocky headlands of Devon and Cornwall to the west. On the whole, the northern coast is more rugged, the cliffs dropping dramatically to tiny coves and beaches, whereas the south coast shelters many more resorts and wider expanses of sand. The crowds gravitate to the southern shore, but there are many remote inlets and estuaries, and you don't need to go far to find a degree of seclusion. The national parks of Exmoor on the northern part of the pen- insula and Dartmoor, with their wilder landscapes, add even more variety.

3 **Plymouth and Dart- moor.** Though modern in appearance, Plymouth has some important historical sights. To the northeast, the open heath and wild moor- land of Dartmoor National Park invites walking and horseback riding; towns such as Chagford make a good base for exploring.

4 **Exeter, Torbay, Totnes, and Dartmouth.** Exeter's sturdy cathedral dominates the historic city, from which you can make an easy foray to Topsham. South of Exeter, relaxed Totnes and bustling Dartmouth lie close to the English Riviera resorts of Torquay and Brixham.

WEST COUNTRY BEACHES

When the British travel to Cornwall and Devon, they're heading for the beach. This region has the best beaches in the country, whether on the Atlantic or the English Channel: crescents of ivory sand at the foot of plunging cliffs, all washed by clear, deep blue water. Bring your swimsuit and join the fun.

Clear turquoise water adds appeal at some of Cornwall's beaches (above); granite cliffs at Porthcurno Beach (right, top); boats add coastal charm (right, bottom)

Carved out by ancient volcanic activity or by the creative erosion of wind and waves, the beaches here are often uniquely beautiful. North Cornwall beaches are rugged and often pounded by surf: those near Newquay are beloved by the young surfer crowd. South Cornwall beaches tend to be sandier and less crowded, and they are also popular with families due to the calmer waves. In Devon the beaches can be a bit wilder and equally spectacular, although the best are often off the beaten track—and well worth the drive. Most beaches are free (but you may pay to park), and rare is the beach that doesn't have an ice cream truck nearby. Expect to bring your own towels, chairs, and floats.

GOOD TO KNOW

The waters off the coasts of England are very cold: brace yourself. Undertows are common due to the nature of the shoreline; beware of fast-moving tides. At most beaches, red-and-yellow flags show the limits of safe swimming. A blue flag means that the beach is excellent. The Blue Flag plan grades cleanliness, water quality, access, and facilities; it's used in Europe and parts of North America.

These Devon and Cornwall beaches include top picks for families, surfers, and those who love stunning landscapes.

WOOLACOMBE BAY

One of the most famous beaches in the country, North Devon's Woolacombe is hugely popular with families because of its soft sand, rolling dunes, and tidal pools for the kids to explore. This beach has all you could need for a dreamy day: cafés, chairs and surfing equipment to rent, lifeguards, ice cream—you name it. But if you're not looking for crowds and kids, you may want to go elsewhere. The beach is 17 mi west of Lynton: to get here, take A361 and follow signs.

BLACKPOOL SANDS

Near Dartmouth on Start Bay in South Devon, this privately managed beach sits at the edge of an extraordinary natural setting of meadows and forest. It's favored for its gentle surf; clear water; and long, wide stretch of sand. Great for swimming (not so great for surfing), the beach is big enough that you can always find a quiet stretch. Take A379 south of Dartmouth for about 3 mi and look for signs.

FISTRAL BAY

This favorite of serious surfers near Newquay in North Cornwall is a long stretch of flat, soft sand, renowned for its powerful tides and strong currents. Surf shops rent equipment and offer

lessons on the beach, or you can just check the scene. Lifeguards watch the water in summer, and there are cafés and shops selling beach supplies. The beach is off Headland Road at the western edge of Newquay.

PORTHCURNO

A protected, turquoise bay in South Cornwall, Porthcurno has a crescent moon of white sand (from crushed shells) at the foot of imposing dark, blocklike granite cliffs. The extraordinary Minack Theatre—carved from solid rock—is on one side, and there are plenty of pubs and cafés nearby. A steep slope can make swimming a challenge at times, but one area near a stream is good for families. The town and beach are signed off B3315, about 3 mi southeast of Land's End.

SENNEN COVE

Located in the aptly named Whitesand Bay, Sennen Cove is a gorgeous expanse of creamy soft sand on the southern tip of Cornwall. When the tide is coming in, the waves are good enough to attract surfers (and it's not too rough). When the tide's out, kids paddle in the tidal pools and the sand stretches as far as you can see. Cafés are nearby, and surfing equipment is for rent on the beach. Sennen is off A30 less than 2 mi north of Land's End: follow signs.

—*by Christi Daugherty*

GREAT COASTAL DRIVES

The best way to explore the West Country is by car. The coast and countryside here are wondrously varied, but the area is not well traversed by buses or trains. A drive can take you from spectacular ocean views to mysterious moors in an hour, and the routes are nearly endless.

Exploring coastal towns such as Tintagel is a West Country pleasure (above); romantic sunset at Tintagel (right, top); coastal view in Cornwall (right, below).

Choose your ideal coastal tour based on the scenery that appeals to you. For plunging cliffs and crashing seas, you'll want the north Devon and Cornwall coast. For creamy white beaches carved out of rocky shores, southern Cornwall is the place for you. You can combine your driving route with breaks for sightseeing or for bike riding, walking on the South West Coast Path, or even surfing. If you prefer a more relaxed option, stop at a café for a cup of tea and a scone; treat yourself to the clotted cream. Stretch your coastal tour out over days, or pack it all into one busy afternoon: your route can fit your own plans. Either way, you're bound to see something beautiful along the way.

BE PREPARED

Gas stations (called petrol stations here) are fairly frequent on major roads but rare on rural lanes. Don't let your tank get low if you're spending your time on small country roads. Coastal roads will be more crowded on summer weekends than weekdays, as you might expect. Heavy traffic is generally limited to the most popular towns and beaches. Outside towns, there are few lights at night—it gets very dark.

THE ATLANTIC HIGHWAY

Length and driving time: 55 mi one-way; about 5 hours with stops, 2 hours without stops

Difficulty: Moderate, with some steep, narrow roads

Running from the top of Devon down to the tip of Cornwall, A39, known as the Atlantic Highway, takes a handy route along the peninsula's northern coast, and you can hop off and on it to see the sights. Starting at the charming, hillside town of Clovelly, you can explore the steep streets and adorable cottages before driving south on A39 to Boscastle (30 mi; turn off on B3266 and follow signs), a stone-built village at the foot of a steep, forested ravine. Stop for tea and spend some time browsing Boscastle's pottery shops before driving four miles (on B3263) to Tintagel with its cliff-top castle ruins (linked to King Arthur). The ocean views are breathtaking. Back on A39, drive 20 mi to the beachfront town of Padstow, a perfect place to stop for the day, and perhaps indulge in a meal at one of Rick Stein's famous seafood restaurants.

ST. IVES TO CAPE CORNWALL, VIA PENZANCE

Length and driving time: 44 mi; about 4 hours with stops, 1.5 hours without stops

Difficulty: Low; mostly wide, easy roads

You can spend hours in St. Ives looking through its art galleries and relaxing on the beach, but when you're ready to

explore, strike out for Penzance, 8 miles south on B3311. Park in the lots near the entrance of town; explore the shops and marinas before heading to Mousehole 3 mi away on the seafront, down Mousehole Lane. In this tiny town, the Lilliputian cottages are crammed into very little space on the side of a steep cliff.

From Mousehole, the winding B3315 road will take you the 10 mi to Land's End, the tip of Cornwall: you can either join in the tourist-fest of the shopping and amusement park there, or drive on to the peace of stunning Sennen Cove a few miles away, off A30.

It's less than 10 mi from Sennen to Cape Cornwall on B3306, but the road twists and turns. It can take time to get there, particularly if you're lured by awesome coastal views along the way. Cape Cornwall is a promontory where Atlantic currents split, heading south to the English Channel or north toward Bristol. The dramatic, rocky shoreline has spectacular views and makes a great picnic spot; there's plenty of well-marked parking.

From Cape Cornwall, you're only 14 mi from St. Ives on B3306, completing your coastal loop.

—by Christi Daugherty

5

Updated
by Robert
Andrews

England's West Country is a land of granite promontories, windswept moors, hideaway hamlets, and—above all— the sea. Leafy, narrow country roads lead through miles of buttercup meadows and cider-apple orchards to heathery heights and mellow villages. With their secluded beaches and dreamy backwaters, Somerset, Devon, and Cornwall can be some of England's most relaxing regions to visit.

The counties of the West County each have their own distinct flavor, and each comes with a regionalism that borders on patriotism. Somerset is noted for its rolling green countryside; Devon's wild and dramatic moors—bare, boggy, upland heath dominated by heathers and gorse— contrast with the restfulness of its many sandy beaches and coves; and Cornwall has managed to retain a touch of its old insularity, despite the annual invasion of thousands of people lured by the Atlantic waves or the ripples of the English Channel.

The historic port of Bristol is where you come across the first unmistakable burrs of the western brogue. Its Georgian architecture and a dramatic gorge create a backdrop to what has become one of Britain's most dynamic cities. To the south lie the cathedral city of Wells and Glastonbury, with its ruined abbey and Arthurian associations. Abutting the north coast is heather-covered Exmoor National Park.

There is more wild moorland in Devon, where Dartmoor is famed for its ponies roaming amid an assortment of strange tors: rocky outcroppings eroded into weird shapes. Devon's coastal towns are as interesting for their cultural and historical appeal—many were smugglers' havens— as for their scenic beauty. Parts of south Devon resemble some balmy Mediterranean shore—hence its soubriquet, the English Riviera.

Cornwall, England's southernmost county, has always regarded itself as separate from the rest of Britain, and the Arthurian legends really took root here, not least at Tintagel Castle, the legendary birthplace of Arthur. The south coast, Janus-like, is filled with sunny beaches, delightful coves, and popular resorts.

WEST COUNTRY PLANNER

WHEN TO GO

In July and August, traffic chokes the roads leading into the West Country. Somehow the region squeezes in all the "grockles," or tourists, and the chances of finding a remote oasis of peace and quiet are severely curtailed. The beaches and resort towns are either bubbling with zest or unbearably tacky, depending on your point of view. In summer, your best option is to find a secluded hotel and make brief excursions from there. Avoid traveling on Saturday, when weekly rentals start and finish and the roads are jammed. Most properties that don't accept business year-round open for Easter and close in late September or October. Those that remain open have reduced hours. Winter has its own appeal: the Atlantic waves crash dramatically against the coast, and the austere Cornish cliffs are at their most spectacular.

The most notable festivals are Padstow's Obby Oss, a traditional celebration of the arrival of summer that takes place around May 1; the Cornish-themed, weeklong Golowan Festival in Penzance in late June; and the St. Ives September Festival of music and art in mid-September. In addition, many West Country maritime towns host regattas over summer weekends. The best times to visit Devon are late summer and early fall, during the end-of-summer festivals, especially popular in the towns of eastern Dartmoor.

PLANNING YOUR TIME

The elongated shape of Britain's southwestern peninsula means that you may well spend more time traveling than seeing the sights. The key is to base yourself in one or two places and make day trips to the surrounding region. The cities of Bristol, Exeter, and Plymouth make handy bases from which to explore the region, but they can also swallow up a lot of time, at the expense of smaller, less demanding places. The same is true of the resorts of Torquay, Newquay, and Falmouth, which can get very busy. Choose instead towns and villages such as Wells, Lynmouth, Port Isaac, St. Mawes, and Fowey to soak up local atmosphere. If you stick to just a few towns in Somerset and Devon (Bristol, Wells, and Exeter) you could get a taste of the area in four or five days. If you intend to cover Cornwall, at the end of the peninsula, you'll need at least a week. Allow time for aimless rambling—the best way to explore the moors and the coast—and leave enough free time for doing nothing at all.

GETTING HERE AND AROUND

AIR TRAVEL

Bristol International Airport, a few miles southwest of the city, has frequent flights from London, as well as from Dublin, Amsterdam, and other international cities. Exeter International Airport is 5 mi east of the city. Newquay Cornwall Airport, 5 mi northeast of town, has daily flights to London Stansted and London Gatwick.

Airport Information Bristol International Airport (✉ *Lulsgate Bottom* ☎ *0871/334–4444* ⊕ *www.bristolairport.co.uk*). **Exeter International Airport** (✉ *Clyst Honiton* ☎ *01392/367433* ⊕ *www.exeter-airport.co.uk*). **Newquay Cornwall Airport** (✉ *St. Mawgan* ☎ *01637/860600* ⊕ *www.newquaycornwallairport.com*).

BUS TRAVEL

National Express buses leave London's Victoria Coach Station for Bristol (2½ hours), Exeter (4–5 hours), Plymouth (5½ hours), and Penzance (8–9 hours). Megabus (book online to avoid premium-line costs) offers cheap service to Bristol, Exeter, Plymouth, Newquay, and Penzance. There's also a good network of regional bus services. First has service to Somerset, Devon, and Cornwall, and Stagecoach South West covers mainly south Devon and the north Devon coast. Western Greyhound operates mostly in North Cornwall. First and Stagecoach South West's money-saving one- and seven-day passes are good for unlimited bus travel. Traveline can help you plan your trip.

Bus Contacts First (☎ 0845/600–1420 ⊕ www.firstgroup.com). **Megabus** (☎ 0900/160–0900 ⊕ www.megabus.com). **National Express** (☎ 0871/781–8178 ⊕ www.nationalexpress.com). **Stagecoach South West** (☎ 01392/427711 ⊕ www.stagecoachbus.com). **Traveline** (☎ 0871/200–2233 ⊕ www.travelinesw.com). **Western Greyhound** (☎ 01637/871871 ⊕ www.westerngreyhound.com).

CAR TRAVEL

Unless you confine yourself to a few towns—for example, Exeter, Penzance, and Plymouth—you will be at a huge disadvantage without your own transportation. The region has a few main arteries, but you should take minor roads whenever possible, if only to see the real West Country at a leisurely pace.

The fastest route from London to the West Country is via the M4 and M5 motorways. Allow at least two hours to drive to Bristol, three to Exeter. The main roads heading west are the A30 (burrowing through the center of Devon and Cornwall all the way to the tip of Cornwall), the A39 (near the northern shore), and the A38 (near the southern shore, south of Dartmoor and taking in Plymouth).

TRAIN TRAVEL

Rail travelers can make use of a fast service connecting Exeter, Plymouth, and Penzance. First Great Western and South West Trains serve the region from London's Paddington and Waterloo stations. Average travel time to Exeter is 2¼ hours, to Plymouth 3¼ hours, and to Penzance about 5¼ hours. Once you've arrived, however, you'll find trains to be of limited use in the West Country, as only a few branch lines leave the main line between Exeter and Penzance.

Regional Rail Rover tickets provide three days' unlimited travel throughout the West Country in any seven-day period, or eight days in any 15-day period; localized Rangers cover Devon or Cornwall.

Train Contacts National Rail Enquiries (☎ 0845/748–4950 ⊕ www.nationalrail.co.uk).

RESTAURANTS

The last few years have seen a food renaissance in England's West Country. In the top restaurants, the accent is firmly on local and seasonal products. Seafood is the number one choice along the coasts, from Atlantic pollock to Helford River oysters, and it's available in places from haute restaurants to harborside fish shacks. Celebrity chefs have marked their pitch all over the region, including Michael Caines in Exeter and Dartmoor, the Tanner brothers in Plymouth, Rick Stein in Padstow and Falmouth, and Jamie Oliver in Newquay. Better-known establishments are often completely booked on Friday or Saturday, so reserve well in advance.

HOTELS

Availability can be limited on the coasts during August and during the weekend everywhere, so book well ahead. Accommodations include national hotel chains, represented in all of the region's principal centers, as well as ancient inns and ubiquitous bed-and-breakfast places. Many farmhouses also rent out rooms—offering tranquillity in rural surroundings—but these lodgings are often difficult to reach without a car. If you have a car, though, renting a house or cottage with a kitchen may be ideal. It's worth finding out about weekend and winter deals that many hotels offer.

WHAT IT COSTS IN POUNDS					
	£	££	£££	££££	£££££
Restaurants	under £10	£10–£14	£15–£19	£20–£25	over £25
Hotels	under £70	£70–£120	£121–£160	£161–£220	over £220

Restaurant prices are per person for a main course or equivalent combination of smaller dishes at dinner excluding tax. Hotels prices reflect the rack rate of a standard double room for two people in high season, including 20% V.A.T. Check online for off-season rates and special deals or discounts.

VISITOR INFORMATION

Contacts South West Tourism (⊕ www.visitsouthwest.co.uk). **VisitCornwall** (✉ Pydar House, Pydar St., Truro ☎ 01872/322900 ⊕ www.visitcornwall.com). **Visit Devon** (⊕ www.visitdevon.co.uk). **Visit Somerset** (✉ Somerset County Council, County Hall, Taunton ☎ 01934/750833 ⊕ www.visitsomerset.co.uk).

BRISTOL, WELLS, AND NORTH DEVON

On the eastern side of this region is the vibrant city of Bristol. From here, you might head south to the pretty cathedral city of Wells and continue on via Glastonbury, which just might be the Avalon of Arthurian legend. Proceed west along the Somerset coast into Devon, skirting the moorlands of Exmoor and tracing the northern shore via Clovelly.

BRISTOL

120 mi west of London, 46 mi south of Birmingham, 45 mi east of Cardiff, 13 mi northwest of Bath.

The West Country's biggest city (population 420,000), Bristol has in recent years become one of the country's most vibrant centers, with a thriving cultural scene encompassing some of the best contemporary art, theater, and music. Buzzing bars, cafés, and restaurants, and a largely youthful population make it an attractive place to spend time.

Now that the city's industries no longer rely on the docks, the historic harbor along the River Avon has been given over to recreation. Arts and entertainment complexes, museums, and galleries fill the quayside. The pubs and clubs here draw the under-25 set and make the area fairly boisterous (and best avoided) on Friday and Saturday nights.

Bristol also trails a great deal of history in its wake. It can be called the "birthplace of America" with some confidence, for John Cabot and his son Sebastian sailed from the old city docks in 1497 to touch down on the North American mainland, which he claimed for the English crown. The city had been a major center since medieval times, but in the 17th and 18th centuries it became the foremost port for trade with North America. Bristol was the home of William Penn, developer of Pennsylvania, and a haven for John Wesley, whose Methodist movement played an important role in colonial Georgia.

GETTING HERE AND AROUND

Bristol has good connections by bus and train to most cities in the country. From London, calculate about 2½ hours by bus or 1¾ hours by train. From Cardiff, it's about 50 minutes by bus or train. By train, make sure you get tickets for Bristol Temple Meads Station (not Bristol Parkway), which is a short bus or taxi ride (or a 20-minute walk) from the center. The bus station is more central, near the Broadmead shopping center. Most sights can be visited on foot, though a bus or a taxi is necessary to reach the Clifton neighborhood.

ESSENTIALS

Visitor Information Bristol (⊠ *E Shed, Canon's Rd.* ☎ *0333/321–0101* ⊕ *www.visitbristol.co.uk*).

EXPLORING
TOP ATTRACTIONS

☺ **At-Bristol**. One of the country's top family-friendly museums, this multimedia attraction provides a "hands-on, minds-on" exploration of science and technology in more than 300 interactive exhibits and displays. New on the scene is "All About Us," dedicated to the inner workings of the human body. A planetarium in a gleaming stainless-steel sphere takes you on a 25-minute voyage through the galaxy. There are up to 10 shows a day, bookable when you buy your ticket. Allow two to three hours to see it all. ⊠ *Anchor Rd.* ☎ *0845/345–1235* ⊕ *www. at-bristol.org.uk* ☐ *£12.50, planetarium £1* ☉ *Weekdays 10–5; weekends, national holiday Mon., and school vacations 10–6.*

QUICK BITES | The excellent café-restaurant upstairs at Watershed (⊠ *1 Canon's Rd.* ☎ *0117/927–5100* ⊕ *www.watershed.co.uk*) overlooks part of the harbor side. Sandwiches and hot snacks are served during the day, along with coffees and cakes.

OFF THE BEATEN PATH | **Berkeley Castle.** In the sleepy village of Berkeley (pronounced *bark*-ley), this castle is perfectly preserved, down to its medieval turrets, and full of family treasures. It witnessed the murder of King Edward II in 1327—the cell in which it occurred can still be seen. Edward was betrayed by his French consort, Queen Isabella, and her paramour, the earl of Mortimer. Roger De Berkeley, a Norman knight, began work on the castle in 1153, and it has remained in the family ever since. Magnificent furniture, tapestries, and pictures fill the state apartments, but even the

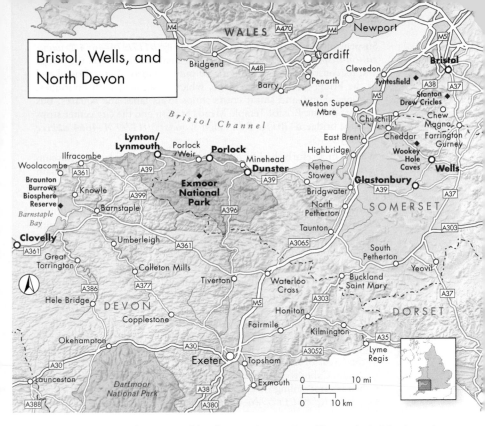

Bristol, Wells, and North Devon

ancient buttery and kitchen are interesting. The castle is 20 mi north of Bristol, accessed from M5. ☒ Off A38, Berkeley ☎ 01453/810332 ⊕ www.berkeley-castle.com ☑ £9.50; gardens only, £4.50; Butterfly House only, £2.50 ☉ Apr.–Oct., Thurs., Sun., and national holidays 11–5:30; last admission at 4:30.

★ **Church of St. Mary Redcliffe.** Built by Bristol merchants who wanted a place in which to pray for the safe (and profitable) voyages of their ships, the rib-vaulted, 14th-century church was called "the fairest in England" by Queen Elizabeth I. High up on the nave wall hang the arms and armor of Sir William Penn, father of the founder of Pennsylvania. The church is a five-minute walk from Temple Meads train station toward the docks. ☒ Redcliffe Way ☎ 0117/929–1487 ⊕ www. stmaryredcliffe.co.uk ☑ Free ☉ Mon.–Sat. 9–5 (until 4 in winter), Sun. 8–7:30.

Clifton Suspension Bridge. In the Georgian district of Clifton—a sort of Bath in miniature—you can take in a monument to Victorian engineering, the 702-foot-long bridge that spans the Avon Gorge. Work began on Isambard Kingdom Brunel's design in 1831, but the bridge was not completed until 1864. Free hour-long guided tours usually take place at 3 on Sunday between April and October, departing from the tollbooth at the Clifton end of the bridge. At the far end of the bridge, the **Clifton**

Suspension Bridge Interpretation Centre (☎ *0117/974–4664* ⊕ *www. clifton-suspension-bridge.org.uk*) has a small exhibition on the bridge and its construction, including a 10-minute video. At the Bristol end of the bridge lies **Clifton Village,** which is studded with boutiques, antiques shops, and smart crafts shops in its lanes and squares. Bus number 8 from Bristol Temple Meads Station and the city center stops near the bridge. ⊠ *Bridge Rd., Leigh Woods* ☎ *0117/974–4664* 🖼 *Free* ☉ *Daily 10–5.*

M Shed. In a refurbished transit shed on the harbor side, this museum is dedicated to the city's history. The collection comprises three main galleries—Bristol People, Bristol Places, and Bristol Life—that focus on everything from the slave trade to scientific inventions to cultural innovations associated with the city. Check out the archives of photos, films, and sound recordings of and by Bristolians, all jazzed up with the latest interactive technology. ⊠ *Wapping Rd.* ☎ *0117/352–6600* ⊕ *www.mshed.org* 🖼 *Free* ☉ *Tues.–Fri. 10–5, weekends 10–6.*

★ **SS *Great Britain.*** On view in the harbor is the first iron ship to cross the Atlantic. Built by the great English engineer Isambard Kingdom Brunel in 1843, it remained in service until 1970, first as a transatlantic liner and ultimately as a coal storage hulk. On board, everything from the galley to the officers' quarters comes complete with sounds and smells of the time. You can descend into the ship's dry dock for a view of the hull and propeller. Your ticket admits you to an exhibit on the history of the *Great Britain.* A replica of the *Matthew,* the tiny craft that carried John Cabot to North America in 1497, may be moored alongside (when it's not sailing on the high seas). ⊠ *Great Western Dockyard, Gas Ferry Rd.* ☎ *0117/926–0680* ⊕ *www.ssgreatbritain.org* 🖼 *£12.50* ☉ *Apr.–Oct., daily 10–5:30; Nov.–Mar., daily 10–4:30; last entry 1 hr before closing.*

WORTH NOTING

Ⓒ **Bristol Zoo Gardens.** Alongside the leafy expanse of Clifton Downs is one of the country's most famous zoos. More than 450 animal species live in 12 acres of gardens; the Seal and Penguin coasts, with underwater viewing, are rival attractions for Gorilla Island, Bug World, and Twilight World. Take Bus 8 or 9 from Temple Meads Station or the city center. ⊠ *Clifton Down* ☎ *0117/974–7399* ⊕ *www.bristolzoo.org.uk* 🖼 *£12.72* ☉ *Apr.–Oct., daily 9–5:30; Nov.–Mar., daily 9–5; last entry 1 hr before closing.*

New Room. John Wesley and Charles Wesley were among the Dissenters from the Church of England who found a home in Bristol, and in 1739 they built the New Room, a meeting place that became the first Methodist chapel. Its simplicity contrasts with the style of Anglican churches and with the modern shopping center hemming it in. Upstairs you can visit the Preachers' Rooms, now containing a small museum. ⊠ *Broadmead* ☎ *0117/926–4740* ⊕ *www.newroombristol. org.uk* 🖼 *Free* ☉ *Mon.–Sat. and national holidays 10–4.*

OFF THE
BEATEN
PATH

Stanton Drew Circles. Three rings, two avenues of standing stones, and a burial chamber make up the Stanton Drew Circles, one of the largest and most mysterious monuments in Britain, dating from 3000 to 2000 BC. It's far less well known than Stonehenge and other circles, however. The size of the circles suggests that the site was once as important as Stonehenge for its ceremonial functions, although little of great visual impact remains. ■ **TIP→** You have to walk through a farmyard to reach the field where the site lies, so wear sturdy shoes. English Heritage supervises the stones, which stand on private land. Access is given at any reasonable time, and a small admission fee may be requested. To get here from Bristol, head south on the A37 and turn right after about 5 mi onto the B3130, marked Stanton Drew. The circles are just east of the village. ⊠ *B3130, Stanton Drew* ☎ *0117/975–0700* ⊕ *www.english-heritage.org.uk.*

Tyntesfield. The National Trust is gradually restoring this extravagant, 35-bedroom Victorian–Gothic Revival mansion. You can see the house, garden, and chapel at your own pace; entry, by timed ticket, can't be guaranteed on the busiest days. Every ornate detail of this decorative-arts showcase compels attention. Besides magnificent woodwork, stained glass, tiles, and original furniture and fabrics, the house contains the modern conveniences of the 1860s, such as a heated billiards table, and the servants' quarters are equally absorbing. There's a restaurant and family play area, too. Tyntesfield is 7 mi southwest of Bristol; take Bus 354 or 361 from the city every day except Sunday. ⊠ *B3128, Wraxall* ☎ *0844/800–4966* ⊕ *www.nationaltrust.org.uk* ⊠ *£12.20; gardens only, £9* ☉ *House late Mar.–Oct., Sat.–Wed. 11–5; early Nov.–late Nov., weekends 11–3; gardens late Mar.–Dec., daily Sat.–Wed. 10–6 or dusk.*

WHERE TO EAT

£££££
MEDITERRANEAN

✕ **Bell's Diner.** A local institution, this bistro occupies a former grocery shop and has polished wood floors and pale gray walls lined with shelves. The inventive fixed-price Mediterranean menu (£37.50) includes locally sourced poultry, rabbit, and seafood, as well as toothsome desserts such as rhubarb-and-hibiscus soufflé. In the Montpelier area, Bell's is rather hard to find. To get here, take A38 north, then turn right on Ashley Road and immediately left at Picton Street, which will lead you to York Road. Alternatively, from Broadmead, board any bus heading up Gloucester Road, or take a taxi. ⊠ *1 York Rd.* ☎ *0117/924–0357* ⊕ *www.bellsdiner.com* ☉ *Closed Sun. No lunch Sat. and Mon.*

££££
MODERN BRITISH

✕ **Bordeaux Quay.** This converted riverside warehouse is the place for modern, sophisticated dining in Bristol. In the more formal upstairs dining room, where a large skylight and harbor views set the scene, you can select from such locally sourced dishes as pork loin and belly with cauliflower puree, red peppers, and sherry jus, as well as desserts like plum pudding with spiced yogurt cream. Sharing the space downstairs with a delicatessen and bar is a rough-and-ready brasserie—recommended for breakfast on weekends. ⊠ *Canon's Way* ☎ *0117/943–1200* ⊕ *www.bordeaux-quay.co.uk* ☉ *Restaurant closed Mon. No lunch in restaurant Tues.–Sat. No dinner in restaurant or brasserie Sun.*

5

EATING WELL IN THE WEST COUNTRY

Sheer indulgence: a cream tea with scones, clotted cream, and jam is compulsory in the West Country.

From cider to cream teas, many specialties tempt your palate in the West Country. Lamb, venison, and, in Devon and Cornwall, seafood are favored in restaurants, which have improved markedly, notably through the influence of Rick Stein's seafood-based culinary empire in Padstow, in Cornwall. Seafood is celebrated at fishy frolics that include the Newlyn Fish Festival (late August) and Falmouth's Oyster Festival (early or mid-October).

WHAT TO EAT

Cheddar. Somerset is the home of Britain's most famous cheese—the ubiquitous cheddar, originally from the Mendip Hills village of the same name. Make certain that you sample a real farmhouse cheddar, made in the traditional barrel shape known as a truckle.

Cream teas. Devon's caloric cream teas consist of a pot of tea, home-made scones, and lots of strawberry jam and thickened clotted cream (clotted, or specially thickened cream, is a regional specialty and is sometimes called Devonshire cream).

Pasties. Cornwall's specialty is the pasty, a pastry shell filled with

chopped meat, onions, and potatoes. The pasty was devised as a handy way for miners to carry their dinner to work; today's versions are generally pale imitations of the original, though you can still find delicious home-cooked pasties if you're willing to search a little.

Seafood. In many towns in Devon and Cornwall, the day's catch is unloaded from the harbor and transported directly to eateries. The catch varies by season, but lobster is available year-round, as is crab, stuffed into sandwiches at quayside stalls and in pubs.

WHAT TO DRINK

Perry. This is similar to cider but made from pears.

Scrumpy. For liquid refreshment, try scrumpy, a homemade dry cider that is refreshing but carries a surprising kick.

Wine and mead. English wine, similar to German wine, is made in all three counties (you may see it on local menus), and in Devon and Cornwall you can find a variant of age-old mead made from local honey.

£   ✕**Boston Tea Party**. Despite the name, this laid-back and vaguely eccen-
BRITISH   tric place is quintessentially English, and ideal for a relaxed lunch away
from the nearby rigors of the Park Street shopping scene. Good sandwiches can be taken out or eaten in the terraced backyard or the upstairs
sofa salon. Generous salads and burgers are also available. Get here
early, as the restaurant closes at 8. ⊠ *75 Park St.* ☎ *0117/929–8601*
⊕ *www.bostonteaparty.co.uk.*

WHERE TO STAY

For expanded hotel reviews, visit Fodors.com.

£   ☷ **Hotel24seven**. Bristol's best budget option has furnishings and decor
HOTEL   that are basic but modern and well maintained. **Pros:** good value; clean
rooms; self-catering. **Cons:** no reception; no breakfast. ⊠ *1 Sean La., at
15 Acramans Rd., Southville* ☎ *0844/770–9411* ⊕ *www.hotel24seven.
com* ↝ *30 rooms* ⚄ *In-room: no a/c, kitchen (some), Wi-Fi. In-hotel:
parking* ⫯◯⫯ *No meals.*

£££   ☷ **Hotel du Vin**. This hip chain has brought high-tech flair to six former
HOTEL   sugar-refining warehouses built in 1728 when the River Frome ran
outside the front door. **Pros:** tastefully restored old building; great bathrooms; excellent food. **Cons:** traffic-dominated location; some noise on
weekends; service can be poor. ⊠ *Narrow Lewins Mead* ☎ *0117/925–
5577* ⊕ *www.hotelduvin.com* ↝ *40 rooms* ⚄ *In-room: a/c, Wi-Fi. In-
hotel: restaurant, bar, parking* ⫯◯⫯ *No meals.*

££££–£££££   ☷ **Thornbury Castle**. An impressive lodging, Thornbury has everything a
HOTEL   genuine 16th-century Tudor castle needs: huge fireplaces, moody paint-
Fodor's Choice   ings, mullioned windows, and a large garden. **Pros:** grand medieval
★   surroundings; sumptuous rooms. **Cons:** many steps to climb; village
is dull. ⊠ *Castle St., off A38, Thornbury* ☎ *01454/281182* ⊕ *www.
thornburycastle.co.uk* ↝ *22 rooms, 5 suites* ⚄ *In-room: no a/c, Internet. In-hotel: restaurant, bar, some pets allowed* ⫯◯⫯ *Breakfast.*

££   ☷ **Victoria Square Hotel**. In two mellow Victorian buildings overlook-
HOTEL   ing one of Clifton's leafiest squares, this hotel makes an excellent base
for exploring Bristol. **Pros:** good advance-booking deals; pleasant
location. **Cons:** numerous steps; some rooms need sprucing up; occasional street noise. ⊠ *Victoria Sq., Clifton* ☎ *0843/357–1490* ⊕ *www.
victoriasquarehotel.co.uk* ↝ *41 rooms* ⚄ *In-room: no a/c, Wi-Fi. In-
hotel: restaurant, bar, parking* ⫯◯⫯ *Breakfast.*

NIGHTLIFE AND THE ARTS

The **Arnolfini**, in a prime waterfront position, is one of the country's most
prestigious contemporary-art venues, known for uncovering innovative
yet accessible art. There's a cinema and a lively bar and bistro. ⊠ *16
Narrow Quay* ☎ *0117/917–2300* ⊕ *www.arnolfini.org.uk.*

St. George's (⊠ *Great George St. off Park St.* ☎ *0845/402–4001*), a
church built in the 18th century, now serves as one of the country's
leading acoustic venues for classical, jazz, and world music. Stop by
for lunchtime concerts.

Watershed (⊠ *1 Canon's Rd.* ☎ *0117/927–5100*), a contemporary art
center by the harbor, also has a movie theater that shows excellent
international films.

Harmonious and serene, Wells Cathedral has a monumental west front decorated with medieval statues of kings and saints.

WELLS

22 mi south of Bristol, 132 mi west of London.

England's smallest cathedral city, with a population of 10,000, lies at the foot of the Mendip Hills. Although set in what feels like a quiet country town, the great cathedral is a masterpiece of Gothic architecture—the first to be built in the Early English style. The city's name refers to the underground streams that bubble up into St. Andrew's Well within the grounds of the Bishop's Palace. Spring water has run through High Street since the 15th century. Seventeenth-century buildings surround the ancient marketplace, which hosts market days on Wednesday and Saturday.

GETTING HERE AND AROUND

Regular First buses from Bristol take an hour to reach Wells; the bus station is a few minutes' walk south of the cathedral. Drivers should take A37, and park outside the compact and eminently walkable center.

ESSENTIALS

Visitor Information Wells (✉ *Wells Museum, 8 Cathedral Green* ☎ *01749/671770* ⊕ *www.wellssomerset.com*).

EXPLORING

Bishop's Palace. The Bishop's Eye gate leading from Market Place takes you to the magnificent, moat-ringed Bishop's Palace, which retains parts of the original 13th-century residence. Most rooms are closed to the public, but you can see the private chapel, the gatehouse, and the ruins of a late-13th-century great hall in the peaceful grounds. The hall lost its roof in the 16th century because Edward VI needed the lead it contained. ⊠ *Market Pl.* ☏ *01749/677698* ⊕ *www.bishopspalacewells. co.uk* ⊡ *£5.45* ☉ *Mid-Feb.–late-Feb., daily 10:30–4:30; Apr.–Oct., daily 10:30–6; last admission 1 hr before closing.*

★ **Cathedral Church of St. Andrew.** The great west towers of this medieval structure, the oldest surviving English Gothic church, can be seen for miles. Dating from the 12th century, the cathedral derives its beauty from the perfect harmony of all of its parts, the glowing colors of its original stained-glass windows, and its peaceful setting among stately trees and majestic lawns. To appreciate the elaborate west-front facade, approach the building from the cathedral green, accessible from Market Place through a great medieval gate called "penniless porch" (named after the beggars who once waited here to collect alms from worshippers). The cathedral's west front is twice as wide as it is high, and some 300 statues of kings and saints adorn it. Inside, vast inverted arches—known as scissor arches—were added in 1338 to stop the central tower from sinking to one side. The cathedral also has a rare and beautiful medieval clock, the second-oldest working clock in the world, consisting of the seated figure of a man called Jack Blandifer, who strikes a bell on the quarter hour while mounted knights circle in a joust. Near the clock is the entrance to the Chapter House—a small wooden door opening onto a great sweep of stairs worn down on one side by the tread of pilgrims over the centuries. Free guided tours lasting up to an hour begin at the back of the cathedral. A cloister restaurant serves snacks and teas. ⊠ *Cathedral Green* ☏ *01749/674483* ⊕ *www.wellscathedral. org.uk* ⊡ *£6 suggested donation* ☉ *Apr.–Sept., daily 7–7; Oct.–Mar., daily 7–6. Tours Apr.–Sept., Mon.–Sat. at 10, 11, 1, 2, and 3; Oct.–Mar., Mon.–Sat. at 11 and 2.*

QUICK BITES

Sadler Street Café (⊠ *5 Sadler St.* ☏ *01749/673866*), a little French café and patisserie near the cathedral, serves exquisite cakes and pastries, chocolate concoctions, and excellent coffee. Soups and sandwiches are also available. The café also offers a Mediterranean-style menu Wednesday through Saturday evenings, and a delicatessen and a good seafood restaurant share the premises. It's closed Sunday.

Vicar's Close. To the north of the cathedral, the cobbled Vicar's Close, one of Europe's oldest streets, has terraces of handsome 14th-century houses with strange, tall chimneys. A tiny medieval chapel here is still in use.

OFF THE BEATEN PATH

Wookey Hole Caves. These limestone caves in the Mendip Hills, 2 mi northwest of Wells, may have been the home of Iron Age people. Here, according to ancient legend, the Witch of Wookey turned to stone. You can tour the caves, dip your fingers in an underground river (artful lighting keeps things lively), and visit a museum, a working paper mill (that once supplied banknotes for the Confederate States of America), and a penny arcade full of Victorian amusement machines. There's plenty for kids. ⊠ *Wookey Hole* ☏ *01749/672243* ⊕ *www.wookey.co.uk* ⊡ *£16* ☉ *Apr.–Oct., daily 10–6; Nov.–Mar., daily 10–5; last tour 1 hr before closing.*

WHERE TO EAT AND STAY

For expanded hotel reviews, visit Fodors.com.

££££–£££££

MODERN BRITISH

✕ **The Old Spot.** For relaxed but top-notch dining in the heart of Wells, this sociable bistro with wood paneling and creamy white walls hits all the right notes. The Modern British and Mediterranean dinner menu (£28.50 for three courses) varies seasonally, but might include cured mackerel salad with avocado, bacon, and crème fraîche for starters, and a main course of roast pheasant with caramelized apples and cider cream. Arrive early for a table at the back, where there are views of the west front of the cathedral. ✉ *12 Sadler St.* ☎ *01749/689099* ⊕ *www. theoldspot.co.uk* ⊘ *Closed Mon. No lunch Tues. No dinner Sun.*

££

B&B/INN

🛏 **Ancient Gate House.** This venerable hostelry makes a convenient base for exploring the area. **Pros:** richly atmospheric; cathedral views. **Cons:** steps to climb; cramped rooms; traffic noise in front rooms. ✉ *20 Sadler St.* ☎ *01749/672029* ⊕ *www.ancientgatehouse.com* ⇆ *9 rooms* ⟵ *In-room: no a/c, Wi-Fi. In-hotel: restaurant, bar, some pets allowed* ⦿*Breakfast.*

£££

HOTEL

🛏 **Swan Hotel.** A former coaching inn built in the 15th century, the Swan faces the cathedral. **Pros:** friendly, professional service; some great views; good restaurant. **Cons:** some rooms need updating; some noise problems; parking lot tricky to negotiate. ✉ *11 Sadler St.* ☎ *01749/836300* ⊕ *www.swanhotelwells.co.uk* ⇆ *48 rooms, 1 suite* ⟵ *In-room: no a/c, Wi-Fi. In-hotel: restaurant, bar* ⦿*Breakfast.*

GLASTONBURY

5 mi southwest of Wells, 27 mi south of Bristol, 27 mi southwest of Bath.

★ A town steeped in history, myth, and legend, Glastonbury lies in the lea of Glastonbury Tor, a grassy hill rising 520 feet above the drained marshes known as the Somerset Levels. The Tor is supposedly the site of crossing ley lines (hypothetical alignments of significant places), and, in legend, Glastonbury is identified with Avalon, the paradise into which King Arthur was reborn after his death. Partly because of these associations but also because of its world-class rock-music festival, the town has acquired renown as a New Age center, mixing crystal gazers with druids, yogis, and hippies, variously in search of Arthur, Merlin, Jesus— and even Elvis. ∎TIP➔ Between April and September, a shuttle bus runs every half hour between all of Glastonbury's major sights. Tickets are £3, and are valid all day.

GETTING HERE AND AROUND

Frequent buses link Glastonbury to Wells and Bristol, pulling in close to the abbey. Drivers should take the A39. You can walk to all the sights or take the shuttle bus, though you'll need a stock of energy for ascending the tor.

ESSENTIALS

Visitor Information Glastonbury (✉ *The Tribunal, 9 High St.* ☎ *01458/832954* ⊕ *www.glastonburytic.co.uk*).

EXPLORING

Glastonbury Abbey. The ruins of this great abbey, in the center of town, are on the site where, according to legend, Joseph of Arimathea built a church in the 1st century. A monastery had certainly been erected here by the 9th century, and the site drew many pilgrims. The ruins are those of the abbey completed in 1524 and destroyed in 1539, during Henry VIII's dissolution of the monasteries. A sign south of the Lady Chapel marks the sites where Arthur and Guinevere were supposedly buried. The visitor center has a scale model of the abbey as well as carvings and decorations salvaged from the ruins. ⊠ *Magdalene St.* ☎ *01458/832267* ⊕ *www.glastonburyabbey.com* ⬚ *£6* ⊗ *Mar.–May, daily 9–6; June–Aug., daily 9–9; Sept.–Nov., daily 9–5; Dec.–Feb., daily 9–4; last admission 30 mins before closing.*

Glastonbury Tor. At the foot of Glastonbury Tor is **Chalice Well,** the legendary burial place of the Grail. It's a stiff climb up the tor, but your reward is the fabulous view across the Vale of Avalon. At the top stands a ruined tower, all that remains of **St. Michael's Church,** which collapsed after a landslide in 1271. Take the Glastonbury Tor bus to the base of the hill.

Somerset Rural Life Museum. Occupying a Victorian farmhouse and a 14th-century abbey tithe barn, this museum tells the story of life in Somerset. More than 90 feet in length, the barn once stored the one-tenth portion of the town's produce that was owed to the church. Exhibits illustrate 19th-century farming practices, and there's a cider-apple orchard nearby. Events designed for children take place most weekends during school holidays. ■**TIP→** For a good walk, take the scenic footpath from the museum that leads up to the tor, a half mile east. ⊠ *Chilkwell St.* ☎ *01458/831197* ⊕ *www.somerset.gov.uk/museums* ⬚ *Free* ⊗ *Tues.– Sat. and national holiday Mon. 10–5.*

WHERE TO EAT AND STAY

For expanded hotel reviews, visit Fodors.com.

££

BRITISH

✕ **Who'd a Thought It.** As an antidote to the natural-food cafés of Glastonbury's High Street, try this traditional backstreet inn for some more-down-to-earth fare that doesn't compromise on quality. Bar classics such as beer-battered cod appear alongside more-ambitious dishes like glazed medallions of beef with garlic mash, and fillet of black bream and king prawns with wilted spinach. The beers are local, and the pub's quirky decor—including ancient radios, a red telephone box, and

The hugely popular Glastonbury Festival attracts music lovers and free spirits from all over the world.

a bicycle on the ceiling—has a definite entertainment quotient. ⊠ *17 Northload St.* ☎ *01458/834460* ⊕ *www.whodathoughtit.co.uk.*

££
HOTEL
⛉ **George and Pilgrim Hotel.** Pilgrims en route to Glastonbury Abbey stayed here in the 15th century. **Pros:** historic surroundings; steps from the abbey. **Cons:** no parking; service can be poor; some rooms are drab. ⊠ *1 High St.* ☎ *01458/831146* ⊕ *www.relaxinnz.co.uk* ⟿ *14 rooms* ⛂ *In-room: no a/c, Wi-Fi. In-hotel: restaurant, bar* ℩◎℩ *Breakfast.*

£
B&B/INN
⛉ **The White House.** You'll receive warm hospitality from the owners of this eco-friendly B&B a few minutes' walk from High Street. **Pros:** friendly hosts; flexible breakfasts. **Cons:** one room on the small side; not great for families. ⊠ *21 Manor House Rd.* ☎ *01458/830886* ⊕ *www. theglastonburywhitehouse.com* ⟿ *2 rooms* ⛂ *In-room: no a/c, Wi-Fi. In-hotel: some age restrictions* ▭ *No credit cards* ℩◎℩ *No meals.*

NIGHTLIFE AND THE ARTS

Held annually a few miles away in Pilton, the **Glastonbury Festival** (⊕ *www. glastonburyfestivals.co.uk*) is England's biggest and perhaps best rock festival. For five days over the last weekend in June, it hosts hundreds of bands—established and up-and-coming—on five stages. Tickets are steeply priced—around £200—and sell out months in advance; they include entertainment, a camping area, and service facilities.

DUNSTER

35 mi west of Glastonbury, 43 mi north of Exeter.

Lying between the Somerset coast and the edge of Exmoor National Park, Dunster is a picture-book village with a broad main street. The eight-sided yarn-market building on High Street dates from 1589.

GETTING HERE AND AROUND

To reach Dunster by car, follow the A39. By bus, there are frequent departures from nearby Minehead and Taunton. Dunster Castle is a brief walk from the village center. The visitor information center is closed weekdays between November and Easter.

ESSENTIALS

Visitor Information Dunster (✉ *Dunster Steep* ☎ *01643/821835* ⊕ *www.exmoor-nationalpark.gov.uk*).

EXPLORING

Dunster Castle. A 13th-century fortress remodeled in 1868, Dunster Castle dominates the village from its site on a hill. Parkland and unusual gardens with subtropical plants surround the building, which has fine plaster ceilings, stacks of family portraits (including one by Joshua Reynolds), 17th-century Dutch leather hangings, and a magnificent 17th-century oak staircase. The climb to the castle from the parking lot is steep. ✉ *Off A39* ☎ *01643/823004* ⊕ *www.nationaltrust.org.uk* 🎫 *£8.50; gardens only, £4.70* ⊙ *Castle mid-Mar.–early Apr., late Apr.–mid-July, and late Aug.–Oct., Fri.–Wed. 11–5; early Apr.–late Apr. and mid-July–late Aug., daily 11–5. Gardens mid-Mar.–Oct., daily 10–5; Nov.–mid-Mar., daily 11–4.*

WHERE TO STAY

For expanded hotel reviews, visit Fodors.com.

££ 🏨 **Luttrell Arms.** In style and atmosphere, this classic inn harmonizes
B&B/INN perfectly with Dunster village and castle; it was used as a guesthouse by the abbots of Cleeve in the 14th century. **Pros:** central location; historic trappings. **Cons:** standard rooms are mostly small and viewless; no parking. ✉ *High St.* ☎ *01643/821555* ⊕ *www.luttrellarms.co.uk* 🛏 *28 rooms* ⚅ *In-room: no a/c. In-hotel: restaurant, bar, business center, some pets allowed* 🍽 *Breakfast.*

EXMOOR NATIONAL PARK

16 mi southwest of Dunster.

GETTING HERE AND AROUND

A car is usually necessary for getting around the inner reaches of Exmoor. Between April and October, one bus traces the coast between Minehead and Lynmouth, and another—a vintage double-decker bus—follows the coast between Minehead and Porlock then circles inland through Exmoor. Both buses are open-top in fine weather and are run by Quantock Motor Services.

ESSENTIALS

Bus Contacts Quantock Motor Services (☎ *01823/430202* ⊕ *www.quantockmotorservices.co.uk*).

Visitor Information Combe Martin (⊠ *Cross St.* ☎ *01271/883319* ⊕ *www.visitcombemartin.co.uk*). **Dulverton** (⊠ *7–9 Fore St.* ☎ *01398/323841*). **Exmoor National Park Authority** (⊠ *Exmoor House, Dulverton* ☎ *01398/323665* ⊕ *www.exmoornationalpark.gov.uk*). **Lynmouth** (⊠ *Lyndale Car Park* ☎ *01598/752509*).

EXPLORING

Exmoor National Park. Less wild and forbidding than Dartmoor to its south, 267-square-mi Exmoor National Park is no less majestic for its bare heath and lofty views. The park extends right up to the coast and straddles the county border between Somerset and Devon. Some walks offer spectacular views over the Bristol Channel. Taking one of the more than 700 mi of paths and bridle ways through the bracken and heather (at its best in fall), you might glimpse the ponies and red deer for which the region is noted. ■ TIP→ Be careful: the proximity of the coast means that mists and squalls can descend with alarming suddenness.

The national park visitor centers at Dulverton, Dunster, and Lynmouth have information and maps. Guided walks, many of which have themes (archaeology or deer, for example), cost £3 to £5. If you're walking on your own, check the weather, take water and a map, and tell someone where you're going. ⊠ *Exmoor National Park Authority, Exmoor House, Dulverton* ☎ *01398/323665* ⊕ *www.exmoor-nationalpark.gov.uk.*

> ### SOUTH WEST COAST PATH
>
> Britain's longest national trail, the South West Coast Path, wraps around the coast of the peninsula for 630 mi from Minehead (near Dunster, Somerset) to South Haven Point, near Poole (Dorset). To complete the trail takes 50 to 60 days.
>
> The **South West Coast Path Association** (⊕ *www.southwestcoastpath.com*) has information about the route and suggests short walks.

PORLOCK

6 mi west of Dunster, 45 mi north of Exeter.

Buried at the bottom of a valley, with the slopes of Exmoor all about, the small, unspoiled town of Porlock lies near "Doone Country," setting for R.D. Blackmore's swashbuckling saga *Lorna Doone.* Porlock had already achieved a place in literary history by the late 1790s, when Samuel Taylor Coleridge declared it was a "man from Porlock" who interrupted his opium trance while the poet was composing "Kubla Khan."

GETTING HERE AND AROUND

Porlock is best reached via the A39 coastal route. Quantock Motor Services operates several buses between Porlock and Minehead. The village can be easily explored by foot.

ESSENTIALS

Bus Contacts Quantock Motor Services (☎ *01823/430202* ⊕ *www.quantockmotorservices.co.uk*).

Visitor Information Porlock (⊠ *The Old School, High St.* ☎ *01643/863150* ⊕ *www.porlock.co.uk*).

EXPLORING

Coleridge Way. The 36-mi Coleridge Way passes through the Quantock and Brendon hills and part of Exmoor, from Nether Stowey (site of Coleridge's home) to Porlock. ⊕ *www.coleridgeway.co.uk.*

Porlock Hill. As you're heading west from Porlock to Lynton, the coast road A39 mounts Porlock Hill, an incline so steep that signs encourage drivers to "keep going." The views across Exmoor and north to the Bristol Channel and Wales are worth it. A less steep but quieter and equally scenic route up the hill on a toll road is accessed from Porlock Weir.

Porlock Weir. Two miles west of Porlock, this tiny harbor is the starting point for an undemanding 2-mi walk along the coast through chestnut and walnut trees to **Culbone church,** reputedly the smallest and most isolated church in England. Saxon in origin, it has a small Victorian spire and is lighted by candles. It would be hard to find a more enchanting spot.

WHERE TO EAT

£££ ✗ **Andrew's on the Weir.** Calling itself a restaurant with rooms, this
MODERN BRITISH waterfront Georgian hotel is pure, relaxed, English country house with touches of glamour. The ambitious contemporary restaurant takes advantage of fresh seafood and local specialties like Exmoor lamb. You can expect such choice desserts as rhubarb cheesecake with vanilla ice cream, and excellent local cheeses. Five guest rooms (££–£££) have print drapes and patchwork quilts. ⊠ *Porlock Weir* ☎ *01643/863300* ⊕ *www.andrewsontheweir.co.uk* ⊙ *Closed Mon. and Tues.*

LYNTON AND LYNMOUTH

13 mi west of Porlock, 60 mi northwest of Exeter.

A steep hill separates this pretty pair of Devonshire villages, which are linked by a Victorian cliff railway you can still ride. Lynmouth, a fishing village at the bottom of the hill, crouches below 1,000-foot-high cliffs at the mouths of the East and West Lyn rivers; Lynton is higher up. The poet Percy Bysshe Shelley visited Lynmouth in 1812, in the company of his 16-year-old bride, Harriet Westbrook. During their nine-week sojourn, the poet found time to write his polemical *Queen Mab.* The grand landscape of Exmoor lies all about, with walks to local beauty spots: Watersmeet, the Valley of the Rocks, or Hollerday Hill, where rare feral goats graze.

GETTING HERE AND AROUND

These towns are best reached via the A39. Lynton is a stop on Quantock Motor Services Bus 300, which runs daily from Minehead between April and October. Lynton and Lynmouth are both walkable, but take the cliff railway to travel between them.

ESSENTIALS

Visitor Information Lynton (⊠ *Lee Rd.* ☎ *0845/660–3232* ⊕ *lynton-lynmouth-tourism.co.uk*).

EXPLORING

Exmoor Coast Boat Cruises. Cruise around the dramatic Devon coast on these boats that depart from Lynmouth Harbour. A one-hour excursion goes as far as Woody Bay, allowing you to experience the clamorous birdlife on the cliffs. Other cruises include mackerel-fishing trips (£10) between May and August. ☎ 01598/753207 ☒ £10 ☉ Easter–Sept.

Lynton with Lynmouth Cliff Railway. Water and a cable system power the 862-foot cliff railway that connects these two towns. As they ascend a rocky cliff, riders get fine views over the harbor. Inaugurated in 1890, it was the gift of publisher George Newnes, who also donated Lynton's imposing town hall, near the top station on Lee Road. ☒ The Esplanade, Lynmouth ☎ 01598/753908 ⊕ www.cliffrailwaylynton.co.uk ☒ £3 round-trip ☉ Mid-Feb.–early Apr. and early Oct.–late Oct., daily 10–5; early Apr.–early May, late May–late July, and late Aug.–mid-Sept., daily 10–7; early May–late May and mid-Sept.–late Sept., daily 10–6; late July–late Aug., daily 10–9; late Oct.–early Nov., daily 10–4.

OFF THE BEATEN PATH

Braunton Burrows Biosphere Reserve. Bird-watching and miles of trails through the dunes are the draws at this sanctuary on the north side of the Taw estuary, the core of a UNESCO-designated biosphere reserve. Empty stretches of sand dunes have vistas of marram grass and the sea, and bird-watching is first-class, especially in winter. The flora is most colorful between May and August. Talks are held in the **Countryside Centre** (☒ Caen parking lot, Braunton ☎ 01271/817171 ☉ Apr.–Oct., Mon.–Sat. 10–4). The reserve is 18 mi southwest of Lynton. ☒ Off B3231, 2 mi west of Braunton ⊕ www.northdevonbiosphere.org.uk ☒ Free ☉ Daily 24 hrs.

WHERE TO EAT AND STAY

For expanded hotel reviews, visit Fodors.com.

£££

MODERN BRITISH

✗ **Rising Sun.** A 14th-century inn and a row of thatched cottages make up this restaurant with great views over the Bristol Channel. The kitchen specializes in local cuisine with European influences such as veal schnitzel with warm dill potato salad and roast shellfish with ginger and coriander, and there's a superb game menu December through February. In the attached hotel, corridors and creaking staircases lead to cozy guest rooms (£££) decorated in stylish print or solid fabrics. ☒ Harbourside, Lynmouth ☎ 01598/753223 ⊕ www.risingsunlynmouth.co.uk.

£££

HOTEL

★

🏠 **Shelley's Hotel.** Centrally located, this well-maintained hotel has bright and spacious rooms with generous windows and excellent views. **Pros:** harbor views from most rooms; good breakfasts; hospitable owners. **Cons:** some rooms overlook public car park; no restaurant. ☒ 8 Watersmeet Rd., Lynmouth ☎ 01598/753219 ⊕ www.shelleyshotel.co.uk ⟳ 11 rooms ⚘ In-room: no a/c, Wi-Fi (some). In-hotel: bar, some age restrictions ❡❍❡ Breakfast.

SPORTS AND THE OUTDOORS

West of Lynton, the Atlantic-facing beaches of Saunton Sands, Croyde Bay, and Woolacombe Bay are much beloved of surfers, with plenty of outlets renting equipment and offering lessons. Croyde Bay and Woolacombe Bay are more family-friendly.

Clovelly may have it all: cobbled streets, quaint houses, and the endless blue sea.

CLOVELLY

40 mi southwest of Lynton, 60 mi northwest of Exeter.

Fodor's Choice
★

Lovely Clovelly always seems to have the sun shining on its flower-lined cottages and stepped and cobbled streets. Alas, its beauty is well known, and day-trippers can overrun the village in summer. Perched precariously among cliffs, a steep, cobbled road—tumbling down at such an angle that it's closed to cars—leads to the toylike harbor with its 14th-century quay. Allow about two hours (more if you stop for a drink or a meal) to take in the village. Hobby Drive, a 3-mi cliff-top carriageway laid out in 1829 through thick woods, gives scintillating views over the village and coast.

GETTING HERE AND AROUND

To get to Clovelly by bus, take Stagecoach service 319 from Barnstaple or Bideford. If you're driving, take the A39 and park at the Clovelly Visitor Centre for £5.95. The center of town is steep and cobbled. The climb from the harbor to the parking lot can be exhausting, but from Easter through October a reasonably priced shuttle service brings you back.

EXPLORING

Clovelly Visitor Centre. Here you'll see a 20-minute film that puts Clovelly into context. In the village you can see a fisherman's cottage in the style of the 1930s and an exhibition about Victorian writer Charles Kingsley, who lived here as a child. ■ TIP→ To avoid the worst crowds, arrive early or late in the day. ⊠ Off A39 ☎ 01237/431781 ⊕ *www.clovelly. co.uk* ⊗ *June–Sept., daily 9–6; Apr., May, and Oct., daily 9:30–5:15; Nov.–Mar., daily 9:30– 4.*

WHERE TO STAY

For expanded hotel reviews, visit Fodors.com.

£££   🖬 **Red Lion Hotel.** One of only two
HOTEL   hotels in this coastal village, the
18th-century Red Lion sits right on
the harbor. **Pros:** superb location;
clean and comfortable; good service. **Cons:** some rooms are small;
food is inconsistent. ⊠ *The Quay*
☎ *01237/431237* ⊕ *www.clovelly.*
co.uk ⤙ *11 rooms* ⅙ *In-room: no*
a/c, Wi-Fi (some). In-hotel: res-
taurant, bars, some pets allowed
🍽 *Breakfast.*

DONKEYS AT WORK

Donkey stables, donkey rides
for kids, and abundant donkey
souvenirs in Clovelly recall the
days when these animals played
an essential role in town life, carrying food, packages, and more
up and down the village streets.
Even in the 1990s, donkeys helped
carry bags from the hotels. Today
sledges do the work, but the animals' labor is remembered.

5

CORNWALL

Cornwall stretches west into the sea, with plenty of magnificent coastline to explore, along with tranquil towns and some bustling resorts. One way to discover it all is to travel southwest from Boscastle and the cliff-top ruins of Tintagel Castle, the legendary birthplace of Arthur, along the north Cornish coast to Land's End. This predominantly cliff-lined coast, interspersed with broad expanses of sand, has many tempting places to stop, including Padstow (for a seafood feast), Newquay (a surfing and tourist center), or St. Ives (a delightful artists' colony).

From Land's End, the westernmost tip of Britain, known for its savage land- and seascapes and panoramic views, return to the popular seaside resort of Penzance, the harbor town of Falmouth, and the river port of Fowey. The Channel coast is less rugged than the northern coast, with more sheltered beaches. Leave time to visit the excellent Eden Project, with its surrealistic-looking conservatories in an abandoned clay pit, and to explore the boggy, heath-covered expanse of Bodmin Moor.

BOSCASTLE

15 mi north of Bodmin, 30 mi south of Clovelly.

In tranquil Boscastle, some of the stone-and-slate cottages at the foot of the steep valley date from the 1300s. A good place to relax and walk, the town is centered on a little harbor and set snug within towering cliffs. Nearby, 2 mi up the valley of the Valency, is St. Juliot's, the "Endelstow" referred to in Thomas Hardy's *A Pair of Blue Eyes*—the young author was involved with the restoration of this church while he was working as an architect.

GETTING HERE AND AROUND

Drivers can reach Boscastle along A39 and B3263. There are regular Western Greyhound buses from Bodmin Parkway, the nearest rail connection. The village is easily explored on foot.

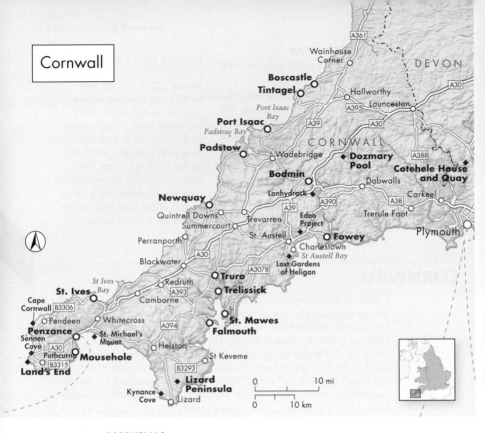

Cornwall

ESSENTIALS

Visitor Information Boscastle (✉ The Harbour ☎ 01840/250010 ⊕ www.visitboscastleandtintagel.com).

WHERE TO STAY

For expanded hotel reviews, visit Fodors.com.

££ 🖼 **The Old Rectory.** Thomas Hardy stayed here, in what is now a
B&B/INN delightful B&B, while restoring St. Juliot's Church. **Pros:** secluded
Fodor'sChoice setting; romantic ambience; helpful hosts. **Cons:** a little hard to find;
★ minimum stay might be required. ✉ Off B3263, St. Juliot, Boscastle
☎ 01840/250225 ⊕ www.stjuliot.com ⤳ 4 rooms ⚲ In-room: no a/c,
Wi-Fi. In-hotel: some pets allowed, some age restrictions ⊘ Closed mid-
Nov.–mid-Feb. ⦿ Breakfast.

TINTAGEL

3 mi southwest of Boscastle.

The romance of Arthurian legend thrives around Tintagel's ruined castle
on the coast. Ever since the somewhat unreliable 12th-century chroni-
cler Geoffrey of Monmouth identified Tintagel as the home of Arthur,
son of Uther Pendragon and Ygrayne, devotees of the legend cycle have
revered the site. In the 19th century Alfred, Lord Tennyson described

Tintagel's Arthurian connection in *The Idylls of the King*. Today the village has its share of tourist junk—including Excaliburgers. Never mind: the headland around Tintagel is splendidly scenic.

GETTING HERE AND AROUND

To drive to Tintagel, take the A39 to the B3263. Numerous parking lots are found in the village center. There's a bus stop near the tourist office for Western Greyhound buses from Bodmin Parkway, the nearest train station. Between April and October a shuttle service brings passengers to the castle.

ESSENTIALS

Bus Contacts Western Greyhound (☎ *01637/871871* ⊕ *www.westerngreyhound.com*).

Visitor Information Tintagel (✉ *Bossiney Rd.* ☎ *01840/779084* ⊕ *www.visitboscastleandtintagel.com*).

EXPLORING

Old Post Office. A 14th-century stone manor house with yard-thick walls, smoke-blackened beams, and an undulating slate-tile roof has been restored to its Victorian appearance. One room originally served as a post office. ✉ *Fore St.* ☎ *01840/770024* ⊕ *www.nationaltrust.org.uk* ☞ *£3.80* ☉ *Mid-Mar.–early Apr. and Oct.–early Nov., daily 11–4; early Apr.–Sept., daily 10:30–5:30.*

Fodor's Choice ★

Tintagel Castle. Although all that remains of the ruined cliff-top Tintagel Castle, legendary birthplace of King Arthur, is the outline of its walls, moats, and towers, it requires only a bit of imagination to conjure up a picture of Sir Lancelot and Sir Galahad riding out in search of the Holy Grail over the narrow causeway above the seething breakers. Archaeological evidence, however, suggests that the castle dates from much later—about 1150, when it was the stronghold of the earls of Cornwall. Long before that, Romans may have occupied the site. The earliest identified remains here are of Celtic (AD 5th century) origin, and these may have some connection with the legendary Arthur. Legends aside, nothing can detract from the castle ruins, dramatically set off by the wild, windswept Cornish coast, on an island joined to the mainland by a narrow isthmus. Paths lead down to the pebble beach and a cavern known as **Merlin's Cave.** Exploring Tintagel Castle involves some arduous climbing on steep steps, but even on a summer's day, when people swarm over the battlements and a westerly Atlantic wind sweeps through Tintagel, you can feel the proximity of the distant past. ✉ *Castle Rd., ½ mi west of village* ☎ *01840/770328* ⊕ *www.english-heritage.org.uk* ☞ *£5.50* ☉ *Apr.–Sept., daily 10–6; Oct., daily 10–5; Nov.–Mar., daily 10–4.*

PORT ISAAC

6 mi southwest of Tintagel.

A mixture of granite, slate, and whitewashed cottages tumbles precipitously down the cliff to the tiny harbor at Port Isaac, still dedicated to the crab-and-lobster trade. Low tide reveals a pebbly beach and rock pools. Relatively unscathed by tourists, it makes for a peaceful and

CLOSE UP

All About King Arthur

Legends about King Arthur have resonated through the centuries, enthusiastically taken up by writers and poets from 7th-century Welsh and Breton troubadours to Tennyson and Mark Twain in the 19th century and T.H. White in the 20th century.

WHO WAS ARTHUR?

The historical Arthur was probably a Christian Celtic chieftain battling against the heathen Saxons in the 6th century, although most of the tales surrounding him have a much later setting, thanks to the vivid but somewhat fanciful chronicles of his exploits by medieval scholars.

The virtuous warrior-hero of popular myth has always been treated with generous helpings of nostalgia for a golden age. For Sir Thomas Malory (circa 1408–71), author of Le Morte d'Arthur, the finest medieval prose collection of Arthurian romance, Arthur represented a lost era of chivalry and noble romance before the loosening of the traditional bonds of feudal society and the gradual collapse of the medieval social order.

FINDING KING ARTHUR

Places associated with Arthur and his consort, Guinevere, the wizard Merlin, the knights of the Round Table, and the related legends of Tristan and Isolde (or Iseult) can be found all over Europe, but the West Country claims the closest association. Arthur was said to have had his court of Camelot at Cadbury Castle (17 mi south of Wells) and to have been buried at Glastonbury.

Cornwall holds the greatest concentration of Arthurian links, notably his supposed birthplace, Tintagel, and the site of his last battle, on Bodmin Moor. However tenuous the links—and, barring the odd, somewhat ambiguous inscription, there is nothing in the way of hard evidence of Arthur's existence—the Cornish have taken the Once and Future King to their hearts, and his spirit is said to reside in the now-rare bird, the Cornish chough.

---

secluded stay. For an extra slice of authentic Cornwall life, you can hear the local choir sing shanties at the harbor side on Friday nights in summer.

GETTING HERE AND AROUND

If you're driving, Port Isaac is reached via the A39, then the B3314. Park at the lot at the top of the village rather than attempting to drive into the center. By bus, take Western Greyhound service 555 from the train station at Bodmin Parkway, changing to 584 at Wadebridge.

WHERE TO STAY

For expanded hotel reviews, visit Fodors.com.

££–£££   **Slipway Hotel.** This 16th-century inn on the harbor front has low
HOTEL   ceilings, exposed timbers, and steep staircases that lead to rooms with simple but stylish modern furnishings. **Pros:** friendly staff; great location; tasty food. **Cons:** some rooms are small and viewless; steep staircases; remote parking. ⊠ *Harbourfront* ☎ *01208/880264* ⊕ *www. portisaachotel.com* ⇘ *8 rooms, 2 suites* ⟁ *In-room: no a/c, Wi-Fi. In-hotel: restaurant, bar, some pets allowed* ¦◎¦ *Breakfast.*

Ruined Tintagel Castle has a magical setting on the wild Cornish coast.

PADSTOW

10 mi southwest of Port Isaac.

A small fishing port at the mouth of the Camel River, Padstow attracts attention and visitors as a center of culinary excellence, largely because of the presence here since 1975 of pioneering seafood chef Rick Stein. Stein's empire includes two restaurants, a café, a fish-and-chips joint, a delicatessen, a patisserie, and a cooking school where classes fill up months in advance.

Even if seafood is not your favorite fare, Padstow is worth visiting. The cries of seagulls fill its lively harbor, a string of fine beaches lies within a short ride—including some choice strands highly prized by surfers—and two scenic walking routes await: the Saints Way across the peninsula to Fowey, and the Camel Trail, a footpath and cycling path that follows the river as far as Bodmin Moor. If you can avoid peak visiting times—summer weekends—so much the better.

GETTING HERE AND AROUND

Regular buses connect Padstow with Bodmin, the main transportation hub hereabouts, and on the main Plymouth–Penzance train line. From Port Isaac, change buses at Wadebridge. There are numerous direct buses on the Newquay–Padstow route. Drivers should take A39/A389 and park in the waterside parking lot before reaching the harbor.

ESSENTIALS

Visitor Information Padstow (✉ *North Quay* ☎ *01841/533449* ⊕ *www.padstowlive.com*).

Eating seafood is a must in Cornwall: celebrity chef Rick Stein's outposts in Padstow are excellent options.

WHERE TO EAT AND STAY

For expanded hotel reviews, visit Fodors.com.

£££££
SEAFOOD
Fodor's Choice
★

✕**The Seafood Restaurant.** Rick Stein's flagship restaurant, just across from where the lobster boats and trawlers unload their catches, has built its reputation on the freshest fish and the highest culinary artistry. The exclusively fish and shellfish menu includes everything from Padstow lobster grilled with fines herbes to monkfish in an Indonesian-style curry sauce. Choose between sitting formally at a table or grabbing a stool at the Seafood Bar in the center of the modern, airy restaurant (no reservations for bar). Don't want to move after your meal? Book one of the sunny, individually designed guest rooms (£££–££££) overlooking the harbor. ✉ *Riverside* ☎ *01841/532700* ⊕ *www.rickstein.com* ⚓ *Reservations essential.*

££££
FRENCH

✕**St. Petroc's Bistro.** Part of chef Rick Stein's empire, this bistro with contemporary art adorning its walls has a more secluded feel. In fine weather you can dine in the sunny walled garden. The French-inspired menu features such dishes as rib-eye steak with béarnaise sauce and *pommes frites* (french fries). Also here are spacious bedrooms (£££–££££), which are individually decorated with stylish modern pieces. ✉ *4 New St.* ☎ *01841/532700* ⊕ *www.rickstein.com.*

£££££
B&B/INN

▢ **St. Edmund's House.** The most luxurious Rick Stein venture has a sophisticated minimalist style. **Pros:** stylish bedrooms; select ambience. **Cons:** inflated prices; short walk to breakfast. ✉ *St. Edmund's La.* ☎ *01841/532700* ⊕ *www.rickstein.com* ⌁ *6 rooms* ⚐ *In-room: Internet, Wi-Fi* ¶◉¶ *Breakfast.*

ITINERARY: FOUR DAYS IN CORNWALL

Here's a trip if you want to see some highlights of Cornwall. Traveling down along the North Devon coast, stop at the harbor village of **Boscastle** before steeping yourself in Arthurian legends at **Tintagel**, ideally taking a coastal walk here. Overnight in **Padstow** and dine on excellent seafood. The next day, head for **St. Ives**, popular with art lovers and beach fans, and push on to the dramatic scenery of the country's westernmost tip, **Land's End**. Stay in **Penzance** for your second night; from here you can visit the island castle of **St. Michael's**

Mount. Then either follow the coast around to tour the scenic **Lizard Peninsula**, or head straight for Pendennis Castle in **Falmouth**. Across the Carrick Roads estuary basin, explore the Roseland Peninsula, spending your third night in **St. Mawes**, which has a fine castle. Start early the next day to visit the **Eden Project**, a must for anyone with even a passing interest in greenery, and then choose between two superb country piles: Victorian **Lanhydrock**, near Bodmin, and **Cotehele House**, a Tudor manor house.

5

SPORTS AND THE OUTDOORS

BIKING

Bikes of all shapes and sizes can be rented at **Trail Bike Hire** (✉ *South Quay* ☎ *01841/532594* ⊕ *www.trailbikehire.co.uk*), at the start of the Camel Trail.

SURFING

Harlyn Surf School (✉ *23 Grenville Rd.* ☎ *01841/533076* ⊕ *www. harlynsurfschool.co.uk*) can arrange two-hour to four-day surfing courses.

WALKING

The **Saints Way**, a 30-mi inland path between Padstow and the Camel Estuary on Cornwall's north coast to Fowey on the south coast, follows a Bronze Age trading route, later used by Celtic pilgrims to cross the peninsula. Several relics of such times can be seen along the way. Contact the tourist offices in Padstow or Fowey for information.

NEWQUAY

14 mi southwest of Padstow, 30 mi southwest of Tintagel.

The biggest, most developed resort on the north Cornwall coast is a fairly large town established in 1439. It was once the center of the trade in pilchards (a small herringlike fish), and on the headland you can still see a white hut where a lookout known as a "huer" watched for pilchard schools and directed the boats to the fishing grounds. Newquay has become Britain's surfing capital, and in summer young California-dreamin' devotees can pack the wide, cliff-backed beaches.

GETTING HERE AND AROUND

A branch line links Newquay with the main Plymouth–Penzance train line at Par, and there are regular buses from Padstow, Bodmin, and St. Austell. Train and bus stations are both in the center of town. Newquay has good road connections with the rest of the peninsula via the A30 and A39. The best beaches are quite a walk from the center.

ESSENTIALS

Visitor Information Newquay (✉ *Marcus Hill* ☎ *01637/854020* ⊕ *www.visitnewquay.org*).

WHERE TO EAT

£££££ ✕ **Fifteen Cornwall.** Bright and modern, this Italian restaurant has won
ITALIAN plaudits both for its fabulous food and for its fine location overlooking
★ magnificent Watergate Bay, a broad beach much beloved of water-sports
enthusiasts. It's run by one of Britain's culinary heroes, Cockney chef
Jamie Oliver, who trains local young people for careers in catering.
To provide the staff with the widest possible repertoire, the frequently
changing sampling menu (£58) lists five courses that might include a
starter of tortellini of squash and buffalo ricotta with lemon-butter
sauce and toasted walnuts, followed by seared scallops for a main
course, and a white chocolate panna cotta to finish. A fixed-price lunch
is a cheaper option at £27. Watergate Bay lies 3 mi east of Newquay.
✉ *Watergate Bay* ☎ *01637/861000* ⊕ *www.fifteencornwall.co.uk*.

SPORTS AND THE OUTDOORS

Surfing is Newquay's raison d'être for many of the enthusiasts who flock
here throughout the year. Great Western and Tolcarne beaches are most
suitable for beginners, while Fistral Beach is better for those with more
experience. There are dozens of surf schools around town, many offering accommodation packages, and rental outlets are also ubiquitous.

Extreme Academy (✉ *Watergate Bay Hotel, Watergate Bay* ☎ *01637/860543*
⊕ *www.watergatebay.co.uk*) is one of the West Country's water-sports
specialists, offering courses in wave-skiing, kite-surfing, kite-buggying,
paddle-surfing, and just plain old surfing, as well as equipment for hire.

ST. IVES

25 mi southwest of Newquay, 10 mi north of Penzance.

James McNeill Whistler came here to paint his landscapes, Barbara
Hepworth to fashion her modernist sculptures, and Virginia Woolf to
write her novels. Today sand, sun, and superb art continue to attract
thousands of vacationers to the fishing village of St. Ives, named after
Saint Ia, a 5th-century female Irish missionary said to have arrived on a
floating leaf. The town has long played host to a well-established artists'
colony, and there are plenty of craftspeople, too. ■**TIP→** Day-trippers
often crowd St. Ives, so it's best to park away from the center. Many come
to St. Ives for the sheltered beaches; the best are Porthmeor, on the
northern side of town, and, facing east, Porthminster—the choice for
those seeking more space to spread out.

GETTING HERE AND AROUND

St. Ives has good bus and train connections with Bristol, Exeter, and
Penzance. Train journeys usually involve a change at St. Erth (the brief
St. Erth–St. Ives stretch is one of the West Country's most scenic train
routes). The adjacent bus and train stations are within a few minutes'
walk of the center. Drivers should avoid the center—parking lots are
well marked in the higher parts of town.

ESSENTIALS

Visitor Information St. Ives (✉ *The Guildhall, Street-an-Pol* ☎ *01736/796297* ⊕ *www.visit-westcornwall.com*).

EXPLORING

Barbara Hepworth Museum and Sculpture Garden. The studio and garden of Dame Barbara Hepworth (1903–75), who pioneered abstract sculpture in England, are now a museum and sculpture garden. London's prominent Tate gallery runs the museum. The artist lived here for 26 years. ✉ *Trewyn Studio, Barnoon Hill* ☎ *01736/796226* ⊕ *www.tate.org.uk* 🎟 *£5.25, combined ticket with Tate St. Ives £9.75* ⊙ *Mar.–Oct., daily 10–5:20; Nov.–Feb., Tues.–Sun. 10–4:20.*

☪ **Geevor Tin Mine.** The winding B3306 coastal road southwest from St. Ives passes through some of Cornwall's starkest yet most beautiful countryside. Barren hills crisscrossed by low stone walls drop abruptly to granite cliffs and wide bays. Evidence of the ancient tin-mining industry is everywhere. Now a fascinating mining heritage center, the early-20th-century Geevor Tin Mine employed 400 men, but in 1985 the collapse of the world tin market wiped Cornwall from the mining map. Wear sturdy footwear for the surface and underground tours. A museum, shop, and café are on the site. ✉ *B3306, Pendeen* ☎ *01736/788662* ⊕ *www.geevor.com* 🎟 *£9.75* ⊙ *Mar.–Oct., Sun.–Fri. 9–5; Nov.–Feb., Sun.–Fri. 9–4; last admission 1 hr before closing.*

St. Ives Society of Artists Gallery. Local artists display selections of their current work for sale at this gallery in the former Old Mariners' Church. The Crypt Gallery in the basement is also used for private exhibitions. ✉ *Norway Sq.* ☎ *01736/795582* ⊕ *www.stisa.co.uk* ⊙ *Mar.–Easter and Oct.–early Jan., Mon.–Sat. 10:30–5:30; Easter–Sept., Mon.–Sat. 10:30–5:30, Sun. 2:30–5:30.*

★ **Tate St. Ives.** The spectacular sister of the renowned London museum displays the work of artists who lived and worked in St. Ives, mostly from 1925 to 1975, and has selections from the rich collection of the Tate in London. It occupies a modernist building—a fantasia of seaside deco-period architecture with a panoramic view of rippling ocean. The rooftop café is excellent for the food and views. ✉ *Porthmeor Beach* ☎ *01736/796226* ⊕ *www.tate.org.uk* 🎟 *£6.25, combined ticket with Barbara Hepworth Museum and Sculpture Garden £9.75* ⊙ *Mar.–Oct., daily 10–5:20; Nov.–Feb., Tues.–Sun. 10–4:20.*

QUICK BITES

One of Cornwall's oldest pubs, the **1312 Sloop Inn** (✉ *The Wharf* ☎ *01736/796584*) serves simple lunches as well as evening meals in wood-beam rooms that display the work of local artists. If the weather's good, you can eat at the tables outside and watch the harbor.

WHERE TO EAT

££££–£££££
MODERN BRITISH

✕ **Garrack Restaurant.** This family-run restaurant is known for the panoramic sea views from its hilltop location and for relaxed and undemanding fine dining. The set-price menus (£23 and £26.50) specialize in local fish and seafood, including steamed local mussels, as well as Cornish beef. Breads are made on the premises, and the wine list features some Cornish vineyards. Some rooms (£££–££££) at the attached hotel are furnished in traditional style; others are more modern. ☒ *Burthallan La.* ☎ *01736/796199* ⊕ *www.garrack. com* ⊘ *No lunch Mon.–Sat.*

££££　✕ **Gurnard's Head**. This gastro-pub
MODERN BRITISH　with bright, homey furnishings and a relaxed ambience overlooks green fields to the Atlantic beyond.

The frequently changing menu features fresh, inventively prepared meat and seafood dishes; look for duck with a carrot and cardamom puree, and plaice with fennel and crushed new potatoes. Seven smallish rooms provide guest accommodations (££–£££). The inn sits near the curvy coast road 6 mi west of St. Ives. ☒ *B3306, Treen, near Zennor* ☎ *01736/796928* ⊕ *www. gurnardshead.co.uk* ☚ *Reservations essential.*

£££　✕ **Porthminster Café**. Unbeatable for its location alone—on the broad,
SEAFOOD　golden sands of Porthminster Beach—this sleek, modern eatery prepares imaginative lunches, teas, and evening meals you can savor while you take in the marvelous vista across the bay. Typical choices are Parmesanbattered sardines, monkfish curry, and hake fillets with crab-and-spinach cannelloni. The sister Porthgwidden Beach Café, in the Downalong neighborhood, has a smaller and cheaper menu that's equally strong on fish. ☒ *Porthminster Beach* ☎ *01736/795352* ⊕ *www.porthminstercafe. co.uk* ☚ *Reservations essential* ⊘ *Closed Mon. Nov.–Easter.*

WHERE TO STAY

For expanded hotel reviews, visit Fodors.com.

££　⊞ **Cornerways**. Everything in St. Ives seems squeezed into the tiniest
B&B/INN　of spaces, and this cottage B&B in the quiet Downalong quarter is no exception. **Pros:** friendly owners and staff; stylish decor; excellent cooked breakfast. **Cons:** rooms are small; narrow stairways to climb; very limited parking. ☒ *1 Bethesda Pl.* ☎ *01736/796706* ⊕ *www. cornerwaysstives.com* ☚ *6 rooms* ☖ *In-room: no a/c, Wi-Fi. In-hotel: parking* ⊟ *No credit cards* ⍾ *Breakfast.*

£££–££££　⊞ **Primrose Valley Hotel**. Blending the elegance of an Edwardian villa
HOTEL　with clean-lined modern style, this family-friendly hotel has the best of
★　both worlds. **Pros:** close to beach and train and bus stations; friendly atmosphere; attention to detail. **Cons:** difficult to find; some rooms lack views; many steps to negotiate. ☒ *Porthminster Beach* ☎ *01736/794939* ⊕ *www.primroseonline.co.uk* ☚ *8 rooms, 1 suite* ☖ *In-room: no a/c, Wi-Fi. In-hotel: bar, parking, some age restrictions* ⍾ *Breakfast.*

LAND'S END

17 mi southwest of St. Ives, 9 mi southwest of Penzance.

The coastal road, B3306, ends at the western tip of Britain at what is, quite literally, Land's End.

GETTING HERE AND AROUND

Frequent buses serve Land's End from St. Ives (taking around one hour, 40 minutes) and Penzance (around 50 minutes). In summer, an open-top double-decker tracks the coast between St. Ives and Penzance, taking in Land's End en route.

EXPLORING

★ **Land's End.** The sea crashes against the rocks at Land's End and lashes ships battling their way around the point. ■ TIP→ Approach from one of the coastal footpaths for the best panoramic view. Over the years, sightseers have caused some erosion of the paths, but new ones are constantly being built, and Cornish "hedges" (granite walls covered with turf) have been planted to prevent erosion. The scenic grandeur of Land's End remains diminished. The Land's End Hotel here is undistinguished, though the restaurant has good views.

Land's End Experience. A low-key theme park, Land's End Experience runs a poor second to nature. There are films, exhibits, and a virtual aquarium filled with prehistoric creatures. (☎ 0871/720–0044 ⊕ *www.landsend-landmark.co.uk*).

Porthcurno Beach, 3 mi east of Land's End, has a stunning strip of cliff-backed sand that's good for both walkers (the coastal path is nearby) and anyone ready to relax on a beach. ✉ *Off B3315, Porthcurno.*

Sennen Cove is less than 2 mi north of Land's End by car; this lovely bay can also be reached by a walk on the South West Coast Path. You can enjoy the view or try the surfing. ✉ *Off A30, Sennen.*

MOUSEHOLE

7 mi east of Land's End, 3 mi south of Penzance.

★ Between Land's End and Penzance, Mousehole (pronounced *mow*-zel, the first syllable rhyming with "cow") merits a stop—and plenty of people do stop—to see this archetypal Cornish fishing village of tiny stone cottages. It was the home of Dolly Pentreath, supposedly the last person to speak solely in Cornish, who died in 1777.

GETTING HERE AND AROUND

Frequent buses take 20 minutes to travel from Penzance to Mousehole. From Land's End, change buses at Newlyn. Drivers should take the B3315 coastal route and park in one of the lots before entering the village.

WHERE TO EAT

£££ ✕ **2 Fore Street.** Within view of Mousehole's tiny harbor, you can
MODERN BRITISH dine on the freshest seafood in this popular bistro. The seasonal, Mediterranean-inspired menu takes in everything from shell-roasted Newlyn scallops to wild sea bass in fennel and fish stew. Meat eaters are also well catered to. The bright, white-walled dining room has a maritime flavor, and there are tables in the sheltered back garden. ✉ 2

Fore St. ☎ *01736/731164* ⊕ *www.2forestreet.co.uk* ⛵ *Reservations essential* ⊘ *Closed Jan.–mid-Feb.*

⬛ EN
ROUTE About 2 mi north of Mousehole on B3315, **Newlyn** has long been Cornwall's most important fishing port. The annual Fish Festival takes over the town for a weekend at the end of August. Newlyn became the magnet for artists at the end of the 19th century, and a few of the fishermen's cottages that first attracted them remain. Today the village has a good gallery of contemporary art.

PENZANCE

3 mi north of Mousehole, 1½ mi north of Newlyn, 10 mi south of St. Ives.

Superb views over Mount's Bay are one lure of this popular, unpretentious seaside resort. Even though it does get very crowded in summer, Penzance makes a good base for exploring the area. The town's isolated position has always made it vulnerable to attack from the sea. During the 16th century, Spanish raiders destroyed most of the original town, and the majority of old buildings date from as late as the 18th century. The main street is Market Jew Street, a folk mistranslation of the Cornish expression Marghas Yow, which means "Thursday Market." Where Market Jew Street meets Causeway Head is Market House, constructed in 1837, an impressive, domed granite building that now serves as a bank.

In contrast to arty St. Ives, Penzance is a no-nonsense working town. Though lacking the traffic-free lanes and quaint cottages of St. Ives, Penzance preserves pockets of handsome Georgian architecture.

GETTING HERE AND AROUND

The main train line from Plymouth terminates at Penzance, which is also served by National Express buses. Bus and train stations are next to each other at the east end of town. A car is an encumbrance here, so use one of the parking lots near the tourist office and the bus and train stations.

ESSENTIALS

Visitor Information Penzance (✉ *Station Approach* ☎ *01736/362207* ⊕ *www.visit-westcornwall.com*).

EXPLORING

Chapel Street. The former main street and one of the prettiest thoroughfares in Penzance, Chapel Street winds down from Market House to the harbor. Its predominantly Georgian and Regency houses suddenly give way to the extraordinary **Egyptian House,** whose facade recalls the Middle East. Built around 1830 as a geological museum, today it houses vacation apartments. Across Chapel Street is the 17th-century **Union Hotel,** where in 1805 the death of Lord Nelson and the victory of Trafalgar were first announced. Near the Union Hotel on Chapel Street is the **Turk's Head,** an inn said to date from the 13th century.

Penlee House Gallery and Museum. A small collection in this gracious Victorian house in Penlee Park focuses on paintings by members of the so-called Newlyn School from about 1880 to 1930. These works evoke the life of the inhabitants of Newlyn, mostly fisherfolk. The museum also covers 5,000 years of West Cornwall history through archaeology, decorative arts, costume, and photography exhibits. ⊠ *Morrab Rd.* ☎ *01736/363625* ⊕ *www.penleehouse.org.uk* ⊠ *£4.50, Sat. free* ⊙ *Easter–Sept., Mon.–Sat. 10–5; Oct.–Easter, Mon.–Sat. 10:30–4:30; last admission 30 mins before closing.*

★ **St. Michael's Mount.** Rising out of Mount's Bay just off the coast, this spectacular granite-and-slate island is one of Cornwall's greatest natural attractions. The 14th-century castle perched at the highest point—200 feet above the sea—was built on the site of a Benedictine chapel founded by Edward the Confessor. In its time, the island has served as a church (Brittany's island abbey of Mont St. Michel was an inspiration), a fortress, and a private residence. The castle rooms you can tour include the Chevy Chase Room—a name probably associated with the Cheviot Hills or the French word *chevaux* (horses), after the hunting frieze that decorates the walls of this former monks' refectory. Don't miss the wonderful views from the battlements. Around the base of the rock are buildings from medieval to Victorian, but they appear harmonious. Fascinating gardens surround the Mount, and many kinds of plants flourish in its microclimate. To get to the island, walk the cobbled causeway from the village of Marazion or, when the tide is in during summer, take the ferry. There are pubs and restaurants in the village, but the island also has a café and restaurant. ■TIP➜ Wear stout shoes for your visit to this site, which requires a steep climb. Visits may be canceled in severe weather. ⊠ *A394, 3 mi east of Penzance, Marazion* ☎ *01736/710507* ⊕ *www.stmichaelsmount.co.uk* ⊠ *Castle £7, garden £3.50, castle and garden £8.75, £1.50 for ferry each way* ⊙ *Castle Apr.–June, Sept., and Oct., Sun.–Fri. 10:30–5; July and Aug., Sun.–Fri. 10:30–5:30; Nov.–Mar., tours Tues. and Fri. 11 and 2, call to check. Garden mid-Apr.–June, weekdays 10:30–5; July–late Aug., Thurs. and Fri. 10:30–5:30; Sept., Thurs. and Fri. 10:30–5; last admission 45 mins before closing.*

OFF THE BEATEN PATH

Isles of Scilly. Fondly regarded in folklore as the lost land of Lyonesse, this compact group of more than 100 islands 30 mi southwest of Land's End is equally famed for the warm summer climate and ferocious winter storms. In fair weather you can find peace, flowers—wild, cultivated, and subtropical—swarms of seabirds, and unspoiled beaches galore. If you have time, take the 2½-hour ferry service from Penzance; otherwise, there's plane and helicopter service. These all arrive at the largest of the five inhabited islands, St. Mary's, which has the bulk of the lodgings, though the most palatial retreats are on the islands of Tresco and St Martin's.

WHERE TO EAT

££ ✕ **Admiral Benbow.** One of the town's most famous inns, the 17th-
BRITISH century Admiral Benbow was once a smugglers' pub—look for the
★ figure of a smuggler on the roof. Seafaring memorabilia, a brass cannon, model ships, and figureheads fill the place. In the family-friendly restaurant area, decorated to resemble a ship's galley, you can dine on seafood or a steak-and-ale pie. ⊠ *46 Chapel St.* ☎ *01736/363448.*

££££ ✕ **Harris's.** Seafood is the main event in the two small, boldly colored
SEAFOOD rooms of this restaurant off Market Jew Street. The menu showcases whatever the boats bring: crab Florentine, grilled on a bed of spinach

The stunning ocean setting of the open-air Minack Theatre near Penzance may distract you from the on-stage drama.

with a Parmesan sauce, is usually available. Meat dishes might include noisettes of Cornish lamb with fennel puree and rosemary sauce in spring and summer, or medallions of venison in winter. An inexpensive brasserie menu is also available for lunch or dinner. The semiformal style is intimate, elegant, and traditional. ✉ *46 New St.* ☎ *01736/364408* ⊕ *www.harrissrestaurant.co.uk* ✷ *Closed Sun. Closed Mon. Nov.–June and 4 wks Nov.–Mar.*

WHERE TO STAY

For expanded hotel reviews, visit Fodors.com.

£££–££££
HOTEL
★
Abbey Hotel. Co-owned by former 1960s model-icon Jean Shrimpton, this Wedgwood-blue-color hotel off Chapel Street is marvelously homey. **Pros:** full of character; inspiring views; solicitous staff. **Cons:** some rooms slightly cramped; limited parking. ✉ *Abbey St.* ☎ *01736/366906* ⊕ *www.theabbeyonline.co.uk* ✷ *6 rooms, 2 apartments* ♿ *In-room: no a/c, Wi-Fi. In-hotel: parking, some pets allowed* ✷ *Closed late Dec.–mid-Feb.* ¶ *Breakfast.*

££
B&B/INN
Camilla House. This flower-bedecked Georgian house stands on a road parallel to the promenade, close to the harbor. **Pros:** friendly management; quiet location near seafront; great breakfasts. **Cons:** some rooms are small; far from bus and train stations. ✉ *12 Regent Terr.* ☎ *01736/363771* ⊕ *www.camillahouse-hotel.co.uk* ✷ *8 rooms* ♿ *In-room: no a/c, Wi-Fi. In-hotel: restaurant, bar, business center* ¶ *Breakfast.*

£
HOTEL
Union Hotel. Strong on historical and nautical details, this central lodging housed the town's assembly rooms, where news of Admiral Nelson's victory at Trafalgar and of the death of Nelson himself were first

announced from the minstrels' gallery in 1805. **Pros:** historic character; spacious rooms; good value for the money. **Cons:** feels dowdy; sparse staff; no elevator. ⊠ *Chapel St.* ☎ *01736/362319* ⊕ *www.unionhotel. co.uk* ⇆ *28 rooms* ⚬ *In-room: no a/c. In-hotel: restaurant, bars, parking* ❍ *Breakfast.*

NIGHTLIFE AND THE ARTS

★ The open-air **Minack Theatre** perches high above a beach 3 mi southeast of Land's End and about 6 mi southwest of Penzance. The slope of the cliff forms a natural amphitheater, with bench seats on the terraces and the sea as a magnificent backdrop. Different companies present plays from classic dramas to modern comedies afternoons and evenings between late May and late September. An exhibition center tells the story of the theater's creation. ⊠ *Off B3315, Porthcurno* ☎ *01736/810181* ⊕ *www.minack.com* ⊠ *Exhibition center £4, performances £8–£9.50* ⊗ *Apr.–Oct., daily 9:30–5:30; Nov.–Mar., daily 10–4.*

SPORTS AND THE OUTDOORS

Many ships have foundered on Cornwall's rocky coastline, resulting in an estimated 3,600 shipwrecks. The area around Land's End has some of the best diving in Europe, in part because the convergence of the Atlantic and the Gulf Stream here results in impressive visibility and unusual subtropical marine life.

Silver Dolphin (⊠ *Trinity House, Wharf Rd.* ☎ *01736/364860* ⊕ *www. silverdolphinmarineconservationanddiving.co.uk*) offers courses and guided dives for beginners and experts.

LIZARD PENINSULA

23 mi southwest of Penzance.

★ The southernmost point on mainland Britain, this peninsula is a government-designated Area of Outstanding Natural Beauty, named so for the rocky, dramatic coast rather than the flat and boring interior. The huge, eerily rotating dish antennae of the Goonhilly Satellite Communications Earth Station are visible from the road as it crosses Goonhilly Downs, the backbone of the peninsula. There's no coast road, unlike Land's End, but the coastal path offers marvelous opportunities to explore on foot—and is often the only way to reach the best beaches. With no large town (Helston at the northern end is the biggest, and is not a tourist center), it's far less busy than the Land's End peninsula.

GETTING HERE AND AROUND

If you're driving, take A394 to reach Helston, gateway town to the Lizard Peninsula. From Helston, A3083 heads straight down to Lizard Point. Helston is the main public transport hub, but bus service to the villages is infrequent.

EXPLORING

Kynance Cove. A path close to the tip of the peninsula plunges down 200-foot cliffs to this tiny cove dotted with a handful of pint-size islands. The sands here are reachable only during the 2½ hours before and after low tide. The peninsula's cliffs are made of greenish serpentine rock, interspersed with granite; souvenirs of the area are carved out of the stone.

FALMOUTH

8 mi northeast of Lizard Peninsula, 12 mi south of Truro.

The bustle of this resort town's fishing harbor, yachting center, and commercial port only adds to its charm. In the 18th century Falmouth was the main mail-boat port for North America, and in Flushing, a village across the inlet, you can see the slate-covered houses built by prosperous mail-boat captains. A ferry service now links the two towns. On Custom House Quay, off Arwenack Street, is the King's Pipe, an oven in which seized contraband was burned.

GETTING HERE AND AROUND

Falmouth can be reached from Truro on a branch rail line or on frequent buses, and it is also served by local and National Express buses from other towns. Running parallel to the seafront, the long, partly pedestrianized main drag links the town's main sights. Visitors to Pendennis Castle traveling by train should use Falmouth Docks Station, from which it's a short walk. Alternatively, drive or take a local bus to the castle to save legwork.

ESSENTIALS

Visitor Information Falmouth (✉ *11 Market Strand, Prince of Wales Pier* ☎ *01326/312300* ⊕ *www.discoverfalmouth.co.uk*).

EXPLORING

☾ **National Maritime Museum Cornwall.** The granite-and-oak-clad structure by the harbor is an excellent place to come to grips with Cornish maritime heritage, weather lore, and navigational science. You can view the collection of 140 or so boats, examine the tools associated with Cornish boatbuilders, and study the prospect across to Flushing from the lighthouselike lookout, which is equipped with maps, telescopes, and binoculars. In the glass-fronted Tidal Zone below sea level, you come face-to-face with the sea itself. ✉ *Discovery Quay* ☎ *01326/313388* ⊕ *www.nmmc.co.uk* 🎫 *£9.50* ☾ *Daily 10–5.*

☾ **Pendennis Castle.** At the end of its own peninsula stands this formidable castle, built by Henry VIII in the 1540s and improved by his daughter Elizabeth I. You can explore the defenses developed over the centuries. In the Royal Artillery Barracks, the Pendennis Unlocked exhibit explores the castle's history and its connection to Cornwall and England. The castle has sweeping views over the English Channel and across to St. Mawes Castle, designed as a companion fortress to guard the roads. Call about events such as concerts, plays, jousting, and shows for kids. ✉ *Pendennis Head* ☎ *01326/316594* ⊕ *www.english-heritage.org.uk* 🎫 *£6.30* ☾ *Apr.–June and Sept., Sun.–Fri. 10–5, Sat. 10–4; July and Aug., Sun.–Fri. 10–6, Sat. 10–4; Oct.–Mar., daily 10–4.*

WHERE TO EAT AND STAY

For expanded hotel reviews, visit Fodors.com.

££   ✗ **Gylly Beach Café.** For views and location, this beachside eatery with
MODERN BRITISH   a crisp, modern interior and deck seating cannot be beat. By day, it's a breezy café offering burgers, salads, and sandwiches, while the evening menu presents a judicious balance of meat, seafood, and vegetarian dishes, from lamb ragout to smoked-paprika-and-haricot-bean

cassoulet. There are barbecues in summer, and live-music evenings. ⊠ *Cliff Rd., Gyllyngvase Beach* ☎ *01326/312884* ⊕ *www.gyllybeach. com* ◷ *No dinner Mon.–Wed. Nov.–mid-Feb.*

££   ✗ **Pandora Inn.** This thatched pub on a creek 4 mi north of Falmouth is a
BRITISH   great retreat, with both a patio and a moored pontoon for summer dining. Maritime memorabilia and fresh flowers provide decoration, and you can eat in the bar, in the formal Upper Deck room upstairs, or outside. The menu highlight is fresh seafood—try the grilled sea bream—though there's a good selection of game in winter. ⊠ *Restronguet Creek, Mylor Bridge* ☎ *01326/372678* ⊕ *www.pandorainn.com.*

££   ✗ **Rick Stein's Fish & Chips.** Celebrity chef Rick Stein has expanded his sea-
SEAFOOD   food empire to Falmouth, where this no-frills takeaway and restaurant opposite the National Maritime Museum makes a welcome addition to the local dining scene. The mackerel, plaice, and monkfish are grilled, fried to a golden hue, or charcoal-roasted and served with polenta and salad. Local oysters and squid are also on the menu in the white-tiled dining room. There's a shorter, mainly shellfish menu at the small Seafood Bar upstairs. Across the square, Stein's Deli stocks all the fixings for a picnic. ⊠ *Discovery Quay* ☎ *01841/532700* ⊕ *www.rickstein.com.*

££££–£££££   ⛤ **St. Michael's Hotel.** Colorful gardens front this seaside hotel overlook-
HOTEL   ing Falmouth Bay. **Pros:** excellent facilities; enthusiastic and amiable staff. **Cons:** some rooms are small; poor soundproofing; uneven service. ⊠ *Stracey Rd.* ☎ *01326/312707* ⊕ *www.stmichaelshotel.co.uk* ⤴ *57 rooms, 4 suites* ⅃ *In-room: a/c (some), Wi-Fi. In-hotel: restaurant, bar, pool, gym, spa, business center* �◉⦀ *Breakfast.*

TRELISSICK

6 mi northeast of Falmouth, 5 mi south of Truro.

Trelissick is known for the colorful Trelissick Garden, owned by the National Trust.

GETTING HERE AND AROUND

Between May and October, the most rewarding way to arrive at Trelissick is by ferry from Falmouth, St. Mawes, or Truro. There are also frequent year-round buses from these towns. By car, it's on B3289, between A39 and A3078.

EXPLORING

King Harry Ferry. A chain-drawn car ferry, the King Harry runs to the scenically splendid Roseland Peninsula each day three times an hour. From its decks you can see up and down the Fal, a deep, narrow river with steep, wooded banks. The river's great depth provides mooring for old ships waiting to be sold; these mammoth shapes lend a surreal touch to the riverscape. On very rare occasions, you may even spot deer swimming across. ⊠ *B3289* ☎ *01872/862312* ⊕ *www.kingharryscornwall. co.uk* ⌲ *£5* ◷ *Apr.–Sept., Mon.–Sat. 7:20 am–9:20 pm, Sun. 9 am–9:20 pm; Oct.–Mar., Mon.–Sat. 7:20 am–7:20 pm, Sun. 9 am–7:20 pm.*

Trelissick Garden. Cornwall's mild climate has endowed it with some of the country's most spectacular gardens, among which is the Trelissick Garden on the banks of the Rivre Fal. Famous for its camellias, azaras, and photinias, the terraced garden is set within 375 acres of wooded parkland, offering wonderful panoramic views and making this a paradise for walkers. ✉ *Feock* ☎ *01872/862090* ⊕ *www.nationaltrust.org. uk* ✍*£7* ☉ *Mid-Feb.–Oct., daily 10:30–5:30 or dusk; Nov.–mid-Feb., daily 11–4 or dusk; last admission 30 mins before closing.*

ST. MAWES

6 mi south of Trelissick, 11 mi south of Truro, 16 mi east of Falmouth.

At the tip of the Roseland Peninsula is the quiet, unspoiled village of St. Mawes, where subtropical plants thrive. The peninsula itself is a lovely backwater with old churches, a lighthouse, and good coast walking. One or two sailing and boating options are available in summer, but most companies operate from Falmouth.

GETTING HERE AND AROUND

By road, St Mawes lies at the end of A3078. The village is connected to Truro by bus or ferry. You could drive from Falmouth, but it's easier to hop on a ferry crossing the estuary. Shuttling passengers between the ports in Falmouth and St. Mawes, the St. Mawes Ferry passes by two atmospheric castles along the way. It runs from Falmouth's Prince of Wales Pier and the Custom House Quay.

ESSENTIALS

Ferry Contacts St. Mawes Ferry (☎ *01872/861910* ⊕ *www.falriver.co.uk/smf*).

EXPLORING

★ **St. Just in Roseland.** North of St. Mawes on the A3078 is St. Just in Roseland, one of the most beautiful spots in the West Country. This tiny hamlet made up of stone cottage terraces and a 13th-century church is set within a subtropical garden, often abloom with magnolias and rhododendrons on a summer's day.

St. Mawes Castle. Outside the village, the well-preserved Tudor-era St. Mawes Castle has a cloverleaf shape that makes it seemingly impregnable, yet during the Civil War its Royalist commander surrendered without firing a shot. (In contrast, Pendennis Castle in Falmouth held out at this time for 23 weeks before submitting to a siege.) ✉ *A3078* ☎ *01326/270526* ⊕ *www. english-heritage.org.uk* ✍ *£4.30* ☉ *Apr.–June and Sept., Sun.–Fri. 10–5; July and Aug., Sun.–Fri. 10–6; Oct., daily 10–4; Nov.–Mar., Fri.–Mon. 10–4.*

WHERE TO STAY

For expanded hotel reviews, visit Fodors.com.

RENT A COTTAGE

There are plenty of opportunities for experiencing rural peace in a rented cottage amid the meadows and moors of England's West Country. However, the best places are often booked up from year to year in the high season (school vacation). Ask at the information centers, or try any of the following specialist companies: **Classic Cottages** (☎ *01326/555555* ⊕ *www. classic.co.uk*). **Cornish Cottage Holidays** (☎ *01326/573808* ⊕ *www.cornishcottageholidays. co.uk*). **Cornish Traditional Cottages** (☎ *01208/821666* ⊕ *www.corncott.com*). **Helpful Holidays** (☎ *01647/433593* ⊕ *www.helpfulholidays.com*).

££££–£££
HOTEL

Lugger Hotel. It's worth the winding drive on some of Cornwall's narrowest roads to get to this waterfront hideaway in a tiny fishing village. **Pros:** unforgettable location; outstanding food; attentive staff. **Cons:** remote and isolated; some rooms are cramped. ⊠ *Portloe* ☎ *01872/501322* ⊕ *www.luggerhotel.co.uk* 🛏 *22 rooms* ⏚ *In-room: no a/c, Wi-Fi (some). In-hotel: restaurant, spa* ⫶⊙⫶ *Breakfast.*

£££££
HOTEL
★

Tresanton Hotel. It's the Cornish Riviera, Italian style: this former yachtsman's club, owned by Olga Polizzi, daughter of grand hotelier Charles Forte, makes for a luxuriously relaxed stay. **Pros:** family-friendly; terrific views; stylishly luxurious setting. **Cons:** some steps to climb; some rooms are small; distant parking lot. ⊠ *Lower Castle Rd.* ☎ *01326/270055* ⊕ *www.tresanton.com* 🛏 *27 rooms, 2 suites* ⏚ *In-room: no a/c, Wi-Fi (some). In-hotel: restaurant, bar, business center* ⫶⊙⫶ *Breakfast.*

EN
ROUTE

The shortest route from St. Mawes to Truro is via the King Harry Ferry. The longer way swings in a circle on A3078 for 19 mi through countryside where subtropical shrubs thrive. It takes you past Portloe and the 123-foot-tall church tower in Probus, which flaunts gargoyles and pierced stonework.

5

TRURO

8 mi north of St. Mawes, 8 mi north of Falmouth.

The county seat and Cornwall's only real city, Truro is a good option mostly for food and shopping, and for cathedral and museum buffs. For an overview of the Georgian houses, take a stroll down steep, broad Lemon Street. The elegant 18th-century facades are of pale stone—unusual for Cornwall, where granite predominates. Like Lemon Street, Walsingham Place is a typical Georgian street, a curving, flower-lined pedestrian oasis. The city nestles in a crook of the River Truro.

GETTING HERE AND AROUND

Truro is on the main rail line between Penzance and Plymouth, and is served by local and National Express buses. The compact center can be easily walked from the bus and train stations.

ESSENTIALS

Visitor Information Truro (⊠ *City Hall, Boscawen St.* ☎ *01872/274555* ⊕ *tourism.truro.gov.uk*).

EXPLORING

Cathedral Church of St. Mary. Although built between 1880 and 1910, this cathedral evokes a medieval church, with an exterior in Early English Gothic style. The interior is filled with relics from the 16th-century parish church that stood on this site, part of which has been incorporated into a side chapel. An open, cobbled area called High Cross lies in front of the west porch, and the city's main shopping streets fan out from here. ⊠ *14 St. Mary's St.* ☎ *01872/276782* ⊕ *www.trurocathedral. org.uk* 💷 *£3 suggested donation* ⊙ *Mon.–Sat. 7:30–6, Sun. 9–7; tours Apr.–Oct., Mon.–Thurs. and Sat. at 11, Fri. at 11:30, also weekdays at 2 during school vacations.*

Royal Cornwall Museum. In a Georgian building, this museum displays some fine examples of Cornwall-inspired art, a sampling of Cornish archaeology, an absorbing hodgepodge of local history, and an extensive collection of minerals. There's also a shop and a small café. ⊠ *River St.* ☎ *01872/272205* ⊕ *www.royalcornwallmuseum.org.uk* ✉ *Free* ☼ *Tues.–Sat. 10–4:45.*

FOWEY

22 mi east of Truro.

Nestled in the mouth of a wooded estuary, Fowey (pronounced Foy) is still very much a working china-clay port as well as a focal point for the sailing fraternity. Increasingly, it's also a favored home of the rich and famous. Good and varied dining and lodging options abound; these are most in demand during Regatta Week in mid-August and the annual Daphne du Maurier Festival in mid-May. The Bodinnick Ferry takes cars as well as foot passengers across the river for the coast road on to Looe.

A few miles west of Fowey are a pair of very different gardens: the Eden Project, a futuristic display of plants from around the world, and the Lost Gardens of Heligan, a revitalized reminder of the Victorian age.

GETTING HERE AND AROUND
Fowey is not on any train line, but the town is served by frequent buses from St. Austell. Don't attempt to drive into the steep and narrow-lane town center, which is ideal for strolling around. Parking lots are signposted on the approach roads.

ESSENTIALS
Visitor Information Fowey (⊠ *5 South St.* ☎ *01726/833616* ⊕ *www.fowey.co.uk*).

EXPLORING

OFF THE BEATEN PATH

Charlestown. Seven miles west of Fowey, Charlestown has a Georgian harbor so well preserved that it often appears in period film and television productions. This port was built by a local merchant in 1791 to export the huge reserves of china clay from nearby St. Austell. It was also one of the ports from which 19th-century emigrants left for North America.

Fodor's Choice
★
☾

Eden Project. Spectacularly set in a former china-clay pit, this garden presents the world's major plant systems in microcosm. The crater contains more than 70,000 plants—many of them rare or endangered species—from three climate zones. Plants from the temperate zone are outdoors, and those from other zones are housed in hexagonally paneled geodesic domes. In one dome, olive and citrus groves mix with cacti and other plants indigenous to warmer climates. The tropical dome steams with heat, resounds to the gushing of a waterfall, and blooms with exotic flora. The emphasis is on conservation and ecology, but is free of any editorializing. A free shuttle helps the footsore, and well-informed guides provide information. An entertaining exhibition in the visitor center gives you the lowdown on the project, and the Core, an education center, provides amusement and instruction for children. Extra attractions include open-air concerts in summer and an ice-skating rink in winter. The Eden Project is 3 mi northeast of Charleston.

■**TIP→** To save money, order tickets at least a week in advance online. You'll need at least a half day to see everything. The Eden Project is 5 mi northwest of Fowey via the A3082. There's frequent bus service from Fowey to St. Austell. ⊠ *Bodelva, signposted off A30, A390, and A391, St. Austell* 🕾 *01726/811911* ⊕ *www.edenproject.com* 🖃 *£18, £14 if arriving by bike or on foot* ⊙ *Apr.–late Oct., daily 9:30–6; late Oct.–Mar., daily 9:30–4:30; last admission 1½ hrs before closing.*

★ **Lost Gardens of Heligan.** These sprawling grounds have something for all garden lovers, as well as an intriguing history. Spruced up in the early 1990s by former rock music producer Tim Smit (the force behind the Eden Project garden), they were begun by the Tremayne family in the late 18th century. In Victorian times the gardens displayed plants from around the British Empire. The Jungle Zone contains surviving plants from this era, including a lone Monterey pine, as well as giant redwood and clumps of bamboo. The Italian Garden and walled Flower Gardens are delightful, but don't overlook the Fruit and Vegetable gardens or Flora's Green, bordered by a ravine. It's easy to spend half a day here. ■**TIP→** Travel via St. Austell to avoid confusing country lanes, then follow signs to Mevagissey. ⊠ *B3273, Pentewan* 🕾 *01726/845100* ⊕ *www. heligan.com* 🖃 *£10* ⊙ *Apr.–Sept., daily 10–6; Oct.–Mar., daily 10–5; last entry 1½ hrs before closing.*

WHERE TO EAT AND STAY

For expanded hotel reviews, visit Fodors.com.

££ ✕ **Sam's.** This small and buzzing bistro has a rock-and-roll flavor, thanks
AMERICAN to the walls adorned with posters of music icons. Diners squeeze onto benches and into booths to savor dishes made with local seafood, including a majestic bouillabaisse, or just a simple "Samburger." You may have to wait for a table, but there's a slinky lounge-bar upstairs for a preprandial drink. ⊠ *20 Fore St.* 🕾 *01726/832273* ⊕ *www.samsfowey. co.uk* ⌖ *Reservations not accepted.*

£££££ 🖃 **Fowey Hall.** A showy Victorian edifice, all turrets and elaborate plas-
HOTEL terwork, this hotel with 5 acres of gardens is a great place for fami-
☺ lies. **Pros:** grand manorial setting; family-friendly rates. **Cons:** could do with a revamp; erratic housekeeping and service. ⊠ *Hanson Dr.* 🕾 *01726/833866* ⊕ *www.foweyhallhotel.co.uk* ⤳ *24 rooms, 12 suites* ⌂ *In-room: no a/c, Wi-Fi (some). In-hotel: restaurants, bar, pool, spa, some pets allowed* ⍥*Breakfast.*

SPORTS AND THE OUTDOORS

Between June and September, **Fowey River Expeditions** (⊠ *17 Passage St.* 🕾 *01726/833627* ⊕ *www.foweyriverexpeditions.co.uk*) runs daily canoe trips up the tranquil River Fowey, the best way to observe the abundant wildlife. Kayaks are also available to rent.

BODMIN

12 mi north of Fowey.

Bodmin was the only Cornish town recorded in the 11th-century Domesday Book, William the Conqueror's census. During World War I the Domesday Book and the Crown Jewels were sent to Bodmin Prison for safekeeping. From the Gilbert Memorial on Beacon Hill, you can see both of Cornwall's coasts. Lanhydrock, a stately home, is also near Bodmin.

GETTING HERE AND AROUND

At the junction of A38 and A30, Bodmin is a major transport hub for north Cornwall. Trains stop at Bodmin Parkway, 3 mi southeast of the center. A car is your best bet for touring Bodmin Moor and visiting Lanhydrock.

ESSENTIALS

Visitor Information Bodmin (✉ *The Shire Hall, Mount Folly* ☎ *01208/76616* ⊕ *www.bodminlive.com*).

EXPLORING

Dozmary Pool. For a taste of Arthurian legend, follow A30 northeast out of Bodmin across the boggy, heather-clad granite plateau of Bodmin Moor. After about 10 mi, turn right at Bolventor to get to Dozmary Pool. A lake rather than a pool, it was here that King Arthur's legendary magic sword, Excalibur, was supposedly returned to the Lady of the Lake after Arthur's final battle.

Fodor's Choice
★

Lanhydrock. One of Cornwall's greatest country piles, Lanhydrock gives a look into the lives of the upper classes in the 19th century. The former home of the powerful, wealthy Robartes family was originally constructed in the 17th century but was totally rebuilt after a fire in 1881. Its granite exterior remains true to the house's original form, however, and the long picture gallery in the north wing, with its barrel-vaulted plaster ceiling depicting 24 biblical scenes, survived the devastation. A small museum in the north wing shows photographs and letters relating to the family. The house's endless pantries, sculleries, dairies, nurseries, and linen cupboards bear witness to the immense amount of work involved in maintaining this lifestyle. About 900 acres of wooded parkland border the River Fowey, and in spring the gardens present an exquisite ensemble of magnolias, azaleas, and rhododendrons. Allow two hours to see the house and more time to stroll the grounds. ✉ *Signposted off A30, A38, and B3268, 3 mi southeast of Bodmin* ☎ *01208/265950* ⊕ *www.nationaltrust.org.uk* 🖾 *£10.40; grounds only, £6.10* 🕐 *House Apr.–Sept., Tues.–Sun. 11–5:30; Mar. and Oct., Tues.–Sun. 11–5; garden daily 10–6; last admission 30 mins before closing.*

PLYMOUTH AND DARTMOOR

Just over the border from Cornwall is Plymouth, an unprepossessing city but one with a historic old core and splendid harbor that recall a rich maritime heritage. North of Plymouth, you can explore the vast, boggy reaches of hilly Dartmoor, the setting for the Sherlock Holmes classic *The Hound of the Baskervilles*. This national park is a great place to hike or go horseback riding away from the crowds.

Upstairs, downstairs: at Lanhydrock you can tour both the elegant picture gallery and the vast pantries and sculleries.

PLYMOUTH

48 mi southwest of Exeter, 124 mi southwest of Bristol, 240 mi southwest of London.

Devon's largest city has long been linked with England's commercial and maritime history. The Pilgrims sailed from here to the New World in the *Mayflower* in 1620. Although much of the city center was destroyed by air raids in World War II and has been rebuilt in an uninspiring style, there are worthwhile sights. A harbor tour is also a good way to see the city.

GETTING HERE AND AROUND

Frequent trains arrive from Bodmin, Penzance, and Exeter. From London Paddington, trains take around three hours, 20 minutes; National Express buses from London's Victoria Coach Station take five hours, 20 minutes. The train station is 1 mi north of the seafront, connected by frequent buses. Long-distance buses stop at the centrally located bus station off Royal Parade. Drivers can leave their cars in one of the numerous parking lots, including a couple right by the harbor. The seafront and central city areas are best explored on foot.

ESSENTIALS

Visitor Information Plymouth (✉ *Plymouth Mayflower, 3–5 The Barbican* ☎ *01752/306330* ⊕ *www.visitplymouth.co.uk*).

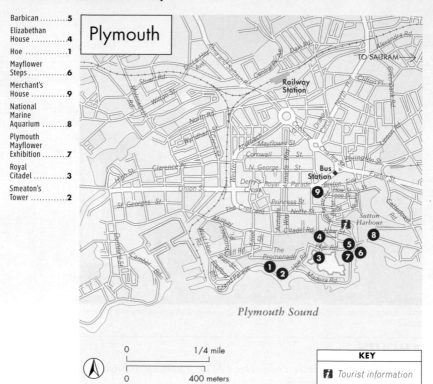

Plymouth Sound

	KEY
🛈	*Tourist information*

EXPLORING
TOP ATTRACTIONS

Barbican. East of the Royal Citadel is the Barbican, the oldest surviving section of Plymouth. Here Tudor houses and warehouses rise from a maze of narrow streets leading down to the fishing docks and harbor. Many of these buildings have become antiques shops, art shops, and bookstores. It's well worth a stroll for the atmosphere.

Elizabethan House. In the heart of the Barbican section, this former sea captain's home offers a fascinating insight into how well-to-do Plymothians lived during the city's golden age. The three floors of the timber-frame house are filled with 16th- and 17th-century furnishings, and there's a reconstructed kitchen and a spiral staircase built around a ship's mast. ⊠ *32 New St.* ☎ *01752/304774* 💷 *£2.50* ⏲ *Apr.–Sept., Tues.–Sat. and national holidays 10–noon and 1–5.*

Hoe. From the Hoe, a wide, grassy esplanade with crisscrossing walkways high above the city, you can take in a magnificent view of the inlets, bays, and harbors that make up Plymouth Sound.

★ **National Marine Aquarium.** This excellent aquarium, on a central harbor-
☁ side site, presents aqueous environments, from a freshwater stream to a seawater wave tank and a huge "shark theater." Not to be missed is the extensive collection of sea horses, part of an important breeding

program, and the chance to walk under sharks in the Mediterranean tank. Explorocean highlights undersea technology with demonstrations and hands-on gizmos, and there's a 3-D cinema. ⊠ *Rope Walk, Coxside* ☎ *0844/893-7938* ⊕ *www.national-aquarium.co.uk* 🎫 *£11.50* ⊙ *Apr.–Sept., daily 10–6; Oct.–Mar., daily 10–5; last admission 1 hr before closing.*

Plymouth Mayflower Exhibition. On three floors, this interactive exhibition narrates the story of Plymouth, from its beginnings as a fishing and trading port to the modern industrial city it is today. Along the way, you'll take in the stories of various expeditions that embarked from here to the New World, including the *Mayflower* itself. The city's tourist office is also in this building. ⊠ *3–5 The Barbican* ☎ *01752/306330* ⊕ *www. visitplymouth.co.uk* 🎫 *£2* ⊙ *Apr.–Oct., Mon.–Sat. 10–4, Sun. 11–3; Nov.–Mar., weekdays 10–4, Sat. 11–3; last admission 1 hr before closing.*

Saltram. An exquisite 18th-century home with many of its original furnishings, Saltram was built around the remains of a late-Tudor mansion. Its jewel is one of Britain's grandest neoclassical rooms, a vast, double-cube salon designed by Robert Adam and adorned with paintings by Sir Joshua Reynolds, first president of the Royal Academy of Arts, who was born nearby in 1723. Fine plasterwork adorns many rooms, and three have original Chinese wallpaper. The outstanding garden includes rare trees and shrubs, and there's a restaurant and a cafeteria. Saltram is 3½ mi east of Plymouth city center. ⊠ *South of A38, Plympton* ☎ *01752/333503* ⊕ *www.nationaltrust.org.uk* 🎫 *£9.10; garden only, £4.70* ⊙ *House mid-Mar.–Oct., Sat.–Thurs. noon–4:30; last admission at 3:45. Garden Jan.–mid-Mar., Sat.–Thurs. 11–4; mid-Mar.–Oct., daily 11–5; Nov. and Dec., daily 11–4.*

WORTH NOTING

Mayflower Steps. By the harbor you can visit the Mayflower Steps, where the Pilgrims embarked in 1620; the **Mayflower Stone** marks the exact spot. They had sailed from Southampton but had to stop in Plymouth because of damage from a storm. ⊠ *3–5 The Barbican.*

Merchant's House. Near the Barbican, just off the Royal Parade, this largely 17th-century house is a museum of local history. ⊠ *33 St. Andrew's St.* ☎ *01752/304774* 🎫 *£2* ⊙ *Apr.–Sept., Tues.–Sat. and national holidays 10–noon and 1–5.*

Royal Citadel. This huge citadel was built by Charles II in 1666 and still operates as a military center. ⊠ *End of the Hoe* ☎ *01752/306330* ⊕ *www.english-heritage.org.uk* 🎫 *£5* ⊙ *May–Sept., Tues. and Thurs. 1¼-hr guided tours at 2:30.*

Smeaton's Tower. This lighthouse, transferred here at the end of the 19th century from its original site 14 mi out to sea, provides a sweeping vista over Plymouth Sound and the city as far as Dartmoor. ⊠ *Hoe Rd.* ☎ *01752/304774* 🎫 *£2.50* ⊙ *Apr.–Sept., Tues.–Fri. 10–noon and 1–4:30, Sat. 10–noon and 1–4; Oct.–Mar., Tues.–Sat. 10–noon and 1–3.*

WHERE TO EAT AND STAY

For expanded hotel reviews, visit Fodors.com.

£££   ✗ **Piermasters.** Fresh seafood landed at nearby piers, notably squid, mus-
SEAFOOD   sels, and oysters, appears high on the menu at this Barbican eatery.
Blending modern decor in a traditional setting, the downstairs dining area has a tile floor, wooden tables, and sails on the ceiling, and
upstairs is wood paneled with contemporary art on the walls. Choose
from one of the excellent fixed-price lunchtime and evening menus,
or order à la carte. ⊠ *33 Southside St.* ☎ *01752/229345* ⊕ *www.
piermastersrestaurant.com.*

££££   ✗ **Tanners.** One of the city's oldest buildings, the 15th-century Prys-
MODERN BRITISH   ten House, is the setting for the highly regarded, inventive cuisine of
brothers Chris and James Tanner. The menus (fixed-price at lunchtime)
include such options as ham-hock-and-leek pie, or roast brill with curried mussels and bok choy. One of the two lattice-windowed dining
rooms has a well in it, and the other is hung with tapestries. A canopied
courtyard is ideal for alfresco dining. The brothers also operate the
Barbican Kitchen, a more relaxed, less pricey offshoot of the restaurant at the Black Friars Distillery on Southside Street. ⊠ *Finewell St.*
☎ *01752/252001* ⊕ *www.tannersrestaurant.com* ⌁ *Reservations essential* ☉ *Closed Sun. and Mon.*

££   ▥ **The Bowling Green.** Friendly and unpretentious, this Georgian house
B&B/INN   overlooks Sir Francis Drake's bowling green on Plymouth Hoe. **Pros:**
convenient base for sightseeing; welcoming owner/manager. **Cons:** low
shower pressure in some rooms; limited parking. ⊠ *9–10 Osborne Pl.,
Lockyer St.* ☎ *01752/209090* ⊕ *www.thebowlinggreenplymouth.com*
⇱ *12 rooms* ⌂ *In-room: no a/c, Wi-Fi. In-hotel: parking* ▮◎▮ *Breakfast.*

££   ▥ **Holiday Inn.** Grandly sited in a tall block overlooking Plymouth Hoe,
HOTEL   this modern chain hotel has a businesslike tone but doesn't skimp
on comforts. **Pros:** excellent location; large rooms; fantastic views.
Cons: impersonal feel; dated decor; tight parking. ⊠ *Armada Way*
☎ *01752/639988* ⊕ *www.holidayinn.com* ⇱ *211 rooms* ⌂ *In-room:
a/c, Wi-Fi. In-hotel: restaurant, bar, pool, gym, business center, parking* ▮◎▮ *Breakfast.*

NIGHTLIFE AND THE ARTS

Plymouth's **Theatre Royal** (⊠ *Royal Parade* ☎ *01752/668282* ⊕ *www.
theatreroyal.com*) presents ballet, musicals, and plays by some of Britain's best companies.

HARBOR AND RIVER TOURS

Sound Cruising. This company runs harbor and river sightseeing trips all
year; boats depart every 45 minutes in peak season from Phoenix Wharf
(call to check November through March). ⊠ *Madeira Rd., Barbican*
☎ *01752/408590* ⊕ *www.soundcruising.com.*

Tamar Cruising. Harbor cruises and longer scenic trips on the rivers
Tamar and Yealm leave from the Mayflower Steps and Cremyll Quay
between Easter and October. ⊠ *Cremyll Quay, Cremyll, Torpoint*
☎ *01752/822105* ⊕ *www.tamarcruising.com.*

Pony trekking in Dartmoor National Park lets you get off the beaten path.

SHOPPING

At the **Black Friars Distillery** (✉ *60 Southside St.* ☎ *01752/665292* ⊕ *www. plymouthgin.com*), where Plymouth's most famous export, gin, has been distilled since 1793, you can purchase bottles of sloe gin, damson liqueur, fruit cup, or the fiery "Navy Strength" gin that traditionally was issued to the Royal Navy.

▌ EN ROUTE From Plymouth you have a choice of routes northeast to Exeter. If rugged, desolate, moorland scenery appeals to you, take A386 and B3212 northeast across Dartmoor. There is plenty to stir the imagination.

DARTMOOR NATIONAL PARK

10 mi north of Plymouth, 13 mi west of Exeter.

GETTING HERE AND AROUND

Public transport services are extremely sparse on Dartmoor, making a car indispensable for anywhere off the beaten track. The peripheral towns of Okehampton and Tavistock are well served by bus from Exeter and Plymouth, and Chagford also has direct connections to Exeter, but central Princetown has only sporadic links with the outside world.

EXPLORING

Dartmoor National Park. Even on a summer's day, the brooding hills of this sprawling wilderness appear a likely haunt for such monsters as the hound of the Baskervilles, and it seems entirely fitting that Sir Arthur Conan Doyle set his Sherlock Holmes thriller in this landscape.

Sometimes the wet, peaty wasteland of Dartmoor National Park vanishes in rain and mist, although in clear weather you can see north to Exmoor,

Plymouth, Exeter, and South Devon

---

south over the English Channel, and west far into Cornwall. Much of Dartmoor consists of open heath and moorland, unspoiled by roads—wonderful walking and horseback-riding territory but an easy place to lose your bearings. Dartmoor's earliest inhabitants left behind stone monuments and burial mounds that help you envision prehistoric man roaming these pastures. Ponies, sheep, and birds are the main animals to be seen.

Several villages scattered along the borders of this 368-square-mi reserve—one-third of which is owned by Prince Charles—make useful bases for hiking excursions. Accommodations include simple inns and some elegant havens. **Okehampton** is a main gateway, and **Chagford** is a good base for exploring north Dartmoor. Other scenic spots include **Buckland-in-the-Moor,** a hamlet with thatch-roof cottages; **Widecombe-in-the-Moor,** whose church is known as the Cathedral of the Moor; and **Grimspound,** the Bronze Age site featured in Conan Doyle's most famous tale. Transmoor Link buses connect most of Dartmoor's towns and villages. Park information centers include the main **High Moorland Visitor Centre** in Princetown and centers in Postbridge and Haytor. The park also works with tourist information centers in Ivybridge, Okehampton, Moretonhampstead, Tavistock, and Buckfastleigh. ⊠ *High Moorland Visitor Centre, Tavistock Rd., Princetown* ☎ *01822/890414* ⊕ *www.dartmoor-npa.gov.uk.*

SPORTS AND THE OUTDOORS

Tourist information centers can help you decide what to do here; another source is the **Dartmoor National Park Authority** (✉ *Parke, Haytor Rd., Bovey Tracey, Newton Abbot* ☎ *01626/832093* ⊕ *www.dartmoor-npa.gov.uk*). This is a great area for horseback riding; many towns have stables for guided rides. Hiking is popular, but longer hikes in the bleak, unpeopled region of Dartmoor—for example, the tors south of Okehampton—are appropriate only for the most experienced walkers. The areas around Widgery Cross, Becky Falls, and the Bovey Valley, and the short but dramatic walk along Lydford Gorge, have wide appeal, as do the many valleys around the southern edge of the moors. Guided hikes (£3–£8) are available through the park; reservations are not needed for most, but you can check with the High Moorland Visitor Centre in Princetown.

TAVISTOCK AND ENVIRONS

5

13 mi north of Plymouth.

On the River Tavy, the ancient town of Tavistock historically owed its importance to its Benedictine abbey (dissolved by Henry VIII in the 16th century) and to its status as a stannary town, where tin was weighed, stamped, and assessed. Today the town of 11,000 preserves a prosperous, predominantly Victorian appearance, especially at the bustling indoor Pannier Market off central Bedford Square. Tavistock makes a useful base for exploring a scattering of nearby sights—Buckland Abbey, Cotehele House, and Morwellham Quay—and for touring Dartmoor's western reaches.

GETTING HERE AND AROUND

Tavistock, on A386 and A390, is easily accessed via the frequent buses from Plymouth, which take about an hour. You'll need your own transportation to visit the attractions scattered around it, however.

ESSENTIALS

Visitor Information Tavistock (✉ *The Archway, Bedford Sq.* ☎ *01822/612938* ⊕ *www.dartmoor.co.uk*).

EXPLORING

Buckland Abbey. A 13th-century Cistercian monastery, Buckland Abbey became the home of Sir Francis Drake in 1581. Today it is filled with mementos of Drake tpanish Armada and has a restaurant. The house is 6 mi south of Tavistock; to get here, ake A386 south to Crapstone and then head west. ✉ *Yelverton* ☎ *01822/853607* ⊕ *www.nationaltrust. org.uk* 🎫 *£8.05; grounds only, £4.05* ⊙ *Late Feb.–early Mar. and early Nov.–mid-Dec., Fri.–Sun. 11–4:30; mid-Mar.–Oct., daily 10:30–5:30; last admission 45 mins before closing.*

★ **Cotehele House and Quay.** About 4 mi west of Buckland Abbey, Cotehele House and Quay was formerly a busy port on the River Tamar, but it is now usually visited for the well-preserved, atmospheric late-medieval manor, home of the Edgcumbe family for centuries. The house has original furniture, tapestries, embroideries, and armor, and you can also visit the impressive gardens, a quay museum, and a restored mill (usually in operation on Tuesday and Thursday). A limited number of visitors are allowed per day, so arrive early and be prepared to wait during busy periods. Choose a bright day, because the rooms have no electric light. Shops, crafts studios, a gallery, and a restaurant provide other diversions. ■TIP➜ Take advantage of the shuttle bus that runs every half hour between the house, quay, and mill. ⊠ *St. Dominick, north of Saltash, signposted off A390* ☎ *01579/351346* ⊕ *www.nationaltrust. org.uk* ✏ *£9; gardens and mill only, £5.40* ⊙ *House mid-Mar.–Oct., Sat.–Thurs. 11–4:30. Mill mid-Mar.–Oct., daily 11–4:30. Gardens daily dawn–dusk.*

🐾 **Morwellham Quay.** In the 19th century, Morwellham (pronounced More-*wel*-ham) was England's main copper-exporting port, and it has been carefully restored as a working museum, with quay workers and coachmen in costume. Visitors can board a special train that goes along the River Tamar and into the Charlotte and George Copper Mine. The site lies 2 mi east of Cotehele House and 5 mi southwest of Tavistock. ⊠ *Off A390, on minor road off B3257* ☎ *01822/832766* ⊕ *www. morwellham-quay.co.uk* ✏ *£7.95, mine train £3.50* ⊙ *July–mid-Sept., daily 10–5:30; mid-Sept.–June, daily 10–4:30.*

WHERE TO EAT AND STAY

For expanded hotel reviews, visit Fodors.com.

££££ **✕ Horn of Plenty.** The restaurant within this Georgian house has mag-
MODERN BRITISH nificent views across the wooded, rhododendron-filled Tamar Valley.
★ The sophisticated menu favors local and seasonal ingredients. Loin of lamb with polenta, balsamic onions, and Madeira sauce is a typical main course. There are several fixed-price menus (lunch £19.50 and £24.50, dinner £49.50); the best value is Monday evening's potluck menu (£29). A converted coach house and the main house contain 10 sumptuously furnished guest rooms (£££). It's 3 mi west of Tavistock. ⊠ *A390, Gulworthy* ☎ *01822/832528* ⊕ *www.thehornofplenty.co.uk.*

££–£££ **⌷ Browns.** With its mustard-and-brown color scheme, plush furnish-
HOTEL ings, and fresh-feeling conservatory, this former coaching inn feels contemporary, but its country furnishings, lattice windows, and exposed stone walls suggest a longer pedigree. **Pros:** professional staff; delicious food. **Cons:** some rooms and bathrooms are small; soundproofing can be inadequate. ⊠ *80 West St.* ☎ *01822/618686* ⊕ *www.brownsdevon. co.uk* ⇨ *21 rooms* ⌂ *In-room: no a/c, Wi-Fi, Internet. In-hotel: restaurants, bars, business center, some pets allowed* ⦿ *Breakfast.*

LYDFORD GORGE

7 mi north of Tavistock, 24 mi north of Plymouth.

GETTING HERE AND AROUND

The gorge is easily accessed on Holsworthy buses from Tavistock (which has frequent bus connections to Plymouth) and Okehampton (connected to Exeter). By car, take A386 between Tavistock and Okehampton.

EXPLORING

★ **Lydford Gorge.** The River Lyd has carved a spectacular 1½-mi-long chasm through the rock at Lydford Gorge, outside the pretty village of Lydford, midway between Oke-hampton and Tavistock on the edge of Dartmoor. Two paths follow the gorge past gurgling whirlpools and waterfalls with evocative names such as the Devil's Cauldron and the White Lady. Sturdy footwear is recommended. Although the walk can be quite challenging, the paths can still get congested during busy periods. In winter, access is restricted to the main waterfall and the top of the gorge. ✉ *Off A386, Lydford* ☎ *01822/820320* ⊕ *www. nationaltrust.org.uk* 🎫 *£5.80, free in winter* 🕐 *Mid-Mar.–early Oct., daily 10–5; early–late Oct., daily 10–4; Nov.–mid-Mar., daily 10:30–3:30.*

> ### STAY ON A FARM
>
> Do you plan to travel by car and want to be far from resorts, traffic jams, and hubbub? One way to experience the authentic rural life in Somerset, Devon, and Cornwall is to stay on a farm. **Cartwheel Holidays'** Web site (⊕ *www. cartwheelholidays.co.uk*) gives details about working farms that supply accommodations—including bed-and-breakfasts and house rentals—throughout the region. Other reference points are **Visit Devon** (⊕ *www.visitdevon. co.uk*), for farms in Devon, and **Cornish Farm Holidays** (⊕ *www.cornishfarmholidays. co.uk*), for Cornwall.

WHERE TO EAT AND STAY

For expanded hotel reviews, visit Fodors.com.

£££
MODERN BRITISH

✗ **Dartmoor Inn.** Locals and visitors alike make a beeline for this gastro-pub in a 16th-century building with a number of small dining spaces done in spare, contemporary country style. Dishes may include fish casserole with a ragout of leeks and saffron sauce, or fillet of duck with vanilla-apple puree, prunes, and toasted almonds. There's also a sepa-rate vegetarian menu. Set-price menus are available daily for under £10. Three spacious guest rooms (££) make it possible to linger. ✉ *A386, Lydford* ☎ *01822/820221* ⊕ *www.dartmoorinn.com* 🍴 *Reservations essential* 🕐 *No dinner Sun. No lunch Mon.*

£–££
B&B/INN

🏨 **Castle Inn.** The heart of Lydford village, this 16th-century inn sits next to Lydford Castle. **Pros:** antique character; peaceful rural setting. **Cons:** shabby in places; some small rooms. ✉ *1 mi off A386, Lyd-ford* ☎ *01822/820241* ⊕ *www.castleinndartmoor.co.uk* 🛏 *8 rooms* ⚙ *In-room: no a/c, Wi-Fi. In-hotel: restaurant, bar, some pets allowed* 🍴 *Breakfast.*

SPORTS AND THE OUTDOORS

Cholwell Riding Stables (✉ *Mary Tavy* ☎ *01822/810526* ⊕ *www. cholwellridingstables.co.uk*) has one- and two-hour horseback rides through some of Dartmoor's wilder tracts. Riders of all abilities are escorted, and equipment is provided. The stables are about 6 mi south of Lydford; call for directions.

A walk in Lydford Gorge takes you through lush forest.

OKEHAMPTON

8 mi northeast of Lydford Gorge, 28 mi north of Plymouth, 23 mi west of Exeter.

This town at the confluence of the rivers East and West Okement is a good base for exploring north Dartmoor. It has numerous pubs and cottage tearooms—take time to indulge in a classic, rich Devon cream tea—as well as a helpful tourist office.

GETTING HERE AND AROUND

There's good bus service to Okehampton from Tavistock and Exeter, and on summer Sundays you can travel by train from Exeter. If you're driving, the town is on A30 and A386; parking is easy in the center of town.

ESSENTIALS

Visitor Information Okehampton (✉ *Okehampton Museum Yard, West St.* ☎ *01837/53020* ⊕ *www.okehamptondevon.co.uk*).

EXPLORING

Museum of Dartmoor Life. The three floors of this informative museum contain models, a working waterwheel, and photos of traditional farming methods. ✉ *3 West St.* ☎ *01837/52295* ⊕ *www.museumofdartmoorlife. eclipse.co.uk* ✐ *£3.50* ☉ *Apr.–Oct., weekdays 10:15–4:15, Sat. 10:15–1; Nov.–mid-Dec., Mon.–Sat. 11–3.*

Okehampton Castle. On the riverbank a mile southwest of the town center, the jagged ruins of this Norman castle occupy a verdant site with a picnic area and woodland walks. ✉ *Castle Lodge, off B3260* ☎ *01837/ 52844* ⊕ *www.english-heritage.org.uk* ✐ *£3.70* ☉ *Apr.–June and Sept., daily 10–5; July and Aug., daily 10–6.*

WHERE TO STAY

For expanded hotel reviews, visit Fodors.com.

££££ 🛏 **Lewtrenchard Manor.** Paneled rooms, stone fireplaces, leaded-glass
HOTEL windows, and handsome gardens outfit this spacious 1620 manor
house on the northwestern edge of Dartmoor. **Pros:** beautiful Jacobean setting; conscientious service; outstanding food. **Cons:** dated in
parts; not very child-friendly. ⊠ *Between Launceston and Okehampton,
Lewdown* ☏ *01566/783222* ⊕ *www.lewtrenchard.co.uk* ⮐ *9 rooms, 5
suites* ⚓ *In-room: no a/c, Internet, Wi-Fi (some). In-hotel: restaurant,
bar, some pets allowed* ⚏ *Breakfast.*

SPORTS AND THE OUTDOORS

Skaigh Stables Farm (⊠ *Skaigh La., Belstone, near Okehampton*
☏ *01837/840917* ⊕ *www.skaighstables.co.uk*) arranges horseback
rides by the hour, half day, and full day from Easter through October.

CHAGFORD

9 mi southeast of Okehampton, 30 mi northeast of Plymouth.

Chagford, once a tin-weighing station, was an area of fierce fighting between the Roundheads and the Cavaliers during the Civil War.
Although officially a "town" since 1305, Chagford is more of a village,
with old taverns grouped around a seasoned old church and a curious
"pepper-pot" market house on the site of the old Stannary Court. With
a handful of cafés and shops to browse around, it makes a convenient
base from which to explore north Dartmoor.

GETTING HERE AND AROUND

Infrequent local buses connect Chagford with Okehampton and Exeter
(except on Sunday, when there's no service). The village is located off
A382; a car or bicycle is the best way to see its far-flung sights.

EXPLORING

Castle Drogo. Northeast of Chagford, this castle looks like a medieval
fortress, complete with battlements, but construction actually took
place between 1910 and 1930. Designed by noted architect Sir Edwin
Lutyens for Julius Drewe, a wealthy grocer, the castle is only half finished (funds ran out). Inside, this magisterial pile combines medieval
grandeur and early-20th-century comforts like the large bathrooms.
■ TIP➔ Between June and September, you can play croquet on the lawn
while taking in awesome views over Dartmoor. Take the A30 Exeter–Okehampton road to reach the castle. ⊠ *Off A30 and A382, Drewsteignton*
☏ *01647/433306* ⊕ *www.nationaltrust.org.uk* 🎟 *£8.20; grounds only,
£5.10* ⏰ *Castle late Feb., daily 11–4; mid-Mar.–Oct., daily 9–5; Nov.–
mid-Dec., weekends 11–4:30.*

★ **Devon Guild of Craftsmen.** The southwest's most important contemporary
arts-and-crafts center, the Devon Guild is in a converted 19th-century
coach house in the village of Bovey Tracey, 10 mi southeast of Chagford
and 14 mi southwest of Exeter. The center has excellent exhibitions
of local, national, and international crafts as well as a shop and café.
⊠ *Riverside Mill, B3344 (Fore St.), Bovey Tracey* ☏ *01626/832223*
⊕ *www.crafts.org.uk* 🎟 *Free* ⏰ *Daily 10–5:30.*

5

QUICK BITES

The Old Cottage Tea Shop (✉ *20 Fore St., Bovey Tracey* ☎ *01626/833430*) is the real deal, perfect for a light lunch or, even better, a cream tea served on bone china. Warm scones come in baskets, with black currant and other homemade jams and plenty of clotted cream. It's closed Wednesday afternoon and all day Sunday.

WHERE TO EAT AND STAY

For expanded hotel reviews, visit Fodors.com.

££££ ✕ **Gidleigh Park.** One of England's foremost country-house hotels,
MODERN BRITISH Gidleigh Park occupies an enclave of landscaped gardens and streams.
★ It's reached via a lengthy, winding country lane and private drive at the edge of Dartmoor. The extremely pricey contemporary restaurant, directed by chef Michael Caines, has been showered with culinary awards. You may see why when you dig into the turbot and scallops with leeks, wild mushrooms, and chive butter sauce. The locally pumped spring water is like no other. Antiques fill the long, halftimber building, built in 1928 in Tudor style; there are 24 luxurious guest rooms. ✉ *Gidleigh Park* ☎ *01647/432367* ⊕ *www.gidleigh.com* ⌂ *Reservations essential.*

£££££ ⊡ **Bovey Castle.** With the grandeur of a country estate and the amenities
HOTEL of a modern hotel, Bovey Castle, built in 1906 for Viscount Hambledon,
★ has it all. **Pros:** baronial splendor; efficient service; range of activities. **Cons:** ground-floor rooms can be noisy; costly extras. ✉ *Off B3212, North Bovey* ☎ *0844/474–0077* ⊕ *www.boveycastle.com* ↩ *63 rooms, 14 self-catering lodges* ⌂ *In-room: no a/c, Wi-Fi (some). In-hotel: restaurants, bar, golf course, pool, tennis courts, spa, business center, some pets allowed* ⦿ *Breakfast.*

££ ⊡ **Easton Court.** Discerning travelers such as C.P. Snow, Margaret Mead,
B&B/INN John Steinbeck, and Evelyn Waugh—who completed *Brideshead Revisited* here—made this their Dartmoor home-away-from-home. **Pros:** helpful hosts; quiet environment. **Cons:** rooms lack much character; need to drive to get anywhere. ✉ *A382, Easton Cross* ☎ *01647/433469* ⊕ *www.easton.co.uk* ↩ *5 rooms* ⌂ *In-room: no a/c, Wi-Fi (some). In-hotel: some pets allowed, some age restrictions* ⦿ *Breakfast.*

EXETER AND SOUTH DEVON

The ancient city of Exeter, Devon's county seat, has preserved some of its historical character despite wartime bombing. From Exeter you can explore southeast to the estuary port of Topsham. Sheltered by the high mass of Dartmoor to the west, the coastal resort area of Torbay, known as the English Riviera, enjoys a mild, warm climate that allows for subtropical vegetation, including palm trees. To the east, on the banks of the River Dart, is the pretty market town of Totnes, while the well-to-do yachting center of Dartmouth lies south of Torbay at the river's estuary.

EXETER

18 mi east of Chagford, 48 mi northeast of Plymouth, 85 mi southwest of Bristol, 205 mi southwest of London.

Exeter has been the capital of the region since the Romans established a fortress here 2,000 years ago. Evidence of the Roman occupation remains in the city walls. Although it was heavily bombed in 1942, Exeter retains much of its medieval character, as well as examples of the gracious architecture of the 18th and 19th centuries. It's convenient to both Torquay and Dartmoor.

GETTING HERE AND AROUND

Train service (leaving roughly hourly) from London Paddington takes about two hours, 15 minutes; the cheaper Megatrain service takes three hours, 20 minutes and leaves London Waterloo four times daily. National Express buses depart every two hours from London's Victoria Coach Station and take around four hours, 30 minutes. Exeter is a major transportation hub for Devon. Trains from Bristol, Salisbury, and Plymouth stop at Exeter St. David's, and connect to the center by frequent buses. Some trains also stop at the more useful Exeter Central. The bus station is off Paris Street near the tourist office. Cars are unnecessary in town, so park yours as soon as possible—all the sights are within an easy walk.

TOURS Free 90-minute walking tours of Exeter by Red Coat guides take place daily all year, focusing on different aspects of the city. See ⊕ *www.exeter. gov.uk/guidedtours* for details, or contact the tourist office. You can also pick up a leaflet on self-guided walks from here.

ESSENTIALS

Visitor Information Exeter (✉ *Dix's Field* ☎ *01392/665700* ⊕ *www.heartofdevon.com*).

EXPLORING
TOP ATTRACTIONS

★ **Cathedral of St. Peter.** At the heart of Exeter, the great Gothic cathedral was begun in 1275 and completed almost a century later. Its twin towers are even older survivors of an earlier Norman cathedral. Rising from a forest of ribbed columns, the nave's 300-foot stretch of unbroken Gothic vaulting is the longest in the world. Myriad statues, tombs, and memorial plaques adorn the interior. In the minstrels' gallery, high up on the left of the nave, stands a group of carved figures singing and playing musical instruments, including bagpipes. The **Close,** a pleasant green space for relaxing, surrounds the cathedral. Don't miss the 400-year-old door to No. 10, the bishop of Crediton's house, ornately carved with angels' and lions' heads. ✉ *Cathedral Close* ☎ *01392/285983* ⊕ *www.exeter-cathedral.org.uk* 🔲 *£5* ⊙ *Mon.–Sat. 9–4:45, Sun. open for services only. Guided tours weekdays at 11, 12:30, and 2:30, Sat. at 11 and 12:30.*

OFF THE
BEATEN
PATH
Powderham Castle. Seat of the earls of Devon, this notable stately home 8 mi south of Exeter and 5 mi south of Topsham is famed for its staircase hall, a soaring fantasia of white stuccowork on a turquoise background, constructed in 1739–69. Other sumptuous rooms, adorned with family portraits by Sir Godfrey Kneller and Sir Joshua Reynolds,

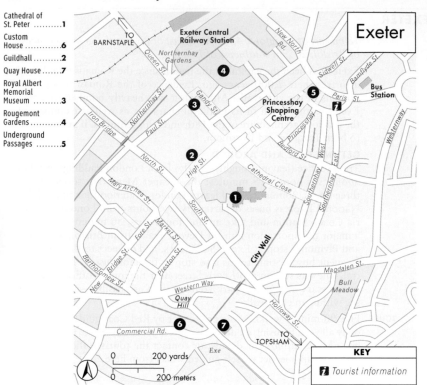

were used in the Merchant-Ivory film *Remains of the Day.* A tower built in 1400 by Sir Philip Courtenay, ancestor of the current owners, stands in the deer park. "Safari" rides (a tractor pulls a trailer) to see the 650 fallow deer depart daily at 1:45 and 3:15, and in summer falconry displays are offered daily at 3:30. The restaurant serves light lunches, and there's a children's play area, a farm shop, and a plant center. ⊠ *A379, Kenton* ☎ *01626/890243* ⊕ *www.powderham.co.uk* ☜ *£9.80, deer park £2* ⊘ *Apr.–late July, Sept., and Oct., Sun.–Fri. 11–4:30; late July–Aug., Sun.–Fri. 11–5:30.*

Royal Albert Memorial Museum. This museum houses natural-history displays, superb Exeter silverware, and the work of some West Country artists. There is also an excellent international gallery and a fine archaeological section. The property has recently benefitted from a major refurbishment. ⊠ *Queen St.* ☎ *01392/665858* ⊕ *www.rammuseum.org. uk* ☜ *Free* ⊘ *Mon.–Sat. 10–5.*

WORTH NOTING

Custom House. Exeter's historic waterfront on the River Exe was the center of the city's medieval wool industry, and the Custom House, built in 1682 on the quay, attests to the city's prosperity. Victorian warehouses flank the city's earliest surviving brick building. ⊠ *The Quay.*

Guildhall. Just behind the Close, this is said to be the oldest municipal building in the country still in use. The current hall, with its Renaissance portico, dates from 1330, although a guildhall has occupied this site since at least 1160. Its timber-braced roof, one of the earliest in England, dates from about 1460. The building is frequently closed for civic functions—call to check. ⊠ *High St.* ☎ *01392/665500* ⬚ *Free* ☺ *Weekdays 10:30–1 and 1:30–4, Sat. 10:30–12:30.*

Quay House. This late-17th-century stone warehouse houses a visitor center, with documents on the city's maritime history and an audiovisual display. ⊠ *The Quay* ☎ *01392/271611* ⬚ *Free* ☺ *Apr.–Oct., daily 10–5; Nov.–Mar., weekends 11–4.*

QUICK
BITES

At the **Prospect Inn** (⊠ *The Quay* ☎ *01392/273152*) you can contemplate the quayside comings and goings over a pint of real ale and a hot or cold meal. The nautical theme comes through in pictures and the ship's wheel hanging from the ceiling.

5

Rougemont Gardens. These gardens behind the Royal Albert Memorial Museum were laid out at the end of the 18th century. The land was once part of the defensive ditch of Rougemont Castle, built in 1068 by decree of William the Conqueror. The gardens contain the original Norman gatehouse and the remains of the Roman city wall, the latter forming part of the ancient castle's outer wall. ⊠ *Off Queen St.*

Underground Passages. Exeter's Underground Passages, which once served as conduits for fresh water, are the only medieval vaulted passages open to the public in Britain. They date to the mid-14th century, although some were enlarged by the Victorians. An exhibition and video precede the 25-minute guided tour. Many of the passages are narrow and low: be prepared to stoop. The tours often sell out during school vacations, so come early. Children under five are not permitted. ⊠ *2 Paris St.* ☎ *01392/665887* ⊕ *www.exeter.gov.uk* ⬚ *£5.50* ☺ *June–Sept. and school vacations, Mon.–Sat. 9:30–5:30, Sun. 10:30–4; Oct.–May, Tues.–Fri. 11:30–5:30, Sat. 9:30–5:30, Sun. 11:30–4; last tours 1 hr before closing.*

WHERE TO EAT

£ ⤫ **Ask.** This outpost of an Italian chain has secured an enviable site in a ITALIAN part-medieval, part-Georgian building opposite the cathedral. There are three dining areas. The large-windowed rooms offer superb views across the Close, the back room is older and has more atmosphere, and the courtyard is perfect for warm days. Although the food is unadventurous, with a generous choice of pizzas and pastas, everything is prepared to high standards, including good antipasti and salads. ⊠ *5 Cathedral Close* ☎ *01392/427127* ⊕ *www.askrestaurants.com.*

£ ⤫ **Herbie's.** A mellow stop, this friendly vegetarian bistro with wood VEGETARIAN floors and simple tables is ideal for unwinding over leisurely conversa-
★ tion. You can snack on pita bread with hummus, or tackle the spicy vegetable satay or spinach-and-mushroom lasagna. All the wines and the superb ice cream are organic. ⊠ *15 North St.* ☎ *01392/258473* ☺ *Closed Sun. No dinner Mon.*

££££ ✕ **Michael Caines Restaurant.** Perfectly located within the Cathedral Close,
MODERN BRITISH this ultrachic restaurant is in the centuries-old building that is now
★ the Abode Exeter. Run by master chef Michael Caines, the kitchen
serves eclectic contemporary fare such as roast loin of lamb with fennel
puree, or slow-poached Brixham brill with stir-fried snow peas, shiitake
mushrooms, and lemongrass foam. Alternatively, a more relaxed (and
more affordable) café-bar next door serves meals all day, including
good fixed-price lunches; there's live jazz on alternate Friday evenings.
⊠ *Cathedral Yard* ☎ *01392/223638* ⊕ *www.michaelcaines.com* ☯ *Restaurant closed Sun.*

£ ✕ **Ship Inn.** Here you can lift a tankard of stout in the very rooms where
BRITISH Sir Francis Drake and Sir Walter Raleigh enjoyed their ale. Drake, in
fact, once wrote, "Next to mine own shippe, I do most love that old
'Shippe' in Exon." The pub dishes out casual bar fare, from curries to
sausage and mash, either in the bar or the more secluded upstairs restaurant (lunchtime only). ⊠ *St. Martin's La.* ☎ *01392/272040.*

WHERE TO STAY

For expanded hotel reviews, visit Fodors.com.

£££ ⬚ **ABode Exeter.** Claimed to be the first inn in England to be described as a
HOTEL "hotel," the 1769 Royal Clarence (the old name still appears outside) has
been transformed into a modern boutique hotel. **Pros:** superb location;
superior bedrooms are very comfortable. **Cons:** no lounge; some rooms
are small and viewless; no parking. ⊠ *Cathedral Yard* ☎ *01392/319955*
⊕ *www.abodehotels.co.uk* ⌦ *53 rooms* ♿ *In-room: a/c, Internet. In-
hotel: restaurants, bar, gym, business center* ⍨ *Breakfast.*

££££–£££££ ⬚ **Combe House.** Rolling parkland surrounds this luxurious Elizabethan
HOTEL manor house 16 mi east of Exeter. **Pros:** beautiful rural surroundings;
★ romantic ambience; attentive but informal staff. **Cons:** rather remote;
minimum stay on weekends. ⊠ *Off A30, Gittisham* ☎ *01404/540400*
⊕ *www.thishotel.com* ⌦ *13 rooms, 2 suites, 1 cottage* ♿ *In-room: no
a/c, Internet, Wi-Fi (some). In-hotel: restaurant, business center, some
pets allowed* ⍨ *Breakfast.*

££ ⬚ **Raffles.** A 10-minute walk from the center, this quirky B&B in a quiet
B&B/INN neighborhood makes an ideal base for a night or two in town. **Pros:** peaceful location; antique style. **Cons:** not very central for sights. ⊠ *11 Blackall
Rd.* ☎ *01392/270200* ⊕ *www.raffles-exeter.co.uk* ⌦ *7 rooms* ♿ *In-room:
no a/c, Wi-Fi (some). In-hotel: parking, some pets allowed* ⍨ *Breakfast.*

£££ ⬚ **St. Olaves Court Hotel.** In a hushed enclave in an unattractive part of
HOTEL Exeter's center, this hotel occupies a Georgian house with a walled garden. **Pros:** secluded location in city center; excellent food. **Cons:** some
rooms are noisy and viewless; some facilities are dated. ⊠ *Mary Arches
St.* ☎ *01392/217736* ⊕ *www.olaves.co.uk* ⌦ *13 rooms, 2 suites* ♿ *In-
room: no a/c, Wi-Fi (some). In-hotel: restaurant, bar, parking.*

££ ⬚ **White Hart.** Guests have been welcomed to this inn since the 15th
HOTEL century, and it is said that Oliver Cromwell stabled his horses here.
Pros: close to center; friendly service. **Cons:** public areas look tired; can
be noisy. ⊠ *66 South St.* ☎ *01392/279897* ⊕ *www.whitehartpubexeter.
co.uk* ⌦ *55 rooms* ♿ *In-room: no a/c, Wi-Fi. In-hotel: restaurant, bar,
parking* ⍨ *Breakfast.*

NIGHTLIFE AND THE ARTS

The **Exeter Festival of South West Food and Drink** (⊕ *www.exeterfood anddrinkfestival.co.uk*) showcases local producers, chefs, and their gastronomic specialties, taking place in Rougemont Gardens and Northernhay Gardens over three days in April or May.

Some of London's best companies often stage plays at the **Northcott Theatre** (⊠ *Stocker Rd.* ☎ *01392/493493* ⊕ *www.exeternorthcott.co.uk*).

SHOPPING

Many of Exeter's most interesting shops are along Gandy Street, off the main High Street drag, with several good food and clothes outlets. Exeter was the silver-assay office for the West Country, and the earliest example of Exeter silver (now a museum piece) dates from 1218; Victorian pieces are still sold. The Exeter assay mark is three castles.

Bruford's of Exeter (⊠ *17 The Guildhall Centre, Queen St.* ☎ *01392/254901* ⊕ *www.brufords.co.uk*) stocks antique jewelry and silver.

SPORTS AND THE OUTDOORS

Saddles and Paddles (⊠ *4 Kings Wharf, the Quay* ☎ *01392/424241* ⊕ *www.sadpad.com*) rents bikes, kayaks, and canoes and is handily placed for a 7-mi route along the scenic Exeter Canal Trail, which follows the River Exe and the Exeter Ship Canal.

TOPSHAM

4 mi southeast of Exeter on B3182.

This town full of narrow streets and hidden courtyards was once a bustling port, and it remains rich in 18th-century houses and inns.

GETTING HERE AND AROUND

Frequent bus service connects Topsham with Exeter; the village is also a stop for twice-hourly trains running between Exmouth and Exeter. Topsham is best negotiated on foot.

EXPLORING

Topsham Museum. Occupying a 17th-century Dutch-style merchant's house beside the river, this museum has period-furnished rooms and displays on local and maritime history. One room has memorabilia belonging to the late actress Vivien Leigh, who spent much time in the region. (⊠ *25 The Strand* ☎ *01392/873244* ⊒ *Free* ⊙ *Apr.–July, Sept., and Oct., Mon., Wed., and weekends 2–5; Aug., Mon., Wed., Thurs., and weekends 2–5.*

★ **A la Ronde.** The 16-sided, nearly circular A la Ronde was built in 1798 by two cousins inspired by the Church of San Vitale in Ravenna, Italy. Among the 18th- and 19th-century curiosities here is an elaborate display of feathers and shells. The house is 5 mi south of Topsham. (⊠ *Summer La. on A376 near Exmouth* ☎ *01395/265514* ⊕ *www.nationaltrust.org.uk* ⊒ *£7* ⊙ *Mid-Mar.–June, Sept., and Oct., Sat.–Wed. 11–5; July and Aug., Fri.–Wed. 11–5; Nov.–mid-Dec., guided tours only weekends noon–4.*

EN
ROUTE
The **Jurassic Coast** (⊕ *www.jurassiccoast.com*), from Exmouth to Stud-land Bay in Dorset, 95 mi to the east, has been designated a World Heritage Site because of the rich geological record of ancient rocks and fossils exposed here. The reddish, grass-topped cliffs of the region are punctuated by quiet seaside resorts such as Budleigh Salterton, Sid-mouth, and Seaton. *For more information, see Chapter 4, The South.*

TORQUAY

26 mi south of Topsham, 23 mi south of Exeter.

The most important resort area in South Devon, Torquay envisions itself as the center of the "English Riviera." Since 1968 the towns of Paignton and Torquay (pronounced tor-*kee*) have been amalgamated under the common moniker of Torbay. Torquay is the supposed site of the hotel in the popular British television comedy *Fawlty Towers* and was the home of mystery writer Agatha Christie. Fans should check out the exhibit devoted to Christie at the town museum. Torre Abbey holds one of Devon's best collections of 19th-century art.

The town has shed some of its old-fashioned image in recent years, with modern hotels, luxury villas, and apartments that climb the hillsides above the harbor. Still, Torquay is more like Brighton's maiden aunt in terms of energy and fizz, though a pubs-and-clubs culture makes an appearance on Friday and Saturday nights. Palm trees and other semitropical plants (a benefit of being near the warming Gulf Stream) flourish in the seafront gardens; the sea is a clear and intense blue.

GETTING HERE AND AROUND

Buses arrive near Torquay's harbor and the tourist office. The train station is close to Torre Abbey, but other points in town are best reached on local buses or by taxi. Drivers should take A38 and A380 from Exeter.

ESSENTIALS

Visitor Information Torquay (⊠ *Vaughan Parade* ☎ *0844/474–2233* ⊕ *www.englishriviera.co.uk*).

EXPLORING

Beaches. Torbay's beaches, a mixture of sand and coarse gravel, have won awards for their water quality and facilities, and can get very crowded in summer. Apart from the central Torre Abbey Sands, they are scattered around town, often separated by the crumbly red cliffs characteristic of the area. To sun and swim, head for Anstey's Cove, a favorite spot for scuba divers, with more beaches farther along at neighboring Babbacombe.

Cockington. Just a mile outside the heart of Torbay by bus or car lies this chocolate-box village with thatched cottages, a 14th-century forge, and the square-tower Church of St. George and St. Mary. Repair to the Old Mill for a café lunch or head to the Drum Inn, designed by Sir Edwin Lutyens to be an archetypal pub. On the village outskirts lies Cock-ington Court—a grand estate with crafts studios, shops, and an eatery. Cockington has, however, more than a touch of the faux: cottages that don't sell anything put up signs to this effect.

★ ☺ **Torre Abbey.** For lovers of fine things, Torquay's chief attraction is Torre Abbey, surrounded by parkland but close to the seafront. The abbey itself, founded in 1196, was razed in 1539, though you can still see traces of the old construction. The mansion that now occupies the site was the home of the Cary family for nearly 300 years, and it was later converted into a museum and art gallery. Artistic riches lie within the main building: marine paintings, Victorian sculptures, Pre-Raphaelite window designs, and drawings by William Blake. Children can have fun in the brass-rubbing center. ⊠ *King's Dr.* ☎ *01803/293593* ⊕ *www.torre-abbey.org.uk* 🎟 *£5.85* ⊙ *Mar.–Oct., daily 10–5; last admission at 4.*

FAWLTY TOWERS

John Cleese was inspired to write the TV series *Fawlty Towers* after he and the Monty Python team stayed at a hotel in Torquay while filming the series *Monty Python's Flying Circus* in the early 1970s. The "wonderfully rude" owner became the model for Basil Fawlty, the exasperated, accident-prone manager in the series. The owner died in 1981, but his hotel, the Gleneagles, is still going strong—though happily nothing like the chaotic Fawlty Towers.

5

WHERE TO EAT AND STAY

For expanded hotel reviews, visit Fodors.com.

£££££
MODERN BRITISH
★

✕ **The Elephant.** Set back from Torquay's harbor, this elegant eatery offers sophisticated but relaxed dining, either in the dining room upstairs with views over Tor Bay or in the less formal street-level brasserie. In the latter, you can tuck into such dishes as steamed Brixham mussels, pork fillet with sage polenta and shallots, and suet pudding. Upstairs, with its high-back chairs, antique lighting fixtures, and polished floorboards, has more-innovative concoctions, available on fixed-price menus, which may include local crab in chive mayonnaise with watermelon and fennel as a starter, and breast of duckling with beetroot and spiced honey jus for a main course. ⊠ *3–4 Beacon Terr.* ☎ *01803/200044* ⊕ *www.elephantrestaurant.co.uk* ⊙ *Closed Sun., Mon., and 2 wks early Jan; upstairs restaurant closed Oct.–mid-Apr. No lunch in upstairs restaurant.*

£££
SEAFOOD

✕ **Number 7 Fish Bistro.** Seafood fans can indulge their passion at this unpretentious, convivial spot near the harbor; wood floors, white walls, and plenty of maritime knickknacks set the mood. Fresh, locally caught fish is brought to your table for inspection before being simply but imaginatively prepared. The extensive menu offers dishes ranging from humble—but abundant and beautifully cooked—fish-and-chips to lobster and crab grilled with garlic and brandy. ⊠ *7 Beacon Terr.* ☎ *01803/295055* ⊕ *www.no7-fish.com* ⌲ *Reservations essential* ⊙ *Closed Sun. Oct.–June, Mon. Nov.–May. No lunch Sun.–Tues.*

£££–££££
HOTEL

🛏 **Barceló Torquay Imperial Hotel.** This enormous pile perched above the sea, overlooking Torbay, exudes slightly faded Victorian splendor. **Pros:** grand setting; great views. **Cons:** renovation overdue; erratic service. ⊠ *Park Hill Rd.* ☎ *01803/294301* ⊕ *www.barcelo-hotels.co.uk* ⤳ *139 rooms, 13 suites* ⚭ *In-room: no a/c, Internet, Wi-Fi (some). In-hotel: restaurants, bar, pools, tennis court, gym, spa, parking, some pets allowed* ❢⚬❢ *Breakfast.*

££
B&B/INN
Lanscombe House. Located in the postcard-pretty village of Cockington, a rural hideaway within Torquay, this family-run Victorian guesthouse offers spacious bedrooms with floral wallpaper and period furnishings, and a walled garden where you can try your hand at croquet. **Pros:** quiet, traditional setting; pleasant garden. **Cons:** touristy environment; car necessary for local sights. ⊠ *Cockington La., Cockington* ☎ *01803/606938* ⊕ *www.lanscombehouse.co.uk* ⬩ *8 rooms* ⬩ *In-room: no a/c, Wi-Fi (some). In-hotel: bar, parking* ⊗ *Closed Nov.–Easter* ⊙| *Breakfast.*

TOTNES

8 mi west of Torquay, 28 mi southwest of Exeter.

This busy market town on the banks of the River Dart preserves plenty of its medieval past, and on summer Tuesdays some shopkeepers dress in Elizabethan costume. Market days proper are Friday and Saturday, when the town's status as a center of alternative medicine and culture becomes especially clear, with an abundance of crafts stalls. The historic buildings include a guildhall and St. Mary's Church.

GETTING HERE AND AROUND

Totnes is on a regular fast bus route between Plymouth and Torbay, and is a stop for main-line trains between Plymouth and Exeter. Buses pull into the center, and the train station is a few minutes' walk north of the center. Drivers should take A38 and A385 from Plymouth or A385 from Torbay.

ESSENTIALS

Visitor Information Totnes (⊠ *The Town Mill, Coronation Rd.* ☎ *01803/863168* ⊕ *www.totnesinformation.co.uk*).

EXPLORING

Brixham. At the southern point of Tor Bay, Brixham has kept much of its original charm, partly because it is still an active fishing village. Much of the catch goes straight to restaurants as far away as London. Sample fish-and-chips on the quayside, where there is a (surprisingly petite) full-scale reproduction of the vessel on which Sir Francis Drake circumnavigated the world. The village is 10 mi southeast of Totnes by A385 and A3022.

South Devon Railway. Steam trains of this railway run through 7 mi of the wooded Dart Valley between Totnes and Buckfastleigh, on the edge of Dartmoor. There are special trips around Christmas. ⊠ *Near Totnes, Littlehempston* ☎ *0845/345–1420* ⊕ *www.southdevonrailway.co.uk* ⬩ *£10 round-trip* ⊙ *Late Mar.–Oct., daily; call for winter operation.*

Totnes Castle. You can climb up the hill in town to the ruins of this castle—a fine Norman motte and bailey design—for a wonderful view of Totnes and the River Dart. ⊠ *Castle St.* ☎ *01803/864406* ⊕ *www.english-heritage.org.uk* ⬩ *£3.40* ⊙ *Apr.–June and Sept., daily 10–5; July and Aug., daily 10–6; Oct., daily 10–4.*

WHERE TO STAY

For expanded hotel reviews, visit Fodors.com.

£££ HOTEL ☰ **Royal Seven Stars Hotel.** Conveniently located at the bottom of the main street, this centuries-old coaching inn has counted Daniel Defoe and Edward VII among its former guests. **Pros:** central location; friendly staff; spotless rooms. **Cons:** occasional noise; busy public areas. ⊠ *The Plains* ☎ *01803/862125* ⊕ *www.royalsevenstars.co.uk* ↩ *16 rooms* ⚭ *In-room: no a/c, Wi-Fi. In-hotel: restaurant, bars, parking, some pets allowed* ⎧⊘⎫ *Breakfast.*

NIGHTLIFE AND THE ARTS

★ One of the foremost arts centers of the West Country, **Dartington Hall** (⊠ *Off A384 and A385, Dartington* ☎ *01803/847070* ⊕ *www. dartington.org/arts*) lies 2 mi northwest of Totnes. There are concerts, a respected summer school of classical music with master classes and performances, film screenings, and exhibitions. The gardens, free year-round, are the setting for outdoor performances of Shakespeare in summer. There's a café, and you can stay overnight in rooms in the hall.

SHOPPING

Near Dartington Hall, 15 stores and two restaurants in and around an old cider press make up **Shops at Dartington** (⊠ *Shinners Bridge, Dartington* ☎ *01803/847500* ⊕ *www.dartington.org/shops*), open daily, which markets handmade Dartington crystal glassware, kitchenware, high-quality crafts, books, and toys from Devon and elsewhere. The farm shop sells fudge, ice cream, and cider, and Cranks is an excellent vegetarian restaurant.

DARTMOUTH

13 mi southeast of Totnes, 35 mi east of Plymouth, 35 mi south of Exeter, 5 mi southwest of Brixham.

An important port in the Middle Ages, Dartmouth is today a favorite haunt of yacht owners. Traces of its past include the old houses in Bayard's Cove near Lower Ferry, the 16th-century covered Butterwalk, and the two castles guarding the entrance to the River Dart. The Royal Naval College, built in 1905, dominates the town. A few miles south of Dartmouth on Start Bay there are a number of pretty beaches including Blackpool Sands, popular with families.

GETTING HERE AND AROUND

Frequent buses connect Dartmouth with Plymouth and Totnes. Drivers coming from the west should follow A381 and A3122. Approaching from the Torbay area via A3022 and A379, you can save mileage by using the passenger and car ferries crossing the Dart. Travelers on foot can take advantage of a vintage steam train service operating between Paignton and Kingswear, where there are ferry connections with Dartmouth. River ferries also link Dartmouth with Totnes.

ESSENTIALS

Visitor Information Dartmouth (⊠ *The Engine House, Mayors Ave.* ☎ *01803/834224* ⊕ *www.discoverdartmouth.com*).

EXPLORING

C **Dartmouth Steam Railway.** These lovingly restored trains chug along on tracks beside the River Dart between Paignton and Kingswear (across the river from Dartmouth). You can combine a train ride with a river excursion between Dartmouth and Totnes and a bus between Totnes and Paignton on a Round Robin ticket. ⊠ *5 Lower St.* ☎ *01803/555872* ⊕ *www.dartmouthrailriver.co.uk* ✆ *£10, Round Robin £21* ☉ *Apr.– Oct., call about daily departures.*

Greenway. A rewarding way to experience the River Dart is to join a cruise from Dartmouth's quay to visit Greenway, the 16th-century riverside home of the Gilbert family (Sir Humphrey Gilbert claimed Newfoundland on behalf of Elizabeth I), more famous today for its association with the crime writer Agatha Christie. Mrs. Mallowan (Christie's married name) made it her holiday home beginning in 1938 and the house displays collections of archaeological finds, china, and silver. The gorgeous gardens are thickly planted with magnolias, camellias, and rare shrubs, and richly endowed with panoramic views. Beware, however, that the grounds are steeply laid out, and those arriving by boat face a daunting uphill climb. Allow three hours to see everything; timed tickets for the house are given on arrival. **Greenway Cruises** (☎ *01803/882811* ⊕ *www.greenwayferry.co.uk*) runs ferries from Dartmouth; a round-trip ticket costs £8. Parking spaces here are restricted and must be booked in advance. Alternatively, ask at the tourist office about walking and cycling routes to reach the house (non-car-users get discounted entry). ⊠ *Galmpton* ☎ *01803/842382* ⊕ *www.nationaltrust. org.uk* ✆ *£8.75* ☉ *Early Mar.–Oct., Wed.–Sun. 10:30–5.*

WHERE TO EAT AND STAY

For expanded hotel reviews, visit Fodors.com.

£££ ✕**The Seahorse.** In a prime riverside location, this seafood restaurant
SEAFOOD epitomizes the region's ongoing food revolution. The knowledgeable staff will guide you through the Italian-inspired menu, which primarily depends on the day's catch: look for scallops with garlic and port, cuttlefish with polenta, and roasted skate with capers. The meat dishes are equally enticing. A few doors down, the same team operates Rockfish, a more casual venue for first-class fish-and-chips. ⊠ *5 S. Embankment* ☎ *01803/835147* ⊕ *www.seahorserestaurant.co.uk* ☉ *Closed Mon. No dinner Sun., no lunch Tues.*

£££–££££ 🛏 **Royal Castle Hotel.** This hotel has truly earned the name "Royal"—sev-
HOTEL eral monarchs have slept here. **Pros:** historical resonance; superb central location; great service. **Cons:** occasional noise; no elevator. ⊠ *11 The Quay* ☎ *01803/833033* ⊕ *www.royalcastle.co.uk* ✆ *25 rooms* ⚹ *Inroom: no a/c, Wi-Fi (some). In-hotel: restaurant, bars, parking, some pets allowed* ⊺⊙⊺ *Breakfast.*

The Thames Valley

WORD OF MOUTH

"Oxford's probably the most unsuitable city in Europe for hop-on, hop-off buses. Buses aren't allowed into most of the areas where there are interesting buildings. The official city walking tours are far, far better, and concentrate on the historic core."

—flanneruk

WELCOME TO THE THAMES VALLEY

TOP REASONS TO GO

★ **Windsor Castle:** The mystique of eight successive royal houses of the British monarchy permeates Windsor and its famous castle, where a fraction of the current Queen's vast wealth is displayed.

★ **Mapledurham House:** This is the house that inspired Toad Hall from *The Wind in the Willows;* you can picnic here on the grounds and drink in the views.

★ **Oxford:** While scholars' noses are buried in their books, you get to sightsee among Oxford University's ancient stone buildings and memorable museums.

★ **Blenheim Palace:** The only British historic home to be named a World Heritage Site has magnificent baroque architecture, stunning parkland, and remembrances of Winston Churchill.

★ **Boating on the Thames:** Life is slower on the river, and renting a boat or taking a cruise is an ideal way to see verdant riverside pastures and villages. Windsor, Marlow, Henley, and Oxford are good options.

1 **Windsor, Marlow, and Environs.** Gorgeous Windsor has its imposing and battlemented castle, stone cottages, and tea shops, and nearby Eton is also charming. The meadows and villages around Marlow and Henley are lovely in summer when the flowers are in bloom. Mapledurham House near Henley-on-Thames is an idyllic stop; you can take a boat here.

2 **Oxford.** Wonderfully walkable, this university town has one handsome, golden-stone building and museum after another to explore. Take a punt on the local waterways for a break. Oxford's good bars, pubs, and restaurants keep you going late at night as well.

3 **Oxfordshire and Environs.** So many grand manor houses, so little time: around the Thames Valley are many intriguing stops. Blenheim is a vast, ornate, extraordinary place that takes the better part of a day to see. Althorp, home of the late Princess Diana, seems almost small by comparison, although it's actually enormous.

GETTING ORIENTED

An ideal place to begin any exploration of the Thames Valley is the town of Windsor, about an hour's drive west of central London. From there you can follow the river to Marlow and to Henley-on-Thames, site of the famous regatta, and then make a counterclockwise sweep west to the area around Henley-on-Thames. To the north is Oxford, with its pubs, colleges, and museums; it can make a good base for exploring some of the area's charming towns and notable stately homes. If you're extending your itinerary, west of the region but nearby are both the Cotswolds and Stratford-upon-Avon.

6

BOATING ON THE THAMES

Whether you're drifting lazily along in your own boat or taking a sightseeing cruise past crucial points of English history, you will see the River Thames from a new and delightful vantage point when you're out on the water.

Views of tranquil countryside are one pleasure of boating on the Thames (above); riverside towns add interest (right, top); colorful boats in Henley (right, bottom).

"There is nothing—absolutely nothing—half so much worth doing as simply messing about in boats." So says the Water Rat in Kenneth Grahame's timeless children's novel *The Wind in the Willows*. So take Ratty's advice: it's hard to beat gliding peacefully on the river, water meadows on either side of you, and then tying up for a picnic or lunch at a riverside pub. You can just potter about in a rowboat for an hour or so, or hire a boat and organize your own itinerary a few days. If this doesn't appeal, go on a romantic lunch cruise or take one of the many organized trips. There are 125 mi of navigable water to explore, quieter nearer the source of the Thames in the Cotswolds, perhaps most picturesque between Pangbourne and Marlow, and busiest nearer London. Wherever you go, your pace of life will slow right down: boats are not allowed to travel above 5 mph.

CHOOSE A BOAT

Most boats rented by the hour accommodate four people. Motorboats are noisy, but you can opt for electric canoes or launches that have the benefit of canopies. Punts (flat-bottom wooden boats) require a strong arm so you can maneuver the long wooden pole and push the boat along. Narrowboats carried freight on canals but are now well equipped for pleasure trips. For information, see ⊕ www.visitthames.co.uk.

MESS ABOUT ON THE RIVER

The main hubs for hiring self-drive boats on the Thames are at Windsor, Henley-on-Thames, Oxford, and Lechlade. The cost varies from £15 an hour for a rowboat, £25 for an electric boat, £60 for half a day with a punt to £125 a day for a motor cruiser. A short break for four on a narrowboat from Oxfordshire Narrowboats ranges from around £200 for a few days to £1,000 in July.

Cotswold Boat Hire (✉ *Faringdon Rd, Lechlade* ☎ 01793/727083 ⊕ *www.cotswoldboat.co.uk*). **Hobbs of Henley** (✉ *Station Rd., Henley-on-Thames* ☎ 01491/572035 ⊕ *www.hobbs-of-henley.com*). **John Logie Motorboats** (✉ *Barry Ave, Windsor* ☎ 07774/ 983809). **Oxford River Cruises** (✉ *Folly Bridge, Oxford* ☎ 01865/304022 ⊕ *www.oxfordrivercruises.com*). **Oxfordshire Narrowboats** (✉ *Station Rd, Bicester* ☎ 01869/340348 ⊕ *www.oxfordshire-narrowboats.co.uk*).

PUSH THE BOAT OUT IN STYLE

Hire an Edwardian electric launch with your own skipper (£90 per hour) and hamper from the Compleat Angler in Marlow; take a vintage boat (from £165) or champagne cruise (£45) from Cliveden; climb aboard the gleaming Victorian steam launch *Nuneham* for afternoon tea (£46.50) or lunch (£55) cruises from Windsor on weekends in summer from French Brothers.

Compleat Angler (✉ *Marlow Bridge, Bisham Rd., Marlow* ☎ 0844/879–9128 ⊕ *www.macdonaldhotels.co.uk/compleatangler*). **Cliveden** (✉ *Off 404 near Maidenhead, Taplow* ☎ 01628/668561 ⊕ *www.clivedenhouse.co.uk*). **French Brothers** (✉ *The Promenade, Windsor* ☎ 01753/851900 ⊕ *www.boat-trips.co.uk*).

PICK AN ORGANIZED CRUISE

Windsor Castle, Runnymede, and Henley, where you can stop for the River and Rowing Museum, and Mapledurham, the inspiration for Toad Hall in *The Wind in the Willows*, all lie on the banks of the Thames. Thames River Cruise has outings to Mapledurham from Caversham on weekends. Salter's Steamers runs short round-trips out of Windsor, Henley, Oxford, and Marlow, and French Brothers *(see above)* offers round-trips from Windsor. Oxford River Cruises *(see above)* offers a one-hour cruise from Folly Bridge in Oxford and a longer trip (2.5 hours) up to Godstow.

Salter's Steamers (✉ *Folly Bridge, Oxford* ☎ 01865/243421 ⊕ *www.salterssteamers.co.uk*). **Thames River Cruise** (✉ *Bridge St., Caversham, Reading* ☎ 0118/948–1088 ⊕ *www.thamesrivercruise.co.uk*).

—by Kate Hughes

6

Updated by
Kate Hughes

Easy proximity to London made the Thames Valley enormously popular with the rich and powerful throughout the country's history. They built the lavish country estates and castles, including Windsor, that form the area's most popular tourist attractions today. Some of these, as well as Oxford and its university, are easy day trips from London. Consider exploring this stretch of the River Thames by boat, either jumping aboard a cruiser or getting behind the oars. Windsor, Henley, and Marlow all make good starting points.

Once an aquatic highway connecting London to the rest of England and the world, the Thames was critical to the power of the city when the sun never set on the British Empire. By the 18th century the Thames was one of the world's busiest water systems, declining in commercial importance only when the 20th century brought other means of transportation to the forefront. Traditionally, the area west of London is known as the Thames Valley, and the area to the east is called the Thames Gateway.

Anyone who wants to understand the mystique of the British monarchy should visit Windsor, home to the medieval and massive Windsor Castle. Farther upstream, the green quadrangles and graceful spires of Oxford are the hallmarks of one of the world's most famous universities. Within 10 mi of Oxford the storybook village of Woodstock and gracious Blenheim Palace, one of the grandest houses in England, are both well worth your time.

The railroads and motorways carrying traffic to and from London have turned much of this area into commuter territory, but you can still find timeless villages and miles of relaxing countryside. The stretches of the Thames near Marlow, Henley, and Henley-on-Thames are lovely, with rowing clubs, piers, and sturdy waterside cottages and villas. It all conspires to make the Thames Valley a wonderful find, even for experienced travelers.

THAMES VALLEY PLANNER

WHEN TO GO

High summer is lovely, but droves of visitors have the same effect on some travelers as bad weather. Consider visiting in late spring or early fall, when the weather is not too bad and the crowds have headed home. Book tickets and accommodations well in advance for Henley's Royal Regatta at the cusp of June and July; Ascot's Royal Meeting in mid-June; and, in late July and early August of 2012, the Olympic rowing and canoeing events at Eton Dorney near Windsor. Visiting at Eton and the Oxford colleges is much more restricted during term time (generally September to late March and late April to mid-July). Most stately homes are open March through September or October only—call in advance if you're planning an itinerary. Avoid any driving in the London area during afternoon and morning rush hours.

PLANNING YOUR TIME

The major towns of the Thames Valley are easy to visit on a day trip from London. A train to Windsor, for example, takes about an hour, and you can fully explore Windsor and its environs in a day. Base yourself in Oxford for a couple of days, though, if you want to make a thorough exploration of the town and the surrounding countryside. To visit the great houses and the rural castles you'll need to either rent a car or join an organized tour. Blenheim Palace and Waddesdon Manor require at least half a day to do them justice, as do Stowe Landscape Gardens and Woburn Abbey.

GETTING HERE AND AROUND

BUS TRAVEL

Oxford and the area's main towns are convenient by bus from London, as is Windsor (although trains are faster), but St. Albans is best reached by train.

You can travel between the major towns by local bus, but it's complicated and can require changing more than once. For information, contact Traveline. If you want to see more than one town in this area in a day, it would be best to rent a car or join a tour.

Contacts Arriva (☎ 0871/200–2233 ⊕ www.arriva.co.uk). **First** (☎ 01344/782222 ⊕ www.firstgroup.com). **Megabus** (⊕ www.megabus.co.uk). **Oxford Bus Company** (☎ 01865/785400 ⊕ www.oxfordbus.co.uk). **Reading Buses** (☎ 0118/959–4000 ⊕ www.reading-buses.co.uk). **Stagecoach Oxford Tube** (☎ 01865/772250 ⊕ www.oxfordtube.com). **Traveline** (☎ 0871/200–2233 ⊕ www.traveline.org.uk).

CAR TRAVEL

Most towns in this area are within a one- or two-hour drive of central London—except during rush hour, of course. Although the roads are good, this wealthy section of the commuter belt has heavy traffic, even on the secondary roads. Parking in towns can be a problem, so take advantage of public parking lots near the outskirts of town centers.

TRAIN TRAVEL

Trains to Oxford (one hour) and the region depart from London's Paddington Station. Trains bound for Ascot (50 minutes) leave Waterloo on the half hour. Trains to St. Albans (20 minutes) leave from St. Pancras Station. A number of lines, including Chiltern and First Great Western, serve the area; National Rail Enquiries has information.

Contacts National Rail Enquiries (☎ 0845/748–4950 ⊕ *www.nationalrail. co.uk*).

RESTAURANTS

Londoners weekend here, and where they go, stellar restaurants follow. Bray (near Windsor), Marlow, and Great Milton (near Oxford) claim some excellent tables. Simple pub food, as well as classic French cuisine, can be enjoyed in waterside settings at many restaurants beside the Thames. Even in towns away from the river, well-heeled commuters and Oxford professors support top-flight establishments. Reservations are often not required but are strongly recommended, especially on weekends.

HOTELS

From converted country houses to refurbished Elizabethan inns, the region's accommodations are rich in history and distinctive in appeal. Many hotels cultivate traditional gardens and retain a sense of the past with impressive collections of antiques. Book ahead, particularly in summer; you're competing for rooms with many Londoners in search of a getaway.

WHAT IT COSTS IN POUNDS					
	£	££	£££	££££	£££££
Restaurants	under £10	£10–£14	£15–£19	£20–£25	over £25
Hotels	under £70	£70–£120	£121–£160	£161–£220	over £220

Restaurant prices are per person for a main course or equivalent combination of smaller dishes at dinner excluding tax. Hotels prices reflect the rack rate of a standard double room for two people in high season, including 20% V.A.T. Check online for off-season rates and special deals or discounts.

VISITOR INFORMATION

Contacts River Thames Alliance (⊕ *www.visitthames.co.uk*) **Tourism Southeast** (☎ 0238/062–5400 ⊕ *www.visitsoutheastengland.com*)

WINDSOR, MARLOW, AND ENVIRONS

Windsor Castle is one of the jewels of the area known as Royal Windsor, but a journey around this section of the Thames has other classic pleasures. The town of Eton holds the eponymous public school, Ascot has its famous racecourse, and Cliveden is a stately home turned into a grand hotel.

The stretch of the Thames Valley from Marlow to Henley-on-Thames is enchanting. Walking through its fields and along its waterways, it's easy to see how it inspired Kenneth Grahame's classic 1908 children's book *The Wind in the Willows*. Whether by boat or on foot, you can discover some of the region's most delightful scenery. On each bank are fine wooded hills, with spacious homes, greenhouses, flower gardens, and neat lawns that stretch to the water's edge. Grahame wrote his book in Pangbourne, and his illustrator, E.H. Shepard, used the great house at Mapledurham as the model for Toad Hall. It all still has the power to inspire.

WINDSOR

21 mi west of London.

Only a small part of old Windsor—the settlement that grew up around the town's famous castle in the Middle Ages—has survived. The town isn't what it was in the time of Sir John Falstaff and the *Merry Wives of Windsor*, when it was famous for its convivial inns—in 1650, it had about 70 of them. Only a handful remain, with the others replaced, it seems, by endless cafés. Windsor can feel overrun by tourists in summer, but even so, romantics will appreciate cobbled Church Lane and noble Queen Charlotte Street, opposite the castle entrance.

GETTING HERE AND AROUND

Fast Green Line buses leave from the Colonnades opposite London's Victoria Coach Station every half hour for the 70-minute trip to Windsor. National Express and First Group have frequent services from Heathrow Airport's Terminal 5; the journey takes less than an hour. First Group also offers regional bus services to small towns and villages near Windsor.

Trains travel from London Waterloo every 30 minutes, or you can catch a more frequent train from Paddington and change at Slough. The trip takes less than an hour from Waterloo and around 30 minutes from Paddington. If you're driving, take the M4 from London; journey time is around an hour. Park in one of the public lots near the edge of the town center.

TOURS   Orchard Poyle Carriage Rides offers 30-minute (£40) and one-hour (£80) horse-drawn carriage rides around the historic district. Tours leave from the Harte & Garter Hotel in central Windsor and tour the town and Windsor Great Park. City Sightseeing has hop-on, hop-off tours of Windsor and Eton, though it's easy to explore compact Windsor on foot; the price is £8.

TIMING

Windsor is at its best in winter and fall when it's not as crowded with tour groups. In summer it can be uncomfortably packed. Queen Elizabeth is in residence when her banner flies above the palace—everybody perks up a bit when that happens.

ESSENTIALS

Bus Contacts First Group (☎ 0175/352–4144 ⊕ www.firstgroup.com). **Green Line** (☎ 0844/801–7261 ⊕ www.greenline.co.uk). **National Express** (☎ 0871/781–8181 ⊕ www.nationalexpress.com).

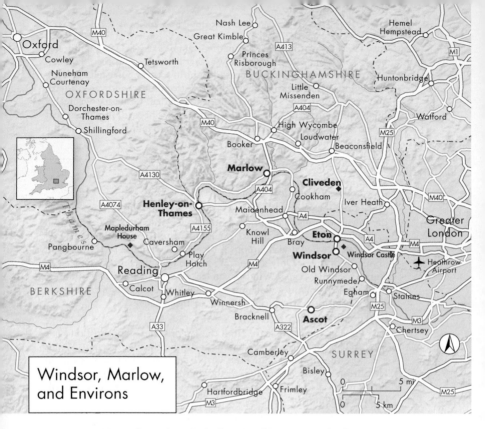

Windsor, Marlow,
and Environs

Tour Information City Sightseeing (☎ 01708/866000 ⊕ www.city-sightseeing.
com). Orchard Poyle Carriage Rides (☎ 01784/435983 ⊕ www.orchardpoyle.
co.uk).

Visitor Information Windsor (✉ Old Booking Hall, Windsor Royal Station,
Thames St. ☎ 01753/743900, 01753/743907 for accommodations ⊕ www.
windsor.gov.uk).

EXPLORING

Fodor's Choice
★

Windsor Castle. From William the Conqueror to Queen Victoria, the
kings and queens of England added towers and wings to this brooding,
imposing castle, visible for miles and now the largest inhabited castle
in the world. Despite the multiplicity of hands involved in its design,
the palace manages to have a unity of style and character. The most
impressive view of Windsor Castle is from the A332 road, coming into
town from the south. Admission includes an audio guide and, if you
wish, a guided tour of the castle precincts. Entrance lines can be long in
season and you're likely to spend at least half a day here, so come early.

William the Conqueror began work on the castle in the 11th century,
and Edward III modified and extended it in the mid-1300s. One of
Edward's largest contributions was the enormous and distinctive **Round
Tower.** Later, between 1824 and 1837, George IV transformed the still

essentially medieval castle into the fortified royal palace you see today. Most of England's kings and queens have demonstrated their undying attachment to the castle, the only royal residence in continuous use by the Royal Family since the Middle Ages.

As you enter the castle, **Henry VIII's gateway** leads uphill into the wide castle precincts, where you are free to wander. Across from the entrance is the exquisite **St. George's Chapel** (closed Sunday). Here lie 10 of the kings of England, including Henry VI, Charles I, and Henry VIII (Jane Seymour is the only one of his six wives buried here). One of the noblest buildings in England, the chapel was built in the Perpendicular style popular in the 15th and 16th centuries, with elegant stained-glass windows; a high, vaulted ceiling; and intricately carved choir stalls. The colorful heraldic banners of the Knights of the Garter—the oldest British Order of Chivalry, founded by Edward III in 1348—hang in the choir. The ceremony in which the knights are installed as members of the order has been held here with much pageantry for more than five centuries.

The **North Terrace** provides especially good views across the Thames to Eton College, perhaps the most famous of Britain's exclusive "public" boys' schools. From the terrace, you enter the **State Apartments,** which are open to the public most days, except when being used by the Queen (check in advance). Queen Elizabeth uses the castle far more than any of her predecessors did, as a sort of country weekend home.

■**TIP**➔ To see the castle come magnificently alive, check out the Changing of the Guard, which takes place at 11 am Monday to Saturday from April through July and on alternate weekdays and Saturday from August through March. Confirm the exact schedule before traveling to Windsor. When the Queen is in town, the guard and a regimental band parade through town to the castle gate; when she is away, a drum-and-fife band takes over.

Although a fire in 1992 gutted some of the State Apartments, hardly any works of art were lost. Phenomenal repair work brought to new life the **Grand Reception Room,** the **Green and Crimson Drawing Rooms,** and the **State and Octagonal Dining Rooms.** A green oak hammer-beam (a short horizontal roof beam that projects from the tops of walls for support) roof looms magnificently over the 600-year-old **St. George's Hall,** where the Queen gives state banquets. The State Apartments contain priceless furniture, including a magnificent Louis XVI bed and Gobelin tapestries; and paintings by Canaletto, Rubens, Van Dyck, Holbein, Dürer, and Bruegel. The tour's high points are the **Throne Room** and the **Waterloo Chamber,** where Sir Thomas Lawrence's portraits of Napoléon's victorious foes line the walls. You can also see arms and armor—look out for Henry VIII's ample suit. ■**TIP**➔ A visit between October and March also includes the Semi-State rooms, the private apartments of George IV, resplendent with gilded ceilings.

♻ **Queen Mary's Dolls' House,** on display to the left of the entrance to the State Apartments, is a perfect miniature Georgian palace-within-a-palace, created in 1923. Electric lights glow, the doors all have tiny little keys, and a miniature library holds Lilliputian-size books especially

Chef Heston Blumenthal and molecular gastronomy rule the roost at the Fat Duck in Bray, near Windsor: quail jelly and truffle toast, anyone?

written for the young queen by famous authors of the 1920s. Five cars, including a Daimler and Rolls-Royce, stand at the ready. In the adjacent corridor are exquisite French couturier–designed costumes made for the two Jumeau dolls presented to the Princesses Elizabeth and Margaret by France in 1938. ⊠ *Castle Hill* ☎ *020/7766–7304 tickets, 01753/831118 recorded information* ⊕ *www.royalcollection.org.uk* ⬚ *£16.50 for Precincts, State Apartments, Gallery, St. George's Chapel, and Dolls' House; £9 when State Apartments are closed* ☉ *Mar.–Oct., daily 9:45–5:15, last admission at 4; Nov.–Feb., daily 9:45–4:15, last admission at 3.*

Jubilee Garden. Created in 2002, Jubilee Garden has a stone bandstand used for concerts on summer Sunday afternoons. The garden begins at the main gates and extends to St. George's Gate on Castle Hill.

Windsor Great Park. The remains of an ancient royal hunting forest, this park stretches for some 5,000 acres south of Windsor Castle. Much of it is open to the public and can be seen by car or on foot, including its geographical focal points, the romantic 3-mi **Long Walk**, designed by Charles II to join castle and park, and **Virginia Water**, a 2-mi-long lake. A spectacular visitor center offers a good introduction to the surrounding landscape. The park contains one of Queen Victoria's most treasured residences, the sprawling white mansion called **Frogmore House.** It's only open for a few days in May and August. The main horticultural delight of Windsor Great Park, the exquisite **Savill Garden** (⊠ *Wick La., Englefield Green, Egham* ☎ *01784/435544* ⊕ *www.theroyallandscape.co.uk* ⬚ *£8.50 Mar.–Oct., £6.25 Nov.–Feb.* ☉ *Mar.–Oct., daily 10–6; Nov.–Feb., daily 10–4:30*), is about 4 mi from

Windsor Castle. It contains a lovely rose garden and a tremendous diversity of trees and shrubs. ✉ *Entrances on A329, A332, B383, and Wick La.* ☎ *01784/435544* ⊕ *www.theroyallandscape.co.uk or www.thecrownestate.co.uk/windor_great_park* ✉ *Free* ☉ *Daily dawn–dusk.*

WHERE TO EAT

Bray, a tiny village 6 mi outside Windsor, is known for its restaurants more than anything else.

£££££

MODERN BRITISH

Fodor's Choice

★

✗ **Fat Duck**. One of the top restaurants in the country, and ranked by some reviewers among the best in the world, this extraordinary, discreet (there's no sign; look for the duck-inspired implements hanging outside) Bray establishment packs in fans of hyper-creative, hyper-expensive cuisine. "Culinary alchemist" Heston Blumenthal is famed for bizarre taste combinations—scrambled-egg-and-bacon ice cream, for example—and the laboratory-like kitchen in which this advocate of molecular gastronomy creates his dishes. The 12 items on the menu (£180) include such dishes as snail porridge, salmon in licorice gel with vanilla mayonnaise, and whisky wine gums. Like the food, the interior blends traditional and contemporary elements—modern art, exposed-brick walls, and ancient wooden beams. Reserve a table two months in advance. ✉ *High St., Bray-on-Thames* ☎ *01628/580333* ⊕ *www.fatduck.co.uk* ✍ *Reservations essential* ☉ *Closed Mon. No dinner Sun.*

£££

MODERN BRITISH

✗ **Hinds Head**. Fat Duck's esteemed chef Heston Blumenthal owns this traditional pub across the road, where he sells less-extreme dishes at more-reasonable prices. The atmosphere and dress code are relaxed, and the look of the place is historic, with low beams, polished wood-panel walls, and brick fireplaces. A brilliant modern take on traditional English cuisine, the food includes salmon with hay-smoked pollock and Aberdeenshire rump steak with bone-marrow sauce and triple-cooked fries. Bar snacks and sandwiches are available for weekday lunches. ✉ *High St., Bray-on-Thames* ☎ *01628/626151* ⊕ *www.hindsheadbray.com* ☉ *No dinner Sun.*

££££

MODERN BRITISH

✗ **Strok's**. In Sir Christopher Wren's House Hotel—a mansion built in 1676 by the architect who designed St. Paul's Cathedral—Strok's offers an ever-changing Modern British menu and a Thames-side wooden terrace that swells with crowds in summer. Dishes may include terrine of smoked halibut followed by saddle of lamb with Jerusalem artichoke mousseline and sautéed celery. ✉ *Thames St. at Eton Bridge* ☎ *01753/861354* ⊕ *www.sirchristopherwren.co.uk.*

££

BRITISH

✗ **Two Brewers**. Locals congregate in the two small, low-ceiling rooms of this 17th-century pub, right by the gates of Windsor Great Park. Children under 18 are not welcome

6

TIME FOR A CUPPA

This is a tea-and-scones town, so having some in one of Windsor's many charming tearooms simply feels right. After taking in the castle and wandering the town's winding medieval lanes, a nice "cuppa," as the locals call it, is just perfect.

Crooked House of Windsor (✉ *51 High St.* ☎ *01753/857534* ⊕ *www.crooked-house.com*), with two tiny rooms in a 300-year-old house, is a traditional favorite for tea and plates of cakes and scones for £8. It's open daily until 5:30.

inside (though they can be served at a few outdoor tables in season), but adults will find a suitable collection of wine, espresso, and local beer, plus an excellent menu with such dishes as ham carved off the bone, wild rabbit burgers, and fish pie. Reservations are essential on Sunday, when the pub serves a traditional lunchtime roast. Friday and Saturday are tapas nights. ⊠ *34 Park St.* ☎ *01753/855426* ⊕ *www. twobrewerswindsor.co.uk* ☾ *No dinner Sun.*

WHERE TO STAY

For expanded hotel reviews, visit Fodors.com.

££
B&B/INN

🏠 **Alma Lodge.** This friendly little bed-and-breakfast in an early-Victorian house retains some of the original features, including ornate ceilings and ornamental fireplaces. **Pros:** very welcoming; beautiful fireplaces. **Cons:** few frills; can be too quiet for some. ⊠ *58 Alma Rd.* ☎ *01753/855620* ⊕ *www.almalodge.co.uk* ⮑ *4 rooms* ♿ *In-room: no a/c, Wi-Fi. In-hotel: parking* ⫯⊙⫯ *Breakfast.*

££
HOTEL
☾

🏠 **Langton House.** A former residence for representatives of the crown, this Victorian mansion on a quiet, leafy road is a 10-minute walk from Windsor Castle. **Pros:** soothing decor; family-friendly environment. **Cons:** not for those who prefer their privacy; a little out of town. ⊠ *46 Alma Rd.* ☎ *01753/858299* ⊕ *www.langtonhouse.co.uk* ⮑ *5 rooms* ♿ *In-room: no a/c, Wi-Fi. In-hotel: parking* ⫯⊙⫯ *Breakfast.*

£££–££££
HOTEL

🏠 **Mercure Castle Hotel.** You get an exceptional view of Windsor Castle's changing of the guard from this former coaching inn, parts of which date back to the 16th century. **Pros:** excellent location; wonderful afternoon tea. **Cons:** older rooms are small; you can get a good bump on the head from the low beams. ⊠ *High St.* ☎ *01753/851577* ⊕ *www. mercure.com* ⮑ *108 rooms, 4 suites* ♿ *In-room: a/c, Internet, Wi-Fi. In-hotel: restaurant, bar, parking* ⫯⊙⫯ *Breakfast.*

£££
HOTEL

🏠 **Oakley Court.** A romantic getaway on the Thames, this Victorian-era mansion stands on landscaped grounds 3 mi west of Windsor. **Pros:** stunning mansion; lots of pampering; friendly staff. **Cons:** many rooms in modern wings; river views cost more. ⊠ *Windsor Rd., Water Oakley* ☎ *01753/609988* ⊕ *www.oakleycourt.co.uk* ⮑ *106 rooms, 12 suites* ♿ *In-room: a/c, Wi-Fi. In-hotel: restaurant, bar, golf course, pool, tennis courts, gym, spa, parking* ⫯⊙⫯ *Breakfast.*

££
HOTEL

🏠 **Rainworth House.** Ducks come knocking at the door of this country house with an expansive green lawn 2 mi from Windsor. **Pros:** peaceful setting; tennis court. **Cons:** out of town. ⊠ *Oakley Green Rd.* ☎ *01753/856749* ⊕ *www.rainworthhouse.com* ⮑ *7 rooms* ♿ *In-room: no a/c, Wi-Fi. In-hotel: parking, tennis court* ⫯⊙⫯ *Breakfast.*

£££££
HOTEL
★

🏠 **Stoke Park.** On a 350-acre estate, Stoke Park's neoclassical grandeur can make Windsor Castle, visible in the distance, seem almost humble in comparison. **Pros:** luxurious rooms; sweeping grounds; wonderful for antiques lovers. **Cons:** not for those lukewarm about golf. ⊠ *Park Rd., Stoke Poges* ☎ *01753/717171* ⊕ *www.stokeparkclub.com* ⮑ *77 rooms* ♿ *In-room: a/c, Internet, Wi-Fi. In-hotel: restaurants, bars, golf course, pool, tennis courts, gym, spa* ⫯⊙⫯ *Breakfast.*

No t-shirts here: at Eton College, students wear the school's traditional shirts, coats, and pinstripe pants.

NIGHTLIFE AND THE ARTS

Windsor's **Theatre Royal** (✉ *Thames St.* ☎ *01753/853888*), where productions have been staged since 1910, is one of Britain's leading provincial theaters. It puts on plays and musicals year-round, including a pantomime for six weeks around Christmas.

Concerts, poetry readings, and children's events highlight the two-week **Windsor Festival** (☎ *01753/740121* ⊕ *www.windsorfestival.com*), held in September, with events occasionally taking place in the castle. A similar festival is held over a weekend in March.

SHOPPING

Check out Peascod Street, opposite the castle, for a good selection of independent stores selling gifts, jewelry, toiletries, chocolates, and more. **Windsor Royal Station** (✉ *5 Goswell Hill* ☎ *01753/797070*), in a Victorian-era train station, includes Jaeger, Viyella, and Hobbs.

SPORTS AND THE OUTDOORS

From Easter to September, **John Logie Motorboats** (✉ *Barry Ave.* ☎ *07774/983809*) rents motorboats and rowboats by the half hour and hour.

ETON

23 mi west of London.

Some observers may find it symbolic that almost opposite Windsor Castle—which embodies the continuity of the royal tradition—stands Eton, a school that for centuries has educated many future leaders of the country. With High Street, its single main street, leading from the river to the famous school, the old-fashioned town of Eton is much quieter than Windsor.

GETTING HERE AND AROUND

Eton is linked by a footbridge across the Thames to Windsor. Most visitors barely notice passing from one to the other.

EXPLORING

★ **Eton College.** The splendid Tudor-style buildings of Eton College, founded in 1440 by King Henry VI, border the north end of High Street; signs warn drivers of "Boys Crossing." During the college semesters, the schoolboys dress in their distinctive pin-striped trousers, swallow-tailed coats, and stiff collars (top hats have not been worn by the boys since the 1940s) to walk to class, and it's all terrifically photogenic. The Gothic **Chapel** rivals St. George's at Windsor in size and magnificence, and is both impressively austere and intimate. Beyond the cloisters are the school's playing fields where, according to the duke of Wellington, the Battle of Waterloo was really won, since so many of his officers had learned discipline and strategy during their school days there. The **Museum of Eton Life** has displays on the school's history. ⊠ *Main entrance, Brewhouse Yard* ☎ *01753/671177* ⊕ *www.etoncollege.com* 🖃 *£6.50* ⊙ *Guided tours at 2 and 3:15: mid-Mar.–mid-Apr. and July–early Sept., daily; mid-Apr.–June and mid-Sept.–early Oct., Wed. and Fri.–Sun.*

WHERE TO EAT AND STAY

For expanded hotel reviews, visit Fodors.com.

£££   ✕ **Gilbey's Bar & Restaurant.** Just over the bridge from Windsor, this
BRITISH   restaurant at the center of Eton's Antiques Row serves a fine, changing menu of imaginative fare, from pumpkin-seed pancakes with wild mushrooms and spinach to braised pork with haggis and star anise. There's a fixed-price lunch and early dinner menu for £17.50. Well-priced French wines are a specialty, as are the savories—think British cheeses, liver pâtés, and such—served with afternoon tea. The conservatory, with its colorful scattering of cushions, is a pleasant place to sit. ⊠ *82–83 High St.* ☎ *01753/854921* ⊕ *www.gilbeygroup.com.*

£££–££££   🛏 **Christopher Hotel.** This former coaching inn on Eton's main shopping
HOTEL   street has spacious rooms in the main building as well as in the courtyard mews. **Pros:** a nice mix of modern and historic; good restaurant. **Cons:** steep stairs; restaurant can get booked up early. ⊠ *110 High St.* ☎ *01753/852359* ⊕ *www.thechristopher.co.uk* ↗ *34 rooms* ⚐ *In-room: a/c (some), Internet, Wi-Fi. In-hotel: restaurant, bar, parking, some pets allowed* ¶◯¶ *Breakfast.*

SHOPPING

JaM (⊠ *81 High St.* ☎ *01753/622333*) has a lovely selection of ceramic and jewelry pieces by contemporary artists.

ASCOT

8 mi southwest of Windsor, 28 mi southwest of London.

The posh town of Ascot (pronounced *as*-cut) has for centuries been famous for horse racing and for style. Queen Anne chose to have a racecourse here, and the first race meeting took place in 1711. The impressive show of millinery for which the Royal Meeting, or Royal Ascot, is also known was immortalized in *My Fair Lady*, in which osprey feathers and black-and-white silk roses transformed Eliza Doolittle into a grand lady. Betting on the races at England's most prestigious course is as important as dressing up; it's all part of the fun.

GETTING HERE AND AROUND

If you're driving, leave M4 at Junction 6 and take A332. Trains from London leave Waterloo Station every half hour, and the journey takes 50 minutes. The racecourse is a seven-minute walk from the train station.

EXPLORING

Ascot Racecourse. The races run regularly throughout the year, and Royal Ascot takes place annually in mid-June. ■ TIP→ Purchase tickets well in advance. Tickets for Royal Ascot generally go on sale from the previous November. Prices range from £17 for standing room on the heath to £69 for seats in the stands. ☒ *A329* ☎ *0870/727–1234* ⊕ *www.ascot.co.uk*

WHERE TO STAY

For expanded hotel reviews, visit Fodors.com.

£££££
HOTEL
Fodor'sChoice
★

🖫 **Coworth Park.** Much imagination and thoughtful renovation has transformed this 18th-century mansion, set in 240 acres of parkland, into a playful and contemporary lodging. **Pros:** country-house atmosphere; attentive and friendly service; free activities for kids. **Cons:** bathrobes weigh you down. ☒ *Blacknest Rd.* ☎ *01344/876600* ⊕ *www. coworthpark.com* ⌖ *55 rooms, 15 suites* ⌕ *In-room: a/c, Wi-Fi. In-hotel: restaurant, bar, pool, gym, spa, some pets allowed* ⦿ *Breakfast.*

6

CLIVEDEN

8 mi northwest of Windsor, 16 mi north of Ascot, 26 mi west of London.

GETTING HERE AND AROUND

If you're driving, take the M4 to the A4, where brown signs lead you to the entrance off the A4094.

EXPLORING

Cliveden. Described by Queen Victoria as a "bijou of taste," Cliveden is a magnificent country mansion that has for more than 300 years lived up to its Georgian heritage as a bastion of aesthetic delights. The house, set in 376 acres of gardens and parkland above the River Thames, was rebuilt for the duke of Sutherland by Sir Charles Barry in 1861; the Astors, who purchased it in 1893, made it famous. In the 1920s and '30s the Cliveden Set met here at the strongly conservative (not to say fascist) salon presided over by Nancy Astor, an American who nevertheless was the first woman to sit in Parliament. The public can visit the spectacular grounds, including a yew tree maze, that run down to bluffs overlooking the Thames, as well as three rooms in the house. ☒ *Off A404, Taplow* ⌖ *Near Maidenhead* ☎ *01628/605069, 01494/755562 recorded information* ⊕ *www.nationaltrust.org.uk* 🎟 *Grounds £8.15, woodlands £3.60, house £1.50* ⊙ *Grounds mid-Feb.–Oct., daily 10–5.30; Nov. and Dec., daily 10–4. House Apr.–Oct., Thurs. and Sun. 3–5:30. Last admission 30 mins before closing.*

The horses at Royal Ascot are beautiful, and so is the formal attire of the memorably dressed spectators.

WHERE TO STAY

For expanded hotel reviews, visit Fodors.com.

££££–£££££
HOTEL

Cliveden. If you've ever wondered what it would feel like to be an Edwardian grandee, splurge on a stay at this stately home, one of Britain's grandest hotels. **Pros:** like stepping back in time; outstanding sense of luxury. **Cons:** can be rather stuffy; you might feel underdressed if you don't have designer duds. ⊠ *Off A404 near Maidenhead, Taplow* ☎ *01628/668561* ⊕ *www.clivedenhouse.co.uk* ⇗ *38 rooms, 1 cottage* ⟐ *In-room: a/c (some), Wi-Fi. In-hotel: restaurants, bar, pool, tennis courts, gym, spa, some pets allowed* ⟐ *Breakfast.*

OUTDOORS

Cliveden Boathouse (⊠ *Off A404 near Maidenhead, Taplow* ☎ *01628/ 668561*) at Cliveden hotel has two vintage boats and a vintage electric canoe that ply the Thames. The 45- minute champagne sunset cruise (most days April through September at 5 and 6) is the most affordable at £45 per person; you can rent the boats, too.

MARLOW

7 mi west of Cliveden, 15 mi northwest of Windsor.

Just inside the Buckinghamshire border, Marlow and the surrounding area overflow with Thames-side prettiness. The unusual suspension bridge was built in the 1830s by William Tierney Clark, architect of the bridge linking Buda and Pest. Marlow has a number of striking old buildings, particularly the privately owned Georgian houses along Peter and West streets. In 1817 the Romantic poet Percy Bysshe Shelley stayed with friends at 67 West Street and then bought **Albion House** on the same street. His second wife, Mary, completed her Gothic novel *Frankenstein* here. Ornate **Marlow Place,** on Station Road, dating from 1721 is reputedly the finest building.

Marlow hosts its own one-day regatta in mid-June. The town is a good base from which to join the **Thames Path** to Henley-on-Thames. On summer weekends, tourism can often overwhelm the town.

GETTING HERE AND AROUND
Hourly trains leave London from Paddington and involve a change at Maidenhead; the journey takes an hour. By car, leave M4 at Junction 8/9, following A404 and then A4155. From M40, join A404 at Junction 4.

ESSENTIALS
Visitor Information Marlow (⊠ *55 High St.* ☎ *01628/483597* ⊕ *www. visitbuckingamshire.org).*

EXPLORING
Swan-Upping. This traditional event, which dates back 800 years, takes place in Marlow during the third week of July. By bizarre ancient laws, the Queen owns the country's swans, so each year swan-markers in skiffs start from Sunbury-on-Thames, catching the new cygnets and marking their beaks to establish ownership. The Queen's Swan Marker, dressed in scarlet livery, presides over this colorful ceremony. ☎ *01628/ 523030.*

WHERE TO EAT AND STAY
For expanded hotel reviews, visit Fodors.com.

££££££
FRENCH

✗ **Vanilla Pod.** Discreet and intimate, this restaurant is a showcase for French-inspired cuisine by chef Michael Macdonald. Some of the best choices on the fixed-price menu are the ravioli of woodland mushrooms and steamed sea bass with fennel cream. For dessert, indulge in mango ravioli with ginger cream. The three-course £19.50 fixed-price lunch menu offers a fantastic bargain, and the seven-course *menu gourmand* for £50 is a tour de force. Vegetarians have a separate menu. ⊠ *31 West St.* ☎ *01628/898101* ⊕ *www.thevanillapod.co.uk* ⌁ *Reservations essential* ☉ *Closed Sun. and Mon.*

£££–££££
HOTEL

▥ **Macdonald Compleat Angler.** Although fishing aficionados consider this luxurious 17th-century Thames-side inn the ideal place to stay, the place is stylish enough to attract those with no interest in casting a line. **Pros:** gorgeous rooms; great views of the Thames. **Cons:** nonanglers might find dinner conversation dull; need a car to get around. ⊠ *Marlow Bridge, Bisham Rd.* ☎ *0844/879–9128* ⊕ *www.macdonaldhotels.co.uk/ compleatangler* ⇗ *61 rooms, 3 suites* ⌂ *In-room: a/c, Internet, Wi-Fi. In-hotel: restaurants, bars, some pets allowed* ⫿◯⫿ *Breakfast.*

6

HENLEY-ON-THAMES

7 mi southwest of Marlow, 8 mi north of Reading, 36 mi west of central London.

Henley's fame is based on one thing: rowing. The Henley Royal Regatta, held at the cusp of June and July on a long, straight stretch of the River Thames, has made the little riverside town famous throughout the world. Townspeople launched the Henley Regatta in 1839, initiating the Grand Challenge Cup, the most famous of its many trophies. The best amateur oarsmen from around the globe compete in crews of eight, four, or two, or as single scullers. For many spectators, however, the event is on par with Royal Ascot and Wimbledon.

The town is set in a broad valley between gentle hillsides. Henley's historic buildings, including half-timber Georgian cottages and inns (as well as one of Britain's oldest theaters, the Kenton), are all within a few minutes' walk. The river near Henley is alive with boats of every shape and size, from luxury cabin cruisers to tiny rowboats.

GETTING HERE AND AROUND

Frequent First Great Western trains depart for Henley from London Paddington; journey time is around an hour. If you're driving from London or from the west, leave M4 at Junction 8/9; follow A404(M) and then A4130 to Henley Bridge. From Marlow, Henley is a 7-mi drive southwest on A4155.

ESSENTIALS

Visitor Information Henley-on-Thames (✉ *Henley Town Hall, Market Pl.* ☎ *01491/578034* ⊕ *www.henley-on-thames.org*).

EXPLORING

★ **Mapledurham House.** This section of the Thames inspired Kenneth Grahame's 1908 *The Wind in the Willows*, which began as a bedtime story for Grahame's son Alastair while the family lived at Pangbourne. Some of E.F. Shepard's illustrations are of specific sites along the river—none more fabled than this Elizabethan mansion, bristling with tall chimneys, mullioned windows, and battlements. It became the inspiration for Shepard's vision of Toad Hall. Family portraits, magnificent oak staircases, and Tudor plasterwork ceilings abound. There's also a 15th-century working grain mill on the river. The house is 10 mi southwest of Henley-on-Thames. On summer weekends you can reach the house by a **Thames River Cruise** (☎ *0118/948–1088*

WALK THE CHILTERNS

Part of the Chiltern Hills is an **Area of Outstanding Beauty** (⊕ *www.chilternsaonb.org*), a nature reserve that stretches over 320 square mi, taking in chalk hills, valleys, forests, lakes, and pretty towns. Its springtime bluebell woods are famed, and its autumn colors are glorious. The distinctive chestnut-color birds soaring above you will be red kites. You'll likely drive in and out of the Chilterns as you explore, or you could walk part of the circular 124-mi Chiltern Way. A 13-mi section starts in Henley, runs north through the Hambleden Valley, and returns to Henley via the Assendons.

⊕ *www.thamesrivercruise.co.uk*) boat from Caversham Promenade in Reading. Departures are at 2 pm, and travel time is 45 minutes. ⊠ *Off A074, Mapledurham* ☎ *0118/948–1088* ⊕ *www.mapledurham. co.uk* ⊠ *House and mill £7; house only, £4.50; grounds and mill £3.50* ⊙ *Easter–Sept., weekends and national holidays Mon. 2–5:30; Oct., Sun. 2–5:30.*

River & Rowing Museum. This absorbing museum focuses not just on the history and sport of rowing but on the Thames and the town itself. One gallery interprets the Thames and its surroundings as the river flows from its source to the ocean; another explores Henley's history and the regatta. Galleries devoted to rowing display models, and actual boats, from a Saxon log boat to an elegant Victorian steam launch. A *Wind in the Willows* exhibit evokes the settings of the famous children's book. ⊠ *Mill Meadows* ☎ *01491/415600* ⊕ *www.rrm.co.uk* ⊠ *£8* ⊙ *May–Aug., daily 10–5:30; Sept.–Apr., daily 10–5.*

St. Mary's Church. With a 16th-century "checkerboard" tower, St. Mary's overlooks Henley's bridge on Hart Street. The adjacent, yellow-washed **Chantry House,** built in 1420, is one of England's few remaining merchant houses from the period. It is an unspoiled example of the rare timber-frame design, with upper floors jutting out. ⊠ *Hart St.* ☎ *01491/577340* ⊠ *Free* ⊙ *By appointment.*

WHERE TO EAT AND STAY
For expanded hotel reviews, visit Fodors.com.

£££ ✕**Crooked Billet.** It's worth negotiating the maze of lanes leading to this
MODERN BRITISH cozy 17th-century country pub, which likes to swap local homegrown produce for lunch. You could be eating slow-roasted pork belly with cider potatoes, or hare braised with red wine and juniper. Unusual British cheeses and homemade fudge and ice cream round off the meal. There's a garden for alfresco dining and regular music evenings. It's popular, so book ahead. Fixed-price lunches are another option. ⊠ *New-lands La., Stoke Row* ✛ *6 mi west of Henley-on-Thames, off B481* ☎ *01491/681048* ⊕ *www.thecrookedbillet.co.uk.*

££ ⊡**Falaise House.** The rooms in this B&B, a Georgian town house in the
B&B/INN center of Henley, are individually furnished in a soft and warm contemporary style that mixes antiques and modern pieces. **Pros:** family-run; great breakfasts; fluffy towels. **Cons:** on the main road; two-night minimum on summer weekends. ⊠ *37 Market Pl.* ☎ *01491/573388* ⊕ *www. falaisehouse.com* ⇝ *6 rooms* ⚬ *In-room: no a/c, Wi-Fi. In-hotel: some age restrictions* ⍾ *Breakfast.*

£££–££££ ⊡**Hotel du Vin.** A sprawling brick brewery near the river has been
HOTEL transformed into a distinctively modern architectural showplace. **Pros:** striking decor; lovely river views from upper floors; good for oenophiles. **Cons:** won't thrill traditionalists; a charge for parking. ⊠ *New St.* ☎ *01491/848400* ⊕ *www.hotelduvin.com* ⇝ *41 rooms, 2 suites* ⚬ *In-room: a/c, Internet, Wi-Fi. In-hotel: restaurant, bar* ⍾ *Breakfast.*

6

The rowing competitions at the Henley Royal Regatta draw spectators all along the river.

NIGHTLIFE AND THE ARTS

A floating stage and spectacular musical events from classical to folk, as well as some art activities, draw a dress-code-abiding crowd to the upscale **Henley Festival** (☎ 01491/843404 ⊕ www.henley-festival.co.uk) during the week after the regatta in July. Book tickets ahead.

SPORTS AND THE OUTDOORS

Henley Royal Regatta (☎ 01491/572153 ⊕ www.hrr.co.uk), a series of rowing competitions that draws participants from many countries, takes place in late June and early July each year. Large tents are erected along both sides of the unique straight stretch of river here known as Henley Reach, and every surrounding field becomes a parking lot. There is plenty of space on the public towpath from which to watch the early stages of the races. ■TIP→ If you want to attend, book a room months in advance. After all, 500,000 people turn out for the event.

OXFORD

With arguably the most famous university in the world, Oxford has been a center of learning since 1167, with only the Sorbonne preceding it. It doesn't take more than a day or two to explore its winding medieval streets, photograph its ivy-covered stone buildings and ancient churches and libraries, and even take a punt down one of its placid waterways. The town center is compact and walkable, and at its heart is Oxford University. Alumni of this prestigious institution include 48 Nobel Prize winners, 25 British prime ministers (including former Prime Minister Tony Blair), and 28 foreign presidents (including former U.S.

president Bill Clinton), along with poets, authors, and artists such as Percy Bysshe Shelley, Oscar Wilde, and W.H. Auden.

Oxford is 55 mi northwest of London, at the junction of the rivers Thames and Cherwell. The city is more interesting and more cosmopolitan than Cambridge, and although it's also bigger, its suburbs are not remotely interesting to visitors. The interest is all at the center, where the old town curls around the grand stone buildings, good restaurants, and historic pubs. Victorian writer Matthew Arnold described Oxford's "dreaming spires," a phrase that has become famous. Students rush past you on the sidewalks on the way to their exams, clad with marvelous antiquarian style in their requisite mortar caps, flowing dark gowns, stiff collars, and crisp white bow ties. ■TIP➜ Watch your back when crossing roads, as bikes are everywhere.

GETTING HERE AND AROUND

Megabus, Oxford Bus Company, and Stagecoach Oxford Tube all have buses traveling from London 24 hours a day; the trip takes about one hour and 40 or 50 minutes. In London, Megabus and Oxford Bus Company depart from Victoria Coach Station, and Oxford Tube has pickup points near Victoria Train Station and Marble Arch Underground stations. Oxford Bus Company also offers round-trip shuttle service from Gatwick (£32) every hour and Heathrow (£24) every half hour. Most of the companies have multiple stops in Oxford, with Gloucester Green, the final stop, being the most convenient for most travelers. You can easily traverse the town center on foot, but the Oxford Bus Company offers a one-day ticket (£6) and seven-day (£19) passes for unlimited travel in and around Oxford.

Trains to Oxford depart from London's Paddington Station for the one-hour trip. Oxford Station is just at the western edge of the historic town center on Botley Road.

To drive, take the M40 northwest from London. It's an hour's drive, except during rush hour when it can take twice as long. In-town parking is notoriously difficult, so use one of the five park-and-ride lots (free) and pay for the bus to the city. The Thornhill Park and Ride and the St. Clement's parking lot before the roundabout that leads to Magdalen Bridge are convenient for the M40.

TOURS The Oxford Tourist Information Centre has information on the many guided walking tours of the city. The best way of gaining access to the collegiate buildings is to take the two-hour university and city tour, which leaves the Tourist Information Centre daily at 10:45 and 2. City Sightseeing offers hop-on, hop-off bus tours (£12.50) with 20 stops around Oxford; your ticket, purchased from the driver, is good for 24 hours.

TIMING

You can explore major sights in town in a day or so, but it takes more than a day to spend an hour in each of the key museums and absorb the scene at the colleges. Some colleges are open only in the afternoons during university terms. When the undergraduates are in residence, access is often restricted to the chapels, dining rooms, and libraries, too, and

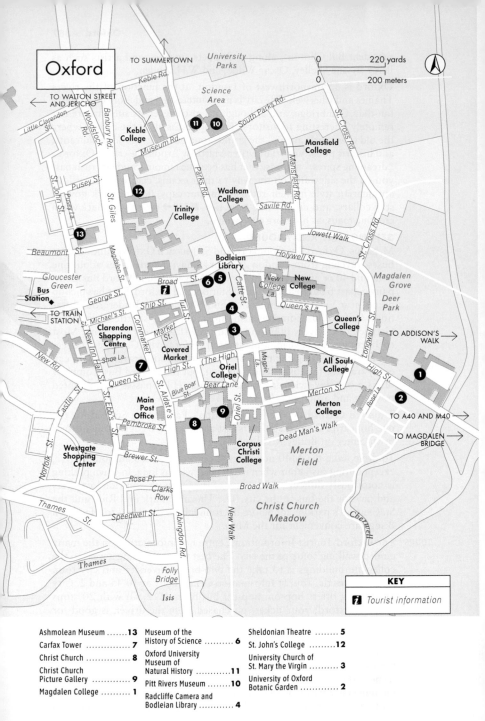

Oxford

TO SUMMERTOWN

University Parks

0   220 yards
0   200 meters

TO WALTON STREET
AND JERICHO

Little Clarendon St.

Keble Rd.

Woodstock Rd.

Banbury Rd.

Science Area

11 **10**

Mansfield College

St. Cross Rd.

Keble College

Museum Rd.

Parks Rd.

Pusey St.

12

St. Giles

Trinity College

Wadham College

Mansfield Rd.

Savile Rd.

Jowett Walk

St. John St.
Pusey La.

13

Magdalen St.

Beaumont St.

Bodleian Library

Holywell St.

St. Cross Rd.

Gloucester Green

Broad   St.

6 **5**

Catte St.

New College La.

New College

Magdalen Grove
Deer Park

Bus Station

George St.

i

Ship St.

Queen's La.

TO TRAIN STATION

St. Michael's St.

Cornmarket

Market St.

4

3

Queen's College

TO ADDISON'S WALK

New Rd.

Clarendon Shopping Centre

Covered Market

(The High)

All Souls College

Longwall St.

High St.

1

Shoe La.

7

High St.

Oriel College

Merton St.

Rose La.

2

New Inn Hall St.

Queen St.

St. Aldate's

Blue Boar St.

Bear Lane

Magpie La.

Oriel St.

Merton College

TO A40 AND M40

Castle St.

St. Ebbe's

Main Post Office

9

Dead Man's Walk

TO MAGDALEN BRIDGE

Norfolk St.

Pembroke St.

8

Corpus Christi College

Merton Field

Westgate Shopping Center

Brewer St.

Rose Pl.

Clarks Row

Broad Walk

Christ Church Meadow

Cherwell

Thames St.

Speedwell St.

Abingdon Rd.

New Walk

Thames

Folly Bridge

Isis

KEY

i Tourist information

you are requested to refrain from picnicking in the quadrangles. All are closed certain days during exams, usually from mid-April to late June.

ESSENTIALS

Bus Contacts Megabus (⊕ www.megabus.com). **Oxford Bus Company** (☎ 01865/785400 ⊕ www.oxfordbus.co.uk). **Stagecoach Oxford Tube** (☎ 01865/772250 ⊕ www.oxfordtube.com).

Visitor and Tour Information City Sightseeing (☎ 01865/790522 ⊕ www.citysightseeingoxford.com). **Oxford Tourist Information Centre** (✉ 15/16 Broad St. ☎ 01865/252200 ⊕ www.visitoxfordandoxfordshire.com).

EXPLORING

Oxford University is not one easily identifiable campus, but a sprawling mixture of 38 colleges scattered around the city center, each with its own distinctive identity and focus. Oxford students live and study at their own college, and also use the centralized resources of the overarching university. The individual colleges are deeply competitive. Most of the grounds and magnificent dining halls and chapels are open to visitors, though the opening times (displayed at the entrance gates) vary greatly.

The **city center** of Oxford is bordered by High Street, St. Giles, and Longwall Street. Most of Oxford University's most famous buildings are within this area. **Jericho,** the neighborhood where many students live, is west of St. Giles, just outside the city center. Its narrow streets are lined with lovely cottages. The area north of the center around Banbury and Marston Ferry roads is called **Summertown,** and the area east of the center, along St. Clement's Street, is known as **St. Clement's.**

TOP ATTRACTIONS

★ **Ashmolean Museum.** Britain's oldest public museum, completely redesigned in 2009, displays its rich and varied collections from the Neolithic to the present day over five floors. Innovative and spacious galleries on the theme of "Crossing Cultures, Crossing Time" explore connections between the priceless Egyptian, Greek, Roman, Chinese, and Indian artifacts, and also display a superb art collection. Among the highlights are drawings by Raphael, the shell-encrusted mantle of Powhatan (father of Pocahontas), the lantern belonging to Guy Fawkes, and the Alfred Jewel. This ancient piece features a large semiprecious stone set in gold carved with the words "*Aelfred mec heht gewyrcan,*" which translates from old English as "Alfred ordered me to be made." The piece dates from the reign of King Alfred the Great (ruled 871–899). ■TIP➔ There's too much to see in one visit. If you have time, dip in and out; it's free. The Ashmolean Dining Room, Oxford's first rooftop restaurant, is a good spot for refreshments. ✉ *Beaumont St.* ☎ *01865/278000* ⊕ *www.ashmolean.org* 🎟 *Free* ⊙ *Tues.–Sun. 10–6.*

Christ Church. Built in 1546, the college of Christ Church is referred to by its members as "The House." This is the site of Oxford's largest quadrangle, Tom Quad, named after the huge bell (6¼ tons) that hangs in the Christopher Wren–designed gate tower and rings 101 times at five past nine every evening in honor of the original number of Christ

Church scholars. The vaulted, 800-year-old chapel in one corner has been Oxford's cathedral since the time of Henry VIII. The college's medieval dining hall, re-created for the Harry Potter films, contains portraits of many famous alumni, including 13 of Britain's prime ministers. ■TIP➔ Plan carefully, as the dining hall is only open weekdays 10–11:45 and 2:15–4:30 and weekends 2:15–4:30. Lewis Carroll, author of *Alice in Wonderland,* was a teacher of mathematics here for many years; a shop opposite the meadows on St. Aldate's sells Alice paraphernalia. ⊠ *St. Aldate's* ☎ *01865/276492* ⊕ *www.chch.ox.ac.uk* ⊠ *£7.50* ⊗ *Mon.–Sat. 9–5, Sun. 2–5; last admission 30 mins before closing.*

Christ Church Picture Gallery. This connoisseur's delight in Canterbury Quadrangle exhibits works by the Italian masters as well as Hals, Rubens, and Van Dyck. Drawings in the 2,000-strong collection are shown on a changing basis. ⊠ *Oriel Sq.* ☎ *01865/276172* ⊕ *www.chch. ox.ac.uk* ⊠ *£3* ⊗ *May–Sept., Mon.–Sat. 10:30–5, Sun. 2–5; Oct.–Apr., Mon.–Sat. 10:30–1 and 2–4:30, Sun. 2–4:30.*

★ **Magdalen College.** Founded in 1458, with a handsome main quadrangle and a supremely monastic air, Magdalen (pronounced *maud*-lin) is one of the most impressive of Oxford's colleges and attracts its most artistic students. Alumni include such diverse people as P.G. Wodehouse, Edward Gibbon, and Oscar Wilde. The school's large, square tower is a famous local landmark. ■TIP➔ A stroll around the Deer Park and along Addison's Walk is a good way to appreciate the place. ⊠ *High St.* ☎ *01865/276000* ⊕ *www.magd.ox.ac.uk* ⊠ *£4.50* ⊗ *July–Sept., daily noon–6; Oct.–June, daily 1–6 or dusk.*

⟳ **Oxford University Museum of Natural History.** This highly decorative Victorian Gothic creation of cast iron and glass, more a cathedral than a museum, is worth a visit for its architecture alone. Among the eclectic collections of entomology, geology, mineralogy, and zoology are the towering skeleton of a *Tyrannosaurus rex* and casts of a dodo's foot and head. There's plenty for children to explore and touch. ⊠ *Parks Rd.* ☎ *01865/272950* ⊕ *www.oum.ox.ac.uk* ⊠ *Free* ⊗ *Daily 10–5.*

⟳ **Pitt Rivers Museum.** More than half a million archaeological and
Fodor's Choice anthropological items from around the globe, based on the collection
★ bequeathed by Lieutenant-General Augustus Henry Lane Fox Pitt Rivers in 1884, are crammed into glass cases and drawers. Items are organized thematically rather than geographically, an eccentric approach but actually thought-provoking. Labels are handwritten, and children are given flashlights to explore the farthest corners and spot the world's smallest dolly. Give yourself plenty of time to wander through the displays of shrunken heads, Hawaiian feather cloaks, and fearsome masks. Children will have a field day. ⊠ *S. Parks Rd.* ☎ *01865/270927* ⊕ *www. prm.ox.ac.uk* ⊠ *Free* ⊗ *Mon. noon–4:30, Tues.–Sun. 10–4:30.*

Radcliffe Camera and Bodleian Library. A vast library, the domed Radcliffe Camera is Oxford's most spectacular building, built in 1737–49 by James Gibbs in Italian baroque style. It's usually surrounded by tourists with cameras trained at its golden-stone walls. The Camera contains part of the Bodleian Library's enormous collection, which was begun in 1602. Much like the Library of Congress in the United States, the

Bodleian contains a copy of every book printed in Great Britain and grows by 4,000 books and leaflets a week. Tours reveal the magnificent Duke Humfrey's Library, which was the original chained library and completed in 1488. (The ancient tomes are dusted once a decade.) Guides will show you the spots used for Hogwarts School in the Harry Potter films. ■ TIP➜ Arrive early to secure tickets for the three to five daily tours, which are sold on a first-come, first-served basis (except for the extended tour, which can be prebooked). Audio tours, the only tours open to kids under 11, don't require reservations. Call ahead to confirm tour times. ⊠ *Broad St.* ☎ *01865/277224* ⊕ *www.www.bodleian. ox.ac.uk* ⊠ *Audio tour £2.50, standard tour £6.50, extended tour £13* ⊙ *Bodleian and Divinity School weekdays 9–5, Sat. 9–4:30, Sun. 11–5.*

St. John's College. One of Oxford's most attractive campuses, St. John's has seven quiet quadrangles surrounded by elaborately carved buildings. You enter the first through a low wooden door. This college dates to 1555, when Sir Thomas White, a merchant, founded it. His heart is buried in the chapel (by tradition, students curse as they walk over it). The Canterbury Quad represented the first example of Italian Renaissance architecture in Oxford, and the Front Quad includes the buildings of the old St. Bernard's Monastery. ⊠ *St. Giles* ☎ *01865/277300* ⊕ *www.sjc.ox.ac.uk* ⊠ *Free* ⊙ *Daily 1–dusk.*

QUICK BITES

Close to St. John's College, the **Eagle and Child pub** (⊠ *49 St. Giles* ☎ *01865/302925*) is a favorite not only for its good ales (try the local Old Hooky) and sense of history, but also for its literary associations. From the 1930s to the 1960s this was the meeting place of C.S. Lewis, J.R.R. Tolkien, and their circle of literary friends who called themselves the "Inklings."

Sheldonian Theatre. This fabulously ornate theater is where Oxford's impressive graduation ceremonies are held, conducted almost entirely in Latin. Dating to 1663, it was the first building designed by Sir Christopher Wren when he served as professor of astronomy. The D-shape auditorium has pillars, balconies, and an elaborately painted ceiling. The stone pillars outside are topped by 18 massive stone heads. ⊠ *Broad St.* ☎ *01865/277299* ⊕ *www.sheldon.ox.ac.uk* ⊠ *£2.50* ⊙ *Apr.–Oct., Mon.–Sat. 10–12:30 and 2–4:30; Nov.–Mar., Mon.–Sat. 10–12:30 and 2–3:30. Closed for 10 days at Christmas and Easter and for degree ceremonies and events.*

WORTH NOTING

Carfax Tower. Passing through Carfax, the center of Oxford and where four roads meet, you can spot this tower. It's all that remains of **St. Martin's Church,** where Shakespeare stood as godfather for William Davenant, who himself became a playwright. Every 15 minutes, little mechanical "quarter boys" mark the passage of time on the tower front. ■ TIP➜ Climb up the 99 steps of the dark stairwell for a good view of the town center. ⊠ *Corner of Queen St. and Cornmarket* ☎ *01865/792653* ⊠ *£2.20* ⊙ *Apr.–Sept., daily 10–5:30; Oct.–Mar., daily 10–dusk.*

Museum of the History of Science. The Ashmolean, the world's oldest public museum, was originally housed in this 1638 building, which now holds scientific and mathematical instruments, from astrolabes to quadrants to medical equipment. Here you'll find Lewis Carroll's camera box and the chalkboard Einstein used in a lecture on the theory of relativity. ⊠ *Broad St.* ☎ *01865/277280* ⊕ *www.mhs.ox.ac.uk* ⊠ *Free* ⊙ *Tues.–Fri. noon–5, Sat. 10–5, Sun. 2–5.*

Rousham Park House and Garden. Fifteen miles north of Oxford and wonderfully uncommercialized, Rousham has an expansive 18th-century English landscape park as well as the austere, gray Dormer family mansion, built in 1635. The design of gardener William Kent (1685–1748) is preserved almost unaltered in the groves, meadows, and walled gardens. Longhorn cattle add an exotic touch to the English landscape. The house is only open to groups that book in advance, but the remarkable gardens are open all year. ■**TIP→** There's no food, so bring a picnic and plenty of water. Children under 15 are not allowed, nor are dogs. ⊠ *Off B4030, Rousham* ✛ *Near Steeple Aston* ☎ *01869/347110* ⊕ *www. rousham.org* ⊠ *£5* ⊙ *Gardens daily 10–4:30.*

University Church of St. Mary the Virgin. Seven hundred years' worth of funeral monuments crowd this church, including the tombstone of Amy Robsart, the wife of Robert Dudley, Elizabeth I's favorite. One pillar marks the site of Thomas Cranmer's trial under Queen Mary for his marital machinations on behalf of Henry VIII. ■**TIP→** The top of the 14th-century tower has a panoramic view of the city's skyline. It's worth the 127 steps. The Vaults Café and Garden, a part of the church accessible from Radcliffe Square, serves generous portions. ⊠ *High St.* ☎ *01865/279111* ⊕ *www.university-church.ox.ac.uk* ⊠ *Church free, tower £3* ⊙ *Sept.–June, Mon.–Sat. 9–5, Sun. noon–5; July and Aug., Mon.–Sat. 9–6, Sun. noon–6; last admission to tower 30 mins before closing.*

University of Oxford Botanic Garden. Founded in 1621 as a healing garden, this is the oldest of its kind in the British Isles. Set on the river, the diverse garden displays 6,000 species ranging from lilies to citrus trees. There's a spacious walled garden and some unusual sights, including interesting rock and bog gardens. ⊠ *Rose La.* ☎ *01865/286690* ⊕ *www. botanic-garden.ox.ac.uk* ⊠ *£3.80* ⊙ *Mar., Apr., Sept., and Oct., daily 9–5; May–Aug., daily 9–6; Nov.–Feb., daily 9–4:30.*

WHERE TO EAT

The city's pubs offer more options for a quick bite.

£££
FRENCH
★
✕ **Brasserie Blanc.** Raymond Blanc's sophisticated brasserie in the Jericho neighborhood, a hipper cousin of Le Manoir aux Quat' Saisons in Great Milton, is one of the best places to eat in Oxford. Wood floors, pale walls, and large windows keep the restaurant open and airy. The changing menu always lists innovative, visually stunning adaptations of bourgeois French fare, sometimes with Mediterranean or Asian influences. Try the pork and leek sausages with chive-and-mustard butter sauce, and leave room for the seasonal French cheeses. The fixed-price lunch menu (£11.90) is a good value. ⊠ *71–72 Walton St.* ☎ *01865/510999* ⊕ *www.brasserieblanc.com.*

££
SEAFOOD
✕ **Fishers.** Everything is remarkably fresh at what is widely viewed as the city's best fish restaurant. Seafood is prepared with a European touch

and frequently comes with butter, cream, and other sauces: calamari with dill mayonnaise, for instance. Hot and cold shellfish platters are popular, as are the oysters with red wine and shallot vinegar. The interior has a casual nautical theme with wooden floors and tables, porthole windows, and red sails overhead. Bustling but relaxed, this place is often fully booked. Lunches are a very good value. ⊠ *36–37 St. Clement's St.* ☎ *01865/243003* ⊕ *www.fishers-restaurant.com.*

£££
BRITISH
✕ **Gee's.** With its glass-and-steel framework, this former florist's shop just north of the town center makes a charming conservatory dining room. The constantly changing menu features locally raised meats and vegetables in modern versions of traditional English dishes, such as pigeon breast with beetroot sauce and smoked eel with horseradish potatoes. Bakewell tart and lemon meringue pie make fine desserts. ⊠ *61 Banbury Rd.* ☎ *01865/553540* ⊕ *www.gees-restaurant.co.uk.*

£
CAFÉ
✕ **Grand Café.** Golden-hue tiles, towering columns, and antique marble tables make this café both architecturally impressive and an excellent spot for sandwiches, salads, or other light fare. It's packed with tourists and the service can be slow, but this is still a pretty spot for afternoon tea. At night it transforms into a popular cocktail bar. ⊠ *84 High St.* ☎ *01865/204463* ⊕ *www.thegrandcafe.co.uk.*

££
ITALIAN
✕ **Jamie's Italian.** Gazing through the window at the shelves of freshly made pasta, the basket of multicolor gourds, and the abundant hams hanging from the ceiling is enough to entice you into this buzzing eatery. Chef Jamie Oliver's mission is to re-create the best rustic Italian dishes, such as wild truffle tagliatelle or buffalo ricotta ravioli with creamy panna cotta. The lively crowd appreciates the results. There are no reservations, so get here early or be prepared to wait in line for a table. ⊠ *24–26 George St.* ☎ *01865/838383* ⊕ *www.jamiesitalian.com.*

£££££
FRENCH
Fodor's Choice
★
✕ **Le Manoir aux Quat' Saisons.** Standards are high at this 15th-century stone manor house, a hotel with a cooking school and one of the country's finest kitchens. Chef Raymond Blanc's epicurean touch shows at every turn. Decide from among such innovative French creations as duck breast with chicory, jasmine tea, and raisin sauce. Try one of the fixed-price menus ranging from £95 to £135; the set-price lunch can be a good deal at £62.50. A stroll through the hotel's herb and Japanese tea gardens is de rigueur. The pretty town of Great Milton is 7 mi southeast of Oxford. ⊠ *Church Rd., Great Milton* ☎ *01844/278881* ⊕ *www.manoir.com* ⌀ *Reservations essential.*

£££
BRITISH
✕ **Trout Inn.** More than a century ago, Lewis Carroll took three children on a Thames picnic. "We rowed up to Godstow, and had tea beside a haystack," he told a friend at Christ Church; "I told them the fairy tale of Alice's adventures in Wonderland." The haystacks are gone, but you can stop at the creeper-covered pub 2 mi north of the city center. Expect stone-baked pizzas, fresh pastas and salads, and a range of daily specials. This place is at the heart of the tourist trail and can get crowded; service may falter. ⊠ *195 Godstow Rd., Wolvercote* ☎ *01865/510930* ⊕ *www.thetroutoxford.co.uk.*

6

WHERE TO STAY

Oxford is pricey; for the cheapest lodging, contact the tourist information center for bed-and-breakfasts in locals' homes.

For expanded hotel reviews, visit Fodors.com.

££–£££
HOTEL

🖭 **Bath Place Hotel.** Down a cobbled alleyway off Holywell Street, these 17th-century weavers' cottages have been converted into a small hotel. **Pros:** quaint building and location; steeped in history. **Cons:** a few scuffed corners; fee for parking; some very steep stairs. ✉ *4–5 Bath Pl.* ☎ *01865/791812* ⊕ *www.bathplace.co.uk* 🛏 *15 rooms* 🚻 *In-room: no a/c, Wi-Fi. In-hotel: bar, parking, some pets allowed* ⑩ *Breakfast.*

££
B&B/INN

🖭 **Brown's Guest House.** At the southern edge of central Oxford, this redbrick Victorian house is a good bet in a town that has precious few affordable guesthouses. **Pros:** comfortable rooms; friendly owners. **Cons:** a long walk to the center; some rooms without private bathroom. ✉ *281 Iffley Rd.* ☎ *01865/246822* ⊕ *www.brownsguesthouse. co.uk* 🛏 *11 rooms, 7 with bath* 🚻 *In-room: no a/c, Wi-Fi. In-hotel: parking* ⑩ *Breakfast.*

££
B&B/INN

🖭 **Burlington House.** This Victorian guesthouse in Summertown, on the outskirts of Oxford, shows flair in its decoration, breakfasts, and attentive, helpful service. **Pros:** friendly; superior breakfasts; double-glazed windows throughout. **Cons:** 10-minute bus ride to the center; main road location. ✉ *374 Banbury Rd.* ☎ *01865/513513* ⊕ *www.burlington-house.co.uk* 🛏 *12 rooms* 🚻 *In-room: no a/c, Wi-Fi. In-hotel: parking, some age restrictions* ⑩ *Breakfast.*

£££–££££
HOTEL

🖭 **Macdonald Randolph.** A 19th-century neo-Gothic landmark, this hotel is ideally situated near both the Ashmolean and the Martyrs' Memorial. **Pros:** handy location; grand building. **Cons:** on a busy street; formality can be a bit daunting. ✉ *Beaumont St.* ☎ *0844/879–9132* ⊕ *www. macdonaldhotels.co.uk/randolph* 🛏 *151 rooms* 🚻 *In-room: a/c, Wi-Fi. In-hotel: restaurant, bar, spa, parking, some pets allowed* ⑩ *Breakfast.*

£££–££££
HOTEL

🖭 **Malmaison Oxford Castle.** Housed in what was a 19th-century prison, this high-concept boutique hotel remains true to its unusual history by showing off the original metal doors and exposed-brick walls. **Pros:** modern luxury; historic building; great bar and restaurant. **Cons:** prison life isn't for everyone; expensive parking. ✉ *3 Oxford Castle* ☎ *01865/248432* ⊕ *www.malmaison.com* 🛏 *86 rooms, 8 suites* 🚻 *In-room: a/c, Internet, Wi-Fi. In-hotel: restaurant, bar, parking* ⑩ *Breakfast.*

£–££
B&B/INN

🖭 **Newton House.** This handsome Victorian mansion, a five-minute walk from all of Oxford's action, is a sprawling, friendly place on three floors. **Pros:** great breakfasts; parking lot. **Cons:** on a main road; no elevator. ✉ *82 Abingdon Rd.* ☎ *01865/240561* ✐ *newton.house@btinternet. com* 🛏 *11 rooms, 10 with bath* 🚻 *In-room: no a/c, Internet, Wi-Fi. In-hotel: parking* ⑩ *Breakfast.*

££££–£££££
HOTEL

🖭 **Old Bank Hotel.** From its sleek lobby to the modern artwork on display and the sleek furnishings in the guest rooms, this stately converted bank offers contemporary style in a city that favors the traditional. **Pros:** excellent location; great city views. **Cons:** standard rooms can be small; breakfast costs extra. ✉ *91–94 High St.* ☎ *01865/799599*

⊕ *www.oldbank-hotel.co.uk* ⟿ *42 rooms* ⟨⟩ *In-room: a/c, Internet, Wi-Fi. In-hotel: restaurant, bar, parking* ⦿ *No meals.*

££££–£££££
HOTEL
★

🛏 **Old Parsonage.** A 17th-century gabled stone house in a small garden next to St. Giles Church, the Old Parsonage is a dignified retreat. **Pros:** interesting building; complimentary walking tours. **Cons:** pricey given what's on offer; some guest rooms on small side. ⊠ *1 Banbury Rd.* ☎ *01865/310210* ⊕ *www.oldparsonage-hotel.co.uk* ⟿ *26 rooms, 4 suites* ⟨⟩ *In-room: a/c (some), Wi-Fi. In-hotel: restaurant, bar, parking* ⦿ *No meals.*

£££
HOTEL

🛏 **Royal Oxford Hotel.** This efficiently run hotel, a few steps from the train station, has bright, light, and modern rooms with simple contemporary furniture. **Pros:** comfortable rooms; good for travelers. **Cons:** not many amenities. ⊠ *17 Park End St.* ☎ *01865/248432* ⊕ *www.royaloxfordhotel.co.uk* ⟿ *26 rooms* ⟨⟩ *In-room: a/c, Internet, Wi-Fi. In-hotel: restaurant* ⦿ *Breakfast.*

££
B&B/INN

🛏 **Tilbury Lodge.** What this modern house on the city's western outskirts lacks in history it makes up for in hospitality; the homemade tea and scones that greet you on arrival set just the right tone. **Pros:** quiet location; free Wi-Fi; well-appointed bathrooms. **Cons:** away from the attractions; not good for families with young kids. ⊠ *5 Tilbury La., Botley* ☎ *01865/862138* ⊕ *www.tilburylodge.com* ⟿ *9 rooms* ⟨⟩ *In-room: no a/c, Wi-Fi. In-hotel: parking, some age restrictions* ⦿ *Breakfast.*

NIGHTLIFE AND THE ARTS

NIGHTLIFE AND PUBS

Nightlife in Oxford centers around student life, which in turn focuses on the local pubs, though you may find a few surprises, too. The popular Jericho area, around Walton Street north of the old city walls and within walking distance of the center of town, has good restaurants and pubs.

Freud (⊠ *119 Walton St.* ☎ *01865/311171*), in a renovated neoclassical church, serves light meals and cocktails and offers nightly live jazz or funk.

The terrace at the **Head of the River** (⊠ *St Aldate's* ☎ *01865/721600*) by Folly Bridge is the perfect location for watching life on the river. You can also enjoy a pint in the clubby interior.

The **Kings Arms** (⊠ *40 Holywell St.* ☎ *01865/242369*), popular with students and fairly quiet during the day, carries excellent local brews as well as inexpensive pub grub.

Raoul's (⊠ *32 Walton St.* ☎ *01865/553732*) is a trendy cocktail bar in the equally trendy Jericho neighborhood.

Turf Tavern (⊠ *Bath Pl.* ☎ *01865/243235*), off Holywell Street, includes a higgledy-piggledy collection of little rooms and outdoor space good for a quiet drink and inexpensive pub food.

A LITTLE NIGHT MUSIC

Choral music at the city's churches is a calming way to spend the early evening. Drop by weekdays during term time at 6 pm at Magdalen (except Monday), New College (except Wednesday), or Christ Church to hear evensong.

6

The cozy **White Horse** (⊠ *52 Broad St.* ☎ *01865/728318*), one of the city's oldest pubs, serves real ales and traditional food all day.

THE ARTS

CONCERTS **Blenheim Palace** (⊠ *Woodstock* ☎ *01993/811091* ⊕ *www.blenheimpalace.com*) in nearby Woodstock puts on marvelous classical and pop concerts in summer, sometimes combined with fireworks displays.
■**TIP**➔ Pack a picnic of Champagne, Kent strawberries, and fresh Henley cream, and head out for an elegant summertime experience.

Music at Oxford (☎ *01865/305305* ⊕ *www.musicatoxford.com*), an acclaimed series of weekend classical concerts, takes place October through June in such surroundings as Christ Church Cathedral and Sir Christopher Wren's Sheldonian Theatre.

At **Oxford Coffee Concerts** (⊠ *Holywell Music Room, Holywell Rd.* ☎ *01865/305305* ⊕ *www.coffeeconcerts.co.uk*), a program of Sunday-morning chamber concerts, string quartets, piano trios, and soloists presents baroque and classical pieces in a 1748 hall.

THEATER **New Theatre** (⊠ *George St.* ☎ *0844/847–1585* ⊕ *www.newtheatreoxford.org.uk*), Oxford's main theater, stages popular shows, comedy acts, and musicals.

OFS Studio Theatre (⊠ *40 George St.* ☎ *0870/534–4444* ⊕ *www.ofsstudio.org.uk*), an alternative theater, showcases student productions, small-scale opera, and new musicals.

The **Oxford Playhouse** (⊠ *Beaumont St.* ☎ *01865/305305* ⊕ *www.oxfordplayhouse.com*) presents classic and modern dramas as well as dance and music performances.

SHOPPING

Small shops line High Street, Cornmarket, and Queen Street; the Clarendon and Westgate shopping centers, leading off them, have branches of several nationally known stores.

Alice's Shop (⊠ *83 St. Aldate's* ☎ *01865/723793*) sells all manner of *Alice in Wonderland* paraphernalia.

Bicester Village Outlet Centre (⊠ *Pringle Dr., Bicester* ☎ *01869/366266* ⊕ *www.bicestervillage.com*) has bargains from more than 120 top-name fashion and home-furnishing designers, including Ralph Lauren, Prada, and Versace. It's 15 mi northeast of Oxford, from where there are regular X5 and S5 buses to make the 30-minute journey.

Blackwell's (⊠ *48–51 Broad St.* ☎ *01865/792792*), family-owned and family-run since 1879, stocks an excellent selection of books.

★ The **Covered Market** (⊠ *Off High St.*) is a fine place for a cheap sandwich and a leisurely browse; the smell of pastries and coffee follows you from cobbler to jeweler to cheesemonger.

Scriptum Fine Stationery (⊠ *3 Turl St.* ☎ *01865/200042*) sells prints and secondhand books as well as leather-bound journals, quills, sealing wax, and handmade paper.

Shepherd & Woodward (⊠ *109–113 High St.* ☎ *01865/249491*), a traditional tailor, specializes in university gowns, ties, and scarves.

Continued on page 402

SEE YOU AT THE PUB

Pubs have been called "England's living rooms": more than just a bar or a place to drink, they are gathering places, conversation zones. A trip to a pub ranks high on most visitors' list of things to do, and that's not surprising: in many ways, pubs *are* England. You simply haven't experienced the country properly until you've been to one.

Pubs started appearing in the late 15th century, when whole communities would gather at the pub to meet and swap news. The very name—pub is short for "public house"—sums up their role. As towns grew into cities, the humble pub came to be seen as an antidote to the anonymity of modern life. "The local," as Brits call it, is a place to relax and socialize. It's not all about drinking. Pubs can be good places for lunch as well, and during the day they're often family environments, before giving way to a lively, adults-only crowd at night.

Despite all this, the pub industry faces changing times and tastes, and competition from modern entertainment. In early 2011 pubs were closing at the rate of around 40 per week. Although the adage about English town centers having a pub on every corner still just about rings true, times are tough—but still, the pub endures.

—by Jack Jewers

(Top) People gather outside the Market Porter pub at Borough Market in London, (bottom) Discovery Blonde Beer, Fuller's

CHOOSING A PUB

Pubs vary enormously, and that's a wonderful thing: in cities you may find splendid Victorian survivors; in the country there are ancient pubs with atmospheric wood beams and warm fires. Or perhaps a simple pub with a sincere welcome is all you need.

To find a pub, ask the locals: everyone knows the good ones. Otherwise, if a pub looks attractive and well kept, check it out. Telltale signs that it's probably not the best include banners advertising lagers and "2-for-1" deals, or TV sports channels. Some basic definitions are useful:

A **freehouse** is a pub that is not tied to a single brewery, which means it can sell as many varieties of beer and wine as it likes. **Chain pubs** affiliated with particular breweries are middle-of-the-road, inexpensive franchises that serve decent food and drink. Bass, Chef & Brewer, Courage, and Whitbread are chains; you will see their names on the pub's sign. The **gastropub** serves very high-quality food, but a pub with good food isn't necessarily a gastropub: the name implies culinary aspirations, and some expense. Another useful term is **"the local,"** shorthand for a favorite pub in your town. Everybody has a "local"—but the term is also used generally to refer to any pub that's good for cozy, convivial conversation.

CAN I TAKE MY KIDS TO THE PUB?

As pubs emphasize what's coming out of the kitchen rather than what's flowing out of the tap, whether to bring the kids has become a question. By law, patrons must be 18 in order to drink alcohol in a pub. Children 14 to 17 may enter a pub, but, children under 14 are not permitted in the bar area of a pub unless it has a "children's certficate" and they are accompanied by an adult. In general, however, some pubs have a section set aside for families—especially during the day. Check with the bartender. Some pubs actively encourage families and have play areas and a kid-friendly menu.

(Left) The Flask, Hampstead, London, (Right) Lamb and Flag pub, Covent Garden, London

PUB ETIQUETTE AND BASICS

Ordering: You order drinks from the bartender, known in England as the "barman" or "barmaid"—and pay up front. Don't be put off by a crowd at the bar. Never be impatient; wait as close to the bar as possible and they'll get to you. At most pubs you also order food from the bar and it is brought to you. Credit cards are common but likely require a minimum of £10.

Tipping: If you're only buying drinks, don't tip.

The round: If you're with friends, generally everyone takes turns buying drinks for the group. This is called a "round."

Smoking: Sorry, no: smoking has been banned since 2007.

Hours: In small towns, most pubs stick to the traditional hours of 11 am–11 pm (10:30 pm on Sunday), with the exception of Friday and Saturday nights. In large towns and cities, a few stay open past midnight, sometimes as late as 2 am. A handful are open 24 hours, but they are invariably dives.

Music: Some pubs have live music, usually local bands that vary in quality; but even big stars started out like this. You're not usually expected to pay.

Conversation: People don't generally get involved in a stranger's discussions, but for the best chance to chat with locals, hang out at the bar.

"Last order, please!": This is the traditional call of a landlord 20 minutes before closing, usually accompanied by a bell and a final rush to buy drinks. When 20 minutes is up, they'll yell "Time please!" Then you have a few minutes to finish up.

DO I HAVE TO DRINK?
It's fine to go to a pub and not drink alcohol. They're social places first, watering holes second. All pubs serve soft drinks and most have tea and coffee. Other popular alternatives include lime and soda water; orange juice and lemonade; and a St. Clement's, a mixture of orange and bitter lemon (like lemonade, only more sour).

WHEN TO GO?
The English take their drink seriously, and pubs are where people go to hang out and, sometimes, drink heavily. Unless you're checking a place out on recommendation (a good idea), you may want to pick a midweek night for your first pub experience. On Friday and Saturday nights, rowdy young drinkers can take over some pubs.

KNOW YOUR BEER

Whether you're ordering a pint (the usual quantity), or a "half" (for half-pint), you have plenty of options, including imported beers. You can discuss your choice with the barman and then turn to your neighbor, raise your glass, and utter that amiable toast, "Cheers!"

ALE. The most quintessentially English type of beer is brewed from barley and hops and usually served at cellar (cooler than room, but not chilled) temperature. The term *real ale* distinguishes the traditionally made product, containing only authentic ingredients and no carbonation, from mass-produced alternatives; real ales have a devoted following. The flavor of ales varies greatly, from nutty and bitter to light and sweet. *Common varieties include Adnams Broadside; Greene King I.P.A.; Newcastle Brown Ale; Well's Waggle Dance.*

Adnams Broadside

BITTER. This is the generic name given to bitter types of ale. They vary greatly in strength; bitters with the word "best" after their name are medium; "premium," "strong," or "special" are the strongest. *Bitters to try include London Pride and Courage Directors.*

LAGER. Often imported, these carbonated, light, pale beers are usually mass produced, and they're extremely popular. Lager is always served chilled. What Americans call beer, the British call lager, including beers from continental Europe.

London Pride

STOUT. Something of an acquired taste, stouts are dark beers made with roasted barley or malt. A stronger variant, known as porter, was popular in the 18th and 19th centuries, and a handful of bottled kinds are sold in pubs today. *Try Guinness (the Irish favorite) or Fuller's London Porter.*

WHEAT BEER. These beers brewed from wheat are mostly imported from Europe. They are often white in color and have a malty taste. *Try Hoegaarden or Erdinger.*

Fuller's London Porter

MORE CHOICES

CIDER. Made with apples, cider is like its American namesake—but alcoholic. Ciders can be sweet or dry. Try Magners or Strongbow.

LAGER TOPS. A pint of lager with a splash of lemonade on top is a lager top. A 50/50 version of the same thing is called a shandy; this traditional summer afternoon drink is worth a try.

SNAKEBITE. Half lager and half cider, snakebite is usually served with a splash of blackcurrant cordial as a "snakebite and black."

(top) Magners cider, (bottom) Newcastle Brown Ale

EATING AT THE PUB

(left) Traditional ploughman's lunch, (right) Steak and kidney pie

In the 1980s, the best you might hope for in a pub was a sandwich or a plate of cold meats and cheese. The gastropub revolution of the 1990s forced everybody to raise their game. Popular chain pubs, such as Wetherspoons and The Slug and Lettuce, offer decent meals, especially at lunchtime. Don't want a full meal? Most pubs will fix you a bowl of chips (thick-cut French fries) or other hot nibbles. If pubs have specials boards or a menu prominently displayed outside, they're probably worth a shot for a meal. Pub fare includes anything from lasagna to burgers, but look for these traditional favorites:

■ Savory pies, such as steak and ale or chicken and bacon. Just make sure they're homemade.

■ Bangers and mash (sausage links and mashed potato), especially if the sausages are "butchers" or "local."

■ Ploughman's lunch, with cheese, fruit, and crackers.

■ Fish and chips may seem like a good pick, but avoid it in city pubs because proper fish and chips shops are usually better. Near the coast, though, pubs that advertise local seafood may be the best place for fish and chips.

■ Sunday roasts, another culinary tradition, are hearty feasts—and pubs are usually the best places to sample them. Even pubs not noted for their food can pull out excellent roasts at Sunday lunchtime, and the best places get packed; you may need a reservation. The centerpiece is roast beef, chicken, pork, or lamb, served with roast potatoes and vegetables, covered in thin, rich, dark gravy. Each meat has its traditional accompaniment; Yorkshire pudding (light, fluffy batter, resembling a soufflé) and horseradish sauce with beef; mint jelly with lamb. It's a treat to savor.

PUB QUIZZES AND GAMES

Many pubs hold general knowledge quizzes on a weekday evening, and anybody can enter. It's usually a pound each, which goes into a pot as prize money. Quizzes are a fun and relaxed way to socialize with locals, although it helps to know some British sports and pop culture.

Video gaming machines are a common, if jarringly modern feature, in many pubs. They're the latest additions to a longtime custom, though. Traditional pub games include darts, dominoes, and chess—plus more arcane pastimes now found only rarely in the countryside. These include bar billiards, a miniature version of pool crossed with skittles; and Nine Men's Morris, similar to backgammon.

6

IN FOCUS SEE YOU AT THE PUB

If you're planning a picnic, **Taylors Deli** (⊠ *31 St. Giles* ☎ *01865/558853*) has everything you need. There are cakes and pastries, as well as first-rate teas and coffees.

The **University of Oxford Shop** (⊠ *106 High St.* ☎ *01865/247414*), run by the university, sells authorized clothing, ceramics, and tea towels, all emblazoned with university crests.

SPORTS AND THE OUTDOORS

BIKING

Bikes can be rented at **Summertown Cycles** (⊠ *200–202 Banbury Rd.* ☎ *01865/316885*), north of the city center in Summertown.

PUNTING

Fodor's Choice ★ You may choose, like many an Oxford student, to spend a summer afternoon **punting**, while dangling your champagne bottle in the water to keep it cool. Punts—shallow-bottom boats that are poled slowly up the river—can be rented in several places, including at the foot of the Magdalen Bridge.

From mid-March through mid-October, **Cherwell Boathouse** (⊠ *Bardwell Rd.* ☎ *01865/515978* ⊕ *www.cherwellboathouse.co.uk*), a punt station and stylish restaurant a mile north of the heart of Oxford, will rent you a boat and, if you wish, someone (usually an Oxford student) to punt it. Rentals are £14 per hour or £70 per day, and should be booked ahead.

At the St. Aldates Road end of Folly Bridge, **Salter's Steamers** (☎ *01865/243421* ⊕ *www.salterssteamers.co.uk*) rents out punts and skiffs (rowboats) for £20 per hour, £60 per half day, and £100 per day. Its chauffeured punts are £60 per hour, booked in advance.

SPECTATOR SPORTS

At the end of May, during Oxford's **Eights Week**, men and women rowers from the university's colleges compete to be "Head of the River." Because the river is too narrow for the eight-member teams to race side by side, the boats set off one behind another. Each boat tries to catch and bump the one in front.

Oxford University Cricket Club (⊕ *www.cricketinthe parks.org.uk*) competes against leading county teams in late spring and summer and also, each summer, the major foreign teams visiting Britain. In the middle of the sprawling University Parks—itself worthy of a walk—the club's playing field is truly lovely.

OXFORDSHIRE AND ENVIRONS

The River Thames takes on a new graciousness as it flows along the borders of Oxfordshire for 71 mi; each league it increases in size and importance. Three tributaries swell the river as it passes through the landscape: the Windrush, the Evenlode, and the Cherwell. Tucked among the hills and dales are one of England's impressive stately homes, an Edenic little town, and a former Rothschild estate. Closer to London in Hertfordshire is St. Albans, with its cathedral and Roman remains.

WOODSTOCK AND BLENHEIM PALACE

8 mi northwest of Oxford on A44.

★ Handsome 17th- and 18th-century houses line the trim streets of Woodstock, at the eastern edge of the Cotswolds. It's best known for nearby Blenheim Palace, and in summer, tour buses clog the village's ancient streets. On a quiet fall or spring afternoon, however, Woodstock is a sublime experience: a mellowed 18th-century church and town hall mark the central square, and along its backstreets you can find flower-bedecked houses and quiet lanes right out of a 19th-century etching.

GETTING HERE AND AROUND

The public bus service S3 runs (usually every half hour) between Oxford and Woodstock and costs £3.40 one way.

ESSENTIALS

Visitor Information Woodstock (✉ *Oxfordshire Museum, Park St.* ☎ *01993/813276*).

EXPLORING

Fodor's Choice **Blenheim Palace.** This grandiose palace was named a World Heritage
★ Site, the only historic house in Britain to receive the honor. Designed by Sir John Vanbrugh in the early 1700s in collaboration with Nicholas Hawksmoor, Blenheim was given by Queen Anne and the nation to General John Churchill, first duke of Marlborough, in gratitude for his military victories (including the Battle of Blenheim) against the French in 1704. The exterior is mind-boggling, with its huge columns, enormous pediments, and obelisks, all exemplars of English baroque. Inside, lavishness continues in monumental extremes: you can join a free guided tour or simply walk through on your own. In most of the opulent rooms family portraits look down at sumptuous furniture, elaborate carpets, fine Chinese porcelain, and immense pieces of silver. Exquisite tapestries in the three state rooms illustrate the first duke's victories. ■TIP➔ Book a tour of the current duke's private apartments for a more intimate view of ducal life. For some visitors, however, the most memorable room is the small, low-ceiling chamber where Winston Churchill (his father was the younger brother of the then-duke) was born in 1874; he is buried in nearby Bladon.

Sir Winston wrote that the unique beauty of Blenheim lay in its perfect adaptation of English parkland to an Italian palace. Its 2,000 acres of grounds, the work of Capability Brown, 18th-century England's best-known landscape gardener, are arguably the best example of the "cunningly natural" park in the country. Blenheim's formal gardens include notable water terraces and an Italian garden with a mermaid fountain, all built in the 1920s.

The Pleasure Gardens, reached by a miniature train that stops outside the palace's main entrance, contain some child-pleasers, including a butterfly house, a hedge maze, and giant chess set. The herb-and-lavender garden is also delightful. It's easy to spend half a day or more here. ✉ *Off A4095, Woodstock* ☎ *0870/060–2080* ⊕ *www.blenheimpalace. com* 🏛 *Palace, park, and gardens £19; park and gardens £11* ⊘ *Pal-*

6

*ace mid-Feb.–Oct., daily 10:30–4:45; Nov.–mid-Dec., Wed.–Fri. 10:30–
4:45; park mid-Feb.–mid-Dec., daily 9–4:45.*

WHERE TO EAT AND STAY

For expanded hotel reviews, visit Fodors.com.

££
BRITISH
Fodor's Choice
★

✕ **Falkland Arms.** It's worth detouring a bit for this supremely appealing pub on the village green at Great Tew, about 8 mi northwest of Woodstock. The bar has impressive malt whiskies, and mugs and jugs hang from the beams. The small restaurant chalks up a traditional but creative menu, which includes such items as roast pork with applesauce risotto and slow-cooked lamb shank. If you can't bear to leave, a spiral stone staircase leads to five guest rooms. ⊠ *19–21 The Green, Great Tew, Chipping Norton* ☎ *01608/683653* ⊕ *www.falklandarms.org.uk* ⌲ *Reservations essential.*

££
B&B/INN

⌂ **Blenheim Guest House & Tea Rooms.** Small and unassuming, this prettily furnished three-story guesthouse stands in the quiet village cul-de-sac that leads to the back gates of Blenheim Palace. **Pros:** handy tearoom downstairs; good location. **Cons:** no frills; floors are a bit creaky. ⊠ *17 Park St.* ☎ *01993/813814* ⊕ *www.theblenheim.com* ⌁ *6 rooms* ⌂ *In-room: no a/c, Wi-Fi* ⍾ *Breakfast.*

££££
HOTEL
★

⌂ **The Feathers.** Antiques-bedecked guest rooms fill this stylish inn, which was cobbled together from five 17th-century houses in the heart of town. **Pros:** beautiful modern decor; great food. **Cons:** pricey; two-night minimum stay on weekends in summer. ⊠ *Market St.* ☎ *01993/812291* ⊕ *www.feathers.co.uk* ⌁ *16 rooms, 5 suites* ⌂ *In-room: no a/c, Wi-Fi. In-hotel: restaurants, bar* ⍾ *Breakfast.*

£££–££££
HOTEL

⌂ **Macdonald Bear.** Tudoresque wood paneling, beamed ceilings, wattle-and-daub walls, and blazing fireplaces help define this as an archetypal English coaching inn. **Pros:** true luxury; historic house. **Cons:** creaky floors; you can knock yourself silly on those old beams. ⊠ *Park St.* ☎ *0844/879–9143* ⊕ *www.macdonaldhotels.co.uk/bear* ⌁ *46 rooms, 8 suites* ⌂ *In-room: a/c (some), Wi-Fi (some). In-hotel: restaurant, bar* ⍾ *Breakfast.*

EN
ROUTE

After taking in Blenheim Palace, stop by **Bladon,** 2 mi southeast of Woodstock on A4095 and 6 mi northwest of Oxford, to see the small, tree-lined churchyard that is the burial place of Sir Winston Churchill. His grave is all the more impressive for its simplicity.

DORCHESTER-ON-THAMES

16 mi southeast of Woodstock, 15 mi east of Uffington, 9 mi southeast of Oxford.

An important center in Saxon times, when it was the seat of a bishopric, Dorchester merits a visit chiefly because of its ancient abbey, but also because it's a charming little town. The main street, once a leg of the Roman road to Silchester, has timber houses, thatched cottages, ancient inns, and what must be the longest wisteria in the country (on the Old College building). Crossing the Thames at Day's Lock and turning left at Little Wittenham takes you on a bucolic and historic walk past the remains of the village's Iron Age settlements. The town is known for its alluring, but pricey, antiques shops.

Fountains and formal Italian gardens set off the monumental baroque pile that is Blenheim Palace.

GETTING HERE AND AROUND

Thames Travel runs a regular hourly bus service from Oxford (40 minutes). Drivers from Oxford should take A4074, which also connects with A4130 and Junction 8/9 of M4 for London.

ESSENTIALS

Bus Contacts Thames Travel (☎ *0871/200–2233* ⊕ *www.thames-travel.co.uk*).

EXPLORING

Dorchester Abbey. In addition to secluded cloisters and gardens, the abbey has a spacious church (1170) with a rare lead baptismal font from the Norman period and two unique items from the 14th century: a sculptured stone Tree of Jesse window and a wall painting of the Crucifixion with an unusual cross design. The great tower was rebuilt in 1602, but incorporated the old 14th-century spiral staircase. ⊠ *Off A4074* ☎ *01865/340007* ⊕ *www.dorchester-abbey.org.uk* ✉ *Free* ⊙ *May–Sept., daily 8:30–6; Oct.–Apr., daily 8:30–dusk, except during services.*

OFF THE BEATEN PATH **Vale of the White Horse.** Stretching up into the foothills of the Berkshire Downs between Swindon and Oxford is a wide fertile plain known as the Vale of the White Horse. Here, off B4507, cut into the turf of the hillside to expose the underlying chalk, is the 374-foot-long, 110-foot-high **figure of a white horse,** an important prehistoric site. Some historians believed that the figure might have been carved to commemorate King Alfred's victory over the Danes in 871, whereas others dated it to the Iron Age, around 750 BC. More-current research suggests that it is at least 1,000 years older, created at the beginning of the second millennium BC. **Uffington Castle,** above the horse, is a prehistoric fort. English Heritage maintains these sites. To reach the Vale of the White

Oxfordshire and Environs

Horse from Oxford (about 20 mi), follow A420, then B4508 to the village of Uffington.

WHERE TO STAY

For expanded hotel reviews, visit Fodors.com.

££
HOTEL

George Hotel. Overlooking Dorchester Abbey, this 500-year-old hotel was built as a coaching inn—there's an old coach parked outside—and it retains whitewashed walls, exposed beams, and fireplaces. **Pros:** lovely building; comfortable rooms. **Cons:** modern rooms are rather dull; small bathrooms. ⊠ *23 High St.* ☎ *01865/340404* ⊕ *www. thegeorgedorchester.co.uk* ⇆ *17 rooms* ♻ *In-room: no a/c, Wi-Fi. In-hotel: restaurant, bar, parking* ❍*Breakfast.*

AYLESBURY

22 mi east of Oxford, 46 mi northwest of London.

Aylesbury makes a good base for exploring the surrounding country-side, including stately homes and gardens. It's a pretty, historic place with a 13th-century church surrounded by small Tudor lanes and cottages. This market town has been associated with the Aylesbury duck since the 18th century, when flocks were walked 40 mi to the London markets. Kids will appreciate a visit to the Roald Dahl's Children's Gallery, which is open all year.

GETTING HERE AND AROUND

From London, Chiltern Railways runs frequent trains from Marylebone Station (one hour). The town is easily accessible from Oxford by Arriva Bus 280, which runs every 30 minutes; travel time is 80 minutes. If you're driving from Oxford, take A40 and A418. From London, follow M1 and A41 and allow 90 minutes.

ESSENTIALS

Visitor Information Aylesbury (⊠ *King's Head Passage, off Market Sq.* ☎ *01296/330559* ⊕ *www.visitbuckinghamshire.org*).

EXPLORING

★ **Stowe Landscape Gardens.** This superb example of a Georgian garden was created for the Temple family by the most famous gardeners of the 18th century. Capability Brown, Charles Bridgeman, and William Kent all worked on the land to create 980 acres of pleasing greenery in the valleys and meadows. More than 40 striking monuments, follies, and temples dot the landscape of lakes, rivers, and pleasant vistas; this is a historically important place, but it's not for those who want primarily a flower garden. Allow at least half a day if you want to explore the grounds. Stowe House, at its center, is now a fancy school with some magnificently restored rooms; it's closed to the public, apart from irregular tours throughout the year. The gardens are about 3 mi northwest of Buckingham, which is 14 mi northwest of Aylesbury. You enter the gardens through the New Inn, transformed into a visitor center, with period parlor rooms to explore. ⊠ *Stowe Ave. off 422 Buckingham–Banbury Rd., Buckingham* ☎ *01280/822850, 01280/818166 house tours* ⊕ *www.nationaltrust.org.uk* ⊠ *Gardens only, £8; house and gardens £12.70; house £5.20* ⊙ *Mar.–Oct., Wed.–Sun. and national holidays Mon. 10:30–5:30; Nov.–mid-Dec., Jan., and Feb., weekends 10:30–4; last admission 90 mins before closing.*

Fodor's Choice **Waddesdon Manor.** Many of the regal residences created by the Rothschild family throughout Europe are gone now, but this one is still a
★ vision of the 19th century at its most sumptuous. G.H. Destailleur built the house in the 1880s for Baron Ferdinand de Rothschild in the style of a 16th-century French château, with perfectly balanced turrets and towers and walls of creamy stone. Although intended only for summer weekend house parties, it was lovingly furnished over the course of 35 years with Savonnerie carpets, Sèvres porcelain, furniture made by Riesener for Marie Antoinette, and paintings by Guardi, Dutch and Flemish masters, Gainsborough, and Reynolds. An exquisite 21st-century broken porcelain chandelier by Ingo Maurer in the Blue Dining Room brings the collection up to date. The gardens are equally extraordinary, with an aviary, colorful plantings, and winding trails that provide panoramic views. In the restaurant you can dine on English or French fare and order excellent Rothschild wines if your pocketbook can take the hit. Admission prices are a bit higher on weekends. ■TIP→ Admission is by timed ticket; arrive early or book in advance. ⊠ *Waddesdon* ✢ *On A41 west of Aylesbury* ☎ *01296/653226* ⊕ *www.waddesdon.*

6

THAMES VALLEY HIKING AND BIKING

The Thames Valley is a great area to explore by foot or bike. It's not too hilly, and pubs and easily accessible lodgings dot the riverside and small towns. The Thames is almost completely free of car traffic along the Thames Path, a 184-mi national trail that traces the river from the London flood barrier to the river's source near Kemble, in the Cotswolds. The path follows towpaths from the outskirts of London, through Windsor, to Oxford and Lechlade.

Good public transportation in the region makes it possible to start and stop easily anywhere along this route. In summer the walking is fine and no special gear is necessary, but in winter the path often floods—check before you head out.

The Countryside Agency has been charting and preserving Thames paths for years, and through its Natural England branch it offers publications and information about them. For maps and advice, contact the National Trails Office or the Ramblers' Association. The Chiltern Conservation Board promotes walking in the Chilterns peaks.

Biking is perhaps the best way to see the Chilterns. Routes include the 99-mi Thames Valley Cycle Route from London to Oxford, the 200-mi Oxfordshire Cycleway around the county's countryside, and the 87-mi Ridgeway Path from Uffington that follows the Chilterns; the National Trails Office has information. The Thames Path also has plenty of biking opportunities.

CONTACTS AND RESOURCES

Chiltern Conservation Board (☎ 01844/355500 ⊕ www. chilternsaonb.org).

Chiltern Way (☎ 01494/771250 ⊕ www.chilternsociety.org.uk).

National Trails Office (☎ 01242/603307 ⊕ www. nationaltrail.co.uk).

Natural England (☎ 0845/600–3078 ⊕ www.naturalengland.org.uk).

Ramblers' Association (☎ 020/7339–8500 ⊕ www.ramblers. org.uk).

Sustrans (Thames Valley Cycle Route) (☎ 0845/113–0065 ⊕ www. sustrans.org.uk).

org.uk ⌨ *House and gardens £13.60–£15.40; gardens only, £5.90–£7.20* ⊗ *House Apr.–Oct., Wed.–Fri. noon–4, weekends and national holidays Mon. 11–4; gardens Jan.–Mar., weekends 10–5; Apr.–Oct., Wed.–Sun. and national holidays Mon. 10–5. Last admission 45 mins before closing.*

WHERE TO STAY

For expanded hotel reviews, visit Fodors.com.

££–£££
HOTEL
Five Arrows. Fancifully patterned brick chimneys and purple gables decorate this elegant building next to the main entrance of Waddesdon Manor. **Pros:** historic building; lovely grounds. **Cons:** some rooms are small; on a busy main road. ⌨ *High St., Waddesdon* ☎ *01296/651727* ⊕ *www.waddesdon.org.uk/five_arrows* ⇆ *9 rooms, 2 suites* ⚄ *In-room: no a/c, Internet, Wi-Fi. In-hotel: restaurant, bar* ⏹*Breakfast.*

££££–£££££
HOTEL
Hartwell House. Part Jacobean, part Georgian, this magnificent stately home offers formal luxury in an opulent country setting. **Pros:** truly

elegant; soothing views of the gardens. **Cons:** may feel too formal; spa is open to the public. ⊠ *Oxford Rd.* ☎ *01296/747444* ⊕ *www. hartwell-house.com* ↪ *33 rooms, 13 suites* ♿ *In-room: a/c (some), Internet, Wi-Fi. In-hotel: restaurant, bar, pool, tennis courts, gym, spa, some pets allowed, some age restrictions* ⦿| *Breakfast.*

ST. ALBANS

25 mi east of Aylesbury, 20 mi northwest of London.

A lively town on the outskirts of London, St. Albans is known for its historic cathedral, and it also holds reminders of a long history. From AD 50 to 440, the town then known as Verulamium was one of the largest communities in Roman Britain. You can explore this past in the Verulamium Museum and splendid Roman sites around the area. For activities more focused on the present, every Wednesday and Saturday the Market Place on St. Peter's Street bustles with traders from all over England, selling everything from fish and farm produce to clothing and CDs.

GETTING HERE AND AROUND

About 20 mi northwest of London, St. Albans is off the M1 and M25 highways, about an hour's drive from the center of the capital. First Capital Connect has frequent trains from London's St. Pancras Station, arriving in St. Albans in 30 minutes. The main train station is on Victoria Street, in the town center. A second station on the south side of town, St. Albans Abbey Station, serves smaller towns in the surrounding area. Bus service is slow and not direct. Central St. Albans is small and walkable. There's a local bus service, but you're unlikely to need it. Taxis usually line up outside the train stations.

ESSENTIALS

Train Contacts First Capital Connect (☎ *0845/026–4700* ⊕ *www. firstcapitalconnect.co.uk*)

Visitor Information St. Albans (⊠ *Town Hall, Market Pl.* ☎ *01727/864511* ⊕ *www.stalbans.gov.uk*).

EXPLORING

TOP ATTRACTIONS

Hatfield House. Six miles east of St. Albans, this outstanding brick mansion surrounded by lovely formal gardens stands as a testament to the magnificence of Jacobean architecture. Robert Cecil, earl of Salisbury, built Hatfield in 1611, and his descendants still live here. The interior, with its dark-wood paneling, lush tapestries, and Tudor and Jacobean portraits, reveals much about the era. Perhaps the finest feature is the ornate Grand Staircase, with carved wooden figures on the banisters. By the knot garden is the Old Palace (not open to the public), built around 1485, with its medieval brickwork. Wednesday is the only day on which the East Garden, with topiaries, parterres, and rare plants, is open. The **Elizabethan Banquet** (☎ *01707/262055* ⊕ *www.hatfield-house.co.uk*) is a hearty five-course dinner accompanied by kitschy entertainment from the minstrels. ⊠ *Off A1, Hatfield* ☎ *01707/287010* ⊕ *www.hatfield-house.co.uk* 🖾 *House, gardens, and park £12.50; East*

6

Gardens £4; park £3; farm and adventure playground £6 ☉ Easter–
Sept., mansion Wed.–Sun. and national holidays Mon. noon–5; West
Garden Wed.–Sun. and national holiday Mon. 11–5; East Garden Wed.
11–5, farm and adventure playground Tues.–Sun. and national holiday
Mon. 10–5:30.

St. Albans Cathedral. Medieval pilgrims came from far and wide to hilltop St. Albans Cathedral to honor its patron saint, a Roman soldier
turned Christian martyr. His red-canopied shrine beyond the choir
has a rare watching loft from where guard was kept over gifts that
were left. Construction of the mainly Norman cathedral began in the
early 11th century, but the nearly 300-foot-long nave dates from 1235;
the pillars are decorated with 13th- and 14th-century paintings. The
tower is even more historic, and contains bricks from ancient Roman
buildings. ⊠ Holywell Hill at High St. ☎ 01727/860780 ⊕ www.
stalbanscathedral.org.uk ✉ Donations welcome ☉ Daily 8:30–5:45;
guided tours weekdays 11:30 and 2:30, Sat. 11:30 and 2, Sun. 2:30.

Ⓒ **Verulamium Museum.** With exhibits on everything from Roman food to
burial practices, the Verulamium Museum, on the site of the ancient
Roman city, explores life 2,000 years ago. The re-created Roman rooms
contain colorful mosaics that are some of the finest in Britain. Every
second weekend of the month, "Roman soldiers" invade the museum
and demonstrate the skills of the Imperial Army. ⊠ St. Michael's St.
☎ 01727/751810 ⊕ www.stalbansmuseums.org.uk ✉ £3.80 ☉ Mon.–
Sat. 10–5:30, Sun. 2–5:30.

WORTH NOTING

Roman Theater. Imagination can take you back to AD 130 and to a
Roman stage drama as you walk around the ruins of the 2,000-seat
Roman Theater, one of the few in this country. Next to the theater are
the ruins of a Roman town house, shops, and a shrine. ⊠ Bluehouse Hill
☎ 01727/835035 ⊕ www.romantheatre.co.uk ✉ £2.50 ☉ Easter–Nov.,
daily 10–5; Dec.–Easter, daily 10–4.

Shaw's Corner. From 1906 to his death in 1950, the famed Irish playwright George Bernard Shaw lived in the small village of Ayot St. Lawrence, 9 mi northeast of St. Albans. Today his small Edwardian home,
Shaw's Corner, remains much as he left it. The most delightful curiosity
is his little writing hut in the garden, which can be turned to face the
sun. ⊠ Off Hill Farm La., Ayot St. Lawrence ☎ 01438/820307 ⊕ www.
nationaltrust.org.uk ✉ £5.80 ☉ House mid-Mar.–Oct., Wed.–Sun. 1–5;
gardens mid-Mar.–Oct., Wed.–Sun. noon–5:30.

Ⓒ **Verulamium Park.** Adjacent to the Verulamium Museum, this park contains the usual—playground, wading pool, lake—and the unusual—
Roman ruins that include part of the Roman town hall and a hypocaust,
a central-heating system. The hypocaust dates to AD 200 and included
one of the first heated floors in Britain. Brick columns supported the
floor, and hot air from a nearby fire was drawn underneath the floor
to keep bathers warm. ⊠ St. Michael's St. ☎ 01727/751810 ⊕ www.
stalbansmuseums.org.uk ✉ Free ☉ Hypocaust Apr.–Sept., Mon.–Sat.
10–4:30, Sun. 2–4:30; Oct.–Mar., Mon.–Sat. 10–3:45, Sun. 2–3:45.

WHERE TO EAT AND STAY

For expanded hotel reviews, visit Fodors.com.

£
BELGIAN
✕ **Waffle House.** Indoors or outside, you can enjoy a great budget meal at the 16th-century Kingsbury Watermill, near the Verulamium Museum. The organic flour for the high-quality, sweet-and-savory Belgian waffles comes from Redbournbury Watermill just north of the city. In the main dining room you can see the wheel churn the water of the River Ver. Waffle House is open 10 to 5 in winter, to 6 in summer. ⊠ *Kingsbury Watermill, St. Michael's St.* ☎ *01727/853502* ⊕ *www.wafflehouse.co.uk* ⊗ *No dinner.*

££
BRITISH
✕ **Ye Olde Fighting Cocks.** Some claim this is England's oldest pub, although that's a contentious category. Still, this octagonal building certainly looks suitably aged. The building was moved to this location in the 16th century, but the foundations date back to the 8th century. The small rooms with low ceilings make a cozy stop for a pint and good home-cooked food. Be prepared for crowds. ⊠ *16 Abbey Mill La.* ☎ *01727/869152* ⊕ *www.yeoldefightingcocks.co.uk.*

£££–££££
HOTEL
⊡ **St. Michael's Manor.** In the same family for three generations, this luxurious 16th-century manor house close to the center of St. Albans is set in 5 acres of sweeping grounds. **Pros:** spacious rooms; excellent food; beautiful grounds. **Cons:** a little too grand for some. ⊠ *Fishpool St.* ☎ *01727/864444* ⊕ *www.stmichaelsmanor.com* ⇆ *30 rooms* ⚙ *In-room: a/c (some), Internet, Wi-Fi. In-hotel: restaurant, bar* ⦿ *Breakfast.*

6

WOBURN ABBEY

30 mi west of St. Albans, 10 mi northeast of Aylesbury.

GETTING HERE AND AROUND

Woburn Abbey is easily accessible for drivers from M1 at Junction 12 or 13; a car is needed to tour the safari park. The nearest train station, Flitwick, is a 15-minute taxi ride away. Frequent trains connect with St. Albans and London's King's Cross and St. Pancras Station.

ESSENTIALS

Train Contacts First Capital Connect (☎ *0845/026–4700* ⊕ *www. firstcapitalconnect.co.uk*)

EXPLORING

☾ **Woburn Abbey.** Still the ancestral residence of the duke of Bedford, Woburn Abbey houses countless Grand Tour treasures and old master paintings, including 20 stunning Canalettos that practically wallpaper the crimson dining salon, and excellent works by Gainsborough and Reynolds. The Palladian mansion contains a number of etchings by Queen Victoria, who left them behind after she stayed here. Outside, 10 species of deer roam grounds that include an antiques center and small restaurant. The adjacent **Woburn Safari Park** is a popular drive-through wildlife experience, home to big game from around the world. Be prepared for fearless monkeys who like to go for a ride on your car. There are plenty of play areas, a boating lake with swan boats, and walkabouts with small animals such as wallabies. ■ **TIP→** Allow at least half a day for the safari park. If you buy a joint ticket with the house, you can use it on another day. ⊠ *A4012, off A5, Woburn* ☎ *01525/290333* *abbey, 01525/290407 safari park ⊕ www.woburn.co.uk ⊠ House, gardens, and deer park £12.95; safari park £19.95; house, gardens, deer park, and Safari Park £24.95 ⊙ House Apr.–Sept., daily 11–4; Mar. and Oct., weekends 11–4. Safari Park Mar.–Oct., daily 10–5; Nov. and Feb., weekends 11–3. Gardens and deer park daily 10–5.*

WHERE TO STAY

For expanded hotel reviews, visit Fodors.com.

££££–££££　⊡ **The Inn at Woburn.** In the center of Woburn, a small Georgian town,
HOTEL　　this former coaching inn has uncluttered and comfortable bedrooms.
Pros: close to Woburn Abbey; light-filled spaces. **Cons:** some decor lacks
character; small bathrooms. ⊠ *George St., Woburn* ☎ *01525/290441*
⊕ *www.theinnatwoburn.com* ↪ *50 rooms, 7 suites* ⌂ *In-room: no a/c,
no safe (some). In-hotel: restaurant, bar, some pets allowed.*

ALTHORP

5 mi west of Northampton, 27 mi northwest of Woburn Abbey.

GETTING HERE AND AROUND

Signposted at Junction 16 of M1, Althorp is most easily reached by car.
However, if you ask the driver, Stagecoach bus 96 from Northampton's
train station will drop you here (Monday through Saturday). Buses run
every two hours.

ESSENTIALS

Train Contacts Stagecoach (☎ *01604/676060* ⊕ *www.stagecoachbus.com*)

EXPLORING

Althorp. Deep in the heart of Northamptonshire sits the ancestral home
of the Spencers, the family of Diana, Princess of Wales. Here, on a tiny
island, is Diana's final resting place. Diana and her siblings found the
house too melancholy, calling it "Deadlock Hall." What the house does
have are rooms filled with Van Dycks, Reynoldses, and Rubenses—all
portraits of the Spencers going back 500 years—and an entry hall that
architectural historian Nikolaus Pevsner called "the noblest Georgian
room in the country." Two paintings by contemporary artist Mitch
Griffiths stand out in complete contrast. To these attractions, Diana's
brother, Earl Spencer, has added a visitor center devoted to her, which
includes her wedding dress, childhood memorabilia, and an exhibition
on her charitable work. A literary festival takes place here in mid-June.
On the west side of the estate park is Great Brington, the neighboring
village where the church of **St. Mary the Virgin** (⊙ *Daily noon–5*) holds
the Spencer family crypt; it's best reached by the designated path from
Althorp. ⊠ *Rugby Rd. off A428* ☎ *01604/770107* ⊕ *www.althorp.com*
⊠ *£13* ⊙ *July and Aug., daily 11–5.*

Bath and the Cotswolds

WORD OF MOUTH

"Bath is excellent for a long weekend. Just walking around the city is a top experience; add to that afternoon tea in the Pump Room (don't forget to try the water) or an afternoon at the Thermae Bath Spa taking the waters as the Romans did 2,000 years ago."

—tjhome1

WELCOME TO BATH AND THE COTSWOLDS

TOP REASONS TO GO

★ **Architecture of Bath:** Bath is perhaps the most perfectly preserved and harmonious English city. Close up, the elegance and finesse of the Georgian buildings is a perpetual delight.

★ **Cotswold pubs:** The classic pubs here press all the right buttons— low wooden beams, horse brasses, and inglenook fireplaces.

★ **Perfect villages:** With their stone cottages, Cotswold villages tend to be improbably picturesque; the hamlets of Upper and Lower Slaughter are among the most seductive.

★ **Hidcote Manor Gardens:** In a region rich with imaginative garden displays, Hidcote lays good claim to eminence. Exotic shrubs from around the world and the famous "garden rooms" are the highlights of this Arts and Crafts masterpiece.

★ **Roman Baths, Bath:** Take a break from the town's Georgian elegance and return to its Roman days on a tour around this ancient bath complex.

1 Bath and Environs. With the Roman Baths— renovated and embellished in the 18th century—and the late-medieval Bath Abbey at its heart, Bath is one of the country's comeliest towns. You can also soak up its thriving cultural scene and many shops.

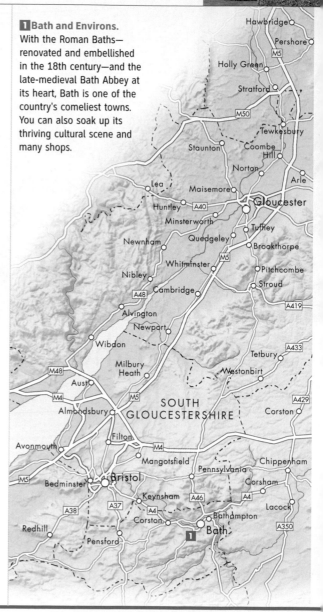

GETTING ORIENTED

The major points of interest in this part of west-central England—Bath, the Cotswolds, and Cheltenham—are one way to organize your explorations. Bath, in the southwestern corner of this area, is a good place to start; it can also be visited on a day trip out from London. The Cotswolds, about two hours northwest of London by car, cover some of southern England's most beautiful terrain. The area's small roads make for wonderful exploring, but public transportation is limited. To the west of the Cotswolds lies the city of Cheltenham, an elegant former spa town.

7

The Cotswolds. With a scattering of picture-postcard towns and villages separated by rolling dales and woods, the Cotswolds are rural England at its best. Nearby Cheltenham, a larger town, with busy cafés and shops, provides a lively counterpoint.

GREAT WALKS IN THE COTSWOLDS

The gentle Cotswolds countryside, designated an Area of Outstanding Natural Beauty, is threaded with more than 3,000 miles of pleasant walking routes that enable you to appreciate these upland tracts at their best. It's easy to plan an afternoon walk or a multiday exploration.

The Cotswold Way traverses some of England's loveliest countryside (above); stone bridge at Lower Slaughter (right, top); helpful sign on the Cotswold Way (right, below).

The Cotswolds are a delight: wherever you turn, green areas are dotted with church steeples and thatched roofs, restful on the eye and nourishing for the soul. To enjoy them to the fullest, do as the locals do—hoist on some walking shoes, don a sun (or rain) hat, and set forth on foot. Waymarked routes crisscross the area, and none of them is too challenging. No specialized equipment is required; it's healthy and it's free. Walks come in all lengths, but unless you decide to tackle one of the more ambitious regional trails, it may be easiest to pick a circular route. Just look for the "Public Footpath" and "Public Bridleway" signs, which indicate a right of way even when this passes through private property. Before you know it, you'll be opening gates and crossing stiles on the trails along with everyone else.

BRING WITH YOU

Light walking shoes or boots are essential, as are rain gear (even if it's sunny out), water, and a map. The walks may not be strenuous, but wear pants you won't mind getting dirty as you pass through fields. A fleece will keep the wind at bay, though in cold weather, bundle up as needed. Carry a day pack for anything you don't want to hold or wear; you'll need your hands free to open gates along the trails.

CHOOSE YOUR WALKING ROUTE

The most celebrated route traversing the area is the **Cotswold Way** (⊕ *www.nationaltrail.co.uk*), a 102-mi national trail that traces the escarpment marking the western edge of the Cotswolds, stretching north to south between Chipping Campden and Bath, and taking in Broadway, Winchcombe, and Painswick, among many other villages. The trail has incomparable views across the Severn Vale to the Malvern Hills and takes you through varied scenery: limestone grasslands crossed by dry-stone walls, beech woodlands, and stone-built villages with ancient churches. You can select a route rather than walk the entire trail, which might take 7–10 days.

The **Heart of England Way** (⊕ *www.heartofenglandway.org*) runs a linear route from Bourton-on-the-Water north to Lower Slaughter, Bourton-on-the-Hill, and Chipping Campden, and continues north into the West Midlands. It's 100 mi in all, and the Cotswold section takes in hills and deep wooded valleys.

The **Warden's Way** and the **Windrush Way** both run between Winchcombe and Bourton-on-the-Water, 14-mi rambles that link the Cotswold Way (at Winchcombe) with the Oxfordshire Way (at Bourton-on-the-Water). The Warden's Way takes you through Upper and Lower Slaughter; the Windrush Way follows the meandering River Windrush and touches on Sudeley Castle, but without entering any village en route. You could make a circular walk of this, one day per leg.

Part of the Cotswold Way can be incorporated into an easy circular route between **Chipping Campden and Broadway**, along mostly level ground but including the elevated viewpoints of Dover's Hill and Broadway Tower. The circular route adds up to around 12 mi.

One of the most scenic Cotswolds walks explores the **Coln Valley**, a 6-mile (10-km) circular route beginning and ending at Bibury. The path follows the banks of the lovely River Coln for part of the way, through meadows and woodland.

RESOURCES

Tourist information centers carry local walking maps and publications describing longer trails. The most useful map for walkers in the area is Ordnance Survey Explorer OL45 (1:25,000). The **National Trail** website (⊕ *www.nationaltrail.co.uk*) outlines circular walks of 2–6 mi that can be made from the Cotswold Way. **Cotswold Voluntary Wardens** conduct free guided walks of 2–10 mi with informative commentary (no booking needed). *The Cotswold Lion* free newspaper at tourist offices lists these, or look on ⊕ *www.cotswoldsaonb. org.uk*, the Web site of the Cotswolds Area of Outstanding National Beauty. **Walk the Landscape** (⊕ *www.walkthelandscape. co.uk*) organizes guided and self-guided hikes with luggage transfer and accommodation. **Compass Holidays** (⊕ *www. compass-holidays.com*) arranges short walking trips in the Cotswolds, and **Sherpa Van** (⊕ *www. sherpavan.com*) offers a luggage transfer and accommodation booking service.

7

Updated
by Robert
Andrews

The rolling uplands of the Cotswolds represent the quintes-
sence of rural England, as immortalized in countless books,
paintings, and films. In eloquently named settlements from
Bourton-on-the-Water to Stow-on-the-Wold, you can taste the
glories of the old English village—its stone slate roofs, low-
ceiling rooms, and gardens; the atmosphere is as thick as
honey, and equally as sweet. On the edge of the Cotswolds
is Bath, among the most alluring small cities in Europe.

The blissfully unspoiled Cotswolds, deservedly popular with visitors and
convenient to London, occupies much of the county of Gloucestershire, in
west-central England. It also takes in slices of neighboring Oxfordshire,
Worcestershire, and Somerset. Together these make up a sweep of land
stretching from close to Stratford-upon-Avon and Shakespeare Country
in the north almost as far as the Bristol Channel in the south. On the edge
of the area, two historic towns have absorbed, rather than compromised,
the flavor of the Cotswolds: Bath, offering up "18th-century England
in all its urban glory," to use a phrase by writer Nigel Nicolson, and
Regency-era Cheltenham, like Bath, a spa town with elegant architecture.

Bath rightly boasts of being the best-planned town in England. Although
the Romans founded the city when they discovered here the only true
hot springs in England, its popularity during the 17th and 18th centuries
luckily coincided with one of Britain's most creative architectural eras.
Today people come to walk in the footsteps of Jane Austen, visit Bath
Abbey and the excavated Roman baths, shop in an elegant setting, or
have a modern spa experience at the stunning Thermae spa.

North of Bath are the Cotswolds—a region that more than one writer
has called the very soul of England. This idyllic region, which from
medieval times grew prosperous on the wool trade, remains a vision of
rural England. Here are time-defying churches, sleepy hamlets, sequestered ancient farmsteads, and such fabled abodes as Sudeley Castle. The
Cotswolds can hardly claim to be undiscovered, but the area's poetic
appeal has survived the tour buses and antiques shops.

BATH AND THE COTSWOLDS PLANNER

WHEN TO GO

This area contains some of England's most popular destinations, and it's best to avoid weekends in the busier areas of the Cotswolds. During the week, even in summer, you may hardly see a soul in the more remote spots. Bath is particularly congested in summer, when students flock to its language schools. On the other hand, Cheltenham is a relatively workaday place that can absorb many tour buses comfortably.

Book your room well ahead if you visit during the two weeks in May and June when the Bath International Music Festival hits town, or if you visit Cheltenham during the National Hunt Festival (horse racing) in mid-March. Note that the private properties of Hidcote Manor, Snowshill Manor, and Sudeley Castle close in winter; Hidcote Manor Garden is at its best in spring and fall.

PLANNING YOUR TIME

Bath and Cheltenham are the most compelling larger towns in the region, and the obvious centers for an exploration of the Cotswolds. Cheltenham is closer to the heart of the Cotswolds and is far less touristy, but it has less immediate appeal. Bath is 29 mi from Cirencester in the southern Cotswolds, and 45 mi from Stow-on-the-Wold in the north. It's also worth finding accommodation in the smaller Cotswold settlements, though overnight stops in this well-heeled area can be costly. Good choices include Cirencester, Stow-on-the-Wold, and Broadway.

You can get a taste of Bath and the Cotswolds in three hurried days; a weeklong visit gives you plenty of time for the slow wandering this small region deserves. Near Bath, it's an easy drive to Lacock and Castle Combe, two stately villages on the southern edge of the Cotswolds, and Winchcombe makes a good entry into the area from Cheltenham. At the heart of the Cotswolds, Stow-on-the-Wold, Bourton-on-the-Water, and Broadway should on no account be missed. Within a short distance of these, Chipping Campden and Moreton-in-Marsh are less showy, with a more relaxed feel. Northleach is fairly low-key but boasts a fine example of a Cotswold wool church, while Bibury and Upper and Lower Slaughter are tiny settlements that can easily be appreciated on a brief passage. On the southern fringes of the area, Burford, Tetbury, and Cirencester have antiques and tea shops galore while avoiding the worst of the crowds.

GETTING HERE AND AROUND

AIR TRAVEL

This area is about two hours from London; Bristol and Birmingham have the closest regional airports.

BUS TRAVEL

National Express buses head to the region from London's Victoria Coach Station. Megabus, a budget bus company best booked online, also serves Cheltenham and Bath from London. It can take about three hours to get to Cheltenham, three to four hours to get to Bath. Bus service between some towns can be extremely limited. The First company covers the area around Bath. Stagecoach, Castleways, Johnson's Coaches, Cotswold Green, Swanbrook, Pulham's Coaches, and Wessex Connect operate in the Cotswolds region. Traveline has comprehensive information about all public transportation.

Contacts Castleways (☏ 01242/602949 ⊕ www.castleways.co.uk). **Cotswold Green** (☏ 01453/835153 ⊕ www.cotswoldgreen.com). **First** (☏ 0845/606–4446 ⊕ www.firstgroup.com). **Johnson's Coaches** (☏ 01564/797070 ⊕ www. johnsonscoaches.co.uk). **Megabus** (☏ 0871/266–3333 for general inquiries, 0900/160–0900 premium-rate number for bookings ⊕ www.megabus.com). **National Express** (☏ 0871/781–8178 ⊕ www.nationalexpress.com). **Pulham's Coaches** (☏ 01451/820369 ⊕ www.pulhamscoaches.com). **Stagecoach** (☏ 01452/418630 ⊕ www.stagecoachbus.com). **Swanbrook** (☏ 01452/712386 ⊕ www.swanbrook.co.uk). **Traveline** (☏ 0871/200–2233 ⊕ www.traveline.org. uk). **Wessex Connect** (☏ 0845/838–7080 ⊕ wessexconnect.com).

CAR TRAVEL

A car is the best way to make a thorough tour of the area, given the limitations of public transportation. M4 is the main route west from London to Bath and southern Gloucestershire; expect about a two-hour drive. From Exit 18, take A46 south to Bath. From Exit 20, take M5 north to Cheltenham; from Exit 15, take A419 to A429 north to the Cotswolds. From London you can also take M40 and A40 to the Cotswolds, where a network of minor roads link the villages.

TRAIN TRAVEL

First Great Western trains serve the region from London's Paddington Station; First Great Western and CrossCountry trains connect Cheltenham and Birmingham. Travel time from Paddington to Bath is about 90 minutes. Most trains to Cheltenham (two hours and 20 minutes) involve a change at Swindon or Bristol. Train service within the Cotswold area is extremely limited, with Kemble (near Cirencester) and Moreton-in-Marsh being the most useful stops, both serviced by daily trains from London Paddington. A three-day or seven-day Heart of England Rover pass is valid for unlimited travel within the region. National Rail Enquiries can help with schedules and other information.

Contacts National Rail Enquiries (☏ 0845/748–4950 ⊕ www.nationalrail. co.uk).

RESTAURANTS

Good restaurants dot the region, thanks to a steady flow of fine chefs seeking to cater to wealthy locals and waves of demanding visitors. The country's food revolution is in full evidence here. Restaurants have never had a problem with a fresh food supply: excellent regional produce, salmon from the rivers Severn and Wye, local lamb and pork, venison from the Forest of Dean, and pheasant, partridge, quail, and grouse in season. Also look for Gloucestershire Old Spot pork, bacon (try a delicious Old Spot bacon sandwich), and sausage on area menus.

HOTELS

The hotels of this region are among Britain's most highly rated—from bed-and-breakfasts in village homes and farmhouses to luxurious country-house hotels. Many hotels present themselves as deeply traditional rural retreats, but some have opted for a sleeker, fresher style, with boldly contemporary or minimalist furnishings. Spas are becoming increasingly popular at these hotels. Book ahead whenever possible and brace yourself for some high prices. B&Bs are a cheaper alternative to the fancier hotels, and most places offer two- and three-day packages. Note that the majority of lodgings in Bath and many in the Cotswolds require a two-night minimum stay on weekends and holidays; rates are often higher on weekends. Accommodation in Cheltenham and the Cotswolds is especially hard to find during the week of Cheltenham's National Hunt Festival in March.

There are numerous possibilities for renting a cottage in and around Bath and the Cotswolds, usually available by the week. Check out Manor Cottages or Jigsaw Holidays for a range of self-catering options.

Contacts Jigsaw Holidays (☎ *01993/849484* ⊕ *www.jigsawholidays.co.uk*). **Manor Cottages** (☎ *01993/824252* ⊕ *www.manorcottages.co.uk*).

WHAT IT COSTS IN POUNDS					
	£	££	£££	££££	£££££
Restaurants	under £10	£10–£14	£15–£19	£20–£25	over £25
Hotels	under £70	£70–£120	£121–£160	£161–£220	over £220

Restaurant prices are per person for a main course or equivalent combination of smaller dishes at dinner excluding tax. Hotels prices reflect the rack rate of a standard double room for two people in high season, including 20% V.A.T. Check online for off-season rates and special deals or discounts.

VISITOR INFORMATION

The South West Tourism Web site has information about the entire region; the Cotswolds site is a government one that has a useful section on tourism. The major towns have Tourist Information Centres that provide advice and help with accommodations.

Contacts Cotswolds (⊕ *www.cotswolds.com*). **South West Tourism** (⊕ *www. visitsouthwest.co.uk*).

BATH AND ENVIRONS

On the eastern edge of the county of Somerset, the city of Bath has strong links with the Cotswolds stretching north, the source of the wool that for centuries underpinned its economy. The stone mansions and cottages of that region are recalled in Bath's Georgian architecture and in the mellow stone that it shares with two of the villages lying across the Wiltshire border, Lacock and Castle Combe.

BATH

13 mi southeast of Bristol, 115 mi west of London.

Fodor's Choice ★ "I really believe I shall always be talking of Bath. Oh! who can ever be tired of Bath," enthuses Catherine Morland in Jane Austen's *Northanger Abbey,* and today plenty of people agree with these sentiments. In Bath,

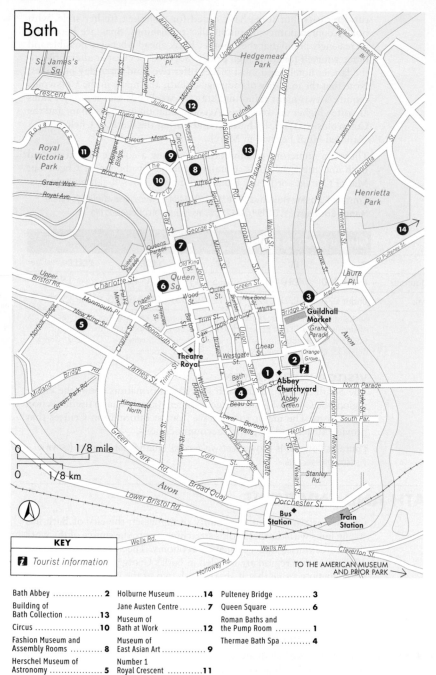

Bath

KEY

i *Tourist information*

TO THE AMERICAN MUSEUM
AND PRIOR PARK →

a UNESCO World Heritage Site, you are surrounded by magnificent 18th-century architecture, a lasting reminder of the vanished world described by Austen. In the 19th century the city lost its fashionable luster and slid into a refined gentility that still remains. Bath is no museum, though: it's lively, with good dining and shopping, excellent art galleries and museums, the remarkable excavated Roman baths, and theater, music, and other performances all year. Many people rush through Bath in a day, but there's enough to do to merit an overnight stay—or more. In summer, the sheer volume of sightseers may hamper your progress on a stroll.

The Romans put Bath on the map in the 1st century when they built a temple here, in honor of the goddess Minerva, and a sophisticated network of baths to make full use of the mineral springs that gush from the earth at a constant temperature of 116°F (46.5°C). ■TIP➔ Don't miss the remains of these baths, one of the city's glories. Visits by Queen Anne in 1702 and 1703 brought attention to the town, and soon 18th-century "people of quality" took it to heart. Assembly rooms, theaters, and pleasure gardens were built to entertain the rich and titled when they weren't busy attending the parties of Beau Nash (the city's master of ceremonies and chief social organizer, who helped increase Bath's popularity) and having their portraits painted by Gainsborough.

GETTING HERE AND AROUND

Frequent trains from Paddington and National Express buses from Victoria connect Bath with London. The bus and train stations are close to each other south of the center. By car from London, take M4 to Exit 18, from which A46 leads 10 mi south to Bath.

Drivers should note that parking is extremely limited within the city, and any car illegally parked is likely to be ticketed. Fees for towed cars can be hundreds of pounds. Public parking lots in the historic area fill up early, but the park-and-ride lots on the outskirts provide inexpensive shuttle service into the center, which is pleasant to stroll around.

TOURS   Free, two-hour walking tours of Bath are offered year-round by the Mayor of Bath's Honorary Guides. Individuals can just show up outside the main entrance to the Pump Room. Tours are Sunday through Friday at 10:30 and 2, Saturday at 10:30. There's also a tour at 7 pm Tuesday and Friday from May to September. The Jane Austen Centre arranges Jane-themed walking tours on weekends. City Sightseeing runs 50-minute guided tours of Bath on open-top buses year-round, leaving two to four times an hour from High Street, near the abbey. Tickets, valid for 24 hours, give discounts on entry to some of Bath's top attractions. Mad Max Tours runs full-day tours from Bath through the Cotswolds on Tuesday, Thursday, and Sunday, stopping at Tetbury, Upper Slaughter and Lower Slaughter, and either Bourton-on-the-Water or Stow-on-the-Wold. The departure point is the Glass House Shop on Orange Grove, near Bath Abbey, at 8:45 am. The company also has tours to Castle Combe, Lacock, Avebury, and Stonehenge.

The remains of the Roman Baths evoke the days when the Romans gathered here to socialize and bathe.

TIMING

Schedule a visit to Bath during the week, as weekends see an influx of visitors. The city gets similarly crowded during its various festivals, though the added conviviality and cultural activity during these events are big draws in themselves.

ESSENTIALS

Visitor and Tour Information Bath Tourist Information Centre (✉ *Abbey Chambers, Abbey Churchyard* ☎ *0906/711–2000 [premium rate], +44 844/ 847–5257 from abroad, 0844/847–5256 booking accommodation service* ⊕ *www.visitbath.co.uk).* **City Sightseeing** (☎ *01225/444102 in Bath* ⊕ *www. city-sightseeing.com).* **Mad Max Tours** (☎ *0799/050–5970* ⊕ *www.madmax. abel.co.uk).* **Mayor of Bath's Honorary Guides** (☎ *01225/477411* ⊕ *www. bathguides.org.uk).*

EXPLORING
TOP ATTRACTIONS

Bath Abbey. Dominating Bath's center, this 15th-century edifice of golden, glowing stone has a splendid west front, with carved figures of angels ascending ladders on either side. Notice, too, the miter, olive tree, and crown motif, a play on the name of the building's founder, Bishop Oliver King. More than 50 stained-glass windows fill about 80% of the building's wall space, giving the interior an impression of lightness. The abbey was built in the Perpendicular (English late-Gothic) style on the site of a Saxon abbey, and the nave and side aisles contain superb fan-vaulted ceilings. There are six services on Sunday, including choral evensong at 3:30. Forty-five-minute **tower tours**, allowing close-up views of the massive bells and panoramic cityscapes from the roof, take place most days; the 212 dizzying steps demand a level of fitness. ⊠ *Abbey Churchyard* ☎ *01225/422462* ⊕ *www.bathabbey.org* ᗴ *Abbey £2.50 donation suggested, tower tours £5, Heritage Vaults free* ⊙ *Abbey Apr.–Oct., Mon.–Sat. 9–6, Sun. 1–2:30 and 4:30–5:30; Nov.–Mar., Mon.–Sat. 9–4:30, Sun. 1–2:30 and 4:30–5:30. Tower tours Apr., May, Sept., and Oct., Mon.–Sat. 10–4 hourly; June–Aug., Mon.– Sat. 10–5 hourly; Nov. and Jan.–Mar., Mon.–Sat. 11, noon, and 2; call for Dec. hrs.*

★ **Circus.** John Wood designed the masterful Circus, a circle of curving, perfectly proportioned Georgian houses interrupted just three times for intersecting streets. Wood died shortly after work on the Circus began; his son, the younger John Wood, completed the project. Notice the carved acorns atop the houses: Wood nurtured the myth that Prince Bladud founded Bath, ostensibly with the help of an errant pig rooting for acorns (this is one of a number of variations of Bladud's story), and the architect adopted the acorn motif in a number of places. A garden fills the center of the Circus. The painter Thomas Gainsborough (1727–88) lived at No. 17 from 1760 to 1774.

QUICK BITES

After a visit to the Royal Crescent and the Circus, nip into the Lime Lounge (⊠ **11 Margaret's Bldgs., off Brock St.** ☎ **01225/421251** ⊕ **www. limeloungebath.co.uk**), a convivial spot for breakfasts, soups, sandwiches, and light lunches. It stays open for afternoon teas and evening meals, too.

7

★ **Fashion Museum and Assembly Rooms.** In its role as the **Assembly Rooms,** this neoclassical building was one of the leading centers for social life in 18th-century Bath, with a schedule of dress balls, concerts, and choral nights. Jane Austen came here often, and it is in the Ballroom that Catherine Morland has her first, disappointing encounter with Bath's beau monde in *Northanger Abbey;* the Octagon Room is the setting for an important encounter between Anne Elliot and Captain Wentworth in *Persuasion.* Built by John Wood the Younger in 1771, the building was badly damaged by wartime bombing in 1942 but was faithfully restored. Its stunning chandeliers are the 18th-century originals. Throughout the year, classical concerts are given here, just as they were in bygone days. The Assembly Rooms are also known today for the entertaining **Fashion Museum**, displaying apparel from Jacobean times up to the present (audio guide included). You might see displays of wedding dresses or punk fashions in changing exhibits. ⊠ *Bennett St.* ☎ *01225/477173* ⊕ *www.museumofcostume.co.uk* ᗴ *£7.25 for Assembly Rooms and Fashion Museum, £2 Assembly Rooms only; combined ticket with Roman Baths (valid 7 days), £15.50* ⊙ *Mar.–Oct., daily 10:30–6; Nov.–Feb., daily 10:30–5; last admission 1 hr before closing.*

★ **Holburne Museum.** One of Bath's gems, this elegant 18th-century building houses a superb collection of 17th- and 18th-century decorative arts, ceramics, and silverware. Highlights include paintings by Gainsborough (*The Byam Family,* on indefinite loan) and George Stubbs (*Reverend Carter Thelwall and Family*), and a hilarious collection of caricatures of the Georgian city's fashionable elite. In its original incarnation as the Sydney Hotel, the house was one of the pivots of Bath's high society, which came to perambulate in the pleasure gardens (Sydney Gardens) that still lie behind it. One visitor was Jane Austen, whose main Bath residence was No. 4 Sydney Place, a brief stroll across the road from the museum. The museum reopened in spring 2011 following a major renovation, adding a bold modern extension and a tea garden. ⊠ *Great Pulteney St.* ☎ *01225/466669* ⊕ *www.holburne. org* ☜ *Free* ☉ *Mon.–Sat. 10–5, Sun. and national holidays 11–5.*

Jane Austen Centre. The one place in Bath that gives Austen any space provides a briefly diverting exhibition about the influence of Bath on her writings; *Northanger Abbey* and *Persuasion* are both set primarily in the city. There's a 15-minute introductory talk, and displays give

a pictorial overview of life in Bath around 1800. The cozy Georgian house, a few doors up from where the writer lived in 1805 (one of several addresses she had in Bath), also includes the Austen-themed Regency Tea Rooms, open to the public. ■TIP→ Buy tickets here for Jane Austen walking tours, which leave from the Abbey Churchyard at 11 on weekends and holidays (also at 4 on Friday and Saturday in July and August). A tour ticket entitles you to a 10% reduction for entry to the exhibition. ⊠ *40 Gay St.* ☎ *01225/443000* ⊕ *www.janeausten.co.uk* ☜ *£7.45, tours £6* ☉ *Late Mar.–June, Sept., and Oct, daily 9:45–5:30; July and Aug., Sun.–Wed. 9:45–5:30, Thurs.–Sat. 9:45–7; Nov.–late Mar., Sun.–Fri. 11–4:30, Sat. 9:45–5:30.*

Fodor's Choice **Number 1 Royal Crescent.** The majestic arc of the Royal Crescent, much
★ used as a film location, is the crowning glory of Palladian architecture in Bath; Number 1 offers you a glimpse inside this splendor. The work of John Wood the Younger, the 30 houses fronted by 114 columns were laid out between 1767 and 1774. A house in the center is now the Royal Crescent Hotel. On the corner of Brock Street and the Royal Crescent, Number 1 Royal Crescent has been turned into a museum and furnished as it might have been in the 18th century. The museum crystallizes a view of the English class system—upstairs is elegance, and downstairs is a kitchen display. However, a renovation planned for completion in 2013 will move the kitchen to its original location in the servants' annex, whose incorporation into the museum will double the number of rooms on view. Parts of the museum will be inaccessible during the work. ⊠ *Royal Crescent* ☎ *01225/428126* ⊕ *www.bath-preservation-trust.org.uk* ☜ *£6.50* ☉ *Mid-Feb.–late Oct., Tues.–Sun. and national holidays 10:30–5; late Oct.–mid-Dec., Tues.–Sun. 10:30–4; last admission 30 mins before closing.*

Pulteney Bridge. Florence's Ponte Vecchio inspired this 18th-century span, one of the most famous landmarks in the city and the only work of Robert Adam in Bath. It's unique in Great Britain because shops line both sides of the bridge.

Queen Square. Palatial houses and the Francis Hotel surround the garden in the center of this square designed by the older John Wood. An obelisk financed by Beau Nash celebrates the 1738 visit of Frederick, prince of Wales.

Fodor'sChoice
★

Roman Baths and the Pump Room. The hot springs have drawn people here since prehistoric times, so it's quite appropriate to begin an exploration of Bath at this excellent museum on the site of the ancient city's temple complex and primary "watering hole." Roman patricians would gather to immerse themselves, drink the mineral waters, and socialize. With the departure of the Romans, the baths fell into disuse and were partially covered. When bathing again became fashionable at the end of the 18th century, this magnificent Georgian building was erected. Almost the entire Roman bath complex was rediscovered and excavated in the 19th century, and the museum displays relics that include a memorable mustachioed, Celtic-influenced Gorgon's head, fragments of colorful curses invoked by the Romans against their neighbors, and information about Roman bathing practices. The **Great Bath** is now roofless, and the statuary and pillars belong to the 19th century, but much remains from the original complex, and the steaming, somewhat murky waters are undeniably evocative. Free tours of the baths take place hourly, and you can visit after 6:30 pm in July and August to experience the baths lighted by torches. Adjacent to the Roman bath complex is the famed **Pump Room,** built in 1792–96, a rendezvous for members of 18th-century and 19th-century Bath society. Here Catherine Morland and Mrs. Allen "paraded up and down for an hour, looking at everybody and speaking to no one," to quote from Jane Austen's *Northanger Abbey.* Today you can take in the elegant space—or you can simply, for a small fee, taste the fairly vile mineral water. Charles Dickens described it as tasting like warm flatirons. ■**TIP**→ The tourist office offers a Spas Ancient and Modern package for £61.50 that includes a ticket to the Roman Baths, a voucher for a three-course lunch or champagne afternoon tea in the Pump Room, and a voucher for a two-hour spa session at Thermae Bath Spa. ⊠ *Abbey Churchyard* ☏ *01225/477785* ⊕ *www. romanbaths.co.uk* ⊠ *Pump Room free, Roman Baths £12 with audio guide, £12.50 in July and Aug.; combined ticket with Fashion Museum and Assembly Rooms (valid 7 days) £15.50* ☉ *Mar.–June, Sept., and Oct., daily 9–6; July and Aug., daily 9 am–10 pm; Nov.–Feb., daily 9:30–5:30; last admission 1 hr before closing.*

7

QUICK
BITES

Tucked away in a quiet courtyard, Le Parisien (⊠ *Milsom Pl. off Broad St.* ☏ *01225/447147*) is handy for coffee or a lunchtime baguette. Mussels, quiches, and children's dishes also appear on the menu.

You can linger in the **Pump Room** (⊠ *Abbey Churchyard* ☏ *01225/444477*) for morning coffee or afternoon tea after seeing the Roman Baths.

Thermae Bath Spa. The only place in Britain where you can bathe in natural hot-spring water, and in an open-air rooftop location as well, this striking complex designed by Nicholas Grimshaw consists of a Bath-stone building surrounded by a glass curtain wall. The only difficulty is in deciding where to spend more time—in the sleekly luxurious, light-filled Minerva Bath, with its curves and gentle currents, or in the smaller, open-air rooftop pool for the unique sensation of bathing with views of Bath's operatic skyline. Two 18th-century thermal baths, the Cross Bath and the Hot Bath, are back in use, too (the latter for treatments only). End your session in the crisp third-floor café and restaurant. ■TIP➔ It's essential to book spa treatments ahead. Towels, robes, and slippers are available for rent. Weekdays are the quietest time to visit. Note that children under 16 are not admitted into the Minerva and rooftop baths, and under-12s cannot use the Cross Bath; you must be 18 or over to book a spa treatment. A separate, free **Visitor Centre** (April through October, Monday through Saturday 10–5, Sunday 11–4) opposite the entrance gives an overview of the project and provides audio guides (£2) for a brief tour of the exterior. ⊠ *Hot Bath St.* ☎ *0844/888–0844* ⊕ *www.thermaebathspa.com* ✉ *£25 for 2 hrs, £35 for 4 hrs, £55 all day; extra charges for treatments* ☉ *Daily 9 am–10 pm; last admission at 7:30.*

WORTH NOTING

American Museum in Britain. A Greek Revival (19th-century) mansion in a majestic setting on a hill 2½ mi southeast of the city holds the only museum of American decorative arts outside the United States. Rooms are furnished in historical styles, such as a 17th-century keeping room from Massachusetts and a richly red New Orleans bedroom from the 1860s. Other galleries explore historical themes (the settlement of the West, the Civil War) or contain rugs and quilts, porcelain, and Shaker objects; a separate building is devoted to folk art. The parkland includes a reproduction of George Washington's garden at Mount Vernon. Take a bus headed to the University of Bath and get off at the Avenue, where signs point to the museum, half a mile away, or take a City Sightseeing bus. ⊠ *Claverton Manor off A36* ☎ *01225/460503* ⊕ *www.americanmuseum.org* ✉ *Museum, special exhibitions, and grounds £8* ☉ *Mid-Mar.–July, Sept., and Oct., Tues.–Sun. and national holidays noon–5; Aug., daily noon–5; late Nov.–mid-Dec., Tues.–Sun. and national holidays noon–4:30; last admission 1 hr before closing.*

Building of Bath Collection. This absorbing museum in the Georgian Gothic-style Countess of Huntingdon's Chapel is an essential stop on any exploration of Bath, particularly for fans of Georgian architecture. It explains and illustrates the evolution of the city, with examples of everything from window design and wrought-iron railings to marbling and other interior decoration. ⊠ *The Paragon* ☎ *01225/333895* ⊕ *www.bath-preservation-trust.org.uk* ✉ *£4* ☉ *Mid-Feb.–Nov., Sat.–Mon. 10:30–5; last admission at 4:30.*

Herschel Museum of Astronomy. In this modest Bath town house, using a handmade telescope of his own devising, William Herschel (1738–1822) identified the planet Uranus. This small museum devoted to his studies and discoveries contains his telescopes, the workshop where he cast his speculum metal mirrors, musical instruments of his time (Herschel was the organist at Bath's Octagon Chapel), and the tiny garden where the discovery of Uranus was made. ⊠ *19 New King St.* ☎ *01225/446865* ⊕ *www.bath-preservation-trust.org.uk* 🎫*£5* ⊙ *Feb.– mid-Dec., Mon., Tues., Wed. (during school holidays only), Thurs. and Fri. 1–5, weekends and national holidays 11–5; last admission at 4:30.*

Museum of Bath at Work. The core of this industrial-history collection, which gives a novel perspective on the city, is an engineering works and fizzy drinks factory, relocated to this building. It once belonged to Bath entrepreneur Jonathan Bowler, who started his many businesses in 1872. The collection includes the original clanking machinery and offers glimpses into Bath's stone industry and cabinetmaking. ⊠ *Julian Rd.* ☎ *01225/318348* ⊕ *www.bath-at-work.org.uk* 🎫*£5 including audioguide* ⊙ *Apr.–Oct., daily 10:30–5; Nov. and Jan.–Mar., weekends 10:30–5; last admission at 4.*

Museum of East Asian Art. Intimate galleries on three floors finely display ancient and modern pieces, mostly from China but with other exhibits from Japan, Korea, and Southeast Asia. Highlights are a graphic 19th-century watercolor depicting the Chinese idea of hell, Chinese ivory figures, Buddhist objects, and Japanese lacquerware and prints. ⊠ *12 Bennett St.* ☎ *01225/464640* ⊕ *www.meaa.org.uk* 🎫*£5* ⊙ *Tues.–Sat. 10–5, Sun. noon–5; last admission at 4:30.*

Prior Park. A vision to warm Jane Austen's heart, Bath's grandest house lies a mile or so southeast of the center, with splendid views over the Georgian townscape. Built around 1738 by John Wood the Elder of honey-color limestone, the Palladian mansion was the home of quarry owner and philanthropist Ralph Allen (1693–1764), whose guests included such luminaries as poet Alexander Pope and novelists Henry Fielding and Samuel Richardson. Today it is a Roman Catholic school and the interior is not open to the public, but you may wander through the beautiful grounds, designed by Capability Brown and embellished with a Palladian bridge and lake. A leisurely circuit of the park should take around an hour. ■**TIP**➔ The parking here is only for people with disabilities: unless you relish the uphill trudge, take a taxi or bus from the center. ⊠ *Ralph Allen Dr.* ☎ *01225/833422* ⊕ *www.nationaltrust.org. uk* 🎫*£5.25* ⊙ *Mid-Feb.–Oct., daily 11–5:30 or dusk; early Nov.–early Feb., weekends 11–5:30 or dusk; last admission 1 hr before closing.*

🅒 **Royal Victoria Park.** Originally designed as an arboretum, this tidy expanse of lawns and shady walks just west of the Royal Crescent provides the perfect setting for pleasant strolls and leisurely picnics. The park has a pond, an aviary, a **Botanic Garden,** and an adventure playground with plenty for kids. Hot-air balloon launches and open-air shows at festival time enliven the atmosphere. ⊠ *Upper Bristol Rd.* 🎫*Free* ⊙ *Daily 24 hrs.*

WHERE TO EAT
Among hotel restaurants, the Dower House in the Royal Crescent Hotel is outstanding; the Cavendish in Dukes Hotel is noteworthy.

££ ✕**Firehouse Rotisserie.** California comes to Bath. Tex-Mex, Pacific Rim,
AMERICAN and creole influences are also evident on a menu that showcases dishes

A GOOD WALK IN BATH

For an hour-long stroll that takes in Bath's architectural showpieces, start in the traffic-free Abbey Churchyard, a lively piazza (often filled with musicians and street artists) dominated by Bath Abbey and the Roman Baths complex. Work your way east to Grand Parade and look out over flower-filled gardens and the River Avon, crossed by the graceful, Italianate Pulteney Bridge.

Stroll over the shop-lined bridge to gaze up the broad thoroughfare of Great Pulteney Street; then cross back over the bridge and head east up Bridge Street, turning right at High Street to follow up Broad Street and its northern extension, Lansdown Road. Turn left onto Bennett Street, passing the 18th-century Assembly Rooms and the Fashion

Museum. Bennett Street ends at the Circus, an architectural tour de force compared by some to an inverted Colosseum.

The graceful arc of Bath's most dazzling terrace, the Royal Crescent, embraces a swath of green lawns at one end of Brock Street. Return to the Circus and walk south down Gay Street, which brings you past dignified Queen Square, with its obelisk, to the Theatre Royal. Wander east from here along tiny alleys packed with stores, galleries, and eating places, back to your starting point at Abbey Churchyard, where you could have a well-earned sit-down and tea at the Pump Room. Alternatively, end your perambulation with a soak at Thermae Bath Spa.

from the rotisserie and grill, such as spice-rubbed rib-eye steak with a fiery sauce, and crab and salmon cakes with tomato-and-basil salsa. Brick-fired pizzas entice with creative toppings; try goat cheese, pesto, and artichokes. White walls and casual wood tables and chairs, an open-view kitchen, and an easy, sociable vibe set the scene. ⊠ *2 John St.* ☏ *01225/482070* ⊕ *www.firehouserotisserie.co.uk* ⊘ *Closed Sun.*

£££
MODERN BRITISH

✕ **Hole in the Wall.** Escape from Bath's busyness at this relaxed eatery serving sophisticated modern English fare in an 18th-century town house. At the bottom of a flight of stairs, the unfussy, stone-tile dining area—warmed by a generous open fire in winter—exudes calm and poise. (The piped-in music can be intrusive, however.) It's a great environment to indulge in such dishes as roasted guinea fowl with mushroom and truffled leek pie. While you wait for your order, nibble on the complimentary freshly baked bread. Lunches and pretheater meals are a good value. ⊠ *16 George St.* ☏ *01225/425242* ⊕ *www.theholeinthewall.co.uk* ⊘ *No dinner Sun., no lunch Mon.*

££
ITALIAN

✕ **Jamie's Italian.** Part of a chain owned by celebrity chef Jamie Oliver, this buzzing brasserie is a cheerful counterpoint to Bath's predominantly sedate tone. The dining areas, spread over two floors and including a rooftop terrace, have a contemporary, slightly industrial feel. Expect dishes typical of Oliver's straightforward Italian rustic style, such as bruschetta; lavish antipasti; garlicky prawn linguine; and prosciutto, pear, and Pecorino salad. Desserts include *affogato* (vanilla ice cream with espresso) and baked walnut tart. There's always a line outside at busy times, but you can take advantage of the all-day service by coming

CLOSE UP

Bath's Georgian Architecture

Bath wouldn't be Bath without its distinctive 18th-century Georgian architecture, much of which was conceived by John Wood the Elder (1704–54), an antiquarian and architect. Wood saw Bath as a city destined for almost mythic greatness. Arriving in Bath in 1727, he sought a suitable architectural style, and found it in the Palladian style, made popular in Britain by Inigo Jones.

ELEMENTS OF STYLE
Derived from the Italian architect Andrea Palladio (1508–1580), who in turn was inspired by ancient Roman architecture, Palladianism accentuated symmetry and proportion. The plain facades of buildings, dignified with columns, pilasters, and pediments over doors and windows, often contrasted with rich interiors. The Building of Bath Collection has more information.

BUILDINGS TO SEE
Wood created a harmonious city, building graceful terraces (row houses), crescents (curving rows of houses), and villas of the same golden local limestone used by the Romans. Influenced by nearby ancient stone circles as well as round Roman temples, Wood broke from convention in his design for Bath's Circus, a circle of houses broken only three times for intersecting streets.

After the death of Wood the Elder, John Wood the Younger (1728–82) carried out his father's plans for the Royal Crescent, a regal crescent of 30 houses. Today you can stop in at No. 1 Royal Crescent for a look at one of these homes—it's like eavesdropping on the 18th century. He also built the Assembly Rooms, now open to the public.

7

during off-peak hours. ✉ *10 Milsom Pl.* ☎ *01225/432340* ⊕ *www. jamieoliver.com* ⌖ *Reservations not accepted.*

£
ECLECTIC
✕ **Jazz Café.** Snack to a background of jazz classics in this cramped but cozy café. Famous for its all-day breakfasts, the café is also a good spot for a quick lunch, with soups, salads, sandwiches, and fine mezes. Daily specials might include spicy beef chili, cassoulet, or Moroccan pork. It closes at 5 pm (4 on Sunday). ✉ *Kingsmead Sq.* ☎ *01225/329002* ⊕ *www.bathjazzcafe.co.uk* ☾ *No dinner.*

£££
FRENCH
✕ **No. 5 Restaurant.** An ideal spot for a light lunch or romantic dinner, this airy bistro decorated with pretty plants and framed posters is just over Pulteney Bridge from the center of town. The menu changes daily but lists soups and such dishes as pork tenderloin with fondant potato, and rib of beef with caramelized shallots, confit tomatoes, and spinach. There are good-value set-price lunch and early-evening menus. ✉ *5 Argyle St.* ☎ *01225/444499* ⊕ *www.no5restaurant.co.uk.*

££££
MODERN BRITISH
★
✕ **Olive Tree.** A sleek space in the basement of the Queensberry Hotel makes a calm, contemporary setting for top-notch English and Mediterranean dishes. The range of seductive, sophisticated choices includes crab risotto for starters and such main courses as Creedy Carver duck breast with duck leg spring roll and Alsace cabbage, and Cornish brill with shrimp and parsley butter. Some dessert picks are dark chocolate fondant with ice cream and malted milk, and apple mousse with

blackberry salad and sorbet. Fixed-price menus are available at lunch-time. ⊠ *Russel St.* ☎ *01225/447928* ⊕ *www.thequeensberry.co.uk* ⊘ *No lunch Mon.*

££
BRITISH
✗ **Pump Room.** The 18th-century Pump Room, with views over the Roman Baths, serves morning coffee, lunches of sandwiches and meat, vegetarian, and seafood dishes, and afternoon tea, often to music by a pianist or string trio. Its stately setting is the selling point rather than the food, but do sample the West Country cheese board and home-made cakes and pastries. There are fixed-price menus at lunchtime, and it's usually open for fixed-price dinners in July, August, and December and during the major festivals (reservations are essential). Be prepared to wait in line for a table during the day. ⊠ *Abbey Churchyard* ☎ *01225/444477* ⊕ *www.romanbaths.co.uk* ⊘ *No dinner except during July, Aug., Dec., and festivals.*

££
BRITISH
✗ **Sally Lunn's.** Small and slightly twee, this tourist magnet near Bath Abbey occupies the oldest house in Bath, dating to 1482. It's famous for the Sally Lunn bun, actually a semisweet bread served here since 1680. You can choose from more than 40 sweet and savory toppings to accompany your bun, or turn it into a meal with such dishes as duck with orange-and-cinnamon sauce. There are also economical lunch and early-evening menus. Daytime diners can view the small kitchen museum in the cellar (30p for nondining visitors). ⊠ *4 N. Parade Passage* ☎ *01225/461634* ⊕ *www.sallylunns.co.uk.*

££
ITALIAN
✗ **Strada.** The former home of Richard "Beau" Nash—the dictator of fashion for mid-18th-century society in Bath—and his mistress Juliana Popjoy provides an elegant setting for this outpost of a reliable chain of Italian eateries. Modern wooden furnishings blend smoothly with the Georgian tone of the dining areas on two levels. Pizzas and pasta vie for space on the menu with classics like *saltimbocca di maiale* (fillet of pork in a sage-and-butter sauce). ⊠ *Beau Nash House, Saw Close* ☎ *01225/337753* ⊕ *www.strada.co.uk.*

£££
FRENCH
✗ **Tilleys Bistro.** This intimate, bow-windowed French eatery presents alluring meat and vegetarian dishes offered in small, medium, and large portions. Choices include medallions of pork *à la dijonnaise* (fried tenderloin and mushrooms in a brandy, cream, and mustard sauce), roasted *aubergine à la Tunisienne* (eggplant cooked with chickpeas, dates, and apricots), and sautéed Gressingham duck breast. Pretheater meals are available weekdays between 6 and 7 pm. ⊠ *3 N. Parade Passage* ☎ *01225/484200* ⊕ *www.tilleysbistro.co.uk* ⊘ *No lunch Sun.*

WHERE TO STAY

For expanded hotel reviews, visit Fodors.com.

££
B&B/INN
🛏 **Albany Guest House.** Homey and friendly, this Edwardian house close to the Royal Crescent has simply furnished rooms decorated with neutral, beige, and cream colors. **Pros:** spotless rooms; convenient location; excellent breakfasts. **Cons:** some rooms are very small; limited parking. ⊠ *24 Crescent Gardens* ☎ *01225/313339* ⊕ *www.albanybath.co.uk* 🛏 *5 rooms* ⏶ *In-room: no a/c, Wi-Fi. In-hotel: parking* ⍾❙ *Breakfast.*

£££–££££
B&B/INN
🛏 **Bath Paradise House.** Don't be put off by the 10-minute uphill walk from the center of Bath—you'll be rewarded by a wonderful view of the city from the garden and upper stories of this Georgian guesthouse. **Pros:**

great attention to detail; spectacular views from some rooms. **Cons:** uphill walk; books up far in advance. ✉ *88 Holloway* ☎ *01225/317723* ⊕ *www.paradise-house.co.uk* ⤴ *11 rooms* ⚬ *In-room: no a/c, Wi-Fi (some). In-hotel: bar, business center, parking* ⦿ *Breakfast.*

££ ⊡ **Cranleigh.** In a quiet location on the hill above the city center, this
B&B/INN Victorian guesthouse has wonderful views of the Avon Valley and richly decorated rooms; three rooms have four-poster beds. **Pros:** quiet rooms; period furnishings; many choices at breakfast. **Cons:** far from center; along a busy road; steps to climb. ✉ *159 Newbridge Hill* ☎ *01225/310197* ⊕ *www.cranleighguesthouse.com* ⤴ *9 rooms* ⚬ *In-room: no a/c, Wi-Fi. In-hotel: business center, parking, some age restrictions* ⦿ *Breakfast.*

£££–££££ ⊡ **Dukes Hotel.** True Georgian grandeur is evident in the refurbished
HOTEL rooms of this Palladian-style mansion–turned–elegant small hotel. **Pros:** excellent central location; superb restaurant; friendly and helpful service. **Cons:** some rooms are small; steps to climb; service occasionally slips. ✉ *53–54 Great Pulteney St. (entrance on Edward St.)* ☎ *01225/787960* ⊕ *www.dukesbath.co.uk* ⤴ *11 rooms, 6 suites* ⚬ *In-room: no a/c, Wi-Fi. In-hotel: restaurant, bar, business center, some pets allowed* ⦿ *Breakfast.*

£££ ⊡ **Harington's Hotel.** It's rare to find a compact hotel in the cobblestone
HOTEL heart of Bath, and this informal three-story lodging converted from a group of Georgian town houses fits the bill nicely. **Pros:** good breakfasts; helpful staff. **Cons:** occasional street noise from revelers; steps to climb; many small rooms. ✉ *Queen St.* ☎ *01225/461728* ⊕ *www.haringtonshotel.co.uk* ⤴ *13 rooms* ⚬ *In-room: no a/c, Wi-Fi (some). In-hotel: bar, parking* ⦿ *Breakfast.*

££–£££ ⊡ **Marlborough House.** A warm, informal welcome greets all who stay
B&B/INN at this Victorian establishment close to the Royal Crescent, where each room charms with period furniture, fresh flowers, and antique beds. **Pros:** obliging and helpful hosts; immaculate rooms. **Cons:** some traffic noise; the walk to the center is along a busy road. ✉ *1 Marlborough La.* ☎ *01225/318175* ⊕ *www.marlborough-house.net* ⤴ *6 rooms* ⚬ *In-room: no a/c, Wi-Fi. In-hotel: some pets allowed* ⦿ *Breakfast.*

£££–££££ ⊡ **Queensberry Hotel.** Intimate and elegant, this boutique hotel in a resi-
HOTEL dential street near the Circus occupies three 1772 town houses built
Fodor's Choice by John Wood the Younger for the marquis of Queensberry; it's a per-
★ fect marriage of chic sophistication, homey comforts, and attentive service. **Pros:** efficient service; tranquil ambience; valet parking. **Cons:** occasional street noise; no tea/coffee-making facilities in rooms; breakfast extra. ✉ *Russel St.* ☎ *01225/447928* ⊕ *www.thequeensberry.co.uk* ⤴ *26 rooms, 3 suites* ⚬ *In-room: no a/c, Wi-Fi (some). In-hotel: restaurant, bar, parking* ⦿ *No meals.*

££–£££ ⊡ **Three Abbey Green.** Just steps away from Bath Abbey, a gorgeous
B&B/INN square dominated by a majestic plane tree is home to this welcoming B&B. **Pros:** superb location; airy rooms. **Cons:** some noise from pub goers; only one suite has a bathtub; no parking. ✉ *3 Abbey Green* ☎ *01225/428558* ⊕ *www.threeabbeygreen.com* ⤴ *7 rooms* ⚬ *In-room: no a/c, Wi-Fi. In-hotel: business center* ⦿ *Breakfast.*

NIGHTLIFE AND THE ARTS

BARS AND PUBS　The **Porter** (⊠ *2 Miles's Buildings, George St.* ☎ *01225/424104*), the city's only vegetarian pub, features nightly music and comedy performances in its grungy cellar bar.

Pub aficionados will relish the friendly, unspoiled ambience of the **Raven** (⊠ *Queen St.* ☎ *01225/425045*), a great spot for a pint, with regular poetry readings, storytelling nights, and live music upstairs.

FESTIVALS　**Bath Comedy Festival** (⊠ *Bath Festivals Box Office, 2 Church St., Abbey Green* ☎ *01225/463362* ⊕ *www.bathcomedyfestival.co.uk*) kicks off on April Fool's Day (April 1) for 11 days of comedy events at venues throughout the city.

★　The **Bath International Music Festival** (⊠ *Bath Festivals Box Office, 2 Church St., Abbey Green* ☎ *01225/463362* ⊕ *www.bathmusicfest.org. uk*), held over 12 days in May and June, presents concerts (classical, jazz, and world music), dance performances, and exhibitions in and around Bath, many in the Assembly Rooms and Bath Abbey.

The weeklong **Bath Literature Festival** (⊠ *Bath Festivals Box Office, 2 Church St., Abbey Green* ☎ *01225/463362* ⊕ *www.bathlitfest.org.uk*) in late February and early March features readings and talks by writers, mostly in the 18th-century Guildhall on High Street.

The **Jane Austen Festival** (☎ *01225/443000* ⊕ *www.janeausten.co.uk/ festival*) celebrates the great writer with films, plays, walks, and talks over eight days in late September. It's a feast for Janeites.

THEATER　The **Theatre Royal** (⊠ *Box Office, Saw Close* ☎ *01225/448844*), a gemlike Regency playhouse from 1805, has a year-round program that often includes pre- or post-London tours. You must reserve the best seats well in advance, but you can line up for same-day standby seats or standing room. Tours usually take place at 11 am on the first Wednesday and the following Saturday of the month (booking not required). ■ **TIP**→ Take care with your seat location—sight lines can be poor.

SHOPPING

Bath has excellent small, family-run, and specialty shops; many close Sunday. The shopping district centers on Stall and Union streets and the new SouthGate shopping center near the train station (modern stores), Milsom Street (traditional stores), and Walcot Street (arts and crafts). Leading off these main streets are alleyways and passages lined with galleries and antiques shops.

For 18 days in late November and early December, the outdoor **Bath Christmas Market** (⊠ *Abbey Green, Abbey Gate St., and Kingston Parade* ☎ *01225/396417*) sells gift items—from handcrafted toys to candles, cards, and edible delights—in stalls around the abbey and Roman Baths.

★　**Bartlett Street Antiques Centre** (⊠ *Bartlett St.* ☎ *No phone*) has more than 50 showcases and stands selling every kind of antique imaginable, including silver, porcelain, and jewelry.

Bath Sweet Shop (⊠ *8 N. Parade Passage* ☎ *01225/428040*), the city's oldest candy store, boasts of stocking some 350 different varieties, including traditional licorice torpedoes, pear drops, and aniseed balls. Sugar-free treats are available.

Beaux Arts Ceramics (✉ *12–13 York St.* ☎ *01225/464850*) carries the work of prominent potters.

The covered **Guildhall Market** (✉ *Entrances on High St. and Grand Parade*), open Monday through Saturday 9–5, is the place for everything from jewelry and gifts to delicatessen food, secondhand books, bags, and batteries; there's a café, too.

Margaret's Buildings (✉ *Halfway between the Circus and Royal Crescent*) is a pretty lane with shops selling antiques and secondhand and antiquarian books.

SPORTS AND THE OUTDOORS

To explore the River Avon by rented skiff, punt, or canoe, head for the **Bath Boating Station** (✉ *Forester Rd.* ☎ *01225/312900*), behind the Holburne Museum. It's open Easter to September.

CASTLE COMBE

12 mi northeast of Bath, 5 mi northwest of Chippenham.

Fodor's Choice ★ This Wiltshire village lived a sleepy existence until 1962, when it was voted the "prettiest village" in England—without any of its inhabitants knowing that it had even been a contender. The village's magic is that it's so toylike, so delightfully all-of-a-piece: you can see almost the whole town at one glance from any one position. Castle Combe consists of little more than a brook, a pack bridge, a street (which is called the Street) of simple stone cottages, a market cross from the 13th century, and the Perpendicular-style church of St. Andrew. The grandest house in the village (on its outskirts) is the Upper Manor House, built in the 15th century by Sir John Fastolf and now the Manor House Hotel.

GETTING HERE AND AROUND

All buses from Bath to Castle Combe involve one or two changes and take 70 to 100 minutes, so it's best to drive or join a tour.

WHERE TO STAY

£££££–£££££ HOTEL ★ 🖬 **Manor House Hotel.** This secluded, partly 14th-century manor house, in a 23-acre park on the edge of the village, has guest rooms—some in mews cottages—that brim with antique character. **Pros:** romantic getaway; rich historical setting; good golf course. **Cons:** mews cottages lack authentic antique ambience; room decor occasionally jars. ✉ *Castle Combe* ☎ *01249/782206* ⊕ *www.manorhouse.co.uk* ⤳ *48 rooms* ⌂ *In-room: no a/c, Wi-Fi. In-hotel: restaurant, bar, golf course, tennis court, business center, some pets allowed.*

LACOCK

Fodor's Choice ★ *8 mi southeast of Castle Combe, 12 mi east of Bath.*

Owned by the National Trust, this lovely Wiltshire village is the victim of its own charm, its unspoiled gabled and stone-tile cottages drawing tour buses aplenty. Off-season, however, Lacock slips back into its profound slumber, the mellow stone and brick buildings little changed in 500 years and well worth a wander. Besides Lacock Abbey, there is the handsome church of St. Cyriac (built with money earned in the

The charm of tiny Castle Combe, with its one main street of stone cottages, far exceeds its size.

wool trade) and a 14th-century tithe barn, and, in the village, a few antiques shops and a scattering of pubs that serve bar meals in atmospheric surroundings.

GETTING HERE AND AROUND

All buses from Bath to Lacock involve a change and take 60 to 110 minutes, so it's best to drive or join a tour.

EXPLORING

Lacock Abbey. Well-preserved Lacock Abbey reflects the fate of many religious establishments in England—a spiritual center became a home. The abbey, at the town's center, was founded in the 13th century and closed down during the dissolution of the monasteries in 1539, when its new owner, Sir William Sharington, demolished the church and converted the cloisters, sacristy, chapter house, and monastic quarters into a private dwelling. His last descendant, Mathilda Talbot, donated the property as well as Lacock itself to the National Trust in the 1940s. The abbey's grounds are also worth a wander, with a Victorian woodland garden and an 18th-century summerhouse. Harry Potter fans, take note: Lacock Abbey was used for some scenes at Hogwarts School in the film *Harry Potter and the Sorcerer's Stone.*

The **Fox Talbot Museum,** in a 16th-century barn at the gates of Lacock Abbey, illustrates the early history of photography with works by pioneers in the field and also exhibits contemporary artists. The museum commemorates the work of William Henry Fox Talbot (1800–77), who developed the first photographic negative at Lacock Abbey, showing an oriel window in his family home. ✉ *Just east of A350* ☎ *01249/730459* ⊕ *www.nationaltrust.org.uk* ✆ *Abbey, museum, gardens, and cloisters*

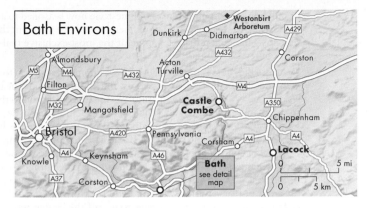

£10.40; *museum, gardens, and cloisters* £7.70 ☉ *Abbey mid-Feb.–Oct.,*
Wed.–Mon. 11–5; early Nov.–mid-Feb., weekends noon–4. Cloisters,
gardens, and museum mid-Feb.–Oct., daily 10:30–5:30; Nov.–mid-
Feb., daily 11–4. Last admission 30 mins before closing.

WHERE TO EAT

£££ ✕ **Sign of the Angel.** An inn since the 15th century, this atmospheric res-
BRITISH taurant is known for its roasts, casseroles, and specialties like Stilton
and walnut pâté. Don't pass up the homemade ice creams and sor-
bets. There are also somewhat cramped accommodations (£££)—some
rooms are in comfortable older buildings, others are in a newer annex.
✉ *6 Church St.* ☎ *01249/730230* ⊕ *www.lacock.co.uk* ☉ *Closed last*
wk of Dec.

THE COTSWOLDS

A gently undulating area of limestone uplands, the Cotswolds are
among England's best-preserved rural districts, and the quiet but lovely
grays and ambers of the stone buildings here are truly unsurpassed.
Much has been written about the area's age-mellowed towns, but the
architecture of the villages actually differs little from that of villages
elsewhere in England. Their distinction lies in their surroundings: the
valleys are lush and rolling, and cozy hamlets appear covered in foliage from church tower to garden gate. Beyond the town limits, you can
explore, on foot or by car, the "high wild hills and rough uneven ways"
that Shakespeare wrote about.

Over the centuries, quarries of honey-color stone have yielded building
blocks for many Cotswold houses and churches and have transformed
little towns into realms of gold. Make Chipping Campden, Moreton-
in-Marsh, or Stow-on-the-Wold your headquarters and wander for a
few days. Then ask yourself what the area is all about. Its secret seems
shared by two things—sheep and stone. These were once the great
sheep-rearing areas of England, and during the peak of prosperity in
the Middle Ages, Cotswold wool was in demand the world over. This
made the local merchants rich, but many gave back to the Cotswolds
by restoring old churches (the famous "wool churches" of the region)

or building rows of almshouses of limestone now seasoned to a glorious golden-gray. These days, the wool merchants have gone but the wealth remains—the region includes some of the most exclusive real-estate in the country.

One possible route is to begin with Cheltenham—the largest town in the area and a gateway to the Cotswolds, but slightly outside the boundaries and more of a small city in atmosphere—then move on to the beauty spots in and around Winchcombe. Next are Sudeley Castle, Stanway House, and Snowshill Manor, among the most impressive houses of the region; the oversold village of Broadway; Chipping Campden—the Cotswold cognoscenti's favorite; and Hidcote Manor, one of the most spectacular gardens in England. Then circle back south, down through Moreton-in-Marsh, Stow-on-the-Wold, Upper Slaughter, Lower Slaughter, and Bourton-on-the-Water, and end with Bibury and Tetbury. This is definitely a region where it pays to go off the beaten track to take a look at that village among the trees.

CHELTENHAM

50 mi north of Bath, 13 mi east of Gloucester, 99 mi west of London.

Although Cheltenham has acquired a reputation as snooty—the population (around 110,000) is generally well-heeled and conservative—it's also cosmopolitan. The town has excellent restaurants and bars, fashionable stores, and a thriving cultural life. Its primary claim to renown, however, is its architecture, rivaling Bath's in its Georgian elegance, with wide, tree-lined streets, crescents, and terraces with row houses, balconies, and iron railings.

Like Bath, Cheltenham owes part of its fame to mineral springs. By 1740 the first spa was built, and after a visit from George III and Queen Charlotte in 1788, the town dedicated itself to idleness and enjoyment. "A polka, parson-worshipping place"—in the words of resident Lord Tennyson—Cheltenham gained its reputation for snobbishness when stiff-collared Raj majordomos returned from India to find that the springs—the only purely natural alkaline waters in England—were the most effective cure for their "tropical ailments."

Great Regency architectural set pieces—Lansdown Crescent, Pittville Spa, and the Lower Assembly Rooms, among them—were built solely to adorn the town. The Rotunda building (1826) at the top of Montpellier Walk—now a bank—contains the spa's original "pump room," in which the mineral waters were on tap. More than 30 statues adorn the storefronts of Montpellier Walk. Wander past Imperial Square, with its ironwork balconies, past the ornate Neptune's Fountain, and along the Promenade. In spring and summer lush flower gardens enhance the town's buildings, attracting many visitors.

GETTING HERE AND AROUND

Trains from London Paddington and buses from London Victoria head to Cheltenham. The train station is west of the center, and the bus station is centrally located off Royal Well Road. Drivers should leave their vehicles in one of the numerous parking lots. The town center is easily

A tour of Gloucester Cathedral provides a visual lesson in architectural styles from Norman through Perpendicular Gothic.

negotiable on foot. Cheltenham's tourist office arranges walking tours (£4) of the town at 11:30 on Saturday April through October, also on Sunday in July and August.

ESSENTIALS

Visitor Information Cheltenham (✉ *77 Promenade* ☎ *01242/522878* ⊕ *www.visitcheltenham.com*)

EXPLORING

OFF THE BEATEN PATH

★**Gloucester Cathedral.** In the center of Gloucester, magnificent Gloucester Cathedral, with its soaring, elegant exterior, was originally a Norman abbey church, consecrated in 1100. Reflecting different periods, the cathedral mirrors perfectly the slow growth of ecclesiastical taste and the development of the Perpendicular style. The interior has largely been spared the sterilizing attentions of modern architects and is almost completely Norman, with the massive pillars of the nave left untouched since their completion. The fan-vaulted roof of the 14th-century cloisters is the finest in Europe, and the cloisters enclose a peaceful garden (used in the filming of *Harry Potter and the Sorcerer's Stone*). ■**TIP→** Don't miss the Whispering Gallery, which has a permanent exhibition devoted to the splendid, 14th-century stained glass of the Great East Window. Tours of the tower (269 steps up) are also available. Gloucester is 13 mi southwest of Cheltenham and reachable from there on frequent buses and trains. ✉ *Westgate St.* ☎ *01452/528095* ⊕ *www. gloucestercathedral.org.uk* ▦ *£5 donation requested, photography permit £5, tower tours £3, exhibition £2* ☉ *Daily 7:30–6, except during services and special events. Tower tours Apr.–Oct., Wed.–Fri. 2:30, Sat. 1:30 and 2:30, national holidays 11:30, 1:30, and 2:30; also Mon. and*

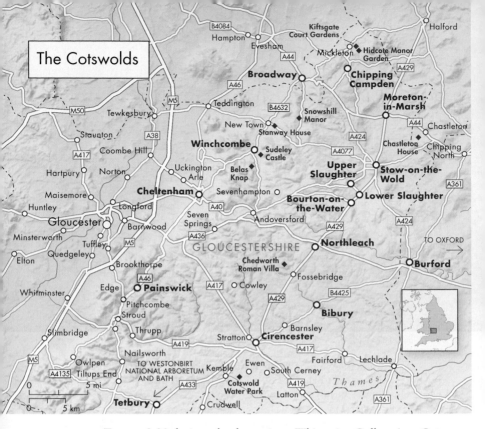

The Cotswolds

Tues. at 2:30 during school vacations. Whispering Gallery Apr.–Oct., weekdays 10:30–4, Sat. 10:30–3:30.

Pittville Pump Room. The grandest of the remaining spa buildings, the pump room is set amid parkland, a 20-minute walk from the town center. The classic Regency structure, built in the late 1820s, now serves mainly as a concert hall and a theatrical venue but still offers its musty mineral waters to the strong of stomach. Note that the venue is not open for visits during events—call first to check. ⊠ *E. Approach Dr., Pittville* ☎ *01242/521621* ⊕ *www.pittvillepumproom.org.uk* ⊠ *Free* ⏱ *Wed.–Sun. 10–4.*

WHERE TO EAT

£££

MODERN BRITISH

✗ **The Daffodil.** This restaurant proves that turning up the wow quotient doesn't always mean a drop in culinary standards. Housed in a former art deco cinema, the place is themed along 1920s lines. It's dimly lighted, with sweeping staircases and an open kitchen where the screen once stood; the best view is from the Circle Bar. The menu features grills of lamb, monkfish, and calves' liver, as well as fillet steak *au poivre* (with black pepper), duck breast, and braised pork belly. Afterwards, indulge in homemade ice cream, lime and lemongrass panna cotta, or a platter of local cheeses. There's live jazz on Monday evenings. Lunchtime and early-evening menus are a good deal. ⊠ *18–20 Suffolk*

Parade ☎ *01242/700055* ⊕ *www.
thedaffodil.com* ⚼ *Reservations
essential* ⊗ *Closed Sun.*

£££ ✕**Montpellier Wine Bar.** In Chel-
BRITISH tenham's fashionable Montpellier
shopping district, this busy, informal wine bar is a perfect place for
a lunchtime snack or a full evening
meal. The menu includes sirloin
steak, swordfish, and roast duck
breast. Seating is on two floors—
upstairs is casual and downstairs is
more formal. Get in early for speed-
ier service. ⊠ *Bayshill Lodge, Montpellier St.* ☎ *01242/527774* ⊕ *www.
montpellierwinebar.com.*

WHERE TO STAY

For expanded hotel reviews, visit Fodors.com.

££££–£££££ ▦ **Cowley Manor.** Good-bye, floral prints: this Georgian mansion on 55
HOTEL acres brings country-house style into the 21st century with a mellow
atmosphere and modern fabrics and furniture. **Pros:** beautiful grounds;
excellent spa facilities; relaxed vibe. **Cons:** slightly corporate feel; food
and service do not always justify the steep prices. ⊠ *Off A435, Cowley*
☎ *01242/870900* ⊕ *www.cowleymanor.com* ⇆ *30 rooms* ⚹ *In-room:
Internet, Wi-Fi (some). In-hotel: restaurant, pools, gym, spa, business
center* ⦿| *Breakfast.*

££ ▦ **Hanover House.** Centrally located, this guesthouse dating from 1848
B&B/INN brims with character, and richly colored cushions and myriad books
enliven the bright and airy rooms. **Pros:** convenient location; award-
winning breakfasts. **Cons:** all guests share one large table at breakfast.
⊠ *65 St. George's Rd.* ☎ *01242/541297* ⊕ *www.hanoverhouse.org* ⇆ *3
rooms* ⚹ *In-room: no a/c, no TV, Wi-Fi. In-hotel: parking, some age
restrictions* ▭ *No credit cards* ⦿| *Breakfast.*

££–£££ ▦ **Lypiatt House.** A short walk from central Cheltenham in the chic
B&B/INN Montpellier area, this splendid Victorian villa offers attentive service
in elegant surroundings. **Pros:** clean and elegant; capacious parking;
excellent breakfasts. **Cons:** occasionally impersonal service; slight traffic noise. ⊠ *Lypiatt Rd.* ☎ *01242/224994* ⊕ *www.lypiatt.co.uk* ⇆ *10
rooms* ⚹ *In-room: no a/c, Wi-Fi. In-hotel: bar, parking, some age
restrictions* ⦿| *Breakfast.*

NIGHTLIFE AND THE ARTS

The late-Victorian **Everyman Theatre** (⊠ *Regent St.* ☎ *01242/572573*)
is an intimate venue for opera, dance, concerts, and plays. ■**TIP**➔ You
can often catch pre– or post–West End productions here, at a fraction of
big-city prices.

For information on the town's ambitious lineup of festivals, contact the
Festivals Box Office (⊠ *Unit 77, Regent Arcade, High St.* ☎ *01242/505444*
⊕ *www.cheltenhamfestivals.com*).

The **Cheltenham Jazz Festival** (☎ *01242/505444* ⊕ *www.cheltenhamfestivals.
com*), held over a week in late April/early May, presents noted musicians.

7

October's Literature Festival brings plenty of authors—and their books— to Cheltenham.

★ The 10-day **Literature Festival** (☎ *01242/505444* ⊕ *www.cheltenhamfestivals.com*) in October brings together world-renowned authors, actors, and critics for hundreds of readings and events.

Cheltenham's famous **Music Festival** (☎ *01242/505444* ⊕ *www.cheltenhamfestivals.com*), in late June–mid-July, highlights new compositions, often conducted by the composers, and classical pieces.

The **Science Festival** (☎ *01242/505444* ⊕ *www.cheltenhamfestivals.com*), which takes place over five days in early June, attracts leading scientists and writers.

SHOPPING

This is serious shopping territory. A stroll along Montpellier Walk and then along the flower-bedecked Promenade brings you to high-quality specialty stores and boutiques. A bubble-blowing Wishing Fish Clock, designed by Kit Williams, dominates the Regent Arcade, a modern shopping area behind the Promenade. A farmers' market enlivens the Promenade on the second and last Friday of the month, and local produce vendors set up stall there on the first Saturday of the month.

Cavendish House (✉ *32–48 The Promenade* ☎ *01242/521300*) is a high-end department store with designer fashions.

Feva (✉ *20 Regent St.* ☎ *01242/222998*) sells eye-catching lines of clothes for women in bright, splashy colors, as well as shoes, belts, and handbags. More-formal wear is sold on the upper floor.

Martin (✉ *19 The Promenade* ☎ *01242/522821*) carries a good stock of classic and modern jewelry.

Q and C Militaria (✉ *22 Suffolk Rd.* ☎ *01242/519815*), a treasure trove for military buffs, offers badges and medals, breastplates, helmets, coats of arms, and books.

SPORTS

Important steeplechase races take place at **Cheltenham Racecourse** (✉ *Prestbury Park* ☎ *0844/579–3003*), north of the town center. The Gold Cup awards crown the last day of the National Hunt Festival in mid-March.

WINCHCOMBE

7 mi northeast of Cheltenham.

The sleepy, unspoiled village of Winchcombe (population 4,500), once the capital of the Anglo-Saxon kingdom of Mercia, has some attractive half-timber and stone houses, as well as a clutch of appealing old inns serving food. A good place to escape the crowds, it's near Sudeley Castle and is also on several walking routes: the Cotswold Way; the Warden's Way and Windrush Way, both linking Winchcombe with Bourton-on-the-Water; and the Winchcombe Way, a 42-mi figure-eight trail around the northern Cotswolds. A three-day walking festival (⊕ *www.winchcombewelcomeswalkers.com*) takes place here in late May.

GETTING HERE AND AROUND

Hourly Castleways buses take 20 minutes to get to Winchcombe from Cheltenham (no Sunday service). By car, take B4632, leading over the steep and panoramic Cleeve Hill.

ESSENTIALS

Visitor Information Winchcombe (✉ *Town Hall, High St.* ☎ *01242/602925* ⊕ *www.visitcotswoldsandsevernvale.gov.uk*)

EXPLORING

Gloucestershire and Warwickshire Railway. Less than a mile north of Winchcombe, at Greet, you can board a steam-hauled train that chugs its way along the foot of the Cotswolds between Greet and Cheltenham Racecourse. The 14-mi round-trip journey takes around 25 minutes each way, with a 15–25-minute pause at Cheltenham (you can start your journey in Cheltenham, too). ✉ *Greet* ☎ *01242/621405* ⊕ *www.gwsr.com* 🎫 *£12 (valid all day)* ☉ *Late-Apr.–Oct., Sun.–Thurs. 10–5; Nov., weekends and Dec. 26–31, 10–5.*

Humblebee Wood. A bracing 2-mi walk south of Winchcombe on the **Cotswold Way**, one of Britain's national walking trails, leads to the hilltop site of **Belas Knap**, a Neolithic long barrow, or submerged burial chamber, above Humblebee Wood. ■ TIP➔ The site isn't much to see, but you hike next to and through one of the most enchanting natural domains in England, with views stretching over to Sudeley Castle. If you have a car, take the scenic Humblebee Wood road down to the villages of Sevenhampton and Brockhampton.

St. Peter's Church. Almost 40 outlandish gargoyles adorn this mid-15th-century Perpendicular-style building, a typical Cotswold wool church.

The interior also displays some of the original tile flooring, a pair of stone coffins, and an ancient rustic cello. ⊠ *Gloucester St.*

★ **Sudeley Castle.** One of the grand showpieces of the Cotswolds, Sudeley Castle was the home and burial place of Catherine Parr (1512–48), Henry VIII's sixth and last wife, who outlived him by one year. Here Catherine undertook, in her later years, the education of the ill-fated Lady Jane Grey and the future queen, Princess Elizabeth. Sudeley, for good reason, has been called a woman's castle. The term "castle" is misleading, though, for it looks more like a Tudor-era palace, with a peaceful air that belies its turbulent history. In the 17th century Charles I took refuge here, causing Oliver Cromwell's army to besiege the castle. It remained in ruins until the Dent-Brocklehurst family stepped in with a 19th-century renovation.

The 14 acres of gardens, which include the spectacular roses of the Queen's Garden and a Tudor knot garden, are the setting for Shakespeare performances, concerts, and other events in summer. During 2012, a program of events will mark the 500th anniversary of the birth of Catherine Parr. Inside the castle, though, visitors see only the West Wing, with the Long Room and temporary exhibitions that focus on such subjects as the Tudors, the Civil War, and the Victorians. The private apartments of Lord and Lady Ashcombe, where you can see paintings by Van Dyck, Rubens, Turner, and Reynolds, are viewable only on Connoisseur Tours on Tuesday, Wednesday, and Thursday (£12, including entry to the public rooms). The 11 cottages on the grounds are booked for a minimum of three-night stays. The castle is a mile southeast of Winchcombe. ⊠ *Off B4632* ☎ *01242/602308* ⊕ *www.sudeleycastle.co.uk* ⏎*£7.20* ⏲ *Late Mar.–early Nov., daily 10:30–5.*

WHERE TO EAT

£££
MODERN BRITISH

✕ **Wesley House.** Wooden beams and stone walls distinguish this 15th-century half-timber building, where the red-carpeted dining room makes a fine backdrop for superior Modern British dishes. The seasonal menu might include Hereford beef fillet with forest mushrooms and red-wine sauce, and roast partridge with butternut squash. Fixed-price lunch and evening menus are a good value. You can eat and drink less formally in the adjoining bar and grill, with a choice of pastas, steaks, and seafood. Upstairs, five small guest rooms (££) have twisted beams and sloping ceilings, including the Preacher's Room, where John Wesley used to stay. ⊠ *High St.* ☎ *01242/602366* ⏲ *No dinner Sun.*

BROADWAY

8 mi north of Winchcombe, 17 mi northeast of Cheltenham.

The Cotswold town to end all Cotswold towns, Broadway has become a favorite of day-trippers. William Morris first discovered the delights of this village, and J.M. Barrie, Vaughan Williams, and Edward Elgar soon followed. Today you may want to avoid Broadway in summer, when it's clogged with cars and buses. Named for its handsome, wide main street (well worth a stroll), the village includes numerous antiques shops, tea parlors, and boutiques. Step off onto Broadway's back-roads

As enchanting as the house, the gardens at Sudeley Castle provide a perfect backdrop for outdoor events in summer.

and alleys and you can discover any number of honey-color houses and colorful gardens.

GETTING HERE AND AROUND

Broadway can be reached by car via A44; drivers should park in one of the parking lots signposted from the main street. Johnson's Coaches connects the town with Stratford-upon-Avon, Chipping Campden, and Moreton-in-Marsh; Castleways connects Broadway with Winchcombe and Cheltenham. No services run on Sunday. You'll need a car to reach Broadway Tower, Stanway House, and Snowshill Manor.

ESSENTIALS

Visitor Information Broadway (✉ *Russell Sq.* ☎ *01386/852937* ⊕ *www. beautifulbroadway.com*).

EXPLORING

Broadway Tower Country Park. Among the attractions of this park, on the outskirts of town, is its **tower**, an 18th-century "folly" built by the sixth earl of Coventry and later used by William Morris as a retreat. Exhibits describe the tower's past and the local Arts and Crafts movement, and the view from the top takes in three counties. (The tower normally stays open longer than the advertised times in fine weather.) Peaceful countryside surrounds you on the nature trails and picnic grounds. ✉ *Off A44* ☎ *01386/852390* ⊕ *www.broadwaytower.co.uk* 🎫 *Park free, tower £4.50* ⊙ *Tower Apr.–Oct., daily 10:30–5; Nov.–Mar., weekends 11–3.*

★ **Snowshill Manor.** Snowshill, 3 mi south of Broadway and 13 mi northeast
☺ of Cheltenham, is one of the most unspoiled of all Cotswold villages. Snuggled beneath Oat Hill, with little room for expansion, the hamlet

is centered around an old burial ground, the 19th-century St. Barnabas Church, and Snowshill Manor, a splendid 17th-century house that brims with the collections of Charles Paget Wade, gathered between 1919 and 1956. Over the door of the house is Wade's family motto, *Nequid pereat* ("Let nothing perish"). The rooms are bursting with Tibetan scrolls, spinners' tools, ship models, Persian lamps,

> ## SEEKING SHAKESPEARE
>
> The country delights of the area lure you to linger, but keep in mind that in the northern part of the Cotswolds, you're less than 15 mi from Stratford-upon-Avon. It's easy to detour to visit the Shakespeare sights or even see a play at the Royal Shakespeare Theatre.

and bric-a-brac; the Green Room displays 26 suits of Japanese samurai armor. Children love the place. Outside, an imaginative terraced garden provides an exquisite frame for the house. ■ TIP➜ Admission is by timed tickets issued on a first-come, first-served basis, so arrive early in peak season. ⊠ *Off A44, Snowshill* ☎ *01386/852410* ⊕ *www.nationaltrust.org. uk* ☜ *£8.10; garden only, £4.40* ⊘ *House mid-Mar.–Oct., Wed.–Sun. noon–5. Garden mid-Mar.–Oct., Wed.–Sun. 11–5:30.*

★ **Stanway House.** This perfect Cotswold manor of glowing limestone, in the small village of Stanway, dates from the Jacobean era. Its triple-gabled gatehouse is a Cotswold landmark, and towering windows dominate the house's Great Hall. They illuminate a 22-foot-long shuffleboard table from 1620 and an 18th-century bouncing exercise machine. The other well-worn rooms are adorned with family portraits, tattered tapestries, vintage armchairs, and, at times, Lord or Lady Neidpath themselves, the current owners. The partly restored baroque water garden has a fountain, built in 2004, that shoots up 300 feet. The tallest in Britain, it shoots at 2:45 and 4. To get to Stanway, about 5 mi south of Broadway, take B4632 south from town, turning left at B4077. ⊠ *Off B4077, Stanway* ☎ *01386/584469* ⊕ *www.stanwayfountain.co.uk* ☜ *House and fountain £7; fountain only, £4.50* ⊘ *House and fountain June–Aug., Tues. and Thurs. 2–5.*

WHERE TO EAT

£££ ✕ **Russell's.** With a courtyard at the back and a patio at the front, this
MODERN BRITISH chic "restaurant with rooms" is perfect for a light lunch at midday or a full meal in the evening. The restaurant, in a former furniture factory belonging to local designer George Russell, is modern and stylish. Menus concentrate on Modern British dishes, with such temptations as warm salad of grilled ox heart with pickled walnuts, mushrooms, and sautéed potatoes; corn-fed chicken with basmati rice and cauliflower fritters; and panfried hake. There's also an outstanding cheese board. Seven boutique-style rooms upstairs (££–£££) are very sleek. ⊠ *20 High St.* ☎ *01386/853555* ⊕ *www.russellsofbroadway.co.uk* ⊘ *No dinner Sun.*

££ ✕ **The Swan.** In the center of Broadway, this pub-restaurant makes a
MODERN BRITISH handy stop for a snack lunch, a drink, or something more substantial. Service may be occasionally slapdash and the place can get congested, but on a weekday it's cozy and convivial, with an open fire in winter

and comfortable seating. The imaginative decor blends the traditional and trendy with large mirrors, log walls, and eye-catching knick-knacks. Among the hot dishes are fillet steak, duck breast with a port-and-plum sauce, and bouillabaisse; light bites include chicken ciabattas and jacket potatoes. Choose among the areas to eat in, including a garden. ⊠ *2 The Green* ☎ *01386/852278* ⊕ *www.theswanbroadway.co.uk.*

WHERE TO STAY

For expanded hotel reviews, visit Fodors.com.

£££££
HOTEL
★

🔲 **Buckland Manor.** As an alternative to the hustle and bustle of Broadway, you can splurge at this exceptional traditional country-house hotel 2 mi away in the idyllic hamlet of Buckland. **Pros:** beautiful setting; elegant guest rooms; large bathrooms with high-quality toiletries. **Cons:** service can be spotty; some rooms are small; restaurant very formal. ⊠ *Off B4632, Buckland* ☎ *01386/852626* ⊕ *www.bucklandmanor. co.uk* ⊅ *13 rooms* ⅁ *In-room: no a/c, Internet. In-hotel: restaurant, bar, tennis courts, business center, some age restrictions* ⏧ *Breakfast.*

££££
HOTEL
★

🔲 **Dormy House Hotel.** Luxury rules at this converted 17th-century farmhouse overlooking the Vale of Evesham from high on the Cotswolds ridge—one of the region's most celebrated vistas. **Pros:** professional staff; good food; attractive packages. **Cons:** slightly bland decor; some standard rooms are small and dark; isolated. ⊠ *Willersey Hill* ☎ *01386/852711* ⊕ *www.dormyhouse.co.uk* ⊅ *45 rooms* ⅁ *In-room: no a/c, Internet (some), Wi-Fi (some). In-hotel: restaurants, bars, golf course, gym* ⏧ *Breakfast.*

£££
B&B/INN

🔲 **Mill Hay House.** If the rose garden, trout-filled pond, and pet sheep at this 18th-century Queen Anne house aren't appealing enough, then the stone-flagged floors, leather sofas, and grandfather clocks should satisfy. **Pros:** delightful owners; beautifully landscaped gardens; gourmet breakfasts. **Cons:** books up quickly; no young children admitted. ⊠ *Snowshill Rd.* ☎ *01386/852498* ⊕ *www.millhay.co.uk* ⊅ *2 rooms, 1 suite* ⅁ *In-room: no a/c, Wi-Fi. In-hotel: some age restrictions* ⏧ *Breakfast.*

££
B&B/INN

🔲 **Old Stationhouse.** This former stationmaster's home on an acre of lawns and gardens makes a peaceful refuge from the tourist traffic of Broadway, a 10-minute walk away. **Pros:** thoughtful extras in rooms; welcoming and knowledgeable hosts. **Cons:** outside the village; lacks old-world ambience. ⊠ *Station Rd.* ☎ *01386/852659* ⊕ *www. oldstationhousebroadway.co.uk* ⊅ *6 rooms* ⅁ *In-room: Wi-Fi (some), no a/c. In-hotel: business center* ⏧ *Breakfast.*

££
B&B/INN

🔲 **The Olive Branch.** Right on the main drag, this 16th-century cottage has authentic period charm and is strewn with antique knickknacks and black-and-white photos. **Pros:** cottage character; central location; hospitable hosts. **Cons:** small bathrooms; narrow stairs; low ceilings. ⊠ *78 High St.* ☎ *01386/853440* ⊕ *www.theolivebranch-broadway.com* ⊅ *8 rooms* ⅁ *In-room: no a/c, Wi-Fi (some). In-hotel: business center, some pets allowed* ⏧ *Breakfast.*

Continued on page 457

GLORIOUS ENGLISH GARDENS

by Kate Hughes

The English have been masters of the garden for centuries; gardening is in the blood. No one, from the owner of vast acres in the country to a town dweller with a modest window box, is able to resist this pull. Since the 18th century they have also been inveterate garden visitors, with people from around the world following. Here's how to make the most of your garden visit, from the variety of styles you'll see to the best bets for all tastes around England.

Magnificent vista of the Pantheon and lake at Stourhead

For many people the quintessential English garden conjures up swaths of close-clipped lawns (the landscape garden), beds of roses, or colorful flowers (the herbaceous border) lining a path to a cottage door framed with honeysuckle.

This is not the whole story, however. Cathedrals and colleges yield up their sequestered cloister gardens; grand houses their patterned beds of flowers by the thousand; manor houses their amusing topiary shapes, orchards, and wildflower meadows; sweeping landscaped parks their classical temples and serpentine lakes; a Cornish ravine its jungle tumbling down to the sea. And this is not to mention the magnificent glasshouses and biomes of the botanical gardens housing spectacular plant treasures. Around the country, gardens large and small invite exploration.

GARDEN STYLES THROUGH THE AGES

In the gardens you'll be visiting, one theme remains constant no matter the style: the combination of usefulness and beauty. Gardens were larders as well as ornaments; plants were grown and birds and animals kept both for decoration and for eating. Behind each great garden was wealth, and gardens became as great a status symbol as the houses they surrounded. Growing the best pineapple, building the most elaborate terraces, flooding a valley to make a lake were all signs that you had made it in the world.

Clockwise from top left: Stowe Landscape Gardens; Chatsworth; Hidcote Manor Garden; Hampton Court Palace (formal Privy Garden)

SYMBOLS AND PATTERNS: TUDOR GARDENS

Since Tudor times the rose has been the emblem of England, and it still is the most loved English flower. Musk roses entwine the arbors in the garden created to impress Queen Elizabeth I on her visit to Kenilworth Castle in 1575, now magnificently restored. Here the formal arrangement of trellises, obelisks, fountain, statues, and aviary set in gravel paths and overlooked by a viewing platform exemplify gardens of the time. Also here is the first uniquely English garden feature—the knot garden. Low evergreen hedges, most famously planted with box, were interlaced in geometric patterns, the spaces filled with flowers and herbs. Good examples of knot gardens can be found at Hampton Court Palace and Hatfield House.

See it: *Hampton Court Palace* (Ch. 2), *Hatfield House* (Ch. 6), *Kenilworth Castle* (Ch. 8)

WEALTH AND POWER: THE 17TH-CENTURY FORMAL GARDEN

Landed gentry with time on their hands took gardening to their hearts. After the ravages of the Civil War (1642–49) and the Great Fire of London (1666) they felt the lure of the rural idyll, and country houses with small estates proliferated. The garden rectangle in front of the house was divided into smaller rectangles—the forerunner of garden "rooms" as at Sissinghurst and Hidcote Manor—and filled with formal walkways, fishponds, and fountains. Topiary gardens (Levens Hall and Packwood House) became popular, and an increase in foreign travel led to the introduction of a greater variety of bulbs and flowers. In 1621 the first botanic garden was set up in Oxford.

See it: *Hidcote Manor* (Ch. 7), *Levens Hall* (Ch. 10), *Packwood House* (Ch. 8), *Sissinghurst* (Ch. 3), *University of Oxford Botanic Garden* (Ch. 6)

7

IN FOCUS GLORIOUS ENGLISH GARDENS

Knot garden at Hatfield House

GEOMETRY TO LANDSCAPE: THE 18TH CENTURY

Gradually the formal approach gave way. One product of the fashionable Grand Tour, when aristocratic young bloods were exposed to new landscapes and ideas, was William Kent (1685–1748), the "father of modern gardening." His innovative genius was his English take on the Italian garden, converting the natural landscape into a pleasure ground for the rich, dotting it with statues, obelisks, and classical temples and ornamenting it with trees and serpentine lakes (Rousham and Stowe).

Kent was eclipsed by Lancelot "Capability" Brown (1715–83), who created 100 gardens between 1750 and 1780 (Stowe, Stourhead, Petworth, Kew Gardens). He brought the landscape right to the front door and created lakes and parkland that also provided timber, cover for game, and grazing for sheep and deer.

See it: *Kew Gardens* (Ch. 2), *Petworth* (Ch. 3) *Rousham and Stowe* (Ch. 6), *Stourhead* (Ch. 4)

SHOW AND TECHNOLOGY: THE VICTORIAN PERIOD

This was an age of new technology, variety, and the return of flowers. Wealthy industrialists could afford to move out of town and create rose gardens, ferneries, and rockeries, and display showier flowers such as chrysanthemums, dahlias, and rhododendrons. The invention of the lawn mower in 1830 made the English obsession with close-clipped lawns accessible to all. Bedding schemes and patterns reappeared in the new public parks of the 1830s and 1840s. One spectacular scheme is the parterre (ornamental flower garden with paths) at Waddesdon Manor, planted with 200,000 plants each summer. Joseph Paxton (1803–1865) head gardener at Chatworth, created the first greenhouse, which started a fashion for conservatories and the growing of exotic fruit such as figs and peaches.

See it: *Chatsworth* (Ch. 9), *Waddesdon Manor* (Ch. 6)

The parterre at Waddesdon Manor

ARTS AND CRAFTS: INTO THE 20TH CENTURY

The Arts and Crafts movement drew inspiration from medieval romance and nature and preferred the informal cottage garden look, seen particularly in the Cotswolds (Hidcote Manor, Kiftsgate, Rodmarton Manor). Female gardeners came to the fore. Gertrude Jekyll (pronounced Jee-kill; 1843–1932), often working with the architect Edwin Lutyens (1869–1944), set the fashion for using drifts of single color, and Vita Sackville West (1892–1962) created the enduringly romantic Sissinghurst.

See it: *Hidcote Manor, Kiftsgate,* and *Rodmarton Manor (Ch. 7), Sissinghurst* (Ch. 3)

ANYTHING GOES: MODERN TIMES

The reaction to the drab years of the Second World War was to create garden cities and increasingly versatile gardens using all modern materials available. The bold approach and strong colors of Christopher Lloyd (1921–2006) at Great Dixter has remained influential. Even bolder is Diarmid Gavin, whose suspended Garden in Sky astonished the 2011 Chelsea Flower Show. Environmental awareness has led to more educational gardens, such as the spectacular Eden Project in Cornwall.

See it: *Great Dixter* (Ch. 3), *Eden Project* (Ch. 5)

Overview of part of Sissinghurst (top); house and garden at Great Dixter (bottom)

BEST IN SHOW AROUND THE COUNTRY

Rousham Park

Practically every house or stately home you visit will be surrounded by a lovingly tended garden, but you will find a profusion of outstanding examples in the Cotswolds (Oxfordshire and Gloucestershire), Kent, and Cornwall. Kent is known as the "Garden of England" for its abundance of orchards and hop gardens; Cornwall's mild climate produces lush gardens, many by the sea; and the mellow honey-colored stone of the Cotswolds makes a perfect backdrop for floral ornament.

FLOWER GARDENS

The first three gardens, created in the 20th century, come top of the garden-visiting league. All show flair for harmonious planting in choice of color, form, and texture within a strong framework. Here flowers hold court.

❶ Hidcote Manor Garden (Bath and the Cotswolds). The pioneer of "garden rooms" and influential ever since, this garden blends the scent of old roses, long avenues with vistas, and the famous Red Borders, especially vibrant from July.

❷ Sissinghurst (Southeast). Inspired by Hidcote Manor, it's divided into themed spaces: the Purple Border, the Rose Garden, the Cottage Garden, and, most famously, the White Garden.

❸ Great Dixter (Southeast). Vibrant color combinations surround the delightful 16th-century, half-timbered manor

house, also open. The Exotic Garden is at its best in late summer and early autumn.

❹ Rose Garden in the Savill Garden at Windsor (Thames Valley). The very contemporary Rose Garden (2010) has a viewing promontory for the 2,500 headily scented roses in their swaths of pinks, yellows, and reds.

BOTANIC AND TEACHING GARDENS

If you're thinking endless paths of plants and reading labels, think again. These gardens share their expertise through stunning architecture, hands-on activities, and fantastic displays.

❺ Kew Gardens (London). An 18th-century Chinese Pagoda is the landmark for Kew Gardens and its magnificent 19th-century greenhouses, housing a tropical rain forest and the world's tallest plant. There's also a treetop walkway.

❻ Eden Project (West Country). Cornwall's "global garden" explores man's relationship with plants with great imagination and a sense of fun. Huge biomes, like see-through golf balls, contain different plants from all climates.

❼ Wisley (Southeast). Flagship garden for the Royal Horticultural Society, it has a huge modern, elegant glasshouse, full of plants from around the world, plus flower and vegetable gardens and a unique interactive Root Zone.

Ayr

SCOTLAND

Dumfries

Carlisle

Keswick

Douglas

Isle of Man

Barrow-in-Furness

Blackpool

Isle of Anglesey

Holyhead

Caernarfon

Liverpool

Irish Sea

Aberystwyth

WALES

Swansea

Cardiff

Bristol Channel

Barnstaple

Lyme Regis

Exeter

Bodelva
215mi

Plymouth

Falmouth

Kew Gardens

Stourhead

LANDSCAPE GARDENS

The 18th-century English landscape garden has much more to offer than sweeping Capability Brown parkland. Adopt an aristocratic air and give yourself time to walk and admire the vistas.

❽ Stowe Landscape Gardens (Thames Valley). The grandest stop on the garden visiting circuit for over 200 years, it has no less than 40 temples, enormous grand avenues, a serpentine lake, and even Elysian Fields.

❾ Stourhead (South). Quite simply, this masterpiece of a garden set in a valley encompassing a lake is one of the finest landscape gardens in the world. Summer rhododendrons and trees in the fall add to the picture.

❿ Rousham Park (Thames Valley). More intimate than Stowe or Stourhead, it makes for an idyllic walk. The walled garden blooms with flowers.

FAMILY FAVORITES

For kids, choose the bigger gardens; they will have special attractions and activities for them. The Eden Project and Kew Gardens are also family friendly.

⓫ Alnwick Garden (Northeast). This contemporary garden was created with families in mind. Kids will be fascinated by the poison garden, water jets, and Bamboo Maze, and won't forget eating in the wooden Treehouse Café.

⓬ Chatsworth (Lancashire and the Peaks). The grand water Cascade falling the 200-foot length of the steps and the Emperor Fountain shooting 300 feet into the sky provide entertainment, along with the maze, farmyard, and woodland adventure playground.

⓭ Westonbirt National Arboretum (Bath and the Cotswolds). Play zones are hidden throughout the arboretum. Kids can clamber into a bird's nest, crawl through trunk tunnels, make dens, and, of course, climb trees.

Map labels

Alnwick ⓫ 270mi
Newcastle
Sunderland
Penrith
Hartlepool
Darlington
Middlesbrough
Kendal
York
Lancaster
Leeds
Bradford
Manchester
Sheffield
Chester
Bakewell ⓬ 135mi
Stoke
Nottingham
Boston
The Wash
Newcastle
Grantham
Shrewsbury
King's Lynn
Norwich
Wolverhampton
Leicester
Birmingham
Peterborough
Lowestoft
Stratford upon-Avon
Coventry
ENGLAND
Ipswich
Hidcote Bartrim ❶ 85mi
Rousham ❿ 60mi
Buckingham ❽ 45mi
Colchester
Harwich
Cheltenham
Luton
Gloucester
Oxford
Kew ❺ 10mi
Tetbury ⓭ 95mi
Englefield Green ❹ 13 mi
LONDON 0mi
Bristol
Reading
Canterbury
Bath
Woking ❼
20mi
Maidstone
Cranbrook ❷ 35mi
Dover
Stourton ❾ 100mi
Salisbury
Northiam ❸ 50mi
Southampton
Brighton
Rye
Bournemouth
Portsmouth
Weymouth
Isle of Wight
English Channel
* Approximate travel distance from London
Dieppe
FRANCE

❀ MAKING THE MOST OF YOUR GARDEN VISIT

SEASONAL SPLENDOR

The best gardens will have something of interest year-round, though many close in winter. Spring through September yield the most rewards, and each season will have its special offerings: early spring offers snowdrops, followed by daffodils and bluebells. May is the month for azaleas and rhododendrons, roses are in full bloom in June, and by July herbaceous borders of lupins, delphiniums, and foxgloves are showing their true colors. August sees hydrangeas and dahlias coming to the fore, while in September there's a second flowering of roses. The oranges and reds of the fall last through October.

Eden Project

TOURING TIPS

The bigger houses have separate, often less expensive tickets for the gardens and the grounds only, so do ask. Depending on your itinerary, buying a Great British Heritage Pass (⊕ www. britishheritagepass.com) or joining the National Trust (⊕ www.nationaltrust. org.uk) may save you money on garden admissions.

A car is preferable, as many places are not accessible by train or bus; Web sites often have information on public transportation options if they are available. The most popular gardens, such as Sissinghurst, get very crowded, especially on weekends, so come early or late in the day for a more peaceful visit. Most gardens have a café or restaurant, and nothing is more delightful than a cream tea in an English country garden in June.

Gardens associated with the National Trust are closed in winter, but their grounds remain open.

GOING DEEPER

The indispensable Yellow Book (£9.99) is published annually by the National Gardens Scheme (⊕ www.ngs.org.uk);

it is also available in sections by county (free, with donation). The directory lists public and private gardens that are normally closed to the public but have open days for charity throughout the year. Many of them offer teas as well.

FLOWER SHOWS

London claims the two main flower shows, both knockouts that last several days. The Chelsea Flower Show, five days in late May (£47; no kids under 5), and, outside the city, Hampton Court Palace Flower Show, six days in early July (£30), represent the cutting edge of design and cover every aspect of gardening (☎ 0121/767–4063 or ☎ 0844/338–7505, ⊕ www.rhs.org.uk).

MORE RESOURCES

Two useful Web sites are ⊕ www. gardenvisit.org, a mine of information on gardens by county, garden hotels, tours self-guided and led, and garden history; and ⊕ www.greatbritishgardens.co.uk, which has a good directory of gardens.

Good books to read are *The Gardens of Britain and Ireland* by Patrick Taylor (Dorling Kindersley), *The Good Gardens Guide*, edited by Katherine Lambert (Readers Digest), and *Great Gardens to Visit* by Tony Russell (Amberley Publishing).

CHIPPING CAMPDEN

4 mi east of Broadway, 18 mi northeast of Cheltenham.

Undoubtedly one of the most beautiful towns in the area, Chipping Campden, with its population of about 2,500, is the Cotswolds in a microcosm. It has St. James, the region's most impressive church; frozen-in-time streets; a silk mill that was once the center of the Guild of Handicrafts; and pleasant, untouristy shops. One of the area's most seductive settings unfolds before you as you travel on B4081 through sublime English countryside and happen upon the town, tucked in a slight valley. North of town is lovely Hidcote Manor Garden. ■TIP→ Chipping Campden can easily be reached on foot along a level section of the Cotswold Way from Broadway Tower, outside Broadway; the walk takes about 75 minutes.

GETTING HERE AND AROUND

By car, Chipping Campden can be reached on minor roads from A44 or A429. There's a small car park in the center and spaces on the outskirts of the village. By bus, take Johnson's Coaches from Stratford-upon-Avon, Broadway, and Moreton-in-Marsh, or Pulham's Coaches from Bourton-on-the-Water and Cheltenham, changing at Moreton-in-Marsh (no Sunday service).

ESSENTIALS

Visitor Information Chipping Campden (⌧ *The Old Police Station, High St.* ☎ *01386/841206* ⊕ *www.chippingcampdenonline.org*).

EXPLORING

TOP ATTRACTIONS

Fodor's Choice ★ **Hidcote Manor Garden.** Laid out around a Cotswold manor house, Hidcote Manor Garden is arguably the most interesting and attractive large garden in Britain. Crowds are large at the height of the season, but it's worthwhile anytime. A horticulturist from the United States (a naturalized British citizen), Major Lawrence Johnston, created the garden in 1907 in the Arts and Crafts style. Johnston was an imaginative gardener and avid traveler who brought back specimens from all over the world. The formal part of the garden is arranged in "rooms" separated by hedges and often with fine topiary work and walls. Besides the variety of plants, what's impressive are the different effects created, from calm open spaces to areas packed with flowers. ■TIP→ Look out for one of Johnston's earliest schemes, the red borders of dahlias, poppies, fuchsias, lobelias, and roses; the tall hornbeam hedges; and the Bathing Pool garden, where the pool is so wide there's scarcely space to walk. The White Garden was probably the forerunner of the popular white gardens at Sissinghurst and Glyndebourne. If you have time, explore tiny Hidcote Bartrim with its thatched stone houses; it borders the garden and fills a storybook dell. The garden is 4 mi northeast of Chipping Campden. ⌧ *Off B4081, Hidcote Bartrim* ☎ *01386/438333* ⊕ *www.nationaltrust. org.uk* ⌸ *£9.05* ⊙ *Mid-Mar.–June and Sept., Mon.–Wed. and weekends 10–6; July and Aug., daily 10–6; Oct.–early Nov., Mon.–Wed. and weekends 10–5; early Nov.–mid-Dec., Mon.–Wed. and weekends 11–4; last admission 1 hr before closing.*

7

St. James. The soaring pinnacled tower of St. James, a prime example of a Cotswold wool church (it was rebuilt in the 15th century with money from wool merchants), announces Chipping Campden from a distance; it's worth stepping inside to see the lofty nave. The church recalls the old saying, which became popular because of the vast numbers of houses of worship in the Cotswolds, "As sure as God's in Gloucestershire." ⊠ *Church St.* ☎ *01386/841927* ⊕ *www.stjameschurchcampden.co.uk* ⊠ *£1 donation suggested* ⊙ *Mar.–Oct., Mon.–Sat. 10–5, Sun. 2–6; Nov. and Feb., Mon.–Sat. 11–4, Sun. 2–4; Dec. and Jan., Mon.–Sat. 11–3, Sun. 2–3.*

WORTH NOTING

Court Barn Museum. Near the church of St. James, the museum occupies an old agricultural building that has been smartly renovated to showcase the area's prominence in the fields of craft and design. You can admire examples of silverware, bookbinding, printing, furniture, and jewelry. Opposite the barn is an important row of almshouses dating from the reign of King James I. ⊠ *Church St* ☎ *01386/841951* ⊕ *www.courtbarn.org.uk* ⊠ *£4* ⊙ *Apr.–Sept., Tues.–Sun. 10–5; Oct.–Mar., Tues.–Sun. 10–4.*

Kiftsgate Court Gardens. While not so spectacular as Hidcote Manor Garden, this intimate, privately owned garden, just a five-minute stroll away, still captivates. It's skipped by the majority of visitors to Hidcote, so you won't be jostled by the crowds. The interconnecting gardens present harmonious arrays of color. Don't miss the prized Kiftsgate rose, supposed to be the largest in England, flowering gloriously in mid-July. ⊠ *Off B4081, Mickleton* ☎ *01386/438777* ⊕ *www.kiftsgate. co.uk* ⊠ *£7* ⊙ *Apr. and Sept., Mon., Wed., and Sun. 2–6; May–July, Sat.–Wed. noon–6; Aug., Sat.–Wed. 2–6.*

Market Hall. The broad High Street, lined with stone houses and shops, follows a captivating curve; in the center, on Market Street, is the Market Hall, a gabled Jacobean structure built by Sir Baptiste Hycks in 1627 "for the sale of local produce."

Silk Mill. In 1902 the Guild of Handicrafts took over the Silk Mill, and Arts and Crafts evangelist Charles Robert Ashbee (1863–1942) brought 150 acolytes here from London, including 50 guildsmen, to revive and practice such skills as cabinetmaking and bookbinding. The operation folded in 1920, but the refurbished building still houses the workshops of a silversmith, jeweler, and stone carver, and has a café and gallery on the ground floor. ⊠ *Sheep St.* ☎ *No phone* ⊠ *Free* ⊙ *Workshops weekdays 9–5, Sat. 9–1; café and gallery weekdays 8:30–5, weekends 10–5.*

WHERE TO EAT

££
BRITISH

✕ **Churchill Arms.** In this small country pub just outside Chipping Campden, plain wooden tables and benches, a flagstone floor, and a roaring fire provide the backdrop for excellent food. Daily specials—grilled sea bass on a bed of spinach, and sirloin steak with fries—appear on the blackboard. If you feel like staying overnight, upstairs are four traditionally furnished bedrooms (££). ⊠ *Off B4035, Paxford* ☎ *01386/594000* ⊕ *www.thechurchillarms.com.*

££ ✕**Eight Bells.** Close to St. James Church, this traditional tavern has low
BRITISH beams, a flagstone floor, and a small courtyard. The long menu includes
such enticing dishes as pea and honey-roasted ham risotto, medallions
of pork with caramelized apples, and baked fillet of salmon. Fixed-
price menus at lunchtime are easy on the wallet. Service is swift, and
good local ales are dispensed. ⊠ *Church St.* ☎ *01386/840371* ⊕ *www.*
eightbellsinn.co.uk.

WHERE TO STAY
For expanded hotel reviews, visit Fodors.com.

££ ⛏**Badgers Hall.** Expect a friendly welcome at this antique B&B above
B&B/INN a tearoom just across from the Market Hall, where the spacious,
spotless rooms have beamed ceilings and exposed stonework. **Pros:**
atmospheric building; attentive hosts; delicious breakfasts. **Cons:** low
ceilings; entrance is through tea shop. ⊠ *High St.* ☎ *01386/840839*
⊕ *www.badgershall.com* ⮌ *3 rooms* ⚅ *In-room: Wi-Fi. In-hotel: some*
age restrictions ⛨ *Breakfast.*

£££ ⛏**Charingworth Manor.** Views of the countryside are limitless from this
HOTEL 14th-century manor house hotel just outside town; mullioned windows and oak beams enhance the sitting room, and bedrooms have
antique furniture. **Pros:** helpful and friendly staff; great breakfasts; lots
of amenities. **Cons:** disappointing restaurant experience; occasional
housekeeping issues; spa facilities need updating. ⊠ *Charingworth*
☎ *01386/593555* ⊕ *www.classiclodges.co.uk* ⮌ *23 rooms, 3 suites*
⚅ *In-room: no a/c, Wi-Fi. In-hotel: restaurant, pool, spa, tennis court,*
gym, some pets allowed ⛨ *Breakfast.*

££££–£££££ ⛏**Cotswold House.** This luxury hotel in the center of Chipping Camp-
HOTEL den injects contemporary design into a stately 18th-century manor
house, and from the swirling staircase in the entrance to the guest
rooms studded with contemporary art and high-tech gadgetry, it's a
winning formula. **Pros:** faultless service; plenty of pampering; pleasant
garden. **Cons:** expensive for what you get; some bathrooms are small;
restaurant lacks atmosphere. ⊠ *The Square* ☎ *01386/840330* ⊕ *www.*
cotswoldhouse.com ⮌ *21 rooms, 7 suites* ⚅ *In-room: no a/c (some),*
Internet, Wi-Fi. In-hotel: restaurant, bars, spa, parking, business center,
some pets allowed ⛨ *Breakfast.*

££–£££ ⛏**Noel Arms Hotel.** Dating to the 14th century, Chipping Campden's old-
HOTEL est inn was built to accommodate foreign wool traders, and even though
it has been enlarged, the building retains its exposed beams and stonework. **Pros:** traditional character; friendly staff. **Cons:** rooms can be
noisy and overheated; annex overlooks car park; Wi-Fi in public areas
but not in rooms. ⊠ *High St.* ☎ *01386/840317* ⊕ *www.noelarmshotel.*
com ⮌ *27 rooms* ⚅ *In-room: no a/c. In-hotel: restaurant, bar, parking,*
some pets allowed ⛨ *Breakfast.*

SHOPPING
At **Hart** (⊠ *The Silk Mill, Sheep St.* ☎ *01386/841100*), descendants of
an original member of the Guild of Handicrafts specialize in fashioning
lovely items from silver.

Martin Gotrel (⊠ *Camperdene House, High St.* ☎ *01386/841360*) crafts
fine traditional and contemporary jewelry.

CLOSE UP

Arts and Crafts in the Cotswolds

The Arts and Crafts movement flourished throughout Britain in the late-19th and early-20th centuries, but the Cotswolds are most closely associated with it. The godfather of the movement was designer William Morris (1834–96), whose home for the last 25 years of his life, Kelmscott Manor in Gloucestershire, became the headquarters of the school. A lecture by Morris, "The Beauty of Life," delivered in Birmingham in 1880, included the injunction that became the guiding principle of the movement: "Have nothing in your houses which you do not know to be useful or believe to be beautiful."

Driven by the belief that the spirit of medieval arts and crafts was being degraded and destroyed by the mass production and aggressive capitalism of the Victorian era, and aided by a dedicated core of artisans, Morris revolutionized the art of house design and decoration. His work with textiles was particularly influential.

WHERE TO SEE IT

Many of Morris's followers were influenced by the Cotswold countryside, such as the designer and architect Charles Robert Ashbee, who transferred his Guild of Handicrafts from London to Chipping Campden in 1902. The village holds the small Court Barn Museum dedicated to local craftwork, including a permanent exhibition of pieces by the original group and those who followed in their wake.

Their work can also be seen at the Cheltenham Art Gallery and Museum (closed through 2012), and, in its original context, at Rodmarton Manor outside Tetbury—which Ashbee declared the finest application of the movement's ideals. (Farther afield, Blackwell in the Lake District is a notable Arts and Crafts house.)

To see the Arts and Crafts ethic applied to horticulture, visit Hidcote Manor Garden, near Chipping Campden.

MORETON-IN-MARSH

5 mi south of Chipping Campden, 18 mi northeast of Cheltenham, 5 mi north of Stow-on-the-Wold.

In Moreton-in-Marsh, the houses have been built not around a central square but along a street wide enough to accommodate a market. The village has fine views across the hills. One local landmark, St. David's Church, has a tower of honey-gold ashlar. This town of about 3,500 also possesses one of the last remaining curfew towers, dated 1633; curfew dates to the time of the Norman Conquest, when a bell was rung to "cover-fire" for the night against any invaders.

GETTING HERE AND AROUND

Moreton-in-Marsh is on the A429 north of Cirencester. Park along the main street or in the lot on Station Road. The town has a train station with daily connections to London Paddington. Pulham's Coaches arrive here from Cirencester or Cheltenham (neither on Sunday). There's also service to and from Stratford-upon-Avon, Stow-on-the-Wold, and Bourton-on-the-Water. For Sezincote, a car is necessary.

ESSENTIALS

Visitor Information Moreton-in-Marsh (✉ *High St.* ☎ *01608/650881* 🌐 *www.cotswolds.com*).

EXPLORING

Sezincote. It comes as somewhat of an architectural surprise to see the blue onion domes and miniature minarets of Sezincote, a mellow stone house and garden tucked into a valley near Moreton-in-Marsh. Created in the early 19th century, Sezincote (pronounced *see*-zinct) was the vision of Sir Charles Cockerell, who made a fortune in the East India Company. He employed his architect brother, Samuel Pepys Cockerell, to "Indianize" the residence with Hindu and Muslim motifs. Note the peacock-tail arches surrounding the windows of the first floor. The exotic garden, Hindu temple folly, and Indian-style bridge were favorites of the future George IV, who was inspired to create that Xanadu of Brighton, the Royal Pavilion. If you come in spring, glorious aconites and snowdrops greet you. Note that children are allowed indoors only at the owners' discretion. ✉ *Off A44* ☎ *01386/700444* 🌐 *www.sezincote.co.uk* 🎫 *House and grounds £10; grounds only, £5* ⏲ *House May–Sept., Thurs., Fri., and national holidays 2:30–5:30; grounds Jan.–Nov., Thurs. and Fri. and national holidays 2–6 or dusk.*

Tuesday Market. Supposed to be the largest street market in the Cotswolds, the Tuesday Market takes over the center of the main street between 8 am and 2:30 pm, with a mix of household goods, fruits and vegetables, and some arts-and-crafts and jewelry stalls. Check out this market, which is no newcomer: it was chartered in 1227.

7

WHERE TO EAT AND STAY

For expanded hotel reviews, visit Fodors.com.

£ ITALIAN ✕ **Ask.** Two stone Cotswold cottages have been tastefully converted to form this warm, relaxed eating space in the center of Moreton. Part of a chain specializing in Italian standards, the restaurant has flagstone floors, modern art on the walls, and a menu that ranges from stone-baked pizzas to *pollo Marsala* (roast chicken with mushroom and wine sauce). Antipasti, salads, and espresso coffee complete the meal. ✉ *High St.* ☎ *01608/651119* 🌐 *www.askcentral.co.uk.*

£££–££££ HOTEL 🏨 **Manor House Hotel.** Secret passageways and a priest's hole testify to the age of this 16th-century building, set back from the main thoroughfare, but the mullioned windows, original stonework, and log fires in winter are tastefully balanced by smart contemporary furnishings in the public areas. **Pros:** accommodating staff; historical ambience; stylish decor. **Cons:** smallish rooms; some noise intrusion. ✉ *High St.* ☎ *01608/650501* 🌐 *www.cotswold-inns-hotels.co.uk* *35 rooms* *In-room: no a/c, no safe (some), Wi-Fi (some). In-hotel: restaurants, bar, some pets allowed* 🍽 *Breakfast.*

STOW-ON-THE-WOLD

5 mi south of Moreton-in-Marsh, 15 mi east of Cheltenham.

At an elevation of 800 feet, Stow is the highest town in the Cotswolds— "Stow-on-the-Wold, where the wind blows cold" is the age-old saying. Built around a wide square, Stow's imposing golden stone houses have been discreetly converted into high-quality antiques stores. The Square, as it is known, has a fascinating history. In the 18th century Daniel Defoe wrote that more than 20,000 sheep could be sold here on a busy day; such was the press of livestock that sheep runs, known as "tures," were used to control the sheep, and these narrow streets still run off the main square. Today pubs and antiques shops fill the area.

Also here are St. Edward's Church and the Kings Arms Old Posting House, its wide entrance still seeming to wait for the stagecoaches that used to stop here on their way to Cheltenham.

GETTING HERE AND AROUND

Stow-on-the-Wold is well connected by road (A429, A424, and A436) and bus (from Moreton-in-Marsh, Bourton-on-the-Water, Northleach, Cirencester, and Cheltenham). There are car parks off Sheep Street and Fosseway (A429). Chastleton House is only reachable by car.

ESSENTIALS

Visitor Information Stow-on-the-Wold (✉ *12 Talbot Ct., off Sheep St.* ☎ *01451/870150* ⊕ *www.go-stow.co.uk*).

EXPLORING

★ **Chastleton House.** One of the most complete Jacobean properties in Britain opts for a beguilingly lived-in appearance, taking advantage of almost 400 years' worth of furniture and trappings accumulated by many generations of the single family that owned it until 1991. The house was built between 1605 and 1612 for William Jones, a wealthy wool merchant, and has an appealing authenticity: bric-a-brac is strewn around, wood and pewter are unpolished, upholstery is uncleaned. The top floor is a glorious, barrel-vaulted long gallery, and throughout the house you can see exquisite plasterwork, paneling, and tapestries. The gardens include rotund topiaries and the first croquet lawn (the rules of croquet were codified here in 1865). ■TIP➔ Admission is by timed ticket on a first-come, first-served basis, so it's a good idea to arrive early before the day's allocation is complete. You can join a private tour on Wednesday at 10, and themed events take place on the last Saturday of the month (both during the open season only). Chastleton is 6 mi northeast of Stow, signposted off A436 between Stow and A44. ✉ *Off A436, Moreton-in-Marsh* ☎ *01608/674981, 01494/755560 (info line)* ⊕ *www.nationaltrust.org.uk* ✍ *£8.25* ☼ *Mid-Mar.–late Mar. and Oct., Wed.–Sat. 1–4; Apr.–Sept., Wed.–Sat. 1–5.*

WHERE TO EAT AND STAY

For expanded hotel reviews, visit Fodors.com.

£   ✕ **Queen's Head.** An excellent stopping-off spot for lunch or dinner, this
BRITISH   pub has a courtyard out back that's a quiet retreat on a summer day. The bench in front, under a climbing rose, makes a relaxing spot for imbibing outdoor refreshment. Besides standard pub grub, including

CLOSE UP

Which Cotswold Garden Is Right for You?

Perhaps it's the sheer beauty of this area that has inspired the creation of so many superb gardens. Gardening is an English passion, and even nongardeners may be tempted by the choices large and small. Here's a guide to your options.

Hidcote Manor Garden. The Arts and Crafts movement in Britain transformed not only interior design but also the world of gardening; in this large, influential, much-visited masterpiece of the style, hedges and walls set off vistas and surround distinct themed garden rooms.

Kiftsgate Court Gardens. Three generations of women gardeners created this intimate but charming garden that has traditional and modern features with harmonious colors.

Painswick Rococo Garden. This 18th-century garden, with its Gothic screen and other intriguing structures, has a pleasant intimacy; it's a rare survivor of the rococo style.

Rodmarton Manor. Here you can tour an Art and Crafts–style house and notable garden rooms that reflect this style.

Sezincote. England wouldn't be England without a touch of eccentricity, and in the Cotswolds the garden at this Indian-style manor, with its temple to a Hindu god, supplies a satisfying blend of the stately and the exotic.

Sudeley Castle. In England, gardens often complement a stately home and deserve as close a look as the house. At the home of Catherine Parr (Henry VIII's last wife), the 19th-century Queen's Garden is beloved for its roses.

Westonbirt National Arboretum. The magnificent collection of trees here spreads over 600 acres; late spring and fall are colorful.

For more about English gardens, see the feature "Glorious English Gardens" in this chapter.

7

---

ploughman's lunches, sandwiches, sausage and mash, and chicken pie, there are daily specials such as homemade fish pie. ⊠ *The Square* ☎ *01451/830563.*

£–££

B&B/INN

🛏 **Number Nine.** Beyond the traditional stone-and-creeper exterior of this former coaching inn—now a bed-and-breakfast—are unfussy, spacious bedrooms done in soothing white and pale colors. **Pros:** helpful and amiable hosts; amazing breakfasts; close to pubs and restaurants. **Cons:** two bathrooms have tubs, not showers; low ceilings; steps to climb. ⊠ *9 Park St.* ☎ *01451/870333* ⊕ *www.number-nine.info* ⬦ *3 rooms* ⚭ *In-room: no a/c, Wi-Fi. In-hotel: business center* ❋❖*| Breakfast.*

£££

HOTEL

🛏 **Stow Lodge.** An ex-rectory, this stately, welcoming, and well-maintained hotel couldn't be better placed, separated from Stow's main square by a tidy garden. **Pros:** central location; hospitable service. **Cons:** would benefit from general refurbishment; chiming church clock can be disturbing; steep steps to top-floor rooms. ⊠ *The Square* ☎ *01451/830485* ⊕ *www. stowlodgehotel.co.uk* ⬦ *19 rooms, 1 suite* ⚭ *In-room: no a/c, no safe, Wi-Fi (some). In-hotel: restaurant, bar, business center, parking, some age restrictions* ❋❖*| Breakfast.*

SHOPPING

Stow-on-the-Wold is the leading center for antiques stores in the Cotswolds, with more than 40 dealers centered on the Square, Sheep Street, and Church Street.

Baggott Church St. Limited (✉ *Church St.* ☎ *01451/830370*) displays fine old furniture, portraits and landscape paintings, and architectural items **Durham House Antiques** (✉ *Sheep St.* ☎ *01451/870404)* includes more than 30 purveyors of jewelry, ceramics, antiquarian books, and period furniture, who display their wares in this complex of showrooms. It's open daily.

Roger Lamb Antiques (✉ *The Square* ☎ *01451/831371*) specializes in objets d'art and small pieces of furniture from the Georgian and Regency periods, with Regency "faux bamboo," tea caddies, and antique needlework the particular fortes.

BOURTON-ON-THE-WATER

4 mi southwest of Stow-on-the-Wold, 12 mi northeast of Cheltenham.

Bourton-on-the-Water, off A429 on the eastern edge of the Cotswolds, is deservedly famous as a classic Cotswold village. Like many others, it became wealthy in the Middle Ages because of wool. The little River Windrush runs through Bourton, crossed by low stone bridges; it's as pretty as it sounds. This village makes a good touring base and has a collection of quirky small museums, but in summer it can be overcrowded. A stroll through Bourton takes you past stone cottages, many converted to small stores and coffee shops.

GETTING HERE AND AROUND

Bourton-on-the-Water is served by Pulham's Coaches from Stow-on-the-Wold, Moreton-in-Marsh, Cirencester, and Cheltenham. By car, take A40 and A436 from Cheltenham. You may find parking in the center, but if not use the lot outside the village.

ESSENTIALS

Visitor Information Bourton-on-the-Water (✉ *Victoria St.* ☎ *01451/820211* ⊕ www.bourtoninfo.com).

EXPLORING

♻ **Cotswold Motoring Museum and Toy Collection.** Housed in an old mill, the museum contains more than 30 vintage motor vehicles and a collection of old advertising signs (supposedly the largest in Europe), as well as two caravans (trailers) from the 1920s, ancient bicycles, and children's toys. ✉ *Sherborne St.* ☎ *01451/821255* ⊕ *www.cotswold-motor-museum.co.uk* £4.35 ☉ *Mid-Feb.–early Dec., daily 10–6.*

♻ **Model Railway Exhibition.** On display are more than 40 British and Continental trains running on 500 square feet of scenic layout. There are plenty of trains and toys to buy in the shop. ✉ *Box Bush, High St.* ☎ *01451/820686* ⊕ *www.bourtonmodelrailway.co.uk* £2.75 ☉ *June–Aug., daily 11–5; Sept.–May, weekends 11–5 (call ahead in Jan.).*

Cotswold shopping isn't just fancy antiques: towns such as Bourton-on-the-Water sell some quirky collectibles as well.

Model Village. An outdoor reproduction of Bourton, the model was built in 1937 to a scale of one-ninth; you can walk through it. ⊠ *Old New Inn* ☎ *01451/820467* ⊕ *www.theoldnewinn.co.uk* ☑ *£3.60* ☉ *Late Mar.–Oct., daily 10–6:15; Nov.–late Mar., daily 10–4:15; last admission 30 mins before closing.*

WHERE TO EAT AND STAY
For expanded hotel reviews, visit Fodors.com.

££ ✕ **Rose Tree.** Plain wooden tables and understated decor are the setting BRITISH for the wholesome English dishes served in this traditional restaurant beautifully sited on the banks of the Windrush. Try the game terrine or fish cakes for starters, moving on to tender lamb shank or calves' liver with crispy bacon. Desserts include profiteroles, raspberry pavlova, and lemon sorbet. Candlelight adds atmosphere in the evenings. Sip a cocktail on the riverside terrace while you wait for your order. ⊠ *Victoria St.* ☎ *01451/820635.*

££ ⊞ **Chester House Hotel.** Just steps from the River Windrush, this tra-HOTEL ditional stone building has been tastefully adapted with contemporary fittings and style. **Pros:** friendly staff; stylish rooms. **Cons:** busy on weekends; coach house rooms overlook car park. ⊠ *Victoria St.* ☎ *01451/820286* ⊕ *www.chesterhousehotel.com* ☑ *22 rooms* ⌂ *In-room: no a/c, Wi-Fi (some). In-hotel: restaurant, bar, parking, some pets allowed* ⑩ *Breakfast.*

SHOPPING
The **Cotswold Perfumery** carries many perfumes that are manufactured here, and also stocks perfume bottles and jewelry. You can exercise your olfactory skills in the Perfumed Garden, part of a prebooked factory

CLOSE UP

Antiques and Markets in the Cotswolds

The Cotswolds contain one of the largest concentrations of art and antiques dealers outside London. The famous antiques shops here are, it is sometimes whispered, "temporary storerooms" for the great families of the region, filled with tole-ware, treen, faience firedogs, toby jugs, and silhouettes, plus country furniture, and ravishing 17th- to 19th-century furniture. The center of antiquing is Stow-on-the-Wold, in terms of volume of dealers. Other towns that have a number of antiques shops are Burford, Cirencester, Tetbury, and Moreton-in-Marsh. The Cotswolds have few of those "anything in this tray for £10" shops, however.

For information about dealers and special events, contact the **Cotswold Antique Dealers' Association** (*CADA* ✉ *Broadwell House, Sheep St., Stow-on-the-Wold* ☎ *07789/968319* ⊕ *www.cotswolds-antiques-art.com*),

which represents more than 40 dealers in the area.

As across England, many towns in the region have market days, when you can purchase local produce (including special treats ranging from Cotswold cheeses to fruit juices), crafts, and items such as clothes, books, and toys. Attending a farmers' market or a general market is a great way to mingle with the locals and perhaps find a special treasure or a tasty treat.

Head for Moreton-in-Marsh on Tuesday and Cirencester on Friday and some Saturdays; tourist information offices have information on market days, or check out **Country Markets** (⊕ *www. country-markets.co.uk*).

For information about farmers' markets in the area, check with tourist information offices or with **Certified Farmers' Markets** (⊕ *www. farmersmarkets.net*).

tour that takes in the laboratory, compounding room, and bottling process. ✉ *Victoria St.* ☎ *01451/820698* 🖵 *Factory tour £5* ⊙ *Mon.–Sat. 9:30–5:30, Sun. 10:30–5:30 (closes at 5 in winter).*

LOWER SLAUGHTER AND UPPER SLAUGHTER

2 mi north of Bourton-on-the-Water, 15 mi east of Cheltenham.

Fodor'sChoice
★

To see the quieter, more typical Cotswold villages, seek out the evocatively named Lower Slaughter and Upper Slaughter (the names have nothing to do with mass murder, but come from the Saxon word *sloh*, which means "a marshy place"). Lower Slaughter is one of the "water villages," with Slaughter Brook running down the center road of the town. Little stone footbridges cross the brook, and the town's resident gaggle of geese can often be seen paddling through the sparkling water. Nearby, Lower and Upper Swell are two other quiet towns to explore.

GETTING HERE AND AROUND

There's only a once-weekly bus service linking the Slaughters with the rest of the world; drivers should follow indications from A429 or B4068.

EXPLORING

Warden's Way. Connecting the two Slaughters is the Warden's Way, a mile-long pathway that begins in Upper Slaughter at the town-center parking lot and passes stone houses, green meadows, ancient trees, and a 19th-century corn mill with a waterwheel and brick chimney. The Warden's Way continues south to Bourton-on-the-Water; the full walk from Winchcombe to Bourton is 14 mi. You can pick up maps and itineraries from local tourist offices.

WHERE TO STAY

For expanded hotel reviews, visit Fodors.com.

£££–£££££   ⊞ **Lords of the Manor Hotel.** You'll find refinement and a warm welcome
HOTEL   in this rambling 17th-century manor house with Victorian additions, tucked away in a quintessential Cotswold village. **Pros:** heavenly setting; understated elegance; outstanding food. **Cons:** expensive extras; hushed, slightly starchy ambience; few leisure or business facilities. ⊠ *Upper Slaughter* ☎ *01451/820243* ⊕ *www.lordsofthemanor.com* ⟿ *26 rooms* ♿ *In-room: no a/c. In-hotel: restaurant, bar* ⏹ *Breakfast.*

NORTHLEACH

7 mi southwest of Lower and Upper Slaughter, 14 mi southeast of Cheltenham.

Just off the Fosse Way (and bypassed by the busy A40), little Northleach—population around 2,000—has remained one of the least spoiled of Cotswold towns. Trim cottages, many with traditional stone-tile roofs, line the streets that converge on the spacious central square. By the 13th century Northleach had acquired substantial wealth thanks to the wool trade. The wool of the local Cotswold Lion sheep (so called because of their thick, manelike fleece) was praised above all other by weavers in Flanders, to whom it was exported.

GETTING HERE AND AROUND

Pulham's Coaches links Northleach with Bourton-on-the-Water, and Swanbrook buses run from Cheltenham. It's an out-of-the-way village—signposted from A40 and A429—where you should be able to park near the central square and walk to the sights.

EXPLORING

Keith Harding's World of Mechanical Music. At this shop, the diverting tour lets you hear pianolas, music boxes, and other mechanical instruments from times past. You can even listen to the maestros Grieg, Paderewski, Rachmaninov, and Gershwin on piano rolls. The shop stocks antique and modern music boxes, mechanical toys, and more. ⊠ *The Oak House, High St.* ☎ *01451/860181* ⊕ *www.mechanicalmusic.co.uk* ⟐ *£8* ◷ *Daily 10–5; last tour at 4.*

St. Peter and St. Paul. Besides its soaring pillars and clerestory windows, this 15th-century church contains notable memorial brasses, monuments to the merchants who endowed the church; each merchant has a wool sack and sheep at his feet. ⊠ *Mill End* ☎ *01451/860314* ⟐ *Free* ◷ *Apr.–Oct., daily 9–6; Nov.–Mar., daily 9–dusk.*

7

WHERE TO EAT AND STAY

For expanded hotel reviews, visit Fodors.com.

£££
MODERN BRITISH

✕**Wheatsheaf Inn.** This traditional pub has a cool, modern coffee lounge and adjoining restaurant specializing in Modern British fare. On the menu you might see such light dishes as deviled kidneys on toast or celeriac and apple soup, and more-substantial fare might include roast rump of lamb with artichoke and potato gratin, and red cabbage. The inn also offers 13 stylish, uncluttered bedrooms (£££). ✉ *West End* ☎ *01451/860244* ⊕ *www.cotswoldswheatsheaf.com.*

££
B&B/INN

⬚**Yew Tree Cottage.** For a peaceful stay in a traditional Cotswold cottage, you can't beat this guesthouse. **Pros:** full of character; charming hostess. **Cons:** a bit remote; dogs in the house. ✉ *Turkdean* ☎ *01451/860222* ⊕ *www.bestcotswold.com* ⬒ *2 rooms* ⬙ *In-room: no a/c, Wi-Fi. In-hotel: business center, some pets allowed* ⦿*Breakfast.*

BURFORD

9 mi east of Northleach, 18 mi north of Swindon, 18 mi west of Oxford.

Burford's broad main street leads steeply down to a narrow bridge across the River Windrush. The village served as a stagecoach stop for centuries and has many historic inns; it's now a popular stop for tour buses and seekers of antiques.

GETTING HERE AND AROUND

Burford can be easily reached by bus from Oxford—you may need to change at Witney—and Northleach. Once here, it's easy to stroll around. Drivers should park as soon as possible; there are possibilities on and off the High Street.

ESSENTIALS

Visitor Information Burford (✉ *The Brewery, Sheep St.* ☎ *01993/823558* ⊕ *www.oxfordshirecotswolds.org*).

EXPLORING

St. John. Hidden away at the end of a lane at the bottom of High Street is the splendid parish church of St. John, its interior a warren of arches, chapels, and shrines. The church was remodeled in the 15th century from Norman beginnings. Among the monuments is one dedicated to Henry VIII's barber, Edmund Harman, that depicts four Amazonian Indians; it's said to be the first depiction of native people from the Americas in Britain. Look also for the elaborate Tanfield monument and its poignant widow's epitaph. ✉ *Church Green* ☎ *01993/822275* ⬚ *Free* ⦿ *Mon.–Sat. 9–5, Sun. 9–10 and 1–5.*

WHERE TO EAT AND STAY

For expanded hotel reviews, visit Fodors.com.

£££
MODERN BRITISH

✕**The Angel at Burford.** Contemporary dishes you might see at the farmhouse-style tables of this informal brasserie in a 16th-century coaching inn include seared scallops with chorizo and spinach and breast of pheasant wrapped in Parma ham. Upstairs, the three delightful guest rooms (££) are furnished in different styles: Indian in rich reds,

Blue skies, stone buildings, a peaceful brook: villages such as Upper Slaughter demonstrate the enduring appeal of the Cotswolds.

French with wooden sleigh bed, or cool-blue contemporary Italian. ⊠ *14 Witney St.* ☎ *01993/822714* ⊕ *www.theangelatburford.co.uk.*

££££ 🏨 **Burford House**. Family photographs, old books, and toys scattered
HOTEL throughout this 17th-century building make it feel more like home than a hotel. **Pros:** friendly, unobtrusive service; comfortable public rooms; great dinners. **Cons:** housekeeping sometimes lapses; poor soundproofing; piped music. ⊠ *99 High St.* ☎ *01993/823151* ⊕ *www. burford-house.co.uk* ⟿ *8 rooms* ⚥ *In-room: no a/c, Wi-Fi. In-hotel: restaurant, bar* ⦿ *Breakfast.*

BIBURY

10 mi southwest of Burford, 6 mi northeast of Cirencester, 15 mi north of Swindon.

The tiny town of Bibury, with a population of less than 1,000, sits idyllically beside the little River Coln on B4425; it was famed Arts and Crafts designer William Morris's choice for Britain's most beautiful village. Fine old cottages, a river meadow, and the church of St. Mary's are some of the delights here.

GETTING HERE AND AROUND

There are buses to Bibury operated on weekdays only by Cotswold Green from Cirencester; otherwise public transport links are sparse. You'll need a car to reach Chedworth Roman Villa.

EXPLORING

Arlington Row. The town has a famously pretty and much-photographed group of 17th-century weavers' cottages made of stone.

⑤ **Chedworth Roman Villa.** The remains of a mile of walls are what's left of one of the largest Roman villas in England, beautifully set in a wooded valley on the eastern fringe of the Cotswolds. Thirty-two rooms, including two complete bath suites, have been identified, and the colorful mosaics are some of the most complete in England. Audio guides are available, and the visitor center and museum give a detailed picture of Roman life in Britain. ■**TIP**➜ Look carefully for the signs for the villa: from Bibury, go across A429 to Yanworth and Chedworth. The villa is also signposted from A40. The site is 6 mi northwest of Bibury and 10 mi southeast of Cheltenham. ⊠ *Yanworth* ☎ *01242/890256* ⊕ *www. nationaltrust.org.uk* ⊠ *£6.30* ☉ *Early Mar.–late Mar., Wed.–Sun. 10–4; late Mar.–Oct., Wed.–Sun. 10–5.*

For a fireside pint, a sandwich, or a hearty meal, the **Seven Tuns** (⊠ *Queen St., Chedworth* ☎ *01285/720242*) fits the bill—a traditional pub with a strong menu and outdoor seating. It sits just a short drive from Chedworth Roman Villa, by a splashing stream and a handsome Perpendicular church.

WHERE TO STAY

For expanded hotel reviews, visit Fodors.com.

£££–££££
HOTEL
▦ **Swan Hotel.** Crystal chandeliers and displays of plates and glassware adorn this mid-17th-century coaching inn on the banks of the River Coln, where guest rooms blend traditional and modern style. **Pros:** idyllic spot; helpful staff. **Cons:** busy with day-trippers and wedding parties on weekends; restaurant can be disappointing; most standard rooms are at the back without views. ⊠ *Off B4425* ☎ *01285/740695* ⊕ *www.cotswold-inns-hotels.co.uk* ⇒ *18 rooms, 4 suites* ⬡ *In-room: no a/c, Wi-Fi. In-hotel: restaurants, bar, some pets allowed* ¶⊙¶ *Breakfast.*

CIRENCESTER

6 mi southwest of Bibury, 9 mi south of Chedworth, 14 mi southeast of Cheltenham.

Cirencester (pronounced *sirensester*) has been a hub of the Cotswolds since Roman times, when it was called Corinium; the town was second only to Londinium (London) in importance. Today this old market town is the area's largest, with a population of 19,000. It sits at the intersection of two major Roman roads, the Fosse Way and Ermin Street (now A429 and A417). In the Middle Ages Cirencester grew rich on wool, which funded its 15th-century parish church. It preserves many mellow stone buildings dating mainly from the 17th and 18th centuries, and bow-fronted shops that still have one foot in the past.

GETTING HERE AND AROUND

Cirencester has hourly bus service from Cheltenham, and less frequent service from Moreton-in-Marsh, Stow-on-the-Wold, Tetbury, and Kemble (for rail links). By road, the town can be accessed on A417, A419, and A429. Its compact center is easily walkable.

ESSENTIALS

Visitor Information Cirencester (⊠ *Corinium Museum, Park St.* ☎ *01285/654180* ⊕ *www.cotswold.gov.uk*).

EXPLORING

★ **Corinium Museum.** Not much of the Roman town remains visible, but the museum displays an outstanding collection of Roman artifacts, including jewelry and coins, as well as mosaic pavements and full-scale reconstructions of local Roman interiors. Spacious galleries explore the town's history in Roman and Anglo-Saxon times and in the 18th century; they include plenty of hands-on exhibits. ⊠ *Park St.* ☎ *01285/655611* ⊕ *www.cotswold.gov.uk* ⊠ *£4.50* ☉ *Mon.–Sat. 10–5, Sun. 2–5; Mon.–Sat. 10–4, Sun. 2–4.*

St. John the Baptist. At the top of Market Place is this magnificent Gothic parish church, known as the cathedral of the "woolgothic" style. Its elaborate, three-tier, three-bay south porch, the largest in England, once served as the town hall. The chantry chapels and many coats of arms bear witness to the importance of the wool merchants as benefactors of the church. A rare example of a 15th-century wineglass pulpit sits in the nave. ⊠ *Market Pl.* ☎ *01285/659317* ⊠ *Free, £3 donation suggested* ☉ *Mon.–Sat. 10–4:45 (10–4 in winter), Sun. 2–5.* .

WHERE TO EAT AND STAY

For expanded hotel reviews, visit Fodors.com.

£££
BRITISH

✕ **Wild Duck Inn.** The deep-red dining room of this Elizabethan inn 3 mi southwest of Cirencester has an abundance of wood beams and oil portraits. Steaks and fresh fish are strong suits on the frequently changing menu—including organic meat from Prince Charles's nearby Highgrove Estate—and there are some tasty vegetarian choices, as well as an impressive wine list. The garden is pleasant for alfresco dining. Upstairs are 12 small but comfortable guest rooms (££–£££), individually styled and with handmade black lacquered four-posters. ⊠ *Off A429, Ewen* ☎ *01285/770310* ⊕ *www.thewildduckinn.co.uk.*

£
B&B/INN

⊞ **Ivy House.** Delicious breakfasts and friendly owners enhance a stay at this stone Victorian house, close to the center of town. **Pros:** homemade granola at breakfast; child-friendly atmosphere. **Cons:** on a main road; rooms have a functional feel. ⊠ *2 Victoria Rd.* ☎ *01285/656626* ⊕ *www.ivyhousecotswolds.com* ⬅ *4 rooms* ⚬ *In-room: no a/c, Wi-Fi. In-hotel: parking* ⚬ *Breakfast.*

£
HOTEL

⊞ **Barnsley House.** A honey-and-cream Georgian mansion, the former home of garden designer Rosemary Verey, has been discreetly modernized and converted into a pricey retreat without sacrificing its essential charm. **Pros:** romantic setting; great attention to detail. **Cons:** some rooms are at the top of three flights of stairs; service occasionally disappoints. ⊠ *B4425 Barnsley* ☎ *01285/740000* ⊕ *www.barnsleyhouse.com* ⬅ *9 rooms, 9 suites* ⚬ *In-room: a/c (some), Wi-Fi. In-hotel: restaurant, bar, tennis court, spa* ⚬ *Breakfast.*

NIGHTLIFE AND THE ARTS

New Brewery Arts (⊠ *Brewery Ct.* ☎ *01285/657181*) includes a theater, an exhibition space, and a café.

SHOPPING

The **Corn Hall** (⊠ *Market Place*) is the venue for a food market on Thursday, an antiques market on Friday, and a crafts market on Saturday.

CLOSE UP

That Special Cotswold Stone

If there's one feature of the Cotswold landscape that sums up its special flavor, it's the oolitic limestone that is the area's primary building material. This stone can be seen in everything from drystone walls (whose total length in the region is said to equal or exceed that of the Great Wall of China) to snug cottages and manor houses. Even roof tiles are fashioned from the stone, contributing to a harmonious ensemble despite the different ages of the buildings.

Malleable when first quarried, and gradually hardening with age, the stone lends itself to every use. During the late-medieval heyday of the great churches funded by wool merchants, it was used to brilliant effect in the mullions, gargoyles, and other intricate decorations on ecclesiastical buildings. Some quarries are still active, producing stone that is used mainly for restoration and repair purposes. The varying colors of the stone are caused by impurities in the rock. They include the honey hues of the northern reaches of the Cotswolds, and modulate to a more golden tone in the central area, with a paler hue in and around Bath.

Writer and commentator J.B. Priestley, however, wrote of Cotswold stone that "the truth is that it has no color that can be described. Even when the sun is obscured and the light is cold, these walls are still faintly warm and luminous, as if they knew the trick of keeping the lost sunlight of centuries glimmering about them." Walk or drive around Cotswold villages and towns for even a day, and you will know what he meant.

Every Monday and Friday, Cirencester's central **Market Place** is packed with stalls selling a motley assortment of goods, mainly household items but some local produce and crafts, too. A farmers' market takes place here every second and fourth Saturday of the month.

William H. Stokes (✉ *6–8 Dollar St.* ☎ *01285/653907*) specializes in oak furniture from the 16th and 17th centuries.

SPORTS AND THE OUTDOORS

Ⓒ You can indulge in water sports such as waterskiing and windsurfing at the **Cotswold Water Park**, 4 mi south of Cirencester. This group of 150 lakes covers 40 square mi and has multiple entrances. There's swimming May through September; the park also draws wildlife enthusiasts, walkers, cyclists, and kayakers. You pay individual charges for the activities, and you can rent equipment on-site. ✉ *Gateway Centre, B4696 (off A419), South Cerney* ☎ *01793/752413* ⊕ *www.waterpark.org* ✉ *Free* ☉ *Individual operators have varying opening hrs.*

PAINSWICK

16 mi northwest of Cirencester, 8 mi southwest of Cheltenham, 5 mi south of Gloucester.

An old Cotswold wool town of around 2,000 inhabitants, Painswick has become a chocolate-box picture of quaintness, attracting day-trippers and tour buses. But come during the week and you can discover the place in relative tranquillity. The huddled gray-stone houses and inns date from as early as the 14th century and include a notable group from the Georgian era. It's worth a stroll through the churchyard of St. Mary's, renowned for its table tombs and monuments and its 100 yew trees planted in 1792. The Cotswold Way passes near the center of the village, making it easy to take a pleasant walk in the countryside.

GETTING HERE AND AROUND

Painswick is on A46 between Stroud and Cheltenham. The village has hourly bus connections with Stroud (15 minutes) and Cheltenham (35 minutes), with reduced service on Sunday.

ESSENTIALS

Visitor Information Painswick (⊠ *Town Hall, Victoria St.* ☎ *0750/351–6924* ⊕ *www.visitthecotswolds.org.uk*).

EXPLORING

Painswick Rococo Garden. This garden, ½ mi north of town, is a delightful, rare survivor from the exuberant rococo period of English garden design (1720–60). After 50 years in its original form, the 6-acre garden became overgrown with woodland. Beginning in 1984, after the rediscovery of a 1748 painting of the garden by Thomas Robins, the garden was restored. Now you can view the original architectural structures—such as the vaguely Gothic Eagle House and Exedra—and asymmetrical vistas. There are also a restaurant and a shop. ⊠ *B4073* ☎ *01452/813204* ⊕ *www.rococogarden.org.uk* 🎫 *£6* ⊙ *Early Jan.– Oct., daily 11–5; last admission at 4.*

WHERE TO EAT AND STAY

For expanded hotel reviews, visit Fodors.com.

££
BRITISH

✕ **Falcon Inn.** Right opposite the church of St Mary's, this pub dating from 1554 offers a reassuringly traditional milieu for food and refreshment. Snacks are available at lunchtime, teas in the afternoon, and the evening menu includes wood-smoked mackerel pâté for starters, baked pork tenderloin with a honey-and-mustard sauce for main course, and "spotted dick" (warm sponge pudding with dried fruit and custard) for dessert. There are views of St Mary's from the front, and the inn's grounds hold what is claimed to be the world's oldest bowling green. ⊠ *New St.* ☎ *01452/814222* ⊕ *www.falconinn-cotswolds.co.uk.*

££
HOTEL
★

🖼 **Cardynham House.** In the heart of the village, this 15th- to 16th-century former wool merchant's house, which retains its beamed ceilings, Jacobean staircase, and Elizabethan fireplace, has four-poster beds in almost all of its rooms. **Pros:** friendly welcome; romantic and quirky; great food in restaurant. **Cons:** some low ceilings; slightly worn around the edges. ⊠ *The Cross, Tibbiwell St.* ☎ *01452/814006, 01452/810030 restaurant* ⊕ *www.cardynham.co.uk* 🛏 *9 rooms* ☖ *In-room: no a/c, Wi-Fi (some). In-hotel: restaurant* ⊘ *Breakfast.*

7

With its majestic trees, Westonbirt National Arboretum is the perfect place to take in fall's splendor.

TETBURY

12 mi south of Painswick, 8 mi southwest of Cirencester.

With about 5,300 inhabitants, Tetbury claims right royal connections. Indeed, the soaring spire of the church that presides over this Elizabethan market town is within sight of Highgrove House, the Prince of Wales's abode; the house is not open to the public, but you can prebook a tour to see the gardens. Tetbury is known as one of the area's antiques centers.

GETTING HERE AND AROUND

Tetbury is well connected to Cirencester by Stagecoach and to Bath by Wessex Connect, which also runs to Westonbirt National Arboretum. There are no Sunday services. It's easy to stroll around the compact town.

ESSENTIALS

Visitor Information Tetbury (✉ *33 Church St.* ☎ *01666/503552* ⊕ *www.visittetbury.co.uk*).

EXPLORING

Highgrove House. Prince Charles and the late Princess Diana made their home at Highgrove House, 1½ mi southwest of Tetbury, in 1981, where Charles set about making the 37-acre estate a showcase for traditional and organic growing methods. The estate includes rare plant and animal species, and a set of interlinked gardens that are open to the public on prebooked tours. Here you can appreciate the amazing industry on the part of the royal gardeners who have created the orchards, kitchen garden, and woodland garden almost from nothing.

You can sample the estate's produce in the restaurant and shop, or from Highgrove's retail outlet in Tetbury. Allow three to four hours for a visit, and book well in advance; under-12s are not permitted. ⊠ *Doughton* ☎ *01666/503203, book tours at 020/7766–7310* ⊕ *www. highgrovegardens.com* ✉ *£16.50; £20 at weekends* ⊙ *Early Apr.–late Oct., weekdays plus some weekends in Aug. (various times)*

Market House. In the center of the village, look for the eye-catching, white-painted stone Market House on Market Square, dating from 1655 and built up on rows of Tuscan pillars. Various markets are held here during the week.

Rodmarton Manor. One of the last English country houses constructed using traditional methods and materials, Rodmarton Manor (built 1909–29) is furnished with specially commissioned pieces in the Arts and Crafts style. Ernest Barnsley, a follower of William Morris, worked on the house and gardens. The notable gardens—wild, winter, sunken, and white—are divided into "rooms" bounded by hedges of holly, beech, and yew. The manor is 5 mi northeast of Tetbury. ⊠ *Off A433, Rodmarton* ☎ *01285/841253* ⊕ *www.rodmarton-manor.co.uk* ✉ *£8; garden only, £5* ⊙ *May–Sept., Wed., Sat., and national holidays 2–5.*

St. Mary the Virgin. This church (⊠ *Church St.* ☎ *01666/502333*), in 18th-century neo-Gothic style, has a galleried interior with pews.

QUICK BITES

Just steps from Market House and at the heart of village life, the Snooty Fox (⊠ *Market Pl.* ☎ *01666/502436* ⊕ *www.snooty-fox.co.uk*) is a bustling inn and restaurant with an open fire in winter and a patio to use in summer. Real ales and local ciders are served at the bar, and teas, coffees, and hot and cold meals are available all day.

7

★ **Westonbirt National Arboretum.** Spread over 600 acres, this arboretum, 3 mi southwest of Tetbury (and about 10 mi north of Bath), contains one of the most extensive collections of trees and shrubs in Europe; it's a lovely place to spend an hour or two. The best times to come for color are in late spring, when the rhododendrons, azaleas, and magnolias are blooming, and in fall, when the maples come into their own. A gift shop, café, and restaurant are on the grounds. Open-air concerts take place in summer, and there are exhibitions throughout the year. ⊠ *Off A433, near Tetbury* ☎ *01666/880220* ⊕ *www.forestry.gov.uk/westonbirt* ✉ *£8 Mar.–Sept., £9 Oct. and Nov., £6 Dec.–Feb.* ⊙ *Apr.–Nov., weekdays 9–8 or dusk, weekends 8–8 or dusk; Dec.–Mar., weekdays 9–5 or dusk, weekends 8–5 or dusk.*

WHERE TO EAT AND STAY

For expanded hotel reviews, visit Fodors.com.

£££
MODERN BRITISH
✕ **The Chef's Table.** On Tetbury's Antiques Alley, this trendy eatery is a blend of farmhouse kitchen and designer chic, with a few tables and chairs next to an open kitchen. You can come for breakfast, snack lunches, or more-substantial fare such as truffle-and-Parmesan soufflé or crab thermidor. Reserve ahead because of the limited dining space. If you can't get a seat, however, do not despair—all dishes are available for a takeout lunch, and cheeses, hams, and organic bread are sold at

the downstairs delicatessen. ⊠ *49 Long St.* ☎ *01666/504466* ⊕ *www. thechefstable.co.uk* ⊗ *Closed Sun. No dinner Mon. and Tues.*

£££££

HOTEL

Ċ

Fodor's Choice

★

▣ **Calcot Manor.** In an ideal world everyone would sojourn in this oasis of opulence at least once; the luxury never gets in the way of the over-all air of relaxation, however, a tribute to the warmth and efficiency of the staff. **Pros:** delightful rural setting; excellent spa facilities; chil-dren love it. **Cons:** all but 12 rooms are separate from main build-ing; not all rooms have separate shower units; some patchy service. ⊠ *A4135* ☎ *01666/890391* ⊕ *www.calcotmanor.co.uk* ⤳ *26 rooms, 9 suites* ♨ *In-room: no a/c, Wi-Fi. In-hotel: restaurants, bars, pool, tennis courts, gym, spa* ⦾| *Breakfast.*

SHOPPING
Tetbury is home to more than 30 antiques shops, some of which are incorporated into small malls.

Highgrove Shop (⊠ *10 Long St.* ☎ *01666/505666* ⊕ *www.highgroveshop. com*) sells organic products and gifts inspired by Prince Charles's interests.

House of Cheese (⊠ *13 Church St.* ☎ *01666/502865* ⊕ *www.houseofcheese. co.uk*) retails fine, farm-produced cheeses, all wonderfully fresh and fla-vorsome. Pâtés and preserves are other goodies at this tiny shop.

Long Street Antiques (⊠ *14 Long St.* ☎ *01666/500850* ⊕ *www. longstreetantiques.com*) houses more than 40 dealers specializing in everything from jewelry to oak and mahogany furniture.

Stratford-upon-Avon and the Heart of England

WORD OF MOUTH

"You have been to Warwick Castle, but there is so much else in the area—Baddesley Clinton, Packwood House, and Charlecote Park are National Trust houses with a lovely mix of periods and styles. You could easily combine some of these with a visit to Stratford-uponAvon."

—spiral

WELCOME TO STRATFORD-UPON-AVON AND THE HEART OF ENGLAND

TOP REASONS TO GO

★ **Shakespeare in Stratford:** To see a play by Shakespeare in the town where he was born—and perhaps after you've visited his birthplace or other sites—is a magical experience.

★ **Warwick Castle:** Taking in the history—and some modern kitsch—at this sprawling medieval castle is a fun day out and great for the whole family.

★ **The city of Birmingham:** The revamped city center shows off its superb art collections and cultural facilities, international cuisine, and renowned Jewellery Quarter.

★ **Half-timber architecture:** Black-and-white half-timber houses are a mark of pride throughout the region; there are concentrations of buildings from medieval times to the Jacobean era in Chester, Shrewsbury, and Ludlow.

★ **Ironbridge Gorge:** Recall the burgeoning of England's Industrial Revolution at this fine complex of industrial-heritage museums.

1 **Stratford-upon-Avon.** The birthplace of Shakespeare, the bustling historic town of Stratford-upon-Avon is liberally dotted with 16th-century buildings the playwright would recognize.

2 **Around Shakespeare Country.** Warwickshire—the county of which Stratford is the southern nexus—has sleepy villages and thatch-roof cottages, as well as stately homes and sprawling Warwick Castle.

3 **Birmingham.** Britain's second-largest city, once known as "the city of 1,001 trades," now recalls its past through excellent museums and a network of canals. Business sets the pace here, but so do an adventurous arts program, buzzing nightlife, and an excellent restaurant scene.

4 **Great Malvern, Hereford, and Environs.** This region includes the cathedral town of Hereford and bucolic villages set amid lush orchards. Providing a backdrop to it all are the volcanic ridges of the Malvern Hills, where you'll find genteel Great Malvern and Ledbury.

5 **Shrewsbury, Chester, and Environs.** The northern, most varied part of the region, studded with its characteristic half-timber buildings, embraces the World Heritage Site of Ironbridge Gorge, the Shropshire hills, and ancient Shrewsbury and Chester, as well as Ludlow with its gastronomic delights.

GETTING ORIENTED

Stratford-upon-Avon is northwest of London in the midland county of Warwickshire, known as Shakespeare Country. Tiny villages surround it; to the north lie two magnificent castles, Warwick and Kenilworth. A little farther northwest is the region's main city, Birmingham. To the southwest, along the Malvern Hills, lie the peaceful spa town of Great Malvern and the prosperous agricultural city of Hereford. The western part of the region, bordering Wales, is hugged by the River Severn. The small city of Shrewsbury is here, close to Ironbridge with its industrial-heritage museums. To its south lies Ludlow, an architectural and culinary hot spot; at the northwestern edge of the region is the ancient city of Chester.

8

GREAT INDIAN FOOD IN ENGLAND

"Going for an Indian" or "going for a curry"— the two are synonymous—is part of English life. On any self-respecting town's main street there's at least one Indian restaurant or take-out place, from inexpensive to high-end.

Chilies add heat to Indian food; you can cool things down with some bread (above); rogan josh, a spicy choice (right, top); chicken tikka masala, a favorite (right, below).

British trade with, and subsequent rule over, India for the two centuries before 1947 has ensured an enduring national appetite for spices. The town of Cheltenham used to be known as an Anglo-Indian paradise since so many "curry-eating colonels" used to retire there. Immigration from Pakistan and Bangladesh in the mid-20th century led to a concentration of restaurants in Birmingham, Manchester, and London. Today you can also find South Indian, Nepalese, and Sri Lankan establishments. The exotic mix of herbs and spices gives Indian food its distinctive appeal. Typically, ginger, garlic, cilantro, cumin, cardamom, fenugreek and cayenne enhance fresh vegetables and meat (chicken or lamb), fish, or cheese (paneer). Fresh cilantro is a common garnish. But it's the addition of chilis that makes things hot: feel free to ask advice when ordering.

ACCOMPANIMENTS

Starters include lime pickle, mango chutney, and *raita* (diced cucumber in minty yogurt), all scooped up with *pappadams* (crispy, thin, fried tortilla-like disks made from chickpea flour). For the main course, there's plain or pilaf Basmati rice, *naan* bread from the tandoor, or *chapatis* (flat bread). Side dishes include onion or eggplant *bhajis* (spiced fritters), and *sag aloo* (potato with spinach). Try Indian beer, too.

Curry is a general term for dishes with a hot, spicy sauce. The strength of each dish is given in italics after the description.

BALTI

Literally meaning "bucket," a *balti* dish is a popular Birmingham invention dating to the 1970s. Different combinations of meat, spices, and vegetables are stir-fried and served at the table in a small wok with handles. Naan bread or chapatis are accompaniments. *Mild to Medium.*

BIRYANI

Made with stir-fried chicken or lamb, almonds, and golden raisins, this rice-based dish has a dry texture. It can be served with a vegetable curry. *Medium.*

DHANSAK

Meat or prawns are combined with a thick sweet-and-sour sauce and a red or yellow *dal* (lentil stew) in a dish that originated in Persia. *Medium to hot.*

DOPIAZA

The name means two or double onions, so expect lots of onions, mixed with green bell peppers. The sauce is reduced, producing concentrated flavors. *Medium hot.*

JALFREZI

This dish derived from British rule in India, when the Indian cook would heat up leftover cold roast meat and

potatoes. Fresh meat is cooked with green bell peppers, onions, and plenty of green chilis in a little sauce. *Hot.*

KORMA

Mild and sweet, this curry is very popular. Chicken or lamb is braised in a creamy or yogurt-based sauce to which almonds and coconut are added. *Mild.*

ROGAN JOSH

A staple dish, rogan josh is quite highly spiced. Its deep red color originally came from dried red Kashmiri chilis, but now red bell peppers and tomatoes are used. *Medium hot.*

TANDOORI CHICKEN

Chicken pieces are marinated in a yogurt and spice paste, and then cooked in a *tandoor* (barrel-shape clay oven). The red color comes from cayenne pepper, chili powder, or food coloring. It's served dry with slices of lemon or lime, naan bread, and salad. *Mild.*

CHICKEN TIKKA MASALA

A British-Bangladeshi invention, this is reputedly the nation's favorite dish. Boneless chunks of chicken breast are marinated in yogurt and *garam masala* (dry-roasted spices), threaded on a skewer, and cooked in a tandoor. The accompanying creamy, tomato-based sauce is either orange-red from turmeric and paprika, or deep red from food coloring. *Mild.*

–by Kate Hughes

8

Updated by Kate Hughes and Paul Cannon

The lyricism of England's emotional and geographical heartland is found in the remote, half-timber market towns of the Welsh borders and the bucolic villages of Warwickshire. It melts away around the edges of one of the country's most culturally vibrant cities, Birmingham—historically the smoldering furnace of the Industrial Revolution—but this region, forever associated with England's greatest literary figure, still does much to embody the spirit of Olde England.

You get new insight into William Shakespeare when you visit the stretch of country where he was born and raised. The sculpted, rolling farmland of Warwickshire may look nothing like the forested countryside of the 16th century, but some sturdy Tudor houses that Shakespeare knew survive to this day. You can walk streets he might have traveled, cross streams where, as a child, he might have dangled his feet. There's beauty in this—and the possibility of tourist overkill. Stratford-upon-Avon, with its Shakespeare sites and the theaters of the Royal Shakespeare Company, is in danger of becoming "Shakespeare World."

Still, it's a fascinating place, and there's much more to see—castles, churches, and countryside—in this famously lovely part of England. Stop in at Charlecote, a grand Elizabethan manor house, and Baddesley Clinton, a superb example of late-medieval domestic architecture. The huge fortresses of Warwick Castle and Kenilworth Castle provide glimpses into past pleasures and pastimes.

To the west, some of England's prettiest countryside lies along the 108-mi border with Wales in the counties of Herefordshire, Shropshire, and southern Cheshire. The Welsh borders are remote and tranquil, dotted with small villages and market towns full of 13th- and 14th-century black-and-white, half-timber buildings, the legacy of a forested countryside. The Victorians were responsible for the more recent fashion of painting these structures black and white. The more elaborately decorated half-timber buildings in market towns such as Shrewsbury and Chester are monuments to wealth, dating mostly from the early 17th century. More half-timbered structures are found in Ludlow, now a culinary center nestled in the lee of its majestic ruined castle.

In the 18th century, in a wooded stretch of the Severn Gorge in Shropshire, the coke blast furnace was invented and the first iron bridge was erected (1779), heralding the birth of the Industrial Revolution. You can get a sense of this history at the museums at Ironbridge Gorge.

The ramifications of that technological leap led to the growth of Britain's second-largest city, Birmingham, the capital of the Midlands. Birmingham has transcended its reputation as one of the country's least attractive cities. Its industrial center inspired the heavy metal sound of Black Sabbath and haunted JRR Tolkien's childhood enough for him to create the dark realm of Mordor in *The Lord of the Rings*. Today an imaginative makeover and active, varied cultural life are draws for anyone interested in modern urban Britain.

STRATFORD-UPON-AVON AND THE HEART OF ENGLAND PLANNER

WHEN TO GO

The Shakespeare sights get very crowded on weekends and school vacations; Warwick Castle usually brims with visitors, so arrive early in the day. Throughout the region, some country properties fill up quickly on weekends. Most rural sights have limited opening hours in winter, and the majority of attractions close at 5. Some stately homes have limited hours even in summer, which is when the countryside is at its most appealing. The open-air performances at Ludlow Castle take place at the end of June; the Autumn in Malvern Festival happens on weekends in October.

PLANNING YOUR TIME

Stratford-upon-Avon is ideal for day visits from London or as a base for exploring nearby; depending on your love of Shakespeare, you probably won't need more than a day or two here. Warwick can be explored in an hour or two, but castle lovers could spend half a day in the many lines at busy Warwick Castle. A drive through the area's country lanes is a pleasant way to spend a day; a stop at any stately home (check hours) will take a few hours. You're also near the northern Cotswolds if you want to explore the countryside further.

Birmingham, where the museums and sights take a full day to explore, makes a logical base if you want cosmopolitan city life. It's easy to reach the countryside from the smaller cities of Hereford, Shrewsbury, and Chester, but if you want to walk the hills, Ludlow is a good gateway for Wenlock Edge, as is Great Malvern or Ledbury for the Malvern Hills. In the north of the region, Ironbridge Gorge and Chester demand a full day each. Ludlow and Shrewsbury take less time, though it would be a shame to leave Ludlow without sampling its fine dining, and Shrewsbury makes a good central base. Once you've gone as far north as this, you might consider going on to Liverpool, if the Beatles and maritime history have any appeal, or to north Wales.

8

GETTING HERE AND AROUND
AIR TRAVEL
The region is served by Birmingham International Airport, 6 mi east of the city center, and the country's second-busiest airport. It has connections to all of Britain's major cities, and limited service to the United States.

Contacts **Birmingham International Airport** (✉ *A45, off Junction 6 of M42* ☎ *0870/733–5511* ⊕ *www.bhx.co.uk*).

BUS TRAVEL
The cheapest way to travel is by bus, and National Express serves the region from London's Victoria Coach Station. You can reach Birmingham in less than three hours; Hereford and Shrewsbury take between four and five hours. It also operates services from London's Heathrow (2¾ hours) and Gatwick (4 hours) airports to Birmingham.

Stagecoach serves local routes throughout the Stratford and Birmingham areas. Megabus, a budget service booked online, runs double-decker buses from Victoria Station in London to Birmingham. The First bus company has service between Birmingham, Hereford, and Ludlow.

Contacts **First** (☎ *0871/200–2233* ⊕ *www.firstgroup.com*). **Megabus** (⊕ *www.megabus.co.uk*). **National Express** (☎ *0871/781–8181* ⊕ *www.nationalexpress.com*). **Stagecoach** (☎ *01788/535555 or 0845/600–1314* ⊕ *www.stagecoachbus.com*).

CAR TRAVEL
To reach Stratford (100 mi), Birmingham (120 mi), Shrewsbury (150 mi), Ludlow (140 mi), and Chester (180 mi) from London, take M40. For the farther areas, keep on it until it becomes M42, or take M1/M6. M4 and then M5 from London take you to Hereford in just under three hours. Driving can be difficult in the region's western reaches—especially in the hills and valleys west of Hereford, where steep, twisting roads often narrow down into mere trackways.

Around Stratford, one pleasure of this rural area is driving the smaller "B" roads, which lead deep into the countryside. Local public bus service is not sufficient for most sightseeing journeys around Warwickshire. Renting a car or taking a tour bus are the two best options, although trains serve the major towns.

TRAIN TRAVEL
Stratford has good train service and can be seen as a day trip from London if your time is limited (a matinee is your best bet if you want to squeeze in a play). Chiltern Railways trains leave from London Marylebone Station and also go to Warwick, and they offer a one-day (£30) or four-day (£45) Shakespeare Explorer ticket for the region. London Midland serves the area from Birmingham (about 40 mi from Stratford).

From London, First Great Western and Arriva trains serve Birmingham and the western parts of the region from Paddington Station, and Virgin, Central, and Silverlink trains leave from Euston (call National Rail Enquiries for information). Travel times are Paddington to Hereford, 3 hours, and Ludlow, 3¼ hours (both changing at Newport); Euston to Birmingham, 1½ hours; Euston to Shrewsbury, with a change at Crewe or Birmingham, 2¾ hours; or to Chester, with a change at Crewe, 2¾ hours. West Midlands Day Ranger tickets (£16.80) and three- and seven-day Heart of England Rover tickets (£65.20 and £84.80) allow unlimited travel on trains throughout the region.

Contacts National Rail Enquiries (☎ *0845/748–4950* ⊕ *www.nationalrail. co.uk).* **Chiltern Railways** (☎ *0845/600–5165* ⊕ *www.chilternrailways. co.uk).* **London Midland** (☎ *0121/634–2040 or 0844/811–0133* ⊕ *www. londonmidland.com).*

RESTAURANTS

Stratford has many reasonably priced bistros and unpretentious eateries offering a broad choice of international fare; Warwick and Kenilworth both have good restaurant options. Birmingham has splendid international restaurants but is probably most famous for its Indian and Pakistani eateries; you'll find good choices both in the city center and out of town. The city hosts the annual Taste of Birmingham Festival in July. In the rest of the area, casual spots dominate, though Ludlow is a culinary center.

HOTELS

Stratford and Warwick have accommodations to fit every wallet. Because Stratford is *so* popular with theatergoers, book well ahead. Most hotels offer discounted two- and three-day packages. Near Stratford, a number of top-notch country hotels guarantee discreet but attentive service—at fancy prices. Birmingham's hotels, geared to the convention crowd and often booked well in advance, are mostly bland and impersonal, but sophisticated; look for weekend discounts. In the countryside, many ancient inns and venerable Regency-style houses have been converted into hotels.

WHAT IT COSTS IN POUNDS					
	£	££	£££	££££	£££££
Restaurants	under £10	£10–£14	£15–£19	£20–£25	over £25
Hotels	under £70	£70–£120	£121–£160	£161–£220	over £220

Restaurant prices are per person for a main course or equivalent combination of smaller dishes at dinner excluding tax. Hotels prices reflect the rack rate of a standard double room for two people in high season, including 20% V.A.T. Check online for off-season rates and special deals or discounts.

VISITOR INFORMATION

Traveline can field all general transportation inquiries. Local tourist offices can recommend day or half-day tours of the region and will have the names of registered Blue Badge guides.

Contacts Heart of England Tourist Board (⊕ *www.visittheheart.co.uk).* **Shakespeare Country** (☎ *0870/160–7930* ⊕ *www.shakespeare-country.co.uk).* **Traveline** (☎ *0871/200–2233* ⊕ *www.traveline.org.uk).*

With its thatch roof, half-timbering, and countryside setting, Anne Hathaway's Cottage is a vision from the past.

STRATFORD-UPON-AVON

Even under the weight of busloads of visitors, Stratford, on the banks of the slow-flowing River Avon, has somehow hung on to much of its ancient character and can, on a good day, still feel like an English market town. It doesn't take long to figure out who's the center of attention here. Born in a half-timber, early-16th-century building in the center of Stratford on April 23, 1564, William Shakespeare died on April 23, 1616, his 52nd birthday, in a more imposing house at New Place. Although he spent much of his life in London, the world still associates him with "Shakespeare's Avon."

Here, in the years between his birth and 1587, he played as a young lad, attended grammar school, and married Anne Hathaway; and here he returned, as a prosperous man. You can see Shakespeare's whole life here: his birthplace on Henley Street; his burial place in Holy Trinity Church; Anne Hathaway's Cottage; the home of his mother, Mary Arden, at Wilmcote; New Place; and the neighboring Nash's House, home of Shakespeare's granddaughter.

By the 16th century Stratford was a prosperous market town with thriving guilds and industries. Half-timber houses from this era have been preserved, and they are set off by later architecture, such as the elegant Georgian storefronts on Bridge Street, with their 18th-century porticoes and arched doorways.

Most sights cluster around Henley Street (off the roundabout as you come in on the A3400 Birmingham road), High Street, and Waterside, which skirts the public gardens through which the River Avon flows. Bridge Street and Sheep Street (parallel to Bridge) are Stratford's main thoroughfares and the site of most banks, shops, and eating places. Bridgefoot, between the canal and the river, is next to Clopton Bridge—"a sumptuous new bridge and large of stone"—built in the 15th century by Sir Hugh Clopton, once lord mayor of London and one of Stratford's richest and most philanthropic residents.

GETTING HERE AND AROUND

Stratford lies about 100 mi northwest of London; take M40 to Junction 15. The town is 37 mi southeast of Birmingham by A435 and A46 or by M40 to Junction 15.

Chiltern Railways serves the area from London's Marylebone Station. Five direct trains a day take just over two hours to reach Stratford; other trains require up to three changes. London Midland operates direct routes from Birmingham's Snow Hill Station (journey time under an hour). From Stratford's train station at the edge of the town center on Alcester Road you can take a taxi or walk the short distance into town.

Stratford's center is small and easily walkable—it's unlikely you'd need to use the local bus service. City Sightseeing runs hop-on, hop-off guided tours of Stratford (£11.75), and you can combine the tour (about an hour with no stops) with entry to either three (£23.25) or five (£25.75) Shakespeare houses. In summer, the same company's Heart of Warwickshire tour includes Compton Verney, Charlecote Park, and Warwick (four trips on weekends in June and July, daily in August). The Stratford Town Walk runs all year and also offers ghost-themed walks and cruises. Note that at the time of this writing Stratford's tourist office was considering a move.

The Shakespeare Birthplace Trust runs the main places of Shakespearean interest: Anne Hathaway's Cottage, Hall's Croft, Mary Arden's House, Nash's House and New Place, and Shakespeare's Birthplace. ■TIP➜ You can buy a money-saving combination ticket to all five properties for £19.50, or pay separate entry fees if you're visiting only one or two. Family tickets are an option, too, and advance booking online gives you a 10% saving. Tickets for Hall's Croft and Nash's House and New Place are available only as a rather pricey (£12.50) joint ticket that includes the birthplace.

PLANNING YOUR TIME

If you have only a day here, arrive early and confine your visit to two or three Shakespeare Birthplace Trust properties, a few other town sights, a pub lunch, and a walk along the river, capped off by a stroll to the cottage of Anne Hathaway. If you don't like crowds, avoid visiting on weekends and school vacations, and take in the main Shakespeare shrines in the early morning to see them at their least frenetic. One high point of Stratford's calendar is the Shakespeare Birthday Celebrations, usually on the weekend nearest to April 23.

ESSENTIALS

Tour Information City Sightseeing (☎ 01789/412680 ⊕ www.city-sightseeing. com). **Shakespeare Birthplace Trust** (☎ 01789/204016 ⊕ www.shakespeare. org.uk). **Stratford Town Walk** (☎ 01789/292478 or 0785/576–0377 ⊕ www. stratfordtownwalk.co.uk).

Visitor Information Stratford-upon-Avon (✉ 62 Henley St. ☎ 01789/264293 ⊕ www.stratford-upon-avon.co.uk).

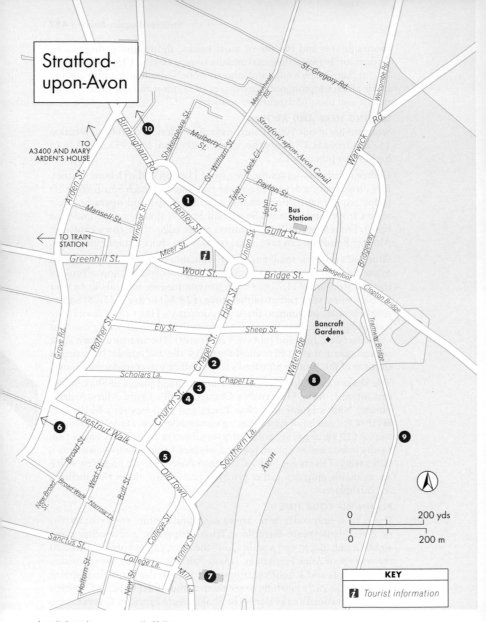

Stratford-upon-Avon

TO
A3400 AND MARY
ARDEN'S HOUSE

TO TRAIN
STATION

Birmingham Rd.

Arden St.

Mansell St.

Windsor St.

Shakespeare St.

Mulberry St.

Gt. William St.

Tyler St.

John St.

Lock Cl.

Payton St.

Maidenhead Rd.

St. Gregory Rd.

Welcombe Rd.

Warwick Rd.

Stratford-upon-Avon Canal

Bus
Station

Guild St.

Henley St.

Meer St.

Greenhill St.

Wood St.

Bridge St.

Union St.

Bridgefoot

Bridgeway

Clopton Bridge

Grove Rd.

Rother St.

Ely St.

High St.

Chapel St.

Sheep St.

Bancroft
Gardens

Waterside

Tramway Bridge

Scholars La.

Chapel La.

Church St.

Southern La.

Avon

Chestnut Walk

Broad St.

West St.

Bull St.

Old Town

New Broad St.

Broad Walk

Narrow La.

Sanctus St.

College St.

College La.

Mottram St.

New St.

Trinity St.

Mill La.

10 **1** **i** **2** **3** **4** **5** **6** **7** **8** **9**

| 0 | 200 yds |
| 0 | 200 m |

KEY
i *Tourist information*

EXPLORING

TOP ATTRACTIONS

★ **Anne Hathaway's Cottage.** The most picturesque of the Shakespeare Trust properties, on the western outskirts of Stratford, was the family home of the woman Shakespeare married in 1582. The "cottage," actually a substantial Tudor farmhouse, has latticed windows and a grand thatch roof. Inside is period furniture, including the settle where Shakespeare reputedly conducted his courtship, and a rare carved Elizabethan bed; outside is a garden planted in lush Victorian style with herbs and flowers. In a nearby field the **Shakespeare Tree Garden** has 40 trees mentioned in the playwright's works, a yew maze, and sculptures with Shakespearean themes. ■TIP➔ The best way to get here is to walk, especially in late spring when the apple trees are in blossom. There are two main footpaths, one via Greenhill Street by the railroad bridge, the other leaving from Holy Trinity Church up Old Town and Chestnut Walk. ✉ *Cottage La., Shottery* ☎ *01789/292100* ⊕ *www.shakespeare.org.uk* 🎟 *£7.50, Shakespeare Trust 5-property ticket £19.50* ⊗ *Apr.–Oct., daily 9–5; Nov.–Mar., daily 10–4; last admission 30 mins before closing.*

Charlecote Park. A celebrated house in the village of Hampton Lucy, Charlecote Park was built in 1572 by Sir Thomas Lucy to entertain Queen Elizabeth I (in her honor, the house is shaped like the letter "E"). Shakespeare knew the house and may even have poached deer here. Standing at the edge of a glassy lake, the redbrick manor is striking and sprawling. It was renovated in neo-Elizabethan style by the Lucy family during the mid-19th century; a carved ebony bed is one of many spectacular pieces of furniture. The Tudor gatehouse is unchanged since Shakespeare's day, and a collection of carriages, a Victorian kitchen, and a small brewery occupy the outbuildings. Indulge in a game of croquet near the quirky, thatched, Victorian-era summer hut, or explore the deer park landscaped by Capability Brown. Interesting themed tours and walks take place in summer—call in advance to find out what's on offer. From Stratford by car take the B4086, or sign up there for City Sightseeing's Heart of Warwickshire tour. The house is 6 mi northeast of Stratford. ✉ *B4086, off A429, Hampton Lucy* ☎ *01789/470277* ⊕ *www.nationaltrust.org.uk* 🎟 *£8.63; grounds only, £4.36* ⊗ *House Mar.–Oct., Fri.–Tues. 11–4:30; Nov.–mid-Dec., weekends noon–4. Conservation tour Mar., Apr., and Oct., Fri.–Tues. 11–noon. Park and gardens daily 10–dusk.*

Holy Trinity Church. The burial place of William Shakespeare, this 13th-century church sits on the banks of the Avon, with a graceful avenue of lime trees framing its entrance. Shakespeare's final resting place is in the chancel, rebuilt in 1465–91 in the late Perpendicular style. He was buried here not because he was a famed poet but because he was a lay rector of Stratford, owning a portion of the township tithes. On the north wall of the sanctuary, over the altar steps, is the famous marble bust created by Gerard Jansen in 1623 and thought to be a true likeness of Shakespeare. The bust offers a more human, even humorous, perspective when viewed from the side. Also in the chancel are the graves of Shakespeare's wife, Anne; his daughter Susanna; his son-in-law John

8

Hall; and his granddaughter's husband, Thomas Nash. Nearby, the Parish Register is displayed, containing Shakespeare's baptismal entry (1564) and his burial notice (1616). Today the church needs to raise £2 million for restoration work. ⊠ *Trinity St.* ⊕ *www.stratford-upon-avon. org* ⊞ *£2 for chancel* ⊙ *Mar. and Oct., Mon.–Sat. 9–5, Sun. 12:30–5; Apr.–Sept., Mon.–Sat. 8:30–6, Sun. 12:30–5; Nov.–Feb., Mon.–Sat. 9–4, Sun. 12:30–5; last admission 20 mins before closing.*

Mary Arden's House. A working farm, where food is grown using methods common in the 16th century, is the main attraction at Mary Arden's House (the childhood home of Shakespeare's mother) and Palmer's Farm. This bucolic stop is great for kids, who can see the lambs, listen as the farmers explain their work in the fields, and watch the cooks prepare food in the Tudor farmhouse kitchen. It all brings the past to life. There are crafts exhibits, a café, and a garden. The site is 3 mi northwest of Stratford; you need to walk or drive here, or else go with a tour. ⊠ *Off A3400, Wilmcote* ☎ *01789/293455* ⊕ *www.shakespeare. org.uk* ⊞ *£9.50, Shakespeare Trust 5-property ticket £19.50* ⊙ *Apr.– Oct. daily 10–5.*

Royal Shakespeare Theatre. The Stratford home of the Royal Shakespeare Company (RSC), set amid gardens along the River Avon, reopened in March 2011 after an extensive renovation. Highlights of the new theater are better sightlines, better seating, and better acoustics; a viewing tower and rooftop restaurant are other amenities. The company, which presents some of the world's finest productions of Shakespeare's plays, has existed since 1879. Shows are also staged in the Swan. ■**TIP**➔ Book ahead for the popular backstage tour; times vary. *See Nightlife and the Arts for more information.* ⊠ *Waterside* ☎ *0844/800–1114 ticket hotline* ⊕ *www.rsc.org.uk.* ⊞ *Theater tours £6.50, tower visit £2.50*

Shakespeare's Birthplace. A half-timber house typical of its time, the playwright's birthplace is a much-visited shrine that has been altered and restored since he lived here. Entering through the modern visitor center, you are immersed in a good but basic introduction to Shakespeare through a "Life, Love, and Legacy" visual and audio exhibition; this can be crowded. You can see a First Folio and what is reputedly Shakespeare's signet ring, listen to the sounds of the Forest of Arden, and watch snippets of contemporary Shakespearean films. The house itself is across the garden from this large modern center. Colorful wall decorations and the furnishings in the actual house reflect comfortable, middle-class Elizabethan domestic life. Shakespeare's father, John, a glove maker and wool dealer, purchased the house;

BARD'S REVENGE?

According to tradition, Shakespeare was caught poaching deer at Charlecote Park soon after his marriage and fled to London. Years later he supposedly retaliated by portraying Sir Thomas Lucy in *Henry IV, Part 2* and the *Merry Wives of Windsor* as the foolish Justice Shallow. Some historians doubt the reference, but Shakespeare does mention the "dozen white luces"—which figure in the Lucy coat of arms—and Shallow does tax Falstaff with killing his deer. Luce is another name for the pike fish.

a reconstructed workshop shows the tools of the glover's trade. Mark Twain and Charles Dickens were earlier pilgrims here, and you can see the signatures of Thomas Carlyle and Walter Scott scratched into Shakespeare's windowpanes. In the garden, actors present excerpts from the plays. ⊠ *Henley St.* ☎ *01789/204016* ⊕ *www.shakespeare.org.uk* ✉ *£12.50, includes entry to Hall's Croft and Nash's House; 5-property ticket £19.50* ⊙ *Apr.– Oct., daily 9–5; Nov.–Mar., daily 10–4.*

> QUICK BITES
>
> Visitors and locals alike head for the half-timber **Hobsons Patisserie** (*1 Henley St* ☎ *01789/293330*) to indulge in their famous savory pies or scrumptious afternoon teas.

WORTH NOTING

Butterfly Farm. Europe's largest displays of exotic butterflies, spiders, caterpillars, and insects from all over the world are housed in a tropical greenhouse, a two-minute walk past the Bridgefoot footbridge. You can watch as butterflies emerge from pupae or take a look at the toxic black widow spider. ⊠ *Swan's Nest La.* ☎ *01789/299288* ⊕ *www.butterflyfarm.co.uk* ✉ *£6.25* ⊙ *Apr.–Sept., daily 10–6; Oct.–Mar., daily 10–dusk.*

Compton Verney. A neoclassical country mansion remodeled in the 1760s by Robert Adam has been repurposed by the Peter Moores Foundation as an art museum with more than 800 works. The house is set in 120 acres of rolling parkland landscaped by Capability Brown. The works of art are intriguingly varied and beautifully displayed in restored rooms: British folk art and portraits, textiles, Chinese pottery and bronzes, southern Italian art from 1600 to 1800, and German art from 1450 to 1600 are the main focus. From Stratford by car, take the B4086, or sign up in Stratford for City Sightseeing's Heart of Warwickshire tour; it's 9 mi east of Stratford. ⊠ *Off B4086, near Kineton* ☎ *01926/645500* ⊕ *www.comptonverney.org.uk* ✉ *£4; extra charge for exhibitions* ⊙ *Late Mar.–mid-Dec., Tues.–Sun. and national holidays 11–5.*

Guild Chapel. This chapel is the noble centerpiece of Stratford's Guild buildings, including the Guildhall, the Grammar School, and the almshouses—all well-known to Shakespeare. The ancient structure was rebuilt in the late Perpendicular style in the first half of the 15th century, thanks to the largesse of Stratford resident Hugh Clopton. Its otherwise plain interior includes fragments of a remarkable medieval fresco of the Last Judgment painted over in the 16th century and uncovered in a 20th-century reconstruction. The bell, also given by Sir Hugh, still rings as it did to tell Shakespeare the time of day. ⊠ *Chapel La. at Church St.* ☎ *01789/207111* ✉ *Free, donations welcome* ⊙ *Daily 10–4.*

Guildhall. Dating to 1416–18, the Guildhall is occupied by **King Edward's Grammar School,** which Shakespeare probably attended as a boy; it's still used as a school. On the first floor is the Guildhall proper, where traveling acting companies performed. Many historians believe that it was after seeing the troupe known as the Earl of Leicester's Men in 1587 that Shakespeare got the acting bug and set off for London. Visits are by prior arrangement only, usually on weekends during vacation time; contact the tourist information office. Immediately beyond the

8

Guildhall on Church Street is a row of 15th-century timber-and-daub almshouses, built for the poor and now serving as housing for pensioners. ⊠ *Church St.*

Hall's Croft. One of the finest surviving Jacobean (early 17th-century) town houses, this impressive residence has a delightful walled garden. Hall's Croft was the home of Shakespeare's elder daughter, Susanna, and her husband, Dr. John Hall, a physician who, by prescribing an herbal cure for scurvy, was well ahead of his time. His medical dispensary is on view along with the other rooms, all containing Jacobean furniture of heavy oak and some 17th-century portraits. ⊠ *Old Town* ☎ *01789/292107* ⊕ *www. shakespeare.org.uk* ⊠ *£12.50, includes admission to Shakespeare's Birthplace and New Place; 5-property ticket £19.50* ⊙ *Apr.–Oct., daily 10–5; Nov.–Mar., daily 11–4.*

SHAKESPEARE FOR SALE

In 1847 two widowed ladies were maintaining Shakespeare's birthplace in a somewhat ramshackle state. With the approach of the tercentennial of the playwright's birth, and in response to a rumor that the building was to be purchased by P. T. Barnum and shipped across the Atlantic, the city shelled out £3,000 for the relic. It was tidied up and opened to a growing throng of Shakespeare devotees.

Nash's House and New Place. This is the home of Thomas Nash, who married Shakespeare's last direct descendant, his granddaughter Elizabeth Hall. The heavily restored house has been furnished in 17th-century style, and it also contains a local museum. In the gardens (note the Elizabethan knot garden) are the foundations of **New Place,** the house in which Shakespeare died in 1616. Built in 1483 "of brike and tymber" for a lord mayor of London, New Place was Stratford's grandest piece of real estate when Shakespeare bought it in 1597 for £60; it was torn down in 1759 by the Reverend Francis Gastrell, who was angry at the hordes of Shakespeare-related sightseers. ⊠ *Chapel St.* ☎ *01789/292325* ⊕ *www.shakespeare.org.uk* ⊠ *£12.50, includes admission to Shakespeare's Birthplace and Hall's Croft; 5-property ticket £19.50* ⊙ *Apr.– Oct., daily 10–5; Nov.–Mar., daily 11–4.*

QUICK BITES

Duck into the quaint **Hathaway Tea Rooms** (⊠ **19 High St.** ☎ **01789/ 292404**), above the shops on the busy High Street in a 17th-century building, for wonderful tea and scones. It can be packed in summer.

WHERE TO EAT

£

BRITISH

★

✕ **The Black Swan/The Dirty Duck.** The only pub in Britain to be licensed under two names (the more informal one came courtesy of American GIs who were stationed here during World War II), this is one of Stratford's most celebrated pubs—it has attracted actors since the 18th-century thespian David Garrick's days. A little veranda overlooks the theaters and the river here. Along with your pint of bitter, you can dig into English grill specialties as well as bar meals such as mussels and chips. Few people come for the food, which is mediocre: the

Stratford-upon-Avon has plenty of pubs and restaurants when you need a break from the Shakespeare trail.

real attraction is the ambience and the other customers. ⊠ *Waterside* ☎ *01789/297312* ⊗ No *dinner Sun.*

££ ✕ **Church Street Town House.** Theatergoers tucking into an early supper
BRITISH in the Blue Bar to the strains of the grand piano, grandmas enjoying
afternoon tea in the Library, and couples lingering over their candlelit
suppers can all happily be found here. Plush armchairs, red drapes, oil
paintings, and bookshelves add to the intimacy and refinement of this
18th-century town house. The chef aims to keep flavors to the fore and
uses local food sources; sample dishes might be mushroom-and-tarragon
pâté, braised lamb with caramelized baby onions, and sticky toffee
pudding with clotted cream ice cream. Twelve bedrooms replete with
silvered French furniture (£££) are available should you wish to linger.
16 Church St. ☎ *01789/262222* ⊕ *www.churchstreettownhouse.com.*

££ ✕ **Lambs of Sheep Street.** Sit downstairs to appreciate the hardwood floors
BRITISH and oak beams of this local epicurean favorite; upstairs, the look is a
bit more contemporary. The updates of tried-and-true dishes include
salmon cakes with sorrel sauce, and Cotswold lamb shank with creamed
potatoes. Desserts are fantastic here, and daily specials keep the menu
seasonal. The two- and three-course fixed-price menus (£11.50 and
£15) for lunch or pretheater dining on weekdays are good deals. ⊠ *12
Sheep St.* ☎ *01789/292554* ⊕ *www.lambsrestaurant.co.uk* ⌂ *Reservations essential* ⊗ No *dinner Sun. in winter.*

££ ✕ **Le Bistrot Pierre.** There's always a satisfied hum in the air at this large,
FRENCH modern, and bustling bistro, part of a small chain, that's close to the
river. It's French and make no mistake about it: olives from Provence,
pâtés, free-range chickens from the Janzé region of Brittany, 21-day
aged Scottish beef cooked overnight in Bordeaux wine, and rustic

cheeses all appear on the menu. Vegetarians are well catered for and service is amicable and attentive. ⊠ *Swan's Nest La.* ☎ *01789/264804* ⊕ *www.lebistrotpierre.co.uk.*

££ ✕ **Opposition.** Hearty, warming meals are offered at this informal,
BRITISH family-style restaurant in a 16th-century building on the main dining street near the theaters. The English and international dishes—chicken roasted with banana and served with curry sauce and basmati rice, for instance—win praise from the locals. There's a good range of lighter and vegetarian options as well. Make reservations a month ahead in summer. ⊠ *13 Sheep St.* ☎ *01789/269980* ⊕ *www.theoppo.co.uk.*

££ ✕ **Sorrento.** Family-run, this Italian restaurant takes a respectable, old-
ITALIAN fashioned approach to service. Upon arrival, guests can choose to sip an aperitif in the lounge before they're escorted to their tables for a silver-service, white-tablecloth meal. The menu of traditional favorites is cooked from family recipes, and includes mozzarella fried in bread crumbs with Parma ham (a starter), and guinea fowl, chicken breast in Marsala wine, and a risotto of the day. Pretheater dinners are a good value. ⊠ *8 Ely St.* ☎ *01789/297999* ⊕ *www.sorrentorestaurant.co.uk* ☾ *Closed Sun. No lunch Mon.*

££ ✕ **Thai Boathouse.** Make for a window seat and you'll have the best inside
THAI view of the river, boats, and swans in Stratford, though the furnishings at this informal spot give you a small taste of Thailand. If the chicken, pork, or duck dishes don't grab you, try the king prawns or the sea bass; all are served with a judicious mix of Thai herbs, spices, or creamy curry sauce. ⊠ *Swan's Nest La.* ☎ *01789/297733* ⊕ *www.thaigroup.co.uk.*

££ ✕ **Thespian's Indian Restaurant.** A buzzing crowd of regulars frequents this
INDIAN casual Indian restaurant, drawn by its extensive menu of spicy dishes from the subcontinent and its friendly atmosphere. Choose from dishes like the creamy lamb *saqi* (barbecued lamb simmered in coconut milk with ginger and mint), the tandooris, or fish specials. It's an excellent option when you're bored with meat and potatoes. ⊠ *26 Sheep St.* ☎ *01789/267187.*

££ ✕ **The Vintner.** The imaginative, bistro-inspired menu varies each day
BISTRO at this café and wine bar. Pork fillet with caper butter is a popular main course, as is the steak; a children's menu is available. To dine before curtain time, arrive early or make a reservation. The building, largely unaltered since the late 1400s, has lovely flagstone floors and oak beams. ⊠ *5 Sheep St.* ☎ *01789/297259* ⊕ *www.the-vintner.co.uk.*

WHERE TO STAY

For expanded hotel reviews, visit Fodors.com.

£££–££££ ⊡ **Arden Hotel.** All is the best of classic contemporary style in this red-
HOTEL brick boutique hotel right across the road from the Royal Shakespeare Theatre. **Pros:** convenient to the Shakespeare theater; crisp and modern style; large bathrooms. **Cons:** can be crowded; plastic, not real, orchids. ⊠ *Waterside* ☎ *01789/298682* ⊕ *www.theardenhotelstratford. com* ⇨ *45 rooms* ⌂ *In-room: no a/c, Wi-Fi. In-hotel: restaurants, bars, parking* ⦿ *Breakfast.*

££
B&B/INN
🎬 **Cherry Trees.** Although it's nothing fancy from the outside, this modern house offers three beautifully and individually furnished suites in a tranquil location near the river. **Pros:** welcoming hosts; great breakfasts; convenient to in-town sights. **Cons:** too small for some. ✉ *Swan's Nest La.* ☎ *01789/292989* ⊕ *www.cherrytrees-stratford.co.uk* ⇥ *3 suites* ⚖ *In-room: no a/c, Wi-Fi. In-hotel: parking* ❖ *Breakfast.*

£££
HOTEL
🎬 **Ettington Park Hotel.** Victorian Gothic in style and with a sympathetic modern wing, this mansion built on land owned by the Shirley family since the 12th century is a soothing retreat for theatergoers who don't want to cope with Stratford's crowds; it's 6 mi south of town. **Pros:** gorgeous building; spacious rooms; relaxing lounge. **Cons:** a bit too formal for some; well out of Stratford; many wedding guests at weekends. ✉ *Off A3400, Alderminster* ☎ *0845/072–7454* ⊕ *www.handpicked. co.uk* ⇥ *42 rooms, 6 suites* ⚖ *In-room: a/c, Wi-Fi. In-hotel: restaurant, bar, pool, tennis courts, gym* ❖ *Breakfast.*

££
B&B/INN
🎬 **Fox & Goose.** A quirky style and fabulous fresh food make this place in the wee, unspoiled village of Armscote, 8 mi south of Stratford, more than just a pub with rooms. **Pros:** relaxing rooms; great restaurant. **Cons:** restaurant gets booked up; room decor can be bright and a bit quirky. ✉ *Middle St., Armscote* ☎ *01608/682635* ⊕ *www. foxandgoosearmscote.co.uk* ⇥ *4 rooms* ⚖ *In-room: no a/c, Wi-Fi. In-hotel: restaurant, bar* ❖ *Breakfast.*

£
B&B/INN
🎬 **Heron Lodge.** Just a mile outside Stratford town center, this B&B combines budget accommodation in a family home with high-quality service and breakfasts to match. **Pros:** welcoming and relaxing place; excellent service. **Cons:** outside town. ✉ *260 Alcester Rd.* ☎ *01789/299169* ⊕ *www.heronlodge.com* ⇥ *5 rooms* ⚖ *In-room: no a/c, Wi-Fi. In-hotel: parking, some age restrictions* ❖ *Breakfast.*

££–£££
↻
HOTEL
🎬 **Holiday Inn Stratford-upon-Avon.** This good-value, modern chain hotel's best selling points are an excellent location very near the center of the historic district, on the banks of the Avon, and views across the river and town center. **Pros:** good location; handy for families; free dinners for kids under 14. **Cons:** modern and featureless; big and impersonal. ✉ *Bridgefoot* ☎ *0871/942–9270* ⊕ *www.holidayinn.com* ⇥ *259 rooms, 2 suites* ⚖ *In-room: a/c, Wi-Fi. In-hotel: restaurant, bar, pool, gym, parking* ❖ *Breakfast.*

££–£££
HOTEL
🎬 **Legacy Falcon Hotel.** Licensed as an alehouse since 1640, this black-and-white timber-frame hotel in the center of town has an excellent location as well as a light, airy interior that looks out to a pleasant garden. **Pros:** great location; old portion of the building is charming. **Cons:** some rooms in old part are a bit cramped; so-so restaurant. ✉ *Chapel St.* ☎ *0844/411–9005* ⊕ *www.legacy-hotels.co.uk* ⇥ *83 rooms* ⚖ *In-room: no a/c, Wi-Fi. In-hotel: restaurant, bars, parking* ❖ *Breakfast.*

£££–££££
HOTEL
🎬 **Macdonald Alveston Manor.** This redbrick Elizabethan manor house across the River Avon from central Stratford has plenty of historic details, as well as a modern spa. **Pros:** nice mix of historic and modern; good spa facilities; you can warm yourself by a fire in winter. **Cons:** modern rooms are less interesting; there's no elevator and lots of stairs. ✉ *Clopton Bridge* ☎ *0844/879–9138* ⊕ *www.macdonald-hotels. co.uk* ⇥ *110 rooms, 4 suites* ⚖ *In-room: a/c, Internet, Wi-Fi. In-hotel:*

8

restaurant, bar, pool, spa, parking, some pets allowed ❙O❙ Breakfast.

££–£££ 🖼 **Shakespeare Hotel.** Built in the
HOTEL 1400s, this Elizabethan town house
★ in the heart of town is a vision right
out of *The Merry Wives of Windsor*,
with its nine gables and long, stunning, black-and-white half-timber
facade. **Pros:** historic building; great
lounge to relax in. **Cons:** prices are
quite high for what's on offer; some
very small bedrooms. ✉ *Chapel St.*
☎ *01789/294997* ⊕ *www.mercure.
com* 🛏 *63 rooms, 10 suites* ⚘ *In-
room: a/c, Internet, Wi-Fi. In-hotel:
restaurant, bar, parking, some pets allowed ❙O❙ Breakfast.*

££–£££ 🖼 **The Stratford, a QHotel.** Although this modern hotel may lack the
HOTEL period charm of older hotels, its up-to-date facilities, spacious rooms,
and ample grounds make it a good option for those for whom Tudor
beamed ceilings are not that important. **Pros:** friendly; handy location very near train station; lots of modern conveniences. **Cons:**
largely used as a conference hotel; rooms lack personality. ✉ *Arden St.*
☎ *01789/271000* ⊕ *www.qhotels.co.uk* 🛏 *102 rooms* ⚘ *In-room: a/c,
Internet, Wi-Fi. In-hotel: restaurant, bar, gym, parking* ❙O❙ *Breakfast.*

£ 🖼 **Victoria Spa Lodge.** This good-value B&B lies 1½ mi outside town,
B&B/INN within view of the Stratford Canal; the grand, clematis-draped build-
★ ing dates from 1837. **Pros:** beautiful building; full of character; family
friendly. **Cons:** away from the town center. ✉ *Bishopton La., Bishopton*
☎ *01789/267985* ⊕ *www.victoriaspa.co.uk* 🛏 *7 rooms* ⚘ *In-room: no
a/c, Wi-Fi. In-hotel: parking* ❙O❙ *Breakfast.*

££ 🖼 **White Swan.** Exposed beams, low ceilings, and winding corridors
HOTEL make this cozy hotel a delight for those who like a little authenticity; it
claims to be the oldest building in Stratford, and the look of the exterior (circa 1450) reinforces that boast. **Pros:** great for those who like
ancient buildings; unique decor; popular pub. **Cons:** most rooms in
newer part of hotel; some rooms are small; some bathrooms are even
tinier. ✉ *Rother St.* ☎ *01789/297022* ⊕ *www.pebblehotels.com* 🛏 *41
rooms* ⚘ *In-room: no a/c, Internet, Wi-Fi. In-hotel: restaurant, parking* ❙O❙ *Breakfast.*

NIGHTLIFE AND THE ARTS

FESTIVALS

The **Shakespeare Birthday Celebrations** (☎ *01789/415536* ⊕ *www.
shakespeare.org.uk*) take place on and around the weekend closest to
April 23 (unless Easter occurs during that time). The events, spread
over several days, include lectures, free concerts, processions, and
impromptu performances.

THEATER

If you're suffering from a surfeit of Shakespeare, head for **Cox's Yard** (✉ *Bridgefoot* ☎ *01789/404600* ⊕ *www.coxsyard.co.uk*), which hosts live music, comedy, and plays (for young children, too), as well as being a family pub and café.

Fodor's Choice
★
The **Royal Shakespeare Company** (✉ *Waterside* ☎ *0844/800–1110 ticket hotline, 01789/403444 general information* ⊕ *www.rsc.org.uk*) performs Shakespeare plays year-round in Stratford, as well as in other venues around Britain. Stratford's Royal Shakespeare Theatre is the home of the RSC, one of the finest repertory troupes in the world and long the backbone of the country's theatrical life. The company's stunningly renovated theater, with a thrust stage remodeled on the lines of the original Globe Theater in London, reopened in March 2011. The Swan Theatre, part of the theater complex and also built in the style of Shakespeare's Globe, stages plays by Shakespeare and contemporaries such as Christopher Marlowe and Ben Jonson, as well as works by contemporary playwrights. Prices usually are £5 to £58. ■**TIP→** Book ahead through the RSC, as seats go fast, but day-of-performance and returned tickets are often available. You can book tickets from London with **Ticketmaster** (☎ *0870/534–4444* ⊕ *www.ticketmaster.co.uk*), operating 24 hours a day.

SHOPPING

Chain stores and shops sell tourist junk, but this is also a good place to shop for high-quality (and high-price) silver, jewelry, and china. There's an open **market** (great for bargains) every Friday in the Market Place at Greenhill and Meer streets.

The **Antiques Centre** (✉ *60 Ely St.*) contains 50 stalls displaying jewelry, silver, linens, porcelain, and memorabilia.

B&W Thornton (✉ *23 Henley St.* ☎ *01789/269405*), above Shakespeare's Birthplace, stocks Moorcroft pottery and glass.

Chaucer Head Bookshop (✉ *21 Chapel St.* ☎ *01789/415691*) is the best of Stratford's many secondhand bookshops.

Lakeland (✉ *4/5 Henley St.* ☎ *01789/262100*) sells a great range of kitchen and home wares.

The **Shakespeare Bookshop** (✉ *39 Henley St.* ☎ *01789/292176*), run by the Shakespeare Birthplace, carries Elizabethan plays, Tudor history books, children's books, and general paraphernalia.

SPORTS AND THE OUTDOORS

From Easter to October, **Avon Boating** (✉ *The Boatyard, Swan's Nest La.* ☎ *01789/267073*) rents boats and punts and provides half-hour river excursions (£4.50) for a welcome escape from the crowds. A Venetian gondola can be rented for £80 for 45 minutes.

Bancroft Cruises (✉ *Moathouse, Bridgefoot* ☎ *01789/269669*) runs regular 45-minute guided cruises daily (£5.50), departing from the Holiday Inn landing stage.

8

AROUND SHAKESPEARE COUNTRY

This section of Warwickshire is marked by gentle hills, green fields, slow-moving rivers, quiet villages, and time-burnished halls, castles (Warwick and Kenilworth are the best examples, and well worth visiting), and churches. Historic houses such as Baddesley Clinton and Packwood House Court are another reason to explore. All the sights are close enough to Stratford-upon-Avon that you can easily use the town as a base if you wish.

HENLEY-IN-ARDEN

8 mi northwest of Stratford.

A brief drive out of Stratford will take you under the Stratford-upon-Avon Canal aqueduct to pretty Henley-in-Arden, whose wide main street is an architectural pageant of many periods. This area was once the Forest of Arden, where Shakespeare set one of his greatest comedies, *As You Like It.* Among the buildings to look for are the former Guildhall, dating from the 15th century, and the White Swan pub, built in the early 1600s. Near Henley-in Arden are two stately homes worth a stop, Packwood House and Baddesley Clinton.

GETTING HERE AND AROUND

The town is on the A3400. London Midland trains for Henley-in-Arden depart every hour from Stratford; the journey takes about 15 minutes. Train service from Birmingham takes about 40 minutes, and trains leave every hour. The town heritage center is not an official Tourist Information Centre but does have brochures; it's open Easter through October but is closed Monday.

ESSENTIALS

Visitor Information Henley-in-Arden Heritage and Visitors Center
(⊠ *Joseph Hardy House, 150 High St.* ☎ *01564/795919* ⊕ *www.heritagehenley. org.uk).*

EXPLORING

★ **Baddesley Clinton.** The eminent architectural historian Sir Nikolaus Pevsner described this as "the perfect late medieval manor house. The entrance side of grey stone, the small, creeper-clad Queen Anne brick bridge across the moat, the gateway with a porch higher than the roof and embattled—it could not be better." Set off a winding back-road, this grand manor dating from the 15th century retains its great fireplaces, 17th-century paneling, and three priest holes (secret chambers for Roman Catholic priests, who were hidden by sympathizers when Catholicism was banned in the 16th and 17th centuries). The café is an idyllic spot. Admission to the house is by timed ticket; Baddesley Clinton is 2 mi east of Packwood House and 15 mi north of Stratford-upon-Avon. ⊠ *Rising La., off A4141 near Chadwick End* ☎ *01564/783294* ⊕ *www.nationaltrust.org.uk* ⊠ *£8.80; garden only, £5.90. Combined ticket with Packwood House: houses £12.40, gardens £6.30* ⊙ *House and grounds Feb.–Dec., Tues.–Sun. 11–5; last admission 30 mins before closing.*

Packwood House. Garden enthusiasts are drawn to Packwood's re-created 17th-century gardens, highlighted by an ambitious topiary Tudor garden in which yew trees depict Jesus's Sermon on the Mount. The house combines redbrick and half-timbering, and its tall chimneys are also typical of the period. Exquisite collections of 16th-century furniture and textiles in the interior's 20th-century version of Tudor architecture make this one of the area's finest historic houses open to the public. It's 5 mi north of Henley-in-Arden and 12 mi north of Stratford-upon-Avon. ⊠ *Off B4439, 2 mi east of Hockley Heath* ☎ *01564/782024* ⊕ *www. nationaltrust.org.uk* ✉ *£7.90; garden only, £4.50. Combined ticket with Baddesley Clinton: houses £12.40, gardens £6.30* ☉ *House and garden Feb.–Oct., Tues.–Sun. 11–5; last admission 30 mins before closing.*

> ## COUNTRY WALKS
>
> The gentle countryside rewards exploration on foot. Ambitious walkers can try the 26-mi Arden Way loop (⊕ *www.ardenway.org*) that takes in Henley-in-Arden and the Forest of Arden. On the 3-mi walk from Stratford to Wilmcote and Mary Arden's House, you can see beautiful scenery. Parkland with trails surrounds stately homes such as Charlecote Park. Even Stratford can be the base for easy walks along the River Avon or on the path bordering the Stratford-upon-Avon Canal. Stratford's Tourist Information Centre has pamphlets with walks.

WARWICK

8 mi east of Henley-in-Arden, 4 mi south of Kenilworth, 9 mi northeast of Stratford-upon-Avon.

Most famous for Warwick Castle—that vision out of the feudal ages— the town of Warwick (pronounced *war*-ick) is an interesting architectural mix of Georgian redbrick and Elizabethan half-timbering.

GETTING HERE AND AROUND
Frequent trains from London to Warwick leave London's Marylebone Station; travel time is about 90 minutes. National Express coaches make the same journey in three hours or more five times a day from Victoria Coach Station. The journey between Stratford-upon-Avon and Warwick takes around 30 minutes by train or bus. Stagecoach bus 16 is more frequent, running every hour.

ESSENTIALS
Visitor Information Warwick (⊠ *Court House, Jury St.* ☎ 01926/492212 ⊕ *www.visitwarwick.co.uk*).

EXPLORING
★ **Collegiate Church of St. Mary.** Crowded with gilded, carved, and painted tombs, the **Beauchamp Chapel** of this church is the essence of late-medieval and Tudor chivalry—although it was built (1443–64) to honor the somewhat-less-than-chivalrous Richard Beauchamp, who consigned Joan of Arc to the flames. Alongside his impressive effigy in gilded bronze lie the fine tombs of Robert Dudley, earl of Leicester, adviser and

8

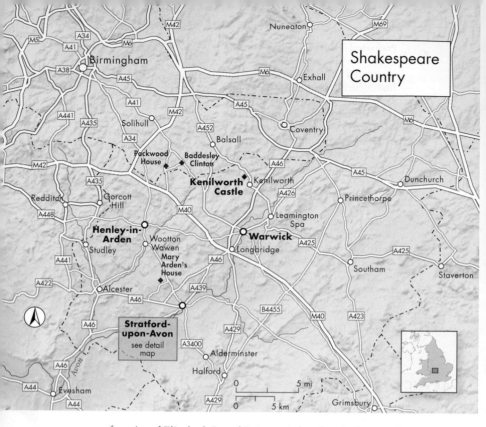

favorite of Elizabeth I, and Leicester's brother Ambrose. The church's chancel, distinguished by its flying ribs, a feature unique to a parish church, houses the alabaster table tomb of Thomas Beauchamp and his wife; the adjacent tiny Dean's chapel has exquisite miniature fan vaulting. In the Norman crypt, look for the rare ducking stool (a chair in which people were tied for public punishment). There's a brass-rubbing center, and you can climb the tower in summer. It's a five-minute walk from Warwick Castle. ⊠ *Church St., Old Sq.* ☎ *01926/403940* ⊕ *www. saintmaryschurch.co.uk* ✉ *£2 donation requested; tower £2.50* ☽ *Apr.–Oct., daily 10–6; Nov.–Mar., daily 10–4:30.*

Lord Leycester Hospital. Unattractive postwar development has spoiled much of Warwick's town center, but look for the 15th-century half-timber Lord Leycester Hospital, a home for old soldiers since the earl of Leicester dedicated it to that purpose in 1571. Within the complex are a chapel, an impressive beamed hall containing a small museum, and a fine courtyard with a wattle-and-daub balcony and 500-year-old gardens. Try a cream tea in the Brethren's Kitchen. ⊠ *High St.* ☎ *01926/491422* ⊕ *www.lordleycester.com* ✉ *£4.90* ☽ *Apr.–Sept., Tues.–Sun. 10–5; Oct.–Mar., Tues.–Sun. 10–4.30.*

☙ **St. John's House.** Kids as well as adults appreciate the well-thought-out St. John's House, a Jacobean building near the castle; beautiful gardens surround it. Inside are period costumes and scenes of domestic life, as well as a Victorian schoolroom and kitchen. ⊠ *Smith St.* ☎ *01926/412132* ⊠ *Free* ☉ *Apr.–Sept., Tues.–Sat. 10–5, Sun. 2:30–5; Oct.–Mar., Tues.–Sat. 10–5.*

☾ **Warwick Castle.** The vast bulk of this medieval castle rests on a cliff
★ overlooking the Avon—"the fairest monument of ancient and chivalrous splendor which yet remains uninjured by time," to use the words of Sir Walter Scott. Today the company that runs the Madame Tussauds wax museums owns the castle, and the exhibits and diversions can occupy a full day. Warwick is a great castle experience for kids, though it's pricey (there are family prices). Warwick's two soaring towers, bristling with battlements, can be seen for miles: the 147-foot-high Caesar's Tower, built in 1356, and the 128-foot-high Guy's Tower, built in 1380. The castle's most powerful commander was Richard Neville, earl of Warwick, known during the 15th-century Wars of the Roses as the Kingmaker. Warwick Castle's monumental walls enclose an impressive armory of medieval weapons, as well as state rooms with historic furnishings and paintings by Peter Paul Rubens, Anthony Van Dyck, and other old masters. Twelve rooms are devoted to an imaginative wax exhibition, "A Royal Weekend Party—1898." Other exhibits display the sights and sounds of a great medieval household as it prepares for an important battle, and of a princess's fairy-tale wedding; in the Dragon Tower, Merlin and a talking dragon breathe life into the Arthurian legend. At the Mill and Engine House, you can see the turning water mill and the engines used to generate electricity early in the 20th century. In the spooky dungeon exhibit, you can wander by wax re-creations of decaying bodies, chanting monks, executions, and "the labyrinth of lost souls"—a modern mirror maze. Elsewhere, falconry displays and rat-throwing (stuffed, not live) games add to the atmosphere. Below the castle, along the Avon, strutting peacocks patrol 60 acres of grounds elegantly landscaped by Capability Brown in the 18th century. ■**TIP→** The castle is popular; arrive early to beat the crowds but expect some lines. If you book online, you can save on ticket prices. Lavish medieval banquets (extra charge) and special events, including festivals, jousting tournaments, and a Christmas market, take place throughout the year, and plenty of food stalls serve lunches. ⊠ *Castle La. off Mill St.* ☎ *01926/495421, 0871/265–2000 24-hr information line* ⊕ *www. warwick-castle.co.uk* ⊠ *£20 without dungeon, £27.50 with dungeon, parking £5–£8* ☉ *Apr.–Sept., daily 10–6; Oct.–Dec. and Jan.–Mar., daily 10–5.*

QUICK BITES After a vigorous walk around the ramparts at Warwick Castle, you can drop by the cream-, crimson-, and gold-vaulted 14th-century **Undercroft** (☎ **01926/495421**) for a spot of tea or a hot meal from the cafeteria.

WHERE TO EAT AND STAY

££ ✕ **The Art Kitchen.** You are encouraged to share the creative Thai dishes
THAI sold by "bytes" (small plates and larger portions) at this chic and contemporary restaurant. The green and red curries are favorites, especially the chicken or lamb Masaman curry; or try the prawn-and-coriander dumplings on lemongrass. Service is always courteous, and the art that

8

Now in impressive ruins, mighty Kenilworth Castle once hosted Queen Elizabeth I. Today it has gardens, exhibitions, and a great setting.

peppers the walls is for sale. ✉ *7 Swan St.* ☎ *01926/494303* ⊕ *www.theartkitchen.com* ⊙ *Closed Sun.*

££
BRITISH

✗ **Rose & Crown.** Stripped pine floorboards, red walls, big wooden tables, and solidly good food and drink set the tone at this contemporary gastro-pub with rooms on the town's main square; it's very popular with locals. The owners take pride in offering seasonal food that mixes British and international influences. Marinated anchovies and smoked mackerel pâté appear on the deli board; other options are salmon in a mustard crust, and 28-day dry-aged Aberdeen rump steak and chips. Five moderately priced bedrooms provide simple but clean and modern lodging. ✉ *30 Market Pl.* ☎ *01926/411117.*

££££–£££££
HOTEL

▦ **Mallory Court Hotel.** This elegant country-house hotel 6 mi southeast of Warwick makes a quiet, luxurious getaway; it has 30 rooms but still manages to feel as if you're just visiting wealthy friends, and there's even a helipad. **Pros:** good for pampering; excellent restaurant. **Cons:** outside town; lots of weekend weddings. ✉ *Harbury La., Bishops Tachbrook* ☎ *01926/330214* ⊕ *www.mallory.co.uk* ⇆ *30 rooms* ⌂ *In-room: no a/c, Internet, Wi-Fi. In-hotel: restaurants* ❖ *Breakfast.*

KENILWORTH CASTLE

5 mi north of Warwick.

GETTING HERE AND AROUND

The local Stagecoach company offers services between Stratford on the 16 bus and Warwick on the X17 route The castle is a 1½ mi from the town center.

ESSENTIALS

Visitor Information Kenilworth (✉ *Kenilworth Library, 11 Smalley Pl.*
☎ *01926/748900* ⊕ *www.kenilworthweb.co.uk*).

EXPLORING

★ **Kenilworth Castle.** The sprawling, graceful red ruins of the castle loom
over the green fields of Warwickshire, surrounded by the low grassy
impression of what was once a lake that surrounded it completely. The
top of the keep (central tower) has commanding views of the countryside, one good indication of why this was such a formidable fortress
from 1120 until it was dismantled by Oliver Cromwell after the civil
war in the mid-17th century. Still intact are its keep, with 20-foot-
thick walls; its great hall built by John of Gaunt in the 14th century;
and its curtain walls, the low outer walls forming the castle's first line
of defense. Even more than Warwick Castle, these ruins reflect English
history. In 1326 King Edward II was imprisoned here and forced to
renounce the throne, before he was transferred to Berkeley Castle and
allegedly murdered with a red-hot poker. Here the ambitious Robert
Dudley, earl of Leicester, one of Elizabeth I's favorites, entertained her
four times, most notably in 1575 with 19 days of revelry. An excellent
exhibition in the restored gatehouse discusses the relationship between
Leicester and Elizabeth, and a stunning re-created Elizabethan garden
with arbors, aviary, and an 18-foot high Cararra marble fountain provides further interest for a visit for an hour or two. This is a good
place for a picnic and contemplation of the passage of time. The fine
gift shop sells excellent replicas of tapestries and swords. ✉ *Off A452,
Kenilworth* ☎ *01926/852078* ⊕ *www.english-heritage.org.uk* ⌑£8
☉ *Mar.–Oct., daily 10–5; Nov.–Feb., daily 10–4.*

8

WHERE TO EAT

£   ✕ **Clarendon Arms.** A location close to Kenilworth Castle helps make this
BRITISH pub a good spot for lunch and some good hand-pulled ales. You can
order fine home-cooked food including steaks and grills from the bar
here. Another option is to sample more-upmarket fare with an international slant at the next-door Harrington's restaurant, under the same
management. ✉ *44 Castle Hill, Kenilworth* ☎ *01926/852017* ⊕ *www.
clarendonarmspub.co.uk.*

££   ✕ **Petit Gourmand.** Locals and those from farther afield are drawn to
FRENCH this relaxed, plush restaurant that has the look of an upscale modern French brasserie. The menu is a creative mixture of classic British dishes prepared with French flair. Seasonal and local produce and
meats are well represented in dishes such as pork belly with applesauce,
Scottish beef bourguignon with green beans, and salmon or free-range
chicken served with your choice of sauce or butter. ✉ *101 Warwick Rd.,
Kenilworth* ☎ *01926/864567* ⊕ *www.petit-gourmand.co.uk* ☉ *Closed
Sun. and Mon.*

BIRMINGHAM

The dynamic cultural life of Birmingham—the result of the museums, art galleries, theater, ballet, and symphony that thrive here—comes as a refreshing surprise. The city's visual appeal, thanks to heavy industry, German bombing during World War II, and some unfortunate late-20th-century civic architecture, may be less than instantly evident, but treasures and historic civic architecture remain. Creative redevelopment and public art are increasingly making areas more attractive, too. The redeveloped Bullring shopping center, part of which has a striking, curving facade of 15,000 aluminum disks, is one creation that has won praise.

Birmingham, with a metropolitan area population of 2.6 million, lies 25 mi north of Stratford-upon-Avon and 120 mi northwest of London. "Brum," as it's known, is one of the country's most ethnically diverse urban areas, with nearly a third of its residents from minority groups. The city first flourished in the boom years of the 19th century's Industrial Revolution. Its inventive citizens accumulated enormous wealth, and at one time the city had some of the finest Victorian buildings in the country. It still has some of the most ravishingly beautiful Pre-Raphaelite paintings, on view in the Birmingham Museum and Art Gallery.

GETTING HERE AND AROUND

Bus 900 runs from the airport to the city center every 20 minutes; a taxi will cost you around £20. Try to avoid the city's convoluted road network. Drivers are often surprised that Birmingham's inner ring road twists through the city center. Parking in the center is free from 6 pm to 8 am.

New Street train station is right in the center of the city, close to the Bullring shopping center. The bus station is at Oxford Street, a few minutes' walk from the Bullring.

Most of the central sights, which are well signposted, form a tight-knit group. The easiest way to get around the city is by foot, though you'll need a bus for the Barber Institute and Cadbury World, and a short Metro (tram) trip for the Jewellery Quarter. A Daytripper ticket covering bus, train, and Metro travel costs £5.50. The tourist information center, the best place to pick up a map, is close to public bus and rail stations. It has details of heritage walks.

PLANNING YOUR TIME

A full day gives you time to linger in the Jewellery Quarter and browse the art museums. Much of Birmingham is now pedestrian-friendly, the downtown shopping area transformed into arcades and buses-only streets. You can also explore restored canals and canal towpaths.

ESSENTIALS

Transportation Contacts Traveline (☎ 0870/200–2233 ⊕ *www.traveline. org.uk*).

Visitor Information Birmingham (✉ *The Rotunda, 150 New St.* ☎ 0844/888–3883 ⊕ *www.visitbirmingham.com*).

EXPLORING

TOP ATTRACTIONS

★ **Barber Institute of Fine Art.** Part of the University of Birmingham, the museum has a small but astounding collection of European paintings, prints, drawings, and sculpture, including works by Bellini, Holbein, Poussin, Turner, Whistler, Degas, Monet, and van Gogh. The museum is 3 mi from the city center; to get here, take a train from New Street Station south to University Station, or Bus 61, 62, or 63 from the city center. ⊠ *Off Edgbaston Park Rd. near East Gate, Edgbaston* ☎ *0121/414–7333* ⊕ *www.barber.org.uk* ☐ *Free* ☉ *Mon.–Sat. 10–5, Sun. noon–5.*

Birmingham Back to Backs. Of the 20,000 courts of back-to-back houses (constructed around a courtyard and thus backing onto each other) built in the 19th century for the city's expanding working-class population, this is the only survivor. Three houses tell the stories of families, headed by a watchmaker, a locksmith, and a glassworker, who lived here between the 1840s and the 1930s. A few houses are available for overnight stays. Admission is by timed ticket, booked in advance; allow one hour for the tour and be prepared for steep stairs. The houses are closed the Tuesday after a national holiday. ⊠ *Hurst St., City Centre* ☎ *0121/666–7671* ⊕ *www.nationaltrust.co.uk* ☐ *£6.60* ☉ *Feb.–Dec., Tues.–Sun. and national holidays 10–5.*

Fodor's Choice **Birmingham Museum and Art Gallery.** Vast and impressive, this museum ★ holds a magnificent collection of Victorian art and is known internationally for its works by the Pre-Raphaelites. All the big names are here—William Holman Hunt, John Everett Millais, and Dante Gabriel Rossetti—reflecting the enormous wealth of 19th-century Birmingham and the aesthetic taste of its industrialists. Galleries of metalwork, silver, and ceramics reveal some of the city's history, and works from the Renaissance, the Arts and Crafts movement, and the present day are also well represented. Also on view may be some of the Anglo-Saxon treasures (coins, helmets, and more) of the Staffordshire Hoard, discovered in 2009. Allow a couple of hours to visit, and consider a stop in the Edwardian Tea Room. ⊠ *Chamberlain Sq., City Centre* ☎ *0121/303–2834* ⊕ *www.bmag.org.uk* ☐ *Free* ☉ *Mon.–Thurs. and Sat. 10–5, Fri. 10:30–5, Sun. 12:30–5.*

8

★ **Black Country Living Museum.** It was in the town of Dudley, in the 17th ☺ century, that coal was first used for smelting iron. The town became known as the capital of the Black Country, a term that arose from the resulting air pollution. The 26-acre Black Country Living Museum consists of an entire village made up of buildings from around the region, including a chain maker's workshop; a trap-works where animal snares were fashioned; his-and-hers hardware stores (pots and pans for women, tools and sacks for men); a druggist; and a general store where costumed women describe life in a poor industrial community in the 19th century. You can also sit on a hard bench and watch Charlie Chaplin in the 1920s cinema, peer into the depths of a mine, or ride on a barge through a tunnel to experience the canal travel of yesteryear. For sustenance there are two cafés, the 1930s-era Fried Fish Shop that serves

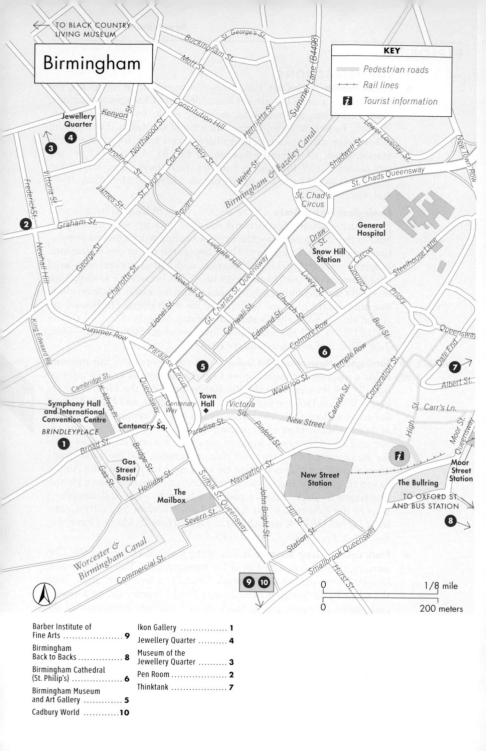

TO BLACK COUNTRY
LIVING MUSEUM

Birmingham

Jewellery
Quarter

St. George's St.

Buckingham St.

Mott St.

St. Chads Queensway

Kenyon St.

Constitution Hill

Northwood St.

Henrietta St.

Summer Lane (B4498)

Birmingham & Fazeley Canal

Lower Loveday St.

New Town Row

Caroline St.

Vittoria St.

Frederick St.

Water St.

Livery St.

Cox St.

Shadwell St.

St. Chad's
Circus

General Hospital

St. Chads Queensway

Steelhouse Lane

Graham St.

St. Paul's

Square

James St.

Newhall Hill

George St.

Charlotte St.

Ludgate Hill

Newhall St.

Draw St.

Snow Hill
Station

Livery St.

Colmore Circus

Priory

Queensway

Summer Row

Lionel St.

Gt. Charles St. Queensway

Cornwall St.

Edmund St.

Church St.

Colmore Row

Temple Row

Bull St.

Date End

King Edward Rd.

Cambridge St.

Paradise Circus

Queensway

Centenary
Way

Waterloo St.

Corporation St.

Albert St.

Cannon St.

High St.

Carr's Ln.

Moor St. Queensway

Symphony Hall
and International
Convention Centre

BRINDLEYPLACE

Centenary Sq.

Town
Hall

Victoria
Sq.

New Street

Broad St.

Bridge St.

Gas St.

Gas
Street
Basin

Holliday St.

The
Mailbox

Paradise St.

Suffolk St. Queensway

Navigation St.

John Bright St.

Pinfold St.

New Street
Station

i

The Bullring

TO OXFORD ST.
AND BUS STATION

Moor
Street
Station

Severn St.

Worcester &
Birmingham Canal

Commercial St.

Hill St.

Station St.

Smallbrook Queensway

Hurst St.

0   1/8 mile

0   200 meters

Cruising Birmingham's Canals

Canal near the Gas Street Basin

With eight canals and 34 mi of waterways, Birmingham has more canals in its center than Venice. The city is at the heart of a system of waterways built during the Industrial Revolution to connect inland factories to rivers and seaports—by 1840 the canals extended more than 4,000 mi throughout the British Isles. These canals, which carried 9 million tons of cargo a year in the late 19th century and helped make the city an industrial powerhouse, have undergone extensive cleanup and renovation, and are now a tourist attraction.

A walk along the Birmingham Canal Main Line near the Gas Street Basin will bring you to modern shops, restaurants, and more developments such as Brindleyplace in one direction and the Mailbox in the other, and you can see the city from an attractive new perspective. Contact the city tourist offices for maps of pleasant walks along the towpaths and canal cruises on colorfully painted barges.

You can take an hour ride on a canal barge from **Sherborne Wharf** (⊠ Sherborne St., City Centre ☏ 0121/455–6163 ⊕ www. sherbornewharf.co.uk). Trips leave daily April through October at 11:30, 1, 2:30, and 4, and on weekends the rest of the year, departing from the International Convention Centre Quayside.

8

fish-and-chips cooked in beef drippings, and the Bottle & Glass pub for ales and drinks. ■TIP→ To avoid the numerous school parties, visit on the weekend or during school vacations. The museum, 3 mi from the M5, is best reached by car. Leave M5 at Junction 2 by A4123, and then take A4037 at Tipton. Trains from Birmingham New Street to Tipton Station take 16 minutes; buses from the train station run past the museum, which is 1 mi away. ⊠ Tipton Rd., Dudley ☏ 0121/557–9643 ⊕ www. bclm.co.uk ☒ £13.60, barge trip £5.50, parking £2 ⊙ Mar.–Oct., daily 10–5; Nov.–Feb., Wed.–Sun. 10–4.

Jewellery Quarter. For more than two centuries, jewelers have worked in the district of Hockley, northwest of the city center; today around 200 manufacturing jewelers continue the tradition, producing more than a third of the jewelry made in Britain. ■TIP→ The Jewellery Quarter is a great place to shop for jewelry. A free booklet from the tourist office gives you the lowdown on the area. The city's Assay Office hallmarks 12 million items each year with the anchor symbol denoting Birmingham origin. The ornate green and gilded Chamberlain Clock, at the intersection of Vyse Street, Warstone Lane, and Frederick Street, marks the center of the district. Shops are closed Sunday. The quarter is two stops along Metro Line 1 from Snow Hill Station. ⊠ *Hockley* ⊕ *www. the-quarter.com.*

Museum of the Jewellery Quarter. The museum is built around the workshops of Smith & Pepper, a firm that operated here for more than 80 years until 1981; little has changed since the early 1900s. A factory tour (about an hour) and exhibits explain the history of the neighborhood and the jeweler's craft, and you can watch demonstrations of jewelry being made in the traditional way. ⊠ *75–79 Vyse St., Jewellery Quarter* ☎ *0121/554–3598* ⊕ *www.bmag.org.uk* ⊠ *£3.50* ⊙ *Tues.–Sat. and national holidays 11:30–4; last admission 1 hr before closing.*

Ⓒ **Thinktank.** This interactive museum in the state-of-the-art Millennium Point center allows you to explore science and the history of Birmingham over four floors of galleries. You can watch giant steam engines at work, explore deep space, program a robot to play the drums, and help perform a hip operation; it's great for families. The IMAX cinema and planetarium put on shows throughout the day. The museum is a 10-minute walk from Moor Street railway station. ⊠ *Curzon St., Digbeth* ☎ *0121/202–2222* ⊕ *www.thinktank.ac* ⊠ *£12.25, IMAX cinema £10.60, planetarium £2.45* ⊙ *Daily 10–5; last admission at 4.*

WORTH NOTING

Birmingham Cathedral. The early-18th-century Cathedral of St. Philip, a few blocks from Victoria Square, contains some lovely plasterwork in its elegant, gilded Georgian interior. The stained-glass windows behind the altar, designed by the Pre-Raphaelite Edward Burne-Jones (1833–98) and executed by William Morris (1834–96), glow with sensuous hues. ⊠ *Colmore Row, City Centre* ☎ *0121/262–1840* ⊕ *www. birminghamcathedral.com* ⊠ *Suggested donation £2* ⊙ *Daily 8:30–5.*

Ⓒ **Cadbury World.** The village of Bournville (4 mi south of the city center) contains this museum devoted to—what else?—chocolate. In 1879 the Quaker Cadbury brothers moved the family business from the city to this "factory in a garden." The museum traces the history of the cocoa bean and the Cadbury dynasty. The rain-forest walk, Cadabra ride, and exhibits may seem kitschy, and some are perhaps tired, but Cadbury World is extremely popular. You can watch (and smell) chocolates being made by hand, enjoy free samples, and then stock up from the cut-price shop. The restaurant has specialty chocolate cakes as well as lunches. ⊠ *Off A38 (take train from New St. to Bournville Train Station), Bournville* ☎ *0844/880–7667* ⊕ *www.cadburyworld.co.uk* ⊠ *£14.30* ⊙ *Feb.–Oct., daily; late Jan., Nov., and Dec., Tues.–Thurs. and weekends; times vary; reservations strongly advised, and essential at busy times.*

Ikon Gallery. Converted from a Victorian Gothic–style school, this gallery serves as the city's main venue for exhibitions of contemporary art from Britain and abroad. The bright, white interior is divided into comparatively small display areas, making the shows easily digestible. If you need fortifying, however, try the attached tapas bar. ⊠ *1 Oozells Sq., Brindleyplace, City Centre* ☎ *0121/248–0708* ⊕ *www.ikon-gallery. co.uk* ⊠ *Free* ⊙ *Tues.–Sun. and national holiday Mon. 11–6.*

QUICK BITES

The balcony of the redbrick **Malt House** (⊠ *75 King Edward's Rd.* ☎ *0121/633–4171*) is just the place to linger over a drink as you watch canal life go by.

Pen Room. During the 19th century Birmingham was the hub of the world pen trade. This compact museum in a former factory illustrates that heyday through an overwhelming and decorative array of nibs, quills, fountain pens, inks, and all the paraphernalia of the pre-ballpoint era. You can try your hand at calligraphy and make your own nib. ⊠ *60 Frederick St., Jewellery Quarter* ☎ *0121/236–9834* ⊕ *www.penroom.co.uk* ⊠ *Free* ⊙ *Mon.–Sat. 11–4, Sun. 1–4.*

EAT BALTI IN BRUM

Birmingham is home to the balti, a popular cuisine created in the mid-1970s by the Pakistani community. The food is cooked and brought to the table in a woklike dish and eaten with naan bread, not rice. Curry and other spices season the meat and vegetables. The more than 30 restaurants in the "Balti Triangle" of the Moseley and Sparkbrook districts include the highly rated **Al Frash** (⊠ *186 Ladypool Rd.Sparkhill* ☎ *0121/753–3120* ⊕ *www.alfrash. com*). Buses 6, 12, 13, and 37 go to this area a few miles south of the center.

WHERE TO EAT

£
CHINESE

✕ **Henry's.** A popular lunch spot, this traditional Cantonese restaurant on the edge of the Jewellery Quarter is a great place to stop during a shopping spree. The menu lists more than 170 items and also includes a good-value fixed-price menu and a Sunday buffet. The sizzling dishes, which arrive at your table on a metal plate, are a good choice. ⊠ *27 St. Paul's Sq., City Centre* ☎ *0121/200–1136* ⊕ *www.henrysrestaurant. co.uk.*

££
INDIAN

✕ **Itihaas.** Birmingham has some of the country's finest Indian restaurants, and this is one upbeat choice. The style is traditional and colonial; potted palms and portraits rub shoulders with antiques. Cooking concentrates on north Indian dishes, and some good choices are *koila murgh*, chicken marinated in yogurt and seared over charcoal, or *hara bara gosth*, a casserole of lamb cooked with garlic, chili, and spinach. The weekday lunchtime tapas menu is a deal at £8.95. ⊠ *18 Fleet St., City Centre* ☎ *0121/212–3383* ⊕ *www.itihaas.co.uk* ⊙ *No lunch weekends.*

£££££
MODERN BRITISH

✕ **Love's.** Overlooking a spruced-up stretch of canal bobbing with barges, this contemporary eatery takes you on an imaginative journey through the British culinary landscape. Chef Steve Love accompanies his belly of Gloucestershire pork with pease pudding and cider jelly, while his wild black sea bream comes with smoked almond gnocchi. Many of the highlights appear between courses, with a well-chosen mango puree or leek-and-ginger foam with goat's cheese. The three-course lunch menu offers good value at £25; the tasting menu is £65. ⊠ *3 Canal Sq., City Centre* ☎ *0121/454–5151* ⊕ *www.loves-restaurant. co.uk* ⊙ *Closed Sun. and Mon.*

8

£££ MODERN BRITISH **Opus.** The best seasonal ingredients are freshly prepared for discerning diners—anyone from ladies out on the town to intimate couples—enjoying this modern, light space. The accent is on local and British, so expect quince, pumpkins, wild mushrooms, and air-dried Cumbrian ham. Meat is free range and fish is wild caught. The weekday three-course fixed-price menu offers an excellent value at £24.50; you can also go the whole hog and treat yourself to a ringside seat at the chef's table, where five courses cost £75. *54 Cornwall St., City Centre 0121/200–2323 www.opusrestaurant.co.uk Closed Sun.*

£££££ MODERN BRITISH **Purnell's.** Business moguls and sophisticated foodies can be found sampling an aperitif in a comfy armchair before moving to the sleek, slate-floor dining room. This high spot in the business district, in a Victorian terra-cotta and redbrick building, is where chef Glyn Purnell creates his adventurous Modern British fare. Pigeon comes with roast duck liver and savoy cabbage; brill is slow-cooked in coconut milk. Set-price dinners (two courses for £38, three courses for £46) are complemented by a tasting menu (£75). Lunches (£22 for two courses) are a good value. *55 Cornwall St., City Centre 0121/212–9799 www.purnellsrestaurant.com Closed Sun. and Mon. No lunch Sat.*

££££ FRENCH Fodor's Choice ★ **Simpsons.** Choose between the conservatory with garden views or the inner dining space of this elegant and gleaming Georgian villa known for French-influenced cuisine. Either way, the light and immaculate surroundings and assured and welcoming service make it easy to savor specialties such as wood pigeon with snails and pearl barley risotto or pear tarte tatin with Roquefort ice cream. There are four luxurious theme guest rooms (££££) for those who wish to stray no farther, and a cooking school. It's a mile south of the city center. *20 Highfield Rd., Edgbaston 0121/454–3434 www.simpsonsrestaurant.co.uk No dinner Sun.*

££ THAI **Thai Edge.** This elegant, contemporary eatery is perfectly at home in fashionable Brindleyplace. Dishes such as *gaeng keow waan* (green curry cooked in coconut milk with eggplant, lime leaves, and basil) and sea bass in banana leaves are excellent. Lunches are a good value. *7 Oozells Sq., City Centre 0121/643–3993 www.thaiedge.co.uk.*

WHERE TO STAY

For expanded hotel reviews, visit Fodors.com.

££££ HOTEL **Hotel du Vin & Bistro.** A Victorian hospital in the city center got a makeover from a *très* hip chain but retains such original details as the ironwork double stairway and marble columns. **Pros:** good for celebrity spotting; central location. **Cons:** no private parking; breakfast costs extra. *25 Church St., City Centre 0121/200–0600 www.hotelduvin.com 56 rooms, 10 suites In-room: no a/c, Wi-Fi. In-hotel: restaurant, bars, gym, spa, parking No meals.*

£££–££££ HOTEL **Macdonald Burlington Hotel.** Housed in one of the city's grand Victorian buildings, this traditional hotel's pedigree is confirmed by an impressive roll call of prime ministers who have spent a night here. **Pros:** close to New Street Station and shops; very good weekend rates. **Cons:** attracts a mainly business clientele. *Burlington Arcade, 126*

New St., City Centre ☎ *0844/879–9019* ⊕ *www.burlingtonhotel.com* ⟿ *112 rooms* ⟁ *In-room: a/c, Wi-Fi. In-hotel: restaurant, bar, gym, parking, some pets allowed* ⊠⊙⟊ *Breakfast.*

£££ HOTEL

Malmaison. Retail therapy is on your doorstep at this chic, up-to-the-minute hotel in the Mailbox shopping center; large windows make the guest rooms light and airy by day, and there's subtle lighting by night. **Pros:** handy for shopping and dining; near canal-side attractions; good online specials. **Cons:** expensive parking (cheaper alternatives are close by); breakfast not included. ⊠ *1 Wharfside St., City Centre* ☎ *0121/246–5000* ⊕ *www.malmaison.com* ⟿ *189 rooms, 10 suites* ⟁ *In-room: a/c, Internet. In-hotel: restaurant, bar, gym, spa, parking* ⊙⟊ *No meals.*

££ HOTEL

Mint Hotel. An excellent central location near the waterside nightlife scene is a perk to staying at this smoothly run hotel, formerly known as the City Inn. **Pros:** free Wi-Fi; windows open to catch the breeze. **Cons:** mostly for business travelers; watching TV on a computer isn't ideal. ⊠ *1 Brunswick Sq., Brindleyplace, City Centre* ☎ *0121/643–1003* ⊕ *www.cityinn.com* ⟿ *238 rooms* ⟁ *In-room: a/c, Internet, Wi-Fi. In-hotel: restaurant, gym, parking* ⊙⟊ *No meals.*

££ HOTEL ★

New Hall Hotel & Spa. A tree-lined drive leads through 26 acres of gardens and open land to this moated, 12th-century manor house, where the public rooms reflect the hotel's long history with touches such as the 16th-century oak paneling and Flemish glass, 18th-century chandeliers, and a stone fireplace from the 17th century. **Pros:** historic building; beautiful grounds; plenty of sports facilities. **Cons:** a little difficult to locate; away from city center. ⊠ *Walmley Rd., Sutton Coldfield* ☎ *0121/378–2442* ⊕ *www.handpickedhotels.co.uk* ⟿ *49 rooms, 10 suites* ⟁ *In-room: no a/c (some), Wi-Fi. In-hotel: restaurant, bar, golf course, pool, tennis court, gym, spa, parking* ⊙⟊ *Breakfast.*

£££–££££ RENTAL

Staying Cool. The 19th and 20th floors of the Rotunda, an iconic, cylindrical office building from 1965, now contain spacious one- and two bedroom apartments, designed to the hilt in sleek '60s style. **Pros:** well-stocked kitchens; dreamy beds; iMacs with free Wi-Fi. **Cons:** no designated parking. ⊠ *150 New St., City Centre* ☎ *0121/285–1250* ⊕ *www.stayingcool.com* ⟿ *15 apartments* ⟁ *In-room: no a/c, kitchen, Internet, Wi-Fi* ⊙⟊ *No meals.*

££ RENTAL

Totel. These large apartments, 1½ mi from Birmingham's center and off the main A456, make for a secluded and peaceful retreat. **Pros:** plenty of room; free, secure parking; frequent buses to center. **Cons:** not in city center; no nearby shops or restaurants. ⊠ *Asquith House, 19 Portland Rd., Edgbaston* ☎ *0121/454–5282* ⊕ *www.toteluk.com* ⟿ *10 apartments* ⟁ *In-room: no a/c, kitchen, Wi-Fi. In-hotel: parking* ⊙⟊ *Breakfast.*

NIGHTLIFE AND THE ARTS

NIGHTLIFE

The city's thriving nightlife scene is concentrated around Broad Street and Hurst Street, as well as the Brindleyplace and Mailbox areas.

Colorful **Asha's** (⊠ *12–22 Newhall St., City Centre* ☎ *0121/200–2767*), a bar and restaurant, has superb fresh fruit cocktails and Asian cuisine.

Bar Epernay (⊠ *171 Wharfside St., City Centre* ☎ *0121/632–1430*), a champagne bar and brasserie in the Mailbox, has a revolving piano and a warming brazier, making it perfect for relaxing after a day's sightseeing.

The **Jam House** (⊠ *3–5 St. Paul's Sq., Jewellery Quarter* ☎ *0121/200–3030*), an excellent drinking, dining, and dancing venue, benefits from nightly live entertainment—jazz, soul, or funk.

The spacious and high-domed **Old Joint Stock** (⊠ *4 Temple Row W, off Colmore Row, City Centre* ☎ *0121/200–1892*) serves good ales and pies, and there's a theater attached.

The bar at the **Vaults** (⊠ *Newhall Pl., Newhall Hill, Jewellery Quarter* ☎ *0121/212–9837*) is perfect for an intimate drink. Another option is to reserve your own private, brick-vaulted booth, draw the curtain, adjust the music, and settle down.

THE ARTS

Birmingham's performing arts companies are well regarded throughout the country. Catch a performance if you can.

BALLET The **Birmingham Royal Ballet** (⊠ *Hurst St., City Centre* ☎ *0870/730–1234*), the second company of the Royal Ballet, is based at the Hippodrome Theatre, which also plays host to visiting companies such as the Welsh National Opera.

CONCERTS The **National Exhibition Centre** (⊠ *M42, Junction 6, close to airport* ☎ *0121/780–4141*) promotes top names in rock and pop.

Symphony Hall (⊠ *International Convention Centre, Broad St., City Centre* ☎ *0121/780–3333*) is the home of the distinguished City of Birmingham Symphony Orchestra and a venue for jazz, pop, and world as well as classical concerts.

The splendidly refurbished neoclassical **Town Hall Birmingham** (⊠ *Paradise St., City Centre* ☎ *0121/780–3333*) holds a wide range of events, including organ recitals, opera, and folk concerts.

THEATER The **Alexandra Theatre** (⊠ *Station St., City Centre* ☎ *0870/607–7533*) welcomes touring companies on their way to or from London's West End.

The **Birmingham Repertory Theatre** (⊠ *Centenary Sq., Broad St., City Centre* ☎ *0121/245–4455*), founded in 1913, is equally at home with modern or classical work as one of England's oldest and most esteemed theater companies.

FILM The **Electric Cinema** (⊠ *47–49 Station St., City Centre* ☎ *0121/643–7879*), the country's oldest working cinema if not the smartest, has sofas and waiter service to enhance the viewing experience at this individualistic art deco survivor.

Worcester Cathedral has a blissfully English setting near the River Severn and the county cricket ground.

SHOPPING

SHOPPING CENTERS

The glass-roof **Bullring** (✉ *Between New St. and High St., City Centre* ☎ *0121/632–1526*) has three floors of retail enticement, including two department stores, Debenhams and the stunningly curved Selfridges, covered with aluminum disks. Don't miss Selfridges's awesome Food Hall.

The **Mailbox** (✉ *150 Wharfside St., City Centre* ☎ *0121/632–1000*), once a Royal Mail sorting office, entices with trendy shops and designer outlets such as Harvey Nichols and Armani, restaurants, and hotels.

JEWELLERY QUARTER

The **Jewellery Quarter** (✉ *Hockley* ☎ *0121/604–7700*) has more than 100 shops that sell and repair gold and silver handcrafted jewelry, clocks, and watches. The Information Centre at 120 Vyse Street provides information on artisans and retail outlets.

Crescent Silver (✉ *83–85 Spencer St., Jewellery Quarter* ☎ *0121/236–9006*) sells a range of interesting silver jewelry and gifts.

St. Paul's Gallery (✉ *94–108 Norwood St., Jewellery Quarter* ☎ *0121/236–5800*), an entertaining treasure trove, specializes in hand-signed fine-art prints of album covers, past and present.

GREAT MALVERN, HEREFORD, AND ENVIRONS

In the arc of towns to the west of Birmingham and around the banks of the River Wye to the south, history and tradition rub up against deepest rural England. Great Malvern or the cathedral town of Hereford is a great base from which to soak up the bucolic flavor of the Malvern Hills and Elgar country, or to view the spectacular swing of the Wye at Symonds Yat.

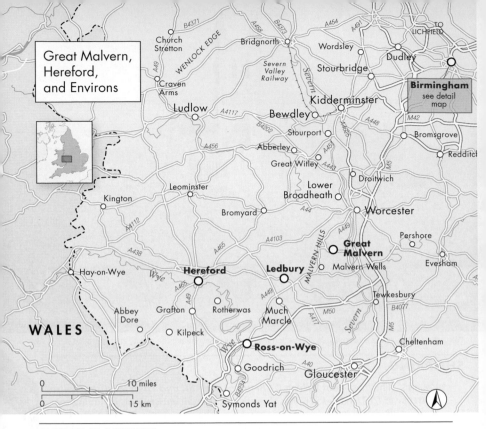

GREAT MALVERN

47 mi southwest of Birmingham, 18 mi northeast of Hereford.

Great Malvern feels a bit like a seaside resort, though instead of the ocean your eyes plunge into an expanse of green meadows rolling away into the Vale of Evesham. Off the A449, this attractive Victorian spa town's architecture has changed little since the mid-1800s. Its Winter Gardens complex with a theater, cinema, and gardens makes Great Malvern a good base for walks in the surrounding Malvern Hills. These hills, with their long, low, purple profiles rising from the surrounding plain, inspired much of the music of Sir Edward Elgar (1857–1934), who composed "Pomp and Circumstance." They also inspired his remark that "there is music in the air, music all around us."

GETTING HERE AND AROUND

To get here from Hereford will take 30 minutes or so by car. There are also frequent trains and buses run by First (29 minutes by train, one hour by bus). Birmingham is an hour away by car and rail.

ESSENTIALS

Visitor Information Great Malvern (✉ *21 Church St.* ☎ *01684/892289*
⊕ *www.malvernhills.gov.uk*).

EXPLORING

Elgar Birthplace Museum. The composer Sir Edward Elgar was born in the village of Lower Broadheath—on B4204, 2 mi west of Worcester and 8 mi north of Great Malvern—in this tiny brick cottage. Set in a peaceful little garden, the museum contains personal memorabilia, and the Elgar Centre exhibits photographs, musical scores, and letters. ⊠ *Crown East La., Lower Broadheath* ☎ *01905/333224* ⊕ *www.elgarfoundation.org* ⊠ *£7* ☉ *Feb.–Dec., daily 11–5; last admission 45 mins before closing.*

Priory. A solidly built early-Norman Benedictine abbey with later Perpendicular elements, the Priory dominates the steep streets downtown. The fine glass spans from the 15th century—including a magnificent east window and the vibrantly blue Magnificat window in the north transept—to the evocative Millennium Windows. There's a splendid set of misericords (the elaborately carved undersides of choir seats). ⊠ *Church St.* ☎ *01684/561020* ⊕ *www.greatmalvernpriory.org.uk* ⊠ *Free* ☉ *Daily 9–5.*

Three Counties Show. During three days in mid-June, this agricultural show presents rare animal breeds, equestrian events, competitions for the best cows, pigs, and sheep, and plenty of food. (☎ *01684/584900* ⊕ *www.threecounties.co.uk*).

OFF THE BEATEN PATH

★**Worcester Cathedral.** There are few more quintessentially English sights than that of Worcester Cathedral, its towers overlooking the green expanse of the county cricket ground, and its majestic image reflected in the swift-flowing—and frequently flooding—waters of the River Severn. A cathedral has stood on this site since 680, and much of what remains dates from the 13th and 14th centuries. Notable exceptions are the Norman crypt (built in the 1080s), the largest in England, and the ambulatory, a cloister built around the east end. The most important tomb in the cathedral is that of King John (1167–1216), one of the country's least-admired monarchs, who alienated his barons and subjects through bad administration and heavy taxation and in 1215 was forced to sign that great charter of liberty, the Magna Carta. Worcester is 7 mi north of Great Malvern. ■TIP➜ Don't miss the beautiful decoration in the vaulted chantry chapel of Prince Arthur, Henry VII's elder son, whose body was brought to Worcester after his death at Ludlow in 1502. The wealthy endowed the chantry chapels so priests could celebrate Masses there for the souls of the deceased. ⊠ *College Yard at High St., Worcester* ☎ *01905/732900* ⊕ *www.worcestercathedral. co.uk* ⊠ *Donations welcome, tours £3* ☉ *Daily 7:30–6, tours Apr.– Oct., Mon.–Sat. at 11 and 2:30.*

WHERE TO STAY

For expanded hotel reviews, visit Fodors.com.

£££–££££
HOTEL
🏨 **Cottage in the Wood.** On shady grounds, this family-run hotel sits high up the side of the Malvern Hills, with splendid views of the landscape. **Pros:** family run; tremendous views; good food. **Cons:** three separate buildings; steep and narrow approach. ⊠ *Holywell Rd.* ☎ *01684/588860* ⊕ *www.cottageinthewood.co.uk* ⟱*30 rooms* ⚘ *In-room: no a/c, Wi-Fi (some). In-hotel: restaurant, bar, some pets allowed* ⎮⊙⎮ *Breakfast.*

8

EATING WELL IN THE HEART OF ENGLAND

"The Malvern water," said John Wall in 1756, "is famous for containing nothing at all." The famously pure water is still bottled in the town and exported worldwide; it is said that the Queen never travels without it.

Outside Birmingham, this area is rich farming country where the orchards have produced succulent fruit, especially apples and plums. Hereford cider is popular because it tastes much sweeter than the cider brewed farther south in Devon.

The meat and milk products, which come from the local red-and-white Hereford breed of cattle, are second to none. Cheshire cheese, one of the country's oldest cheeses, is noted for its rich, crumbly texture; blue-veined Shropshire cheese is more unusual and worth trying. Ludlow produces a formidable assortment of local meat products and is noted for its sausages.

£–££

B&B/INN

🔲 **Sidney House.** In addition to having stunning views, this dignified early-19th-century bed-and-breakfast, run by a friendly husband-and-wife team, is near the town center. **Pros:** great views; easy access to Malvern Hills. **Cons:** on busy road, so ask for room at the back. ✉ *40 Worcester Rd.* ☎ *01684/574994* ⊕ *www.sidneyhouse.co.uk* 🛏 *8 rooms* ♿ *In-room: no a/c. In-hotel: parking, some pets allowed* ⦿ *Breakfast.*

NIGHTLIFE AND THE ARTS

Malvern has links with Sir Edward Elgar as well as with George Bernard Shaw, who premiered many of his plays here.

The **Autumn in Malvern Festival** (☎ *01684/892277 or 01684/892289* ⊕ *www.malvernfestival.co.uk*) takes place on weekends throughout October and concentrates on classical music, including Elgar, as well as literary events.

LEDBURY

10 mi southwest of Great Malvern on A449.

Among the black-and-white half-timber buildings that make up the market town of Ledbury, take special note of two late-16th-century ones: the Feathers Hotel and the Talbot Inn. The cobbled Church Lane, almost hidden behind the 17th-century market house, is crowded with medieval half-timber buildings and leads to St. Michael's Church.

GETTING HERE AND AROUND

If you're driving, Ledbury is 25 minutes from Hereford via the A438, and 15 minutes from Great Malvern via the A449. There are local buses from both Hereford and Great Malvern, which has rail links with the rest of the country.

ESSENTIALS

Visitor Information Ledbury (✉ *The Master's House, St. Katherine's* ☎ *01531/636147* ⊕ *www.visitherefordshire.co.uk*).

EXPLORING

★ **Eastnor Castle.** Completed in 1820, Eastnor Castle, a turreted Norman Revival extravaganza on the eastern outskirts of Ledbury, includes some magnificent neo-Gothic salons designed by 19th-century architect Augustus Pugin. The Hervey-Bathurst family has restored other grand rooms, full of tapestries, gilt-framed paintings, Regency chandeliers, and Auntie's old armchairs and enormous sofas, making Eastnor a must-see for lovers of English interior decoration. In the Little Library, look out for the rare game of Life Pool, originally played on the billiards table. Eastnor hosts the innovative Big Chill arts festival each August. ⊠ *A438* ☎ *01531/633160* ⊕ *www. eastnorcastle.com* ✉ *House and grounds £8.75; grounds only, £5.75* ☉ *Mid-July and Aug., Sun.–Thurs. 11–4:30; June and Sept., Sun. and national holiday Mon. 11–4:30; last admission 30 mins before closing.*

WALKS AND DRIVES IN THE MALVERNS

The Malvern Hills have climbs and walks of varying length and difficulty; the seasonal Malvern Hills Hopper bus gives useful access on weekends April through August. The best places to start are Great Malvern and Ledbury. The Elgar Route, a drive, extends for 45 mi and touches on Malvern and Worcester as it threads through the Malverns. The hilltop vistas across the countryside are spectacular—isolated hills rise up from the fairly flat plain. The area around Ross-on-Wye has ideal walks with scenic river views. For information on hiking the Malverns, contact the Malvern or Ross-on-Wye tourist office.

Hellens. Just outside the village of Much Marcle, 4 mi southwest of Ledbury, lies the beautiful 17th-century manor of Hellens, still in authentic condition. Part of the house dates from the 13th century and contains fine old-master paintings. The gloom and dust are part of the experience of visiting; candles illuminate the house, and central heating has been scorned. Take a walk in the gardens and, if you have time, also check out the 13th-century village church. The house is ½ mi east of A449. ⊠ *Off B4024 and Monks Walk, Much Marcle* ☎ *01531/660504* ⊕ *www.hellensmanor.com* ✉ *£6* ☉ *Apr.–Sept., Wed., Thurs., Sun., and national holiday Mon. 2–5; tours at 2, 3, and 4.*

Ledbury Heritage Centre. In the old grammar school, this museum traces the history of the building, town, railroad, and canal, mostly through local postcards. It also has displays on two literary celebrities linked to the area, John Masefield and Elizabeth Barrett Browning. ⊠ *Church La.* ☎ *01531/635680* ✉ *Free* ☉ *Easter–Oct., daily 10–4.*

WHERE TO STAY

For expanded hotel reviews, visit Fodors.com.

£££ ⚬ **Feathers Hotel.** You can't miss the striking black-and-white facade of
HOTEL this centrally located hostelry, which dates from the 16th century; its interior has a satisfyingly antique flavor, with creaking staircases and ancient floorboards, and some rooms have four-posters. **Pros:** guest rooms retain wooden beams; period feel; indoor heated pool. **Cons:** some guest rooms on the small side; some steps to climb. ⊠ *High St.*

8

☎ *01531/635266* ⊕ *www.feathers-ledbury.co.uk* ↩*22 rooms* ⚄ *In-room: no a/c, Wi-Fi. In-hotel: restaurants, bar, pool, gym, some pets allowed* ⑩ *Breakfast.*

ROSS-ON-WYE

10 mi southwest of Ledbury.

Perched high above the River Wye in the Malvern Hills, Ross-on-Wye seems oblivious to modern-day intrusions and remains at heart a small market town. Its steep streets come alive on Thursday and Saturday—market days—but they're always a happy hunting ground for antiques. Nearby towns have sights from a castle to a scenic overlook on the river.

GETTING HERE AND AROUND

A449 connects Ross-on-Wye with Great Malvern and Ledbury, and M50 leads directly to Ross from Junction 8 of M5. Stagecoach buses run from Ledbury (30 minutes) and have frequent connections with Hereford (50 minutes) and Gloucester (45 minutes).

ESSENTIALS

Visitor Information Ross-on-Wye (⊠ *Swan House, Edde Cross St.* ☎ *01989/562768* ⊕ *www.visitherefordshire.co.uk).*

EXPLORING

Goodrich Castle. Looming dramatically over the River Wye at Kerne Bridge, the castle from the south looks like a fortress from the Rhineland amid the green fields; you quickly see its grimmer face from the battlements on its north side. Dating from the late 12th century, the red sandstone castle is surrounded by a deep moat carved out of solid rock, from which its walls appear to soar upward. Built to repel Welsh raiders, it was destroyed in the 17th century during the Civil War. The town of Goodrich is 3 mi south of Ross-on-Wye on the B4234. ⊠ *Off A40, Goodrich* ☎ *01600/890538* ⊕ *www.english-heritage.org.uk* ☎ *£5.80, parking charge* ⊙ *Mar.–June, Sept., and Oct., daily 10–5; July and Aug., daily 10–6; Nov.–Feb., Wed.–Sun. 10–4.*

Symonds Yat. Six miles south of Ross-on-Wye, outside the village of Symonds Yat ("gate"), the 473-foot-high Yat Rock commands superb views of the River Wye as it winds through a narrow gorge and swings around in a great 5-mi loop. It's best approached from the south on B4432, from which it's a short walk. A small ferry takes passengers across the river (80p).

SPORTS AND THE OUTDOORS

Symonds Yat Canoe Hire rents canoes and kayaks by the hour or for full days or more; it's a popular way to experience the River Wye. ⊠ *The Leisure Park, Symonds Yat West* ☎ *01600/891069* ⊕ *www.canoehire. com.*

WHERE TO STAY

For expanded hotel reviews, visit Fodors.com.

£££–££££
HOTEL
🔲 **Chase Hotel.** The public areas in this nicely renovated Georgian-style country-house hotel retain some original elements. **Pros:** 11 acres of peaceful grounds; country-house appeal. **Cons:** conventional

furnishings. ⊠ *Gloucester Rd.* ☎ *01989/763161* ⊕ *www.chasehotel. co.uk* ⇌ *36 rooms* ⚭ *In-room: no a/c, Wi-Fi. In-hotel: restaurant, bar, gym* ⦿ *Breakfast.*

HEREFORD

9 mi northwest of Ross-on-Wye, 56 mi southwest of Birmingham, 54 mi northeast of Cardiff.

It's an important cathedral city, and the massive Norman building towers proudly over the River Wye. Before 1066 Hereford was the capital of the Anglo-Saxon kingdom of Mercia and, earlier still, the site of Roman, Celtic, and Iron Age settlements. Today people come primarily to see the cathedral but quickly discover the charms of this busy country town. Hereford is the center of a wealthy agricultural area known for its cider, fruit, and cattle—the white-faced Hereford breed has spread across the world.

GETTING HERE AND AROUND

The bus and train stations are about half a mile northeast of the center. A train from Birmingham will take around 1¾ hours. Traveling by car, take M50 at Junction 8 of M5, then A417 and A438 to Hereford. First buses cover the local area, and the city is compact enough to cover on foot.

ESSENTIALS

Visitor Information Hereford (⊠ *1 King St.* ☎ *01432/268430* ⊕ *www. visitherefordshire.co.uk*).

EXPLORING

TOP ATTRACTIONS

Hereford Cathedral. Built of local red sandstone, Hereford Cathedral retains a large central tower and some fine 11th-century Norman carvings but suffered considerable "restoration" in the 19th century. Inside, its greatest glories include a 12th-century chair, to the left of the high altar, one of the earliest pieces of furniture in the country and reputedly used by King Stephen, and some exquisite contemporary stained-glass windows by Tom Denny commemorating local 17th-century literary figure Thomas Traherne in the Audley Chapel. ⊠ *Cathedral Close* ☎ *01432/374200* ⊕ *www.herefordcathedral.org* ⬗ *Suggested donation £5, garden tours £5* ⊗ *Mon.–Sat. 9:15–5:30, Sun. 8–3:30; cathedral tours Apr.–Oct., Mon.–Sat. at 11 and 2; garden tours Apr.–Oct., Wed. and Sat. at 3.*

★ **Mappa Mundi and Chained Library Exhibition.** This extraordinary double attraction includes the more than 20-square-foot parchment Mappa Mundi. Hereford's own picture of the medieval world shows the Earth as flat, with Jerusalem at its center. It's thought that the map was originally the central section of an altarpiece dating from 1290. The chained library contains some 1,500 books, among them an 8th-century copy of the Four Gospels. Chained libraries, in which books were attached to cupboards to discourage theft, are extremely rare: they date from medieval times, when books were as precious as gold. ⊠ *Cathedral Close* ☎ *01432/374219* ⊕ *www.herefordcathedral.org* ⬗ *£4.50* ⊗ *Apr.–late*

8

May, Sept., and Oct., Mon.–Sat. 10–5; late May–Aug., Mon.–Sat. 10–5, Sun. 11–4; Nov., Dec., Feb., and Mar., Mon.–Sat. 10–4; last admission 30 mins before closing.

Old House. The half-timber Old House is a fine example of domestic Jacobean architecture, furnished in 17th-century style on three floors. You can see a kitchen, dining hall, parlor, and bedrooms. Look for the dog's door between the nursery and master bedroom. ⊠ *High Town* ☎ *01432/260694* ☒ *Free* ☉ *Apr.–Sept., Tues.–Sat. 10–5, Sun. and national holiday Mon. 10–4; Oct.–Mar., Tues.–Sat. 10–5.*

WORTH NOTING

All Saints Church. On the west side of High Town, this 13th-century church contains superb canopied choir stalls and misericords, as well as unusual Queen Anne renovations in the south chapel. It also has an excellent coffee bar and restaurant. ⊠ *High St.* ☎ *01432/370414.*

Cider Museum. A farm cider house and a cooper's workshop have been re-created at the Cider Museum, where you can tour ancient cider cellars with huge oak vats. Cider brandy is made here, and the museum sells its own brand, along with other cider items. ⊠ *Pomona Pl. at Whitecross Rd.* ☎ *01432/354207* ⊕ *www.cidermuseum.co.uk* ☒ *£4* ☉ *Apr.–Oct., Tues.–Sat. and national holiday Mon. 10–5; Nov.–Mar., Tues.–Sat. 11–3; last admission 1 hr before closing.*

WHERE TO EAT AND STAY

£
VEGETARIAN
★
✕ **Café @ All Saints.** Open 8 to 5 and a good spot for lunch, a coffee bar and restaurant occupy the western end and gallery of this community-minded church, granting a rare opportunity to indulge body and spirit at one sitting. The imaginative vegetarian menu is worth every penny and the shepherd's pie is a winner, but for something lighter, try the tasty sandwiches (roast mushroom and tofu, for example), salads, cakes, and local ice creams. Or come for breakfast or coffee—scrambled eggs and smoked salmon is one option. ⊠ *High St.* ☎ *01432/370415* ⊕ *www. cafeatallsaints.co.uk* ☉ *Closed Sun. No dinner.*

££££
HOTEL
⌂ **Castle House.** These conjoined Georgian villas next to the moat (all that remains of Hereford Castle) offer luxury, a warm welcome, and good food. **Pros:** close to cathedral; quiet setting; lovely garden. **Cons:** not cheap; some report slow service. ⊠ *Castle St.* ☎ *01432/356321* ⊕ *www.castlehse.co.uk* ↵ *10 suites, 5 rooms* ☖ *In-room: no a/c, Internet. In-hotel: restaurant, bar, parking, some pets allowed* ¶◯¶ *Breakfast.*

££
HOTEL
⌂ **Sink Green Farm.** Benefits of staying on this informal working farm, which dates back to the 16th century, include views of the Wye Valley and use of the barbecue and outdoor hot tub in a summerhouse. **Pros:** friendly and casual; lovely garden, river walks. **Cons:** car needed to get around. ⊠ *B4399, Rotherwas* ☎ *01432/870223* ⊕ *www.sinkgreenfarm. co.uk* ↵ *4 rooms* ☖ *In-room: no a/c, Wi-Fi. In-hotel: parking, some pets allowed* ▤ *No credit cards* ¶◯¶ *Breakfast.*

SHOPPING

Hereford has a market for livestock on Wednesday and for general retail on Saturday.

The stores in **Capuchin Yard** (⊠ *Off 29 Church St.*) display crafts, including handmade shoes and knitwear; other outlets sell haberdashery and ceramics.

SHREWSBURY, CHESTER, AND ENVIRONS

Rural Shropshire, one of the least populated English counties, is far removed from most people's preconceptions of the industrial Midlands. Within its spread are towns long famed for their beauty, such as Ludlow. Two important cities of the region, Shrewsbury and Chester, are both renowned for their medieval heritage and their wealth of half-timber buildings. The 6-mi stretch of the Ironbridge Gorge, however, gives you the chance to experience the cradle of the Industrial Revolution with none of the reeking smoke that gave this region west of Birmingham its name—the Black Country—during the mid-19th century. Now taken over by the Ironbridge Gorge Museum Trust, the bridge, the first in the world to be built of iron and opened in 1781, is the centerpiece of this vast museum complex.

SHREWSBURY

55 mi north of Hereford, 46 mi south of Chester, 48 mi northwest of Birmingham.

One of England's most important medieval towns, Shrewsbury (pronounced *shrose*-bury), the county seat of Shropshire, lies within a great horseshoe loop of the Severn. It has numerous 16th-century half-timber buildings—many built by well-to-do wool merchants—plus elegant ones from later periods. Today the town retains a romantic air (indeed, there are many bridal shops, along with churches), and it can be a lovely experience to stroll the Shrewsbury "shuts." These narrow alleys overhung with timbered gables lead off the central market square, which was designed to be closed off at night to protect local residents. You can also relax in Quarry Park on the river.

A good starting point for exploring the city is the small square between Fish Street and Butcher Row. These streets are little changed since medieval times, when some of them took their names from the principal trades carried on there, but Peacock Alley, Gullet Passage, and Grope Lane clearly got their names from somewhere else.

GETTING HERE AND AROUND

The train station is at the neck of the river that loops the center, a little farther out than the bus station on Raven Meadows. A direct train service runs here from Hereford (50 minutes) and Birmingham (one hour). If you're coming from London by car, take M40 and M42 north, then M6 and M54, which becomes A5 to Shrewsbury; it's 150 mi. The streets are full of twists, but it's small enough not to get lost. Walking tours of Shrewsbury depart daily from the tourist office at 2:30 from May through September and on Saturday the rest of the year (£4).

ESSENTIALS

Visitor Information Shrewsbury (✉ *Rowley's House, Barker St.* ☎ *01743/281200* ⊕ *www.visitshrewsbury.com*).

EXPLORING

TOP ATTRACTIONS

Attingham Park. Built in 1785 by George Steuart (architect of the church of St. Chad in Shrewsbury) for the first Lord Berwick, this elegant stone mansion has a three-story portico, with a pediment carried on four tall columns. The building overlooks a sweep of parkland, including a deer park landscaped by Humphrey Repton (1752–1818). Inside the house are painted ceilings and delicate plasterwork, a fine picture gallery designed by John Nash (1752–1835), and 19th-century Neapolitan furniture. Attingham Park is 4 mi southeast of Shrewsbury. ✉ *B4380, off A5, Atcham* ☎ *01743/708123* ⊕ *www.nationaltrust.org.uk* 🎫 *£9.90; park and grounds only, £4.50* ☉ *House early Mar., weekends 1–4; mid-Mar.–Oct., Thurs.–Tues. 1–5:30, national holiday Mon. 11–5:30; last admission 1 hr before closing. Park and grounds mid-Feb.–Oct., daily 9–6; Nov.–mid-Feb., daily 9–5.*

St. Chad. On a hilltop west of the town center, this church designed by George Steuart, the architect of Attingham Park, is one of England's most original ecclesiastical buildings. Completed in 1792, the round Georgian church is surmounted by a tower that is in turn square, octagonal, and circular—and finally topped by a dome. When being built, it provoked riots among townsfolk averse to its radical style. The interior has a fine Venetian east window and a brass Arts and Crafts pulpit. ✉ *St. Chad's Terr.* ☎ *01743/365478* 🎫 *Free* ☉ *Apr.–Oct., daily 8–5; Nov.–Mar., daily 8–1.*

Shrewsbury Abbey. Now unbecomingly surrounded by busy roads, the abbey was founded in 1083 and later became a powerful Benedictine monastery. The abbey church has survived many vicissitudes and retains a 14th-century west window above a Norman doorway. A more recent addition is a memorial to the World War I poet, Wilfred Owen. To reach the abbey from the center, cross the river by the English Bridge. ✉ *Abbey Church, Abbey Foregate* ☎ *01743/232723* ⊕ *www.shrewsburyabbey. com* 🎫 *Donations welcome* ☉ *Mon.–Sat. 10:30–3, Sun. 9:30–2:30.*

Shrewsbury Castle. Guarding the northern approaches to the town, the sandstone castle rises over the River Severn at the bottom of Pride Hill. Originally Norman, it was dismantled during the civil war and later rebuilt by Thomas Telford, the Scottish engineer who designed many notable buildings and bridges in the early 19th century. The castle holds the **Shropshire Regimental Museum,** containing enough social history to engage the non–military buff. ■**TIP→** The numerous benches in the gardens are good for a quiet sit-down. ✉ *Shrewsbury Castle, Castle Gates* ☎ *01743/358516* ⊕ *www.shrewsburymuseums.com* 🎫 *£2.50* ☉ *Mid-Feb.–May and mid-Sept.–Dec., Tues.–Sat. and national holiday Mon. 10:30–4; June–mid-Sept., Tues.–Sun. and bank holiday Mon. 10:30–5. Castle grounds Mon.–Sat. 9–5, Sun. 10:30–5.*

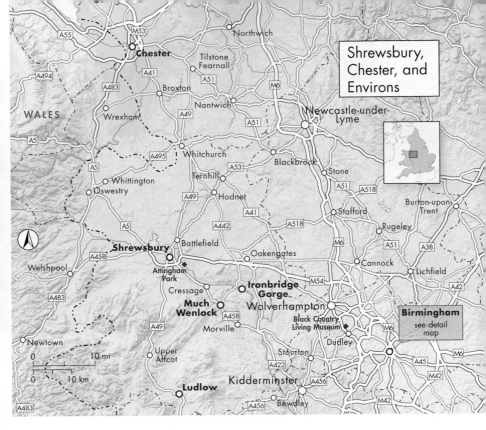

WORTH NOTING

Ireland's Mansion. The cluster of restored half-timber buildings that link Fish Street with Market Square is known as Bear Steps; this mansion, built in 1575 with elaborate Jacobean timbering and richly decorated with quatrefoils, is the most notable. It's not open to the public.

Shrewsbury Museum and Art Gallery. The museum holds Shropshire pottery and ceramics, as well as items of local history and Roman finds, such as a unique silver mirror from nearby Wroxeter. A reconstructed 17th-century paneled bedroom showcases an elaborate four-poster bed (1593), enlivened with richly embroidered silk and velvet hangings. The Darwin Exhibition explores the life of Shrewsbury's famous son, Charles Darwin. ⊠ *Barker St.* ☎ *01743/281205* ⊕ *www. shrewsburymuseums.com* ✉ *Free* ☉ *May–Sept., Mon.–Sat. 10–5, Sun. 10–4; Oct.–Apr., Mon.–Sat. 10–4.*

WHERE TO EAT

£££
MODERN BRITISH

✕ **Draper's Hall.** The dark-wood paneling, antique furniture, and intimate lighting of this 16th-century hall make it a distinctive dining spot for up-to-date Modern British cuisine. You might try the slow-roasted crispy duck with Cointreau or a fish risotto with lemon shavings; leave room for desserts such as red berry pavlova and Chantilly cream. There are plenty of cheeses and salads, as well as good fish and vegetarian

The sprawling Ironbridge Gorge Museum interprets the country's industrial history and includes a recreated Victorian town.

choices; special diets are accommodated. Another option is the lighter brasserie menu. The establishment also has four guest rooms. ⊠ *10 St. Mary's Pl.* ☎ *01743/344679* ⊕ *www.drapershallrestaurant.co.uk* ⊗ *No dinner Sun.*

£££   ✕ **Mad Jack's.** Whether you eat in the sleek, dark-wood restaurant or
BRITISH   the foliage-filled courtyard, you'll be tucking into good local and seasonal produce. Look out for the Shropshire lamb and, in winter, local venison sausages with Shropshire blue cheese mash. It's a good spot for plump sandwiches at lunchtime, or afternoon tea or cocktails later in the day. Four contemporary rooms are available should you wish to linger longer. ⊠ *15 St. Mary's St.* ☎ *01743/358870* ⊕ *www.madjacks. uk.com* ⊗ *No dinner Sun.*

WHERE TO STAY

For expanded hotel reviews, visit Fodors.com.

£££–££££   ⊞ **Albright Hussey Hotel.** Lovely gardens surround this Tudor manor
HOTEL   house, originally the home of the Hussey family, which dates back to 1524; black-and-white half-timbering combines with a later redbrick-and-stone extension. **Pros:** friendly service; beautiful grounds. **Cons:** popular venue for weddings; books up for weekends. ⊠ *Ellesmere Rd.* ☎ *01939/290523* ⊕ *www.albrighthussey.co.uk* ⟿ *22 rooms, 4 suites* ⚴ *In-room: no a/c, Wi-Fi. In-hotel: restaurant, bar, parking, some pets allowed* ⏐⊚⏐ *Breakfast.*

££–£££   ⊞ **The Lion Hotel.** The myriad corridors of this famous coaching inn in
HOTEL   the heart of town creak with more than 600 years of history; rooms are small and traditionally furnished, but the glorious lounge, with its high ceiling, oil paintings, and carved-stone fireplace, sets the Lion apart.

Pros: historic appeal; good breakfasts. **Cons:** prone to wedding parties on weekends; smallish rooms. ☒ *Wyle Cop* ☎ *01743/353107* ⊕ *www.thelionhotelshrewsbury.co.uk* ⥲ *59 rooms* ☖ *In-room: no a/c. In-hotel: restaurant, bar* ❄ *Breakfast.*

NIGHTLIFE AND THE ARTS

The **Theatre Severn** (☒ *Frankwell Quay* ☎ *01743/281281*) covers all the performance arts: music, both classical and popular; dance; and drama.

SHOPPING

The **Parade** (☒ *St. Mary's Pl.* ☎ *01743/343178*), just behind St. Mary's church, is a shopping center created from the neoclassical former Royal Infirmary, built in 1830. One of the most appealing malls in England, it has 25 attractive boutiques, a coffee shop, and a river terrace.

MUCH WENLOCK

12 mi southeast of Shrewsbury.

Much Wenlock, a town on A458, is full of half-timber buildings, including a 16th-century guildhall. Nearby are popular places to walk; ask the tourist office for information. The town has held the Wenlock Olympian Games most years since 1850, when Dr. William Penny Brookes founded the Wenlock Olympian Society. The games were an inspiration for the modern Olympic Games; the town museum has some information.

GETTING HERE AND AROUND

The town is a half hour by car from Shrewsbury on A458, or you can take the Arriva bus service that runs hourly (35 minutes).

ESSENTIALS

Visitor Information Much Wenlock (☒ *The Museum, High St.* ☎ *01952/727679* ⊕ *www.muchwenlockguide.info*).

Bus Contact Arriva (☎ *0871/200–2233* ⊕ *www.arrivabus.co.uk*).

EXPLORING

Wenlock Priory. The romantic ruins of this Norman priory, with their elaborate decoration, are in a topiary garden. ☒ *High St.* ☎ *01952/727466* ⊕ *www.english-heritage.org.uk* ⛁ *£4* ☉ *Late Mar.–Apr., Sept., and Oct., Wed.–Sun. and national holiday Mon. 10–5; May–Aug., daily 10–5; Nov.–Feb., Thurs.–Sun. 10–4.*

SPORTS AND THE OUTDOORS

The high escarpment of **Wenlock Edge** runs southwest from Much Wenlock and provides a splendid view. This is hiking country, and if a healthful walk sounds inviting, turn off B4371 through Church Stretton into Cardingmill Valley, or to the wide heather uplands on top of Long Mynd. You can park and set off on foot.

8

IRONBRIDGE GORGE

4 mi east of Much Wenlock, 15 mi east of Shrewsbury, 28 mi northwest of Birmingham.

The River Severn and its tree-cloaked banks make an attractive backdrop to this cluster of villages; within a mile of the graceful span of the world's first iron bridge are a cluster of fascinating museums exploring the area's industrial past and the reasons it has been described as the "cradle of the Industrial Revolution."

GETTING HERE AND AROUND

To drive here from Shrewsbury, take the A5 east, the A442 south, and then the A4169 west before following the brown signs for Ironbridge. On weekends and bank holidays from Easter to late October, the Gorge Shuttle Bus shuttles passengers between Ironbridge's museums; it's free of charge to museum passport holders.

ESSENTIALS

Visitor Information Ironbridge Visitor Information (⊠ *The Toll House* ☎ *01952/884391* ⊕ *www.ironbridge.org.uk*).

EXPLORING

★ The 10 sections of the **Ironbridge Gorge Museum,** spread over 6 square
ℭ mi, preserve the area's fascinating industrial history. ■TIP→ Allow at least a full day to appreciate all the major sights, and perhaps to take a stroll around the famous iron bridge or hunt for Coalport china in the stores clustered near it. On weekends and national holidays from April through October, a shuttle bus takes you between sites. The best starting point is the **Museum of the Gorge,** which has a good selection of literature and an audiovisual show on the gorge's history. In nearby Coalbrookdale, the **Museum of Iron** explains the production of iron and steel. You can see the blast furnace built by Abraham Darby, who developed the original coke process in 1709. The adjacent **Enginuity** exhibition is a hands-on, feet-on, interactive exploration of engineering; it's good for kids. From here, drive the few miles along the river until the arches of the **Iron Bridge** come into view. Designed by T.F. Pritchard, smelted by Darby, and erected between 1777 and 1779, this graceful arch spanning the River Severn can best be seen—and photographed or painted—from the towpath, a riverside walk edged with wildflowers and shrubs. The tollhouse on the far side houses an exhibition on the bridge's history and restoration.

A mile farther along the river is the **Jackfield Tile Museum,** a repository of decorative tiles from the 19th and 20th centuries. Another half mile brings you to the **Coalport China Museum.** Exhibits show some of the factory's most beautiful wares, and craftspeople give demonstrations; visit the restrooms for the unique communal washbasins. Above Coalport is **Blists Hill Victorian Town,** where you can see old mines, furnaces, and a wrought-iron works. But the main draw is the re-creation of the "town" itself, with its doctor's office, bakery, grocer's, candle maker's, sawmill, printing shop, and candy store. At the entrance you can change some money for specially minted pennies and make purchases from the shops. Shopkeepers, the bank manager, and the doctor's wife are on hand to give you advice. If you don't fancy the refreshments at the Fried Fish shop, drop into the **New Inn** pub (in Blists Hill) for a traditional ale or ginger beer, and join in the sing-along around the piano at 1 and 3:30 (3 in winter), or tuck into a steak-and-kidney pudding from the butcher next door. ✉ *B4380, Ironbridge, Telford* 🕾 *01952/884391* ⊕ *www.ironbridge.org.uk* 🎫 *£22.50* ⊘ *Daily 10–5; Blists Hill Apr.–Oct., daily 10–5; Nov.–Mar., daily 10–4.*

WHERE TO EAT AND STAY

££££
MODERN BRITISH

✕ **Restaurant Severn.** This discreet eatery, set back from the main road in the center of Ironbridge, delivers fine quality food prepared with care and attention. Fixed-price dinner menus (around £25) of up-to-date English fare might feature wild mushroom soufflé, or duckling with damson plum compote; pear-and-almond tart rounds off the meal well. The warm yellow walls cast a glow on elegant surroundings. ✉ *33 High St.* 🕾 *01952/432233* ⊕ *www.restaurantseven.co.uk* ⊘ *Closed Mon. and Tues. No dinner Sun. No lunch Wed.–Sat.*

££
HOTEL

🛏 **Hundred House Hotel.** The low beams, stained glass, wood paneling, and patchwork cushions that greet you as you enter this Georgian inn set the tone for the whimsical guest rooms. **Pros:** full of nooks and corners; good food. **Cons:** not for those who favor the plain and simple. ✉ *A442, Norton* 🕾 *01952/580240* ⊕ *www.hundredhouse.co.uk* 🛏 *10 rooms* ⚘ *In-room: no a/c, Wi-Fi. In-hotel: restaurant, bar, some pets allowed* ⍟ *Breakfast.*

££
B&B/INN
★

🛏 **Library House.** At one time the village's library, this small guesthouse on the hillside near the Ironbridge museums (and a few steps from the bridge) has kept its attractive Victorian style while allowing for modern-day luxuries—a DVD library, for instance. **Pros:** welcoming hosts; good location; free parking passes for the town. **Cons:** not for families with young children. ✉ *11 Severn Bank, Telford* 🕾 *01952/432299* ⊕ *www. libraryhouse.com* 🛏 *4 rooms* ⚘ *In-room: no a/c, Wi-Fi. In-hotel: bar, some age restrictions* ⍟ *Breakfast.*

LUDLOW

22 mi south of Ironbridge Gorge, 29 mi south of Shrewsbury, 24 mi north of Hereford.

Fodor's Choice
★

Medieval, Georgian, and Victorian buildings jostle for attention in pretty Ludlow, which has a finer display of black-and-white half-timber buildings than even Shrewsbury. Dominating the center is the Church of St. Lawrence, its extravagant size a testimony to the town's prosperous wool trade. Cross the River Teme and climb Whitcliffe for a spectacular view of the church and the Norman castle.

Several outstanding restaurants have given the town of 10,000 a reputation as a culinary hot spot. Ludlow is now the national headquarters of the Slow Food movement, which focuses on food traditions and responsible production.

GETTING HERE AND AROUND

Ludlow has good train connections. From London Paddington, the journey time is 3¼ hours (changing at Newport), from Birmingham 1¾ hours, and from Shrewsbury 30 minutes. The train station is a

15-minute walk southwest to the center. Driving from London, take M40, M42, and then A448 to Kidderminster, A456, and A4117 to Ludlow. The town has good parking and is easily walkable.

ESSENTIALS

Visitor Information Ludlow (✉ *Castle St.* ☎ *01584/875053* ⊕ *www.ludlow.org.uk*).

EXPLORING

Ludlow and the Marches Food Festival. The festival takes place over a weekend in mid-September and has demonstrations and tastings of local sausages, ale, and cider. ☎ *01584/873957* ⊕ *www.foodfestival.co.uk*.

Ludlow Castle. The "very perfection of decay," according to author Daniel Defoe, the ruins of this red sandstone castle date from 1085. No wonder the massive structure dwarfs the town: it served as a vital stronghold for centuries and was the seat of the Marcher Lords who ruled "the Marches," the local name for the border region. The two sons of Edward IV—the little princes of the Tower of London—spent time here before being dispatched to London and their death in 1483. Follow the terraced walk around the castle for a lovely view of the countryside. ✉ *Castle Sq.* ☎ *01584/873355* ⊕ *www.ludlowcastle.com* ⬚ *£5* ⊙ *Jan. and Dec., weekends 10–4; Feb., Mar., Oct., and Nov., daily 10–4; Apr.–July and Sept., daily 10–5; Aug., daily 10–7; last admission 30 mins before closing.*

OFF THE BEATEN PATH
Stokesay Castle. This 13th-century fortified manor house built by a wealthy merchant is arguably the finest of its kind in England. Inside the main hall, the wooden cruck roof and timber staircase (a rare survival) demonstrate state-of-the-art building methods of the day. Outside, the cottage-style garden creates a bewitching backdrop for the magnificent Jacobean timber-frame gatehouse. ✉ *Craven Arms* ✛ *Off A49 Shrewsbury road, 7 mi northwest of Ludlow* ☎ *01588/672544* ⊕ *www.english-heritage.org.uk* ⬚ *£5.50* ⊙ *Mar. and Oct., Wed.–Sun. and national holidays 10–5; Apr.–Sept., daily 10–5; Nov.–Feb., Thurs.–Sun. 10–4.*

WHERE TO EAT

Ludlow is known for some pricier fine-dining establishments, but options from excellent tearooms to pubs and ethnic restaurants are also available.

££££££
FRENCH
✕ **La Bécasse.** Dip into the past—the intimate building dates to 1349, the warm oak paneling merely to the 17th century—as you savor a fixed-price menu (£54–£60) of French food that's bang up to the minute. Rose-color glass chargers on crisp white table linen signal the artistry with which dishes such as smoked pigeon with beetroot-infused spaghetti and horseradish-flavored ice cream are presented. Vegetarians are well served with a separate menu. The two-course lunch menu is a good value at £26. Reservations are essential on weekends. ✉ *17 Corve St.* ☎ *01584/872325* ⊕ *www.labecasse.co.uk* ⊙ *Closed Mon. No dinner Sun. No lunch Tues.*

££££££
MODERN BRITISH
✕ **Mr. Underhill's.** Occupying a converted mill building beneath the castle, this secluded establishment looks onto the wooded River Teme and is stylish, light, and informal. The superb Modern British, fixed-price

menus (£54–£62) take advantage of fresh seasonal ingredients. For a main dish you might choose local venison with caper-and-raisin sauce, and for dessert, pear jelly with pistachio-scented rice pudding. Book well ahead, especially on weekends; rooms and suites available should you want to make a night of it. ✉ *Dinham Weir* ☎ *01584/874431* ⊕ *www.mr-underhills.co.uk* ✆ *Closed Mon. and Tues. No lunch.*

WHERE TO STAY

For expanded hotel reviews, visit Fodors.com.

£££–££££
HOTEL
🔲 **Dinham Hall.** This 1792 hotel near Ludlow Castle formerly served as a boys' dormitory for the local grammar school; guest rooms preserve the Georgian spirit with graceful period furniture and traditional print fabrics. **Pros:** light and intimate; great views over walled garden; good restaurant. **Cons:** no Internet access; can be chilly in winter. ✉ *Off Market Sq.* ☎ *01584/876464* ⊕ *www.dinhamhall.co.uk* ☞ *10 rooms, 3 suites* ⚒ *In-room: no a/c. In-hotel: restaurant, bar, some pets allowed* ⍾ *Breakfast.*

£££–££££
HOTEL
🔲 **The Feathers.** Even if you're not staying here, take time to admire the extravagant half-timber facade of this hotel, described by the architectural historian Nicholas Pevsner as "that prodigy of timber-framed houses." **Pros:** ornate plasterwork; unpretentious feel. **Cons:** most guest rooms lack antique look. ✉ *The Bull Ring* ☎ *01584/875261* ⊕ *www. feathersatludlow.co.uk* ☞ *40 rooms* ⚒ *In-room: no a/c. In-hotel: restaurant, bar, some pets allowed* ⍾ *Breakfast.*

££
B&B/INN
✆
🔲 **Timberstone.** The Read family has made a rambling stone cottage in the Clee Hills into a welcoming haven. **Pros:** relaxing and hospitable; geared to families; great food. **Cons:** out of center of Ludlow; twisty lanes. ✉ *B4363, Clee Stanton* ☎ *01584/823519* ⊕ *www. timberstoneludlow.co.uk* ☞ *4 rooms* ⚒ *In-room: no a/c, no TV (some), Wi-Fi. In-hotel: some pets allowed* ⍾ *Breakfast.*

NIGHTLIFE AND THE ARTS

The two-week **Ludlow Festival** (☎ *01584/872150* ⊕ *www.ludlowfestival. co.uk*), starting in late June, includes Shakespeare performed near the ruined castle, and opera, dance, and concerts around town.

CHESTER

75 mi north of Ludlow, 46 mi north of Shrewsbury.

Cheshire's thriving center is Chester, a city similar in some ways to Shrewsbury, though it has many more black-and-white half-timber buildings (some built in Georgian and Victorian times), and its medieval walls still stand. History seems more tangible in Chester than in many other ancient cities, and modern buildings have not been allowed to intrude. A negative result of this perfection is that Chester has become a favorite bus-tour destination, with gift shops, noise, and crowds.

Chester has been a prominent city since the late 1st century, when the Roman Empire expanded north to the banks of the River Dee. The original Roman town plan is still evident: the principal streets, Eastgate, Northgate, Watergate, and Bridge Street, lead out from the Cross—the site of the central area of the Roman fortress—to the four

8

city gates, and the partly excavated remains of what is thought to have been the country's largest Roman amphitheater lie to the south of Chester's medieval castle.

GETTING HERE AND AROUND

There's a free shuttle bus to the center if you arrive by train, and buses pull up at Vicar's Lane in the center. Chester is 180 mi from London, and about 2¾ hours by train (change at Crewe). If you're driving and here for a day only, use the city's Park and Ride lots, as central parking lots fill quickly, especially in summer.

Guided walks leave the town hall daily at 10:30, and City Sightseeing operates daily tours in open-top buses from May to September.

ESSENTIALS

Visitor and Tour Information Chester (✉ *Town Hall, Northgate St.* ✉ *Vicar's La.* ☎ *01244/402111* ⊕ *www.visitchester.com*). **City Sightseeing** (☎ *01244/381461* ⊕ *www.city-sightseeing.com*).

EXPLORING

TOP ATTRACTIONS

Chester Cathedral. Tradition has it that a church of some sort stood on the site of what is now Chester Cathedral in Roman times, but records indicate construction around AD 900. The earliest work traceable today, mainly in the north transept, is that of the 11th-century Benedictine abbey. After Henry VIII dissolved the monasteries in the 16th century, the abbey church became the cathedral church of the new diocese of Chester. The misericords in the choir stalls reveal carved figures of people and animals, both real and mythical, and above is a gilded and colorful vaulted ceiling. In the inner garden, a striking modern bronze statue depicts the woman of Samaria offering water to Jesus. ✉ *St. Werburgh St., off Market Sq.* ☎ *01244/324756* ⊕ *www.chestercathedral. com* ✉ *£5, includes audio guide* ✆ *Mon.–Sat. 9–5, Sun. 12:30–4.*

City walls. The city walls, accessible from several points, provide splendid views of the city and its surroundings. The whole circuit is 2 mi, but if your time is short, climb the steps at Newgate and walk along toward Eastgate to see the great ornamental **Eastgate Clock,** erected to commemorate Queen Victoria's Diamond Jubilee in 1897. Lots of small shops near this part of the walls sell old books, old postcards, antiques, and jewelry. Where the **Bridge of Sighs** (named after the enclosed bridge in Venice that it closely resembles) crosses the canal, descend to street level and walk up Northgate Street into Market Square.

★ **Rows.** Chester's unique Rows, which originated in the 12th and 13th centuries, are essentially double rows of stores, one at street level and the other on the second floor with galleries overlooking the street. The Rows line the junction of the four streets in the old town. They have medieval crypts below them, and some reveal Roman foundations.

WORTH NOTING

ChesterBoat. This company runs excursions on the River Dee every 30 minutes daily (April through October) and hourly on weekends (November through March). Saturday evening cruises in summer feature discos. ✉ *Boating Station, Souters La., The Groves* ☎ *01244/325394* ⊕ *www. chesterboat.co.uk.*

Lined with handsome brick, stone, and half-timber buildings, Chester's compact center is perfect for shopping and strolling.

Chester Zoo. Well-landscaped grounds and natural enclosures make the 80-acre zoo one of Britain's most popular, as well as the largest. Highlights include Chimpanzee Island, the jaguar enclosure, and the Islands in Danger tropical habitat. Baby animals are often on display. Eleven miles of paths wend through the zoo, and you can use the waterbus boats or the overhead train to tour the grounds. ⊠ *A41, 2 mi north of Chester* ☎ *01244/380280* ⊕ *www.chesterzoo.org* ✉ *Apr.–Oct. £16.90, Nov.–Mar. £15.40; waterbus £2, train £2* ☼ *Daily 10–dusk.*

Grosvenor Museum. Start a visit with a look at Roman Chester, particularly in the Roman Stones Gallery, which houses tombstones previously used to repair the walls; look out for the wounded barbarian. Then skip a few centuries to explore the period house for a tour from 1680 to the 1920s. ⊠ *27 Grosvenor St.* ☎ *01244/402033* ✉ *Free* ⊕ *www. grosvenormuseum.co.uk* ☼ *Mon.–Sat. 10:30–5, Sun. 1–4.*

WHERE TO EAT

£ ✕**Albion.** You feel as if you're stepping back in time at this Victorian
BRITISH pub; the posters, advertisements, flags, and curios tell you the idiosyncratic landlord keeps it as it would have been during World War I. The candlelit restaurant forms one of the three snug rooms and, unsurprisingly, serves up traditional fare such as corned beef hash, Staffordshire oatcakes, and gammon (thick-sliced ham) with pease pudding. You can stay overnight here as well. ⊠ *Park St.* ☎ *01244/340345* ⊕ *www. albioninnchester.co.uk* ▭ *No credit cards* ☼ *No dinner Sun.*

££ ✕**Chez Jules.** Once a fire station, this bustling bistro is now unasham-
BISTRO edly French and rustic, with red-and-white-check tablecloths and a menu chalked up on the blackboard. Start perhaps with a tomato tarte

tatin, and then follow with poached trout fillet with white wine–and–blue cheese sauce, or rabbit stew with truffle-infused dumplings. ⊠ *71 Northgate St.* ☎ *01244/400014* ⊕ *www.chezjules.com.*

£££££ ✕ **Simon Radley at the Chester Grosvenor.** Named for its noted chef, this
FRENCH   restaurant has a sophisticated panache and prices to match. Expect the seasonal but not the usual, including named dishes: Montmorency is duck with fondant liver and liquid cherries, and Coffee is a chocolate cup with iced latte, espresso jelly, and coffee-bean brittle. There's a fixed-price dinner (£69) as well as a daily tasting menu (£90). The wine cellar has more than 1,000 bins. Reservations are essential on weekends, and children must be at least 12. ⊠ *Chester Grosvenor Hotel, Eastgate St.* ☎ *01244/895618* ⊕ *www.chestergrosvenor.com* ☯ *No dinner Mon. and Sun. Closed 1st 3 wks in Jan.*

WHERE TO STAY

For expanded hotel reviews, visit Fodors.com.

£££££ 🏨 **Chester Grosvenor Hotel.** Handmade Italian furniture and French silk
HOTEL   furnishings fill this deluxe downtown hotel in a Tudor-style building.
★   **Pros:** pampering luxury; superb food; excellent service and facilities. **Cons:** no private parking. ⊠ *Eastgate St.* ☎ *01244/324024* ⊕ *www.chestergrosvenor.com* ⬩ *66 rooms, 14 suites* ⬩ *In-room: Internet. In-hotel: restaurants, bar, gym, spa* ⍾ *Breakfast.*

££ 🏨 **Chester Recorder House.** This Georgian redbrick house has the perfect
B&B/INN   location right on the city wall and overlooking the River Dee. **Pros:** within easy reach of the center; excellent breakfasts. **Cons:** no elevator. ⊠ *19 City Walls* ☎ *01244/326580* ⊕ *www.recorderhotel.co.uk* ⬩ *11 rooms* ⬩ *In-room: no a/c, Wi-Fi. In-hotel: parking* ⍾ *Breakfast.*

££–£££ 🏨 **Frogg Manor.** Leave the modern world behind, dance foxtrots after
HOTEL   dinner in the party room, and sleep in sumptuous tranquillity; lavishly
★   furnished with antiques, drapes, and ornaments (frogs in particular), this hotel makes its individualist statement and never fails its devotees. **Pros:** English eccentricity at its best; frills and furbelows. **Cons:** not for minimalists; outside town. ⊠ *A534, Nantwich Rd., Broxton* ☎ *01829/782629* ⊕ *www.froggmanorhotel.co.uk* ⬩ *8 rooms* ⬩ *In-room: no a/c, Wi-Fi. In-hotel: restaurant, bar, parking* ⍾ *Breakfast.*

£££££ 🏨 **Green Bough Hotel.** Chester's leafy outskirts are the setting for this memora-
HOTEL   ble small hotel a mile from the town center. **Pros:** attentive service; well-designed rooms. **Cons:** no young children allowed. ⊠ *60 Hoole Rd.* ☎ *01244/326241* ⊕ *www.greenbough.co.uk* ⬩ *8 rooms, 7 suites* ⬩ *In-room: no a/c, Wi-Fi. In-hotel: restaurant, bar, parking, some age restrictions* ⍾ *Breakfast.*

NIGHTLIFE AND THE ARTS

Oddfellows (⊠ *20 Lower Bridge St.* ☎ *01244/400001*) is the swankiest bar in town. Sip champagne cocktails or afternoon tea and admire the big wallpaper and big candelabra. You can dine (and stay) here, too.

SHOPPING

Chester has an **indoor market** in the Forum, near the Town Hall, every day except Sunday. Watergate Street hosts antiques shops with anything from ceramics to furniture.

Bluecoat Books (⊠ *1 City Walls* ☎ *01244/318752*) specializes in travel, art, architecture, and history.

Lancashire and the Peaks

WORD OF MOUTH

"Liverpool is the home of the Beatles. Go into the Beatles Story at the Albert Dock. A 3-D exhibition down at Pier Head is included in the ticket. It's where you would take the ferry across the Mersey, which you could do. The actual Cavern was pulled down—although there is a pub/club of the same name on the site."

—Hastobe_Katt

WELCOME TO
LANCASHIRE AND THE PEAKS

TOP REASONS
TO GO

★ **The Beatles:** Liverpool is the place to visit the Fab Four's haunts and see their childhood homes.

★ **Museums in Manchester and Liverpool:** Take history lessons at the Museum of Science and Industry and the Imperial War Museum North in Manchester, and the Merseyside Maritime Museum in Liverpool. Then opt for art appreciation in the cities' galleries.

★ **Manchester nightspots:** Catch the city at night in any of its humming café-bars and pubs; or just enjoy a good beer in an ornate Victorian-era pub.

★ **Chatsworth House and Haddon Hall:** Engage the past and imagine yourself as a country landowner roaming the great pile that is Chatsworth, or as a Tudor noble exercising in the paneled long gallery of English Haddon Hall.

★ **Walking in the Peak District:** Even a short walk in Edale or High Peak reveals the rocky yet intimate scenery that is unique to the area.

1 Manchester. The skies may be gray, but the vibrant city of Manchester is known for its modern urban design and its thriving music and club scenes. Great museums justify its status as the leading city of the Northwest.

2 Liverpool. Now in the midst of a postindustrial rebirth, this city is more than the Beatles. The imposing waterfront, the pair of cathedrals, and the grand architecture make this clear. But the museums don't forget to mention the city's place in rock-and-roll history.

GETTING ORIENTED

Manchester lies at the heart of a tangle of motorways in the northwest of England, about a half hour across the Pennines from Yorkshire. It's 70 mi from the southern edge of the Lake District. The city spreads west toward the coast and the mouth of the River Mersey, where Liverpool is still centered on its port. For the Northwest's most dramatic scenery—indeed, its only real geological feature of interest—you must travel to the Peak District, a national park less than an hour's drive southeast of Manchester. England at its grandest and most ducal can be seen in the great houses of Derbyshire's Wye Valley.

9

3 The Peak District.
Britain's first national park, the Peak District is studded with an array of stately homes, the most impressive being Chatsworth House. Dramatic moors, intimate dales, and limestone caverns invite exploration.

THE BEATLES IN LIVERPOOL

This distinctive northern English city was the birthplace of the Beatles, who changed rock music forever using recording techniques unheard of at the time. The Fab Four became counterculture icons who defined the look and sound of the 1960s; but despite their international success, they remained true sons of Liverpool.

The Beatles' music and style—and their haircuts—rocked the 1960s (above); Mendips, John's childhood home and now a National Trust site (right, top); the rebuilt Cavern (right, bottom).

Reinvigorated by its stint as European Capital of Culture in 2008, the city remains a site of pilgrimage for fans more than half a century after the Beatles' early gigs here. Liverpool may no longer be the rough, postwar city the Beatles grew up in, but it makes the most of its connections to Paul McCartney, John Lennon, George Harrison, and Ringo Starr. John's and Paul's childhood homes, Mendips and 20 Forthlin Road, are in south Liverpool; both are National Trust sites. You can take in a show at Mathew Street's (re-created) Cavern Club, where the band played in its early days, or tour Penny Lane, Strawberry Fields, and other mop-top nostalgia spots. On the waterfront at Albert Dock, the Beatles Story museum provides a state-of-the-art overview of the group's career.

THEIR WORDS

"I knew the words to 25 rock songs, so I got in the group. 'Long Tall Sally' and 'Tutti Frutti,' that got me in. That was my audition."
—Paul McCartney

"Paul wasn't quite strong enough, I didn't have enough girl appeal, George was too quiet, and Ringo was the drummer. But we thought that everyone would be able to dig at least one of us, and that's how it turned out."
—John Lennon

FOLLOW IN THE FOOTSTEPS

SEE THE MAIN SIGHTS
The three key shrines of Beatle-dom in Liverpool are John's and Paul's childhood homes in south Liverpool and the legendary Cavern Club on Mathew Street downtown where the Beatles were discovered by their future manager Brian Epstein in 1961. A combined ticket for both Beatle homes includes a bus between the city center and the two sites.

CHECK OUT THE BEATLES STORY
At this attraction in the Albert Dock, entertaining scenes re-create stages in the Fab Four's lives, from early gigs in Germany and the Cavern Club to each member's solo career, with 3-D computer animations, band artifacts, and more.

CHOOSE THE RIGHT TOUR
The two-hour Magical Mystery Tour departing from the Albert Dock Visitor Centre is a great way to zoom around Penny Lane, Strawberry Field, and other landmarks it would be difficult to find. Liverpool Beatles Tours can cram in every Beatles haunt, on four-hour or full-day tours. Other options are private guides or personalized tours.

SLEEP WITH THE BEATLES . . . AND SHOP TOO
Within earshot of the Cavern on the corner of Mathew Street is the Hard Day's Night Hotel, with Lennon- and McCartney-themed suites, Yellow Submarine jukeboxes, and an inviting bar. It's done with pizzazz. At 31 Mathew Street, the Beatles Shop packs in memorabilia and souvenirs from vintage posters and vinyls to mugs.

GO TO BEATLES WEEK
The annual **International Beatle Week** (⊕ *www.cavernclub. org*) is usually held the last week in August. Attend John and Yoko fancy-dress parties, listen to Beatles tribute bands, and attend record fairs, exhibitions, and conventions.

TAKING STOCK

When these four local rapscallions appeared on the Liverpool pop circuit in the early 1960s, they were just another group of lads struggling to get gigs on the city's "Merseybeat" scene. What followed was extraordinary; Beatlemania swept over fans around the world, including the United States, which the group first visited in 1964. Before their 1969 breakup, the Beatles achieved phenomenal commercial and creative success, bringing bohemianism to the masses and embodying a generation's ideals of social liberation and peace. They reinvented pop music, bridging styles and genres as diverse as Celtic folk, psychedelia, and Indian raga, starring in epoch-making movies such as *A Hard Day's Night* and *Help*, and causing such hysteria they couldn't even hear their own guitars on stage. Though adulation followed them everywhere, the Beatles remained obstinate "Scousers," showing a grounded charm and irreverent humor characteristic of their native city.

9

Updated by
Paul Cannon

For those looking for the postcard England of little villages, the northwest region of England might not appear at the top of a sightseeing list. Manchester, Britain's third-largest city, today bustles with redevelopment, and Liverpool is undergoing significant revitalization. However, the 200 years of smokestack industry that abated only in the 1980s have taken a toll on the east Lancashire landscape. The region does have some lovely scenery inland, in Derbyshire (pronounced *Dar*-byshire)—notably the spectacular Peak District, a national park at the southern end of the Pennine range.

Manchester and Liverpool, the economic engines that propelled Britain in the 18th and 19th centuries, are sloughing off their mid-20th-century decline and celebrating their rich industrial and maritime heritage in excellent museums—in imposing Victorian edifices, or, in Manchester's case, in strikingly modern buildings.

The cities, each with a population of about 450,000, have reestablished themselves as centers of sporting and musical excellence, and as nightlife hot spots. Since 1962 the Manchester United, Everton, and Liverpool football (soccer in the United States) clubs have won everything worth winning in Britain and Europe. The Beatles launched the Mersey sound of the '60s; contemporary Manchester groups ride both British and U.S. airwaves. On the classical side of music, Manchester is also the home of Britain's oldest leading orchestra, the Hallé (founded in 1857)—just one legacy of 19th-century industrialists' investments in culture.

The Peak District is a wilder part of England, a region of crags that rear violently out of the plain. The Pennines, a line of hills that begins in the Peak District and runs as far north as Scotland, are sometimes called the "backbone of England." In this landscape of rocky outcrops and vaulting meadowland, you'll see nothing for miles but sheep, drystone (without mortar) walls, and farms, interrupted—spectacularly—by 19th-century villages and treasure houses. In and around this area are Victorian-era spas such as Buxton, prettytowns such as Bakewell, and magnificent houses such as Chatsworth, Hardwick Hall, and Haddon Hall. The delight of the Peak District is being able to ramble for days in rugged countryside but still enjoy the pleasures of civilization.

LANCASHIRE AND THE PEAKS PLANNER

WHEN TO GO

Manchester has a reputation as one of the wettest cities in Britain, and visiting in summer won't guarantee fine weather. Nevertheless, wet or cold weather shouldn't spoil a visit because of the many indoor sights and cultural activities here and in Liverpool. Summer is the optimum time to see the Peak District, especially because traditional festivities take place in many villages at its start. The *only* time to see the great houses of Derbyshire's Wye Valley is from spring through fall.

PLANNING YOUR TIME

It's possible to see the main sights of Manchester or Liverpool in a day, but you'd have to take the museums at a gallop. In Manchester, the Museum of Science and Industry and the Imperial War Museum could easily absorb a day, as could the Albert Dock and waterfront area of Liverpool, where the Beatles Story, Tate Liverpool, Merseyside Maritime, and International Slavery museums, as well as the new Museum of Liverpool, all vie for your attention. In Liverpool, an additional half day is needed to see the homes of John Lennon and Paul McCartney. The buzzing nightlife of each city demands at least an overnight stay. You can explore the Peak District on a day trip from Manchester in a pinch, but allow longer to visit the stately homes or to hike.

GETTING HERE AND AROUND

AIR TRAVEL

Both Manchester and Liverpool are well served by their international airports. Manchester, the third-largest airport in the country, has the greater number of flights, including some from the United States.

Airports Manchester Airport (☎ *0871/271–0711* ⊕ *www.manchesterairport. co.uk*). **Liverpool John Lennon Airport** (☎ *0871/521–8484* ⊕ *www. liverpoolairport.com*).

BUS TRAVEL

National Express buses serve the region from London's Victoria Coach Station. Average travel time to Manchester or Liverpool is five hours. To reach Matlock, Bakewell, and Buxton you can take a bus from London to Derby and change to the TransPeak bus service, though you might find it more convenient to travel first to Manchester.

Bus Contacts National Express (☎ *0871/781–8181* ⊕ *www.nationalexpress. com*). **TransPeak** (☎ *01733/712265* ⊕ *www.transpeak.co.uk*). **Traveline** (☎ *0871/200–2233* ⊕ *www.traveline.org.uk*).

CAR TRAVEL

If you're traveling by road, expect heavy traffic out of London on weekends. Travel time to Manchester or Liverpool from London via the M6 is 3 to 3½ hours. Although a car may not be an asset in touring the centers of Manchester and Liverpool, it is helpful in getting around the Peak District. Bus service there is quite good, but a car allows the most flexibility.

Roads within the region are generally very good. In Manchester and Liverpool, try to sightsee on foot to avoid parking problems. In the Peak District, park in signposted parking lots whenever possible. In summer, Peak District traffic is very heavy; watch out for speeding motorbikes, especially on the A6. In winter, know the weather forecast, as moorland roads can quickly become impassable.

TRAIN TRAVEL

Virgin Trains serves the region from London's Euston Station. Direct service to Manchester and Liverpool takes 2½ hours. There are trains between Manchester's Piccadilly Station and Liverpool's Lime Street every half hour during the day; the trip takes 50 minutes. Get schedules and other information through National Rail Enquiries.

To reach Buxton, in the Peak District, from London, take the Manchester train; switch at Stockport. Local service—one train an hour—from Manchester to Buxton takes one hour. Call National Rail Enquiries for timetable information.

Train Contacts National Rail Enquiries (☎ *0845/748–4950* ⊕ *www. nationalrail.co.uk*).

TRANSPORTATION DISCOUNTS AND DEALS

A Wayfarer ticket (£10), which covers a day's travel on all forms of transport in Manchester and the Peak District, is a good deal. Contact National Rail Enquiries for information.

RESTAURANTS

Dining options in Manchester and Liverpool vary from smart cafés offering Modern British and Continental fare to excellent ethnic restaurants. Manchester has one of Britain's biggest Chinatowns, and locals also favor the 40-odd Bangladeshi, Pakistani, and Indian restaurants along Wilmslow Road in Rusholme, a mile south of the city center, known as Curry Mile.

One local dish that has survived is Bakewell pudding (*never* called "tart" in these areas, as its imitations are elsewhere in England). Served with custard or cream, the pudding—a pastry covered with jam and a thin layer of almond-flavor filling—is the joy of Bakewell. Another regional creation is Lancashire hot pot, a hearty meat stew.

HOTELS

Because the larger city-center hotels in Manchester and Liverpool rely on business travelers during the week, they may markedly reduce their rates on weekends. Smaller hotels and guesthouses abound in nearby suburbs, many just a short bus ride from downtown. The Manchester and Liverpool visitor centers operate room-booking services. Also worth investigating are serviced apartments, which are becoming more popular in the cities. The Peak District has inns, bed-and-breakfasts, and hotels, as well as a network of youth hostels. Local tourist offices have details; reserve well in advance for Easter and summer.

WHAT IT COSTS IN POUNDS					
	£	££	£££	££££	£££££
Restaurants	under £10	£10–£14	£15–£19	£20–£25	over £25
Hotels	under £70	£70–£120	£121–£160	£161–£220	over £220

Restaurant prices are per person for a main course or equivalent combination of smaller dishes at dinner excluding tax. Hotels prices reflect the rack rate of a standard double room for two people in high season, including 20% V.A.T. Check online for off-season rates and special deals or discounts.

VISITOR INFORMATION
England's Northwest (⊕ *www.visitenglandsnorthwest.com*).

MANCHESTER

Today Manchester's center hums with the vibe of cutting-edge popular music and a swank café culture. The city's once-grim industrial landscape, redeveloped since the late 1980s, includes tidied-up canals, cotton mills transformed into loft apartments, and stylish contemporary architecture that has pushed the skyline ever higher. Beetham Tower, the second-tallest building in Britain after London's Canary Wharf, can't be overlooked. Bridgewater Hall and the Lowry, as well as the Imperial War Museum North, are outstanding cultural facilities. Sure, it still rains here, but the rain-soaked streets are part of the city's charm, in a bleak, northern kind of way.

The now-defunct Haçienda Club marketed New Order to the world, and Manchester became the clubbing capital of England. Joy Division, The Smiths, Stone Roses, Happy Mondays, and Oasis rose to the top of the charts. The extraordinary success of the Manchester United football club (which now faces a stiff challenge from its newly rich neighbor, Manchester City, owing to a stupendous injection of cash from its oil-rich Middle Eastern owners) has kept the eyes of sports fans fixed firmly on Manchester.

GETTING HERE AND AROUND
Manchester Airport has many international flights, so you might not even have to travel through London. There are frequent trains from the airport to Piccadilly Railway Station (15–20 minutes) and buses to Piccadilly Gardens Bus Station (one hour). A taxi from the airport to Manchester city center costs between £18 and £20. For details about public transportation in Manchester, call the Greater Manchester Passenger Transport Executive information line.

Driving to Manchester from London (3 to 3½ hours), take M1 north to M6, then the M62 east, which becomes M602 as it enters Greater Manchester. Trains from London's Euston Station drop passengers at the centrally located Piccadilly Railway Station. The journey takes 2½ hours. Chorlton Street Coach Station, a few hundred yards west of Piccadilly Railway Station, is the main bus station for regional and long-distance buses.

Most local buses leave from Piccadilly Gardens Bus Station, the hub of the urban bus network. Metroshuttle operates three free circular routes around the city center; service runs every 5 to 10 minutes Monday to Saturday 7 to 7 and Sunday 10 to 6.

Metrolink electric tram service runs through the city center and out to the suburbs. The Eccles extension has stops for the Lowry (Harbour City) and for the Manchester United Stadium (Old Trafford). Major extensions to the service will see routes added to Droylsden, Chorlton, Media City UK, and Oldham and Rochdale by 2012. Buy a ticket from the platform machine before you board. A £6.30 one-day tram and bus ticket is a good value.

Blue Badge Guides can arrange dozens of different tours of the city, and City Centre Cruises offers a three-hour Sunday lunch round-trip on a barge to the Manchester Ship Canal.

ORIENTATION

Manchester is compact enough that you can easily walk across the city center in 40 minutes, but buses and trams make it easy to navigate. Deansgate and Princess Street, the main thoroughfares, run roughly north–south and west–east; the lofty terra-cotta Victorian **Town Hall** sits in the middle, close to the visitor center and the fine **Manchester Art Gallery.** Dominating the skyline at the southern end of Deansgate is Manchester's newest and highest building, Beetham Tower, which houses a Hilton Hotel and marks the beginning of the **Castlefield Urban Heritage Park,** with the Museum of Science and Industry and the canal system. The **Whitworth Art Gallery** is a bus ride from downtown; otherwise, all other central sights are within easy walking distance of the Town Hall. Take a Metrolink tram 2 mi south for the Salford Quays dockland area, with the **Lowry** and the **Imperial War Museum;** you can spend half a day or more in this area. ■TIP➜ Keep in mind that the museums are both excellent and free.

ESSENTIALS

Transportation Contacts Greater Manchester Passenger Transport Executive (☎ 0161/244–1000 ⊕ www.gmpte.com). **Metrolink** (☎ 0161/205–2000 ⊕ www.metrolink.co.uk). **Metroshuttle** (☎ 0161/244–1000 ⊕ www.tfgm.com/buses/metroshuttle.cfm). **Tour Information Blue Badge Guides** (☎ 0161/440–0277 ⊕ www.blue-badge-guides.com/northwest.html). **City Centre Cruises** (☎ 0161/902–0222 ⊕ www.citycentrecruises.co.uk).

Visitor Information Manchester Visitor Centre (✉ Town Hall Extension, Lloyd St., City Centre ☎ 0871/222–8223 ⊕ www.visitmanchester.com).

EXPLORING

TOP ATTRACTIONS

Castlefield Urban Heritage Park. Site of an early Roman fort, the district of Castlefield was later the center of the city's industrial boom, which resulted in the building of Britain's first modern canal in 1764 and the

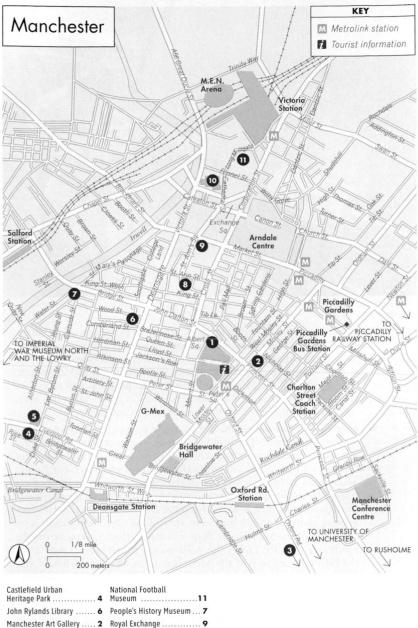

Manchester

KEY	
M	Metrolink station
i	Tourist information

M.E.N. Arena

Victoria Station

Salford Station

Exchange Sq.

Arndale Centre

Piccadilly Gardens

Piccadilly Gardens Bus Station

TO PICCADILLY RAILWAY STATION

TO IMPERIAL WAR MUSEUM NORTH AND THE LOWRY

Chorlton Street Coach Station

G-Mex

Bridgewater Hall

Bridgewater Canal

Deansgate Station

Oxford Rd. Station

Manchester Conference Centre

TO UNIVERSITY OF MANCHESTER

TO RUSHOLME

0   1/8 mile
0   200 meters

9

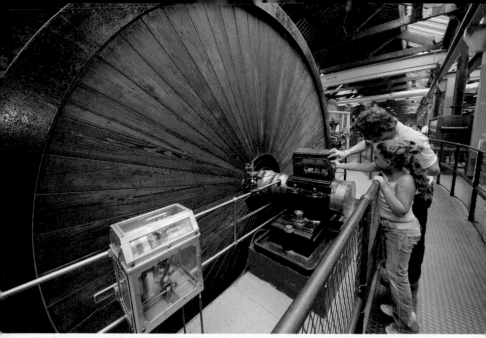

Manchester was an industrial powerhouse; learn all about this history at the engaging Museum of Science and Industry.

world's first railway station in 1830. What had become an urban waste-land has been beautifully restored into an urban park with canal-side walks, landscaped open spaces, and refurbished warehouses. The 7-acre site contains the reconstructed gate to the Roman fort of Mamucium, the buildings of the **Museum of Science and Industry,** and several of the city's hippest bars and restaurants. You can spend half a day here, including the museum. ⊠ *Off Liverpool Rd., Castlefield.*

★ **Imperial War Museum North.** The thought-provoking exhibits in this striking, aluminum-clad building, which architect Daniel Libeskind described as representing three shards of an exploded globe, present the reasons for war and show its effects on society. Three Big Picture audiovisual shows envelop you in the sights and sounds of conflicts from 1914 to the present, and a storage system has trays of objects to examine, including artifacts from the 2003 war in Iraq. A 100-foot viewing platform gives a bird's-eye view of the city. The museum is on the banks of the Manchester Ship Canal in Salford Quays, across the footbridge from the Lowry. It's a 10-minute (often breezy) walk from the Harbour City stop of the Metrolink tram. ⊠ *Trafford Wharf Rd., Salford Quays* ☎ *0161/836–4000* ⊕ *www.iwm.org.uk* ⊠ *Free* ⊘ *Mar.–Oct., daily 10–6; Nov.–Feb., daily 10–5; last admission 30 mins before closing.*

The Lowry. Clad in perforated steel and glass and fronted by an illumi-nated canopy, this impressive arts center in Manchester is one of the highlights of the Salford Quays waterways. L.S. Lowry (1887–1976) was a local artist, and one of the few who painted the industrial land-scape. Galleries showcase Lowry's and other contemporary artists' work. The theater, Britain's largest outside London, presents an impressive lineup of touring companies. The nearest Metrolink tram stop is Harbour City, a 10-minute walk from the Lowry. ⊠ *Pier 8, Salford Quays* ☎ *0843/208–2000* ⊕ *www.thelowry.com* ✉ *Free, prices vary for shows, tours £3* ☉ *Building Sun. and Mon. 10–6, Tues.–Sat. 10–8, or last performance; galleries Sun.–Fri. 11–5, Sat. 10–5.*

★ **Manchester Art Gallery.** Behind its impressive classical portico, this splendid museum presents its collections in both a Victorian and contemporary setting. Don't miss the outstanding collection of vibrant paintings by the Pre-Raphaelites and their circle, notably Ford Madox Brown's masterpiece *Work* and Holman Hunt's *The Hireling Shepherd*. British artworks from the 18th century—*Cheetah and Stag with Two Indians* by George Stubbs, for instance—and the 20th century are also well represented. The Manchester Gallery illustrates the city's contribution to art, and the second-floor Craft and Design Gallery shows off the best of the decorative arts in ceramics, glass, metalwork, and furniture. ⊠ *Mosely St., City Centre* ☎ *0161/235–8888* ⊕ *www.manchestergalleries.org.uk* ✉ *Free* ☉ *Tues.–Sun. and national holidays 10–5.*

Fodor's Choice **Museum of Science and Industry.** The museum's five buildings, one of ★ which is the world's oldest passenger rail station (1830), hold marvelous collections relating to the city's industrial past and present. You can walk through a reconstructed Victorian sewer, be blasted by the heat and noise of working steam engines, see cotton looms whirring in action, and watch a planetarium show. The Air and Space Gallery fills a graceful cast-iron-and-glass building, constructed as a market hall in 1877. ■ TIP→ Allow at least half a day to get the most out of all the sites, which are in the Castlefield Urban Heritage Park. ⊠ *Liverpool Rd., main entrance on Lower Byrom St., Castlefield* ☎ *0161/832–2244* ⊕ *www.mosi.org.uk* ✉ *Free, charges vary for special exhibits* ☉ *Daily 10–5.*

☾ **People's History Museum.** Not everyone in 19th-century Manchester owned a cotton mill or made a fortune on the trading floor. This museum recounts powerfully the struggles of working people in the city since the Industrial Revolution. It tells the story of the 1819 Peterloo Massacre and has an unrivaled collection of trade-union banners, tools, toys, utensils, and photographs, all illustrating the working lives and pastimes of the city's people. ⊠ *Left Bank, City Centre* ☎ *0161/838–9190* ⊕ *www.phm.org.uk* ✉ *Free* ☉ *Daily 10–5.*

NEED A BREAK? The brick-vaulted **Mark Addy pub** (⊠ **Stanley St. off Bridge St., City Centre** ☎ **0161/832–4080**) is a good spot to have a drink and sample an excellent spread of pâtés and cheeses. The waterside pub is named for the 19th-century boatman who rescued more than 50 people from the River Irwell.

Royal Exchange. Throughout its commercial heyday, this was the city's most important building—the cotton market. Built with Victorian exuberance in 1874, the existing structure accommodated 7,000 traders. The giant glass-dome roof was restored after a 1996 IRA bombing. Visit to see the lunar module–inspired Royal Exchange Theatre, have a drink in the café, and browse the crafts shop or the clothes outlets in the arcade. ✉ *St. Ann's Sq., City Centre* ☏ *0161/833–9833* ⊕ *www. royalexchange.co.uk.*

Town Hall. Manchester's imposing Town Hall, with its 280-foot-tall clock tower, speaks volumes about the city's 19th-century sense of self-importance. Alfred Waterhouse designed the Victorian Gothic building (1867–76); extensions were added just before World War II. Over the main entrance is a statue of Roman general Agricola, who founded Mamucium in AD 79. Above him are Henry III, Elizabeth I, and St. George, the patron saint of England. Murals of the city's history, painted between 1852 and 1865 by the Pre-Raphaelite Ford Madox Brown, decorate the Great Hall, with its emblazoned hammer-beam roof. Guided tours (twice a month) include the murals, but ask at the front desk: if the rooms aren't being used, you may be allowed to wander in. ✉ *Albert Sq., public entrance on Lloyd St., City Centre* ☏ *0161/234–5000* ▤ *Free, guided tours £6* ⊙ *Mon.–Sat. 8:45–5.*

Whitworth Art Gallery. This University of Manchester–run art museum has strong collections of British watercolors, old-master drawings, and postimpressionist works, as well as wallpapers. The excellent textile gallery—befitting a city built on textile manufacture—demonstrates the meaning and power of clothing in such items as a 16th-century Spanish funeral cope, 18th-century babies' vests, and a modern-day Turkish circumcision suit. A good bistro and a gift shop are also here. To get to the museum, catch any southbound bus with a number in the 40s (except 47) on Oxford Road, or from St. Peter's Square or Piccadilly Gardens. ✉ *Oxford Rd., University Quarter* ☏ *0161/275-7450* ⊕ *www. whitworth.manchester.ac.uk* ▤ *Free* ⊙ *Mon.–Sat. 10–5, Sun. noon–4.*

WORTH NOTING

John Rylands Library. Owned by the University of Manchester, this Gothic Revival masterpiece designed by Alfred Waterhouse was built by Enriqueta Augustina Rylands as a memorial to her husband, a cotton magnate. Constructed of red sandstone in the 1890s, the library resembles a cathedral and contains outstanding collections of illuminated manuscripts and personal papers of famous writers. ✉ *150 Deansgate, City Centre* ☏ *0161/400–9434* ⊕ *www.library.manchester.ac.uk* ⊙ *Tues.– Sat. 10–5, Sun. and Mon. noon–5.*

Manchester Cathedral. The city's sandstone cathedral, set beside the River Irwell and originally a medieval parish church dating in part from the 15th century, is unusually broad for its length and has the widest medieval nave in Britain. Inside, angels with gilded instruments look down from the roof of the nave, and misericords (the undersides of choristers' seats) in the early-16th-century choir stalls reveal intriguing carvings. The octagonal chapter house dates from 1485. ✉ *Victoria St., Millennium Quarter* ☏ *0161/833–2220* ⊕ *www.manchestercathedral.org* ▤ *Free* ⊙ *Weekdays 8:30–7, Sat. 8:30–5, Sun. 8:30–7:30.*

National Football Museum. The striking, glass-skinned triangle of a building is slated to reopen as the National Football Museum in 2012; call or check the Web site before visiting. Exhibits will include sacred memorabilia such as the ball from the 1966 World Cup Final and the signed shirts of legendary players such as Bobby Moore and Sir Stanley

Manchester's History: Cottonopolis

Manchester's spectacular rise from a small town to the world's cotton capital—with the nickname Cottonopolis—in only 100 years began with the first steam-powered cotton mill, built in 1783. Dredging made the rivers Irwell and Mersey navigable to ship coal to the factories. The world's first passenger railway opened in 1830, and construction of the Manchester Ship Canal in 1894 provided the infrastructure for Manchester to dominate the industrial world. Check out ⊕ *www.modernhistory.co.uk* for information about seeing more of this industrial heritage.

A few people acquired great wealth, but factory hands worked under appalling conditions. Working-class discontent came to a head in 1819 in the Peterloo Massacre, when soldiers killed 11 workers at a protest meeting. The conditions under which factory hands worked were later recorded by Friedrich Engels (co-author with Karl Marx of the *Communist Manifesto*), who managed a cotton mill in the city. More-formal political opposition to the government emerged in the shape of the Chartist movement (which campaigned for universal suffrage) and the Anti–Corn Law League (which opposed trade tariffs), forerunners of the British trade unions. From Victorian times until the 1960s, daily life for the average Mancunian was so oppressive that it bred the desire to escape, although most stayed put and endured the harsh conditions.

Matthews. There will also be interactive exhibits exploring soccer's role in British popular culture. ⊠ *Cathedral Gardens, Millennium Quarter* ☎ *0161/870–9275* ⊕ *www.nationalfootballmuseum.com.*

St. Ann's Church. Built in 1712 and sometimes wrongly attributed to Christopher Wren, St. Ann's is Manchester's oldest surviving classical building. The plain, elegant interior has a gallery supported by Tuscan columns, and light from the clear windows enhances the dark-wood pews and chancel. ⊠ *St. Ann's Sq., City Centre* ☎ *0161/834–1161* 💳 *Free* ⊕ *www.stannsmanchester.com* ⊙ *Mon.–Sat. 9:45–4:45, Sun. 8:45–4:45 and 6–7:30.*

9

WHERE TO EAT

The city's dining scene, with everything from Indian (go to Rusholme) to Modern British fare, is lively. The Manchester Food & Drink Festival, held the first two weeks of October, showcases the city's chefs and regional products with special events. The city's pubs are also good options for lunch or dinner.

£ ✕ **Akbar's.** Locals line up for this big, bright, and buzzing contemporary
INDIAN restaurant just opposite the Museum of Science and Industry. If they're not tucking into sizzling, stir-fried balti dishes (a don't-miss), they might be enjoying a mild and creamy korma, *rogan josh* (with tomatoes and coriander) or a sweet-and-sour *dhansak* dish (with pineapple and lentils)—all popular staples. Vegetarians have plenty of choices, too. Be prepared to wait at busy times. ⊠ *73–83 Liverpool Rd., Castlefield*

☎ *0161/834–8444* ⊕ *www.akbars. co.uk* ⌀ *Reservations not accepted.*

£
INDIAN

✕ **Lal Haweli.** One of Rusholme's string of Indian restaurants, this bright and spacious establishment specializes in tandoori chicken and other staples. What sets it apart are Nepalese offerings such as chicken *sultani* (with orange, pineapple, and chilis) and stir-fried balti dishes. This mostly Asian (mainly Pakistani) area is full of bright neon signs and waiters trying to lure you into their restaurants. A mile south of the city center, it's easily accessible by Buses 41, 42, 43, 44, and 45, or a short taxi ride. ✉ *68–72 Wilmslow Rd., Rusholme* ☎ *0161/248–9700.*

$$$
MODERN BRITISH

✕ **The Lime Tree.** Chef Patrick Hannity's unstuffy restaurant offers a seductive British menu with a hint of northern bohemia in the leafy suburb of West Didsbury. Expect Cheshire lamb in the exotic company of moussaka, couscous, and mint yogurt, or Morecambe Bay scallops in cannelloni. If you don't mind eating between 5:30 and 6:30 pm, the early-evening three-course menu is superb value at £15.95. Wine can be ordered by the glass to suit each dish. You might need to book a week in advance. ✉ *8 Lapwing La., West Didsbury* ☎ *0871/811–4873* ⊕ *www.thelimetreerestaurant.co.uk* ⌀ *Reservations essential.*

££
BRITISH

✕ **Mr. Thomas's Chophouse.** The city's oldest restaurant, dating from 1872, dishes out good old British favorites such as brown onion soup, steak-and-kidney pudding, Lancashire hot pot, and corned-beef hash to crowds of city types and shoppers. This hearty food is served in a Victorian-style room with a black-and-white-checked floor and green tiling. The wine list is exceptional. Mr. Sam's Chophouse in Chapel Walks serves similar fare. ✉ *52 Cross St., City Centre* ☎ *0161/832–2245* ⊕ *tomsmanchester.thevictorianchophousecompany.com.*

££
JAPANESE

✕ **Sapporo Teppanyaki.** The emphasis is on riotous good fun at this modern Japanese restaurant in Castlefield. Take your place around the chef's iron griddle and the theater begins; once you've had potato fritters tossed into your mouth and seen other morsels caught and balanced on the chef's spatula, you can enjoy your choice of dishes such as yummy teriyaki beef and sizzling scallops. For a quieter, lighter meal, take a private table and peruse the sushi menu. Curiosity might tempt you to try a Manchester roll, made of smoked swordfish with Lancashire cheese and crabmeat. ✉ *91–93 Liverpool Rd., Castlefield* ☎ *0161/831–9888* ⊕ *www.sapporo.co.uk.*

£££
ITALIAN

✕ **Stock.** The Edwardian building that houses this busy Italian restaurant was once the city's stock exchange—hence its name and grand domed setting. Chef Enzo Mauro emphasizes the flavors of southern Italy on a menu that might include fish and shellfish broth on a garlicky bruschetta or black-squid-ink linguine with cuttlefish. You can accompany this with a fine-quality wine. Bonuses are a good-value lunch deal, jazz on Friday, and occasional opera nights. ⊠ *4 Norfolk St., City Centre* ☎ *0161/839–6644* ⊕ *www.stockrestaurant.co.uk* ☿ *Closed Sun.*

££   ✕ **Sweet Mandarin.** Warm neon lighting and floor-to-ceiling windows
CHINESE invite you into this contemporary Chinese restaurant from the hip streets of the Northern Quarter. Deliciously simple family recipes have earned it a growing reputation; locals flock to enjoy the famous salt-and-pepper ribs, clay-pot chicken, Lily Kwok's curry, and crispy Szechuan beef, all of which come on the banquet menu at £19.50 per head. On the à la carte menu, try General Tse's sweet-and-sour chicken, named after a late uncle said to have been almost militant in nurturing his cherished recipe. ⊠ *19 Copperas St., Northern Quarter* ☎ *0161/832–8848* ⊕ *www.sweetmandarin.com* ☿ *Closed Mon.*

WHERE TO STAY

For expanded hotel reviews, visit Fodors.com.

£££–££££ ▦ **Arora International.** The centrally located Arora International, oppo-
HOTEL site the Manchester Art Gallery, occupies one of the city's grand Victorian buildings. **Pros:** fun theme rooms; historic building; good deals on weekends. **Cons:** no parking; smallish rooms. ⊠ *18–24 Princess St., City Centre* ☎ *0161/236–8999* ⊕ *www.arorainternational.com* ⤳ *141 rooms* ⚬ *In-room: no a/c, Internet. In-hotel: restaurant, bar, gym* ⍾ *No meals.*

££–£££ ▦ **Castlefield Hotel.** This popular modern hotel near the water's edge in
HOTEL the Castlefield Basin, opposite the Museum of Science and Industry, has cheery and traditional public rooms. **Pros:** excellent leisure facilities; reasonable rates. **Cons:** rooms can feel stuffy; slightly removed from city center. ⊠ *Liverpool Rd., Castlefield* ☎ *0161/832–7073* ⊕ *www. castlefield-hotel.co.uk* ⤳ *48 rooms* ⚬ *In-room: no a/c, Wi-Fi. In-hotel: restaurant, bar, pool, gym, parking* ⍾ *Breakfast.*

£££££ ▦ **Great John Street.** Once a Victorian schoolhouse, this plush boutique
HOTEL hotel next to the Granada TV studios now attracts well-heeled business executives, television stars, and anyone seeking something truly special. **Pros:** luxurious rooms; unique design. **Cons:** expensive valet parking. ⊠ *Great John St., City Centre* ☎ *0161/831–3211* ⊕ *www. greatjohnstreet.co.uk* ⤳ *14 rooms, 16 suites* ⚬ *In-room: a/c, Internet, Wi-Fi. In-hotel: bar, gym, parking* ⍾ *No meals.*

££££–£££££ ▦ **The Lowry Hotel.** The strikingly modern design of this glass edifice
HOTEL overlooking the River Irwell and Santiago Calatrava's Trinity Bridge exudes luxury and spaciousness. **Pros:** luxury at every turn; spacious rooms. **Cons:** you feel swallowed up in the vast lobby; view is less than inspiring. ⊠ *50 Dearman's Pl., Chapel Wharf, City Centre* ☎ *0161/827–4000* ⊕ *www.thelowryhotel.com* ⤳ *157 rooms, 7 suites* ⚬ *In-room: a/c, Internet, Wi-Fi. In-hotel: restaurant, bar, pool, gym, spa, parking* ⍾ *Breakfast.*

£££ ▦ **The Midland Hotel.** The Edwardian splendor of the hotel's public rooms
HOTEL manages to shine through a contemporary makeover, evoking the days

9

when this was the city's railroad station hotel. **Pros:** central location; tasty restaurant; good for business travelers. **Cons:** impersonal feel; rooms facing road can be noisy. ✉ *Peter St., City Centre* ☎ *0161/236–3333* ⊕ *www.qhotels.co.uk* ↪ *298 rooms, 14 suites* ⚐ *In-room: a/c, Internet, Wi-Fi. In-hotel: restaurants, bars, pool, gym, parking, some pets allowed* ❧ *Breakfast.*

£
HOTEL

⊡ **The Oxnoble.** Friendly and relaxed, this gastro-pub with rooms has accommodations that are simple, creamy cool and modern in style. **Pros:** friendly staff; bargain prices. **Cons:** no-frills decor; noise from the bar reaches some of the rooms. ✉ *71 Liverpool Rd., Castlefield* ☎ *0161/839–7740* ⊕ *www.theox.co.uk* ↪ *9 rooms* ⚐ *In-room: no a/c. In-hotel: restaurant, bar* ❧ *No meals.*

££–£££
RENTAL

⊡ **RoomZZZ.** Although the stylishly modern serviced apartments in this old cotton warehouse are all about self-contained autonomy, the lobby and corridors have the jazzed-up feel of a boutique hotel. **Pros:** bang in the center of town; on Chinatown's doorstep; smoothly run. **Cons:** some bathrooms lack privacy. ✉ *36 Princess St., Chinatown* ☎ *0161/236–2121* ⊕ *www.roomzzz.co.uk* ↪ *48 apartments* ⚐ *In-room: a/c, no safe (some), kitchen, Wi-Fi* ❧ *No meals.*

£££–££££
RENTAL

⊡ **Staying Cool.** A stay with this trendy chain, which has 11 serviced apartments in three locations across the city center, could mean a designer studio on the 30th floor of the Beetham Tower or a corner duplex in a converted dye works overlooking a stretch of Castlefield canal. **Pros:** high-tech gadgets; helpful staff; impressive range of options. **Cons:** some maintenance issues. ✉ *216 Box Works, Worsley St., Castlefield* ☎ *0161/832–4060* ⊕ *www.stayingcool.com* ↪ *11 apartments* ⚐ *In-room: a/c, kitchen, Wi-Fi* ❧ *No meals.*

NIGHTLIFE AND THE ARTS

Manchester vies with London as Britain's capital of youth culture, but has vibrant nightlife and entertainment options for all ages. Spending time at a bar, pub, or club is definitely an essential part of any trip. For event listings, check out the free *Manchester Evening News* or *Manchester Metro News*, both widely available.

NIGHTLIFE

The action after dark centers on the Deansgate and Northern Quarter areas.

CAFÉ-BARS

Barça (✉ *8–9 Catalan Sq., Castlefield* ☎ *0161/839–7099*) is a hip canalside bar-restaurant that has won awards for its interesting architecture.

Cloud 23 (✉ *Beetham Tower, 303 Deansgate, City Centre* ☎ *0161/870–1688*) in the Hilton has a stunning 360-degree view of the city that you'll pay for; but at 23 floors up, this swanky bar is not for the vertiginous. Book well ahead.

Dry Bar (✉ *28–30 Oldham St., Northern Quarter* ☎ *0161/236–9840*), the Northern Quarter's original café-bar opened by Factory Records, is full of young people dancing and drinking.

Manchester's pubs and café-bars, whether Victorian or modern, are well worth a stop.

Whether you come to see or be seen, the **Living Room** (✉ *80 Deansgate, City Centre* ☎ *0161/832–0083*) is the city's top spot; a pianist plays in the early evening.

Obsidian (✉ *18–24 Princess St., City Centre* ☎ *0161/238–4348*) has a huge frosted-glass bar and great cocktails.

With striped rubber floors and surreal wallpaper, psychedelic **Walrus** (✉ *78-88 High St., Northern Quarter* ☎ *0161/828–8700*) serves cocktails and Asian cuisine.

PUBS

Fodor's Choice
★

The **Britons Protection** (✉ *50 Great Bridgewater St., Peter's Fields* ☎ *0161/236–5895*) is a relaxed pub with stained-glass windows, cozy back rooms, and a mural of the Peterloo Massacre. You can sample more than 230 whiskies and bourbons.

Dukes 92 (✉ *18 Castle St., Castlefield* ☎ *0161/839–3522*) has a perfect canal-side setting for a summer pub lunch or drink.

Peveril of the Peak (✉ *127 Great Bridgewater St., Peter's Fields* ☎ *0161/236–6364*), a throwback Victorian pub with a green-tile exterior, draws a crush of locals to its tiny rooms.

Sinclair's Oyster Bar (✉ *2 Cathedral Gates, Millennium Quarter* ☎ *0161/834–0430*), a half-timber pub built in the 17th century, specializes in fresh oyster dishes.

DANCE CLUBS

Off Deansgate, **42nd Street** (✉ *2 Bootle St., City Centre* ☎ *0161/831–7108*) plays retro, indie, sing-along anthems, and classic rock.

9

Sankey's (⌗ *Beehive Mill, Jersey St., Ancoats* ☎ *0161/236–5444*) covers electro, techno, and hard-core music.

GAY CLUBS

★ The **Gay Village,** which came to television in the British series *Queer as Folk,* has stylish bars and cafés along the Rochdale Canal; Canal Street is its heart. The area is not only the center of Manchester's good-size gay scene but also the nightlife center for the young and trendy. **Lammars** (⌗ *57 Hilton St., Northern Quarter* ☎ *0161/237–9058*) is a popular place with stand-up comedy and live music.

LIVE MUSIC

Band on the Wall (⌗ *25 Swan St., Northern Quarter* ☎ *0161/834–1786*), a famous venue recently revamped, has a reputation for both established and pioneering music. Past performers include Joy Division, Simply Red, and Björk.

Manchester Apollo (⌗ *Stockport Rd., Ardwick Green* ☎ *0844/847–2277*) showcases live performances for all musical tastes.

Major rock and pop stars appear at the **Manchester Evening News Arena** (⌗ *21 Hunt's Bank, Hunt's Bank* ☎ *0844/847–8000*).

The **Roadhouse** (⌗ *8 Newton St., City Centre* ☎ *0161/237–9789*), an intimate band venue, also hosts funk and indie nights.

THE ARTS

PERFORMING ARTS VENUES

★ Dramatically modern **Bridgewater Hall** (⌗ *Lower Mosley St., Peter's Fields* ☎ *0161/907–9000*) has concerts by Manchester's renowned Hallé Orchestra and hosts both classical music and a varied light-entertainment program.

The **Lowry** (⌗ *Pier 8, Salford Quays* ☎ *0870/787–5780*) contains two theaters and presents everything from musicals to dance and performance poetry.

The **Opera House** (⌗ *Quay St., City Centre* ☎ *0161/828–1700*) is a venue for West End musicals, opera, and classical ballet.

The **Palace Theatre** (⌗ *Oxford St., City Centre* ☎ *0844/245–6600*) presents large touring shows—major plays, ballet, and opera.

Royal Northern College of Music (⌗ *124 Oxford Rd., University Quarter* ☎ *0161/907–5555*) hosts classical and contemporary music concerts, jazz, and opera.

THEATER

Royal Exchange Theatre (⌗ *St. Ann's Sq., City Centre* ☎ *0161/833–9833*) serves as the city's main venue for innovative contemporary theater.

SHOPPING

The city is nothing if not fashion conscious; take your pick from glitzy department stores, huge retail outlets, designer shops, and idiosyncratic boutiques. Famous names are centered on Exchange Square, Deansgate, and King Street; the Northern Quarter provides style for younger trendsetters.

Afflecks Palace (✉ *52 Church St., Northern Quarter* ☎ *0161/839–0718*) attracts young Mancunians with four floors of bohemian glam, ethnic crafts and jewelry, and innovative gift ideas.

Barton Arcade (✉ *51–63 Deansgate, City Centre* ☎ *No phone*) has specialty shopping inside a lovely Victorian arcade.

★ **Harvey Nichols** (✉ *21 New Cathedral St., City Centre* ☎ *0161/828–8888*), an outpost of London's chic luxury department store, is packed with designer goods and has an excellent second-floor restaurant and brasserie.

The **Lowry Designer Outlet** (✉ *11 The Quays, Salford Quays* ☎ *0161/848–1850*), with 80 stores, has good discounts on top brands at stores such as Nike and Karen Millen.

The **Manchester Craft and Design Centre** (✉ *17 Oak St., Northern Quarter* ☎ *0161/832–4274*) houses two floors of workshop-cum-retail outlets.

The world's largest **Marks & Spencer** (✉ *7 Market St., City Centre* ☎ *0161/831–7341*) department store offers its own brand of fashion and has an excellent food department.

Oldham Street, in the Northern Quarter, is littered with urban hip-hop boutiques and music shops.

The **Triangle** (✉ *Millennium Quarter* ☎ *0161/834–8961*), a stylish mall in the Victorian Corn Exchange, has more than 30 stores, including independent designer shops.

FOOTBALL

Football (soccer in the United States) is *the* reigning passion in Manchester. Locals support the local club, Manchester City, and glory seekers come from afar to root for Manchester United, based in neighboring Trafford. Matches for both clubs are usually sold out months in advance, though you have more of a chance with Manchester City.

Manchester City (✉ *Rowsley St., SportCity* ☎ *0870/062–1894*) plays at the City of Manchester Stadium.

At the **Manchester City Museum and Stadium Tours** (✉ *Rowsley St., Sport-City* ☎ *0870/062–1894*) you can see club memorabilia, visit the players' changing rooms, and go down the tunnel to pitch side. Excluding match days, there are three tours daily Monday through Saturday, two on Sunday; admission is £8.50.

★ **Manchester United** (✉ *Sir Matt Busby Way, Trafford Wharf* ☎ *0161/868–8000*) has home matches at Old Trafford.

You can take a trip to the Theatre of Dreams at the **Manchester United Museum and Tour** (✉ *Sir Matt Busby Way, Trafford Wharf* ☎ *0161/868–8000*), which tells the history of the football club. It's best to prebook the tour (not available on match days), which takes you behind the scenes, into the changing rooms and players' lounge, and down the tunnel. The museum is open daily 9:30–5; admission for the museum and tour is £13.50; for the museum only, £10.50. Take the tram to the Old Trafford stop and walk five minutes.

9

LIVERPOOL

A city lined with one of the most famous waterfronts in England, celebrated around the world as the birthplace of the Beatles, and still the place to catch that "Ferry 'Cross the Mersey," Liverpool reversed a downturn in its fortunes with developments in the late 1980s, such as the impressively refurbished Albert Dock area and Tate Liverpool. Its stint as the European Union's Capital of Culture in 2008, when £3 billion was invested in the city, acted as a catalyst for further regeneration. UNESCO named six historic areas in the city center a World Heritage Site, in recognition of its maritime and mercantile achievements during the height of Britain's global influence. This heritage, together with the renowned attractions and a legacy of cultural vibrancy, now draw in an ever-increasing number of visitors.

The 1960s produced Liverpool's most famous export—the Beatles. The group was one of hundreds that copied the rock and roll they heard from visiting American GIs and merchant seamen in the late 1950s, and one of many that played local venues such as the Cavern (demolished but rebuilt nearby). All four Beatles were born in Liverpool, but the group's success dates from the time they left for London. Nevertheless, the city has milked the group's Liverpool connections for all they are worth, with a multitude of local attractions such as Paul McCartney's and John Lennon's childhood homes.

GETTING HERE AND AROUND

Liverpool John Lennon Airport, about 8 mi southeast of the city, receives mostly domestic and European flights. The Airlink 500 bus service runs to the city center every 30 minutes, and a taxi to the center of Liverpool costs around £15.

Long-distance National Express buses, including service from London, use the Norton Street Coach Station, and local buses depart from Sir Thomas Street, Queen Square, and the Paradise Street Interchange. Traveline has information on long-distance and local routes. Train service on Virgin Trains from London's Euston Station takes 2½ hours.

If you're walking (easier than driving), you'll find the downtown sights well signposted. Take care when crossing the busy inner ring road separating the Albert Dock from the rest of the city. The circular C4 bus links Queen Square bus station with the Albert Dock (Gower Street stop).

TOURS   Blue Badge Guides can arrange dozens of different tours, which can be booked through the tourist office. Cavern City Tours offers a Beatles Magical Mystery Tour of Liverpool, departing from the Albert Dock visitor center. The two-hour bus tour, which costs £14.95, runs past Penny Lane, Strawberry Field, and other mop-top landmarks. Liverpool Beatles Tours has personalized tours of Beatles sites from two hours to all day. The oddly named Yellow Duckmarines runs daily tours on amphibious vehicles from World War II. The trips, which cost between £9.95 and £12.95, leave from the Gower Street bus stop in Albert Dock.

ORIENTATION

Liverpool has a fairly compact center, and you can see most of the city highlights on foot. The skyline helps with orientation: the Radio City tower on **Queen Square** marks the center of the city. The Liver Birds, on top of the **Royal Liver Building,** signal the waterfront and River Mersey. North of the Radio City tower lie Lime Street Station and William Brown Street, a showcase boulevard of municipal buildings, including the outstanding **Walker Art Gallery** and **World Museum Liverpool.** The city's other museums and the **Beatles Story** are concentrated westward on the waterfront in the **Albert Dock** area, a 20-minute walk or 5-minute bus ride away. **Hope Street,** to the east of the center, connects the city's two cathedrals, both easily recognizable on the skyline. On nearby Berry Street the red, green, and gold **Chinese Arch,** the largest outside China, marks the small Chinatown area. ■TIP→ Allow extra time to visit the childhood homes of Paul McCartney and John Lennon (viewable only on a tour), as they lie outside the city center.

DISCOUNTS AND DEALS

If you're staying in Liverpool, you could make use of Your Ticket for Liverpool, a visitor card that gives free admission to selected sights, free bus travel in the city, and restaurant discounts over three consecutive days. It costs £24.99 and is available from tourist offices and online at ⊕ *www.yourticketforliverpool.com.*

ESSENTIALS

Bus Contacts **Airlink 500** (☎ *0871/200–2233* ⊕ *www.arrivabus.co.uk*). **Traveline** (☎ *0871/200–2233* ⊕ *www.traveline.org.uk*).

Tour Contacts **Blue Badge Guides** (☎ *0796/451–5681 or 0791/865–5113* ⊕ *www.blue-badge-guides.com*). **Cavern City Tours** (✉ *Mathew St., City Centre* ☎ *0151/236–9091* ⊕ *www.cavernclub.org*). **Liverpool Beatles Tours** (✉ *25 Victoria St., City Centre* ☎ *0151/281–7738* ⊕ *www.beatlestours.co.uk*). **Yellow-Duckmarines** (☎ *0151/708–7799* ⊕ *www.theyellowduckmarine.co.uk*).

Visitor Information **Liverpool** (✉ *36–38 Whitechapel, City Centre* ☎ *0151/233–2008, 0844/870–0123 for accommodations* ✉ *Anchor Courtyard, Albert Dock* ☎ *0151/707–0729* ✉ *Arrival Hall, South Terminal, John Lennon Airport* ☎ *0151/907–1057* ⊕ *www.visitliverpool.com*).

9

EXPLORING LIVERPOOL

TOP EXPERIENCE: BEATLES SIGHTS

20 Forthlin Road. From 1955 to 1964, Paul McCartney lived with his family in this modest 1950s council house (a building rented from the local government). A number of the Beatles' songs, including "Love Me Do" and "When I'm Sixty-Four," were written here. The house is viewable only on a tour, leaving from the Jurys Inn next to Albert Dock (mornings) or Speke Hall (afternoons). ✉ *20 Forthlin Rd., Allerton* ☎ *0844/800–4791* ⊕ *www.nationaltrust.org.uk* 💷 *£20, includes Mendips and Speke Hall gardens* ☉ *Mid-Mar.–Oct., Wed.–Sun., 4 departures a day; early Mar. and Nov., Wed.–Sun., 3 departures a day.*

 Beatles Story. You can follow in the footsteps of the Fab Four at one of the more popular attractions in the Albert Dock complex. Entertaining scenes re-create stages in their career, from the enthusiastic early days in Germany and the Cavern Club to the White Room, where "Imagine" seems to emanate from softly billowing curtains. Artifacts included are the glasses John Lennon wore when he composed "Imagine" and the blue felt bedspread used in the famous "Bed-in" in 1969. The "Going Solo" section follows the members' separate careers. ■TIP→ Avoid the crowds of July and August by visiting in the late afternoon. You can purchase tickets, good for two days, online in advance. A shop sells everything from wallets to alarm clocks emblazoned with the Beatles logo. Admission to a second location at the Mersey Ferries Terminal at Pier Head is included in the price: Fab4D, a 3-D show with computer animation, and special exhibits are highlights. ⊠ *Britannia Vaults, Albert Dock, Waterfront* ☏ *0151/709–1963* ⊕ *www.beatlesstory.com* ☐ *£12.95* ⊙ *Daily 9–7; last admission 2 hrs before closing.*

Mathew Street. It was at the Cavern on this street that Brian Epstein, the Beatles' manager, first heard the group in 1961. The Cavern had opened at No. 10 as a jazz venue in 1957, but beat groups, of whom the Beatles were clearly the most talented, had taken it over. Epstein became their manager a few months after first visiting the club, and within two years the group was the most talked-about phenomenon in music. The club was demolished in 1973; it was rebuilt a few yards from the original site. At No. 5 is the Cavern Pub, opened in 1994, with Beatles memorabilia and plenty of nostalgia. ■TIP→ At No. 31, check out the well-stocked Beatles Shop.

QUICK BITES

Not far from Mathew Street, Delifonseca (⊠ *12 Stanley St., City Centre* ☏ *0151/255–0808*) offers reviving coffee and cake, as well as excellent sandwiches and salads. You could also stock up on munchies from the capacious downstairs deli.

Mendips. The National Trust (overseers of such landmarks as Blenheim Palace) maintains the 1930s middle-class, semidetached house that was the home of John Lennon from 1946 to 1963 and is a must-see for Beatles pilgrims. After his parents separated, John joined his aunt Mimi here; she gave him his first guitar but banished him to the porch, saying, "The guitar's all very well, John, but you'll never make a living out of it." The house can be seen only on a tour, leaving from the Jurys Inn next to Albert Dock (mornings) or Speke Hall (afternoons). ⊠ *251 Menlove Ave., Woolton* ☏ *0844/800–4791* ⊕ *www.nationaltrust.org.uk* ☐ *£20, includes 20 Forthlin Road and Speke Hall gardens* ⊙ *Mid-Mar.– Oct., Wed.–Sun., 4 departures a day; early Mar. and Nov., Wed.–Sun., 3 departures a day.*

TOP ATTRACTIONS

★ **Albert Dock.** To understand the city's prosperous maritime past, head for waterfront Albert Dock, 7 acres of restored warehouses built in 1846. Named after Queen Victoria's consort, Prince Albert, the dock provided storage for silk, tea, and tobacco from the Far East until it was closed in 1972. The fine colonnaded brick warehouse buildings are England's largest heritage attraction, containing the **Merseyside Maritime Museum**, the **International Slavery Museum**, **Tate Liverpool**, and

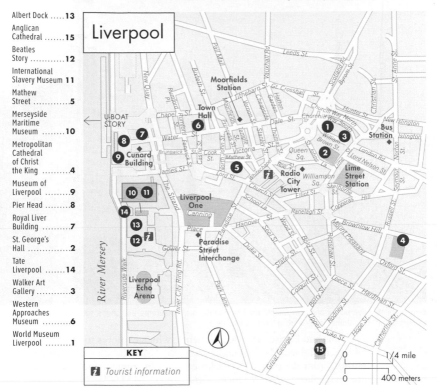

the **Beatles Story.** When weather allows, sit at an outdoor café over-looking the dock or take a boat trip through the docks and onto the river. Albert Dock is part of the area known as **Liverpool's Historic Waterfront.** ■TIP→ Much of the pedestrian area of the Albert Dock and waterfront area is cobblestone, so wear comfortable shoes. ✉ *Waterfront* ⊕ *www.albertdock.com.*

International Slavery Museum. On the third floor of the Maritime Museum, this museum's three dynamic galleries recount the history of transatlantic slavery and trace its significance in contemporary society. "Life in West Africa" reproduces a Nigerian Igbo compound; all the shackles of slavery are shown in the "Enslavement" section; and many stories, some never heard before, are told in "Legacies of Slavery." ✉ *Albert Dock, Waterfront* ☎ *0151/478–4499* ⊕ *www.liverpoolmuseums.org. uk* ✉ *Free* ☉ *Daily 10–5.*

Fodor's Choice
★
☺
Merseyside Maritime Museum. Part of the Albert Dock complex, this is a wonderful place to explore the role of the sea in the life of the city. The museum captures the triumphs and tragedies of Liverpool's seafaring history over five floors. Besides exhibits of maritime paintings, models, ceramics, and ships in bottles, the main museum brings to life the ill-fated stories of the *Titanic* and *Lusitania*, the Battle of the Atlantic, and the city's role during World War II. The basement is home to the

Once a major shipping center and now transformed with museums, restaurants, and shops, the Albert Dock has views of the large dome of the Port of Liverpool Building.

Customs and Excise National Museum, which explores the heroes and villains of the world of smuggling, together with the story of mass emigration from the port in the 19th century. In summer full-size vessels are on display. ⊠ *Albert Dock, Waterfront* ☎ *0151/478–4499* ⊕ *www. liverpoolmuseums.org.uk* 🖃 *Free* ⊙ *Daily 10–5.*

Pier Head. Here you can take a ferry across the River Mersey to Birkenhead and Seacombe. Boats leave regularly and offer fine views of the city—a journey celebrated in "Ferry 'Cross the Mersey," Gerry and the Pacemakers' 1964 hit song. It was from Pier Head that 9 million British, Irish, and other European emigrants set sail between 1830 and 1930 for new lives in North America, Australia, and Africa. The ferry terminal is also home to a number of Beatles Story attractions; you might want to make it the last stop on your Beatles tour. ■TIP➜ Take a short ferry ride or the longer cruise with commentary; the city views are worth the time and money. "Scousers," as locals are called, are famous for their patter. ⊠ *Pier Head Ferry Terminal, Mersey Ferries, Waterfront* ☎ *0151/330–1444* ⊕ *www.merseyferries.co.uk* 🖃 *£2.50 round-trip, cruises £6.70* ⊙ *Ferries every 30 mins weekdays 7:30–9:30 AM (Seacombe only) and 4:15–6:45; cruises hourly weekdays 10–3, weekends 10–6.*

Royal Liver Building. Best seen from the ferry, the 322-foot-tall Royal Liver (pronounced lie-ver) Building with its twin towers is topped by two 18-foot-high copper birds. They represent the mythical Liver Birds, the town symbol; local legend has it that if they fly away, Liverpool will cease to exist. For decades Liverpudlians looked to the Royal Liver Society for assistance—it was originally a burial club to which families paid contributions to ensure a decent send-off. ⊠ *Water St., Waterfront.*

CLOSE UP

Liverpool's History: Shipping Center

Liverpool, on the east bank of the Mersey River estuary, at the point where it merges with the Irish Sea, developed from the 17th century through the slave trade. It became Britain's leading port for ferrying Africans to North America and for handling sugar, tobacco, rum, and cotton, which began to dominate the local economy after the abolition of the slave trade in 1807.

Because of its proximity to Ireland, the city was also the first port of call for those fleeing famine, poverty, and persecution in that country. Similarly, Liverpool was often the last British port of call for thousands of mostly Jewish refugees fleeing Eastern Europe.

Many of the best-known liner companies were based in Liverpool, including Cunard and White Star, whose best-known vessel, the *Titanic,* was registered in Liverpool. The city was dealt an economic blow in 1894 with the opening of the Manchester Ship Canal, which allowed traders to bypass Liverpool and head to Manchester, 35 mi east. Britain's entry into the European Common Market saw more trade move from the west coast to the east, and the postwar growth of air travel diverted passengers from the sea. But as a sign of the city's revival, oceangoing liners returned to the city in 2008 after the building of a new cruise liner terminal at the Pier Head.

Tate Liverpool. A handsome conversion of Albert Dock warehouses by the late James Stirling, one of Britain's leading 20th-century architects, hosts an offshoot of the London-based art galleries of the same name. Galleries display changing exhibits of challenging modern art. A free introductory tour begins daily at 12:30. The excellent shop sells art books, prints, and posters, and there's a children's play area and a dockside café-restaurant. ⊠ *The Colonnades, Albert Dock, Waterfront* ☎ *0151/702–7400* ⊕ *www.tate.org.uk* ☜ *Free, charge for special exhibitions* ⊙ *Apr.–Sept., daily 10–5:50; Oct.–Mar., Tues.–Sun. 10–5:50.*

Fodor'sChoice
★
Walker Art Gallery. With a superb display of British art and some outstanding Italian and Flemish works, the Walker maintains its position as one of the best British art collections outside London. Don't miss the unrivaled collection of paintings by 18th-century Liverpudlian equestrian artist George Stubbs, and works by J.M.W. Turner, John Constable, Sir Edwin Henry Landseer, and the Pre-Raphaelites. Modern artists are included, too; on display is one of David Hockney's typically Californian pool scenes. Other excellent exhibits showcase china, silver, and furniture that once adorned the mansions of Liverpool's industrial barons. The Tea Room holds center stage in the airy museum lobby. ⊠ *William Brown St., City Centre* ☎ *0151/478–4199* ⊕ *www.liverpoolmuseums.org.uk* ☜ *Free* ⊙ *Daily 10–5.*

World Museum Liverpool. You can travel from the prehistoric to the space age through stunning displays in these state-of-the-art galleries. Ethnology, the natural and physical sciences, and archaeology all get their due on five floors. The World Cultures gallery colorfully illustrates the cosmopolitan history of the city. If the kids aren't grabbed by the monster bugs in the Bug House or afternoon shows in the Treasure House The-atre and Planetarium, they'll find plenty to do in the hands-on cen-ters. ✉ *William Brown St., City Centre* ☎ *0151/478–4393* ⊕ *www.liverpoolmuseums.org.uk* ✉ *Free* ⊙ *Daily 10–5.*

WORTH NOTING

Anglican Cathedral. The largest church in northern Britain overlooks the city and the River Mersey. Built of local sandstone, the Gothic-style cathe-dral was begun in 1903 by architect Giles Gilbert Scott; it was finally finished in 1978. Take a look at the grand interior on your own or expe-rience the Great Space film and audio tour to help you appreciate the building. The 331-foot-tall tower is a popular climb; two elevators and 108 steps take you to breathtaking views. View the Embroidery Gallery on your way up. A refectory serves light meals and coffee. ✉ *St. James's Mount, City Centre* ☎ *0151/709–6271* ⊕ *www.liverpoolcathedral.org.uk* ✉ *£3 suggested donation; combination ticket for tower, film, and audio tour £5* ⊙ *Daily 8–6. Tower Mar.–Sept., Mon.–Sat. 10–4:30; Oct.–Feb., Mon.–Sat. 10–3:30. Film and audio tour Mon.–Sat. 9–4, Sun. noon–2:30.*

Another Place. A hundred naked, life-size, cast-iron figures by sculptor Antony Gormley stand proudly on the 2 mi of foreshore at Crosby Beach, weathered by sand and sea. Unlike most other statues, you are permitted to interact with these and even clothe them as you wish. Check tide times before you go and be aware that it's not safe to walk out to the farthest figures. The site is 6 mi north of Liverpool center; to get here, take the Merseyrail train to Waterloo from Moorfields Station. A taxi will cost around £15. ✉ *Mariners Rd., Crosby Beach* ☎ *0151/237–3945, 0151/934–2967 for tide times* ⊕ *www.visitsouthport.com* ✉ *Free.*

Metropolitan Cathedral of Christ the King. Consecrated in 1967, this Roman Catholic cathedral is a modernistic, funnel-like structure of concrete, stone, and mosaic, topped with a glass lantern. Long, narrow, blue-glass windows separate chapels, each with modern works of art. An earlier design by classically inspired architect Edwin Lutyens was abandoned when World War II began (the current design is by Frederick Gibberd), but you can still take a look at Lutyen's vast brick-and-granite crypt and barrel-vaulted ceilings. ✉ *Mount Pleasant, City Centre* ☎ *0151/709–9222* ⊕ *www.liverpoolmetrocathedral.org.uk* ✉ *£3 suggested donation* ⊙ *Mon.–Sat. 8–6, Sun. 8–5.*

Museum of Liverpool. This ambitious new attraction on the waterfront at Pier Head tells the story of the city beginning with its earliest settlement in the Neolithic Age. Highlights include an extraordinary 3-D map with different perspectives of the city as you move around it, an engrossing film about soccer fan culture, and an interactive time line peeling away layers of Liverpool's history. ✉ *Albert Dock, Waterfront* ☎ *0151/478–4545* ✉ *Free* ⊙ *Daily 10–5* ⊕ *www.liverpoolmuseums.org.uk.*

St. George's Hall. Built between 1839 and 1847, St. George's Hall is among the world's finest examples of Greek Revivalist architecture. When Queen Victoria visited Liverpool in 1851, she declared it "worthy of ancient Ath-ens." Today the hall serves as a home for music festivals, concerts, and fairs. Self-guided tours tell the story of the building as a Crown court and cultural venue. ✉ *Lime St., City Centre* ☎ *0151/225–6909* ⊙ *Daily 10–5.*

Speke Hall and Gardens. This black-and-white mansion 6 mi from downtown Liverpool is one of the best examples of half-timbering in Britain. Built around a cobbled courtyard, the great hall dates to 1490; an elaborate western bay with a vast chimneypiece was added in 1560. The house, owned by the National Trust, was heavily restored in the 19th century, though a Tudor priest hole and Jacobean plasterwork remain intact. Speke Hall is on the east side of the airport; the Airlink 500 bus drops you a pleasant 10-minute walk away. ⊠ *The Walk, Speke* ☎ *0151/427–7231* ⊕ *www.nationaltrust.org.uk* 🖃 *£7.99; gardens only, £4.77; £20 combination ticket includes 20 Forthlin Road and Mendips* ⊙ *House mid-Mar.–Oct., Wed.–Sun. 11–5; Nov.–early Dec., weekends 11–4:30. Gardens daily 11–5:30 or dusk. Last admission 30 mins before closing.*

U-Boat Story. Explore the claustrophobic world of life onboard a German World War II submarine, one of only four left in the world. Sunk in 1945 by RAF depth charges, U-534 was hauled off the sea bed in 1993. Now she is docked at Birkenhead, beside the Woodside Ferry Terminal. As well as listening to interviews with crew members, you can decode enemy messages on an Enigma machine and take charge of a model submarine. ⊠ *Woodside Ferry Terminal, Birkenhead* ☎ *0151/330–1000* ⊕ *www.u-boatstory.co.uk* 🖃 *£5* ⊙ *Daily 10–5:30.*

Western Approaches Museum. Be taken right back to the 1940s when you explore the warren of rooms under the city streets, once the top-secret headquarters for the Battle of the Atlantic during World War II. The lofty Operations Room, full of the state-of-the-art technology of the time, is especially evocative. ⊠ *1–3 Rumford St., off Chapel St., City Centre* ☎ *0151/227–2008* ⊕ *www.liverpoolwarmuseum.co.uk* 🖃 *£6* ⊙ *Mar.–Oct., Mon.–Thurs. and Sat. 10:30–4:30.*

WHERE TO EAT

9

££££
MODERN BRITISH
✕ **60 Hope Street**. The combination of a ground-floor restaurant and a more informal basement bistro makes this a popular choice. A light, polished-wood floor and blue-and-cream walls help create an uncluttered backdrop for updated British dishes (sea bream is served with a confit of lemon gnocchi and pancetta, for example), but found only on British shores are rhubarb and custard and deep-fried jam sandwiches with condensed-milk ice cream. ⊠ *60 Hope St., City Centre* ☎ *0151/707–6060* ⊕ *www.60hopestreet.com* ⊙ *Closed Sun. No lunch Sat. in restaurant.*

££
JAPANESE
✕ **Etsu**. Minimalist decor, friendly staff, and a polished Japanese menu greet you at this inconspicuous street-corner locale just off the Strand (entrance on Brunswick Street). Along with the traditional sushi, noodle soups, and tempuras, all served with the freshest ingredients, are some witty East-meets-West creations, including sushi pizzas and tuna burgers made of rice blocks. The bento box meals provide great value at lunchtime in between museum visits. Make sure you try a *shochu*, a stronger version of sake, served neat or with oolong tea. ⊠ *25 The Strand, City Centre* ☎ *0151/236–7530* ⊕ *www.etsu-restaurant.co.uk* ⊙ *Closed Mon. No lunch Wed. and weekends.*

£ ✕**Everyman Bistro.** A cosmopolitan crowd can always be found at the
BRITISH simple wooden tables in the crypt of the Everyman Theatre. The hearty,
★ varied menu changes twice daily and might include lamb scouse (stew)
with beetroot and red cabbage, or smoked haddock with horseradish and pea-fish cakes, with apple-and-almond pudding for a notable
dessert. Vegetarians have plenty of choices, and there are good soups,
cheeses, and salads for lunch. ⊠ *5–9 Hope St., City Centre* ☎ *0151/708–
9545* ⊕ *www.everyman.co.uk* ⊘ *Closed Sun.*

££ ✕**Matou.** Expansive views of the historic waterfront are joined by the
ASIAN scent of Eastern spicesat this popular spot on the second floor of the
Mersey Ferry Terminal. The menu sticks to pan-Asian classics, such as
Thai green curry, Malaysian lamb satay, and rib-eye steak in a black-
bean sauce. Within a swoop of the Royal Liver birds, the terrace is a win-
ner in warmer weather. Contemporary dark-wood furnishings sit beside
huge slanting windows in the dining room. ⊠ *Mersey Ferry Terminal,
Georges Parade, Pier Head* ☎ *0151/236–2928* ⊕ *www.matou.co.uk.*

££ ✕**Side Door.** You'll often find couples enjoying a meal before a play or
BRITISH concert at this intimate and unpretentious bistro. The menu changes
every week, but there is always plenty of fish, such as hake with rosemary potatoes or sea bass cannelloni with butternut squash. Sticky
toffee pudding is a don't-miss dessert here. Pretheater fixed-price meals
are good value, and service is attentive. ⊠ *29A Hope St., City Centre*
☎ *0151/707–7888* ⊕ *www.thesidedoor.co.uk* ⊘ *Closed Sun.*

£££ ✕**Simply Heathcote's.** This chic contemporary restaurant, an outpost
MODERN BRITISH of chef Paul Heathcote's empire, has a curved glass front, cherry furnishings, and a granite floor. The menu has a local accent—lamb hot
pot with pickled red cabbage, braised ox cheek (from the face) with
horseradish foam, and bread-and-butter pudding—along with dishes
from warmer climes. Vegetarians are well served, too. The restaurant
is opposite the Royal Liver and Cunard buildings. ⊠ *25 The Strand,
Waterfront* ☎ *0151/236–3536* ⊕ *www.heathcotes.co.uk.*

£ ✕**Tate Café.** The Tate Liverpool's café-bar is a winner for daytime sus-
BRITISH tenance whether or not you're visiting the museum. Dockside seats
are great on warm summer days, and you can choose from among the
salads and open sandwiches including steak with Wirral watercress, as
well as main dishes such as chicken breast with Savoy cabbage. Fruit
scones with jam and cream also make an appearance. ⊠ *The Colonnades, Albert Dock, Waterfront* ☎ *0151/702–7581* ⊕ *www.tate.org.uk*
⊘ *Closed Mon. in winter. No dinner.*

WHERE TO STAY

For expanded hotel reviews, visit Fodors.com.

££–£££ ▦ **Crowne Plaza Liverpool.** Many of the city's main sights are at the
HOTEL doorstep of this modern hotel on the waterfront next to the Royal
Liver Building. **Pros:** on waterfront; friendly staff; plenty of activities.
Cons: chain-hotel furnishings; no Wi-Fi in rooms. ⊠ *St. Nicholas Pl.,
Waterfront* ☎ *0151/243–8000* ⊕ *www.cpliverpool.com* ⇥ *159 rooms*
△ *In-room: a/c, Internet. In-hotel: restaurants, bar, pool, gym, parking*
⏀ *No meals.*

£££–££££
HOTEL
Fodor's Choice
★

Hard Day's Night Hotel. "Everything seems to be right" since the marble-columned office block on the corner of Mathew Street was transformed into a hotel in homage to the Beatles. **Pros:** welcoming staff; sophisticated rooms; close to Beatles attractions. **Cons:** rumbling trains and street noise heard in some rooms; no parking. ⊠ *Central Bldgs., N. John St., City Centre* ☎ *0151/236–1964* ⊕ *www.harddaysnighthotel. com* ⌨ *108 rooms, 2 suites* ♿ *In-room: a/c, Wi-Fi. In-hotel: restaurant, bars* ¶○¶ *No meals.*

£££
HOTEL
★

Hope Street Hotel. Liverpool's first boutique hotel is in a converted carriage warehouse built in the style of a Venetian palazzo. **Pros:** beautiful design; plenty of space. **Cons:** service can be inconsistent; parking difficult to find; rooms face a busy street. ⊠ *40 Hope St., City Centre* ☎ *0151/709–3000* ⊕ *www.hopestreethotel.co.uk* ⌨ *41 rooms, 7 suites* ♿ *In-room: no a/c, Internet. In-hotel: restaurant, bars, parking* ¶○¶ *No meals.*

££££
HOTEL

Malmaison. The only purpose-built hotel in this chic chain—most are in recycled older buildings— combines extreme glamour with sleek industrial modernity and a great sense of space. **Pros:** buzzy atmosphere; rich decor. **Cons:** dim lighting in guest rooms; no parking; views to the back are disappointing. ⊠ *Princes Dock Waterfront* ☎ *0151/229–5000* ⊕ *www.malmaison.com* ⌨ *128 rooms, 2 suites* ♿ *In-room: a/c, Internet, Wi-Fi. In-hotel: restaurant, bar, gym* ¶○¶ *No meals.*

££–£££
RENTAL

Premier Apartments. These recently built apartments in Liverpool's glossy Garden Quarter in the heart of downtown have everything you need for an independent stay—including groceries, which can be delivered to your door. **Pros:** great for travelers who don't need hotel services; plenty of room; breakfast delivered every morning (extra charge). **Cons:** more expensive on weekends; limited parking. ⊠ *11 Hatton Gardens, City Centre* ☎ *0151/227–9467 or 0845/070–0907* ⊕ *www. premierapartments.com* ⌨ *62 apartments* ♿ *In-room: no a/c, kitchen, Internet, Wi-Fi. In-hotel: laundry facilities, parking* ¶○¶ *No meals.*

££–£££
RENTAL
★

Staybridge Apartments. These up-to-the-minute and well-fitted apartments close to the Liverpool Echo Arena make for a great stay on the waterfront. **Pros:** upbeat atmosphere; complimentary receptions on weekday evenings; public spaces for socializing. **Cons:** limited parking; no river views. ⊠ *21 Keel Wharf, Waterfront* ☎ *0151/703–9700* ⊕ *www.staybridge.co.uk* ⌨ *132 apartments* ♿ *In-room: a/c, kitchen, Internet, Wi-Fi. In-hotel: gym, laundry facilities, parking* ¶○¶ *Breakfast.*

9

NIGHTLIFE AND THE ARTS

NIGHTLIFE

The many bars, clubs, and pubs of Liverpool are an experience in themselves, from the trendy to the traditional.

Fodor's Choice
★

Alma de Cuba (⊠ *Seel St., City Centre* ☎ *0151/702–7394*), a church transformed into a luxurious bar, uses a huge mirrored altar and hundreds of dripping candles to great effect.

Baby Cream (⊠ *Atlantic Pavilion, Albert Dock, Waterfront* ☎ *0151/709–1004*) is known for its weekend DJs. The ladies can pamper themselves in the glitzy black powder room.

The **Cavern Club** (✉ *8–10 Mathew St., City Centre* ☎ *0151/236–1965*) draws many on the Beatles trail, some of whom don't realize it's not the original spot—that was demolished years ago.

The **Cavern Pub** (✉ *5 Mathew St., City Centre* ☎ *0151/236–4041*) merits a stop for nostalgia's sake; here are recorded the names of the groups and artists who played in the Cavern Club between 1957 and 1973.

Opposite Philharmonic Hall, the **Philharmonic** (✉ *36 Hope St., City Centre* ☎ *0151/707–2837*) is a Victorian-era extravaganza decorated in colorful marble. Make sure to check out the ornate loos (toilets).

Ye Cracke (✉ *13 Rice St., off Hope St., City Centre* ☎ *0151/709–4171*), one of the city's oldest pubs, was much visited by John Lennon in the 1960s.

THE ARTS

FILM

The **FACT Centre** (✉ *88 Wood St., City Centre* ☎ *0151/707–4444*) of the Foundation for Art and Creative Technology shows art-house and independent films on three screens; galleries display experimental film, video, and new media.

PERFORMING ARTS VENUES

Bluecoat (✉ *School La., City Centre* ☎ *0151/702–5324*) features contemporary visual and performing arts.

★ The well-regarded Royal Liverpool Philharmonic Orchestra plays its concert season at **Philharmonic Hall** (✉ *Hope St., City Centre* ☎ *0151/709–3789*). The venue also hosts contemporary music, jazz, and world concerts, and shows classic films.

The **Liverpool Empire** (✉ *Lime St., City Centre* ☎ *0844/847–2525*) presents major ballet, opera, drama, and musical performances.

THEATER

Everyman Theatre (✉ *5–9 Hope St., City Centre* ☎ *0151/709–4776*) focuses on works by British playwrights as well as experimental productions from around the world.

Royal Court Theatre (✉ *1 Roe St., City Centre* ☎ *0870/787–1866*), an art deco building, is one of the city's most appealing sites for stand-up comedy and theater.

SHOPPING

Circa 1900 (✉ *11–13 Holts Arcade, India Bldgs., Water St., City Centre* ☎ *0151/236–1282*) specializes in authentic art nouveau and art deco pieces, from ceramics and glass to furniture.

From Me to You (✉ *Cavern Walks, Mathew St., City Centre* ☎ *0151/227–1963*) may stock the mop-top knickknack of your dreams.

Liverpool One (✉ *Off Paradise St., City Centre* ☎ *0151/232–3100*), the city's largest shopping complex, has more than 160 stores, including John Lewis.

Metquarter (✉ *35 Whitechapel, City Centre* ☎ *0151/224–2390*), with more than 40 stores, is the place for designer names and the latest fashions.

The **Stanley Dock Sunday Market** (✉ *Great Howard St. and Regent Rd., City Centre*) operates each Sunday, selling bric-a-brac, clothes, and toys.

Liverpool claims its share of stylish bars and restaurants such as Alma de Cuba, housed in a converted church.

SPORTS AND THE OUTDOORS

FOOTBALL

Football (soccer) matches are played on weekends and, increasingly, weekdays. Tickets for Liverpool are sold out months in advance, but you should have more luck with Everton.

Everton (⊠ *Anfield Rd., Anfield* ☎ *0870/442–1878*), now reestablishing its historic competitiveness, plays at Goodison Park, about ½ mi north of Anfield.

Liverpool (⊠ *Goodison Park* ☎ *0844/844–0844*), one of England's top clubs, plays at Anfield, 2 mi north of the city center.

The **Liverpool Museum and Stadium Tour** (⊠ *Anfield Rd., Anfield* ☎ *0151/260–6677* ⚓ *£14* ⊙ *Daily 10–3*) takes you into the dressing rooms and down the tunnel, and gives you a sense of match day. There are no tours on match days.

HORSE RACING

★ Britain's most famous horse race, the Grand National steeplechase, has been run at Liverpool's **Aintree Racecourse** (⊠ *Ormskirk Rd., Aintree* ☎ *0844/579–3001*) almost every year since 1839. The race is held in March or April; book well ahead. Admission on most race days is £18.

THE PEAK DISTRICT

Heading southeast, away from the urban congestion of Manchester and Liverpool, it's not far to the southernmost contortions of the Pennine Hills. Here, about an hour from Manchester, sheltered in a great natural bowl, is the spa town of Buxton: at an elevation of more than 1,000 feet, it's the second-highest town in England. Buxton makes a convenient base for exploring the 540 square mi of the Peak District, Britain's oldest—and, some say, most beautiful—national park. About 38,000 people live in the towns throughout the park.

"Peak" is perhaps misleading; despite being a hilly area, it contains only gentle rises that don't reach much higher than 2,000 feet. Yet a trip around destinations such as Bakewell, Matlock, Castleton, and Edale, and the grand estates of Chatsworth House, Haddon Hall, and Hardwick Hall involves negotiating fairly perilous country roads, each of which repays the effort with enchanting views. Outdoor activities are popular in the Peaks, particularly caving (or "potholing"), walking, and hiking. Bring all-weather clothing and waterproof shoes.

BUXTON

25 mi southeast of Manchester.

Buxton makes a good base for Peak District excursions, but it has its own attractions as well. The town's spa days left a notable legacy of 18th- and 19th-century buildings, parks, and open spaces that give the town an air of faded grandeur. The Romans arrived in AD 79 and named Buxton Aquae Arnemetiae, loosely translated as "Waters of the Goddess of the Grove." The mineral springs, which emerge from 3,500 to 5,000 feet below ground at a constant 82°F, were believed to cure assorted ailments; in the 18th century the town became established as a popular spa, a minor rival to Bath. You can still drink water from the ancient St. Anne's Well, and it's also sold throughout Britain.

GETTING HERE AND AROUND

Both the National Express and TransPeak bus services from Manchester stop at Buxton. There are departures every two to three hours from Manchester's Chorlton Street Bus Station. If you're driving from Manchester, take A6 southeast to Buxton. The journey takes one hour. The hourly train from Manchester to Buxton takes an hour.

Visitor Information Buxton (✉ *Pavilion Gardens, St. John's Rd.* ☎ *01298/25106* ⊕ *www.visitpeakdistrict.com*).

EXPLORING

TOP ATTRACTIONS

The Crescent. Almost all out-of-town roads lead toward this central green with its curving semicircle of buildings. The three former hotels that make up the Georgian-era Crescent, with its arches, colonnades, and 378 windows, were built in 1780 by fashionable architect John Carr for the fifth duke of Devonshire (of nearby Chatsworth House). The thermal baths at the end of the Crescent now house a shopping center. It's where High Street meets A53.

OFF THE
BEATEN
PATH

★ **Little Moreton Hall.** The epitome of "magpie" black-and-white half-timber buildings, Little Moreton Hall, in the words of Olive Cook's *The English Country House,* "exaggerates and exalts the typical and humble medieval timber-framed dwelling, making of it a bizarre, unforgettable phenomenon." Covered with zigzags, crosses, and lozenge shapes

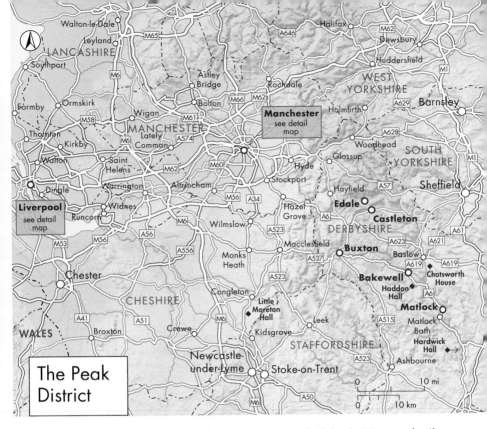

The Peak District

crafted of timber and daub, the house was built by the Moreton family between 1450 and 1580. The long gallery and colorful Tudor-era wall paintings are spectacular, and the staggered lavatories are intriguing. Little Moreton Hall lies to the west of the Peak District; to get here from Liverpool, take the M6 to the A534 east to Congleton. The house is 20 mi southwest of Buxton. ✉ *A34, Congleton* ☎ *01260/272018* ⊕ *www. nationaltrust.org.uk* 🎟 *£6.70* ☾ *Early–mid-Mar. and mid-Nov.–late Nov., weekends 11–4; late Mar.–early Nov., Wed.–Sun. 11–5; early to mid-Dec., weekends 11–4.*

Pavilion Gardens. Surrounded by 25 acres of pretty gardens, the Pavilion, with its ornate iron-and-glass roof, was originally a concert hall and ballroom. Erected in the 1870s, it remains a lively place that hosts local events, and also has a plant-filled conservatory, two cafés, and a restaurant. The Pavilion is adjacent to the Crescent and the Slopes on the west; the tourist office is here, too, with a food-and-crafts shop. ✉ *St. John's Rd., Pavilion Gardens* ☎ *01298//23114* ⊕ *www.paviliongardens.co.uk.*

WORTH NOTING

Buxton Museum and Art Gallery. The museum, on the eastern side of the Slopes, contains a collection of Blue John stone, a semiprecious mineral found only in the Peak District. It also displays local archaeological finds and pieces made from Derbyshire black marble, and there's a

small art gallery. ⊠ *Terrace Rd.* ☎ *01629/533540* ⊕ *www.derbyshire.
gov.uk/leisure* 🖃 *Free* ☉ *Oct.–Mar., Tues.–Fri. 9:30–5:30, Sat. 9:30–5;
Apr.–Sept., Tues.–Fri. 9:30–5:30, Sat. 9:30–5, Sun. 10:30–5.*

Poole's Cavern. The Peak District's extraordinary geology is revealed close
to Buxton at this large limestone cave far beneath the 100 wooded acres of
Buxton Country Park. The cave was inhabited in prehistoric times and contains, in addition to the standard stalactites and stalagmites, the source of
the River Wye, which flows through Buxton. ⊠ *Green La.* ☎ *01298/26978*
⊕ *www.poolescavern.co.uk* 🖃 *£8, including 50-min guided tour; park
and visitor center free* ☉ *Daily 9:30–5. Tours every 20 mins.*

WHERE TO EAT

££   ✗**Columbine.** The husband-and-wife team behind Columbine always
BRITISH   goes for local ingredients and flavors, no matter if the dishes are traditional, such as pork tenderloin with poached pear in mild Stilton sauce,
or more experimental, like duckling with oranges and Grand Marnier.
The cozy venue, with upstairs and downstairs seating, is a good spot for
pre- and post-theater meals. ⊠ *7 Hall Bank* ☎ *01298/78752* ☉ *Closed
Sun. Closed Tues. Nov.–Apr. No lunch Aug.–June.*

WHERE TO STAY

For expanded hotel reviews, visit Fodors.com.

££   ▦ **Buxton's Victorian Guesthouse.** One of a group of row houses built
B&B/INN   by the duke of Devonshire in 1860, this handsomely decorated house
★   stands in the center of Buxton. **Pros:** peaceful location on Pavilion
Gardens; family suite available. **Cons:** many stairs to climb; surcharge for credit cards. ⊠ *3A Broad Walk* ☎ *01298/78759* ⊕ *www.
buxtonvictorian.co.uk* ⋈ *7 rooms, 1 suite* ⚬ *In-room: no a/c. In-hotel:
parking, some age restrictions* ❘❍❘ *Breakfast.*

££–£££   ▦ **Old Hall.** In a refurbished 16th-century building rumored to have
B&B/INN   once accommodated Mary Queen of Scots, this hotel overlooks the
city's ornate Opera House. **Pros:** unpretentious atmosphere; good
dining choices. **Cons:** conventional furnishings; no private parking.
⊠ *The Square* ☎ *01298/22841* ⊕ *www.oldhallhotelbuxton.co.uk* ⋈ *38
rooms* ⚬ *In-room: no a/c. In-hotel: restaurant, bar, some pets allowed*
❘❍❘ *Breakfast.*

££   ▦ **Stoneridge.** Built of stone, this Edwardian B&B has been richly
B&B/INN   restored. **Pros:** excellent food choices; secluded and tranquil garden.
Cons: no tubs in bathrooms; credit cards not accepted. ⊠ *9 Park Rd.*
☎ *01298/26120* ⊕ *www.stoneridge.co.uk* ⋈ *4 rooms* ⚬ *In-room: no
a/c, Wi-Fi. In-hotel: parking, some pets allowed, some age restrictions*
▭ *No credit cards* ❘❍❘ *Breakfast.*

NIGHTLIFE AND THE ARTS

★   **Buxton Opera House** (⊠ *Water St.* ☎ *0845/127–2190*), bedecked with
carved cupids, presents excellent theater, ballet, and jazz performances
year-round; in late February it also hosts the annual Four-Four Time
festival of world, jazz, blues, and folk music.

The renowned **Buxton Festival** (⊠ *The Square* ☎ *01298/70395* ⊕ *www.
buxtonfestival.co.uk*), held for two weeks during mid-July each year,
includes opera, drama, and concerts.

SHOPPING

Buxton has many kinds of stores, especially around Spring Gardens, the main shopping street.

Stores in the beautifully tiled **Cavendish Arcade** (⊠ *The Crescent*), on the site of the old thermal baths, sell antiques, jewelry, fashions, and leather goods in stylish surroundings.

A **market**, selling mainly food and clothes, is held in Buxton every Tuesday and Saturday.

EN ROUTE As you head southeast from Buxton on the A6, you pass through the spectacular valleys of Ashwood Dale, Wyedale, and Monsal Dale before reaching Bakewell.

BAKEWELL

12 mi southeast of Buxton, 32 mi northeast of Little Moreton Hall.

In Bakewell, a medieval bridge crosses the winding River Wye in five graceful arches, and the 9th-century Saxon cross that stands outside the parish church reveals the town's great age. Narrow streets and houses built out of the local gray-brown stone also make the town extremely appealing. Ceaseless traffic through the streets can take the shine off—though there's respite down on the quiet riverside paths.

This market town is the commercial hub of the Peak District, for locals and visitors. The crowds are really substantial on market day (Monday), attended by area farmers. For a self-guided hour-long stroll, pick up a map at the tourist office, where the town trail begins. A small exhibition upstairs explains the landscape of the Peak District.

GETTING HERE AND AROUND

National Express and TransPeak offer bus services from Manchester's Chorlton Street Bus Station to Bakewell. By car, Bakewell is a one-hour, 30-minute drive southeast on the A6 from Manchester.

ESSENTIALS

Visitor Information Bakewell (⊠ *Old Market Hall, Bridge St.* ☎ *01629/816558* ⊕ *www.visitpeakdistrict.com*).

EXPLORING

★ **Chatsworth House.** Glorious parkland leads to the ancestral home of the dukes of Devonshire and one of England's greatest country houses. The vast expanse of greenery, grazed by deer and sheep, sets off the Palladian-style elegance of "the Palace of the Peak." Originally an Elizabethan house, Chatsworth was conceived on a monumental scale. It was altered over several generations starting in 1686, and the architecture now has a hodge-podge look, though the Palladian

BAKEWELL PUDDING

Bakewell is the source of Bakewell pudding, said to have been created inadvertently when, sometime in the 19th century, a cook at the town's Rutland Arms Hotel (which is still in business) dropped some rich cake mixture over jam tarts and baked it. Every local bakery and tearoom claims an original recipe, so it's easy to spend a gustatory afternoon tasting rival puddings.

9

CLOSE UP

Stoke-on-Trent: The Potteries

The area known as the Potteries, about 55 mi southeast of Liverpool, is still the center of Britain's ceramics industry, though production is increasingly being transferred overseas. There are, in fact, six towns, now administered as "the city of Stoke-on-Trent." Famous names such as Wedgwood, Royal Doulton, Spode, and Coalport carry on, though they have been taken over by other companies.

The most famous manufacturer, Josiah Wedgwood, established his pottery works at Etruria, near Burslem, in 1759, and created the cream-color ware (creamware), which so pleased Queen Charlotte that in 1762 she appointed him royal supplier of dinnerware. More recent innovators include the very collectible Clarice Cliff, who strove to brighten plain whiteware in the 1920s with her colorful geometric and floral designs. Also bold and colorful were the classic art deco pieces of Susie Cooper. Museums portray the history of this area, and there's still plenty of shopping, with good prices for seconds.

Ceramica occupies an ornate former town hall and uses displays, videos, and interactive technology to explore the area's history, the process of creating china, and some noted companies. In Bizarreland (the name comes from Clarice Cliff's art deco designs), kids can dig for relics from the past and take a virtual ride over the Potteries. A shop sells local wares. ✉ *Market Pl., Burslem* ☎ *01782/832001* ⊕ *www.ceramicauk.com* 🎟 *£4.10* 🕒 *Tues.–Sat. 10:30–4:30.*

While others are being taken over by big corporations, **Emma Bridgewater** continues to run her very successful pottery firm, known for its whimsical

designs including Polka Dots, Union Jack, and Figs. The factory tour shows how she adapted 200-year-old pottery techniques. There's a gift shop, a shop with seconds, and a little café. ✉ *Lichfield St., Hanley* ☎ *01782/201328* ⊕ *www.emmabridgewaterfactory.com* 🎟 *£2.50* 🕒 *Mon.–Sat. 9:30–5:30, Sun. 10–4.*

The **Gladstone Pottery Museum**, the city's only remaining Victorian pottery factory, contains examples of the old bottle kilns, surrounded by original workshops where you can watch the traditional skills of throwing, casting, and decorating. The Flushed with Pride galleries tell the story of the toilet from the 1840s onward. ✉ *Uttoxeter Rd., Longton* ☎ *01782/237777* ⊕ *www.stokemuseums.org.uk* 🎟 *£6.95* 🕒 *Daily 10–5; last admission at 4.*

The modern **Potteries Museum and Art Gallery** displays a 5,000-piece ceramic collection of international repute, and is recognized worldwide for its unique Staffordshire pottery. ✉ *Bethesda St., Hanley* ☎ *01782/232323* ⊕ *www.stoke.gov.uk* 🎟 *Free* 🕒 *Mar.–Oct., Mon.–Sat. 10–5, Sun. 2–5; Nov.–Feb., Mon.–Sat. 10–4, Sun. 1–4.*

At the **Wedgwood Museum and Visitor Centre** you can learn about the history of Wedgwood, and see samples of its ware. The visitor center has craft demonstrations and also displays Doulton and Minton ware. Both the museum and visitor center have shops where you can buy firsts and seconds. ✉ *Off A5035, Barlaston* ☎ *01782/371900* ⊕ *www.wedgwoodmuseum.org.uk* 🎟 *£10 joint ticket, £6 museum only* 🕒 *Weekdays 9–5, weekends 10–5.*

facade remains splendid. The house is surrounded by woods, elaborate gardens, greenhouses, rock gardens, and the most famous water cascade in the kingdom—all designed by two great landscape artists, Capability Brown in the 18th century and, in the 19th century, Joseph Paxton, an engineer as well as a brilliant gardener. The gravity-fed Emperor Fountain can shoot as high as 300 feet. Perennially popular with children, the farmyard area has milking demonstrations at 3 and an adventure playground. ■TIP➔ Plan on at least a half day to explore the grounds; avoid Sunday if you prefer not to be with the heaviest crowds.

Inside are intricate carvings, Van Dyck portraits, superb furniture, and a few fabulous rooms, including the Sculpture Gallery, the library, and the Blue Drawing Room, where you can see two of the most famous portraits in Britain, Sir Joshua Reynolds's *Georgiana, Duchess of Devonshire, and Her Baby,* and John Singer Sargent's enormous *Acheson Sisters.* Chatsworth is 4 mi northeast of Bakewell. ⊠ *Off B6012* ☎ *01246/582204* ⊕ *www.chatsworth.org* ✉ *House, gardens, and farmyard £16; house and gardens £12; gardens only, £7.75; parking £2* ⊙ *Mid-Mar.–late Dec., house daily 11–5:30, gardens daily 11–6, farmyard daily 10:30–5:30; last admission 1 hr before closing.*

Fodor's Choice **Haddon Hall.** Stately house scholar Hugo Montgomery-Massingberd
★ has called this storybook medieval manor set along the River Wye 2 mi southeast of Bakewell, "the *beau idéal* of the English country house." Unlike other trophy homes that are marble Palladian monuments to a European grand tour, Haddon Hall remains quintessentially English in appearance, bristling with crenellations and stepped roofs and landscaped with rose gardens.

The house, built between 1180 and 1565, passed into the ownership of the dukes of Rutland and remained largely unaltered until the early 20th century, when the ninth duke undertook a superlative restoration. This revealed a series of early decorative 15th-century frescoes in the chapel. The finest of the intricate plasterwork and wooden paneling is best seen in the superb Long Gallery on the first floor. Baking is still done in the bread ovens in the well-preserved Tudor kitchen. Here, too, is the unique collection of Gothic dole cupboards, some original to the house, which would have been filled with food and placed outside for those in need. The wider world saw the hall in *Pride and Prejudice* (2005) and *The Other Boleyn Girl* (2008). ⊠ *A6* ☎ *01629/812855* ⊕ *www.haddonhall.co.uk* ✉ *£9.50, parking £1.50* ⊙ *May–Sept., daily noon–5; Apr. and Oct., Sat.–Mon. noon–5; last admission 1 hr before closing.*

WHERE TO EAT AND STAY
For expanded hotel reviews, visit Fodors.com.

£££ ✗ **Devonshire Arms.** This stone 18th-century coaching inn, which counts
BRITISH Charles Dickens as one of its many famous visitors, is divided into a cozy bar area and a modern brasserie, both serving great homemade fare. Typical dishes include beef fillet with a morel-and-Madeira sauce, and rice pudding with raisins and orange marmalade. There's an excellent snack menu, too. The inn is 2 mi south of Chatsworth and also has eight bedrooms. ⊠ *B6012, Beeley* ☎ *01629/733259* ⊕ *www.devonshirebeeley.co.uk.*

The Emperor Fountain enhances the bucolic landscape at Chatsworth, one of England's most magnificent stately homes.

££££££ ✕ **Fischer's.** The Fischer family bought this stately Edwardian manor on
BRITISH the edge of the Chatsworth estate, 4 mi north of Bakewell, to house
★ their restaurant. Intimate and formal, the restaurant takes pride in using
high-quality local products; on the fixed-price menus you'll find wild
venison, Derbyshire pork and lamb, and Yorkshire rhubarb, all presented with care and aplomb. If you can't decide, there's a six-course
tasting menu of specialty dishes (£68). With 11 elegant bedrooms here
as well, you might consider staying the night. Sunday dinner is for overnight guests only. ⌧ *Baslow Hall, Calver Rd., Baslow* ☎ *01246/583259*
⊕ *www.fischers-baslowhall.co.uk.*

£ ✕ **The Old Original Bakewell Pudding Shop.** Given the plethora of local
BRITISH rivals, it takes a bold establishment to claim its Bakewell puddings
as "original," but there's certainly nothing wrong with those served
here, eaten hot with custard or cream. The oak-beam dining room also
turns out commendable main courses of Yorkshireman (batter pudding with meat and vegetables) and steak-and-ale pie. ⌧ *The Square*
☎ *01629/812193* ⊕ *www.bakewellpuddingshop.co.uk.*

££ ⌾ **Haddon House Farm.** This may be a working farm, but there's noth-
B&B/INN ing workaday about the fresh and imaginatively designed rooms (with
★ themes such as Monet and Shakespeare) that the Nicholls husband-
and-wife team created. **Pros:** charming and obliging hosts; outdoor hot
tub; easily accessible by bus. **Cons:** no credit cards; no single rooms.
⌧ *Haddon Rd.* ☎ *01629/814024* ⊕ *www.great-place.co.uk* ⇄ *4 rooms*
⌂ *In-room: no a/c, Wi-Fi. In-hotel: parking, some age restrictions* ▭ *No
credit cards* ⎢⊙⎢ *Breakfast.*

MATLOCK

8 mi southeast of Bakewell, 5 mi south of Haddon Hall.

In the heart of the Derbyshire Dales, Matlock and its near neighbor Matlock Bath are former spa towns compressed into a narrow gorge on the River Derwent. Some surviving Regency buildings in Matlock testify to its former importance, although it's less impressive an ensemble than that presented by Buxton. The surroundings, however, are particularly beautiful.

The Matlock River Illuminations, a flotilla of lighted boats, shimmers after dark along the still waters of the Derwent. The festival takes place on weekends September to late October.

GETTING HERE AND AROUND

Matlock is served by National Express and TransPeak buses from Manchester's Chorlton Street Bus Station. The town is about a one-hour, 40-minute drive southeast on the A6 from Manchester.

ESSENTIALS

Visitor Information Matlock (⊠ *Crown Sq.* ☎ *01629/583388* ⊕ *www. visitpeakdistrict.com*).

EXPLORING

★ **Hardwick Hall.** Few houses in England evoke the late Elizabethan era as vividly as Hardwick Hall, a beautiful stone mansion and treasure trove. The facade glitters with myriad windows, making it easy to see why the house came to be known as "Hardwick Hall, more glass than wall." ■ TIP→ Choose a sunny day to see the rooms and their treasures at their best. The vast state apartments well befit their original chatelaine, Bess of Hardwick. By marrying a succession of four rich husbands, she had become second only to Queen Elizabeth in her wealth when work on this house began. She took possession in 1597, and four years later made an inventory of the important rooms and their contents—furniture, tapestries, and embroideries. Unique patchwork hangings, probably made from clerical copes and altar frontals taken from monasteries and abbeys, grace the entrance hall, and superb 16th- and 17th-century tapestries cover the walls of the main staircase and first-floor High Great Chamber. The collection of Elizabethan embroideries—table carpets, cushions, bed hangings, and pillowcases—is second to none. There are also fine examples of plasterwork, painted friezes, and ornamental chimneypieces. Outside, you can visit the walled gardens. Hardwick Hall is 10 mi east of Matlock. Access is signposted from Junction 29 of the M1 motorway. ⊠ *Doe Lea, Chesterfield* ☎ *01246/850430* ⊕ *www. nationaltrust.org.uk* ⊠ *£9.98; gardens only, £5.04* ⊙ *House mid-Mar.–Oct., Wed.–Sun. noon–4:30; Dec., weekends noon–3. Gardens mid-Mar.–Oct., Wed.–Sun. noon–4:30; Dec. weekends 11–3; last admission 30 mins before closing. Grounds daily 8–dusk.*

☺ **Heights of Abraham Country Park and Caverns.** At Matlock Bath, 2 mi south of Matlock, river and valley views unfold from the curving line of buildings that makes up the village. Aside from riverside strolls, the major attraction is the cable-car ride across the River Derwent that takes you to this park on the crags above, with a visitor center and café. The all-inclusive ticket allows access to the woodland walks and nature

9

Well Dressing

Unique to the Peak District is the custom of well dressing, when certain wells or springs are decorated with elaborate pictures made of flowers. Frames up to 4 feet wide and 6 feet high, covered with a base of clay, are filled with a colorful mosaic of seeds, grasses, berries, and moss as well as flowers and flower petals, a process that involves a team of workers and takes about a week to complete. Although the designs usually incorporate religious themes such as biblical stories, they are a Christian veneer over an ancient pagan celebration of the water's life-giving powers. The well dressing and blessing ceremony, usually accompanied by a brass band, heralds the start of several days of festivities.

Of the 70 or so towns and villages that continue this summertime tradition, Tissington (May), south of Matlock; Bakewell (early July); and, near Chatsworth, Eyam (late August) are among the most popular. Check with local tourist offices for information.

trails of the 60-acre park, as well as entry to a cavern and a guided descent into an old lead mine, where workers toiled by candlelight. ⊠ *A6, Matlock Bath* ☎ *01629/582365* ⊕ *www.heightsofabraham.com* 🎟 *£12.50* 🕙 *Mid-Feb.–late Feb. and Oct., daily 10–4:30; early to mid-Mar., weekends 10–4:30; late Mar.–Sept., daily 10–5.*

WHERE TO STAY

For expanded hotel reviews, visit Fodors.com.

££
B&B/INN
Dower House. This charming 16th-century stone structure sitting at the head of the pretty village of Winster, about 6 mi west of Matlock, has all you expect from a small country-house stay. **Pros:** country house character; very peaceful; beautifully furnished. **Cons:** no credit cards; minimum stay on weekends; not easily accessible without a car. ⊠ *Main St., Winster* ☎ *01629/650931* ⊕ *www.thedowerhousewinster.com* 🛏 4 *rooms* ⚹ *In-room: no a/c. In-hotel: some age restrictions* ⊟ *No credit cards* 🍽 *Breakfast.*

SPORTS AND THE OUTDOORS

One of the major trails in the Peak District, **High Peak Trail** runs for 17 mi from Cromford (south of Matlock Bath) to Dowlow, following the route of an old railroad. For information, guidebooks, guide services, and maps, contact any Peak District National Park Office.

Red House Stables (⊠ *Old Rd., Darley Dale* ☎ *01629/733583* ⊕ *www. workingcarriages.com*) arranges carriage trips through the local countryside. An hour-long ride costs £30.

CASTLETON

24 mi northwest of Matlock, 10 mi northwest of Chatsworth, 9 mi northeast of Buxton.

The area around Castleton, in Hope Valley, contains the most famous manifestations of the geology of the Peak District. A number of caves and mines are open to the public, including some former lead mines and Blue John mines (amethystine spar; the unusual name is a corruption of the French *bleu-jaune* (meaning "blue yellow"). The limestone caverns attract many people, which means that pretty Castleton shows a certain commercialization. Summer brings the crowds, many of which poke around in the numerous shops displaying Blue John jewelry and wares.

GETTING HERE AND AROUND

Hope Rail Station, 1½ mi from the center of Castleton, is served by the Manchester–Sheffield railroad line. By car, Castleton is a one-hour drive southeast on the A6 from Manchester.

ESSENTIALS

Visitor Information Castleton (✉ *Castle St.* ☎ *01433/620679* ⊕ *www. visitpeakdistrict.com*).

EXPLORING

Peak Cavern. Caves riddle the entire town and the surrounding area, and in the massive Peak Caverns—reputedly Derbyshire's largest natural cave—rope making has been done on a great ropewalk for more than 400 years. You can still see the remains of the 17th-century rope makers' village. ✉ *Off Goosehill* ☎ *01433/620285* ⊕ *www.devilsarse.com* ▭ *£8.25, £14 joint ticket with Speedwell Cavern* ⊙ *Apr.–Oct., daily 10–5; Nov.–Mar., weekends 10–5, call ahead for weekday hrs.*

Peveril Castle. In 1176 Henry II added the square tower to this Norman castle, whose ruins occupy a dramatic crag above the town. The castle has superb views—from here you can still clearly see a curving section of the medieval defensive earthworks in the town center below. Peveril Castle is protected on its west side by a 230-foot-deep gorge formed by a collapsed cave. Park in the town center, from which it's a steep climb up. ✉ *Market Pl.* ☎ *01433/620613* ⊕ *www.english-heritage.org. uk* ▭ *£4.30* ⊙ *Apr.–June, Sept., and Oct., daily 10–5; July and Aug., daily 10–6; Nov.–Mar., Thurs.–Mon. 10–4.*

Speedwell Cavern. The area's most exciting cavern by far is Speedwell Cavern, where 105 slippery steps lead down to old lead-mine tunnels, blasted out by 19th-century miners. Here you transfer to a small boat for the claustrophobic ¼-mi chug through an illuminated access tunnel to the cavern itself. At this point you're 600 feet underground, in the deepest public-access cave in Britain, with views farther down to the so-called Bottomless Pit, a water-filled cavern. A shop on-site sells items made of the Blue John mineral. Speedwell Cavern is at the bottom of Winnats Pass, 1 mi west of Castleton. ✉ *Winnats Pass* ☎ *01433/620512* ⊕ *www.speedwellcavern.co.uk* ▭ *£8.75; £14 joint ticket with Peak Cavern* ⊙ *Daily 10–5; last tour 1 hr before closing.*

WHERE TO STAY

For expanded hotel reviews, visit Fodors.com.

£   ▣ **Bargate Cottage.** Dating to 1650, this cottage at the top of Market Place below the castle is one of Castleton's B&B treasures. **Pros:** peaceful location; great breakfasts. **Cons:** small rooms; no credit cards. ✉ *Market Pl.* ☎ *01433/620201* ⊕ *www.bargatecottage.co.uk* ⬅3

B&B/INN

9

rooms 丛 *In-room: no a/c. In-hotel: some age restrictions* ➡ *No credit cards* ¦○¦ *Breakfast.*

££   ⊡ **Underleigh House.** Peaceful is the word for the location of this
B&B/INN   creeper-clad cottage and barn at the end of a lane in lovely walking
country. **Pros:** superb views; ample breakfasts. **Cons:** minimum stays
on weekends; surcharge for credit cards. ✉ *Off Edale Rd., Hope*
☎ *01433/621372* ⊕ *www.underleighhouse.co.uk* ⤵ *3 rooms, 2 suites*
丛 *In-room: no a/c. In-hotel: parking, some pets allowed, some age*
restrictions ¦○¦ *Breakfast.*

EN ROUTE   Heading northwest to Edale, the most spectacular driving route is over
Winnats Pass, through a narrow, boulder-strewn valley. Beyond are the
tops of Mam Tor (where there's a lookout point) and the hamlet of
Barber Booth, after which you run into Edale.

EDALE

5 mi northwest of Castleton.

At Edale, an extremely popular hiking center, you're truly in the Peak
District wilds. This sleepy, straggling village, in the shadow of Mam
Tor and Lose Hill and the moorlands of the high plateau known as
Kinder Scout (2,088 feet), lies among some of the most breathtaking
scenery in Derbyshire. England can show little wilder scenery than
Kinder Scout, with its ragged edges of grit stone and its interminable
leagues of heather and peat.

GETTING HERE AND AROUND

Edale Rail Station has service to Manchester and Sheffield. By car, Edale
is a one-hour drive southeast on the A6 from Manchester.

ESSENTIALS

Visitor Information Moorlands Centre (✉ *Fieldhead* ☎ *01433/670207*
⊕ *www.visitpeakdistrict.com).*

EXPLORING

National Park Information Centre. In the village, this visitor center has
maps, guides, and information on all the walks in the area. There's limited accommodation in the village (all B&B-style), but the information
center can provide a list or point you in the right direction. ✉ *Fieldhead*
☎ *01433/670207* ⊕ *www.peakdistrict.com* ☉ *Apr.–Oct., daily 9:30–5;*
Nov.–Mar., weekdays 10–3:30, weekends 9:30–4:30.

Old Nag's Head. This pub at the top of the village has marked the official
start of the Pennine Way since 1965. Call in at the Hiker's Bar, sit by the
fire, and tuck into hearty bar meals and hot toddies. On Monday and
Tuesday in winter, when this pub is closed, the Ramblers' Inn, at the
other end of the village, is open. ✉ *Grinsbrook Booth* ☎ *01433/670291.*

SPORTS AND THE OUTDOORS

Edale is the starting point of the 250-mi-long **Pennine Way** (⊕ *www.*
nationaltrail.co.uk), which crosses Kinder Scout. If you plan to attempt
this, seek local advice first, because bad weather can make the walk
treacherous. However, several much shorter routes into the Edale Valley,
like the 8-mi route west to Hayfield, give you a taste.

The Lake District

WORD OF MOUTH

"Kendal is considered the gateway to the southern lakes. The rule of thumb is that the northern Lake District (including Keswick) has the wilder, more dramatic scenery, while the southern area is more chocolate-box pretty. Ambleside is also a possibility in the south. My favorite way to stay in the Lakes is a farm bed-and-breakfast."

—Morgana

WELCOME TO THE LAKE DISTRICT

TOP REASONS TO GO

★ **Hiking the trails:**
Whether it's a demanding trek or a gentle stroll, walking is the way to see the Lake District at its best.

★ **Mucking around in boats:** There's nowhere better for renting a small boat or taking a cruise. The Coniston Boating Centre and Derwentwater Marina near Keswick are possible places to start.

★ **Literary landscapes:**
The Lake District has a rich literary history, in the children's books of Beatrix Potter, in the writings of John Ruskin, and in the poems of Wordsworth. Stop at any of the writers' homes to enrich your experience.

★ **Pints and pubs:** A pint of real ale in one of the region's inns, such as the Drunken Duck near Hawkshead, may never taste as good as after a day of walking.

★ **Sunrise at Castlerigg:**
The stone circle at Castlerigg, in a hollow ringed by peaks, is a reminder of the region's ancient history.

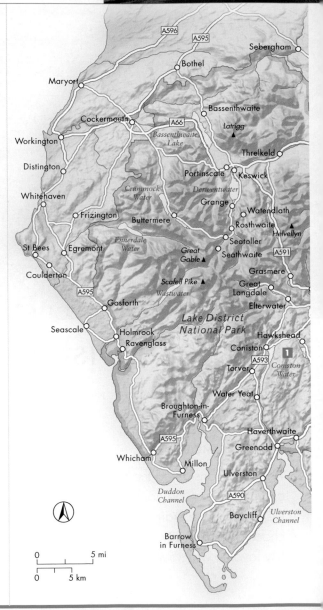

1 The Southern Lakes. The southern lakes and valleys contain the park's most popular, and thus most overcrowded in summer, destinations, incorporating the largest body of water, Windermere, as well as most of the quintessential Lakeland towns and villages: Bowness, Ambleside, Grasmere, Elterwater, Coniston, and Hawkshead. To the east and west of this cluster of habitation, the valleys and fells climb to some beautiful upland country.

2 Penrith and the Northern Lakes. In the north, the landscape opens out across the bleaker fells to reveal challenging, spectacular walking country. Here, in the northern lakes, south of Keswick and Cockermouth, you have the best chance to get away from the crowds. This region's northwestern reaches are largely unexplored, while the northeast is home to Penrith, a bustling market town.

GETTING ORIENTED

The Lake District is in northwest England, some 70 mi north of the industrial belt that stretches from Liverpool to Manchester, and south of Scotland. The major gateway from the south is Kendal, and from the north, Penrith. Both are on the M6 motorway. Main-line trains stop at Oxenholme, near Kendal, with a branch linking Oxenholme to Kendal and Windermere. Windermere, in the south, is the most obvious starting point and has museums, cafés, and gift shops. But the farther (and higher) you can get from the southern towns, the more you'll appreciate the area's spectacular landscapes. The Lake District National Park breaks into two reasonably distinct sections: the gentler, rolling south and the craggier, wilder north.

10

CLASSIC ENGLISH DESSERTS

The English love to round off lunch or dinner with something sweet. British food is experiencing an ongoing revival that has cooks bringing back favorites such as fool, trifle, spotted dick, and sticky toffee pudding, and making the most of seasonal fruits and traditional spices.

A dense texture and toffee sauce make sticky toffee pudding perfect for winter (above); trifle variation with strawberries and mascarpone (right, top); Eton mess (right, bottom) can use mixed berries.

"Sweet," "afters," "pudding," "dessert": all these refer informally to dessert; "sweets" are simply candies, though. In England dessert is as likely to be a delicate creamy confection as a warming fruit pie or a rich, hearty pudding. Winter is the perfect time for steamed puddings, made with currants, dried fruits, and spices such as cinnamon, nutmeg, cloves and ginger, or for hot fruit crumbles with custard. The warmer months bring an avalanche of fresh berries, and with them light, creamy desserts such as syllabub and fool come into their own. For many, the classic desserts such as sticky toffee pudding and spotted dick capture memories of growing up in the 20th century, even though rationing during and after World War II kept sweet things off the menu. No longer: dessert bars are becoming a trend in cities including London.

SPECIAL INGREDIENTS

Desserts may use wine and brandy, and other special items. These include **currants**—dried small black grapes—as well as dried fruits, candied fruit peel, and spices such as cinnamon, cloves, nutmeg, and ginger. **Quinces**, hard, apple-like fruits, can be combined with apples in a crumble or turned into a paste to accompany cheese. **Damsons** are acidic plums, made into jams, jellies, or wine.

HOT STEAMED PUDDINGS

These puddings are cooked slowly over boiling water. Sticky toffee pudding is a dark sponge cake, made with finely chopped dates or prunes and covered in a thick toffee sauce. The oddly named spotted dick is traditionally made with suet and steamed in a hot cloth, "spotted" with currants and other dried fruits, and served with custard. Another classic, Christmas pudding, dates from medieval times. Also known as plum pudding, it contains brandy, currants, and dried fruit, and is strong-flavored. Before the pudding steams for many hours, each family member stirs the mixture and makes a wish.

FRUIT CRUMBLES

Crumbles, similar to American crisps, were invented during wartime rationing when butter, flour, and sugar were too scarce to make pastry for pie. Tart Bramley apples native to England work well with cinnamon and cloves. Don't pass up rhubarb crumble, especially around February when the delicate bright pink forced variety of rhubarb from Yorkshire makes its brief appearance.

TRIFLE, FOOL, AND SYLLABUB

Dating from Tudor times, fool is simply a sharp fruit, usually gooseberry, swirled with whipped cream and a little sugar. Trifle evolved from fool, and begins with a layer of sponge (soaked in port, sherry, or Madeira wine) and Jell-O or

jam, topped with custard and whipped cream. Light but flavorful, syllabub is made from wine or brandy infused overnight with lemon and sugar and whipped with cream.

ETON MESS

Invented at the famous Eton College, after, it is said, a Labrador dog accidentally sat on a picnic basket, Eton Mess is still served at the annual prize-giving ceremony. This unfussy summer dessert consists of strawberries mixed with whipped cream and crushed meringue.

SUMMER PUDDING

Fresh summer berries, bread, and a little sugar are all that should go into a summer pudding. Left for several hours so that the sweet and sharp flavors develop, the pudding turns out a deep red color, and is often served with a touch of cream.

MORE FAVORITES

Grasmere gingerbread from the Lake District is a dense spicy cake flavored with ginger and golden syrup. Eccles cakes, from Eccles in Lancashire, are round pastry cases, slashed three times for the Holy Trinity and filled with syrupy currants. Bakewell pudding or tart has a layer of jam and almond sponge, topped with flaked almonds or white icing.

—by Sarah Christie

10

Updated by
Julius Honnor

"Let nature be your teacher." Wordsworth's ideal comes true in this popular region of jagged mountains, waterfalls, wooded valleys, and stone-built villages. No mountains in Britain give a greater impression of majesty; deeper and bluer lakes can be found, but none that fit so readily into the surrounding scene. Outdoors enthusiasts flock to this region for boating or hiking, while literary types visit the homes of Beatrix Potter and other favorite writers.

In 1951 the Lake District National Park was created here from parts of the counties of Cumberland, Westmorland, and Lancashire. The Lake District is a contour map come to life, covering an area of approximately 885 square mi and holding 16 major lakes and countless smaller stretches of water. The scenery is key to all the park's best activities: you can cross it by car in about an hour, but this is an area meant to be walked or boated or climbed. The mountains are not high by international standards—Scafell Pike, England's highest peak, is only 3,210 feet above sea level—but they can be tricky to climb. In spring, many higher summits remain snowcapped long after the weather below has turned mild.

The poets Wordsworth and Coleridge, and other English writers, found the Lake District an inspiring setting for their work, and visitors have followed ever since, to walk, go boating, or just relax and take in the views. Seeing the homes and other sights associated with these writers can occupy part of a trip.

This area can be one of Britain's most appealing reservoirs of calm, though in summer the lakeside towns, however appealing, can lose their charm when cars and tour buses clog the narrow streets. Similarly, the walks and hiking trails that crisscross the region seem less inviting when you share them with a crowd. Despite the challenges of popularity, the Lake District has managed tourism and the landscape in a manner that retains the character of the villages and the natural environment.

Explore beyond Windermere and Keswick to discover little farming communities eking out a living from the occasionally harsh conditions.

Today, too, a new generation of hotel and restaurant owners is making more creative use of the edible and other assets of the Lakeland fells, and chic modern or foodie-oriented establishments are springing up next to traditional tearooms and chintz-filled inns.

Off-season visits can be a real treat. All those inns and bed-and-breakfasts that turn away crowds in summer are eager for business the rest of the year (and their rates drop accordingly). It's not an easy task to find a succession of sunny days in the Lake District—some malicious statisticians allot to it about 250 rainy days a year—but when the sun breaks through and brightens the surfaces of the lakes, it is an away-from-it-all place to remember.

LAKE DISTRICT PLANNER

WHEN TO GO

The Lake District is one of the rainiest areas in Britain, but June, July, and August hold the best hope of fine weather and are the time for all the major festivals. You will, however, be sharing the lakes with thousands of other people. If you must travel at this time, turn up early at popular museums and attractions, and expect to work to find parking. April and May, as well as September and October, are good alternatives. Later and earlier in the year there will be even more space and freedom, but many attractions close, and from December to March, snow on high ground may preclude serious hill walking without heavy-duty equipment.

PLANNING YOUR TIME

You could spend months tramping the hills, valleys, and fells of the Lake District, or, in three days you could drive through the major towns and villages. The key is not to do too much in too short a time. If you are traveling by public transportation, many places will be off-limits. As a base, Windermere has the best transport links, but it can be crowded and it has less character than some of the smaller towns. Ambleside and Keswick also have plenty of sleeping and eating options; for a more intimate version of village life, try Coniston, Hawkshead, or Grasmere. Keep in mind that the northern and western lakes have the most dramatic scenery and offer the best opportunity to escape the summertime hordes.

The Lake District may be compact, but it is not a place to hurry. Allow plenty of time for walking: paths can be steep and rocky, and in any case you'll want to stop frequently to look at the great views. A good day's walking with a picnic can be done from nearly anywhere. Driving brings its own speed inhibitors, from sheep on the roads to slow tractors.

You're likely to be based down near lake level, but try to experience the hills, too. If you're short of time, a drive over one of the high passes such as Honister will give you a glimpse of the enormity of the landscape.

10

GETTING HERE AND AROUND

AIR TRAVEL

Manchester Airport has its own rail station with direct service to Carlisle, Windermere, and Barrow-in-Furness. Manchester is 70 mi from the southern part of the Lake District.

Contact **Manchester Airport** (⊠ *Near Junctions 5 and 6 of M56* ☎ *08712/710711* ⊕ *www.manchesterairport.co.uk*).

BOAT TRAVEL

Whether you rent a boat or take a ride on a modern launch or vintage vessels, getting out on the water is a fun (and often useful) way to see the Lake District. Windermere, Coniston Water, and Derwentwater all have boat rental facilities.

BUS TRAVEL

National Express serves the region from London's Victoria Coach Station and from Manchester's Chorlton Street Station. Average travel time to Kendal is just over 7 hours from London; to Windermere, 7½ hours; and to Keswick, 8¼ hours. From Manchester there's one bus a day to Windermere via Ambleside, Grasmere, and Keswick. There's direct bus service to the Lake District from Carlisle, Lancaster, and York. Traveline handles public transportation inquiries.

Stagecoach in Cumbria provides local service between Lakeland towns and through the valleys and high passes. Contact Traveline for an up-to-date timetable. Bus service between main tourist centers is fairly frequent on weekdays, but much reduced on weekends and bank holidays. Don't count on reaching the more remote parts of the area by bus. Off-the-beaten-track touring requires a car or strong legs. A one-week Cumbria Goldrider ticket (£23.50), available on the bus, is valid on all routes. Explorer tickets (£9.75) are valid for a day on all routes.

Contacts **National Express** (☎ *08717/818178* ⊕ *www.nationalexpress.com*). **Traveline** (☎ *0871/200–2233* ⊕ *www.traveline.org.uk*).

CAR TRAVEL

A car is almost essential in the Lake District; bus service is limited and trains can get you to the edge of the national park but no farther. You can rent cars in Penrith and Kendal. Roads within the region are generally good, although minor routes and mountain passes can be steep and narrow. Warning signs are often posted if snow or ice has made a road impassable; check local weather forecasts in winter before heading out. In July and August and during the long public holiday weekends, expect heavy traffic. The Lake District has plenty of parking lots; use them to avoid blocking narrow lanes.

To reach the Lake District by car from London, take M1 north to M6, getting off either at Junction 36 and joining A590/A591 west (around the Kendal bypass to Windermere) or at Junction 40, joining A66 direct to Keswick and the northern lakes region. Travel time to Kendal is about four to five hours, to Keswick five to six hours. Expect heavy traffic out of London on weekends.

TRAIN TRAVEL

There are direct trains from Manchester and Manchester airport to Windermere. For schedule information, call National Rail Enquiries. Two train companies serve the region from London's Euston Station: take a Virgin or Northern Rail train bound for Carlisle, Edinburgh, or Glasgow and change at Oxenholme for the branch line service to Kendal and Windermere. Average travel time to Windermere (including the change) is 4½ hours. If you're heading for Keswick, you can either take the train to Windermere and continue from there by Stagecoach bus (Bus 554/555/556; 70 minutes), or stay on the main London–Carlisle train to Penrith Station (four hours), from which Stagecoach buses (Bus X5) also run to Keswick (45 minutes). Direct trains from Manchester depart for Windermere five times daily (travel time two hours). First North Western runs a local service from Windermere and Barrow-in-Furness to Manchester Airport. National Rail can handle all questions about trains.

Train connections are good around the edges of the Lake District, but you must take the bus or drive to reach the central Lakeland region. Trains they are reduced, or nonexistent, on Sunday.

Contacts National Rail Enquiries (☎ 0845/748–4950 ⊕ www.nationalrail. co.uk). **Northern Rail** (☎ 0845/000–0125 ⊕ www.northernrail.org). **Virgin Trains** (☎ 08719/774222 ⊕ www.virgintrains.co.uk).

NATIONAL PARK

The Lake District National Park head office (and main visitor center) is at Brockhole, north of Windermere. It's closed November through mid-February. Helpful regional national-park information centers sell books and maps, book accommodations, and provide walking advice.

Contacts Lake District National Park (✉ Brockhole, A591, Ambleside Rd., near Windermere ☎ 015394/46601 ⊕ www.lake-district.gov.uk). **Bowness Bay** (✉ Glebe Rd., Bowness-on-Windermere ☎ 015394/42895). **Keswick** (✉ Moot Hall, Main St. ☎ 017687/72645). **Ullswater** (✉ Beckside Car Park, Glenridding ☎ 017684/82414).

TOURS

Mountain Goat and Lakes Supertours provide minibus sightseeing tours with skilled local guides. Half- and full-day tours, some of which really get off the beaten track, depart from Bowness, Windermere, Ambleside, and Grasmere.

Walks range from gentle, literary-oriented strolls to challenging ridge hikes. The Lake District National Park or tourist information centers can put you in touch with qualified guides. Blue Badge Guides can provide experts on the area. English Lakeland Ramblers organizes single-base and inn-to-inn guided tours of the Lake District. Lake District Walker offers guided day hikes for different abilities. Go Higher will take you on challenging routes and provides technical gear and courses on mountaineering skills.

Contacts Blue Badge Guides (☎ 020/7403–1115 ⊕ www.blue-badge.org.uk). **English Lakeland Ramblers** (☎ 703/680–4276, 800/724–8801 in U.S. ⊕ www. ramblers.com). **Go Higher** (✉ High Dyon Side, Distington ☎ 01946/830476

10

⊕ *www.gohigher.co.uk*). **Lake District Walker** (☎ *01900/822448* ⊕ *www. lakedistrict walker.co.uk*). **Lakes Supertours** (✉ *1 High St., Windermere* ☎ *015394/42751* ⊕ *www.lakes-supertours.co.uk*). **Mountain Goat** (✉ *Victoria St., Windermere* ☎ *015394/45161* ⊕ *www.mountain-goat.com*).

RESTAURANTS

Lakeland restaurants increasingly reflect a growing British awareness of good food. Local sourcing and international influences are common, and even old Cumberland favorites are being creatively reinvented. Pub dining in the Lake District can be excellent—the hearty fare often makes use of local ingredients such as Herdwick lamb, and real ales are a good accompaniment. If you're going walking, ask your hotel or B&B about making you a packed lunch. Some local delicatessens also offer this service.

HOTELS

Your choices include everything from small country inns to grand lakeside hotels; many hotels offer the option of paying a higher price that includes dinner as well as breakfast. The regional mainstay is the bed-and-breakfast, from the house on Main Street to isolated farmhouses. Most country hotels and B&Bs gladly cater to hikers and can provide on-the-spot information. Wherever you stay, book well in advance for summer visits, especially those in late July and August. In winter many accommodations close for a month or two. On weekends and in summer it may be hard to get a reservation for a single night. Internet access is improving, and an increasing number of hotels and cafés offer Wi-Fi access.

WHAT IT COSTS IN POUNDS					
	£	££	£££	££££	£££££
Restaurants	under £10	£10–£14	£15–£19	£20–£25	over £25
Hotels	under £70	£70–£120	£121–£160	£161–£220	over £220

Restaurant prices are per person for a main course or equivalent combination of smaller dishes at dinner excluding tax. Hotels prices reflect the rack rate of a standard double room for two people in high season, including 20% V.A.T. Check online for off-season rates and special deals or discounts.

VISITOR INFORMATION

Contacts Cumbria Tourism (✉ *Windermere Rd., Staveley, Kendal* ☎ *015398/22222* ⊕ *www.golakes.co.uk*).

THE SOUTHERN LAKES

Among the many attractions here are the small resort towns clustered around Windermere, England's largest lake, and the area's hideaway valleys, rugged walking centers, and monuments rich in literary associations. This is the easiest part of the Lake District to reach, with Kendal, the largest town, just a short distance from the M6 motorway. An obvious route from Kendal takes in Windermere, the area's natural touring center, before moving north through Ambleside and Rydal Water to Grasmere. Some of the loveliest Lakeland scenery is to be found by then turning south, through Elterwater, Hawkshead, and Coniston.

The design of the famous, fanciful topiary garden at Levens Hall dates back to the 17th century.

KENDAL

70 mi north of Manchester.

The southern gateway to the Lake District is the "Auld Gray Town" of Kendal, outside the national park and less touristy than the towns to the north. You may want to stay closer to the action, but the town has some worthwhile sights. Nearby hills frame Kendal's gray stone houses and provide some delightful walks; you can also explore the ruins of Kendal Castle. ■TIP➜ Pack a slab of Kendal mint cake, the local peppermint candy that British walkers and climbers swear by. It's on sale around the region.

10

The town's motto, "Wool Is My Bread," refers to its importance as a textile center in northern England before the Industrial Revolution. It was known for manufacturing woolen cloth, especially Kendal Green, which archers favored. Away from the main road are quiet courtyards and winding medieval streets known as "ginnels." Wool merchants used these for easy access to the River Kent.

GETTING HERE AND AROUND

Kendal is just off the M6, about 70 mi north of Manchester. It has train service via a branch line from Oxenholme, and National Express bus service from London as well. It's the largest town in the area but is still plenty small enough to walk around.

ESSENTIALS

Visitor Information Kendal (✉ *Town Hall, Highgate* ☎ *01539/725758*).

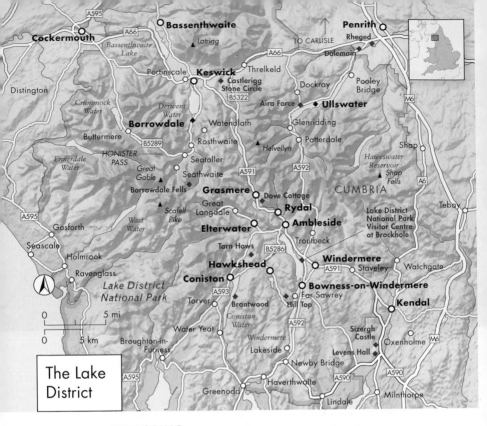

The Lake District

EXPLORING

★ **Abbot Hall.** One of the region's finest art galleries, Abbot Hall occupies a Palladian-style Georgian mansion built in 1759. In the permanent collection are works by Victorian artist and critic John Ruskin, who lived near Coniston, and by 18th-century portrait painter George Romney, who worked (and died) in Kendal. The gallery also owns some good contemporary British art and mounts a changing calendar of high-profile exhibits of 20th- and 21st-century art. There's an excellent café. Abbot Hall is on the River Kent, next to the parish church. The **Museum of Lakeland Life,** with exhibits on blacksmithing and wheelwrighting and a wonderful re-creation of a period pharmacy, is in the former stable block of the hall, on the same site. ✉ *Off Highgate* ☎ *01539/722464* ⊕ *www.abbothall.org.uk* ✉ *Abbot Hall £6, Museum of Lakeland Life £5, combined ticket £7.50* ☉ *Apr.–Oct., Mon.–Sat. 10:30–5; Nov.–mid-Dec. and Jan.–Mar., Mon.–Sat. 10:30–4.*

★ **Levens Hall.** An Elizabethan house and the home of the Bagot family, Levens Hall is famous for its topiary garden, probably the most distinctive in the world. Laid out in 1694, the garden retains its original design, and the yew and beech hedges, cut into complex shapes that resemble enormous chess pieces, rise among a profusion of flowers. The house contains a stunning medieval hall with oak paneling, ornate plasterwork, Jacobean furniture, and Cordova goat-leather wallpaper. You can easily spend a couple of hours here admiring the place or getting lost in the living willow labyrinth. There's a play area for children. Levens Hall is 4 mi south of Kendal. ⊠ *Off A590, Levens* ☎ *015395/60321* ⊕ *www. levenshall.co.uk* ✎ *£11.50; gardens only, £8.50* ⊘ *Mid-Apr.–mid-Oct., Sun.–Thurs., house noon–4:30, last admission at 4; gardens 10–5.*

Sizergh Castle. One of the Lake District's finest fortified houses, Sizergh Castle has a 58-foot-tall defensive peel tower that dates from 1340, when Scottish raids were feared. It has been the home of the Strickland family for more than 760 years. Expanded in Elizabethan times, the castle includes outstanding oak-paneled interiors with intricately carved chimneypieces and oak furniture. The estate has a rock garden with a large collection of ferns, two lakes, an orchard, and an ancient woodland; there are good walks here, too. Sizergh is 3½ mi south of Kendal. ⊠ *Off A591, Sizergh* ☎ *015395/60951* ⊕ *www.nationaltrust. org.uk* ✎ *£7.15; gardens only, £4.65* ⊘ *Castle mid-Mar.–Oct., Sun.– Thurs. 1–5 (also noon–1 by guided tour); gardens mid-Mar.–Oct., Mon.–Sun. 11–5.*

WAINWRIGHT'S GUIDES

Alfred Wainwright (1907-91), an accountant, became one of travel writing's most famous authors. First published in the 1950s and 1960s, his handwritten, illustrated guides have sold more than 2 million copies; these classics are still sold in area bookstores. The gruff Wainwright seemed to want the hills to himself, yet he lovingly created 49 books that continue to introduce people to the Lakeland mountains.

WHERE TO EAT AND STAY

The Brewery Arts Centre has other good dining options in Kendal, including the Grain Store restaurant and the theatrical Warehouse Café.

For expanded hotel reviews, visit Fodors.com.

££
MODERN BRITISH

✕ **The New Moon.** Small but sleek, this restaurant with an open fire and artfully battered floorboards has won a good local reputation for high-quality dishes. The vegetarian selections are always worthwhile, and the sometimes-adventurous Modern British cooking shows Mediterranean flourishes. Damson plum-and-pork sausages come with mashed potatoes and a red wine jus, and the fresh mussels are cooked in a curry sauce. Excellent lunches and the fixed-price early dinners (5:30–7 weekdays) are especially good value. ⊠ *129 Highgate* ☎ *01539/729254* ⊕ *www.newmoonrestaurant.co.uk* ⊘ *Closed Sun. and Mon.*

£
VEGETARIAN

✕ **Waterside Wholefoods Café.** In summer, grab one of the outdoor picnic tables overlooking the River Kent and order from the delicious, filling vegetarian (and mostly organic) menu of soups, buckwheat burgers, curried green lentil pie, salads, and cakes and scones. Don't miss the moist chocolate, walnut, and pear tart. ⊠ *2 Kent View, Waterside* ☎ *01539/729743* ⊕ *www.watersidewholefood.co.uk* ⊘ *Closed Sun. No dinner.*

££
B&B/INN
★

🏠 **Beech House.** Old-fashioned charm combines with modern luxuries like heated bathroom floors in this comfortable, ivy-clad town house.

10

Pros: homey rooms; locally made toiletries; private parking. **Cons:** steep walk up the hill to get here; two-night minimum on weekends. ⊠ *40 Greenside* ☎ *01539/720385* ⊕ *www.beechhouse-kendal.co.uk* 🛏 *6 rooms* ⚬ *In-room: no a/c, Wi-Fi* �🍽 *Breakfast.*

NIGHTLIFE AND THE ARTS

★ The **Brewery Arts Centre,** a contemporary complex in a converted brewery, includes an art gallery, theater, cinemas, and workshop spaces. The Grain Store, overlooking lovely gardens, serves lunch and dinner, the Warehouse Café offers savory crepes and occasional live performances, and Vats Bar has good beer and wine. In November the Mountain Film Festival presents productions aimed at climbers and walkers. ⊠ *Highgate* ☎ *01539/725133* ⊕ *www.breweryarts.co.uk* 🎫 *Free, except for special exhibitions* ⊙ *Mon.–Sat. 9 am–11 pm.*

SHOPPING

Kendal has a pleasant mix of chains, factory outlet stores, specialty shops, and traditional markets. The most interesting stores are tucked away in the quiet lanes and courtyards around Market Place, Finkle Street, and Stramongate. There's been a **market** in Kendal since 1189, and outdoor market stalls still line the center of town along Stramongate and Market Place every Wednesday and Saturday.

Henry Roberts Bookshop (⊠ *7 Stramongate* ☎ *01539/720425*), in Kendal's oldest house (a 16th-century cottage), stocks a superb selection of regional books.

K Village (⊠ *20 Stricklandgate* ☎ *01539/732363*), an outlet shopping center, sells some brand names at a discount: look for clothing, shoes, china, and more.

Peter Hall & Son (⊠ *Danes Rd., Staveley* ☎ *01539/821633*), a woodcraft workshop 5 mi north of Kendal along A591, sells ornamental bowls and gifts.

WINDERMERE AND BOWNESS-ON-WINDERMERE

10 mi northwest of Kendal.

For a natural touring base for the southern half of the Lake District, you don't need to look much farther than Windermere, though it does get crowded in summer. The resort became popular in the Victorian era when the arrival of the railway made the remote and rugged area accessible. Wordsworth and Ruskin opposed the railway, fearing an influx of tourists would ruin the tranquil place. Sure enough, the railway terminus in 1847 brought with it Victorian day-trippers, and the original hamlet of Birthwaite was subsumed by the new town of Windermere, named after the lake.

The town has continued to flourish, despite being a mile or so from the water; the development now spreads to envelop the slate-gray lakeside village of Bowness-on-Windermere. Bowness is the more attractive, but they are so close it doesn't matter where you stay.

Walk through an underwater tunnel and learn about the Lake District's fish and wildlife at the Lakes Aquarium near Windermere.

GETTING HERE AND AROUND

Windermere is easily reached by car, less than a half hour off the M6. There's also a train station at the eastern edge of town; change at Oxenholme for the branch line to Kendal and Windermere.

Bus 599, leaving every 20 minutes in summer (hourly the rest of the year) from outside the Windermere train station, links the town with Bowness.

ESSENTIALS

Visitor Information Windermere (✉ *Victoria St.* ☎ *015394/46499* ⊕ *www.southlakeland.gov.uk/tourism*).

EXPLORING
TOP ATTRACTIONS

Fodor's Choice ★ **Blackwell.** From 1898 to 1900, architect Mackay Hugh Baillie Scott (1865–1945) designed Blackwell, a quintessential Arts and Crafts house with carved paneling, delicate plasterwork, and a startling sense of light and space. Originally a retreat for a Manchester brewery owner, the house is a refined mix of modern style and the local vernacular. Lime-washed walls and sloping slate roofs make it fit elegantly into the landscape above Windermere, and the artful integration of decorative features into stained glass, stonework, friezes, and wrought iron gives the house a sleekly contemporary feel. Accessibility is wonderful here: nothing is roped off and you can even play the piano. Peruse the shop and try the honey-roast ham in the excellent tearoom. ✉ *B5360, Windermere* ☎ *015394/46139* ⊕ *www.blackwell.org.uk* ✐ *£7* ⊙ *Apr.–Oct., daily 10:30–5; Nov., Dec., and mid-Jan.–Mar., daily 10:30–4.*

★ **Lakes Aquarium.** On the quayside at the southern end of Windermere,
☺ this excellent aquarium has wildlife and waterside exhibits that focus
mostly on the region. The highlight is an underwater tunnel walk along
a re-created lake bed, complete with diving ducks, though the piranhas
and the bumblebee poison arrow frogs also have their fans. Friendly
staff are eager to talk about the exhibits. ■**TIP➔** Tickets are cheaper if
booked in advance online. ✉ *C5062, Lakeside* ☎ *015394/30153* ⊕ *www.*
lakesaquarium.co.uk ✍ *£9.15* ⊙ *Apr.–Oct., daily 9–6; Nov.–Mar., daily 9–5.*

OFF THE
BEATEN
PATH

Orrest Head. To escape the traffic and have a view of Windermere, set
out on foot and follow the signs to the left of the Windermere Hotel
(across from the train station) to Orrest Head. The shady, uphill path
winds through Elleray Wood, and after a 20-minute hike you arrive at a
rocky little summit (784 feet) with a panoramic view that encompasses
the Yorkshire fells, Morecambe Bay, and the beautiful Troutbeck Valley
(up which walks can be extended), toward the high passes to the north.

★ **Windermere.** No sights in Windermere or Bowness compete with that
of Windermere itself. At 11 mi long, 1½ mi wide, and 220 feet deep,
the lake is England's largest and stretches from Newby Bridge almost
to Ambleside, filling a rocky gorge between steep, thickly wooded hills.
The cold waters are superb for fishing, especially for Windermere char,
a rare lake trout. In summer, steamers and pleasure craft travel the lake,
and a trip across the island-studded waters, particularly the round-
trip from Bowness to Ambleside or down to Lakeside, is wonderful.
Although the lake's marinas and piers have some charm, you can bypass
the busier stretches of shoreline (in summer they can be packed solid) by
walking beyond the boathouses. Here, from among the pine trees, are
fine views across the lake. The **car ferry**, which also carries pedestrians,
crosses from Ferry Nab on the Bowness side of the lake to reach Far
Sawrey and the road to Hawkshead. A ferry has been running this route
since the 15th century. ☎ *01228/227653* ✍ *Car ferry £4 cars, 50p foot*
passengers ⊙ *Ferries every 20 mins Mon.–Sat. 6:50 am–9:50 pm, Sun.*
9:10 am–9:50 pm; Nov.–Mar. until 8:50 pm.

WORTH NOTING

☺ **Lake District National Park Visitor Cen-**
tre at Brockhole. Brockhole, a lakeside 19th-century mansion with 30
acres of terraced gardens sloping
down to the water, serves as the
park's official visitor center and
has exhibits about the local ecology, flora, and fauna. It's a good
stop at the start of your visit. The
gardens, designed in the Arts and
Crafts style by Thomas Mawson,
are at their best in spring, when
daffodils cover the lawns and azaleas burst into bloom. Among the
park activities are lectures, guided
walks, and demonstrations of traditional crafts. Some programs are

ARTS AND CRAFTS TRAIL

The Arts and Crafts movement of
the late 19th century flourished in
the Lake District, inspired by the
landscape as well as the writings
of John Ruskin, who lived here.
The search for meaningful style
produced many artistic gems
in the area's houses, churches,
and hotels. At Blackwell you can
purchase an Arts and Crafts Trail
map and explore the best of them.
Blackwell's Web site, ⊕ *www.*
blackwell.org.uk, has extensive
information about trail sites.

geared to children, who appreciate the adventure playground here. The bookstore carries hiking guides and maps, and you can picnic here or eat at the café-restaurant. Bus 555/559 goes to the visitor center from Windermere. **Windermere Lake Cruises** (☎ *015394/43360* ⊕ *www. windermere-lakecruises.co.uk*) runs a seasonal ferry service to the center from Waterhead in Ambleside. ✉ *Ambleside Rd., Windermere* ☎ *015394/46601* ⊕ *www.lake-district.gov.uk* 🎫 *Free, parking £2.50* ⊙ *Mid-Feb.–Oct., daily 10–5. Gardens daily dawn–dusk.*

○ **Lakeside & Haverthwaite Railway Company.** Vintage steam trains run on the 4-mi branch line between Lakeside and Haverthwaite along the lake's southern tip; you can add on a lake cruise. Departures from Lakeside coincide with ferry arrivals from Bowness and Ambleside; you can also depart from Haverthwaite. ✉ *A590, Haverthwaite* ☎ *015395/31594* ⊕ *www.lakesiderailway.co.uk* 🎫 *£6.20 round-trip* ⊙ *Apr.–Oct., daily 10:30–6.*

○ **World of Beatrix Potter.** A touristy attraction aimed at kids interprets the author's 23 tales with three-dimensional scenes of Peter Rabbit and more. Skip it if you can and visit Potter's former home at Hill Top and the Beatrix Potter Gallery in Hawkshead. ✉ *The Old Laundry, Crag Brow, Bowness-on-Windermere* ☎ *015394/88444* ⊕ *www.hop-skip-jump.com* 🎫 *£6.75* ⊙ *Easter–Sept., daily 10–5:30; Oct.–Easter, daily 10–4:30.*

WHERE TO EAT

££
BRITISH
✕ **Angel Inn.** Up the steep slope from the water's edge in Bowness, this spacious, stylish pub serves good home-cooked fare as well as a fine collection of beers that includes its own Hawkshead brew. Specials, chalked on a board, might be grilled sole with crushed crab and char-grilled steak with thyme-roasted tomatoes. Leather sofas and open fires make the Angel a cozy place; service is low-key and friendly, and the decoration is bright, minimal, and contemporary, with wooden floors and off-white walls. Thirteen comfortable, good-value bedrooms complete the picture. ✉ *Helm Rd., Bowness-on-Windermere* ☎ *015394/44080* ⊕ *www.the-angelinn.com.*

£££
MODERN BRITISH
✕ **Jerichos at the Waverley.** The town's most stylish restaurant occupies an 1870 Victorian building near the center of town and has 10 smart bedrooms upstairs; staying here means you'll also get a high-quality breakfast. An open kitchen, bare wood, stone, and candles give the place a contemporary look and make for a sophisticated evening out. Choices from the brief, frequently changing Modern British menu might include lamb on onion, rosemary, and cream baked potatoes, or halibut with roast scallops and local herbs. ✉ *College Rd., Windermere* ☎ *015394/42522* ⊕ *www.jerichos.co.uk* ⊙ *Closed Thurs., last 2 wks of Nov., and 1st wk of Dec. No lunch.*

££
BRITISH
✕ **Lazy Daisy's.** Wooden floors, a big window onto the main street, displays of hops, and the smell of homemade bread: it's a Lakeland kitchen with a contemporary twist. Try the daily roast, slow cooked with herbs, or great sandwiches such as melted Brie, bacon, and tomato, and homemade soup. Good all day are cakes such as "lumpy bumpy"—a caloric mix of peanuts, sugar, and chocolate. This friendly and cozy coffee shop opens for breakfast and serves a full dinner menu, and there's Wi-Fi,

10

too. ⊠ *31–33 Crescent Rd., Windermere* ☎ *015394/43877* ⊕ *www. lazydaisyslakelandkitchen.co.uk.*

£££ ✕ **The Queen's Head Hotel.** An unpretentious 17th-century inn 3 mi north
BRITISH of Windermere, the Queen's Head is renowned for innovative pub
★ food such as *bobotie* (a curried South African dish with minced lamb, almonds, and apricots). It's also noted for real ales served from what was once an Elizabethan four-poster bed. The intimate dining rooms have oak beams, flagged floors, and log fires. Lunches can be less hearty than the excellent evening meals. If you want to stay overnight, the 15 guest rooms have splendid views. ⊠ *A592, Troutbeck* ☎ *015394/32174* ⊕ *www.queensheadhotel.com.*

WHERE TO STAY

For expanded hotel reviews, visit Fodors.com.

££ 🛏 **1 Park Road.** On a quiet street, this upmarket boutique B&B has
B&B/INN spacious guest rooms with carefully chosen fabrics and contempo- rary touches such as iPod docking stations. **Pros:** welcoming and stylish; good-size family room; good food, wine, and beer. **Cons:** a 15-minute walk to the lake. ⊠ *1 Park Rd., Windermere* ☎ *015394/ 42107* ⊕ *www.1parkroad.com* ⟳ *6 rooms* ♿ *In-room: no a/c, Wi-Fi. In-hotel: restaurant* ❖❘ *Breakfast.*

£ 🛏 **Archway Guesthouse.** A chef and a restaurant manager make a fine
B&B/INN team running this excellent little guesthouse in a Victorian building near the train station. **Pros:** great value; uncluttered sitting area; friendly ser- vice; rooms at front have good views. **Cons:** not as much space as you might find in more-expensive places. ⊠ *13 College Rd., Windermere* ☎ *015394/45613* ⊕ *www.the-archway.co.uk* ⟳ *4 rooms* ♿ *In-room: no a/c, Wi-Fi. In-hotel: parking* ❖❘ *Breakfast.*

£££££ 🛏 **Gilpin Lodge.** Hidden in 22 acres of grounds with meandering paths
HOTEL and five resident llamas, this rambling country-house hotel 2 mi east of
★ Windermere pampers its guests in a low-key way. **Pros:** high-class but laid-back pampering with a smile; notable food; a policy of no wed- dings or conferences. **Cons:** location is beautiful, but it's a little out of the way if you want to eat out; expensive. ⊠ *Crook Rd. off B5284, Bowness-on-Windermere* ☎ *015394/88818* ⊕ *www.gilpinlodge.co.uk* ⟳ *14 rooms, 11 suites* ♿ *In-room: no a/c. In-hotel: restaurant, bars, business center, some age restrictions* ❖❘ *Some meals.*

££ 🛏 **Ivy Bank.** One of Windermere's smarter bed-and-breakfasts, Ivy Bank
B&B/INN is in a quiet, leafy part of town. **Pros:** bike storage; near good walks. **Cons:** no bathtub in most rooms (shower only). ⊠ *Holly Rd., Winder- mere* ☎ *015394/42601* ⊕ *www.ivy-bank.co.uk* ⟳ *5 rooms* ♿ *In-room: no a/c, Wi-Fi* ❖❘ *Breakfast.*

£££££ 🛏 **Miller Howe.** Location, lake views, and superb service help set this
HOTEL luxurious Edwardian country-house hotel apart. **Pros:** more than 5
Fodor'sChoice acres of grounds; great lake views; staff that take care of the little extras.
★ **Cons:** sometimes closes for a couple of weeks in winter. ⊠ *Rayrigg Rd., Bowness-on-Windermere* ☎ *015394/42536* ⊕ *www.millerhowe. com* ⟳ *15 rooms* ♿ *In-room: no a/c. In-hotel: restaurant, some pets allowed, some age restrictions* ❖❘ *Some meals.*

£££–££££ 🛏 **The Punch Bowl.** An outstanding inn and restaurant, the Punch Bowl
HOTEL is a pleasantly modern retreat in the peaceful Lyth Valley, between
★

Windermere and Kendal. **Pros:** contemporary-yet-relaxed design will make you look at beer and Lakeland lodgings in a new light; excellent food. **Cons:** a little way from the area's main sights. ✉ *Off A5074, Crosthwaite, Lyth Valley* ☎ *015395/68237* ⊕ *www. the-punchbowl.co.uk* ⤳ *9 rooms* ☞ *In-room: no a/c, Wi-Fi (some). In-hotel: restaurant* ♚ *Breakfast.*

> **STAY ON A FARM**
>
> The Cumbrian Web site, ⊕ *www. luxuryinafarm.co.uk*, is a good place to start checking out farm stays, whether B&B-style or with kitchens; ⊕ *www.golakes.co.uk* has a wider selection of less luxurious options. Prices can be reasonable, but you'll need a car for most.

£££££
HOTEL
★

☷ **The Samling.** On its own sculpture-dotted 67 acres above Windermere, this place oozes exclusivity from every carefully fashioned corner. **Pros:** you'll feel like a star, and may sit next to one at breakfast, too. **Cons:** exclusivity doesn't come cheap. ✉ *Ambleside Rd., Windermere* ☎ *015394/31922* ⊕ *www.thesamling.com* ⤳ *11 suites* ☞ *In-room: no a/c, Internet. In-hotel: restaurant* ♚ *Breakfast.*

SHOPPING

The best selection of shops is at the Bowness end of Windermere, on Lake Road and around Queen's Square: clothing stores, crafts shops, and souvenir stores of all kinds.

At **Lakeland Jewellers** (✉ *Crag Brow, Bowness-on-Windermere* ☎ *015394/42992*) the local experts set semiprecious stones in necklaces and brooches.

More? The Artisan Baker, between Kendal and Windermere, is the place to stop for mouthwatering, award-winning bread, cakes, and sandwiches. It also brews fine coffee. ✉ *Mill Yard, Staveley* ☎ *015398/22297.*

SPORTS AND THE OUTDOORS

BIKING

Windermere Cycle Hire (✉ *Railway station, Windermere* ☎ *015394/44544*) rents a variety of bikes from £5 per hour or £16 per day, and is right next to the train station. There's another branch at Lakeside, at the southern tip of Windermere.

BOATING

Windermere Lake Holidays (✉ *Mereside, Ferry Nab, Bowness-on-Windermere* ☎ *015394/43415*) rents boats, from small sailboats to houseboats.

AMBLESIDE

7 mi northwest of Windermere.

Unlike Kendal and Windermere, Ambleside seems almost part of the hills and fells. Its buildings, mainly of local stone and many built in the traditional style that forgoes the use of mortar in the outer walls, blend perfectly into their setting. The small town sits at the northern end of Windermere along A591, making it a popular center for Lake District excursions. It has a better choice of restaurants than Windermere or Bowness, and the numerous outdoor shops are handy for fell walkers.

10

Ambleside does, however, suffer from overcrowding in high season. Wednesday, when the local market takes place, is particularly busy.

GETTING HERE AND AROUND

An easy drive along A591 from Windermere, Ambleside can also be reached by ferry.

ESSENTIALS

Visitor Information Ambleside (⊠ *Central Bldgs., Market Cross, Rydal Rd.* ☎ *015394/32582* ⊕ *www.amblesideonline.co.uk*).

EXPLORING

Armitt Museum. Ambleside's fine local-history gallery and library explores the town's past and its surroundings through the eyes of local people such as Beatrix Potter. A large collection of Beatrix Potter's natural-history watercolors and a huge number of photographic portraits can be viewed by appointment in the excellent library upstairs. Temporary exhibitions of art with a local connection are widely lauded. ⊠ *Rydal Rd.* ☎ *015394/31212* ⊕ *www.armitt.com* ⊠ *£2.50* ⊗ *Mon.–Sat. 10–5; last admission at 4:30.*

Bridge House. A tiny 17th-century stone former apple store perches on an arched stone bridge that spans Stone Beck. It may have been built here to avoid land tax. This much-photographed building holds a National Trust shop and information center. ⊠ *Rydal Rd.* ☎ *015394/35599* ⊠ *Free* ⊗ *Easter–Oct., daily 10–5.*

QUICK BITES **Cozy Sheila's Cottage** (⊠ *The Slack* ☎ *015394/33079*), serving great homemade cakes and desserts, is a good place to gather the strength for a walk or to relax after one by the fire. Try a good-value afternoon tea with tea bread or, for full calorie replenishment, go for a hot chocolate loaded with cream.

Windermere Lake Cruises. With year-round service between Ambleside, Bowness, Brockhole, and Lakeside, this company is a pleasant way to experience the lake. ☎ *015394/43360* ⊕ *www.windermere-lakecruises.co.uk.*

WHERE TO EAT

££
VEGETARIAN

✕ Fellinis. Styling themselves "Vegeterranean" to reflect Mediterranean culinary influence, Fellinis is Cumbria's newest foodie destination. Upstairs a plush studio cinema shows art-house releases, while downstairs the restaurant rustles up sumptuous concoctions for a sophisticated crowd. The menu's imaginative dishes might start with goat cheese and chive soufflé and continue with mushroom, red wine, and juniper bourguignon with horseradish mash. A large, open, rectangular dining room has soft seating, bold patterns, and oversize lamp shades, and a chill, jazzy soundtrack plays. White tablecloths, contemporary art, and fresh flowers enhance the modern sensibility. ⊠ *Church St.* ☎ *01539/433845* ⊕ *www.fellinisambleside.com* ⊗ *No lunch.*

££
MODERN BRITISH
★

✕ Glass House. A converted medieval mill with a working waterwheel is an atmospheric setting for this restaurant serving Modern British cuisine. Look for an international twist in dishes such as chicken liver parfait with toasted brioche or braised lamb with potatoes. You can have an elegant dinner or just sip a cappuccino in the courtyard beside the stream. ⊠ *Rydal Rd.* 🕾 *015394/32137* ⊕ *www.theglasshouserestaurant. co.uk* ⚄ *Reservations essential.*

£££
BRITISH
★

✕ **Lucy's on a Plate.** Ambleside's favorite informal eatery is the perfect spot to relax, whether with mushroom stroganoff for lunch, a chocolate almond torte for afternoon tea, or grilled char for dinner by candlelight. One room has scrubbed pine tables; a conservatory provides additional seating. Lucy's is famous for its puddings (desserts), and on the first Wednesday of every month the "up the duff" pudding night includes a menu with at least 30 choices. Lucy's delicatessen, on nearby Compston Road, sells high-class Cumbrian foods: sticky toffee pudding, farm cheeses, Cumberland sausage, jams, chutneys, and biscuits. Lucy's culinary empire also includes a wine bar on nearby St. Mary's Lane called Lucy4. ⊠ *Church St.* 🕾 *015394/31191* ⊕ *www.lucysofambleside.co.uk.*

WHERE TO STAY

For expanded hotel reviews, visit Fodors.com.

£–££
B&B/INN

🏠 **3 Cambridge Villas.** It's hard to find a more welcoming spot than this lofty Victorian house right in the center of town, thanks to the hosts who know a thing or two about local walks. **Pros:** especially good value for single travelers; warm family welcome; central. **Cons:** some rooms are a little cramped; can occasionally be noisy. ⊠ *3 Church St.* 🕾 *015394/32307* ⊕ *www.3cambridgevillas.co.uk* ⮌ *7 rooms, 5 with bath* ⚄ *In-room: no a/c, Wi-Fi* �🍽 *Breakfast.*

££
B&B/INN
★

🏠 **The Old Vicarage.** A quiet edge of Ambleside's old center is the peaceful setting for this excellent-value B&B in a large Victorian former vicarage. **Pros:** friendly welcome; heated indoor pool. **Cons:** some rooms are on the plain side of stylish; cuddly owls won't be to everybody's taste. ⊠ *Vicarage Rd.* 🕾 *015394/33364* ⊕ *www.oldvicarageambleside.co.uk* ⮌ *15 rooms* ⚄ *In-room: no a/c, Wi-Fi. In-hotel: pool* �🍽 *Breakfast.*

SPORTS AND THE OUTDOORS

The fine walks in the vicinity include routes north to Rydal Mount or southeast over Wansfell to Troutbeck. Each walk will take up to a half day, there and back. Ferries from Bowness-on-Windermere dock at Ambleside's harbor, called Waterhead. ■**TIP➜** To escape the crowds, rent a rowboat at the harbor for an hour or two.

Biketreks (⊠ *Rydal Rd.* 🕾 *015394/31245*), a good source for bike rentals, charges £20 per day.

RYDAL

1 mi northwest of Ambleside.

The village of Rydal, on the small glacial lake called Rydal Water, is rich with Wordsworthian associations.

EXPLORING

Dora's Field. One famous beauty spot linked with Wordsworth is Dora's Field, below Rydal Mount next to the church of **St. Mary's** (where you can still see the poet's pew). In spring the field is awash in yellow daffodils, planted by William Wordsworth and his wife in memory of their beloved daughter Dora, who died in 1847.

10

One of the Lake District's literary landmarks, Dove Cottage near Grasmere was where poet William Wordsworth wrote many famous works.

Rydal Mount. If there's one poet associated with the Lake District, it is Wordsworth, who made his home at Rydal Mount from 1813 until his death. Wordsworth and his family moved to these grand surroundings when he was nearing the height of his career, and his descendants still live here, surrounded by his furniture, books, and portraits. You can see the study in which he worked, the family dining room, and the 4½-acre garden, laid out by the poet himself, that gave him so much pleasure. ■TIP→ Wordsworth's favorite footpath can be found on the hill past White Moss Common and the River Rothay. Spend an hour or two walking the paths and you may understand why the great poet composed most of his verse in the open air. A tearoom in the former saddlery provides cakes and drinks. ⊠ *A591* ☎ *015394/33002* ⊕ *www.rydalmount.co.uk* 🖼 *£6.50; garden only, £4* ⊙ *Mar.–Oct., daily 9:30–5; Nov., Dec., and Feb., Wed.–Sun. 11–4.*

WHERE TO STAY
For expanded hotel reviews, visit Fodors.com.

£££–££££
B&B/INN

🏠 **Cote How Organic Guest House.** Elegant, peaceful, and with a focus on organic and sustainable fare, Cote How is a cut above most of the B&Bs in the lakes. **Pros:** beautiful gardens; great organic food; spacious rooms. **Cons:** location is great for walks and privacy, less so if you want other amenities. ⊠ *Rydal* ☎ *015394/32765* ⊕ *www.cotehow. co.uk* 🛏 *3 rooms* ⚿ *In-room: no a/c, no TV, Wi-Fi. In-hotel: laundry facilities* 🍽 *Breakfast.*

GRASMERE

3 mi north of Rydal, 4 mi northwest of Ambleside.

Lovely Grasmere, on a tiny, wood-fringed lake, is made up of crooked lanes in which Westmorland slate–built cottages hold shops and galleries. The village is a focal point for literary and landscape associations because this area was the adopted heartland of the Romantic poets, notably Wordsworth and Coleridge. The Vale of Grasmere has changed over the years, but many features Wordsworth wrote about are still visible. Wordsworth lived on the town's outskirts for almost 50 years and described the area as "the loveliest spot that man hath ever known."

GETTING HERE AND AROUND

On the main A591 between Ambleside and Keswick, Grasmere is easily reached by car.

EXPLORING

★ **Dove Cottage.** William Wordsworth lived in Dove Cottage from 1799 to 1808, a prolific and happy time for the poet. During this time he wrote some of his most famous works, including "Ode: Intimations of Immortality" and *The Prelude*. Built in the early 17th century as an inn, this tiny, dim, and, in some places, dank, house is beautifully preserved, with an oak-paneled hall and floors of Westmorland slate. It first opened to the public in 1891 and remains as it was when Wordsworth lived here with his sister, Dorothy, and wife, Mary. Bedrooms and living areas contain much of Wordsworth's furniture and many personal belongings. Coleridge was a frequent visitor, as was Thomas De Quincey, best known for his 1822 autobiographical masterpiece *Confessions of an English Opium-Eater*. De Quincey moved in after the Wordsworths left. You visit the house on a timed guided tour, and the ticket includes admission to the spacious, modern **Wordsworth Museum and Art Gallery,** which documents the poet's life and the literary contributions of Wordsworth and the Lake Poets. The museum includes space for major art exhibitions. The **Jerwood Centre,** open to researchers by appointment, houses 50,000 letters, first editions, and manuscripts. Afternoon tea is served at **Villa Colombina.** ⊠ *A591, 1 mi south of Grasmere* ☎ *015394/35544* ⊕ *www.wordsworth.org.uk* 🎫 *£7.50* ⊙ *Mar.–Nov., daily 9:30–5:30; Dec. and Feb., daily 9:30–4:30..*

QUICK
BITES

Heidi's (⊠ *Red Lion Sq.* ☎ *015394/35248* ⊕ *www.heidisgrasmerelodge. co.uk*) is a bustling, cozy little café and deli lined with jars of locally made jams and chutneys. Bang in the center of Grasmere, it's great for coffee and a homemade pastry or flapjack (bars made with syrup, butter, and oats).

St. Oswald's. Wordsworth, his wife Mary, his sister Dorothy, and four of his children are buried in the churchyard of this church on the River Rothay. The poet planted eight of the yew trees here. As you leave the churchyard, stop at the Gingerbread Shop, in a tiny cottage, for a special local treat. ⊠ *Stock La.* ⊕ *www.grasmereandrydal.org.uk*

Poetry, Prose, and the Lakes

The Lake District's beauty has whetted the creativity of many a famous poet and artist over the centuries. Here's a quick rundown of some of the writers inspired by the area's vistas.

William Wordsworth (1770–1850), one of the first English Romantics, redefined poetry by replacing the mannered style of his predecessors with a more conversational style. Many of his greatest works, such as *The Prelude,* draw directly from his experiences in the Lake District, where he spent the first 20 and last 50 years of his life. Wordsworth and his work had an enormous effect on Coleridge, Keats, Shelley, Byron, and countless other writers. Explore his homes in Rydal and Grasmere, among other sites.

John Ruskin (1819–1900), writer, art critic, and early conservationist, was an impassioned champion of new ways of seeing. He defended contemporary artists such as William Turner and the Pre-Raphaelites. His five-volume masterwork, *Modern Painters,* changed the role of the art critic from that of approver or naysayer to that of interpreter. Stop by Coniston to see his home and the Ruskin Museum.

Thomas De Quincey (1785–1859) wrote essays whose impressionistic style influenced many 19th-century writers, including Poe and Baudelaire. His most famous work, *Confessions of an English Opium-Eater* (1822), is an imaginative memoir of his young life, which indeed included opium addiction. He settled in Grasmere in 1809.

Beatrix Potter (1866–1943) never had a formal education; instead, she spent her childhood studying nature. Her love of the outdoors, and Lakeland scenery in particular, influenced her delightfully illustrated children's books, including *The Tale of Peter Rabbit* and *The Tale of Jemima Puddle-Duck.* Potter also became a noted conservationist who donated land to the National Trust. The story of her life was made into the 2006 film *Miss Potter,* starring Renée Zellweger and Ewan McGregor. Today you can visit Hill Top, the writer-artist's home in Hawkshead.

WHERE TO EAT

£££   ✕ **The Jumble Room.** A small stone building dating to the 18th century,
BRITISH   Grasmere's first shop is now a friendly, fashionable, and colorful place,
★   with children's books, bold animal paintings, and hanging lamps. A dedicated local fan base means the place always buzzes, and the owners' enthusiasm is contagious. The food is an eclectic mix of international and traditional British: excellent fish-and-chips and beefsteak appear on the menu with crab and cucumber soup and Catalan fish stew with paprika and almonds. Lunches are lighter and cheaper, with good soups and homemade puddings. Note: hours can change frequently. ✉ *Langdale Rd.* ☎ *015394/35188* ⊕ *www.thejumbleroom.co.uk* ⊙ *Closed Mon. and Tues.*

£££   ✕ **Tweedies Bar.** Attached to the Dale Lodge Hotel, Tweedies is one of
BRITISH   the region's best gastro-pubs and attracts many locals as well as visitors.
★   Delicious updated British food such as slow-roasted pork belly with caramelized apple and duck with apricots and parsnip puree is served in a smart, cozy, wood-filled contemporary pub with mellow music

and a fireplace. Several of Cumbria's best beers are on tap alongside a good selection of world beers; you can also try a number of real ales. ⊠ *Langdale Rd.* ☎ *15394/35300* ⊕ *www.tweediesbargrasmere.co.uk.*

WHERE TO STAY

For expanded hotel reviews, visit Fodors.com.

££
B&B/INN
★
Banerigg House. A cozy country estate less than a mile south of the village, Banerigg House has unfussy, well-appointed rooms, most with lake views. **Pros:** very welcoming hosts; good value for single rooms; canoes available. **Cons:** a little out of town; the house has an awkward, and potentially dangerous, turn onto the road. ⊠ *Lake Rd.* ☎ *015394/35204* ⊕ *www.baneriggguesthouse.co.uk* ⇆ *6 rooms, 5 with bath* ⚭ *In-room: no a/c, no TV, Wi-Fi. In-hotel: parking* ▭ *No credit cards* ◎ *Breakfast.*

£££
B&B/INN
Heidi's Grasmere Lodge. Small but sumptuous, this lodging has a distinctly feminine sensibility, with floral wallpaper, curly steel lamps, and painted woodwork. **Pros:** chic bathrooms with whirlpool tubs; warm welcome. **Cons:** not good for families; so pristine you may worry about your muddy boots. ⊠ *Red Lion Sq.* ☎ *015394/35248* ⊕ *www. harwoodhotel.co.uk* ⇆ *6 rooms* ⚭ *In-room: no a/c, Internet. In-hotel: restaurant, some age restrictions* ◎ *Breakfast.*

£££££
B&B/INN
Moss Grove. A Victorian building in the heart of Grasmere, Moss Grove has been refurbished impressively, with an emphasis on its environmental credentials. **Pros:** plenty of room; huge chunky furniture; modern design with a conscience. **Cons:** tight parking; not the place for a big fry-up breakfast. ⊠ *Red Lion Sq.* ☎ *015394/35251* ⊕ *www. mossgrove.com* ⇆ *11 rooms* ⚭ *In-room: no a/c, Internet (some). In-hotel: some pets allowed* ◎ *Breakfast.*

SHOPPING

★
The smells wafting across the churchyard draw many people to the **Grasmere Gingerbread Shop** (⊠ *Church Cottage* ☎ *015394/35428*). Since 1854 Sarah Nelson's gingerbread has been sold from this cramped 17th-century cottage, which was once the village school. The delicious treats, still made from a secret recipe, are available in attractive tins for the journey home or to eat right away.

10

SPORTS AND THE OUTDOORS

The most panoramic views of lake and village are from the south of Grasmere, from the bare slopes of **Loughrigg Terrace**, reached along a well-signposted track on the western side of the lake or through the woods from parking lots on the A591 between Grasmere and Rydal Water. It's less than an hour's walk from the village, though your stroll can be extended by continuing around Rydal Water, passing Rydal Mount and Dove Cottage before returning to Grasmere, a 4-mi (three-hour) walk in total.

ELTERWATER

2½ mi south of Grasmere, 4 mi west of Ambleside.

The delightful village of Elterwater, at the eastern end of the Great Langdale Valley on B5343, is a good stop for hikers. It's barely more than a cluster of houses around a village green, but from here you can choose from a selection of excellent circular walks.

Continued on page 609

HIKING IN THE LAKE DISTRICT

by Julius Honnor

From easy strolls around lakes to mountain climbs, the Lake District has some of England's best hiking. The landscape is generally accessible but also spectacular, with crashing streams cascading from towering mountains into the rivers and lakes that define the region. The scenery that inspired Wordsworth and Ruskin, among many others, is best experienced on an exhilarating walk.

With its highest mountain topping out at just 3,209 feet, the Lake District has peaks that are sometimes sniffed at by hardcore hikers, but they provide a stunning and not always benevolent setting. In winter the peaks are often ice- and snow-bound, and even routes at lower levels can occasionally be impassable.

There is plenty of variety to suit all abilities and enthusiasms, and almost everywhere you go in the national park you'll come across wooden footpath signs pointing the way over stiles and across fields. Paths are usually well maintained and, especially in summer, the most popular trails can be busy with booted walking hordes. Many people don't venture far from their cars, however, and peace and solitude are usually only a hillside or two away.

Many lakes and tarns (small mountain lakes) have paths that skirt their edges, though to see the best of the region you should head upward into the fells (mountains) and valleys, where the landscape becomes increasingly grand. Some of the best routes combine a boat ride with a walk up a fellside. When your walk is over, be sure to reward yourself with a pint at the pub.

Above: View of Troutbeck Park, a farm near Troutbeck that writer Beatrix Potter left to the National Trust

CHOOSE YOUR BEST DAY HIKE

Trails are abundant in the Lake District: you can walk just about anywhere, but a little planning will be rewarded. It's worthwhile to buy a good Ordnance Survey map, too. The routes included here, from 90 minutes to 5 hours, all show the national park at its best, from the southern lakes to the wilder, bleaker northern lakes. A couple of the trails are fairly popular, well-trodden routes; others take you off the most beaten paths. Several include a boat trip for extra enjoyment— just don't miss the last boat home.

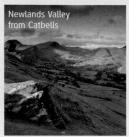

Newlands Valley from Catbells

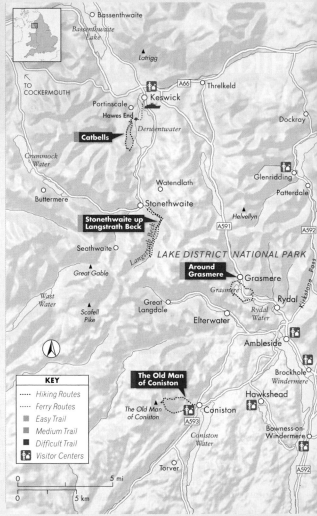

CATBELLS

Medium; 3.6 miles walking, plus boat ride to and from Keswick; 1 hour, 30 minutes walking
Starting point: Hawes End

This classic, popular Lakes route climbs the long, fairly gently sloping hill of Catbells, above Derwentwater. You'll need to catch the ferry from Keswick to the beginning of the route at Hawes End. The Keswick-on-Derwentwater Launch Co (☎ *017687/72263*, ⊕ *www. keswick-launch.co.uk*) runs a boat every hour in summer, less frequently in winter.

From the ferry landing stage, climb straight uphill before heading right (south) along the spine of the hill to the summit. From Catbells, the views over Derwentwater and beyond to the high fells of Skiddaw and

Borrowdale

On Pillar mountain, western Lake District

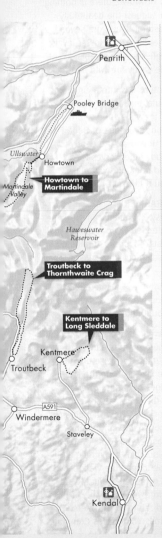

Blencathra are breathtaking. Take the lower path, nearer the lake, on the return in order to make this a circular route. The route can be shortened by catching a boat back from High Brandelhow or Low Brandelhow (other landing stages) instead of Hawes End.

STONETHWAITE UP LANGSTRATH BECK
Easy; 6 miles; 2 hours, 30 minutes
Starting point: Stonethwaite

In the high valleys in the middle of the Lake District, rivers become streams and wind through a wonderfully wild, largely treeless landscape away from the lakes themselves.. Running south from Derwentwater, Borrowdale is one of the most beautiful valleys around, but for even more spectacular walking country continue to the hamlet of Stonethwaite, from where the road becomes a track and then

Red deer

a path as it leads up beside the beck, the valley opening out into moorland. At the bottom of the valley, the climb is a fairly gentle one. About 3 miles upstream, cross a bridge and return on the other side of the stream. The Langstrath Inn makes a good food and drink spot at the end of the walk.

TROUTBECK TO THORNTHWAITE CRAG
Difficult; 9.8 miles; 4–5 hours
Starting point: Troutbeck

Windermere is more known for its boating, but you can find great mountain routes. Starting in the village of Troutbeck, 3 miles north of Windermere, this walk drops down into the valley, following the stream of Hagg Gill and climbing around a hill known as the Troutbeck Tongue. The trail then rises onto the ridge of Thornthwaite Crag, from where there are vertiginous views. Parts of this upper section are steep. For the return to Troutbeck, head west into the valley of the Trout Beck (stream) itself. Back in the village of Troutbeck, the Queen's Head Hotel is a great pub for food and drink.

10

Looking into the valley of Martindale

KENTMERE TO LONG SLEDDALE

Medium; 4.5 miles; 2 hours, 30 minutes
Starting point: Kentmere

Easily accessible from popular centers in the south of the region such as Windermere or Kendal, Kentmere and Long Sleddale are nevertheless in a part of the national park that many visitors bypass in their haste to

LAKELAND LINGO

If someone tells you to walk along the "beck" to the "force" and then climb the "fell" to the "tarn," you've just been told to hike along the stream or river (beck) to the waterfall (force) before climbing the hill or mountain (fell) to reach a small mountain lake (tarn).

You should also keep in mind that town or place names in the Lake District can be the same as the name of the lake on which the town stands. For example, Windermere is both the town and the lake itself—a "mere" is a lake in Old English.

get to the lakes—and that's a shame. These two valleys are beautiful examples of rural Cumbria, and the easy climb from one to another has some great views.

For a circular route, head south along the road from the village of Kentmere before heading left up the hill and across high moorland and down into the grand valley of Long Sleddale. The trail is a pleasant loop.

■TIP→ Stop off at More? The Artisan Baker (⊕ www. moreartisan.co.uk), in Mill Yard in Staveley, to stock up on cakes and sandwiches to fortify you along the way. You have to pass through Staveley to get to the starting point of the walk.

HOWTOWN TO MARTINDALE

Medium; 7.6 miles plus optional boat ride from Pooley Bridge; 3 hours, 30 minutes plus 25-minute boat ride
Starting point: Howtown

To get to Howtown, you can drive the long, narrow road down the eastern side of Ullswater; but to arrive at this spot in style, catch an

antique Ullswater Steamer (⊕ *www.ullswater-steamers. co.uk*) from Pooley Bridge at the lake's northern end.

Martindale is a magically hidden valley, enclosed on all sides by large fells. Climbing the steep switchback road up the bare hillside of Hallin Fell to the pass from the hamlet of Howtown, there is nothing to suggest the beautifully pastoral landscape beyond. Sheep graze at lower levels; higher up the steep sides of the valley are wild and rocky.

To turn this into a circular route, turn left at the top of the valley and return along the ridge of Beda Fell. In Howtown, the eponymous hotel serves food and drink and will make you a take-out lunch.

GRASMERE

Easy; 3.4 miles (can easily be extended to go around Rydal Water); 1 hour, 30 minutes
Starting point: Grasmere village

Rich with literary and artistic traditions, Grasmere is a bijou little lake easily walked around in an afternoon.

Starting in the village, where there is parking, head counter-clockwise around the lake, skirting the lower edge of Loughrigg Terrace. At the southeastern end of the lake, follow the stream through woods that link Grasmere to Rydal Water. If you want something a little longer, the walk can be extended around Rydal before you cross the A591 and return to Grasmere across White Moss Common.

Snow in the Lake District

View of the Langdale Fells

In Grasmere, Tweedies Bar is a good place for a post-stroll pint.

OLD MAN OF CONISTON
Difficult; 4.6 miles; 2 hours, 30 minutes to 3 hours
Starting point:
Coniston village

Of all the area's classic peaks, the Old Man of Coniston is one of the most accessible. Though it's a fairly steep climb that can be difficult in winter, the paths are well-trodden and well-maintained and it doesn't require any climbing to reach the summit, 2,634 feet up. From the top on a clear day, there are extraordinary views down to Coniston Water and around and beyond the Furness Fells.

Set off from the center of the village of Coniston, where the Black Bull Inn offers good hearty food and some excellent ales. Multiple paths to the summit make it easy to turn the walk into a circular route.

PREPARING FOR YOUR HIKE

CHOOSING A HIKE
A glance at a map of the Lake District National Park (🌐 www.lakedistrict.gov.uk) reveals a lacework mesh of footpaths; stop your car at random on a country road and there will probably be a path somewhere nearby. In the Lake District meticulous planning is not necessarily required in order to go for a walk: possibilities for short strolls abound.

The walks suggested offer good options; for other choices and for maps, stop in any town visitor information office or at the Lake District National Park Visitor Centre at Brockhole.

There are trails from this visitor center. You can also join a guided hike. *(For more information on these offices, see the towns in this chapter and the Lake District Planner.)*

WHAT TO WEAR
Check the weather, but expect the unexpected. Good clothing, and clothing for rain, is essential: even at the height of summer, wet weather can roll in from the west and spoil a sunny day. Higher up, too, temperatures are noticeably colder than at lake level, and it's usually much breezier. Generally a good pair of walking boots will suffice, and for lakeside walks you'd probably get by with flat-soled shoes. For the highest routes, snow and ice in winter can linger until spring and a set of slip-on spikes can be useful. The national park is overflowing with shops selling walking clothes, maps, and equipment.

WHAT TO BRING
Carry plenty of water and lightweight, high-energy food—or whatever you want for a picnic. Kendal mint cake is a favorite snack. Don't forget sunscreen and insect repellent. Bring a map: Ordnance Survey maps, available in area bookstores and visitor centers, are the best.

A WALK TO THE PUB

Kirkstone Pass Inn

It sometimes feels as if the entire Lake District economy revolves around walkers and walking, and the national park's pubs are no exception. The area has some of the finest exponents of that most English of institutions, the hiker's pub. To get the true flavor of the Lake District, join the locals and drink up.

Most of these pubs offer a hot fire to warm your feet by in cool weather, and some calorie-rich sustenance to send you on your way or replenish energy when you return from your walk. Few have any frills, and the stone floors are meant to be walked on with muddy boots. All offer local Cumbrian ales (some even brew their own), which will never taste as good as after a long hard stride up a steep fell. These pubs usually have their own parking, making them good starting and finishing places for a Lake District walk.

Here's a guide to some of the best, and some of the best placed, pubs.

Britannia Inn. Facing onto the village green in Elterwater, the Britannia is a destination as much as a stopping-point for many ramblers, who spill out onto the terrace of this cozy old pub on sunny days. *Elterwater, ⊕ www. britinn.net*

Drunken Duck Inn. Too stylish to be considered an archetypal walkers' pub, the inn has a superb isolated setting and fantastic home-brewed beers that nevertheless make it a great stopping place. A terrace opposite the pub has great views of the central fells and attracts many walkers who might otherwise feel put off by the gastropub interior. *Barngates, near Hawkshead, ⊕ www.drunkenduckinn.co.uk*

Kirkstone Pass Inn. At around 1,500 feet above sea level, this old coaching inn is the highest in the Lake District, and well placed for a satisfying pint after a walk on one of the nearby fells. *A592, Kirkstone Pass, ⊕ www. kirkstonepassinn.com*

Old Dungeon Ghyll. Isolated at the top of Great Langdale, this 300-year old hotel serves homemade soup and flapjacks (a bar cookie) to waves of passing walkers. *Elterwater, ⊕ www.odg.co.uk*

Queen's Head Hotel. Troutbeck's best pub is an excellent all-rounder, serving delicious food in a comfortable atmosphere and good beers from a distinctive bar. It's handily placed for walks up the Troutbeck valley toward Thornthwaite Crag. *Troutbeck, near Windermere, ⊕ www.queensheadhotel.com*

WHERE TO EAT AND STAY
For expanded hotel reviews, visit Fodors.com.

££
BRITISH

✗ **Britannia Inn**. At this 500-year-old pub, restaurant, and inn in the heart of superb walking country, antiques, comfortable chairs, and prints and oil paintings furnish the cozy, beamed public rooms. The whole family can relax with a bar meal and Cumbrian ale on the terrace while taking in the village green and the rolling scenery beyond. The hearty traditional British food—from grilled sea bass fillet to chicken, ham, and leek pie—is popular with locals, as are the many ales and whiskies. It's mainly a traditional pub, though the nine smallish guest rooms are more modern in style, with new pine furniture. Ask about discounts for midweek stays. ✉ *B5343* ☎ *015394/37210* ⊕ *www.britinn.net.*

££
HOTEL
★

🖵 **Old Dungeon Ghyll Hotel**. There's no more comforting stop after a day outdoors than the Hiker's Bar of this 300-year-old hotel at the head of the Great Langdale Valley. **Pros:** ideally situated for walking; wonderfully isolated; spectacular views all around. **Cons:** no-nonsense approach not to everyone's taste. ✉ *Off B5343, Great Langdale* ☎ *015394/37272* ⊕ *www.odg.co.uk* 🛏 *13 rooms, 8 with bath* ⟁ *In-room: no a/c, no TV. In-hotel: restaurant, bars* ⑩ *Breakfast.*

SPORTS AND THE OUTDOORS
There are access points to Langdale Fell from several spots along B5343, the main road; look for information boards at local parking places. You can also stroll up the river valley or embark on more-energetic hikes to Stickle Tarn or to one of the summits of the Langdale Pikes. Beyond the Old Dungeon Ghyll Hotel, the Great Langdale Valley splits in two around a hill known as the Band—a path up its spine has particularly good views back down over the valley and can be continued to the summit of Scafell Pike.

CONISTON

5 mi south of Elterwater.

This small lake resort and boating center attracts climbers to the steep peak of the **Old Man of Coniston** (2,635 feet), which towers above the slate-roof houses. It also has sites related to John Ruskin. Quieter than Windermere, Coniston is a good introduction to the pastoral and watery charms of the area, though the small town itself can get crowded in summer.

10

ESSENTIALS
Visitor Information Coniston (✉ *Ruskin Ave.* ☎ *015394/41533* ⊕ *www.conistontic.org*).

EXPLORING
★ **Brantwood**. On the eastern shore of Coniston Water, Brantwood was the cherished home of John Ruskin (1819–1900), the noted Victorian artist, writer, critic, and social reformer, after 1872. The rambling, white, 18th-century house (with Victorian alterations) is on a 250-acre estate that stretches high above the lake. Here, alongside mementos such as his mahogany desk, are Ruskin's own paintings, drawings, and books. On display is art that this great connoisseur collected, and in cerebral

corners such as the Ideas Room visitors are encouraged to think about meaning and change. A video on Ruskin's life shows the lasting influence of his thoughts, and the Severn Studio has rotating art exhibitions. Ruskin himself laid out the extensive grounds; take time to explore the gardens and woodland walks. Brantwood hosts a series of classical concerts on some Saturdays as well as talks, guided walks, and study days. The **Coniston Launch** (☎ *017687/75753* ⊕ *www.conistonlaunch. co.uk*) connects Coniston Pier with Ruskin's home at Brantwood, offering hourly service (£9.50) on its wooden *Ruskin* and *Ransome* launches. ✉ *Off B5285* ☎ *015394/41396* ⊕ *www.brantwood.org.uk* 🖃 *£6.30; gardens only, £4.50* ⊙ *Mid-Mar.–mid-Nov., daily 11–5:30; mid-Nov.– mid-Mar., Wed.–Sun. 11–4:30.*

Coniston Water. The lake came to prominence in the 1930s when Arthur Ransome made it the setting for *Swallows and Amazons,* one of a series of novels about a group of children and their adventures. The lake is about 5 mi long, a tempting stretch that drew boat and car racer Donald Campbell here in 1959 to set a water-speed record of 260 mph. He was killed when trying to beat it in 1967. His body and the wreckage of *Bluebird K7* were retrieved from the lake in 2001. Campbell is buried in St. Andrew's church in Coniston, and a stone memorial on the village green commemorates him.

Ruskin Museum. A favorite destination in Coniston, this interesting repository holds fascinating and thought-provoking manuscripts, personal items, and watercolors by John Ruskin that illuminate his thinking and influence. There is also a focus on Donald Campbell; the tail fin of his *Bluebird K7,* dragged up from Coniston Water, is here. A new Bluebird wing has been built to house the speedboat. Good local-interest exhibits include copper mining, geology, lace, and more. ✉ *Yewdale Rd.* ☎ *015394/41164* ⊕ *www.ruskinmuseum.com* 🖃 *£5.25* ⊙ *Mid-Mar.– mid-Nov., daily 10–5:30; mid-Nov.–mid-Mar., Wed.–Sun. 10:30–3:30.*

Steam Yacht *Gondola*. The National Trust's luxurious Victorian steam yacht (originally launched in 1859 and restored in the 1970s) runs between Coniston Pier, Brantwood, and Park-a-Moor at the south end of Coniston Water, daily from April through October (£9.90). A stop at Monk Coniston jetty connects to the footpaths through the Monk Coniston Estate, linking Coniston Water to the beauty spot of **Tarn Hows.** ☎ *015394/41288* ⊕ *www.nationaltrust.org.uk.*

WHERE TO EAT

££
BRITISH
✕ **Black Bull Inn.** Attached to the Coniston Brewing Company, whose ales are on tap here, the Black Bull is an old-fashioned pub in the heart of the village: a little gruff but a good pick for simple, hearty food and exemplary beer. Old photos of Donald Campbell's boat *Bluebird* decorate the walls, and there are wooden beams and benches. The menu lists daily specials as well as sandwiches for lunch or shrimp from Morecambe Bay. ✉ *Coppermines Rd.* ☎ *015394/41335* ⊕ *www. conistonbrewery.com.*

£
BRITISH
✕ **Jumping Jenny's.** Named after Ruskin's beloved boat, the woodbeamed tearoom at Brantwood occupies the converted coach house. It has an open-log fire and mountain views, and serves morning coffee,

lunch (sophisticated soups, pastas, sandwiches, and salads), and afternoon tea with homemade cakes. You can sit on the terrace in season. ⊠ *Off B5285* ☎ *015394/41715* ⊕ *www.jumpingjenny.com* ⊘ *Closed Mon. and Tues. Also closed Wed.–Fri. in Jan. No dinner.*

WHERE TO STAY

For expanded hotel reviews, visit Fodors.com.

££   ⬚ **Bank Ground Farm.** Used by Arthur Ransome as the model for the
HOTEL   setting for *Swallows and Amazons*, 15th-century Bank Ground is beautifully situated on the eastern shore of Coniston Water, opposite the village of Coniston on the western shore. **Pros:** stunning lake views; homey; traditional welcome. **Cons:** a fair walk from the village; no Internet access. ⊠ *East of the Lake, Coniston* ☎ *015394/41264* ⊕ *www. bankground.com* ⥢ *7 rooms, 5 cottages* ☖ *In-room: no a/c, kitchen (some), no TV. In-hotel: parking* ⦿❘ *Breakfast.*

£   ⬚ **Beech Tree Guest House.** Some of the individually furnished guest rooms
B&B/INN   at this Victorian stone house look out over a garden with an ancient
★   beech tree. **Pros:** cozy, family atmosphere; excellent breakfast. **Cons:** not for those wanting all the mod cons. ⊠ *Yewdale Rd.* ☎ *015394/413717* ⥢ *8 rooms, 4 with bath* ☖ *In-room: no a/c, no TV. In-hotel: some pets allowed* ▭ *No credit cards* ⦿❘ *Breakfast.*

££–£££   ⬚ **Yew Tree Farm.** Homemade cakes on arrival set the scene for this
B&B/INN   friendly, working farm B&B 5 mi north of Coniston toward Skelwith Bridge. **Pros:** pretty location; bacon from the farm for breakfast. **Cons:** not in town; often booked up far in advance; no small children unless you book whole house. ⊠ *A593* ☎ *015394/41433* ⊕ *www.yewtree-farm.com* ⥢ *3 rooms* ☖ *In-room: no a/c, no TV, Wi-Fi. In-hotel: some pets allowed* ⦿❘ *Breakfast.*

SPORTS AND THE OUTDOORS

BOATING

★   **Coniston Boating Centre** (⊠ *Lake Rd.* ☎ *015394/41366*) can help you get out on the water. You can rent launches, canoes, kayaks, and wooden rowboats, or even take a sailing lesson. A picnic area and café are near the center, too. Rowboats are £10 an hour, while motorboats are £20 an hour.

HIKING

Steep tracks lead up from the village to the **Old Man of Coniston.** The trail starts near the Sun Hotel on Brow Hill and goes past an old copper mine to the peak, which you can reach in about two hours. It's one of the Lake District's most satisfying—not too arduous but high enough to feel a sense of accomplishment and get fantastic views (west to the sea, south to Morecambe Bay, and east to Windermere). Experienced hikers include the peak in a seven-hour circular walk from the village, also taking in the heights and ridges of Swirl How and Wetherlam.

HAWKSHEAD

3 mi east of Coniston.

In the Vale of Esthwaite, this small market town, with a pleasing hodge-podge of tiny squares, cobbled lanes, and whitewashed houses (and a

10

pedestrianized center), is perhaps the Lake District's most picturesque village. There's a good deal more history here than in most local villages, however. The Hawkshead Courthouse, just outside town, was built by the monks of Furness Abbey in the 15th century. Hawkshead later derived much wealth from the wool trade, which flourished here in the 17th and 18th centuries.

As a thriving market center, Hawkshead could afford to maintain the **Hawkshead Grammar School,** at which William Wordsworth was a pupil from 1779 to 1787; he carved his name on a desk inside, now on display. In the village, Ann Tyson's House claims the honor of having provided the young William with lodgings. The twin draws of Wordsworth and Beatrix Potter—apart from her home, Hill Top, there's a Potter gallery—conspire to make Hawkshead crowded year-round.

GETTING HERE AND AROUND

Hawkshead is east of Coniston on B5285 and south of Ambleside via B5286. An alternative route is to cross Windermere via the car ferry from Ferry Nab, south of Bowness. Local buses link the village to others nearby.

ESSENTIALS

Visitor Information Hawkshead (✉ *Main St.* ☎ *015394/36946* ⊕ *www. hawksheadtouristinfo.org.uk*).

EXPLORING

Beatrix Potter Gallery. In the solicitor's offices formerly used by Potter's husband, the Beatrix Potter Gallery displays an annually changing selection of the artist-writer's original watercolors and drawings, as well as information on her interests as a naturalist. Potter was a conservationist and an early supporter of the National Trust. The house looks almost as it would have in her day. Admission is by timed ticket. ✉ *Main St.* ☎ *015394/36355* ⊕ *www.nationaltrust.org.uk* ✑ *£4.60* ☽ *Mid-Feb.–mid-Mar., Sat.–Thurs. 11–3:30; mid-Mar.–May, Sept., and Oct., Sat.–Thurs. 11–5; June–Aug., Sat.–Thurs. 10:30–5.*

Hill Top. Children's author and illustrator Beatrix Potter (1866–1943), most famous for her *Peter Rabbit* stories, called this place home. The house looks much the same as when Potter bequeathed it to the National Trust, and fans will recognize details such as the porch and garden gate, old kitchen range, Victorian dollhouse, and four-poster bed, which were depicted in the book illustrations. ■TIP➜ Admission to this often-crowded spot is by timed ticket; book in advance and avoid summer weekends and school vacations. Hill Top lies 2 mi south of Hawkshead by car or foot, though you can also approach via the car ferry from Bowness-on-Windermere.

LAKE DISTRICT BIKING

Cycling along the numerous bicycle paths and quiet forest roads in Cumbria is pleasurable and safe. Some flat paths are beside the lakes, but the best routes involve plenty of ups and downs. The Cumbria Cycle Way circles the county, and for local excursions guided bike tours are often available, starting at about £25 per day. Contact local tourist offices or bike-rental places for details on cycle routes.

Children's writer Beatrix Potter used details from her house at Hill Top, near Hawkshead, in the illustrations for her stories.

✉ *Off B5285, Near Sawrey* ☎ *015394/36269* ⊕ *www.nationaltrust.org.*
uk ✉ *£6.20, gardens free when house is closed* ☉ *House mid-Feb.–Mar.,*
Sat.–Thurs. 10:30–3:30; Apr., May, Sept., and Oct., Sat.–Thurs. 10:30–
4:30; June–Aug., Sat.–Thurs. 10–5. Gardens and shop mid-Feb.–Mar.,
daily 10:15–4; Apr., May, Sept., and Oct., daily 10–5; June–Aug., daily
9:45–6:30; Nov. and Dec., daily 10–4.

Tarn Hows. Two miles northwest of Hawkshead (follow signs on B5285)
is this small mountain lake, one of the Lake District's most celebrated
beauty spots. Scenic overlooks let you drink it all in, or you can take
an hour to putter along the paths. A free National Trust bus runs here
from Hawkshead and Coniston (Easter through October, Sunday only).

10

WHERE TO EAT AND STAY
For expanded hotel reviews, visit Fodors.com.

$ ✕ **Tower Bank Arms.** With a porch that appears in a Beatrix Potter story
BRITISH   and a location just a rabbit's hop from the author's home, you might
expect this pub to be something of a tourist trap. It's anything but.
There's a slate floor, a crackling open fire, and a bar that stocks some of
the best beers around, usually including some of the great ales from the
nearby Barngates Brewery. There's a friendly welcome and the meals are
tasty and copious, making use of local ingredients; the beef-and-ale stew
is especially good. Four bedrooms upstairs offer a good-value alternative to pricier lodgings. ✉ *Off B5285, Near Sawrey* ☎ *015394/36334*
⊕ *www.towerbankarms.com.*

££–£££   🛏 **Drunken Duck Inn.** After four centuries, this friendly old coaching inn
HOTEL   remains an outstanding place for both food and lodging. **Pros:** superchic
Fodor's Choice   rural style; excellent dining and drinking. **Cons:** hunting paraphernalia
★

The Grizedale Forest Park has adventures including the Go Ape aerial challenge—or you can just walk through the sculpture park.

may put you off your beer; can feel isolated. ✉ *Off B5286, Barngates* ☎ *015394/36347* ⊕ *www.drunkenduckinn.co.uk* 🛏 *16 rooms* ⚹ *In-room: no a/c, Wi-Fi. In-hotel: restaurant, bar* 🍽 *Some meals.*

££££
B&B/INN ▦ **Randy Pike.** Built in the 19th century as the shooting lodge for Wray Castle, Randy Pike is filled with stylish, imaginative, and personal touches. **Pros:** space; style; good food; big garden. **Cons:** a little out of the way; pricey. ✉ *Off B5286 between Outgate and Clappersgate* ☎ *015394/36088* ⊕ *www.randypike.co.uk* 🛏 *2 rooms* ⚹ *In-room: no a/c* 🍽 *Breakfast.*

££
B&B/INN ▦ **Yewfield.** With the laid-back friendliness of a B&B but with most of the style of a fancier country-house hotel, this is a very good value for the money—especially if you can get one of the rooms with a great view across the valley from the front of the house. **Pros:** a great out-of-the-way location; garden; apartments a convenient option for week-long stays. **Cons:** laid-back service can occasionally be too relaxed; not good for families with young kids. ✉ *Hawkshead Hill* ☎ *015394/36765* ⊕ *www.yewfield.co.uk* 🛏 *10 rooms, 2 apartments* ⚹ *In-room: no a/c, Wi-Fi (some). In-hotel: bar, some age restrictions* ⊗ *Closed Dec. and Jan.* 🍽 *Breakfast.*

SPORTS AND THE OUTDOORS

Stretching southwest from Hawkshead and blanketing the hills between Coniston and Windermere, **Grizedale Forest Park** (✉ *Off B5286* ☎ *01229/860010* ⊕ *www.forestry.gov.uk/grizedaleforestpark*) has a thick mix of oak, pine, and larch woods crisscrossed with biking and walking paths. Ninety-two outdoor sculptures are scattered

What's Real About Real Ale?

The English can be passionate about their drink, as the growing interest in real ale shows. It differs from other ales by the use of natural ingredients and the fact that it is matured by fermentation in the barrel from which the ale is served. The process doesn't use carbon dioxide, so pure taste wins out over fizz.

The **Directory of U.K. Real Ale Breweries** (⊕ *www.quaffale.org.uk*) lists 28 operating real-ale breweries in Cumbria, of which the Coniston Brewing Company, Barngates Brewery (at the Drunken Duck Inn), and Hawkshead (in Staveley, between Kendal and Windermere) are three of the best. Most real ales are caramel in color and hoppy, malty, and slightly bitter to taste. A pint of ale is the usual quantity to be consumed, though a half is acceptable; you can also find it in bottles.

Most pubs in the Lake District offer some sort of local brew—the better ones take enormous pride in their careful tending of the beer, from barrel to glass. Interested in the subject, or just in the taste? Check out the Web site of the **Campaign for Real Ale** (⊕ *www.camra.org.uk*).

beside the trails. The **visitor center** has information, maps, a café, and an adventure playground.

Grizedale Mountain Bikes (✉ *Old Hall Car Park, Grizedale Forest Park Visitor Centre, off B5286* ☎ *01229/860369* ⊕ *www.grizedalemountainbikes. co.uk*) rents bicycles.

PENRITH AND THE NORTHERN LAKES

The scenery of the northern lakes is considerably more dramatic—some would say bleaker—than much of the landscape to the south, a change that becomes apparent on your way north from Kendal to Penrith. Your easiest approach is a 30-mi drive on the A6 that takes you through the wild and desolate Shap Fells, which rise to a height of 1,304 feet. This is one of the most notorious moorland crossings in the country: even in summer it's a lonely place to be, and in winter, snow on the road can be dangerous. From Penrith the road leads to Ullswater, possibly the grandest of all the lakes; then there's a winding route west past Keswick, south through the marvelous Borrowdale Valley, and on to Cockermouth. Outside the main towns such as Keswick, it can be easier to escape the summer crowds in the northern lakes.

10

PENRITH

30 mi north of Kendal.

The red-sandstone town of Penrith was the capital of Cumbria, part of the Scottish kingdom of Strathclyde in the 9th and 10th centuries. It was rather neglected after the Normans arrived, and the Scots sacked it on several occasions. Penrith has been a thriving market town for centuries; the market still takes place on Tuesday, and it continues to be known for good shopping.

The tourist information center, in the Penrith Museum, has information about the historic town trail, which takes you through narrow byways to the plague stone on King Street, where food was left for the stricken, to St. Andrew's churchyard and its 1,000-year-old "hog back" tombstones (stones carved as stylized "houses of the dead"), and finally to the ruins of Penrith Castle.

GETTING HERE AND AROUND
Penrith is just off the M6, 30 mi north of Kendal and 100 mi north of Manchester. Both the M6 and the alternative A6 cross the Pennines spectacularly at Shap Fells. From Windermere, you can reach Penrith by going over the Kirkstone Pass to Ullswater. There are some direct trains from Euston Station in London to Penrith; sometimes it's necessary to change.

ESSENTIALS
Visitor Information Penrith (⊠ *Penrith Museum, Middlegate* ☎ *01768/867466* ⊕ *www.eden.gov.uk*).

EXPLORING
Dalemain. Home of the Hasell family since 1679, Dalemain, 3 mi southwest of Penrith, began with a 12th-century peel tower built to protect the occupants from raiding Scots, and is now a delightful hodgepodge of architectural styles. An imposing Georgian facade of local pink sandstone encompasses a medieval hall and extensions from the 16th through the 18th century. Inside are a magnificent oak staircase, furniture dating from the mid-17th century, a Chinese drawing room, a 16th-century room with intricate plasterwork, and many fine paintings, including masterpieces by Van Dyck. The gardens are worth a look, too, and deer roam the estate. ⊠ *A592* ☎ *01768/486450* ⊕ *www.dalemain. com* ⊆ *£9.50; gardens only, £6.50* ☉ *House Apr.–Sept., Sun.–Thurs. 11:15–4; Oct., Sun.–Thurs. 11:15–3. Gardens Apr.–Oct., Sun.–Thurs. 10:30–5; Nov.–mid-Dec., Sun.–Thurs. 11–3.*

Penrith Castle. The evocative remains of this 15th-century redbrick castle stand high above a steep, now-dry moat. Home of the maligned Richard, duke of Gloucester (later Richard III), who was responsible for keeping peace along the border, it was one of England's first lines of defense against the Scots. By the civil war the castle was in ruins, and the townsfolk used some of the fallen stones to build their houses. The ruins stand across from the town's train station. ⊠ *Off Castlegate* ☎ *No phone* ⊕ *www.english-heritage.org.uk* ⊆ *Free* ☉ *June–Sept., daily 7:30 am–9 pm; Oct.–May, daily 7:30–4:30.*

Penrith Museum. In a 16th-century building that served as a school from 1670 to the 1970s, this museum contains displays on the history of the Eden Valley, including Roman pottery and a medieval cauldron. The Penrith Tourist Information Centre is here. ⊠ *Robinson's School, Middlegate* ☎ *01768/865105* ⊕ *www.eden.gov.uk* ⊆ *Free* ☉ *Apr.–Oct., Mon.–Sat. 10–5, Sun. 1–4:45; Nov.–Mar., Mon.–Sat. 10–4.*

🕒 **Rheged.** Named for the Celtic kingdom of Cumbria, Rheged is the theme of this grass-covered visitor center with activities for kids and some interesting free exhibits about the history, culture, and other aspects of the Lake District. A new gallery opened in 2011 with rotating exhibitions. Its centerpiece, a large-format cinema (fee), shows 50-minute 3-D movies such as *Dolphins and Whales 3-D* and *Secrets of the Mummies*. Shops showcase Cumbrian produce and crafts, and the Rheged Café and Café Pod and Taste Food Bar all offer drinks and light meals. Rheged is 2 mi southwest of Penrith and 1 mi west of Junction 40 on the M6. ✉ *A66* ☎ *01768/868000* ⊕ *www.rheged.com* 🖃 *Free, movie £6.50* ⊙ *Daily 10–5:30.*

WHERE TO EAT AND STAY

For expanded hotel reviews, visit Fodors.com.

££   ✗ **George and Dragon.** Just south of Penrith, this freshly updated pub
BRITISH owned by the nearby Lowther estate makes good use of the local produce for its tasty traditional organic dishes. Sausages come from up the Eden Valley, brown trout from the River Lowther. The inn is also a well-tended spot for a pint of local beer, with handsome slate floors and hanging hops. Bonnie Prince Charlie was once involved in a battle here, and the remains of 12 Scottish rebels were discovered in the pub's back garden. For an overnight stay, choose from 10 smart, individually designed guest rooms with furnishings from the Lowther family's collection. ✉ *A6, Clifton* ☎ *01768/865381* ⊕ *www.georgeanddragonclifton.co.uk* ⊙ *No lunch Mon.*

£   ✗ **No. 15.** Red walls and comfy sofas set the tone for this laid-back, spa-
CAFÉ cious contemporary gallery and café. There's a large range of teas and coffees, as well as such dishes as homemade soups, savory pancakes, and huge slabs of chocolate cake. Wi-Fi can be used for 30 minutes for £2, and there's monthly live music in the evening. ✉ *15 Victoria Rd.* ☎ *01768/867453.*

££   🛏 **Brooklands.** Decorated in soothing tones, this Victorian terraced
B&B/INN house is one of a cluster of B&Bs on Portland Place, a short walk north of Penrith's center. **Pros:** well-looked-after B&B; bathrobes in room; fancy toiletries. **Cons:** a drive from the spectacular Lakeland scenery. ✉ *2 Portland Pl.* ☎ *01768/863395* ⊕ *www.brooklandsguesthouse.com* 🛏 *8 rooms* ⚬ *In-room: no a/c, Wi-Fi* ¶◯¶ *Breakfast.*

SHOPPING

Penrith is a diverting place to shop, with its narrow streets and arcades chockablock with family-run specialty shops. Major shopping areas include Devonshire Arcade, with its brand-name stores; the pedestrian-only Angel Lane and Little Dockray; and Angel Square.

The stalls of the outdoor **market** line Dockray, Corn Market, and Market Square every Tuesday and sell fine local produce and original crafts.

The excellent **Bluebell Bookshop** (✉ *8 Angel La.* ☎ *01768/866660*) sometimes hosts special events and readings.

James & John Graham of Penrith Ltd. (✉ *Market Sq.* ☎ *01768/862281*) has a great bakery and a well-stocked delicatessen that specializes in cheese and local products.

The **Toffee Shop** (✉ *7 Brunswick Rd.* ☎ *01768/862008*), where the Queen buys her toffee, may also have England's best fudge.

10

ULLSWATER

6 mi southwest of Penrith.

Hemmed in by towering hills, Ullswater, the region's second-largest lake, is one of the least developed, drawing people for its calm waters and good access to the mountain slopes of Helvellyn. The A592 winds along the lake's pastoral western shore, through the adjacent hamlets of **Glenridding** and **Patterdale** at the southern end. Lakeside strolls, great views, tea shops, and rowboat rentals provide the full Lakeland experience.

ESSENTIALS

Visitor Information Ullswater (⊠ *Main Car Park, Glenridding* ☎ *017684/82414*).

EXPLORING

Aira Force. A spectacular 65-foot waterfall pounds under a stone bridge and through a wooded ravine to feed into Ullswater. From the parking lot it's a 10-minute walk to the falls, with more-serious walks on Gowbarrow Fell and to the village of Dockray beyond. Bring sturdy shoes, especially in wet or icy weather, when the paths can be treacherous. Just above Aira Force in the woods of Gowbarrow Park is the spot where, in 1802, William Wordsworth's sister Dorothy observed daffodils that, as she wrote, "tossed and reeled and danced and seemed as if they verily laughed with the wind that blew upon them." Two years later Wordsworth transformed his sister's words into the famous poem "I Wandered Lonely as a Cloud." And two centuries later, national park wardens patrol Gowbarrow Park in season to prevent tourists from picking the few remaining daffodils. ⊠ *Off A592, 5 mi north of Patterdale* 🚗 *Parking £3.50–£5.50.*

★ **Helvellyn.** West of Ullswater's southern end, the brooding presence of Helvellyn (3,118 feet), one of the Lake District's most formidable mountains, recalls the region's fundamental character. It's an arduous climb to the top, especially via the challenging ridge known as Striding Edge, and the ascent shouldn't be attempted in poor weather or by inexperienced hikers. Signposted paths to the peak run from the road between Glenridding and Patterdale and pass by **Red Tarn,** at 2,356 feet the highest small mountain lake in the region.

Ullswater Steamers. These antique vessels, including a 19th-century steamer (claimed to be the oldest working passenger vessel in the world), run the length of Ullswater between Glenridding in the south and Pooley Bridge in the north. It's a pleasant tour and combines well with a lakeside walk. The service operates from the pier at Glenridding. A one-way trip the full length of the lake is £8, or you can do any three stages for £11. ☎ *017684/82229* ⊕ *www.ullswater-steamers.co.uk.*

WHERE TO STAY

For expanded hotel reviews, visit Fodors.com.

£££ 🏠 **Howtown Hotel.** Near the end of the road on the isolated eastern side
HOTEL of Ullswater, this gloriously quiet, always welcoming, family-run hotel is low-key and low-tech. **Pros:** exceptionally quiet; spectacular location; dinner included in price. **Cons:** not for those who must be plugged in;

The most expert climbers will attempt an ascent of Helvellyn on the difficult Striding Edge even in winter.

a bit remote. ✉ *4 mi south of Pooley Bridge* ☎ *017684/86514* ⊕ *www. howtown-hotel.com* ⇄ *12 rooms, 4 cottages* ♿ *In-room: no a/c, no TV. In-hotel: restaurant, bars, some pets allowed* ▭ *No credit cards* ⊙ *Closed Nov.–Mar.* ◯◯ *Some meals.*

£££££
HOTEL
★

🏨 **Sharrow Bay**. Sublime views and exceptional service and cuisine add distinction to this country house on the shores of Ullswater. **Pros:** great views across Ullswater; pretty garden. **Cons:** not for the faint of wallet; some distance from other facilities. ✉ *Howtown Rd., Pooley Bridge* ☎ *017684/86301* ⊕ *www.sharrowbay.co.uk* ⇄ *16 rooms, 8 suites* ♿ *In-room: no a/c (some), Wi-Fi. In-hotel: restaurants, bars, some age restrictions* ◯◯ *Some meals.*

10

KESWICK

14 mi west of Ullswater.

The great mountains of Skiddaw and Blencathra brood over the gray slate houses of Keswick (pronounced *kezz*-ick), on the scenic shores of Derwentwater. The town is a natural base for exploring the rounded, heather-clad Skiddaw range to the north, while the hidden valleys of Borrowdale and Buttermere (the latter reached by stunning Honister Pass) take you into the rugged heart of the Lake District. Nearby, five beautiful lakes are set among the three highest mountain ranges in England. The tourist information center here has regional information and is the place to get fishing permits for Derwentwater.

Keswick's narrow, cobbled streets have a grittier charm compared to the refined Victorian elegance of Grasmere or Ambleside. However, it

CLOSE UP

Festivals and Folk Sports

With everything from rushbearing to Westmorland wrestling to traditional music, the Lake District hosts some of Britain's most unusual country festivals as well as some excellent but more typical ones.

MAJOR EVENTS

Major festivals include the Keswick Film Festival (February), Words by the Water (a literary festival in Keswick, March), Keswick Jazz Festival (May), Cockermouth and Keswick carnivals (June), Ambleside rushbearing (August) and sports (July), Grasmere rushbearing (August) and sports (August), and Lake District Summer Music (regionwide, in August)—but there are many others.

SPECIAL ACTIVITIES

Rushbearing dates back to medieval times, when rushes covered church floors; today processions of flower-bedecked children and adults bring rushes to churches in a number of villages. Folk sports, often the highlights at local festivals, include Cumberland and Westmorland wrestling, in which the opponents must maintain a grip around each other's body. Fell running, a sort of cross-country run where the route goes roughly straight up and down a mountain, is also popular.

A calendar of events is available at tourist information centers or on the Cumbria Tourism Web site, ⊕ *www.golakes.co.uk*.

---

is the best spot in the Lake District to purchase mountaineering gear and outdoor clothing. There are also many hotels, guesthouses, restaurants, and pubs.

GETTING HERE AND AROUND

It's easily reached along A66 from Penrith, though you can get to Keswick more scenically via Grasmere in the south. Buses run from the train station in Penrith to Keswick. The town center is pedestrianized.

■ TIP→ Traffic can be horrendous in summer, so consider leaving your car in Keswick. The open-top Borrowdale bus service between Keswick and Seatoller (to the south) runs frequently, and the Honister Rambler minibus is perfect for walkers aiming for the high fells of the central lakes; it makes stops from Keswick to Buttermere. The Keswick Launch service on Derwentwater links to many walks as well as the Borrowdale bus service.

ESSENTIALS

Visitor Information Keswick (⊠ *Moot Hall, Market Sq.* ☎ *017687/72645* ⊕ *www.keswick.org*).

EXPLORING

★ **Castlerigg Stone Circle.** A Neolithic monument about 100 feet in diameter, this stone circle lies in a brooding natural hollow called St. John's Vale, ringed by magnificent peaks and ranged by sheep. The 38 stones aren't large, but the site makes them particularly impressive. Wordsworth described them as "a dismal cirque of Druid stones upon a forlorn moor." A marked route leads to a 200-foot-long path through a pasture. You can visit at any time, no charge. ⊠ *Off A66, 4 mi east of Keswick.*

🐛 **Cumberland Pencil Museum.** Legend has it that shepherds found graphite on Seathwaite Fell after a storm uprooted trees in the 16th century. The Derwent company still makes pencils here, and the museum contains the world's longest pencil, a pencil produced for World War II spies that contains a rolled-up map, and displays about graphite mining and pencil making. There's a café and quizzes for kids. ✉ *Southey Works* ☎ *017687/73626* ⊕ *www.pencilmuseum.co.uk* 🎫 *£3.75* ⊙ *Daily 9:30–5; last admission at 4.*

★ **Derwentwater.** To understand why Derwentwater is considered one of England's finest lakes, take a short walk from Keswick's town center to the lakeshore and past the jetty, and follow the **Friar's Crag** path, about a 15-minute level walk from the center. This pine-tree-fringed peninsula is a favorite vantage point, with its view of the lake, the ring of mountains, and many tiny islands. Ahead, crags line the **Jaws of Borrowdale** and overhang a mountain ravine—a scene that looks as if it emerged from a Romantic painting.

Keswick-on-Derwentwater Launch Co. For the best lake views, take a wooden-launch cruise around Derwentwater. Between late March and November, cruises set off every hour in each direction from a dock at the shore; there is also a limited winter timetable. You can also rent a rowboat here. Buy a hop-on, hop-off Around the Lake ticket (£9) and take advantage of the seven landing stages around the lake that provide access to hiking trails, such as the two-hour climb up and down Cat Bells, a celebrated lookout point on the western shore of Derwentwater. ☎ *017687/72263* ⊕ *www.keswick-launch.co.uk.*

WHERE TO EAT

£ ✕ **Café Bar 26.** A metropolitan bar in the rural Lake District, where cozy
BRITISH tearooms are more the norm, Café Bar 26 has Wi-Fi, wooden beams, mellow brick-color walls, candlelight, and live music every Saturday. The wine list is on the short side, but there are good nibbles at night, though no dinner. During the day light lunches are served, including a "warm tart of the day." The three bedrooms upstairs are an excellent value for an overnight. ✉ *26 Lake Rd.* ☎ *017687/80863* ⊕ *www. cafebar26.co.uk* ⊙ *No dinner.*

£ ✕ **Lakeland Pedlar.** Colorful and cheerful, this café and bike shop serves
VEGETARIAN inspired international vegetarian and vegan cuisine such as spanakopita (Greek spinach pie) and chickpea tagine, and a filling, homemade soup. You can check out the fresh juices, espresso, and homemade cakes, and hearty breakfasts are a specialty. Admire the fells from the outdoor tables, or take food with you for the trail. ✉ *Henderson's Yard, Bell Close* ☎ *017687/74492* ⊕ *www.lakelandpedlar.co.uk* ⊙ *Closed Wed. No dinner Sept.–June.*

£££ ✕ **Morrels.** One of the town's better eating places has cinematically
BRITISH themed art and wooden floors that give a contemporary edge to the bar and dining area. Updated British fare is the specialty at this mellow restaurant: a tomato, olive, and pine-nut compote complements the mackerel fillet, and the fish cakes come spiced with a bean-and-corn salsa. A couple of equally stylish apartments upstairs are available for short-term rentals. ✉ *34 Lake Rd.* ☎ *017687/72666* ⊕ *www.morrels. co.uk* ⊙ *Closed Mon.*

10

The setting of the Castlerigg Stone Circle, ringed by stunning mountains, makes this Neolithic monument deeply memorable.

£ ✕ **Square Orange Café Bar.** Young locals and windblown walkers gather
CAFÉ here for excellent coffee, tea, cordials, and some serious hot chocolate;
★ cakes, paninis, and tapas are served as well. Music is laid-back, the
walls have paintings and photos, and there are games, pizza (some
days and nights), and snacks, and pints of local beer for long rainy days
or cold winter nights. ⊠ *20 St. John's St.* ☎ *017687/73888* ⊕ *www.
thesquareorange.co.uk.*

WHERE TO STAY
For expanded hotel reviews, visit Fodors.com.

£–££ ⊟ **Ferndene.** Exceptionally friendly, this spotless B&B is carefully tended
B&B/INN by its kindly owners. **Pros:** family-focused; good value; bicycle stor-
♻ age. **Cons:** lacks style of more expensive lodgings. ⊠ *6 St. John's Terr.*
☎ *017687/74612* ⊕ *www.ferndene-keswick.co.uk* ⇨ *6 rooms, 3 with
bath* ⚐ *In-room: Wi-Fi* ⚑ *Breakfast.*

££££–£££££ ⊟ **Highfield Hotel.** Slightly austere on the outside but exceptionally
HOTEL charming within, this Victorian hotel overlooks the lawns of Hope
★ Park and has lodging with great character, including rooms in the turret
rooms and the former chapel. **Pros:** good service and food; great views.
Cons: some small downstairs bedrooms. ⊠ *The Heads* ☎ *017687/72508*
⊕ *www.highfieldkeswick.co.uk* ⇨ *18 rooms* ⚐ *In-room: no a/c. In-hotel:
restaurant, bar, business center* ⊙ *Closed Jan.–mid-Feb.* ⚑ *Some meals.*

££ ⊟ **Howe Keld.** In a town that overflows with B&Bs, this comfortable town
B&B/INN house stands out because of its contemporary flair and pampering touches.
Pros: famously good breakfasts; good ecological practices; one room accessible for people with disabilities. **Cons:** a short distance from the heart
of town; backs onto a busy road. ⊠ *5–7 The Heads* ☎ *017687/72417*

⊕ *www.howekeld.co.uk* ⇆ *14 rooms* ⚓ *In-room: no a/c. In-hotel: restaurant, bar, some pets allowed* ❂ *Closed Jan.* ❒ *Breakfast.*

NIGHTLIFE AND THE ARTS

The **Keswick Film Club** (☎ *017687/72398*) has an excellent festival in February and a program of international and classic films, screened at the old redbrick Alhambra Cinema on St. John's Street and at the Theatre by the Lake.

The popular **Keswick Jazz Festival** (☎ *017687/74411*), held each May, consists of four days of music. Reservations are taken as early as before Christmas.

The company at the **Theatre by the Lake** (✉ *Lake Rd.* ☎ *017687/74411*) presents classic and contemporary productions year-round. The Keswick Music Society season runs from September through January, and the Words on the Water literary festival takes place in March.

SHOPPING

Keswick has a good choice of bookstores, crafts shops, and wool-clothing stores tucked away in its cobbled streets, as well as excellent outdoor shops.

Keswick's market is held Saturday.

George Fisher (✉ *2 Borrowdale Rd.* ☎ *017687/72178*), the area's largest and best outdoor equipment store, sells sportswear, travel books, and maps. Daily weather information is posted in the window.

Needle Sports (✉ *56 Main St.* ☎ *017687/72227*) supplies equipment for mountaineering and for rock and ice climbing.

Northern Lights Gallery (✉ *22 St. John's St.* ☎ *01768/775402*) carries a good selection of contemporary paintings, photography, sculpture, jewelry, and ceramics by around 80 local artists.

Thomasons (✉ *8–10 Station St.* ☎ *017687/80169*), a butcher and delicatessen, sells some very good meat pies—just the thing for putting in your pocket before you climb a Lakeland fell.

SPORTS AND THE OUTDOORS

BIKING

Keswick Mountain Bike Centre (✉ *Southey Hill* ☎ *017687/75202*) rents bikes and provides information on trails. Guided tours can be arranged with advance notice.

WATER SPORTS

Derwentwater Marina (✉ *Portinscale* ☎ *017687/72912*) offers boat rentals in all shapes and sizes, and instruction in canoeing, sailing, windsurfing, and rowing as well as in other water-related activities such as ghyll scrambling—the fine art of walking up a steep Lakeland stream. A two-day sailing or windsurfing course costs £185.

EN ROUTE The most scenic route from Keswick, B5289 south, runs along the eastern edge of Derwentwater, past turnoffs to natural attractions such as Ashness Bridge, the idyllic tarn of Watendlath, the Lodore Falls (best after a good rain), and the precariously balanced Bowder Stone. Farther south is the tiny village of **Grange,** a walking center at the head of Borrowdale, where there's a riverside café.

10

BORROWDALE

7 mi south of Keswick.

Fodor's Choice ★ South of Keswick and its lake lies the valley of Borrowdale, whose varied landscape of green valley floor and surrounding crags has long been considered one of the region's most magnificent treasures. **Rosthwaite**, a tranquil farming village, and **Seatoller**, the southernmost settlement, are the two main centers (both are accessible by bus from Keswick), though they are little more than clusters of aged buildings surrounded by glorious countryside.

GETTING HERE AND AROUND
The valley is south of Keswick on B5289. The Borrowdale bus service between Keswick and Seatoller runs frequently.

EXPLORING
Borrowdale Fells. These steep fells rise up dramatically behind Seatoller. Get out and walk whenever inspiration strikes. Trails are well signposted, or you can pick up maps and any gear in Keswick.

Scafell Pike. England's highest mountain at 3,210 feet, Scafell (pronounced *scar*-fell) Pike is visible from Seatoller. One route up the mountain, for experienced walkers, is from the hamlet of Seathwaite, a mile south of Seatoller.

WHERE TO STAY
For expanded hotel reviews, visit Fodors.com.

£££ **B&B/INN** ⊡ **Hazel Bank Country House.** Hikers and others of a less energetic bent appreciate the comforts of this stately, carefully restored Victorian home, which retains such original elements as the stained-glass windows. **Pros:** serene location; immaculate gardens; packed lunches on request. **Cons:** some distance from a lake; not for families with younger children. ⊠ *Off B5289, Rosthwaite* ☎ *017687/77248* ⊕ *www.hazelbankhotel.co.uk* ⇗ *8 rooms, 1 cottage* ⚲ *In-room: no a/c. In-hotel: restaurant, bar, business center, some age restrictions* ⊺◎⊺ *Some meals.*

££ **HOTEL** ⊡ **The Langstrath Country Inn.** Set in the tranquil hamlet of Stonethwaite at the top of Borrowdale, the Langstrath was originally built as a miner's cottage in the 16th century but has expanded into a spacious inn. **Pros:** great walks right out the door and up the Langstrath Valley; wonderfully peaceful. **Cons:** little or no choice of other places to eat nearby. ⊠ *Stonethwaite* ☎ *017687/77239* ⊕ *www.thelangstrath.com* ⇗ *8 rooms* ⚲ *In-room: no a/c, Wi-Fi. In-hotel: restaurant, bar* ⊗ *Closed Dec. and Jan.* ⊺◎⊺ *Breakfast.*

EN ROUTE **Honister Pass.** Beyond Seatoller, B5289 turns westward through Honister Pass (1,176 feet) and Buttermere Fell. Boulders line the road, which is one of the most dramatic in the region; at times it channels through soaring rock canyons. The road sweeps down from the pass to the village of Buttermere, sandwiched between Buttermere (the lake) and Crummock Water at the foot of high, craggy fells. Just beyond the pass toward Buttermere, Syke House Farm sells fantastic ice cream.

COCKERMOUTH

15 mi northwest of Borrowdale, 14 mi northwest of Seatoller.

This small but bustling town, at the confluence of the rivers Derwent and Cocker, has a maze of narrow streets that are a delight to wander. It's a bit off the usual tourist path, and a bit bohemian. The ruined 13th-century castle is open only on special occasions. Over a weekend in September the town holds the Taste Cumbria Food Festival.

GETTING HERE AND AROUND

The most straightforward access to the town is along the busy A66 from Penrith. For a more scenic, roundabout route, head over the Whinlatter or Honister passes from Keswick.

ESSENTIALS

Visitor Information Cockermouth (⌧ *The Town Hall, Market St.* ☎ *01900/822634* ⊕ *www.cockermouth.org.uk*).

EXPLORING

★ **Castlegate House Gallery.** One of the region's best galleries, Castlegate displays and sells an outstanding collection of contemporary works, many by Cumbrian artists. Changing exhibitions focus on paintings, sculpture, glass, ceramics, and jewelry. ⌧ *Castlegate* ☎ *01900/822149* ⊕ *www.castlegatehouse.co.uk* ☉ *Mar.–Dec., Fri., Sat., and Mon. 10:30–5; Jan. and Feb., Sat. 10:30–4.*

Jennings Brewery. Learn how real ales are made on a tour that includes the history of the company and allows you to see inside the fermentation casks, which hold up to 150 barrels of beer. It finishes up in the bar for some tastes of the product. There are one or two tours a day (more in summer), but no Sunday tours except in July and August. ⌧ *Castle Brewery* ☎ *0845/129–7190* ⊕ *www.jenningsbrewery.co.uk* ☒£6.50 tour ☉ *Shop Sept.–June, Mon.–Sat. 10–4; July and Aug., daily 10–4.*

Wordsworth House. Cockermouth was the birthplace of William Wordsworth (and his sister Dorothy), whose childhood home was this 18th-century town house. You see it complete with clutter, costumed interpreters, and period cooking in the kitchen; young visitors can also dress up in period costumes. Live harpsichord recitals take place regularly. Wordsworth's father is buried in the All Saints' churchyard, and the church has a stained-glass window in memory of the poet. ⌧ *Main St.* ☎ *01900/824805* ⊕ *www.nationaltrust.org.uk* ☒£6.50 ☉ *Mid-Mar.–Oct., Sat.–Thurs. 11–5; last admission at 4.*

10

WHERE TO EAT AND STAY

For expanded hotel reviews, visit Fodors.com.

££   ✕ **Bitter End.** Flocked floral wallpaper, old lamps, an open fire, and a
BRITISH   handsome wooden floor set the tone at this appealing pub attached to Cumbria's smallest brewery, whose beers it sells. In contrast to big brother Jennings nearby, this outfit is homey, intimate, and steadfastly independent, serving big, tasty portions of traditional British food such as lamb cobbler and fish-and-chips. Excellent Sunday lunches are especially popular with locals. ⌧ *15 Kirkgate* ☎ *01900/828993* ⊕ *www.bitterend.co.uk.*

£££
VEGETARIAN
★
✕ **Quince & Medlar.** Sophisticated and imaginative vegetarian cuisine, served by candlelight, is the specialty at this refined, wood-paneled Georgian town house. Diners are offered a drink in the sitting room before being called to their table; you choose from at least six main courses, such as smoked Cumberland cheese and mushroom roulade, all served with seasonal vegetables. Desserts are delicious, especially the lemon-and-almond sponge. ⊠ *13 Castlegate* ☎ *01900/823579* ⊕ *www. quinceandmedlar.co.uk* ⊗ *Closed Sun. and Mon. No lunch.*

£
B&B/INN
★
🏠 **Six Castlegate.** After a day of exploring, relax in stylish accommodation in an elegant B&B in a Georgian town house. **Pros:** modern facilities and antique style blend nicely; near galleries and attractions; exceptional value for money. **Cons:** some road noise in some rooms. ⊠ *6 Castlegate* ☎ *01900/826786* ⊕ *www.sixcastlegate.co.uk* ⇆ *6 rooms* ⚷ *In-room: no a/c, Wi-Fi* ⵔ *Breakfast.*

BASSENTHWAITE LAKE

5 mi east of Cockermouth, 3 mi north of Keswick.

Bassenthwaite is the only body of water officially called a lake in the Lake District; the others are known as "meres" or "waters." Bird-watchers know this less-frequented lake well because of the many species of migratory birds found here, including ospreys (check out ⊕ *www. ospreywatch.co.uk*). The shoreline habitat is the best preserved in the national park—in part because most of it is privately owned, and also because motorboats are not allowed. Posh accommodations and good restaurants dot the area, and popular walks include the climb up Skiddaw (3,054 feet), which, on a clear day, has panoramic views of the Lake District, the Pennines, Scotland, and the Isle of Man from its summit.

WHERE TO STAY

For expanded hotel reviews, visit Fodors.com.

££££
HOTEL
★
🏠 **The Pheasant.** Halfway between Cockermouth and Keswick at the northern end of Bassenthwaite Lake, this traditional 18th-century coaching inn exudes English coziness without the usual Lakeland fussiness. **Pros:** atmosphere of a well-loved local inn; fantastic bar. **Cons:** a little out of the way. ⊠ *Off A66, Bassenthwaite Lake* ☎ *017687/76234* ⊕ *www.the-pheasant.co.uk* ⇆ *15 rooms, 3 suites* ⚷ *In-room: no a/c. In-hotel: restaurant, bar, some pets allowed* ⵔ *Some meals.*

East Anglia

WORD OF MOUTH

"You can do a nifty 'self-tour' of King's College in Cambridge. Things are marked pretty clearly. The chapel was built by Kings Henry VI, VII, VIII, and Richard III. There's also a pretty cool little round Norman church."

—uhoh_busted

WELCOME TO EAST ANGLIA

TOP REASONS TO GO

★ **Cambridge:** A walk though the colleges is grand, but the best views of the university's colleges and immaculate lawns (and some famous bridges) are from a punt on the river.

★ **Constable Country:** In the area where Constable grew up, you can walk or row downstream from the pastel-shaded village of Dedham straight into the setting of one of the English landscape painter's masterpieces at Flatford Mill.

★ **Lincoln's old center:** The ancient center of the city has a vast, soaring cathedral, a proper rampart-ringed castle, and winding medieval streets.

★ **Wild North Sea coast:** North Norfolk has enormous sandy beaches (great for walking) and opportunities to see seals and birdlife, especially on the salt marshes around Blakeney.

★ **Lavenham:** This medieval town is the most comely of the tight-knit cluster of places that did well from the wool trade, with architecture including timber-frame houses gnarled into crookedness by age.

1 Cambridge. The home of the ancient university is East Anglia's liveliest town. The city center is perfect for ambling around the colleges, museums, and King's College Chapel, one of England's greatest monuments.

2 Ely and Central Suffolk. The villages within a short drive of Cambridge remain largely unspoiled. Ely's lofty cathedral dominates the surrounding flatlands, and Sudbury, Long Melford, Lavenham, and Bury St. Edmunds preserve their rich historical flavor.

3 The Suffolk Coast. Idyllic villages such as Dedham and Flatford form the center of what's been dubbed "Constable Country," while the nearby Suffolk Coast includes such atmospheric seaside towns as Woodbridge and Aldeburgh.

Map labels: TO LINCOLN · The Wash · Houghton Hall · A149 · Spalding · A17 · Sutton Crosses · Sandringham · King's Lynn · 5 · LINCOLNSHIRE · Stamford · Wisbech · Burghley House · Downham Market · A141 · Peterborough · CAMBRIDGESHIRE · Chatteris · A10 · Ely · A1(M) · Huntingdon · A142 · A14 · Newmarket · A1 · A11 · 1 · Cambridge · M11 · ESSEX · M11 · Braintree · A120 · A131

11

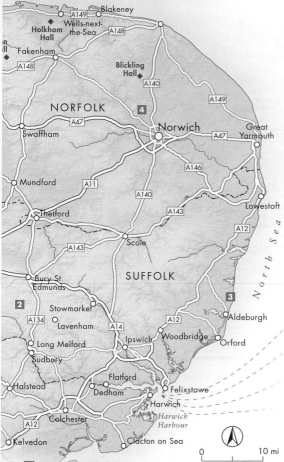

GETTING ORIENTED

East Anglia, in southeastern England, can be divided into distinct areas for sightseeing: the central area surrounding the ancient university city of Cambridge and including Ely, with its magnificent cathedral rising out of the flatlands, and the towns of inland Suffolk; the Suffolk Heritage Coast, with its historic small towns and villages; and the northeast, with the region's capital, Norwich, the waterways of the Broads, and the beaches and salt marshes of the North Norfolk coast. Farther north, in Lincolnshire, are the city of Lincoln, landmarked by its tall, fluted cathedral towers, and the historic town of Stamford.

0 ——— 10 mi
0 ——— 10 km

4 Norwich and North Norfolk. Sights in Norwich include its cathedral and castle. To the north and west you'll find the stately homes of Blickling Hall, Houghton Hall, and Sandringham, plus quiet coastal resorts such as Blakeney and Wells-next-the-Sea.

5 Stamford and Lincoln. On the western fringes of East Anglia, Lincoln is worth visiting for its Norman cathedral, whereas Stamford is best known for Burghley House, an impressive Elizabethan mansion.

EAST ANGLIA'S SEAFOOD BOUNTY

Perhaps unsurprisingly in an island nation, the harvest of the rivers and the sea forms an essential part of the British culinary tradition. Few regions are so closely associated with a love of good seafood as East Anglia.

Fish and chips taste perfect during a day by the sea in East Anglia (above); Cromer crab dressed with lemon mayonnaise (right, top); potted shrimp, a tasty appetizer (right, bottom).

The coastlines of Essex, Suffolk, and Norfolk overflow with towns that specialize in one type of seaborne bounty or another. Shrimp, crab, and oysters are still caught using centuries-old methods; and lobsters, crabs, and mussels from Norfolk are sent to the top restaurants in London. Changing tastes tell a kind of social history of their own: oysters, now an expensive luxury, were once considered peasant food; and a new generation of chefs, eager to reconnect with forgotten ingredients or preparations, is rediscovering old-fashioned flavors such as eel and samphire. Then there's that most famous of British seafood dishes—humble fish and chips. Some of the best in the country can be found in Suffolk towns such as Aldeburgh, where savvy fish-and-chip shop owners have installed webcams so customers can check how far the line stretches down the street.

SEA SALT

Evidence suggests that sea salt has been harvested in East Anglia for 2,000 years. It's popular today—but only one regional company still produces sea salt in the local style. Based in and named after the harbor town of Maldon in Essex, Maldon Crystal Salt Company uses a distinctive method that yields thin, flaky crystals with a delicate piquancy. Praised by chefs, Maldon salt is widely available at English supermarkets.

CROMER CRAB
Known for their juicy flesh and higher-than-average white meat content, the best East Anglian crab comes from the area around Cromer in Norfolk. It's often served in salads and pasta dishes, or in savory crab cakes.

EEL
A staple of the East Anglian diet for centuries but long out of favor, the humble eel is making a comeback at fashionable restaurants. Eels are usually served smoked (on their own, or in soups or salads) or jellied in a flavored stock with the consistency of aspic.

MUSSELS
This type of small clam is particularly associated with the towns of Brancester and Stiffkey. Cheap and versatile, mussels can be served on their own; with other seafood; or in soups and stews.

OYSTERS
The Essex coast has been producing oysters since Roman times. A luxury item, oysters are usually served raw by the dozen, with few accompaniments, as a main course, or as a starter by the half dozen.

SAMPHIRE
A green sea vegetable that grows wild on shores and marshland, samphire is abundant in East Anglia, where it is an accompaniment to local seafood. Crisp and slightly salty, it is often described as "tasting like the sea."

SHERINGHAM LOBSTER
This well-regarded lobster is usually served with melted butter, or with fries as a kind of upper-class cousin of fish and chips. Lobster bisque—a rich, creamy soup—is also popular.

SHRIMP
Caught primarily off the coasts of Lancashire and East Anglia, the British shrimp is a type of shellfish similar to, but much smaller than, prawns. Potted shrimp is a traditional starter, made with butter, mace, and nutmeg.

YARMOUTH BLOATERS
A form of cured herring produced in Great Yarmouth, near Norwich, the fat, slightly salted fish are not gutted before being smoked. This gives them a particularly strong, almost gamey flavor.

CHOOSING YOUR FISH AND CHIPS
The key word is simplicity: very fresh fish, deep-fried in batter, served immediately. Chips (slices of potato) must be thick cut and slightly soft, not crisp like fries, and sprinkled with salt and vinegar. The kind you get in fish and chip shops is almost always better than pub offerings. Cod, plaice, and haddock are the most popular choices, but the concern about cod overfishing means that you may see pollock, coley, or skate as alternatives.

Updated by
Jack Jewers

One of those beautiful English inconsistencies, East Anglia has no spectacular mountains or rivers to disturb the storied, quiet land, full of rural delights. Occupying an area of southeastern England that pushes out into the North Sea, its counties of Essex, Norfolk, Suffolk, Lincolnshire, and Cambridgeshire feel cut off from the pulse of the country. Among its highlights is Cambridge, a lovely and ancient university city. East Anglia also has four of the country's greatest stately homes: Holkham Hall, Blickling Hall, Houghton Hall, and Sandringham—where the Queen spends Christmas.

In times past, East Anglia was one of the most important centers of power in northern Europe. Towns like Lincoln were major Roman settlements, and the medieval wool trade brought huge prosperity to the higgledy-piggledy streets of tiny Lavenham. Thanks to its relative lack of thoroughfares and canals, however, East Anglia was mercifully untouched by the Industrial Revolution. The area is rich in idyllic, quintessentially English villages: sleepy, sylvan settlements in the midst of otherwise deserted lowlands. Even the towns feel small and manageable; the biggest city, Norwich, has a population of just 125,000. Cambridge, with its ancient university, is the area's most famous draw. There are incomparable cathedrals, at Ely and Lincoln particularly, and one of the finest Gothic buildings in Europe, King's College Chapel.

And yet, despite all of these treasures, the real joy of exploring East Anglia is making your own discoveries. Spend a couple of days exploring the hidden byways of the fens, or just taking in the subtle beauties of the many England-like-it-looks-in-the-movies villages. If you find yourself driving down a small country lane and an old church or mysterious, ivy-covered ruin peeks out from behind the trees, give in to your curiosity and look inside. Such hidden places are East Anglia's best-kept secret. There are real treasures to be found within those walls.

EAST ANGLIA PLANNER

11

WHEN TO GO

Summer and late spring are the best times to visit East Anglia. Late fall and winter can be cold, windy, and rainy, though this is England's driest region and crisp, frosty days here are beautiful. To escape crowds, avoid the popular Norfolk Broads in late July and August. You can't visit most of the Cambridge colleges during exam period (late May to mid-June), and the competition for hotel rooms heats up during graduation week (late June). The Aldeburgh Festival of Music and the Arts, one of the biggest events on the British classical music calendar, takes place in June.

PLANNING YOUR TIME

Cambridge is the region's most interesting city, and ideally you should allow two or three days to absorb its various sights. (In a pinch you could do it as a day trip from London, but only with an early start and a good pair of walking shoes.) You could easily use the city as a base for exploring Ely, Bury St. Edmunds, Lavenham, Long Melford, and Sudbury, although you will also find accommodations in these towns. The Suffolk Coast offers enticing overnight stops in such small towns as Dedham and Aldeburgh. In the northern part of the region, Norwich makes a good place to stop for the night, and has enough sights to keep you interested for a day. If you're here to see the coast, you'd do better staying in villages such as Blakeney or Wells. Allow a full day for seeing large houses such as Blickling Hall, near Norwich, and Burghley House, outside Stamford. Lincoln, notable for its cathedral, and Stamford are west and north of Norfolk if you want to work them into an itinerary.

GETTING HERE AND AROUND

AIR TRAVEL

Norwich International Airport serves a limited number of domestic and international destinations, though not the United States. London Stansted Airport, 30 mi south of Cambridge, is used mainly for European flights. The vast majority of travelers to the region arrive by train, car, or bus.

Airports London Stansted Airport (✉ *Bassingbourn Rd., A140, Bishop's Stortford* ☎ *0844/335/1803* ⊕ *www.stanstedairport.com).* **Norwich International Airport** (✉ *Amsterdam Way, A140, Norwich* ☎ *01603/411923* ⊕ *www. norwichairport.co.uk).*

BUS TRAVEL

National Express buses serve the region from London's Victoria Coach Station. Average travel times are 3 hours to Cambridge, 2½ hours to Bury St. Edmunds, 5 hours (with one transfer) to Norwich, and 4 hours to Lincoln.

Long-distance buses are useful for reaching the region and traveling between its major centers, but for smaller hops, local buses are best. First and Stagecoach buses cover the Cambridge, Lincolnshire, and Norwich areas. Information about local Norfolk service and county service is available from the Norfolk Bus Information Centre. Traveline can answer public transportation questions.

636 < **East Anglia**

A FirstDay ticket from First for a day's unlimited bus travel around Norwich and the Norfolk coast costs £13, while a FirstWeek pass, good for seven days, costs £28. These tickets cover all buses except the Park and Ride shuttles that link parking lots with the town center. There are also various local passes that cost between £2 and £18. You can buy any of these tickets from the driver.

Bus Contacts First (☎ *0845/602–0121* ⊕ *www.firstgroup.com*). **National Express East Anglia** (☎ *0845/600–7245* ⊕ *www.nationalexpresseastanglia. com*). **Norfolk Bus Information Centre** (☎ *0845/300–6116*). **Stagecoach** (☎ *01223/423578* ⊕ *www.stagecoachbus.com/cambridge*). **Traveline** (☎ *0871/200–2233* ⊕ *www.traveline.org.uk*).

CAR TRAVEL

If you're driving from London, Cambridge (54 mi) is off M11. At Exit 9, M11 connects with A11 to Norwich (114 mi); A14 off A11 goes to Bury St. Edmunds. A12 from London goes through east Suffolk via Ipswich. For Lincoln (131 mi), take A1 via Huntingdon, Peterborough, and Grantham to A46 at Newark-on-Trent. A more scenic alternative is to leave A1 at Grantham and take A607 to Lincoln.

East Anglia has few fast main roads besides those mentioned here. Once off the A roads, traveling within the region often means taking country lanes that have many twists and turns, and going even just a few miles can take much longer than you think.

TRAIN TRAVEL

The entire region is well served by trains from London's Liverpool Street, King's Cross, and St. Pancras stations. The quality and convenience of these services varies enormously, however. Cambridge trains leave from King's Cross and Liverpool Street, take around one hour, and cost £20. On the other hand, getting to Lincoln from St. Pancras entails at least one transfer, takes two to three hours, and costs £55 to £80. ■TIP➜ Tickets for trains between London and Lincoln are a fraction of the price if you buy online in advance. A good way to save money on local trains in East Anglia is to buy an Anglia Plus Ranger Pass. It costs £15 for one day or £30 for three days, and allows unlimited rail travel in Norfolk, Suffolk, and part of Cambridgeshire. You can add kids for an extra £2.

Train Contacts East Midlands Trains (☎ *0845/712–5678* ⊕ *www. eastmidlandstrains.co.uk*). **First Capital Connect** (☎ *0845/026–4700* ⊕ *www. firstcapitalconnect.co.uk*). **National Express** (☎ *0845/600–7245* ⊕ *www. nationalexpresseastanglia.com*). **National Rail Enquiries** (☎ *0845/748–4950* ⊕ *www.nationalrail.co.uk*).

RESTAURANTS

In summer the coast gets so packed with people that reservations are essential at restaurants. Getting something to eat at other than regular mealtime hours is not always possible in small towns; look for cafés if you want a midmorning or after-lunch snack. Look for area specialties, such as duckling, Norfolk black turkey, hare, and partridge, on menus around the region. In Norwich, there's no escaping the hot, bright-yellow Colman's mustard, which is perfect smeared gingerly on some sausage and mash.

HOTELS

The region is full of centuries-old, half-timber inns with rooms full of roaring fires and cozy bars. Bed-and-breakfasts are a good option in pricey Cambridge. It's always busy in Cambridge and along the coast in summer, so reserve well in advance.

WHAT IT COSTS IN POUNDS					
	£	££	£££	££££	£££££
Restaurants	under £10	£10–£14	£15–£19	£20–£25	over £25
Hotels	under £70	£70–£120	£121–£160	£161–£220	over £220

Restaurant prices are per person for a main course or equivalent combination of smaller dishes at dinner excluding tax. Hotel prices reflect the rack rate of a standard double room for two people in high season, including 20% V.A.T. Check online for off-season rates and special deals or discounts.

VISITOR INFORMATION

Broads Authority (✉ *Dragonfly House, 2 Gilders Way, Norwich* ☎ *01603/610734* ⊕ *www.broads-authority.gov.uk*). **East of England Tourism** (✉ *Dettingen House, Dettingen Way, Bury St. Edmunds* ☎ *01284/727470* ⊕ *www. visiteastofengland.com*).

CAMBRIDGE

With the spires of its university buildings framed by towering trees and expansive meadows, its medieval streets and passages enhanced by gardens and riverbanks, the city of Cambridge is among the loveliest in England. The city predates the Roman occupation of Britain, but there's confusion over exactly how the university was founded. The most widely accepted story is that it was established in 1209 by a pair of scholars from Oxford, who left their university in protest over the wrongful execution of a colleague for murder.

Today Cambridge embodies a certain genteel, intellectual, and sometimes anachronistically idealized image of Englishness. Think William Wordsworth, Thackeray, Byron, Tennyson, E.M. Forster, and C.S. Lewis. The exquisite King's College choir defines the traditional English Christmas, when the *Festival of Nine Lessons and Carols* is broadcast live on Christmas Eve. On top of all this tradition and history, Cambridge remains a lively city and an extraordinary center of learning and research where innovation and discovery still happen behind its ancient walls.

Keep in mind there is no recognizable campus: the scattered colleges *are* the university. The town reveals itself only slowly, filled with tiny gardens, ancient courtyards, imposing classic buildings, alleyways that lead past medieval churches, and wisteria-hung facades. Perhaps the best views are from the Backs, the green parkland that extends along the River Cam behind several colleges. This sweeping openness, a result of the larger size of the colleges and from the lack of industrialization in the city center, is what distinguishes Cambridge from Oxford.

GETTING HERE AND AROUND

Good bus (three hours) and train (one hour) services connect London and Cambridge. The train station is a mile or so southeast of the center and is connected by the frequent Citi 3 bus service, run by Stagecoach, to Emmanuel Street, which is just around the corner from the long-distance bus terminus on Drummer Street. If you're driving, don't attempt to venture very far into the center—parking is scarce and pricey. The center is amenable to explorations on foot, or you could join the throng by renting a bicycle.

Stagecoach sells Dayrider (£3.50) tickets for all-day bus travel within Cambridge, and Megarider tickets (£11.50) for seven days of travel within the city. You can extend these to cover the whole county of Cambridgeshire (£5.40 and £21.50, respectively). Buy any of them from the driver.

City Sightseeing operates open-top bus tours of Cambridge—the Backs, the colleges, the Imperial War Museum in Duxford, and the Grafton shopping center. Tours can be joined at marked bus stops in the city. Tickets are £13. Also ask the tourist office about tours.

TIMING

In summer and over the Easter and Christmas holidays, Cambridge is devoid of students, its heart and soul. To see the city in full swing, visit from October through June. In summer there are arts and music festivals, notably the Strawberry Fair and the Arts Festival (both June) and the Folk Festival (late July to early August). The May Bumps, intercollegiate boat races, are, confusingly, held the first week of June. This is also the month when students celebrate the end of exam season, so expect to encounter some boisterous nightlife.

ESSENTIALS

Bus Contacts First (☎ *0845/602–0121* ⊕ *www.firstgroup.com*). **Stagecoach** (☎ *01223/423578* ⊕ *www.stagecoachbus.com/cambridge*).

Visitor and Tour Information Cambridge (✉ *Peas Hill* ☎ *0871/226–8006, 44/1223-464732 from abroad* ⊕ *www.visitcambridge.org*). **Cambridge University** (☎ *01223/337733* ⊕ *www.cam.ac.uk*). **City Sightseeing** (✉ *Cambridge Train Station, Station Rd.* ☎ *01223/423578* ⊕ *www.city-sightseeing.com*).

EXPLORING

Exploring the city means, in large part, exploring the university. Each of the 25 oldest colleges is built around a series of courts, or quadrangles, framing manicured, velvety lawns. Because students and fellows (faculty) live and work in these courts, access is sometimes restricted, and at *all* times you are asked not to picnic in the quadrangles.

Visitors are not normally allowed into college buildings other than chapels, dining halls, and some libraries; some colleges charge admission for certain buildings. The university's Web site (⊕ *www.cam.ac.uk*) has information about the colleges and related institutions. Public visiting hours vary from college to college, depending on the time of year, and it's best to call or to check with the city tourist office. Colleges close to visitors during the main exam time, late May to mid-June. Term

Cricket, anyone? Audley End, a 17th-century house, serves as an idyllic backdrop for a cricket match.

time (when classes are in session) means roughly October to December, January to March, and April to June; summer term, or vacation, runs from July to September. ■ TIP→ Bring a pair of binoculars, as some college buildings have highly intricate details, such as the spectacular ceiling at King's College Chapel. When the colleges are open, the best way to gain access is to join a walking tour led by an official Blue Badge guide—many areas are off-limits unless you do. The two-hour tours (£12.50–£14.50) leave up to four times daily from the city tourist office. The other traditional view of the colleges is gained from a punt—the boats propelled by pole on the River Cam.

TOP ATTRACTIONS

OFF THE BEATEN PATH

Audley End House and Gardens. A famous example of early-17th-century architecture, Audley End was once owned by Charles II, who bought it as a convenient place to break his journey on the way to the Newmarket races. Although the palatial building was remodeled in the 18th and 19th centuries, the Jacobean style is still on display in the magnificent Great Hall. You can walk in the park, landscaped by Capability Brown in the 18th century, and the fine Victorian gardens. Two newer exhibits focus on the lives of domestic servants in the late 19th century. The Service Wing lets you look "below stairs" at the kitchen, scullery (where fish were de-scaled and chickens were plucked), and game larder (where pheasants, partridges, and rabbits were hung), while the stables give kids the chance to see old saddles and tack and don Victorian riding costumes. The house is in Saffron Waldon, 14 mi south of Cambridge. ✉ *B1383* ☎ *01799/522842* ⊕ *www.english-heritage.org.uk* 🎫 *£12.50; gardens and Service Wing only, £8.70* ⊗ *House: Apr.–Sept., Wed.–Sun.*

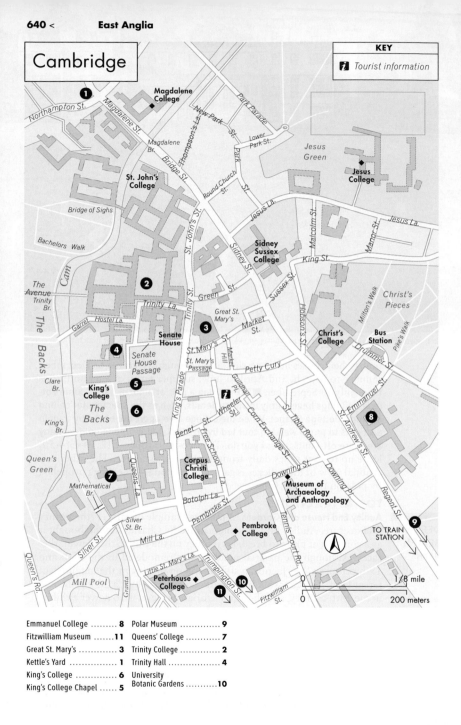

Cambridge

KEY

i *Tourist information*

noon–5; Oct., Wed.–Sun. noon–4. Stables, Service Wing, and gardens: Apr.–Sept., Wed.–Sun. 10–6; Oct., Wed.–Sun. 11–5; Nov.–late Dec. and early Feb., weekends 10–4; late Feb.–Mar, Wed.–Sun. 10–4. Winter hrs can vary; call ahead.

Emmanuel College. The master hand of architect Christopher Wren (1632–1723) is evident throughout much of Cambridge, particularly at Emmanuel, built on the site of a Dominican friary, where he designed the chapel and colonnade. A stained-glass window in the chapel has a likeness of John Harvard, founder of Harvard University, who studied here. The college, founded in 1584, was an early center of Puritan learning; a number of the Pilgrims were Emmanuel alumni, and they remembered their alma mater in naming Cambridge, Massachusetts. ✉ *St. Andrew's St.* ☎ *01223/334200* ⊕ *www.emma.cam.ac.uk* ☉ *Daily 9–6, except exam period.*

Fodor's Choice
★

Fitzwilliam Museum. In a Classical Revival building renowned for its grand Corinthian portico, the Fitzwilliam, founded by the seventh viscount Fitzwilliam of Merrion in 1816, has one of Britain's most outstanding collections of art and antiquities. Highlights include two large Titians, an extensive collection of French impressionist painting, and many paintings by Matisse and Picasso. The opulent interior displays its treasures to marvelous effect, from Egyptian pieces such as inch-high figurines and painted coffins to sculptures from the Chinese Han dynasty of the 3rd century BC. Besides its archaeological collections, the Fitzwilliam contains English Staffordshire and other pottery, as well as a fascinating room of armor and muskets. Guided tours beginning at 2:30 pm on Saturday cost £4; buy tickets that day or in advance from the tourism office. ✉ *Trumpington St.* ☎ *01223/332900* ⊕ *www.fitzmuseum.cam.ac.uk* ✉ *Free* ☉ *Tues.–Sat. 10–5, Sun. noon–5.*

Great St. Mary's. Known as the "university church," Great St. Mary's has its origins in the 11th century, although the current building dates from 1478. The main reason to visit is to climb the 113-foot tower, which has a superb view over the colleges and marketplace. Also here is the **Michaelhouse Centre,** a small café, gallery, and performing arts venue with frequent free lunchtime concerts. Guided tours of the church and tower depart Saturday at 11:55, 1:25, and 2:55. ✉ *Market Hill, King's Parade* ☎ *01223/741716* ⊕ *www.gsm.cam.ac.uk* ✉ *Free, tower £2.50, guided tours £10* ☉ *May–Aug., Mon.–Sat. 9:30–5, Sun. 12:30–5; Sept.–Apr., Mon.–Sat. 9:30–4, Sun. 12:30–4.*

OFF THE BEATEN PATH

Imperial War Museum Duxford. The buildings and grounds of this former airfield, now Europe's leading aviation museum, house a remarkable collection of 180 aircraft from Europe and the United States. It's effectively a complex of several museums under one banner. The **Land Warfare Hall** features tanks and other military vehicles. The striking **American Air Museum,** honoring the 30,000 Americans killed in action flying from Britain during World War II, contains the largest display of American fighter planes outside the United States. (Duxford was the headquarters of the American 78th Fighter Group.) **AirSpace** contains a vast array of military and civil aircraft in a 3-acre hangar. Directly underneath is the **Airborne Assault Museum,** which chronicles

A must-see at Cambridge is King's College Chapel, a masterpiece of Perpendicular Gothic style.

the history of airborne forces, such as the British Parachute Regiment, which played a pivotal role in the Normandy Landings. There are also hangars where you can watch restoration work on World War II planes and exhibitions on maritime warfare and the Battle of Britain. ✉ *A505, Duxford* ☎ *01223/835000* ⊕ *duxford.iwm.org.uk* ✉ *£16.50* ⊙ *Mid-Mar.–late Oct., daily 10–6; late Oct.–mid-Mar., daily 10–4. Last admission 1 hr before closing.*

King's College. Founded in 1441 by Henry VI, King's College's most famous landmark is its late-15th-century chapel. Other architecture of note is the neo-Gothic Porters' Lodge, facing King's Parade, which was a relatively recent addition in the 1830s, and the classical Gibbs building. ■**TIP→** Head down to the river, from where the panorama of college and chapel is one of the university's most photographed views. Past students of King's College include the novelist E.M. Forster, the economist John Maynard Keynes, and the World War I poet Rupert Brooke. ✉ *King's Parade* ☎ *01223/331100* ⊕ *www.kings.cam.ac.uk* ✉ *£6.50, includes chapel* ⊙ *Term time, weekdays 9:30–3:30, Sat. 9:30–3:15, Sun. 1:15–2:15; out of term, Mon.–Sat. 9:30–4:30, Sun. 10–5.*

Fodor's Choice
★

King's College Chapel. Based on Sainte-Chapelle, the 13th-century royal chapel in Paris, this house of worship is the final, perhaps most glorious flowering of Perpendicular Gothic in Britain. Henry VI, the king after whom the college is named, oversaw the work. From the outside, the most prominent features are the massive flying buttresses and the fingerlike spires that line the length of the building. Inside, the most obvious impression is of great space—the chapel has been described as "the noblest barn in Europe"—and of light flooding in from its huge windows. The brilliantly colored bosses (carved panels at the intersections of the roof ribs) are particularly intense, although hard to see without binoculars. An exhibition in the chantries, or side chapels, explains more about the chapel's construction. Behind the altar is *The Adoration of the Magi,* an enormous painting by Peter Paul Rubens. ■TIP➔ The chapel, unlike the rest of King's College, stays open during exam periods. Every Christmas Eve, a festival of carols is sung by the chapel's famous choir. To compete for the small number of tickets available, join the line at the college's main entrance early—doors open at 7 am. ✉ *King's Parade* ☎ *01223/331212* ⊕ *www.kings. cam.ac.uk* 🖱 *£6.50, includes college and grounds* ⊗ *Term time, weekdays 9:30–3:30, Sat. 9:30–3:15, Sun. 1:15–2:15; out of term, Mon.–Sat. 9:30–4:30, Sun. 10–5; hrs vary, so call ahead.*

A GIFT FOR SCIENCE

For centuries Cambridge has been among the country's greatest universities, rivaled only by Oxford. Since the time of its most famous alumnus, Sir Isaac Newton, it has outshone Oxford in the natural sciences. The university has taken advantage of this prestige, sharing its research facilities with high-tech industries. Surrounded by technology companies, Cambridge has been dubbed "Silicon Fen," a comparison to California's Silicon Valley.

QUICK BITES The 600-year-old **Pickerel Inn** (✉ *30 Magdalene St.* ☎ *01223/355068*), one of the city's oldest pubs, makes for a good stop for an afternoon pint of real ale or lager and a bowl of potato wedges. Watch for the low beams.

★ **Polar Museum.** Beautifully designed, this museum at the university's Scott Polar Research Institute chronicles the history of polar exploration. There's a particular emphasis on the British expeditions of the 20th century, including the ill-fated attempt by Robert Falcon Scott to be the first to reach the South Pole in 1912. Norwegian explorer Roald Amundsen reached the pole first; Scott and his men perished on the return journey, but his story became legendary. There are also collections devoted to the indigenous people of northern Canada, Greenland, and Alaska. ✉ *Scott Polar Research Institute, Lensfield Rd.* ☎ *01223/336540* ⊕ *www.spri. cam.ac.uk/museum* 🖱 *Free* ⊗ *Tues.–Sat. 10–4.*

Queens' College. One of the most eye-catching colleges, Queens' is named after Margaret, queen of Henry VI, and Elizabeth, queen of Edward IV. Founded in 1448, the college is tucked away on Queens' Lane, next to the wide lawns that lead down from King's College to the Backs. The secluded "cloister court" looks untouched since its completion in the 1540s. Queens' masterpiece is the **Mathematical Bridge,** the original version of which is said to have been built without any fastenings. The current bridge (1902) is securely bolted. The college is closed for visitors late May to late June. ✉ *Queens' La.* ☎ *01223/335511* ⊕ *www. quns.cam.ac.uk* 🖱 *£2.50* ⊗ *Mid-Mar.–mid-May, daily 10–4:30; late June–early Oct., daily 10–4:30; early Oct.–late Oct., weekdays 2–4, weekends 10–4:30; Nov.–mid-Mar., daily 2–4.*

Trinity College. Founded in 1546 by Henry VIII, Trinity replaced a 14th-century educational foundation and is the largest college in either

Cambridge or Oxford, with nearly 700 undergraduates. Many of the buildings match its size, not least its 17th-century "great court." Here the massive gatehouse holds "Great Tom," a giant clock that strikes each hour with high and low notes. The college's greatest masterpiece is Christopher Wren's **library,** colonnaded and seemingly constructed with as much light as stone. Here you can see A.A. Milne's handwritten manuscript of *The House at Pooh Corner.* Alumni include Isaac Newton, William Thackeray, George Byron, Alfred Tennyson, and 31 Nobel Prize winners. ⊠ *St. John's St.* ☎ *01223/338400* ⊕ *www.trin.cam.ac.uk* 🎫 *£1* ⊙ *College and chapel daily 10–4, except exam period and event days; library weekdays noon–2, Sat. in term time 10:30–12:30; hall weekdays 3–5, except during services and rehearsals.*

WORTH NOTING

Kettle's Yard. Originally a private house owned by a former curator of London's Tate galleries, Kettle's Yard contains a fine collection of 20th-century art, sculpture, furniture, and decorative arts, including works by Henry Moore, Barbara Hepworth, and Henri Gaudier-Brzeska. One gallery shows changing exhibitions of modern art and crafts, and weekly concerts and lectures attract an eclectic mix of enthusiasts. Ring the bell for admission. ⊠ *Castle St.* ☎ *01223/748100* ⊕ *www. kettlesyard.co.uk* 🎫 *Free* ⊙ *House early Apr.–Sept., Tues.–Sun. and Mon. holidays 1:30–4:30; Oct.–early Apr., Tues.–Sun. and Mon. holidays 2–4. Gallery Tues.–Sun. 11:30–5.*

Trinity Hall. Not one of the university's standout buildings, Trinity Hall does have one of its most quintessential viewpoints. Beside the river is a wall where you can sit and watch students in punts maneuver under the ancient ornamental bridges of Clare and King's. Access to the river is down Trinity Lane, off Trinity Street. ⊠ *Trinity La.* ☎ *01223/332500* ⊕ *www.trinhall.cam.ac.uk* ⊙ *Daily 9:15–noon and 2–5:30, except exam period and summer term.*

University Botanic Gardens. Laid out in 1846, these gardens contain rare specimens, conservatories, and a rock garden. They are a five-minute walk from the Fitzwilliam Museum. ⊠ *Cory Lodge, Bateman St.* ☎ *01223/336265* ⊕ *www.botanic.cam.ac.uk* 🎫 *£4, free Nov.–Feb.* ⊙ *Apr.–Sept., daily 10–6; Nov.–Jan., daily 10–4; Feb., Mar., and Oct., daily 10–5. Conservatories close ½ hr before gardens.*

WHERE TO EAT

££

ITALIAN

✕ **Jamie's Italian.** Run by celebrity chef Jamie Oliver, this is possibly the busiest restaurant in Cambridge. In truth, the long queues probably have more to do with his star power and the no-reservations policy, but the food also deserves praise. The menu is a combination of authentic Italian flavors and modern variations on the classics; you could opt for the pasta *arrabiata,* made with bread crumbs and fiery peppers, or a plate of shell-roasted scallops with pancetta and tomato salsa. The gorgeous building, a former library, is an attraction in itself. The atmosphere is relaxed and casual, and the prices are lower than you'd expect. ⊠ *Old Library, Wheeler St.* ☎ *01223/654094* ⊕ *www.jamieoliver.com/ italian* 🍴 *Reservations not accepted.*

££
SEAFOOD
✕ **Loch Fyne.** Part of a Scottish chain that harvests its own oysters, this airy, casual place across the street from the Fitzwilliam Museum is deservedly popular. The mussels and salmon are fresh and well prepared, and line-caught tuna is served with a mint-and-caper salsa. Try the Bradan Rost smoked salmon flavored with Scotch whisky. The place is open for breakfast, lunch, and dinner. ✉ *37 Trumpington St.* ☎ *01223/362433* ⊕ *www.lochfyne.com.*

£££££
FRENCH
★
✕ **Midsummer House.** An elegant restaurant beside the River Cam on the edge of Midsummer Common, this gray-brick building has a comfortable conservatory and a handful of tables in a lush secluded garden under fruit trees. Fixed-price menus for lunch and dinner include innovative French and Mediterranean dishes. Choices might include braised turbot or roast venison. ✉ *Midsummer Common* ☎ *01223/369299* ⊕ *www.midsummerhouse.co.uk* ⚑ *Reservations essential* ⊘ *Closed Sun. and Mon. No lunch Tues.*

££
BRITISH
✕ **The Oak.** This charming, intimate restaurant has fast become a local favorite. It's near an unpromisingly busy intersection, but the friendliness of the staff and classic bistro food more than make up for it. Typical mains include sea bream fillet with tomato-and-basil dressing, or rib-eye steak with truffle butter and fries. Ask to be seated in the lovely walled garden if the weather's fine. ✉ *6 Lensfield Rd.* ☎ *01223/323361* ⊕ *www.theoakbistro.co.uk.*

£££££
BRITISH
✕ **Restaurant 22.** Pretty stained-glass windows separate this sophisticated little restaurant from bustling Chesterton Road. The setting, in a terrace of houses, is low-key, but the food is creative and eye-catching. The fixed-price menu changes monthly and features such dishes as pork belly with bubble and squeak (a traditional dish made of fried potatoes and onions), and twice-baked-ricotta-and-baba-ghanoush soufflé. ✉ *22 Chesterton Rd.* ☎ *01223/351880* ⊕ *www.restaurant22.co.uk* ⊘ *Closed Sun. and Mon. No lunch.*

£££
ITALIAN
★
✕ **Three Horseshoes.** This early-19th-century pub-restaurant in a thatched cottage has an elegant dining space in the conservatory and more-casual tables in the airy bar. The tempting, beautifully presented, and carefully sourced dishes are modern Italian with a British accent. Appetizers include scallops with cauliflower puree, and among the main courses is turbot with local cockles and roast chicken served with crayfish, mushrooms, and truffles. The wine list is enormous and predominantly Italian, but there are also some good New World choices. It's 5 mi west of Cambridge, about a 10-minute taxi ride. ✉ *High St., Madingley* ☎ *01954/210221* ⊕ *www.threehorseshoesmadingley.co.uk.*

££
MODERN BRITISH
✕ **The Willow Tree.** Plenty of Cambridge residents are happy to drive 20 minutes to this stylish pub in the sleepy village of Bourn. The seasonal menu serves classic British and European dishes with a flourish. Typical dishes include sea bass with saffron sauce, or oxtail pie with parsnip and vanilla puree. There's also a selection of pizzas and tapas. For dessert try the deliciously zingy lemon meringue with lemon jelly, or the sticky toffee pudding with toffee sauce and ice cream. Best of all, prices are very reasonable. Bourn is 10 mi east of Cambridge; take the B1046 for the prettiest drive. ✉ *29 High St., Bourn* ☎ *01954/719775* ⊕ *www. thewillowtreebourn.com.*

WHERE TO STAY

There aren't many hotels downtown. For more (and cheaper) options, consider one of the numerous guesthouses on the arterial roads and in the suburbs. These average around £30 to £70 per person per night and can be booked through the tourist information center.

For expanded hotel reviews, visit Fodors.com.

££££–£££££
HOTEL

⊡ **Doubletree by Hilton.** Many rooms have sweeping views of the surrounding area at this modern establishment that makes the most of its peaceful riverside location. **Pros:** central position; good facilities; spacious rooms. **Cons:** occasionally poor service; disappointing breakfasts. ⊠ *Granta Pl. and Mill La.* ☎ *01223/259988* ⊕ *www.doubletreebyhilton. co.uk* ⇨ *118 rooms, 4 suites* ⚷ *In-room: no a/c (some), Wi-Fi. In-hotel: restaurant, bar, pool, gym, parking* ¶◯¶ *Breakfast.*

££–£££
HOTEL

⊡ **Duxford Lodge.** A short drive from the Imperial War Museum in Duxford, this family-run hotel sits off the main road between Cambridge and Saffron Walden. **Pros:** off the beaten path; good food. **Cons:** need a car to get around; prices go up air show weekends. ⊠ *Ickleton Rd., Duxford* ☎ *01223/836444* ⊕ *www.duxfordlodgehotel.co.uk* ⇨ *11 rooms* ⚷ *In-room: no a/c (some), Wi-Fi. In-hotel: restaurant* ¶◯¶ *Breakfast.*

££
B&B/INN

⊡ **Finches Bed and Breakfast.** Although it's in a rather inauspicious building, Finches is a well-run little B&B and an excellent value. **Pros:** cheerful staff; quiet location; good level of service. **Cons:** away from the action; no tubs in bathrooms. ⊠ *144 Thornton Rd.* ☎ *01223/276653* ⊕ *www.finches-bnb.com* ⇨ *3 rooms* ⚷ *In-room: no a/c, Wi-Fi. In-hotel: parking* ⊟ *No credit cards* ¶◯¶ *Breakfast.*

££££–£££££
HOTEL

⊡ **Hotel Felix.** From the outside, this hotel looks like a genteel and quaint Victorian manor house; inside it's been converted into a stylish, contemporary lodging. **Pros:** up-to-the-minute furnishings; quiet location; easy to reach from motorway. **Cons:** impersonal feel; spotty service; can be noisy. ⊠ *Whitehouse La. off Huntingdon Rd.* ☎ *01223/277977* ⊕ *www. hotelfelix.co.uk* ⇨ *52 rooms* ⚷ *In-room: no a/c, Wi-Fi. In-hotel: restaurant, bar, parking, some pets allowed* ¶◯¶ *Breakfast.*

££–£££
HOTEL

⊡ **Regent Hotel.** A rare small hotel in central Cambridge, this handsome Georgian town house has wooden sash windows that look out over a tree-lined park called Parker's Piece. **Pros:** good view from top rooms; close to bars and restaurants. **Cons:** no parking; a tad scruffy; disappointing breakfasts. ⊠ *41 Regent St.* ☎ *01223/351470* ⊕ *www. regenthotel.co.uk* ⇨ *22 rooms* ⚷ *In-room: a/c, Wi-Fi. In-hotel: bar* ¶◯¶ *Breakfast.*

££££–£££££
HOTEL

⊡ **The Varsity.** This stylish boutique hotel and spa has wide windows that flood the place with light. **Pros:** beautiful location; stylish design. **Cons:** cheaper rooms don't share the romantic views. ⊠ *Thompson's La. off Bridge St.* ☎ *01223/306030* ⊕ *www.thevarsityhotel.co.uk* ⇨ *48 rooms* ⚷ *In-room: a/c (some), Wi-Fi. In-hotel: restaurant, bar, gym, spa.*

££
B&B/INN

⊡ **Warkworth House.** The location of this sweet B&B could hardly be better, as the Fitzwilliam Museum and several of Cambridge's colleges are within a 15-minute walk. **Pros:** excellent location; lovely hosts; some free parking. **Cons:** few frills. ⊠ *Warkworth Terr.* ☎ *01223/363682* ⊕ *www. warkworthhouse.co.uk* ⇨ *5 rooms* ⚷ *In-room: no a/c* ¶◯¶ *Breakfast.*

NIGHTLIFE AND THE ARTS

NIGHTLIFE

The city's pubs provide the mainstay of Cambridge's nightlife and shouldn't be missed.

The **Eagle** (✉ *8 Benet St.* ☎ *01223/505020*), first among equals, is a 16th-century coaching inn with several bars and a cobbled court-yard that's lost none of its old-time character. It's extremely busy on weekends.

Fort St. George (✉ *Midsummer Common* ☎ *01223/354327*), which over-looks the university boathouses, gets the honors for riverside views.

The **Free Press** (✉ *7 Prospect Row* ☎ *01223/368337*) is a small pub with an excellent selection of traditional ales. It's a favorite of student rowers.

THE ARTS

CONCERTS Cambridge supports its own symphony orchestra, and regular musical events are held in many colleges, especially those with large chapels.

The **Cambridge Folk Festival** (☎ *01223/357851* ⊕ *www.cambridgefolkfes-tival.co.uk*), spread over a weekend in late July or early August at Cherry Hinton Hall, attracts major international folk singers and groups.

The beautifully restored **Corn Exchange** (✉ *Wheeler St.* ☎ *01223/357851* ⊕ *www.cornex.co.uk*) presents classical and rock concerts, stand-up comedy, musicals, opera, and ballet.

During regular terms, **King's College Chapel** (☎ *01223/331155* ⊕ *www. kings.cam.ac.uk*) has evensong services Monday through Saturday at 5:30, Sunday at 3:30.

THEATER The **ADC Theatre** (✉ *Park St.* ☎ *01223/300085* ⊕ *www.adctheatre.com*) hosts mainly student and fringe theater productions, including the famous Cambridge Footlights revue.

The **Arts Theatre** (✉ *6 St. Edward's Passage* ☎ *01223/503333* ⊕ *www. cambridgeartstheatre.com*), the city's main repertory theater, was built by economist John Maynard Keynes in 1936 and supports a full pro-gram of plays and concerts. It also has a good ground-floor bar and two restaurants.

SHOPPING

Cambridge has all the usual chain stores, many in the Grafton Centre and Lion's Yard shopping precincts. More interesting are the specialty shops in the center of town, especially in and around Rose Crescent and King's Parade. Bookshops, including antiquarian stores, are Cam-bridge's pride and joy.

All Saints Garden Art & Craft Market (✉ *Trinity St.* ⊕ *www.cambridge-art-craft.co.uk*) displays the wares of local artists outdoors on Saturday. It's also open Friday from June to August and Wednesday to Friday in December (weather permitting).

Ryder & Amies (✉ *22 King's Parade* ☎ *01223/350371* ⊕ *www.ryderamies. co.uk*) carries official university wear and even straw boaters.

CLOSE UP

Punting on the Cam

To punt is to maneuver a flat-bottom, wooden, gondola-like boat—in this case, through the shallow River Cam along the verdant Backs behind the colleges of Cambridge. One benefit of this popular activity is that you get a better view of the ivy-covered walls from the water. Mastery of the sport lies in your ability to control a 15-foot pole, used to propel the punt. With a bottle of wine, some food, and a few friends, you may find yourself saying things such as, "It doesn't get any better than this." One piece of advice: if your pole gets stuck, let go. You can use the smaller paddle to go back and retrieve it. Hang on to a stuck punt for too long and you'll probably fall in with it.

The lazier-at-heart may prefer chauffeured punting, with food supplied. Students from Cambridge often do the work, and you get a fairly informative spiel on the colleges. For a romantic evening trip, there are illuminated punts.

One university punting society once published a useful "Bluffer's Guide to Punting" featuring detailed instructions and tips on how to master the art. It can still be found online at ⊕ *duramecho. com/Misc/HowToPunt.html.*

BOOKS **Cambridge University Press bookshop** (⊠ *1 Trinity St.* ☎ *01223/333333* ⊕ *www.cambridge.org/uk/bookshop*) is where books have been sold since at least 1581.

G. David (⊠ *16 St. Edward's Passage* ☎ *01223/354619*), near the Arts Theatre, sells antiquarian books.

The **Haunted Bookshop** (⊠ *9 St. Edward's Passage* ☎ *01223/312913* ⊕ *www.sarahkeybooks.co.uk*) carries a great selection of old, illustrated books and British classics.

Heffer's (⊠ *20 Trinity St.* ☎ *01223/568568* ⊕ *bookshop.blackwell.co.uk*) stocks many rare and imported books, and boasts a particularly extensive arts section.

SPORTS AND THE OUTDOORS

BIKING

It's fun to explore by bike. **City Cycle Hire** (⊠ *61 Newnham Rd.* ☎ *01223/365629* ⊕ *www.citycyclehire.com*) charges supercheap rates of £10 per day and £22 for a week. Advance reservations are essential in July and August.

PUNTING

You can rent punts at several places, notably at Silver Street Bridge–Mill Lane, at Magdalene Bridge, and from outside the Rat and Parrot pub on Thompson's Lane on Jesus Green. Hourly rental costs £15 to £20. Chauffeured punting, usually by a Cambridge student, is also popular. It costs around £12 per person.

Scudamore's Punting Co. (⊠ *Mill La. and Quayside* ☎ *01223/359750* ⊕ *www.scudamores.com*) rents chauffeured and self-drive punts. It also offers various tours, ranging from a **Ghost Tour** to a **Punt & Cream Tea Tour**, for about £17.50 per person.

ELY AND CENTRAL SUFFOLK

This central area of towns and villages within easy reach of Cambridge is testament to the amazing changeability of the English landscape. The town of Ely is set in an eerie, flat, and apparently endless marsh, or fenland. (A medieval term, "the fens," is still used informally to describe the surrounding region.) Only a few miles south and east into Suffolk, however, all this changes to pastoral landscapes of gently undulating hills, and clusters of villages including pretty Sudbury and Lavenham.

ELY

16 mi north of Cambridge.

Known for its magnificent cathedral, Ely is the "capital" of the fens, the center of what used to be a separate county called the Isle of Ely (literally "island of eels"). Until the land was drained in the 17th century, Ely was surrounded by treacherous marshland, which inhabitants crossed wearing stilts. Today Wicken Fen, a nature reserve 9 mi southeast of town (off A1123), preserves the sole remaining example of fenland in an undrained state.

Enveloped by fields of wheat, sugar beets, and carrots, Ely is a small, dense town that fails to live up to the high expectations created by its big attraction, its cathedral. The shopping area and market square lie to the north and lead down to the riverside, and the medieval buildings of the cathedral grounds and the King's School (which trains cathedral choristers) spread out to the south and west. Ely's most famous resident was Oliver Cromwell, whose house is now a museum.

GETTING HERE AND AROUND

The 9 and X9 buses leave twice an hour from the Drummer Street bus station in Cambridge. The journey to Ely takes about 45 minutes. To drive there from Cambridge, simply take the A10 road going north out of the city. Ely is quite small, so find somewhere to park and walk to the center. Trains from Cambridge to Ely leave three times an hour and take 15 minutes.

ESSENTIALS

Visitor Information Ely (✉ *Oliver Cromwell's House, 29 St. Mary's St.* ☏ *01353/662062* ⊕ *visitely.eastcambs.gov.uk*).

EXPLORING

★ **Ely Cathedral.** Known affectionately as the Ship of the Fens, Ely Cathedral can be seen for miles, towering above the flat landscape on one of the few ridges in the fens. In 1083 the Normans began work on the cathedral, which stands on the site of a Benedictine monastery founded by the Anglo-Saxon princess Etheldreda in 673. In the center of the cathedral you see a marvel of medieval construction—the unique octagonal **Lantern Tower,** a sort of stained-glass skylight of colossal proportions, built to replace the central tower that collapsed in 1322. The cathedral's **West Tower** is even taller; the view from the top (if you can manage the 288 steps) is spectacular. Tours of both towers are daily between April and October and on weekends between November and

March. The cathedral is also notable for its 248-foot-long **nave,** with its simple Norman arches and Victorian painted ceiling. Much of the decorative carving of the 14th-century **Lady Chapel** was defaced during the Reformation (mostly by knocking off the heads of the statuary), but enough traces remain to show its original beauty. Ely Cathedral is a popular location for films; it doubled for Westminster Abbey in *The King's Speech.* Guided tours begin daily at 10:45, 1, and 2, with an additional tour at 3 on weekends and also weekdays between April and October. ■**TIP→** Always call ahead about tours, as times are subject to change. The cathedral houses a superior **Stained Glass Museum** (☎ *01353/660347* ⊕ *www.stainedglassmuseum.com* ✉ *£4* ☉ *Easter–Oct., weekdays 10:30–5, Sat. 10:30–5:30, Sun. noon–6; Nov.–Easter, Mon.–Sat. 10:30–5, Sun. noon–4:30*), up a flight of 42 steps. Exhibits trace the history of stained glass from medieval to modern times. ✉ *The Gallery* ☎ *01353/667735* ⊕ *www.cathedral.ely.anglican.org* ✉ *£6.50, free on Sun; Lantern Tower £5.50; West Tower £5.50; tower tour and Stained Glass Museum £9.40* ☉ *May–Oct., daily 7–6:30; Nov.–Apr., Mon.–Sat. 7:30–6:30, Sun. 7:30–5:30.*

Oliver Cromwell's House. This half-timber medieval building stands in the shadows of Ely Cathedral. During the 10 years he lived here, Cromwell (1599–1658) was leading the rebellious Roundheads in their eventually victorious struggle against King Charles I in the English Civil War. The house contains an exhibition about its controversial former occupant, who was Britain's Lord Protector from 1653 to 1658. It's also the site of Ely's tourist information center. ✉ *29 St. Mary's St.* ☎ *01353/662062* ⊕ *www.visitely.org.uk* ✉ *£4.50* ☉ *Apr.–Oct., daily 10–5; Nov.–Mar., weekdays 11–4, Sat. 10–5, Sun. 11–4.*

WHERE TO EAT AND STAY

For expanded hotel reviews, visit Fodors.com.

£££
BRITISH
★

✗ **Old Fire Engine House.** Scrubbed pine tables fill the main dining room of this converted fire station near Ely Cathedral. Another room, used only for overflow, has an open fireplace and a polished wood floor, and also serves as an art gallery. Among the English dishes are such traditional fenland recipes as pike baked in white wine, as well as eel pie and game in season. Desserts include syllabub, a traditional dish made from cream, sugar, and wine. Reserve ahead for the fine afternoon tea (£15.50). ✉ *25 St. Mary's St.* ☎ *01353/662582* ⊕ *www.theoldfireenginehouse.co.uk* ☉ *Closed 2 wks at Christmas. No dinner Sun.*

££
HOTEL

🏠 **Cathedral House.** This Georgian house, full of interesting period details, makes a pleasant overnight stop in Ely. **Pros:** heaps of character; steps from the cathedral; free parking. **Cons:** small bathrooms; on a busy road. ✉ *17 St. Mary's St.* ☎ *01353/662124* ⊕ *www.cathedralhouse. co.uk* 🛏 *3 rooms, 1 cottage* ♿ *In-room: no a/c. In-hotel: parking* ▭ *No credit cards* ¶⊘ *Breakfast.*

SUDBURY

32 mi southeast of Ely, 16 mi south of Bury St. Edmunds.

An early silk-weaving industry (still in existence, on a smaller scale) as well as the wool trade brought prosperity to Sudbury, which has three fine Perpendicular Gothic churches and some half-timber houses.

Thomas Gainsborough, one of the greatest English portrait and landscape painters, was born here in 1727; a statue of him holding his palette stands on Market Hill. In Charles Dickens's first novel, *The Pickwick Papers*, Sudbury was the model for the fictional Eatanswill, where Mr. Pickwick stands for Parliament.

GETTING HERE AND AROUND
From Cambridge, driving to Sudbury requires a circuitous route that takes about an hour. The A14 is slightly quicker, but the A3107 is more picturesque. There are no practical bus or train connections from Cambridge or Ely.

ESSENTIALS
Visitor Information Sudbury (✉ *Town Hall, Market Hill* ☎ *01787/881320* ⊕ *www.sudbury.org.uk*).

EXPLORING
Gainsborough's House. The birthplace and family home of Thomas Gainsborough (1727–88) contains many paintings and drawings by the artist and his contemporaries. Although it presents a Georgian facade, with touches of the 18th-century neo-Gothic style, the building is essentially Tudor. The walled garden has a mulberry tree planted in 1620 and a printmaking workshop. The entrance is through the café and shop on Weavers Lane. ✉ *46 Gainsborough St.* ☎ *01787/372958* ⊕ *www. gainsborough.org* 🎟 *£4.50, free Tues. 1–5* ⏰ *Mon.–Sat. 10–5.*

> ### DRAINING EAST ANGLIA
>
> Large areas of East Anglia were originally barely inhabited, swampy marshes. Drainage of the wetlands by the creation of waterways was carried out most energetically in the 17th and 18th centuries. The process was far from smooth. Locals, whose fishing rights were threatened, sometimes destroyed the work. Also, as the marshland dried out, it shrank and sank, requiring pumps to stop renewed flooding. Hundreds of windmills were used to pump water away; some of them can still be seen today.

LONG MELFORD

2 mi north of Sudbury, 14 mi south of Bury St. Edmunds.

It's easy to see how this village got its name, especially if you walk the full length of its 2-mi-long main street, which gradually broadens to include green squares and trees and finally opens into the large triangular green on the hill. Long Melford grew rich on its wool trade in the 15th century, and the town's buildings are an appealing mix, mostly Tudor half-timber or Georgian. Many house antiques shops. Away from the main road, Long Melford returns to its resolutely late-medieval roots.

GETTING HERE AND AROUND
Long Melford is just off the main A134. If you're driving from Sudbury, take the smaller B1064; it's much quicker than it looks on the map. There are several bus connections with Sudbury, Bury St. Edmonds, and Ipswich. The nearest train station is in Sudbury.

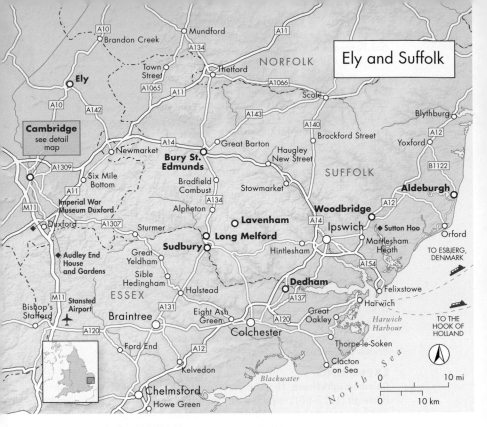

EXPLORING

Holy Trinity Church. This largely 15th-century church, founded by the rich clothiers of Long Melford, stands on a hill at the north end of the village. Close up, the delicate flint flush-work (shaped flints set into a pattern) and huge Perpendicular Gothic windows that take up most of the church's walls have great impact, especially because the nave is 150 feet long. The Clopton Chapel, with an ornate ceiling, predates the rest of the church by 150 years. The beautiful Lady Chapel has an unusual cloister; the stone on the wall in the corner is an ancient multiplication table, used when the chapel served as a school in the 17th and 18th centuries. ✉ *Main St.* ☎ *01787/310845* ⊕ *www.stedmundsbury.anglican. org/longmelford* ☉ *Apr.–Oct., daily 10–6; Nov.–Mar., daily 10–5.*

☝ **Kentwell Hall.** A wide moat surrounds this redbrick Tudor manor house with tall chimneys and domed turrets. Built between 1520 and 1550, it was heavily restored inside after a fire in the early 19th century. On some weekends from mid-April through September, costumed "servants" and "farmworkers" perform reenactments of Tudor life or life during World War II. The house and farm are a half mile north of Long Melford Green. Always call ahead, as this place has notoriously variable opening times—and a frustrating habit of not sticking to them.

✉ *Off A134* ☎ *01787/310207* ⊕ *www.kentwell.co.uk* 🖾 *£10; farm and garden only, £7* ⊙ *Feb.–Oct., call ahead for days and times.*

Melford Hall. Distinguished from the outside by its turrets and topiaries, Melford Hall is an Elizabethan house with its original banqueting room, a fair number of 18th-century additions, and pleasant gardens. Much of the porcelain and other fine pieces here come from the *Santissima Trinidad,* a ship loaded with gifts from the emperor of China and bound for Spain that was captured in the 18th century. Children's writer Beatrix Potter, related to the owners, visited often; there's a small collection of Potter memorabilia. ✉ *Off A134* ☎ *01787/376395* ⊕ *www. nationaltrust.org.uk* 🖾 *£6.60* ⊙ *Early–mid Apr. and Oct., weekends 1:30–5; late Apr.–Sept. Wed.–Mon. 1:30–5.*

WHERE TO STAY

For expanded hotel reviews, visit Fodors.com.

££–£££

HOTEL

🛏 **The Bull.** This half-timber Elizabethan building reveals its long history with stone-flagged floors, bowed and twisted oak beams, and heavy antique furniture. **Pros:** historic atmosphere; comfortable bedrooms; friendly staff. **Cons:** minimum stay on summer weekends; popular with wedding parties. ✉ *Hall St.* ☎ *01787/378494* ⊕ *www.thebull-hotel.com* 🛏 *25 rooms* 🛁 *In-room: no a/c. In-hotel: restaurant, bar* ❏ *Some meals.*

LAVENHAM

4 mi northeast of Long Melford, 10 mi southeast of Bury St. Edmunds.

Fodor's Choice

★

Virtually unchanged since the height of its wealth in the 15th and 16th centuries, Lavenham is one of the most perfectly preserved examples of a Tudor village in England. The weavers' and wool merchants' houses occupy not just one show street but most of the town. The houses are timber-frame in black oak, the main posts looking as if they could last another 400 years, though their walls are often no longer entirely perpendicular to the ground. The town has many examples of Suffolk pink buildings, in hues from pale pink to apricot, and many of these house small galleries selling paintings and crafts.

GETTING HERE AND AROUND

Lavenham is on the A1141 and B1071. Take the latter if possible, as it's a prettier drive. There are hourly buses from Sudbury and Bury St. Edmunds and slightly less frequent buses from Ipswich. The nearest train station is in Sudbury.

ESSENTIALS

Visitor Information Lavenham (✉ *Lady St.* ☎ *01787/248207* ⊕ *www. southandheartofsuffolk.org.uk*).

EXPLORING

Church of St. Peter and St. Paul. Set apart from the village on a hill, this grand 15th-century church was built between 1480 and 1520 by cloth merchant Thomas Spring. The height of its tower (141 feet) was meant to surpass those of the neighboring churches—and perhaps to impress rival towns. The rest of the church is perfectly proportioned, with intri-

Colorful and ancient, the timbered houses in pretty towns such as Lavenham recall the days when these buildings housed weavers and wool merchants.

cately carved wood. ⊠ *Church St.* ☎ *01787/247244* 🎫 *Free* 🕒 *Daily; hrs vary but usually 10–5.*

Guildhall of Corpus Christi. The timber-frame guildhall (1529) dominates Market Place, a square with barely a foot in the present. Upstairs is a rather dull exhibition on the Wool Trade, although looking around the building itself is worth the admission charge. ⊠ *Market Pl.* ☎ *01787/247646* ⊕ *www.nationaltrust.org.uk* 🎫 *£4.30* 🕒 *Early Mar.–late Mar., Wed.–Sun. 11–4; late Mar.–Oct., daily 11–5; Nov., weekends 11–4.*

Little Hall. This timber-frame wool merchant's house shows the building's progress from its creation in the 14th century to its subsequent "modernization" in the 17th century. Don't leave without seeing the beautiful garden at the back. ⊠ *Market Pl.* ☎ *01787/247019* ⊕ *www.littlehall. org.uk* 🎫 *£3* 🕒 *Apr.–Oct., Wed., Thurs., and weekends 2–5:30, bank holidays 11–5:30.* Last admission at 4:30.

QUICK BITES

In a haphazardly leaning old house, the **Tickled Pink Tea Room** (⊠ **17 High St.** ☎ **01787/248438**) serves fresh cakes and coffee as well as soup and sandwiches.

WHERE TO EAT

££££
CONTINENTAL
★

✗ **Great House.** The town's finest "restaurant with rooms" occupies a 15th-century building on the medieval market square. Run by Régis and Martine Crépy, the dining room serves European fare with a French touch. The five spacious bedrooms have sloping floors, beamed ceilings, well-appointed bathrooms, and antique furnishings. ⊠ *Market Pl.*

☎ *01787/247431* ⊕ *www.greathouse.co.uk* ⊘ *Closed Mon. and Jan. No dinner Sun. No lunch Tues.*

££
INDIAN
Fodor'sChoice
★

✕**Memsaab.** In a town ready to burst with cream teas, it's a bit of a surprise to find an Indian restaurant, let alone such an exceptional one. Among the classics one would expect from a curry house—from mild kormas to spicy *madrases* and *jalfrezies* (traditional curries made with chili and tomato)—are some finely executed specialties, including Nizami chicken (a fiery dish prepared with yogurt and fresh ginger) and duck *bhujon* (a fusion dish made with orange and Madeira sauce). The menu also contains regional specialties from Goa and Hyderabad. ✉ *2 Church St.* ☎ *01787/249431* ⊕ *www.memsaboflavenham.co.uk.*

WHERE TO STAY

For expanded hotel reviews, visit Fodors.com.

££
B&B/INN

🏠 **Guinea House.** Still a private home after 600 years, Guinea House attracts travelers seeking more authenticity than your average B&B. **Pros:** quiet central location; intimate feel; one-of-a-kind atmosphere. **Cons:** hobbit-size doorways; no common areas; credit-card payment must be arranged in advance. ✉ *16 Bolton St.* ☎ *01787/249046* ⊕ *www. guineahouse.co.uk* 🛏 *2 rooms* ⚬ *In-room: no a/c* 🍴 *Breakfast.*

££–£££
B&B/INN

🏠 **Lavenham Priory.** You can immerse yourself in Lavenham's Tudor history at this sprawling house that dates back to the 13th century. **Pros:** historic ambience; charming rooms; lovely garden. **Cons:** sloping floors; no locks on room doors; service can be surly. ✉ *Water St.* ☎ *01787/247404* ⊕ *www.lavenhampriory.co.uk* 🛏 *5 rooms, 1 suite* ⚬ *In-room: no a/c, Wi-Fi. In-hotel: bar, some age restrictions* 🍴 *Breakfast.*

££££–£££££
HOTEL

🏠 **Swan Hotel.** This half-timber 14th-century lodging has rambling public rooms, roaring fireplaces, and corridors so low that cushions are strategically placed on beams. **Pros:** lovely building; atmospheric rooms. **Cons:** creaky floors; lots of steps to climb. ✉ *High St.* ☎ *01787/247477* ⊕ *www.theswanatlavenham.co.uk* 🛏 *47 rooms, 2 suites* ⚬ *In-room: no a/c, Internet. In-hotel: restaurant, bar, some pets allowed.* 🍴 *Some meals.*

BURY ST. EDMUNDS

★

10 mi north of Lavenham, 28 mi east of Cambridge.

The Georgian streetscape helps make the town one of the area's prettiest, and the nearby Greene King Westgate Brewery adds the smell of sweet hops to the air. Robert Adam designed the town hall in 1774.

Bury St. Edmunds owes its name, and indeed its existence, to Edmund, the last king of East Anglia and medieval patron saint of England, who was hacked to death by marauding Danes in 869. He was subsequently canonized, and his shrine attracted pilgrims, settlement, and commerce. In the 11th century the erection of a great Norman abbey (now only ruins) confirmed the town's importance as a

A HALF-PINT PUB?

While you're in Bury St. Edmunds, pop in for a pint of the local Greene King ale at the **Nutshell** (✉ *17 The Traverse* ☎ *01284/764867*), which claims to be Britain's smallest pub, measuring just 16 feet by 7½ feet.

religious center. The tourist office has a leaflet about the ruins and can arrange a guided tour.

GETTING HERE AND AROUND

The 11 bus from Cambridge's Drummer Street bus station takes about an hour to reach Bury St. Edmunds. By car, the town is a short drive from either Lavenham or Cambridge. Trains from Cambridge to Bury St. Edmunds leave once or twice an hour and take 40 minutes.

ESSENTIALS

Visitor Information Bury St. Edmunds (✉ *6 Angel Hill* ☎ *01284/764667* ⊕ *www.visit-burystedmunds.co.uk*).

EXPLORING

TOP ATTRACTIONS

Abbey Ruins and Botanical Gardens. This is all that remain of the Abbey of Bury St. Edmunds, which fell during Henry VIII's dissolution of the monasteries. The Benedictine abbey's enormous scale is evident in the surviving Norman Gate Tower on Angel Hill; besides this, only the fortified Abbot's Bridge over the River Lark and a few ruins remain. There are explanatory plaques amid the ruins, which are now the site of the Abbey Botanical Gardens, with roses, elegant hedges, and rare trees, including a Chinese tree of heaven planted in the 1830s. There's also an aviary, a putting green, and a children's play area on-site. ✉ *Angel Hill* ⊠ *Free* ⊙ *Mon.–Sat. 7:30 am–dusk, Sun. 9 am–dusk.*

St. Edmundsbury Cathedral. Although the cathedral dates from the 15th century, its brilliant ceiling and gleaming stained-glass windows are the result of 19th-century restoration by architect Sir Gilbert Scott. Don't miss the memorial (near the altar) to an event in 1214, when the barons of England took an oath here to force King John to grant the Magna Carta. The cathedral's original Abbey Gate was destroyed in a riot, and it was rebuilt in the 14th century with defense in mind—you can see the arrow slits. Guided tours are available every day except Sunday during the summer months. There's also a small but popular café. ✉ *Angel Hill* ☎ *01284/748720* ⊕ *www.stedscathedral.co.uk* ⊠ *Free, suggested donation £3* ⊙ *Daily 8:30–6.*

WORTH NOTING

Angel Hill. A walk here is a journey through the history of Bury St. Edmunds. Along one side, the Abbey Gate, cathedral, Norman Gate Tower, and St. Mary's church make up a continuous display of medieval architecture. Elegant Georgian houses line Angel Hill on the side opposite St. Mary's Church; these include the Athenaeum, an 18th-century social and cultural meeting place that has a fine Adam-style ballroom.

Angel Hotel. This splendid lodging is the scene of Sam Weller's meeting with Job Trotter in Dickens's *The Pickwick Papers*. Dickens stayed here while he was giving readings at the Athenaeum. ✉ *3 Angel Hill* ☎ *01284/71400* ⊕ *www.theangel.co.uk.*

Moyse's Hall. This 12th-century building, probably the oldest building in East Anglia, is a rare surviving example of a Norman house. The rooms hold local history and archaeological collections. One macabre display relates to the Red Barn murder, a local case that gained notoriety in a 19th-century play. ⊠ *Cornhill* ☎ *01284/757160* ⊕ *www.stedmundsbury.gov.uk* ⊒ *£4* ◷ *Daily 10–5; last entry at 4.*

St. Mary's Church. Built in the 15th century, St. Mary's has a blue-and-gold embossed "wagon" (barrel-shape) roof over the choir. Mary Tudor, Henry VIII's sister and queen of France, is buried here. ⊠ *Angel Hill at Honey Hill* ☎ *01284/754680* ⊕ *www.stmarystpeter.net* ◷ *Apr.–Oct., daily 10–4; Nov.–Mar., daily 10–3; call to confirm times.*

WHERE TO EAT

£

CAFÉ

✗**Harriet's Café Tearooms.** In an elegant dining room, Harriet's brings back the tearooms of yesteryear. Munch on a savory sandwich or have a full cream tea while listening to hits from the 1940s. ⊠ *57 Cornhill Bldgs.* ☎ *01284/756256* ⊕ *www.harrietscafetearooms.co.uk* ◷ *No dinner.*

£££

FRENCH

✗**Maison Bleue.** This stylish French restaurant, with the same owners as the Great House in nearby Lavenham, specializes in locally caught seafood and serves some tasty meat dishes, too. The seafood depends on the day's catch, but grilled sole and roast cod are always available, as are cheeses imported from Paris. ⊠ *31 Churchgate St.* ☎ *01284/760623* ⊕ *www.maisonbleue.co.uk* ⊗ *Reservations essential* ◷ *Closed Sun. and Mon.*

WHERE TO STAY

For expanded hotel reviews, visit Fodors.com.

£££££

HOTEL

★

☾

▦ **Ickworth Hotel.** You can live like nobility in the east wing of the Italianate Ickworth House, a National Trust property with 1,800 acres of grounds 5 mi southwest of Bury St. **Pros:** gorgeous grounds; relaxed atmosphere; family-friendly vibe. **Cons:** inconsistent service; some rooms are small; minimum stay on weekends. ⊠ *Off A143, Horringer* ☎ *01284/735350* ⊕ *www.ickworthhotel.co.uk* ⇝*24 rooms, 11 apartments* ⟐ *In-room: no a/c, kitchen (some), Wi-Fi. In-hotel: restaurants, bar, pool, tennis court, spa, some pets allowed* ⎛⎞*Breakfast.*

£££

B&B/INN

★

▦ **Ounce House.** Small and friendly, this Victorian B&B has a great deal of charm. **Pros:** spotlessly clean; spacious and comfortable rooms; generous breakfasts. **Cons:** fussy decor; booked up far in advance. ⊠ *Northgate St.* ☎ *01284/761779* ⊕ *www.ouncehouse.co.uk* ⇝*4 rooms* ⟐ *In-room: no a/c, Internet. In-hotel: bar* ⎛⎞*Breakfast.*

NIGHTLIFE AND THE ARTS

The **Theatre Royal** (⊠ *6 Westgate St.* ☎ *01284/7551275* ⊕ *www.theatreroyal.org*), which presents touring shows, was built in 1819 and is an outstanding example of Regency design. Guided tours in spring and summer can be booked at the box office.

THE SUFFOLK COAST

The 40-mi Suffolk Heritage Coast, which wanders northward from Felixstowe up to Kessingland, is one of the most unspoiled shorelines in the country. The lower part of the coast is the most impressive; however, some of the loveliest towns and villages, such as Dedham and the older part of Flatford, are inland. The best way to experience the countryside around here is to be willing to get lost along its tiny, ancient back-roads. Try to avoid the coastal area between Lowestoft and Great Yarmouth; it has little to offer but run-down beach resorts.

DEDHAM

62 mi southeast of Cambridge, 15 mi southeast of Bury St. Edmund.

Fodor's Choice
★

Dedham is the heart of Constable Country. Here gentle hills and the cornfields of Dedham Vale, set under the district's delicate, pale skies, inspired John Constable (1776–1837) to paint some of his most celebrated canvases. He went to school in Dedham, a picture-book village that did well from the wool trade in the 15th and 16th centuries and has retained a well-off air ever since. The 15th-century church looms large over handsomely sturdy, pastel-color houses.

Nearby towns have several other sites of interest to Constable fans. About 2 mi from of Dedham is Flatford, where you can see Flatford Mill, one of the two water mills owned by Constable's father. Northeast of Dedham, off A12, the Constable trail continues in East Bergholt, where Constable was born in 1776. Although the town is mostly modern, the older part has some atmospheric buildings like the church of St. Mary-the-Virgin.

GETTING HERE AND AROUND
From the main A12, Dedham is easily reached by car via the B1029. Public transportation is extremely limited; there is no nearby train station.

EXPLORING
Bridge Cottage. On the north bank of the Stour, this 16th-century home in East Bergholt has a shop and an exhibition about Constable's life. You can also rent rowboats from here. ⊠ *Off B1070, East Bergholt* ☎ *01206/298260* ⊕ *www.nationaltrust.org.uk* ☒ *Free, guided tours £2.50* ☉ *Jan. and Feb., weekends 11–3:30; Mar., Wed.–Sun. 11–4; Apr., daily 11–5; May–Sept., daily 10:30–5:30; Oct., daily 11–4:30; Nov. and Dec., Wed.–Sun. 11–3:30. Guided tours Apr.–Oct., daily at 11:30, 1:30, and 2:30.*

OFF THE BEATEN PATH

Colchester. Nobody knows whether Colchester is, as it claims, the oldest town in Britain. What is certain, however, is that it was a major stronghold during the Roman occupation. History buffs enjoy the impressive Roman amphitheater, where parts of the walls and floor are visible. Sections of the original Roman walls are also still standing. Colchester Castle was built on the foundations of the huge Roman Temple of Claudius. Colchester is off the A12, 9 mi southwest of Dedham.

St. Mary-the-Virgin. One of the most remarkable churches in the region,

CONSTABLE'S FAME

Constable's landscape paintings may be popular today, but *The Hay Wain*, now in London's National Gallery, did not sell after the Royal Academy displayed it. The artist sold only 20 paintings in England during his lifetime. He was elected to the Royal Academy with a majority of one vote at age 52.

The area around Flatford is Constable Country: you may feel you are in one of the artist's paintings as you explore the area in a rowboat.

St. Mary-the-Virgin was started just before the Reformation. The doors underneath the ruined archways outside (remnants of a much older church) contain a coded message left by Catholic sympathizers of the time. The striking interior is full of little treasures, including an ancient wall painting of the Virgin Mary in one of the rear chapels, a 14th-century chest, and an extraordinary series of florid memorial stones on the nave wall opposite the main entrance. ⊠ *Flatford Rd., East Bergholt* ☎ *01206/298932* 🔁 *Free* ⊙ *Daily; hrs vary but usually 10–5.*

Willy Lott's House. A five-minute stroll down the path from Bridge Cottage brings you to this 16th-century structure that is instantly recognizable from Constable's painting *The Hay Wain* (1821). Although the house itself is not open to the public, the road is a public thoroughfare, so you don't have to buy a ticket to see the famous—and completely unchanged—view for yourself. Just stand across from the two trees on the far bank, with the mill on your right, and look upstream. ■ TIP➔ The display board on the outside wall of the mill contains a handy reproduction of *The Hay Wain* to help you compose your own photo. ⊠ *Off B1070, East Bergholt.*

WHERE TO EAT

££££
BRITISH
★

✕ **Le Talbooth.** A longtime favorite, this sophisticated restaurant in a Tudor house is idyllically set beside the River Stour. There are floodlighted terraces where food and drinks are served in summer and where jazz and steel bands play on summer Sunday nights. Inside, original beams, leaded-glass windows, and a brick fireplace add to the sense of age. The superb British fare at lunch and dinner may include loin of venison, local sea bass, or duck breast. From June to September there are Sunday-night barbecues on the river. ⊠ *Gun Hill* ☎ *01206/323150* ⊕ *www.milsomhotels.com/letalbooth* ⚒ *Reservations essential* ⊘ *No dinner Sun. Nov.–May.*

££ ✕ **Marlborough Head.** This friendly, 300-year-old pub across from Con-
BRITISH stable's school in Dedham serves traditional bar food with a flourish. Dishes such as venison pie and Lincolnshire sausages share the menu with fish-and-chips, pizzas, and burgers. There are also rooms available (one with a four-poster bed) for £55–£100 per night, depending on the season. ⊠ *Mill La.* ☎ *01206/323250* ⊕ *www.marlborough-head.co.uk.*

SPORTS AND THE OUTDOORS

From Dedham, on the banks of the River Stour, you can rent a rowboat from the **Boathouse Restaurant** (⊠ *Mill La.* ☎ *01206/323153* ⊕ *www. dedhamboathouse.com* ⚒ *£12 per hr* ⊘ *Easter–Sept., daily 10–5*).

WOODBRIDGE

18 mi northeast of Dedham.

One of the first good ports of call on the Suffolk Heritage Coast, Wood-bridge is a town whose upper reaches center on a fine old market square, site of the 16th-century Shire Hall. Woodbridge is at its best around its old quayside, where boatbuilding has been carried out since the 16th century. The most prominent building is a white-clapboard mill, which dates from the 18th century and is powered by the tides.

GETTING HERE AND AROUND

Woodbridge is on A12. There are local buses, but they mostly serve commuters. By train, Woodbridge is 1½ hours from London, and just under 2 hours from Cambridge (with connections).

ESSENTIALS

Visitor Information Woodbridge (⊠ *The Station* ☎ *01394/382240* ⊕ *www. suffolkcoastal.gov.uk/tourism/tics*).

EXPLORING

Sutton Hoo. The visitor center at Sutton Hoo tells the story of one of Britain's most significant Anglo-Saxon archaeological sites. In 1938 a local archaeologist excavated a series of earth mounds and discovered a 7th-century burial ship, probably that of King Raedwald of East Anglia. A replica of the 90-foot-long ship stands in the visitor center, which has artifacts and displays about Anglo-Saxon society. Trails around the 245-acre site explore the area along the River Deben. ⊠ *Signposted on the B1083, 2 mi east of Woodbridge* ☎ *01394/389700* ⊕ *www. nationaltrust.org.uk* ⚒ *£5.90* ⊘ *Mar., Wed.–Sun. 10:30–5; Apr.–Oct., daily 10:30–5; Nov.–mid-Dec. and Jan.–mid Feb., weekends 11–4; late Feb., daily 11–4.*

WHERE TO EAT AND STAY

For expanded hotel reviews, visit Fodors.com.

££ ✕ **Butley-Orford Oysterage.** What started as a little café that sold oysters
SEAFOOD and cups of tea is now a bustling restaurant. It has no pretenses to grandeur but serves some of the best smoked fish you're likely to taste anywhere, accompanied with simple plates of buttered brown bread.

Traditional English desserts are also exceptional. The actual smoking (of fish, cheese, and much else) takes place in the adjacent smokehouse, and products are for sale in a shop around the corner. ⊠ *Market Hill, Orford* ☏ *01394/450277* ⊕ *www.butleyorfordoysterage.co.uk* ⊗ *No dinner Sun.–Thurs. Nov.–Mar.*

£££–££££
B&B/INN
★

🏠 **Crown and Castle**. Artsy, laid-back, and genuinely friendly, this little gem occupies an 18th-century building in the village of Orford, 10 mi east of Woodbridge. **Pros:** warm service; good restaurant. **Cons:** need a car to get around. ⊠ *Market Hill, Orford* ☏ *01394/450205* ⊕ *www. crownandcastle.co.uk* ⌁ *19 rooms* ⚲ *In-room: no a/c. In-hotel: restaurant, bar, parking, some pets allowed* ❍|*Breakfast.*

£££–££££
HOTEL
Fodor's Choice
★

🏠 **Seckford Hall**. The sense of history at this delightfully old-school hotel comes from more than just the magnificent Tudor architecture. **Pros:** antique charm; lovely setting; great atmosphere. **Cons:** no elevator; creaky old beds; fussy service in restaurant; minimum stay on weekends. ⊠ *Signposted off the A12 outside Woodbridge* ☏ *01394/385678* ⊕ *www.seckford.co.uk* ⌁ *32 rooms* ⚲ *In-room: no a/c, Wi-Fi. In-hotel: restaurants, bar, pool, gym, spa, some pets allowed* ❍|*Breakfast.*

ALDEBURGH

15 mi northeast of Woodbridge.

Aldeburgh (pronounced *orl*-bruh) is a quiet seaside resort, except in June, when the town fills up with people attending the noted Aldeburgh Festival. Its beach is backed by a promenade lined with candy-color dwellings. The 20th-century composer Benjamin Britten lived here for some time. He was interested in the story of Aldeburgh's native son, poet George Crabbe (1754–1832), and turned his life story into *Peter Grimes*, a celebrated opera that perfectly captures the atmosphere of the Suffolk Coast.

GETTING HERE AND AROUND

You have little choice but to drive to Aldeburgh; turn off the A12 near Farnham and follow signs. Bus connections are few: the 563 from Norwich takes 2½ hours, but only leaves twice a day on weekdays not at all on weekends. There is no train station.

ESSENTIALS

Visitor Information Aldeburgh (⊠ *High St.* ☏ *01728/453637* ⊕ www.visit-suffolkcoast.co.uk).

EXPLORING

Moot Hall. The Elizabethan Moot Hall, built of flint and timber, stood in the center of a thriving 16th-century town when first erected. Now it's just a few steps from the beach, a mute witness to the erosive powers of the North Sea. It's the home of the Aldeburgh Museum, a low-key collection that includes finds from an Anglo-Saxon ship burial. ⊠ *Market Cross Pl., Sea Front* ☏ *01728/454666* ⊕ *www.aldeburghmuseum.org. uk* 🎫 *£1* ⊗ *Easter–Apr., weekends 2:30–5; May, Sept., and Oct., daily 2:30–5; June–Aug., daily noon–5.*

WHERE TO EAT

£ ✕**Fish and Chip Shop.** When frying time approaches, Aldeburgh's most
BRITISH celebrated fish-and-chip shop always has a long line of eager custom-
Fodor's Choice ers. Popularity ensures a high turnover, so you know the fish is always
★ fresh. The batter melts in your mouth, and the chips are satisfyingly
chunky. Upstairs you can bring your own wine or beer and sit at tables.
For the full experience, join a line for the paper-wrapped version. The
deep-fried delicacies are equally good at the **Golden Galleon**, on the
same road and run by the same team. ✉ *226 High St.* ☎ *01728/452250*
⊟ *No credit cards.*

££ ✕**The Lighthouse.** An excellent value, this low-key brasserie with tightly
MODERN BRITISH packed wooden tables relies exclusively on local products. The menu
focuses on seafood, including oysters and Cromer crabs. All the contemporary British dishes are imaginatively prepared. Desserts, such as
the chocolate–and–Grand Marnier fudge cake, are particularly good.
✉ *77 High St.* ☎ *01728/453377* ⊕ *www.lighthouserestaurant.co.uk.*

NIGHTLIFE AND THE ARTS

★ East Anglia's most important arts festival, and one of the best known
in Great Britain, is the **Aldeburgh Festival** (☎ *01728/687110* ⊕ *www.
aldeburgh.co.uk*). It's held for two weeks in June in the small village
of Snape, 5 mi west of Aldeburgh. Founded by Benjamin Britten, the
festival concentrates on music but includes related exhibitions, poetry
readings, and even walks. A less hectic calendar of events continues
through the year.

It's well worth a stop to take in the peaceful River Alde location of the
Snape Maltings cultural center. It includes art galleries and crafts shops in
distinctive large brick buildings once used to malt barley. You can pause
at the tea shop or the Plough & Sail pub. Snape Maltings has special
events year-round, such as the Britten Festival in October. Leisurely
river cruises (£6) leave from the quayside during high tide. ✉ *Snape*
✛ *Near Saxmundham* ☎ *01728/688303* ⊕ *www.snapemaltings.co.uk*
☉ *Daily Apr.–July and Sept. and Oct., 10–5:30; Aug., daily 10–6;
Nov.–Mar., daily 10–5.*

NORWICH AND NORTH NORFOLK

Norwich, unofficial capital of East Anglia, is dominated by the 15th-
century spire of its impressive cathedral. Norfolk's continuing isolation
from the rest of the country, and its unspoiled landscape and architecture—largely bypassed by the Industrial Revolution—have proved to be
a draw. Many of the flint-knapped (decorated with broken flint) houses
in North Norfolk's newly trendy villages are now weekend or holiday
homes. Windmills, churches, and waterways are the area's chief defining
characteristics. A few miles inland from the Norfolk coast, the Broads
begin, a national park made up of a network of shallow, reed-bordered
lakes, many linked by wide rivers. Boating and fishing are great lures;
rent a boat for a day or a week and the waterside pubs, churches, villages, and nature reserves are all within easy reach.

Continued on page 670

ENGLAND THROUGH THE AGES

English unflappability can cover up a multitude of dark deeds. A landscape, village scene, or ruined castle may present itself as a serene, untroubled canvas, but this is mere show. Trauma and passion are the underlying reality of history; dynastic ambitions, religious strife, and sedition are the subtext. Dig deeper, and what might appear to be a vast, nation-wide museum turns out to be a complex tapestry of narratives and personalities.

On a far-flung corner of Europe, England's geographical position can account for many things: its slowness in absorbing technological and cultural influences from the great Mediterranean civilizations, its speedy adaptation to the global explosion of trade in the early modern era, and its separate, rather aloof identity. But other factors have molded English history too, not least the waves of immigration, settlement and conquest, by Celts, Romans, Danes, and Normans among numerous others. Perhaps the greatest factor of all has been the unforeseen events, accidental meetings, and random coincidences that history delights in throwing up. The careful—sometimes over-zealous—custodianship of England's heritage may pretend otherwise, but behind every object and beneath every ruin lies a tangle of interconnected events. With some context, history is lifted out of the realm of show and into biting reality.

—*by Robert Andrews*

On stage at Shakespeare's Globe Theatre, London

(clockwise from top left) Avebury Stone Circles in Wiltshire; Roman Baths, Bath; Illuminated manuscript, *Liber Vitae*, 1031; Iron Age coins from Yorkshire

Early Arrivals

5000 BC–55 BC

The British Isles had already assumed their current shape by 5000 BC, after the final thawing of the last ice age had resulted in a substantial northwestern promontory being detached from the rest of mainland Europe. However, the influx of different peoples and cultures from the east continued as before. It may have been one of these waves of immigrants that brought agriculture to the islands. Numerous burial sites, hill forts, and stone circles have survived from these early societies, notably in the soft chalk downs of southern England.

■ Visit: Stonehenge and Avebury (⇨ Ch. 4).

Roman Britain

55 BC– AD 450

The emperor Claudius declared Colchester Rome's first British colony soon after the invasion of AD 43, and legionary fortresses in the north were established by AD 75. Resistance included Queen Boudicca's uprising, during which Londinium (London) was razed. However, a Romano-British culture was forged with its northern limit at Hadrian's Wall, built in AD 128. To the south, Celtic Britain became integrated into the Roman Empire with the construction of villas, baths, fortifications, and roads.

■ Visit: Fishbourne Roman Palace (⇨ Ch. 3). Roman Baths, Bath (⇨ Ch. 7).

Anglo-Saxons

450–1066

Following the withdrawal of the Roman legions, Britain fell prey to invasions by Jutes, Angles, and Saxons from the mainland. The native Celts were pushed back to the fringes of Britain: Cornwall, Wales, northern England, and Scotland. Eventually seven Anglo-Saxon kingdoms emerged, all of which had adopted Christianity by 650. In the 8th century, the Anglo-Saxon kingdoms faced aggressive incomers from Scandinavia, halted only when Alfred the Great, king of Wessex, unified the English against the Viking invaders.

■ Visit: Bede's World (⇨ Ch. 13). Jorvik Viking Centre (⇨ Ch. 12).

597 St. Augustine arrives in Canterbury to Christianize Britain	1066 William of Normandy defeats King Harold at the Battle of Hastings	1086 Domesday Book completed, a survey of all taxpayers in England	1215 King John signs Magna Carta at Runnymede

AD 1000   AD 1100   AD 1200   AD 1300   **11**

IN FOCUS ENGLAND THROUGH THE AGES

(clockwise from top left) Tower of London; Bayeux Tapestry, scene where the English flee from Normans; Sculpture of King William I on the exterior of Lichfield Cathedral; Reliquary of St. Thomas à Becket, 12th century

1066-1381 Middle Ages: Normans and Plantagenets

The course of England's history altered radically when William, duke of Normandy, invaded and became king of England in 1066. A Norman military and feudal hierarchy was established, French became the language of government, and the country became more centralized. Trading and dynastic links with Europe meant that military campaigns abroad absorbed resources, while artistic innovations were more easily absorbed at home—for example, the introduction of Gothic architecture in England's churches and cathedrals. The Plantagenet dynasty came to power in 1154 with the accession of Henry II. A power struggle with the church led to the murder of Henry's archbishop Thomas à Becket in Canterbury Cathedral, which became a center for pilgrimage. The autocratic ambitions of Henry's son John were similarly stymied when he was forced to sign the Magna Carta, promulgating basic principles of English law: no taxation except through Parliament, trial by jury, and property guarantees. In 1348–49, the Black Death (bubonic plague) reduced Britain's population from 4.25 million to 2.5 million.

■ Visit: Tower of London ($\Rightarrow$ Ch. 2). Canterbury Cathedral ($\Rightarrow$ Ch. 3). Wells Cathedral ($\Rightarrow$ Ch. 5).

1381-1485 Twilight of the Middle Ages

English kings invested resources in the Hundred Years War, a struggle to increase their territories in France, but Henry V's gains at Agincourt in 1415 were reversed following the succession of the infant Henry VI. In the domestic Wars of the Roses, the House of York, with a white rose as emblem, triumphed over the House of Lancaster (red rose as emblem), when Edward IV seized the crown. But Edward's brother Richard III was defeated by Henry Tudor, who became Henry VII.

■ Visit: St. James, Chipping Campden ($\Rightarrow$ Ch. 7). King's College Chapel, Cambridge ($\Rightarrow$ Ch. 4).

(clockwise from top left) Hampton Court Palace; Elizabeth I; English ships and the Spanish Armada; Queen Mary I; Henry VIII

Tudor Renaissance

1485–1603

The Tudor era saw the political consolidation of the kingdom but a deep religious divide. Henry VIII's break with Rome in order to obtain a divorce from Catherine of Aragon coincided with the Reformation, and he pursued his attack on the church with the dissolution of the monasteries. Protestantism became further entrenched under the short reign of Henry's son, Edward VI, but Catholicism was again in the ascendant under Mary. Elizabeth I strove to heal the sectarian divisions while upholding the supremacy of a Protestant Church of England. Her position was further imperiled by the threat of invasion by Spain, which abated with

the defeat of the Spanish Armada in 1588. Elizabeth encouraged piratical attacks on the Spaniards throughout the Atlantic, as well as voyages to the New World, with Walter Raleigh leading expeditions to Virginia in the 1580s. A major flourishing of arts and letters took place during the reign of Good Queen Bess, with such figures as Edmund Spenser and William Shakespeare. When Elizabeth died without an heir, her chief minister, Robert Cecil, invited the Stuart James VI of Scotland to occupy the throne as James I of England.

■ Visit: Hampton Court Palace (⇨ Ch. 2). Burghley House (⇨ Ch. 11). Longleat (⇨ Ch. 4).

Stuart England

1603–1660

The Stuarts' attempts to rule independently of Parliament led to disaster. Religious tensions persisted, and Puritans and other dissenters began to seek refuge in the New World. Those who stayed were persecuted under James's son Charles I, who alienated the gentry and merchant classes until war was declared between king and Parliament. The Civil War ended with Charles's trial and execution in 1649 and an interregnum in which Oliver Cromwell, the general who became Parliamentarian leader, was declared Lord Protector.

■ Visit: Banqueting House, London (⇨ Ch. 2).

1620 Pilgrims sail from Plymouth on the *Mayflower*	1660 The Restoration: Charles II restored to the throne	1689 Bill of Rights: Parliament established as England's primary governing body	1795-1815 Napoleonic Wars: Britain and its allies defeat France
1650	1700	1750	1800

11

IN FOCUS ENGLAND THROUGH THE AGES

(clockwise from top left) *The Great Fire of London* by Turner; George III; West front entrance of St. Paul's Cathedral; Charles II; Chippendale mahogany bonnet-top highboy, 1770s

Restoration

1660-1714

In an uneasy pact with Parliament, Charles I's son was invited back from exile to reign as Charles II. The Restoration led to a revival of the arts, especially in the fields of theater and literature, and a wave of church building. Old divisions resurfaced when Charles was succeeded by James II, whose conversion to Catholicism led to the Glorious Revolution (1688), when Parliament offered the English crown to William of Orange and Mary Stuart, James II's daughter. The thrones of England and Scotland were united in the Act of Union (1707).

■ Visit: St. Paul's Cathedral (⇨ Ch. 2). Blenheim Palace (⇨ Ch. 6).

Georgian England
1714-1837

With the death of Queen Anne, the Stuart monarchy came to an end and the succession of the new kingdom of Great Britain passed to the Protestant German House of Hanover. But real power now lay with Parliament. George I spent most of his reign in Germany; George II leaned heavily on Robert Walpole (the first "prime minister"); George III was intermittently mad; and George IV's life was marked by dissipation. However, despite losing the Thirteen Colonies in the American Revolution, Britain had by now become the leading European power in the Indian subcontinent.

It demonstrated martial supremacy over France in the wars that simmered throughout this period, finally ending in Britain's two victories against Napoleon at Trafalgar and Waterloo. The growing empire, combined with engineering and technical advances at home, helped bring about an early Industrial Revolution in Britain. The process accelerated urbanization, especially in the Midlands and north, and created an urban working class. Partly in response, a new sentimental view of rural England emerged, reflected in the building of stately homes with landscaped estates.

■ Visit: Bath (⇨ Ch. 7). Stourhead (⇨ Ch. 4).

(clockwise from top left) Edward VII in coronation robes; Queen Victoria in characteristic mourning clothes; Trellis wallpaper design by William Morris, 1862; British troops in France, World War I

Victorian Age of Empire
1837-1901

Victoria's reign coincided with the high-water mark of the British Empire, expanding into Africa and consolidating in India. Two parties dominated politics: the Liberals and the Conservatives. These parties supplied such prime ministers as Benjamin Disraeli (Conservative) and William Gladstone (Liberal), who left their mark in reformist measures relating to working conditions, policing, education, health, welfare provision, and the extension of suffrage—all areas highlighted in the literature of the time, notably in the works of Charles Dickens. A network of railways and a nationwide postal service enhanced infrastructure and the growth of industry. In other spheres, the Victorian age harked back to the past, whether in art, as in the Arts and Crafts and Pre-Raphaelite movements, or in architecture, which revived old forms of building from classical to Gothic and Tudor. After Prince Albert's death in 1861, Victoria became a recluse in her Isle of Wight palace, Osborne House, though her golden and diamond jubilees restored her popularity while glorifying the achievements of her long reign.

■ Visit: Houses of Parliament (⇨ Ch. 2). Black Country Living Museum (⇨ Ch. 8). Osborne House (⇨ Ch. 4).

Edwardian England and World War I
1901-1918

Edward VII, Victoria's son, was a keen sportsman, gambler, and society figure who embodied the blinkered spirit of the country in the aftermath of the Victorian age. The election to Parliament of 29 members of the newly formed Labour Party in 1906 signaled a realignment of politics, though the eruption of World War I sidetracked domestic concerns. The intense fighting across Europe brought about huge loss of life and economic meltdown.

■ Visit: Royal Liver Building (⇨ Ch. 9). Great Dixter (⇨ Ch. 3).

| 1939-45 World War II | 1952 Queen Elizabeth II accedes to the throne | 1994 Channel Tunnel opened | 2012 Olympics in London |

1940　　　1965　　　1990　　　2015

11

(clockwise from bottom left) Winston Churchill; London Aquatics Centre for the 2012 Olympics; The Beatles; The wedding of Prince William and Catherine Middleton, April 2011

1918-1945

Depression and World War II

The interwar period was one of social upheaval, and the unemployment caused by the Great Depression rose to 70% in a few areas. At the start of World War II, Hitler's forces pushed the British army into the sea at Dunkirk. The aerial Blitz that followed devastated cities. Winston Churchill's rousing leadership and the support of United States and Commonwealth forces helped turn the tide, with Britain emerging triumphant—but bankrupt.

■ Visit: Imperial War Museum, London (⇨ Ch. 2). Manchester (⇨ Ch. 9), and Duxford (⇨ Ch. 11).

1945-PRESENT

To Present Day

Elected in 1945, the new Labour government introduced important reforms in welfare and healthcare and initiated the dismantling of the British empire, starting with independence for India and Pakistan in 1947. The years of austerity lasted until the late 1950s, but the following decade saw a cultural explosion that covered every field, from art (David Hockney and Peter Blake) to music (the Beatles and Rolling Stones at the forefront) to fashion (Twiggy, Mary Quant, and the Carnaby Street look), reflecting a new consumer confidence. British industry had never recovered its former, pre-war strength,

however, and inflation and industrial strife marked the 1970s. Britain's entry into the European Economic Community (later to become the European Union) in 1973 did not immediately slow the economic decline. Manufacturing was largely forsaken by Margaret Thatcher (Conservative) and Tony Blair (Labour) in favor of service industries, but Britain's heavy reliance on finance meant that the economy was hit hard by the crash of 2009. In 2010, the Conservative party established a coalition government with the Liberal Democrats.

■ Visit: Beatles attractions, Liverpool (⇨ Ch. 9). Tate Modern, London (⇨ Ch. 2). Angel of the North (⇨ Ch. 13).

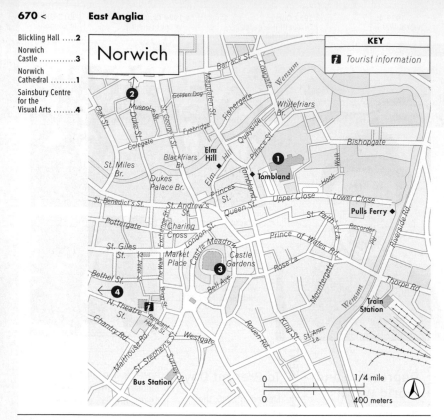

NORWICH

63 mi northeast of Cambridge.

It used to be said that Norwich had a pub for each day of the year and a church in which to repent for every Sunday. Although this is no longer true, real ales and steeples (including that of its grand cathedral) are still much in evidence in this pleasant city of 130,000. The University of East Anglia brings a cosmopolitan touch, including a lively arts scene, to an otherwise remote urban area. It's a good base from which to explore the Norfolk Broads and the coast.

Established by the Saxons because of its prime trading position on the rivers Yare and Wensum, the town sits in the triangle between the two waterways. The inner beltway follows the line of the old city wall, much of which is still visible. It's worth walking or driving around after dark to see the floodlit buildings. By the time of the Norman Conquest, Norwich was one of the largest towns in England, although much was destroyed by the Normans to create a new town. You can see the old flint buildings as you walk down the medieval streets and alleyways. Despite some industrial sites and many modern shopping centers, the town remains engaging.

GETTING HERE AND AROUND

There are regular bus and train connections from London; the trip takes about three hours. The bus and train stations are a 10-minute walk from the center. If you're driving, leave your car in any of the numerous lots scattered around the center.

City Sightseeing operates 45-minute open-top bus tours of Norwich, leaving hourly (starting at 10) from Theatre Street. Tours cost £9.

ESSENTIALS

Visitor and Tour Information City Sightseeing (✉ *Theatre St. across from Theatre Royal* ☎ *01263/587005* ⊕ *www.city-sightseeing.com*). **Norwich** (✉ *The Forum, Millennium Plain* ☎ *01603/213999* ⊕ *www.visitnorwich.co.uk*).

EXPLORING

★ **Blickling Hall.** Behind the wrought-iron entrance gate to Blickling Hall, two mighty yew hedges form a magnificent frame for this perfectly symmetrical Jacobean masterpiece. The redbrick mansion, 15 mi north of Norwich, has towers and chimneys, baroque Dutch gables, and, in the center, a three-story timber clock tower. The grounds include a formal flower garden and parkland with woods that conceal a temple, an orangery, and a pyramid. Blickling belonged to a succession of historic figures, including Sir John Fastolf, the model for Shakespeare's Falstaff; Anne Boleyn's family; and finally, Lord Lothian, ambassador to the United States at the outbreak of the Second World War. The Long Gallery (127 feet) has an intricate plasterwork ceiling with Jacobean emblems. ✉ *B1354, Blickling* ☎ *01263/738030* ⊕ *www.nationaltrust. org.uk* ✉ *£10.75; gardens only, £7.25* ☉ *House late Feb.–late July and mid-Sept.–late Oct., Wed.–Sun. 11–5; late July–mid Sept., Wed.–Mon. 11–5. Gardens Nov. and Dec., daily 11–4; Jan–late Feb., Thurs.–Sun. 11–4; late Feb.–Oct., daily 10–5:30.*

☽ **Norwich Castle.** The decorated stone facing of this castle, now a museum on the hill in the center of the city, makes it look like a children's-book illustration. The castle is Norman (1130), but a stone keep replaced the original wooden bailey (wall). The thick walls and other defenses attest to its military function. Interactive displays explore topics from ancient Egypt to life in Norman times. The art section includes a gallery devoted to the Norwich School of painters who, like John Constable, focused on the everyday landscape and seascape. Daily tours explore the castle's battlements or dungeons. ✉ *Castle Meadow* ☎ *01603/495897* ⊕ *www.museums.norfolk.gov.uk* ✉ *Gallery, museum, and castle £6.20 (£1 last hr before closing and noon–1 weekdays); special exhibitions £3.30; tours of battlements or dungeons £2.10* ☉ *Oct.–June, Mon.–Sat. 10–4:30, Sun. 1–4:30; July–Sept., Mon.–Sat. 10–5, Sun. 1–5.*

★ **Norwich Cathedral.** The grandest example of Norman architecture in Norwich has the second-largest monastic cloisters in Britain (only Salisbury's are bigger). Although its 315-foot-tall spire is visible from everywhere in the city, you cannot see the building itself until you pass through St. Ethelbert's Gate. The cathedral was begun in 1096 by Herbert de Losinga, who had come from Normandy in 1091 to be its first bishop; his splendid tomb is by the high altar. The remarkable length of the nave is immediately impressive; the similarly striking height of the

CLOSE UP

Experiencing Norfolk's Broads

Breathtakingly lovely, The Broads are a network of rivers and canals that stretch for about 150 mi across East Anglia, mostly in North Norfolk. It's a unique landscape of glassy waters, reed-covered marshlands, and impossibly photogenic windmills. At sunset, the whole area turns the color of honey.

The Broads can be seen from your car window, but it's nothing compared to floating through them on a boat. **Broads Tours** (✉ *The Bridge, Wroxham* ☎ *01603/782207* ⊕ *www.broads. co.uk*) offers day cruises around the area, as well as half-day and full-day

boat rentals. The company is based in Wroxham, 7 mi northeast of Norwich.

You can also see much of the Broads by bike. **Broadland Cycle Hire** (✉ *The Rhond, Hoveton* ☎ *07887/480331* ⊕ *www. norfolkbroadscycling.co.uk*), 8 mi northeast of Norwich, charges £15 per day for rental (with discounts for couples and families). The company can recommend several good bike routes.

For more information visit ⊕ *www. enjoythebroads.com*, where you can download a useful leaflet from the tourist board.

---

vaulted ceiling makes it a strain to study the delightful colored bosses, which illustrate Bible stories with great vigor and detail. (Binoculars are handy.) The grave of Norfolk-born nurse Edith Cavell, the British World War I heroine shot by the Germans in 1915, is at the east end of the cathedral. There's also a small medieval-style herb garden, plus a restaurant and coffee shop. Guided tours are offered Monday to Saturday at 11, noon, 1, 2, and 3. ■**TIP→** There are two excellent interactive guides online, including clickable maps. The Cathedral Close (grounds) is one of the most idyllic places in Norwich; past the mixture of medieval and Georgian houses, a path leads down to the ancient water gate, Pulls Ferry. ✉ *62 The Close* ☎ *01603/218300* ⊕ *www.cathedral.org. uk* ◻ *Free* ☉ *Cathedral daily 7:30–6; herb garden Tues.–Thurs. 9–5.*

Sainsbury Centre for the Visual Arts. A hangarlike building designed by Norman Foster on the University of East Anglia campus holds the collection of the Sainsbury family, owners of a supermarket chain. It includes a remarkable quantity of tribal art and 20th-century works, especially art nouveau, and has pieces by Pablo Picasso and Alberto Giacometti. Rotating exhibitions include big-name photography and art shows. Buses 22, 25, 26, and 27 run from downtown Norwich to the university. ✉ *Earlham Rd.* ☎ *01603/593199* ⊕ *www.scva.org.uk* ◻ *Free; special exhibits vary* ☉ *Tues.–Sun. 10–5.*

WHERE TO EAT AND STAY

For expanded hotel reviews, visit Fodors.com.

£   ✕ **Adam and Eve.** Said to be Norwich's oldest pub, this place dates back
BRITISH   to at least 1249. From noon until 7, the kitchen serves such hearty pub staples as chicken-and-ham pie or cheese-and-ale soup from the short but solid bar menu. Theakston's and Adnams beer are available

To get the most from your visit to Blickling Hall, a Jacobean mansion, take time to explore the gardens and grounds.

on tap, as is Aspall's cider. ⊠ *Bishopsgate* ☎ *01603/667423* ⊕ *www.adamandevenorwich.co.uk.*

££
BRITISH
★

✕ **Britons Arms**. A converted pub, this cozy, thatched café and eatery has famously good homemade cakes as well as some pies and tarts. The 15th-century building has low ceilings, a garden in summer, and an open fire in winter. ⊠ *9 Elm Hill* ☎ *01603/623367* ▭ *No credit cards* ⊗ *Closed Sun.*

£
BELGIAN
☾

✕ **Waffle House**. The perfect antidote to all those heavy English breakfasts, this is the kind of place where walking through the door is enough to make you salivate with anticipation. It's waffles, waffles, and more waffles on the menu, although the selection shows imagination. Breakfast choices include such savory concoctions as smoked salmon waffles; later in the day you can order waffles topped with anything from tuna salad to guacamole and salsa. Or you could skip to dessert and waffles topped with pecan and butterscotch or *banoffee* sauce (a mix of banana and toffee). ⊠ *39 St. Giles St.* ☎ *01603/612790* ⊕ *www.wafflehouse.co.uk.*

£££
HOTEL

▦ **The Old Rectory**. This gorgeous, ivy-covered Georgian manor house overlooking manicured lawns and rolling hills is a real find. **Pros:** lovely old building; peaceful setting; friendly staff. **Cons:** away from the action; minimum stay at weekends. ⊠ *103 Yarmouth Rd., Thorpe St. Andrew* ☎ *01603/700772* ⊕ *www.oldrectorynorwich.com* ⇗ *7 rooms* ♨ *In-room: no a/c, Internet. In-hotel: restaurant, pool* ⃫⃝ *Breakfast.*

NIGHTLIFE AND THE ARTS

The **Maddermarket Theatre** (⊠ *St. John's Alley* ☎ *01603/620917* ⊕ *www. maddermarket.co.uk*), patterned after Elizabethan theaters, has been the base of amateur and community theater in Norwich since 1911.

Norwich Arts Centre (⊠ *St. Benedict's St.* ☎ *01603/660352* ⊕ *www. norwichartscentre.co.uk*) puts on an eclectic program of live music, dance, and comedy. Its café has free Internet access.

Norwich Playhouse (⊠ *Gun Wharf, St. George's St.* ☎ *01603/598598* ⊕ *www.norwichplayhouse.org.uk*), a professional repertory group, performs everything from Shakespeare to world premieres of new plays.

Norwich's biggest and best-known theater, the **Theatre Royal** (⊠ *Theatre St.* ☎ *01603/630000* ⊕ *www.theatreroyalnorwich.co.uk*) hosts touring companies staging musicals, ballet, opera, and plays.

SHOPPING

The medieval lanes of Norwich, around Elm Hill and Tombland, contain the best antiques, book, and crafts stores.

Colman's Mustard Shop (⊠ *15 Royal Arcade* ☎ *01603/627889* ⊕ *www. colmansmustardshop.com*) pays homage to Colman's Mustard, a somewhat iconic local company founded in the early 19th century. It sells collectibles and more than 15 varieties of mustard.

Norwich Market (⊠ *Market Pl., Gentleman's Walk* ☎ *01603/213537* ⊕ *www.norwich-market.co.uk*), the city's main outdoor market, is open daily; it sells everything from jewelry to clothes and food and has been the heart of the city for 900 years.

SPORTS AND THE OUTDOORS

Traffic on the River Yare is now mostly for pleasure rather than commerce, and a summer trip with **City Boats** (⊠ *Highcraft Marina, Griffin La.* ☎ *01603/701701* ⊕ *www.cityboats.co.uk*) gives a fresh perspective on Norwich. Longer trips are available down the rivers Wensum and Yare to the nearer Broads.

BLAKENEY

28 mi northwest of Norwich.

The Norfolk coast begins to feel wild and remote near Blakeney, 14 mi west of Cromer. Driving the coast road from Cromer, you pass marshes, sandbanks, and coves, as well as villages. Blakeney is one of the most appealing, with harbors for small fishing boats and yachts. Once a bustling port town exporting corn and salt, it enjoys a quiet existence today, and a reputation for wildlife viewing at Blakeney Point.

GETTING HERE AND AROUND

A48 passes through the center of Blakeney. There are few bus connections, though the 46 and CH1 Coasthopper connect the town with Wells-next-the-Sea.

EXPLORING

Blakeney Point. These 1,000 acres of grassy dunes are home to nesting terns and about 500 common and gray seals. You can walk 3½ mi from Cley Beach to get here, but a boat trip from Blakeney or Morston

11

Walking Paths in East Anglia

East Anglia is a walker's dream, especially if a relatively flat trail appeals to you. The regional Web site ⊕ *www.visiteastofengland.com* has further details about these paths.

The long-distance footpath known as the Peddars Way follows the line of a pre-Roman road, running from near Thetford through heathland, pine forests, and arable fields, and on through rolling chalk lands to the Norfolk coast near Hunstanton.

The Norfolk Coastal Path then continues eastward along the coast, joining at Cromer with the delightfully varied Weaver's Way, which passes through medieval weaving villages and deeply rural parts of the Norfolk Broads on its 56-mi route from Cromer to Great Yarmouth. Anyone interested in birds should carry binoculars and a field guide, as both of these routes have abundant avian life—both local and migratory.

Quay is fun and educational. **Bishop's Boats** (⊠ *Blakeney Quay opposite junction with High St.* ☎ *01263/740753* ⊕ *www.norfolksealtrips.co.uk*) runs one- or two-hour trips daily between February and October from Morston Quay and Blakeney harbor for £8 per person. An information center and a tearoom at Morston Quay are open according to tides and weather. ⊠ *A149* ☎ *01263/740241* ⊕ *www.nationaltrust.org.uk* ⊠ *Free.*

WHERE TO EAT AND STAY
For expanded hotel reviews, visit Fodors.com.

£
SEAFOOD
★
✕ **Anchor Inn.** This delightful little gastro-pub in Morston, 1½ mi west of Blakeney, has a cozy, coastal atmosphere. The menu doesn't consist solely of seafood, but why would you order anything else when the local catch is this good? Platters of mussels and oysters are popular, and prawns are served the way purists like them—in a pint glass, shells on, with a twist of lemon and a pot of homemade mayo. The tasty fish-and-chips draw crowds. ⊠ *22 The Street, Morston* ☎ *01263/741392.*

£££
MODERN BRITISH
✕ **White Horse at Blakeney.** Fine food is the draw at this former coaching inn. Roast whiting with gnocchi appears on the menu along with such classics as fish-and-chips. You can dine in the bar, an airy conservatory, or the more intimate Long Room. There are also a few simply furnished guest rooms with sea views that are worth the extra pence. ⊠ *4 High St.* ☎ *01263/740574* ⊕ *www.blakeneywhitehorse.co.uk.*

£££–££££
HOTEL
★
🛏 **Byfords.** In a market town 5 mi southeast of Blakeney, Byfords epitomizes the increasing trendiness of North Norfolk. **Pros:** plush rooms; amiable staff; relaxed atmosphere. **Cons:** minimum stay on weekends. ⊠ *1–3 Shirehall Plain, Holt* ☎ *01263/711400* ⊕ *www.byfords.org.uk* 🛏 *16 rooms* ⚬ *In-room: no a/c. In-hotel: restaurant* ⏐⊙⏐ *Breakfast.*

SPORTS AND THE OUTDOORS
Temples Seal Watching Trips (☎ *01263/740791* ⊕ *www.sealtrips.co.uk*) organizes two-hour boat trips out to Blakeney Point, where you can watch seals in their natural environment. Tours cost £9; there are usually two or three daily departures in high season. The ticket office is located in the Anchor Inn in Morston, 1½ mi west of Blakeney.

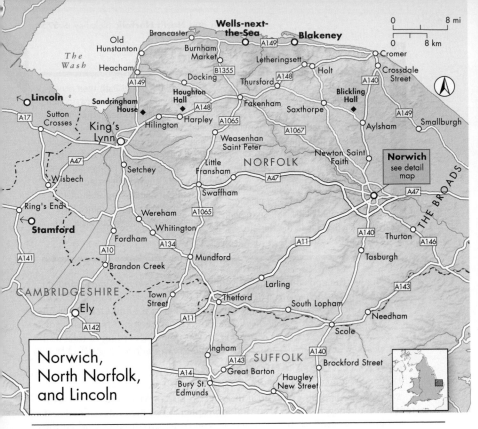

Norwich
see detail
map

Norwich,
North Norfolk,
and Lincoln

WELLS-NEXT-THE-SEA

10 mi west of Blakeney, 34 mi northwest of Norwich.

A quiet base from which to explore other nearby towns, the harbor town of Wells-next-the-Sea and the nearby coastline remain untouched, with many excellent places for bird-watching and walking on the sandy beaches of Holkham Bay, near Holkham Hall. Today the town is a mile from the sea, but in Tudor times, when it was closer to the ocean, it served as one of the main ports of East Anglia. The remains of a medieval priory point to the town's past as a major pilgrimage destination in the Middle Ages. Along the nearby beach a narrow-gauge steam train makes the short journey to Walsingham between Easter and October.

GETTING HERE AND AROUND

Wells-next-the-Sea is on the main A149 coastal road, but can also be reached via the B1105 from Fakenham. The nearest train station is about 16 mi away in Sheringham. There are regular buses from Sheringham, Fakenham and Norwich.

ESSENTIALS

Visitor Information Wells-next-the-Sea (✉ *Staithe St.* ☎ *01328/711885* ⊕ *www.wells-guide.co.uk*).

EXPLORING

Fodor's Choice
★

Holkham Hall. One of the most splendid mansions in Britain, Holkham Hall is the seat of the Coke family, the earls of Leicester. In the late 18th century, Thomas Coke went on a grand tour of the Continent, returning with art treasures and determined to build a house according to the new Italian ideas. Centered by a grand staircase and modeled after the Baths of Diocletian, the 60-foot-tall Marble Hall (mostly alabaster, in fact), may be the most spectacular room in Britain. Beyond are salons filled with works from Coke's collection of masterpieces, including paintings by Gainsborough, Van Dyck, Rubens, and Raphael. Surrounding the house is parkland landscaped by Capability Brown in 1762. You'd be hard-pressed to walk through it without spotting several deer. A good way to see the grounds is a half-hour-long lake cruise. The original walled kitchen gardens have been restored and once again provide produce for the estate. The **Bygones Museum,** in the old stable block, displays everything from gramophones to fire engines. ⌧ *Off A149* ☎ *01328/710227* ⊕ *www.holkham.co.uk* ⌧ *Hall £9, museum £4, combined ticket £11; lake cruise £3.50; grounds free* ☉ *Hall Apr.–Oct., Sun., Mon., and Thurs. noon–4. Museum Apr.–Oct., daily 10–5. Walled gardens Apr.–Oct., daily noon–4. Park daily 7–7.*

Houghton Hall. Built by the first British prime minister, Sir Robert Walpole, in the 1720s, this grand Palladian pile has been carefully restored by its current owner, the seventh marquess of Cholmondeley. The double-height Stone Hall and the sumptuous rooms reveal designer William Kent's preference for gilt, plush fabrics, stucco, and elaborate carvings. The Common Parlour, one of the original family rooms, is elegant but far simpler. Stroll in the 5-acre walled garden. The house is 14 mi southwest of Wells-next-the-Sea. ⌧ *Off A148, near Harpley* ☎ *01485/528569* ⊕ *www.houghtonhall.com* ⌧ *£8.80; park and grounds only, £6* ☉ *House Apr.–Sept., Wed., Thurs., Sun., and bank holidays 1:30–5 (last admission at 4:30); grounds Apr.–Sept., Wed., Thurs., Sun., and bank holidays 11–5:30.*

Sandringham House. Not far from the old-fashioned seaside resort of Hunstanton, Sandringham House is where the Royal Family traditionally spends Christmas. The redbrick Victorian mansion was clearly designed for enormous country-house parties, with a ballroom, billiard room, and bowling alley, as well as a shooting lodge on the grounds. The house and gardens close when the Queen is in residence, but the woodlands, nature trails, and museum of royal memorabilia in the old stables remain open, as does the church, medieval but in heavy Victorian disguise. Tours access most rooms but steer clear of personal effects of current royals. The house is 20 mi southwest of Wells-next-the-Sea. It's closed for about a week in late July for a royal visit. ⌧ *Sandringham* ☎ *01553/612908* ⊕ *www.sandringhamestate.co.uk* ⌧ *House, gardens, and museum £11; gardens and museum only, £7.50* ☉ *Easter–late July and early Aug.–Oct., daily 11–5 (last admission at 4:30). Gardens open 30 mins early.*

WHERE TO STAY

For expanded hotel reviews, visit Fodors.com.

££££–££££ ⊡ **Victoria at Holkham.** A colorful, whimsical hideaway, this hotel on the
HOTEL Holkham Hall estate is managed by the earl of Leicester's family. **Pros:**
Fodor's Choice original character; excellent location; outstanding food. **Cons:** mini-
★ mum stay on weekends; extremely busy in summer; no elevator. ⊠ *Park*
ℭ *Rd., Holkham* ☎ *01328/711008* ⊕ *www.holkham.co.uk/victoria* ⌨ *9*
rooms, 1 suite, 4 self-contained lodges ⚿ *In-room: no a/c (some). In-*
hotel: restaurant, bar ◯ *Breakfast.*

SPORTS AND THE OUTDOORS

On Yer Bike Cycle Hire (⊠ *The Laurels, Nutwood Farm, Wighton*
☎ *01328/820719* ⊕ *www.norfolkcyclehire.co.uk*) will deliver and collect bikes; rentals are £13 per day. Reservations are required.

STAMFORD AND LINCOLN

The fens of northern Cambridgeshire pass imperceptibly into the three
divisions of Lincolnshire: Holland, Kesteven, and Lindsey are parts of
the county, divided administratively. Holland borders the Isle of Ely
and the Soke of Peterborough. This marshland spreads far and wide
south of the Wash. The chief attractions are two towns: Stamford, to
the southwest, and Lincoln, with its magnificent cathedral.

STAMFORD

48 mi northwest of Cambridge.

Serene, honey-hued Stamford, on a hillside overlooking the River
Welland, has a well-preserved center, in part because in 1967 it was designated England's first conservation area. This unspoiled town, which
grew rich from the medieval wool and cloth trades, has a delightful,
harmonious mixture of Georgian and medieval architecture.

GETTING HERE AND AROUND

Stamford is on the A43 and A1. Trains from London and Lincoln depart
every 50 minutes (with connections). The journey from London takes
between one and two hrs, slightly longer from Lincoln.

ESSENTIALS

Visitor Information Stamford (⊠ *Stamford Tourist Information Centre, St.
Mary's St.* ☎ *01780/755611* ⊕ www.stamford.co.uk).

EXPLORING

★ **Burghley House.** Considered one of the grandest houses of the Elizabethan age, this architectural masterpiece is celebrated for its roof-scape
bristling with pepper-pot chimneys and slate-roof towers. It was built
between 1565 and 1587 to the design of William Cecil, first Baron
Burghley, when he was Elizabeth I's high treasurer; his descendants still
occupy the house. The interior was remodeled in the late 17th century
with treasures from Europe. On view are 18 sumptuous rooms, with
carvings by Grinling Gibbons and ceiling paintings by Antonio Verrio
(including the dramatic Heaven Room and the Hell Staircase), as well
as innumerable paintings and priceless porcelain. You can tour on your
own or join a free 80-minute guided tour beginning daily at 3:30. In

the 18th century Capability Brown landscaped the grounds (where deer roam and open-air concerts are staged in summer), dug the lake, and added the Gothic Revival orangery, where today you can take tea or lunch. In early September Burghley is host to the international Burghley Horse Trials. The house is a mile southeast of Stamford. ✉ *Off A1* ☎ *01780/752451* ⊕ *www.burghley.co.uk* ✉ *House and gardens £12.20; gardens only, £7* ⊙ *Late Mar.–Oct., Sat.–Thurs. 11–4:30.*

LINCOLN

53 mi north of Stamford, 93 mi northwest of Cambridge, 97 mi northwest of Norwich.

★ Celts, Romans, and Danes all had important settlements here, but it was the Normans who gave Lincoln its medieval stature after William the Conqueror founded Lincoln Castle as a stronghold in 1068. Four years later William appointed Bishop Remigius to run the huge diocese stretching from the Humber to the Thames, resulting in the construction of Lincoln Cathedral, the third largest in England after York Minster and St. Paul's. Since medieval times Lincoln's status has declined. However, its somewhat remote location (there are no major motorways or railways nearby) has helped preserve its traditional character.

The cathedral is on the aptly named Steep Hill; to its south, narrow medieval streets cling to the hillside. Jew's House, on the Strait, dating from the early 12th century, is one of several well-preserved domestic buildings in this area. The name is almost as old as the house itself—it refers to a former resident, Belaset of Wallingford, a Jewish woman who was murdered by a mob in 1290, the same year the Jews were expelled from England. The River Witham flows unobtrusively under the incongruously named High Bridge, a low, vaulted Norman bridge topped by timber-frame houses from the 16th century. West from here you can rent boats, or, in summer, go on a river cruise.

GETTING HERE AND AROUND

There are direct buses (four hours) from London, but most rail journeys (two to three hours) involve changing trains. The bus and train stations are south of the center, and it's a steep walk uphill to the cathedral and castle. You can avoid the climb by taking the Walk & Ride electric bus service from the stop on St. Mary's Street. Purchase tickets on board. Drivers will find parking lots around the bus and train stations and in the center at the Lawn and Westgate.

ESSENTIALS

Visitor Information Lincoln (✉ *9 Castle Hill* ☎ *01522/545458* ⊕ www. visitlincolnshire.com).

EXPLORING

★ **Cathedral of St. Mary.** Lincoln's crowning glory, this great cathedral was for hundreds of years the tallest building in Europe. The Norman bishop Remigius began work in 1072. The Romanesque church he built was irremediably damaged, first by fire, then by earthquake, but you can still see parts of the ancient structure at the west front. The next great phase of building, initiated by Bishop Hugh of Avalon, is mainly 13th

century in character. The west front, topped by two strikingly tall towers, gives tremendous breadth to the entrance. It is best seen from the 14th-century Exchequer Gate arch in front of the cathedral, or from the castle battlements beyond.

Inside, a breathtaking impression of space and unity belies the many centuries of building and rebuilding. The 13th-century stained-glass window at the north end of the transept, known as the Dean's Eye, is one of the earliest traceried windows, whereas its opposite number at the south end shows a 14th-century sophistication in its interlaced designs. ■TIP➜ Look for the Lincoln Imp on the pillar nearest St. Hugh's shrine; according to legend, an angel turned this creature to stone. Through a door on the north side is the chapter house, a 10-sided building that sometimes housed the medieval Parliament of England during the reigns of Edward I and Edward II. The chapter house is connected to the 13th-century cloister, notable for its amusing ceiling bosses. The cathedral library, a restrained building by Christopher Wren, was built onto the north side of the cloisters after the original library collapsed. Tours of the cathedral roof and tower are fascinating, but no children under 14 are allowed. ✉ *Minster Yard* ☎ *01522/561600* ⊕ *www.lincolncathedral. com* ✉ *£6* ☉ *Late June–Aug., weekdays 7:15 am–8 pm, weekends 7:15–6; Sept.–late June, Mon.–Sat. 7:15–6, Sun. 7:15–5.*

QUICK BITES | After climbing Steep Hill, you'll need at least one of the 23 different teas or 15 coffees available at Pimento Tearooms (✉ *27 Steep Hill* ☎ *01522/544880*). Choose a cake or snack to go along with your pick-me-up.

⌚ **Lincoln Castle.** Facing the cathedral across Exchequer Gate, this castle was built on two great mounds by William the Conqueror in 1068, incorporating part of the remains of Roman garrison walls. The castle was a military base until the 17th century, after which it operated as a prison. In the extraordinary prison chapel you can see the cagelike stalls in which Victorian convicts listened to sermons. ■TIP➜ One of the four surviving copies of the Magna Carta, signed by King John at Runnymede in 1215, is on display. ✉ *Castle Hill* ☎ *01522/511068* ⊕ *www.lincolnshire. gov.uk/lincolncastle* ✉ *£5* ☉ *Apr. and Sept., daily 10–5; May–Aug., daily 10–6; Oct.–Mar., daily 10–4; last entry 45 mins before closing.*

Medieval Bishop's Palace. On the south side of Minster Yard, this building has exhibits about the former administrative center of the diocese, plus a garden and working vineyard. ✉ *Minster Yard* ☎ *01522/527468* ⊕ *www.english-heritage.org.uk* ✉ *£4.40* ☉ *Apr.–Oct., daily 10–5; Nov.–Mar., Thurs.–Mon. 10–4.*

Minster Yard. Surrounding the cathedral on three sides, Minster Yard contains buildings of different periods, including graceful Georgian architecture. A statue of Alfred, Lord Tennyson, who was born in Lincolnshire, stands on the green near the chapter house.

WHERE TO EAT AND STAY

For expanded hotel reviews, visit Fodors.com.

££££ ✗ **Brown's Pie Shop.** More than you might imagine from the modest
BRITISH   name, Brown's Pie Shop serves the best of traditional British cuisine:

succulent beef, great desserts, and some very good, freshly made savory pies. There are also fish specials, steaks, and a small selection of vegetarian dishes. This restaurant, close to the cathedral, serves an economical early-evening menu. ⊠ *33 Steep Hill* ☎ *01522/527330* ⊕ *www.brownspieshop.co.uk.*

£££ ✕ **Jew's House.** This intimate restaurant, with restrained tones and open
MODERN BRITISH stonework, is in one of Lincoln's oldest buildings, a rare survivor of
★ 12th-century Norman domestic architecture. The cosmopolitan menu has a modern flair; typical main dishes include wild sea bass with linguine and crab in a shellfish-and-orange sauce, or spiced duck breast with butternut squash and sloe gin. ⊠ *15 The Strait* ☎ *01522/524851* ⊕ *www.jewshouserestaurant.co.uk* ☉ *Closed Sun. and Mon.*

££–£££ 🖭 **Bailhouse & Mews.** In a 14th-century baronial hall near the cathedral,
B&B/INN the welcoming Bailhouse & Mews has flagstone floors and wooden beams. **Pros:** good value; views of cathedral and castle; convenient parking. **Cons:** some street noise; beds are rather creaky. ⊠ *34 Bailgate* ☎ *01522/541000* ⊕ *www.bailhouse.co.uk* ☜ *10 rooms, 3 cottages, 1 house* ⚭ *In-room: no a/c, Wi-Fi. In-hotel: bar, pool* ❙◎❙ *Breakfast.*

££–£££ 🖭 **White Hart.** Luxuriously furnished with a wealth of antiques, among
HOTEL them some fine clocks and china, the White Hart has been a hotel
★ for 600 years. **Pros:** excellent location; blend of period and modern furnishings. **Cons:** slow service; rooms could use a face-lift. ⊠ *Bailgate* ☎ *01522/526222* ⊕ *www.whitehart-lincoln.co.uk* ☜ *39 rooms, 11 suites* ⚭ *In-room: no a/c, Internet. In-hotel: restaurant, bar, some pets allowed* ❙◎❙ *Breakfast.*

SHOPPING

The best stores are on Bailgate, Steep Hill, and the medieval streets leading directly down from the cathedral and castle.

Just off Steep Hill, the **Cheese Society** (⊠ *1 St. Martin's La.* ☎ *01522/511003*) has a great selection of English and French cheeses and an attached café.

Cobb Hall Craft Centre (⊠ *St. Paul's La. off Bailgate* ☎ *No phone*), filled with shops and workshops, sells clocks, candles, and ornaments.

Steep Hill has good bookstores, antiques shops, and crafts and art galleries, including **Harding House Galleries** (⊠ *Steep Hill* ☎ *01522/523537*).

Yorkshire

WORD OF MOUTH

"I would give York two days. Walk around the walls, see York Minster, the Castle Museum, the National Railway Museum, etc. We did an evening ghost walk—fun for the kids, but the grown-ups quite liked it too. Beyond York, Rievaulx Abbey is wonderful: you really get a sense of what it was like in days gone by."

—TaniaP

WELCOME TO YORKSHIRE

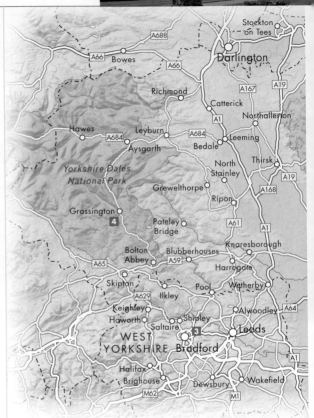

TOP REASONS TO GO

★ **York Minster:** The largest Gothic cathedral in England helps make York one of the country's most visited towns. The building's history is told in its crypt, brilliantly converted into a museum.

★ **North York Moors:** There's enough space in this national park for walkers to experience isolation amid the heather-covered hills that glow crimson and purple in late summer and early fall.

★ **Rievaulx Abbey:** Heading down the tiny lane that leads to the ruins of one of the great Cistercian abbeys only serves to make it all the more dramatic when its soaring arches appear out of the trees.

★ **Coastal towns:** Seafront Whitby inspired Bram Stoker to write *Dracula*. Robin Hood's Bay, a village set in a ravine, has an outstanding beach.

★ **Haworth:** Looking as if it were carved from stone, this picture-perfect hillside town in the dales is a lovely place to learn about the Brontë sisters.

1 York. Still wrapped up in its medieval city walls, this beautifully preserved city makes the perfect introduction to Yorkshire. Its towering Minster and crooked little streets entrance history buffs.

2 York Environs. This rural region holds the exquisite Victorian spa town, Harrogate, as well as charming villages like Knaresborough, tucked away in a steep valley. Baroque Castle Howard is also near York.

3 Leeds and Brontë Country. Rocky and bleak, this windswept stretch of country makes sense of all those tragedies penned by the Brontë sisters in prettily gloomy Haworth. Leeds is a reviving former industrial center worth a stop.

12

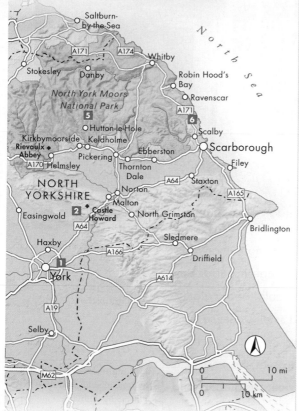

GETTING ORIENTED

Yorkshire is the largest English region to explore (its fiercely proud inhabitants would say it's the only English region *worth* exploring). At the heart of it all is the ancient city of York, with its cathedral and medieval city walls. To the west is the busy city of Leeds, while a few miles away are the wild hills that form what the tourist office calls Brontë Country—Haworth, erstwhile home of the Brontë family, and the valleys and villages of the Yorkshire Dales. North of York is the North York Moors National Park. Isolated stone villages, moorland walks, and Rievaulx Abbey are within easy reach. Along the east coast of Yorkshire, fine beaches and a fascinating history await you in the resort of Scarborough, the former whaling port of Whitby, and Robin Hood's Bay.

4 The Yorkshire Dales. This mountainous region, a bit off the beaten track, has windswept moors and valleys that offer extraordinary views. Gorgeous villages like Bolton Abbey and Grassington are well worth exploring.

5 The North York Moors. A short drive north from York, these heather-covered hills are a perfect place to wander. Hutton-le-Hole and Helmsley are pleasant towns, and the ruins of Rievaulx Abbey are nearby.

6 The North Yorkshire Coast. Along this part of the coast, tiny fishing villages cling to the cliffs where the earth rushes down to meet the cold sea. Scarborough and adorable Robin Hood's Bay make ideal getaways.

GREAT ENGLISH CHEESES

England's lush pastures yield more than 700 types of cheese, which the English eat at any time except breakfast. Smooth and creamy, nutty and tasty, or blue and smelly, cheese turns up in sandwiches and soups, on toast, as a topping, and on cheese boards at the end of a meal. You can ask for advice; restaurants and cheese counters let you try before you buy.

You can buy pieces of cheese both small and large around England (above); Wensleydale cheese (right, top); strong-flavored Blue Stilton is a classic (right, bottom).

Cheeses come in three strengths: mild, medium, and mature. Young cheese is mild and crumbly; as it ages, the flavor gets sharper and the texture firmer. Protected Designation of Origin (PDO) applies to 14 cheeses. An increasing number of small artisan makers produce distinctive and organic cheeses as well as those made from the milk of goats (Quickes) or sheep (Blacksticks); they aren't afraid to experiment. Cornish Yarg is covered with nettles, Stinking Bishop is washed in perry (an alcoholic drink made from pears) and White Stilton is often stuffed with fruit. Most pubs serve a ploughman's lunch—cheese served with crusty bread or a roll, and salad vegetables.

ACCOMPANIMENTS

For **ploughman's lunches,** look for fruit chutneys made from raisins, apples, onions, vinegar, and sugar. Branston pickle is a crunchy, spicy-sweet mix of chopped vegetables. Small pickled onions and gherkins are common; piccalilli consists of cauliflower florets pickled in a thick yellow spicy sauce. **Cheese boards** have three or four cheeses; grapes, apples, and pears; and biscuits and crackers.

These cheeses are made from cows' milk.

CHEDDAR
Originally matured only in caves at Cheddar in Somerset, this is the most well-known of all English cheeses. Ranging from mild to extra-mature, it's firm in texture. If you're looking for the best, aim for West Country Farmhouse Cheddar, which has PDO status when it is made traditionally in Devon, Cornwall, Somerset, and Dorset. For the nuttiest flavor, go for the extra-mature.

CHESHIRE
The oldest named English cheese has appeared on the menu since Roman times. Usually white in color, it has a crumbly texture and salty tang, and is sometimes colored with annatto, a derivative of the achiote tree that gives a yellow to orange color.

DOUBLE AND SINGLE GLOUCESTER
Both varieties have a smooth, dense texture and creamy flavor. Double is more common, and its buttery color is due to annatto. Single Gloucester has PDO status; this requires the cheese to be made in Gloucestershire, to be wheel-shaped, and to be natural in color.

LANCASHIRE
This cheese comes in three strengths according to age: creamy, crumbly, and tasty. The creamy, young cheese is ideal for cheese on toast (Welsh rarebit); the crumbly goes well with fruitcake or an apple, or is good in a salad. The tasty (matured longer) often turns up in a ploughman's lunch.

SHROPSHIRE BLUE
Contrary to expectation, this cheese has never been made in Shropshire. Now produced exclusively in the East Midlands, it's a soft, mellow, orange-colored cheese with blue veins, caused by the injection of the penicillum mold.

BLUE STILTON
This has been the king of English cheeses since the 18th century. With a strong taste and scent, it's now the traditional cheese for Christmas, served with port. Distinguished by blue veins and a crusty exterior, the whole cheeses are wheel-shape and become softer and creamier as they age. As a condition of its PDO status, it must be made in Nottinghamshire, Derbyshire and Leicestershire. White Stilton is milder, younger, crumbly, and creamy; it's a good dessert cheese often combined with dried fruit.

WENSLEYDALE
Made all over the country, the cheese is traditionally made at Hawes in Wensleydale in Yorkshire. It has a white, crumbly texture and is salty; it's best eaten when young and fresh. Wensleydale is often served with fruitcake, fresh apples, or hot apple dishes.

—by Kate Hughes

Updated
by Christi
Daugherty

A hauntingly beautiful region, Yorkshire is known for its wide-open spaces and dramatic landscapes. The hills of the North York Moors and the Yorkshire Dales glow pink with heather in summer, and turn black with it in winter. Hearty fishing villages like Robin Hood's Bay cling to the edges of cliffs in one of England's last remaining wildernesses. In towns like York, Whitby, and Harrogate, historic buildings line narrow streets, and ancient cathedrals, abbeys, and castles create a majestic backdrop to day-to-day life.

Many of the region's biggest attractions are the result of human endeavor: the towering cathedral in medieval York; Castle Howard, a baroque masterpiece near York; and the old haunts of the Brontë sisters in the hillside town of Haworth.

In Yorkshire, though, the landscape is just as big a draw. The most rugged land is the North York Moors, a vast, lonely area free of fences, and dotted with fluffy sheep that wander at will in summer. Between the bleak moors and the rocky Pennine hills lie lush, green valleys known as the Yorkshire Dales, where the high rainfall produces luxuriant vegetation, swift rivers, and sparkling streams. The villages here, immortalized in the books of the Brontës, are constructed of gray stone. These are wonderfully peaceful places, bursting into life in summer as hundreds of hikers (or "ramblers," as they're known in England) appear over the hills.

The area is not all green fields and perfect villages—there's also a gritty, urban aspect to the region. In West Yorkshire, once down-at-the-heels Leeds has remade itself with trendy restaurants and cafés, and its buzzing music industry and nightlife scene.

YORKSHIRE PLANNER

WHEN TO GO

To see the heather at its lushest, visit in summer (but despite the season, be prepared for some chilly days). It's also the best time for the coast, when colorful regattas and arts festivals are under way. York Minster makes a splendid focal point for the prestigious York Early Music Festival in early July. Spring and fall bring their own rewards: far fewer crowds and crisp, clear days, although there's an increased risk of rain and fog. The harsh winter is hard to call: with snow and bright days, the coast, moors, and dales are beautiful, but storms and blizzards set in quickly. The moorland roads become impassable, and villages can be cut off entirely. In winter, stick to York and the main towns.

PLANNING YOUR TIME

Yorkshire is a vast region; it's difficult to explore in a short amount of time. If you're in a hurry, you could see the highlights of York or Leeds as a day trip from London; the fastest trains take just two hours. But it's an awful lot to pack into one day, and you're bound to leave out places you'll probably regret missing. Proper exploration—especially of the countryside—requires time and effort. In a few days you could explore York and some highlights such as Castle Howard and Studley Royal. You'd need the better part of a week to take in the small towns, abandoned abbeys, and inspiring moors and coast. It's well worth it: this is the path less traveled. The Yorkshire Pass (⊕ *www.yorkshirepass. co.uk*), good for one, two, three, or six days, can save you money on more than 70 attractions, but check it against your itinerary.

GETTING HERE AND AROUND

AIR TRAVEL

Leeds Bradford Airport, 8 mi northwest of Leeds, has frequent flights from other cities in England and Europe. Look for cheap fares from London on bmi baby, easyJet, Jet2, or Ryanair. Another good choice for this region is Manchester Airport, about 40 mi southwest of Leeds. This larger airport is well served by domestic and international carriers.

Airports Leeds Bradford International Airport (✉ *A658, Yeadon* ☎ *0871/288–2288* ⊕ *www.lbia.co.uk*). **Manchester Airport** (✉ *Near Junctions 5 and 6 of M56* ☎ *0871/271–0711* ⊕ *www.manairport.co.uk*).

BUS TRAVEL

National Express and Megabus both have numerous daily departures from London's Victoria Coach Station to major cities in Yorkshire. Average travel times are 4¼ hours to Leeds, 6 hours to York, and 8 hours to Scarborough. Once you're in the region, local bus companies take over the routes. There are Metro buses from Leeds and Bradford into the more remote parts of the Yorkshire Dales. Other companies are Harrogate & District for services to Ripon, Harrogate, and Leeds; Yorkshire Coastliner for Castle Howard, Scarborough, Whitby, Malton, and Leeds; Arriva for Whitby, Scarborough, and Middlesbrough; and York Pullman for Hawes and other destinations. In York the main local bus operator is First. Traveline has route information.

Bus Contacts Arriva (📞 0844/800–4411 ⊕ www.arriva.co.uk). **First** (📞 0845/604–5460 ⊕ www.firstgroup.com). **Harrogate & District** (📞 01423/566061 ⊕ www.harrogatebus.co.uk). **Megabus** (📞 0900/160–0900 ⊕ www.megabus.co.uk). **Metroline** (📞 0113/245–7676 ⊕ www.wymetro. com). **National Express** (📞 0871/781–8178 ⊕ www.nationalexpress.com). **Traveline** (📞 08711/200–2233 ⊕ www.traveline.org.uk). **Yorkshire Coastliner** (📞 01653/692556 ⊕ www.yorkshirecoastliner.co.uk). **York Pullman** (📞 01904/622992 ⊕ www.yorkpullmanbus.co.uk).

CAR TRAVEL

If you're driving, the M1 is the principal route north from London. This major thoroughfare gets you to Leeds in about two hours. For York (193 mi) and the Scarborough areas, stay on M1 to Leeds (189 mi), and then take A64. For the Yorkshire Dales, take M1 to Leeds, then A660 to A65 north and west to Skipton. For the North York Moors, take either B1363 north from York to Helmsley, or the A64 through Malton to Whitby. The trans-Pennine motorway, the M62, between Liverpool and Hull, crosses the bottom of this region. North of Leeds, A1 is the major north–south road, although narrow stretches, roadwork, and heavy traffic make this route slow going at times.

Some of the steep, narrow roads in the countryside off the main routes are difficult drives and can be perilous (or closed altogether) in winter. Main roads often closed by snowdrifts are the moorland A169 and the coast-and-moor A171. If you plan to drive in the dales or moors in winter, check the weather forecast in advance.

TRAIN TRAVEL

East Coast trains travel to York and Leeds from London's King's Cross Station. Average travel times from King's Cross are 2 hours to York and 2½ hours to Leeds. Northern Rail trains operate throughout the region. Contact National Rail for train times, and to find out if any discounted Rover tickets are available for your journey.

Train Contacts East Coast (📞 0845/722–5111 ⊕ www.eastcoast.co.uk). **National Rail Enquiries** (📞 0845/748–4950 ⊕ www.nationalrail.co.uk). **Northern Rail** (📞 0845/000–0125 ⊕ www.northernrail.org).

RESTAURANTS

Yorkshire is known for hearty food, though bacon-based breakfasts and lunches of pork pies do tend to pale fairly quickly. Increasingly, though, in the larger towns and cities, particularly in Leeds, a foodie culture of sorts has developed. Indian eateries (called "curry restaurants") can be very good in northern cities. Out in the countryside, pubs are your best bet for dining. Many offer excellent home-cooked food and locally reared meat (especially lamb) and vegetables. Roast beef dinners generally come with Yorkshire pudding, the tasty, light bread that is called a popover in the United States and Canada. It's generally served with lots of gravy. Be sure to sample local cheeses, especially Wensleydale, which has a delicate flavor and honeyed aftertaste.

HOTELS

Traditional hotels are limited primarily to major towns and cities; those in the country tend to be guesthouses. Many of the better guesthouses are at the edge of town, but some proprietors will pick you up at the main station if you're relying on public transportation—verify before booking. Rooms fill quickly at seaside resorts in July and August, and some places in the moors and dales close in winter. Always call ahead to make sure a hotel is open and has space available.

12

WHAT IT COSTS IN POUNDS				
£	££	£££	££££	£££££
Restaurants	under £10	£10–£14	£15–£19	£20–£25	over £25
Hotels	under £70	£70–£120	£121–£160	£161–£220	over £220

Restaurant prices are per person for a main course or equivalent combination of smaller dishes at dinner excluding tax. Hotels prices reflect the rack rate of a standard double room for two people in high season, including 20% V.A.T. Check online for off-season rates and special deals or discounts.

VISITOR INFORMATION

Contact Yorkshire Tourist Board (*0113/322–3500* ⊕ *www.yorkshire.com*).

YORK

For many people, the first stop in Yorkshire is the historic cathedral city of York. Much of the city's medieval and 18th-century architecture has survived, making York a delight to explore. It's one of the most popular short-stay destinations in Britain, and only two hours by train from London's King's Cross Station.

Named "Eboracum" by the Romans, York was the military capital of Roman Britain, and traces of garrison buildings survive throughout the city. After the Roman Empire collapsed in the 5th century, the Saxons built "Eoforwic" upon the ruins of a fort, but were soon defeated by Vikings who called the town "Jorvik" and used it as a base from which to subjugate the countryside. The Normans came in the 11th century and emulated the Vikings by using the town as a military base. It was during Norman times that the foundations of York Minster, the largest medieval cathedral in England, were laid. The only changes the 19th century brought were large houses, built mostly on the outskirts of the city center.

GETTING HERE AND AROUND

If you're driving, take the M1 north from London. Stay on it to Leeds, and then take the A64 to York; York is 25 mi northeast of Leeds. The journey should take around three hours. National Express and Megabus have motor coaches departing from London's Victoria Coach Station every hour. The journey takes 4½ hours. National Express trains run from London's King's Cross Station about every 30 minutes during the week. The trip takes about two hours. York Station, just outside the city walls, has a line of taxis out front to take you to your hotel. If you don't have bags, the walk to town takes eight minutes.

York's city center is mostly closed to traffic and is very walkable. The old center is a compact, dense web of narrow streets and tiny medieval alleys called "snickleways." These provide shortcuts across the city center, but they're not on maps, so you never quite know where you'll end up, which in York is often a pleasant surprise.

TOURS   City Sightseeing runs frequent bus tours of York that stop at the Castle Museum, the Shambles, and Jorvik. You can get on and off as often as you please. York Association of Voluntary Guides arranges short walking tours around the city, which depart daily at 10:15. There are additional tours at 2:15 April through October and at 6:45 July and August. The tours are free, but tips are appreciated.

TIMING

In July and August tourists choke the narrow streets and form long lines at the Minster. April, May, June, and September are less crowded, but the weather can be unpredictable. April is also the time to see the embankments beneath the city walls filled with the pale gold ripple of daffodils.

ESSENTIALS

Tour Information City Sightseeing (☎ 01904/655585 ⊕ www.citysightseeing. co.uk). **York Association of Voluntary Guides** (✉ De Grey Rooms, Exhibition Sq. ☎ 01904/640780).

Visitor Information York (✉ 1 Museum St. ☎ 01904/550099 ⊕ www.visityork. org ✉ York Train Station ☎ 01904/621756).

EXPLORING

TOP ATTRACTIONS

★ **City walls.** York's almost 3 mi of ancient stone walls are among the best preserved in England. A walk on the narrow paved path along the top leads you through 1,900 years of history, from the time the earthen ramparts were raised by the Romans and York's Viking kings to repel raiders, to their fortification by the Normans, to their current colorful landscaping by the city council. The walls are crossed periodically by York's distinctive "bars," or fortified gates: the portcullis on Monk's Bar on Goodramgate is still in working order, and Walmgate Bar in the east is the only gate in England with an intact barbican. It also has scars from the cannon balls hurled at it during the Civil War. Bootham Bar in Exhibition Square was the defensive bastion for the north road, and Micklegate Bar, in the city's southwest corner, was traditionally the monarch's entrance. Fees for these gates range from £1.85 to £2.50. To access the path and the lookout towers, find a staircase at one of the many breaks in the walls. ◻ *Free* ☉ *Daily 8 am–dusk.*

☾ **Dig.** This venture from the people behind the Jorvik Viking Centre is a great way to get young people inspired about history and archaeology. It's an ongoing archaeological dig in and beneath an old church; kids, supervised by knowledgeable experts, dig in the dirt and "find" Roman or Viking artifacts. After your exploration, head to the lab to learn what

12

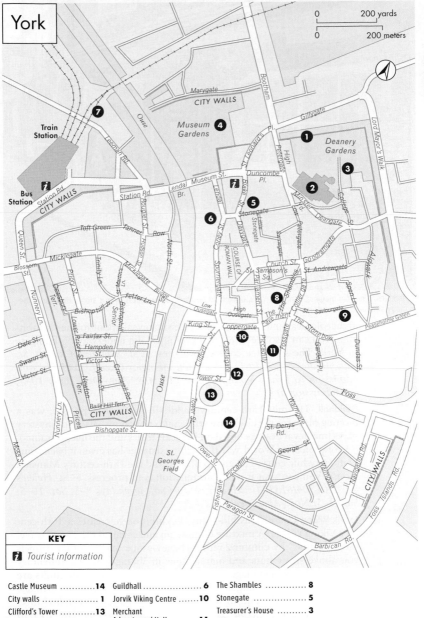

York

Train Station

Bus Station

CITY WALLS

Museum Gardens **4**

Deanery Gardens

7

1

3

2

5

6

8

9

10

11

12

13

14

St. Georges Field

CITY WALLS

0   200 yards
0   200 meters

The Shambles, a narrow medieval street in York, once held butchers' shops but now has stores that serve the city's many shoppers and visitors.

archaeological finds discovered on the site reveal about former inhabitants. You can also see a real archaeological dig underway on Hungate in York. The same fee covers both sites. ✉ *St. Saviour's Church, St. Saviourgate* ☎ *01904/615505* ⊕ *www.vikingjorvik.com* ✉ *£5.50; joint admission to Jorvik Viking Centre £13.50* ⊗ *Apr.–Oct., daily 10–5, last admission at 4.*

Guildhall. The mid-15th-century guildhall, by the River Ouse, was a meeting place for the city's powerful guilds. It was also used for mystery plays (medieval dramas based on biblical stories and the lives of saints). Restoration after World War II bombing damage has given it back some of its erstwhile glory. The guildhall is behind the 18th-century Mansion House; you can visit it when no function is in progress. ✉ *St. Helen's Sq.* ☎ *01904/613161* ✉ *Free* ⊗ *May–Oct., weekdays 9–5, Sat. 10–5, Sun. 2–5; Nov.–Apr., weekdays 9–5.*

☺ **Jorvik Viking Centre.** This kid-focused exhibition re-creates a 10th-century Viking village. A mixture of museum and carnival ride, you "travel through time" by climbing into a Disney-esque machine that propels you above straw huts and mannequins in Viking garb. Commentary is provided in 10 languages. Kids will get a lot out of it, but adults are unlikely to learn anything new. A small collection of Viking-era artifacts is on display at the end of the ride. ✉ *Coppergate* ☎ *01904/615505* ⊕ *www.vikingjorvik.com* ✉ *£9.25; joint admission to Dig £13.50* ⊗ *Apr.–Oct., daily 10–5; Nov.–Mar., daily 10–4.*

☺ **National Railway Museum.** For train-lovers one and all: here Britain's national collection of locomotives forms part of a massive train museum. Among the exhibits are gleaming giants of the steam era, including the *Mallard*, holder of the world speed record for a steam engine (126 mph). Passenger cars used by Queen Victoria are on display, as well as the only Japanese bullet train to be seen outside Japan. You can clamber aboard the trains, some of which are started up regularly to keep the engines working. ✉ *Leeman Rd.* ☎ *08448/153139* ⊕ *www.nrm.org.uk* ✉ *Museum free* ☉ *Daily 10–6.*

The Shambles. York's best-preserved medieval street has half-timber stores and houses with overhangs so massive you could almost reach across the street from one second-floor window to another. Once filled with butcher shops (meat hooks are still fastened outside some of the doors), today it's filled with touristy shops of scant interest to most visitors. Still, it's beautiful to walk down for the atmosphere.

WHERE ARE THE GATES?

The Viking conquerors of northern England held the region for more than a century and made York their capital. *Gate* was the Viking word for "street," hence the street names such as Goodramgate and Micklegate. Adding to the confusion, the city's entrances, or gates, are called "bars," from an Old English term. As local tour guides like to say, "In York, our streets are called gates, our gates are called bars, and our bars are called pubs."

12

Stonegate. This narrow, pedestrian-only street of Tudor and 18th-century storefronts and courtyards retains considerable charm. It has been in daily use for almost 2,000 years, since first being paved in Roman times. Today it's lined with jewelry stores, knickknack shops, tea shops, and ancient pubs. A passage just off Stonegate, at 52A, leads to the remnants of a 12th-century Norman stone house attached to a more recent structure. You can see the old Norman wall and window. ■TIP→ Look out for the little red devil that once announced a printer's shop. At the intersection of Stonegate and High Petergate, Minerva lounges on a stack of books. She once advertised a bookseller.

NEED A BREAK? At the opposite end of Stonegate from the Minster, Betty's (✉ *6–8 Helen's Sq., off Stonegate* ☎ *01904/659142*) has been a York institution since 1912. This tea-and-cakes salon in an attractive art nouveau building is more beloved for its history and ambience than for its so-so food. Still, it's a piece of history, and a good place to take a rest. There's always a line out front, so expect a short wait for a table.

Fodor's Choice **York Minster.** *For information about the cathedral, see the feature York Minster: Gothic Grandeur in this chapter.*

★

WORTH NOTING

Castle Museum. A former 18th-century debtors' prison, this quirky museum of everyday items presents detailed exhibitions and re-creations, including a Victorian street complete with crafts shops and a working water mill, as well as notable domestic, costume, and arms and armor displays. One treasure is the Coppergate Helmet, an extremely rare 1,200-year-old Anglo-Saxon helmet discovered during excavations of the city. You can also visit the cell where Dick Turpin, the 18th-century highwayman and folk hero, spent the night before his execution.

Continued on page 701

DID YOU KNOW?

York Minster is the largest
Gothic cathedral in England.
The towers of its west front
rise 174 feet, and its nave is
an imposing 138 feet wide
and 276 feet long. The west
front includes the window
known as the Heart of Yorkshire because of the shape of
the tracery near its top.

YORK MINSTER
GOTHIC GRANDEUR by Christi Daugherty

You can see this vast cathedral from 10 miles away, the tall Gothic towers rising over the flat horizon. The focal point of York, it encompasses centuries of the city's history, and its treasures include 128 dazzling medieval glass windows. The Minster today is a tranquil place, but over the centuries it has survived structural threats and political upheaval.

The present York Minster is the fourth attempt to build a church on this site. The first, a Saxon minster from the 7th century, was built of wood. In the 8th century it was rebuilt in stone. Norman invaders badly damaged the first stone church in 1069 as they conquered the recalcitrant north. They later rebuilt it in their own style, and you can see Norman elements—foundations, masonry, columns—in the undercroft. Marauding Vikings, however, damaged that building. Much of the limestone building you see is the result of the vision of one 13th-century archbishop, Walter de Gray. He wanted to build one of the world's greatest cathedrals, on the scale of Canterbury, with vaulted ceilings soaring hundreds of feet high. York Minster was finally completed in 1472. De Gray stayed with his beloved building beyond the end. He died in 1255, and his effigy lies atop his tomb inside the south transept near the main entrance.

(top left) York Minster interior, (top right) A stone gargoyle, (bottom right) Chapter House ceiling

MINSTER ORIENTATION AND HIGHLIGHTS

The Minster is designed in cruciform, meaning in the shape of a cross. As you walk through the main doors, you're entering one of the arms of the cross, or transepts. These transepts were built in Archbishop de Gray's time in the 13th century. Ahead of you, the grand, soaring, light-filled nave stretches out to your left and right, with massive stained-glass windows at both ends. Across the nave is the northern transept—the other arm of the cross—and off of it a corridor leads to the octagonal Chapter House. The nave's ceiling is held up through the use of flying buttresses on the exterior of the building. In the 13th and 14th centuries, this sort of architecture was so experimental that the builders could not be certain the structure would not simply collapse.

Nave

❶ Nave. The 14th-century builders of the nave used painted wood for the nave's soaring ceilings out of practicality: they feared stone would be too heavy. A fire in 1840 destroyed the roof, but the vaulting and bosses are exact replicas. Giant stained-glass windows glow from each end: the Heart of Yorkshire to the west, and opposite it the great East Window. ⚠ The East Window is being restored.

❷ Heart of Yorkshire. The heart-shaped tracery in the window that dominates the west end of the nave dates to 1338, and is remarkable both for its shape and its intricate, delicate design.

❸ Rose Window. This extraordinary stained-glass window in the south transept dates to the 13th century but has early 16th-century glass in which white and red Tudor roses show the union of the houses of York and Lancaster. It was nearly lost when lightning struck the building in 1984, causing a fire.

❹ The Five Sisters. At the end of the north transept, these five tall, blade-shaped windows from around 1250 are rare pieces of medieval glass art made of 50,000 pieces of glass. Each blade is more than five feet wide and towers 52 feet high. All were painted using a French technique (grisaille), rather than stained, giving them a pale gray tinge.

❺ Chapter House. With a beautifully painted and gilded ceiling (restored in 1845), the octagonal 13th-century Chapter House is a marvel, lined with exquisite stained glass and decorated with fanciful animals and gargoyles with human faces that could be caricatures of early monks.

❻ Choir Screen. Stretching along one section of the nave, an elegantly carved 15th-century stone panel, known as the choir screen, contains almost life-size sculptures of 15 kings of England from William the Conqueror to Henry VI.

The Rose Window

Choir Screen

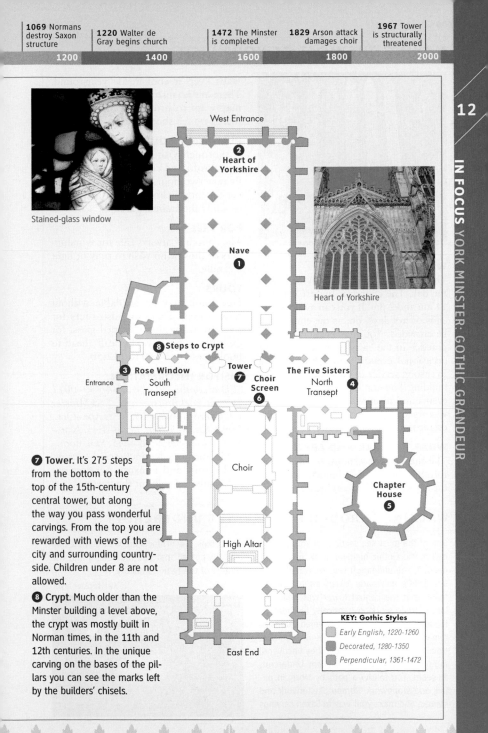

1069 Normans destroy Saxon structure

1220 Walter de Gray begins church

1472 The Minster is completed

1829 Arson attack damages choir

1967 Tower is structurally threatened

1200   1400   1600   1800   2000

Stained-glass window

West Entrance

2 Heart of Yorkshire

Nave

1

Heart of Yorkshire

8 Steps to Crypt

3 Rose Window
South Transept

Entrance

Tower
7 Choir Screen
6

The Five Sisters
North Transept
4

Choir

Chapter House
5

High Altar

East End

7 Tower. It's 275 steps from the bottom to the top of the 15th-century central tower, but along the way you pass wonderful carvings. From the top you are rewarded with views of the city and surrounding countryside. Children under 8 are not allowed.

8 Crypt. Much older than the Minster building a level above, the crypt was mostly built in Norman times, in the 11th and 12th centuries. In the unique carving on the bases of the pillars you can see the marks left by the builders' chisels.

KEY: Gothic Styles

Early English, 1220-1260

Decorated, 1280-1350

Perpendicular, 1361-1472

MAKING THE MOST OF YOUR VISIT

Five Sisters

WHEN TO VISIT

The best time to visit is early or late in the day. The church is busiest between 11 am and 2 pm. If you can avoid weekends or holidays, do, as the church can be crowded. You may encounter choir practice in the early evening. Look for occasional evening concerts; attending Evensong service can also be lovely. The building sometimes closes for church events and meetings, and it is closed to visitors (except those attending services) on most major religious holidays.

WHAT TO WEAR AND BRING

The church is enormous, so wear comfortable shoes. Bring binoculars to see the glass and higher carvings. The stone walls keep it cool inside year-round. There are no restrictions on attire. You may want to bring a bottle of water; there's no tea shop.

PLANNING YOUR TIME

A thorough visit, including the crypt, undercroft, and central tower, can easily take two hours, and could take longer for those who read all the displays or study the stained glass.

FOR FREE

The church is always free for worshippers or those who wish to pray or light a candle.

TOURS

Free tours may be available without reservations. There are also tours for a fee (to learn about stained glass, for example) some days, but call ahead to book; fees are £7.50 to £12.50.

VISITOR INFORMATION

✉ *Duncombe Pl.* ☎ *0844/939–0011* ⊕ *www.yorkminster.org* ✉ *Minster £9, Central Tower £5.50* ☉ *Apr.–Oct., Mon.–Sat. 9–5, Sun. noon–3:45; Nov.–Mar., Mon.–Sat. 9:30–4:45, Sun. noon–3:45. Entrance fee includes the crypt, undercroft, and treasury. Services are held daily throughout the day.*

WALKING THROUGH HISTORY: THE UNDERCROFT

One of the must-see sections of York Minster isn't in the Gothic building at all, but underneath it. The undercroft was excavated in the late 1960s and early 1970s after a survey found that the central tower was near collapse. While working frantically to shore up the foundations, builders uncovered extensive remains of previous structures on this site. Now the ruins and remnants they uncovered form the basis for the excellent Undercroft Museum. You follow a path by Norman pillars and stonework, Roman plasterwork and statues, and make your way to Saxon carvings and coffins. The artifacts are well-lighted, and displays put all that you are seeing into the context of the region's history.

York Minster crypt

✉ *Clifford St.* ☎ *01904/687687*
🌐 *www.yorkcastlemuseum.org.uk*
🎟 *£8* ⊘ *Daily 9:30–5.*

Clifford's Tower. Apart from the city walls, this rather battered-looking keep at the top of a steep mound is all that remains of the old York castle. The stone tower, which sits on a grassy mound surrounded by a parking lot, dates from the mid-12th century. The Norman tower that preceded it, built in 1068 by William the Conquerer, was destroyed in 1190 when more than 150 Jews locked themselves inside to protect themselves from a violent mob. Trapped with no food or water, they committed mass suicide by setting their own prison aflame. From the top of the tower you have good views of the city. ✉ *Tower St.* ☎ *01904/646940* 🌐 *www.cliffordstower.com* 🎟 *£4* ⊘ *Apr.–June and Sept., daily 10–6; July and Aug., daily 9:30–7; Oct.–Mar., daily 10–4.*

A WALK IN YORK

York is a fine city for walking, especially along the walls embracing the old center. Start at the Minster and head down the medieval lane, Stonegate, which is lined with shops and leads directly to Betty's tea shop. From there you can swing right to find antiques shops, or left for more-modern shops, and eventually the shopping area known as the Shambles and the remains of the old castle. At any point, climb the steps to the top of the city walls for perspective on where you are in town. The Ouse River, bordered in places by walking paths, makes for a pleasant stroll.

Fairfax House. This 1762 Georgian town house is a museum of decorative arts. The house is beautifully decorated with period furniture, crystal chandeliers, and silk wallpaper. Entrance on Monday is restricted to guided tours at 11 and 2. ✉ *Castlegate* ☎ *01904/655543* 🌐 *www.fairfaxhouse.co.uk* 🎟 *£6* ⊘ *Feb.–Dec., Tues.–Thurs. and Sat. 10–5, Sun. 12:30–4; Mon. by appt.; last admission 30 mins before closing.*

Merchant Adventurers' Hall. Built between 1357 and 1368 by a wealthy medieval guild, this is the largest half-timber hall in York. Portraits, silver, and furniture are on display, and the house itself is much of the attraction. A riverfront garden lies behind the hall. On most Saturdays, antiques fairs are held inside the building. ✉ *Fossgate* ☎ *01904/654818* 🌐 *www.theyorkcompany.co.uk* 🎟 *£6* ⊘ *Apr.–Sept., Mon.–Thurs. 9–5, Fri. and Sat. 9–3:30, Sun. 11–4; Oct.–Mar., Mon.–Sat. 9–3:30; closed 1st wk in Dec.*

Treasurer's House. Surprises await inside this large 17th-century house, the home from 1897 to 1930 of industrialist Frank Green. With a fine eye for texture, decoration, and pattern, Green created period rooms—including a medieval great hall—as a showcase for his collection of antique furniture. Delft tiles decorate the kitchen, copies of medieval stenciling cover the vibrant Red Room, and 17th-century stumpwork adorns the Tapestry Room. The cellar has displays about the hard lives of the servants. ✉ *Minster Yard* ☎ *01904/624247* 🌐 *www.nationaltrust.org.uk* 🎟 *House and garden £5.70, £7 with cellar tour* ⊘ *Mar.–Oct., Sat.–Thurs. 11–4:30; Feb. and Nov., Sat.–Thurs. 11–3; last admission 30 mins before closing.*

12

TOURS OF HAUNTED YORK

Given its storied history, dark streets, and atmospheric buildings, it's no surprise that York feels as if it could be haunted. What might startle you is that York *is* haunted, at least according to the Ghost Research Foundation International. Because of York's 500 recorded cases of ghostly encounters, the foundation has determined that it is the most haunted city in England, and one of the most haunted in the world.

Not everybody believes in earthbound spirits, but it seems that just about every tour company does. Here are a few options, should you choose to explore the town's spookier side.

Ghost Creeper (☎ 07947/325239 ⊕ www.ghostdetective.com) runs "bloodcurdling" tours weekend nights from November to June and nightly from July through Halloween, starting at 7:30 pm outside the Jorvik Viking Centre. Tickets are £5 per person.

Ghost Hunt (☎ 01904/608700 ⊕ www.ghosthunt.co.uk) guides take a slightly tongue-in-cheek approach to the ghouls. The tours start at 7:30 pm nightly in the Shambles and cost £5 per person.

Ghost Trail of York (☎ 01904/633276 ⊕ www.ghosttrail. co.uk) explores the city's spectral species. It takes a straightforward approach to ghosts—telling you what other people have heard or seen, and what they have seen themselves. The hour-long tours commence at 7:30 pm by the Minster and cost £4 per person.

The **Original Ghost Walk of York** (☎ 017947/603159 ⊕ www. theoriginalghostwalkofyork.co.uk), a long-timer among the tour groups, presents the city's ghost tales as fascinating unexplained mysteries. The tours depart at 8 pm from in front of the King's Arms Pub on Ouse Bridge and cost £4.50 per person.

Yorkshire Museum. The natural and archaeological history of the county, including material on the Roman, Anglo-Saxon, and Viking aspects of York, is the focus of this museum. The museum is divided into themed galleries focusing on the different time periods. On display in the solid, Doric-style building is the 15th-century Middleham Jewel, a pendant gleaming with a large sapphire. The museum lies just outside the walled city, through Bootham Bar (one of York's old gates), on the site of the medieval St. Mary's Abbey. ⊠ *Museum Gardens, Museum St.* ☎ *01904/687687* ⊕ *www.yorkshiremuseum.org.uk* ⊠ *£7* ☉ *Daily 10–5.*

WHERE TO EAT

££££ ✕ **Blue Bicycle.** One of York's best restaurants is in a building that once
BRITISH served as a brothel. Downstairs are intimate walled booths, and at
★ street level is a lively room lighted with candles. The menu changes with the seasons and concentrates on local beef and seafood. Typical dishes include pan-seared scallops with horseradish puree, seared sea bass with truffle-crushed potatoes, or grilled beef sirloin with pink peppercorn mash. The wine list is impressive, and the service couldn't be

friendlier. The restaurant has launched a small guesthouse—a handful of luxury rooms in a mews nearby—called Blue Rooms. ✉ *34 Fossgate* ☎ *01904/673990* ⊕ *www.thebluebicycle.com* ⚓ *Reservations essential.*

££ | ✕ **Café Concerto.** Music is the theme at this relaxed, intimate bistro
MODERN BRITISH | in sight of York Minster where sheet music serves as wallpaper. The kitchen serves updated versions of British classics. Dinner favorites include braised lamb shank with caramelized onion mash, panfried pork fillet with a Madeira cream sauce, or sirloin steak with field mushrooms and roast potatoes. Lunch is mostly salads and sandwiches, and you can always pop in for tea and cake. ✉ *21 High Petergate* ☎ *01904/610478* ⊕ *www.cafeconcerto.biz* ▭ *No credit cards.*

12

£££ | ✕ **Melton's.** Once a private house, this unpretentious restaurant has local
MODERN BRITISH | art on the walls, but you'll more likely be watching the open kitchen. The excellent seasonal menus are highly imaginative with modern English and European fare, such as chicken with apples and parsley mashed potatoes, venison in a red wine sauce with fondant potatoes, or fish-and-mussel stew with potato and fennel. Melton's is a 10-minute walk from York Minster. ✉ *7 Scarcroft Rd.* ☎ *01904/634341* ⊕ *www. meltonsrestaurant.co.uk* ⚓ *Reservations essential* ☉ *Closed 3 wks at Christmas, and 1 wk in Aug. No lunch Mon. No dinner Sun.*

£ | ✕ **Spurriergate Centre.** Churches are not just for services, as this 15th-cen-
BRITISH | tury house of worship proves. Resurrected as a cafeteria, St. Michael's is a favorite spot for travelers and mothers with strollers to refuel spiritually as well as gastronomically. You may end up eating bean-and-cabbage hot pot on the spot where John Wesley prayed in 1768. Don't pass up the cream scones. ✉ *Spurriergate* ☎ *01904/629393* ⊕ *www. thespurriergatecentre.com* ☉ *Closed Sun. No dinner.*

WHERE TO STAY

For expanded reviews, visit Fodors.com.

££££–£££££ | 🏨 **Cedar Court Grand Hotel.** This historic hotel near the train station is
HOTEL | lovely—mosaics cover walls and ceilings, black-and-white tiles stretch across the floors, and carved wood paneling is polished until it shines. **Pros:** beautiful building; some rooms have views. **Cons:** a 10-minute walk to the center; standard rooms are quite basic. ✉ *Station Rise* ☎ *01904/380038* ⊕ *www.cedarcourtgrand.co.uk* ⤴ *107 rooms* ⚭ *In-room: a/c, Wi-Fi. In-hotel: restaurant, bar, pool, gym, spa, parking* ⑩ *Breakfast*

££ | 🏨 **Dairy Guest House.** Victorian stained glass, fine woodwork, and intri-
B&B/INN | cate plaster cornices are original features of this former dairy near the city walls. **Pros:** interesting building; nice period details. **Cons:** a bit of a walk to the center; minimum stay required in summer; few amenities. ✉ *3 Scarcroft Rd.* ☎ *01904/639367* ⊕ *www.dairyguesthouse.co.uk* ⤴ *5 rooms* ⚭ *In-room: no a/c. In-hotel: some pets allowed* ⑩ *Breakfast.*

£££–££££ | 🏨 **Grange Hotel.** Built in the early 19th century as a home for high-
HOTEL | ranking clergy from York Minster, this luxurious boutique hotel is remi-
★ | niscent of a grand country home. **Pros:** spacious rooms; lovely decor. **Cons:** can feel a bit fussy; 10-minute walk from most sights. ✉ *1 Clifton*

The Vikings occupied York, and the city recalls this era enthusiastically during the Viking Festival each February.

☎ 01904/644744 ⊕ www.grangehotel.co.uk ⇆ 30 rooms ⚷ In-room: no a/c, Wi-Fi. In-hotel: restaurant, bar, gym, parking ⦿ Breakfast.

££ **B&B/INN** ⛨ **The Hazelwood.** Close to York Minster, this tall and elegant Victorian town house stands in a peaceful cul-de-sac, away from the hustle and bustle. **Pros:** near the Minster; lovely building. **Cons:** not much privacy; few amenities. ⊠ 24–25 Portland St. ☎ 01904/626548 ⊕ www.thehazelwoodyork.com ⇆ 14 rooms ⚷ In-room: no a/c. In-hotel: parking, some age restrictions ⦿ Breakfast.

£££–££££ **HOTEL** ⛨ **Hotel Du Vin.** An orphanage in the 19th century, this historic building has been converted into a swanky hotel that preserves the original exposed brick walls and arched doorways. **Pros:** makes great use of the space; jovial staff; comfortable beds. **Cons:** minimum stay on weekends; 10-minute walk to most sights. ⊠ 89 The Mount ☎ 01904/557350 ⊕ www.hotelduvin.com ⇆ 44 rooms ⚷ In-room: Internet. In-hotel: restaurant, bar, parking ⦿ Breakfast.

££££–£££££ **HOTEL** ★ ⛨ **Middlethorpe Hall & Spa.** Antiques, paintings, and fresh flowers fill the traditionally decorated rooms in this splendidly restored 18th-century mansion, about 1½ mi from the city center. **Pros:** traditional splendor; gorgeous grounds. **Cons:** some rooms are getting a bit worn; has an old-fashioned approach; well outside the city center. ⊠ Bishopthorpe Rd. ☎ 01904/641241 ⊕ www.middlethorpe.com ⇆ 23 rooms, 8 suites ⚷ In-room: no a/c, Internet. In-hotel: restaurant, bar, pool, gym, spa, parking, some age restrictions ⦿ Breakfast.

£££–££££ **HOTEL** ⛨ **Mount Royale Hotel.** In a quiet country house in the upscale residential part of west York, this hotel offers excellent service that is both professional and friendly. **Pros:** country-club feel; large rooms; lovely pool and garden. **Cons:** well outside the town center; parking can be an issue. ✉ *117–119 The Mount* ☎ *01904/628856* ⊕ *www.mountroyale. co.uk* ⬅ *23 rooms* ⚴ *In-room: no a/c, Wi-Fi. In-hotel: restaurant, bar, pool* ⊠ *Breakfast.*

NIGHTLIFE AND THE ARTS

NIGHTLIFE

York is full of historic pubs where you can while away an hour over a pint.

The **Black Swan** (✉ *Peasholme Green* ☎ *01904/686911* ⊕ *www. blackswanyork.com*), in a 16th-century Tudor building, serves good British food. It's said to be haunted by a young girl who sits by the fireplace.

The **Old White Swan** (✉ *Goodramgate* ☎ *01904/540911*) is vast, spreading across five medieval, half-timber buildings on busy Goodramgate. It's known for good pub lunches and its ghosts—it claims to have more than the Black Swan.

The **Snickleway Inn** (✉ *Goodramgate* ☎ *01904/656138*) is in a 15th-century building with open fireplaces and a real sense of history.

THE ARTS

The **Early Music Festival** (☎ *01904/658338 festival office, 01904/621756 Tourist Information Centre* ⊕ *www.ncem.co.uk*), featuring pre-18th-century music, is held each July and again in December

The **Viking Festival** (✉ *Jorvik, Coppergate* ☎ *01904/543402* ⊕ *www. vikingjorvik.com*) takes place each February. The celebrations, including a parade and long-ship regatta, end with the Jorvik Viking combat reenactment, when Norsemen confront their Anglo-Saxon enemies.

In a lovely 18th-century building, the **York Theatre Royal** (✉ *St. Leonard's Pl.* ☎ *01904/623568*) presents plays, music, poetry readings, and art exhibitions.

SHOPPING

Stonegate is the city's main shopping street. Winding down from the Minster toward the river, it's lined with a mix of unique shops and boutiques. Other good shopping streets include Petergate, which has mostly chain stores. The Shambles is another prime shopping area, with an eclectic mix of mostly tourist shops.

The **Minster Gate Bookshop** (✉ *8 Minster Gate* ☎ *01904/621812*) sells secondhand books, old maps, and prints.

Mulberry Hall (✉ *Stonegate* ☎ *01904/620736*) is a sales center for all the famous names in fine bone china and crystal. It also has a neat café.

The **York Antiques Centre** (✉ *2 Lendal* ☎ *01904/641445*) has 25 shops selling antiques, bric-a-brac, books, and jewelry.

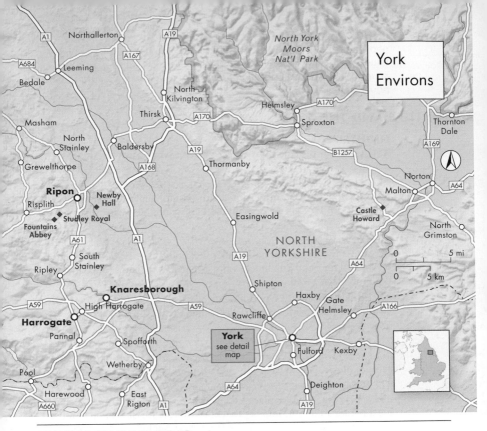

YORK ENVIRONS

West and north of York a number of sights make easy, appealing day trips from the city: the spa town of Harrogate, atmospheric Knaresborough, the ruins of Fountain Abbey, the market town of Ripon, and nearby Newby Hall. If you're heading northwest from York to Harrogate, you might take the less direct B1224 across Marston Moor, where, in 1644, Oliver Cromwell won a decisive victory over the Royalists during the Civil War. A few miles beyond, at Wetherby, you can cut northwest along the A661 to Harrogate. Also nearby, northeast of York, is Castle Howard, a magnificent stately home.

HARROGATE

21 mi west of York, 11 mi south of Ripon, 16 mi north of Leeds.

★ During the Regency and early-Victorian periods, it became fashionable for the noble and wealthy to retire to a spa to "take the waters" for relaxation. In Yorkshire the trend reached its grandest heights in Harrogate, an elegant town that flourished during the 19th century. Today the Regency buildings, parks, and spas built during that time make Harrogate an absorbing getaway.

12

GETTING HERE AND AROUND

Trains from York leave every hour or so, and the journey takes about 30 minutes. There are no direct trains from London. National Express buses leave from York every hour most days; the journey takes about 40 minutes. By car, Harrogate is off A59, and is well marked. It's a walkable town, so you can park in one of its central parking lots and explore on foot.

Within and around Harrogate, the Harrogate and District bus company provides area services, and taxis are plentiful.

ESSENTIALS

Visitor Information Harrogate (⊠ *Royal Baths, Crescent Rd.* ☎ *0845/389–3223* ⊕ *www.yorkshire.com/harrogate*).

EXPLORING

Royal Pump Room Museum. This octagonal structure was built in 1842 over the original sulfur well that brought great prosperity to the town. You can still drink the evil-smelling (and nasty-tasting) spa waters here. The museum displays some equipment of spa days gone by, alongside a somewhat eccentric collection of fine 19th-century china, clothes, and bicycles. ⊠ *Crown Pl.* ☎ *01423/556188* ⊕ *www.harrogate.gov.uk* ⌐*£3.50* ⊙ *Apr.–Oct., Mon.–Sat. 10–5, Sun. 2–5; Nov.–Mar., Mon.–Sat. 10–4, Sun. 2–4.*

★ **Turkish Baths.** Dating from 1897, the exotic and fully restored Turkish Baths allow you to experience what brought so many Victorians to Harrogate. After changing into your bathing suit, you can relax on luxurious lounge chairs in the stunning mosaic-tile warming room. Move on to increasingly hot sauna rooms, and then soak up eucalyptus mist in the steam room before braving the icy plunge pool. You can also book a massage or facial. Open hours are divided into women-only, men-only, and couples-only nights, so book in advance. ⊠ *Parliament St.* ☎ *01423/556746* ⊕ *www.harrogate.gov.uk/turkishbaths* ⌐*£13.50–£19 per bath and sauna session* ⊙ *Daily; call for schedules.*

Stray. At the edge of the town center, this 200-acre grassy parkland is a riot of color in spring. It contains many of the mineral springs that first made Harrogate famous.

Valley Gardens. Southwest of the town center, Valley Gardens include a boating lake, tennis courts, and a little café.

WHERE TO EAT AND STAY

£ ✕ **Betty's.** The celebrated Yorkshire tearoom began life in Harrogate
CAFÉ in 1919, when a Swiss restaurateur brought his Alpine pastries and chocolates to England. The elegant surroundings have changed little since then, and the cakes, pastries, and extensive array of teas not at all. A pianist plays nightly. ⊠ *1 Parliament St.* ☎ *01423/814070* ⊕ *www. bettys.co.uk.*

££ 🏨 **Balmoral Hotel.** Luxurious contemporary furnishings and antique
HOTEL pieces, patterned wallpapers, and colorful ornaments fill this mock-Tudor edifice. **Pros:** spacious rooms; attractive restaurant. **Cons:** a bit old-fashioned; very formal atmosphere. ⊠ *Franklin Mt.* ☎ *01423/508208*

You can paddle on the River Nidd in the pretty town of Knaresborough.

www.balmoralhotel.co.uk *17 rooms, 3 suites* *In-room: no a/c. In-hotel: restaurant, bar, some pets allowed* *Breakfast.*

£££ HOTEL **Hotel du Vin.** This hip hotel sprawls through eight Georgian houses, using stripped-wood floors, clubby leather armchairs, and a purple billiard table to set the tone. **Pros:** relaxed lounge; wonderful wine list; modern vibe. **Cons:** a bit battered around the edges; the bar can take over the lounge. *Prospect Pl.* *01423/856800* *www.hotelduvin.com* *40 rooms, 8 suites* *In-room: no a/c, Wi-Fi. In-hotel: restaurant, bar, gym.*

NIGHTLIFE AND THE ARTS

★ Harrogate's annual **International Festival** (*01423/562303* *www.harrogate-festival.org.uk*) of ballet, music, contemporary dance, film, comedy, street theater, and more takes place during two weeks at the end of July and beginning of August.

KNARESBOROUGH

3 mi northeast of Harrogate, 17 mi west of York.

At the bottom of a precipitously deep rocky gorge along the River Nidd, the little town of Knaresborough couldn't be more photogenic. It's best seen from a train, crossing the high Victorian viaduct above. In summer you can rent a boat and paddle down the slow-moving river and wander the town's little marketplace, and year-round you can climb to the hilltop ruins of the castle where Richard II was imprisoned in 1399.

12

GETTING HERE AND AROUND

Northern Rail trains leave from Harrogate and York every hour or so, taking 12 and 20 minutes. Local buses travel here from nearby towns, but they are less frequent. By car, the village is on A59, and well signposted.

The village lies on a precipitous hill. The town is easily walkable, although it helps to be in good shape. There are clearly marked public parking areas.

EXPLORING

☺ **Mother Shipton's Cave.** Across the river from the main riverside attractions, this tourist place is tucked in a pleasant park. The cave is, according to local lore, the birthplace of the titular 16th-century prophetess. Events supposedly foretold by her include the defeat of the Spanish Armada. The mineral-rich well beside her cave is famed for its ability to turn any object to stone in just a few hours. ⊠ *Prophesy House, High Bridge* ☎ *01423/864600* ⊕ *www.mothershipton.co.uk* ⊠ *£6* ☉ *Apr.– Oct., daily 10–5:30; Nov., Feb., and Mar., weekends 10–4:30.*

RIPON

12 mi north of Knaresborough, 24 mi northwest of York.

Ripon was thriving as early as the 9th century as an important market center. A relatively small church has been designated a cathedral since the mid-19th century, which makes Ripon, with only about 15,000 inhabitants, technically a city. Market day, Thursday, is probably the best day to stop by.

GETTING HERE AND AROUND

Ripon is just off A1, 12 mi north of Harrogate. There is no train service to Ripon, but local buses run from Harrogate several times a day.

EXPLORING

☺ **Newby Hall.** An early-18th-century house redecorated later in the same century by Robert Adam for his patron William Weddell, Newby Hall contains fine decorative art of its period, particularly ornamental plasterwork and Chippendale furniture. The domed Sculpture Hall with Roman works, and the Tapestry Hall, with its priceless Gobelin tapestries, are gorgeous. The 25 acres of gardens are justifiably famous; a double herbaceous border, which runs down to the river, separates garden "rooms," each flowering during a different season. A miniature railroad, playground, and pedal boats amuse kids. The house is 5 mi southeast of Ripon. Entry to the house is restricted to guided tours, given every hour in April, May, June, September, and October, and every half hour in July and August. ⊠ *Skelton-on-Ure* ☎ *0845/450–4068* ⊕ *www.newbyhall.co.uk* ⊠ *£12; gardens only, £8.70* ☉ *Apr.–June and Sept., Tues.–Sun., Mon., 11–5:30; July and Aug. daily 11–5:30; last admission 30 mins before closing.*

Ripon Cathedral. Successive churches here were destroyed by the Vikings and the Normans, and the current cathedral, dating from the 12th and 13th centuries, is notable for its finely carved choir stalls. The Saxon crypt (AD 672), now an empty series of chambers, housed sacred relics.

✉ *Minster Rd.* ☎ *01765/603462* ⊕ *www.riponcathedral.org.uk* ✉*£3 donation requested* ⊘ *Daily 8:30–6.*

★ **Studley Royal Water Garden & Fountains Abbey.** You can easily spend a day at this World Heritage Site, an 822-acre complex made up of an 18th-century water garden and deer park and the majestic ruins of medieval Fountains Abbey. Here a neoclassical vision of an ordered universe—with spectacular terraces, classical temples, and a grotto—blends with the glories of English Gothic architecture. The abbey, on the banks of the River Skell, was founded in 1132 and completed in the early 1500s. The Cistercian monks here, called "White Monks" for the color of their robes, devoted their lives to silence, prayer, and work. Of the surviving buildings, the lay brothers' echoing refectory and dormitory impresses most. Fountains Mill, with sections dating back to 1140, displays reconstructed mill machinery (wool was the abbey's profitable business). The 17th-century Fountains Hall, partially built with stones taken from the abbey, has an exhibition and video display. The water garden and Fountains Abbey is 9 mi northwest of Knaresborough, 4 mi southwest of Ripon. ✉ *Off B6265* ☎ *01765/608888* ⊕ *www.fountainsabbey.org. uk* ✉*£9* ⊘ *Apr.–Sept., daily 10–5; Oct. and Mar., daily 10–4. Nov.–Jan., Sat.–Thurs. 10–4.*

WHERE TO EAT AND STAY

£££ ✕ **Perk Up.** This attractive eatery on the market square started as a cof-
BRITISH fee shop when the owner couldn't find a good cup anywhere in town. It then expanded to a café, and now to a respected restaurant. During the day it offers tasty sandwiches on fresh-baked bread. At night it offers sophisticated takes on classic British dishes using local meats and produce. The menu changes constantly, but usually includes grilled Yorkshire steaks with chunky fries. There are also fresh fish and vegetarian options. The atmosphere is informal and friendly. ✉ *43 Market Pl. S* ☎ *01765/698888* ⊘ *Closed Sun. and Mon.*

££££–£££££ 🏨 **Swinton Park.** The Cunliffe-Lister family operates part of its ances-
HOTEL tral castle—a stately pile rebuilt in the 18th and 19th centuries with battlements and a turret—as a hotel. **Pros:** eye-popping castle; gorgeous rooms. **Cons:** some rooms have better views than others; atmosphere is very formal. ✉ *Off A1, Swinton Park, Masham* ☎ *01765/680900* ⊕ *www.swintonpark.com* ⇆ *26 rooms, 4 suites* & *In-room: no a/c, Internet. In-hotel: restaurant, gym, some pets allowed* ❦ *Breakfast.*

CASTLE HOWARD

15 mi northeast of York, 12 mi southeast of Helmsley.

GETTING HERE AND AROUND

There is no easy public transportation to Castle Howard, which is well outside any town and several miles off any public road. The nearest train stop is Malton, and you can take a taxi from there. By car, follow signs off A64 from York.

At Castle Howard, a baroque masterpiece, the splendor of the grounds matches the opulence of the sprawling house.

EXPLORING

Castle Howard. Standing serene among the Howardian Hills to the west of Malton, Castle Howard is an opulent, stately home whose magnificent profile is punctuated by stone chimneys and a graceful central dome. Many people know it best as Brideshead, the home of the Flyte family in Evelyn Waugh's tale of aristocratic woe, *Brideshead Revisited,* because much of the 1981 TV series was filmed here. The house was designed by Sir John Vanbrugh (1664–1726) for the Howard family. This was Vanbrugh's first building design; he later went on to create opulent Blenheim Palace.

The audacity of this great baroque house proclaimed the wealth and importance of the Howards. A magnificent central hallway spanned by a hand-painted ceiling dwarfs all visitors, and there is no shortage of grandeur: vast family portraits, delicate marble fireplaces, immense and fading tapestries, huge pieces of Victorian silver on polished tables, and a great many marble busts. Outside, the neoclassical landscape of carefully arranged woods, lakes, bridges, and obelisks led Horace Walpole, the 18th-century bon vivant, to comment that a pheasant at Castle Howard lives better than a duke elsewhere. The grounds sprawl for miles, and hidden away among the hills and lakes (there's even a fanciful playground for children) are the Temple of the Four Winds and a grand mausoleum. Hourly tours, included in the admission price, fill you in on more background and history. ⊠ *Off A64 and B1257, Coneysthorpe* ☎ *01653/648333* ⊕ *www.castlehoward.co.uk* ✉ *£13; gardens only, £8.50* ☉ *House late Mar.–Oct., daily 11–6; last admission at 4. Grounds daily 10–6:30 or dusk; last admission at 4:30.*

LEEDS AND BRONTË COUNTRY

The busy city of Leeds provides an obvious starting point for a tour of West Yorkshire. From here you can strike out for the traditional wool towns, such as Saltaire, a UNESCO-protected gem, and the Magna museum at Rotherham, which draws long lines for its surprisingly interesting exploration of steel. But the main thrust of many visits to West Yorkshire is to the west of Leeds, where the gaunt hills north of the Calder Valley and south of the River Aire form the district immortalized by the mournful writings of the Brontë sisters. Haworth, a gray-stone village, might have faded into obscurity were it not for the magnetism of the literary sisters. Every summer, thousands toil up the steep main street to visit their hometown, but to truly understand their writing you need to go farther afield to the ruined farm of Top Withins, which is by legend, if not fact, Wuthering Heights.

LEEDS

25 mi southwest of York, 43 mi northeast of Manchester.

One of the cultural centers of the north, Leeds has successfully transformed itself. Its Victorian buildings have been polished and restored, its old factories and warehouses converted into pricey loft housing and modern offices. Everywhere are cafés with outdoor tables defying the northern weather, sleek bars, modern hotels, and upscale restaurants. Leeds University keeps the town young and hip, supporting the city's good music shops and funky clothing and jewelry boutiques.

GETTING HERE AND AROUND

Leeds Bradford Airport, 8 mi northwest of the city, is the main gateway to this part of the country. National Express and Megabus have frequent buses here from London's Victoria Coach Station. The journey takes about four hours. East Coast trains depart from London's King's Cross Station to Leeds Station about every 30 minutes during the week. The trip takes about 2½ hours. Leeds Station is in the middle of central Leeds and usually has a line of taxis waiting out front.

A city of nearly half a million people, Leeds has an efficient local bus service. Most visitors will never use it, as most sights are in the easily walkable downtown.

ESSENTIALS

Visitor Information Leeds (✉ *Leeds City Station* ☎ *0113/242–5242* ⊕ *www. visitleeds.co.uk*).

EXPLORING

TOP ATTRACTIONS

The Calls. East of Granary Wharf, the Calls has converted old riverfront warehouses into snazzy bars and restaurants that enliven the cobbled streets and quayside. This is definitely the area to wander at lunchtime and when you're craving an afternoon coffee.

City Square. One of the city's best examples of Victorian architecture is City Square, right in front of the train station. Busy streets surround the traffic-free oasis where benches make a good place to get your bearings

12

as you take in the 19th-century statues. On the east side is the 18th-century Mill Hill Chapel.

★ **Harewood House.** The home of the earl of Harewood, a cousin of the
⟳ Queen, Harewood House (pronounced *har*-wood) is a spectacular neoclassical mansion, built in 1759 by John Carr of York. Highlights include Robert Adam interiors, important paintings and ceramics, and a large, ravishingly beautiful collection of Chippendale furniture (Chippendale was born in nearby Otley), notably the magnificent State Bed. The Old Kitchen and Below Stairs exhibition illustrates life from the servants' point of view. Capability Brown designed the handsome grounds, and Charles Barry created a notable Italian garden with fountains in the 1840s. Also here are a bird garden with 120 rare and endangered species, a playground, and a butterfly house. The house is 7 mi north of Leeds; you can take Harrogate & District Bus 36. ■**TIP→** Ticket prices are discounted in spring and fall. ⊠ *Junction of A61 and A659, Harewood* ☎ *0113/218–1010* ⊕ *www.harewood.org* ⊠ *£13* ⊗ *House Apr.–Oct., daily noon–4. Gardens Apr.–Oct., daily 10–6; Nov., Feb., and Mar., weekends 10–4.*

★ **Leeds Art Gallery.** Next door to the Victorian Town Hall, the Leeds Art Gallery is Yorkshire's most impressive art museum, with a strong core collection of works by Courbet, Sisley, Constable, Crome, and the internationally acclaimed Yorkshire sculptor Henry Moore, who studied at the Leeds School of Art. The graceful statue on the steps outside the gallery is Moore's *Reclining Woman*. More works by Moore are at the adjacent **Henry Moore Institute**, which also has regular exhibitions of modern sculpture. The **Craft Centre and Design Gallery**, also in the museum, exhibits and sells fine contemporary crafts. ⊠ *The Headrow* ☎ *0113/247–8256* ⊕ *www.leeds.gov.uk/artgallery* ⊠ *Free* ⊗ *Mon., Tues., and Thurs.–Sat. 10–5, Wed. noon–5, Sun. 1–5.*

**QUICK
BITES**

Step down to the cozy, book-lined **New Conservatory** (⊠ *The Albions, Albion Pl., off Briggate* ☎ *0113/246–1853*) for fresh sandwiches, wraps, and cakes. You can also sit and relax with a cup of tea or a glass of wine.

WORTH NOTING

Granary Wharf. Once the center of Leeds's decayed industrial area, two adjacent neighborhoods along the River Aire are now a trendy area of chic bars and pleasant cafés. Granary Wharf, in the Canal Basin, reached via the Dark Arches where the River Aire flows under City Station, is a good place to go exploring design and crafts shops, music shops, and a regular market.

**OFF THE
BEATEN
PATH**

Magna. A 45-minute drive south from Leeds to Rotherham brings you squarely in view of Yorkshire's industrial past, embodied by a former steelworks that houses Magna, a widely respected science museum. Smoke, flames, and sparking electricity bring one of the original six arc furnaces roaring to life in a sound-and-light show. Steelworkers lost their jobs in the 1970s and '80s when the British coal and steel industries collapsed, and a permanent exhibit explores what happened to those workers afterward. Four pavilions engagingly illustrate the use of fire, earth, air, and water in the production of steel. ⊠ *Junction*

33 or 34 off M1, Sheffield Rd., Rotherham ☎ *01709/720002* ⊕ *www. visitmagna.co.uk* 🎫 *£11* ⊙ *Daily 10–5.*

⟳ **Royal Armouries.** Much of the legendary arms and armor originally collected in the Tower of London fills the Royal Armouries, which occupies a redeveloped 13-acre dockland site, a 15-minute walk from the city center. Five themed galleries—War, Tournament, Self-Defense, Hunting, and Arms and Armor of the Orient—trace the history of weaponry. The state-of-the-art building is stunningly designed: expect a full-size elephant in armor, warriors on horseback, and floor-to-ceiling tents, as well as spirited interactive displays and live demonstrations. Shoot a crossbow, direct operations on a battlefield, experience an Elizabethan joust: it's your choice. ⊠ *Armouries Dr. off M1 or M621* ☎ *0113/220– 1999* ⊕ *www.armouries.org.uk* 🎫 *Free* ⊙ *Daily 10–5.*

Temple Newsam. The Leeds City Council uses Temple Newsam, a huge Elizabethan and Jacobean building, to display its impressive collections of furniture, paintings, and ceramics. The house was the birthplace in 1545 of Lord Darnley, the doomed husband of Mary, Queen of Scots. Surrounding the house is a public park with rose gardens, greenhouses, and miles of woodland walks, all laid out by Capability Brown in 1762. Temple Newsam is 4 mi east of Leeds on A63; Buses 18, 40, 88, and 163–165 leave from Leeds Central Bus Station every 30 minutes and

Artistic Renaissance in Wakefield

The workaday West Yorkshire town of Wakefield, 12 mi south of Leeds off M1, seems an unlikely arts center. Once bustling because of the coal and textile industries, the downtown feels worn around the edges today. Lately, thanks to art, Wakefield is having a renaissance of sorts. You can get here easily from Leeds by train or car.

Hepworth Wakefield. In 2011, this gallery opened, stocked with exceptional works by Yorkshire native Henry Moore and sculptor Barbara Hepworth (who was born in Wakefield), among other esteemed international artists. The unique design of slightly skewed concrete building blocks, combined with the powerful permanent collection focused on modern British art, drew interest from art lovers around

the world. It will ultimately be the largest purpose-built British gallery outside of London. *Gallery Walk, Wakefield* ☎ *01924/247360* ⊕ *www. hepworthwakefield.org* ⌨ *Free* ☉ *Tues.-Sat. 10–6, Sun. 11–5.*

Yorkshire Sculpture Park. On the edge of Wakefield, this outdoor gallery sprawls across 100 acres of an 18th-century estate. The park and garden are filled with a carefully curated collection including works by Henry Moore and Barbara Hepworth, as well other respected artists including Antony Gormley, Anthony Caro, and David Nash. Changing exhibitions round out the displays. *West Bretton, Wakefield* ☎ *01924/832631* ⊕ *www. ysp.co.uk* ⌨ *Free* ☉ *Grounds daily 10–6, galleries daily 10–5.*

stop at the Irwin Arms, a 10-minute walk from the site. ✉ *Off Selby Rd.* ☎ *0113/264–5535* ⊕ *www.leeds.gov.uk/templenewsam* ⌨ *House £3.70, farm £3.30, joint ticket £6, parking £4* ☉ *Apr.–Oct., Tues.– Sun. 10:30–5; Nov.–Mar., Tues.–Sun. 10:30–4. Last admission 45 mins before closing.*

WHERE TO EAT

£££
MODERN BRITISH
✕ **Anthony's.** The chef in this intimate basement restaurant takes a lot of chances, and the results are hugely rewarding to lovers of daring food. Main courses change daily but can include venison loin carpaccio with prawns, or braised pig cheek with baby squid and orzo. These unusual combinations work well in the formal setting. Other Anthony's outposts are a lunch spot at Flannels on Vicar Lane, a larger restaurant in the Corn Exchange, and a patisserie in the Victoria Quarter shopping arcade. ✉ *19 Boar La.* ☎ *0113/245–5922* ⊕ *www.anthonysrestaurant. co.uk* ☉ *Closed Sun. and Mon.*

£££
MODERN BRITISH
✕ **Brasserie Forty 4.** Within the elegant 42 The Calls hotel, the Brasserie is one of the city's best restaurants. The atmosphere, like the menu, is modern and upscale, but not snobby. The dining room has exposed stone walls and arched windows overlooking the canal. In summer there's a balcony for alfresco dining. The often-changing menu usually features appetizers like smoked chicken tart with lavender-honey dressing, and duck with spiced rhubarb chutney. Elegant main courses include fish stew with lobster sauce, and duck confit with braised red cabbage. For dessert try the chocolate fondue with marshmallows and fruit. ✉ *42–44 The Calls* ☎ *0113/234–3232* ⊕ *www.brasserie44.com.*

£

BRITISH

✕**Crosskeys.** A former watering hole for foundry workers, this lovely old inn is now a warm and sunny restaurant known for its use of fresh, local ingredients. The food is unfussy and reliably good. The menu includes hearty dishes like lamb pie, sausages and mashed potatoes, or beer-battered fish with fries. Enjoy a glass of wine from the good wine list, or a pint of local ale. Best of all, prices are very reasonable. ✉ *107 Water La.* ☎ *0113/243–3711* ⊕ *www.crosskeys.com.*

£

DELI

✕**Salts.** This attractive deli is done in proper Victorian style: the walls are lined with wooden shelves, stacked high with sparkling bottles and colorful cans. The affordable menu is classic British deli food using locally produced meats and vegetables. Locals stop by for salads (chicken and avocado, tomato, or arugula and blue cheese), quiches, and made-to-order sandwiches. It's open early for breakfast weekdays. There's plenty of seating at rustic wooden tables in a comfortable dining room flooded with light from the tall windows. ✉ *14 Swinegate* ☎ *0113/243–2323* ⊕ *www.saltsdeli.co.uk* ☯ *Closed Sun.*

£

BRITISH

✕**Whitelocks.** The city's oldest pub, dating from 1715, is tucked away in an alley in the city center. It's been known for years for traditional pub food, including bangers and mash, meat pies, and real ale. The long, narrow bar has all the trappings of the Victorian era—stained glass, etched mirrors, copper-top tables, and red-plush banquettes. Service is brisk and friendly, and during the day the emphasis is more on food than drink. ✉ *Turks Head Yard off Briggate* ☎ *0113/245–3950.*

WHERE TO STAY

For expanded reviews, visit Fodors.com.

£££–££££

HOTEL

▥ **42 The Calls.** This high-tech, high-concept hotel in the trendy waterfront area was once a grain mill, and each room shows creative flair but retains such original elements as exposed beams and atmospheric brickwork. **Pros:** laid-back vibe; luxurious rooms; clever use of space. **Cons:** some find it too trendy; rather pricey. ✉ *42 The Calls* ☎ *0113/244–0099* ⊕ *www.42thecalls.co.uk* ↜ *41 rooms* ⚹ *In-room: no a/c, Wi-Fi. In-hotel: restaurant, bar, some pets allowed* ▯⦿▯ *Breakfast.*

£££–££££

HOTEL

★

▥ **Malmaison.** Passengers who once used this building as a tram and bus terminal could hardly have envisioned its rebirth as a chic hotel exuding contemporary class and comfort. **Pros:** beautiful design; spacious rooms; comfortable beds. **Cons:** restaurant is often booked up; overly trendy. ✉ *1 Swinegate* ☎ *0113/398–1000* ⊕ *www.malmaison. com* ↜ *100 rooms* ⚹ *In-room: no a/c, Wi-Fi. In-hotel: restaurant, bar, gym, spa* ▯⦿▯ *Breakfast.*

££££

HOTEL

▥ **Quebecs.** This elegant boutique hotel has real Victorian verve, especially the sweeping oak staircase lighted by tall stained-glass windows. **Pros:** gorgeous building; spacious rooms; great bar. **Cons:** a bit too formal; some rooms are better than others. ✉ *9 Quebec St.* ☎ *0113/244– 8989* ⊕ *www.theetoncollection.com* ↜ *45 rooms, 6 suites* ⚹ *In-room: no a/c, Internet. In-hotel: restaurant, bar* ▯⦿▯ *Breakfast.*

12

NIGHTLIFE AND THE ARTS
NIGHTLIFE
At fashionable café-bars all over Leeds, you can grab a bite or sip cappuccino or designer beer until late into the night. There's no shortage of clubs, either: Leeds has one of the best party scenes outside London. **Bar Norman** (⊠ *36 Call La.* ☎ *0113/234–3988*) has won the local in-crowd with its weird and wonderful design, including curved walls. Japanese food and music are other draws.

Cuban Heels (⊠ *The Arches, 28–30 Assembly St.* ☎ *0113/234–6115*) kicks out salsa sounds most nights.

Mojo (⊠ *18 Merrion St.* ☎ *0113/244–6387*) is a real rock-and-roll bar, with the music and the look to match.

Around for 300 years, **The Ship** (⊠ *71A Briggate* ☎ *0113/246–8031*) is a friendly place to stop in for a quick drink or a tasty pub lunch.

THE ARTS
Opera North, a leading provincial opera company, has its home in Leeds at the **Grand Theatre** (⊠ *46 New Briggate* ☎ *0113/222–6222*); the opulent auditorium is modeled on that of La Scala. Opera North also plays for free each summer at Temple Newsam.

The Victorian **Town Hall** (⊠ *The Headrow* ☎ *0113/224–3801*) hosts an international concert season (October through May) that attracts top performers and conductors. In September it is the site of the fourth and final stage of the prestigious Leeds International Piano Competition.

The ultramodern **West Yorkshire Playhouse** (⊠ *Playhouse Sq., Quarry Hill* ☎ *0113/213–7700* ⊕ *www.wyp.org*) was built on the slope of an old quarry. Its adaptable staging makes it eminently suitable for new and classic productions.

SHOPPING
★ For upscale items for the home, visit the shops inside the historic **Corn Exchange** (⊠ *Call La.* ☎ *0113/234–0363*). The circular structure is also a good place to grab a coffee or stop for lunch.

The city has some excellent markets, notably **Kirkgate Market** (⊠ *34 George St.* ☎ *0113/214–5162* ⊙ *Closed Wed. morning and Sun.*), an Edwardian beauty that's the largest in the north of England.

The glistening **Victoria Quarter** (⊠ *Briggate* ☎ *0113/245–5333*), with its 70 stores, epitomizes fin de siècle style and 21st-century chic. It's on Briggate Street, one of the city's best shopping strips.

SALTAIRE

12 mi east of Leeds, 8 mi east of Haworth.

GETTING HERE AND AROUND
Saltaire is 4 mi north of Bradford, an old wool-market town. There are regular bus and train services to Saltaire from Bradford. Drivers should take A650 from Bradford and follow the signs.

ESSENTIALS
Visitor Information Saltaire Tourist Information Center (⊠ *2 Victoria Rd.* ☎ *01274/774993* ⊕ *www.saltaire-village.co.uk*).

EXPLORING

★ **Saltaire.** A UNESCO World Heritage Site, the former model town of Saltaire was built in the mid-19th century by textile magnate Sir Titus Salt, who was trying to create the ideal industrial world. When he decided to relocate his factories from the dark mills of Bradford to the countryside, he hoped to create a beautiful environment in which his workers would be happy. The Italianate town is remarkably well preserved, its former mills and houses now turned into shops, restaurants, and galleries. Salt's Mill, built in 1853, resembles a palazzo and was the largest factory in the world when it was built. Today it holds an art gallery and crafts and furniture shops. One-hour guided tours (£3.75) depart weekends at 2 pm from the **tourist information center** (⊠ *2 Victoria Rd.* ☎ *01274/599887* ⊕ *www.saltaire-village.info*). The **1853 Gallery** (⊠ *Salt's Mill, Victoria Rd.* ☎ *01274/531163* ⊠ *Free* ☉ *Daily 10–6*) holds a remarkable exhibition of 400 works by Bradford-born artist David Hockney. There are two restaurants on-site.

OFF THE BEATEN PATH

Ⓒ **National Media Museum.** Bradford, 10 mi west of Leeds, is known for this renowned museum, which traces the history of photographic media. It's a huge and hugely entertaining place, with five galleries displaying the world's first photographic negative, the latest digital imaging, and everything between. ■**TIP➜** It's popular with children, so come early or late in the day. ⊠ *Pictureville, Prince's Way* ☎ *01274/202030 or 0870/701–0200* ⊕ *www.nationalmediamuseum.org.uk* ⊠ *Free* ☉ *Tues.–Sun. and bank holidays 10–6.*

HAWORTH: HEART OF BRONTË COUNTRY

8 mi west of Saltaire.

★ Whatever Haworth might have been in the past, today it is Brontë country. This old stone-built textile village on the edge of the Yorkshire Moors long ago gave up its own personality and allowed itself to be taken over by the doomed sisters, their powerful novels, and their legions of fans. In 1820, when Anne, Emily, and Charlotte were very young, their father moved them and their other three siblings away from their old home in Bradford to Haworth. The sisters—Emily (author of *Wuthering Heights,* 1847), Charlotte (*Jane Eyre,* 1847), and Anne (*The Tenant of Wildfell Hall,* 1848) were all affected by the stark, dramatic countryside.

These days it seems that every building they ever glanced at has been turned into a memorial, shop, or museum. The Haworth Visitor Center has good information about accommodations, maps, books on the Brontës, and inexpensive leaflets to help you find your way to such outlying *Wuthering Heights* sites as Ponden Hall (Thrushcross Grange) and Ponden Kirk (Penistone Crag).

GETTING HERE AND AROUND

To reach Haworth by bus or train, buy a Metro Day Rover for bus and rail (£6.60) and take the Metro train from Leeds train station to Keighley, where you change to a Keighley and District bus to Haworth. On weekends you can opt to take the Keighley and Worth Valley Railway to continue on to Haworth.

The streets and houses of Haworth look much as they did when the Brontë sisters lived and wrote their famous novels in this village near the moors.

By car, Haworth is an easy drive 3 mi south on A629 from Leeds; it's well signposted, and there's plenty of cheap parking in town.

ESSENTIALS

Visitor Information Haworth Visitor Center (⊠ *Main St.* ☏ *01535/642329*).

EXPLORING

★ **Brontë Parsonage Museum.** The best of the Brontë sights in Haworth is this museum. In the somber Georgian house in which the sisters grew up, it displays original furniture (some bought by Charlotte after the success of *Jane Eyre*), portraits, and books. The Brontës moved to this simple house when the Reverend Patrick Brontë was appointed to the local church, but tragedy soon struck—his wife, Maria, and their two eldest children died within five years. They were done in, along with hundreds of others, by water wells tainted by seepage from the neighboring graveyard. The museum explains the family's tragic life story and makes it real with a strong collection of enchanting mementos of the four children, including tiny books they made when they were still very young; Charlotte's wedding bonnet; and the sisters' spidery, youthful graffiti on the nursery wall. Branwell, the Brontës' only brother, painted several of the portraits on display. ⊠ *Church St.* ☏ *01535/642323* ⊕ *www. bronte.info* ▣ *£7* ⊙ *Apr.–Sept., daily 10–5:30; Oct.–Mar., daily 11–5; last admission 30 mins before closing.*

Brontë Waterfall. If you have the time, you can pack a lunch and walk an hour or so along a field path, a lane, and a moorland track to the lovely, isolated waterfall that has, inevitably, been renamed in honor of the sisters. It was a favorite of theirs, and they wrote about it in poems and letters.

⟲ **Keighley and Worth Valley Railway.** Haworth is on this gorgeous 5-mi-long branch line, along which steam engines run between Keighley and Oxenhope. On special days, family fairs en route add to the fun. ⊠ *Railway station, Keighley* ☎ *01535/645214* ⊕ *www.kwvr. co.uk* ☐ *£10 round-trip, £14 Day Rover ticket* ☉ *Sept.–June, weekends; July and Aug., daily; call for schedules.*

Main Street. Haworth's steep, cobbled high street has changed little in outward appearance since the early 19th century, but today acts as a funnel for the people who crowd into the points of interest: the **Black Bull** pub, where the reprobate Branwell Brontë drank himself into an early grave; the **post office** from which Charlotte, Emily, and Anne sent their manuscripts to their London publishers; and the **church,** with its gloomy graveyard (Charlotte and Emily are buried inside the church; Anne is buried in Scarborough).

Top Withins. A ruined, gloomy house on a bleak hilltop farm 3 mi from Haworth, Top Withins is often taken to be the inspiration for Heathcliff's gloomy mansion, Wuthering Heights. Brontë scholars say it probably isn't; the ruins never looked the way the book describes them. Still, it's an inspirational walk across the moors. There and back from Haworth is a two-hour walk. ■**TIP➔** If you've read *Wuthering Heights,* you don't need to be reminded to wear sturdy shoes and protective clothing.

LANDSCAPE AS MUSE

The rugged Yorkshire Moors helped inspire Emily Brontë's 1847 *Wuthering Heights*; if ever a work of fiction grew out of the landscape in which its author lived, it was surely this. "My sister Emily loved the moors," wrote Charlotte. "Flowers brighter than the rose bloomed in the blackest of the heath for her; out of a sullen hollow in a livid hillside her mind could make an Eden. She found in the bleak solitude many and dear delights; and not the least and best loved was liberty."

WHERE TO EAT AND STAY

£££ ✗**Weavers.** This restaurant serves traditional, organic Yorkshire fare
BRITISH in a cozy dining room. Dinner options change with the seasons, but include dishes like pork with pancetta and chutney, roast cod with braised leeks, or slow-cooked lamb with an orange-and-currant sauce. Whatever you choose, it's served with warm, home-baked bread. Although Weavers is known primarily as a restaurant, upstairs there are a few spacious, chintz-filled rooms with antique French beds. Should you spend the night you'll find that breakfasts are amazing, including oatcakes with melted Wensleydale cheese and black pudding. ⊠ *15 West La.* ☎ *01535/643822* ⊕ *www.weaversmallhotel.co.uk* ☉ *Closed Sun. and Mon. No lunch Tues. or Sat.*

£ ⊞ **Aitches.** This intimate 19th-century stone house, situated very close
HOTEL to the Brontë Parsonage, has modern guest rooms decorated with pine furnishings and colorful quilts. **Pros:** intimate building; friendly staff. **Cons:** the rustic decor won't appeal to everyone. ⊠ *11 West La.* ☎ *01535/642501* ⊕ *www.aitches.co.uk* ➴ *5 rooms* ☖ *In-room: no a/c. In-hotel: restaurant* ⃝⃝ *Breakfast.*

£££–££££ ⊞ **Ashmount Country House.** A short walk from the Parsonage, this
B&B/INN charming stone building was once home to the Brontë sisters' physician,

Amos Ingham. **Pros:** lovely old building; ideal location; great views. **Cons:** books up in advance; it's one of the priciest places in town. ⊠ *Mytholmes La.* ☎ *01535/646726* ⊕ *www.ashmounthaworth.co.uk* ⚲ *8 rooms* ⚭ *In-room: no a/c, Wi-Fi* ❑ *Breakfast.*

12

THE YORKSHIRE DALES

The western equivalent of the North York Moors, the Yorkshire Dales are just as beautiful and nearly as wild. The word "dale" comes from the Viking word for valley, which gives you an indication that, although the moors have steep hills, the dales are more rugged, with sharper, higher hills culminating in the mountains Pen-y-ghent, Ingleborough, and Whernside. These river valleys fall south and east from the Pennines, and beyond Skipton they present an almost wholly rural aspect. Ruined priories, narrow roads, drystone walls made without mortar, and babbling rivers make for a quintessentially English landscape, full of paths and trails to explore.

BOLTON ABBEY

12 mi north of Haworth, 24 mi northwest of Leeds.

A leafy, picturesque village amid the rolling hills of the Yorkshire Dales, Bolton Abbey is a famously attractive town with a stone church and evocative priory ruins. Much of the area is still technically owned by the duke of Devonshire, who has a huge estate nearby—a lingering remnant of the country's feudal past.

GETTING HERE AND AROUND

Bolton Abbey, off the A59 between Skipton and Harrogate, is best reached by car. Buses are infrequent, but you can take the 883, 884, or 850 from Skipton, Shipley, or Bradford.

EXPLORING

★ **Bolton Priory.** Some of the loveliest Wharfedale scenery comes into view around Bolton Priory, the ruins of an Augustinian priory, which sits on a grassy embankment inside a great curve of the River Wharfe. The priory is just a short walk or drive from the village of Bolton Abbey. You can wander through the 13th-century ruins or visit the priory church. The duke of Devonshire owns the Bolton Abbey estate, including the ruins. John Ruskin, the Victorian art critic, rated it the most beautiful of all English ruins. Close to Bolton Priory, surrounded by romantic woodland scenery, the River Wharfe plunges between a narrow chasm in the rocks (called the Strid) before reaching **Barden Tower,** a medieval hunting lodge. This lodge is now a ruin and can be visited just as easily as Bolton Priory, in whose grounds it stands. ⊠ *B6160 off A59* ☎ *01756/718009* ⊕ *www.boltonabbey.com* ⚲ *Free, parking £6* ☉ *Daily 9–dusk.*

Embsay and Bolton Abbey Steam Railway. You can ride this scenic 4-mi railway, which has a station in Bolton Abbey (£8) (☎ *01756/710614,* *01756/795189 recorded timetable* ⚲ *£8).*

The imposing ruins of Bolton Priory provide a scenic backdrop for a walk along the River Wharfe.

WHERE TO STAY

For expanded reviews, visit Fodors.com.

£££££
★
HOTEL
🏨 **Devonshire Arms**. Originally an 18th-century coaching inn, and still belonging to the duke of Devonshire, this luxurious country-house hotel is near the River Wharfe, an easy walk from Bolton Abbey. **Pros:** one of the region's best hotels; real manor-house style. **Cons:** you pay for all that charm; you need a car to get here. ✉ *Bolton Abbey* ☎ *01756/710441* ⊕ *www.thedevonshirearms.co.uk* 🛏 *37 rooms, 3 suites* *In-room: no a/c, Internet. In-hotel: restaurants, bars, pool, tennis court, gym, spa, some pets allowed* 🍴 *Breakfast.*

SKIPTON

6 mi west of Bolton Abbey, 12 mi north of Haworth, 22 mi west of Harrogate.

Skipton in Airedale, capital of the limestone district of Craven, is a typical dales market town with as many farmers as visitors milling in the streets. There are markets Monday, Wednesday, Friday, and Saturday, and shops selling local produce predominate.

GETTING HERE AND AROUND

Skipton is off A59 and A65 at the edge of the Yorkshire Dales. From Leeds, First Leeds buses run regularly to Skipton. Dales buses depart regularly from Harrogate. There are regular trains from Leeds; the journey takes about 40 minutes.

ESSENTIALS

Visitor Information Skipton (✉ *35 Coach St.* ☎ *01756/792809* ⊕ *www. skiptononline.co.uk*).

EXPLORING

★ **Skipton Castle.** Built by the Normans in 1090 and unaltered since the 17th century, Skipton Castle is a remarkably well-preserved medieval castle. After the Battle of Marston Moor during the Civil War, it remained the only Royalist stronghold in the north of England. So sturdy was the squat little fortification with its rounded battlements (in some places the walls are 12 feet thick) that Oliver Cromwell ordered that the roof be removed, as it had survived one bombardment after another during a three-year siege. When the castle's owner, Lady Anne Clifford, later asked if she could replace the roof, he allowed her do so, as long as it was not strong enough to withstand cannon fire. In the central courtyard a yew tree, planted more than 300 years ago by Lady Anne herself, flourishes. ✉ *High St.* ☎ *01756/792442* ⊕ *www.skiptoncastle. co.uk* ⌑ *£6.50* ⊙ *Mar.–Sept., Mon.–Sat. 10–6, Sun. noon–6; Oct.–Feb., Mon.–Sat. 10–4, Sun. noon–4.*

Yorkshire Dales National Park Centre. This visitor center 10 mi north of Skipton has guidebooks, maps, and bus schedules to help you enjoy a day in the Yorkshire Dales National Park. Grassington is deep in the Dales on the tiny B6265, also known as the Grassington Road; buses travel here from nearby towns. A small, stone village, it makes a good base for exploring Upper Wharfedale. The Dales Way footpath passes through the village, and there are stores, pubs, and cafés. In summer it becomes overwhelmed by day-trippers and walkers, but you can escape them on the many local walks. ✉ *Colvend, Hebdon Rd., Grassington* ☎ *01756/752774* ⊕ *www.yorkshiredales.org.uk* ⊙ *Apr.–Oct., daily 10–5; Nov.–Mar., Wed. and Fri.–Sun. 10–4.*

WHERE TO EAT AND STAY

£££ ✕ **Angel Inn.** Diners at the Angel clog the hidden-away hamlet of Hetton
BRITISH with their vehicles, such is the attraction of this place with its casual brasserie and more formal restaurant. Roasted lamb and duck are specialties, and they are beautifully prepared. The ancient stone barn across the road has five well-equipped guest rooms decorated in unfussy country styles (£140). The inn is 5 mi north of Skipton. ✉ *Off B6265, Hetton* ☎ *01756/730263* ⊕ *www.angelhetton.co.uk.*

££ ✕ **Devonshire.** This traditional inn makes a comfortable rural dining
BRITISH spot, with its oak-paneled dining room aglow with flickering candles. Local lamb, beef, and dishes such as creamy fish pie appear on the menu with fresh local vegetables. There are also seven beautifully decorated rooms with a mix of antiques and modern furniture (£70). The inn is 10 mi north of Skipton in the town of Grassington. ✉ *Main St., Grassington* ☎ *01756/752525* ⊕ www.*thedevonshirehotel*.co.uk.

££ ⊡ **Ashfield House.** Three converted 17th-century stone cottages, once the
B&B/INN homes of Grassington lead miners, make up this well-run small hotel off the main street. **Pros:** charming cottages; gorgeous gardens. **Cons:** decor isn't always subtle; not a lot of amenities; it's 10 mi north of Skipton in Grassington. ✉ *Summers Fold, Grassington* ☎ *01756/752584* ⊕ *www.*

ashfieldhouse.co.uk 🔍 *7 rooms* ♿ *In-room: no a/c. In-hotel: restaurant, business center, some age restrictions* ⊘ *Breakfast.*

HAWES

30 mi north of Skipton.

The best time to visit the so-called cheesiest town in Yorkshire is on Tuesday, when farmers crowd into town for the weekly market. Crumbly, white Wensleydale cheese has been made in the valley for centuries, and it is sold in local stores and at the market. Allow yourself time to wander the cobbled side streets, some of which are filled with antiques shops and tearooms.

GETTING HERE AND AROUND

Hawes is high in the moors on A684. To get here from Grassington, take the Beggerman's Road north for 23 mi. There's no train service, but buses travel from Leeds throughout the day.

EXPLORING

Dales Countryside Museum. The Yorkshire Dales National Park Information Centre in the old train station contains this museum, which gives a picture of dales life in past centuries. A traditional rope-making shop here also welcomes visitors. ✉ *Station Yard* ☎ *01969/666210* ⊕ *www. yorkshiredales.org.uk* 🏛 *Museum £3.50* ⊘ *Daily 10–5.*

Wensleydale Creamery Visitor Centre. In a working dairy farm, this museum tells the story of the famed local cheese so beloved by the cartoon characters Wallace and Gromit. You can watch production (best seen between 10 and 2) from the viewing gallery, and then taste (and buy) the output in their excellent cheese shop. A restaurant on-site has plenty of cheese samples as well, such as smoked, with ginger, or with apple pie. ✉ *Gayle La.* ☎ *01969/667664* ⊕ *www.wensleydale.co.uk* 🏛 *Tour £2.50* ⊘ *Mon.–Sat. 9:30–5:30, Sun. 10–4:30.*

RICHMOND

22 mi northeast of Hawes.

Richmond tucks itself into a curve above the foaming River Swale, with a network of narrow Georgian streets and terraces opening onto a large cobbled marketplace. Despite all the Georgian architecture, the town is actually very old. The Normans swept in during the late 11th century, determined to subdue the local population and establish their rule in the north. This they did by building a mighty castle, around which the town grew, and throughout the Middle Ages Richmond was effectively a garrison town.

GETTING HERE AND AROUND

East Coast Trains run regularly from Leeds and from London's King's Cross to the town of Darlington, where you must change to a local train to Richmond. The journey from London takes around 3½ hours, from Leeds it takes about 1½ hours. By car, Richmond is on the rural B6274—follow signs off A1.

ESSENTIALS

Visitor Information Richmond (✉ *Friary Gardens, Victoria Rd.* ☎ *01748/828742* ⊕ *www.yorkshiredales.org*).

EXPLORING

Richmond Castle. The immense keep of this Norman castle towers above the river, providing excellent views of the countryside. Built around 1071 by Alan Rufus, first earl of Richmond, it was used as a prison for William "the Lion" of Scotland 100 years later. The castle retains its thick curtain wall and chapel, and a great hall that has been restored to its medieval splendor; even the 14th-century graffiti remains. There's a heritage garden, and a path along the river leads to the ruins of golden-stone Easby Abbey. One historical note: when Henry Tudor (son of Edmund Tudor, earl of Richmond) became Henry VII in 1485, he began calling his palace in southwest London by the name Richmond after his family seat in Richmond. The name gradually came to be used to describe that area of London. ☎ *01748/822493* ⊕ *www.english-heritage.org.uk* ✉ *£4.60* ☉ *Apr.–Sept., daily 10–6; Oct.–Mar., Thurs.–Mon. 10–4.*

Theatre Royal. A jewel box built in 1788, this Georgian structure retains original features such as the wooden seating from the days of the 18th-century Shakespearean actor David Garrick. The museum holds scenery dating from 1836. There are hourly tours of the theater Monday to Saturday, between 10 and 4. ✉ *Victoria Rd.* ☎ *01748/823710* ⊕ *www.georgiantheatreroyal.co.uk* ✉ *Museum £3 suggested donation* ☉ *Museum mid-Feb.–Dec., Mon.–Sat. 10–4:30.*

WHERE TO EAT AND STAY

££ ✕ **Black Bull.** Over the years the Black Bull has grown from a small place
BRITISH popular with locals to a sprawling operation that attracts visitors from throughout the area. The broad and varied menu of French-influenced British cuisine includes medallions of venison with goat-cheese mash, monkfish thermidor with skewered prawns, and duck confit with fondant potatoes. Less-fussy food (sausages and mash, Brie sandwiches) is served in the pub. The friendly staff doesn't mind if you just want a drink. ✉ *Back La., Moulton* ☎ *01325/377289* ⊕ *www.blackbullmoulton.com* ☉ *No dinner Sun.*

£££ ⌕ **Frenchgate Hotel.** This three-story Georgian town house on a quiet
HOTEL cobbled street has a bright and welcoming interior and a secluded walled garden for summer days. **Pros:** lovely gardens; quiet neighborhood. **Cons:** restaurant can be a bit noisy; not a lot of amenities. ✉ *59–61 Frenchgate* ☎ *01748/822087* ⊕ *www.thefrenchgate.co.uk* ⇨ *11 rooms* ☐ *In-room: no a/c. In-hotel: restaurant, bar* ⦿\ *Breakfast.*

£££ ⌕ **Millgate House.** This 18th-century house in the center of Richmond
B&B/INN has been beautifully restored, as you'll note from the elegant dining room and lounge. **Pros:** in the middle of town; grand historic house. **Cons:** rooms can be a bit chilly; not the bargain it once was. ✉ *Millgate* ☎ *01748/823571* ⊕ *www.millgatehouse.com* ⇨ *5 rooms, 2 apartments.* ☐ *In-room: no a/c, kitchen (some)* ⦿\ *Breakfast.*

HIKING IN MALHAM

Gordale Scar, a mile from Malham, is a popular destination for walkers.

Avid summer hikers descend in droves on Malham, 11 mi northeast of Skipton, to tour the remarkable limestone formations Malham Cove and Gordale Scar, and Malham Tarn. The three sites are on a circular walk of 8 mi that takes most people four to five hours. Those with less time should cut out the tarn (a small lake): a circular walk from the village to the limestone formations Malham Cove and Gordale Scar can be completed in just over two hours.

Malham's **National Park Centre** (☎ 01969/652380 ⊕ www.yorkshiredales.org.uk ⊘ Apr.–Oct., daily 10–5; Nov.–Mar., Fri.–Sun. 10–4) has displays and will give you ideas of what to do locally and in Yorkshire Dales National Park. You can get a list of bed-and-breakfast and pub accommodations, too.

Malham Cove, a huge, 300-foot-high natural rock amphitheater, is a mile north of the village and provides the easiest local walk. Following the path up to the top is a brutal climb, though rewarded by magnificent views.

At **Gordale Scar,** a deep natural chasm between overhanging limestone cliffs, the white waters of a moorland stream plunge 300 feet. It's a mile northeast of Malham by a lovely riverside path.

A walk of more than 3 mi leads north from Malham to **Malham Tarn,** an attractive lake in windswept isolation. There's a nature reserve on the west bank and an easy-to-follow trail on the east bank. Malham is 10 mi west of Grassington: take B6265 south 2 mi through Cracoe, then branch west onto the minor road past Hetton and Calton. Malham is also 12 mi northwest of Skipton, off A65.

THE NORTH YORK MOORS

The North York Moors are a dramatic swath of high moorland starting 25 mi north of the city of York and stretching east to the coast and west to the Cleveland Hills. Once covered in forest, of which a few pockets survive, the landscape changed when the monks at Rievaulx and Whitby abbeys began raising huge flocks of sheep in medieval times. Over the course of centuries, the sheep have kept the moors deforested, and still ensure that the pink heather on which they feed spreads lushly across the hills. A series of isolated, medieval "standing stones" that once acted as signposts on the paths between the abbeys are now handy for hikers.

For more than four decades the area has been a national park, ensuring the protection of the bleak moors and grassy valleys that shelter brownstone villages and hamlets. Minor roads and tracks crisscross the hills, and there's no single, obvious route through the region. You can approach from York; another approach is from the coast at Whitby, along the Esk Valley to Danby, which is also accessible on the Esk Valley branch-train line between Middlesbrough and Whitby. From Danby, minor roads run south over the high moors reaching Hutton-le-Hole, beyond which main roads lead to interesting towns on the moors' edge, such as Helmsley. Completing the route in this direction leaves you with an easy side trip to Castle Howard before returning to York.

DANBY

49 mi northeast of York, 15 mi west of Whitby.

The old stone village of Danby nestles in a green valley, just a short walk from the tops of the moors. It's been settled since Viking times—Danby means "village where the Danes lived"—and these days it bumbles along in a semi-touristed way. There's a pub, and a cozy bakery with a tearoom, and if you bring hiking boots, within 10 minutes you can be above the village looking down, surrounded by moorland.

GETTING HERE AND AROUND

From York, take A64 to A169 and then follow the signs across the moor. Northern Rail travels to Danby station throughout the day from nearby towns. To get here from Whitby, take A171 west and turn north for Danby after 12 mi, after which it's a 3-mi drive over Danby Low Moor to the village.

ESSENTIALS

Bus Information Moorsbus (☎ *01845/597000* ⊕ *www.northyorkmoors.org.uk*).

EXPLORING

Moors Centre. In a house on the eastern outskirts of Danby, the North York Moors National Park's Moors Centre will interest gardeners with its extensive displays on the flora and fauna of the moors. There's a tearoom, a picnic area, and a beautiful play area for kids. The summer Moorsbus operates from the center for the 30-minute journey south to Hutton-le-Hole. ⊠ *Danby Lodge* ☎ *01439/772737* ⊕ *www.northyorkmoors.co.uk* ⊠ *Free, parking £2* ⊗ *Jan. and Feb., weekends 11–4; Mar., Nov., and Dec., daily 11–4; Apr.–Oct., daily 10–5.*

EN ROUTE

From Danby take the road due west for 2 mi to Castleton, and then turn south over the top of the moors toward Hutton-le-Hole. The narrow road offers magnificent views over North York Moors National Park, especially at the old stone **Ralph Cross** (5 mi), which marks the park's highest point. Drive carefully: sheep dodging is a necessary art.

HUTTON-LE-HOLE

13 mi south of Danby.

Sleepy Hutton-le-Hole is a charming little place based around a wide village green, with fluffy sheep snoozing in the shade of stone cottages. Unfortunately, it can be unbearably crowded in summer. You can always keep driving to either the charming nearby burg of Thorton-le-Dale or to the medieval market towns of Helmsley or Pickering.

GETTING HERE AND AROUND

Hutton-le-Hole is in the moors off A170. It has no train station, and is only accessible by bus in summer when the Yorkshire Coastliner travels between the small towns in the region.

EXPLORING

Ryedale Folk Museum. The excellent open-air Ryedale Folk Museum interprets life in the dales from prehistory onward through craft demonstrations and 13 historic buildings, including a medieval kiln, 16th-century cottages, and a 19th-century blacksmith's shop. ☎ *01751/417367* ⊕ *www.ryedalefolkmuseum.co.uk* ✉ *£5.50* ☉ *Early Mar.–Oct., daily 10–5:30; Nov.–Feb., daily 10–dusk.*

HELMSLEY

8 mi southwest of Hutton-le-Hole, 27 mi north of York.

The market town of Helmsley, with its flowering window boxes, stone cottages, arched bridges across streams, and churchyard, is the perfect place to spend a relaxing afternoon. You can while away a few hours lingering in its tea shops and tiny boutiques, and exploring the craggy ruins of its Norman castle. Market day is Friday. Nearby are the impressive ruins of Rievaulx Abbey.

GETTING HERE AND AROUND

There is no train station in Helmsley, and it has no major bus service. The Moorsbus stops in Helmsley in summer. By car, Helmsley is on A170.

Visitor Information Helmsley (✉ *Town Hall, Market Pl.* ☎ *01439/770173* ⊕ *www.ryedale.gov.uk*).

EXPLORING

Fodor's Choice ★

Rievaulx. The perfect marriage of architecture and countryside, Rievaulx (pronounced ree-*voh*) Abbey has a dramatic setting 2 mi northwest of Helmsley; its sweeping arches soar at the precise point where a forested hillside rushes down to the River Rye. A French Cistercian sect founded this abbey in 1132, and though its monks led a life of isolation and silence, they were active in the wool business. By the end of the 13th century the abbey was massively wealthy. The evocative ruins give a good indication of how vast the abbey once was. Medieval mosaic tiling

The ruins of Rievaulx Abbey, which was enormously wealthy in medieval times because of the wool trade, show how large the abbey was.

can still be seen here and there, and part of the symmetrical cloisters remains. The Chapter House retains the original shrine of the first abbot, William, by the entrance. By the time of Henry VIII the abbey had shrunk dramatically; only 20 or so monks lived here when the king's soldiers arrived to destroy the building in 1538. After that, the earl of Rutland owned Rievaulx, and he demolished what was left to the best of his ability. What remains is a beautiful ghost of the magnificent building that once stood here. If you're up for walking, the abbey is a 1½-hour walk from Helmsley. ⊠ *Off B1257* ☎ *01439/798228* ⊕ *www.english-heritage.org.uk* ✉ *£5.60* ⏱ *Apr.–Sept., daily 10–6; Oct., daily 10–5; Nov.–Mar., Thurs.–Mon. 10–4.*

OFF THE BEATEN PATH

Rievaulx Terrace and Temples. From Rievaulx Abbey it's a short walk or drive up to the hill where Rievaulx Terraces have a magnificent view of the abbey. The long, grassy walkway on the hillside ends at the remains of several Tuscan- and Ionic-style classical temples, once maintained by the earl of Rutland. ⊠ *Off B1257* ☎ *01439/798340* ⊕ *www.nationaltrust.org.uk* ✉ *£5* ⏱ *Mid-Feb.–Oct., daily 11–5; last admission 1 hr before closing.*

WHERE TO STAY

For expanded reviews, visit Fodors.com.

£££–££££

HOTEL

▣ **Black Swan.** A splendid base for exploring the area, this ivy-covered property sits on the edge of Helmsley's market square. **Pros:** historic charm; great location. **Cons:** decor is a bit old-fashioned; bathrooms need updating. ⊠ *Market Pl.* ☎ *01439/770466* ⊕ *www.blackswan-helmsley.co.uk* ⇆ *45 rooms* ⚭ *In-room: no a/c, Internet. In-hotel: restaurant, bar, some pets allowed* ⑪ *Breakfast.*

Visiting Yorkshire's Monastic Past

Today the ruined abbeys at Fountains, Rievaulx, and Whitby are top attractions where you can learn about the religious and business worlds of the great monasteries of Yorkshire, and the political machinations that destroyed them. They serve as vivid reminders of what life was like in the Middle Ages.

THE FALL OF THE MONASTERIES
The sheer number of once richly decorated monastic buildings here is a testament to the power of the Catholic monks of medieval Yorkshire. They became some of the richest in Europe by virtue of the international wool trade that they conducted, with the help of lay workers, from their vast religious estates. The buildings lie mostly in romantic ruins, a result of the dissolution of the monasteries during the 16th century, part of Henry VIII's struggle with the Catholic Church over finances and his divorce request (the rejection of which he perceived as a calculated way to deny him a male heir). Henry's break with Rome was made official in 1534 with the Act of Supremacy, which made him head of the Church of England. By 1540 no monasteries or abbeys remained; the king confiscated all their property, distributed the lands, and destroyed or gave away many buildings.

££   No. 54. Tea and cakes provide a tasty welcome in this stone cottage
B&B/INN   just off market square. **Pros:** tea and cakes for everyone; comfy beds. **Cons:** small rooms; not much privacy. ⌂ *Bondgate* ☎ *01439/771533* ⊕ *www.no54.co.uk* ⇆ *3 rooms* ♢ *In-room: no a/c. In-hotel: some pets allowed* ⊟ *No credit cards* ⊙ *Breakfast.*

SPORTS AND THE OUTDOORS
Helmsley, on the southern edge of the moors, is the starting point of the **Cleveland Way** (⊕ *www.nationaltrail.co.uk*), the long-distance moor-and-coastal footpath. Boots are donned at the old cross in the market square; it's 50 mi or so across the moors to the coast and then a similar distance south to Filey along the cliff tops. The footpath is 110 mi long and takes around nine days start to finish. The trail passes close to Rievaulx Abbey, a few miles outside town.

THE NORTH YORKSHIRE COAST

The North York Moors plummet down to the sea in spectacular cliffs that stretch down the coastline, creating a dramatic view of pink heather and white cliffs hundreds of feet above the dark sea. The red roofs of Robin Hood's Bay, the sharply curved bay at Whitby, and the gold-and-white buildings of Scarborough capture the imagination at first sight. Most coastal towns still support an active fishing industry, and every harbor offers fishing and leisure trips throughout summer. Beaches at Scarborough, Whitby, and Filey have patrolled areas: swim between the red-and-yellow flags, and don't swim when a red flag is flying. All the North Sea beaches are ideal for fossil hunting and seashell collecting.

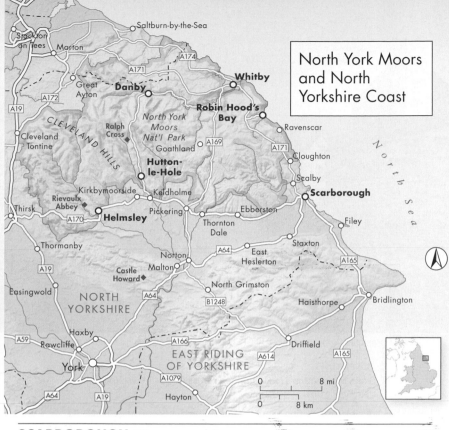

North York Moors
and North
Yorkshire Coast

North Sea

SCARBOROUGH

34 mi northeast of York.

There is no Scarborough Fair, and historians are divided on whether there ever was one, but don't let that stop you from heading to this classic English seaside resort, where lemon-hue Victorian houses top cliffs overlooking the dark blue sea. The older, more genteel side of Scarborough is in the southern half of town, with carefully laid-out crescents and squares, the ruins of its castle, and views across Cayton Bay. The northern side is a riot of tacky seaside arcades, ice-cream stands, bingo halls, and stores selling "rock" (luridly colored hard candy). The huddle of streets, alleyways, and red-roof cottages around the harbor gives an idea of what the town was like before the resort days.

GETTING HERE AND AROUND

Scarborough is difficult to reach by public transportation. There are no direct trains from London, and a bus from London takes all day. Transpennine Express trains leave from York every hour or so; the journey takes just under an hour. The journey from Leeds by National Express bus takes about four hours. By car, Scarborough is on the coastal A165 road.

A former smuggling center, the village of Robin Hood's Bay is known for its red-roof cottages as well as its beach.

ESSENTIALS

Train Information Transpennine Express (☎ 0845/600–1671 ⊕ www.tpexpress.co.uk).

Visitor Information Scarborough (✉ Pavilion House, Valley Bridge Rd. ☎ 01723/383636 ⊕ www.discoveryorkshirecoast.com).

EXPLORING

Rotunda Museum. The extraordinary circular building that holds this museum was constructed in 1829 for William Smith of the Scarborough Philosophical Society to display his geological collection. It now contains important archaeological and local history collections. ✉ Vernon Rd. ☎ 01723/374753 ⊕ www.rotundamuseum.co.uk ⚑ £4.50 ☉ Tues.–Sun. 10–5.

St. Mary. Most visitors to this little medieval church are attracted by the churchyard's most famous occupant: Anne, the youngest Brontë sister. She was taken to Scarborough from Haworth when suffering from tuberculosis in a futile effort to save her life by exposing her to the sea air. She died in 1849. The church is near the castle on the way into town. ✉ Castle Rd. ☎ 01723/500541.

Scarborough Castle. For nearly 900 years the rambling ruins of this castle have dominated the northern headland. The Romans used the site as a signaling station in the 4th century, and archaeological digs have uncovered evidence that people lived here in the Bronze Age. The current structure dates to 1136, when it was built by William de Gros to replace a wooden fort. Henry II later took the castle for himself because he believed it was impossible to invade. He was right: although the castle was repeatedly besieged, it was never taken by force. ■TIP➜ The castle has spectacular views across the North Bay and the shore gardens.

✉ *Castle Rd.* ☎ *01723/372451* ⊕ *www.english-heritage.org.uk* 🎟 *£5* ⊘ *Apr.–Sept., daily 10–6; Oct.–Mar., Thurs.–Mon. 10–4.*

🐣 **Scarborough Sea Life Centre.** Recognizable by its white pyramids, this aquarium is a great—if expensive—way to entertain the kids for an afternoon. The underwater world is presented in an engaging way, with all the marine habitats native to Great Britain accounted for. ✉ *Scalby Mills, North Bay* ☎ *01723/373414* ⊕ *www.sealifeeurope.com* 🎟 *£15* ⊘ *Mar.–Oct., daily 10–6; Nov.–Feb., daily 10–4; last admission 1 hr before closing.*

WHERE TO EAT AND STAY

£ ╳ **The Golden Grid.** Everyone has to
SEAFOOD have fish-and-chips at least once in Scarborough, and this harborfront spot is a classic of its kind. Choose an upstairs window table and tuck into freshly fried cod or haddock. ✉ *4 Sandside* ☎ *01723/360922* ⊕ *www.goldengrid.co.uk* ⊘ *No dinner Sun.–Thurs. Sept.–Mar.*

£££ ╳ **Lanterna.** This unpretentious restaurant prides itself on *not* being mod-
ITALIAN ern. Instead it offers classic Italian dishes, including tender steak cooked with ham and cheese, and seafood chosen fresh off the boats in the harbor. Opt for seasonal specials using fresh vegetables, fish, and white truffles (October to January). ✉ *33 Queen St.* ☎ *01723/363616* ⊕ *www.lanterna-ristorante.co.uk* ⊘ *Closed Sun. and 2 wks late Oct. No lunch.*

££–£££ 🏨 **The Crown Spa.** The centerpiece of the Regency Esplanade, this 19th-
HOTEL century hotel overlooks South Bay and the castle headland. **Pros:** pure Victorian style; modern amenities. **Cons:** small bathrooms. ✉ *The Esplanade* ☎ *01723/357426* ⊕ *www.crownspahotel.com* ↩ *87 rooms* ⌂ *In-room: no a/c, Wi-Fi. In-hotel: restaurant, bar, pool, gym, spa, some pets allowed* ⍾ *Breakfast.*

NIGHTLIFE AND THE ARTS

Scarborough is one of England's busy theater towns, especially for summer repertory, with most of the activity buzzing around the **Stephen Joseph Theatre** (✉ *Westborough* ☎ *01723/370541* ⊕ *www.sjt.uk.com*). It presents productions on two stages and also has a cinema, a restaurant, and a bar.

A SPA IS BORN

In 1626 Elizabeth Farrow came upon a stream of acidic water running from a cliff south of Scarborough. This led to the town's establishment as a hugely popular spa on a par with Harrogate. By the 18th century, when icy sea bathing came into vogue, no beaches were busier than Scarborough's. Donkeys and horses drew wheeled cabins called bathing machines into the surf and anchored there. The city's prosperity manifested itself in the handsome Regency and early-Victorian residences and hotels you see today.

ROBIN HOOD'S BAY

15 mi northwest of Scarborough.

★ This tiny fishing village squeezed into a steep narrow ravine is absolutely adorable, from its name right down to its little red-roof cottages and cobbled roads. The village has no connection to the famous medieval outlaw, though. It was once a smuggling center that passed contraband up the streambed beneath the cottages, linked to one another by secret passages. The attraction here is the town itself, with its winding stone staircases that eventually wander off across the headland. ■TIP➔ Park in the pay lots at the top of the hill. Do not attempt to drive down the hill.

GETTING HERE AND AROUND

Robin Hood's Bay is 5 mi south of Whitby off A171. Park in the public lots at the top of the hill. Robin Hood's Bay has no train station, but buses arrive from Scarborough and Whitby throughout the day.

EXPLORING

Robin Hood's Bay Beach. The beach is lovely, but mercurial—the tide rushes in quickly, so take care not to get cut off. Provided the tide is out, you can stroll for a couple of hours south from the town, along a rough stone shore full of rock pools, inlets, and sandy strands. A few stretches of sand are suitable for sunbathers. To the south, at the curiously named **Boggle Hole,** a ravine nestles an old water mill, now an atmospheric youth hostel (signs mark the way on the cliff-top path from Robin Hood's Bay). Farther south is **Ravenscar,** a Victorian village that now consists of little more than a hotel, which can be reached by a hazardous but exhilarating path up the cliff.

WHERE TO EAT AND STAY

£   ✕ **Bay Hotel.** The village's most favored pub is this friendly Victorian retreat,
SEAFOOD   perfectly positioned at the bottom of the village. It sits on a rocky outcrop lapped by the sea, so there are nice views. The bar is festooned with oak and brass; in winter, a roaring fire warms all comers. Whitby scampi and savory meat pies are often on the menu. ⊠ *The Dock* ☎ *01947/880278.*

£££–££££   ⊡ **Raven Hall Hotel.** This Georgian hotel with landscaped grounds offers
HOTEL   unrivaled coastal views from the headland of Ravenscar, 3 mi southeast of Robin Hood's Bay. **Pros:** breathtaking coastal views; great for sports fanatics. **Cons:** a bit off the beaten track; need a car to get around. ⊠ *Ravenscar* ☎ *01723/870353* ⊕ *www.ravenhall.co.uk* ↵ *53 rooms* ♨ *In-room: no a/c, Internet. In-hotel: restaurant, bar, golf course, pool, tennis courts, gym* ⦿| *Breakfast.*

SPORTS AND THE OUTDOORS

Several superb long-distance walks start at, finish in, or run through Robin Hood's Bay.

The coastal part of **Cleveland Way** (⊕ *www.nationaltrail.co.uk*) runs north to Whitby and south to Scarborough.

The village marks one end of the 190-mi **Coast-to-Coast Walk**; the other is at St. Bees Head on the Irish Sea. Walkers finish at the Bay Hotel, above the harbor.

The trans-moor **Lyke-Wake Walk** (⊕ *www.lykewakewalk.co.uk*) finishes 3 mi away at Ravenscar.

WHITBY

7 mi northwest of Robin Hood's Bay, 20 mi northeast of Pickering.

Fodor's Choice   A scenic seaside town with a Gothic edge, Whitby is a busy tourist
★   hub, but it handles that fact so well you might not notice (except at

The ruins of Whitby Abbey rise above the pretty town of Whitby and the River Esk.

dinnertime, when it's hard to get a seat in a restaurant). Whitby curves around its symmetrical harbor and winds its way up the cliffs. The glassy waters of the slow-moving River Esk cut through the town. Fine Georgian houses dominate the west side of the river (known as West Cliff), and across the swing bridge smaller 17th-century buildings mark the old town (known as East Cliff). Here cobbled Church Street is packed in summer with people exploring the shop-lined alleyways.

Whitby came to prominence as a whaling port in the mid-18th century. Whaling brought wealth, and shipbuilding made it famous: Captain James Cook (1728–79), explorer and navigator, sailed on his first ship from Whitby in 1747, and all four of his subsequent discovery vessels were built here.

GETTING HERE AND AROUND

A car is a must, as there are no direct buses or trains from London. National Express and Megabus have buses to the region, but you must change at least once, and the journey can take up to 10 hours. National Express trains from London's King's Cross Station go to Leeds, where you can change to a local train. The entire journey takes around six hours.

Whitby has a very small town center, and it's easily walkable. The train station is in the town center, between its two cliffs. If you're looking for a taxi, they tend to line up outside the station.

ESSENTIALS

Visitor Information Whitby (✉ Langbourne Rd. ☎ 01723/383636 ⊕ www. whitbyonline.co.uk).

Whitby Jet

In the 19th century Whitby became famous around the Western world for jet, a very hard, black form of natural carbon, found in thin seams along the coast here and worked into jewelry and ornaments. Known since prehistoric times and sometimes used to ward off the evil eye, it reached the peak of its popularity in the 1850s when 1,400 men and boys, supplied by 200 miners, made a good living in jewelry workshops all over the town.

The queen of Bavaria was impressed enough to order a chain more than 4 feet long. On the death of her husband, Queen Victoria introduced jet into court circles and set the fashion for mourning memorabilia.

You can see fine examples in the Whitby Museum on St. Hilda's Terrace and in the shop displays in the old town along Church Street and parallel to Sandgate. If you buy a piece, keep it shiny with baby oil.

EXPLORING

Captain Cook Memorial Museum. Filled with exhibits relating to the man and explorer, this museum is in the 18th-century house belonging to ship owner John Walker. Cook lived here as an apprentice from 1746 to 1749. On display are mementos of his epic expeditions, including maps, diaries, and drawings. ⊠ *Grape La.* ☎ *01947/601900* ⊕ *www. cookmuseumwhitby.co.uk* ☜ *£4.50* ⊙ *Apr.–Oct., daily 9:45–5; Mar., daily 11–3.*

OFF THE BEATEN PATH

Goathland. This moorland village, 8 mi southwest of Whitby, has a cute 1865 train station that served as Hogsmeade Station for students arriving at the school of wizardry in the film *Harry Potter and the Sorcerer's Stone*. The 18-mi **North Yorkshire Moors Railway** (⊠ *Pickering Station, Park St., Pickering* ☎ *01751/472508* ⊕ *www.nymr.co.uk* ☜ *£16* ⊙ *Late Mar.–early Nov., daily; early Nov.–Feb., some weekends and holiday periods*), between Grosmont and Pickering, passes through neat towns and moorland. Steam-powered trains provide a great outing.

St. Mary. On top of the East Cliff—reached by climbing 199 stone steps—this Gothic church overlooks the town, while it in turn is watched over by the gaunt ruins of Whitby Abbey. Bram Stoker lived in Whitby briefly and later said the image of pallbearers carrying coffins up the church's long stone staircase inspired him to write *Dracula*. The unusual-looking church with its ship's-deck roof, triple-decker pulpit, and enclosed box pews dates from the 12th century, although almost everything else you see today is the result of 19th- and 20th-century renovations. The weather-beaten churchyard is filled with the crooked old gravestones of ancient mariners. ■TIP➔ Rather than walking the 199 steps, you can drive to the hilltop and park in the abbey's large parking lot for a small fee. ⊠ *Church La., East Cliff* ☎ *01947/603421* ☜ *Free* ⊙ *Apr., daily 10–4; May–Aug., daily 10–5; Sept. and Oct., daily 10–3; Nov.–Mar., daily 10–2.*

★ **Whitby Abbey.** The glorious ruins of this abbey, high on the East Cliff, dominate the area. The skeletal remains of the once grand church can

All aboard! You can take North Yorkshire Moors Railway steam trains to stations including Goathland.

even be seen from the hills of the moors miles away. St. Hilda founded the abbey in AD 657. It was one of very few founded by a woman, and operated with a mixed population of monks and nuns. Sacked by the Vikings in the 9th century, the monastery was refounded in the 11th century and enlarged in the 13th century. It flourished until Henry VIII destroyed it. The visitor center is excellent, with exhibits on Hilda and Bram Stoker, artifacts from the site, interactive displays on the medieval abbey, and a tea shop. ⊠ *Abbey La., East Cliff* ☎ *01947/603568* ⊕ *www.english-heritage.org.uk* ✉ *£6* ☉ *Apr.–Sept., daily 10–6; Oct.– Mar., Thurs.–Mon. 10–4.*

Whitby Museum. Exhibits in this quirky museum wander from local geology and natural history to archaeology, whaling, and trade routes in Asia. It's interesting for its old-fashioned approach—displays have handwritten cards. ⊠ *St. Hilda's La., Pannett Park* ☎ *01947/602908* ⊕ *www.whitbymuseum.org.uk* ✉ *£4* ☉ *Tues.–Sun. 9:30–4:30.*

WHERE TO EAT

£££
SEAFOOD
✕ **Greens of Whitby.** Greens specializes in fresh local seafood served with a Continental flair. The restaurant is two eateries in one: downstairs a more casual bistro, upstairs a white-linen restaurant. The menu changes constantly, but downstairs grilled and fried seafood lead the way. Upstairs the catch of the day might be served with shellfish linguine, or Yorkshire beef might be grilled and topped with a creamy blue cheese sauce. ⊠ *13 Bridge St.* ☎ *01947/600284* ⊕ *www.greensofwhitby.com.*

££
SEAFOOD
✕ **Magpie Café.** Whitby is full of fish-and-chips places, but this is the one that draws the biggest crowd with a well-stocked menu that includes plaice, cod, and haddock along with grilled fish and meat platters. The

food is good and fans say it's worth the wait, which can stretch to an hour on busy nights. ⊠ *14 Pier Rd.* ☎ *01947/602058* ⌂ *Reservations not accepted* ⊙ *Closed Jan.*

WHERE TO STAY

For expanded reviews, visit Fodors. com.

££   🖼 **Broom House.** Tucked away in the
B&B/INN tiny village of Egton Bridge, about 5 mi outside Whitby, this two-story stone house sits beside a babbling brook at the base of forested hills. **Pros:** gorgeous setting; beautifully decorated rooms. **Cons:** far from Whitby; need a car to get around. ⊠ *Broom House La., Egton Bridge* ☎ *01947/895279* ⊕ *www.egton-bridge.co.uk* 🛏 *10 rooms* ⌂ *In-room: no a/c* ⦿ *Breakfast.*

£   🖼 **Shepherd's Purse.** This splendid little complex in the cobbled old town
HOTEL   consists of boutique-style guest rooms, an organic café, and a health-food store. **Pros:** quirky style; comfortable rooms. **Cons:** some rooms are quite small; no breakfast. ⊠ *95 Church St.* ☎ *01947/820228* 🛏 *9 rooms, 5 with bath* ⌂ *In-room: no a/c. In-hotel: restaurant, some pets allowed.* ⦿ *Breakfast.*

££   🖼 **White Horse and Griffin.** When looking for the perfect inn, you want
HOTEL   an old building with character, a roaring fire, and food to thrill. **Pros:** lots of character; tasty food. **Cons:** old-fashioned style; few amenities. ⊠ *Church St.* ☎ *01947/604857* ⊕ *www.whitehorseandgriffin.co.uk* 🛏 *10 rooms* ⌂ *In-room: no a/c. In-hotel: restaurant, bar, some pets allowed* ⦿ *Breakfast.*

NIGHTLIFE AND THE ARTS

★ The **Whitby Regatta** (⊕ *www.whitbyregatta.co.uk*), held each August, is a three-day jamboree of boat races, fair rides, lifeboat rescue displays, fireworks, and music.

Music (but also traditional dance and storytelling) predominates during **Whitby Folk Week** (⊕ *www.whitbyfolk.co.uk*), usually held the week before the late-August bank holiday, when pubs, sidewalks, and halls become venues for more than 600 traditional folk events by British performers.

A LOCAL HAUNT

Locals know well that St. Mary's church is an eerie sight—at night it is chillingly illuminated. In Bram Stoker's *Dracula*, the count claimed Lucy as his victim in the churchyard. Even though the tale is fiction, few linger up there after dark.

The Northeast

WORD OF MOUTH

"For Hadrian's Wall, we did Housesteads and Vindolanda and found both very interesting. Housesteads is a fort on the wall. Vindolanda was a fortress town near, not on, the wall. There we took a tour of the town (mostly foundation stones), led by an archaeologist."

—Mimar

WELCOME TO THE NORTHEAST

TOP REASONS TO GO

★ **Hadrian's Wall:** The ancient Roman wall is a true wonder for the wild countryside around it and the resiliency of its stones and forts.

★ **Castles, castles, castles:** Fought over by the Scots and the English, and prey to Viking raiders, the Northeast was heavily fortified. Durham, Alnwick, and Dunstanburgh castles are spectacular remnants of this history.

★ **Medieval Durham:** A splendid Norman cathedral that dates back to the 11th century is just one of the city's charms. Take a stroll on its ancient winding streets or along the River Wear.

★ **Lindisfarne (Holy Island):** To get to this historic island, you drive across a causeway that floods at high tide. This remote spot includes the ruins of Lindisfarne Priory.

★ **Alnwick Castle and Gardens:** The inland seat of the dukes of Northumberland is fascinating with its formidable walls, luxurious interiors, and gardens.

1 Durham, Newcastle, and Environs. The historic city of Durham, set on a rocky spur, has a stunning castle and cathedral. South and west are scenic towns with castles and industrial heritage sites. Newcastle, to the north, is a sprawling metropolis with a lively regional arts scene.

2 Hadrian's Wall Country. England's wildest countryside is traversed by the remains of the wall that marked the northern border of the Roman Empire. Hexham is a useful base, and Housesteads Roman Fort is a key site. It's stunning country for walking or biking.

3 The Far Northeast Coast. In this dramatic landscape, rocky hillsides plunge into the sea. The ruins of castle towers such as Dunstanburgh and Bamburgh stand guard over windswept beaches, and Lindisfarne has a long religious history. Alnwick, inland, has spectacular gardens.

Cornhill-on-Tweed

Rochester
Elishaw

West Woodburn

Northumberland National Park

Hadrian's Wall **2**

Greenhead Henshaw Hexham
Br

Ireshopeburn

0 ____ 10 mi
0 ____ 10 km

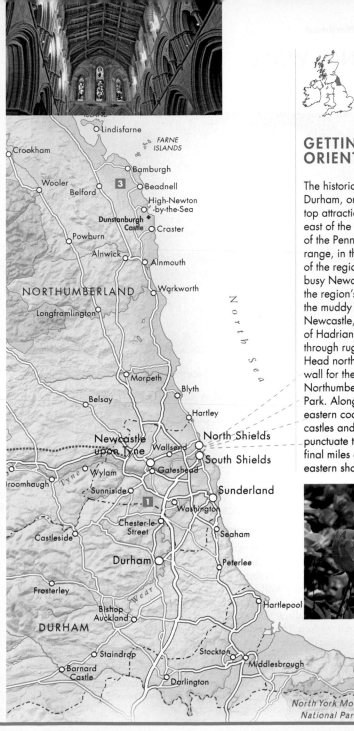

GETTING ORIENTED

The historic cathedral city of Durham, one of the region's top attractions, sits to the east of the wooded foothills of the Pennines mountain range, in the southern part of the region. Farther north, busy Newcastle straddles the region's main river, the muddy Tyne. West of Newcastle, the remains of Hadrian's Wall snake through rugged scenery. Head northwest of the wall for the wilderness of Northumberland National Park. Along the far northeastern coast, towering castles and misty islands punctuate the stunning, final miles of England's eastern shoreline.

Lindisfarne

FARNE ISLANDS

Crookham

Bamburgh

Wooler

Belford

Beadnell

High-Newton -by-the-Sea

Dunstanburgh Castle

Craster

Powburn

Alnwick

Alnmouth

NORTHUMBERLAND

Warkworth

Longframlington

North Sea

Morpeth

Blyth

Belsay

Hartley

Newcastle upon Tyne

Wallsend

North Shields

Broomhaugh

Tyne

Wylam

Gateshead

South Shields

Sunniside

Sunderland

Washington

Chester-le-Street

Seaham

Castleside

Durham

Peterlee

Frosterley

Wear

Bishop Auckland

Hartlepool

DURHAM

Staindrop

Stockton

Barnard Castle

Middlesbrough

Darlington

North York Moors National Park

HADRIAN'S WALL

Winding through the wild and windswept Northumberland countryside, Hadrian's Wall is Britain's most important Roman relic. It once formed the northern frontier of the Roman Empire—its most remote outpost and first line of defense against raiders from the north. Even today, as a ruin, the wall is an awe-inspiring structure.

The wall is a dramatic sight in the countryside (above); Roman writing tablet from Vindolanda (right, top); remains of a fort near Housesteads (right, bottom).

One of the most surprising things about visiting the 73-mi-long wall is its openness and accessibility. Although many of the best-preserved sections are within managed tourist sites, Hadrian's Wall is also part of the landscape, cutting through open countryside. Signposted trails along the entire route allow you to hike or cycle along most of the wall for free. The area around the wall is also rich in archaeological treasures that paint a picture of a thriving, multicultural community. The soldiers and their families who were stationed here came from as far away as Spain and North Africa, and recent discoveries provide insight into their daily lives. Artifacts displayed at the wall's museums provide fascinating perspective.

POSTCARDS FROM THE PAST

"Oh, how much I want you at my birthday party. You'll make the day so much more fun. Good-bye, sister, my dearest soul."

"I have sent you two pairs of sandals and two pairs of underpants. Greet all your messmates, with whom I pray you live in the greatest good fortune."

—*From 1st-century writing tablets unearthed at Vindolanda*

SEEING THE WALL'S HIGHLIGHTS

Hadrian's Wall has a handful of Roman-era forts, the best of which are concentrated near Housesteads, Vindolanda, and Chesters. Housesteads is the most complete, although getting there involves a quarter-mile walk up a hill; Chesters and Vindolanda have excellent museums. The separate Roman Army Museum near Greenhead offers a good overview of the wall's history and is very near one of the best sections in open countryside, at Walltown Crags.

WHEN TO GO

The best time to visit is midsummer, when the long hours of daylight allow time to see a few of the wall's major attractions and fit in a short hike on the same day. Winter brings icy winds; not all the forts and museums stay open, but those that do can be all but deserted. The weather can change suddenly at any time of year, so always bring warm clothes.

GETTING AROUND BY CAR OR BUS

The tiny, winding B6318 road passes within a stone's throw of most of the forts. It's a true back-road, so don't expect to get anywhere fast. Public transport is limited; the special AD 122 bus covers the highlights (but only during summer), and local buses 10, 185, 602, and 681 follow parts of the same route.

EXPLORING BY FOOT OR BIKE

Hadrian's Wall Path meanders along the wall's entire length; it's a seven-day hike. Joining it for a mile or so is a great way to see the wall and stunning scenery. Try the section around Walltown, or at Corbridge where the path goes by the remains of a Roman garrison town. Hadrian's Cycleway, for bicyclists, follows roughly the same route.

SIGHTSEEING RESPONSIBLY

The wall is accessible but vulnerable. Don't climb on it, and never break off or remove anything. In muddy weather you're encouraged not to stand directly next to the wall, as over time this can make the soil unstable.

WALL TIMELINE

13

55 BC Julius Caesar invades what is now southern England, but does not stay. He names the island Britannia.

AD 41–50 Full-scale invasion. The Romans establish fortified towns across the south, including London.

75–79 The conquest of northern England is completed—but the Romans fail to take Caledonia (Scotland).

122 Emperor Hadrian orders the construction of a defensive wall along the territory's northern border.

208 After the Romans make another disastrous attempt to invade Caledonia, Hadrian's Wall is expanded.

410 The Romans leave Britain. Local tribes maintain the wall for at least a century.

1700s Stones from the ruined wall are plundered for road building.

1830s Local philanthropist John Clayton buys land around the wall to save it from further destruction.

1973 First Vindolanda tablets are found.

1987 Hadrian's Wall becomes a UNESCO World Heritage Site.

Updated by
Jack Jewers

For many Britons, the words "the Northeast" provoke a vision of near-Siberian isolation. But although there are wind-hammered, wide-open spaces and empty roads threading the wild high moorland, the Northeast also has simple fishing towns, small villages of remarkable charm, and historic abbeys and castles that are all the more romantic for their often-ruinous state. This is also where you'll find two of England's most iconic sights: the medieval city of Durham and the stark remains of Hadrian's Wall.

Even the remoteness can be relative. Suddenly, around the next bend of a country road, you may come across an imposing church, a tall monastery, or a Victorian country house. The value found in the shops and accommodations, the uncrowded beaches ideal for walking, and the friendliness of the people also add appeal. Still, outside of a few key sights, the Northeast is off the well-trodden tourist path.

Mainly composed of the two large counties of Durham and Northumberland, the Northeast includes English villages adjacent to the Scottish border area, renowned in ballads and romantic literature for feuds, raids, and battles. Fittingly, Durham Cathedral, the seat of bishops for nearly 800 years, has been described as "half church of God, half castle 'gainst the Scot." Hadrian's Wall, which marked the northern limit of the Roman Empire, stretches across prehistoric remains and moorland in this region. Not far north of Hadrian's Wall are some of the most interesting parts of Northumberland National Park. Steel, coal, railroads, and shipbuilding made prosperous towns such as Newcastle upon Tyne, which is now re-creating itself as a cultural center.

The region's 100 mi of largely undeveloped coast is one of the least visited and most dramatic shorelines in all Europe. Several outstanding castles perch on headlands and promontories along here, including Bamburgh, which according to legend was the site of Joyous Garde, the castle of Sir Lancelot du Lac.

NORTHEAST PLANNER

13

WHEN TO GO

The best time to see the Northeast is in summer. This ensures that the museums—and the roads—will be open, and you can take advantage of the countryside walks that are one of the region's greatest pleasures. Rough seas and inclement weather make it dangerous to swim at any of the beaches except in July and August; even then, don't expect warm water. At the end of June, Alnwick hosts its annual fair, with a medieval market, art shows, and concerts. The Durham Regatta also takes place in June. The Northumberland Traditional Music Festival runs over two weeks in October. Winter here is not for the fainthearted. The weather is terrible, but there's nowhere else in England so beautiful and so remote.

PLANNING YOUR TIME

If you're interested in exploring Hadrian's Wall and the Roman ruins, you will probably want to base yourself at a guesthouse in or around Hexham. From there you can easily take in Housesteads and the other local landmarks. Anywhere in this area is within easy reach of Durham, with its lovely ancient buildings, or Newcastle, with its excellent museums. Romantics will want to spend a day or two driving up the coast to take in the incredible castle views.

GETTING HERE AND AROUND

AIR TRAVEL

Newcastle's airport (a 15-minute drive from the city center) has flights from British and European cities.

Contact Newcastle Airport (✉ *Off A696* ☎ *0871/882–1121* ⊕ *www. newcastleairport.com*).

BUS TRAVEL

National Express and Megabus (book online to avoid premium-line charges) travel to Durham and Newcastle and leave from London's Victoria Coach Station, but the journey takes between six and eight hours, more than twice the time it takes by train. (It can be considerably cheaper, especially if you book months in advance.) Connecting services to other parts of the region leave from those cities. Traveline has information. The Explorer Northeast Pass (£8) allows unlimited one-day travel on most local bus and Metro train services in the region and is available from the bus driver or local bus or Metro stations.

Contacts Explorer Northeast Pass (⊕ *www.explorernortheast.co.uk*). **Megabus** (☎ *0900/160–0900* ⊕ *www.megabus.com/uk*). **National Express** (☎ *0871/781–8178* ⊕ *www.nationalexpress.com*). **Traveline** (☎ *0871/200–2233* ⊕ *www. traveline.org.uk*).

CAR TRAVEL

If you're headed to small villages, remote castles, or Hadrian's Wall, traveling by car is the best alternative. The A1 highway links London and Newcastle (five to six hours). The scenic route is the A697, which branches west off A1 north of Morpeth. For the coast, leave the A1 at Alnwick and follow the minor B1340 and B1339 for Craster, Seahouses, and Bamburgh. Holy Island is reached from the A1.

TRAIN TRAVEL

Within England, the train is still the best way to reach this region. East Coast runs the train service from London to the Northeast. The average travel times from London are three hours to Durham and Newcastle. From Newcastle, you can catch local trains to Alnwick, Corbridge, Hexham, and Carlisle; these journeys take about a half hour. National Rail Enquiries has information.

Contacts **East Coast** (☎ 0845/722–5333 ⊕ www.eastcoast.co.uk). **National Rail Enquiries** (☎ 0845/748–4950 ⊕ www.nationalrail.co.uk).

RESTAURANTS

Make sure to sample fine local meats and produce. Look for restaurants that serve game from the Kielder Forest, local lamb from the hillsides, salmon and trout from the rivers, and shellfish, crab, and oysters from the coast. Outside the cities, the region lags somewhat behind other parts of England in terms of good places to eat, although there are special spots to be found. Aside from the ubiquitous chains, the best bets are often small country pubs that serve the traditional, hearty fare associated with the region. Don't wait until 9 pm to have dinner, though, or you may have a hard time finding a place that is still serving.

HOTELS

The large hotel chains don't have much of a presence in the Northeast, outside the few cities. Instead, you can expect to find country houses converted into welcoming hotels, old coaching inns that still greet guests after 300 years, and cozy bed-and-breakfasts convenient to hiking trails. Many budget accommodations close in winter.

WHAT IT COSTS IN POUNDS					
	£	££	£££	££££	£££££
Restaurants	under £10	£10–£14	£15–£19	£20–£25	Over £25
Hotels	under £70	£70–£120	£121–£160	£161–£220	Over £220

Restaurant prices are per person for a main course or equivalent combination of smaller dishes at dinner excluding tax. Hotels prices reflect the rack rate of a standard double room for two people in high season, including 20% V.A.T. Check online for off-season rates and special deals or discounts.

VISITOR INFORMATION

Contacts **Hadrian's Wall Country** (⊕ www.hadrians-wall.org). **Visit North East England** (☎ 01271/336182 ⊕ www.visitnorthumbria.com).

DURHAM, NEWCASTLE, AND ENVIRONS

Durham—the first major northeastern town on the main road up from London—is by far the region's most interesting historic city. Its cobblestone streets and towering cathedral make it a charming place to visit. The city is surrounded on all sides by scenic countryside, ruined castles, and isolated villages. Newcastle, though, is the region's biggest, liveliest, and most cosmopolitan city. Most other towns in the area made

Rounded arches and columns with zigzag patterns are hallmarks of the Romanesque style at Durham Cathedral.

their fortunes during the Industrial Revolution and have since subsided into slow decline.

DURHAM

250 mi north of London, 15 mi south of Newcastle.

The great medieval city of Durham, seat of County Durham, stands dramatically on a rocky spur, overlooking the countryside. Its cathedral and castle, a World Heritage Site, rise together on a wooded peninsula almost entirely encircled by the River Wear (rhymes with "beer"). For centuries these two ancient structures have dominated Durham—a thriving university town, the Northeast's equivalent of Oxford or Cambridge. Steep, narrow streets overlooked by perilously angled medieval houses and 18th-century town houses make for fun exploring. In the most attractive part of the city, near the Palace Green and along the river, people go boating, anglers cast their lines, and strollers walk along the shaded paths. For great views, take a short stroll along the River Wear and cross the 17th-century Prebends Footbridge. You can return to town via the 12th-century Framwellgate Bridge.

Despite the military advantages of its location, Durham was founded surprisingly late, probably in about the year 1000, growing up around a small Saxon church erected to house the remains of St. Cuthbert. It was the Normans, under William the Conqueror, who put Durham on the map, building the first defensive castle and beginning work on the cathedral. From here, Durham's prince-bishops, granted almost dictatorial local powers by William in 1072, kept a tight rein on the county,

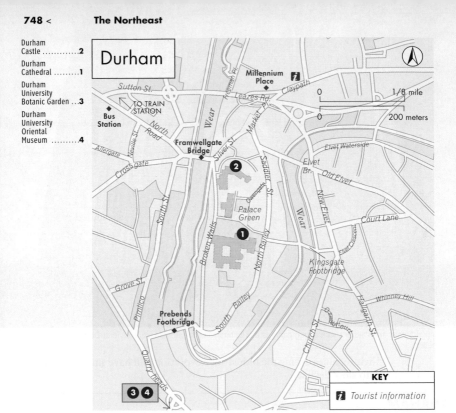

coining their own money and maintaining their own laws and courts; not until 1836 were these rights finally restored to the English Crown.

GETTING HERE AND AROUND

East Coast trains from London's King's Cross Station arrive at the centrally located Durham Station once an hour during the day. The journey takes about three hours. Trains from York arrive three to four times an hour; that journey takes roughly 50 minutes. A handful of National Express and Megabus buses make the seven-hour trip from London daily. Local Bus 40 links parking lots and the train and bus stations with the cathedral. Between 10 and 4 Monday through Saturday, cars are charged £2 (on top of parking charges) to enter the Palace Green area. You pay the charge at an automatic tollbooth on exiting. ■TIP➔ If you don't have change for the tollbooth, press the button and an attendant will take down your information. Pay later, in person or over the phone, at the Parking Shop. Don't forget or you'll be fined by the police.

ESSENTIALS

Visitor Information Durham (✉ *Millennium Pl.* ☎ *0191/384–3720* ⊕ *www. thisisdurham.com*). **Parking Shop** (✉ *56 North Rd.* ☎ *0191/384-6633* ⊕ www. durham.gov.uk).

13

EXPLORING

Durham Castle. Facing the cathedral across Palace Green, the castle commands a strategic position above the River Wear. It has required many renovations and repairs through the ages because of less-than-stable foundations, but it remains an impressive pile. For almost 800 years the castle was the home of successive prince-bishops; from here they ruled large tracts of northern England and kept the Scots at bay. Henry VIII first curtailed the bishops' independence, although it wasn't until the 19th century that the prince-bishops finally had their powers annulled. They abandoned the castle, turning it over to University College, one of several colleges of the University of Durham (founded 1832), the oldest in England after Oxford and Cambridge. You can visit the castle only on a 45-minute guided tour—usually three times daily (times vary, so call ahead). ⊠ *Palace Green* ☎ *0191/334–3800* ⊕ *www.dur.ac.uk/university.college* ☑ *£5* ☉ *Early Oct.–late June, weekdays at 2, 3, and 4; late June–early Oct., weekdays at 10, 11, and 2.*

■ QUICK BITES

Down a narrow alleyway between the castle and the river, the tiny 9 Altars Café (⊠ *River St.* ☎ *0191/374–1120*) is an excellent spot for coffee and sandwiches. Eat on the river terrace if the weather's good—and you're lucky enough to get a seat.

Fodor'sChoice
★

Durham Cathedral. A Norman masterpiece in the heart of the city, the cathedral is an amazing vision of solidity and strength, a far cry from the airy lightness of later, Gothic cathedrals. Construction began in about 1090, and the main body was finished in about 1150. The round arches of the nave and the deep zigzag patterns carved into them typify the heavy, gaunt style of Norman, or Romanesque, building. The technology of Durham, however, was revolutionary. This was the first European cathedral to be given a stone, rather than a wooden, roof. When you consider the means of construction available to its builders—the stones that form the ribs of the roof had to be hoisted by hand and set on a wooden structure, which was then knocked away—the achievement seems staggering.

The origins of the cathedral go back to the 10th century. In 995 monks brought to this site the remains of St. Cuthbert, which had been removed from the monastery at Lindisfarne after a Viking raid in 875. Soon the wealth attracted by Cuthbert's shrine paid for the construction of a cathedral. The bishop's throne here was claimed to be the loftiest in medieval Christendom; the miter of the bishop is the only one to be encircled by a coronet, and his coat of arms is the only one to be crossed with a sword as well as a crosier.

Upon entering the cathedral, it's impossible not to notice the enormous bronze **Sanctuary Knocker,** shaped like the head of a ferocious mythological beast, mounted on the massive northwestern door. By grasping the ring clenched in the animal's mouth, medieval felons could claim sanctuary; cathedral records show that 331 criminals sought this protection between 1464 and 1524. An unobtrusive tomb at the west end of the cathedral, in the Moorish-influenced **Galilee Chapel,** is the final resting place of the **Venerable Bede,** an 8th-century Northumbrian monk whose contemporary account of the English people made him the country's first reliable historian—and one of the most important figures in Early English literature.

While the cathedral itself is free, most of its actual treasures are behind a turnstile. Head down to the undercroft for the **Treasures of St. Cuthburt,** a permanent exhibit that contains **St. Cuthbert's Shrine** as its centerpiece. There's more than enough here to justify the price of admission, including various illuminated manuscripts and the saint's original coffin (his bones now rest beneath a simple marble slab). Admission includes a 20-minute film on the cathedral's history, an exhibit about the building of the cathedral that's aimed at kids, and the medieval monks' dormitory (now a library). In good weather you can climb the tower, although this costs extra. There's also a decent restaurant and a lovely shop. ⊠ *Palace Green* ☎ *0191/386–4266* ⊕ *www.durhamcathedral.co.uk* ✉ *£5 donation requested; Treasures of St. Cuthburt, monks' dormitory, and exhibits £5; tower £5; guided tours £4* ⊙ *Cathedral mid-July–Aug., daily 7:30 am–8 pm; Sept.–mid-July, Mon.–Sat. 7:30–6, Sun. 7:45–5:30. Tower Apr.–Sept., Mon.–Sat. 10–4; Oct.–Mar., Mon.–Sat. 10–3. Treasures of St. Cuthburt Mon.–Sat. 10–4:30, Sun. 2–4:30. Choral evensong service Tues.–Sat. at 5:15, Sun. at 3:30. Guided tours Apr.–Oct., daily at 11 and 2.*

> ## DURHAM'S REGATTA
>
> The pretty River Wear winds through Durham, curving beneath the cathedral and castle. In mid-June each year the city hosts the prestigious Durham Regatta, Britain's oldest rowing event. Three hundred racing crews compete in events, including races for single sculls and teams of eight.

Durham University Botanic Garden. This 18-acre park contains a plethora of plant life from Asia, Africa, and the Americas. The greenhouses shelter rare specimens, such as the giant Amazonian water lily. Almost every weekend in summer there are family-friendly events ranging from picnics to storytelling sessions. ⊠ *South Rd.* ☎ *0191/334–5521* ⊕ *www.dur.ac.uk/botanic.garden* ✉ *£4* ⊙ *Mar.–Oct., daily 10–5; Nov.–Feb., daily 10–4.*

Durham University Oriental Museum. A 15-minute walk from the cathedral, this museum displays fine art- and craftwork from all parts of Asia. A recent renovation project has added the Ancient Egyptian Gallery, expanded the Chinese Gallery (with its notable collection of ceramics), and added a new lobby café. ⊠ *Elvet Hill off South Rd.* ☎ *0191/334–5694* ⊕ *www.dur.ac.uk/oriental.museum* ✉ *£1.50* ⊙ *Weekdays 10–5, weekends noon–5.*

WHERE TO EAT

£££
FRENCH

✕ **Bistro 21.** This fashionable restaurant, a few miles northwest of the center, is known for its eclectic menu of French classics with a modern twist. Signature dishes include sirloin steak with mustard, herbs, and anchovies, and braised Moroccan lamb with fruit-and-nut couscous. You can get here by taxi, or take Bus 43 to Durham Hospital and walk five minutes. ⊠ *Aykley Heads* ☎ *0191/384–4354* ⊕ *www.bistrotwentyone.co.uk* ⊙ *No dinner Sun.*

£££ ✕**Oldfields.** At this convivial restaurant, cheerful raspberry-hue walls
BRITISH and unfussy walnut furnishings create a nicely laid-back vibe that complements the excellent food. Organic vegetables and free-range meat,
sourced mostly from the surrounding region, are a specialty. The seasonal menu features such dishes as roast chicken, mutton hot pot, and
rabbit and crayfish pie. ✉ *18 Clay Path* ☎ *0191/370–9595* ⊕ *www.
oldfieldsrealfood.co.uk.*

£££ ✕**Zen.** The mix-and-match decor of this popular eatery—part classi-
THAI cal Chinese restaurant, part Indonesian nightclub—reflects the variety of the Asian cuisine on the menu. Delicious (and huge) plates of
Thai curries and noodle dishes share the menu with Mongolian duck,
teriyaki beef, and peppered pork with five-spice gravy. There are also
steaks for the less adventurous. ✉ *Court La.* ☎ *0191/384–9588* ⊕ *www.
zendurham.co.uk.*

13

WHERE TO STAY

For expanded reviews, visit Fodors.com.

££ ⊡**Georgian Town House.** At the top of a cobbled street overlooking the
B&B/INN cathedral and castle, this family-run guesthouse has small, snug bedrooms with pleasant city views. **Pros:** great location; jovial owners;
laid-back atmosphere. **Cons:** small rooms; odd design choices. ✉ *11
Crossgate* ☎ *0191/386–8070* ⊕ *www.thegeorgiantownhouse.co.uk* ⇄ *8
rooms* ⚿ *In-room: no a/c* ▭ *No credit cards* ☾ *Closed last wk of Dec.*
⎮○⎮ *Breakfast.*

££–£££ ⊡**Lumley Castle Hotel.** This is a real Norman castle, right down to the
B&B/INN dungeons and maze of dark flagstone corridors. **Pros:** great for antiques
Fodor's Choice lovers; good online deals. **Cons:** it's easy to get lost down the wind-
★ ing corridors. ✉ *B1284, Chester-le-Street* ☎ *0191/389–1111* ⊕ *www.
lumleycastle.com* ⇄ *59 rooms* ⚿ *In-room: no a/c, Wi-Fi. In-hotel: restaurant, bar* ⎮○⎮ *Some meals.*

££ ⊡**Seven Stars Inn.** This early-18th-century coaching inn is cozy and sur-
HOTEL prisingly affordable. **Pros:** cozy lounge; reasonable rates; pleasant staff.
Cons: on a main road; two-night minimum stay in high season; guests
must return by midnight. ✉ *High St. N, Shincliffe Village* ☎ *0191/384–
8454* ⊕ *www.sevenstarsinn.co.uk* ⇄ *8 rooms* ⚿ *In-room: no a/c, Wi-Fi.
In-hotel: restaurant, some pets allowed* ⎮○⎮ *Breakfast.*

£ ⊡**Three Tuns Hotel.** In central Durham, this 16th-century inn has echoes
HOTEL of its solid country past. **Pros:** nice mix of the old and the new; lots of
atmosphere. **Cons:** it's a bit of a walk to use the pool and health club.
✉ *New Elvet* ☎ *0191/386–4326* ⊕ www.swallow-hotels.com/hotels/
three-tuns-hotel ⇄ *50 rooms* ⚿ *In-room: no a/c. In-hotel: restaurant,
bar, parking* ⎮○⎮ *Breakfast.*

NIGHTLIFE AND THE ARTS

Durham's nightlife is geared to university students.

The **Half Moon** (✉ *New Elvet* ☎ *0191/374–1918*) is an atmospheric old
pub with a lively local crowd.

The **Market Tavern** (✉ *27 Market Pl.* ☎ *0191/386–2069*) draws fans of
real ales.

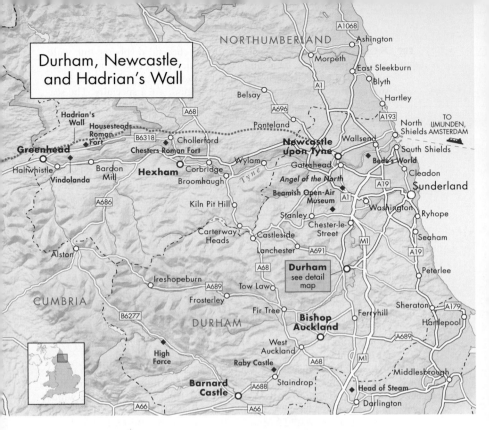

Durham, Newcastle,
and Hadrian's Wall

SHOPPING

Bramwells Jewellers (✉ *24 Elvet Bridge* ☎ *0191/386–8006*) has its own store specialty, a pendant copy of the gold-and-silver cross of St. Cuthbert.

The food and bric-a-brac stalls in **Durham Indoor Market** (✉ *Market Pl.* ☎ *0191/384–6153* ⊕ *www.durhammarkets.co.uk*), a Victorian arcade, are open Monday through Saturday 9–5. A farmers' market is held on the third Thursday of every month.

SPORTS AND THE OUTDOORS

Brown's Boat House (✉ *Elvet Bridge* ☎ *0191/386–3779*) rents rowboats April through early November and offers short cruises all year.

BISHOP AUCKLAND

10 mi southwest of Durham.

For 700 years, between the 12th and 19th century, the powerful prince-bishops of Durham had their country residence in Auckland Castle, in the town of Bishop Auckland. When finally deprived of their powers in 1836, the bishops left Durham and made Bishop Auckland their official home. You can tour the house as well as nearby Raby Castle.

13

GETTING HERE AND AROUND

Bishop Auckland is just off the A1 motorway from London (260 mi) or Durham (13 mi). There's no direct train service here from London or Durham. However, you can take a train from either city to Darlington and change. The journey takes about three hours from London and one hour from Durham. National Express offers a regional bus service between Bishop Auckland and Durham. This trip takes about 30 minutes.

ESSENTIALS

Visitor Information Bishop Auckland (⊠ *Town Hall, Market Pl.* ☎ *01388/604922* ⊕ *www.thisisdurham.com*).

EXPLORING

Auckland Castle. Arguably the greatest of the prince-bishops of Durham's properties is this episcopal palace, which you enter through an elaborate stone arch. Much of what's on view today dates from the 16th century, although the limestone-and-marble chapel, with its dazzling stained-glass windows, was built in 1665 from the ruins of a 12th-century hall. ■**TIP→** Don't miss the paintings by the 17th-century Spanish artist Zurbarán of Jacob and his 12 sons in the Long Dining Room. ⊠ *Off Market Pl.* ☎ *01388/601627* ⊕ *www.auckland-castle.co.uk* ☑ *£4* ⊙ *Easter–June and Sept., Mon. and Sun. 2–5; July and Aug., Mon. and Wed. 11–5, Sun. 2–5; park daily 7 am–sunset.*

☼ ★ **Head of Steam.** A family-friendly museum in nearby Darlington tells the story of the early days of rail travel. The town gained fame in 1825, when George Stephenson piloted his steam-powered *Locomotion* along newly laid tracks the few miles to nearby Stockton, thus kick-starting the railway age. Set in an abandoned 1842 train station, the museum has interactive exhibits and big steam trains that are great for kids; antique engines and scale models help bring history to life. There's also a café and children's activity room. Darlington is 13 mi southeast of Bishop Auckland, on A68. Train connections run roughly every two hours. ⊠ *North Road Station, Station Rd., Darlington* ☎ *01325/460532* ⊕ *www.darlington.gov.uk* ☑ *£5* ⊙ *Apr.–Sept., Tues.–Sun. 10–4; Oct.–Mar., Wed.–Sun. 11–3:30.*

★ **Raby Castle.** The stone battlements and turrets of moated Raby Castle, once the seat of the powerful Nevills and currently the home of the 11th baron Barnard, stand amid a 200-acre deer park and ornamental gardens. Charles Nevill supported Mary, Queen of Scots in the 1569 uprising against Elizabeth I; when the Rising of the North failed, the estate was confiscated. Dating mostly from the 14th century (using stone plundered from Barnard Castle) and renovated in the

UPSTAIRS, DOWNSTAIRS

Gorgeous Raby Castle acts as a living museum for castle life through the centuries. It's especially good at juxtaposing life as a servant with life as a lord. In the lord's dining room, rich red carpets and patterned silk wallpaper glow under a soaring, intricately carved ceiling. Downstairs, the servants had their meals in the bare, low-ceilinged medieval servants' hall, sitting at a rough pine table on hard wooden benches. Ouch!

The 18th-century mechanical silver swan at the Bowes Museum swallows a silver fish each day.

18th and 19th centuries, the luxuriously furnished castle has displays of art and other treasures. Rooms in wonderfully elaborate Gothic Revival, Regency, and Victorian styles are open for viewing. Raby Castle is 7 mi southwest of Bishop Auckland, 19 mi southwest of Durham. ✉ *A688, 1 mi north of Staindrop* ☎ *01833/660202* ⊕ *www.rabycastle. com* ✍ *Castle, park, and gardens £9.50; park and gardens £5* ⊘ *May, June, and Sept., Sun.–Wed. 1–4:30 (park 11–5:30); July and Aug., Sun.–Fri. 1–4:30 (park 11–5:30). Also open Sat. on bank holiday weekends.*

BARNARD CASTLE

14 mi south of Bishop Auckland, 25 mi southwest of Durham.

The handsome market town of Barnard Castle has sights of its own and can also serve as a base for venturing into the Teesdale Valley to the northwest. Its unusual butter-market hall (known locally as Market Cross), surmounted by an old fire-alarm bell, marks the junction of the streets Thorngate, Newgate, and Market Place. Stores, pubs, and cafés line these thoroughfares. In 1838 Charles Dickens stayed at the **King's Head Inn** here while doing research for his novel *Nicholas Nickleby*. The local tourist office has a free "In the Footsteps of Charles Dickens" leaflet.

GETTING HERE AND AROUND

Barnard Castle is about a 20-minute drive from Bishop Auckland on A688. Bus 20 departs from Bishop Auckland at roughly 15 minutes past the hour; the trip to Barnard Castle takes an hour. The town is small, and walking is an easy way to explore.

ESSENTIALS

Visitor Information Barnard Castle (✉ *Woodleigh, Flatts Rd.* ☎ *01833/696356* ⊕ *www.teesdalediscovery.com*).

EXPLORING

Barnard Castle. The substantial ruins of Barnard Castle, which gave its name to the town, cling to an aerie overlooking the River Tees. From the outside it looks satisfyingly complete from the right angle; inside, however, it's mostly just a shell. Inside you can see parts of the 14th-century Great Hall and the cylindrical, 13th-century tower, built by the castle's original owners, the Anglo-Scottish Balliol family. Look for the figure of a carved boar high on the wall of the inner courtyard—it was the family emblem of King Richard III (1452–85), placed there during his reign in honor of the elevated status he bestowed upon the castle. ✉ *Off Galgate* ☎ *01833/638212* ⊕ *www.english-heritage.org. uk* ✍ *£4.30* ⊗ *Apr.–late Sept., daily 10–6; Oct.–Mar., weekends 10–4.*

★ **Bowes Museum.** This vast French-inspired château a mile west of the town center was built between 1862 and 1875 to house the art and artifacts accumulated by philanthropists John and Josephine Bowes. Highlights include paintings by Canaletto, El Greco, Francisco Goya, and François Boucher, and 18th-century French furniture. ∎ **TIP→** Don't miss the extraordinary 18th-century mechanical swan, which catches and swallows a silver fish every day at 2. The café serves light meals and afternoon tea. ✉ *Up Newgate, follow signs from town center* ☎ *01833/690606* ⊕ *www.thebowesmuseum.org.uk* ✍ *£8* ⊗ *Daily 10–5.*

High Force. The Upper Teesdale Valley's elemental nature shows its most volatile aspect in the sprays of England's highest waterfall, the 72-foot High Force. From the roadside parking lot it's a 10-minute walk through woodland to the massive rocks over which the water tumbles. Access is sometimes closed in bad weather. The waterfall is 15 mi northwest of Barnard Castle. ✉ *Off B6277* ☎ *01833/640209* ✍ *£1.50; parking £2* ⊗ *Easter–Oct., daily 9:30–5; Nov.–Easter, open but unattended (honesty box for fee).*

WHERE TO EAT

£ ✗ **Market Place Teashop.** A nicely old-fashioned air pervades this 17th-
BRITISH century building on the main square. Waitresses clad in striped uniforms serve such dishes as cottage pie (made with ground beef and meat gravy, topped with mashed potato). There's also lasagna, sandwiches, and vegetarian options. ✉ *29 Market Pl.* ☎ *01833/690110* ⊕ *www.teashop-barnard-castle.co.uk* ⊗ *Closed Sun. except afternoons Apr.–Oct. No dinner.*

NEWCASTLE UPON TYNE

16 mi north of Durham, 42 mi northeast of Barnard Castle.

Durham may have the glories of its castle, cathedral, and university, but the liveliest city of the Northeast is Newcastle, currently reinventing itself as a regional center for culture and modern architecture after years of decline. Settled since Roman times on the Tyne River, the city made its fortune twice—first by exporting coal and later by shipbuilding. As a 19th-century industrial center, Newcastle had few equals in Britain, showing off its wealth in grand Victorian buildings lining the broad streets. Some of these remain, particularly on Grey Street. The cluster of bridges (older and newer) crossing the Tyne is a quintessential city sight.

Much of the regeneration since the early 1990s has been based around the Gateshead Quays. Here the Baltic Centre for Contemporary Art and the pedestrian-only Millennium Bridge—the world's first tilting bridge, which opens and shuts like an eyelid—have risen from industrial wasteland.

GETTING HERE AND AROUND

Newcastle Airport, a 15-minute drive from the city center, has flights from British and European cities. Metro trains connect to the center. The A1 highway links London and Newcastle (five to six hours).

East Coast trains from London's King's Cross take about three hours. National Express and Megabus have service from London's Victoria Coach Station several times a day for the six- to eight-hour trip.

Newcastle has a good public transportation system. Its Metro light-rail network is easy to use, well signposted, and has stops near most sights. Buses go all the places Metro doesn't reach.

ESSENTIALS

Visitor Information Newcastle upon Tyne (⊠ *8–9 Central Arcade, Market St.* ☎ *0191/277–8000* ⊕ *www.newcastlegateshead.com*).

EXPLORING
TOP ATTRACTIONS

★ ***Angel of the North.*** If you're approaching Newcastle from the south, 8 mi from the city center, at the junction of A1(M) and A1 at Gateshead, stands England's largest—and one of its most popular—sculptures, the *Angel of the North.* Created by Antony Gormley in 1998, the rust-color steel sculpture is a sturdy, abstract human figure with airplane-like wings rather than arms. It stands 65 feet tall and has a horizontal wingspan of 175 feet. There's parking nearby, signposted on A167.

Baltic Centre for Contemporary Art. Formerly a grain warehouse and now the country's largest national gallery for contemporary art outside London, Baltic presents intriguing changing exhibitions. ⊠ *Gateshead Quays, S. Shore Rd.* ☎ *0191/478–1810* ⊕ *www.balticmill.com* ⊠ *Free* ⊗ *Tues. 10:30–6, Wed.–Mon. 10–6.*

★ **Beamish Open-Air Museum.** Made up of buildings moved from elsewhere in the region, this sprawling complex explores the way people in the Northeast lived and worked from the early 1800s to the early 1900s. A streetcar takes you around the site and to a reconstructed 1920s shopping street with a dentist's office, pub, and grocery store. Other attractions include a small manor house, a railroad station, and a coal mine. In summer, a steam train makes a short run. ■TIP➔ Allow at least a half day if you come in summer, less in winter. The museum is about 8 mi south of Newcastle, off the main road to Durham. ⊠ *Off A693, between villages of Chester-le-Street and Stanley* ☎ *0191/370–4000* ⊕ *www.beamish.org.uk* ⊠ *£16 Apr.–Oct., £8 Nov.–Mar.* ⊗ *Apr.–*

Oct., daily 10–5; Nov.– Mar., Tues.–Thurs. and weekends 10–4; last admission at 3.

★ **Great North Museum.** This modern museum contains an impressive collection of ancient archaeological finds, plus galleries on natural history and astronomy. Highlights include artifacts left behind by the Roman builders of Hadrian's Wall, ancient Egyptian mummies, and a reconstruction of the 1st-century Temple of Mithras at Carrawburgh. This place isn't designed for kids, but there's plenty here to amuse them, including a working planetarium and a life-size model of a *Tyrannosaurus rex*. A short walk takes you to the smaller **Hatton Gallery,** which holds artwork by Francis Bacon and Kurt Schwitters. It includes a masterpiece by the latter called *Merzbarn Wall*, commissioned by New York's Museum of Modern Art after World War II to replace an earlier version destroyed in Germany. The museum is just off the Great North Road, and five minutes from the Haymarket Metro station. ⊠ *Barras Bridge* ☎ *0191/222–6765* ⊕ *www.twmuseums.org.uk/greatnorthmuseum* 🖾 *Free* ☉ *Mon.–Sat. 10–5, Sun. 2–5.*

QUICK BITES

The popular, 70-year-old art deco **Tyneside Coffee Rooms** (⊠ **10 Pilgrim St.** ☎ **0191/227-5520**), on the second floor above the Tyneside Cinema, makes an intriguing place to stop for teas, coffee, and a good, unfussy lunch. It's open daily until 10 pm (11 pm on Sunday).

★ **Laing Art Gallery.** One of the Northeast's finest art museums merits at least an hour's visit for its selection of British art. Some of the most extraordinary paintings are those by 19th-century local artist John Martin, who produced dramatic biblical landscapes. The Pre-Raphaelites are on show, too, and the Art on Tyneside exhibition traces 400 years of local arts, highlighting glassware, pottery, and engraving. ⊠ *Higham Pl. near John Dobson St.* ☎ *0191/232–7734* ⊕ *www.twmuseums.org.uk/laing* 🖾 *Free* ☉ *Mon.–Sat. 10–5, Sun. 2–5.*

WORTH NOTING

Bede's World. Four miles east of Newcastle, this site holds substantial monastic ruins, the church of St. Paul, and a small museum reflecting the long tradition of religion and learning that began here in AD 681, when the first Saxon church was established on the site. The Venerable Bede, deemed to be England's earliest historian, moved into the monastery when he was age seven and remained until his death in AD 735. You can gain a sense of medieval life from the reconstructed farm buildings and the rare breeds of pigs and cattle on the 11-acre Anglo-Saxon farm. From the southern exit traffic circle at South Tyne tunnel, take A185 to South Shields and follow signs to St. Paul's Church and Jarrow Hall; or use Bus 526 or 527, or the Bede/Jarrow Metro stop (20-minute walk). ⊠ *Church Bank, Jarrow* ☎ *0191/489–2106* ⊕ *www.bedesworld.co.uk* 🖾 *£5.50* ☉ *Mon.–Sat. 10–5, Sun. noon–5; last admission 1 hr before closing.*

★ **Discovery Museum.** Reconstructed streets and homes lead you from Roman times to the present day in this engaging museum. Kids will like its interactive approach to teaching Newcastle's history, and maritime buffs will be most thrilled by galleries showing off the town's

Sir Norman Foster designed the Sage Gateshead performance venue, an emblem of Newcastle's revival.

maritime and industrial achievements, including the *Turbinia*. Built in 1894, it was once the fastest ship in the world, and the first to be powered by steam turbines. ✉ *Blandford Sq.* ☎ *0191/232–6789* ⊕ *www. twmuseums.org.uk/discovery* 🎫 *Free* ☉ *Mon.–Sat. 10–5, Sun. 2–5.*

Tyne Bridge. By the old quayside, this bridge (built in 1929) is the symbol of Newcastle, and is one of seven bridges spanning the river in the city.

WHERE TO EAT AND STAY

£££
MODERN BRITISH
★

✕ **Café 21.** A Newcastle classic, this sleek brasserie has been a favorite for business lunches and romantic dinners for years. Warm wood, leather banquettes, and crisp white table linens lend a polished look. The menu focuses on modern versions of classic British cuisine, peppered with European and Asian influences; try the confit of duck with Lyonnaise potatoes, or the monkfish and tiger prawn and coconut curry. Desserts such as custard tart with nutmeg ice cream are excellent. The three-course early-bird menu (£20; 5:30–7 and all evening Sunday) is a good way to try it all. ✉ *Trinity Gardens, Quayside* ☎ *0191/222–0755* ⊕ *www.cafetwentyone.co.uk.*

£–££
B&B/INN

🛏 **Clifton House Hotel.** A cozier alternative to the gleaming modern city-center hotels that are rather *en trend* in Newcastle, this friendly B&B offers a touch of quiet, old-fashioned elegance. **Pros:** pleasant Victorian building; sweet hosts; quiet location. **Cons:** too far from the action for some; no restaurant; not wheelchair accessible. ✉ *46 Clifton Rd.* ☎ *0191/273–0407* ⊕ *www.cliftonhousehotel.com* 🛏 *11 rooms* 🖧 *In-room: no a/c, Wi-Fi. In-hotel: bar* 🍽 *Breakfast.*

£££££–£££££
HOTEL
★

🛏 **Jesmond Dene House.** Occupying a sprawling 19th-century mansion in the northeastern part of the city, this hotel is surrounded by lush gardens and filled with polished oak floors, huge windows, and wandering staircases. **Pros:** beautiful light-filled rooms; lovely gardens. **Cons:** the restaurant is popular, so you need to book in advance. ✉ *Jesmend Dene Rd.* ☎ *0191/212–3000* ⊕ *www.jesmonddenehouse.co.uk* ⇆ *40 rooms* ♿ *In-room: a/c, Internet. In-hotel: restaurant, bar, pool, gym, spa* �‖ *Breakfast.*

£££–££££
HOTEL
📷 **Malmaison.** Converted from an old riverside warehouse, this member of a glamorous, design-conscious chain sits right beside the pedestrian Millennium Bridge. **Pros:** interesting building; gorgeous restaurant; irresistible claw-foot tubs. **Cons:** bar and restaurant get very crowded. ✉ *Quayside* ☎ *0191/245–5000* ⊕ *www.malmaison.com* ⇆ *116 rooms* ♿ *In-room: a/c, Wi-Fi. In-hotel: restaurant, bar, gym, spa, some pets allowed.*

13

NIGHTLIFE AND THE ARTS

The upstairs terrace of the **Pitcher and Piano** (✉ *108 Quayside* ☎ *0191/ 232–4110*), a popular pub with floor-to-ceiling windows, is the perfect viewing point for the Millennium Bridge.

★ The **Sage Gateshead** (✉ *West St., Gateshead Quays* ☎ *0191/433–4661* ⊕ *www.thesagegateshead.org*) hosts concerts—jazz, world, pop, classical, folk, and rock—in a curving, modern building designed by Sir Norman Foster.

Theatre Royal (✉ *Grey St.* ☎ *0844/811–2121* ⊕ *www.theatreroyal. co.uk*), the region's most established theater, has high-quality productions and is also a venue for opera and dance.

HADRIAN'S WALL COUNTRY

A formidable line of Roman fortifications, Hadrian's Wall was the Romans' most ambitious construction in Britain. The land through which the old wall wanders is wild and inhospitable in places, but that seems only to add to the powerful sense of history it evokes. Museums and information centers along the wall make it possible to learn as much as you want about the Roman era.

HADRIAN'S WALL

73 mi from Wallsend, north of Newcastle, to Bowness-on-Solway, beyond Carlisle.

GETTING HERE AND AROUND

The A69 roughly follows Hadrian's Hall, although sometimes it's a few miles in either direction. The best sections of the wall are near the narrower B6318, including Vindolanda, Houseteads Roman Fort, and Chesters Roman Fort. There is a small railway station at Hexham, with frequent trains from Newcastle.

A special Hadrian's Wall Bus offers day passes (£8) for service between Wallsend and Carlisle, stopping at Newcastle, Hexham, and the major Roman forts. The service runs daily from April to October and on Sunday throughout the year. Another bus runs daily from Wallsend to Bowness, and another from Hexham to Vindolanda (£3). The aptly named AD122 public bus runs between Newcastle and Carlisle during the summer months, stopping near all the major destinations along the way. Buses 10, 185, 602, and 681 also pass parts of the wall.

ESSENTIALS

Visitor Information Hadrian's Wall Bus (☎ *01434/322002* ⊕ *www.hadrians-wall.org*). **Hexham Tourism Information Centre** (✉ *Wentworth Car Park* ☎ *01434/652220* ⊕ *www.visitnortheastengland.com*). **Once Brewed National Park Visitor Centre** (✉ *In Northumberland National Park, B6318, Once Brewed* ☎ *01434/344396* ⊕ *www.northumberland-national-park.org.uk* ⊗ *Mid-Mar.–Nov., daily 9:30–5*).

EXPLORING

Fodor'sChoice
★

Hadrian's Wall. Dedicated to the Roman god Terminus, the massive span of Hadrian's Wall once marked the northern frontier of the Roman Empire. Today, remnants of the wall wander across pastures and hills, stretching 73 mi from Wallsend ("Wall's End," north of Newcastle) in the east, to Bowness-on-Solway in the west. The wall is a World Heritage Site, and excavating, interpreting, repairing, and generally managing the Roman remains a Northumbrian growth industry. ■TIP→ At Chesters, Housesteads, and Vindolanda, and at the Roman Army Museum near Greenhead, you get a good introduction to the life led by Roman soldiers. In summer most sites sponsor talks, Roman drama, and festivals; local tourist offices and the sites have details.

At Emperor Hadrian's command, three legions of soldiers began building the wall in AD 122, and finished it in four years. It was constructed by soldiers and masons after repeated invasions by troublesome Pictish tribes from what is now Scotland. During the Roman era it was the most heavily fortified wall in the world, with walls 15 feet high and 9 feet thick; behind it lay the vallum, a ditch about 20 feet wide and 10 feet deep. Spaced at 5-mi intervals along the wall were massive forts (such as those at Housesteads and Chesters), which could house up to 1,000 soldiers. Every mile was marked by a thick-walled milecastle (a fort that housed about 30 soldiers), and between each milecastle were two turrets, each lodging four men who kept watch. For more than 250 years the Roman army used the wall to control travel and trade and to fortify Roman Britain against the barbarians to the north.

During the Jacobite Rebellion of 1745, the English dismantled much of the Roman wall and used the stones to pave what is now the B6318 highway. The most substantial stretches of the remaining wall are between Housesteads and Birdoswald (west of Greenhead). Running through the southern edge of Northumberland National Park and along the sheer escarpment of Whin Sill, this section is also an area of dramatic natural beauty. The ancient ruins, rugged cliffs, dramatic vistas, and spreading pastures make it a good area for hiking. For information about the wall, check out ⊕ *www.hadrians-wall.org*.

SPORTS AND THE OUTDOORS

BIKING

Hadrian's Cycleway (⊕ *www.cycle-routes.org/hadrianscycleway*), between Tynemouth and Whitehaven, follows the River Tyne from the east coast until Newcastle, before chasing the entire length of Hadrian's Wall. It then continues west to the Irish Sea. Maps and guides are available at the Tourist Information Centre in Newcastle or online.

Bikes in the **Bike Shop** (✉ *16–17 St. Mary's, Hexham* ☎ *01434/601032* ⊕ *www.thebikeshophexham.com*) cost £15 per day.

Purple Mountain Bike Centre (✉ *Kielder Castle, Kielder* ☎ *01434/250532* ⊕ *www.purplemountain.co.uk*) rents mountain bikes for £15 to £25 per day.

HIKING

Hadrian's Wall Path (☎ *01434/322022* ⊕ *www.nationaltrail.co.uk/ hadrianswall*), one of Britain's national trails, runs the entire 73-mi length of the wall. If you don't have time for it all, take one of the less-challenging circular routes. One of the most scenic but also most rugged sections is the 12-mi western stretch between Sewingshields and Greenhead.

13

HEXHAM

22 mi west of Newcastle, 31 mi northwest of Durham.

The area around the busy market town of Hexham is a popular base for visiting Hadrian's Wall. Just a few miles from the most significant remains, it's a bustling working town, but it has enough historic buildings and winding medieval streets to warrant a stop in its own right. First settled in the 7th century, around a Benedictine monastery, Hexham later became a byword for monastic learning, famous for its book painting, sculpture, and singing.

GETTING HERE AND AROUND

The A1 highway links London and the region (five to six hours). No major bus companies travel here, but the AD122 tourist bus from Newcastle and Carlisle does. East Coast trains take about three hours to travel from London's King's Cross to Newcastle. From there, catch a local train.

Hexham is a small, walkable town. It has infrequent local bus service, but you're unlikely to need it. If you're driving, park in the lot by the tourism office and walk into town. The tourism office has free maps and will point you in the right direction.

ESSENTIALS

Visitor Information Hexham Tourism Information Centre (✉ *Wentworth Car Park* ☎ *01434/652220* ⊕ *www.visitnortheastengland.com*).

EXPLORING

Chesters Roman Fort. This cavalry fort in a wooded valley on the banks of the North Tyne River was known as Cilurnum in Roman times, when it protected the point where Hadrian's Wall crossed the river. You approach the fort directly from the parking lot, and, although the site cannot compete with Housesteads in setting, the recently renovated museum here holds a fascinating collection of Roman artifacts, including statues of river and water gods, altars, milestones, iron tools, weapons, and jewelry. The military bathhouse by the river is supposedly the best-preserved Roman structure of its kind in the British Isles. The fort is 4 mi north of Hexham. ⊠ *B6318, ½ mi southwest of Chollerford* ☎ *01434/681379* ⊕ *www.english-heritage.org.uk* 🎫£5 ⊙ *Apr.–Sept., daily 10–6; Oct.–Mar., daily 10–4.*

★ **Hexham Abbey.** A site of Christian worship for more than 1,300 years, ancient Hexham Abbey forms one side of the town's main square. Inside, you can climb the 35 worn stone "night stairs," which once led from the main part of the abbey to the canon's dormitory, to overlook the whole ensemble. Most of the current building dates from the 12th and 13th centuries, and much of the stone, including that of the Anglo-Saxon crypt, was taken from the Roman fort at Corbridge. Note the portraits on the 16th-century wooden rood screen and the four panels from a 15th-century *Dance of Death* in the sanctuary. In May the abbey is a venue for the **Hexham Book Festival** (⊕ *www.hexhambookfestival. co.uk*), which draws speakers from the worlds of politics and the arts. ⊠ *Beaumont St.* ☎ *01434/602031* ⊕ *www.hexhamabbey.org.uk* 🎫 *Requested donation £3* ⊙ *Daily 9:30–5. Crypt daily at 11 and 3:30.*

Market Place. Since 1239, this has been the site of a weekly market, now held each Tuesday. Crowded stalls are set out under the long slate roof of the Shambles; other stalls, protected only by bright awnings, take their chances with the weather.

Old Gaol. Dating from 1330, Hexham's Old Gaol, across Market Place from the abbey, houses fascinating exhibits about border history. Photographs, models, a house interior, and weapons tell the story of the "Middle March," the medieval administrative area governed by a warden and centered on Hexham. A glass elevator takes you to four floors, including the dungeon. ⊠ *Hallgate* ☎ *01434/652439* 🎫 *£3* ⊙ *Mar.–Oct., daily 10–4:30; Nov. and Feb., Mon., Tues., and Sat. 10–4:30.*

WHERE TO EAT AND STAY

£££££
BRITISH

✕**Langley Castle.** Rescued from decline by a professor from the United States in the mid-1980s, this lavish 14th-century castle hotel with turrets and battlements offers an elegant fine-dining experience. The baronial dining room is romantic, with little candlelit alcoves draped in rich fabric. Choose from an excellent prix fixe menu of traditional English dishes—perhaps the roast lamb rump with pea puree, or pork medallions with foie gras, rhubarb, and ginger jus. There's also a lighter (and cheaper) snack menu. Langley Castle is 6 mi west of Hexham. ⊠ *A686, Langley-on-Tyne* ☎ *01434/688888* ⊕ *www.langleycastle.com.*

£
B&B/INN

🏠 **Dene House.** This former farmhouse on 9 acres of lovely countryside has beamed ceilings and homey rooms with pine pieces and colorful quilts. **Pros:** tasty breakfasts; warm atmosphere. **Cons:** no restaurant. ⊠ *B6303, Juniper* ☎ *01434/673413* ⊕ *www.denehouse-hexham.co.uk* 🛏 *3 rooms, 1 with bath* ♿ *In-room: no a/c, no TV, Wi-Fi. In-hotel: bar* ⏹ *Breakfast.*

££
B&B/INN

🏠 **Montcoffer.** A short hop from Hadrian's Wall, this cozy, whitewashed guesthouse is actually a beautifully converted stable. **Pros:** big rooms; helpful owners. **Cons:** it gets booked up early; no restaurant. ⊠ *Bardon Mill* ☎ *01434/344138* ⊕ *www.montcoffer.co.uk* 🛏 *3 rooms* ♿ *In-room: no a/c* ⏹ *No credit cards* ⏹ *Breakfast.*

££   🖼 **Shieldhall Guesthouse.** This lovely 19th-century farmhouse and its
B&B/INN original outbuildings were once home to the family of landscaper Capa-
★   bility Brown. **Pros:** lots of peace and quiet; dinners are exceptional.
Cons: well outside town; need a car to get around. ⊠ *Off B6342, about
15 mi northeast of Hexham, Wallington* ☎ *01830/540387* ⊕ *www.
shieldhallguesthouse.co.uk* 🛏 *3 rooms* ⚭ *In-room: no a/c. In-hotel:
restaurant* ❨◎❩ *Breakfast.*

NIGHTLIFE AND THE ARTS

The **Queen's Hall Arts Centre** (⊠ *Beaumont St.* ☎ *01434/652477* ⊕ *www.
queenshall.co.uk*) presents theater, dance, and art exhibitions.

13

GREENHEAD

18 mi west of Hexham, 49 mi northwest of Durham.

Tiny Greenhead has the Roman Army Museum, an informative Hadrian's Wall site. Other important sites are nearby, too.

GETTING HERE AND AROUND

Greenhead is on the A69 and B6318. The nearest train station is 3 mi
east, in Haltwhistle.

EXPLORING

Fodor's Choice **Housesteads Roman Fort.** If you have time to visit only one Hadrian's Wall
★   site, Housesteads Roman Fort, Britain's most complete example of a
Roman fort, is your best bet. It includes an interpretive center, views of
long sections of the wall, the excavated 5-acre fort itself, and a small
but interesting museum containing statues and other items uncovered at
the fort. The steep, 10-minute walk up from the parking lot to the site
rewards the effort, especially for the sight of the wall disappearing over
hills and crags into the distance. Excavations have revealed remains of
granaries, gateways, barracks, a hospital, and the commandant's house.
The fort is 11 mi east of Greenhead, and about 35 mi northwest from
Durham. ⊠ *B6318* ☎ *01434/344363* ⊕ *www.english-heritage.org.uk*
🎫 *£5* ⊙ *Apr.–Sept., daily 10–6; Oct.–Mar., daily 10–4.*

Once Brewed National Park Visitor Centre. In Northumberland National
Park, about ½ mi north of Vindolanda, this center has informative displays about Hadrian's Wall and can advise about local walks. ⊠ *Military
Rd. (B6318), Once Brewed* ☎ *01434/344396* ⊕ *www.northumberland-
national-park.org.uk* 🎫 *Free* ⊙ *Apr.–Oct., daily 9:30–5; Nov.–Mar.,
weekends 10–3.*

Roman Army Museum. At the garrison fort of Carvoran, near the village,
this museum makes an excellent introduction to Hadrian's Wall. Full-
size models and excavations bring this remote outpost of the empire to
life; authentic Roman graffiti adorn the walls of an excavated barracks.
A recent renovation has added more artifacts and a 3-D film that puts it
all into historical context. Opposite the museum, at Walltown Crags on
the Pennine Way (one of Britain's long-distance national hiking trails),
are 400 yards of the best-preserved section of the wall. ⊠ *Off B6318,
1 mi northeast of Greenhead* ☎ *01697/747485* ⊕ *www.vindolanda.
com* 🎫 *£5; £10 for joint ticket with Vindolanda* ⊙ *Mar. and Oct., daily
10–5; Apr.–Sept., daily 10–6.*

The rose displays at Alnwick Garden have a romantic view of nearby Alnwick Castle.

Vindolanda. This great garrison fort, 8 mi east of Greenhead, holds the remains of eight successive Roman forts and civilian settlements, which have provided intriguing information about daily life in a military compound. Most of the visible remains date from the 2nd and 3rd centuries, and excavations are always under way. A reconstructed Roman temple, house, and shop provide context, and the museum displays rare artifacts such as writing tablets. A full-size reproduction of a section of the wall gives a sense of its massiveness. ⊠ *Near Bardon Mill* ☎ *01434/344277* ⊕ *www.vindolanda.com* ✉ *£6; £10 for joint ticket with Roman Army Museum* ⊙ *Mid.–late Mar. and Oct., daily 10–5; Apr.–Sept., daily 10–6; call to confirm times in winter. Last admission 45 mins before closing.*

WHERE TO EAT AND STAY

££ ✕ **Milecastle Inn.** The snug traditional bar and restaurant of this remote,
BRITISH peaceful 17th-century pub make an excellent place to dine. Fine local
★ meat goes into its famous pies; take your pick from wild boar, duckling, or turkey, ham, and chestnut. Two cottages (three-night minimum stay) are available for rent. The inn is on the north side of Haltwhistle on B6318. ⊠ *Military Rd., Haltwhistle* ☎ *01434/321372* ⊕ *www.milecastle-inn.co.uk.*

£–££ ▦ **Holmhead Guest House.** Talk about a feel for history—this former
B&B/INN farmhouse in open countryside, graced with stone arches and exposed beams, is not only built *on* Hadrian's Wall but also *of* it. **Pros:** perfect for history buffs; close to Hadrian's Wall. **Cons:** rooms are a bit of a squeeze; you need a car out here. ⊠ *Off A69* ☎ *016977/47402* ⊕ *www.bandbhadrianswall.com* ⌂ *4 rooms, 8 beds, 1 apartment* ⌂ *In-room: no a/c, no TV. In-hotel: restaurant* ⦿ *Breakfast.*

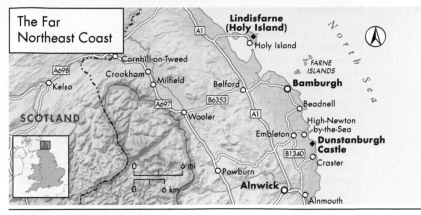

THE FAR NORTHEAST COAST

Extraordinary medieval fortresses and monasteries line the final 40 mi of the Northeast coast before England gives way to Scotland. Northumbria was an enclave where the flame of learning was kept alive during Europe's Dark Ages, most notably at Lindisfarne, home of saints and scholars. Castles abound, including the spectacularly sited Bamburgh and the desolate Dunstanburgh. The region also has some magnificent beaches, though because of the cold water and rough seas, they are far better for walking than swimming. The 3-mi walk from Seahouses to Bamburgh gives splendid views of the Farne Islands, and the 2-mi hike from Craster to Dunstanburgh Castle is unforgettable. A bit inland are a few other pretty towns and other castles.

ALNWICK

30 mi north of Newcastle, 46 mi north of Durham.

Dominated by a grand castle, the little market town of Alnwick (pronounced *ahn*-ick) is the best base from which to explore the dramatic coast and countryside of northern Northumberland.

GETTING HERE AND AROUND
If you're driving, Alnwick is just off the A1. Buses 501, 505 and 518 connect Alnwick with Newcastle, Berwick, and Morpeth. The nearest train station is 4 mi away in Alnmouth; trains travel between here and Newcastle roughly every hour and take 25 minutes.

ESSENTIALS
Visitor Information Alnwick (✉ *2 The Shambles* ☎ *01665/511333* ⊕ *www. visitalnwick.org.uk*).

EXPLORING
★ **Alnwick Castle.** The grandly scaled Alnwick Castle, on the edge of the
☁ town center, is known for its gardens as well as the castle itself. This is still the home of the dukes of Northumberland, whose family, the regal Percys, dominated the Northeast for centuries. Known as "the Windsor of the North," it has been remodeled several times since Henry de Percy adapted the original Norman keep. Nowadays Alnwick is used as a set for films, including the first two Harry Potter movies (the castle grounds

appear as the exterior of Hogwarts School). In contrast with the cold, formidable exterior, the interior has all the opulence of the palatial home it still is. You see only 6 of the more than 150 rooms, but among the treasures are a galleried library, niches with larger-than-life-size marble statues, and Venetian-mosaic floors. Kids appreciate Knights' Quest, a mock training school for knights where they get to dress up and complete interactive challenges, and Dragon's Quest, a labyrinth designed to teach a bit of medieval history while providing a few harmless scares. The castle's gardens (separate admission) include a modern, 260-foot-long stepped water cascade as well as ornamental gardens. ⊠ *Above junction of Narrowgate and Bailiffgate* ☎ *01665/511100* ⊕ *www.alnwickcastle.com* ▨ *£13; combined ticket with gardens £20* ◷ *Late Mar.–late Oct., daily 11–5; last admission at 4:15.*

★ .**Alnwick Garden.** A marvelous flight of fancy, Alnwick Garden represents
℧ the vision of the duchess of Northumberland. Centering on modern terraced fountains by Belgian designers Jacques and Peter Wirtz, the gardens include traditional features (shaded woodland walks, a rose garden) and funkier, kid-appealing elements such as a Poison Garden and a labyrinth of towering bamboo. It's also the location of one of the area's most unique restaurants, the Treehouse. ⊠ *Denwick La.* ☎ *01665/511350* ⊕ *www.alnwickgarden.com* ▨ *Apr.–Oct. £9.50; combined ticket with Alnwick Castle £20; Nov.–Mar. free* ◷ *Apr.–Oct., daily 10–dusk; Nov.–Mar., daily 11–3; last admission 45 mins before closing.*

Market Place. A weekly open-air market (every Saturday) has been held here for more than 800 years. Note the market cross, built on the base of an older cross; the town crier once made his proclamations from here. In the last week of June, this site is host to the **Alnwick Fair,** a festival noteworthy for the enthusiastic participation of locals in medieval costume. ⊠ *Off Market St.*

WHERE TO EAT AND STAY

£££ ✕ **The Treehouse.** You don't have to visit Alnwick Garden to eat at this
BRITISH extraordinary restaurant set among the treetops on the grounds. Though at first glance the location may seem gimmicky, the food exceeds expectations, with a menu strong on British classics. Typical dishes include honey-glazed duck with braised red cabbage and creamed potatoes, and fillet of plaice stuffed with zucchini and fennel. You can also grab a light evening meal at the bar (open the same nights as the restaurant). ⊠ *Alnwick Garden, Denwick La.* ☎ *01665/511852* ⊕ *www.alnwickgarden. com/eat* ◷ *No dinner Tues. and. Wed. No dinner Mon. Oct.–May.*

£–££ ⚏ **The Tower.** More of a "restaurant with rooms" than a guesthouse, this
HOTEL charming place around the corner from Alnwick Castle is a great find. **Pros:** relaxed atmosphere; sweet hosts; good restaurant. **Cons:** double rooms are on the small side. ⊠ *10 Bondgate Within* ☎ *01665/603888* ⊕ *www.tower-alnwick.co.uk* ⤶ *5 rooms* ⚫ *In-room: Wi-Fi, no a/c, no TV. In-hotel: restaurant* ⦿⎮ *Breakfast.*

SHOPPING

The **House of Hardy** (⊠ *A1* ☎ *01665/602771*), just outside Alnwick (from downtown, take A1 south to just beyond the traffic circle on the left, clearly marked), is one of Britain's finest stores for country sports. It has a worldwide reputation for handcrafted fishing tackle.

It's worth the scenic coastal walk to see the remote cliff-top ruins of Dunstanburgh Castle.

DUNSTANBURGH CASTLE

8 mi northeast of Alnwick.

GETTING HERE AND AROUND

The castle is 8 mi northeast of Alnwick, and is accessible only by footpaths from the villages of Craster or Embleton off the B1339 rural road. Follow the signs to the castle. To get here you'll need a car—there is no public transportation to or near the site.

EXPLORING

Dunstanburgh Castle. Perched romantically on a cliff 100 feet above the shore, these castle ruins can be reached along a windy, mile-long coastal footpath that heads north from the tiny fishing village of Craster. Built in 1316 by the earl of Lancaster as a defense against the Scots (or perhaps as a symbol of Lancaster's deteriorating relationship with King Edward II), and later enlarged by John of Gaunt, the powerful duke of Lancaster who virtually ruled England in the late 14th century, the castle is known to many from the popular paintings by 19th-century artist J.M.W. Turner. Several handsome sandy bays indent the coastline immediately to the north. ■TIP→ Take the time to sample the great kippers—salted and smoked herring—served in local pubs. ☎ 01665/576231 ⊕ *www.english-heritage.org.uk* ⊠ £4 ☺ *Apr.–Sept., daily 10–5; Oct., daily 10–4; Nov.–Mar., Thurs.–Mon. 10–4.*

BAMBURGH

14 mi north of Alnwick.

Tiny Bamburgh has a splendid castle, and several beaches are a few minutes' walk away.

GETTING HERE AND AROUND

Bamburgh can be reached by car on B3140, B3141, or B3142. Buses run from Alnwick to Bamburgh every two hours at quarter to the hour. The nearest train station is in Chathill, about 7 mi away.

EXPLORING

Bamburgh Castle. Especially stunning when floodlighted at night, Bamburgh Castle dominates the coastal view for miles. It's set atop a great crag to the north of Seahouses and overlooking a magnificent sweep of sand and sea backed by high dunes. A fortification of some kind has stood here since the 6th century, but the Norman castle was damaged during the 15th century. Much of the castle—the home of the Armstrong family since 1894—was restored during the 18th and 19th centuries, including the Victorian Great Hall, although the great Norman keep (central tower) remains intact. Exhibits include armor, porcelain, jade, furniture, and paintings. Parts of the castle are now rented as apartments. ⊠ *Off B3140, 3 mi north of Seahouses* ☎ *01668/214515* ⊕ *www.bamburghcastle.com* 🖃 *£8.50; parking £1* ☉ *Late Feb.–Oct., daily 10–5; Nov.–mid-Feb., weekends 11–4:30; last admission 1 hr before closing.*

WHERE TO EAT AND STAY

££££ ✕ **Waren House.** Six acres of woodland surround this Georgian house on a quiet bay between Bamburgh and Holy Island. The crisply elegant restaurant has romantic views of Holy Island when the trees are bare; three-course fixed-price dinners might include loin of monkfish with smoked salmon and rosemary cream, pork tenderloin with black pudding, followed by rhubarb mousse with mascarpone. Public areas are furnished comfortably in period style, and there are guest rooms (£££–££££) if you want to linger overnight. ⊠ *B1342, Waren Mill* ☎ *01668/214581* ⊕ *www.warenhousehotel.co.uk.*

BRITISH

££ 🏨 **Lord Crewe Hotel & Restaurant.** This cozy, stone-walled inn with oak beams sits in the heart of the village, close to Bamburgh Castle. **Pros:** in the center of the village; good restaurant. **Cons:** pub can get quite crowded. ⊠ *Front St.* ☎ *01668/214243* ⊕ *www.lordcrewe.co.uk* 📩 *18 rooms* ⅍ *In-room: no a/c. In-hotel: restaurant, bar, some pets allowed, some age restrictions* ☉ *Closed Dec. and Jan.* ⅋ *Breakfast.*

HOTEL

13

WALK AND BIKE

Wide vistas, quiet roads, and fresh air make hikes and bike rides appealing in the Northeast. Long-distance footpaths include the 90-mi Teesdale Way, which follows the River Tees through Barnard Castle and Middleton-in-Teesdale. Otherwise, the russet hills and dales of Northumberland National Park will please any serious walker. Bike routes to explore—in whole or in part—are the 220-mi Northumbria's Cycling Kingdom loop and the 81-mi Coast and Castles cycle route.

LINDISFARNE (HOLY ISLAND)

6 mi north of Bamburgh off the A1, 22 mi north of Alnwick.

★ Cradle of northern England's Christianity and home of St. Cuthbert, Lindisfarne (or Holy Island) has a religious history that dates from AD 635, when St. Aidan established a monastery here. Under its greatest abbot, the sainted Cuthbert, Lindisfarne became one of the foremost centers of learning in Christendom. Today you can explore the atmospheric ruined priory and a castle.

GETTING HERE AND AROUND

By car, the island is reached from the mainland via a long drive on a causeway that floods at high tide, so check when crossing is safe. The times, which change daily, are displayed at the causeway and printed in local newspapers. Traffic can be heavy; allow at least a half hour for your return trip. The only public transportation to Holy Island is run by Perryman's Buses. Bus 477 has limited service (two buses a day in summer, and not every day) from Berwick-upon-Tweed railroad station to the island.

ESSENTIALS

Bus Contacts Perryman's Buses (☏ *01289/308719* ⊕ *www.perrymansbuses. co.uk*).

EXPLORING

Lindisfarne Castle. Reached during low tide via a causeway from the mainland, this castle appears to grow out of the rocky pinnacle on which it was built 400 years ago, looking for all the world like a fairy-tale illustration. In 1903 architect Sir Edwin Lutyens converted the former Tudor fort into a private home that retains the original's ancient features. Across several fields from the castle is a walled garden designed by Gertrude Jekyll. Call ahead for times, as they change with the tides. ⊠ *Lindisfarne* ☏ *01289/389244* ⊕ *www.nationaltrust.org.uk* ⌑ *£6; garden only, £1.30* ☉ *Castle mid-Mar.–Oct., Tues.–Sun., call for hrs (generally 10–3 or noon–5); early Jan.–early Feb., alternate weekends 10–3; mid-Feb.–late Feb., daily 10–3; garden Tues.–Sun. dawn–dusk. Last admission 30 mins before closing.*

Lindisfarne Priory. In the year 875, Vikings destroyed the Lindisfarne community; only a few monks escaped, carrying with them Cuthbert's bones, which they reburied in Durham. The sandstone Norman ruins of Lindisfarne Priory, reestablished in the 11th century by monks from Durham, remain impressive and beautiful. A museum here displays Anglo-Saxon carvings. ⊠ *Lindisfarne* ☏ *01289/389200* ⊕ *www.english-heritage.org.uk* ⌑ *£4.80* ☉ *Feb. and Mar., daily 10–4; Apr.–Sept., daily 9:30–5; Oct., daily 9:30–4; Nov.–Jan., Mon. and weekends 10–2.*

Wales

WORD OF MOUTH

"Look into visiting the Gower Peninsula . . . and then push onward to Pembrokeshire for castles, villages, dramatic coast, and stunning beaches galore. Don't miss St David's for a visit to the smallest cathedral city in the U.K."

—Kate

WELCOME TO WALES

TOP REASONS TO GO

★ **Castle country:** Wales doesn't have a castle in each town, but it has a greater concentration than almost anywhere else in Europe—more than 600 in all.

★ **The Gower Peninsula:** This stretch of coastland near Swansea includes some of the region's prettiest beaches, as well as spectacular coastal views and medieval ruins.

★ **Snowdonia:** The biggest of the country's three national parks contains its highest mountain, Snowdon, as well as villages that recall the past.

★ **Brecon Beacons:** Moorlands, mountains, and valleys make up this rough and wild stretch of the Welsh midlands, as popular with hikers as it is with those who are just happy to take in the stunning views from the road.

★ **Hay-on-Wye:** This pretty village on the Welsh-English border has become world famous as a book lover's paradise; every street is lined with secondhand bookstores.

1 **South Wales.** Cardiff, the lively young capital city, is here, as are two very different national parks: the green, swooping hills of the Brecon Beacons and, in the far west, the sea cliffs, beaches, and estuaries of the Pembrokeshire Coast. Both are excellent for outdoor activities such as walking and mountain biking. Pembrokeshire has some of the region's best beaches.

2 **Mid- Wales.** The quietest part of Wales is home to scenic countryside, from rolling hills to more rugged mountains. Aberystwyth is a Victorian resort town on the coast, and Hay-on-Wye is a magnet for lovers of antiquarian bookstores.

3 **North Wales.** Wales's most famous castles are in its northern region. The cream of the crop is Caernarfon, a medieval palace dominating the waterfront on the Menai Strait. Conwy (castle and town) is popular, too. Snowdonia's mountains are a major draw, as is the quirky, faux-Italian village of Portmeirion.

GETTING ORIENTED

Wales has three main regions: South, mid-, and North. South Wales is the most varied and in just a few miles you can travel from Wales's bustling and cosmopolitan capital city, Cardiff, to the most enchanting old villages and historical sights. Mid-Wales is almost entirely rural (its largest town has a population of just 16,000), and it's fringed on its western shores by the arc of Cardigan Bay. Here you'll find mountain lakes, quiet roads, hill sheep farms, and traditional market towns. North Wales is a mixture of mountains, popular sandy beaches, and coastal hideaways. Although dominated by the rocky Snowdonia National Park, the north has a gentler, greener side along the border with England.

14

CASTLES IN WALES

You can't go far in Wales without seeing a castle: there are more than 600 of them. From crumbling ruins in fields to vast medieval fortresses with rich and violent histories, these castles rank among the most impressive in the world.

The first great wave of castle building arrived in England with the Norman Conquest in 1066. When the descendants of those first Anglo-Norman kings invaded Wales 200 years later, they brought with them their awesome skill and expertise. Through deviousness and brutal force, King Edward I (1239–1307) won control over the Welsh lords in the north and wasted no time in building mighty castles, including Caerphilly and Conwy, to consolidate his power. These became known as his "ring of iron." Wars came and went over the next few centuries, until, rendered obsolete by gunpowder and the changing ways of warfare, castles were destroyed or fell into disrepair. Only in the Victorian age, when castles became hugely fashionable, was there widespread acceptance of how important it was to save these historic structures for the nation.

The marquess of Bute transformed Cardiff Castle into a Victorian extravaganza (above); Caerphilly Castle's romantic moat (right, top); Raglan Castle's impressive ruins (right, bottom).

CASTLE GLOSSARY

Bailey: open grounds within a castle's walls.

Battlements: fortified ledge atop castle walls.

Keep: largest, most heavily defended castle building.

Moat: water-filled ditch around castle.

Motte: steep man-made hill on which a castle was often built.

Portcullis: iron drop-gate over entrance.

With such a dizzying array of castles, it can be hard to know where to start. Here are six of the best to help you decide. At the larger sites, buy a guidebook or take an audio or other tour so that you can best appreciate the remains of a distant era.

CAERNARFON CASTLE

Welsh naturalist Thomas Pennant (1726–98) called Caernarfon Castle "that most magnificent badge of our subjection." Built in 1283 on the site of an earlier castle, it is the most significant symbol of Edward I's conquest of Wales. It is also the best preserved of his "ring of iron" and, along with Edward's Beaumaris, Harlech, and Conwy castles in North Wales, is a UNESCO World Heritage Site. *North Wales*

CAERPHILLY CASTLE

Near Cardiff, this is the largest castle in Wales, and the second largest in Britain after Windsor Castle. Caerphilly's defenses included a man-made island and two huge lakes. The castle was ruined by centuries of warfare, although modern renovations have recaptured much of its former glory: kids love it. *South Wales*

CARDIFF CASTLE

Though the capital's titular castle has medieval sections, most of it is, in fact, a Victorian flight of fancy. Its most famous occupant, the third marquess of

Bute (1847–1900), was once the richest man in the world, and his love of the exotic led to the bizarre mishmash of styles. *South Wales*

CARREG CENNEN CASTLE

The great views over the countryside are worth the steep hike to this bleak, craggy clifftop fortress in the Brecon Beacons. This medieval stronghold was partially destroyed during the Wars of the Roses in the 15th century. Some interior rooms, hollowed out from the mountain itself, survive intact. *South Wales*

CONWY CASTLE

Imposing, if partially ruined, Conwy Castle with its eight towers captures like no other the feeling of sheer dominance that Edward I's citadels must have had over the landscape. The approach by foot over the River Conwy, along a 19th-century suspension bridge designed by Thomas Telford, makes for an awesome view. You can walk the ancient walls of Conwy town, which has places to eat and shop. *North Wales*

RAGLAN CASTLE

The boyhood home of Henry VII, the first Tudor king, Raglan is a small but impressive 15th-century castle, surrounded by a steep moat (one of the few in Wales that is still filled with water). Largely a ruin, it is relatively complete from the front, making for some irresistible, fairytale photo ops. *South Wales*

14

Updated by
Jack Jewers

Not as famous as Ireland, or as feted as Scotland, Wales isn't high on many people's itineraries when they first visit this region. And what a shame that is, for Wales is a land of dramatic national parks, such as the Brecon Beacons and Snowdonia; plunging, unspoiled coastlines, such as the Gower Peninsula and Cardigan Bay; and a host of awe-inspiring medieval castles. You won't encounter hordes of travelers, which is a big part of its appeal.

Vast swaths of Wales were untouched by the industrial boom of the 19th century. Although pockets of the country were given over to industries such as coal mining and manufacturing (both of which have all but disappeared), most of Wales remained unspoiled. The country is largely rural, and there are more than 10 million sheep—but only 3 million people. It has a Britain-as-it-used-to-be feel that can be hugely appealing.

Now is a great time to visit Wales. The country is reveling in a new political autonomy, little more than a decade old, that has brought with it a flourish of optimism and self-confidence. Wales loves being Wales, and that enthusiasm is infectious to the visitor. It also means that the tourism industry has grown in leaps and bounds, including some truly unique and special places to stay.

Although Wales is a small country—on average, about 60 mi wide and 170 mi north to south—looking at it on a map is deceptive. It's quite a difficult place to get around, with a distinctly old-fashioned road network and poor public transportation connections. To see it properly, you really need a car. The good news is that along the way you'll experience some beautiful drives. There are rewards to be found in the gentle folds of its valleys and in the shadow of its mountains.

Were some of the more remote attractions in Wales in, say, the west of Ireland, they'd be world famous, and overrun with millions of visitors. Here, if you're lucky, you can almost have them to yourself.

WALES PLANNER

WHEN TO GO

The weather in Wales, as in the rest of Britain, is a lottery. It can be hot in summer or never stop raining; generally it's cool and wet in spring and autumn, but they can be surprisingly warm and sunny. The only surefire rule is that you should be prepared for the unexpected.

Generally speaking, southwest Wales tends to enjoy a milder climate than elsewhere in Britain, thanks in part to the moderating effects of the Gulf Stream. In contrast, mountainous areas like Snowdonia and the Brecon Beacons can be chilly at any time of the year. Book far ahead for major festivals such as the literary Hay Festival, Brecon Jazz, and the Abergavenny Food Festival.

14

PLANNING YOUR TIME

First-time visitors often try to cover too much ground in too little time. It's not hard to spend half your time traveling between points that look close on the map, but take the better part of a day to reach. From Cardiff, it's easy to visit the Wye Valley, Brecon Beacons, and the Gower Peninsula. Along the North Wales coast, Llandudno or Lake Vyrnwy make good bases for the Snowdonia National Park.

The location of Wales lends itself to a border-hopping trip–in both directions. Well-known locations like Bath (near South Wales) and Chester (near North Wales) are no more than an hour from the Welsh border, and you can even take a ferry to Ireland if you want to go farther afield.

GETTING HERE AND AROUND

AIR TRAVEL

If you're arriving from the United States, London's Heathrow and Gatwick airports are generally the best options because of their large number of international flights. Heathrow (2 hours) is slightly closer than Gatwick (2½ hours), but both have excellent motorway links with South Wales. For North Wales, the quickest access is via Manchester Airport, with a travel time of less than an hour to the Welsh border.

Cardiff International Airport, 19 mi from downtown Cardiff, is the only airport in Wales with international flights, but these are mostly from Europe and Canada. A bus service runs from the airport to Cardiff's central train and bus stations.

Airports Cardiff International Airport (✉ *A4226, Rhoose* ☎ *01446/711111* ⊕ *www.cwlfly.com*). **Manchester Airport** (✉ *Near Junctions 5 and 6 of M56* ☎ *08712/710711* ⊕ *www.manchesterairport.co.uk*).

BUS TRAVEL

Most parts of Wales are accessible by bus, but long-distance bus travel takes a long time. National Express travels to all parts of Wales from London's Victoria Coach Station and also direct from London's Heathrow and Gatwick airports. The company also has routes into Wales from many major towns and cities in England and Scotland. Average travel times from London are 3½ hours to Cardiff, 4 hours to Swansea, 7 hours to Aberystwyth, and 4½ hours to Llandudno.

Wales's three national parks run summer bus services. In the North, the excellent Snowdon Sherpa runs into and around Snowdonia and links with main rail and bus services. The Pembrokeshire Coastal Bus Service operates in the Pembrokeshire Coast National Park, and the Beacons Bus serves the Brecon Beacons National Park.

Bus Contacts **Beacons Bus** (☎ 01874/624437 ⊕ www.breconbeacons.org). **National Express** (☎ 0871/781–8181 ⊕ www.nationalexpress.com). **Pembrokeshire Coastal Bus** (☎ 0845/345–7275 ⊕ www.pembrokeshirecoast.org. uk). **Snowdon Sherpa** (☎ 01766/770274 ⊕ www.eryri-npa.gov.uk).

CAR TRAVEL

To explore the Welsh heartland properly, you really need a car. Be prepared to take the scenic route: there are no major highways north of Swansea (which means virtually all of Wales). For the most part it's all back-roads, all the way. There are some stunning routes to savor: the A487 runs along or near most of the coastline, while the A44 and A470 both wind through mountain scenery with magnificent views.

FERRY TRAVEL

Two ferry ports that connect Britain with Ireland are in Wales. Regular daily ferries sail from Fishguard, in the southwest, and Holyhead, in the northwest. Stena Line and Irish Ferries are the two main companies, but Celtic Link runs some ferries between Rosslare and Cherbourg in France.

Celtic Link (☎ 00353/539–162–688 ⊕ www.irishferries.com).

Irish Ferries (☎ 00353/818–300–400 ⊕ www.irishferries.com).

Stena Line (☎ 0844/770–7070 ⊕ www.stenaline.co.uk).

TRAIN TRAVEL

Travel time on the First Great Western rail service from London's Paddington Station is about two hours to Cardiff and three hours to Swansea. Trains connect London's Euston Station with Mid-Wales and North Wales, often involving changes in cities as Birmingham. Travel times average between three and five hours. Regional train service covers much of South and North Wales but, frustratingly, there are virtually no direct connections between these regions—for example, to make the short trip between Cardiff and Aberystwyth you first have to make a connection to Shrewsbury. North Wales has a cluster of steam railways, but these are tourist attractions rather than a practical way of getting around. The mainline long-distance routes can be very scenic indeed, such as the Cambrian Coast Railway, running between Machynlleth and Pwllheli, and the Heart of Wales line, linking Swansea with London, Bristol, and Manchester.

Train Contacts **National Rail Enquiries** (☎ 0845/748–4950 ⊕ www.nationalrail.co.uk).

DISCOUNTS AND DEALS

For travel within Wales, ask about money-saving unlimited-travel tickets (such as the Freedom of Wales Flexi Pass, the North and Mid-Wales Rover, and the South Wales Flexi Rover), which include the use of bus services. A discount card offering a 20% reduction on each of the steam-driven Great Little Trains of Wales is also available. It costs £10 and is valid for 12 months.

The Cadw/Welsh Historic Monuments Explorer Pass is good for unlimited admission to most of Wales's historic sites. The seven-day pass costs £18 (single adult), £30 (two adults), or £36 (family ticket); the three-day pass costs £11.50, £18.50, and £26.50, respectively. Passes are available at any site covered by the Cadw program. All national museums and galleries in Wales are free.

Discount Information **Cadw/Welsh Historic Monuments** (✉ _Plas Carew, Unit 5–7, Cefn Coed, Parc Nantgarw, Treforest_ ☎ _01443/336000_ ⊕ _www. cadw.wales.gov.uk_). **Flexi Pass information** (☎ _0845/606–1660_ ⊕ _www. walesflexipass.co.uk_). **Great Little Trains of Wales** (✉ _Wharf Station, Tywyn_ ☎ _01654/710472_ ⊕ _www.greatlittletrainsofwales.co.uk_). **National Museums and Galleries of Wales** (⊕ _www.museumwales.ac.uk_).

TOURS

In summer there are day and half-day tour bus excursions to most parts of the country. In major resorts and cities, ask for details at a tourist information center or bus station.

The Wales Official Tourist Guide Association (WOTGA) uses only guides recognized by VisitWales and will create tailor-made tours. You can book a driver-guide or someone to accompany you as you drive.

Tour Information **Wales Official Tourist Guide Association** (☎ _01633/774796_ ⊕ _www.walestourguides.com_).

RESTAURANTS

Wales has developed a thriving restaurant scene over the last decade or so, and not just in major towns. Some truly outstanding food can be found in rural pubs and hotel restaurants. More and more restaurants are creating dishes using fresh local ingredients—Welsh lamb, Welsh Black beef, Welsh cheeses, and seafood from the Welsh coast—that show off the best of the region's cuisine.

HOTELS

A 19th-century dictum, "I sleeps where I dines," still holds true in Wales, where good hotels and good restaurants often go together. Castles, country mansions, and even disused railway stations are being transformed into interesting hotels and restaurants. Traditional inns with low, beamed ceilings, wood paneling, and fireplaces are often the most appealing places to stay. The best ones tend to be off the beaten track. Cardiff and Swansea have some large chain hotels, and, for luxury, some excellent spas have cropped up in the countryside. An added bonus is that prices are generally lower than they are for equivalent properties in the Cotswolds, Scotland, or southeast England.

14

WHAT IT COSTS IN POUNDS					
	£	££	£££	££££	£££££
Restaurants	under £10	£10–£14	£15–£19	£20–£25	over £25
Hotels	under £70	£70–£120	£121–£160	£161–£220	over £220

Restaurant prices are per person for a main course or equivalent combination of smaller dishes at dinner excluding tax. Hotels prices reflect the rack rate of a standard double room for two people in high season, including 20% V.A.T. Check online for off-season rates and special deals or discounts.

VISITOR INFORMATION

Contacts VisitWales Centre (☎ 08708/300306 ⊕ www.visitwales.com). **Wales in Style** (⊕ www.walesinstyle.com).

SOUTH WALES

The most diverse of Wales's three regions, the south covers the area around Cardiff that stretches southwest as far as the rugged coastline of Pembrokeshire. It's the most accessible part of the country, as the roads are relatively good and the rail network is more extensive than it is elsewhere in Wales. Pleasant seaside towns such as Tenby are within a four- to five hour drive of London; from Cardiff and Swansea you're never more than a half hour away from some gorgeous small villages.

Cardiff has had some success in reinventing itself as a cultured, modern capital, but Swansea and neighboring Newport have struggled to find their place in this postindustrial region. With a few exceptions, it's better to stick to the countryside in South Wales. The heart-stopping Gower Peninsula stretches along 14 miles of sapphire-blue bays and rough-hewn sea cliffs, and the Brecon Beacons National Park is an area of grassy mountains and craggy limestone gorges.

CARDIFF CAERDYDD

20 mi southwest of the Second Severn Bridge.

With a population of around 330,000, Cardiff is the largest and most important city in Wales. It's also one of the youngest cities in Europe: although a settlement has existed here since Roman times, Cardiff wasn't declared a city until 1905, and didn't become the capital until 50 years later. This is an energetic, youthful place, keen to show its new-found cosmopolitanism to the world. Cardiff is experiencing something of a cultural renaissance with the opening of the Wales Millennium Centre in Cardiff Bay.

For all its urban optimism, however, Cardiff is still a rather workaday town, with little to detain you for more than a day. See Cardiff Castle, the National Museum, wander Cardiff Bay, and maybe catch a show. Otherwise, it's a convenient base for exploring the nearby countryside.

Castell Coch looks medieval but don't be fooled: it's a delightful Victorian-Gothic fantasy.

GETTING HERE AND AROUND

The capital is a major transportation hub with good connections to other parts of South Wales and with England. Getting to Mid-Wales and North Wales is more difficult, as there's no direct north–south train route (you'll have to connect in Bristol or Shrewsbury) and north–south buses are painfully slow. From London, trains from Paddington to Cardiff Central take about two hours; National Express coaches take about three hours. Cardiff is easily accessible by the M4 motorway. You have to pay a toll of around £6 to cross the Severn Bridge.

TIMING

If you don't like crowds, avoid Cardiff during international rugby tournaments or other major sporting events.

ESSENTIALS

Visitor and Tour Information Cardiff (✉ *The Old Library, The Hayes* ☎ *029/2087–3573*✉ *Wales Millennium Centre, Bute Pl.* ☎ *029/2087–7927* ⊕ *www.visitcardiff.com*).

EXPLORING
TOP ATTRACTIONS

Caerphilly Castle. One of the most impressive fortresses in Wales was remarkable at the time of its construction in the 13th century. Built by an Anglo-Norman lord, the concentric fortification contained powerful inner and outer defenses. It was badly damaged during the English Civil War, although extensive 20th-century renovations have restored much of its former glory. The original Great Hall is still intact, and near the edge of the inner courtyard there's a replica of a trebuchet—a giant catapult used to launch rocks and other projectiles at the enemy.

Kids love exploring this castle, which is 7 mi north of Cardiff. ⊠ *Castle St., Caerphilly* ☎ *029/2088–3143* ⊕ *www.cadw.wales.gov.uk* 🖃 *£3.70* ⊙ *Apr.–June, Sept., and Oct., daily 9:30–5; July and Aug., daily 9:30–6; Nov.–Mar., Mon.–Sat. 10–4, Sun. 11–4.*

Cardiff Bay. Perhaps the most potent symbol of Cardiff's 21st-century rebirth, this upscale district is a 10-minute cab ride from Cardiff Central Station. Its museums and other attractions are clustered around the bay itself. The area can seem rather tranquil during the day, but buzzes with activity at night. Topped by a distinctive redbrick clock tower, the Victorian Gothic **Pierhead** (⊠ *Pierhead St., Cardiff Bay* ☎ *0845/010–5500* ⊕ *www.pierhead.org/en*) contains a good exhibition on Welsh history, including a few artifacts relating to the medieval struggle for independence from England. A large science-discovery center on the waterfront, **Techniquest** (⊠ *Stuart St., Cardiff Bay* ☎ *029/2047–5475* ⊕ *www. techniquest.org* 🖃 *£7* ⊙ *Weekdays 9:30–4:30, weekends 10–5*) has 160 interactive exhibits, a planetarium, and a science theater. Known locally as "The Armadillo" for its scaly exterior, the modern Wales Millennium Centre (⊠ *Bute Pl.* ☎ *029/2063–6400* ⊕ www.wmc.org. uk) is an extraordinary building, inside and out. The materials used in the construction of this arts complex are intended to represent "Welshness." (Slate is for the rocky coastline, for example, while wood is for its ancient forests). The huge words carved into the curving facade read "In These Stones Horizons Sing" in English and Welsh. Guided tours costing £5.50 depart about every hour.

Cardiff Castle. Bizarre but appealing, this castle was begun in the 11th century and has endured additions in every subsequent century. The result is an extraordinary mishmash of styles, from an austere Norman keep to an over-the-top Victorian mansion complete with turreted tower. William Burges (1827–81), an architect obsessed by the Gothic period, transformed the castle into an extravaganza of medieval color for the third marquess of Bute. The result was the Moorish-style ceiling in the Arab Room and the intricately carved shelves lining the Library. Look for the painting of the *Invisible Prince* in the Day Nursery; on first glance it's just a tree, but stare long enough and a man suddenly takes shape in the branches. The vast grounds, which include beautiful rhododendron gardens, are sometimes the setting for jousting in summer. ⊠ *Castle St.* ☎ *029/2087–8100* ⊕ *www.cardiffcastle.com* 🖃 *£11, £14 with guided tour* ⊙ *Mar.–Oct., daily 9–6; Nov.–Feb., daily 9–4.* Last admission 1 hr before closing.

Castell Coch. Perched on a hillside is this fairy-tale castle. The turreted Red Castle was built on the site of a medieval stronghold in the 1870s, about the time that Ludwig II of Bavaria was creating his castles in the mountains of Germany. This Victorian fantasy wouldn't look out of place among them. The castle was another collaboration of the third marquess of Bute and William Burges, who transformed Cardiff Castle. Burges created everything, including the whimsical furnishings and murals, in a remarkable exercise in Victorian-Gothic whimsy. ⊠ *A470, 4 mi north of Cardiff, Tongwynlais* ☎ *029/2081–0101* ⊕ *www.cadw. wales.gov.uk* 🖃 *£3.70* ⊙ Mar.–June, Sept., and Oct., daily 9:30–5; July and Aug., daily 9:30–6; Nov.–Feb., Mon.–Sat. 10–4, Sun. 11–4.

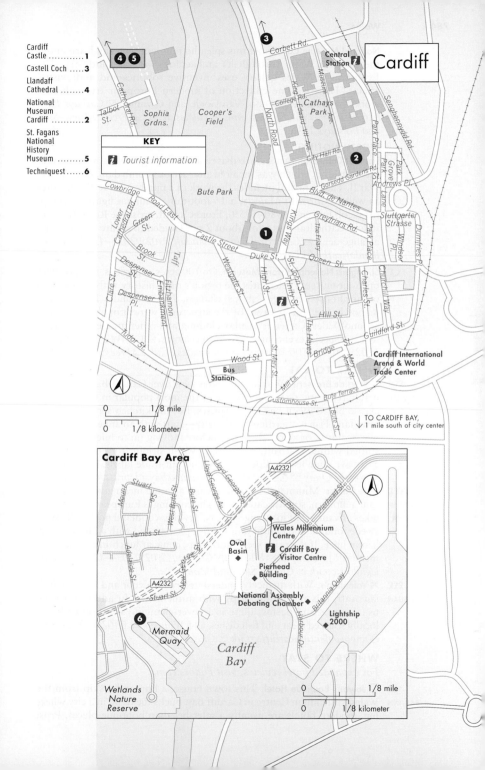

Cardiff

KEY

🛈 *Tourist information*

Corbett Rd.

Central Station 🛈

Cathedral Rd.

Talbot St.

Sophia Grdns.

Cooper's Field

Cathays Park

Sengbennydd Rd.

Museum Ave.

King Edward VII Ave.

College Rd.

North Road

City Hall Rd.

Gorsedd Gardens Rd.

Park Place

Park Grove

Park Lane

St. Andrews Pl.

2

Cowbridge Road East

Bute Park

Blvd. de Nantes

Greyfriars Rd.

Stuttgarter Strasse

Dumfries Pl.

Windsor Pl.

Lower Cathedral Rd.

Green St.

Castle Street

Kings Way

The Friary

Park Place

1

Duke St.

Queen St.

Brook St.

Taff Embankment

Elizhamon Embankment

Westgate St.

High St.

St. John St.

St. Trinity St.

Charles St.

Churchill Way

Despenser St.

Clare St.

Despenser Pl.

Tudor St.

🛈

Hill St.

The Hayes

Guildford St.

Wood St.

Bus Station

St. Mary St.

Bridge St.

Mill La.

Mary Ann St.

Cardiff International Arena & World Trade Center

Customhouse St.

Bute Terrace

Bute St.

↓ TO CARDIFF BAY,
↓ 1 mile south of city center

0   1/8 mile

0   1/8 kilometer

Cardiff Bay Area

A4232

Stuart St.

North Bute St.

Lloyd George Av.

Bute Place

Pierhead St.

Wales Millennium Centre ◆

James St.

Oval Basin

🛈 **Cardiff Bay Visitor Centre**

Pierhead Building ◆

Adelaide St.

A4232

Stuart St.

New George St.

National Assembly Debating Chamber ◆

Harbour Dr.

Britannia Quay

◆ **Lightship 2000**

6

Mermaid Quay

Cardiff Bay

Wetlands Nature Reserve

0   1/8 mile

0   1/8 kilometer

National Museum Cardiff. At this splendid museum, you can learn about the story of Wales through its archaeology, art, and industry. The Evolution of Wales gallery uses inventive robotics and audiovisual effects. There's a fine collection of modern European art, including works by Daumier, Renoir, Van Gogh, and Cézanne. ⊠ *Cathays Park* ☎ *029/2039–7951* ⊕ *www.museumwales.ac.uk* ⊠ *Free* ☉ *Tues.–Sun. and holidays 10–5.*

WORTH NOTING

Llandaff Cathedral. In a suburb that retains its village feeling, you can visit this cathedral, which was repaired after serious bomb damage in World War II. The cathedral includes the work of a number of Pre-Raphaelites as well as *Christ in Majesty,* a 15-foot-tall aluminum figure by sculptor Jacob Epstein (1880–1959). From Cardiff, cross the River Taff and follow Cathedral Road for about 2 mi. Guided tours are available by arrangement. ⊠ *Cathedral Close, Llandaff* ☎ *029/2056–4554* ⊕ *www. llandaffcathedral.org.uk.*

♺ **St. Fagans National History Museum.** On 100 acres of gardens, this excellent open-air museum celebrates the region's rural history with a collection of farmhouses, cottages, shops, chapels, a school, and a 16th-century manor house. All but two of the structures were brought here from around Wales. Galleries display clothing and other articles from daily life, and special events highlight local customs. ⊠ *Off A4232, St. Fagans* ☎ *029/2057–3500* ⊕ *www.museumwales.ac.uk* ⊠ *Free* ☉ *Daily 10–5.*

WHERE TO EAT

£££　✕ **Bayside Brasserie.** With its gorgeous view over Cardiff Bay, this unde-
FRENCH　niably romantic restaurant is one of the most popular in Cardiff. The
★　classic bistro menu has few surprises, but the kitchen serves up some tasty fare. Fish is a particular specialty—start with an appetizer of mussels, scallops, or smoked salmon before moving on to fillet of sea bass stuffed with citrus fruit, or a simple Welsh sirloin from the grill. The extensive wine list includes organic and fair-trade labels. ⊠ *Upper 14, Mermaid Quay* ☎ *029/2035–8444* ⊕ *www.baysidebrasserie.com.*

£££££　✕ **Le Gallois.** Minimalist furnishings and a varied menu give this restau-
MODERN BRITISH　rant a modern, sophisticated vibe. The cooking is European in style and
★　takes advantage of local ingredients. Try the woodland pork belly with swede fondant and chutney, or the fish pie flavored with a hint of zingy lemon juice. If the price seems too steep, come at lunchtime—the same menu is £10 cheaper. ⊠ *8 Romilly Crescent* ☎ *029/2034–1264* ⊕ *www. legallois.co.uk* ☉ *Closed Sun. and Mon.*

£££　✕ **Valentino's.** With its nicely understated rustic decor and friendly Ital-
ITALIAN　ian staff, this restaurant drips with authenticity. In addition to the usual pizzas and pastas, there is an ever-changing selection of fresh, locally sourced meat and fish dishes. ⊠ *5 Windsor Pl.* ☎ *029/2022–9697* ⊕ *www.valentinocardiff.co.uk* ☉ *Closed Sun.*

WHERE TO STAY

For expanded hotel reviews, visit Fodors.com.

££　🛏 **Jolyons Boutique Hotel.** This town house, a hop and a skip from the
B&B/INN　Wales Millennium Centre in Cardiff Bay, bucks the trend in a city where big, modern hotels are usually a safer bet than boutique places. **Pros:**

WALES: COUNTRY WITHIN A COUNTRY

Is Wales a nation, a state, or a country? The answer—confusingly—is yes, kind of, and yes and no. This requires some untangling.

Wales is a country within the United Kingdom, the same as Scotland and England. It has its own language—which you'll see on every signpost, though everybody also speaks English—its own flag, and sends its own teams to international sporting events like soccer's World Cup (but not the Olympics).

While Wales has the right to pass some of its own laws, it is not a sovereign nation. It shares the same head of state and has the same central government as England, Scotland, and Northern Ireland. It uses the same currency, and there are no restrictions for travelers who cross the English border.

In medieval times Wales was an independent nation, but lacked a single government or ruler. It was slowly annexed by England in a drawn-out series of wars and skirmishes. Although the Welsh retained a strong sense of their own national identity, by the middle of the 16th century their land was effectively part of England.

This was the case until 1997, when Tony Blair was elected prime minister on a platform that included semiautonomous legislatures for Wales and Scotland. Two years later, the Welsh Assembly passed the first laws made solely by and for Wales in more than 400 years.

You should always refer to Wales as a separate country. Be respectful of the fact that, when you cross the border, you're entering a place with a rich and proud history of its own.

14

loads of character; comfortable bar; in the heart of Cardiff Bay. **Cons:** 10-minute drive from the city center; no parking. ⊠ *Bute Crescent, Cardiff Bay* 🖀 *029/2048–8775* ⊕ *www.jolyons.co.uk* ⌔ *6 rooms* ⚙ *In-room: no a/c, Wi-Fi. In-hotel: bar, some age restrictions* ⦿ *Breakfast.*

££
B&B/INN

🎔 **Lincoln House Hotel.** Perhaps the best of the B&Bs on Cathedral Road—a handsome enclave of Victorian houses—this place close to the city center is a great find. **Pros:** good service; handy location; free parking. **Cons:** on a busy road; no restaurant; steps to climb. ⊠ *118 Cathedral Rd.* 🖀 *029/2039–5558* ⊕ www.lincolnhotel.co.uk ⌔ *24 rooms* ⚙ *In-room: no a/c, Wi-Fi. In-hotel: bar* ⦿ *Breakfast.*

££–£££
HOTEL

🎔 **Park Plaza.** Just off Cardiff's main shopping street, this contemporary hotel is popular with business travelers for its luxurious feel and convenient downtown location. **Pros:** central location; good spa; stainless-steel pool. **Cons:** a bit sterile. ⊠ *Greyfriars Rd.* 🖀 *029/2011–1111* ⊕ *www.parkplaza.com* ⌔ *129 rooms* ⚙ *In-room: Wi-Fi. In-hotel: restaurant, bar, pool, gym, spa* ⦿ *Breakfast.*

££££–£££££
HOTEL
★

🎔 **St. David's Hotel and Spa.** Natural light from a glass atrium floods this up-to-the-minute luxury hotel overlooking Cardiff Bay. **Pros:** a bit like staying on a cruise ship; relaxing spa. **Cons:** starkly modern decor lacks charm; out-of-the-way location. ⊠ *Havannah St.* 🖀 *029/2045–4045* ⊕ *www.stdavidshotelcardiff.co.uk* ⌔ *132 rooms* ⚙ *In-room: Internet. In-hotel: restaurant, pool, gym, spa, business center.*

NIGHTLIFE AND THE ARTS

NIGHTLIFE **Café Jazz** (✉ *21 St. Mary St.* ☎ *029/2038–7026* ⊕ www.cafejazzcardiff. com) presents live jazz five nights a week and has video monitors in the bar and restaurant so you can enjoy the on-stage action.

Clwb Ifor Bach (✉ *11 Womanby St.* ☎ *029/2023–2199 wwww.clwb.net*), whose name means "Little Ivor's Club," has three floors of eclectic music, from funk to folk to rock.

THE ARTS The huge **Cardiff International Arena** (✉ *Mary Ann St.* ☎ *029/2023–4500*) is Cardiff's premier venue for big-ticket music acts and other touring shows.

New Theatre (✉ *Park Pl.* ☎ *029/2087–8889* ⊕ *www.newtheatrecardiff. co.uk*), a refurbished Edwardian playhouse, presents big names, including the Royal Shakespeare Company, the National Theatre, and the Northern Ballet.

St. David's Hall (✉ *The Hayes* ☎ *029/2087–8500* ⊕ *www.stdavidshallcardiff. co.uk*), a popular venue, presents the Welsh Proms in July, attracting major international orchestras and soloists. It also stages rock, pop, jazz, and folk events.

SHOPPING

Canopied Victorian and Edwardian shopping arcades lined with specialty stores weave in and out of the city's modern shopping complexes.

Cardiff Antiques Centre (✉ *Royal Arcade* ☎ *029/2039–8891*), in an 1856 arcade, is a good place to buy vintage jewelry and accessories.

The traditional **Cardiff Market** (✉ *St. Mary St.* ☎ *029/2087–1214* ⊕ *www. cardiff-market.co.uk*) sells tempting fresh foods beneath its Victorian glass canopy.

Melin Tregwynt (✉ *26 Royal Arcade* ☎ *029/2022–4997* ⊕ *www. melintregwynt.co.uk*) is an elegant shop selling woolen clothing, bags, and cushions woven in an old Pembrokeshire mill.

ABERGAVENNY Y FENNI

28 mi north of Cardiff.

The market town of Abergavenny, just outside Brecon Beacons National Park, is a popular base for walkers and hikers. It has a ruined castle and is near the industrial history sites at Blaenavon.

GETTING HERE AND AROUND

Abergavenny is on the A40 road, about an hour's drive from Cardiff. Direct trains connect with Cardiff about every half hour and take about 45 minutes.

ESSENTIALS

Visitor Information Abergavenny (✉ *24 Monmouth Rd.* ☎ *01873/853254* ⊕ www.visitabergavenny.co.uk).

EXPLORING

Abergavenny Castle. Built early in the 11th century, this castle witnessed a tragic event on Christmas Day, 1176: the Norman knight William de Braose invited the neighboring Welsh chieftains to a feast, and in a crude

South Wales

attempt to gain control of the area, had them all slaughtered as they sat to dine. The Welsh retaliated and virtually demolished the castle. Most of what now remains dates from the 13th and 14th centuries. The castle's 19th-century hunting lodge houses an excellent museum of regional history. The re-creation of a Victorian Welsh farmhouse kitchen includes old utensils and butter molds. ⊠ *Castle St.* ☏ *01873/854282* ⊕ *www.abergavennymuseum.co.uk* ☒ *Free* ☉ *Mar.–Oct., Mon.–Sat. 11–1 and 2–5, Sun. 2–5; Nov.–Feb., Mon.–Sat. 11–1 and 2–4.*

Fodor'sChoice
★

Big Pit: National Coal Museum. For hundreds of years, South Wales has been famous for its mining industry. Decades of decline—particularly during the 1980s—left only a handful of mines in business. The mines around Blaenavon, a small town 7 mi south of Abergavenny, have been designated a UNESCO World Heritage Site, and this fascinating museum is the centerpiece. Ex-miners lead you 300 feet underground into a coal mine. You spend just under an hour examining the old stables, machine rooms, and exposed coalfaces. Afterward you can look around an exhibition housed in the old Pithead Baths, including an extraordinary section on child labor in British mines. ⊠ *Off A4043, Blaenavon* ☏ *01495/790311* ⊕ *www.museumwales.ac.uk* ☒ *Free* ☉ *Feb.–Dec., daily 9:30–5; Jan., weekends 9:30–5; underground tours 10–3. Last admission 1 hr before closing.*

Blaenavon Ironworks. Dating from 1789, Blaenavon Ironworks is a museum that traces the entire process of iron production in the late 18th century. Well-preserved blast furnaces, a water-balance lift used to transport materials to higher ground, and a terraced row of workers' cottages show how the business operated. ⊠ *A4043, Blaenavon* ☎ *01495/792615* ⊕ *www.cadw.wales.gov.uk* ⊠ *Free* ⊙ *Apr.–Oct., daily 10–5; Nov.–Mar., Fri. and Sat. 9:30–4, Sun. 11–4.*

★ **Raglan Castle.** Impressively complete from the front, majestically ruined within, Raglan was built in the 15th century and was the childhood home of Henry Tudor (1457–1509), who seized the throne of England in 1485 and became Henry VII. Raglan's heyday was relatively short-lived. The castle was attacked by Parliamentary forces during the English Civil War, and has lain in ruins ever since. The hexagonal Great Tower survives in reasonably good condition, as do a handful of rooms on the ground floor. ⊠ A40, *Raglan* ☎ *01291/690228* ⊕ *www.cadw. wales.gov.uk* ⊠ *£3.10* ⊙ *Mar.–June, Sept., and Oct., daily 9:30–5; July and Aug., daily 9:30–6; Nov.–Feb., Mon–Sat. 10 – 4, Sun. 11–4.*

WORTH NOTING

Tretower Court. A rare surviving example of a fortified medieval manor house, Tretower Court dates mostly from the 15th century. Buildings such as these were huge status symbols in their day, as they combined the security of a castle with the luxury of a manor house. On the grounds are the ruins of an earlier Norman castle. Tretower Court, restored in the 1930s, is outside the idyllic village of Crickhowell, 5 mi northwest of Abergavenny. ⊠ *A479, Crickhowell* ☎ *01874/730279* ⊕ *www.cadw. wales.gov.uk* ⊠ *£4* ⊙ *Mar.–Oct., daily 10–5; Nov.–Apr., Fri. and Sat. 10–4, Sun. 11–4.*

WHERE TO EAT AND STAY

For expanded hotel reviews, visit Fodors.com.

£££　✕ **Clytha Arms.** On the banks of the River Usk between Abergavenny
MODERN BRITISH　and Raglan, this eatery serves imaginative modern Welsh dishes in a relaxed setting. The menu makes great use of local Welsh ingredients in the leek-and-walnut soufflé and the loin of wild boar with an apple and calvados sauce. If the restaurant seems too pricey, eat at the bar—it's cheaper. ⊠ *Off B4598* ☎ *01873/840206* ⊕ *www.clytha-arms.com* ⊙ *Closed Mon.*

££–£££　 **Bear Hotel.** In the middle of town, this coaching inn is full of character.
HOTEL　**Pros:** friendly bar; good food. **Cons:** some rooms overlook the road; rooms vary in size; can get busy on weekends. ⊠ *A40, Crickhowell* ☎ *01873/810408* ⊕ *www.bearhotel.co.uk* ⤳ *35 rooms* ⚇ *In-room: no a/c, Wi-Fi. In-hotel: restaurant, bar, some pets allowed* ¶⊙∣ *Breakfast.*

£　 **The Lamb and Flag Inn.** This inn on the outskirts of Abergavenny
HOTEL　embodies what the British like to call "cheap and cheerful," meaning good-quality accommodations that cover all the basics. **Pros:** excellent value; good restaurant; free parking. **Cons:** a little way from the town center; few amenities. ⊠ *Brecon Rd.* ☎ *01873/857611* ⊕ *www.lambflag. co.uk* ⤳ *5 rooms* ⚇ *In-room: no a/c, Wi-Fi. In-hotel: restaurant, bar* ¶⊙∣ *Breakfast.*

£££ 🗔 **Llansantffraed Court Hotel.** Dating from 1400, this grand country house
HOTEL 4 mi southeast of Abergavenny is set on 20 acres of well-tended grounds
with lovely views of the Brecon Beacons. **Pros:** excellent food; peaceful
setting; great for anglers. **Cons:** tired decor; out-of-the-way location.
✉ *Old Raglan Rd., Clytha* ☎ *01873/840678* ⊕ *www.llch.co.uk* 🛏 *21
rooms* ☖ *In-room: no a/c, Wi-Fi. In-hotel: restaurant, bar, business center, some pets allowed* ¶⃝ *Breakfast.*

NIGHTLIFE AND THE ARTS
Held over a weekend in September, the **Abergavenny Food Festival**
(⊕ *www.abergavennyfoodfestival.com*) is a celebration for foodies and
a symbol of the growing interest in Welsh cuisine. There are demonstrations, lectures, special events, and, of course, a food market. Be
sure to sample the local cheese called Y Fenni, flavored with a piquant
combination of mustard seeds and ale.

14

BRECON ABERHONDDU

19 mi northwest of Abergavenny, 41 mi north of Cardiff.

The historic market town of Brecon is known for its Georgian buildings,
narrow passageways, and pleasant riverside walks. It's also the gateway
to Brecon Beacons National Park. The town is particularly appealing
on Tuesday and Friday, which are market days. You may want to purchase a hand-carved wooden love spoon similar to those on display in
the Brecknock Museum.

GETTING HERE AND AROUND
Brecon's nearest railway stations are at Merthyr Tydfil and Abergavenny
(both about 19 mi away). Beacons Bus service runs to many parts of
Brecon Beacons National Park. Brecon is a handsome town to explore
on foot—especially the riverside walk along the Promenade.

ESSENTIALS
Visitor Information Brecon (✉ *Market Car Park, Church La.*
☎ *01874/622485* ⊕ *www.breconbeaconstourism.co.uk*).

EXPLORING
TOP ATTRACTIONS
★ **Brecon Beacons National Park.** About
5 mi southwest of Brecon you
encounter mountains and wild,
windswept uplands that are tipped
by shafts of golden light when the
weather's fine, or fingers of ghostly
mist when it's not. This 519-square-
mi park is one of Wales's most
breathtaking areas, perfect for a
hike or scenic drive. Start at the
visitor center on Mynydd Illtyd,
a grassy stretch of upland west of
the A470. It's an excellent source
of information about the park,
including maps and advice on the

LOVE SPOONS

The rural Welsh custom of giving the object of your affection
a "love spoon" dates from the
mid-17th century. Made from
wood, the spoons are elaborately
hand-carved with tokens of love,
including hearts, flowers, doves,
intertwined vines, and chain links.
These days you don't have to
make the effort yourself—you can
barely turn around in a Welsh
souvenir shop without seeing one.

HIKING AND BIKING IN WALES

Hiking and walking are the most popular outdoor activities in Wales, and a great way to see the country. Long-distance paths include the Pembrokeshire Coast Path (which runs all along the spectacular shores of southwest Wales), the south–north Offa's Dyke Path, based on the border between England and Wales established by King Offa in the 8th century, and the Glyndr Way, a 128-mi-long highland route that traverses Mid-Wales from the border town of Knighton via Machynlleth to Welshpool. Signposted footpaths in Wales's forested areas are short and easy to follow. Dedicated enthusiasts might prefer the wide-open spaces of Brecon Beacons National Park or the mountains of Snowdonia.

Wales's reputation as both an on-road and off-road cycling mecca is well established. There's an amazing choice of scenic routes and terrain from challenging off-road tracks (⊕ www.mtbwales.com is for the serious cyclist) to long-distance road rides and gentle family trails; VisitWales has information to get you started.

CONTACTS AND RESOURCES

Cycling Wales (⊕ www.cycling. visitwales.com).

Offa's Dyke Centre (☎ 01547/528753 ⊕ www.offasdyke. demon.co.uk).

Pembrokeshire Coast Path (⊕ www.nationaltrail.co.uk).

Ramblers' Association in Wales (☎ 029/2064–4308 ⊕ www.ramblers. org.uk/wales).

best routes (guided or self-guided). There's also an excellent Tea Room where you can fuel up for the journey or reward yourself with an indulgent slice of cake afterwards. If you want to see it all from your car, any road that crosses the Beacons will reward you with beautiful views, but the most spectacular is the high and undulating A4069, between Brynamman and Llangadog in the park's western end. ■TIP→ To explore the moorlands on foot, come prepared. Mist and rain descend quickly, and the summits are exposed to high winds. ⊠ *Off A470, Libanus* ☎ *01874/623366* ⊕ *www.breconbeacons.org* ☜ *Free, parking £1* ☼ *Mar.–Oct., daily 9:30–5; Nov.–Feb., daily 9:30–4:30.*

Fodor'sChoice
★ **Carreg Cennen Castle.** On the edge of Brecon Beacons National Park, about 30 mi west of Brecon, this decaying cliff-top fortress was built in the 12th century, although remains of earlier defenses have been found dating back to the Iron Age. The castle, though a ruin, has a partially intact barbican (fortified outer section) and some inner chambers hewn dramatically from the bedrock. The climb up is somewhat punishing—you have to trudge up a steep, grassy hill—but the views of the valley, with its patchwork of green fields framed by the peaks of the Black Mountains, are enough to take away whatever breath you have left. ⊠ *Off Derwydd Rd., Trapp* ☎ *01443/336000* ⊕ *www.cadw.wales. gov.uk* ☜ *£4* ☼ *Apr.–Oct., daily 9:30–6:30; Nov.–Mar., daily 9:30–4.*

One of three national parks in Wales, Brecon Beacons offers some panoramic mountain views, whether you're on foot or in a car.

WORTH NOTING

Brecon Cathedral. Modest on the outside but surprisingly cavernous on the inside, this cathedral stands on the hill above the middle of town. Its heritage center does a decent job of telling the building's history, and there's also a handy café. Local choirs perform concerts here regularly. ✉ *Cathedral Close* 🕾 *01874/623857* 💰 *Free* ☉ *Daily 8–6.*

Brecknock Museum. In the colonnaded Shire Hall, built in 1842, this museum holds artifacts of Welsh rural life, including a large collection of carved love spoons and a perfectly preserved 19th-century law court. ✉ *Captain's Walk* 🕾 *01874/624121* 💰 *Free* ☉ *Apr.–Oct., weekdays 10–5, Sat. 10–1 and 2–5, Sun. noon–5; Nov.–Mar., weekdays 10–5, Sat. 10–1 and 2–5.*

National Show Caves of Wales. This underground cave system was discovered by two local men in 1912—make that rediscovered, as one of the caves contained 42 human skeletons that had lain undisturbed for up to 7,000 years. The main cave system, Dan Yr Ogof (Welsh for "beneath the cave"), is an impressive natural wonder, particularly the Cathedral Cave with natural stone archways and a dramatic waterfall. The whole thing is pitched at kids, with dramatic piped music to enhance the atmosphere, and a park featuring life-size models of prehistoric creatures. There's also a petting zoo and playground. The caves are 17 mi southwest of Brecon. ✉ *Off A48 or B4310, Abercrave* 🕾 *01639/730284* ⊕ *www.showcaves.co.uk* 💰 *£13.50* ☉ *Apr.–Oct., daily 10–3.*

WHERE TO EAT AND STAY

For expanded hotel reviews, visit Fodors.com.

£££ ✕**Felin Fach Griffin.** Old and new blend perfectly in this modern country-
BRITISH style inn with old wood floors, comfy leather sofas, and stone walls
hung with bright prints. The excellent menu makes use of fresh local
produce, much of it coming from the Griffin's own organic garden, in
dishes such as monkfish with chicory, Dauphinois potatoes and Pernod
cream, or rib eye with bone-marrow gratin and chips. The inn is in Felin
Fach, 5 mi northeast of Brecon. ⊠ *A470, Felin Fach* ☎ *01874/620111*
⊕ *www.eatdrinksleep.ltd.uk.*

££ ⊡ **The Coach House.** This former coach house in the center of Brecon
HOTEL has been converted into a luxurious place to stay. **Pros:** lovely staff;
central location; private parking. **Cons:** on a main road. ⊠ *Orchard St.*
☎ *01874/620043* ⊕ *www.coachhousebrecon.co.uk* ⇆ *7 rooms* ⚘ *In-
room: no a/c, Wi-Fi. In-hotel: restaurant, bar, some age restrictions*
⦿*| Breakfast.*

££ ⊡ **Felin Glais.** In the 17th century Felin Glais was a barn; enlarged but
B&B/INN without losing its ancient character, it provides spacious and comfortable accommodations. **Pros:** beautiful building; spacious rooms; good
food. **Cons:** dogs allowed in rooms; communal dining table. ⊠ *Abersy-
cir* ☎ *01874/623107* ⊕ *www.felinglais.co.uk* ⇆ *4 rooms* ⚘ *In-room: no
a/c, Wi-Fi. In-hotel: restaurant, some pets allowed* ⊟ No *credit cards*
⦿*| Breakfast.*

NIGHTLIFE AND THE ARTS

For a weekend every August, **Brecon Jazz** (☎ *01497/822629* ⊕ *www.
breconjazz.co.uk*), an international music festival, takes over the town.
It attracts an increasingly high-profile list of performers and includes a
parade through the town on the Sunday morning.

Theatr Brycheiniog (⊠ *Canal Wharf* ☎ *01874/611622* ⊕ *www.brycheiniog.
co.uk*), on the canal, is the town's main venue for music, plays, and comedy. It also has a waterfront bistro.

SPORTS AND THE OUTDOORS

Crickhowell Adventure Gear (⊠ *21 Ship St.* ☎ *01874/611586* ⊕ *www.
crickhowelladventure.co.uk*) sells outdoor gear and climbing equipment.

The Brecon Beacons contain some of the best cycling routes in Britain.
Biped Cycles (⊠ *10 Ship St.* ☎ *01874/622296* ⊕ *www.bipedcycles.co.uk*)
will rent you the right bike and equipment.

MERTHYR MAWR

45 mi south of Brecon, 22 mi west of Cardiff.

As you cross over an ancient stone bridge into Merthyr Mawr, you feel
as if you've entered another world. From stone cottages with beehive
thatched roofs, to the Victorian-era Church of St. Teilo, with the pieces
of its long-gone 5th-century predecessor lined up in its churchyard, it's
an idyllic place to wander around. The picturesque ruin of Ogmore
Castle is just off the B4524, but the most memorable way to reach it is
via the walking path that starts in the car park at the very southern tip
of the village. The mile-long route goes through a farm and a Shetland
pony stables.

GETTING HERE AND AROUND

Merthyr Mawr is signposted from the A48 and B4524, 7 mi southwest of junction 35 on the M4. The nearest train station is in Bridgend. There is no bus service to the village.

EXPLORING

★ **Nash Point.** Just a few miles south of Merthyr Mawr is this stunning promontory overlooking the Bristol Channel. Twin lighthouses stand guard against the elements; one is still operational, but the other is open for tours. This is also a popular picnic spot, and a small snack kiosk is open during summer months. Nothing beats this place at sunset, when the evening sky ignites in a riot of color. It's one of the most romantic spots in South Wales. ■TIP→ There's no guardrail on the cliff, so keep a close eye on children. ✉ *Nash Point, Marcross* ☎ *01225/245011* 💷 *£4* ⊙ *Jan.–early Apr., weekends 2–5; mid-late Apr., Sat. 2–5; May–July, Wed. and weekends 2–5; Aug., Mon., Wed., and Fri.–Sun. 2–5.*

Ogmore Castle. Just south of the village are these atmospheric ruins, nestled by a river that can only be crossed via stepping-stones. A number of legends are associated with the castle, one concerning a ghost that supposedly forces passersby to embrace a large rock known as the "Goblin Stone." When you try to draw back, so the story goes, you find that your hands and feet have become part of the rock. ✉ *Ogmore Rd.*

QUICK BITES

Up a small hill next to Ogmore Castle, **The Pelican in Her Piety** (✉ *Ogmore Rd. [B452]* ☎ *01656/880049* ⊕ *www.pelicanpub.co.uk*) stands like a mirage. This friendly and fabulously named little pub is a welcome spot for a snack or restorative pint after the long walk from Merthyr Mawr.

WHERE TO EAT

££
BRITISH

✕ **The Plough and Harrow.** A short drive from Nash Point is this friendly local pub, on the edge of the tiny cliff-top village of Monknash. The food is delicious and unfussy, mostly pub classics like steaks and grilled fish. Everything is served in a cozy dining room with a fireplace and a hopeful-looking dog. There's a small but decent wine list, and an even better selection of real ales. This place is popular, so call ahead or be prepared to wait. ✉ *Off Hoel Las, Monknash* ☎ *01656/890209* ⊕ *www.theploughmonknash.com.*

SWANSEA ABERTAWE

22 mi northwest of Merthyr Mawr, 40 mi west of Cardiff.

Swansea, the birthplace of poet Dylan Thomas (1914–53), adores its native son. It honors him throughout the year, especially at the Dylan Thomas Festival in October and November. But Swansea no longer seems like a place that would inspire poetry. Heavily bombed in World War II, it was clumsily rebuilt. Today there's little to recommend it apart from a couple of good museums. However, the surrounding countryside tells a different story. The National Botanic Gardens and Neath Abbey make for interesting diversions, and the stunning Gower Peninsula contains some of the region's best beaches.

Stretching west of Swansea, the Gower Peninsula has some stunning beaches, including Rhossili.

GETTING HERE AND AROUND

There's hourly rail service from London's Paddington Station. The city has direct National Express buses arrive from other parts of Wales, as well as from London and other cities.

ESSENTIALS

Visitor Information Swansea (✉ *Plymouth St.* ☎ *01792/468321* ⊕ *www. visitswanseabay.com*).

EXPLORING

TOP ATTRACTIONS

Dylan Thomas Centre. Situated on the banks of the Tawe close to the Maritime Quarter, the Dylan Thomas Centre serves as the National Literature Centre for Wales. The center houses a permanent Dylan Thomas exhibition, art gallery, restaurant, and café-bookshop, and hosts the annual Dylan Thomas Festival. ■TIP→ Those interested in the poet can buy a booklet that outlines the Dylan Thomas Trail around South Wales. ✉ *Somerset Pl.* ☎ *01792/463980* ⊕ *www.dylanthomas. com* ⊟ *Free* ⊙ *Daily 10–4:30.*

Fodor'sChoice
★
☺
Gower Peninsula. This peninsula, which stretches westward from Swansea, was the first part of Britain to be designated an Area of Outstanding Natural Beauty. Its shores are a succession of sheltered sandy bays and awesome headlands. The seaside resort of Mumbles, on the outskirts of Swansea, is the most famous town along the route. It's an elegantly faded place to wander on a sunny afternoon, with an amusement pier and seaside promenade. Farther along the peninsula, the secluded Pwlldu Bay can only be reached on foot from nearby villages like Southgate. A few miles westward is the more accessible (and very

popular) Three Cliffs Bay, with its sweeping views and wide, sandy beach. At the far western tip of the peninsula, Rhossili has perhaps the best beach of all. Its unusual, snaking causeway—known locally as the Worm's Head—is inaccessible at high tide. ⊕ *www.enjoygower.com.*

National Botanic Garden of Wales. This 568-acre, 18th-century estate is dotted with lakes, fountains, and a Japanese garden. The centerpiece is the Norman Foster–designed Great Glass House, the largest single-span greenhouse in the world, which blends into the curving land-forms of the Tywi Valley. The greenhouse's interior landscape includes a 40-foot-deep ravine and thousands of plants from all over the world. The garden, 20 mi northwest of Swansea, is signposted off the main road between Swansea and Carmarthen. ⊠ *Off A48 or B4310, Llan-arthne* ☎ *01558/668–7688* ⊕ *www.gardenofwales.org.uk* ☞ *£8.50* ⊙ *Apr.–Sept., daily 10–6; Oct.–Mar., daily 10–4:30.*

⟳ **National Waterfront Museum.** Housed in a construction of steel, slate, and glass grafted onto a historic redbrick building, the National Waterfront Museum's galleries have 15 theme areas. State-of-the-art interactive technology and a host of artifacts bring Welsh maritime and indus-trial history to a 21st-century audience. ⊠ *Oystermouth Rd., Maritime Quarter* ☎ *01792/638950* ⊕ *www.museumwales.ac.uk* ☞ *Free* ⊙ *Daily 10–5.*

WORTH NOTING

5 Cwmdonkin Drive. Dylan Thomas was born in this suburban Edward-ian house, which remains a place of pilgrimage for the poet's devotees. It's not for casual fans, however; the two-hour tour discusses his life in exhaustive detail. Tours must be booked in advance. ⊠ *5 Cwmdonkin Dr.* ☎ *01792/405331* ⊕ *www.5cwmdonkindrive.com* ☞ *£5* ⊙ *Call ahead for tours.*

Maritime Quarter. Swansea was extensively bombed during World War II, and its old dockland has reemerged as the splendid Maritime Quarter, a modern marina with attractive housing and shops and a seafront that commands views across the sweep of Swansea Bay.

Swansea Museum. Founded in 1841, this museum contains a quirky and eclectic collection that includes an Egyptian mummy, local archaeo-logical exhibits, and the intriguing Cabinet of Curiosity, which holds artifacts from Swansea's past. The museum is close to the Maritime Quarter. ⊠ *Victoria Rd.* ☎ *01792/653763* ⊕ *www.swanseaheritage.net* ☞ *Free* ⊙ *Tues.–Sun. 10–5.*

WHERE TO EAT AND STAY
For expanded hotel reviews, visit Fodors.com.

£££ ✕ **La Braseria.** Lively and welcoming, this spot resembles a Spanish
SPANISH *bodega* (wine cellar), with its flamenco music, oak barrels, and white-washed walls. Among the house specialties are sea bass in rock salt, roast suckling pig, and pheasant (in season, of course). There's a good choice of 140 Spanish and French wines. ⊠ *28 Wind St.* ☎ *01792/469683* ⊕ *www.labraseria.com* ⊙ *Closed Sun.*

£ ✕ **Verdi's.** This family-run ice-cream parlor, café, and restaurant sits
ITALIAN right on the seafront. Homemade pizza is a specialty, or you could just join the queue for the delicious fresh gelato. Every indoor and

outdoor table has panoramic views of Swansea Bay. It's in The Mumbles, a resort town southwest of Swansea. ⊠ *Off Pier Rd., The Mumbles* ☏ *01792/369135* ⊕ *www.verdis-cafe.co.uk.*

££££–£££££   Ⓣ **Fairyhill.** Luxuriously furnished public rooms, spacious bedrooms,
HOTEL   and delicious cooking make this 18th-century country house a restful
★   retreat. **Pros:** peaceful surroundings; good restaurant. **Cons:** weekend stays include two meals a day; restaurant always busy. ⊠ *Off B4295, 11 mi southwest of Swansea, Reynoldston* ☏ *01792/390139* ⊕ *www. fairyhill.net* ⟿ *8 rooms* ⚥ *In-room: no a/c, Wi-Fi. In-hotel: restaurant, bar, business center, some age restrictions* ❧ *Some meals.*

£££–££££   Ⓣ **Morgans.** Now a hotel, the Victorian-era Port Authority building in
HOTEL   the Maritime Quarter has lost none of its period features: moldings, pillars, stained glass, and wood floors. **Pros:** near the marina; short walk to shops; maritime flair. **Cons:** no outdoor space; busy bars; popular for weddings. ⊠ *Somerset Pl.* ☏ *01792/484848* ⊕ *www.morganshotel. co.uk* ⟿ *41 rooms* ⚥ *In-room: no a/c (some), Internet (some), Wi-Fi (some). In-hotel: restaurant, bars, gym, business center.* ❧ *Breakfast.*

TENBY DINBYCH-Y-PYSGOD

53 mi west of Swansea.

Pastel-color Georgian houses cluster around a harbor in this seaside resort, where two golden sandy beaches stretch below the hotel-lined cliff top. Medieval Tenby's ancient town walls still stand, enclosing narrow streets and passageways full of shops, inns, and places to eat. From the harbor you can take a short boat trip to Caldey Island, with its active Cistercian community.

GETTING HERE AND AROUND

Tenby is on the southwest Wales rail route from London's Paddington Station. You have to change trains at Swansea or Newport. The center of Tenby, a maze of narrow medieval streets, has parking restrictions. In summer, downtown is closed to traffic, so park in more-remote lots and take the shuttle buses.

ESSENTIALS

Visitor Information Tenby (⊠ *Unit 2, Upper Park Rd.* ☏ *01834/842402* ⊕ *www. virtualtenby.co.uk*).

EXPLORING

Fodor's Choice   **Caldey Island.** This beautiful little island off the coast at Tenby has white-
★   washed stone buildings that lend it a Mediterranean feel. The island is best known for its Cistercian order, whose black-and-white-robed monks make a famous perfume from the local plants. You can visit tiny St. Illtud's Church to see the Caldey Stone, an early Christian artifact engraved in Latin and ancient Celtic. St. David's Church, on a hill above the village, is a simple Norman chapel noted for its art deco stained glass. The monastery itself is not open to the public, but its church has a public viewing gallery if you want to observe a service. Boats to Caldey Island leave from Tenby's harbor every 20 minutes or so between Easter and September. ⊠ *Caldey Island* ☏ *01834/844453*

⊕ *www.caldey-island.co.uk* ✉ *Free, boats £11 round-trip* ◷ *Boats Easter–Sept., Mon.–Sat. 10–3; Oct., weekdays 10–3.*

Pembroke Castle. Ten miles east of Tenby is this remarkably complete Norman fortress dating from 1190. Its walls remain stout, its gatehouse mighty, and the enormous cylindrical keep proved so impregnable to cannon fire in the Civil War that Cromwell's men had to starve out its Royalist defenders. Climb the towers and walk the walls for fine views. A well-stocked gift shop sells faux-medieval knickknacks. ✉ *Northgate, St. Pembroke* ☎ *01646/681510* ⊕ *www.pembroke-castle.co.uk* ✉ *£5* ◷ *Apr.–Sept., daily 9:30–6; Oct. and Mar., daily 10–5; Nov.–Feb., daily 10–4.*

Ⓒ **Tenby Museum and Art Gallery.** Close to the castle, this small but informative museum recalls the town's maritime history and its growth as a fashionable resort. Kids will appreciate the section on Tenby's role in the golden age of piracy. Two art galleries feature works by local artists. ✉ *Castle Hill* ☎ *01834/842809* ⊕ *www.tenbymuseum.org.uk* ✉ *£4* ◷ *June–Sept., daily 10–4:30; Oct.–Apr., weekdays 10–4:30.*

Ⓒ **Tudor Merchant's House.** This late-15th-century home shows how a prosperous trader would have lived in Tudor times. Kids can try on Tudor-style costumes. ✉ *Quay Hill* ☎ *01834/842279* ⊕ *www.nationaltrust. org.uk* ✉ *£3* ◷ *Late Feb.–early Mar., daily 11–3; mid-Mar.–Oct., Sun.–Fri. 10–5; also mid-Mar.–mid-July and late Aug.–Oct., Sat. 11–5. Last admission 30 mins before closing.*

WHERE TO EAT AND STAY
For expanded hotel reviews, visit Fodors.com.

£££
BRITISH

✕ **Plantagenet House.** Flickering candles, open fireplaces, exposed stone walls, and top-notch locally sourced food are hallmarks of this popular restaurant and bar. The menu contains a selection of Welsh-reared steaks and other meat dishes, but seafood is the specialty. The romantic setting is as much of a draw as the food. Check out the huge stone "Flemish chimney," a distinctive style popularized by immigrants during the 16th century. ✉ *Quay Hill* ☎ *01834/842350* ◷ *Closed Jan.–mid-Feb.*

£–££
B&B/INN

Ivy Bank Guest House. This comfortable and immaculate Victorian house sits across from the train station, a five-minute stroll from the sea. **Pros:** cozy and simple; close to beach. **Cons:** you have to park at the train station; feels dated. ✉ *Harding St.* ☎ *01834/842311* ⊕ *www. ivybanktenby.co.uk* ⇆ *5 rooms* ⚡ *In-room: no a/c. In-hotel: bar* ⦿ *Breakfast.*

££££–£££££
HOTEL

St. Brides Spa Hotel. Between Amroth and Tenby, this luxury hotel perches in a breathtaking location above Carmarthen Bay. **Pros:** amazing view; wonderful spa; displays of contemporary art. **Cons:** steep walk from beach; surrounding area lacks charm; minimum stay on weekends. ✉ *Saundersfoot* ☎ *01834/812304* ⊕ *www.stbridesspahotel.com* ⇆ *35 rooms* ⚡ *In-room: no a/c, Internet (some), Wi-Fi (some). In-hotel: restaurant, bar, pool, spa* ⦿ *Breakfast.*

SPORTS AND THE OUTDOORS

The town's beaches are hugely popular in summertime. North Beach is the most popular, with shops and a little café along the promenade. The adjoining Harbour Beach is prettier and more secluded. Castle Beach is in a little cove where you can walk out to a small island at low tide. Past that is South Beach, which stretches for more than a mile.

ST. DAVID'S TYDDEWI

35 mi northwest of Tenby.

Despite its miniscule size, this community of under 1,800 people is not a village or a hamlet—it's actually Britain's smallest city. Historically, little St. David's has punched above its weight due to the presence of St. David's Cathedral, the resting place of the patron saint of Wales and once a major destination for pilgrims. These days, visitors with time on their hands might want to consider approaching the city via the Pembrokeshire Coast Path, around the St. David's headland from St. Justinian to Caerfai Bay. In May and June the town's hedgerows and coastal paths are ablaze with wildflowers. The town's visitor center also has a small collection of art and artifacts drawn from the collection of the National Museum of Wales.

GETTING HERE AND AROUND

St. David's is on the A487. The nearest train station is 14 mi southeast in Haverfordwest. Bus 411 travels from Haverfordwest to St. David's roughly every hour or so.

ESSENTIALS

Visitor Information St. David's Oriel y Parc (⊠ *1 High St.* ☎ *01437/720392* ⊕ *www.orielyparc.co.uk*).

EXPLORING

★ **St. David's Cathedral.** You must climb down 39 steps (called locally the Thirty-Nine Articles) to enter the cathedral. Its location helped protect the church from Viking raiders by hiding it from the view of invaders who came by sea. Originally founded by St. David himself in around 600 AD, the current building dates from the 12th century, although it has been added to at various times since. Start at the Gatehouse, with its exhibition on the history of the cathedral. Inside the building itself, the 15th-century choir stalls still have original medieval floor tiles, while the Holy Trinity Chapel contains an intricate fan-vaulted ceiling and a casket said to contain the patron saint's bones. ■**TIP**➜ Don't miss the Treasury and its illuminated gospels, silver chalices, and 700-year-old golden bishop's crosier. In August, guided tours costing £4 begin Monday at 11:30 and Friday at 2:30. The cathedral has a good café. At the rear of the grounds of St. David's Cathedral are the ruins of the 13th-century **Bishop's Palace** (☎ *01437/720517* ⊕ *www.cadw.wales. gov.uk* ☞ *£3.10* ☉ *Apr.–June, Sept., and Oct., daily 9:30–5; Nov.–Feb., Mon.–Sat. 10–4, Sun. 11–4*), particularly beautiful at dusk. ⊠ *The Close* ☎ *01437/720202* ⊕ *www.stdavidscathedral.org.uk* ☞ *Free* ☉ *Mon.– Sat. 8:30–5; Sun. 12:30–5.*

OFF THE
BEATEN
PATH

Last Invasion Tapestry. The 100-foot-long Last Invasion Tapestry, on display in the Town Hall in Fishguard, is modeled on the famous Bayeux Tapestry depicting the Norman invasion of 1066. This modern version marks a lesser known, and certainly less successful assault on the country. In 1797, a unit of French soldiers, led by an Irish-American general, landed in Fishguard Harbour. They were defeated by a hastily assembled local militia, which included many women. The impressive tapestry, commissioned to mark the event's 200th anniversary, took 70 local women more than 40,000 hours to complete. Fishguard is 16 mi northeast of St. David's off the A487. ⊠ *Market Sq.* ☎ *01437/776639* 🕾 *Free* 🕙 *Apr.–Sept., Mon.–Wed., Fri., and Sat. 9:30–5, Thurs. 9:30–6:30; Oct.–Mar., Mon.–Wed. and Fri. 9:30–5, Thurs. 9:30–6:30, Sat. 9:30–1.*

14

WHERE TO STAY

For expanded hotel reviews, visit Fodors.com.

££££
HOTEL

🖾 **Warpool Court Hotel.** Overlooking a stunning stretch of coastline, this hotel sits on a bluff above St. Non's Bay. **Pros:** beautiful sea views; peaceful gardens; good food. **Cons:** unattractive entrance; few restaurants nearby. ⊠ *Off Goat St.* ☎ *01437/720300* ⊕ *www.warpoolcourthotel. com* 🗭 *25 rooms* ♿ *In-room: no a/c, Wi-Fi. In-hotel: restaurant, bar, pool, tennis court, gym, business center, some pets allowed* ❗○❙ *Breakfast.*

MID-WALES

Traditional market towns and country villages, small seaside resorts, quiet roads, and rolling landscapes filled with sheep farms, forests, and lakes make up Mid-Wales, the country's green and rural heart. There are no cities here—the area's largest town is barely more than a big village. Outside of one or two towns, such as Aberystwyth and Llandrindod Wells, accommodations are mainly country inns, small hotels, and rural farmhouses. This area also has some splendid country-house hotels.

There are no motorways through Mid-Wales, and nobody preserves the railway lines that once linked this area with Cardiff. Getting around requires a bit of advance planning, but it's worth the trouble. The bibliophilic charms of Hay-on-Wye have made the town world-famous, while the countryside around Abertystwyth is peppered with peaceful sandy beaches and dramatic beauty spots.

HAY-ON-WYE Y GELLI GANDRYLL

57 mi north of Cardiff, 25 mi north of Abergavenny.

Fodor's Choice
★

With its crumbling old castle and low-slung buildings framed by lolloping green hills, Hay-on-Wye is a beautiful little place. In 1961 Richard Booth established a small secondhand bookshop here. Other booksellers soon got in on the act, and now there are dozens of shops. It's now the largest secondhand bookselling center in the world, and priceless 14th-century manuscripts rub spines with "job lots" selling for a few pounds.

For 10 days every May and June, Hay-on-Wye is taken over by its Literary Festival, a celebration of literature that attracts famous writers from all over the world. (Bill Clinton, himself an attendee, once called it "the Woodstock of the mind.") Plan ahead if you want to attend, as hotels get booked several months in advance.

GETTING HERE AND AROUND

You'll need a car to get to Hay. Use one of the public lots of the outskirts of town and walk—the whole town is accessible by foot. The nearest train stations are Builth Wells in Wales (19 mi) and Hereford in England (22 mi).

ESSENTIALS

Visitor Information Hay-on-Wye (⊠ *Oxford Rd.* ☎ *01497/820144* ⊕ *www. hay-on-wye.co.uk/tourism*).

EXPLORING

Hay Castle. On a hilltop are the handsome remains of a 12th-century castle keep, jutting out from behind a 16th-century manor house. ⊠ *Castle St.* 🎫*Free* ⊙ *Late Mar.–Oct., daily 9:30–6; Nov.–late Mar., daily 9:30–5:30.*

NEED A BREAK? The delicious ice cream at Shepherd's (⊠ *9 High Town* ☎ *01497/2189* ⊕ *www.shepherdsicecream.co.uk*) is legendary in these parts. Produced at a local farm, its distinct, creamy flavor comes from the fact that it's made from sheep's milk.

WHERE TO EAT AND STAY

For expanded hotel reviews, visit Fodors.com.

£££
BRITISH
✕**Kilverts Inn.** This Edwardian town house at the back of Hay-on-Wye's covered market is an ideal spot for a lunch break while thumbing through your finds from the local bookstores. The bar serves a seasonal menu of British classics, including a popular traditional roast on Sunday. The selection of real ales is excellent. ⊠ *The Bullring* ☎ *01497/821042* ⊕ *www.kilverts.co.uk.*

£££
BRITISH
✕**Old Black Lion.** A 17th-century coaching inn close to Hay's center is ideal for a lunch break while you're ransacking the bookshops. The oak-beamed bar serves food, and the breakfasts are especially good. The restaurant's sophisticated cooking has an international flavor and emphasizes local meats and produce. You can even opt for an overnight stay in one of the country-style rooms. ⊠ *Lion St.* ☎ *01497/820841* ⊕ *www.oldblacklion.co.uk.*

££££
HOTEL
🏨 **Llangoed Hall.** This magnificent Jacobean mansion on the banks of the River Wye, about 7 mi west of Hay-on-Wye, has beautiful fabrics and furnishings, open fireplaces, a sweeping carved staircase, and a paneled library dating back to 1632. **Pros:** secluded setting by River Wye; wonderful art collection. **Cons:** often filled with wedding parties; minimum stay sometimes required; no attractions within walking distance. ⊠ *Llyswen* ☎ *01874/754525* ⊕ *www.llangoedhall.com* ⤴ *23 rooms* ⚴ *In-room: no a/c, Wi-Fi. In-hotel: restaurant, some age restrictions* ⏍ *Breakfast.*

Mid-Wales

£££-£££ 🏨 **The Swan.** Once a coaching inn, this sophisticated lodging on the edge
HOTEL of town retains its sense of history. **Pros:** atmospheric building; friendly
staff; good food. **Cons:** wedding parties dominate in summer; beds a bit
creaky. ⊠ *Church St.* ☎ *01497/821188* ⊕ *www.swanathay.co.uk* 🛏 *17
rooms* ⚬ *In-room: no a/c, Wi-Fi. In-hotel: restaurant, bar* 🍴 *Breakfast.*

SHOPPING

The Thursday Market takes over much of the town center every Thursday morning. Traders sell everything from antiques to home-baked
cakes.

The kind of dusty old bookshop you see in movies, **Boz Books** (⊠ *13A
Castle St.* ☎ *01497/821613* ⊕ *www.bozbooks.demon.co.uk*) has an
impressive range of 19th-century first editions, including many by
Dickens.

Murder and Mayhem (⊠ *5 Lion St.* ☎ *01497/821613*) specializes in crime
and horror. Head upstairs for a cheaper and more eclectic selection,
including old pulp novellas.

Run by the man who opened Hay-on-Wye's first secondhand bookstore, **Richard Booth Books** (⊠ *44 Lion St.* ☎ *01497/820322* ⊕ *www.
richardbooth.demon.co.uk*) has a huge collection from all over the
world, piled haphazardly across two labyrinthine floors.

Hay-on-Wye's claims to fame are its many secondhand bookstores and the annual Literary Festival.

Easy to spot for its fuchsia-pink front, **Rose's Books** (✉ *14 Broad St.* ☎ *01497/821277* ⊕ *www.rosesbooks.com*) is devoted entirely to children's books, including rare first editions.

LLANDRINDOD WELLS LLANDRINDOD

27 mi north of Hay-on-Wye, 67 mi north of Cardiff.

Also known as Llandod, the old spa town of Llandrindod Wells preserves its Victorian look with turrets, cupolas, loggias, and balustrades everywhere. Cross over to South Crescent, passing the Glen Usk Hotel with its wrought-iron balustrade and the Victorian bandstand in the gardens opposite, and you reach Middleton Street, a Victorian thoroughfare. From there, head to Rock Park and the path that leads to the Pump Room. This historic building is now an alternative health center, but visitors can freely "take the waters."

GETTING HERE AND AROUND

There are a handful of trains daily from Cardiff's Craven Arms Station, and the journey takes around three hours. Direct trains from Swansea and Shrewsbury also stop here, but they are less frequent.

ESSENTIALS

Visitor Information Llandrindod Wells (✉ *Temple St.* ☎ *01597/822600* ⊕ *www.llandrindod.co.uk*).

OFF THE BEATEN PATH

EXPLORING

★ **Powis Castle.** Continuously occupied since the 13th century, Powis Castle rises above the town of Welshpool. One of the most elegant residential castles in Britain, Powis is equally renowned for its magnificent terraced gardens. The interior contains an outstanding art collection, from Greek vases to paintings by Thomas Gainsborough and Joshua Reynolds. The **Clive of India Museum** contains perhaps the most extensive private collection of antique Indian art in Britain. Powis Castle is north of Llandrindod Wells on the A483. ⊠ *Off A483, Welshpool* ☎ *01938/551944* ⊕ *www. nationaltrust.org.uk* ⊠ *£12.40; gardens only, £9.10* ⊙ *Castle and museum Mar.–Oct., Wed.–Mon. 1–4. Castle only, Nov. and Dec., Fri.–Sun. noon–4. Gardens Mar. and Oct., Wed.–Mon. 11–4:30; Apr.–Sept., Wed.–Mon. 11–5:30; Nov. and Dec., Fri.–Sun. 11–4; late Feb., Wed.–Mon. 11–4.*

Radnorshire Museum. In Memorial Gardens, this museum tells the story of the town's development from prehistory onwards, and includes a small collection of Roman and medieval artifacts. The largest and most interesting section is devoted to the town's Victorian heyday, with some of the "cures" at the spa explained in gruesome detail. ⊠ *Temple St.* ☎ *01597/824513* ⊠ *£1* ⊙ *Apr.–Sept., Tues.–Fri. 10–4, Sat. 10–5, Sun. 1–5; Oct.–Mar., Tues.–Fri. 10–4, Sat. 10–1.*

WHERE TO EAT AND STAY

For expanded hotel reviews, visit Fodors.com.

££
BISTRO
✗ **Jules.** Cheerful and family-run, this bar and bistro in the middle of town offers a small but well-edited menu of bistro classics with a Welsh twist, such as local lamb steak with minted potatoes and sea bass roasted in lemon and butter. Traditional Sunday roast lunches are delicious and very popular, as are the regular themed nights, which run the gamut from Mexican to Thai. ⊠ *Temple St.* ☎ *01597/824642* ⊕ *julesrestaurant.blogspot.com.*

£
B&B/INN
🏠 **Brynhir Farm.** A friendly welcome awaits at this cozy farmhouse 2 mi outside Llandrindod. **Pros:** lovely, peaceful location; charming hosts. **Cons:** lacks modern extras; remote location is not walking distance to town. ⊠ *Chapel Rd., Howey* ☎ *01597/822425* ⊕ *www. brynhirfarm.co.uk* ⟿ *3 rooms* ⌂ *In-room: no a/c. In-hotel: restaurant, bar* ⊤⊙⊦ *Breakfast.*

£££
HOTEL
🏠 **Metropole.** This grand looking hotel from 1896 is surprisingly contemporary on the inside, with modern furnishings that complement the original architectural flourishes. **Pros:** very central; good service; inexpensive spa. **Cons:** lacks character; can be taken over by conferences. ⊠ *Temple St.* ☎ *01597/823700* ⊕ *www.metropole.co.uk* ⟿ *120 rooms* ⌂ *In-room: no a/c, Wi-Fi. In-hotel: restaurant, bar, business center, pool, spa* ⊤⊙⊦ *Breakfast.*

FESTIVAL SEASON

The town of Llanelwedd, 7 mi south of Llandrindod, comes to life in late July for the **Royal Welsh Agricultural Show** (☎ *01982/ 553683* ⊕ *www.rwas.co.uk*). The livestock judging, sheepdog competitions, and craft demonstrations haven't changed much since the show debuted in 1904.

The **Victorian Festival** (☎ *01597/823441* ⊕ *www. victorianfestival.co.uk*) takes over Llandrindod Wells for a week in late August. Everyone from shopkeepers to hotel clerks dresses up in period costume for events from tea dances to street parades.

14

ABERYSTWYTH

41 mi northwest of Llandrindod Wells via A44, 118 mi northwest of Cardiff.

A pleasingly eccentric combination of faded Victorian seaside resort and artsy college town, Aberystwyth is the largest community in Mid-Wales, with a population of barely 16,000. When the weather's fine, the beaches along the bay fill up with sunbathers; when it's not, waves crash so ferociously against the sea wall that even the hotels across the street get soaked. To the east of the town are the Cambrian Mountains and the Veil of Rheidol, which can be visited by steam train.

GETTING HERE AND AROUND

All journeys from South Wales are routed through Shrewsbury and take four to five hours. From London, the trip here takes five to six hours. Long-distance buses are infrequent and painfully slow, though the local bus system is good. There are two roads to Aberystwyth, both of them among the most scenic in Wales: the coastal A487 and the mountainous A44.

ESSENTIALS

Visitor Information Aberystwyth (✉ *Lisburn House, Terrace Rd.* ☎ *01970/612125* ⊕ *www.aberystwyth-online.co.uk*).

EXPLORING

TOP ATTRACTIONS

❊ **Constitution Hill.** At the northern end of the beach promenade, Constitution Hill dominates the skyline. If you're feeling hale and hearty, there's a long footpath that zigzags up to the 430-foot summit. From there, a 5-mi-long coastal path stretches to the village of Borth, a smaller, sleepier resort north of Aberystwyth. There's a small café at the top and plenty of space for a picnic. The Victorian-era **Aberystwyth Cliff Railway** (☎ *01970/617642* ⊕ *www.aberystwythcliffrailway.co.uk* ✎ *£3.50 round-trip* ⊗ *Mar.–Oct., daily 10–5; Nov.–Mar. Wed.–Sun. 10–5*) deposits you at the top of Constitution Hill. Opened in 1896, it's the longest electric cliff railway in Britain. From the top you can see much of the Welsh coastline on a clear day (and allegedly, on a very clear day, Ireland). The **Great Aberystwyth Camera Obscura** (☎ *01970/617642* ✎ *£1* ⊗ *Mar.–Oct., daily 10–5; winter hrs vary*), a modern version of a Victorian amusement, is a massive 14-inch lens that gives you a bird's-eye view of Cardigan Bay and 26 Welsh mountain peaks.

National Library of Wales. This massive neoclassical building next to the University of Wales houses notable Welsh and other Celtic literary works among its more than 4.5 million volumes. The cache of public records makes it an invaluable tool if you're tracing your family tree. Also here is the National Screen and Sound Archive of Wales, which hosts lunchtime and evening film screenings. ✉ *Off Penglais Rd.* ☎ *01970/632800* ⊕ *www.llgc.org.uk* ✎ *Free* ⊗ *Weekdays 9:30–6, Sat. 9:30–5.*

★ **Vale of Rheidol Railway.** At Aberystwyth Station you can hop on the
❊ steam-powered Vale of Rheidol Railway for an hour-long ride to the **Devil's Bridge** (*Pont y Gwr Drwg*, or, literally, "the Bridge of the Evil

One") where the rivers Rheidol and Mynach meet in a series of spectacular falls. Clamped between two rocky cliffs where a torrent of water pours unceasingly, there are actually three bridges, one built on top of the other. The oldest bridge is about 800 years old. ⊠ *Park Ave.* ☎ *01970/625819* ⊕ *www.rheidolrailway.co.uk* ⊠ *£14.50 round-trip, bridges £1* ⊙ *Easter–Oct.; call for schedule.*

WORTH NOTING

Aberystwyth Castle. At the southern end of the bay, a little way down from the pier, are the crumbling remains of this castle. Built in 1277, it was one of the key strongholds captured in the early 15th century by Owain Glyndwr, a Welsh prince who led the country's last serious bid for independence from England. Today it's a romantic, windswept ruin.

Ceredigion Museum. Housed in a flamboyant 1905 Edwardian theater, the Ceredigion Museum has collections related to folk history and the building's own music hall past. Highlights include a reconstructed mudwalled cottage from 1850 and items illustrating the region's seafaring, lead-mining, and farming history. ⊠ *Terrace Rd.* ☎ *01970/633088* ⊕ *museum.ceredigion.gov.uk* ⊠ *Free* ⊙ *Apr.–Sept., Mon.–Sat. 10–5; Oct.–Mar., Mon.–Sat. noon–4:30.*

☺ **Llynwenog Silver-Lead Mine.** Outside the village of Ponterwyd, 10 mi east of Aberystwyth, this 200-year-old mine is now an open-air museum where you can wander around reproductions of mining buildings and some original machinery, including working waterwheels. There are also tours of the mines themselves. The experience is very much aimed at kids, who enjoy the chance to pan for precious minerals themselves. ■**TIP**➜ It's cold in the mine, even on hot days, so bring a jacket or sweater. ⊠ *Off A44* ☎ *01970/890620* ⊕ *www.silverminetours.co.uk* ⊠ *£7.50* ⊙ *Apr.–June, Sept., and Oct., daily 10:30–5; July and Aug., daily 10–6; last tour 1 hr before closing.*

WHERE TO EAT

££   ✕ **Gannets.** A simple but friendly bistro, Gannets specializes in hearty
BRITISH   roasts and traditional Welsh-style dishes that use local meat and fish. Organically grown vegetables and a good wine list are further draws for a university crowd. This place is very popular with a local crowd, and you're likely to hear Welsh being spoken at the next table. ⊠ *7 St. James's Sq.* ☎ *01970/617164* ⊙ *Closed Sun.–Tues.*

££   ✕ **Little Italy.** At this homey little restaurant, red checkered tablecloths
ITALIAN   and candles in wine bottles still pass for sophistication—and it's all the sweeter for it. The menu features an extensive selection of traditional Italian classics, from pasta and risotto to pizza. The small dining room is busy on weekends, so call ahead. ⊠ *51 N. Parade* ☎ *01970/625707* ⊕ *www.littleitalyaber.co.uk.*

WHERE TO STAY

For expanded hotel reviews, visit Fodors.com.

££–£££   ▣ **Gwesty Cymru.** This seafront Edwardian house has been converted
HOTEL   into one of Aberystwyth's more stylish lodgings. **Pros:** contemporary design; beautiful location. **Cons:** seafront can be noisy at night; limited parking; small restaurant. ⊠ *19 Marine Terr.* ☎ *01970/612252* ⊕ *www.*

14

gwestycymru.com 🖘 *8 rooms ♿ In-room: no a/c, Wi-Fi. In-hotel: restaurant, bar* ⦿| *Breakfast.*

££   🔝 **Harbourmaster Hotel.** A drive south on the coast road from Aberyst-
HOTEL   wyth brings you to this early-19th-century Georgian-style building,
right on the harbor among colorfully painted structures. **Pros:** good
food; stunning harbor location; friendly hosts. **Cons:** difficult parking;
often booked up; minimum stay on weekends. ✉ *Pen Cei, 15 mi south
of Aberystwyth, Aberaeron* ☎ *01545/570755* ⦿ *www.harbour-master.
com* 🖘 *13 rooms ♿ In-room: no a/c, Wi-Fi. In-hotel: restaurant, bar,
some age restrictions* ⦿| *Breakfast.*

£££££   🔝 **Ynyshir Hall.** This luxurious Georgian mansion is *the* place to stay
HOTEL   in this part of Wales if money is no object—as the photos of its
Fodor's Choice   world-famous guests on the lobby walls will attest. **Pros:** arty ambi-
★   ence; unabashed luxury; great food. **Cons:** isolated location is impos-
sible to reach without a car. ✉ *Off A487, southwest of Machynlleth,
Eglwysfach* ☎ *01654/781209* ⦿ *www.ynyshir-hall.co.uk* 🖘 *9 rooms
♿ In-room: no a/c. In-hotel: restaurant, bar, business center, some age
restrictions* ⦿| *Breakfast.*

NIGHTLIFE AND THE ARTS

★ **Aberystwyth Arts Centre** (✉ *Bridge St.* ☎ *01970/625177* ⦿ www.aberyst-
wythartscentre.co.uk) has a theater, cinema, gallery, shops, and a good
café and bar. The small cinema's program is varied, including an international horror movie festival every fall.

OUTDOORS

To the east of Aberystwyth, the 128-mi **Glyndwr's Way** (⦿*www.
nationaltrail.co.uk/glyndwrsway*) walking route passes through the
Cambrian Mountains before turning north through the town of
Machynlleth. From there it veers east to climb above the River Dovey,
with wonderful views north to Cadair Idris.

DOLGELLAU

34 mi northeast of Aberystwyth.

A solidly Welsh town with dark stone buildings and old coaching inns
made of the local gray dolerite and slate, Dolgellau (pronounced dol-
geth-lee) thrived with the wool trade until the mid-19th century. Prosperity left striking architecture, with buildings of different eras side by
side on crooked streets that are a legacy from Norman times.

Dolgellau has long been a popular base for people eager to walk the
surrounding countryside, which forms the southern tip of Snowdonia
National Park. To the south of Dolgellau rises the menacing bulk of
2,927-foot Cadair Idris. The name means "the Chair of Idris," a reference to a giant from ancient Celtic mythology.

GETTING HERE AND AROUND

Dolgellau's nearest railway station is at the town of Barmouth, about
10 mi away. The town is small and full of interesting nooks and crannies easily explored on foot. To discover the surrounding area you will
need a car.

ESSENTIALS

Visitor Information Dolgellau (✉ *Ty Meirion, Eldon Sq.* ☎ *01341/422888*).

EXPLORING

Museum of the Quakers. In the town square, this museum commemorates the area's strong links with the Quaker movement and the Quakers' emigration to the American colonies. ✉ *Eldon Sq.* ☎ *01341/422888* 🎟 *Free* ⊙ *Easter–Oct., daily 9:30–5:30; Nov.–Easter, Thurs.–Mon. 9:30–4:30.*

🐣 **Ty Siamas.** The National Centre for Welsh Folk Music is in the converted Victorian Market Hall and Assembly Rooms. It has a fascinating interactive folk music exhibition, performance auditorium, and café and bar. ✉ *Neuadd Idris, Eldon Sq.* ☎ *01341/421800* ⊕ *www.tysiamas. com* 🎟 *£3.95* ⊙ *Easter–Sept., Wed.–Fri. 10–4, Sat. 10–1. Call for off-season hrs.*

14

NORTH WALES

Wales masses its most dramatic splendor and fierce beauty in the north. Dominating the area is Snowdon, at 3,560 feet the highest peak in England and Wales. The peak gives its name to the 840 square mi Snowdonia National Park, which extends southward all the way to Machynlleth in Mid-Wales. As in other British national parks, much of the land is privately owned, so inside the park are towns, villages, and farms, in addition to some spectacular mountain scenery.

The mock-Italianate village of Portmeirion is an extraordinary architectural flight of fancy, and the seaside resort of Llandudno is as popular today as it was during its Victorian heyday. And scattered across the countryside are a ring of mighty medieval castles, built by King Edward I (1239–1307) at the end of a bloody war to bring the population under English rule.

Although North Wales is more popular with travelers than Mid-Wales, the road network is even more tortuous. In fact, you haven't really experienced North Wales until you've spent a maddening hour snaking along a narrow mountain road, all the while with your destination in plain view.

LLANGOLLEN

23 mi southwest of Chester, 60 mi southwest of Manchester.

Llangollen's setting in a deep valley carved by the River Dee gives it a typically Welsh appearance. The bridge over the Dee, a 14th-century stone structure, is named in a traditional Welsh folk song as one of the "Seven Wonders of Wales." In July the very popular International Musical Eisteddfod brings crowds to town.

For a particularly scenic drive in this area, head for the Horseshoe Pass. For other views, follow the marked footpath from the north end of the canal bridge up a steep hill to see Castell Dinas Bran, the ruins of a 13th-century castle built by a native Welsh ruler. The views of the town and the Vale of Llangollen are worth the 45-minute (one-way) walk.

WELSH: A SHORT PRIMER

The native language of Wales, Welsh (or *Cymraeg*, as it's properly called) is spoken fluently by around a quarter of the population. (The vast majority, however, speak a little.) Not legally recognized in Britain until the 1960s, it was suppressed beginning in the time of Henry VIII and blamed for poor literacy during the reign of Queen Victoria. Today Welsh children under 17 are required to take classes to learn the language.

Welsh may look daunting to pronounce, but it is a phonetic language; pronunciation is fairly easy once the alphabet is learned.

Remember that "dd" is sounded like "th" in they, "f" sounds like "v" in save, and "ff" is the equivalent of the English "f" in forest. The "ll" sound has no English equivalent; the closest match is the "cl" sound in "close."

Terms that crop up frequently in Welsh are *bach* or *fach* (small), *craig* or *graig* (rock), *cwm* (valley; pronounced cum), *dyffryn* (valley), *eglwys* (church), *glyn* (glen), *llyn* (lake), *mawr* or *fawr* (great, big), *mynydd* or *fynydd* (mountain, moorland), *pentre* (village, homestead), *plas* (hall, mansion), and *pont* or *bont* (bridge).

GETTING HERE AND AROUND
You'll need a car to get here, but once you arrive you can take a trip on the Llangollen Railway. Along the Llangollen Canal longboat tours head both west and east. The town itself is easy to explore on foot.

ESSENTIALS
Visitor Information Llangollen (⊠ *Y Capel, Castle St.* ☎ *01978/860828*).

EXPLORING
Pontcysyllte. From the canal wharf you can take a horse-drawn boat or a narrow boat (a slender barge) along the Llangollen Canal to the longest and highest navigable, cast-iron aqueduct in the world at Pontcysyllte, a UNESCO-designated World Heritage Site. The aqueduct is more than 1,000 feet long. You can also drive there for a view of this early 19th-century marvel, and walk over it: the aqueduct is 3 mi east of Llangollen. ⊠ *Off A5, Froncysyllte.*

Chirk Castle. In the rather sleepy village of Chirk (Y Waun), this impressive medieval fortress has evolved from its 14th-century origins into a grand home complete with an 18th-century servants hall and interiors furnished in 16th- to 19th-century styles. However, it still looks satisfyingly medieval from the outside—and also below ground, where you tour the original dungeons. Surrounding the castle are beautiful formal gardens and parkland. Chirk Castle is 5 mi southeast of Llangollen. ⊠ *Off B4500* ☎ *01691/777701* ⊕ *www.nationaltrust.org.uk* ☜ *£10; garden and medieval tower only, £7.20* ☉ *Castle Mar.–June, Wed.–Sun. 10–5; July–Oct., daily 10–5; early Nov.–mid-Dec. and early–mid-Feb., weekends 10–4; late Feb., daily 10–4.*

ℭ **Llangollen Railway.** This restored standard-gauge steam line runs for 7 mi along the scenic Dee Valley. The terminus is near the town's bridge. ⊠ *Abbey Rd.* ☎ *01978/860979* ⊕ *www.llangollen-railway.co.uk* ☜ *£10 round-trip* ☉ *Apr.–Oct., daily 10:30–5; Nov.–Mar., weekends, limited service.*

Llangollen's yearly International Musical Eisteddfod, a gathering of international choirs and dancers, shows that Wales is truly a land of song.

Plas Newydd. From 1778 to 1828 Plas Newydd (not to be confused with the similarly named Isle of Anglesey estate) was the home of Lady Eleanor Butler and Sarah Ponsonby, the eccentric Ladies of Llangollen, who set up a then-scandalous single-sex household, collected curios and magnificent carvings, and made it into a tourist attraction even during their lifetimes. You can take tea there, as did Wordsworth and the duke of Wellington, and stroll in the attractively terraced gardens. ✉ *Hill St.* ☎ *01978/862834* ⊕ *www.denbighshire.gov.uk* 🎫 *£5.50* 🕐 *Apr.–Oct., daily 10–5.*

Vale of Ceiriog. Near Llangollen is this verdant valley, known locally as "Little Switzerland." The B4500, running between Chirk and the village of Glyn Ceiriog, at the foothills of the Berwyn Mountains, is one of the region's great drives. It's just remote enough that you can often have the road to yourself.

WHERE TO EAT AND STAY

For expanded hotel reviews, visit Fodors.com.

££ ✕ **The Corn Mill.** Right on the river Dee in a converted mill, this pub and
BRITISH restaurant with solidly good food and drink also wins high marks for its soothing setting and use of rustic stone and wood, from the floors to the beams; a water wheel turns behind the bar. Dine on the deck or eat indoors, sampling stylishly updated pub fare and more, from pan-fried scallops with cauliflower puree to deep-fried haddock (and chips) and braised lamb; there are light bites, too, and dessert classics such as sticky toffee pudding. The ales from small breweries are tempting. Service can be slow when things get busy, but this is a good place to unwind. ✉ *Dee La.* ☎ *01978/869555* ⊕ *www.cornmill-llangollen.co.uk.*

££   ⊡ **Cornerstones Guesthouse.** Made up of three 16th-century cottages with
B&B/INN   views over the River Dee, this lodging blends period charm with modern
amenities. **Pros:** spacious bedrooms; free passes for town parking lots.
Cons: directly on the street. ⊠ *Regent St.* ☎ *01978/861569* ⊕ *www.*
cornerstones-guesthouse.co.uk ⤶ *3 rooms, 2 suites* ⏃ *In-room: no a/c,*
Wi-Fi. In-hotel: some pets allowed ⏃⏃*Breakfast.*

NIGHTLIFE AND THE ARTS

★   The six-day **International Musical Eisteddfod** (☎ *01978/862001* ⊕ *www.*
international-eisteddfod.co.uk), held in early July, brings together amateur choirs and dancers—more than 12,000 participants in all—from
all corners of the globe for a colorful folk festival. The tradition of
the *eisteddfod,* held throughout Wales, goes back to the 12th century.
Originally gatherings of bards, the *eisteddfodau* of today are more like
national festivals.

SPORTS AND THE OUTDOORS

There are easy walks along the banks of the River Dee or along part
of the **Offa's Dyke Path** (⊕ *www.offasdyke.demon.co.uk*), which passes
through hills, river valleys, and lowlands. This 177-mi-long National
Trail follows the line of an ancient earthen wall, still surviving in parts,
which was built along the border with England in the 8th century by
King Offa of Mercia to keep out Welsh raiders.

**EN
ROUTE**   The peat-brown water of **Pistyll Rhaeadr,** the highest waterfall in Wales,
thunders down a 290-foot double cascade. When you're driving on
the B4500 between Llangollen and Llanwddyn, take the road leading
northwest from the town of Llanrhaeadr ym Mochnant, in the peaceful
Tanat Valley. It was near here that, in 1588, the Bible was translated
into Welsh—one of the key moments that helped to ensure the survival
of the language. The waterfall is 4 mi up the road.

LAKE VYRNWY LLYN EFYRNWY

18 mi southwest of Llangollen.

This beautiful lake has a sense of tranquillity that doesn't entirely befit
its history. Lake Vyrnwy was created in the 1880s to provide water
for the people of Liverpool, 80 mi north. Unfortunately, this meant
forcibly evicting the residents of a small town—an act that is still controversial in Wales. Today it's a peaceful spot surrounded by a thriving
nature reserve.

The closest settlement is tiny Llanwddyn, and a bit farther away is Bala,
a pretty town with an almost as lovely natural lake of its own.

GETTING HERE AND AROUND

Rural bus service is infrequent, so you need a car to explore the area.
The B4393 circles Lake Vyrnwy itself; from here, Bala is a 14-mi drive
over hair-raising Bwlch y Groes pass or a circuitous drive along the
B4391. Llangollen is 28 mi northeast of Lake Vyrnwy on the B4396.

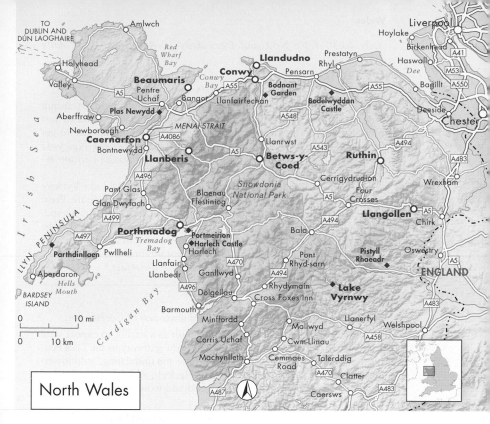

North Wales

EXPLORING

☾ **Bala Lake Railway.** The steam-powered train runs along the southern shores of Bala Lake (Llyn Tegid, or "Lake of Beauty"), a large natural reservoir just northeast of Lake Vyrnwy. Bala Lake is also popular for kayaking and other water sports. ✉ *Off B4403, Llanuwchllyn* ☎ *01678/540666* ⊕ *www.bala-lake-railway.co.uk* 🎫 *Free.*

★ **Bwlch y Groes.** One of the great drives of North Wales, the sweeping, vertiginous panoramas of Bwlch y Groes (*"Pass of the Cross"*) form the highest mountain pass accessible by road in the country. From Lake Vyrnwy, drive for a mile on B4393 before heading west on the mountain road.

★ **Lake Vyrnwy Nature Reserve.** Bordered by lush forest and emerald green
☾ hills, Lake Vyrnwy is a haven for wildlife. It's rich in rare bird species, from falcons to siskins and curlews. Stretching out along the shores of the lake near the visitor center, the Lake Vyrnwy Sculpture Park is a collection of pieces by the talented local artist Andy Hancock. Arranged along a paved walking trail, many of the wooden sculptures resemble oversize versions of the lake's wildlife, including a 15-foot-long dragonfly. It's an extremely popular cycling route, and there's a bike shop and coffee shop near the visitor center. ✉ *Off B4393, Llanwddyn* ☎ *01691/870278* ⊕ *www.rspb.org.uk* 🎫 *Free* ☉ *Apr.–Oct.,*

daily 10:30–5:30; Nov. and Dec., daily 10–4:30; Jan.–Mar., daily 10:30–dusk.

WHERE TO STAY

For expanded hotel reviews, visit Fodors.com.

££
B&B/INN

⊡ Cyfie Farm. This ivy-clad 17th-century farmhouse sits in a tranquil area 5 mi from Lake Vyrnwy. **Pros:** in-room fireplaces; outdoor hot tub; hosts are trained chefs. **Cons:** remote location; need a car to get around. ⊠ *Off B4393, near Llanfyllin, Llanfihangel-yng-Ngwynfa* ☎ *01691/648451* ⊕ *www.cyfiefarm.co.uk* ⟳ *4 suites* ⚮ *In-room: no a/c. In-hotel: some age restrictions* ⦿ *Breakfast.*

£££–££££
B&B/INN
★

⊡ Lake Vyrnwy Hotel. Awesome views of mountain-ringed Lake Vyrnwy are just one asset of this country mansion on a 24,000-acre estate. **Pros:** perfect for outdoor pursuits; dramatic lakeside location; luxurious spa. **Cons:** too remote for some; minimum stay on some summer weekends. ⊠ *Off B4393, Llanwddyn* ☎ *01691/870692* ⊕ *www.lakevyrnwy.com* ⟳ *52 rooms* ⚮ *In-room: no a/c. In-hotel: restaurant, bars, tennis court, gym, spa, water sports, some pets allowed* ⦿ *Breakfast.*

PORTHMADOG

35 mi southeast of Lake Vyrnwy, 16 mi southeast of Caernarfon.

The little seaside town of Porthmadog, built as a harbor to export slate from nearby Blaenau Ffestiniog, stands at the gateway to the Llyn Peninsula, with its virtually unspoiled coastline and undulating, wildflower-covered hills. It's also near the town of Harlech, which contains one of the great castles of Wales, and the weird and wonderful Portmeirion.

GETTING HERE AND AROUND

The picturesque Cambrian Coast Railway runs from Machynlleth, near Aberystwyth, up the coast to Porthmadog. When you arrive you can take a scenic trip on the town's "little railways." Porthmadog is a stop on the excellent Snowdon Sherpa bus service. The town itself is totally walkable and has good access to coastal trails.

ESSENTIALS

Visitor Information Porthmadog (⊠ *High St.* ☎ *01766/512981* ⊕ *www. porthmadog.co.uk*).

EXPLORING

TOP ATTRACTIONS

☾ **Ffestiniog Railway.** Founded in the early 19th century to carry slate, the Ffestiniog Railway starts at the quayside and climbs up 700 feet through a wooded vale, past a waterfall, and across the mountains. The northern terminus is in Blaenau Ffestiniog, where you can visit an old slate mine. The Ffestiniog Railway is perhaps the best of several small steam lines in this part of the country. ☎ *01766/516000* ⊕ *www.festrail.co.uk* 🎫 *£19 round-trip* ⊙ *Apr.–Oct., daily; call for times.*

★ **Harlech Castle.** A wealth of legend, poetry, and song is conjured up by the 13th-century Harlech Castle, built by Edward I to help subdue the Welsh. Its mighty ruins, visible for miles, are as dramatic as its history (though you have to imagine the sea, which used to crash against the

EATING WELL IN WALES

Talented chefs making use of the country's bountiful resources have put Wales firmly on the culinary map. Welsh Black beef and succulent Welsh lamb are world renowned, and the supply of fish and seafood (including mussels and oysters) from coasts and rivers is excellent. Organic products are available to restaurants and the public from specialty companies, farm shops, and farmers' markets.

Ty Nant Welsh spring water graces restaurant tables worldwide, and there are a few small vineyards producing nice whites scattered here and there in the south. There's even a Welsh whisky that has won awards at international tastings.

Cheese making has undergone a remarkable revival. You can try traditionally named cheeses such as Llanboidy and Caws Cenarth or an extra-mature cheddar called Black Bomber.

Contemporary cuisine has the buzz, but traditional dishes are worth seeking out. Cawl, for example, is a nourishing broth of lamb and vegetables, and laverbread is a distinctive-tasting pureed seaweed that's usually fried with eggs and bacon.

14

rocks below but receded in the 19th century). Harlech was occupied by the Welsh Prince Owain Glyndwr from 1404 to 1408 during his revolt against the English. The music of the traditional folk song "Men of Harlech" refers to the heroic defense of this castle in 1468 by Dafydd ap Eynion, who, summoned to surrender, is alleged to have replied: "I held a castle in France until every old woman in Wales heard of it, and I will hold a castle in Wales until every old woman in France hears of it." On a clear day you can climb the battlements for a spectacular view of the surrounding countryside. The castle dominates the coastal town of Harlech, 12 mi south of Porthmadog. ⊠ *Off B4573* ☎ *01443/336000* ⊕ *www.cadw.wales.gov.uk* ⊠ *£3.80* ⊙ *Mar.–June, Sept., and Oct., daily 9:30–5; July and Aug., daily 9:30–6; Nov.–Feb., Mon.–Sat. 10–4, Sun. 11–4.*

Fodor'sChoice ★ **Portmeirion.** One of the true highlights of North Wales is Portmeirion, a tiny fantasy-Italianate village on a private peninsula surrounded by hills, which is said to be loosely modeled after Portofino. Designed in the 1920s by architect Clough Williams-Ellis (1883–1978), the village has a hotel and restaurant among its multicolored buildings, and gift shops sell a distinctive local pottery. On the edge of town is a peaceful woodland trail punctuated here and there by such flourishes as a red iron bridge and a miniature pagoda. William-Ellis called it his "light-opera approach to architecture," and the result is magical, though distinctly un-Welsh. Portmeirion is about 2 mi east of Porthmadog. ⊠ *Off A487, near Minffordd* ☎ *01766/772311* ⊕ *www.portmeirion-village. com* ⊠ *£9* ⊙ *Daily 9:30–5:30.*

WORTH NOTING

☺ **Llechwedd Slate Caverns.** At these caverns you can take two trips: a tram ride through floodlighted tunnels where Victorian working conditions have been re-created, and a ride on Britain's deepest underground

For a touch of whimsy, visit the mock-Italianate village of Portmeirion, set on the coast.

railway to a mine where you can walk by an eerie underground lake. Either tour gives a good idea of the difficult working conditions the miners endured. Above are a re-created Victorian village and slate-splitting demonstrations. ⊠ *Off A470* ☎ *01766/830306* ⊕ *www.llechwedd-slate-caverns.co.uk* 🎫 *Tour £9.50, grounds free* ⊙ *Apr.–Sept., daily 10–5:15; Oct.–Mar., daily 10–4:15.*

🅒 **Welsh Highland Heritage Railway.** You can take a short rail ride, tour the engine sheds, and clamber in the cabs of the locomotives housed here. ⊠ *Tremadog Rd.* ☎ *01766/513402* ⊕ *www.whr.co.uk* 🎫 *£6* ⊙ *Easter–Oct., daily 10:30–4*

WHERE TO EAT AND STAY
For expanded hotel reviews, visit Fodors.com.

£££££ ✕**Castle Cottage.** Close to Harlech's mighty castle, this friendly "restau-
BRITISH rant with rooms" is a wonderful find. The emphasis is on the exceptional cuisine of chef-proprietor Glyn Roberts, who uses ingredients from lobster to lamb to create imaginative, beautifully presented contemporary dishes. There's a fixed-price dinner menu (£36.50). The three spacious, modern rooms in the main house and four more in the annex, a former 16th-century coaching inn. ⊠ *Near B4573, Harlech* ☎ *01766/780479* ⊕ *www.castlecottageharlech.co.uk* ⊙ *No lunch.*

£ ✕**Ty Coch Inn.** In a seafront building in picture-postcard Porthdinllaen,
BRITISH this pub has what is undoubtedly one of the best locations in Wales. The
★ lunches are honest and unpretentious: pies, sandwiches, bangers and mash, or perhaps a plate of local mussels in garlic butter. Everything is delicious and reasonably priced. The atmosphere is friendly and slightly bohemian; this is the kind of place where they're pleasantly surprised

you've managed to find it. ✉ *Porthdinllaen* ☎ *01758/720498* ⊕ *www. tycoch.co.uk* ☾ *No dinner.*

££–£££
B&B/INN
★
🔲 **Hotel Maes-y-Neuadd.** Eight acres of gardens and parkland create a glorious setting for this luxurious manor house dating from the 14th century. **Pros:** magnificent location above Tremadog Bay; great restaurant. **Cons:** breakfast not included; low ceilings in some rooms. ✉ *Off B4573, Talsarnau* ☎ *01766/780200* ⊕ *www.neuadd.com* ➾ *15 rooms* ⅙ *In-room: no a/c, Wi-Fi. In-hotel: restaurant, bar, some pets allowed* ❢◎❢ *Breakfast.*

£££
HOTEL
🔲 **Hotel Portmeirion.** One of the most elegant and unusual places to stay in Wales, this waterfront mansion is located at the heart of Portmeirion. **Pros:** unique location; beautiful building; woodland walks. **Cons:** gets crowded with day-trippers; minimum stay on weekends; some rooms a bit shabby. ✉ *A487, Portmeirion* ☎ *01766/770000* ⊕ *www. portmeirion-village.com* ➾ *42 rooms, 11 suites* ⅙ *In-room: no a/c, Wi-Fi. In-hotel: restaurant, bar, pool, tennis court* ❢◎❢ *Breakfast.*

BETWS-Y-COED

25 mi northeast of Porthmadog, 19 mi south of Llandudno.

The rivers Llugwy and Conwy meet at Betws-y-Coed, a popular village surrounded by woodland with excellent views of Snowdonia. It can be used as a base to explore the national park, although its diminutive size means that it can get overcrowded in summer. The most famous landmark in the village is the ornate iron Waterloo Bridge over the River Conwy, designed in 1815 by Thomas Telford.

GETTING HERE AND AROUND

The town is easy to reach on the Conwy Valley Railway that runs from Llandudno to Blaenau Ffestiniog. Betws-y-Coed is also a hub for the excellent Snowdon Sherpa bus service that covers most of Snowdonia's beauty spots, so it's feasible to explore this part of Wales without a car.

ESSENTIALS

Visitor Information Betws-y-Coed (✉ *Royal Oak Stables* ☎ *01690/710426* ⊕ *www.betws-y-coed.co.uk*).

EXPLORING

★
☾
Snowdonia National Park. Stretching from the Welsh midlands almost to its northern coast, Snowdonia National Park covers a vast swath of North Wales. The park consists of 840 square mi of rocky mountains, valleys clothed in oak woods, moorlands, lakes, and rivers, all guaranteeing natural beauty and, to a varying extent, solitude. Its most famous attraction, by far, is the towering peak of Mt. Snowdon. The view from the top is jaw-dropping: to the northwest you can see the Menai Strait and Anglesey; to the south, Harlech Castle and the Cadair Idris mountain range. To the southwest, on an exceedingly clear day, you can make out the distant peaks of Ireland's Wicklow Mountains. There are six different walking paths to the top, but a far less punishing way is via the Snowdon Mountain Railway, in nearby Llanberis.

Perched at the top of Snowdon is Hafod Eryri, an eco-friendly replacement for the previous visitor center (once described by Prince Charles as "the highest slum in Wales"). The granite-roof building, which blends beautifully into the rocky landscape, has a café and exhibitions about the mountain, its ecology, and its history. If you're planning to make the ascent, the visitor center in Betws-y-Coed is the best place to stop for information.

Swallow Falls. Betws-y-Coed is bordered by Gwydyr Forest, which has several well-marked walking trails. The forest also contains a half dozen or so mines, the last of which was abandoned in the 1940s. On the western approach to the village are Swallow Falls, where the River Llugwy tumbles down through a wooded chasm. Be careful on the footpath though; there's no guardrail. ⊠ *Off A5.*

WHERE TO EAT AND STAY

For expanded hotel reviews, visit Fodors.com.

££££
BRITISH

✕ **Ty Gwyn.** This coaching inn, built in 1636, is one of the best places to eat in Snowdonia. The food is traditional Welsh fare, beautifully prepared with local ingredients: duck breast in a whiskey reduction, for instance, or Aberdaron lobster with cheddar and mustard crème fraiche. Vegetarians are well cared for with such dishes as Thai-style vegetable curry with fresh lime and chili. The inn also has simple, cozy bedrooms starting at £40 per night. ⊠ *A5* ☎ *01690/710383* ⊕ *www. tygwynhotel.co.uk.*

££
B&B/INN

🛏 **Aberconwy House.** This luxurious Victorian house has panoramic views over Betws-y-Coed. **Pros:** beautiful countryside views; great breakfasts. **Cons:** no bar or evening meal. ⊠ *Turn onto Lôn Muriau off A470, then Llanrwst* ☎ *01690/710202* ⊕ *www.aberconwy-house. co.uk* 🛏 *8 rooms* ⌂ *In-room: no a/c, Wi-Fi* ⦿ *Breakfast.*

££
B&B/INN

🛏 **Pengwern Country House.** In Victorian times this stone-and-slate country house on 2 acres of woodland was an artists' colony; today the polished slate floors, high ceilings, and classic color schemes exude charm and country-house sophistication. **Pros:** woodland location; wealth of Victorian details. **Cons:** close to main road; car is essential. ⊠ *A5, Allt Dinas* ☎ *01690/710480* ⊕ *www.snowdoniaaccommodation.co.uk* 🛏 *3 rooms* ⌂ *In-room: no a/c, no TV, Wi-Fi. In-hotel: business center, some age restrictions* ⦿ *Breakfast.*

££££–££££
B&B/INN

🛏 **Tan-y-Foel Country House.** Hidden away on a wooded hillside outside Betws-y-Coed, this quiet, contemporary hideaway has views over the Conwy Valley. **Pros:** strikingly contemporary decor; inventive cuisine. **Cons:** meals by arrangement only; too far to walk into town. ⊠ *Off A5, Capel Garmon* ☎ *01690/710507* ⊕ *www.tyfhotel.co.uk* 🛏 *6 rooms* ⌂ *In-room: no a/c, Wi-Fi. In-hotel: restaurant, bar, some age restrictions* ⦿ *Breakfast.*

LLANBERIS

17 mi west of Betws-y-Coed.

Llanberis, like Betws-y-Coed, is a focal point for people visiting Snowdonia National Park.

The Llanberis Path is one route to the top of Snowdon, the highest peak in Wales, in Snowdonia National Park.

GETTING HERE AND AROUND

Llanberis is accessible by bus. The most convenient service, targeted at visitors, is the Snowdon Sherpa bus route.

ESSENTIALS

Visitor Information Llanberis (✉ *41b High St.* ☎ *01286/870765*).

EXPLORING

★ **Caernarfon Castle.** The grim, majestic mass of Caernarfon Castle, a UNESCO World Heritage Site, looms over the waters of the River Seiont. Numerous bloody encounters were witnessed by these sullen walls, erected by Edward I in 1283 as a symbol of his determination to subdue the Welsh. The castle's towers, unlike those of Edward I's other castles, are polygonal and patterned with bands of different-color stone. In 1284 the monarch thought of a scheme to steal the Welsh throne. Knowing that the Welsh chieftains would accept no foreign prince, Edward promised to designate a ruler who could speak no word of English. Edward presented his infant son to the assembled chieftains as their prince "who spoke no English, had been born on Welsh soil, and whose first words would be spoken in Welsh." The ruse worked, and on that day was created the first prince of Wales of English lineage. In the Queen's Tower, a museum charts the history of the local regiment, the Royal Welsh Fusiliers. The castle is in the town of Caernarfon, 7 mi west of Llanberis. ✉ *Castle Hill, Caernarfon* ☎ *01286/677617* ⊕ *www.caernarfon.com* ⏱ *£5* ⊙ *Mar.–June, Sept., and Oct., daily 9:30–5; July and Aug., daily 9:30–6; Nov.–Feb., Mon.–Sat. 10–4, Sun. 11–4.*

National Slate Museum. In the Padarn Country Park, this museum in the old Dinorwig Slate Quarry is dedicated to what was once an important

Want the view but not the walk up Snowdon? Take the scenic Snowdon Mountain Railway from Llanberis.

industry for the area. The museum has quarry workshops and slate-splitting demonstrations, as well as restored worker housing, all of which convey the development of the industry and the challenges faced by those who worked in it. The narrow-gauge Llanberis Lake Railway runs from here. ⊠ *A4086* 🕾 *01286/870630* ⊕ *www.museumwales. ac.uk* 🖼 *Free* ☉ *Easter–Oct., daily 10–5; Nov.–Easter, Sun.–Fri. 10–4.*

★ **Snowdon Mountain Railway.** One of the region's most famous attractions
🖑 is the rack-and-pinion Snowdon Mountain Railway, with some of its track at a thrillingly steep grade; the train terminates within 70 feet of the 3,560-foot-high summit. Snowdon, *Yr Wyddfa* in Welsh, is the highest peak south of Scotland and lies within the 840-square-mi national park. From May through September, weather permitting, trains go all the way to the summit; on a clear day you can see as far as the Wicklow Mountains in Ireland, about 90 mi away. In 1998 the National Trust bought the mountain, ensuring its long-term protection. ⊠ *A4086* 🕾 *0870/458–0033* ⊕ *www.snowdonrailway.co.uk* 🖼 *£25 round-trip* ☉ *Mar.–Oct., daily; schedule depends on customer demand.*

🖑 **Welsh Highland Railway–Rheilffordd Eryri.** You can take a trip on a coal-fired steam locomotive at this narrow-gauge line that operates on the scenic route of an abandoned railway. The line was extended to Porthmadog in 2011, linking with the Ffestiniog Railway. The terminus is on the quay near Caernarfon Castle. ⊠ *St. Helens Rd., Caernarfon* 🕾 *01766/516000* ⊕ *www.welshhighlandrailway.net* 🖼 *£28 round-trip* ☉ *Apr.–Oct., daily 10–4; Nov.–Mar., limited weekend service.*

WHERE TO STAY
For expanded hotel reviews, visit Fodors.com.

££–£££   🏠 **Meifod Country House.** Former home of the high sheriff of Caernarfon,
HOTEL   this opulent Victorian house has polished tile floors, wood-burning fireplaces, and bedrooms with features such as Victorian claw-foot baths
and chandeliers. **Pros:** authentic atmosphere; good food. **Cons:** often
booked with wedding parties; not walking distance to town. ⊠ *Off
A487, Bontnewydd* ☎ *01286/673351* ⊕ *www.meifodcountryhouse.
co.uk* ⇨ *5 rooms* ⌂ *In-room: no a/c. In-hotel: restaurant, bars, tennis
court* ⫼⊙⫼ *Breakfast.*

BEAUMARIS (BIWMARES) AND ANGLESEY (YNYS MÔN)

14 mi north of Llanberis.

Elegant Beaumaris is on the Isle of Anglesey, the largest island directly
off the shore of Wales and England. It's linked to the mainland by the
Britannia road and rail bridge and by Thomas Telford's remarkable
chain suspension bridge, built in 1826 over the Menai Strait. Though
its name means "beautiful marsh," Beaumaris has become a town of
pretty cottages, Georgian houses, and bright shops; it also has Plas
Newydd, one of the grandest stately homes in Wales.

Around 70% of Anglesey's 60,000 or so inhabitants speak Welsh, so
you'll probably hear it more than English. Anglesey is the home of Prince
William and the Duchess of Cambridge (formerly Kate Middleton),
until William completes his posting as an air ambulance pilot in 2013.

GETTING HERE AND AROUND

Anglesey is linked to the mainland by the A55 and A5. The roads on
the island are in good condition, and there's a relatively extensive bus
network. Ferries and catamarans to Ireland leave from Holyhead, on
the island's western side.

EXPLORING

Beaumaris Castle. The town of Beaumaris dates from 1295, when
Edward I commenced work on this impressive castle, the last and largest link in an "iron ring" of fortifications around North Wales built
to contain the Welsh. Guarding the western approach to the Menai
Strait, the unfinished castle (a World Heritage Site) is solid and symmetrical, with concentric lines of fortification, arrow slits, and a moat:
a superb example of medieval defensive planning. ⊠ *Castle St., Beaumaris* ☎ *01248/810361* ⊕ *www.cadw.wales.gov.uk* ⊠ *£3.60* ⊙ *Apr.–
Oct., daily 9–5; Nov.–Mar., Mon.–Sat. 9:30–4, Sun. 11–4.*

Beaumaris Gaol. To learn about the grim life of a Victorian prisoner,
head to the old jail, built in 1829 by Joseph Hansom (1803–82), who
was also the designer of the Hansom cab. ⊠ *Steeple La., Beaumaris*
☎ *01248/810921* ⊠ *£3.50* ⊙ *Easter–Sept., daily 10:30–5.*

Church of St. Mary and St. Nicholas. Opposite Beaumaris Gaol in Steeple
Lane, this 14th-century church houses the stone coffin of Princess Joan,
daughter of King John (1167–1216) and wife of Welsh leader Llewelyn
the Great. ⊠ *Steeple La., Beaumaris.*

★ **Plas Newydd.** Some historians consider Plas Newydd to be the finest
mansion in Wales. Remodeled in the 18th century by James Wyatt
(1747–1813) for the marquesses of Anglesey (whose descendants still

live here), it stands on the Menai Strait about 7 mi southwest of Beaumaris. The interior has some fine 18th-century Gothic Revival decorations. Between 1936 and 1940 the society artist Rex Whistler (1905–44) painted the mural in the dining room. A museum commemorates the Battle of Waterloo, where the first marquess led the cavalry. The woodland walk and rhododendron gardens are worth exploring, and it's sometimes possible to take boat trips on the strait. ⊠ *Off A4080, southwest of Britannia Bridge, Llanfairpwll* ☎ *01248/715272* ⊕ *www. nationaltrust.org.uk* ⊠ *House £9.30; garden only, £7.30* ⊙ *House mid-Mar.–early Nov., Sat.–Wed. 11:15–5; last admission ½ hr before closing. Garden mid-Mar.–early Nov., Sat.–Wed. 10–5:30.*

WHERE TO STAY
For expanded hotel reviews, visit Fodors.com.

££
B&B/INN
★
Cleifiog. This cozy manor house, mostly Georgian in style, is on the banks of the Menai Strait a short stroll from Beaumaris Castle. **Pros:** seafront location; close to town; interesting history. **Cons:** minimum stay on weekends; a little claustrophobic. ⊠ *A454, Beaumaris* ☎ *01248/811507* ⊕ *www.cleifiogbandb.co.uk* ⊅ *3 rooms* ☊ *In-room: no a/c. In-hotel: business center, some age restrictions* ⦿ *Breakfast.*

££–£££
B&B/INN
Ye Olde Bull's Head and Townhouse. These twin hotels, a stone's throw away from each other, could hardly be more different: one is a restored 15th- century coaching inn, the other a contemporary lodging. **Pros:** lovely blend of historic and contemporary; good food. **Cons:** Bull's Head has low ceilings. ⊠ *Castle St., Beaumaris* ☎ *01248/810329* ⊕ *www.bullsheadinn.co.uk.* ⊅ *13 rooms* ☊ *In-room: no a/c, Wi-Fi (some). In-hotel: restaurants.* ⦿ *Breakfast.*

SPORTS AND THE OUTDOORS
Anglesey is a great place to get outdoors. The **Isle of Anglesey Coastal Path** (⊕ *www.angleseycoastalpath.co.uk*) extends 125 mi around the island, with cliffs, sandy covers, and plenty of scenic variety. Pick up information at tourist offices and choose a section; the west coast has the most dramatic scenery.

CONWY

23 mi east of Beaumaris, 48 mi northwest of Chester.

The still-authentic medieval town of Conwy grew up around its castle on the west bank of the River Conwy. A ring of ancient but well-preserved walls, built in the 13th century to protect the English merchants who lived here, enclose the old town and add to the pervading sense of history. Sections of the walls, with their 21 towers, can still be walked. The impressive views from the top take in the castle and the estuary, with mountains in the distance.

GETTING HERE AND AROUND
The A55 expressway links Conwy into the central U.K. motorway system via the M56. The town is also on the North Wales coast rail route, which ends at Holyhead on Anglesey. The town itself—surrounded by its wonderfully preserved walls—is perfect for pedestrians.

ESSENTIALS

Visitor Information Conwy (⊠ *Castle Bldg.* ☎ *01492/592248* ⊕ www. visitconwytown.co.uk).

EXPLORING

Aberconwy House. Built in the 14th century, Aberconwy House is the only surviving medieval merchant's house in Conwy. Each room in the restored building reflects different eras of its long history. ⊠ *Castle St.* ☎ *01492/592246* ⊕ *www.nationaltrust.org.uk* ⛱ *£3.40* ☉ *Mid-Mar. June, Sept., and Oct., Wed.–Mon. 11–5; July and Aug., Wed.–Mon. 11–5.*

★ **Bodnant Garden.** Undoubtedly one of the best gardens in Wales, Bodnant Garden is something of a pilgrimage spot for horticulturists from around the world. Laid out in 1875, the 87 acres are particularly famed for rhododendrons, camellias, and magnolias. ■TIP➔ Visit in May to see the laburnum arch that forms a huge tunnel of golden blooms. The mountains of Snowdonia form a magnificent backdrop to the Italianate terraces, rock and rose gardens, and pinetum. The gardens are about 5 mi south of Conwy. ⊠ *Off A470, Tal-y-Cafn* ☎ *01492/650460* ⊕ *www.nationaltrust.org.uk* ⛱ *£7.95* ☉ *Mar.–Oct., daily 10–5; early to mid-Nov., daily 10–4.*

★ **Conwy Castle.** Of all Edward I's Welsh strongholds, it is perhaps Conway Castle that best preserves a sheer sense of power and dominance. The eight large round towers and tall curtain wall, set on a rocky promontory, provide sweeping views of the area and the town walls. Although the castle is roofless (and floorless in places), the signage does a pretty good job of helping you visualize how rooms such as the Great Hall must have looked when they were complete. Conwy Castle can be approached on foot by a dramatic suspension bridge completed in 1828; engineer Thomas Telford designed the bridge with turrets to blend in with the fortress's presence. ⊠ *Rose Hill St.* ☎ *01492/592358* ⊕ *www.cadw.wales.gov.uk* ⛱ *£4.80, £7.30 joint ticket with Plas Mawr* ☉ *Mar.–Oct., daily 9.30–5; Nov.–Feb., Mon.–Sat. 9:30–4, Sun. 11–4.*

Plas Mawr. Dating from 1576, Plas Mawr is the best-preserved Elizabethan town house in Britain. Richly decorated with ornamental plasterwork, it gives a unique insight into the lives of the Tudor gentry and their servants. ⊠ *High St.* ☎ *01492/580167* ⊕ *www.cadw.wales.gov.uk* ⛱ *£5.20, £7.30 joint ticket with Conwy Castle* ☉ *Apr.–Sept., Tues.– Sun. 9–5; Oct., Tues.–Sun. 9:30–4.*

Smallest House in Britain. What is said to be Britain's smallest house is furnished in mid-Victorian Welsh style. The house, which is 6 feet wide and 10 feet high, was reputedly last occupied in 1900 by a fisherman who was more than 6 feet tall. ⊠ *Lower Gate St.* ☎ *01492/593484* ⛱ *£1* ☉ *Apr.–Oct., daily 10–4:30.*

WHERE TO EAT AND STAY

For expanded hotel reviews, visit Fodors.com.

£££

MODERN BRITISH

✕ **Le Gallois.** Just off the coast road 4 mi west of Conwy, this small and unpretentious restaurant is a culinary oasis. The chef-proprietor offers a daily menu using the best local produce. Dishes may include

14

juicy scallops with a beurre blanc, Conwy crab au gratin, or local lamb cooked with a mint-and-Madeira sauce. ⊠ *Pant yr Afon, Penmaenmawr* ☎ *01492/623820* ☾ *Closed Mon.–Wed. No lunch.*

££   ✕ **The Mulberry.** This family-run restaurant overlooking the boats bob-
MODERN BRITISH   bing in Conwy Marina is as popular for its jovial atmosphere as it is for its eclectic, unpretentious cooking. The menu consists of classic dishes like rack of lamb, as well as more-inventive fare like crispy duck cooked with hoisin sauce, or sea bass with a saffron-and-red-pepper sauce. Sunday lunch is served buffet style. ⊠ *Morfa Dr.* ☎ *01492/583350* ⊕ www. themulberryconwy.com.

£££   ▦ **Castle Hotel.** Nestled within Conwy's medieval walls, this former
HOTEL   coaching inn has wood beams, stone fireplaces, and plenty of antiques. **Pros:** oozes history; in the heart of Conwy; good food. **Cons:** small rooms; noisy seagulls. ⊠ *High St.* ☎ *01492/582800* ⊕ *www.castlewales. co.uk* ⤴ *28 rooms* ⌂ *In-room: no a/c, Wi-Fi. In-hotel: restaurant, bar, some pets allowed* ⌘ *Breakfast.*

££   ▦ **Sychnant Pass House.** On a peaceful wooded hillside 2 mi west of
HOTEL   Conwy, this country-house hotel has a laid-back atmosphere. **Pros:** great indoor pool and hot tub; beautiful grounds; unforced hospitality. **Cons:** pets allowed in rooms; far outside Conwy. ⊠ *Sychnant Pass Rd.* ☎ *01492/596868* ⊕ *www.sychnant-pass-house.co.uk* ⤴ *12 rooms* ⌂ *In-room: no a/c. In-hotel: restaurant, pool, gym, some pets allowed* ⌘ *Breakfast.*

LLANDUDNO

3 mi north of Conwy, 50 mi northwest of Chester.

This engagingly old-fashioned North Wales seaside resort has a wealth of well-preserved Victorian architecture and an ornate amusement pier with entertainments, shops, and places to eat. Grand-looking small hotels line the wide promenade with a view of the deep-blue waters of the bay. The shopping district beyond retains its original canopied walkways.

GETTING HERE AND AROUND

Llandudno is on the North Wales railway line, with fast access from London and other major cities. By road, it is connected to the motorway system via the A55 expressway. The scenic Conwy Valley rail line runs to Blaenau Ffestiniog, and the town is also on the network covered by the Snowdon Sherpa bus service.

ESSENTIALS

Visitor Information Llandudno (⊠ *Mostyn St.* ☎ *01492/876413* ⊕ *www. visitllandudno.org.uk).*

EXPLORING

Great Orme. Named for the Norse word meaning "sea monster," the 679-foot headland called Great Orme towers over Llandudno, affording extraordinary views over the bay. The **Grand Orme Aerial Cable Car** (⊠ *Happy Valley Rd.* ☎ *01492/879306* 🎫 *£7 round-trip* ☾ *Easter– Sept., daily 10–4:30*) zips you to the top of Grand Orme in no time. At the summit there's an artificial ski slope and a toboggan run, both usable

With plants and trees from around the world, Bodnant Garden, south of Conwy, is colorful in fall.

all year. The most picturesque way to reach the summit of Grande Orme is the **Great Orme Tramway** (✉ *Victoria Station, Church Walks* ☎ *01492/879306* ⊕ *www.greatormetramway.co.uk* 🎫 *£6 round-trip* ⊙ *Late Mar.–late Oct., daily 10–6*). The summit is a sylvan spot, with open grassland, fields of wildflowers, and rare butterflies.

Great Orme Mines. Discovered in 1987, these mines date back 4,000 years to when copper was first mined in the area. You can take a tour and learn about the technology that ancient people used to dig the tunnels, which are thought to be the largest surviving prehistoric mines in the world. ✉ *Great Orme* ☎ *01492/870447* ⊕ *www.greatormemines. info* 🎫 *£6* ⊙ *Mar.–Oct., daily 10–5.*

WHERE TO STAY
For expanded hotel reviews, visit Fodors.com.

£££–££££   🏨 **Bodysgallen Hall.** Tasteful antiques, polished wood, and comfortable
HOTEL   chairs by cheery fires distinguish one of Wales's most luxurious country-
★   house hotels. **Pros:** superb spa and pool; rare 17th-century knot garden; elegant dining. **Cons:** too formal for some; hard to get to without a car. ✉ *Off A470* ☎ *01492/584466* ⊕ *www.bodysgallen.com* 🛏 *15 rooms, 16 cottage suites* ⚒ *In-room: no a/c (some), Wi-Fi. In-hotel: restaurant, bar, pool, gym, spa, business center, some pets allowed, some age restrictions* ⊙| *Breakfast.*

££   🏨 **Bryn Derwen Hotel.** This immaculate Victorian hotel has been reno-
HOTEL   vated into a charming, contemporary place to stay. **Pros:** attractive Victorian building; close to the beach. **Cons:** no sea views. ✉ *34 Abbey Rd.* ☎ *01492/876804* ⊕ *www.bryn-derwen.co.uk* 🛏 *9 rooms* ⚒ *In-*

room: no a/c, Wi-Fi. In-hotel: restaurant, bar, some age restrictions
†Ol *Breakfast.*

£££–££££   🏨 **St. Tudno Hotel.** Perfectly situated on the seafront promenade over-
HOTEL   looking the beach and pier, this hotel has been run by the same fam-
           ily for nearly 40 years. **Pros:** ocean views; swimming pool; good
           food. **Cons:** some rooms are snug; overly fussy decor. ⊠ *Promenade*
           ☎ *01492/874411* ⊕ *www.st-tudno.co.uk* ⤴ *18 rooms* △ *In-room: no a/c
           (some). In-hotel: restaurant, bar, pool, some pets allowed* †Ol *Breakfast.*

RUTHIN RHUTHUN

33 mi southeast of Llandudno, 23 mi southwest of Chester.

Once a stronghold of the rebel Welsh prince Owain Glyndwr (c. 1354–
1416), Ruthin is a delightful market town with elegant shops, good
inns, and a fascinating architectural mix of medieval, Tudor, and Georgian buildings. The town also has a crafts complex with displays of the
artisans' creations.

GETTING HERE AND AROUND

Ruthin is on the A494 and A525 roads. The nearest railway stations
are Rhyl and Wrexham, (both about 20 mi.) Local bus connections are
reasonably good; most useful bus connections go through Rhyl.

EXPLORING

Myddleton Arms. This distinctive 17th-century building in the town
square has seven Dutch-style dormer windows, known as the "eyes of
Ruthin," set into its red-tile roof. ⊠ *St. Peter's Sq.*

Ruthin Gaol. You can tour the local jail, where from 1654 to 1916 thousands of prisoners were incarcerated, and learn about prison conditions
over the centuries. ⊠ *Clwyd St.* ☎ *01824/708281* ⊕ *www.ruthingaol.
co.uk* ⤴ *£3.50* ⊙ *Late Feb.–Mar., daily 10–5; Apr.–Oct., Wed.–Sun.
and bank holidays 10–5. Last admission 1 hr before closing.*

WHERE TO STAY

For expanded hotel reviews, visit Fodors.com.

££   🏨 **Eyarth Old Railway Station.** This Victorian railway station 2 mi south
B&B/INN   of Ruthin has been converted into an outstanding B&B. **Pros:** unique
           building; secluded garden; great views. **Cons:** rooms a little dated. ⊠ *Off
           A525, Llanfair Dyffryn Clwyd* ☎ *01824/703643* ⊕ *www.eyarthstation.
           com* ⤴ *6 rooms* △ *In-room: no a/c, no TV, Wi-Fi. In-hotel: bar, pool,
           business center, some pets allowed* †Ol *Breakfast.*

££–£££ 🏨 **manorhaus.** A Georgian town house in the heart of Ruthin has been
B&B/INN   converted into a gorgeous boutique hotel. **Pros:** cutting-edge design;
   ★   art lover's paradise; trendy bistro. **Cons:** small rooms; limited parking.
           ⊠ *Well St.* ☎ *01824/704830* ⊕ *www.manorhaus.com* ⤴ *8 rooms* △ *In-
           room: Wi-Fi. In-hotel: restaurant, bar, gym, spa* †Ol *Breakfast.*

UNDERSTANDING ENGLAND

ENGLISH ARCHITECTURAL STYLES

BOOKS AND MOVIES

ENGLISH ARCHITECTURAL STYLES

In England you can see structures that go back to the dawn of history, such as the hauntingly mysterious circles of monoliths at Stonehenge or Avebury, or view the surviving remains of the Roman Empire preserved in Bath, Cirencester, and other towns. On the other hand, you can startle your eyes with the very current designs of contemporary architects in areas such as London's Docklands or the City. Knowing a few hallmarks of particular styles can enhance your enjoyment. Here, then, is a primer of a millennium of architectural styles.

Norman
Duke William of Normandy brought the solid Norman style to Britain when he invaded and conquered England in 1066, although William's predecessor, King Edward (the Confessor) used the style in the building of Westminster Abbey a little earlier, in 1042. Until around 1200 it was favored for buildings of any importance, and William's castles and churches soon dominated the countryside.

Norman towers tended to be hefty and square, arches were always round-top, and the vaulting was barrel shape. Decoration was mostly geometrical, but within those limits, ornate. Norman motte-and-bailey castles had two connecting stockaded mounds, with the keep on the higher mound, and other buildings on the lower mound. *Best seen in the Tower of London and in the cathedrals of St. Albans, Ely, Gloucester, Durham, and Norwich.*

Gothic Early English
From 1130 to 1300, pointed arches began to supplant rounded ones, buttresses became heavier than the Norman variety, and windows lost their rounded tops to become more pointed and lancet shape. Buildings climbed skyward and were less squat and heavy, with the soaring effect accentuated by steep roofs and spires. *Best seen in the cathedrals of York, Salisbury, Ely, Worcester, Wells (interior), and Canterbury (east end), and Westminster Abbey's Chapter House.*

Decorated. From the late 1100s until around 1400, elegance and ornament became fully integrated into architectural design, rather than applied to the surface of a solid, basic form. Windows filled more of the walls and were divided into sections by carved mullions. Vaulting grew increasingly complex, with ribs and ornamented bosses proliferating; spires became even more pointed; arches took on the ogee shape, with its unique double curve. This style was one of England's greatest gifts to world architecture. *Best seen at the cathedrals of Wells, Lincoln, Exeter, Durham (east transept), and Ely (Lady Chapel and Octagon).*

Perpendicular. In later Gothic architecture, the emphasis on the vertical grew more pronounced, as shown in features such as slender pillars, huge expanses of glass, and superb fan vaulting resembling the formalized branches of frozen trees. Walls were divided by panels. One of the chief areas in which to see Perpendicular architecture is East Anglia, where towns that grew rich from the wool trade built magnificent churches in the style. Houses, too, began to reflect the prevailing taste. Perpendicular Gothic lasted for well over two centuries from its advent around 1330. *Best seen at St. George's Chapel in Windsor, Gloucester Cathedral (cloister), Henry VII's Chapel in Westminster Abbey, Bath Abbey, and King's College Chapel in Cambridge.*

Tudor
With the great period of cathedral building over, from 1500 to 1560 the nation's attention turned to the construction of spacious homes characterized by this latest fashionable architectural style. The rapidly expanding, newly rich middle class, created by the two Tudor Henrys (VII and VIII) to challenge the power of the aristocracy, built spacious manor houses, often on the foundations of pillaged monasteries. Thus began the era of the great stately homes. Brick replaced stone as the most popular medium, and

plasterwork and carved wood displayed the elaborate motifs of the age.

Timber-frame and plaster buildings were also popular in this period for domestic and commercial use. Many "black-and-white" structures, as they are called, are copies made in later eras, but notable originals survive. (The Victorians are responsible for the fashion of painting half-timber buildings, of whatever era, black and white.) Wealthier individuals could afford to have the exposed wood beams carved or shaped; Little Moreton Hall, in Congleton near the Peak District, has wonderfully intricate patterns. Speke Hall in Liverpool is another notable example, and Shrewsbury and Ludlow in the West Midlands have many half-timber buildings in this style.

Another way the social climbers could make their mark, and ensure their place in the next world, was by building churches. Money earned in the wool trade continued to fund splendid parish churches. Some of the most magnificent are in Suffolk, Norfolk, and the Cotswolds. *Domestic architecture is best seen at Hampton Court and St. James's Palace, London; for wool churches, Lavenham and Long Melford (though its tower is much later) in Suffolk, and Cirencester, Chipping Campden, Northleach, and Winchcombe in the Cotswolds.*

Renaissance Elizabethan

For a short period under Elizabeth I, 1560–1600, this development of Tudor style flourished as Italian influences began to seep into England, seen especially in symmetrical facades. The most notable example was Hardwick Hall in Derbyshire, built in the 1590s by Bess of Hardwick; the jingle that describes it goes "Hardwick Hall, more glass than wall." However grand the houses were, they were still on a human scale, warm and livable, built of a mellow amalgam of brick and stone. *Other great Elizabethan houses are Longleat in Wiltshire and Burghley House in Cambridgeshire.*

Jacobean

At the beginning of the 17th century, for the first 15 years of the reign of James I (the name "Jacobean" is taken from the Latin word for James, Jacobus), architecture did not change noticeably. Windows were still large in proportion to the wall surfaces. Gables, in the style of the Netherlands, were popular. Carved decoration in wood and plaster (especially the geometrical patterning called "strapwork," another element of Dutch origin, which resembled intertwined leather belts) remained exuberant, now even more so.

A change was on the way, though. Inigo Jones (1573–1652), the first great modern British architect, attempted to synthesize the architectural heritage of England with current Italian theories. Two of his finest remaining buildings—the Banqueting House in London and the Queen's House at Greenwich—epitomize his genius, which was to introduce to England the Italian-created Palladian style that would dominate England's architecture for centuries. It uses the classical Greek orders: Doric, Ionic, and Corinthian. The grand classical style that proved so monumentally effective under a hot Mediterranean sun was transformed in England, domesticated and tamed. Columns and pediments decorated the facades, and huge frescoes provided acres of color to interior walls and ceilings, all in the Italian manner.

Two quite distinct styles ran concurrently: the comfortably domestic and the purer classical in public buildings. They were finally fused by the talent of Christopher Wren. *Jacobean is best seen at the Bodleian Library, Oxford; Audley End, near Cambridge; Chastleton House, near Stow-on-the-Wold; Hatfield House, near St. Albans; and Emmanuel College, Cambridge.*

Wren and the English Baroque

The work of Sir Christopher Wren (1632–1723) constituted an architectural era all by itself. Not only was he one of the world's greatest architects, but he was also given an unparalleled opportunity in 1666 when the disastrous Great Fire of London wiped out the center of the capital, destroying no fewer than 89 churches and 13,200 houses. Although Wren's great scheme for a modern city center was rejected, he did build 52 churches in London, the greatest of which was St. Paul's, completed in just 35 years. The range of Wren's designs is extremely wide, from simple classical shapes to the extravagantly dramatic baroque. He was also at home with domestic architecture, where his combinations of brick and stone produced a warm, homey effect.

The influence of the Italian baroque can be seen in Sir John Vanbrugh's Blenheim Palace, where the facade echoes the piazza of St. Peter's in Rome, and at Vanbrugh's exuberant Castle Howard in Yorkshire.

Nicholas Hawksmoor, Wren's pupil, designed some notable London churches and also the baroque mausoleum at Castle Howard. The baroque had only a brief heyday in England; by 1725 the Palladian style was firmly in favor and the vast pile of Blenheim was being mocked by trendsetters. *Wren's ecclesiastical architecture is best seen at St. Paul's Cathedral (baroque with classical touches) and his other remaining London churches, his domestic style at Hampton Court Palace, Kensington Palace, and the Old Royal Naval College in Greenwich. English baroque is best seen at Blenheim Palace (Oxfordshire) and Castle Howard (Yorkshire).*

Palladian

In Britain this style is often referred to as Georgian, so called from the Hanoverian kings George I through IV, although it was introduced as early as Inigo Jones's time. During the 18th century, classical inspiration was thoroughly acclimatized. Though they looked completely at home among the hills, lakes, and trees of the English countryside, Palladian buildings were derived from the Roman-inspired designs of the Italian architectural theorist Andrea Palladio (1508–80), with pillared porticoes, triangular pediments, and strictly balanced windows. In domestic architecture, this large-scale classicism was usually modified to quiet simplicity, preserving mathematical proportions of windows, doors, and the exactly calculated volume of room space, to create a feeling of balance and harmony.

The occasional departures from the classical manner at this time included the over-the-top Indian-style Royal Pavilion in Brighton, built for the prince regent (later George IV) by John Nash. The Regency style comes under the Palladian heading, though strictly speaking it lasted only for the few years of the actual Regency (1811–20).

Architects such as the brilliant Robert Adam, who was born in Scotland but also worked in England, handled the Palladian style with more freedom than their counterparts elsewhere in Europe, and the United States took its cue from the British. *Among the best Palladian examples are Regent's Park Terraces (London), the library at Kenwood (London), the Royal Crescent and other streets in Bath, Stourhead (Wiltshire), and Holkham Hall (Norfolk).*

Victorian

Elements of imaginative fantasy, already seen in the Palladian era, came to the fore during the long reign of Victoria (1837–1901). The country's vast profits made from the Industrial Revolution were spent lavishly. Civic building accelerated in all the major cities, with town halls modeled after castles or French châteaux.

The Victorians plundered the past for styles, with Gothic, about which the scholarly Victorians were very knowledgeable, leading the field. The supreme examples here are the Houses of Parliament by Charles Barry and Augustus Pugin, and the Albert Memorial by George Gilbert Scott, both in London. (To distinguish between the Victorian variety and a version of the style that flourished in the late 1700s, the earlier one is commonly spelled "Gothick.") *Other striking examples of Victorian architecture are Truro Cathedral, Manchester Town Hall, and Ironbridge.*

Edwardian

Toward the end of the Victorian era, in the late 1800s, architecture calmed down considerably, with a return to a solid sort of classicism, and even to a muted baroque. The Arts and Crafts movement, especially the work of William Morris (1834–96) and work inspired by Morris, produced simpler designs, sometimes returning to medieval models. In an age of increasing mechanization, craftsmanship was emphasized. Architectural elements incorporated stylized natural motifs. *Best seen in Buckingham Palace and the Admiralty Arch in London. Rodmarton Manor near Tetbury (the Cotswolds), and Blackwell in Windermere (the Lake District) are notable Arts and Crafts houses.*

Modern

A public debate has raged in Britain for years between traditionalists and the adherents of modernistic architecture. Britons tend to be strongly conservative when it comes to their environment. One reason for the strength of this attitude is that the country suffered from much ill-conceived development after World War II, when large areas of city centers had to be rebuilt after the devastation caused by German bombs. Town planners and architects created badly built and worse-designed towers and shopping areas.

Today, however, there is an increased readiness to embrace the new. In London, Sir Norman Foster's graceful Millennium Bridge became a landmark almost as soon as it opened. Foster's glassy masterpiece, City Hall, near Tower Bridge, has been knocked as a "glass testicle," but it is one of the boldest designs in London. Other buildings, such as Barclays Bank with its

jukebox dome, and Swiss Re's "Gherkin" at 30 St. Mary Axe, the latter by Foster and looking akin to a glittering carousel pole, have begun to push height limitations established because of the proximity of historic buildings.

Other centers of modern architectural innovation include Manchester, with the Imperial War Museum North by Daniel Libeskind. After the city center was bombed by the Irish Republican Army in 1996, Manchester received an impressive face-lift. Also in the north, Gateshead Quays is the spectacularly renovated industrial area around the River Tyne and Newcastle. The tilting Millennium Bridge in Newcastle is as dramatic as London's, and the city has opened the Baltic Centre for Contemporary Art, as well as the Sage, a curvaceous steel-and-glass music venue. Cornwall has the Eden Project, the world's largest conservatories, which are set in a former china-clay pit and massed to make a giant glass crater. Anyone with an interest in architecture should visit the headquarters of the Royal Institute of British Architects (RIBA) in Portland Place, London, for exhibits on buildings great and small, new and old.

What's next? The 2012 Summer Olympics in London have prompted some ambitious building plans. Everyone's waiting for a swimming pool by world-renowned architect Zaha Hadid and the 1,016-foot "Shard" designed by Italian Renzo Piano—it will be the tallest building in London by 2012. *Among other buildings to see are the Clore Building at Tate Britain (in London), the campus of Sussex University (outside Brighton), the Royal Regatta Building (Henley), the Sainsbury Centre for the Visual Arts (Norwich), and the Lowry Centre (Manchester).*

BOOKS AND MOVIES

Fiction and Poetry

Many writers' names have become inextricably linked with the regions in which they set their books or plays. Hardy's Wessex, Daphne Du Maurier's Cornwall, Wordsworth's Lake District, Shakespeare's Arden, and Brontë Country in Yorkshire are now evocative catch-phrases, treasured by local tourist boards. However hackneyed the tags may be, you *can* still get a heightened insight into an area through the eyes of authors of genius, even though they may have written a century or more ago. Here are a few works that may provide you with an understanding of their authors' loved territory.

Thomas Hardy's novels *The Mayor of Casterbridge, Tess of the d'Urbervilles,* and *Far from the Madding Crowd* (and indeed almost everything he wrote) are solidly based on his Wessex (Dorset) homeland. Daphne Du Maurier had a deep love of Cornwall from her childhood; *Frenchman's Creek, Jamaica Inn,* and *The King's General* all capture the county's Celtic mood. The wildness of Exmoor in Devon is captured in the historical novel *Lorna Doone* by R.D. Blackmore. The Brontë sisters' *Wuthering Heights, The Tenant of Wildfell Hall,* and *Jane Eyre* breathe the sharp air of the moors around the writers' Haworth home. William Wordsworth, who was born at Cockermouth in the Lake District, depicts the area's rugged beauty in many of his poems, especially the *Lyrical Ballads.*

Virginia Woolf's visits to Vita Sackville-West at her ancestral home of Knole, in Sevenoaks, inspired the novel *Orlando.* The stately home is now a National Trust property. American writer Henry James lived at Lamb House in Rye, also in East Sussex, as did E.F. Benson, whose delicious Lucia novels take place in a thinly disguised version of the town. Lamb House is a National Trust building.

A highly irreverent and very funny version of academic life, *Porterhouse Blue,* by Tom Sharpe, will guarantee that you look at Oxford and Cambridge with a totally different eye. Also irreverent is *England, England* by Julian Barnes, in which an entrepreneur takes over the Isle of Wight and establishes a theme park based on national clichés. John Fowles's *The French Lieutenant's Woman,* largely set in Lyme Regis, is full of local color about Dorset, and Laurie Lee's *Cider with Rosie* is a poignant reminiscence about Cotswold village life in the 1920s.

Mysteries are almost a way of life, partly because many of the best English mystery writers set their plots in their home territories. Modern whodunits by P.D. James and Ruth Rendell convey a fine sense of place, and Ellis Peters's Brother Cadfael stories re-create life in medieval Shrewsbury with a wealth of telling detail. Colin Dexter's Inspector Morse mysteries capture the flavor of Oxford's town and gown. There are also always the villages, vicarages, and scandals of Agatha Christie's Miss Marple books.

The fans of Arthurian legends can turn to some excellent, imaginative novels that not only tell the stories but also give fine descriptions of the countryside. Among them are *Sword at Sunset,* by Rosemary Sutcliffe, *The Once and Future King,* by T.H. White, and the four Merlin novels by Mary Stewart: *The Crystal Cave, The Hollow Hills, The Last Enchantment,* and *The Wicked Day.* Edward Rutherfurd's historical novels *Sarum, London,* and *The Forest* deal with British history with a grand sweep from the prehistoric past to the present.

An animal's close-to-the-earth viewpoint can reveal all kinds of countryside insights. *Watership Down,* a runaway best seller about rabbits, was written by Richard Adam in the early '70s. *The Wind in the Willows,* by Kenneth Grahame, gives a vivid impression of the Thames Valley almost 100 years ago that still holds largely true today. Devon, the northern part in particular, is the setting of Henry Williamson's *Tarka the Otter,* a beloved nature story published in the 1920s; many paths in the region are signposted as part of the Tarka Trail.

Nonfiction

Those interested in writers and the surroundings that influenced their works should look at *Bloom's Literary Guide to London,* by Donna Dailey, and *The Oxford Literary Guide to the British Isles,* edited by Dorothy Eagle and Hilary Carnell (now out of print). One author currently in vogue is Jane Austen: Janeites will want to read Maggie Lane's *Jane Austen's World* and Nigel Nicolson's wonderful *World of Jane Austen* (now out of print).

Good background books on English history are *The Oxford Illustrated History of Britain,* edited by Kenneth O. Morgan, and *The Story of England,* by Christopher Hibbert. *The Isles,* a long history by Norman Davies, challenges conventional Anglocentric assumptions. *The English: A Portrait of a People,* by Jeremy Paxman, examines the concept of Englishness in a changing world. Simon Schama's three-volume *History of Britain,* with handsome color illustrations, was written to accompany the BBC–History Channel television series. Peter Ackroyd's illustrated *London: A Biography* captures the city's energy and its quirks from prehistory to the present. Ronald Blythe's well-regarded *Akenfield: Portrait of an English Village,* written in the 1960s, gives a perceptive account of life in the English countryside.

The finest book on the country's stately homes is Nigel Nicolson's *Great Houses of Britain,* written for the National Trust (now out of print). Also spectacular is the picture book *Great Houses of Britain and Wales,* by Hugh Montgomery-Massingberd. *The Buildings of England,* written by Nikolaus Pevsner but much updated since his death, is part of a multivolume series, organized by county. Pevsner's *Best Buildings of Britain* is a grand anthology with lush photographs. New Pevsner Architectural Guides continue to be published. For the golden era of Georgian architecture, check out John Summerson's definitive *Architecture in Britain 1530–1830.*

Simon Jenkins's *England's Thousand Best Churches,* with photographs, describes parish churches (not cathedrals) large and small. The same author's delightful *England's Thousand Best Houses* has pithy descriptions (and star ratings) of small and large houses open to the public. Mark Girouard's *Life in the English Country House* focuses on houses over the centuries, and *The Victorian Country House* (out of print) addresses the lifestyles of the rich and famous of the 19th century. For a scenic look at English villages, see *The Most Beautiful Villages of England,* by James Bentley, with ravishing photographs by Hugh Palmer.

Timothy Mowl's entertaining Historic Gardens series, with titles that focus on individual counties, is the gardening equivalent to Pevsner on buildings. The titles are more easily available in Britain, but check an online bookseller.

There are many delightful travel books about Britain. Bill Bryson's *Notes from a Small Island* is perennially popular, though it is a bit dated. Few of today's authors have managed to top the wit and perception of Henry James's magisterial *English Hours.*

Movies

From *Macbeth* to *Jane Eyre,* great classics of literature have been rendered into great classics of film. It's surprising to learn, however, how many of them were creations of Hollywood and not the British film industry (which had its heyday from the 1940s to the 1960s). From Laurence Olivier to Kenneth Branagh, noted director-actors have cross-pollinated the cinema in Britain and the United States.

Films can motivate travelers to visit specific locations and sights in a favorite film. VisitBritain (⊕ *www.visitbritain.com*) has recognized this by including movies on its Web site and producing "movie maps" with the locations for certain films such as the Harry Potter series.

A survey can begin with the dramas of Shakespeare: Olivier gave the world a memorable *Othello* and *Hamlet,* Orson Welles a moody *Macbeth,* and Branagh gave up mod versions of *Hamlet* and *Much Ado About Nothing.* Leonardo DiCaprio graced Australian Baz Luhrmann's contemporary version of *Romeo and Juliet.* Going behind the scenes, so to speak, Tom Stoppard created the Oscar winner *Shakespeare in Love.* Charles Dickens has also provided the foundation for film favorites: David Lean's immortal *Great Expectations,* George Cukor's *David Copperfield,* and *A Christmas Carol,* with Alastair Sim as Scrooge, top this list, which continues to grow with additions such as Douglas McGrath's *Nicholas Nickleby.*

McGrath's *Emma,* starring Gwyneth Paltrow, and Ang Lee's *Sense and Sensibility,* starring Emma Thompson and Kate Winslet, are just two of the recent film versions of Jane Austen's works. Keira Knightley had the role of Elizabeth Bennet in the latest *Pride and Prejudice* (2005). Anne Hathaway played Jane Austen herself in *Becoming Jane,* which imagines an early love affair for the novelist.

Harry Potter and the Sorcerer's Stone (in Britain, *Harry Potter and the Philosopher's Stone*), based on the wildly popular children's books by J.K. Rowling, was filmed in many British locations, including London, Gloucester, the Cotswolds, Northumbria, Yorkshire, and Scotland. The second movie, *Harry Potter and the Chamber of Secrets,* used some of the same settings as the first. *Harry Potter and the Prisoner of Azkaban, Harry Potter and the Goblet of Fire, Harry Potter and the Order of the Phoenix,* and

Harry Potter and the Half-Blood Prince are additional installments; *Harry Potter and the Deathly Hallows* appeared in two installments, in 2010 and 2011, to conclude the saga.

Of the film versions of Agatha Christie's books, one is especially treasured: *Murder, She Said,* which starred the inimitable Margaret Rutherford. With its quiet English village setting, harpsichord score, and the dotty Miss Marple as portrayed by Rutherford, this must be the most English of all Christie films. (Miss Marple remains a fixture on public television, with new shows being produced.)

Lovers of opulence, spectacle, and history (or just juicy costume dramas) have choices that grow each year—including Robert Bolt's classic version of Sir Thomas More's life and death, *A Man for All Seasons.* His *Lady Caroline Lamb* is surely the most beautiful historical film ever made. Richard Harris made a stirring Lord Protector in *Cromwell,* and the miniseries on Queen Elizabeth I, starring Glenda Jackson, is a great BBC addition to a DVD library. Elizabeth's adversary came to breathless life in Vanessa Redgrave's rendition of *Mary, Queen of Scots,* certainly one of her finest performances. More recent and a chilling performance of tortuous times is Cate Blanchett as *Elizabeth*; 2007 saw the release of *The Golden Age,* a sequel.

The historical movies keep coming: Helen Mirren played a dignified Elizabeth II facing the dilemmas caused by the death of Princess Diana in the excellent *The Queen. Miss Potter,* with Renée Zellweger, explored the life of the beloved children's book writer and illustrator Beatrix Potter, who had a home in the Lake District. Keira Knightley starred in *The Duchess,* the story of Georgiana, duchess of Devonshire, a flamboyant 18th-century aristocrat, and Emily Blunt played the young Queen Victoria in *The Young Victoria* (2009). *Sherlock Holmes* (2009) with Robert Downey Jr.

and *Robin Hood* (2010) with Russell Crowe gave these characters a new shot of cinematic life and showed some lovely British scenery. The television series *The Tudors* has won fans on both sides of the Atlantic.

Musicals? Near the top of anyone's list are four films set in England—three of them in Hollywood's England—that rank among the greatest musicals of all time: Walt Disney's *Mary Poppins*, George Cukor's *My Fair Lady*, Carol Reed's Oscar-winner *Oliver!*, and—yeah, yeah, yeah!—the Beatles' *A Hard Day's Night*, a British production.

If you're seeking a look at contemporary England, you might view *My Beautiful Laundrette*, about Asians in London, or *Secrets and Lies*, about a dysfunctional London family. Manchester's rocking music scene from the 1970s to early 1990s is the subject of the well-named *24 Hour Party People*. Mods, New Romantics, and Skinheads feature in *This Is England*, a sensitive tale of working-class life in the Midlands in the early 1980s.

Closer, adapted from Patrick Marber's play, takes a dark look at love in modern London. Woody Allen set his movies *Match Point* and *Scoop* in London; there are gorgeous shots of historic and modern locations in both.

You might lighten up with *The Full Monty*, about six former steelworkers in Sheffield who become strippers, or one of numerous romantic comedies: *Notting Hill*, with Julia Roberts and Hugh Grant; Hugh Grant again in *Four Weddings and a Funeral*; Gwyneth Paltrow in *Sliding Doors*; and Renée Zellweger (and Hugh Grant, again) in *Bridget Jones's Diary* and *Bridget Jones: The Edge of Reason*. *Calendar Girls*, filmed in rural Yorkshire, follows the true story of middle-aged women who raise money for charity with an (almost) bare-all calendar.

Quintessentially British are some comedies of the 1950s and '60s: Alec Guinness's *Kind Hearts and Coronets*, Peter Sellers's *The Mouse That Roared*, and Tony Richardson's Oscar winner and cinematic style setter, *Tom Jones*, starring Albert Finney, are best bets.

In 2001 American director Robert Altman took a biting look at the country's class system in *Gosford Park*, a country-house murder mystery set in the 1930s that stars mostly British actors, including Jeremy Northam and Maggie Smith. *Atonement* (2007), based on Ian McEwan's novel and starring Keira Knightley, also explores class tensions and depicts a small country estate between the world wars. A more staid, upstairs-downstairs look at the class system is the film of Kazuo Ishiguro's novel *The Remains of the Day*, featuring Anthony Hopkins as the stalwart butler, with Emma Thompson. Today some people's visions of turn-of-the-20th-century England have been captured by the Merchant and Ivory films, notably their *Howard's End*, which won many awards.

Travel Smart England

GETTING HERE AND AROUND

■ AIR TRAVEL

The least expensive airfares to England are often priced for round-trip travel and must usually be purchased in advance. Airlines generally allow you to change your return date for a fee; most low-fare tickets, however, are nonrefundable.

Flying time to London is about 6½ hours from New York, 7½ hours from Chicago, 9½ hours from Dallas, 10 hours from Los Angeles, and 21½ hours from Sydney. From London, flights take an hour to Paris or Amsterdam, 1½ hours to cities in Switzerland or Luxembourg, and 2 hours to Rome.

If you're flying from England, plan to arrive at the airport two hours in advance for flights to Europe, three hours for the United States. Security at Gatwick and Heathrow airports is always fairly intense. Most people can expect to be patted down after they pass through metal detectors. Travelers are randomly searched again at the gate before transatlantic flights.

Airline Security Issues Transportation Security Administration (⊕ www.tsa.gov).

AIRPORTS

Most international flights to London arrive at either Heathrow Airport (LHR), 15 mi west of London, or at Gatwick Airport (LGW), 27 mi south of the capital. Most flights from the United States go to Heathrow, with Terminals 3, 4, and 5 handling transatlantic flights (British Airways uses Terminal 5). Gatwick is London's second gateway, serving many U.S. destinations. A third, much smaller airport, Stansted (STN), is 35 mi northeast of the city. It handles mainly European and domestic traffic.

London City Airport (LCY), a small airport inside the city near Canary Wharf, has twice-daily business-class flights to New York on British Airways, as well as flights to European destinations. Luton Airport (LLA), 30 mi north of the city, is also quite small, and serves British and European destinations. Luton is the hub for low-cost easyJet. Manchester (MAN) in northwest England handles some flights from the United States, as does Birmingham (BHX).

Heathrow and Gatwick are enormous and can seem like shopping malls. Both airports have bars and pubs, and dining options. Several hotels are connected to each airport, and both Gatwick and Heathrow are near dozens of hotels that run free shuttles to the airports. Heathrow has a Hotel Hoppa service that runs shuttles between the airport and around 20 nearby hotels for £4 each way. A free, subsidized local bus service operates between the Central Bus Station serving Terminals 1, 2, and 3 and nearby hotels. You can find out more at the Central Bus Station or at the Transport for London (TfL) Information Centre in the Underground station serving Terminals 1, 2, and 3. Yotel has budget pod hotels in both Heathrow and Gatwick with cabin-size rooms to be booked in advance in four-hour blocks or overnight. Prices begin at about £50, depending on how long you stay and the time of day.

In comparison, other British airports have much more limited shopping, hotel, and dining options; a delay of a few hours can seem like years.

Airport Information Birmingham Airport (☎ 0844/576–6000 ⊕ www.birminghamairport. com). **Gatwick Airport** (☎ 0844/335–1802 ⊕ www.gatwickairport.com). **Heathrow Airport** (☎ 0844/335–1801 ⊕ www. heathrowairport.com). **London City Airport** (☎ 0207/646–0088 ⊕ www.londoncityairport. com) **Luton Airport** (☎ 01582/405100 ⊕ www.london-luton.co.uk). **Manchester Airport** (☎ 0871/271–0711 ⊕ www. manchesterairport.co.uk). **Stansted Airport** (☎ 0844/355–1803 ⊕ www.stanstedairport. com).

GROUND TRANSPORTATION

London has excellent bus and train connections between its airports and downtown. Train service can be the fastest, but the downside is that you must get yourself and your luggage to the terminal, often via a series of escalators and connecting trams. Airport buses (generally run by National Express) may be located nearer to the terminals and drop you closer to central hotels, but they're subject to London traffic, which can be horrendous. Taxis can be more convenient than buses, but prices can go through the roof.

The Transport for London Web site has helpful information, as does Airport Travel Line. The official sites for Gatwick, Heathrow, and Stansted are useful resources for transportation options.

FROM HEATHROW TO CENTRAL LONDON		
Travel Mode	Time	Cost
Taxi	1 hour+	£50+
Heathrow Express Train	15 minutes	£16.50 one way
Underground	50 minutes	£4 one way
National Express Bus	1 hour 50 minutes	£7 one way

Heathrow by Bus: National Express buses take around two hours to reach the city center (Victoria Coach Station) and cost from £7 one way and £12 round-trip. Buses leave frequently from 6:30 am to 7:05 pm. National Express also operates other bus services between 6:30 am and 7:05 pm that travel to Earls Court, Kensington, and Hammersmith in west London. Prices are from £7 one way, and the trip takes two to three hours, depending on traffic. The National Express Hotel Hoppa service runs from all terminals to around 20 hotels near the airport (£4). Alternatively, nearly every hotel in London is served by the Hotel By Bus service. Fares to Central London begin at £22.50. SkyShuttle also offers a minibus service between Heathrow and any London hotel. The N9 night bus runs every half hour from midnight to 5 am to Trafalgar Square; it takes an hour and costs £4.

Heathrow by Train: The cheap, direct route into London is via the Piccadilly line of the Underground (London's extensive subway system, or "Tube"). Trains normally run every four to eight minutes from all terminals from early morning until just before midnight. The 50-minute trip into central London costs £4.50 one way and connects with other central Tube lines. The Heathrow Express train is comfortable and very convenient, if costly, speeding into London's Paddington Station in 15 minutes. Standard one-way tickets cost £16.50, or £26 for first class. Book online for the lowest fares. If you arrive without tickets you should purchase them at a kiosk before you board, as they are more expensive on the train. There's daily service from 5:10 am (5:20 am on Sunday) to 11:42 pm (11:40 pm on Sunday), with departures every 15 minutes. A less expensive option is the Heathrow Connect train, which stops at local stations between the airport and Paddington. Daily service is every half hour from 5:20 am (6:05 am on Sunday) to 11:20 pm (11:05 pm on Sunday). The journey takes about 30 minutes and costs £8.50 one way.

Gatwick by Bus: Hourly bus service runs from Gatwick's north and south terminals to Victoria Station with stops at Hooley, Coulsdon, Mitcham, Streatham, Stockwell, and Pimlico. The journey takes two hours and 10 minutes and costs £6.80 one way. Make sure you get on a direct bus not requiring a change; otherwise the journey could take much longer. The easyBus service runs a service to Earls Court in west London from as little as £2; the later the ticket is booked online, the higher the price (up to £10 on board).

Gatwick by Train: The fast, nonstop Gatwick Express leaves for Victoria Station every 15 minutes 4:35 am–1:35 am. The 30-minute trip costs £15.95 one way. Book in advance, as tickets cost more on board. The First Capital Connect rail company's nonexpress services are cheaper; trains runs regularly throughout the day until midnight to St. Pancras International, London Bridge, and Blackfriars stations; daytime departures are every 15 minutes (hourly between 9 pm and 9 am), and the journey takes 30 to 45 minutes. Tickets are from £9.40 one way. You can also reach Gatwick by First Capital Connect coming from Brighton in the opposite direction. First Capital Connect service is on commuter trains, and during rush hour trains can be crowded, with little room for baggage and seats at a premium.

Stansted by Bus: Hourly service on National Express Airport bus A6 (24 hours a day) to Victoria Coach Station costs from £10 one way, and takes about one hour and 45 minutes. Stops include Golders Green, Finchley Road, St. John's Wood, Baker Street, Marble Arch, and Hyde Park Corner. The easyBus service to Victoria via Baker Street costs from £2.

Stansted by Train: The Stansted Express to Liverpool Street Station (with a stop at Tottenham Hale) runs every 15 minutes 5:30 am–12:30 am daily (1:30 pm Friday to Sunday). The 45-minute trip costs £20 one way if booked online. Tickets cost more on board.

Luton by Bus and Train: A free airport shuttle runs from Luton Airport to the nearby Luton Airport Parkway Station, from which you can take a train or bus into London. From there, the First Capital Connect train service runs to St. Pancras, Farringdon, Blackfriars, and London Bridge. The journey takes about 40 minutes. Trains leave every 10 minutes or so from 5 am until midnight. One-way tickets begin at £12. The Terravision Shuttle bus runs from Luton to Victorial Coach Station, with departures every 30 minutes during peak hours. The journey takes around 70 minutes, with fares from £13 one-way. The Green Line 757 bus service from Luton to Victoria Station runs two to three times an hour, takes about 90 minutes, and costs £15, while an easyBus shuttle has tickets starting from £2.

Heathrow, Gatwick, Stansted, and Luton by Taxi: This is an expensive and time-consuming option. The city's congestion charge (£10) will be added to the bill. If you get stuck in traffic, a taxi from the stand will be even more expensive; a cab booked ahead is a set price. A taxi trip from Heathrow to Victoria, for example, can take more than an hour and cost more than £58. Checkercars offers cars from Gatwick, Heathrow, and Stansted for a flat fee—at this writing, the fee to Victoria Station is £50.50 from Heathrow, £101.50 from Gatwick, and £109.50 from Stansted, not including the congestion charge. Another option, if you have friends in the London area, is to have them book a reputable minicab firm to pick you up. The cost of a minicab from Heathrow to central London is approximately £47. Your hotel may also be able to recommend a car service.

TRANSFERS BETWEEN AIRPORTS

Allow at least two to three hours for an interairport transfer. The National Express Airport bus is the most direct option between Gatwick and Heathrow. Buses depart from Gatwick every hour from 5 am to 11:35 pm (more frequently from 10:30 to 11:30 am) and from Heathrow every hour from 3 am to 12:45 am (more frequently 3 am to 6 am). The trip takes around one hour, and the fare is £21.50 one way. Book tickets in advance. National Express buses between Stansted and Gatwick depart every hour and take around three hours. The one-way fare is £30.70. Some airlines may offer shuttle services as well—check with your airline before your journey.

The cheapest option—but most complicated—is public transport: from Gatwick to Stansted, for instance, catch the commuter train from Gatwick to Victoria Station, take the Tube to Liverpool Street Station, then hop on the train to Stansted. To get from Heathrow to Gatwick, take the Tube to King's Cross/St. Pancras, then take the commuter train to Gatwick, or else transfer to the District/Circle Line at South Kensington, head to Victoria Station, and take the Gatwick Express.

Contacts **Airport Travel Line** (☎ *0871/200-2233 or 0870/574-7777*). **Checkercars** (☎ *01293/661-100* ⊕ *www.checkercars.com*). **easyBus** (⊕ *www.easybus.co.uk*). **First Capital Connect** (⊕ *www.firstcapitalconnect.co.uk*). **Gatwick Express** (☎ *0845/850-1530* ⊕ *www.gatwickexpress.com*). **Green Line** (⊕ *www.greenline.co.uk*). **Heathrow Connect** (☎ *0845/678-6975* ⊕ *www.heathrowconnect.com*). **Heathrow Express** (☎ *0845/600-1515* ⊕ *www.heathrowexpress.com*). **Hotel By Bus Heathrow** (☎ *0845/850-1900* ⊕ *www.hotelbybusheathrow.com*). **National Express** (☎ *0871/781-8178* ⊕ *www.nationalexpress.com*). **SkyShuttle** (☎ *0845/481-0960* ⊕ *www.skyshuttle.co.uk*). **Stansted Express** (☎ *0845/850-0150* ⊕ *www.stanstedexpress.com*). **Terravision** (☎ *01279/662-931* ⊕ *www.terravision.eu/London.html*). **Transport for London** (☎ *0843/222-1234* ⊕ *www.tfl.gov.uk*).

FLIGHTS

British Airways offers mostly nonstop flights from 19 U.S. cities to Heathrow, along with flights to Manchester and Birmingham. In addition, it has a vast program of discount airfare–hotel packages. Britain-based Virgin Atlantic is a strong competitor in terms of packages. London is a very popular destination, so many U.S. carriers have flights and packages, too.

Because England is such a small country, internal air travel is much less important than it is in the United States. For trips of less than 200 mi, trains are often quicker because rail stations are more centrally located. Flying tends to cost more, but for longer trips air travel has a considerable time advantage (you need to factor in time to get to and from the airport, though).

British Airways operates shuttle services between Heathrow or Gatwick and Manchester. Bmi/British Midland operates from Heathrow to Leeds and Manchester, as well as to Washington, D.C., Chicago, Las Vegas, and major cities in eastern Canada.

Low-cost airlines such as easyJet, bmi baby, and Ryanair offer flights within the United Kingdom as well as to cities in Ireland and continental Europe. Prices are low, but these airlines usually fly out of smaller British airports such as Stansted and Luton, both near London. Check ⊕ *www.cheapflights.com* for price comparisons.

Major Airline Contacts **American Airlines** (☎ *800/433-7300, 0844/499-7300 in U.K.* ⊕ *www.aa.com*) to Heathrow, Gatwick, Manchester. **British Airways** (☎ *800/247-9297, 0844/493-0787 in U.K.* ⊕ *www.britishairways.com*) to Heathrow. **Continental Airlines** (☎ *800/231-0856 for international reservations* ⊕ *www.continental.com*) to Heathrow, Gatwick. **Delta Airlines** (☎ *800/221-1212 for U.S. reservations, 800/241-4141 for international reservations, 0871/221-1222 in U.K.* ⊕ *www.delta.com*) to Gatwick. **United Airlines** (☎ *800/864-8331 for U.S. reservations, 800/538-2929 for international reservations, 0845/844-4777 in U.K.* ⊕ *www.united.com*) to Heathrow. **US Airways** (☎ *800/428-4322 for U.S. and Canada reservations, 085/600-3300 in U.K.* ⊕ *www.usairways.com*) to Heathrow, Gatwick, Manchester. **Virgin Atlantic** (☎ *800/862-8621, 0800/209-7777 in U.K.* ⊕ *www.virgin-atlantic.com*) to Heathrow, Gatwick.

Within England and to Europe **bmi baby** (☎ *0845/810110 from outside U.K., 0905/828-2828 in U.K.* ⊕ *www.bmibaby.com*). **easyJet** (☎ *0158/244-3330 in U.K.* ⊕ *www.easyjet.com*). **Ryanair** (☎ *03531/248-0856 Ireland office* ⊕ *www.ryanair.com*).

PASSES

The Star Alliance Europe Airpass from bmi is available on the airline's British and European flights. The pass is valid for up to 90 days and allows passengers to travel to a combination of European cities for reduced fares. The Visit Europe Pass from British Airways offers travelers a way to choose from the airline's and its partners' networks.

Air Pass Info **bmi** (☎ *800/788-0555, 0844/848-4888 in U.K.* ⊕ *www.flybmi.com*). **British Airways** (☎ *800/247-9297, 0844/493-0787 in U.K.* ⊕ *www.britishairways.com*).

▌ BOAT TRAVEL

Ferries and other boats travel regular routes to France, Spain, Ireland, and Scandinavia. P&O runs ferries between Belgium, Great Britain, Ireland, France, and the Netherlands. Norfolk Line covers Denmark, Holland, France, Ireland, and Northern Ireland. Stena Line serves Ireland and the Netherlands.

Low-cost airlines and Eurotunnel (which lets you take a car to France on the train) have cut into ferry travel, but companies have responded by cutting fares and upgrading equipment.

Prices vary; booking early ensures cheaper fares, but also ask about special deals. Seaview is a comprehensive online ferry- and cruise-booking portal for Britain and continental Europe. Ferry Cheap is a discount Web site.

Information Ferry Cheap (⊕ *www.ferrycheap. com*). **Norfolk Line** (☎ *0871/521–5522* ⊕ *www.norfolkline.co.uk*). **P&O** (☎ *0871/664– 2020* ⊕ *www.poferries.com*). **Seaview** (⊕ *www. seaview.co.uk*). **Stena Line** (☎ *0844/770–7070* ⊕ *www.stenaline.co.uk*).

TRANSATLANTIC AND OTHER CRUISES

Most cruise ships leave from southern England—particularly Southampton and Portsmouth. Some ships leave from Liverpool and Dover as well, or from Harwich, near London.

Cruise Lines Cunard Line (☎ *800/728–6273 in U.S., 0845/678–0013 in U.K* ⊕ *www.cunard. com*). **Holland America Line** (☎ *0845/351– 0557* ⊕ *www.hollandamerica.com*). **Norwegian Cruise Line** (*0845/201–8900 in U.K or 866/234–7350 in U.S.* ⊕ *www.ncl.com*). **Princess Cruises** (☎ *866/774–6237 in U.S., 0845/355–5800 in U.K.* ⊕ *www.princess.com*). **Royal Caribbean International** (☎ *866/562– 7625 in U.S., 0800/018–2020 in U.K.* ⊕ *www. royalcaribbean.com*).

▌ BUS TRAVEL

Britain has a comprehensive bus (short-haul) and coach (the British term for long-distance buses) network that offers an inexpensive way of seeing England. National Express is the major coach operator, and Victoria Coach Station, near Victoria Station in central London, is its hub. The company serves more than 1,000 destinations within Britain and Ireland (and, via Eurolines, 500 more in continental Europe). There are 2,000 ticket agents nationwide, including offices at London's Heathrow and Gatwick airport coach stations.

Green Line is the second-largest national service, serving airports and major tourist towns. A budget option for long-distance travel, Megabus has double-decker buses that serve cities across Britain. (The company does not accommodate wheelchairs, and limits luggage to one checked piece per person and one piece of hand luggage.) Greyhound has launched low-cost, long-distance bus service to four southern England destinations. In London, all three companies depart from Victoria Coach Station.

Bus tickets can be much less than the price of a train ticket (even lower if you take advantage of special deals). For example, an Oxford Tube bus ticket from London to Oxford is £14, whereas a train ticket is £25. Buses are also just as comfortable as trains. However, buses often take twice as long to reach their destinations. Greyhound and Oxford Tube have onboard Wi-Fi. All bus services forbid smoking.

Double-decker buses, run by private companies, offer local bus service in cities and regions. Check with the local bus station or tourist information center for routes and schedules. Most companies offer day-long or weeklong unlimited-travel tickets, and those in popular tourist areas operate special scenic tours in summer. The top deck of a double-decker bus is a great place from which to view the countryside.

DISCOUNTS AND DEALS

National Express's Discount Coach Card for students age 16 to 26 costs £10 annually and gets 20% to 30% discounts off many fares. Most companies also offer a discount for children under 15. A discount card for the over-60s gets savings of 30% to 50%. Apex tickets (advance-purchase tickets) save money on standard fares, and traveling midweek is cheaper than over weekends and holidays.

FARES AND SCHEDULES

You can find schedules online, pick them up from tourist information offices, or get them by phone from the bus companies. Fares vary based on how close to the time of travel you book—Megabus tickets, for example, are cheaper if ordered in advance online.

PAYING

Tickets for National Express can be bought from the Victoria, Heathrow, or Gatwick coach stations, by phone, online, or from most British travel agencies. Reservations are advised. Tickets for Megabus must be purchased online or by phone (avoid calling, as there is surcharge).

Most companies accept credit cards for advance purchases, but it's cash-only if you're purchasing your tickets on the bus.

RESERVATIONS

Book in advance, as buses on busy routes fill up quickly. With most bus companies (National Express, Megabus, Green Line), advance payment means you receive an email receipt and your name is placed on a list given to the bus driver.

Bus Contacts Green Line (☎ 0871/200–2233 ⊕ www.greenline.co.uk). **Greyhound** (☎ 0900/096–0000 ⊕ www.greyhounduk.com). **Megabus** (☎ 0871/266–3333 ⊕ www.megabus.com). **National Express** (☎ 0871/781–8178 ⊕ www.nationalexpress.com). **Victoria Coach Station** (✉ 164 Buckingham Palace Rd., London ☎ 0207/027–2522 ⊕ www.tfl.gov.uk/vcs).

▌ CAR TRAVEL

Britain can be a challenging place for most foreigners to drive, considering that people drive on the left side of the road, most rental cars have standard transmissions, and the gearshift is on the wrong side entirely.

There's no reason to rent a car for a stay in London, since the city and its suburbs are well served by public transportation, and traffic is desperately congested. Here and in other major cities it's best to rely on public transportation.

Outside the cities, a car can be very handy. Many sights are not easily reached without one—castles, for example, are rarely connected to any public transportation system. Small villages might have only one or two buses a day pass through them. If you are comfortable on the road, the experience of driving between the tall hedgerows or on country roads is a truly English experience.

In England and Wales your own driver's license is acceptable. However, you may choose to get an International Driving Permit (IDP), which can be used only in conjunction with a valid driver's license and which translates your license into 10 languages. Check the Automobile Association of America Web site for more info as well as for IDPs ($15) themselves. These permits are universally recognized, and having one in your wallet may save you a problem with the local authorities.

GASOLINE

Gasoline is called petrol in England and is sold by the liter. The price you see posted at a petrol station is the price of a liter, and there are about 4 liters in a U.S. gallon. Petrol is expensive; it was around £1.35 per liter, or $5.10, at the time of this writing. Supermarket pumps just outside city centers frequently offer the best prices. Premium and superpremium are the two varieties, and most cars run on premium. Diesel is widely used; be sure not to use it by mistake. Along busy motorways, most large stations are open

24 hours a day, seven days a week. In rural areas, hours can vary. Most service stations accept major credit cards, and most are self-service.

PARKING

Parking regulations are strictly enforced. If there are no signs on a street, you can park there. Many streets have centralized "pay and display" machines, in which you deposit the required money and get a ticket allowing you to park for a set period of time. In London's City of Westminster (⊕ *www.westminster.gov.uk*), parking machines have been replaced by a pay-by-phone plan, enabling you to pay by cell phone if you've preregistered. In town centers your best bet is to park in a public lot marked with a square blue sign with a white "P" in the center.

If you park on the street, follow these basic rules: Do not park within 15 yards of an intersection. Do not park in bus lanes, on double yellow lines, or on single yellow lines when parking meters are in effect. On busy roads with red lines painted on the street you cannot park or stop to let a passenger out of the car.

RENTALS

Rental rates are generally reasonable, and insurance costs are lower than in the United States. If you want the car only for country trips, consider renting outside London. Rates are cheaper, and you avoid traversing London's notoriously complex road system. Rental rates vary widely, beginning at £40 a day and £180 a week for a midsize car, usually with manual transmission. As in the United States, prices rise in summer and during holidays. Car seats for children cost about £9, and GPS is usually around £10.

Major car-rental agencies are much the same in Britain as in the United States: Alamo, Avis, Budget, Enterprise, Hertz, and National all have offices in Britain. Europcar is another large company. Companies may not rent cars to people who are under 23 or over 75.

ROAD CONDITIONS

There's a very good network of major highways (motorways) and divided highways (dual carriageways) throughout most of England and Wales. Motorways (with the prefix "M"), shown in blue on most maps, are mainly two or three lanes in each direction. Other major roads (with the prefix "A") are shown on maps in green and red. Sections of fast dual carriageways (with black-edged, thick outlines on maps) have both traffic lights and traffic circles. Turnoffs are often marked by highway numbers, rather than place-names. An exit is called a junction in Britain.

The vast network of lesser roads, for the most part old coach and turnpike roads, might make your trip twice as long but show you twice as much. Minor roads are drawn in yellow or white on maps, the former prefixed by "B," the latter unlettered and unnumbered. Should you take one of these, be prepared to back up into a passing place if you meet an oncoming car.

ROADSIDE EMERGENCIES

On major highways, emergency roadside telephone booths are positioned at regular intervals. Contact your car-rental company or call the police. You can also call the British Automobile Association (AA) toll-free. You can join and receive assistance from the AA or the RAC on the spot, but the charge is higher than a simple membership fee. If you are a member of the American Automobile Association, check before you travel; reciprocal agreements may give you free roadside aid.

Emergency Services Ambulance, fire, police (☎ 999). **Automobile Association** (☎ 0161/333–0044 ⊕ www.theaa.com). **RAC** (☎ 0192/243–7000 ⊕ www.rac.co.uk).

RULES OF THE ROAD

Driving on the left side of the road might be easier than you expected, as the steering and mirrors on British cars are designed for driving on the left. If you have a standard transmission car, you have to shift gears with your left hand. Give yourself time to adjust before leaving the rental-car lot. Seat belts are obligatory in the front and back seats. It is illegal to talk on a handheld cell phone while driving.

Pick up a copy of the official Highway Code (£2.50) at a service station, newsstand, or bookstore, or check it out online by going to ⊕ *www.direct.gov.uk* and putting "Highway Code" in the search bar. Besides driving rules and illustrations of signs and road markings, this booklet contains information for motorcyclists, cyclists, and pedestrians.

Speed limits are complicated, and there are speed cameras everywhere. The speed limit (shown on circular red signs) is generally 20 or 30 mph in towns and cities, 40–60 mph on two-lane highways, and 70 mph on motorways. At traffic circles (called roundabouts), you turn clockwise. As cars enter the circle, they must yield to those already in the circle. If you're taking an exit all the way around the circle, stay to the center until just before your own exit.

Pedestrians have the right-of-way on "zebra" crossings (black-and-white-stripe crosswalks between two orange-flashing globe lights). At other crossings, pedestrians must yield to traffic, but they do have the right-of-way over traffic turning left.

Drunk-driving laws are strictly enforced. The legal limit is 80 milligrams of alcohol per 100 milliliters of blood, which means two units of alcohol—two glasses of wine, one pint of beer, or one glass of whisky— but amounts vary, depending on your weight or what you have eaten that day.

▌ TRAIN TRAVEL

Operated by private companies, the train system in Britain is extensive and useful, though less than perfect. Some regional trains are old, and virtually all lines suffer from occasional delays, schedule changes, and periodic repair work that runs over schedule. All major cities and many small towns are served by trains, and despite the

difficulties, rail travel is the most pleasant way to cover long distances.

On long-distance runs some rail lines have buffet cars; on others you can purchase snacks from a mobile snack cart. Most train companies now have "quiet cars" where mobile-phone use is forbidden and conversation is kept at a low volume.

CLASSES
Most rail lines have first-class and second-class cars. In virtually all cases, second class is perfectly comfortable. First class is quieter and less crowded, has better furnishings, and marginally larger seats. It also costs two to three times the price of second class. Most train operators offer a Weekend First ticket. Available on weekends and holidays, these tickets allow you to upgrade for as little as £5.

FARES AND SCHEDULES
National Rail Enquiries is a helpful, comprehensive, and free service that covers all the country's rail lines. National Rail will help you choose the best train, and then connect you with the right ticket office. You can also book tickets online. A similar service is offered by the Trainline, which provides online train information and ticket booking for all rail services. The Man in Seat 61, a Web site, offers objective information along with booking facilities.

Ticket prices are more expensive during rush hour, so plan accordingly. For long-distance travel, tickets cost more the longer you wait. Book in advance and tickets can be half of what you'd pay on the day of departure. A journey from London to Cardiff costs £12 if you buy a ticket two weeks in advance, but the fare rises to £37 if you wait until the day of your trip.

▌TIP→ Ask the local tourist board about hotel and local transportation packages that include tickets to major events.

Information National Rail Enquiries (☎ *0845/748–4950, 020/7278–5240 outside U.K.* ⊕ *www.nationalrail.co.uk*). **The Man in Seat 61** (⊕ *www.seat61.com*). **Trainline** (☎ *0871/244–1545* ⊕ *www.thetrainline.com*).

PASSES

National Rail Enquiries has information about rail passes such as Rovers, which save you money on individual railroads.

If you plan to travel a lot by train in England and Wales, consider purchasing a BritRail Pass, which gives unlimited travel over the entire British rail network and can save you money. If you don't plan to cover many miles, you may come out ahead by buying individual tickets. Try to buy your BritRail Pass before you leave home, as the only place that sells them in the United Kingdom is the visitor center on London's Regent Street. The passes are available from most U.S. travel agents or from ACP Rail International, Flight Centre, or VisitBritain. Note that Eurail Passes are not honored in Britain.

BritRail passes come in two basic varieties: the Consecutive Pass and the FlexiPass. The Consecutive Pass for 8 consecutive days costs $259 standard and $385 first class; for 15 days, it costs $385 standard and $579 first class. The Flexi-Pass for four days of travel in two months costs $285 standard and $425 first class; for eight days of travel in two months it costs $415 standard and $619 first class.

Don't assume that a rail pass guarantees you a seat on a particular train. You need to book seats even if you are using a rail pass, especially on trains that may be crowded, particularly in summer on popular routes.

Discount Passes ACP Rail International (☎ 866/938–7245 ⊕ www.acprail.com). **BritRail** (☎ 866/274–8724 ⊕ www.britrail. com). **Flight Centre** (☎ 0870/499–0040 ⊕ www.flightcentre.com). **VisitBritain** (⊕ www. visitbritain.com).

PAYING

Cash and credit cards are accepted by all train ticket offices; credit cards are accepted over the phone and online.

RESERVATIONS

Reserving your ticket in advance is recommended. Even a reservation 24 hours in advance can provide a substantial discount. Look into cheap day returns if you plan to travel a round-trip in one day.

CHANNEL TUNNEL

Short of flying, taking the Eurostar through the Channel Tunnel is the fastest way to cross the English Channel. Travel time is 2¼ hours from London's St. Pancras Station to Paris's Gare du Nord.

Early risers can easily take a day trip to Paris if time is short. Book ahead, as Eurostar ticket prices increase as the departure date approaches. If purchased in advance, round-trip tickets start at £144.

Channel Tunnel Car Transport Eurotunnel (☎ 0844/335–3535 in U.K., 08–10–63–03–04 in France ⊕ www.eurotunnel.com). **French Motorail/Rail Europe** (☎ 0844/848–4050 ⊕ www. raileurope.co.uk).

Channel Tunnel Passenger Service Eurostar (☎ 0843/218–6186 in U.K. ⊕ www. eurostar.co.uk). **Rail Europe** (☎ 800/622–8600 in U.S., 0844/848–4064 in U.K. ⊕ www. raileurope.com).

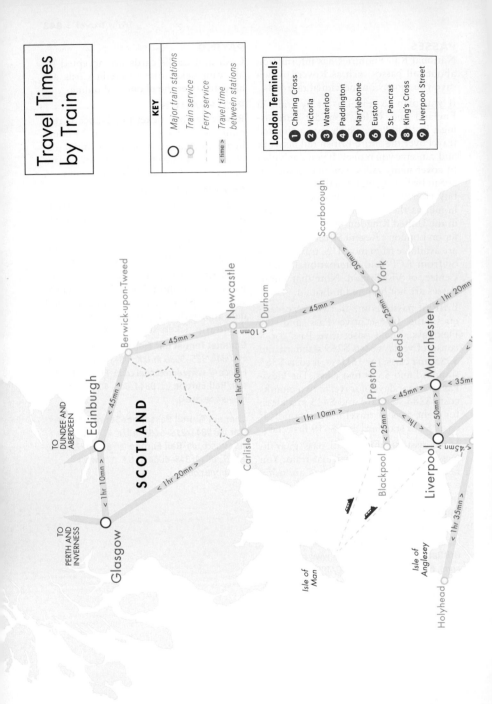

Travel Times by Train

KEY

○ Major train stations

⊙ Train service

- - - Ferry service

< time > Travel time between stations

London Terminals

1. Charing Cross
2. Victoria
3. Waterloo
4. Paddington
5. Marylebone
6. Euston
7. St. Pancras
8. King's Cross
9. Liverpool Street

SCOTLAND

TO PERTH AND INVERNESS

TO DUNDEE AND ABERDEEN

Glasgow

Edinburgh

Berwick-upon-Tweed

< 1hr 10mn >

< 45mn >

< 45mn >

< 1hr 20mn >

Newcastle

< 45mn >

Durham

< 10mn >

Carlisle

< 1hr 30mn >

< 1hr 10mn >

Scarborough

< 50mn >

York

< 25mn >

Leeds

< 45mn >

Preston

< 45mn >

< 25mn >

Blackpool

< 1hr >

Manchester

< 1hr 20mn >

< 35mn >

< 50mn >

Liverpool

< 45mn >

Isle of Man

Isle of Anglesey

Holyhead

< 1hr 35mn >

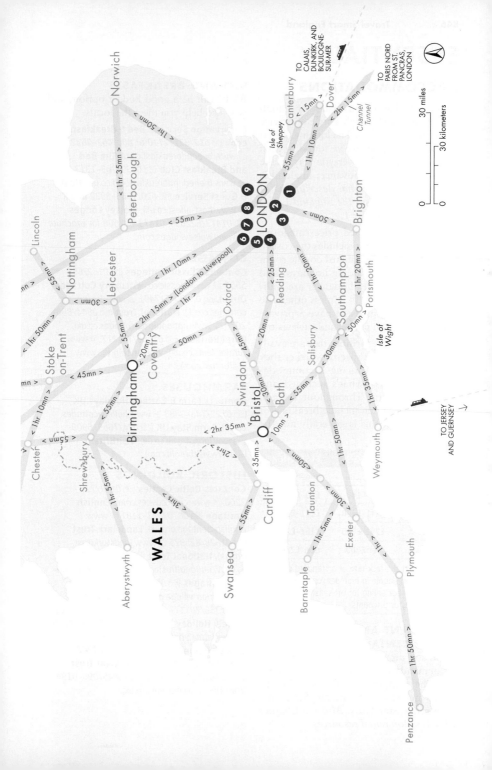

Travel Smart England

845

TO CALAIS, DUNKIRK, AND BOULOGNE-SUR-MER

TO PARIS NORD FROM ST. PANCRAS, LONDON

Canterbury

Dover

Channel Tunnel

15mn

55mn

1hr 10mn

2hr 15mn

Isle of Sheppey

Brighton

50mn

Norwich

1hr 30mn

1hr 35mn

Peterborough

LONDON

9
8 7
2 6
3 5 4
1

55mn

Reading

25mn

1hr 20mn

Southampton

1hr 20mn

Portsmouth

Isle of Wight

Lincoln

55mn

Nottingham

30mn

Leicester

1hr 10mn

(London to Liverpool)

2hr 15mn

1hr

Oxford

50mn

45mn

Swindon

20mn

20mn

30mn

Bath

Salisbury

30mn

50mn

55mn

1hr 35mn

1hr 50mn

Stoke on-Trent

1hr 50mn

55mn

30mn

Birmingham

55mn

Coventry

45mn

Weymouth

TO JERSEY AND GUERNSEY

1hr 10mn

Chester

55mn

Shrewsbury

55mn

1hr 55mn

2hrs

Bristol

10mn

35mn

50mn

Cardiff

55mn

3hrs

WALES

Aberystwyth

Swansea

Taunton

1hr 5mn

Barnstaple

30mn

Exeter

1hr

Plymouth

Penzance

1hr 50mn

30 miles

30 kilometers

0

0

30 miles

30 kilometers

ESSENTIALS

■ ACCOMMODATIONS

Hotels, bed-and-breakfasts, or small country houses—there's a style and price to suit most travelers. The lodgings listed are the best options we've found in each price category. Wherever you stay, make reservations well in advance: England is popular. (*For additional descriptions of kinds of lodgings, see the England Lodging Primer in Chapter 1.*)

Properties are assigned price categories based on a range that includes the cost of the least expensive standard double room in high season (excluding holidays) and the most expensive. Lodgings are indicated in the text by ⛉. Unless otherwise noted, all lodgings listed have a private bathroom, a room phone, and a television.

We always list the facilities that are available—but we don't specify whether they cost extra: when pricing accommodations, always ask what's included and what costs extra. Throughout Britain, lodging prices often include breakfast of some kind, but this is generally not the case in London.

CATEGORY	LONDON	ELSEWHERE
£	under £80	under £70
££	£80–£140	£70–£120
£££	£141–£200	£121–£160
££££	£201–£300	£161–£220
£££££	over £300	over £220

Prices reflect the rack rate of a standard double room for two people in high season, including 20% V.A.T. Check online for off-season rates and special deals or discounts.

APARTMENT AND HOUSE RENTALS

If you deal directly with local agents, get a recommendation from someone who has used the company. Unlike with hotels, there's no accredited system for apartment-rental standards. *Also see Chapter 2 for London rental resources.*

BED-AND-BREAKFASTS

B&Bs can be a good budget option, and will also help you meet the locals.

Reservation Services **Bed & Breakfast. com** (☎ 512/322–2710 or 800/462–2632 ⊕ www.bedandbreakfast.com). **The Bed and Breakfast Club** (☎ 0239/263–1313 ⊕ www.thebedandbreakfastclub.co.uk). **Host & Guest Service** (☎ 020/7385–9922 in U.K. ⊕ www.host-guest.co.uk). **Wolsey Lodges** (☎ 01473/822058, 01473/827500 for brochure ⊕ www.wolseylodges.com).

COTTAGES

Contacts **Classic Cottages** (☎ 0132/655–5555 ⊕ www.classic.co.uk). **Luxury Cottages Direct** (☎ 02920/212491 ⊕ www.luxury-cottages.co.uk). **National Trust** (☎ 0844/800–2070 ⊕ www.nationaltrustcottages.co.uk). **Rural Retreats** (☎ 01386/701177 ⊕ www.ruralretreats.co.uk). **VisitBritain** (⊕ www.visitbritain.com).

FARMHOUSES

Contacts **Farm & Cottage Holidays UK** (☎ 0123/745–9888 ⊕ www.holidaycottages.co.uk). **Farm Stay UK** (☎ 024/7669–6909 ⊕ www.farmstayuk.co.uk). **VisitBritain** (⊕ www.visitbritain.com).

HISTORIC BUILDINGS

Contacts **Celtic Castles** (☎ 0142/223–3200 ⊕ www.celticcastles.com). **English Heritage** (☎ 0870/333–1181 ⊕ www.english-heritage.org.uk). **Landmark Trust** (☎ 01628/825925 ⊕ www.landmarktrust.org.uk). **National Trust** (☎ 0844/800–2070 ⊕ www.nationaltrustcottages.co.uk). **Portmeirion Cottages** (☎ 01766/770000 ⊕ www.portmeirion-village.com). **Rural Retreats** (☎ 01386/701177 ⊕ www.ruralretreats.co.uk). **Stately Holiday Cottages** (☎ 01638/674756 ⊕ www.statelyholidaycottages.co.uk). **Unique Home Stays** (☎ 01637/881942 ⊕ ww.uniquehomestays.com). **Vivat Trust** (☎ 01981/550753 from U.S., 0845/090–0194 from U.K. ⊕ www.vivat.org.uk).

Online Booking Resources

Contacts

The Apartment Service	0208/944–1444	www.apartmentservice.com
At Home Abroad	212/421–9165	www.athomeabroadinc.com
Barclay International Group	516/364–0064 or 800/845–6636	www.barclayweb.com
English Country Cottages	0845/268–0785	www.english-country-cottages.co.uk
In the English Manner	01559/371600 or 213/629–1811	www.english-manner.co.uk
Interhome	800/882–6864	www.interhome.us
Living Architecture	0788/779–1294	www.living-architecture.co.uk
National Trust	0844/800–2070	www.nationaltrustcottages.co.uk
Suzanne B. Cohen & Associates	207/622–0743	www.villaeurope.com
Vacation Rentals By Owner	303/680–9280	www.vrbo.com
Villanet	877/250–4366 or 206/417–3444	www.rentavilla.com
Villas International	415/499–9490 or 800/221–2260	www.villasintl.com

HOME EXCHANGES

With a direct home exchange you stay in someone else's home while they stay in yours. Some outfits handle vacation homes, so you're staying in someone's vacant weekend place. Home Exchange. com offers a one-year membership for $119.40, HomeLink International costs $119 for an annual online membership, which includes a directory listing, and Intervac U.S. offers international membership for $100.

Exchange Clubs Home Exchange.com (☎ 800/877–8723 ⊕ www.homeexchange. com). **HomeLink International** (☎ 800/638–3841 ⊕ www.homelink.org). **Intervac U.S.** (☎ 800/756–4663 ⊕ www.intervacus.com).

HOTELS

Most hotels have rooms with "ensuite" bathrooms—as private bathrooms are called—although some older ones may have only washbasins; in this case, showers and toilets are usually down the hall.

Especially in London, rooms and bathrooms may be smaller than what you find in the United States.

Besides familiar international chains, England has some local chains that are worth a look; they provide rooms from the less expensive (Travelodge, basic but bargain, and Premier Inn are the most widespread; Jurys Inns offer good value in city centers) to the trendy (ABode, Hotel du Vin, Malmaison).

Local Chains ABode (⊕ www.abodehotels. co.uk). **Hotel du Vin** (☎ 0845/365–4438 ⊕ www.hotelduvin.com). **Jurys Inn** (☎ 0870/410–0800 ⊕ www.jurysinn.com). **Malmaison** (☎ 0845/365–4247 ⊕ www. malmaison.com). **Premier Inn** (☎ 0871/527–8000, 1582/567890 outside U.K. ⊕ www. premierinn.com). **Travelodge** (⊕ www. travelodge.co.uk).

LOCAL DOS AND TABOOS

CUSTOMS OF THE COUNTRY

In general, British and American rules of etiquette are much the same. Differences are subtle. British people find Americans' bluntness somewhat startling from time to time, but are charmed by their friendliness.

British people tend to take politeness extremely seriously. They say "thank you" at every stage of a financial transaction.

The famous British stiff upper lip is more relaxed these days, but on social occasions it's best to observe what the others do, and go with the flow. If you're visiting a family home, a gift of flowers is welcome, as is a bottle of wine.

GREETINGS

Older British people will shake hands on greeting old friends or acquaintances; female friends may greet each other with a kiss on the cheek. In Britain, you can never say "please," "thank you," or "sorry" too often; to thank your host, a phone call or thank-you card does nicely. Email and other electronic messages are fine for younger hosts.

SIGHTSEEING

As in the United States, in public places it is considered polite to give up your seat to an elderly person, to a pregnant woman, or to a parent struggling with children and bags. Jaywalking is not illegal in England and everybody does it. However, since driving is on the left in England, the traffic flow may be confusing; use caution.

British people used to take waiting in line (called queuing) incredibly seriously, but, especially in London bus queues, line discipline is breaking down. Nevertheless, many still highly value patience, and will turn on "queue jumpers" who try to cut in line. Complaining while waiting in line is considered wimpy. Enduring the wait with good humor is considered a sign of strong moral character.

The single thing you can do that will most mark you as a tourist—and an impolite one—is fail to observe the written and spoken rule that, on virtually all escalators but especially those in Tube stations, you stand on the right side of the escalator and leave room for people to walk past you on the left.

OUT ON THE TOWN

Etiquette in restaurants is much the same as in any major U.S. city. In restaurants you hail a waiter by saying, "Excuse me . . ." as one passes by, or by politely signaling with subtle hand signals. It is common to have drinks before dinner, and wine with dinner. Friends and co-workers frequently gather in pubs, but you don't have to drink alcohol—some people in the pub drink juice or sodas. Nonetheless, drunkenness can be common in major cities after 10 pm.

You're generally expected to dress "smart casual" for the theater (suits or nice jackets for men, skirts or nice slacks for women), and those going to nightclubs will dress just the same here as they would in New York or Chicago—the flashier the better. Pubs are very casual places, however.

Smoking is forbidden in all public places, including bars and restaurants.

DOING BUSINESS

Punctuality is of prime importance; if you anticipate a late arrival, call ahead. For business dinners, if you proffered the invitation, it's usually assumed that you will pick up the tab. If you're the visitor, however, it's good form for the host to pay the bill. Alternatively, play it safe and offer to split the check.

HOTEL GRADING SYSTEM

Hotels, guesthouses, inns, and B&Bs in the United Kingdom are all graded from one to five stars by the tourism board, VisitBritain. Basically, the more stars a property has, the more amenities it has, and the facilities will be of a higher standard. It's a fairly good reflection of lodging from small B&Bs up to palatial hotels. The most luxurious hotels will have five stars; a simple, clean, acceptable hostelry will have one star.

DISCOUNTS AND DEALS

Hotel rates in major cities tend to be cheapest on weekends, whereas rural hotels are cheapest on weeknights. The lowest occupancy is between November and April, so hotels lower their prices substantially during these months.

Lastminute.com offers deals on hotel rooms all over the United Kingdom. VisitLondon.com, London's official Web site, has some good deals. London Information Centre provides free maps, tourist information, and last-minute hotel bookings in the city, with savings of up to 50%. Its kiosk in Leicester Square is open daily 8 am–midnight.

Local Resources Lastminute.com
((☎ 0871/222–5969 ⊕ www.lastminute. com). **London Information Centre** (✉ Leicester Sq. ☎ 0207/292–2333 ⊕ www. LondonInformationCentre.com).

▮ COMMUNICATIONS

INTERNET

If you're traveling with a laptop, carry a spare battery and adapter. If your hotel has dial-up (a rarity these days), get a telephone cord that's compatible with a British phone jack; these are available in Britain at airports and electronics stores. Wi-Fi is increasingly available in hotels, and broadband coverage is widespread in cities. Outside big cities, wireless access is relatively rare in cafés and coffee shops, but its popularity there is growing.

Contacts Cybercafes (⊕ www.cybercafes.com). **Wi-Fi Freespot** (⊕ www.wififreespot.com).

PHONES

All calls (including local calls) made within the United Kingdom are charged according to the time of day. The standard rate applies weekdays 7 am to 7 pm; a cheaper rate is in effect weekdays 7 pm to 7 am and all day on weekends, when it's even cheaper. As of this writing, a daytime call to the United States will cost about 24p a minute on a regular phone (weekends are cheaper), £1.20 on a pay phone.

A word of warning: 0870 numbers are *not* toll-free numbers in Britain; in fact, numbers beginning with this or the 0871, 0844, or 0845 prefixes cost extra to call. The amount varies and is usually relatively small—except for numbers with the premium-rate 0905 prefix, which cost an eye-watering £1 per minute when dialed from within the country—but can be excessive when dialed from outside Britain.

CALLING ENGLAND

The country code for Great Britain (and thus England) is 44. When dialing an English number from abroad, drop the initial 0 from before the local area code. For example, let's say you're calling Buckingham Palace—020/7839–1377—from the United States. First, dial 011 (the international access code), then 44 (Great Britain's country code), then 20 (London's center-city code—without its initial 0), then the remainder of the number.

CALLING WITHIN ENGLAND

For all calls within England (and Britain), dial the area code (which usually begins with 01, except in London), followed by the telephone number.

There are four types of pay phones: those that accept (a) only coins, (b) only British Telecom phone cards, (c) British Telecom phone cards and credit cards, or (d) phone cards and credit cards from other companies. Most coin-operated phones take 10p, 20p, 50p, and £1 coins. Insert the coins *before* dialing. Minimum charges vary, but generally start around 10p. The indicator panel shows how much money is left; add more whenever you like. If there is no answer, replace the receiver and your money will be returned.

For pay and other phones, if you hear a repeated single tone after dialing, the line is busy; a continuous tone means the number didn't work.

There are several different directory-assistance providers. For information anywhere in Britain, try dialing 118–888 or 118–118; you'll need to know the town and the street (or at least the neighborhood) of the person you're trying to reach. For the operator, dial 100. For genuine emergencies, dial 999.

CALLING OUTSIDE ENGLAND

For direct overseas dialing from England (and Britain), dial 00, then the country code, area code, and number. For the international operator, credit card, or collect calls, dial 155; for international directory assistance, dial 118505. The country code for the United States is 1.

Access Codes AT&T Direct (☎ 0800/890–0011). MCI WorldPhone (☎ 0800/279–5088). Sprint International Access (☎ 0800/890877).

CALLING CARDS

Public card phones operate with special cards that you can buy from post offices or newsstands. Ideal for longer calls, the cards are composed of units of 10p, and come in values of £3, £5, £10, and more. To use a card phone, lift the receiver, insert your card, and dial the number. An indicator panel shows the number of units used. At the end of your call the card will be returned. Where credit cards are taken, slide the card as indicated.

MOBILE PHONES

Any cell phone can be used in Europe if it's tri-band, quad-band, or GSM. Travelers should ask their cell-phone company if their phone fits in this category and make sure it is activated for international calling before leaving their home country. Roaming fees can be steep, however: $1

a minute is considered reasonable. And overseas you normally pay the toll charges for incoming calls. It's almost always cheaper to send a text message than to make a call, since text messages have a low set fee (often less than 25¢).

If you just want to make local calls, consider buying a new SIM card (your provider may have to unlock your phone for you) and a prepaid local service plan. You'll then have a local number and can make local calls at local rates. You can also rent a cell phone from most major car-rental agencies in England. Some upscale hotels now provide loaner cell phones to their guests. Beware, however, of the per-minute rates charged.

Contacts Cellular Abroad (☎ 800/287–5072 ⊕ www.cellularabroad.com). Mobal (☎ 888/888–9162 ⊕ www.mobalrental.com). Planet Fone (☎ 888/988–4777 ⊕ www.planetfone.com). Renta Mobile Phone (☎ 020/7353–7705 ⊕ www.rent-mobile-phone.com).

▌ CUSTOMS AND DUTIES

You're always allowed to bring goods of a certain value back home without having to pay any duty or import tax. But there's a limit on the amount of tobacco and liquor you can bring back duty-free, and some countries have separate limits for perfumes; for exact figures, check with your customs department. The values of so-called "duty-free" goods are included in these amounts. When you shop abroad, save all your receipts, as customs inspectors may ask to see them as well as the items you purchased. If the total value of your goods is more than the duty-free limit, you'll have to pay a tax (most often a flat percentage) on the value of everything beyond that limit.

Fresh meats, plants and vegetables, controlled drugs, and firearms (including replicas) and ammunition may not be brought into the United Kingdom, nor can dairy products from non-EU countries. Pets from the United States with the proper documentation may be brought into the country without quarantine under the U.K. Pet Travel Scheme (PETS). The process takes about six months to complete and involves detailed steps.

You will face no customs formalities if you enter Scotland or Wales from any other part of the United Kingdom.

Information in England HM Revenue and Customs (☎ 0845/010–9000 ⊕ www.hmrc. gov.uk). **Pet Travel Scheme** (☎ 0870/241– 1710 ⊕ www.defra.gov.uk/corporate/contacts/ wildlife-pets-qa).

U.S. Information U.S. Customs and Border Protection (⊕ www.cbp.gov).

▌ EATING OUT

The stereotypical notion of English meals as parades of roast beef, overcooked vegetables, and stodgy puddings is being replaced—particularly in London, other major cities, and some country hot spots—with an evolving picture of the country as foodie territory. From trendy gastro-pubs to the see-and-be-seen dining shrines, England is becoming known for a global palate.

In general, restaurant prices are high. If you're watching your budget, seek out pubs and ethnic restaurants.

CATEGORY	LONDON	ELSEWHERE
£	under £10	under £10
££	£10–£16	£10–£14
£££	£17–£23	£15–£19
££££	£24–£32	£20–£25
£££££	over £32	over £25

Price per person in pounds for a main course or equivalent combination of smaller dishes at dinner excluding tax.

DISCOUNTS AND DEALS

Eating out in England's big cities in particular can be expensive, but you can do it cheaply. Try local cafés, more popularly known as "caffs," where heaping plates of English comfort food (bacon sandwiches and stuffed baked potatoes, for example) are served. England has plenty of the big names in fast food, as well as smaller places selling sandwiches, fish-and-chips, burgers, falafel, kebabs, and the like. For a local touch, check out curry houses; Indian food is popular throughout the country. Marks & Spencer, Sainsbury's, Tesco, and Waitrose are chain supermarkets with outlets throughout the country. They're good choices for groceries, premade sandwiches, or picnic fixings.

MEALS AND MEALTIMES

Cafés serving the traditional English breakfast (called a "fry-up") of eggs, bacon, sausage, beans, half a grilled tomato, and strong tea are often the cheapest—and most authentic—places for breakfast. For lighter morning fare (or for real brewed coffee), try the Continental-style sandwich bars and coffee shops—the Pret-a-Manger chain being one of the largest—offering croissants and other pastries.

At lunch you can grab a sandwich between sights, pop into the local pub, or sit down in a restaurant. Dinner, too, has no set rules, but a three-course meal is standard in most midrange or high-end restaurants. Pre- or post-theater menus, offering two or three courses for a set price, are usually a good value.

Note that most traditional pubs do not have any waitstaff and that you are expected to go to the bar to order a beverage and your meal. Also, in cities many pubs do not serve food after 3 pm, so they're usually a better lunch option than dinner. In rural areas, it's not uncommon for pubs to stop serving dinner after 9 pm.

Breakfast is generally served between 7:30 and 9, lunch between noon and 2, dinner or supper between 7:30 and 9:30, sometimes earlier, seldom later except in large cities. These days tea is rarely a proper meal anymore (it was once served between 4:30 and 6), and tea shops are often open all day in touristy areas (they're not found at all in nontouristy places). So you can have a cup and pastry or sandwich whenever you feel you need it. Sunday roasts at pubs last from 11 am or noon to 3 pm.

Smoking is banned in pubs, clubs, and restaurants throughout Britain.

PAYING

Credit cards are widely accepted in restaurants and pubs, though some require a minimum charge of around £10. Be sure that you don't double-pay a service charge. Many restaurants exclude service charges from the printed menu (which the law obliges them to display outside), and then add 10% to 15% to the check. Others will stamp "Service not included" along the bottom of the bill, in which case you should add 10% to 15%. Cash is always appreciated, as it is more likely to go to the specific waiter.

PUBS

A common misconception among visitors to England is that pubs are simply bars. Pubs are also gathering places, conversation zones, even restaurants. In many pubs the social interaction is as important as the alcohol. Pubs are, generally speaking, where people go to meet their friends and catch up on one another's lives. In small towns pubs act almost as town halls. Traditionally pub hours are 11–11, with last orders called about 20 minutes before closing time, but pubs can choose to stay open until midnight or 1 am, or later.

Though to travelers it may appear that there's a pub on almost every corner, in fact pubs are something of an endangered species, closing at a rate of 39 a week (as of February 2010), with independent, non-chain pubs at particular risk.

Most pubs tend to be child-friendly, but others have restricted hours for children. If a pub serves food, it will generally allow children in during the day with adults. Some pubs are stricter than others, though, and will not admit anyone younger than 18. Some will allow children in during the day, but only until 6 pm. Family-friendly pubs tend to be packed with kids, parents, and all of their accoutrements.

RESERVATIONS AND DRESS

Regardless of where you are, it's a good idea to make a reservation if you can. We mention them specifically only when reservations are essential or when they are not accepted. For popular restaurants, book as far ahead as you can (often 30 days), and reconfirm as soon as you arrive. (Large parties should always call ahead to check the reservations policy.) We mention dress only when men are required to wear a jacket or a jacket and tie.

Online reservation services aren't as popular in England as in the United States, but Toptable and Square Meal have a fair number of listings in England.

Contacts Square Meal (⊕ www.squaremeal. co.uk). **Toptable** (⊕ www.toptable.co.uk).

WINES, BEER, AND SPIRITS

Although hundreds of varieties of beer are brewed around the country, the traditional brew is known as bitter and is not carbonated; it's usually served at room temperature. Fizzy American-style beer is called lager. There are also plenty of other potations: stouts like Guinness and Murphy's are thick, pitch-black brews you'll either love or hate; ciders, made from apples, are an alcoholic drink in Britain

(Bulmer's and Strongbow are the names to remember); shandies (oddly) are a low-alcohol mix of lager and lemon soda. Real ales, which have a natural second fermentation in the cask, have a shorter shelf life (so many are brewed locally) but special flavor; these are worth seeking out. Generally the selection and quality of cocktails is higher in a wine bar or café than in a pub. The legal drinking age is 18.

■ ECOTOURISM

Ecotourism is an emerging trend in the United Kingdom. The Shetland Environmental Agency Ltd. runs the Green Tourism Business Scheme, a program that evaluates lodgings in England, Scotland, and Wales and gives them gold, silver, or bronze ratings. You can find a list of green hotels, B&Bs, and apartments on the GTBS Web site. Also check out the VisitBritain Web site, which has information and tips about green travel in Britain.

Contacts Green Tourism Business Scheme (☎ 01738/632162 ⊕ www.green-business. co.uk). **VisitBritain** (⊕ www.visitbritain.com).

■ ELECTRICITY

The electrical current in Great Britain is 220–240 volts (in line with the rest of Europe), 50 cycles alternating current (AC); wall outlets take three-pin plugs, and shaver sockets take two round, oversize prongs. British bathrooms are not permitted to have 220–240 volt outlets in them. Blackouts and brownouts are rare and are usually fixed in a few hours.

Consider making a small investment in a universal adapter, which has several types of plugs in one lightweight, compact unit. Most laptops and mobile phone chargers are dual voltage (i.e., they operate equally well on 110 and 220 volts), so require only an adapter. These days the same is true of small appliances such as hair dryers. Always check labels and manufacturer instructions. Don't use 110-volt outlets marked "For shavers only"

for high-wattage appliances such as hair dryers.

Contacts Steve Kropla's Help for World Travelers (⊕ www.kropla.com). **Walkabout Travel Gear** (⊕ www.walkabouttravelgear.com).

■ EMERGENCIES

If you need to report an emergency, dial 999 for police, fire, or ambulance. Be prepared to give the telephone number you're calling from. You can get 24-hour treatment in Accident and Emergency at British hospitals, although you should expect to wait hours for treatment. Prescriptions are valid only if made out by doctors registered in the United Kingdom.

Although England has a subsidized National Health Service, free at the point of service for British residents, foreign visitors are expected to pay for any treatment they receive. Expect to receive a bill after you return home. Check with your health-insurance company to make sure you're covered. Some British hospitals now require a credit card or other payment before they'll offer treatment.

U.S. Embassies American Embassy (✉ 24 Grosvenor Sq., London ☎ 0207/499–9000 ⊕ www.usembassy.org.uk). **U.S. Passport Unit** (✉ 55/56 Upper Brook St., London ☎ 0207499–9000).

General Emergency Contacts Ambulance, fire, police (☎ 999).

▌ HEALTH

SPECIFIC ISSUES IN ENGLAND

If you take prescription drugs, keep a supply in your carry-on luggage and make a list of all your prescriptions to keep on file at home while you are abroad. You will not be able to renew a U.S. prescription at a pharmacy in Britain. Prescriptions are accepted only if issued by a U.K.-registered physician.

OVER-THE-COUNTER REMEDIES

Over-the-counter medications in England are similar to those in the United States, with a few significant differences. Medications are sold in boxes rather than bottles, and are sold in small amounts—usually no more than 24 pills. There may also be fewer brands. All headache medicine is usually filed under the "painkillers." You can buy generic ibuprofen or a popular European brand of ibuprofen, Nurofen. Tylenol is not sold in the United Kingdom, but its main ingredient, acetaminophen, is—but it's called paracetamol.

Among sinus and allergy medicines, Clarityn is the main option here; it's spelled slightly differently but is the same brand sold in the United States. Some medicines are pretty much the same as brands sold in the United States—instead of Nyquil cold medicine, there's Night Nurse. The most popular over-the-counter cough medicine is Benylin.

Drugstores are generally called pharmacies, but sometimes referred to as chemists' shops. The biggest drugstore chain in the country is Boots, which has outlets everywhere, except for the smallest towns. If you're in a rural area, look for shops marked with a sign of a green cross.

If you can't find what you want, ask at the counter; many over-the-counter medicines are kept behind the register.

SHOTS AND MEDICATIONS

No special shots are required or suggested for England.

Health Warnings National Centers for Disease Control & Prevention (CDC

☎ 800/232–4646 *international travelers' health line* ⊕ *wwwnc.cdc.gov/travel*). **World Health Organization** (*WHO* ⊕ *www.who.int*).

▌ HOURS OF OPERATION

Most banks are open weekdays from 9:30 until 3:30 or 4:30. Some have Thursday evening hours, and a few are open Saturday morning. Normal office hours for most businesses are weekdays 9 to 5.

The major national museums and galleries are open daily 9–6, including lunchtime, but have shorter hours on Sunday. Regional museums are usually closed Monday and have shorter hours in winter. In London many museums are open late one evening a week.

Independently owned pharmacies are generally open Monday through Saturday 9:30–5:30, although in larger cities some stay open until 10 pm; local newspapers list which pharmacies are open late.

Usual retail business hours are Monday through Saturday 9–5:30, Sunday noon–4. In some small villages, shops may close at 1 pm once a week, often Wednesday or Thursday. They may also close for lunch and not open on Sunday at all. In large cities—especially London—department stores stay open late (usually until 7:30 or 8) one night a week, usually Thursday. On national holidays most stores are closed, and over the Christmas holidays most restaurants are closed as well.

HOLIDAYS

Holidays are January 1, New Year's Day; Good Friday and Easter Monday; May Day (first Monday in May); spring and summer bank holidays (last Monday in May and August, respectively); December 25, Christmas Day; and December 26, Boxing Day (day after Christmas). If these holidays fall on a weekend, the holiday is observed on the following Monday. There will be a special four-day holiday the first weekend in June 2012 to celebrate the Queen's Diamond Jubilee, marking her 60th year on the throne. During the Christmas holidays many restaurants, as well as museums and other attractions, may close for at least a week—call to verify hours. Book hotels for Christmas travel well in advance, and check whether the hotel restaurant will be open.

▌ MAIL

Stamps can be bought from post offices (open weekdays 9–5:30, Saturday 9–noon), from stamp machines outside post offices, and from news dealers' stores and newsstands. Mailboxes, known as post or letter boxes, are painted bright red. Allow 7 days for a letter to reach the United States and about 10 days to two weeks to Australia or New Zealand. The useful Royal Mail Web site has information on everything from buying stamps to finding a post office.

Airmail letters up to 10 grams (0.35 ounce) to North America cost 76p. Letters within Britain are 46p for first class, 36p for second class. Rates for envelopes larger than 353 mm (13.9 inches) long, 250 mm (9.84 inches) wide, and 25 mm (1 inch) deep are higher. All rates are subject to change.

Contact **Royal Mail** (⊕ *www.royalmail.com*).

SHIPPING PACKAGES

Most department stores and retail outlets can ship your goods home. You should check your insurance for coverage of possible damage. Private delivery companies such as Federal Express and DHL offer two-day delivery service to the United States, but you'll pay a considerable amount for the privilege.

Express Services **DHL** (☎ *0844/248–0844* ⊕ *www.dhl.co.uk*). **Federal Express** (☎ *0845/607–0809* ⊕ *www.fedex.com*). **Parcelforce** (☎ *0844/800–4466* ⊕ *www.parcelforce.co.uk*).

▌ MONEY

Prices in England can seem high because of the exchange rate. London remains one of the most expensive cities in the world. But for every yin there's a yang, and travelers can get breaks: staying in bed-and-breakfasts, or renting a city apartment brings down lodging costs, and national museums are free. The chart below gives some ideas of the prices you can expect to pay for day-to-day life.

ITEM	AVERAGE COST
Cup of Coffee	£1.50–£3
Glass of Wine	£3.50 in a pub or wine bar, £5.50 or more in a restaurant
Glass of Beer	£2.70 or more
Sandwich	£3.50
One-Mile Taxi Ride in London	£5.50–£8.60
Museum Admission	National museums free; others £5–£10

Prices throughout this guide are given for adults. Substantially reduced fees—generally referred to as "concessions" throughout Great Britain—are almost always available for children, students, and senior citizens.

▌TIP➜ Banks never have every foreign currency on hand, and it may take as long as a week to order. If you're planning to exchange funds before leaving home, don't wait until the last minute.

ATMS AND BANKS

Make sure before leaving home that your credit and debit cards have been programmed for ATM use abroad—ATMs in England and Wales accept PINs of four or fewer digits only. If you know your PIN as a word, learn the numerical equivalent, since most keypads in England show numbers only, not letters. Most ATMs are on both the Cirrus and Plus networks. ATMs are available at most main-street banks, large supermarkets such as Sainsbury's and Tesco's, some Tube stops in London, and many rail stations. Major banks include Barclays, HSBC, and NatWest.

Your own bank will probably charge a fee for using ATMs abroad; the foreign bank you use may also charge a fee. Nevertheless, you'll usually get a better rate of exchange at an ATM than you will at a currency-exchange office or even when changing money in a bank. And extracting funds as you need them is a safer option than carrying around a large amount of cash.

CREDIT CARDS

The Discover card is not accepted throughout Britain. Other major credit cards, except Diners Club, are accepted virtually everywhere in Britain; however, you're expected to know and use your pin number for all transactions—even for credit cards, so it's a good idea to do some quick memorization for whichever card you intend to use in England.

Keep in mind that most European credit cards store information in microchips, rather than magnetic strips. Although some banks in the United States, such as Chase and Wells Fargo, are starting to adapt this system, you may find some places in England that can't process your credit card. It's a good idea to carry enough cash to cover small purchases.

Inform your credit-card company before you travel, especially if you're going abroad and don't travel internationally very often. Otherwise, the credit-card company might put a hold on your card owing to unusual activity. Record all your credit-card numbers in a safe place. Both MasterCard and Visa have general numbers you can call (collect if you're abroad) if your card is lost, but you're better off calling the number of your issuing bank, since MasterCard and Visa usually just transfer you to your bank; your bank's number is usually printed on your card.

If you plan to use your credit card for cash advances, you'll need to apply for a PIN at least two weeks before your trip. Although it's usually cheaper (and safer) to use a credit card abroad for large purchases (so you can cancel payments or be reimbursed if there's a problem), note that some credit-card companies *and* the banks that issue them add substantial percentages to all foreign transactions, whether they're in a foreign currency or not. Check on these fees before traveling.

Reporting Lost Cards American Express (☎ 01273/696933 in U.K., 715/343-7977 collect from abroad ⊕ www.americanexpress. com). **Diners Club** (☎ 0870/190-0011 in U.K., 303/799-1504 collect from abroad ⊕ www. dinersclubinternational.com). **MasterCard** (☎ 0800/964767 in U.K., 636/722-7111 collect from abroad ⊕ www.mastercard.com). **Visa** (☎ 0800/891725 in U.K., 800/847-2911 collect from abroad ⊕ www.visa.com).

CURRENCY AND EXCHANGE

The unit of currency in Great Britain is the pound sterling (£), divided into 100 pence (p). The bills (called notes in Britain) are 50, 20, 10, and 5 pounds. Coins are £2, £1, 50p, 20p, 10p, 5p, 2p, and 1p. If you are traveling beyond England and Wales, note that Scotland and the Channel Islands have their own bills, and the Channel Islands their own coins, too. Scottish bills are accepted in the rest of Britain, but you cannot use Channel Islands currency outside the islands.

At the time of this writing, the exchange rate was about U.S. $1.64 to £1.

British post offices exchange currency with no fee, and at decent rates.

■TIP→ Even if a currency-exchange booth has a sign promising no commission, rest assured that there's some kind of huge, hidden fee. And as for rates, you're almost always better off getting foreign currency at an ATM or exchanging money at a bank.

Currency Conversion Google (⊕ www. google.com). **Oanda.com** (⊕ www.oanda.com). **XE.com** (⊕ www.xe.com).

■ PACKING

England can be cool, damp, and overcast, even in summer. You'll want a heavy coat for winter and a lightweight coat or warm jacket for summer. There's no time of year when a raincoat or umbrella won't come in handy. For the cities, pack as you would for an American city: coats and ties for expensive restaurants and nightspots, casual clothes elsewhere. If you plan to stay in budget hotels, take your own soap. It's also a good idea to take a washcloth. Pack insect repellent if you plan to hike.

▮ PASSPORTS

U.S. citizens need only a valid passport to enter Great Britain for stays of up to six months. Travelers should be prepared to show sufficient funds to support and accommodate themselves while in Britain (credit cards will usually suffice for this) and to show a return or onward ticket. If you're within six months of your passport's expiration date, renew it before you leave—nearly expired passports are not strictly banned, but they make immigration officials anxious, and may cause you problems. Health certificates are not required.

▮ RESTROOMS

Public restrooms are sparse in England, although most big cities maintain public facilities that are clean and modern. Train stations and department stores have public restrooms that occasionally charge a small fee, usually 30p. Most pubs, restaurants, and even fast-food chains reserve their bathrooms for customers. Hotels and museums are usually a good place to find clean, free facilities. On the road, gas-station facilities are usually clean and free.

Find a Loo **The Bathroom Diaries** (⊕ www. thebathroomdiaries.com).

▮ SAFETY

England has a low incidence of violent crime. However, petty crime, mostly in urban areas, is on the rise, and tourists can be the target. Use common sense: when in a city center, if you're paying at a shop or a restaurant, never put your wallet down or let your bag out of your hand. When sitting on a chair in a public place, keep your purse on your lap or between your feet. Don't wear expensive jewelry or watches. Store your passport in the hotel safe, and keep a copy with you. Don't leave anything in your car.

Although scams do occur in Britain, they are not pervasive. If you're getting money out of an ATM, beware of someone bumping into you to distract you. You may want to use ATMs inside banks rather than those outside them. In London scams are most common at ATMs on Oxford Street and around Piccadilly Circus. Watch out for pickpockets, particularly in London. They often work in pairs, one distracting you in some way.

Always take a licensed black taxi or call a car service (sometimes called minicabs) recommended by your hotel. Avoid drivers who approach you on the street, as in most cases they will overcharge you. Always buy theater tickets from a reputable dealer. If you are driving in from a British port, beware of thieves posing as customs officials who try to "confiscate illegal goods."

While traveling, don't leave any bags unattended, as they may be viewed as a security risk and destroyed by the authorities. If you see an unattended bag on the train, bus, or Tube, find a worker and report it. Never hesitate to get off a Tube, train, or bus if you feel unsafe.

▮ **TIP→** Distribute your cash, credit cards, IDs, and other valuables between a deep front pocket, an inside jacket or vest pocket, and a hidden money pouch. Don't reach for the money pouch once you're in public.

General Information and Warnings Transportation Security Administration (*TSA* ⊕ www.tsa.gov). **U.K. Foreign & Commonwealth Office** (⊕ www.fco.gov.uk/ travel). **U.S. Department of State** (⊕ www. travel.state.gov).

▮ SIGHTSEEING PASSES

DISCOUNT PASSES

If you plan to visit castles, gardens, and historic houses during your stay in England and Wales, look into discount passes or memberships that offer significant savings. Just be sure to match what the pass or membership offers against your itinerary to see if it's worthwhile.

The National Trust, English Heritage, and the Historic Houses Association each encompass hundreds of properties. English Heritage's Overseas Visitors Pass costs £20 for a 7-day pass and £24.50 for a 14-day pass for one adult. You can order it in advance by phone or online or purchase it at a participating property in England. The National Trust Touring Pass, for overseas visitors, must be purchased in advance, either by phone or online. A 7-day pass is £22; a 14-day pass is £27.

VisitBritain's Great British Heritage Pass is £39 for 3 days, £69 for one week, and £89 for 15 days, and includes more than 500 properties belonging to English Heritage and the National Trust. The pass is sold online and at major tourist information centers in Britain. Family passes are available, too.

Annual membership in the National Trust (through the Royal Oak Foundation, the U.S. affiliate) is $55 a year, much cheaper than if you buy one in Britain. English Heritage membership is £46, and the Historic Houses Association is £40. Memberships entitle you to free entry to properties.

For London Pass information, see Chapter 2. For passes specifically for Wales, see Chapter 14.

Information English Heritage (☎ 0870/333–1181 ⊕ www.english-heritage.org.uk). **Great British Heritage Pass** (☎ 0870/242–9988, 0166/448–5020 from U.S. ⊕ www.britishheritagepass.com). **Historic Houses Association** (☎ 0207259–5688 ⊕ www.hha.org.uk). **National Trust** (☎ 0844/800–1895 ⊕ www.nationaltrust.org.uk). **Royal Oak Foundation** (☎ 212/480–2889 or 800/913–6565 in U.S. ⊕ www.royal-oak.org).

▮ SPORTS AND THE OUTDOORS

In addition to the associations listed below, VisitBritain and local Tourist Information Centres can recommend places to enjoy your favorite sport.

BIKING

The national body promoting cycle touring is the Cyclists' Touring Club (£37 a year). Members get free advice and route information and a magazine. The CTC and VisitBritain publish a free guide, "Britain for Cyclists." Both the CTC and VisitBritain provide lists of travel agencies specializing in cycling vacations.

Contacts Cyclists' Touring Club (☎ 0208/891–8451 ⊕ www.ctc.org.uk). **VisitBritain** (⊕ www.visitbritain.com).

BOATING

Boating can be a leisurely way to explore the English landscape, ranging from bucolic rivers to industrial canals, from a unique perspective. For boat-rental operators along Britain's several hundred miles of historic canals and waterways, from the Norfolk Broads to the Lake District, contact the Association of Pleasure Craft Operators or Waterway Holidays. British Waterways has maps and other information. Waterway Holidays arranges boat accommodations from traditional narrow boats to wide-beam canal boats, motorboats, and sailboats; Waterways UK has both brochures and an online reservation service for canal travel.

Contacts Association of Pleasure Craft Operators (☎ 0844/800–9575 ⊕ www.apco.org.uk). **British Waterways** (☎ 01923/201120 ⊕ www.waterscape.com). **Waterway Holidays** (☎ 01252/796400 ⊕ www.waterwaysholidays.com). **Waterways UK** (☎ 01952/79640 ⊕ www.waterways-uk.com).

GOLF

Invented in Scotland, golf is a beloved pastime all over England. Some courses take advantage of spectacular natural settings, from the ocean to mountain backdrops. Most courses are reserved for club members and adhere to strict rules of protocol and dress. However, many famous courses can be used by visiting golfers reserving well in advance. In addition, numerous public courses are open to anyone, though advance reservations are advised. Package tours with companies such as Golf International and Owenoak International Golf Travel allow visitors into exclusive clubs. For further information on courses, fees, and locations, try the Web sites for UK Golf Guide or English Golf Courses.

Contacts English Golf Courses
(☎ 0141/353–2222 ⊕ www.englishgolf-courses.co.uk). **Golf International**
(☎ 212/986–9176 or 800/833–1389 in U.S. ⊕ www.golfinternational.com). **Owenoak International Golf Travel** (☎ 203/854–9000 or 800/426–4498 in U.S. ⊕ www.owenoak.com). **UK Golf Guide** (☎ 0844/826–9088 ⊕ www.uk-golf.com).

WALKING

Walking and hiking, from the slowest ramble to a mountainside climb requiring technical equipment, are enormously popular in England. National Trails, funded by Natural England and the Countryside Counsel for Wales, has great resources online. The Ramblers, a well-known charitable organization promoting walking and care of footpaths, has helpful information, including a list of B&Bs within 2 mi of selected long-distance footpaths. Some of the best maps for walking are the Explorer Maps, published by the Ordnance Survey; check out ⊕ *www.ordnancesurvey.co.uk*.

Contacts National Trails (⊕ www.nationaltrail.co.uk). **The Ramblers**
(☎ 020/7339–8500 ⊕ www.ramblers.org.uk).

▌TAXES

Air Passenger Duty (APD) is a tax included in the price of your ticket. APD fees are divided into four bands: short-haul destinations under 2,000 mi, £12 per person in Economy (£24 all other classes);

medium-haul destinations under 4,000 mi (including the United States), £60 Economy (£120 all others); long-haul destinations under 6,000 mi, £75 Economy (£150 all others); ultra-long-haul destinations over 6,000 mi, £85 Economy (£170 all others).

The British sales tax (Value Added Tax, or V.A.T.) is 20%. The tax is almost always included in quoted prices in shops, hotels, and restaurants. The most common exception is at high-end hotels, where prices often exclude V.A.T. Outside of hotels and rental-car agencies, which have specific additional taxes, there is no other sales tax in England.

Most travelers from outside the EU can get a V.A.T. refund by either the Retail Export or the more cumbersome Direct Export method. Refunds apply for V.A.T. only on goods being taken out of Britain, and purchases must exceed a minimum limit, generally £50 to £100. Many large stores provide a V.A.T.–refund service, but only if you request it.

For the Retail Export method, you must ask the store to complete Form V.A.T. 407, to be given to customs at departure along with a V.A.T. Retail Export scheme invoice. Have the form stamped like any customs form when you leave the country or, if you're visiting several European Union countries, when you leave the EU. Be ready to show customs officials what you've bought. After you're through passport control, take the form to a refund-service counter for an on-the-spot refund, or mail it back after you arrive home.

With the Direct Export method, the goods are mailed directly to your home; you must have a Form V.A.T. 407 certified by customs, police, or a notary public when you get home and then sent back to the store, which will refund your money. Remember, V.A.T. refunds can't be processed after you arrive back home.

Another option is a refund service, which processes refunds for most shops. Global Blue is a Europe-wide service with

270,000 affiliated stores and more than 700 refund counters at major airports and border crossings. Its refund form, called a Tax Free Check, is the most common across the European continent. The service issues refunds in the form of cash, check, or credit-card adjustment. The latter is useful for small purchases as the cost of cashing a foreign-currency check may exceed the amount of the refund.

V.A.T. Refunds Global Blue (☎ *0208/222–0100* ⊕ *www.global-blue.com*). **HM Revenue and Customs** (☎ *0845/010–9000* ⊕ *www. hmrc.gov.uk*).

▮ TIME

England sets its clocks by Greenwich Mean Time, five hours ahead of the U.S. East Coast. British summer time (GMT plus one hour) generally coincides with American daylight saving time adjustments.

Time Zones Timeanddate.com (⊕ *www. timeanddate.com/worldclock*).

▮ TIPPING

Tipping is done in Britain just as in the United States, but at a lower level than you would back home. Tipping more can look like you're showing off. Do not tip bar staff in pubs—although you can always offer to buy them a drink. There's no need to tip at clubs (it's acceptable at posher establishments, though) unless you're being served at your table. Rounding up to the nearest pound or 50p is appreciated.

TIPPING GUIDELINES FOR ENGLAND	
Bartender	£1–£2 per round of drinks, depending on the number of drinks, except in pubs, where tipping is not the custom
Bellhop	£1 per bag, depending on the level of the hotel
Hotel Concierge	£5 or more, if he or she performs a service for you
Hotel Doorman	£1 if he helps you get a cab
Hotel Maid	It's extremely rare for hotel maids to be tipped; £1 or £2 would be generous.
Hotel Room-Service Waiter	Nothing, if a service charge is added to the bill
Porter at Airport or Train Station	£1 per bag
Skycap at Airport	£1 per bag checked
Taxi Driver	10p per pound of the fare, then round up to nearest pound
Tour Guide	Tipping optional: £1 or £2 is generous.
Waiter	10%–15%, with 15% being the norm at high-end London restaurants; nothing additional if a service charge is added to the bill, unless you want to reward particularly good service. Tips in cash preferred.
Other	Restroom attendants in more expensive restaurants expect some small change or £1. Tip coat-check personnel £1 unless there is a fee, then nothing. Hairdressers and barbers get 10%–15%.

▮ TOURS

Visiting London on a fully escorted tour is unnecessary because of its extensive public transport and wide network of taxicabs. Many tour companies offer day tours to the main sights, and getting around is fairly easy.

If you're traveling beyond London, packaged tours can be very useful, particularly if you don't want to rent a car. Because many sights are off the beaten track and not accessible by public transportation—particularly castles, great houses, and small villages—tour groups make the country accessible to all. There are a few downsides to escorted tours: rooms in castles and medieval houses tend to be small and can feel overrun when tour groups roll in.

Dozens of companies offer fully guided tours in Britain. Most of these are full packages including lodging, food, and transportation costs in one flat fee. Do a bit of research before booking. You'll want to know about the hotels you'll be staying in, how big your group is likely to be, how your days will be structured, and who the other people are likely to be.

Among the most reliable tour companies, two U.S.-based companies—Trafalgar Tours and Globus & Cosmos Tours—specialize in moderately priced trips that feature plenty of sights. Tauck is another well-established company. At the high end of the price scale is Abercrombie & Kent, known for luxurious tours that include everything from castle hotels to journeys on vintage railways.

Contacts Abercrombie & Kent (☎ 800/554–7016 ⊕ www.abercrombiekent.com). **Globus & Cosmos Tours** (☎ 866/785–8581 Globus, 800/276–1241 Cosmos ⊕ www.globusandcosmos.com). **Tauck** (☎ 800/788–7885 ⊕ www.tauck.com). **Trafalgar Tours** (☎ 866/544–4434 ⊕ www.trafalgartours.com).

SPECIAL-INTEREST TOURS
CULINARY
Britain's foodie culture is increasingly rich and thriving. Gourmet on Tour, a U.S.-based tour company, offers vacations dominated by cooking, eating, and fine wine.

Contact Gourmet on Tour (☎ 646/461–6088 in U.S., 0207/558–8796 in U.K. ⊕ www.gourmetontour.com).

GARDENS
England is a land of garden lovers, and its gardens are varied and impressive. Adderley and Flora are British companies; the American tour companies Coopersmiths and Lynott Tours also offer tours of gardens around Britain. The Web site ⊕ www.gardenvisit.com is a useful reference site.

Contacts Adderley Travel Ltd. (☎ 01953/606706 ⊕ www.adderleytravel.com). **Coopersmiths** (☎ 415/669–1914 in U.S. ⊕ www.coopersmiths.com). **Flora Garden Tours** (☎ 01366/328946 ⊕ www.flora-gardentours.co.uk). **Lynott Tours** (☎ 800/221–2474 in U.S. ⊕ www.lynotttours.com).

HEALTH
You can relax with yoga- and spa-based holidays throughout the United Kingdom. Lotus Journeys offers some good options.

Contact Lotus Journeys (☎ 0845/170–1747 ⊕ www.lotusjourneys.com).

HIKING AND WALKING
For those who prefer to spend their vacations on the move, Adventureline will keep you on your bike, on your feet, or swinging from hillsides. Country Walkers and England Lakeland Ramblers, based in the United States, have guided walks in Britain. The Wayfarers offer specialized walking tours, such as treks through Brönte Country.

Contacts Adventureline (☎ 01209/820847 ⊕ www.adventureline.co.uk). **Country Walkers** (☎ 800/464–9255 ⊕ www.countrywalkers.com). **England Lakeland Ramblers** (☎ 800/724–8801 ⊕ www.ramblers.com). **The Wayfarers** (☎ 01242/620871 ⊕ www.thewayfarers.com).

HISTORY
England is rich in history and culture, to the point where it has developed what is known as the "heritage industry." Inscape offers tours of four days or less oriented toward fine art and architecture led by knowledgeable academics. Classic England specializes in private tours to castles, cathedrals, and areas of historic interest.

Contacts **Classic England** (☎ 01277/841651 in U.K., 866/464–7389 in U.S. ⊕ www.classic-england.com). **Inscape** (☎ 020/839–3988 ⊕ www.inscapetours.co.uk).

▌ VISITOR INFORMATION

ONLINE TRAVEL TOOLS

ALL ABOUT ENGLAND

Enjoy England (⊕ www.enjoyengland.com), part of VisitBritain, includes a handy list of local Tourist Information Centres. All of England's regions, along with most major towns and cities, have their own dedicated tourism Web sites providing useful information. VisitBritain (⊕ www.visitbritain.com), the official visitor Web site, focuses on information most helpful to England-bound U.S. travelers, from practical information to money-saving deals; you can even find out about movie locations. Visit London (⊕ www.visitlondon.com) is packed with information and can help you book your accommodations.

GARDENS

The National Gardens Scheme opens exceptional gardens attached to private houses and private garden squares to the public on selected weekends.

Contact National Gardens Scheme (⊕ www.ngs.org.uk).

HISTORIC SITES

The British monarchy has an official Web site with practical information about visiting royal homes and more. English Heritage, the National Trust, and VisitBritain all offer discount passes.

Contacts The British Monarchy (⊕ www.royal.gov.uk). **English Heritage** (☎ 0870/333–1181 ⊕ www.english-heritage.org.uk). **National Trust** (☎ 0844/800–1895 ⊕ www.nationaltrust.org.uk).

MUSEUMS AND THE ARTS

The London Theatre Guide, created by the Society of London Theatre, presents what's on and sells tickets. Their half-price ticket booths, tkts, located in London's Leicester Square and Brent Cross

Shopping Centre, offer same-day bargains. Culture 24 is a nonprofit, partly government-funded site packed with information about publicly funded museums (including special exhibits), art galleries, and historic sights. Tokenline sells gift vouchers for theater tickets. The London 2012 Web site (⊕ www.london2012.com) has Olympics-related information from transport to tickets.

Contacts Culture 24 (☎ 01273/623266 ⊕ www.culture24.org.uk). **London Theatre Guide** (☎ 0207/527–6700 ⊕ www.officiallondontheatre.co.uk). **tkts** (⊕ www.tkts.co.uk). **Tokenline** (☎ 0844/887–7878 ⊕ www.theatretokens.com).

VISITOR INFORMATION OFFICES

In many towns there are local and regional tourist information centers; many have Web sites. Offices offer services from discounts for local attractions, to visitor guides, maps, parking information, accommodation advice, and, in several locations, a booking service for local B&Bs.

The Britain and London Visitor Centre (open October to March, Monday 9:30–6, Tuesday to Friday 9–6, and weekends 10–4, and April to September, Monday 9:30–6:30, Tuesday to Friday 9–6:30, and weekends 10–4) provides details about travel, accommodations, and entertainment for London and Britain, but you must visit in person.

In London Britain and London Visitor Centre (✉ 1 Regent St., Piccadilly Circus ☎ 0870/156–6366 ⊕ www.visitlondon.com).

In the U.S. VisitBritain (⊕ www.visitbritain.com).

INDEX

PHOTO CREDITS

1, Adam Woolfitt / age fotostock. 3, Stowe Park, Buckinghamshire by Martin Pettitt http://www.flickr.com/photos/mdpettitt/4663854507/ Attribution License. Chapter 1: Experience England: 8-9, Heeb Christian/age fotostock. 10, David Peta/Shutterstock. 11 (left), London 2012. 11 (right), Morland Abingdon by Jim Champion http://www.flickr.com/photos/treehouse1977/4524995971/ Attribution-ShareAlike License. 12, Monkey Business Images/Shutterstock. 13 (left), ChrisAngove/Wikimedia Commons. 13 (right), redlentil/Wikimedia Commons. 14, Gail Johnson/Shutterstock. 15 (left), Gail Johnson/Shutterstock. 15 (right), Stewart Smith Photography/Shutterstock. 18 (left), StraH/Shutterstock. 18 (top center), Hampton Court Palace, gatehouse by Pavel Medzyun http://www.flickr.com/photos/mad_wraith/3926037589/ Attribution License. 18 (bottom center), Matthew Jacques/Shutterstock. 18 (top right), Tadeusz Ibrom/Shutterstock. 18 (bottom right), Pecold/Shutterstock. 19 (left), Bill Gats/Wikimedia Commons. 19 (top center), Adrian Zenz/Shutterstock. 19 (bottom center), ian woolcock/Shutterstock. 19 (top right), David Hughes/Shutterstock. 19 (bottom right), Kevin Eaves/Shutterstock. 20, [champions] Chelsea x Juventus : 3 by Crystian Cruz http://www.flickr.com/photos/crystiancruz/3310826822/ Attribution-ShareAlike License. 21, Nikki Bidgood/Hemera/Thinkstock. 22, David Hughes/Shutterstock. 23 (left), Dahlia Flower by William Warby http://www.flickr.com/photos/wwarby/4085740597/ Attribution License. 23 (right), Albert Dock by thinboyfatter http://www.flickr.com/photos/1234abcd/227827242/ Attribution License. 24, Matthew Jacques/Shutterstock. 25 (left), Ashdown Park by Caitlin http://www.flickr.com/photos/lizard_queen/110491647/ Attribution License. 25 (right), Kevin Eaves/Shutterstock. 26, IMG_4286 by Leon Brocard http://www.flickr.com/photos/acme/3111148216/ Attribution License. 27 (left), O'Shea Fillet by Simon Doggett http://www.flickr.com/photos/simondee/4886407274/ Attribution License. 27 (right), Elzbieta Sekowska/Shutterstock. 28, Hampton Court Palace by Roberto Arias http://www.flickr.com/photos/roberto8080/4844875392/ Attribution License. 30, David Woods/Shutterstock. 31 (left), JCElv/Shutterstock. 31 (right), Debu55y/Shutterstock. 32, Herbert Ortner/Wikimedia Commons. 34, Peekaboopink/Wikimedia Commons. Chapter 2: London: 35, Doug Pearson/age fotostock. 36 (top), Angelina Dimitrova/Shutterstock. 36 (bottom), jan kranendonk/Shutterstock. 37, Christopher Steer/iStockphoto. 38, Tan, Kim Pin/Shutterstock. 45, ktylerconk/Flickr. 52, Britain on View/photolibrary.com. 61, Jon Arnold/age fotostock. 64, Jarno Gonzalez Zarraonandia/Shutterstock. 71, iStockphoto. 73 (left), Walter Bibikow/viestiphoto.com. 73 (right), Tom Hanley / Alamy. 74, News Team International Ltd. 75, Peter Phipp/age fotostock. 76 (left), Mary Evans Picture Library /Alamy. 76 (center), Reflex Picture Library / Alamy. 76 (right), Classic Image / Alamy. 77, Jan Kranendonk/iStockphoto. 85, Londonstills.com / Alamy. 92, Danilo Donadoni/Marka/age fotostock. 101, Munro http://www.flickr.com/photos/55935853@N00/4476609453/ Attribution ShareAlike License. 106, jason lowe ltd. 112, Harwood Arms. 121 (top left), Claridge's Hotel. 121 (top right), Damian Russell. 121 (bottom left), The Dorchester. 121 (bottom right), The Stafford. 126 (top), Marriott International. 126 (bottom left), Leading Hotels of the World. 126 (bottom right), Generator Hostel London. 133 (top left), Mandarin Oriental. 133 (top right), Church Street Hotel. 133 (center left), The Hoxton. 133 (center right), Firmdale Hotels. 133 (bottom left), VIEW Pictures Ltd / Alamy. 133 (bottom right), RayMain.co.uk. 143, Gianni Muratore / Alamy. 148, Bettina Strenske/age fotostock. 157, Jess Moss. 162, Britain on View/photolibrary.com. Chapter 3: The Southeast: 167, Britain on View/photolibrary.com. 168, Dover White Cliffs_2010 08 14_0077 by Harvey Barrison http://www.flickr.com/photos/hbarrison/4930390553/ Attribution-ShareAlike License. 169 (top), Jake Keup/Wikimedia Commons. 169 (bottom), Sissinghurst Castle, Kent by Allan Harris http://www.flickr.com/photos/50638285@N00/3777894502/ Attribution-ShareAlike License. 170, High Tea by Adam Burt http://www.flickr.com/photos/aburt/3013235854/ Attribution-ShareAlike License. 171 (top), shtukicrew/Shutterstock. 171 (bot-

http://www.flickr.com/photos/mdpettitt/4663854507/ Attribution License. 450 (top right), Britain On View/photolibrary.com. 450 (center), Hidcote Manor gardens by Allan Harris http://www.flickr.com/photos/allan_harris/3811624501/ Attribution-ShareAlike License. 450 (bottom), Andreas Tille/Wikimedia Commons. 451, John Glover / age fotostock. 452, National Trust Photo Library/Britain On View/photolibrary.com. 453 (top), North Light Images / age fotostock. 453 (bottom), David Sellman/Britain On View/photolibrary.com. 454, Paul Felix/Britain On View/photolibrary.com. 455 (left), Targeman/Wikimedia Commons. 455 (right), 20100506Stourhead_Cutler_P1010967 by Wendy Cutler http://www.flickr.com/photos/wlcutler/4586726477/ Attribution License. 456, Peter Packer/Britain On View/photolibrary.com. 465, Jon Bower / age fotostock. 469, Andy Williams / age fotostock. 474, Simon Tranter / age fotostock. Chapter 8: Stratford-Upon-Avon and the Heart of England: 477, John Martin / Alamy. 479 (top), David Benton/Shutterstock. 479 (bottom), Stratford on Avon by Allan Harris. http://www.flickr.com/photos/allan_harris/3941380761/ Attribution-ShareAlike License. 480, Simon Reddy / Alamy. 481 (top), Monkey Business Images/Shutterstock. 481 (bottom), Foodpics/Shutterstock. 482, Ironbridge Gorge Museum Trust. 486, Cotswolds Photo Library/Britain on View/photolibrary.com. 493, Travel Pix Collection / age fotostock. 502, Britain on View/photolibrary.com. 507, Tupungato/Shutterstock. 513, Britain on View/photolibrary.com. 524, Ironbridge Gorge Museum Trust. 531, Chester Street Scene by Nadia http://www.flickr.com/photos/nadiapriestley/177285267/ Attribution-ShareAlike License. Chapter 9: Lancashire and the Peaks: 533, James Osmond/Britain on View/photolibrary.com. 535 (top), Paul Collins/Wikimedia Commons. 535 (bottom left), Jonathan Barton/iStockphoto. 535 (bottom right), Hardwick Hall, National Trust by Sue Hasker. http://www.flickr.com/photos/24481894@N08/2962783462/ Attribution-ShareAlike License. 536, Land of Lost Content / age fotostock. 537 (top), Havaska/Wikimedia Commons. 537 (bottom), Cavern Club by Jennifer Boyer http://www.flickr.com/photos/jenniferboyer/5254721200/ Attribution License. 538, MAISANT Ludovic / age fotostock. 544, Pawel Libera/Britain on View/photolibrary.com. 551, Chris Brink / age fotostock. 558, Britain on View/photolibrary.com. 565, MAISANT Ludovic / age fotostock. 572, Alan Novelli/Britain on View/photolibrary.com. Chapter 10: The Lake District: 577, Rob Carter / Alamy. 578, Kevin Eaves/Shutterstock. 579 (top), Kevin Eaves/Shutterstock. 579 (bottom left), Neil Hanson/Wikimedia Commons. 579 (bottom right), Ashness Bridge by Alan Cleaver http://www.flickr.com/photos/alancleaver/4432415435/Attribution License. 580, Douglas Freer/Shutterstock. 581 (top), sarsmis/Shutterstock. 581 (bottom), Monkey Business Images/Shutterstock. 582, Stones in evening light by Alex Southward http://www.flickr.com/photos/bulletma9net/2272599130/ Attribution-ShareAlike License. 587, Val Corbett. 591, Simon Balson / Alamy. 598, Val Corbett/Britain on View/photolibrary.com. 602, Alan Novelli/Britain On View/photolibrary.com. 603, Roy Shakespeare / age fotostock. 604, Stewart Smith Photography/Shutterstock. 605 (top left), Julius Honnor. 605 (top right), Stewart Smith Photography/Shutterstock. 605 (bottom), Julius Honnor. 606, Britain on View/photolibrary.com. 607 (top left), Lake District (England) by Larra Jungle Princess http://www.flickr.com/photos/larra505/4577901927/ Attribution License. 607 (top right), Mike D Williams/Shutterstock. 608 (top), Alan Novelli/Britain On View/photolibrary.com. 608 (bottom), Drunken Duck Inn - Ambleside by Sarah & Austin Houghton-Bird http://www.flickr.com/photos/houghtonbird/3546801252/ Attribution License. 613, National Trust Photo Library/Britain on View/photolibrary.com. 614, Ashley Cooper / age fotostock. 619, Ashley Cooper / age fotostock. 622, D & S Tollerton / age fotostock. 626-27, Joe Cornish/Britain on View/photolibrary.com. Chapter 11: East Anglia: 629, Alistair Laming / age fotostock. 630, Burghley House Preservation Trusti. 631 (top), Wells Next The Sea 5 August 2007 af032 by Martin Pettitt http://www.flickr.com/photos/mdpettitt/1268905540/ Attribution License. 631 (bottom), Bridge of Sighs by Jared and Corin http://www.flickr.com/photos/redjar/194284319/ Attribution-ShareAlike License. 632, Shane W Thompson/Shutterstock. 633 (top), Monkey Business Images/Shutterstock. 633 (bottom), Roddy Paine / age fotostock. 634, flikr2502 by Kelbv http://www.flickr.com/photos/flikr/2374130579/ Attribution License. 639, Quentin Bargate / age fotostock. 642, Mark Sunderland / age fotostock. 654, Vidler / age fotostock. 659, Richard Surman/Britain on View/photolibrary.com. 663, Duncan Soar / Alamy. 664 (left), Matthew Collingwood/Shutterstock. 664 (top center), Roman_Baths_in_Bath_Spa,_England_July_2006.jpg by http://www.flickr.com/photos/corruptive/4500903016/ Attribution ShareAlike License. 664 (bottom center), A hoard of Iron Age coins from Beverly by Portable Antiquities Scheme http://www.flickr.com/photos/finds/2347635542/ Attribution License. 664 (right), public domain. 665 (left), Jan Kranendonk/iStockphoto. 665 (top right), Public Domain. 665 (bottom center), Marie-Lan Nguyen/Wikimedia Commons. 665 (bottom right), Public Domain. 666 (top left), Rachelle Burnside/Shutterstock. 666 (bottom left, bottom center, top right, and bottom right), Public Domain. 667 (top left), Art Renewal Center. 667 (bottom left), SuperStock/age fotostock. 667 (bottom center and top right), Public domain. 667 (bottom right), jeff gynane/iStockphoto. 668 (top left), Public domain. 668 (bottom left), The Print Collector / age fotostock. 668 (center), The National Archives / age fotostock. 668 (right), Trellis by NinaZed http://www.flickr.com/photos/ninazed/5046017851/ Attribution License. 669 (top left), Zaha Hadid/2012 Olympics. 669 (bot-

NOTES

ABOUT OUR WRITERS

Longtime contributor **Robert Andrews** loves warm beer and soggy moors, but hates shopping malls and the sort of weather when you're not sure if it's raining—all of which he found in abundance while updating the West Country and Bath and the Cotswolds chapters. Rob also wrote the "England Through the Ages" feature. He writes and revises other guidebooks and has penned his own guide to Devon and Cornwall.

Paul Cannon spent his youth following in J.R.R. Tolkien's footsteps, traipsing around the Welsh Borders in search of its secret spots. He likes nothing better than a ramble in the hills of his native Worcestershire. Today he divides his time between Britain and Spain, working for Spanish television and contributing to Fodor's England and Spain guides. Paul covers Lancashire and the Peaks and part of the Stratford-upon-Avon and the Heart of England chapters.

Sarah Christie explored the South for this edition and wrote the "Mysterious Stonehenge" feature, as well as several spotlights. She also leads gastronomic tours of London, and is a freelance writer and photographer. A born and bred Londoner, Sarah returned to England after several years in Washington, D.C., where she contributed to Fodor's guide to the city.

Texan by birth and Anglophile at heart, **Christi Daugherty** has lived in (and written about) England for nearly a decade. Her Fodor's territory included the Southeast and Yorkshire; she also wrote the "Gothic Grandeur" feature on York Minster and a number of spotlights on topics from tea to beaches. She has written and edited guidebooks to Ireland and Paris.

The team of London updaters included **Astrid deRidder, Damian Harper,** and **Michelle Rosenberg,** who updated various neighborhoods, as well as **Erin Huebscher,** the shopping updater.

Julius Honnor lives in London, but his Fodor's beat included rural spots in the Lake District, where he has observed chic new hotels and restaurants popping up alongside more traditional places. This year Julius added the "Hiking in the Lake District" feature. His work for other guidebooks has taken him around the globe.

Writer and editor **Kate Hughes** acquired a liking for the big city when she studied classical literature in Liverpool. Having since indulged her penchant for the country and landed gentry by getting a master's in garden history, she feels qualified to pass judgment on matters both urban and rural. She is responsible for the Thames Valley chapter and the section on Stratford-upon-Avon and Shakespeare Country, and for the "Glories of the Garden" feature. Other contributions for this edition are "Flavors of England" and several food spotlights.

A Londoner since public transportation was cheap, **Jack Jewers** has directed films for the BBC and reviewed pubs for *Time Out.* He updated the East Anglia, Northeast, and Wales chapters, adding various spotlights, as well as the Where to Stay section of London and several London neighborhoods. Jack also wrote the "See You at the Pub" feature.

Ellin Stein has written for publications on both sides of the Atlantic, including the *New York Times,* the *Times of London,* and *InStyle.* She has lived in London for 15 years and is married to a native. For this edition, Ellin updated Travel Smart England and the London chapter Planner.

By day, Londoner and Shoalin kung fu enthusiast **Alex Wijeratna** works as a global hunger activist for ActionAid; by night he hunts down the capital's best food. With his English/Sri Lankan roots, Alex knows that the real flavor of London is found in its ethnic diversity. Alex updated the Where to Eat section of London.